THE NEW
CAMBRIDGE MODERN HISTORY

ADVISORY COMMITTEE
G. N. CLARK   J. R. M. BUTLER   J. P. T. BURY
THE LATE E. A. BENIANS

VOLUME VIII

THE AMERICAN AND
FRENCH REVOLUTIONS
1763-93

THE NEW CAMBRIDGE MODERN HISTORY

VOLUME VIII

THE AMERICAN AND FRENCH REVOLUTIONS

1763–93

EDITED BY

A. GOODWIN

CAMBRIDGE
AT THE UNIVERSITY PRESS
1965

PUBLISHED BY
THE SYNDICS OF THE CAMBRIDGE UNIVERSITY PRESS

Bentley House, 200 Euston Road, London, N.W. 1
American Branch: 32 East 57th Street, New York, N.Y. 10022
West African Office: P.O. Box 33, Ibadan, Nigeria

©

CAMBRIDGE UNIVERSITY PRESS

1965

Printed in Great Britain at the University Printing House, Cambridge
(Brooke Crutchley, University Printer)

LIBRARY OF CONGRESS CATALOGUE
CARD NUMBER: 57-14935

ACKNOWLEDGEMENT

The editor wishes to acknowledge with gratitude his debt to Dr Peter Murray, Dr J. Lynch, Dr J. Roberts and Dr M. S. Anderson who, at a crucial stage in the preparation of this volume, agreed to associate themselves with it at short notice. All of them willingly accepted and fulfilled a rather strictly imposed time schedule, which the editor is conscious may not have given them all the opportunities for the preparation or final revision of their contributions which normally they would have had the right to expect.

CONTENTS

CHAPTER I

INTRODUCTORY SUMMARY

CHAPTER II

POPULATION, COMMERCE AND ECONOMIC IDEAS

By H. J. HABAKKUK, *Fellow of All Souls College and Chichele Professor*
of Economic History in the University of Oxford

CONTENTS

CONTENTS

2. ART AND ARCHITECTURE

By PETER MURRAY, *Witt Librarian, Courtauld Institute of Art,
University of London*

CHAPTER V

SCIENCE AND TECHNOLOGY

By D. McKIE, *formerly Professor of the History and Philosophy of Science
in the University of London*

CONTENTS

CHAPTER VI

EDUCATIONAL IDEAS, PRACTICE AND INSTITUTIONS

By A. V. JUDGES, *Professor of the History of Education in the University of London*

CHAPTER VII

ARMED FORCES AND THE ART OF WAR

I. NAVIES

By CHRISTOPHER LLOYD, *Professor of History, Royal Naval College, Greenwich*

CONTENTS

2. ARMIES

By J. R. WESTERN, *Lecturer in History in the Victoria University*
of Manchester

CHAPTER VIII

EUROPEAN RELATIONS WITH ASIA AND AFRICA

I. RELATIONS WITH ASIA

By K. A. BALLHATCHET, *Reader in Indian History in the University of Oxford*

CONTENTS

2. RELATIONS WITH AFRICA

By J. D. HARGREAVES, *Professor of History in the University of Aberdeen*

CHAPTER IX

EUROPEAN DIPLOMATIC RELATIONS, 1763–1790

By M. S. ANDERSON, *Reader in International History in the London School*
of Economics and Political Science

CONTENTS

CHAPTER X

THE HABSBURG POSSESSIONS AND GERMANY

By E. WANGERMANN, *Lecturer in Modern History in the
University of Leeds*

CONTENTS

CONTENTS

CHAPTER XIII

THE IBERIAN STATES AND THE ITALIAN STATES, 1763–1793

1. THE IBERIAN STATES

By J. LYNCH, *Leverhulme Lecturer in Hispanic and Latin American
History, University College, London*

2. THE ITALIAN STATES

By J. ROBERTS, *Fellow of Merton College, Oxford*

CONTENTS

CHAPTER XIV

THE DEVELOPMENT OF THE AMERICAN COMMUNITIES OUTSIDE BRITISH RULE

By R. A. HUMPHREYS, O.B.E., *Professor of Latin American History in the
University of London*

CONTENTS

CONTENTS

CHAPTER XVII

AMERICAN INDEPENDENCE IN ITS IMPERIAL, STRATEGIC AND DIPLOMATIC ASPECTS

By M. A. JONES, *Senior Lecturer in American History and Institutions in the Victoria University of Manchester*

CONTENTS

CHAPTER XVIII

AMERICAN INDEPENDENCE IN ITS AMERICAN CONTEXT: SOCIAL AND POLITICAL ASPECTS: WESTERN EXPANSION

By ESMOND WRIGHT, *Professor of Modern History in the
University of Glasgow*

CONTENTS

CHAPTER XIX

THE BEGINNINGS OF REFORM IN GREAT BRITAIN: IMPERIAL PROBLEMS: POLITICS AND ADMINISTRATION, ECONOMIC GROWTH

By W. R. WARD, *Senior Lecturer in History in the Victoria University of Manchester*

CHAPTER XX

FRENCH ADMINISTRATION AND PUBLIC FINANCE IN THEIR EUROPEAN SETTING

By J. F. BOSHER, *Associate Professor of History in the University of British Columbia*

CONTENTS

CHAPTER XXI

THE BREAKDOWN OF THE OLD RÉGIME IN FRANCE

By D. DAKIN, *Reader in History, Birkbeck College, University of London*

CHAPTER XXII

THE HISTORIOGRAPHY OF THE FRENCH REVOLUTION

By the Rev. J. McMANNERS, *Professor of Modern History in the University of Sydney*

CONTENTS

CHAPTER XXIII

THE OUTBREAK OF THE FRENCH REVOLUTION

By G. E. RUDÉ, *Senior Lecturer in History in the University of Adelaide*

CONTENTS

CHAPTER XXIV

REFORM AND REVOLUTION IN FRANCE:
OCTOBER 1789–FEBRUARY 1793

By A. GOODWIN, *Professor of Modern History in the Victoria
University of Manchester*

CHAPTER I

INTRODUCTORY SURVEY

BETWEEN the Peace of Paris 1763 and the outbreak, thirty years later, of the war of the first European coalition against revolutionary France, the outlines of a Western civilisation which was recognisably 'modern' in most of its characteristic attitudes and attributes rapidly emerged. A civil war between the English colonists in North America and the imperial government at Westminster, unparalleled industrial and commercial expansion in Britain, radical social and political reforms in France and a steady but uneven increase in population imposed on the western world a momentum of revolutionary change which has never since slackened. On a comparatively minor scale, but with results which helped to determine the trend towards greater social and political equality at this period, there occurred in western Europe another series of revolutions—such as the struggles in the small city republic of Geneva between 1768 and 1789 for the political and economic emancipation of the middle-class *représentants* and the socially inferior and unprivileged *natifs*, the Dutch 'patriotic' movement of 1784-7 and the schismatic revolt of the Belgian democrats in the Austrian Netherlands between 1789 and 1792. Even in conservative England the radicalism inherent in the ambivalent Whig creed received a fresh emphasis in the county 'association' movement of 1779-80 in favour of parliamentary reform and the agitation in 1787-90 for the relief of the Protestant Dissenters from their civic disabilities under the Test and Corporation Acts. The closer study of these radical movements and of their connections with the American and French revolutions has led some historians to see in this period a pattern of radical reform and revolutionary change common to many parts of the western world.[1]

This approach has stemmed from dissatisfaction with the tendency to study the American and French revolutions in isolation, rather than in the wider context of an emergent eighteenth-century 'Atlantic community'. This community was itself the product of the expanding commercial, intellectual and religious contacts between western Europe and the New World. Within this vast complex, whose seaports and urban centres were being linked together more closely by speedier maritime and postal connections, the ideas and concepts of the European Enlightenment

---

[1] See especially R. R. Palmer, *The Age of the Democratic Revolution—A Political History of Europe and America, 1760-1800*, vol. I (Princeton, N.J., 1959), and J. Godechot, *La Grande Nation. L'Expansion Révolutionnaire de la France dans le monde, 1789-1799* (Paris, 1956), vol. I, ch. I.

circulated freely.[1] On both sides of the Atlantic after 1763 supporters of the democratic cause, it is suggested, put their faith in the same philosophy of natural rights, asserted similar notions of popular sovereignty, showed the same preference for written constitutions based on the principle of the 'separation' of powers and contended for the admission of all citizens to public office, irrespective of their social origins or religious professions.[2] A two-way transmission across the Atlantic of these political principles was made possible by the proliferation at this period of literary and philosophical societies, masonic lodges, scientific and learned academies and by a remarkable growth of metropolitan and provincial newspapers. The protagonists of radical views in politics and religion within this community were moved by common sympathies and ideals and in their struggles against established authority in church and state lent each other mutual assistance. This co-operation was evident in the support given to the cause of American independence and later to the French Revolution by the leaders of the English 'philosophical' Dissenters—Price and Priestley, in the compelling republican propaganda of Thomas Paine and in the sympathetic encouragement given by Benjamin Franklin and Thomas Jefferson as successive American ambassadors at Versailles to liberal reform in France. Less successful and more suspect was the close association after 1789 between Lord Lansdowne's Bowood circle of Utilitarian reformers in England and Mirabeau's expatriated Genevan collaborators in Paris and the parallel agitations conducted on both sides of the Channel by the British Society for the Abolition of the Slave Trade and its French counterpart—the Société des Amis des Noirs.[3]

This general movement towards modern democracy, it has been suggested, was essentially a revolt against an aristocratic ascendancy strongly entrenched in the various European 'constituted bodies', such as the national or provincial estates, diets, sovereign judicial courts or established churches and in the colonial assemblies and governors' councils of British North America.[4] After 1763 these centres of aristocratic predominance were under pressure from three main directions. In France the surviving provincial estates and the *parlements* were endangered by the centralising and reforming policies of the Bourbon monarchy; in central and northern Europe the authority of the national or provincial diets was being steadily eroded by the encroaching power of the Enlightened autocracies; in colonial America, Britain, Geneva and the United Provinces legislative assemblies or councils were encountering democratic

---

[1] M. Kraus, *The Atlantic Civilization: Eighteenth-century Origins* (Ithaca, N.Y. 1949), ch. II.

[2] J. Godechot and R. R. Palmer, 'Le Problème de l'Atlantique du XVIIIème au XXème Siècle', *X Congresso Internazionale di Scienze Storiche* (Rome, 1955), *Relazioni*, Vol. v, pp. 219–33.

[3] For Mirabeau's collaborators see J. Bénétruy, *L'Atelier de Mirabeau, Quatre Proscrits Genevois dans la tourmente révolutionnaire* (Geneva, 1962).

[4] See below, ch. xv, p. 432.

pressure or criticism from middle-class or popular radicalism. Under these attacks, and partly under the stress of growing economic difficulties, the privileged orders were provoked into the reassertion of their immunities and corporate exclusiveness. This aristocratic 'reaction' was most pronounced in France, where it took the form of an increasing political solidarity of the lay, clerical and judicial nobility, which culminated in the final attempt to arrest radical reform of the *ancien régime*—the so-called *révolte nobiliaire* of 1787-8. It was also evident, however, in the expulsion of the Genevan 'liberals' after the aristocratic *coup d'état* of 1782, in the revolt of the Magyar nobility and the conservative Belgian estates against the social and administrative reforms of the Emperor Joseph II, and in the suppression of the Dutch 'patriots' in 1787. All this serves to underline the complexity of the evolving revolutionary situation in North America and western Europe by indicating that 'conservatism and counter-revolution were no mere "reactions" against revolution, but eighteenth-century forces against which revolution was itself a reaction'.[1]

Although the concept of a general 'democratic' revolutionary movement in the West is formulated largely in political terms, the absence of a similar impulse outside the ambit of the Atlantic community is explained by the divergent economic and social structure of central and eastern Europe. There was in fact a glaring contrast between western Europe—where in Britain only vestigial traces of former feudalism remained, where in France the vast majority of peasants had long been personally free and their holdings of land increasingly subdivided—and the regions east of the river Elbe—where, except on the crown domains of the king of Prussia, the full rigours of feudalism survived and where, particularly in Hungary, Poland and Russia, vast landed estates (*latifundia*) were still intact. It has long been recognised, however, that the sense of social injustice and the gravity of economic grievances were much more pronounced in the western regions of Europe, where the hold of feudalism had been relaxed and where the French 'feudal reaction' of the latter part of the eighteenth century was all the more bitterly resented. Three other differences between West and East make this superficially paradoxical discontent in the West more intelligible. Firstly, in France, as Tocqueville observed more than a century ago, the impoverished provincial nobility had ceased to perform even the smallest administrative functions at the parochial level, whereas, in the rural areas of central Germany, despite the decay of the provincial diets, the Prussian, Austrian and Magyar nobility were still actively concerned in the work of local government. Secondly, whereas in France the central government showed little disposition to prevent the nobility from reviving obsolete feudal dues at the expense of the peasantry, in Prussia Frederick II made determined efforts to protect the serfs outside the royal domain from undue lordly

[1] R. R. Palmer, *The Age of the Democratic Revolution*, p. 22.

exactions, while in the Habsburg dominions the Empress Maria Theresa regulated the amount of the serfs' obligations to their lords, and Joseph II even tried to replace them by a fixed and reduced percentage of their annual yield calculated in money terms. Thirdly, in central and eastern Europe, where large centres of urban population were few and far between, one of the most important vehicles of radical unrest—a numerous and influential middle-class—was largely absent. This was why France came to be the real crucible of the Western revolutionary movement, because there middle-class resentment against social and political inequality and peasant grievances against surviving feudalism and capitalistic forms of exploitation could profit from the collapse of monarchical authority and the imminence of national bankruptcy.

This concept of a general democratic movement dominating the western world from the end of the Seven Years War is valuable in so far as it emphasises a truth often neglected by historians who confine their attention to particular countries—namely that the institutions, social organisation and economic practices of the old régime, both in America and many parts of western Europe, were being questioned and challenged by like-minded radicals and that the choice between drastic reform from above or revolution from below was one which confronted most European governments of the time and not merely that of France. There can be no doubt that some of the revolutionary disturbances in western Europe in the 1780s owed not a little to the political concepts, example and tactics of the American colonists as well as to indigenous circumstances. The French Revolution in turn owed something to impulses received from the minor European revolutions which preceded it. Further research will probably help to establish more clearly the multiple connections which existed between reformers in many countries in a western world whose cultural unity was sustained by eighteenth-century cosmopolitanism, the cult of the Grand Tour, the prestige of the 'philosophic' movement and by what Sorel described as the 'nomad dynasties'. On the other hand, the thesis tends perhaps to exaggerate the common denominators between the various revolutionary movements and to undervalue their specific differences. American historians have questioned the alleged importance of the role of Enlightenment ideas in shaping the political principles of the American Revolution, English historians find it difficult to assimilate British history at this period even into a quasi-revolutionary pattern, while French historians consider, with some justice, that the concept tends to underrate the unique historical significance of the revolution of 1789.[1]

---

[1] For criticisms of the general thesis see M. Reinhard, 'Sur l'histoire de la Révolution française: Travaux récents et perspectives', *Annales. Économies, Sociétés, Civilisations*, Vol. XIV, 1959, pp. 554–6, and A. Cobban, 'The Age of the Democratic Revolution', *History*, vol. XLV (Oct. 1960), pp. 234–9. For a contrary view that Enlightenment ideas were mainly

Less controversially an introduction to the contents of this volume may perhaps stress the importance of the Seven Years War and of the Peace of Paris of 1763 as determining factors in the history of the western world during most of the subsequent decade. From this source may be traced, for example, a reorientation of international relations which was soon to throw into significant relief the political problems of central and eastern Europe. The material destruction and economic dislocation wrought by the Seven Years War imposed on the former belligerents, victors and vanquished alike, the necessity for financial retrenchment and further administrative reform. In North America the conquest of Canada confronted the British government with urgent and perplexing problems of imperial defence and reconstruction. The immediate destiny of Poland and the ultimate fate of the Ottoman Empire, the trend in most parts of Europe outside the sphere of the Atlantic community towards systems of Enlightened Absolutism and the schism in the first British empire were thus all, directly or indirectly, connected with the outcome of the Seven Years War and the peace settlement which followed it.

The immediate effects of the treaty of Paris were to leave Britain without an ally on the Continent and to confirm France's chief minister, Choiseul, in his determination to seek revenge for the loss of French colonial possessions in North America and India. Britain's diplomatic isolation after 1763 may be attributed, not so much to her alleged desertion of Prussia in order to secure a separate peace with France, but rather to the long-range consequences of the reversal of alliances of 1756–7 and to Frederick II's frankly avowed and wholly intelligible unconcern with the fate of the cod-fisheries of Newfoundland.[1] One result of France's alliance with Austria was the abandonment of her former aggressive designs against the Austrian Netherlands. This automatically weakened the long-standing connection between Britain and the United Provinces and confirmed the recent tendency of the Dutch to be neutralist in continental conflicts. The Franco-Austrian alliance also had the effect of further stabilising the political situation in the Italian peninsula, which before 1748 had been the main arena of Bourbon–Habsburg conflict, and, by so doing, helped to consolidate the Bourbon Family Compact. Lastly, by its apparent incompatibility with France's traditional support of the Ottoman Empire, the Austrian alliance enhanced the tendency of the French government after 1763 to disinterest itself in the affairs of eastern Europe. A similar attitude on the part of the British government also explains its failure at this period to effect a political alliance with Russia.

significant in helping to shape the concepts of the post-revolutionary period of American constitution-making see B. Bailyn, 'Political Experience and Enlightenment Ideas in Eighteenth-century America', *American Historical Review*, vol. LXVII (1962), pp. 339–51.
[1] F. Spencer, 'The Anglo-Prussian Breach of 1762: An Historical Revision', *History*, new series, vol. XLI (1956), pp. 100–12. For the diplomatic revolution see vol. VII of this series, ch. XIX.

Until his fall from office in 1770 Choiseul used his preponderant ministerial position to concentrate all available French resources upon the rebuilding of his country's naval and military strength and upon the vigorous reform of her colonial administration.[1] Though remaining loyal to the Austrian connection, Choiseul took care to restrict its continental commitments and clearly regarded his own creation—the Franco-Spanish offensive and defensive alliance of 1761—as the chief means of wresting from Britain the naval preponderance which had proved France's ruin in the Seven Years War. In contrast with Louis XV's system of secret diplomacy, which still aimed at the maintenance of Bourbon dynastic interests in Poland, French official foreign policy after 1763 was, therefore, mainly geared to a resumption of the maritime and colonial contest with Britain. This policy coincided closely with the paramount interests of Spain—the defence of its colonial possessions and the protection of its commercial monopoly in Latin America.[2] As the French alliance was the only available one for Spain at this period, even the refusal of her ally to support her in her dispute with Britain over the Falkland Islands in 1770 did not seriously affect the close co-operation between the Bourbon powers. Their prospects of defeating Britain in the vital area of Atlantic rivalry depended ultimately, however, upon their ability to restore the balance of power at sea and upon the anticipated deterioration of the relations between the British government and the American colonists.

It was the continuation after 1763 of Anglo-French and Anglo-Spanish colonial and maritime rivalry, the determination of Frederick the Great to disengage Prussia from the Atlantic struggle and the decision of the French and British governments not to be involved in the affairs of central and eastern Europe which almost divided the west and the east of the continent at this period into separate political worlds.[3] Whereas, however, an open rupture between Britain and the Bourbon powers in the Atlantic world was necessarily delayed till the successful revolt of the American colonies, a vacancy on the electoral throne of Poland, owing to the death of Augustus III in October 1763, initiated a prolonged and dangerous crisis in central and eastern Europe, which was only resolved by the first partition of Poland in 1772 and by the conclusion of Russo-Turkish hostilities in the treaty of Kutchuk-Kainardji of 1774.[4] That treaty, which conceded to Russia freedom of navigation on the Black Sea, together with vague and ill-defined rights of protecting the Greek Orthodox Christians in Constantinople and a secure, if restricted, foothold on territory between the rivers Bug and Dnieper, marked the opening of the Near Eastern problem as it was to perplex European statesmen for the

[1] Below, ch. vii(1), 'Navies', and A. Temple Patterson, *The Other Armada, the Franco-Spanish Attempt to Invade Britain in 1779* (Manchester, 1960), ch. ii.
[2] For the successive relaxations of the commercial restrictions within the Spanish colonial empire see below, ch. xiv.   [3] See below, ch. ix, pp. 253 and 266.
[4] For the general causes of Poland's decline at this period see ch. xii below.

rest of the eighteenth and for much of the nineteenth century—for it fore-shadowed the possibility that Turkey might soon fall wholly under the dominion of Russia or suffer partition.[1]

It is equally clear that the domestic policies of the major continental powers after 1763 were partially dictated by the economic and financial effects of the Seven Years War. During the conflict large tracts of central Europe had been devastated, rural populations had been displaced, commerce and industry disrupted. In a world of competing and predatory states, hardly any of the former belligerents felt sufficiently secure, even after the peace, to relax their military preparedness, while those with revisionist aims wished not only to maintain but to increase their military potential. The most pressing problems confronting rulers after 1763 were, therefore, those of economic rehabilitation and retrenchment, and above all the need to ensure increased public revenues. Alone of the major belligerents Prussia had emerged from the war with its public finances intact and Frederick II was thus able to devote large sums from the royal treasury to the financing of rural credit institutions (*Landschaften*), intended to help the impoverished Prussian landowners, to the free distribution of seed-corn and cattle, and to the rebuilding of farms.[2] In the first year of peace seven million thalers were spent on agricultural subsidies of this kind. Currency reform, the establishment of a state discount bank, in January 1765, modelled on the Bank of England, and the introduction of a French *régie* for the collection of the indirect taxes indicate the extent to which the Prussian king was at this period preoccupied with the issues of public finance.[3] More interesting for their social and political consequences were the financial policies adopted in the Habsburg dominions and in France. In Austria the public debt at the end of the Seven Years War amounted to approximately 300,000,000 gulden. By placing the whole of his inherited personal fortune (22,000,000 gulden) at the disposal of the treasury, the young Emperor Joseph II reduced the annual interest on this debt from six to four per cent. The Empress Maria Theresa, guided by the finance minister Hatzfeld, sought more radical remedies by seeking to tap the largely untaxed wealth of the lay nobility and clergy. When the Hungarian nobility resisted these demands in 1764 by defending its fiscal immunities and by pleading that the taxable capacity of the unprivileged orders had already been exceeded, the empress was led in 1767 to interfere in the feudal relationship by regulating the labour services of the Hungarian peasants by royal decree. This policy of protecting the peasants and restricting their obligations to their

---

[1] See below, ch. IX, p. 265.

[2] O. Hintze, *Die Hohenzollern und ihr Werk* (Berlin, 1915), pp. 380–1.

[3] For the view that the essential preoccupations of the enlightened despots at this period were financial, see C. Morazé, 'Finance et despotisme, essai sur les despotes éclairés', *Annales. Économies, Sociétés, Civilisations*, vol. III (1948), pp. 279–96. For Prussian recovery after 1763 see W. O. Henderson, *Studies in the Economic Policy of Frederick the Great* (London, 1963), ch. 3.

7

feudal superiors was subsequently applied, between 1771 and 1778, to Austrian Silesia, Lower Austria, Bohemia, Moravia and Styria.[1] Though this measure was a compromise devised to leave the fiscal exemption of the nobility intact for the time being by making it possible for the unprivileged to sustain a greater weight of state taxation, the empress had thus embarked on a policy of social reform which her son was later to carry to its logical conclusion by the abolition of serfdom. Equally important were the consequences of papal resistance to the government's demands for clerical contributions to public revenues, for from 1768 onwards the Austrian clergy were taxed without papal dispensation and in 1769 the dissolution of the monasteries and the diversion of their endowments first to more general ecclesiastical purposes and then to charitable and educational uses was begun. By these and other means the amount of Austrian state revenues was raised, by 1773, to almost double what it had been ten years earlier. The trend towards greater state absolutism and towards policies of social reform later identified with enlightened absolutism was thus rooted in financial necessity.

In France similar attempts to increase public revenues between 1763 and 1769 by prolonging some of the war taxes to which the privileged orders were subject and by a more equitable reassessment of the *taille* encountered the violent and concerted opposition of the *parlements*. It was at this time and from this reactionary quarter that the first public demands were raised for the summons of the Estates General. To appease the recalcitrant magistrates Louis XV was compelled to emasculate the ministerial projects for financial reform and to agree reluctantly to the expulsion of the Jesuits. Only after the opposition of the *parlement* of Paris had been swept aside by the drastic judicial reforms of the Chancellor Maupeou in 1771 did it prove possible for the abbé Terray, by a series of drastic fiscal expedients, to establish French public finances on a somewhat firmer footing in the last years of Louis XV.[2]

Fiscal considerations were equally, if not more prominent, among the factors which shaped the attitude of the British government to the American colonists after 1763. In general, three main aims seem to have informed British financial policy towards America at this period—the determination to check leakages of customs revenues in the colonies resulting from the widespread evasion of the Navigation laws, the attempt to raise a revenue in America by act of the imperial parliament and the endeavour to remodel and strengthen the executive power in the colonies by making it financially independent of the colonial assemblies. Behind these objectives there lay the intelligible desire to relieve the heavy burden on the British taxpayer of a national debt which had doubled in size in consequence of the Seven Years War, the need, suggested by wartime experience, to provide the American colonies with an adequate system of

[1] See below, ch. x, p. 282.　　　[2] See below, ch. xxi, p. 597.

defence and the urgent necessity of endowing the empire as a whole with a more rational and coherent administrative structure. These policies were not hastily improvised by ill-informed or incompetent ministers, they were not inspired by any covert designs to subordinate or enslave the colonists or to exploit their rising prosperity for the selfish advantage of the mother-country. They were, however, viewed in a very different light by the commercial interests and radical leaders across the Atlantic and thus provoked a resistance culminating in civil war, which ended with the disruption of the first British empire.

To the American colonists this more positive approach of the British government to financial and imperial problems after 1763 appeared as dangerous 'innovation', threatening to restrict their own western expansion, to undermine the sources of their commercial prosperity and to infringe the constitutional rights and privileges of their colonial assemblies.[1] As differences between the colonists and the imperial government deepened and misunderstandings multiplied, the propaganda of the Whig political leaders in America intensified these resentments and made the compromise, which many of them desired, difficult. In a very real sense, however, the American contention that in these years the British government was attempting to implement an imperial policy at variance with its previous practice of 'wise and salutary neglect' was not exaggerated. This policy was the product of bitter wartime experience and also of the advice tendered to the government by conscientious officials at the Board of Trade and by sorely tried soldier-administrators on the American frontier.

The first aspect of this 'new departure' in imperial policy was the attempt to grapple with the complex issues raised by the defence of the western colonial frontiers against the Indians.[2] Here the rising of the north-western tribes under their Ottowa chief Pontiac in the spring of 1763, and the failure of the colonial governments adequately to co-operate in its suppression, reinforced the need both to strengthen the garrisons of British regular forces at strategic points and to reassure the Indians against the westward expansion of the colonials. By the royal proclamation of 7 October 1763 the ministry of George Grenville gave formal expression to the policy, adumbrated two years earlier, of excluding settlers from the territories west of the Appalachian mountains until the Indians had been pacified and until an agreed basis for land settlement in these areas had been devised. By this decision the government not only honoured its obligations arising from a series of wartime treaties with the Indians, but also attempted to redirect the course of colonial expansion away from the fur-trading areas towards Nova Scotia and Canada in the north and towards Florida in the south.[3] Although not unalterably

---

[1] See below, ch. XVIII.
[2] E. Wright, *Fabric of Freedom, 1763–1800* (New York, 1961), pp. 40–8.
[3] J. Steven Watson, *The Reign of George III, 1760–1815* (Oxford, 1960), p. 183.

fixed, the new demarcation line was held in America to be inconsistent with the western land claims contained in some of the colonial charters, and in so far as it was observed, it naturally antagonised the southern land-speculators and the frontiersmen anxious to escape from their limited opportunities in the settled tidewater areas.[1] Though, after 1768, the imperial government had to abandon this restrictive policy, none of the colonial land-settlement projects subsequently sanctioned had time to bear fruit before the outbreak of the revolution. On the eve of that event the government of Lord North, in the effort to placate Canada in the Quebec Act of 1774, revived all the worst fears of the northern seaboard colonies by reverting to the policy of imperial control in the western territories north of the Ohio.

The second element of the 'new' imperial policy after 1763 was the reinvigoration and strict enforcement of the Navigation laws and the attempt to transfer to the colonists some share of the increased costs of colonial defence by levying taxation in America by act of parliament. The Grenville administration, imitating the war measures of Pitt, tightened up the administration of the customs services and, in Massachusetts, made increased use of 'writs of assistance' and of the jurisdiction of the Vice-Admiralty courts. Within a year of taking office the government had more than doubled the number of 'enumerated' articles in the Navigation code and had forbidden the colonial governments to issue paper currencies. Above all, however, in its quest for increased revenue, it provoked the opposition of the powerful New England merchants by the Sugar Act of 1764 and roused a general outcry of the most vocal and influential elements in America by the Stamp Act of March 1765. It was the combination of these measures—the attempt to terminate the lucrative smuggling trade of the New England and middle colonies with the French and Spanish West Indies at a time of post-war economic recession and the decision to abandon the unsatisfactory method of financing the costs of colonial defence by way of requisition that caused the colonists openly to challenge the methods and principles of the new imperial policies.[2] Neither the mob violence employed by the 'Sons of Liberty' against the colonial stamp distributors, which nullified the Stamp Act in America, nor the economic boycott of British goods by the colonial merchants which forced its repeal in 1766, were as significant in the ensuing crisis of Anglo-American relations as the defiance of Patrick Henry in the 'rump' Virginia assembly or the more moderate resolutions of the Stamp Act Congress of October 1765. Though the pattern of

[1] The colonies whose charters did contain western land claims were New Hampshire, Massachusetts, Connecticut, New York, Virginia, North and South Carolina and Georgia.
[2] Requisition was the method revived by Newcastle and Pitt whereby ministers, exercising the prerogative power of the crown, had called on the colonial assemblies to provide for common defence by means of quotas. Parliament subsequently reimbursed the colonies for part, and often most, of the cost.

physical and economic resistance to the British government was to be repeated with success in the recurrent episodes of conflict between 1765 and 1774, the main importance of the Stamp Act crisis was that it forced into the open the fundamental differences on matters of constitutional principle which led to the eventual schism. Hitherto the colonists had tended to rely for the defence of their liberties on their royal charters; henceforth emphasis was placed on their rights, under the English constitution, to be taxed only with their consent, to trial by jury and to petition for the redress of their grievances. Accepting both their subordination to the British crown and the right of the imperial parliament to regulate trade and commerce by means of external customs duties, the colonists now repudiated as 'unconstitutional' the attempt to raise internal taxes for purposes of revenue.[1] When the legislative supremacy of the imperial parliament over the colonies 'in all cases whatsoever' was reasserted in the Declaratory Act, when Townshend attempted, though without success, to force the colonial superior courts to sanction a more extended use of 'writs of assistance', and when he also allocated the revenues from a further series of customs duties to the payment of the salaries of colonial governors, judges and officials, these measures were seen as direct attacks on the status and privileges of the colonial assemblies and as part of a settled design to 'enslave' the colonists.[2] The so-called 'intolerable' acts of 1774, intended to isolate and quell the resistance of Massachusetts to the duty on tea, confirmed these suspicions and indicated that the British government had finally resorted, in the face of repeated colonial opposition, to a policy of coercion.[3] Under this threat the first Continental Congress virtually repudiated the sovereign authority of the imperial parliament.[4] The final rejection of allegiance to the crown and the appeal, in justification, to natural rights came only after the outbreak of hostilities and the realisation of the need for foreign alliances—in the Declaration of Independence.

The struggle of the United States for independence was thus initially a colonial rebellion or, as some historians have described it, a second English civil war. As the Americans themselves were quick to appreciate, however, their chances of successful revolt depended upon foreign intervention, and as the war progressed it developed into an international conflict.[5] Assured from the early months of 1776 of French co-belligerency and of the cautious benevolence of Spain and the United Provinces,

[1] See below, ch. XVI, p. 455.
[2] For the late Sir Lewis Namier's interpretation of the American policy of Townshend see *Crossroads of Power* (London, 1962), pp. 203–12. See also O. M. Dickerson's 'Writs of Assistance as a Cause of the Revolution', in *The Era of the American Revolution*, ed. R. B. Morris (New York, 1939), pp. 40–75.
[3] See below, ch. XVII, p. 484.
[4] C. H. McIlwain, *The American Revolution. A Constitutional Interpretation* (New York, 1923), p. 116.
[5] See below, ch. XVII.

the colonists regarded the war, not merely as one for their political emancipation, but also for the disruption and partition of the British empire.[1] Territorially the ambitions of the 'insurgents' extended, at the outset, to the conquest and absorption of all the other British possessions in North America—Canada, Nova Scotia, Cape Breton island, Newfoundland and the Floridas. Hardly less confident were American designs on the capture of trade outlets in western Europe and on the naval domination of the western Atlantic. The early discomfiture of the attempted conquest of Canada and the increasing need for the financial and naval assistance of France in order merely to survive finally forced the Americans to limit their more immediate objectives to the achievement of a formal alliance with the French as the indispensable means of winning the war.

Fortunately for the colonists the Comte de Vergennes, at the French Ministry of Foreign Affairs, was no less determined than his predecessor Choiseul to restore the commercial and naval balance of power in the Atlantic and, in any case, regarded Franco-British hostilities as inevitable, whatever the outcome of the civil war in America. Even before the Declaration of Independence French secret assistance in the way of military supplies was on its way to the colonies. More important was the decision of the French government in May 1776, despite the strenuous opposition of Turgot, to commit itself to the policy of affording the colonists financial assistance.[2] Owing, however, to Spanish reluctance to assist a rebellion which might excite unrest in its own dependencies in central and southern America and to French fears of a possible collapse of colonial resistance, it was not until after the American victory at Saratoga in October 1777 that Vergennes saw his way open to offer the colonists a formal alliance. By the terms of the treaty signed on 6 February 1778 France recognised the independence of the United States, both countries guaranteed each other's possessions in the New World and undertook to prosecute the war until American sovereignty had been assured. By July Britain and France were at war. French naval participation in the vital Atlantic theatre was, however, considerably delayed, mainly owing to Spanish unwillingness to underwrite American independence and because of Florida Blanca's determination that Britain should be forced to concede substantial advantages to the Bourbon powers either as the price of their joint mediation in the colonial conflict or as a result of a Franco-Spanish invasion. It was only in order to implement this limited strategy and to secure Gibraltar, Minorca and her claims in central America that Spain entered the war in June 1779 as the ally of France.[3] The hostile encirclement of

[1] R. W. Van Alstyne, *The Rising American Empire* (Oxford, 1960), ch. II.

[2] It was disagreement between Vergennes and Turgot on this issue which was one of the major factors in the latter's fall from office on 12 May 1776. H. Glagau, *Reformversuche und Sturz des Absolutismus in Frankreich (1774–1778)*, (Berlin, 1908), pp. 114–32.

[3] A. Temple Patterson, *The Other Armada* (Manchester, 1960), ch. III.

Britain was completed in 1780 by the formation, with French encouragement, of the Armed Neutrality of the northern powers and by Dutch involvement. Though a small French expeditionary force, under Rochambeau, was landed in Rhode Island in the spring of that year, the main French naval effort continued to be concentrated in the West Indies. In these circumstances, the Americans, ably and devotedly led by Washington, came close to defeat towards the end of 1780. In May of the following year however, the French fleet was ordered to co-operate with the colonial armies and the result was the defeat of Graves by de Grasse off the capes of the Chesapeake and the surrender of the British forces under Cornwallis at Yorktown. As Washington himself had always anticipated, it was the financial and, above all, the naval assistance of France which had proved decisive. Equally important, however, for their effects on the peace settlement at Versailles in 1783 were British naval victories against the Bourbon powers in the final stages of the war in the Indian Ocean, the western Mediterranean and the Caribbean. In the event the skilful and imaginative diplomacy of Shelburne was able not only to prevent the complete disintegration of the first British empire, but also to deprive France and Spain of the territorial and economic advantages in Europe and Asia which seemed at that point to be within their grasp.

The essence of this achievement lay in a prior understanding with the American peace commissioners Franklin and Jay, whereby the recognition of American independence was coupled with the admission of the claims of the United States to expansion in the territories of the old north-west, south of the Great Lakes. This settlement involved the sacrifice of Shelburne's visionary hopes for the creation of an Anglo-American federal union and an Atlantic community of free trade, but it allowed Britain to retain its hold on Canada, Nova Scotia and Newfoundland and virtually to undermine the Franco-American alliance.[1] By contrast, though some gains were made by France and Spain and though Britain had been humiliated by the partial collapse of her North American empire, the Bourbon powers accepted settlements which left British gains in the Seven Years War substantially intact. Above all, Vergennes' hopes of converting the United States into an economic satellite of France had been dissipated.

The repercussions of the American revolution on Great Britain and France were profound and far-reaching. Part of the political response in Britain to the disasters of the American war was the highly organised campaign of the middle-class landowners in Yorkshire and of the London radicals for 'economical' and parliamentary reform in 1779–80. Though the agitation confirmed the aversion of the Rockingham Whigs for parliamentary reform and only achieved its more limited objectives, the

---

[1] For Shelburne's imperial policy at the peace settlement see V. T. Harlow, *The Founding of the Second British Empire, 1763–1793* (London, 1952), ch. vi.

'American' methods adopted by the county associations to bring pressure to bear on parliament were not forgotten when the demand for parliamentary reform was raised again by a younger generation of Whig politicians ten years later. Neither in 1780 nor in 1793, however, were these political movements revolutionary in intention. Wartime necessity, the eloquence of Grattan, and the armed demonstrations of the Irish Volunteers induced Rockingham in 1782 to concede legislative independence to the Irish parliament. The loss of the American colonies also made British imperial problems after 1783 not less, but more important. Though the attitude of responsible officials remained stubbornly committed to mercantilist principles in colonial policy, in the following decade Pitt laid the foundations of a wiser and more enduring imperialism. The increased importance of British trading interests in the East in consequence of the American schism and the inadequacy of Lord North's Regulating Act of 1773 made it necessary to establish official relations with India on a more satisfactory footing.[1] Pitt's India Act of 1784 imposed more rigorous standards of commercial behaviour on the East India Company's servants, subjected its directors to a ministerial board of control appointed by the Crown, and, in its amended form, conferred on the Governor General in Calcutta the necessary authority to override his council. It was also because of the closure of the former American colonies to the transportation overseas of British convicts that the first penal settlement was made in 1788 at Sydney. That was the beginning of the colonisation of New South Wales, with all its implications for the future development of Australia and the opening up of the Pacific. Later still, in 1791, the continuing demands of the exiled American Empire Loyalists for representative institutions in Upper Canada resulted in the separation of that province from Lower Canada and the grant to both areas of a semblance of self-government. When Pitt insisted, as he then did, that Canadian taxation should be 'left to the wisdom of their own legislatures', he was clearly recalling, in a different context, the great lesson of 1776. Above all, the financial aftermath of the American War provided the spur to the great series of fiscal, commercial and administrative reforms carried through to success by Pitt between 1784 and 1789.[2] These not only ensured Britain's recovery in the post-war period, but also enabled her to profit from her new and unprecedented opportunities of commercial and industrial expansion.

In France the response to the challenge of financial reform after 1783 came too late. There, as Turgot had predicted, the financial disorders resulting from participation in the American war led within a few years to national insolvency and to the fiscal collapse of the *ancien régime*. Just as the fiscal problems left by the Seven Years War had led the British government to adopt new imperial policies which culminated in the loss

[1] See below, ch. VIII (1).   [2] See below, ch. XIX.

of its American colonies, so the financial legacy of the American war involved France in a situation from which no issue could be found except by the summons of the Estates General. The refusal of the first Assembly of Notables and of the *parlement* of Paris to sponsor the fiscal remedies of Calonne and Brienne and their call for the summons of a national representative assembly amounted, in effect, to a repetition of the American demand for 'no taxation without representation'. In the ensuing contest between the privileged orders and the Third Estate a decisive role was played by the French liberal aristocracy, several of whose most influential members had served as volunteers in the American war. These were reinforced by a group of younger magistrates inside the conservative *parlement* of Paris who, because of their admiration for the new American state constitutions, came to be known as 'the Americans'. By assuming the political leadership of the *parti patriote* and by throwing their weight behind middle-class demands for equality, these dissident groups of the French aristocracy ensured the eventual defeat of the *révolte nobiliaire* in 1787–8 and made a significant, though often forgotten, contribution to the triumph of the popular cause in the crucial struggles of 1789.[1]

The post-war decade in Britain, however, was perhaps mainly significant for the so-called economic 'take-off into self-sustained growth', which a former generation of historians has termed 'the industrial revolution'. Though the chronology of this phenomenon has been one of the most controversial subjects of debate among economic historians, informed opinion is now agreed that the sudden spurt of expansion, which was to transform not only Britain but the whole of the modern world, occurred in the third rather than in the first decade of the reign of George III. The origins of this sudden growth are now sought less in the technological innovations of British inventors—which were, with the exception of Watt's rotary steam-engine, modest rather than revolutionary in scope—and rather more in Britain's pre-eminence throughout the eighteenth century in oversea colonial trade, in her pioneering exploitation of the cotton trade, ideally suited both to command and to supply the mass markets that would ensure ever-expanding capitalistic production, the prevalence in Britain of comparatively low interest rates and the deployment of new entrepreneurial skills.[2] Stress has also rightly been placed on the social and economic conditions which fostered British commercial and industrial growth at this period—a rapidly improving system of land and water communications, the existence since the Act of Union with Scotland of a large area of internal free trade, adequate port facilities and the existence in Britain, and nowhere else in Europe, of a capitalistic and

---

[1] For a brilliant analysis of the social structure of the French nobility at this period see M. Reinhard's article, 'Élite et Noblesse dans la seconde moitié du XVIIIe siècle', *Revue d'Histoire Moderne et Contemporaine*, vol. III (1956), pp. 5–37.
[2] Cf. E. J. Hobsbawm's *The Age of Revolution, Europe 1789–1848* (London, 1962), ch. II.

scientific form of agriculture already equipped to support a rapidly rising urban population, sufficiently profitable not to absorb entirely all the capital it attracted from the world of commerce and drastic enough in its effects on the rural population to provide industry with its needed reserves of labour.[1] Already by 1790 the social structure of Britain was visibly changing into that urbanised and industrialised community which came into being during the next half-century. Even by 1793, however, the growth of the factory system—even in the textile industry—was still in its early stages. The industrial revolution had begun, but had not yet swung into its full momentum.

In most regions of continental Europe outside the sphere of the Atlantic community, the most pronounced political tendency of the period 1763–89 was towards systems of government traditionally known as 'Enlightened Despotism'. Though some historians have questioned the usefulness of this label, owing to its ambiguity, there would seem as yet no need to abandon the description as an outworn and meaningless term of art.[2] What was distinctive about late eighteenth-century continental 'despotism' was that it was based on new theoretical justifications of absolute monarchy, that it employed new administrative techniques and showed some inclination to allow its policies of reform, if not to be shaped, at least to be coloured, by the secular attitudes and the social and economic theories of the European Enlightenment.[3]

Most European sovereigns (or their ministers) were at this period concerned to stimulate the economic growth of their countries in order to maximise their military strength, some wished to achieve the greater administrative cohesion of their dominions by rationalising or abolishing the complex, overlapping and retrograde provincial jurisdictions, which had survived from medieval times. Yet others were moved to seek a solution for the problem of a resurgent, and sometimes anarchical, nobility either in an effective co-partnership in government or in a resolute autocracy. Such aims were severely practical and far from novel, but the methods and policies of the 'Enlightened Despots' were related to contemporary needs and can hardly be understood except in the context of eighteenth-century rationalism, the prevalent preoccupation with theories of natural law and the not wholly altruistic concern of rulers to promote the moral and material welfare of their subjects.

The new concepts of absolutism propounded at this time, to replace the

[1] For the role of English landlords in industrial development (particularly in mining, transport and iron) see ch. VIII of G. E. Mingay's *English Landed Society in the Eighteenth Century* (London, 1963).

[2] The most recent interpretation is by F. Hartung, *Enlightened Despotism*, Historical Association pamphlet (G. 36) (London, 1957)—an English translation of his article in *Historische Zeitschrift*, vol. 180 (1955).

[3] I follow here, in part, the 'working definition' of the concept suggested by Dr J. M. Roberts in his study of 'Enlightened Despotism in Italy' in the symposium *Art and Ideas in Eighteenth-century Italy* (Rome, 1960), pp. 26–7.

discredited notion of divine right, were derived from two main sources—the contractual theory of Locke and the political theories of the Physiocrats. The classical formulation of the theory of enlightened despotism was that given by Frederick the Great in his *Essai sur les Formes de Gouvernement et sur les Devoirs des Souverains*. In this brief work, privately printed for Voltaire and other friends in 1771, the contractual view of monarchy was clearly implied and the obligations of the ruler to his subjects explicitly stated.[1] 'In order that the sovereign should never deviate from these responsibilities', Frederick concluded, 'he should remember that he is a man like the least of his subjects; if he is the first magistrate, the first general, the first financier, the first minister of the community, this is not in order that he should merely symbolise but actually discharge these duties. He is only the first servant of the state, obliged to act with integrity, wisdom and complete disinterestedness as if, at any moment, he were bound to render an account of his administration to his fellow-citizens.'[2] The other source of the new doctrine of absolutism was the physiocratic conception of 'legal despotism'.[3] Evading the full rigours of the social contract, the earlier Physiocrats found a new intellectual sanction for absolute, but not despotic, monarchy, in its functional character. These functions were identified with the defence of liberty and property. In order that the sovereign should be able to fulfil these functions effectively, it was considered that he should possess both legislative and executive powers. In his legislative capacity, however, the sovereign was to be guided by consultative assemblies of elected landowners and confined to the task of 'declaring' and embodying in positive laws the immutable principles of the natural economic order. In practice this meant that the Physiocrats wished to exclude the monarch from interference in the free play of economic forces, and that he should be confined within his 'legitimate' functions by an independent magistracy. It is hardly surprising that few monarchs, with the possible exception of the Emperor Leopold II, were at all impressed with such notions—though Catherine II of Russia in her *Instruction* to the Legislative Commission of 1767 also made plain her rejection of Montesquieu's doctrine of the separation of powers.

In their efforts to modernise the machinery of government the Enlightened Despots resorted to administrative improvements of a quasi-technical character. Documents and records hitherto often regarded as the private property of ministers and officials were accumulated in public archives and used for statistical and planning purposes. Officials who had formerly been dependent on fees, perquisites and the interest on venal

---

[1] *Œuvres*, vol. IX, pp. 195–210.
[2] *Ibid.* p. 208. The use of the word 'citizens' rather than 'subjects' is significant.
[3] L. P. May, 'Despotisme légal et despotisme éclairé d'après Le Mercier de la Rivière', *Bulletin of the International Committee of Historical Sciences*, vol. IX (1937), pp. 56–67.

offices were now increasingly paid fixed salaries from the central treasury. In the interest of economy sinecures and court pensions were pruned and the auditing of public accounts, traditionally used as a judicial check on the integrity of officials, was now expedited and used to reveal the current position of state revenue and expenditure. Systems of treasury and budgetary control were devised. Censuses of population were put in hand, cadastral surveys were undertaken to facilitate fiscal reform, newspapers, foreign and domestic, were utilized as sources of intelligence and technological, agricultural and scientific knowledge was systematically deployed in the service of governments.[1] Forward economic planning, though in its infancy, and resorted to only in emergencies, had at last arrived.[2]

Some of the difficulty in accepting 'enlightened despotism' as a valid or credible political concept has arisen from scepticism about the sincerity of the public professions of autocratic rulers, such as Frederick II or Catherine II, who in private ridiculed as Utopian the 'enlightened' projects of their philosophic confidants and advisers. The 'Enlightenment' of eighteenth-century sovereigns has thus often been equated with specious literary propaganda intended to secure the approval of the educated classes in other countries for systems of government which, in practice, still resorted to the use of repressive censorship, the secret police and arbitrary imprisonment. This can hardly be denied. The 'Enlightenment' which affected the reforming policies of these monarchs was, however, of a different character from what is actually implied when their sponsors are described, inaccurately, as 'philosopher-kings' or as the crowned disciples of the great European intellectual figures. These monarchs showed themselves not so much secular as neutral in their policies of toleration and anti-curialist in their ecclesiastical reforms; their social improvements were inspired partly by humanitarian as well as by utilitarian motives, and their fiscal and commercial policies were often abreast of the latest developments in economic thought.[3] In these respects at least the autocracies of this period were cautiously progressive and 'enlightened' in no pejorative sense. If both Frederick and Catherine were conservative, or even medieval, in the rigidity of their social sympathies, and if neither ventured to tamper with the feudal régime, this was due to their recognition that their autocracies were still dependent on the co-operation and support of their privileged orders. The fate of those who did experiment with radical or revolutionary notions was exemplified in the tragedy of Joseph II. In claiming to make 'philosophy' the legislator of his domi-

[1] See below, ch. xx, pp. 566–7.
[2] The most interesting example of this was the five-year plan (1787–92) submitted by Brienne to the French Assembly of Notables as a way of restoring financial equilibrium and of postponing the meeting of the Estates General. J. Egret, *La Pré-Révolution Française, 1787–1788* (Paris, 1962), pp. 179–85.
[3] For physiocratic and cameralist economic theory see below, ch. ii, pp. 47–54.

nions, Joseph betrayed the true creed of the 'enlightened despots', which was empirical rather than doctrinaire.

The most significant consequences of 'enlightened' reform in Europe were a growing tension in church–state relations, further progress towards the codification and modernisation of civil and criminal law and, in central Germany, increasing public criticism of the social and political pretensions of the nobility, coupled with demands for the mitigation of absolutist government.

The crisis in the relations of church and state was itself the result of the assertion of lay sovereignty in the field of ecclesiastical reform and of the steady development of anti-curialist opinion in Catholic countries. 'Josephism' in Austria drew strength from the cult of Febronianism in the ecclesiastical politics of the Holy Roman Empire, but it was also, to some extent, a legacy from Maria Theresa.[1] In Spain and Italy the historic claims of Regalism were fortified by the spread of eighteenth-century 'political' Jansenism. Both phenomena, however, reflected the same general tendency in Catholic countries towards monarchical and episcopal independence of the Holy See and the same determination that the church itself should contribute to social and economic development. Anti-curialist sentiment achieved its most striking victory in the expulsion of the Jesuits from Portugal, France and Spain between 1759 and 1767 and the dissolution of the order in July 1773, imposed on Clement XIV by the united pressure of the Bourbon princes.[2] In the Habsburg territories toleration for non-Catholics, state-controlled general seminaries, the suppression of the contemplative orders and a replanning of the areas of ecclesiastical administration; in Spain the restriction of the powers of the Inquisition, royal control over episcopal appointments and the emancipation of the universities from clerical control; in Italy itself the sequestration of church land, legislation forbidding mortmain and clerical taxation, and the limitation of the right of sanctuary—all these were reforms imposed by rulers determined to assert their sovereignty against a recalcitrant but powerless papacy.[3] Such were the precedents which, when followed by the Constituent Assembly in revolutionary France, were to produce religious schism in the Gallican church.

The movement towards the codification of law was less an illustration of the progress of humanitarian enlightenment than of the continued emphasis on the supremacy of the state. The Frederician code of 1794, besides embracing the whole field of civil, criminal and administrative law, also redefined the unique position of the sovereign as the sole representative of the state and gave further legal sanction to the social

---

[1] For Febronianism see vol. VII, pp. 21–2.
[2] See below, ch. XIII(2), p. 391.
[3] For the relations of Pope Pius VI with the enlightened despots see ch. II of E. E. Y. Hales, *Revolution and Papacy, 1769–1846* (London, 1960).

and political ascendancy of the nobility.[1] This organic fusion of Roman and Germanic law—the work of the enlightened Silesian jurist Suarez—was applied to the whole complex of the Prussian dominions. It might, without undue injustice, be described as a socially retrograde essay in state-building. In Russia it was not the law itself which was codified, but rather the privileges of the nobility.[2] In the Habsburg dominions the first part of a new civil code, published in 1786, abolished, with certain exceptions, the principle of primogeniture in the law of inheritance, and by instituting civil marriage with the possibility of divorce, enlarged still further the quarrel with the papacy. In 1787 a penal code, reflecting the influence of Beccaria, confirmed the abolition of both torture and capital punishment and mitigated the severe and inhuman punishments of the sixteenth century, which had been largely perpetuated in an earlier code of 1768—the appropriately named *Nemesis Theresiana*.[3]

Recent studies of the impact of enlightened despotism in central Germany have revealed the growth of powerful movements of public opinion directed against the rigidity of the social structure in Prussia, against the retreat from the reforming policies of Joseph II and the repressive activities of the Austrian secret police.[4] One of the unforeseen consequences of enlightened despotism in Austria and Hungary was the political awakening of the Fourth Estate of peasants, students and urban working class, who had been alienated by the fiscal and military burdens of the Turkish war of 1787 and by Joseph II's interference with traditional religious practices. These unprivileged classes were encouraged by the reforms of Joseph II to hanker for that complete social and political emancipation which the emperor had never intended, but which was part of the new gospel of the French revolutionaries.[5]

The attempts of Joseph II to renovate the administrative, legal and social institutions of his dominions, regardless of the susceptibilities and privileges of the nobility, indicated that the moment of greatest danger for the absolutist régimes of Europe would ensue when radical policies of reform were initiated from above. This danger was revealed on a greater scale in the France of Louis XVI, for the revolution that was to overthrow the Bourbon monarchy and to uproot the surviving traces of feudalism in the most populous state of Europe was itself precipitated by reform projects inspired by motives analogous to those of the Enlightened Despots. The study of that revolution, so complex and so far-reaching in its consequences for France and the modern world, has in the last

[1] For Tocqueville's famous analysis of the Code see *L'Ancien Régime et la Révolution*, *Œuvres Complètes*, ed. J. P. Mayer, vol. II (Paris, 1952), pp. 268–71.
[2] For Catherine II's charter of the nobility, 1785, see below, ch. XI, p. 316.
[3] H. Kretschmayr, *Maria Theresia* (Gotha, 1925), p. 187.
[4] H. Brunschwig, *La crise de l'État Prussien à la fin du XVIIIe siècle* (Paris, 1947), and E. Wangermann, *From Joseph II to the Jacobin Trials* (Oxford, 1957).
[5] See below, ch. X, pp. 300–1.

generation attained new dimensions of significance at the hands of scholars who have sought to reinterpret it from the angle of the most dynamic of its participants—the peasantry and urban *sans-culottes*. Some of the findings of these scholars and a survey of the diverse interpretations placed by historians on the larger significance of this cataclysmic upheaval are contained in the later chapters of this volume.[1]

The financial, constitutional and economic problems of the *ancien régime* had for long demanded drastic treatment and when at last, in 1787–8, Calonne and his successor Brienne provided solutions which might, if applied earlier, have averted collapse, the recalcitrance and disunion of the privileged orders provoked an unparalleled crisis of authority. Reform had then to be entrusted, not to a hand-picked quasi-representative body of interested Notables, but to a popularly elected Estates General. The first conquest of the revolution in the spring of 1789 was the crucial transformation of this out-worn institution into the National Assembly endowed with the constituent power and full political sovereignty. The second was the vindication of the assembly's authority, against threats of its forcible dissolution, by the storming of the Bastille. The other 'conquests' of 1789 followed—the partial overthrow of the feudal régime on the night of 4 August, the imperishable Declaration of the Rights of Man and of the Citizen and the final removal of the remaining obstacles to reform by the October days.[2]

By that early date, as Burke realised, the pattern of revolutionary change in France had been established, for though the 'principles of 1789' had been elaborated by the bourgeois members of the National Assembly, and though the construction of the new order was their achievement, it was the direct intervention of the masses in politics which had proved decisive in the struggle with reaction. This pattern was to be repeated throughout the successive phases of a revolution that was, until Thermidor, to move steadily towards the left and it is in this sense that the study of the peasant insurrections of the period and of the activities and crowd psychology of the Parisian working class has proved so significant.[3] The main motivation of mass intervention in revolutionary politics was economic—peasant impatience with the failure of the Constituent Assembly 'totally' to demolish the economic foundations of 'feudalism', the concern of the town populations for adequate and cheap supplies of the staple popular diet—bread, the efforts of the workers in Paris to secure minimum daily wages and, from 1792 onwards, anxiety at the rising cost of living under the stress of inflation and the desire to secure official price control of the articles of common consumption. Sometimes it was the

---

[1] See below, chs. xxi–xxiv.   [2] Ch. xxiii below.
[3] The main pioneer in this respect was the late Professor G. Lefebvre with his definitive studies of *Les Paysans du Nord pendant la Révolution française*, 2 vols. (Paris, 1924), and *La Grande Peur de 1789* (Paris, 1932).

narrow exclusiveness of bourgeois legislation which helped to precipitate revolutionary *journées*—the denial of the franchise to 'passive' citizens, the exclusion of manual workers from the National Guard or the restrictions placed on the right of collective petitioning. On other occasions revolutionary crowds were clearly incited by radical leaders, journalists and popular clubs to take sides on the great political issues of the day—to support the claims of the Third Estate in the Estates General, to agitate against an absolute royal veto, to throw their weight behind the republican petitions of the Cordelier club after the failure of the king's flight, to demonstrate in favour of the Brissotin war policy or of Jacobin pressure for the deposition and execution of Louis XVI.[1] Popular rumours and collective fears—such as those provoked by the recurrent counter-revolutionary plots of the aristocracy, by the subversive activities of imaginary 'brigands', by the engrossment of food supplies by rich speculators, and by 'fifth-column' intrigue at the height of the Prussian invasion also provided powerful stimuli to mass unrest. The response was the prolongation of radical disturbances in town and country and their culmination in the direct democracy of the Parisian sections in 1792-3 and in the punitive aspects of the September massacres.

The indirect political consequences of such mass revolutionary activity were far-reaching. It led, firstly, to repeated schisms in the ranks of the 'patriotic' leadership of the revolutionary assemblies—the earliest being the secession of Mounier and the Moderates from the Constituent Assembly and the conversion of Mirabeau into a crypto-royalist after the October days of 1789. More important shifts to the right were those of the 'constitutional' or Feuillant group after the 'massacre' of the Champ de Mars in July 1791 and of the Brissotin or Girondin connection after the overthrow of the monarchy. These defections to moderate and then to reactionary policies were mainly determined by apprehensions of the social and economic consequences of political radicalism. Those middle-class democrats in the Convention, who in order to retain the political support of the Parisian *sans-culottes*, were prepared to accept their economic demands, were the Jacobins.[2] Secondly, fears of the increasing influence wielded in Paris by the Jacobin and popular clubs prompted their opponents to think in terms of counter-revolution mounted by a military dictatorship. Narbonne, Lafayette and Dumouriez all conceived such plans and aspired to be their executants.[3] These occult ambitions helped to speed France down the path to war with Austria in the spring of 1792, and, after Dumouriez's treason in 1793, brought her near to total defeat. Thirdly, revolutionary France, as the home of Jacobin extremism

---

[1] G. Rudé, *The Crowd in the French Revolution* (Oxford, 1959), *passim*.
[2] For the repetition of these political shifts in the pattern of nineteenth-century revolutions see E. J. Hobsbawm, *The Age of Revolution: Europe from 1789 to 1848* (London, 1962), p. 62.   [3] See below, ch. xxiv, pp. 702-3.

and the Terror, not only drew upon itself the enmity of the autocratic monarchies of Europe, it alienated many of its initial supporters and sympathisers in Britain and it subjected suspected radicals everywhere to witch-hunts and state trials. The spectre of Jacobinism continued to haunt many parts of Europe and America until well into the following century.

Such extremes, it is fair to add, had never been contemplated by those liberal aristocrats and middle-class reformers who had wrested the political initiative from the privileged orders even before the meeting of the Estates General. After the initial popular revolts of 1789 even the most liberal members of the 'patriotic party' wished to preserve the sanctity of private property however tainted with 'feudalism', to retain the social status and honorific privileges of the nobility and clerical control over large areas of the public services. When, however, Louis XVI identified his interests with those of the emigrant nobility and invoked the assistance of foreign powers, Brissotin leaders in the Legislative Assembly determined to confiscate the estates of the *émigrés* and to extirpate clerical influence. The continuance of royal treason after the outbreak of war with Austria enabled Robespierre to invoke the assistance of the Parisian *sectionnaires* and of the provincial *fédérés* in the overthrow of the monarchy. With the advent of universal suffrage and the republic, France at last attained the status of a modern democracy.

In the last resort, however, it was not the lessons drawn by subsequent generations of politicians from the course taken by the revolution, nor the radicalism of its political and social experiments, but rather the ecumenical appeal of its ideology, which was so powerfully to influence the future. Popular sovereignty was to result in the ideals of the lay state, political and social equality in the extinction of feudal and aristocratic privilege, the doctrine of self-determination and the cult of *la patrie* were to give a new and formidable extension to nationalism in the nineteenth and to anti-colonialism in the twentieth century.[1] Some observers have even seen in the Jacobin dictatorship and the social democracy of the year II the remote origins of modern totalitarianism.[2]

The rise of the United States of America and the decline and fall of the *ancien régime* in Europe were accompanied by the revelation of new intellectual, cultural and scientific horizons, which became more distinct as the *siècle des lumières* drew towards its close. In these respects— as in others—the age was one of transition—for, if it still drew inspiration from the republican ideals and aesthetic glories of the ancient world, it was beginning to react against the formalism and rationalism of the earlier Enlightenment and in art, music and literature was reaching out

[1] G. Lefebvre, 'La Révolution française dans l'histoire du monde', *Études sur la Révolution Française* (Paris, 1954), pp. 315–26.
[2] J. L. Talmon, *The Origins of Totalitarian Democracy* (1952).

towards the Romanticism of the future.[1] Here the pervading influences were those of Neoclassicism and of Rousseau. In the field of metaphysical inquiry the transcendental philosophy of Kant brought about yet another and more profound revolution by indicating the boundaries of human reason and by reconciling for the first time the opposing intellectual principles of the rationalists and empiricists.[2] Equally, if not more significant, however, was the renewal of the scientific impulse, which had slackened in the first half of the century, but which now yielded new discoveries of fundamental importance in the physical sciences and in man's knowledge of the material universe.[3]

[1] See below chs. III and IV.   [2] Ch. III.   [3] See below, ch. V.

CHAPTER II

POPULATION, COMMERCE AND ECONOMIC IDEAS

I. POPULATION GROWTH

THE estimates of European population in the eighteenth century are subject to a very wide margin of error; direct censuses were few and imperfect, and most of the figures are derived from enumerations of households, which, besides being incomplete, can be translated into total population only by making necessarily arbitrary assumptions about the size of households. While such estimates give a reasonably reliable indication of the approximate size of a country's population, they are a poor guide to the rates of growth within a country, since they reflect changes in administrative efficiency, and their general effect is probably to exaggerate the speed with which population was increasing. There can, nevertheless, be little doubt that population was growing in most parts of Europe in the eighteenth century and that, for Europe as a whole, it was growing more rapidly after 1760 than before.[1]

It is natural in retrospect to interpret this increase of population as the first stage of the sustained and cumulative increase which has marked the last two hundred years, and to seek an explanation in the operation of new influences, such as higher standards of living or improvements in medicine and public health. It should be observed, however, that the population growth in the second half of the century was rapid only in certain parts of Scandinavia and the Low Countries, in Russia, England and Wales and Ireland, and in parts of Germany. Even in these countries the rate of growth in the later eighteenth century was probably not more than 1 per cent per annum except in Russia, certain Prussian provinces, Finland and Ireland. In Spain, Italy, France and probably in Switzerland, the rates of increase were around or below 0·5 per cent per annum, a rate by no means uncommon in earlier periods— Gregory King, for example, estimated that the population of England and Wales was increasing at 0·4 per cent per annum in the later seventeenth century.

Moreover, in certain of the areas where population was increasing most rapidly in the later eighteenth century, rapid growth was of long standing; in parts of Germany, population had been increasing rapidly since the end of the Thirty Years War and in Russia from the second quarter of the

---

[1] A collection of estimates, of different degrees of reliability, is given in the appendix (p. 715). The figures for some areas, Hungary in particular, are influenced by migration and not only by natural increase.

eighteenth century. In such areas, the population growth of the later eighteenth century did not represent a sudden ascent from a plateau. In Sweden and Finland, population actually increased more rapidly in the two decades after the cessation of the Northern War than it did in the later half of the century. So that though there was an acceleration of growth, especially evident in England and Wales and in Ireland, this was by no means universal. What needs to be explained is not only the acceleration of growth in certain areas in the later eighteenth century but the existence and persistence of higher rates of growth in some areas than in others.

We owe to Malthus the distinction between the preventive and the positive checks on population—deferment or avoidance of marriage on the one hand, and war, famine and disease on the other. In most parts of western Europe before the industrial revolution preventive checks were operative. Responsibility for the care of children rested upon the parents, as opposed to an extended family or kinship group, and, in deciding whether or when to marry, people were influenced by their ability to acquire the means of establishing a separate household. Where it was easy to acquire the means to support a family, marriage was earlier and celibacy less common; where conditions were difficult men tended to postpone marriage or not to marry at all. Thus conventions about marriage tended in the long run to accommodate themselves to the available resources in such a way as to prevent a too rapid growth of population. If population grew in excess of the land and agricultural equipment available, the younger sons of the peasants found it less easy to acquire and stock a farm of their own, and became farm hands, domestic servants or soldiers.

Whether these controls on marriage were reinforced by the limitation of births within marriage is not known. Abortion and primitive techniques of contraception have been practised in all societies, but from the tone of contemporary comment it is probable that their use in this period was rarely widespread enough to reduce fertility significantly, except in France; elsewhere they were resorted to principally in exceptional circumstances, such as years of famine.

Population was also periodically checked by visitations of war, famine and disease. In the absence of adequate supplies of fertiliser and efficient methods of drainage, the fluctuations in the yield of food crops were much greater than at present, and though the direct losses from famine were small in relation to total deaths, a bad harvest tended to intensify the effects of disease. Similarly, though the direct casualties of war were small compared with the losses by epidemics, the movement of troops and the disruption of communications made society more vulnerable to epidemics. In years of exceptionally high mortality from these causes a substantial amount of population growth might be eliminated, especially where, as M. Goubert has suggested for the Beauvais region, mortality was particularly severe, not among the very old and the very young, but among young adults and children above the age of five.[1]

According to Malthus' original view, set out in the first edition of his *Essay on Population* (1798), famine and disease were the penalties imposed upon a population which grew more rapidly than the means of subsistence. The high death-rates were the consequence of malnutrition and over-crowding as the result of too high birth-rates. In Sweden and England, however, which have been examined in detail, it does not seem likely that the high mortality was closely related to population pressure. The frequency and severity of harvest failure were determined by climate rather than by the proportion of people to resources; and, though the urban death-rate was sensitive to fluctuations in the price of grain and the poorer quarters more sensitive than the well-to-do, bad harvests were not often sufficient by themselves to cause a substantial and widespread rise in death-rates. The years of exceptionally high mortality were principally due to epidemic diseases, often accompanied by unusual activity of the diseases endemic to an area. Neither the occurrence of epidemics nor the capacity of the population to resist them were closely related to food supplies, and though certain endemic diseases, such as tuberculosis, may have been influenced by the level of nutrition, the character and virulence of the most deadly endemic diseases was determined by the epidemio-logical factors other than food supply—by climate, particularly tempera-ture and rainfall, and by the extent of urbanisation. At least in England and Sweden, therefore, the preventive checks seem to have adjusted population growth to the supply of land and equipment at a standard of living which, while extremely low by modern standards, was sufficiently above the bare minimum to avoid major famines, and outbreaks of disease directly induced by famine. High death-rates were not a conse-quence of high birth-rates; it would probably be more true to say that the level of the death-rate was high for reasons independent of the food-supply, and that, in the long run, births accommodated themselves to this level, by changes in the age at marriage and in celibacy. Malthus himself, in his later writings, thought this was generally true of those parts of Europe which had been long settled: 'In almost all the more improved countries of modern Europe', he wrote, 'the principal check which at present keeps the population down to the actual level of the means of subsistence is the prudential restraint on marriage.'

These conclusions are not equally true of all parts of western Europe; the responsibility for keeping population in line with resources was not distributed between the preventive and the positive checks in the same proportion in all parts of the Continent. The preventive check was most effective where conventions about the standard of living held to warrant

[1] P. Goubert, 'En Beauvaisis: Problèmes démographiques du XVIIe siècle', in *Annales. Économies, Sociétés, Civilisations*, vol. VII (1952).

marriage were stronger than conventions about the age at marriage. But in some areas, marriage habits which developed when opportunities were abundant did not adjust themselves to the subsequent narrowing of these opportunities. Where, as a result, growth seriously encroached on living-standards, there was too small a margin to cushion the effects of temporary spurts of population or a run of bad harvests. In such circumstances death-rates were more sensitive to harvest deficiency, and the character and incidence of endemic disease were more directly influenced by living-standards. The population of Ireland, for example, was much more vulnerable to poor harvests than the English; and in the Electorate of Saxony the bad years 1770–2 caused such heavy mortality that the population in 1780 was no higher than it had been in 1744.

Whatever the causes of the variations in the death-rate from one country to another, it seems probable that the main differences between the countries where population growth was normally rapid and those where it was slow lay in the level of their birth-rates; and while differences in their birth-rates may have reflected physiology and nutrition they were most often due to differences in the age at marriage and the extent of celibacy. The area of most spectacular growth—as high as 3 per cent per annum—was North America where abundant land afforded opportunities for early marriage. The rapid growth of population in Russia also reflects frontier conditions, accentuated by the weakness of the preventive checks. For the household in Russia consisted of a number of families, and marriage did not involve the setting up of a separate household; moreover the peasant land was periodically redistributed in accordance with the working strength or number of 'eaters' in each family, a practice which developed partly because of increasing population but which also promoted that increase by rewarding rather than, as was often the case in the West, penalising the larger families. In Finland, also, and the eastern parts of Prussia, the high rates of growth reflect the opportunities represented by sparsely populated regions.

The rate of growth in Finland was much more rapid than in the rest of Scandinavia, and the explanation of this can be seen from the following table.

	Birth-rate (%)	Death-rate (%)	Natural increase (%)
Denmark	31·0	28·2	2·8
Norway	32·4	25·0	7·4
Sweden	33·6	27·4	6·2
Finland	41·3	28·1	13·2

The evidence for the other areas of rapid growth is necessarily more circumstantial. The relatively high rate of growth in Ireland even before the acceleration in the closing decades of the century, was probably also due to early marriage and high nuptuality; for the Irish had a reputation of long-standing for marrying, as Petty said, 'upon the first capacity'.

By contrast, the areas where population growth was slowest were those where the means for establishing new households were most restricted, where there were few opportunities outside agriculture and where the opportunities in agriculture were limited by scarcity of land and the prevalence of large estates. Thus in Spain, while the population of Austurias, Galicia and Valencia more than doubled in the course of the century, Estremadura with its many latifundia, and oppressed with the Mesta, was as sparsely populated at the end of the century as at the beginning; and the population of the country as a whole rose by only 50 per cent. The Spanish writer Sarmiento ascribed the 'depopulation' of his country not only to clerical celibacy but to the high proportion of unmarried among the laity, who were unable to maintain a family because of the maldistribution of agricultural property; and the fact that only just over 20 per cent of the population between the ages of sixteen and twenty-five were married in the census of 1768 suggests that the explanation was correct.[1]

In Italy the rate of increase for the country as a whole was only about 0·4 per cent per annum, and it was slowest in Tuscany and the Po valley where population was already densest and the potentialities of intensive agriculture fully exploited. The possibilities of setting up a separate household were restricted, and marriage was deferred; in eighteenth-century Venice the age at first marriage was between 29·9 and 31·7 years for men and between 28·0 and 29·8 years for women. The situation in Austria is more obscure for it included provinces like Upper and Lower Austria and Bohemia which were well populated, and provinces such as Styria and Carinthia which were only half as densely populated. The sparse population of the latter provinces cannot be explained entirely by the nature of the soil, and it has been attributed to the heavy pressure of *Grundherrschaft* and *Gutsherrschaft* on the peasantry and to the existence of a rural proletariat who married late or not at all, partly because they were too poor to maintain a family, and partly because the landlords would not allow men without means to marry.[2] But similar social institutions in Prussia were not incompatible with a very rapid increase of population, and the probable explanation of the contrasting demographic history of the northern and southern frontier regions of Europe is that the latter were not well situated to become large exporters of foodstuffs and were therefore incapable of supporting a rapid growth of population.

In France, according to Levasseur's estimates, population increased between 1770 and 1789 at less than 0·5 per cent per annum and the 1770s saw the beginning of a continuous fall in fertility, brought about not by a change in the age of marriage or in the proportion of people marrying

---

[1] D. Ortiz, *La sociedad española en el siglo XVIII* (Madrid, 1955), pp. 58–61.

[2] K. Schünemann, *Österreichs Bevölkerungspolitik unter Maria Theresia* (Berlin, 1935), pp. 42 ff.

but by control of births within marriage. The desire to limit births is to be associated with the need among the peasantry to protect their holdings against the threat of morcellation as the result of population increase where there were no large reserves of land and no rapid expansion of opportunities outside agriculture. Already in the later eighteenth century the growth of population had led to an increase in the practice of equal division of the family property, a method of providing for children resorted to only when openings outside the family holding are inadequate and which in itself reinforces the need to have small families.

The broad differences in population growth between countries seem therefore to have been principally due to differences in births. But it does not follow that the same agency was responsible for the acceleration evident in certain countries in the later part of the century.

This acceleration was not necessarily due to the operation of entirely new influences. It is probable that in most parts of Europe outside the great towns there was an excess of births over deaths in a year which was free from epidemics and war and in which the yield of the harvest was normal. Any run of years which was fortunate in these respects was therefore likely to enjoy an increase of population. The second half of the eighteenth century seems to have been such a period. The fluctuations in the number of deaths were less violent in the eighteenth century than in the seventeenth, and less violent in the second half of the eighteenth than in the first. The 1720s and 1730s were in most parts of Europe unhealthy decades; there was an outbreak of the plague in the 1720s; in the 1730s a severe influenza pandemic swept across the western hemisphere: and there were also outbreaks of smallpox, typhus, typhoid and dysentery. In the later decades of the century by contrast there were long periods free from serious visitations of disease, in the south as well as in the north of Europe. In Spain, for example, though malaria remained a serious endemic disease in the rural areas, rising to the proportions of an epidemic in 1784–7 and 1790–2, the main epidemics in the latter part of the century were confined to the towns: while the epidemic of 1709 had repercussions throughout the country, that of 1800 was concentrated in Cadiz, Seville and their neighbourhood.

Moreover the years of exceptionally high mortality, though they temporarily reduced the growth of population, might ultimately produce an age structure which was favourable to a rapid spurt of population. In the years of epidemics not only did deaths rise but marriages were deferred; and not only were marriages deferred, and the births which they would have produced, but the births to existing marriages also fell, partly because marriages were broken by death and partly because the conditions which produced the high mortality were unfavourable to conception. But when the causes of high mortality had passed, there was a large increase in the number of births; the deferred marriages were now contracted and many young people were able to marry earlier than had been customary because they succeeded to holdings or occupations earlier than would otherwise have been the case. The stock of marriages depleted by the high mortality was now replenished by new and more fertile marriages. These bulges of births produced very marked fluctuations of age composition, a wave-like effect as the bulge moved forward through time. A generation or so after such a bulge, the population contained an abnormally high proportion of young adults. If then conditions happened to be unusually favourable to marriage, the coincidence of a favourable age composition and earlier marriage was capable of producing for a decade or more a sharp burst of population.

Part of the more rapid growth of English population in the later eighteenth century may be explained in these terms. The smallpox epidemic of 1725–9 was followed by a great surge of births in the 1730s and some twenty-five years later the population contained an unusually high proportion of young adults, and other conditions were favourable to marriage. There was therefore a peak in marriages around 1760 which accounts for some of the population increase in the 1760s and 1770s. From similar causes there were surges of population growth in Sweden from 1750 to 1765, 1774 to 1780 and 1791 to 1798.

The traditional mechanisms of population change are capable, therefore, of explaining much of the more rapid rise of population in the later eighteenth century. Whether entirely new influences were operating and the extent and nature of such influences is still in dispute. Does the lower mortality of the period represent a permanent improvement, or was it simply due to the long interval of peace after 1763, a favourable conjunction of the weather and a fortuitous fall in the frequency of epidemics? The disappearance of the bubonic plague from Europe—the last serious outbreak was in Provence in 1721—certainly represented a permanent gain; but though the plague had caused heavy mortality wherever it had occurred, the outbreaks had always been relatively infrequent and confined to limited areas, so that its disappearance did not contribute a great deal to the explanation of lower mortality. In France, it has been argued, infant mortality was falling at the end of the century; while mortality in the age-groups 5–14 and 15–24 was virtually stationary, that in the age-group 1–4 fell because of the almost complete disappearance of smallpox, which before 1789 had been responsible for about 30 per cent of the deaths in this group.[1] There was also some decline of deaths from smallpox in England, as the result of inoculation in the later eighteenth century and vaccination in the early decades of the nineteenth. But except in the case of smallpox there is no evidence of improvement in medical practice exerting a significant influence on the expectation of life;

[1] J. Bourgeois-Pichat, 'Évolution générale de la population française depuis le XVIIIe siècle', in *Population*, vol. VI (1951).

any increase in medical facilities was confined to the towns and did no more, and may have done less, than countervail the unfavourable effects of urbanisation on death-rates.

A new influence more likely to have had a significant effect on population growth is an improvement in food supply. It has been concluded from French evidence that the correlation between dearth and death was much less clearly marked between 1770 and 1789 than in the later seventeenth and early eighteenth centuries; and the harvests of 1770-2 and 1795 which were deficient in many parts of Europe seem to have had less marked effects on the death-rate than the bad harvests of 1709-10.[1] Any such diminution in the vulnerability of the European population to dearth in the later eighteenth century could not safely be attributed solely to improvements in food supply; bad harvests may have caused fewer deaths because the diseases likely to be exacerbated by shortage of food were less active for independent reasons. But it is possible that in some areas crop failures were fewer as a result of more favourable weather conditions and greater variety of crops and improvements in cultivation; and it is probable that improvements in the organisation in the trade in foodstuffs made it easier to alleviate harvest deficiencies, where local reserves were insufficient, by imports from the regions of surplus. For better nutrition and greater resistance to disease there is little evidence except in the poorer regions where the potato spread; increases in agricultural productivity were absorbed in supporting a larger population rather than in increasing consumption per head; though in the absence of improvements in agricultural productivity, population increase might have provoked the Malthusian positive checks in areas where living-standards were very low.

On balance it seems likely that, though lower mortality did to some extent represent the operation of new influences, it was for the most part the result of temporarily favourable conditions of a kind that occurred in earlier periods and was not the start of the sustained fall in the death-rate which has marked modern times. The death-rate in those areas for which evidence is available rose again in the early nineteenth century.

In some areas the acceleration of population growth in the later eighteenth century may have owed something to the relaxation of the prudential restraints on marriage. The increase of 40 per cent in the population of Brabant in a period of twenty-nine years—all the more remarkable an increase in the rural areas because the population of Brussels, Louvain and Antwerp increased by only 25 per cent and because the area was already among the most densely populated in Europe—reflects in part the favourable effects of expanding foreign trade and improving agriculture on the opportunities for marriage. In Ireland, it has been argued, the sub-

---

[1] C. E. Labrousse, *La Crise de l'Économie française à la fin de l'Ancien Régime* (Paris, 1944), p. 182.

division of existing holdings was facilitated by the spread of the potato and the shift from pasture to arable to meet the growing English demand for grain; and new land was also brought under cultivation. As a result the sons of peasant families found it easier in the later eighteenth century to acquire holdings and marry. In England the acceleration of economic growth after 1760 and particularly the increased demand for agricultural products possibly afforded inducements to marriage similar to those provided by abundant land in frontier regions. In England at least, the view that there were influences favourable to births has contemporary warrant. 'What is essentially necessary', wrote Malthus, 'to a rapid increase of population is a great and continued demand for labour.' Moreover, in the absence of any such favourable influences on the birth-rate, it might have been expected that an increase of population due to low mortality would have produced some corresponding fall in fertility of the sort which occurred in France but not in England. But the view that there were influences sustaining or stimulating the birth-rate has not yet been supported by detailed statistical evidence, and it remains an open question how far population increase of the later eighteenth century was a response to an increase in the ability of the economy to support life, and how far it was an independent development, absorbed without a fall in living-standards where it coincided with rapid economic development, but depressing living-standards where it occurred in stagnant economies.

2. TRADE

The pattern of trade

Before the application of steam to transport the cost of all types of carriage was very high, and therefore trade was small in relation to total output. Moreover, before the building of railways the costs of carriage were much lower by water than by land, so that much more trade was done between regions, even regions far apart, which were linked by sea or river than between regions, even regions of the same country, which were connected only by land. There was some long-distance trade in European products within Europe itself, for example the exchange at Leipzig of the industrial products of Saxony and Silesia for the primary products of eastern Europe, and a substantial trade in Zurich, Basle and Strasbourg which acted as intermediaries between Germany, Italy and southern France. But the main areas of trade were concentrated around the great seas— the Atlantic, the Mediterranean, the Baltic—and the main European trading cities were those which mediated the exchange of goods between the more densely settled areas of western and central Europe and the regions on the periphery.

The most important complex of trade was that between Europe and the Americas. The West Indies had a large surplus of products which were in demand in Europe, principally sugar, coffee and some minor products such as cotton, indigo, pimento and ginger. The hybrid colonies from Maryland to Carolina also had staple crops. The northern colonies had few staples of value in European markets, but a surplus of food and lumber. This distribution of national specialities made possible an elaborate system of exchanges. The exports of British manufactured goods to the southern mainland colonies roughly balanced British imports of primary products from this region. In her trade with the West Indies, Britain ran a substantial unfavourable balance of trade, offset to some extent by invisible payments, and with the northern mainland colonies a smaller, favourable, balance. The northern colonies covered the deficit in their trade with Britain partly by exports of provisions to the western Indies, and partly by a favourable balance with southern Europe; fish, lumber and wheat-products were exported to Spain and Portugal and sold for wine, salt and fruit, which was then shipped to England.

The Spanish and Portugese colonies in South America provided mainly bullion against manufactured goods. Though in law the trade of these areas was a monopoly of the mother-country, a large part of the trade was in fact conducted by the English and French. Most of the manufactured goods imported into Spain, Portugal and their colonies were supplied by England and France. These were partly paid for, in the case of English goods, by imports of wool, fruit and wine; but France and England both had a substantial favourable trade balance with the Iberian peninsula which was settled in bullion. Thus some part of the exports of English goods to North America were ultimately paid for by imports of bullion into England. The settlements of international balances in the international trade of the Atlantic area were never altogether smooth, and the heavy indebtedness of American merchants on the eve of the American Revolution perhaps suggests the presence of some long-term difficulties. But compared with most of the other principal trading areas the difficulties were limited. The European demand for primary products could, in the New World, ultimately be paid for in goods.

In the Far East, the great expansion of the seventeenth century had taken European traders into areas with a low propensity to import European goods. India, principally Bengal, exported to Britain cotton goods, silks, saltpetre, indigo, sugar, and rice and tea and some other products of the China trade. In return Britain exported principally cloth, but also lead, iron and copper. Though in absolute terms these exports were not insignificant, they were only about a third of the official value of Britain's East Indian imports. India, until the British were able to provide cheap cottons, was a reluctant market for European goods, and the same was true of the Dutch East Indies and of China. The balance of European trade with the East was therefore settled by the export of bullion

34

and by remittances of a political character, and in the case of China by the sale of Indian opium.

To a lesser extent, similar difficulties arose in the trade with the Middle and Near East. This trade consisted mainly of an exchange of the natural specialities of the Ottoman empire—textile raw materials (mainly cotton), grain, hides, oil and spices—against cloth and colonial goods; and, principally through the agency of the French, these natural specialities were distributed through northern Europe, though some went more directly through Salonica, Trieste, Venice and Genoa. In this case too there was a balance settled in bullion or coin.

The fourth great complex of trade was the Baltic. The countries bordering the Baltic formed the traditional granary of western Europe on which it drew particularly in years of deficient harvests; except for wheat, Danzig had lost its earlier predominance in this trade and the main area of export had shifted east. The Baltic also provided timber from Finland, Livonia, Estonia and Sweden—there was a very large increase of timber exported through the Sound after 1760—and iron, which came from Sweden and, to an increasing extent during this period, from Russia. Of the ships passing through the Sound in 1784 the major part (37 per cent) traded with German ports and the next largest (26 per cent) with Russia. The bulk of the exports went, initially at least, to England and Holland. Of the exports to Holland the major part were for distribution to other areas, but those to England were retained there. In return the English provided manufactured goods and some colonial goods, and the Mediterranean countries provided salt (French, Italian and some Portuguese), wine, herring, cloths, hides, colonial goods and, especially after 1740, some raw cotton and wool; from the 1740s onwards there was a very rapid increase in the Baltic import of colonial goods. Even so there was a residue, though small and diminishing, which had to be settled in bullion.

Long-distance trade has always consisted partly of an exchange of the natural specialities of one region with those of another, partly of an exchange of manufactures against natural specialities, and partly of an exchange of manufactures with manufactures. All three types of transaction were represented in this period. The trade between the Baltic and the Mediterranean was mainly of the first sort, the trade with America had a large element of the second. There was little trade of the third sort: there was an exchange of specialities between the more advanced areas themselves, and some exchange of western woollens against eastern linen, but probably not a great deal. In bulk and value the exchange of natural specialities was the most important, but the trades which had the greatest potentialities for the future were the exchanges of the manufactured goods of a small number of highly specialised regions against the natural specialities of the periphery. It is significant that English trade was already almost exclusively an exchange of manufactured goods for primary products.

In very broad outline the pattern of international trade was determined by relative costs; in certain branches, for example, the trade in grain, perhaps predominantly so. But in areas where the European countries had political control or influence, the distribution and character of trade was distorted by the various steps they took—navigation acts and monopoly companies—to ensure that the mother-country secured the principal advantages of the trade. There were also the barriers on trade in manufactured goods—for example, those imposed by the French and the English against each other and the various prohibitions on Indian calicoes.

The fact that the colonial powers attempted to maintain a monopoly in their colonial markets is of great economic importance; for the character of the markets which were secured to a country by its politics made a considerable difference to its development. Exactly how far the regulations of the various colonial systems were effective and how far they diverted trade from the channels in which it would otherwise have flowed it is difficult to say. Almost from the start the Spanish monopoly of colonial trade had been subject to heavy inroads, and as a result of the Seven Years War England enlarged her opportunities in the Caribbean areas and virtually eliminated the French as competitors in this region. From 1766 the British made a systematic attempt to establish the British West Indies as an entrepôt for trade with the Spanish colonial empire. From the passage of the first Free Ports Act in 1766, through successive emendations to the revisions of 1787 and 1805, they tried to foster trade between the British West Indies free ports and foreign plantations. The Spaniards attempted to withstand this pressure by relaxing the restrictions on Spaniards in their trade with Spanish America. By the Decree of Free Trade of 1778 Cadiz and Seville were deprived of their monopoly of this trade and all the major ports of Spain and of Central and South America were allowed to trade direct with one another.[1] This was an attempt, by allowing a large measure of free trade to Spanish subjects within the Spanish empire, to lower prices and so render them better able to meet the competition of foreign interlopers. The relaxation of restrictions did, in fact, stimulate a rapid expansion of trade with Spanish America, but it did not succeed in limiting the inroads of the English, who took an increasing share of the trade. At the close of the eighteenth century Spain's monopoly of her colonial trade was still complete in theory, except for the relaxations made to meet the special circumstances of Louisiana, but in practice, according to contemporary estimates, as much as 25 per cent of the trade was in the hands of foreigners. The attempt to maintain a monopoly failed simply because Spanish manufacturers and merchants could not meet the needs of the colonies.

[1] See below, ch. XIV, p. 401.

If the Spanish monopoly of colonial trade crumbled under external pressure, the British was broken by pressure from within. The monopoly which the British attempted to maintain with its colonies in the western hemisphere was much less rigorous than the Spanish. After 1730 the North American colonies were allowed to export rice and after 1739 sugar direct to the Mediterranean, and until the attempt after the Peace of Paris to tighten up the execution of the Acts of Trade and Navigation the old colonial system operated with some flexibility. Moreover, there was a natural complementarity between the economy of England and its colonial possessions. How far the regulations of the old colonial system distorted the pattern of trade is a debatable question. It is sometimes argued that the regulations made little difference to the trade of the British colonies because they coincided with the natural conditions of trade, and it is pointed out that the break-away of the American colonies did not substantially divert the course of Anglo-American trade. But 1783 did, in fact, make some difference. It has been estimated that before the war, if allowance be made for smuggling, some two-thirds to three-quarters of the trade of the American colonies had been within the empire; and that independence had reduced the imperial share of American exports to about one half, and the share of the British Isles from one half to a third.[1] Moreover, American independence certainly led to some decline in London's position as an entrepôt centre, especially for tobacco, although there were other economic forces also working in the same direction.

The argument from American experience is indeed a weak one. After 1783 England was, of course, the best source of supply on strictly economic grounds for most manufactured goods. This was much less true earlier in the century and there is some evidence that, in its early days, the old colonial system did direct demand along lines it would not have taken if left to its own volition. The fact that 1783 made relatively little difference to trade is partly a tribute to the strength of the commercial ties which had been created by the old colonial system; more than a century of regulation, it may reasonably be argued, had developed business links which tied England and the colonies together commercially even after the trade regulations ceased to apply.

One thing seems reasonably certain, that without the provision that certain enumerated colonial products had to be brought first to England, London would not have acquired as rapidly so preponderant a position in merchanting and finance. England was not the best natural entrepôt. Holland, for example, had considerable advantages: how strong can be seen from the hold she retained over the distribution on the Continent of Asian, African and American products, even when she had to acquire them in England. Germany, also, had considerable advantages; for

[1] H. Heaton, 'The American Trade', in *The Trade Winds* (London, 1948), ed. C. N. Parkinson, p. 196.

example, as soon as the navigation laws ceased to apply to America, Bremen became the entrepôt centre for hogshead tobacco and Hamburg established direct commercial contact with the U.S.A.

By the later eighteenth century the mere fact that England was importing, for her own consumption, much larger quantities of most colonial products than other countries gave her exceptional advantages in the entrepôt trade, for larger stocks were held, marketing facilities developed and knowledge of sources accumulated. But, had it not been for the regulations of the old colonial system, the process by which London became a great entrepôt centre would have been much slower, and since the customers who came to London in order to acquire their colonial goods tended to come also for their shipping and commercial finance, the regulations contributed also to its emergence as an international financial centre.

This period saw a further decline of the Dutch as providers of ships and merchanting services. They lost ground in both fields to the English. In the case of cloth, for example, the English share of shipping through the Sound rose significantly at the expense of the Dutch. The absolute volume of Dutch shipping through the Sound continued to increase until the 'sixties or 'seventies, but relatively they lost ground to Britain and the Scandinavian countries. The position of any middleman is precarious, since sooner or later the two parties he serves will tend to make direct contact with each other. It was not only English competition that faced the Dutch. There was a great extension of shipping by the Scandinavian powers themselves, particularly the Swedes. In the case of colonial goods the relative position of both Britain and Holland in the Baltic trade declined, and by 1771–80 other countries, particularly the Baltic countries themselves, carried nearly two-thirds of the imports through the Sound— the Swedish percentage for this decade nearly equals the English. In grain exports from the Baltic, which at the opening of the eighteenth century the Dutch had entirely dominated, it was the Scandinavians and the Balts who encroached in the eighteenth century rather than the English, whose ships had never been of great importance in this trade. In 1771–80 the Dutch had only 41 per cent of the total grain transport through the Sound. Inevitably in time other major staple centres for the distribution of colonial goods arose besides Amsterdam and London— Hamburg did an increasing amount of business after 1740 and in this period became the main intermediary in the growing grain trade from Archangel and the Baltic to England; with the outbreak of the revolutionary wars she took over much of the trade hitherto done by Amsterdam. France developed entrepôt centres for her own colonial trade. The Anglo-Dutch War of 1780–3 had bad effects on both Dutch and British shipping. The Dutch herring fishery declined in the eighteenth century, expelled from the Baltic not only by the Swedes, who in the second half of the century took a larger share of the trade, but by the rise of the herring trade in Göteborg.

There is nothing particularly surprising either about the inroads which the English made upon the Dutch, or about the initiative taken by the traders of Scandinavia and the Baltic. But one of the most curious features of the period is the failure of the French to develop a large mercantile marine. In 1767 of 6495 ships passing the Sound, 203 were bound to and 299 from French ports, but of these only ten were owned by Frenchmen. French shipping, despite the increase in French trade, was being driven out of a number of routes. The Dutch and English and, especially after 1740, the Swedes drove the French out of the trade with the northern countries. The explanation is simple: French freight rates were 20–30 per cent higher than the Danish or Dutch. French shipping kept to the trade with the French colonies, where they had some protection, and to the Levant and eastern trades.

The closing decades of the eighteenth century saw substantial relaxations of restraints on trade. If few of these were prompted by specifically free trade ideas, all of them reflected as well as promoted the increase in trade. The French monopoly of the trade of their West Indian colonies met the same difficulty as beset the English attempt to maintain a colonial monopoly—the complementary nature of the West Indian and North American colonies which made it profitable to exchange the sugar products of the former for the provisions of the latter. And the inability of the French adequately to ensure the provision of the goods required by her colonies led not only to an extensive contraband trade, but to relaxations of the monopoly in 1763, 1767 and 1779, and finally to the decree of 30 August 1784, which created six entrepôts where foreign ships were allowed to trade in a wide range of specified commodities. The Decree of 1778 liberalised trade between Spain and her colonial possessions. By the revolt of the American colonies, the most important part of the first British empire was detached from the old colonial system. There were also relaxations on internal trade. The German lands of the Habsburg dominions formed a single customs area from 1775, which in 1796 was extended to include Galicia. And even in Russia, under pressure from nobles who were large producers of grain and from merchants, internal customs duties were abolished in 1753, and in 1762 arrangements were made to allow free trade in grain; though Catherine's general economic policy was in general restrictive, with high tariffs and various prohibitions on exports and imports, and a reinforcement of guilds in the Artisan Regulations of 1785. Finally, by the Anglo-French commercial treaty of 1786, France reduced duties on textiles, leather, hardware and chinaware—in some cases to 10 per cent—and Great Britain removed the discrimination, in favour of Portugal, against French wines and spirits. There had been so much smuggling between the two countries that it would have been difficult to assess the effects, but in any case the French denounced the treaty in 1793.

The trends in trade

There are no statistics for international trade as a whole in this period, but something may be deduced from the figures for Britain, whose trade was larger and more widely dispersed than that of any other country. British imports through legal channels, after a period of relative stability between 1735 and 1747, increased substantially to 1775; between 1775 and 1782 they fell, under the impact of the war against the American colonies, and then rose to the end of the century. Exports of English products show the general pattern, except that the halt started earlier and lasted longer; after a rise to 1764, exports evened off and there followed two decades in which they were no higher and often lower than in the early 'sixties; then from 1786 there was a spectacular expansion, broken only temporarily by the outbreak of war in 1793. In the last two decades of the century the rate of increase of British imports and exports taken together fell not far short of 5 per cent a year, compared with less than 1 per cent a year in the first half of the century. The areas principally responsible for this increase were North American, and the Indies, East and West. In Holland and Germany, which served the central European markets, England failed to hold the gains she had made in the export boom of the early 'sixties: English exports to Germany were no greater in the later 'eighties than the later 'sixties, and to Holland they were lower.

It is difficult to say how far these changes in Britain's trade reflect the course of international trade as a whole and not simply changes in her share. Except during the American War, the British share must have been increasing; in the shipping passing through the Sound, for example, it rose until in the decade 1770–80 it was over 26 per cent. And there are obvious reasons why there should have been such an increase: Britain's long-term competitive power increased as a result of improvements in technology, and in the 'nineties the French wars, by crippling her major commercial competitors on the Continent and limiting their access to oversea primary producers, opened up new markets for her manufactures and enabled her to take a larger part of the entrepôt trade. The spectacular increase of British trade in the 'nineties must have been predominantly at the expense of her rivals. But British trade was conducted in so many parts of the world that it is probable that the expansion of trade in the 1740s and 1750s and the renewed expansion in the 'eighties were the pattern of trade over a wide area, and that, except when interrupted by specific disturbances such as war, the underlying conditions from the 1740s on were favourable to the expansion of world trade.

After 1740 there was a marked increase in the trade passing through the Sound, and in the decade 1771–80, 712,000 pieces of cloth were carried, compared with an average in the early eighteenth century of about 400,000. French trade with the Levant also started to rise in the 1740s and, with interruptions due to war, continued to increase to the end of the century, and her trade with the West Indies shows a similar trend.

There are several other signs of trade expansion. At the end of the 1760s Nikolaus Ernst Kleeman pioneered the trade down the Danube with the Crimea in textiles, paper and iron wares, and the Willeshavensche Company (1782–4), though it ended as a commercial fiasco, planted the Austrian flag at the mouth of the Dnieper.[1] The Austro-Turkish commercial convention of 1784 opened the Ottoman empire to German textiles, and down to 1788 the Austrian trade with Turkey made good progress.[2] The exports of iron from Russia were expanding, partly under the umbrella of the restrictive policy on iron production pursued by the Swedes. There was a growing international market in grain. The only major area which possibly was not affected by this general expansion was Germany and central Europe, where we may reasonably conclude that the sluggishness of the demand for English goods from the later 'sixties to the later 'eighties reflects the failure of incomes in this area to grow and not simply a diversion of their demand to other foreign or domestic sources of supply.

The expansion of trade had diverse effects: for instance, it made Europe more liable to commercial crises, and less liable to famine. On industrial development the effects were twofold. In the first place it caused an increased demand for European industrial goods, and where it was difficult to increase the supply of these goods within the existing framework of production, it stimulated invention and changes in industrial organisation. It can be objected to this view that the most important changes, initially, came in industries working for the home-market—for example, not in the woollen industry which was heavily dependent on export markets, but in the cotton-textile industry which, initially, was less so. It is, indeed, true that in the early stages of industrialisation developments usually take place first in industries for which there is already an existing home demand hitherto met by imports, since it is natural for industrialists to attempt in the first place to expand the production of goods for which it is known that there is an existing demand. The first step consists of driving foreign goods out of the home-market, and export and expansion abroad come later. In England, and probably in some parts of continental Europe, the low grain prices of the first half of the century had released purchasing power for the simpler manufactures, and industry had grown in response to an increase in domestic demand. Nevertheless, it remains true that foreign demand did sustain expansion even in the case of industries which developed primarily to meet the needs of the

[1] H. Halm, *Habsburgischer Osthandel im 18. Jahrhundert* (Munich, 1954).
[2] N. G. Svoronos, *Le Commerce de Salonique au XVIIIe siècle* (Paris, 1956).

home-market, while in industries in which the most important technical developments occurred expanding foreign demand was of critical importance.

But, in the second place, the expansion of trade influenced the nature of the home-market. Trade not only increased wealth; it also tended to modify the extreme inequalities of income and wealth which were characteristic of the societies of western Europe. Trade acted as a solvent on the distribution of wealth in societies dominated by the land nobility. It increased the relative importance of people with moderate incomes, who provided a better market than either the very poor or the very rich for solid substantial as opposed to fine quality goods—that is, for just the sort of goods most suitable for production by machinery.

In both these ways the expansion of trade was favourable to the development of industry. But there were a number of industrial areas in Europe which, around the middle of the eighteenth century, did not differ very widely in the state of their techniques or in the nature of their organisation: Saxony, Silesia, the mining areas of Germany, the metal-lurgical and metal-processing centres of the Urals, the silk industry at Lyons, textile production in Barcelona. In the event, most of the techniques which ushered in the Industrial Revolution were developed in England, but there were steps in the same direction in other areas, for example, Cugnot's steam-engine. Why did the break-through occur in England?

Partly because the English home-market was more favourable. The natural facilities for moving goods from one part of the country to the other were greatly superior to those of the Continent, and she was the largest free-trade area in Europe. Moreover, because of her geographical position, her foreign trade was large in relation to her total industrial output long before the great increase in exports in the later eighteenth century, and had had the effect of making her social structure more flexible. Because of the importance of trade, internal and foreign, the middle income groups, the men of moderate substance, were more important in England than on the Continent in general. As a result, the home-market facing English manufacturers—the purchasing power and tastes of the individuals who composed it—was more favourable than in most parts of the Continent: average *per capita* incomes were higher; there were relatively more people with a reasonable margin above subsistence for the consumption of manufactured goods, and their preference for leisure as opposed to additional goods was smaller.

But the growth of the English market would hardly, by itself, have been sufficiently rapid to cause the accelerated increase in output which is evident in England in the closing decades of the eighteenth century. Of particular importance was the fact that English exports found substantial markets in North America. This area had special characteristics which made it a powerful stimulus to economic advance. It had little industry of its own—its economy was complementary to that of England; it was a relatively untapped market—that is, the complementaries were not fully exploited; its income per head was higher than in Europe, and its total income was increasing more rapidly as the country was settled. Moreover, it was an area where, by comparison with Europe, there was considerable equality in the distribution of income and where, therefore, the goods in demand were of the solid standard kind, the production of which had best possibilities of technical improvement. In 1788 net export of English goods to the U.S.A. amounted to £1·5 m. and to British America £1·2 m.; exports to the principal European markets came to £3·7 m., but they were expanding much less rapidly. On all points the markets of the New World present a contrast to the markets in the East and Middle East where *per capita* incomes were low, where total incomes were not expanding, and where the propensity to import manufactured goods was small, so that the balance of trade was in their favour and had to be covered by the export to them of bullion. To some extent the circumstances of the Baltic region was similar. Britain's close links with North America were therefore of crucial importance to her development.

French external trade was also expanding. Both France and England were well situated for trade, and there are some similarities. Both had West Indian colonies which enabled them to conduct a substantial entrepôt trade in colonial products. But a much higher proportion of French trade with oversea regions consisted of re-exports which added to mercantile profits but did not directly constitute a demand for French goods; throughout the eighteenth century re-exports from France— mainly re-exports of sugar and coffee to Germany and the north—grew much more rapidly than the export of domestic products.

Moreover, of the French products exported, a substantial proportion consisted of natural products, mainly wines and spirits. Her exports of manufactured goods—almost exclusively textiles—went principally to Germany and the Ottoman empire and the French colonies. The demand of the French colonies in the New World was never comparable, in absolute magnitude, to that of the English colonies, and though French merchants were strongly entrenched in the Levant, this market for manufactured goods was sluggish. From the 1760s on, French imports of Levantine goods increased much more rapidly than French exports to this area. Moreover, after an expansion to 1763–73 the volume of her cloth exports to the Ottoman empire fell and the area served by French exports narrowed under competition from other foreigners: English competition in this area revived; in Greece there was pressure from the Austrians; in the Black Sea area she had to leave the trade to Austria and Russia. After an expansion in the earlier decades of the century in the area served by French exports, they tended in the closing

43

decades to concentrate in the areas served by Constantinople and Smyrna.

The acceleration of English exports in the 1780s is, of course, to some extent, the *result* of technical improvements. But at least in cotton textiles these improvements were in some measure the result of the fact that in the preceding decades England had been linked to markets which, for quite independent reasons, were growing rapidly. The textile industries of the Continent—of Silesia, Saxony and Bohemia—served markets where the growth of demand was much slower, and for this reason they were not faced with the same need to improve their techniques and methods of organisation.

But this difference in the character of the foreign markets available to them was only a matter of degree; there was an increase in demand for the products of all the main industrial areas. The contrasts were also in the way this increased demand was met. Where supplies of labour and natural resources were ample, it was met predominantly by an increase in industry of the existing type, based on the domestic form of organisation. Where labour was abundant and techniques simple, the domestic system had real advantages: it reduced the merchant capitalist's overhead charges and made him less vulnerable to temporary reductions of demand. Where supplies of labour and raw materials were scarce the industry either failed to expand (or migrated) or, if it was in the hands of men of resource and technical ingenuity, it invented new techniques to overcome the scarcities, among them the new technique of organising labour—the factory. In some English industries the expansion of demand was met by an extension of the domestically organised industry, either because new methods were, for technical reasons, difficult to devise, as in the case of woollen textiles, or because additional labour was readily available, as in the manufacture of metal goods in the Black Country. But where shortages emerged—of labour in the manufacture of cotton textiles, of power in the mining industry—necessity proved the mother of invention. It was when the possibilities of increasing production by existing methods were exhausted that attention was concentrated on devising new methods. Home demand, it is true, was also increasing, and in iron and copper, linens and silks, the supply to the home-market probably kept pace with the growth of exports. But in the cotton-textile industry, where the most continuous technical innovation took place, exports increased much more rapidly than sales at home.

In the trade with the Baltic, the Levant and the East Indies, the pace was set by increased European demand for their products. It is tempting to suppose that, in contrast, the expansion of trade with America was dictated by the autonomous growth of American incomes. But the fact that British exports tended to grow most rapidly when their prices were low, compared with the prices of primary products, suggests that, in this case too, commercial expansion generally started with an increase in European demand, principally for West Indian products. Even so, an unusually large part of the consequent rise in income in America was used to buy European, and particularly British goods, and it is for this reason that the Atlantic trade played a crucial part in the industrial development of Europe in this period.

3. ECONOMIC IDEAS

The later eighteenth century saw the emergence of systematic economic analysis of a sort which was to provide the core of economics for the next century. This analysis was, in the main, conducted in the course of attacking practical problems and prescribing measures of policy. Programmes of economic policy were nothing new: what was new was their number, range and connection with a general view of the working of the economy, and with organised thought as opposed to intuition. There were economic writers of intelligence and penetration earlier in the century— Cantillon and Montesquieu for example—but in quality and range the works of the later decades of the eighteenth century are without precedent.

In France, to take the most conspicuous examples, there was Quesnay's *Tableau économique* (1758) and the large volume of physiocratic writing, and Turgot's *Réflexions sur la formation et la distribution des richesses* (written in 1766); in Spain, Campomanes, *Discurso sobre el fomento de la industria popular* (1774), and in Italy, Genovesi's *Lezioni di economia civile* (1765), and *Economia nazionale* (1774) by Ortes.

The development of this body of economic thought was due partly to internal developments, to a cumulative increase in intellectual capacity to analyse economic problems, and partly to the appearance of problems of a complexity which required to be dealt with in an analytical fashion. These two influences interacted; intellectual habits predisposed men to frame explanations in general terms at the same time as the problems of practical administration required to be treated in this way.

The most powerful stimulus to the development of the powers of intellectual analysis was the application to economic events of an idea which had already been applied to (or derived from) the world as a whole by theologians and to the physical world by scientists—the idea of a self-regulating natural order. According to this idea, in its most uncompromising form, there existed behind the apparent confusion of events an order which was maintained, not by deliberate intention, not by the exertion of human effort to this end, but by the operation of instincts planted in men by Providence. This Providence was assumed to be benign and the order so established was favourable to the welfare of men.

This notion of a natural order, all the parts of which were related, was a powerful stimulus to economic investigation; for men will undertake the search for uniformities and patterns in economic behaviour only when they are confident such uniformities exist. Under the influence of this idea men more easily drew, from an examination of particular practical problems, generalisations which illuminated wide areas of experience.

Adam Smith derived this notion from his teacher Francis Hutcheson, and it struck him with the force of a religious conversion. But the transference to the economic sphere of ideas which had already been so fruitful elsewhere—ideas springing fundamentally from scholastic ideas of natural law—was an obvious next step in the development of economic ideas. The same idea occurred independently to the Physiocrats; their 'natural and substantive order of society' was fundamentally a long-term equilibrium to which the natural forces of society tended. And it is to be found, expressed very explicitly, among one of the keenest critics of the Physiocrats, Ferdinando Galiani. 'Nature if left alone', he wrote, 'will lead to equilibrium, the natural state of affairs and the most pleasing to man.'

This idea of a natural equilibrium was held in more extreme form by some economists than others. Quesnay held that it involved the harmony of interests between individuals and between classes. The more empirical Adam Smith, for all his reference to the 'hidden hand', allowed for a good deal of conflict of interest. Economists also differed in the deductions about practical policy which they derived from this notion. But despite these differences, almost all the writers of the period shared an appreciation of the fact that the various economic phenomena were related to each other and that the spontaneous decisions of individuals tended to establish a pattern. It was in the light of these ideas that the most influential English and French writers—and by derivation the Spanish and many of the Italian—considered the practical problems of their day.

The fruitful influence of this general assumption was the principal reason for the increase in this period in the ability to handle economic questions. But the increased ability was also the result of an accumulation of the successful attempts of previous decades to deal with certain limited problems—particularly the problems of foreign trade and public finance thrown up by the economic and political developments of the sixteenth and seventeenth centuries. By the later eighteenth century enough work of this kind had been done to warrant the large works of synthesis which are a characteristic of the period.

Such works were essentially designed to deal with the urgent economic problems of the time. These problems themselves constituted an independent influence on economic thought; in some cases theoretical presuppositions dictated the writers' treatment of a particular problem, but sometimes the exigencies of a specific problem determined the development of a theory or induced a writer to present proposals which were out of line with the general framework of his ideas. Proposals for policy were influenced by the economic facts as well as by the writers' conceptions of the facts and the intellectual tradition they inherited or developed for analysing them; and sometimes writers arrived at the same conclusions on policy—for example, on the internal grain trade—as the result purely of practical considerations and without any common intellectual influence.

The most systematic of the economic writers, and the only ones to constitute a self-conscious group, were the Physiocrats. The two practical problems with which they were principally concerned were a stagnant agriculture and the financial difficulties of the crown. These problems were interrelated in practice, and their treatment at the hands of the Physiocrats sprang from the same theoretical assumptions. Agriculture was the only economic activity which produced a net revenue (that is, a revenue over and above costs), and hence the promotion of a capitalist agriculture (*grande culture*) in place of small-scale *métayage* was the principal practical aim. It was for this reason that the Physiocrats wanted the abolition of restrictions on the internal movement and the export of grain which depressed prices. From the same reasoning followed their proposals for the reform of taxation—the abolition of feudal privileges and the imposition of a single tax on the rent of land; for exemption of the nobility meant that taxation fell on the cultivators and encroached on the outlays necessary to replace equipment. Moreover, because of this exemption, the revenue of the state was inadequate, and the state was forced to concede or maintain fiscal and monopolistic privileges which enabled those who enjoyed them to absorb a large part of the economic surplus, the *produit net*. Hence also followed the direct attack on the privileges of financiers and merchants and the guilds. Thus the problems of fiscal and agricultural rehabilitation were closely linked, and the Physiocrats attacked feudal privilege as well as mercantilist regulation. The essential object of all the items of their programme was to ensure to agriculture a large share of the economic surplus it alone produced, in order to encourage agricultural investment.

Adam Smith's programme had a different orientation, but in his case too it sprang from the belief not merely that existing restrictions and regulations resulted in a wrong distribution of resources, but, more specifically, that they promoted trade and industry, especially the former, at the expense of agriculture. His whole work sprang from the attempt to show why in England, as in Europe generally, private persons often found it more profitable to devote their capital to distant trades than to the improvement of domestic agriculture. And his work contains a fairly specific programme of reform: the removal of restrictions on the free choice of employment, such as the laws on apprenticeship and settlement; the removal of laws and customs which restricted the free sale and private use of land; internal free trade; and the abolition of duties and other restrictions on imports and of duties and bounties on exports.

In the eighteenth century, economic thought was no more a homogeneous whole than in other periods. Between Smith and the Physiocrats there were important differences not merely in emphasis, but in their economic analysis. And there were major French economists—for example, Turgot—whose relations with the Physiocrats were close but who were not strictly members of the group; there were others whose approach to contemporary economic problems was independent of or opposed to the assumptions of the Physiocrats, for example, Forbonnais, who published his *Principes et observations économiques* in 1767. Adam Smith did not completely capture the mind of his generation even in England.

Moreover, even among those whose general presuppositions were those of economic liberalism, there were wide differences in the practical conclusions they drew about policy, variations of emphasis depending partly upon differences in logic and partly on differences in the nature of the problems which faced them. There was nothing in England to correspond to the exemption of the nobility from certain types of taxation which constituted the core of the fiscal problem in most continental countries. The powers of masters and corporations were weaker. The restrictions on the sale and purchase of land were much less rigorous in England, though not in Scotland where the system of permanent entail was comparable in its effects to the *majorat* and the *fidei commisse* on the Continent and made Smith's observations on free trade in land more relevant to his French or Spanish than to English readers. The impediments to the most economic use of land presented by rights of common yielded to private action much more readily in England than in France. Freedom of internal trade in England was not a problem. Above all, freedom of external trade figures more largely in Smith than in the writings of the Physiocrats. Their advocacy of the removal of restrictions on external trade in corn sprang from their desire to maintain good prices for agricultural products. As a practical matter there was no question of protecting French agriculture, and if protection had been necessary their emphasis on agricultural prosperity might have led to different conclusions; and as a matter of theory they ranked trade low in the hierarchy of economic activities. They are, as Rist said, 'to be regarded as the founders of Free Trade not because of any desire to favour trade as such, but because their attitude towards it was one of disdainful *laissez-faire*. They were not, perhaps, altogether free from the belief that *laissez-faire* would lead to the disappearance of commerce altogether.'

Despite all this, on the plane of general economic ideas it was Smith and the Physiocrats who were most widely influential and the general effect of their ideas, as they passed into common currency, was to underpin a programme of practical proposals which was common ground to economic liberals.

It was on this body of ideas that those Spanish writers drew who were concerned to explain and to remedy the economic backwardness of their country. The most important writers, Capmany, Campomanes, Jovellanos, made contributions of their own on specific subjects, but the general framework of their ideas was derivative. They borrowed their fundamental notions from the French—not only from the Physiocrats but from the elder Mirabeau whose l'Ami des hommes had enormous influence, and Turgot—and from Adam Smith. Under these influences they adopted the principles of economic liberty. 'Le premier principe politique', wrote Jovellanos, 'conseille de laisser aux hommes la plus grande liberté possible à l'ombre de laquelle croîtront le commerce, la population et la richesse.' They rejected mercantilist notions of wealth and money, and adopted an essentially physiocratic attitude towards agriculture as the main source of wealth. The most characteristic Spanish works of the period—for example, the two reports of Jovellanos, Informe sobre el libro ejercicio de las artes (1785) and Ley agrario (1794)—were attempts to apply liberal principles, taken at second hand, to Spanish circumstances.

The most important field for the application of these principles was agriculture, and among Spanish writers, as among the French, there was an attack on the great territorial estates and the laws which maintained them, and on the commons and the various common rights. Measures were advocated by Jovellanos for restrictions on mainmorte and for the division of the commons. On the problem presented by the great estates there was a fair degree of unanimity. On the commons there was, as in France, some ambivalence, for respect for the rights of individual property might be urged in favour of existing rights of common as well as in favour of division of the commons into separate individual holdings; and arguments on the lines of Rousseau for property in common are to be found, even in Jovellanos, alongside the advocacy of measures for their division. There is no doubt, however, that the prevailing attitude of Spanish economic writers was in favour of division, and between 1760 and 1780 there was legislation from the king and the local authorities for the division of the commons, and some of the edicts were prepared by Campomanes. In Spain too there was an attack on corporations, on hermandades, and pleas for occupational freedom, particularly in the works of Campomanes and Jovellanos.

Even in Spain, where 'liberal' ideas were influential, they were not, of course, uniformly or consistently influential. Thus, on the question of corporations, the Catalan economist Capmany defended their privileges against the attacks of Campomanes, and they were also defended by Cadalso. And though under physiocratic influence, Spanish writers attacked the arrangements whereby the trade of the American colonies was monopolised by Cadiz, they were not primarily interested in external trade, and even Jovellanos was quite prepared to depart from liberal principles in external trade and proposed a law which permitted importation but was to be suspended when the harvest was abundant. In the case of Campomanes the empiricism went further, for in 1790 he was responsible for revoking the decree of 1765, for which he had agitated, allowing free trade in corn.

In Italy the reception of liberal ideas was less complete, partly because some of the most important Italian thinkers were bureaucrats—several of the Neapolitan *illuministi* were government servants and both Verri and Beccaria were members of the Milanese administration—and more apt therefore to tailor ideas to suit particular situations; partly because of the political fragmentation of the country; and partly because of the independent vitality of economic thinking. The Spanish writers were essentially derivative; the Italians have some claim to be the most original of their time. The emphasis upon agriculture is common. For example, Genovesi was principally concerned with encouraging agriculture, even if this meant restricting industry; Gaetano Filangieri recognised the pre-eminence of agriculture. But a version of economic liberalism represented by several of the Italians was very attenuated. For example, Beccaria, the greatest of them, started with a moderate type of mercantilism, and though he was later influenced by physiocratic views on agriculture, abolition of the guilds and internal free trade, he remained opposed to complete freedom for foreign trade. Indeed, among Italian writers it is quite common to find a programme of internal free trade put forward simultaneously with a programme for protection. Genovesi, for example, distinguished the exports of finished goods and the imports of raw materials —which should be free—from imports of manufactured goods and exports of raw materials—which should be strictly regulated. Verri represents the same combination of internal free trade with restriction of imports and encouragement of exports. Such men selected those items of the 'liberal' programme likely to promote the development of their state, but were too well aware of the economic backwardness of Italy to suppose that a policy of complete and thorough *laissez-faire* would serve their purpose.

Despite these variations, there was much in common in the assumptions and practical recommendations of the writers of France, England, Spain and Italy. Between this programme and that of the German Cameralists there is a marked contrast. The German economic writers of the seventeenth century, Johann Becher and Von Hornigk for example, were, in their emphasis on the positive role of the state, similar to the English and French mercantilists; but whereas in England mercantilist ideas were not developed in a systematic form in the eighteenth century, German Cameralism had a continuous intellectual history both in the university and in the administration. In Germany the tradition survived and developed that the state should accept direct responsibility for the welfare, economic as well as moral, of the population and should undertake measures of social and economic planning to promote the growth of population and employment. Thus Sonnenfels (1738–1817) advocated the promotion of exports and the restriction of imports to raw materials, and Justi (1717–71) was an advocate of state planning to promote industry, of schemes for the organisation of credit, of subsidies and exemptions from taxation to encourage the immigration of foreigners.

The primary concern of the Cameralists was with the proper administration and increase of the prince's revenue. Cameralism was the economics of administrators; it dealt systematically with the wide range of problems faced by the bureaucracy of a state, especially a backward state in which the spontaneous forces making for economic progress were few and in which the system of administration and taxation was weak. The content of cameralist economics was therefore wider than that of French and English economics and the emphasis on topics for discussion was differently placed: it included administration and (often) technology, and paid particular attention to problems of public finance and currency. The Cameralists' general approach to problems was more specific and empirical, as is evident from the contrast between their observations on fiscal policy in the regalian rights controversy and the physiocratic proposal for a single tax upon a single class which was derived directly from their analysis of the net product.

It is as if royal revenue had remained in eighteenth-century England the problem it had been in the early seventeenth century, and English writing on economic matters had developed from such speculations about royal revenue as may be found in Cranfield or Bacon. But English writings on royal finance never showed signs of branching out into an economic science, perhaps because the constitutional, not administrative or economic, aspects of royal insolvency attracted intellectual effort, perhaps because the interests of economic writers were concentrated on foreign trade; and by the later eighteenth century, when systematic economics had arisen in England, public finance was no longer an urgent problem—it had been coped with by national taxation and a long-term debt—and public finance, while still an important subject, did not give its colour to the whole science.

The concern of the Cameralists with the state and its revenue accounts for their emphasis on the growth of population and employment, on industry rather than commerce, and of specific measures to this end, on protection and self-sufficiency and precious metals.

These differences between the programmes of the Cameralists and their western contemporaries partly sprang from the position of the writers, from differences in their degree of responsibility for policy. The Cameralists, though most held academic posts, were advisers to princes in a sense which was true of few of the French and none of the English writers. Partly the differences sprang from the different nature of the practical problems owing to the greater capacity of individual enterprise in the richer countries of the West. Partly they were due to differences in intellectual tradition.

The practical programme of economic liberalism sprang from a view of the way in which the economic order operated, and was derived from, or at any rate defended by, reference to general principles. By contrast, the Cameralists' practical proposals were not derived from a body of fundamental principles; they were the reactions of administrators to practical problems, and as such were much less unified as well as less consciously grounded in theory. And in so far as there was theory, it was to all appearances mercantilist; it took for granted that in many and perhaps most situations there was a conflict between the interests of the private individual and those of the state, and that state intervention was necessary as a normal condition.

Nevertheless, in their fundamental view as to how economic life was ordered the cameralist writers differed less from Smith and the Physiocrats than their language suggests.

In the first place the differences between the economic liberals and their mercantilist predecessors were smaller than the liberals themselves supposed. The most prominent of the ideas of Smith were conceived in the course of an outright attack on mercantilist policies, but several were a natural development of the insights, reservations and corrections which mercantilist writers themselves made. Moreover, some mercantilist ideas survived; for example, populationist ideas retained their full force, not only in Adam Smith, but right down to Malthus. Smith and the Physiocrats alike regarded a growing population as a sign of a healthy economy.

In the second place, a good deal of the attack on regulation sprang in fact, not so much from *laissez-faire* principles, as from objections to specific regulations in force at the time. When Smith and Quesnay took up a critical attitude towards existing economic institutions it was not necessarily or mainly because of ideas of a natural order. Their economic philosophy gave a doctrinaire edge to the expression of views even when the views themselves were not derived from the doctrines. If some writers were more critical of specific regulations because they held *laissez-faire* ideas, others were attached to *laissez-faire* ideas principally because they disliked the operation and character of specific regulations. In Spain, for example, though the guilds were attacked in part because they restricted the rights of man—'droits imprescriptibles de la liberté dont le plus ferme, le plus inviolable, le plus sacré est celui qu'a l'homme de travailler pour vivre'—the case was often argued simply in terms of their effects on economic development.

Sometimes thinkers who had been launched on their criticism of existing institutions by ideas of natural order came ultimately to dispense with this particular basis for their criticisms, and much of Smith's attack on mercantilism is conducted by arguing the detailed disadvantages of specific regulations rather than the general undesirability of interference with economic law. And if in the details of their proposals the economic liberals were sometimes more pragmatic than the tone of their language suggests, the general view of economic phenomena of the most important German Cameralists had more in common with that of the economic liberals than their practical proposals would suggest. Justi and Sonnenfels were, like Smith, deeply influenced in their assumptions about the economic order by ideas of natural law. If their practical proposals were different it was partly because, as administrators in backward countries, they were more keenly aware of short-term difficulties, and took a more pessimistic view of the power and direction of the autonomous forces in the economy.

That there was a wide gulf in their practical programmes it cannot be denied, but even this can be exaggerated. The immediate programme of the economic liberals was very far from being one of pure *laissez-faire*. While the notion of a natural order in general led to a more critical attitude towards existing regulations, the notion was compatible with a variety of attitudes to practical problems; the question was left open how far this order was represented by the existing state of affairs. The most *laissez-faire* of Western writers envisaged an active role for the state in the period of the removal of restrictions of mercantilist origin. In the physiocratic programme a more positive role was envisaged: the state was to undertake public works and make roads. And, as Gide pointed out, the amount of tax which they thought should be paid represents some 12 per cent of the then total gross revenue of France. Justi, for his part, advocated the abolition of government price regulation, of monopolies, and the abrogation of the privileges of trading companies; and the duties he suggested for the limitation of imports were moderate.

The practical proposals of the Cameralists coincided with the policies of Maria Theresa and Joseph II and of Frederick the Great; they confirmed and elaborated the traditional predispositions of the state. By contrast, the proposals of the economic liberals constituted an attack on existing institutions and the question of their influence on policy has therefore to be considered.

How far was policy shaped by such ideas? How far was policy simply the *ad hoc* reactions of practical men to urgent and specific situations within limits narrowly set by the facts of the situation itself. Practical men, thought Keynes, were merely echoing the voices of dead thinkers. On the other hand, there is the view that 'policy...is a set of devices into which a government drifts under the pressure of practical problems, and which gradually acquire the conscious uniformity of a type, and begin, at last, to defend themselves as such'. The debate is perennial and no easier to settle for the late eighteenth century than for any other. Between the ideas and the policy the links sometimes appear close. D'Ormesson's measures against 'vaine pâture' owe something to physiocratic influence. So do some elements in Turgot's policy as Comptroller General of Finances—the abolition of the *jurandes* (craft guilds), the reforms in financial administration and the establishment of internal free trade in grains. Many of the social, economic and institutional reforms of the Constituent Assembly were based on physiocratic thinking.

It was in response to Campomanes' *Réponse fiscale* that the Spanish crown on 11 July 1765 suppressed the tax on grain, allowed internal free trade, and even exportation, up to a specified maximum price. Verri, while a member of the administration of Milan, was responsible for the abolition of tax-farming (1770) and for the reduction and simplification of the tariff in 1786. The Eden Treaty of 1786 has often been ascribed to the influence of Smith's ideas on Pitt.

But even such measures as these were of a kind which purely practical considerations might well have suggested to an intelligent administrator without benefit of theory. Economic liberalism was certainly the dominant intellectual fashion, and in Spain and Italy it was a derived fashion. But policies which accorded with physiocratic notions or were defended in physiocratic language were sometimes dictated by local circumstances and independently arrived at by simple common sense. The influence of economic ideas was less in moulding specific measures of policy than in creating certain presuppositions about policy. The ideas of economic liberalism exerted their power in much the same way, though to different intent, as Keynsian ideas in our own day. At the least, they provided an armoury for the defence of measures which might well have been adopted in any case; at the most, they created a disposition to choose from the limited alternatives set by the facts of a situation those policies which did most to relax restrictions. Their main work was the creation of a presumption in favour of leaving economic forces free play, but the main fruits of this change in the climate of opinion were not garnered till the following century.

CHAPTER III

LITERATURE AND THOUGHT: THE ROMANTIC TENDENCY, ROUSSEAU, KANT

I N the twenty-five years which preceded the outbreak of the French Revolution, the intellectual condition of Europe was one of exceptional complexity. In some of the more backward countries, and also in some of the more backward social strata, old orthodoxies still held sway, such as the belief in the divine right of kings and in the providential character of universal history. Side by side with it there existed a new radicalism which has come to be known as the Enlightenment. It appealed above all to the intelligentsia and to the *grande bourgeoisie*, but made increasing inroads into the thinking of the other social classes. Its watchwords were: rationality, not tradition; happiness in this life, not salvation for the next. It was this movement, with its insistent demand for the revaluation of all social institutions, which prepared the great cataclysm of 1789. But the most interesting feature of this period is the presence within it of yet a third tendency which was both revolutionary and reactionary at the same time: revolutionary in relation to the old orthodoxies, reactionary in relation to the Enlightenment. The philosophy of the Enlightenment was essentially a rationalistic philosophy, that is to say, it regarded man as, in the first place, a rational animal, and, consistently with this, looked to abstract ratiocination for the answer to all human problems, great and small. But man is more than an animated calculating machine. The very one-sidedness of the *philosophes* was bound to evoke, sooner or later, a vigorous reaction which was to emphasise the non-rational elements in human nature, the power of sentiment and passion, the glory of the imaginative faculties, and the need to confront, and indeed to accept, the mysteries of existence which surround us on all sides. This movement achieved its full stature only after the French Revolution, in the first half of the nineteenth century, the period of romanticism; but its foundations were laid before the French Revolution, in the deeply stirred generation of which we are to speak here. Rationalistic on the surface, it carried within it a preromantic undercurrent which may perhaps be described as an incipient intellectual revulsion against the revolutionaries.

Some desire to break away from rationalism in thought and practice was already manifest earlier in the century, especially in the sphere of art, where the mathematical spirit is apt to hamper and deaden the play of imagination. There was, for instance, the music of Carl Philipp Emanuel Bach, which restored natural, unsophisticated melody to its rightful place and refused to be enslaved by the formalistic principles of counterpoint; there was the spirited defence, by Bodmer and Breitinger, of Shakespeare's 'wild' poetic drama against the pedantic poetics of Gottsched which demanded that stage-plays should have a logical structure, that rhythm should be meticulously maintained and verse should always be pure; there was the dawn of a new age in landscape gardening when taste began to abandon the style of Le Nôtre, who had forced flowers and trees into exact geometrical patterns, and attention was increasingly directed to the natural capabilities inherent in the terrain, as it was by the great 'Capability' Brown. This incipient reaction against rationalism was perhaps strongest in religion. To give but one example: Law's *Serious Call* of 1728 'rejected the claims of reason and proclaimed a universe ruled by a mysterious God, who spoke to men...through the profound intuitions of the human heart'.[1] Pietism, in the widest sense of the word, worked, like a leaven, in the depths of European society and tended to permeate and to revivify it in its entirety; and pietism, in this inclusive meaning of the term, was no narrowly Protestant, let alone sectarian, phenomenon. It was much rather an offshoot of the great Franciscan tradition which had, in the sixteenth century, embodied itself afresh in the great Capuchin community which was now reaching the high noon of its power and influence and tended, like Methodism, to evoke a 'religion of the heart'.

All these tendencies came to a head in one great and commanding figure, Jean-Jacques Rousseau. Born in 1712 and living until 1778, he was more in the eighteenth century than of it. His tempestuous personality could not tolerate either the insipid formalities of court life at Versailles, nor the cynical petulance of the Paris *salons*. He was, or rather was forced to be, a typical *bohémien*, a position all the more distressing to him as he had a deep longing for the comforts of friendship and love. In this he constituted something of an archetype, for many leading spirits of his generation found it equally impossible to secure a foothold, or at any rate achieve complete integration, in contemporary society, for instance in Germany Lenz and Hamann, and even Herder, Kant and Schiller, in spite of their appointment to high offices of state. 'I demand as much as I give', Rousseau wrote to Madame d'Houdetot on 1 October 1757, 'and as I do not come upon anybody who would make me a fair return, I retire into myself, pained not to have found a heart which would respond to mine.'[2] In this way, Jean-Jacques became a lonely man, a *solitaire*, to use his own expression, but a *solitaire* who was anything but happy in his solitude. His enforced isolation found its psychological counterpart in a deep yearning which, unlike the cravings of physical passion or of worldly ambition, had no determinate object and so tended

---

[1] Vol. VII, p. 109.   [2] *Correspondance générale* (1924 ff.), vol. III, p. 125.

to become insatiable and even mystical in character. In this, too, Rousseau was typical of his generation rather than an exception to it. 'The whole content of my joy', Goethe makes one of his characters say, 'is a surging longing for something I do not possess, for something I do not know',[1] and, in the same spirit, Lenz felt that no figure symbolised his own being better than the ancient hero Tantalus, hapless victim of a hunger which could never be satisfied.

In his great novel *Die Leiden des jungen Werthers*[2] Goethe drew a poignant picture of a young man caught in the coils of this mental condition, and many recognised in its central character a reflection of their own selves. This state of mind was unfruitful in so far as men's ability to deal with their day-to-day problems was concerned—Werther's suicide was but the logical and well-nigh inevitable conclusion to his whole life— but it created an atmosphere in which all the arts could freely develop. Shut out from contemporary reality which was more petty, cramping and confining than we can easily realise today, men of Rousseau's stamp found refuge in a dream existence in which their imagination could spread its wings. Thus there came into being a grand, if unrealistic, vision of a new society in which goodness reigned and peace was secure. And thus there arose also a new relationship to nature and its beauties, strongly contrasting with the old rationalistic attitude which had seen even in the Alps, for all their grandeur, no more than an inconvenient obstacle in the way of the post-chaises from north to south. 'To commune with nature' was a phrase much used in the age, and one of its most favourite images was that of nature as a great mother to whose bosom her children could flee in their deepest sorrows and joys. When Rousseau was in his blackest moods, when his frustrated love of society had plunged him into the depths of misanthropy and persecution-mania, he found relief in long botanising expeditions, in collecting the flowers of woods and fields.

In the first years of his life, up to about 1744 or 1745, we find Rousseau still speaking in the accents of the *ancien régime*. In a memoir on education which he wrote in 1740[3] there is no trace of the fundamental conviction which we have come to associate with his name, namely the assertion that man is born good. Nor is there as yet any hostility to polite society. On the contrary; Rousseau argues, at this stage, that polite society, by agreeably occupying us with such pastimes as music and painting, light verse and charming women, dissipates the dangerous power of the passions which slumber within us and thereby has a highly positive educational effect. But before long there is a complete revolution in his outlook. The original position is inverted. Man, he now

---

[1] Morris, *Der junge Goethe* (1910 ff.), vol. II, p. 54.
[2] *The Sufferings of Young Werther.*
[3] *Fragment du Mémoire présenté à M. de Sainte-Marie pour l'Éducation de son Fils. Correspondance Générale*, vol. I, pp. 367 ff.

teaches, and is to teach to the end of his life, springs from the hands of nature unspoilt, virtuous and noble. There is upon him no stain of original sin. His true fall comes with his entry into a society which is corrupt, vicious and mean. Society is artificial, both in the sense that it is an arte- fact, a man-made thing, and in the sense that it is not genuine, that it is filled by artifice, permeated in every fibre by convention, pretence, and lying. It must be remodelled so as to come into line with the original and fundamental nature of man, and indeed with the desires of that loving Providence whose beneficent designs have been frustrated by men, and by nobody more than by those who style themselves the servants of the hidden deity. To some extent, this passionate preaching against the wickedness of 'civilised' society was no more than a philosophy of sour grapes. It seems to have been Rousseau's failure to make a success of his office of secretary to the comte de Montaigu, who dismissed him without ceremony on 6 August 1744 for insolence, which finally turned him away from, and against, a world in which he was unable to find a niche. The *Épitre à M. de l'Étang, Vicaire de Marcoussis*, written in 1749, is not only the first impassioned attack against the rottenness of Parisian society to come from Jean-Jacques' pen, but also an early indication that he was turning into a man dominated by resentment, bitterness and spite. But if the inception of his new philosophy was, on the biographical side, a petty personal affair, its consequences on the stage of history were des- tined to be very great indeed.

The last twenty-eight years of Rousseau's career were devoted to the dissemination of these ideas, an enterprise in which he was remarkably successful, for they entered deeply into the European consciousness. But before we speak about the books which were the vehicle of his propaganda, it will be expedient to characterise the social ideal which Rousseau placed alongside the highly coloured picture he drew of con- temporary conditions. Superficially it seems to be, and certainly pretends to be, a description of Genevan society and the Genevan state. When he had left his native city of Geneva and ventured forth into the fashionable world, Rousseau had abandoned the Calvinist creed and embraced Catholicism. Under the lash of his disappointments, he turned back, a penitent, to his domestic gods. He rejoined the Calvinist church, regained the citizenship which he had forfeited through his apostasy, and hence- forth took great pride in describing himself as 'Citoyen de Genève'. Now, with the somewhat transfigured image of Geneva which he cherished and bore in his heart, there fused in his mind a vision of ancient society, and more especially of the Rome of pre-imperial days and of Sparta. Few books had a more penetrating and decisive influence on his thought than Plutarch's *Lives*. Evidently, it was his conviction that there was something in common between Cato's Rome and Calvin's Geneva, and in this something there rested, in his view, the whole secret of a successful community life. It is not altogether easy to say what exactly this all-important something was, for Rousseau was a highly suggestive rather than a concise and clear writer. But perhaps we come near to the core of his conviction when we define the something we are speaking of as 'republican virtue'. Jean-Jacques' ideal citizen was the man of moral integrity, the strong and independent personality tempered by self-education and self-discipline, and this type he thought he saw realised in the three classical centres of republicanism. With it he contrasted both the pleasure-seeker of Versailles and the pleasure-seeker of Paris, the naïve voluptuary of *ancien régime* court society and the more rational and systematic votary of the greatest happiness principle embraced and propagated by the *philosophes*—two types to whom he denied not only human worth but also the capacity of fitting into a sound and abiding social life.

It is not difficult to see that Rousseau, when he speaks of, or rather enthuses about, his pretended historical models, presents us with a picture, not of fact, but of fiction. 'You depict us such as we ought to be and not such as we are', his Genevan fellow-citizen Dupan rightly wrote to him on 20 June 1755, after the appearance of the *Discours sur l'Inégalité*.[1] As so many other social ideals that have been presented in a historical guise, Jean-Jacques', too, was determined by his hopes of the future rather than by any realities of the past. Yet some, at any rate, of the characteristics of Sparta, early Rome and Geneva are pointers to the kind of society which Rousseau envisaged and desired.

There is, first of all, the important fact that these three cities were, comparatively speaking, rather small—that is, small in comparison not only with our modern monster conurbations, but also with the Paris of Rousseau's own days. Geneva, Rousseau himself informs us, had at the time about 24,000 inhabitants.[2] Now, a community of 24,000 souls is not yet entirely divorced from the natural setting of human existence; its members are still embedded in the great matrix of all animate life and can, to that extent, be said to have a 'natural' mode of being. Further-more, country towns of this size tend to be closely knit neighbourhood units within which everybody is known to everybody else and hence there is a good deal of informal, but not ineffectual, moral supervision. Who-ever wishes the world to be peopled by moral and patriotic men—moral and patriotic in the specific form of neighbourliness—must wish for some social setting of this sort. The same conditions will also make for a sound relationship between the rulers and the ruled, and will in this way pro-duce a good form of government, to supplement the good form of society. Not only will there be no yawning gap between the power-holders and those over whom they are set, but the citizens, as electors, will know

[1] *Correspondance Générale*, vol. II, p. 193.
[2] *Lettre à d'Alembert sur les Spectacles*, ed. Fuchs (1948), p. 125.

exactly whom to entrust with power. All candidates will be like open books to the constituents, and so authority will always go to those who deserve it, and are fit to exercise it.

All these are important elements in Jean-Jacques' social and political day-dream. But another feature of republican Rome and contemporary Geneva is even more helpful in the attempt to discern its essence and to understand its impact. Both republican Rome and contemporary Geneva were, by and large, communities of comparative social homogeneity. The impression Rousseau received from such studies of ancient history as he undertook—an impression by no means entirely unjustified—was that Rome was originally inhabited by a sturdy peasant population tilling its ancestral soil and cultivating all the qualities necessary for the assertion of its rights both in relation to its rulers at home and to potential enemies abroad. Now, peasants of this kind will live side by side rather than together; not involved in any highly developed division of labour, not depending on any all-important market, their main preoccupation will be with their own welfare and that of their families, whereas the common weal will only be a background to their work. This is very definitely also part and parcel of Rousseau's social ideal: individual independence is for him the prime *desideratum*, and society as a whole, as he makes it grow out of a social contract, is only a secondary phenomenon to him. Thus *liberty* is one of the key words in Jean-Jacques' political vocabulary. But *equality* is another. Peasant populations do not, as a rule, noticeably differ in wealth, especially not when there is around the cultivated fields still a sizeable unappropriated no-man's-land, out of which additional acres can be carved or additional holdings constituted, if the need arises. Rousseau's bitter condemnation of the first man who erected a fence around a plot of land and said, 'This is mine', is understandable from this point of view, for it was he who took the first step towards that modern monopoly of the soil enjoyed by the aristocracies of Europe which finally destroyed the *de facto* equality which the peasant peoples of old enjoyed.

At first sight it may seem curious that Rousseau equated the social constitution of a town like Geneva with a typically rural community such as that of early Rome, but nothing is more understandable since the two societies really did agree in the decisive characteristics. Geneva, too, was a community of comparative social homogeneity, of comparative liberty and equality. Composed of watch-makers and other artisans, it had a population of independent producers, and though these producers were no doubt competing with each other, yet their well-being depended in the first place on their own industry and on their own skill. Just as the Roman yeomen owned their homesteads and their lands, so they owned their workshops and their tools. The parallel is obvious. If Rousseau's social ideal can be compressed at all into a short formula, we can say that it was a society of liberty and equality, or of peasants and artisans, or a society of independent producers without masters above and without slaves beneath them. 'The laws', he writes in one of his most characteristic utterances, 'are always favourable to those who possess and prejudicial to those who have nothing; whence it follows that the social state is only advantageous to men if everybody has something and nobody too much.'[1]

Clearly, such an ideal is essentially a formulation of the aspirations of the Third Estate as it then existed, or of middle-class ambitions as we should say today when a fourth estate (the proletariat) has come to complicate the social structure and has deprived the whole Rousseauite outlook of its extremist character. Jean-Jacques' appeal was to the petty bourgeoisie of Europe, whereas that of the old orthodoxies was to nobility and clergy, and that of the *philosophes à la* Voltaire to the *grande bourgeoisie* and to the intelligentsia. Rousseau towered above his contemporaries, not only because he had great personal gifts, not only because his physical disabilities and life-experience developed in him the acidity and acerbity which a writer on social and political affairs seems to need if his books and pamphlets are to have the necessary sharp cutting-edge, but also because he looked upon the great problems of social conduct and organisation from a new vantage-point, and that a vantage-point of extraordinary significance within the context of contemporary life.

Rousseau started his grand campaign with the *Discours sur les Sciences et les Arts*. In 1749 the Academy of Dijon had proposed the following subject for their prize essay of the ensuing year: *Le rétablissement des sciences et des arts a-t-il contribué à épurer ou à corrompre les mœurs?* Has the re-establishment of the sciences and the arts tended to purify or to corrupt social morality? When Rousseau chanced to come across this question a strong emotion took hold of him and shook him to his depths. All the turbulent ideas which, for five years or so, had been fermenting in his head, fell with lightning speed into their place and he recognised that there had grown up in him a whole inclusive philosophy. 'The moment I read these words', he tells us in his autobiography, the *Confessions*, 'I saw a new universe and I became a new man.'[2] Civilisation, so he answers the Academy's question, has had a negative, not a positive effect on the virtues: it has corrupted men's *mores*, not purified them. It has extinguished the honest rudeness and rusticity of our ignorant, but innocent forefathers and put in its place a false urbanity which may be pleasing on the surface but is really a cloak for many vices: hypocrisy, treachery, hardness of heart, suspiciousness, fear, hatred and the like. History, Rousseau insists, always repeats the same pattern: civilisation brings with it corruption and moral decay. Egypt, Greece, Rome and

[1] *The Political Writings of Jean-Jacques Rousseau*, ed. Vaughan (1915), vol. II, p. 39.
[2] *Édition de la Pléiade* (1950), p. 344.

Byzantium, all have followed, as if of necessity, the same dismal path. In the second part of his essay, he then tries to show how individual sciences and arts spring from, correspond to, and reinforce, specific human vices: astronomy, for instance, deriving from superstition, rhetoric from flattery, and so on. Of course, not all knowledge is condemned: there were, originally, some great 'preceptors of the human race' who deserve to be remembered with gratitude. But their day is past, and the *littérateurs* of the modern age, animated as they are, not by a desire of true enlightenment, but rather by a selfish craving for publicity, have a baleful, not a beneficial effect on social life. Where they set the tone, cleverness is rewarded, but not manliness.

The tone of this first *Discours* was both challenging and intolerant. In his *Dernière Réponse à M. Bordes*, in which he endeavoured to controvert the arguments of an able critic, Jean-Jacques went so far as to write: 'If I were the head of one of the nations of Nigritia, I declare that I should erect a gallow-tree on the frontier of the country and mercilessly hang the first European who would dare to enter it and the first native who would try to leave.'[1] No wonder that France, and with it the rest of Europe, sat up and listened: such language had never been heard before.

Rousseau followed this first prize essay with a second which appeared in 1755 under the title *Discours sur l'Inégalité*. The subject which the Dijon Academy had set on this occasion was the question: what is the origin of inequality among men, and is it permitted by the law of nature? In order to tackle the first part of this query, Rousseau had to form some opinion on the preliminary question which he saw to be involved: what was man like before inequality came to change him and his society? To find this original of mankind was like finding the pristine form of the statue of Glaucus which had long been under the waters of the ocean and been so corroded by its brine as to resemble no longer a god but a beast. Studying the so-called primitives of 'Nigritia' would not help, for they, too, had some history behind them. Rousseau came to the conclusion that we can best recover the shining image of primitive man, man as nature had fashioned him, by an effort of introspection. We ourselves still bear within us the original of human nature, only that the rubbish of civilisation has increasingly overlaid it and must be taken away, or at least thought away, in order to allow the genuine primitive archetype to show itself in its true outline and colours. This is the fundamental contention of the new *Discours*.

Looking inward in this way, we can sketch out a picture of the life which man must have led in the age of his innocent childhood. His needs were few and simple: he had to eat, to sleep, and to mate, but the means of satisfying these basic desires were always at hand. Neither physical nor mental illness ever distressed him: not physical, because the

[1] *Œuvres*, nouvelle ed. (1819 ff.), vol. I, pp. 141 ff.

weak and sickly were quietly removed before they were beyond the stage of infancy; not mental, because reflection had not yet come to cast its shadow over the human mind. The fear of death was absent, too. And so were the complications which the social habit, as we know it, has introduced into our existence. Not even the family was there to tie man down and deprive him of his independence. Man and woman met casually, and as casually separated; the child had to fend for himself almost as soon as he was weaned. Original man was thus to all intents and purposes a-social. 'Men are not made to be crowded together in ant-hills, but to be scattered over the earth.... The more they congregate, the more they corrupt each other',[1] Rousseau was soon to write in his *Émile*. But the man of nature, though a-social, was not anti-social for he bore in him the sentiment of pity, of sympathy with human suffering in every shape or form. This natural and inborn quality has nothing to do with the intellect; indeed, any undue development of the intellectual faculties will weaken it. It was much more intense before civilisation began to develop, or rather to deprave, man, so that man, paradoxically, was more social and more moral before he began to live in society, and to speculate about morality. In a word, like the animals, our species enjoyed at first a careless existence, of limited horizons certainly, but of unaffected and uncomplicated happiness.

Yet the seeds of future sufferings lay hidden in man from the very beginning. Nature has given him two endowments of great value, but also of potential danger: free will and intellectual perfectibility. They came into their own, as soon as social life began to develop. Why it ever did develop is a great puzzle, a great difficulty, to Rousseau, for he is of the opinion that the social state, with its inherent tendency towards regimentation, cannot have been naturally attractive to our carefree forefathers. In so far as he has any theory at all about the inception of the social habit, he ascribes it to a congeries of unfortunate circumstances, more or less accidental in character, 'which might never have happened',[2] such as climatic changes and the growth of the earth's population. But however obscure the causes of the formation of human society may be, its consequences, Jean-Jacques tells us, are crystal-clear. Men ceased to be nomadic, both in the sense that they no longer roamed from place to place, and in the sense that they no longer changed from mate to mate. But settling down produced the habits which are summed up in the words 'mine' and 'thine'. And as soon as these concepts were in the world, a thousand and one vices followed: jealousy and envy, vanity and contemptuousness, and all the rest. The exclusive appropriation of individual plots of land then set the seal on these developments which play the same part in Rousseau's philosophy as the fall does in the Bible. With property

---

[1] *Émile*, ed. Garnier (1939), p. 37.
[2] *The Political Writings of Jean-Jacques Rousseau*, ed. Vaughan (1915), vol. I, p. 168.

came inequality, and with inequality insecurity. Men, envious of each other, worried about the preservation of what they had and held, and, threatened by all the horrors of fratricidal war, ultimately agreed, egged on by some rich person, to raise property to the level of a legal principle. This was the first social contract, the false social contract, whose dismal results can only be overcome by some new and better *contrat social*.

This brings us to the very heart of Rousseau's political theory. In none of his writings does it show itself more impressively than in his treatise *Du Contrat Social*, published in 1762, the book in which he meditates upon, and idealises, the original constitution of the republic of Geneva, that model state of the small man. Here, as in the second *Discours*, the fundamental conviction from which the argument starts is the thesis that social and political life is not really natural to the human race and must, in consequence, be consciously arranged, that is, instituted by contract, if it is to exist and to continue. The essential submission is that once upon a time there sprang from the united wills of a number of associating individuals a new entity, a new being, the body social and the state. Henceforth there existed not only the personal wills of the men who had joined together, but also, beside and above them, a general will which expresses itself in the commands of the law. Yet this emergence of a general will *of* the community, distinct from, and superior to, the personal wills *in* the community, does not mean the end of individual freedom. Individual freedom certainly perishes where one man is subject to another, that is, where one personal will is subordinated to another personal will. But this is definitely not the situation created by the conclusion of the true *contrat social*, which stands in contrast with the spurious form of law-making discussed in the second *Discours*. For what the founders of state and society submit to is not a personal, but an impersonal will, in other words, an objective rule binding on all alike. This impersonal will, this objective rule, in short, this *law* of state and society is comparable to the laws of nature to which even prehistoric 'natural' man was in thrall, without losing his essential liberty. As the reader can see, Rousseau changes, in this his most important treatise, from a predominantly critical to a much more constructive attitude. By that creative act which brought into being a common life under a common law, we are now told, humanity gained more than it lost. That act put into the place of brute instinct moral rectitude and into the place of the raw independence enjoyed by the savage the rational liberty characteristic of the citizen. Thereby it laid the foundations of a more cultured existence and made 'a stupid and limited animal' into 'an intelligent being', into 'man'.[1]

The situation created by the social contract is thus to be adjudged good, but this does not mean that it is free from difficulties. 'The people always spontaneously desires the good, but it does not always spontaneously

[1] Vaughan, *op. cit.* vol. ii, p. 36.

recognise it.'[1] What is implicit in the unformulated general will must be made explicit in the formulated general law. How can the one be transmuted into the other without losing anything in the process? Rousseau falls back, in the face of this great and difficult task, on two expedients: majority decision where unanimity is unattainable, and the intervention of law-givers à la Solon and Lycurgus. It is inherently probable that the majority decision will coincide with the true public interest, if and in so far as the voters are in possession of the true facts and unswayed by stultifying propaganda. Rousseau evidently assumes that in small communities such as he has in mind, which are also regularly communities of few, simple and transparent needs, conflicts of opinion will turn more on technical matters and method than on questions of principle or content, and the former ought to be amenable to resolution by rational discussion and amicable decision-taking. But however good a guide all this may be to the right line of action, Rousseau, it seems, prefers, especially where fundamental laws are concerned, the intervention of a law-giver who divines what the general will is and puts it into words. He must say what all would say if only they knew how, and so he is merely their mouthpiece and not their master. For this reason his activity does not infringe upon, but rather implements, the sovereignty of the covenanted people. As for the danger that the administration of the laws may fall into the hands of unpatriotic men, Rousseau sees only one remedy, namely the unremitting vigilance of the people at large over those entrusted with the execution of the general will.

This theory, taken as a whole, is a rather typical embodiment of the great tradition in social and political philosophy which is commonly described as individualistic, atomistic or mechanistic. It ascribes primacy of being to the individuals, the man-atoms of society, as it were, and regards society itself as something derived, secondary, and lower in the scale of reality. This is clear from every page of *Du Contrat Social*; and it is clearer still from the article *De l'Économie Politique* which Rousseau contributed to the *Encyclopédie*. For though he likens, in this essay, the activities of agriculture, industry and trade in the body social to the digestive processes in the body physical, and employs more metaphors of this sort, he borrows from the opposing, organical tradition no more than its language and its outer trappings. As far as the substance of his argument is concerned, there can be no doubt that he considers the origin and existence of society as due, not to nature, but to convention. It comes into being, and it continues to function, because the individuals composing it will it so; and they will it so because they find their mutual advantage in a communal mode of life.

And yet, Rousseau felt that society is more, and must be more, than a kind of public utility. He realised that if it is to survive as an organised

[1] *Ibid.* p. 50.

entity, it must be pervaded by a common life-principle, a common set of assumptions and beliefs, without which its coherence would be too weak to withstand the inevitable shifts and shocks of history. That is why he ends *Du Contrat Social* with an investigation of the social role of religion. There is need of a civic faith, to underpin the structure of the state. Christianity will not do, for Christianity—at any rate true Christianity, Christianity as embodied in the Gospels—is too otherworldly. Soldiers who would turn the other cheek will never do, nor will citizens of the same instincts when faced with tyranny or the threat of it. Yet Christianity must not be replaced by another dogmatic system. Men's beliefs should be their own; in the face of the ultimate mysteries, different opinions are possible and should be respected. The civic faith should only concern civic matters. And so Jean-Jacques formulates the main articles of its creed as follows: there is a deity, all-powerful and all-good; there is a life after death with reward for the just and punishment for the wicked; the laws are sacred. Anyone who does not accept these propositions, being anti-social, should be banished. Indeed, Rousseau goes so far as to write: 'If anybody, after having publicly accepted these same dogmas, conducts himself as if he did not believe them, he shall be punished by death; he has committed the greatest of all crimes....'[1] At this point one can, almost bodily, see the stern figure of Robespierre looming up behind that of his master, throwing his shadow before him, and, behind Robespierre, the guillotine.

The words we have quoted bring a somewhat harsh and discordant note into the book and have pained many. Green, for instance, writes: 'That a noble creation like the *Contrat Social* should have been disfigured by such a monstrous appendage is one of the most baffling enigmas recorded in literature.'[2] And, indeed, it is impossible to condone the attitude expressed in this passage. But if it is impossible to condone it, it is not impossible to understand it. Rousseau's ideal, so we must recall, was not the anarchic condition, nor the liberal state, nor yet the civic state as such; it was what, for want of a better word, could perhaps be described as the neighbourhood community. In a small village, or in a closed tribe or town, social pressures have always been strong, and must be so, especially if a high degree of moralisation is to be achieved. Ostracism, in one form or another, has ever been the last word of their laws.

A brief glance at two minor and less speculative essays of Rousseau's will bring our account of his social and political philosophy to a close. The one is his *Considérations sur le Gouvernement de Pologne*, written in 1771 or thereabouts. His main recommendation here is that the country, being rather extended, should be broken up into little self-governing cantons. 'Nearly all the small countries', he writes, 'whether they be republics or monarchies, prosper simply because they are small; because

---

[1] Vaughan, *op. cit.* vol. II, p. 132.   [2] *Jean-Jacques Rousseau* (1955), p. 304.

all the citizens know each other and watch over each other; because the civic heads can see for themselves what goes wrong and what they have to put right; and because their orders are carried out under their very eyes.... God alone can rule the [whole] world; and it would take more than human abilities to govern great nations.'¹ The *Projet de Constitution pour la Corse* of 1765, referring to a state whose boundaries nature herself has drawn narrow, brings out Rousseau's other prime preoccupation: that with the moral perfection of the citizens. The Corsicans, he advises, should stick to the hard and rustic existence which their forefathers had led; they should eschew foreign trade because it brings corruption; they should even be chary of too extended a use of money. If the roads are few, all the better, for then the inhabitants will lead isolated lives and will preserve their manly independence. As for property, the ideal would be that each Corsican should possess only such lands as his labour entitles him to. In practice established rights must be respected, though any further step in the direction of large landed properties must be prevented. In all these arguments it is easy to hear the voice of the Genevan, the Calvinist—and the petty bourgeois.

Apart from the political writings properly so called, Rousseau expressed his vision above all in two novels, both published within a few months of *Du Contrat Social*: *La Nouvelle Héloïse* (1761), and *Émile; ou de l'Éducation* (1762). Between them, they introduced into European thought a new attitude to self, God and nature. Like Freud in this century, Rousseau insisted that we must distinguish in ourselves a human self (which is original and basic) and a social self (which is merely secondary and adventitious). To know ourselves, and to be ourselves, we must find the *moi humain*, and that will be revealed to us only in solitude, never in society. But that self-revealing solitude which we ought to seek should not be the solitude of the chamber and the closet, for there the very walls surrounding us and, as it were, pressing in upon us, will still speak to us of society, obligation, discipline and all the other elements of civilisation and artificiality—it ought to be the solitude of nature. There alone we can be, and there alone we can see, what we really are. And there alone we can receive such knowledge of the Creator as is within our ken. As the words of the dying heroine in *La Nouvelle Héloïse* indicate, there is no room in Jean-Jacques' religious speculations for either the Bible or Jesus Christ— either the revealed word, or the Word Incarnate. His idea of God, as classically set forth in the part of *Émile* entitled *Profession de Foi d'un Vicaire Savoyard* is pure deism, that is, religion without dogma of any kind, with a certain tendency towards pantheism. Like Spinoza before him, Jean-Jacques found it difficult to distinguish between nature and the author of nature. To anyone urging that this was an intellectually unsatisfactory position, indeed, evidence of muddled thinking, he would have

¹ Vaughan, *op. cit.* vol. II, p. 442.

replied that no more is possible in view of the fact that mystery surrounds us on all sides.

. It is not at all surprising that the 'impious' doctrines of *Émile* were condemned by Calvinists and Catholics alike. On 12 May 1763 Rousseau once again cut all connection with his native Geneva, so dear to his heart, by denouncing his citizenship in reply to the condemnation of his book pronounced by the Petit Conseil. But what is much more significant than this hostility of the orthodox is the equal, if not greater, hostility it aroused among the so-called *philosophes,* the intellectuals *à la* Voltaire gathered around the *Encyclopédie.* A very broad and open ditch now divided Rousseau from men like d'Holbach and d'Alembert with whom the public had at one time associated his name: he extolled sentiment, they reason; he was hostile to innovations, they gloried in them; he believed in the historical mutation and mutability of man, they operated with the concept of an eternally unchanging human nature; he thought nature and solitude the true setting of a noble life, they the town and its *salons*; he accepted the existence of a deity, they were to all intents and purposes atheists. These disagreements had found for the first time sharp expression in the winter of 1757–8 when Jean-Jacques had composed his *Lettres Morales.* In them, the whole conflict had come into focus: for the philosophers of Enlightenment, Rousseau explains here, the greatness of man resides in his intellect, but I, he goes on to say, see it in his native goodness. The advancement of cleverness has made us neither wiser nor better nor happier. As a race, 'we are small as far as our lights are concerned', but 'we are great through our feelings'.[1] The publication of *Émile* set the seal as it were on the intellectual, moral and personal estrangement between Jean-Jacques and the *côterie Holbachique* foreshadowed in these pages. Superficially, the war between the two increasingly hostile camps looks like a purely literary squabble, but in reality it is two total philosophies, not to say two classes, which are in conflict. Our whole survey has confirmed the assertion with which we started, namely, that if Voltaire was the spokesman of the *grande bourgeoisie,* still clamouring for reform but already half satisfied with things as they were, Rousseau was the protagonist of the *petite bourgeoisie,* eager for a total revolution and even announcing, to some extent, the proletarian class and the proletarian movement of the future. What embittered Rousseau more than anything against the *philosophes* was, characteristically, their doctrine that there is little to pick and choose between the different social strata so far as happiness is concerned since all human beings become, through habituation, adjusted to their lot. 'No habit', Rousseau writes of the poor man in *Émile,* 'can free him from the physical sensations of tiredness, exhaustion and hunger.'[2] There is a good deal more in this seemingly

---

[1] *Correspondance Générale* (1924 ff.), vol. III, p. 361.
[2] Ed. Garnier (1939), p. 266.

commonplace sentence than meets the eye. It is spoken on the threshold of a new age, the nineteenth century, rather than in the depths of the eighteenth. True, in 1761 the *ancien régime* is still in the saddle; the decisive battle between the privileged orders and the Third Estate is still in the future; but in the conflict between the author of *Émile* and his former friends of the *Encyclopédie* the great social upheavals yet to come are already foreshadowed.

That the true social and historical significance of Rousseauism as a whole consisted precisely in this can be seen from a glance at the developments reminiscent of, and parallel to, it in England and Germany. England was economically far more advanced than France, and for this reason the main carrier of anti-rationalistic sentiment in the country was a typical working-class movement, namely Methodism. Methodism has always, in a favourite term of its founder, been characterised as a 'heart-religion', and this phrase recalls a brief but expressive sentence from *Émile*: 'True worship is worship of the heart.'[1] *Mutatis mutandis*, John Wesley's relation to the clergy of the Established church (whom Edward Young, in his *Night Thoughts*, called 'cold-hearted, frozen formalists'[2]) was not unlike that of Rousseau to the men of the Enlightenment. Both Wesley and Rousseau were protesting passionately against excessive intellectualism, external social conformity and religious indifference. Defending himself against the charge of being a fanatic, Wesley wrote on 12 August 1771 in his *Journal*: 'The very thing Mr Shinstra calls Fanaticism is no other than heart-religion; in other words, righteousness, peace and joy in the Holy Ghost. These must be felt, or they have no being. All therefore who condemn inward feelings in the gross, leave no place either for joy or peace or love in religion, and consequently reduce it to a dry, dead carcase.'

These are the genuine accents of Rousseauism. They are even more clearly heard in the testimonies of John Wesley's followers than in his own for, personally, he still owed much to the old spirit.[3] But he felt the tide and was swept away by it; so much so that in his *Advice to the People called Methodists* he could call the Methodists 'a people who profess to pursue holiness of heart and life', *heart* being the operative word in this definition. Nothing shows better the high emotional tension with which the movement was charged than the hymn literature to which it gave rise; a comparison between the often over-popular but always heart-warming strains of a Charles Wesley and the formally more perfect, yet rather frosty hymns of, for instance, Addison, is most instructive. Another salient feature which English Methodism shared with French Rousseauism was the new relationship it developed between man and nature. Wesley, in his many journeys, always kept an open eye for the beauties of the

[1] Ed. Garnier (1939), p. 381.   [2] Eighth night.
[3] Cf. R. Knox, *Enthusiasm* (1950), esp. pp. 515 ff.

countryside, and it is characteristic of him that he is as struck by the absence of bird-life around Dublin as he is by its abundance on the Isle of Man, facts which the rationalists would never have noticed, let alone mentioned. In his sermon on *Family Religion* he counsels parents to lead their children through the contemplation of nature to the knowledge of Him who made it: 'God, though you cannot see Him, is above the sky, and is a deal brighter than the sun! It is He, it is God that made the sun, and you, and me, and everything. It is He that makes the grass and the flowers grow; that makes the trees green, and the fruit to come upon them.' Clearly, this is a Rousseauesque theme, and though Wesley always remained safely within the bounds of theism and never deviated into pantheism, there is no mistaking his kinship with the man for whom the mystery of creation had always been in the first place a mystery of nature. Both show here their common ancestry: that of Saint Francis, God's troubadour, whose love was lavished on brother Sun and sister Moon, on singing-birds and fishes.

On an intellectually more sophisticated and socially more elevated level, English society shows about this time a reawakening of interest in the primitive and natural, as against that which is refined and artificially contrived. This was a kind of response, definite if perhaps by comparison somewhat cool, to Jean-Jacques' cry of *retournons à la nature*. Books like Robert Lowth's *De Sacra Poesi Hebraeorum* (1753), Robert Wood's *On the Original Genius and Writings of Homer* (1769–1771), and Richard Hurd's *Letters on Chivalry and Romance* (anonymously published in 1762) did much to remove the prejudice which existed in educated circles against the 'wild' and 'coarse' literature of the primitive races and prepared the way for the Ossianic poems whose great success throughout the western world proves how far the public had, in twenty or thirty years, moved away from the contempt of the rationalists for all that was not abstract, quasi-mathematical and new. The Ossianic poems themselves, which made their appearance between 1760 and 1763, were not what they pretended to be, bardic songs of hoary antiquity, but the products of a Scots dominie, James Macpherson, and the fact that they were widely accepted as genuine proves that the public's attitude to primeval literature was as yet more enthusiastic than discerning. But one must not forget that a highlander like Macpherson still had his roots in a living tradition pointing back to proto-historic times; born in 1763, he had spent his childhood in a clan society whose final break-up had not yet begun.

It has become customary to describe men like Lowth and Wood as 'pre-romantics', and the continental countries, too, show figures which deserve to be comprised under this name. Perhaps the greatest of them all was the German Justus Möser whose *Osnabrückische Geschichte*, begun in 1762, was published from 1768 onward. Here again we have before us an intellectual cousin-german of Jean-Jacques Rousseau. The convictions common to the two men were above all their preference for the small unbureaucratic state and for the traditional rustic way of life. However, Möser's advance beyond the rationalist position remained rather limited and partial. We may indeed compare him to Lowth and Wood, but we cannot compare him with the Wesleyans. He allowed the new breath of air that was blowing in Europe to touch and to transform his work, but he did not allow it to revolutionise his life. Yet there was a group of people in Germany who opened their hearts fully and freely to it, and whose whole being was transformed in consequence. These were the so-called *Stürmer und Dränger*, the 'men of stress and strain'.[1] They were, almost without exception, young men who had been born in the 'forties of the century and were now slowly approaching their maturity. Dramatising their revolt against tradition and convention, many of them threw off the powdered wigs on the wearing of which 'refined society' was still insisting, and walked around in their natural hair—an act symbolic of their resolve to 'return to nature'. Characteristically, then, Rousseauism as a movement assumed, east of the Rhine, the form of a youth movement. It is easy to understand why. If England was further advanced economically and socially than France, Germany was rather less advanced; there simply was no working class that could have absorbed and preached the new gospel. And the burghers as a class were far too timid, far too cowed by political authority, far too securely contained by the existing semi-feudal society, to venture forward, to any significant extent, in the direction of a new radical and revolutionary philosophy. There were only the young, especially the university students, to hear the call and respond to it. And among them, indeed, we find many who remind us of the Wesleyans, even if their revolt did not always appear in a specifically religious form.

Often in fact it did. Johann Gottfried Herder was one of this group, and he had accepted Lutheran orders in the same way as John Wesley had Anglican. But, before long, his attitude to his fellow clergymen of the older school had become one of mutual estrangement. Writing to his betrothed on 21 March 1772, he says: 'My sermons are as little clerical as my person: they are human feelings flowing from a full heart.'[2] It was even more dramatically expressed by Reinhold Lenz in his poem *Eduard Allwills einziges geistliches Lied*, in which one stanza, fairly literally translated, runs as follows:

> No, I cry—Redeemer! Father!
> This heart's thirst and longing slake!
> If it cannot be, then rather
> Smash the image Thou didst make!

[1] Originally the title of a play by F. M. Klinger.
[2] *Briefwechsel mit Caroline Flachsland*, ed. Schauer (1926 ff.), vol. II, p. 68.

As these words indicate, some of the young Germans who were caught up in the *Sturm und Drang* movement lived at fever-heat. Passion drove them into positions which they would have eschewed if they had not lost their self-control. Quite a few of them were not unlike the unfortunate Werther of Goethe's novel, men who went to pieces, whether or not they actually committed suicide. The impetus of their revolt as a rule carried them beyond the limits of traditional Christianity, however emotionally reinterpreted, into pantheism. Two of Goethe's early writings, *Brief des Pastors zu...an den neuen Pastor zu...* and *Zwo wichtige bisher unerörterte biblische Fragen* (both of 1773) are clearly inspired by Rousseau's creed of the *Vicaire Savoyard*. Some passages in these essays superficially sound like John Wesley, but the spirit of them is rather that of Jean-Jacques. After some years of searching, Herder, Goethe and many of their friends found a new intellectual haven in neo-platonic philosophy (outwardly manifested by their entry into freemasonry), according to which all that is, is suffused by a divine spirit—a form of mysticism, but no longer a theistic one, as the Creator-Spirit is no longer conceived as a definite person. This is the reason why the same tendency which revivified religion in England left it weaker in Germany—indeed, opened the door to the rabid atheism and materialism of people like Feuerbach or Marx. It was in this period that the equation God = nature was established in many German minds, an equation from which the first term is all too apt to be dropped and lost.

The literary manifestations of the new spirit were far too numerous to be surveyed here in any detail. One of the most characteristic of its expressions was the play *The Robbers*[1] by the youthful Friedrich Schiller which appeared first in 1781, and then again in 1782 showing on its title-page a lion rampant with the legend: 'In Tirannos.' It is the story of two brothers, Karl and Franz. Franz is a typical product of the old society: selfish, vain, weak, but above all calculating and scheming; Karl, on the other hand, is a man as nature made him—somewhat wild, as youths will be, but upright, candid, strong, and generous of heart. It is in the last resort because of these qualities that he is driven out of staid and respectable society and forced to join up with a band of other wild youngsters who become outlaws operating in the Bohemian woods: staid and respectable society has no place for men of his kind. Even this terse characterisation of the main personalities shows what the play is: a presentation, on the stage, of Rousseau's doctrine of man 'natural' and 'unnatural', right and wrong. Similar in theme and tendency are such works as Merck's *Geschichte des Herrn Oheim*, Klinger's *Simsone Grisaldo*, Schiller's *Kabale und Liebe*, Goethe's *Götz von Berlichingen*, and many more. They all discuss, in one form or another, the conflict between the elementary, spontaneous and genuine inner needs and

[1] *Die Räuber.*

strivings of their heroes with the cold, dead and artificial outward manners and conventions of the society within which the drama, as a rule the tragedy, of their life is set.

Enough has now been said to show that Rousseau enunciated a theme which was taken up by all the leading nations of the West and transposed by them into their own key, thus producing a number of variations which reflected and expressed at the same time European unity and national diversities. In surveying its main manifestations, we have again and again been led to speak of it as a revolt, a revolution, anticipating, in a way, the great political crisis of 1789. But revolts and revolutions seem fated to follow a law of exaggeration: they have a tendency to run to excess, to drive, as it were, towards a state of anarchy, and when that happens, a reaction is bound to arise; law and order must needs reassert themselves. So it was with Napoleon in whom we must see both a product of, and a counterblast to, the turbulent last decade of the eighteenth century. Now the history of ideas presents exactly the same pattern as the history of political events. In the 'sixties of the century, the European mind had liberated itself from the fetters which a century of rationalism had forced upon it. In the 'seventies and 'eighties it had enjoyed its new-found freedom and experimented with it. By the 'nineties, the time had come for a return to more disciplined forms of thought and life—indeed for a return to reason (and that in more senses of the word than one). The great philosopher who initiated and effected this calming of the spirit after the storms of the preceding generation was Immanuel Kant (1724–1804). Herder and Goethe, born respectively in 1744 and 1749, ended, as we have seen, as pantheists, men filled with that 'oceanic feeling' which will for ever defy definition and rational restriction; their younger contemporary, Schiller, on the other hand, who was born in 1759, found it not impossible to submit to the austere canons of Kantian thought.

There is hardly a sector of reality in which the forces released about the middle of the century did not ultimately lead to absurd results. The new men rebelled against the hidebound formalism of, for instance, Gottsched's poetics, scornfully saying, with Cowper,[1]

> A poet does not work by square or line,
> As smiths and joiners perfect a design,

but they soon found that poetry without form is apt to degenerate into mere stammering. They rebelled against the petty dictates of a philistine morality, but they soon found that it is impossible for a society to survive without some morality, that is to say, some discipline. They asserted the right of all individuals 'to be themselves', but they soon saw that if this principle is applied to the full, the common life will break up into a disconnected series of private worlds, within which each is a prisoner

[1] Cf. Cowper's poem *Conversation* (1782).

instead of being a free man. How easily this danger could be realised can be seen from the case of J. G. Hamann, Kant's Königsberg compatriot, who has become known as 'the Magus of the North'.[1] 'Magus' in this context means 'the deep one', and it is indeed impossible to read Hamann without being aware that in him we are confronted with a thinker of no common magnitude. But so obscure is his language—a language pregnant with meaning, but delphic and sibylline—that it is very difficult to get his ideas into focus. Holding, as he did, that 'the books of nature and of history' contain nothing but 'cyphers and hidden signs', and demanding that genius should shake off all rules 'as a fig tree its fruit',[2] he allowed himself to drift deeper and deeper into divination, mysticism and eschatology until there was nobody left who could follow him. How different was Kant with his endeavour to find the conditions of true knowledge and the rules of right action binding on all men!

By the rational testing and tempering of the emotional inspirations of *Sturm und Drang*, Kant performed the greatest possible service to his age. He gave permanence to ideas which might otherwise well have proved ephemeral. But his importance as a thinker is by no means confined to the period in which he lived. We must see him, rather, as a companion and counterpart of those great ones who, like Plato or Aquinas, formulated a perennial philosophy. Before speaking of him as a man of the eighteenth century, we must at least indicate wherein his permanent significance consists.

Down to the day of Kant, European philosophy had been divided into two hostile camps: rationalism and empiricism. Just how deep the contrast of the two traditions was, can be seen from the fact that it had made its appearance even in the Middle Ages, yet had always proved irreconcilable, in spite of all earnest endeavours to break the deadlock. In 1781, when Kant's *Critique of Pure Reason* first appeared, it might still have been thought impossible to find a synthesis of principles so utterly disparate. Yet this is precisely what Kant achieved.

Perhaps an example will show best what issues were involved. Men have always spoken of cause and effect, and philosophers have always tried to determine what exactly these words ought to mean. The rationalists saw little difficulty; they asserted that our reason provided all the answers, and therefore Kant described their philosophy as 'dogmatic'. When we think according to the rules of logic, we draw consequences from antecedents, a process which has nothing at all mysterious about it, and, so the argument ran, this connection in our mind between antecedent and consequent reveals to us the nature of the connection between cause and

---

[1] This sobriquet was first applied to him by C. F. von Moser. There is a striking similarity in mental type between Hamann and Blake.

[2] *Schriften*, ed. Roth and Wiener (1821 ff.), vol. I, p. 148, and vol. II, p. 430.

effect in the physical world, outside our mind. The empiricists, on the other hand, maintained that any knowledge of this nexus, if it is to be valid, must spring from the direct observation of the external world. But the external world does not show us the inner workings of the law of causation. All we are able to say is that some facts, x, are succeeded by later facts, y, and when we see this happening repeatedly, we get into the habit of connecting x and y with each other, without ever really seeing the cogency of the concatenation. The most we can assert is that things behave *as if* there was a law of causation. This attitude explains why the empiricist position has also often been described as 'sceptical'. Kant accepted neither the rationalistic-dogmatic argument with its positive, nor yet the empiricist-sceptical argument with its negative, implications, but his own solution is none the less strikingly akin to both. What the connection of cause and effect *in itself* may be, he taught, we do not and cannot know since it is beyond our ken. *We* can never know reality as it is *apart from ourselves*. But our mind is so constituted that it will connect suitable successive phenomena through the pattern of cause and effect; that pattern is *a priori* (before any concrete experience) inherent in our mind (cf. the rationalistic position). On the other hand, it is a pattern—a form of thought—which, before the encounter with concrete experiences, is merely an empty possibility; it is not yet a reality, even a mental reality; it can only be realised—we can only realise it—by observing, in the external world, cases which suggest and fall into that pattern or form (that is, *a posteriori*, after and through experience—the empirical assertion). With such ideas, Kant brought together lines of thought which had, for centuries, run parallel to each other without showing any tendency to converge.

The same principle of reconciliation is applied by Kant to all the basic issues of philosophy. Time and space, for instance, had been to the rationalists innate ideas, whereas the empiricists had regarded them as features of the external world of which we become aware in the same way in which we become acquainted with things in space and events in time. To Kant they are forms of cognition, categories of the human understanding, and given as soon as that understanding itself is given, for they are of the essence of it. Thus far he went with the rationalists. But forms are nothing without content. It can surely be said of them that they find actualisation only when they have some material to form, and that material (of knowledge) comes to us only when we take cognisance of the external world through eye, ear, nose, taste or touch. Hence the salient point of the empiricist position is accepted as well as the basic assertion of the rationalist: 'thoughts without contents are empty, intuitions without concepts are blind.'[1]

[1] *Critique of Pure Reason* (B75), translation by N. Kemp Smith, abridged ed. (1934), p. 61.

Looking upon this technical philosophy from the point of view of history in general, it is easy to recognise wherein its overriding importance consists. Formulating the matter somewhat crudely, we can say that the great philosophers of antiquity and the Middle Ages, such as Plato and St Thomas, had directly concerned themselves with reality, while Kant set out to prove that the decisive as well as exclusively fruitful task of philosophy was to study the *human mind* in its *relation* to reality—to determine how, and how far, true knowledge is at all possible. In other words: before Kant philosophers had always tried to penetrate the mysteries of existence, whereas Kant asked the question: what are the necessary limits of man's knowledge in relation to the mysteries that surround him? This is the famous 'Copernican revolution' in philosophy which Kant claims to have brought about.[1] His philosophy is not concerned with the *transcendent*, that is, that which goes beyond human knowledge and its possibilities, but is a *transcendental* philosophy, that is, one which investigates the *non plus ultra* of all knowing, the dividing line between the area which the arc-lamps of human reason can illumine and those ulterior regions which must for ever remain in darkness. Pushing outward towards the ultimate frontiers imposed upon us by the limited nature of our understanding, we come in the end upon three great 'ideas' whose reality we can indeed assume, because the facts are pointing towards them, but whose reality we can at the same time never adequately attain or grasp or prove, because they are beyond the facts as we know them: God, Freedom and Immortality. These 'ideas' allow us as active beings, beings of 'practical reason', to chart a course for ourselves in the midst of our present uncertainties, but from the point of view of 'pure' reason they are not, and cannot be, certainties, for they transcend its scope.

This brings us to Kant as a moral philosopher, and here we see a man who is within the limits of his age rather than one who towers above it. According to an old tradition, Kant's study had but one adornment, namely a portrait of Rousseau, and there is no doubt that, in his practical philosophy at any rate, the sage of Königsberg was as deeply indebted to, as he was personally enamoured of, the prophet from Geneva. Jean-Jacques' declaration, in his fifth *lettre morale* to Madame d'Houdetot,[2] 'all that is moral in human life lies in man's intention', could almost be described as a summary, by anticipation, of Kant's ethical teaching. True, Kant did not share Rousseau's belief in the native goodness of man; this is an important point which shows that Kantianism, as a system of ethics, was a reaction against, as well as a continuation of, Rousseauism. But this made surprisingly little difference so far as the positive norms of action were concerned. Kant's doctrine, like that of Rousseau, can be subsumed under the twin concepts of liberty and equality.

Man, Kant explains, may be considered from a double point of view.

[1] *Op. cit.* p. 22 (B XVII).   [2] *Correspondance Générale*, vol. III, p. 364.

We can look upon him as a phenomenon like other phenomena, and then he appears subject to the same laws and regularities to which all other phenomena, for instance animals or inanimate objects, are subordinated. This will be the approach natural to, and appropriate for, the scientist, for instance the physiologist. But it is not an approach that will make sense in ethics. When we come to consider ethical conduct, we are at once up against man's intuitive and unshakeable knowledge that he is master of his own action, that he is free. When I ponder whether I should act in this way or in that, whether I should, for instance, prefer my neighbour's happiness to my own or vice versa, I am not involved in the phenomenal world and its causalities and contingencies; I must make my own decision in full independence and responsibility. I can then obey the call of duty and must demand of myself that I do so. This is where for Kant man's true greatness lies. The *Critique of Practical Reason* (1788) is written by a prouder man than the *Critique of Pure Reason*. According to the argument put forward in this most central of all Kant's works, 'good' and 'bad' do not belong to, and show themselves in, the external world, for there everything appears to happen as it must; they are concepts which lie, contend, and operate in men's consciousness—in their intentions, as Rousseau had formulated it. In practice acting according to duty meant for Kant regularly acting in such a way as to resist our sinful native bent and rising superior to it. This, as we have emphasised, is where he disagrees with Rousseau. But it is obvious that the points of agreement between the two thinkers are far more important than the points of disagreement. For what else is Kant's philosophy of practical reason—his 'ethics of pure willing' as Hermann Cohen has called it—but the very same deification of duty which we also find in Rousseau where he speaks of the great men of Rome and Sparta, those heroes who, like Curtius and Cato, always preferred the common weal to private interest? Both Kant and Rousseau followed in the footsteps of the Stoa and of classical Protestantism.

A system of morality such as this, which concentrates all attention on the act of the will, must necessarily be disinterested in the *consequences* of human action, and Kantianism, in fact, accepted the old adage: let justice be done, even if the heavens should fall. It is an unconditional, absolute, rigoristic ethic which it preaches, not a conditional, adjustable and utilitarian one. As Kant himself expressed it, its imperative is 'categorical', not 'hypothetical'. But this means that the rule of conduct which it formulates must be strictly abstract or formal; if it were not, if it were to recommend this or that concrete mode of behaviour, it would unavoidably get caught up in considerations of expediency and thus lose its identity and in the end become subservient to an unprincipled hedonism. The categorical imperative must run something like this: 'Do right, whatever may come of it.' But this formula is too vague. How can it be made more definite? How can it be so elaborated as to give guidance to a being who, like man, must live and move within the circle of his fellows? Always keeping within the frame of formalism, Kant asks, in order to advance his argument, what a society is, if we consider it in the abstract, and answers that it is an assemblage of egos such as my own, each one endowed with that capacity of free decision which is characteristic of man as a moral creature. The social and moral philosopher must then inquire, under what conditions can *all* the associated human beings *equally* assert and live out their inherent freedom? For Kant, the whole problem of social life lay contained in this question. Clearly, the answer to it must be, if they act in such a way that they grant to their fellows the same chance of free and rational decision and deportment which they claim for themselves. Hence the famous formula of Kant's 'categorical imperative': 'Act only on that maxim whereby thou canst at the same time will that it should become a universal law',[1] that is, law for *every* man. It is a formula born of a profound egalitarianism.

This is once again Rousseauite theory presented in a more rational and philosophical guise. The *Critique of Practical Reason* owes an immense debt to *Du Contrat Social* published twenty-six years before, for the chastening agency to which both would subject man is the Law, that 'general will' which is yet the will of nobody in particular, which applies to all alike without respect of person, and which, if it limits our freedom at all, limits it only so that we should have it more abundantly.

In this way, Kant took the invaluable kernel of Rousseau's political and social theory, freed it from the ephemeral husk in which it was originally presented and cast it into a form in which it could last far into the future. Nothing shows better what Kant did for Rousseau than his reinterpretation of the Rousseauan key-concept of *contrat social*. Rightly or wrongly, Rousseau's writings had given the impression that he regarded the social contract as a historical fact. But even the eighteenth century knew that this was nonsense, no more than conjectural history at its worst. Kant left no doubt whatever that he considered the *contrat social* as a historical fiction, as an 'event' which never did nor ever could take place. But he showed to what great practical uses this fiction could be put. It provides an invaluable touchstone for the mental and moral testing of political arrangements in general and legal enactments in particular. If it was to be assumed that all citizens were, after rational consideration, willing to agree to them, if they *could* have become part and parcel of a freely entered and universally accepted *contrat social*, then they were clearly good, in accordance with the demands of the categorical imperative; if not, not. Thus handled, the concept of a social contract ceases to be a piece of historical fancy and becomes a political—a 'regulative'—

[1] *Grundlegung zur Metaphysik der Sitten* (1785), p. 47. Cf. T. K. Abbott, *Kant's Critique of Practical Reason and Other Works on the Theory of Ethics* (ed. 1923), p. 38.

principle of the highest importance, the embodiment of a perennial ideal of public life.

All this goes to show that Kant synthesised and brought to a higher perfection the best thought of the period which we have surveyed. Like the French Revolution, whose 'German philosopher' he has often been called, he marks the end of one epoch and the beginning of another. He marks the end of an epoch because his work brings to reconciliation and completion the main lines of philosophical inquiry which had occupied the leading minds of Europe for hundreds of years. He marks the beginning of another because the final result of his own philosophy was the redirection of human energies from theory to practice, from thought to action. The *Critique of Pure Reason* seemed to say: so far you can go in the exploration of mystery, in the pursuit of truth; further you cannot, and thereby it broke the spring of all metaphysical speculation, the belief in the possibility of one day knowing the apparently unknowable. The *Critique of Practical Reason*, on the other hand, showed that man is never greater than when he acts in pursuit of duty, of the ideal, and this was a lesson which sank deeply into the collective subconsciousness of Europe. The nineteenth century was a century of doers, not of dreamers, and it was not least Immanuel Kant who made it so.

When the French Revolution broke out in 1789, the compass of European history was already firmly set in this direction. True, one of the first and most remarkable literary reactions to it—Edmund Burke's *Reflections on the Revolution in France* (1790)—was an impassioned plea for the preservation of, or a return to, the old order of things. Burke insisted that a libertarian and egalitarian society, such as Rousseau and Kant had envisaged, would lack the necessary social coherence. There is order only where there is organisation; and there is organisation only where there is a division of functions, backed by a firmly established and defended integration such as we find in the healthy organism. Without ranks, making for diversity in unity, and without authority, making for unity in diversity, a society will not be able to survive. Burke sneered at those for whom society was no better than a 'partnership agreement' of the kind concluded 'in a trade of pepper and coffee, calico or tobacco, or some other such low concern', and defined it, for his part, as a community of tradition, 'the ancient order into which we are born'.[1]

But though Burke could deeply impress the first—reactionary—quarter of the new century, the future did not belong to him and those who thought like him. It followed a different prophet, the utilitarian Jeremy Bentham, whose slogan, 'the greatest happiness of the greatest number', was well fitted to become the shibboleth of a materialistic age. Bentham, whose first great work, *An Introduction to the Principles of Morals and Legislation*, had come out in 1789, despised all metaphysics

[1] *Works*, Rivington ed. (1826 ff.), vol. v, p. 184, and vol. vi, p. 207.

as a silly and unrewarding pastime. 'I don't care two straws about liberty and necessity', he wrote to his friend George Wilson. 'Were I to see any...new truths on the subject...lying at my feet, I should hardly think it worth while to stoop to pick them up....'[1] That sort of thing did not matter now; what mattered was the maximisation of pleasure and the minimisation of pain for all members of society. Needless to say, this crude and consistent hedonism raises as many problems, philosophical and otherwise, as any other fundamental attitude, for instance Kant's rigoristic idealism, but the day of such intellectual preoccupations was over. The great advances in technology which had been achieved in the last three decades of the eighteenth century had conjured up before men's eyes the pipe-dream of a world of plenty, and though its progressive realisation since has only led to new disappointments and new yearnings, it is perhaps understandable that it should have dominated history and society for a hundred years.

[1] *Works*, ed. Bowring, vol. x, p. 216.

CHAPTER IV

MUSIC, ART AND ARCHITECTURE

I. MUSIC

OUR acquaintance with musical developments in the closing decades of the Age of Enlightenment has come about only gradually and is still far from complete. Haydn and Mozart are among our best known composers, and Haydn was known internationally in his own time. But in spite of the attraction to scholar and layman alike of this great period in musical history a definitive assessment has, so far, not been achieved. This is not true of German literature, which has elicited excellent monographs on the corresponding decades of the eighteenth century. Among these H. A. Korff's *Der Geist der Goethezeit* makes a conspicuous contribution by stressing the importance of Rousseau and Kant for the work of Herder and Goethe. He would be a churlish musician who would deny the relevance of Goethe's poetics and aesthetics for music, the art which is so peculiarly tied to its own technique. For this reason, Korff's searching quest for the criteria of 'classicism', and his attempt to define the term as a uniquely balanced blend of eighteenth-century 'enlightenment' and nineteenth-century 'romanticism' deserve to be applied to music *in extenso*.

Of the general histories of music written since the first World War, two deal with the period of the Enlightenment.[1] Ernst Bücken's *Die Musik des Rokokos und der Klassik* (Potsdam, 1931) is the relevant volume in the series known as *Handbuch der Musikwissenschaft*, edited by the same author. *Handbuch der Musikgeschichte*, edited by Guido Adler (2nd ed., 2 vols., 1930) contains several chapters on the eighteenth century, notably Adler's 'Die Wiener klassische Schule', Robert Haas' 'Die Oper im 18. Jahrhundert', and Wilhelm Fischer's 'Instrumentalmusik, 1750–1828'.

It was to be expected that the German editor Bücken would emphasise the importance of Mannheim and Berlin, while the Austrian editor Adler naturally extolled the musical glories of Vienna.[2] However, an assertion that the modern sonata-form, the greatest single musical achievement of the age, was invented in a particular locality at any one time—Vienna, Mannheim, Berlin or Milan—could not be supported by any but a biased observer. Upon examination of the primary sources

---

[1] See vol. vi, ch. iii (2). The English and American series of musical histories have not as yet reached the later eighteenth century. P. H. Láng, *Music in Western Civilization* (1941) and O. Strunk, *Source Readings in Music History* (1950) may be found useful.

[2] Italian scholars, among them Fausto Torrefranca, have rightly reminded us of the influence of Giovanni Battista Sammartini and his compatriots.

there emerges a picture of general dissatisfaction with the music of the baroque era among composers and public alike and of a simultaneous groping in various localities for a vocabulary and kind of musical architecture that were appropriate to the mood of the later eighteenth century. In a situation of this sort priority counts for little. It is important, nevertheless, to trace the origins of the four-movement form that dominated the middle and late symphonies of Haydn, a form that was perfected by Beethoven and retained its leadership in subsequent periods to the time of Vaughan Williams. Adler's discovery of a symphony in four movements composed by Georg Matthias Monn, dated Vienna 1740, has been the subject of much discussion. Its significance lay in the fact that between the opening and closing allegros it contained, in addition to the usual slow movement, a minuet. One may assume, then, that this extension of the Italian form of the symphony in three movements was in the air and occurred in Vienna (where Monn was organist at the Karlskirche) before Johann Stamitz took up residence in Mannheim in 1741. On the other hand, while Stamitz and the Mannheimer proceeded to favour the minuet as a symphonic movement (at Paris as well as Mannheim), the Viennese composers Wagenseil and the young Haydn and Monn himself continued to write symphonies in three movements. Moreover, Haydn, in the course of his countless experiments with form, found it agreeable to incorporate the minuet into his symphonies quite independently of Stamitz's influence. This he did in his middle period, and here we have the crux of the matter, for the modern symphony was established by the success of Haydn's works in Paris and London in the 1780s. Haydn's minuet led to Beethoven's scherzo and thus changed the future course of instrumental music. But to name Sammartini, Stamitz or C. P. Emanuel Bach merely as precursors of Haydn would be unfair to these masters. Certain of their works, such as the piano sonatas of Emanuel Bach and the symphonies of Stamitz, are enjoyed today as works of art aside from their historical importance. At the same time, it would be captious to deny that these composers were of lesser stature than Haydn and his younger contemporary Mozart. The superior craftsmanship of a Haydn and his lifetime of experience were necessary to mould and establish a pattern that survived for more than a century. To speak, then, of a Viennese period and of Viennese classicism in music does not imply priority, nor monopoly of artistic birthright; it assumes that, at the turn of the century, Europe's leading composers lived, for better or worse, in the Austrian capital. They may not have been born there, but they resided and died there, as did Gluck (1787), Mozart (1791), Haydn (1809), Beethoven (1827), and Schubert (1828). When Napoleon posted sentries at Haydn's door to honour and protect the dying master, he recognised Vienna as the musical capital of Europe, which, indeed, it remained until the death of Brahms in 1897.

This much will be gleaned from a perusal of the most recent histories of music. Our knowledge is greatly fortified by two other classes of publication: dictionaries and monographs.

Grove's Dictionary of Music was from its inception (1st ed., 4 vols., 1879–89; 5th ed., 9 vols., 1954) an invaluable aid to research on Haydn, Mozart, Beethoven and Schubert; its founder and first editor was a notable authority on the Viennese school. The comprehensive article on Haydn in the latest edition includes the results of original research not elsewhere available. Even more extensive coverage is given in the German encyclopaedia *Die Musik in Geschichte und Gegenwart*. Of the eight volumes which have appeared up to 1960 the articles on 'Klassik' and 'Barock' display an admirable grasp of both cultural and musical history. Its biographical articles on Haydn and Beethoven complement, bibliographically and otherwise, the material in *Grove*.

The modern scholarly monograph, discussing in detail the life as well as the works of a single composer, is a product of the mid-nineteenth century. In 1856 Otto Jahn, a classical scholar, issued the first of his four volumes on *Mozart*. This remarkable work has been translated into many languages;[1] in various revisions it achieved seven German editions within a century. Jahn's exemplary thoroughness was quickly emulated by Chrysander's *Handel*, Spitta's *Bach*, and C. F. Pohl's *Haydn* (2 vols., 1875–82). Much as we may criticise these works of the nineteenth century for their inevitable omissions, their authors' patient labours have not, so far, been wholly superseded. Jahn's *Mozart* suffers chiefly from the fact that, at the time of its writing, the works of the lesser masters were hardly known. Since the symphonies of Monn and Stamitz were not discovered until after Jahn's death, he can hardly be blamed for not discussing them. Similarly, one who lived during the conflict between Wagner's 'music of the future' and Hanslick's 'notion of the beautiful' should not be criticised for stressing unduly the Apollonian and timeless beauty of Mozart. In our own day the demonic and tragic aspects of Mozart's art have been similarly exaggerated by some of Jahn's critics. His enduring contribution to musical scholarship was embodied in the new theory, however imperfectly applied, that a work of art should be put into perspective by a consideration of earlier and related works. This historical and comparative approach bore fruit in the monographs of the twentieth century, of which we may single out three.

In 1912 there appeared the first two volumes of *Mozart, Sa vie musicale...* by G. de Saint-Foix and T. de Wyzewa.[2] Disdaining biographical minutiae, the authors studied Mozart's complete works morphologically and extended this method to the works of many of his contemporaries. They revised the chronology of Mozart's development

---

[1] English translation by P. D. Townsend, 3 vols. (London, 1891).
[2] The fifth and final volume appeared in 1946.

and discussed the models on which he drew in Salzburg, Vienna, Milan, Mannheim, Paris and London. Thus, the French monograph made a new contribution to scholarship—criticism of style. Hardly less basic to our knowledge of the eighteenth century is the complete revision of Jahn's *Mozart* by Hermann Abert (5th ed., 2 vols., 1919–21). Perhaps Abert was, at times, too respectful of Jahn's methods, but the very significant revision and expansion of Jahn's historical 'digressions' are masterly. Abert's discussion of various musical genres up to the time of Mozart, whether opera, symphony or string quartet, still remains the best history of the so-called classical period in music. Although he disagrees with Jahn's notion in regard to the elements of beauty in Mozart's music, Abert's account of its dissonant and tragic aspects is balanced and moderate.

Haydn fared less well. When Jahn died in 1869 the material he had amassed on Haydn passed to C. F. Pohl of Darmstadt and his researches on Beethoven to A. W. Thayer of Boston, Massachusetts. These two scholars had migrated to Austria to study and publish monographs on the music of the Viennese period. Neither man lived to complete his task. In 1927 Hugo Botstiber added a useful third volume to Pohl's uncompleted study.[1] In 1955 there appeared *The Symphonies of Joseph Haydn* by H. C. Robbins Landon, containing a revised chronology of Haydn's 104 symphonies and an assessment of the composer's stylistic development. Landon's results were based on a careful examination of the Haydn manuscripts, which were badly scattered in a variety of Austrian localities, and a study of material in provincial libraries, including autographs, copies and watermarks.

Haydn's position in the mainstream of music comes into perspective when we consider the record of achievement of previous generations. Of the composers born in the 1680s Rameau, Bach, Handel and D. Scarlatti wrote in a style that appeared heavy and old-fashioned for the most part to the later eighteenth century. To be sure, the formal patterns of the Viennese masters were occasionally anticipated by the Italians. Francesco Conti (1681–1732), appointed court composer in Vienna in 1713, prefaced his opera *Pallade Trionfante* (1722) with an overture that has rightly been hailed as a forerunner of the symphony:[2] of its three separate movements which together form the pattern fast–slow–fast, the first and third are, in effect, in sonata form. However, such patterns were the exception rather than the rule. Although the sonatas of D. Scarlatti (1685–1757) were surprisingly ahead of their time in idiom as well as pattern, Scarlatti nevertheless wrote many harpsichord *Esercizi* that

---

[1] At Thayer's death only three volumes of his study of Beethoven (1866–79) had been published. Volumes IV and V were completed and revised by H. Deiters and H. Riemann (1907–8).

[2] G. Adler, *Handbuch der Musikgeschichte*, vol. II, pp. 797 f.; Hugo Botstiber, *Geschichte der Ouvertüre...* (Leipzig, 1913), pp. 82, 258 ff.

showed no concern for the key relationships that became so highly standardized in sonata form after 1750.[1] The same may be said of many of the operatic overtures produced by Conti and others.

Of the next generation, Giovanni Battista Sammartini (1701–75) had the advantage of working in Milan, a city that was important in the schooling of both Gluck and Mozart. For this reason, perhaps, his works have had a more direct influence on the Viennese masters. Not only do his operatic overtures, symphonies, concertos, his quartets and trios exhibit an architectural pattern that is familiar to the modern concert listener, but within its framework a new spirit is revealed: the contrasting sections display real dualism, and there are the beginnings of Haydn's famous thematic development.[2]

It was the second decade of the eighteenth century, however, that produced Haydn's major predecessors: the Vienna composers Gluck (1714–87), Wagenseil (1715–77) and Monn (1717–50); the Mannheimers Richter (1709–89) and Stamitz (1717–57); Pergolesi (1710–36) and Rousseau (1712–78); and, finally, Johann Sebastian Bach's son, Carl Philip Emanuel Bach (1714–88), who divided his career between Berlin and Hamburg.

The joint successes of Pergolesi and Rousseau rang the knell of the type of stately operas that had been composed by Rameau and Handel. The success of *La Serva Padrona* and *Le Devin du Village* (jointly produced in Paris in 1752) was a clear indication that the general audience craved neither grandeur nor serious and rich harmony. Melody, and melody only, was called for; moreover, melody of a special type. Pergolesi's comic masterpiece was originally intended as a mere interlude to be presented at Naples in 1733 in honour of the wife of the Emperor Charles VI. The main entertainment of the evening was the grand opera *Il Prigioner superbo*.[3] But, whereas Pergolesi's serious operas rest quietly on library shelves, *La Serva Padrona*, admired by Rousseau and Goethe, is known and performed even today. The simplicity and modernity of the tunes of *opera buffa* were a direct answer to the battle-cry of the century, 'Back to nature!' The aesthetic cliques in Paris quickly formed themselves into two camps: the 'coin de la reine' which championed the Italians vigorously opposed the 'coin du roi' which favoured native French composers. Pergolesi's melodies followed the inflections of speech more closely and obscured the verbal text much less than did the ornate roulades of grand opera. Though comparisons were unfairly made between the serious *tragédies lyriques*[4] of Lully and Rameau and the comic *opere buffe* of Pergolesi and his fellow Neapolitans no one really

---

[1] The term 'sonata form', denoting an architectural pattern, applies to sonatas for keyboard (or other instruments) as well as to quartets and symphonies.
[2] Cf. E. Bücken, *Die Musik des Rokokos und der Klassik*, pp. 28, 175, 210.
[3] This was the third *opera seria* composed by Pergolesi.   [4] Cf. vol. VI, ch. III(2).

cared whether the genres were comparable. If Jean-Jacques Rousseau's *Devin du Village* could hardly be called Italian, its simple, infectious tunes ensured its survival in the Paris repertory for sixty years. Champions of the Age of Reason and of Enlightenment expected melody unencumbered by counterpoint or thorough bass, melody of a direct, folksong-like appeal that spoke a universal language. In previous centuries composers took pride in the results they were able to achieve with their melodic raw material; now their aim was to choose, to invent, apt melodies from the start. The originality and propriety of the tunes were of primary consideration. The mood of the times was reflected in the enormous vogue on the Continent of Percy's *Reliques of Ancient English Poetry* and the concomitant enthusiasm for folk-song of Herder and Goethe, Walter Scott, Arnim and Brentano. When Herder praised Gluck's grand opera *Orfeo* (1762) he commended the arias for being as plain and simple as the English ballads. And, *mutatis mutandis*, he was right, for the stylistic simplicity of *opéra comique* had an important influence on Gluck, who was criticised by Handel for understanding counterpoint as little as his (Handel's) cook. This criticism was astute enough but little did the great Handel realise that the many-voiced texture of music belonged to the *ancien régime*, and that Gluck's seeming shortcoming served him well in an age that was avid for lucid and intelligible musical speech. 'When you want to know whether a melody is really beautiful', counselled Haydn, 'sing it without accompaniment.'

The historical importance of Gluck's *Orfeo* far transcends its musical excellence. In many respects *Alceste* (1767), *Paride* (1770), *Iphigénie en Aulide* (1774), and particularly *Iphigénie en Tauride* (1779) are more successful works of art. But the spectacular defiance with which Gluck and his librettist Calzabigi challenged the hegemony of the Metastasian type of opera caught the imagination of Europeans. To condemn Metastasio for the shortcomings of Italian opera would be unjust. Audiences then, as now, longed for aria-operas and number-operas; that is to say, operas consisting for the most part of numbers or units which were arias for star-singers. Gluck at Vienna, Hasse at Dresden and Jommelli at Stuttgart satisfied this demand, and Metastasio, court poet of Vienna from 1730 to 1782, supplied these various courts with the kind of tasteful verse and dramatic construction ideally suited to this Italian genre. It was against this background that Gluck surprised the musical world by his declaration that in future he would strive for dramatic truth; his operas would henceforth contain, beside the usual set arias, a generous admixture of choral singing and purely instrumental music (ballets). This practice savoured more of the tradition of the *tragédie lyrique* than of *opera seria*: it was, in fact, the injection of a French ingredient into an essentially Italian form.

Gluck instituted an equally important (though less readily recognised) reform in his significant increase of the time-dimension of the scena. Gone was the choppy, short-breathed structure of the Metastasian style, where the hero (or villain) would exit immediately after his aria, signifying the dramatic and musical conclusion of the basic unit. The Vienna version of *Orfeo* (1762) contained, in the pleading of Orpheus with the Furies, a complex in which ten separate numbers had been welded together into a unified larger whole. This method of construction was destined to influence Mozart, Beethoven and Wagner.

Of Haydn's remaining major predecessors, Stamitz and C. P. E. Bach made significant contributions to the new style of musical composition. Stamitz was twenty-four years old when he joined the court orchestra of the Elector Palatine in Mannheim in 1741. He was born in Habsburg territory, in the Bohemian town of Brod.[1] So far as the rest of Europe was concerned, Stamitz was a German composer, as were his compatriots Richter and Wagenseil, who were active at Mannheim and Vienna respectively. Compositions by these Germans were published in Paris in the 1750s under the collective Italian title, *La Melodia Germanica composte de vari autori*.[2] Italian was (as it still is to some extent) the international language of music, but the German-speaking countries were slowly supplanting Italy as Europe's major purveyor of musicians.[3] In the same way Leipzig was later to supersede Paris as a major centre of music publishing, although London and Amsterdam continued in their favoured positions.

Stamitz's dynamics and formal structures mark an important stage on the road from the early Italian *sinfonia* of less than 100 bars to the gigantic first movement of Beethoven's *Eroica*. He was a singularly efficient trainer of the orchestra; certain effects of the so-called Mannheim school, such as the famous crescendo, were already noted and admired by Burney in the eighteenth century. This crescendo device should not be viewed merely as a contrast to the echo dynamics of Scarlatti and Handel. It was a token of the new kind of symphonic thinking and patterning: the themes (or groups of themes) were more carefully and dramatically prepared and of necessity placed in a more spacious structure.

C. P. Emanuel Bach became harpsichordist to Frederick the Great in 1740. Upon the death of the famous Telemann in 1767 Emanuel Bach was appointed his successor as municipal director of music of the five main churches of Hamburg. He remained in this post until his death in 1788. Bach made his impact primarily through the publication of his compositions, which were among the most important products of the musical printing presses before Haydn's day. The hegemony of vocal

[1] Satirised in the title of F. W. Grimm's pamphlet *Le Petit prophète de Boehmisch-Brode* (Paris, 1753), which championed the modern music of Pergolesi and Rousseau. Grimm was associated with Rousseau and Diderot in the great *Encyclopédie*.

[2] Cf. *Denkmäler deutscher Tonkunst*; Folge II: *Bayern*; Jahrgang III, vol. I, p. xxxiv; Jahrgang VII, vol. II, p. xxvi.   [3] Cf. vol. VI, ch. III (2).

music (primarily opera) over instrumental music still prevailed in the days of Emanuel Bach. The two categories were nearly balanced in the works of Haydn and Mozart, and the scales were not reversed until Beethoven impinged upon the scene in the early nineteenth century. It was primarily through the medium of the keyboard that Emanuel Bach taught the younger composers how to achieve a combination of two objectives, namely, to write in a truly idiomatic instrumental style and at the same time to move the heart by song-like 'cantabile' melodies. Successive series of sonatas demonstrate his teachings from Opus 1, the six 'Prussian' sonatas (Nuremberg, 1742) to the sonatas, rondos and fantasias 'for connoisseurs and amateurs' (Leipzig, 1787). In addition, he wrote the most famous piano manual of the eighteenth century, *Versuch über die wahre Art, das Clavier zu spielen*.[1] His compositions and theoretical writings alike betray a new 'seriousness', a magisterial view of art that is closer to Beethoven than to Haydn and Mozart. Emanuel Bach postulated melodies conceived in song and evocative of poetical ideas. These notions, which clearly echoed Rousseau, Bach passed on to his younger brother Christian and to J. A. P. Schulz.

The ripples occasioned by the weight of Bach's authority expanded considerably when the Austrian ambassador to Berlin, Baron Gottfried Van Swieten, commissioned Bach to write six symphonies, in which the composer's creative imagination might have free rein, unfettered by any regard for technical difficulties. In their serious and intense spirit these remarkable works, written in 1773, anticipate the most profound compositions of Haydn and Beethoven. It is hardly necessary to stress Van Swieten's illustrious benefactions to music in the latter half of the eighteenth century. His home in Vienna, where the scores of Bach's six symphonies were housed, was a veritable hive of musical activity, with its Sunday concerts and the host's unflagging encouragement to young musicians. There Mozart arranged Handel's *Messiah* for performance at one of the musicales. The Baron himself arranged the libretto of Haydn's *Creation* and *Seasons* and made suggestions concerning the musical settings of these oratorios. It was to this Austrian patron of the arts that Beethoven dedicated his first symphony. And it was in this environment that Haydn and Mozart found a rare opportunity to study the works of Emanuel Bach and to discover in them new melodies and a new spirit.[2]

Haydn was born in Lower Austria in 1732; he was taken to Vienna at eight years of age to be a choir-boy at St Stephen's cathedral, and he remained in that city, with few interruptions, for the next twenty years. From 1761 to 1790 his services for the Princes Esterházy required his

[1] 1st and 2nd eds., Berlin, 1753 and 1759; 3rd and 4th eds., Leipzig, 1780 and 1787; ed. W. Niemann (Leipzig, 1906); ed. and trans. W. J. Mitchell (New York, 1948).

[2] Cf. also C. P. E. Bach's *Magnificat*, ed. C. Deis (New York, 1950); *Sinfonie no. 3*, ed. E. F. Schmid (Hanover, 1932); *Sinfonie no. 2*, ed. E. F. Schmid (Hanover, 1933); and *Mozart-Jahrbuch 1953* (Salzburg, 1954), pp. 15–31.

residence either in one of the provincial palaces from twenty-five or fifty miles south-east of Vienna or in Vienna itself. Except for the English journeys in 1790–5 Haydn lived in the capital for the most part until his death in 1809. In contrast to those ceaseless travellers Handel, Gluck and Mozart, Haydn's career was quiet and not very cosmopolitan. As he spent little of his long life outside his native country, he listened to music that was largely composed by Austrians and Italians resident in Austria. These compositions may be termed his models, which he then augmented by studying the scores of Emanuel Bach and, later, the works of Handel and Sebastian Bach. But, essentially, Haydn was self-taught and developed independently. The experiments issuing from his fertile, logical and disciplined mind ultimately produced the string quartet and the symphony as we know them today. Unlike some of his younger contemporaries— Goethe, Mozart—Haydn's genius did not seem to require the challenging stimulus of other great works. Not that he was insensitive to his surroundings: he responded to the music of Mozart, and his experience of Handel's oratorios clearly influenced *The Creation* (1799) and *The Seasons* (1801). Yet, whilst Saint-Foix and Abert have chronicled for Mozart more influences of this kind than there is space to record, Haydn's great models can be counted on one's fingers. After the Mannheim school had perfected the four-movement form to include the minuet, Haydn seems to have worked out the formula for himself again. Another aspect of the independent course of Haydn's development is that he used the famous Mannheim crescendo only rarely in his 104 symphonies.

Until his fortieth year (1772) Haydn concentrated his energies on instrumental music. The earliest symphonies are brief, the three movements together equalling little more than a single first or last movement of one of the majestic London symphonies of the 1790s. Haydn entered the service of Prince Esterházy in 1761. With this new post he inherited an orchestra that was superior to any he had hitherto directed. For this reason he could expand the scope of his ideas to good purpose and in the first year of his residence he composed symphonies nos. 6, 7 and 8. The character of the works, however, wavered between the new symphony and the old concerto grosso. Nor did Haydn seem quite certain whether he wished to write entertainment music in the gallant style, so prevalent in Europe from 1740 to 1770, or whether his symphonies were to be a medium for the expression of sustained and profound meditation. From time to time the more serious attitude prevailed. In the first movement of no. 22 ('The Philosopher', composed 1764), in the key of E flat major, a slow and solemn adagio with a chorale-like theme on the horns and cors anglais is accompanied by muted strings.

The minor mode, where sombre tones are most likely to occur, is wholly absent from Haydn's early symphonies. Between 1765 and 1772, however, he composed the 'Lamentazione' in D minor, 'La passione' in

F minor and the so-called Farewell symphony in the remote key of F sharp minor.

In the late eighteenth century symphonies were composed for amateurs (*Liebhaber*), and only rarely did Haydn violate this general rule. His most serious thought was reserved for the string quartet, a category addressed to connoisseurs and intellectuals. If J. S. Bach's 'Forty-eight' are considered the Gospel of fugue composition, Haydn's 'Eighty-three' may be designated the *locus classicus* of the quartet. The first twelve of these betray their inheritance—the Viennese fondness for out-of-door entertainment in the form of *divertimenti* and serenades. These gay works were full of melody; since it was impracticable to employ a harpsichord in the open they were unencumbered by the thorough-bass of an earlier age. On the whole, instrumental music was intended for dancing, and Haydn's early quartets usually include two minuets in their five movements. But after the composer had worked extensively in the new symphonic spirit at Esterházy—a spirit which is basically opposed to that of the dance—he infused new elements of style into his quartet-writing. In four of the six works comprising Opus 3 (Quartets 13–18) the four-movement form is used and the individual movements show a proportionate growth in stature and length. One wonders whether this unconventional course and the increased brilliance and difficulty of the violin parts made the work sufficiently unusual to cause a delay in publication, for the first set, nos. 1–6, had been published in Paris in 1764, and in Amsterdam the following year, while nos. 7–12, published in Paris in 1766, also appeared in the following year in Amsterdam. But Opus 3, though composed in the middle 'sixties, did not appear in print until 1777 (Paris, Bailleux).[1]

Haydn perfected his quartet writing in three further cycles: nos. 19–24 (1769), 25–30 (1771) and 31–6 (1772). With the completion of the last set the decisive advance had been made, and the classical phase of chamber music in the age of Haydn, Goethe and Mozart had been achieved. The earlier gallant style, with a melody in the treble and mere accompaniment below, was here superseded by a texture of four parts in which the first violin functioned as a *primus inter pares*. With this development a new strictness entered the entire fabric of music-making. 'For myself, this [quartet playing] has always been the most intelligible of instrumental music: one hears the conversation of four sensible people and one expects to learn something from their discourse and to come to know the peculiar character of each instrument', remarked the sage of Weimar.[2] Haydn's *modus operandi* had, in fact, often proved its worth in the history of the arts: by reverting to a style that was obsolete, Haydn was able to

---

[1] The fact that most of Haydn's early publications were unauthorised by him proves the European demand for his works. Sometimes the quartets were published as *divertimenti* with additional horn parts, cf. M. M. Scott, 'Haydn's Opus Two...and Three', *Proceedings of the Royal Musical Association*, vol. LXI (1934–5), pp. 1–19.

[2] H. Abert, *Goethe und die Musik* (1922), p. 54.

perfect the pattern of his quartet writing. For the fugues that loom there so prominently belong to the age of Handel, Rameau and Sebastian Bach. By the 1770s some composers were ready to temper, though by no means abandon, the new style of Rousseau and Pergolesi. A desire for strictness, seriousness and compactness, of which Haydn's string quartet fugues were only one example, resulted in adding depth and craftsmanship to the innovations of Vienna, Mannheim and the other centres of music.

As if conscious of the achievement, Haydn rested on his laurels and left off composing quartets. During nine years he devoted his major energies to vocal music, opera, oratorio and mass. There were many reasons: for one thing, Prince Esterházy found Haydn's new phase too heavy; for another, his patron had built a 'new Versailles' whose beautiful theatre was to provide opera on state occasions. In honour of Maria Theresa's visit to Esterházy in 1773 Haydn composed *L'infedeltà delusa*. *Il mondo della luna* came four years later and in 1779 *L'Isola disabitata*, which was obviously influenced by Gluck's *Orfeo*.

Haydn's fame continued to grow and the composer established himself eventually as the favourite of a general middle-class public. In 1780 the Vienna publisher Artaria printed a set of his piano sonatas and followed this in 1781 with six new quartets (nos. 37–42) which Haydn advertised as being composed in an entirely new and special manner. Actually, they were not so new. Haydn consolidated and expanded the advances of 1772 but did so in a manner acceptable to the public: fugal touches there were, though no movement was learnedly entitled 'fuga'. The success of these authorised publications enhanced Haydn's prestige and income considerably. His trips to Vienna, where he enjoyed the companionship and counsel of the younger Mozart, become more frequent. In 1784, having brought to completion his efforts in the vocal forms—for the time being at least—he abandoned opera and liturgical music and devoted himself once more to instrumental composition. His eye was now fixed on far-off horizons, beyond Vienna, toward Paris and London. Between 1785 and 1788 Haydn wrote eleven symphonies, which became *le dernier cri* in Paris; between 1787 and 1790 he composed the quartets nos. 44–68. When the orchestra at Esterházy was disbanded on Prince Nicholas' death in 1790 Haydn had a choice of offers, including a post at the Neapolitan court. But he now preferred freedom from court life and accepted the proposal of J. P. Salomon to come to London. Haydn would receive £300 for an opera, £300 for six new symphonies, £200 for the copyright of these, £200 for twenty new pieces of various sorts, and £200 for a benefit concert. Mozart tried to counsel his older friend and tutor who knew so little of the world, concerning the difficulties of travelling, and of languages. In reply, Haydn gave the classic formulation of the universal appeal of his art: 'My language is understood all over the world.'[1] He thereupon ministered to the public demand and supplied the kind of music Paris and Europe were ready for. This was not to be Italian *coin de la reine* nor French *coin du roi*, not even Austrian in character. In effect, he had forged a synthesis of these various styles that appealed to the 'sensible' human beings of Goethe's description, regardless of national boundaries. Haydn's late compositions, dating from the London concerts of 1791–2, encompassed the achievement of Mozart and were contemporaneous with Beethoven's initial impact on Vienna.[2]

Mozart's position in the cultural life of Europe is singularly anomalous. Unlike Haydn, who was the son of a wheelwright, Mozart had the good fortune to be born (in Salzburg, 1756) of cultivated parents. His father, Leopold Mozart, was not only a good musician and capable teacher, but he remained Mozart's guide and mentor for most of that restless composer's life. The young prodigy's appearances before royalty and aristocracy from the age of six onwards are well known. His performances before the Elector at Munich and Maria Theresa at Vienna were followed by concert tours in Belgium, France and Germany (where Goethe heard him play). At Christmas 1763 he performed before Madame de Pompadour at Versailles and in April 1764 before George III at St James's. Mozart's violin sonatas were printed in Paris when he was eight years old, in London when he was nine and in Amsterdam a year later. His operas *Mitridate*, *Ascanio*, *Lucio Silla* were successfuly presented at Milan in three consecutive winters (1770–2). Yet Mozart was buried in a pauper's grave in 1791.

Had Mozart been disposed to accommodate the social forces of his age his material future need have caused him no anxiety. But where Haydn emancipated himself slowly from provincial patronage, Mozart combated it. His famous break with the archbishop of Salzburg in 1781 and his subsequent career as a free-lance composer in Vienna were manœuvres both ill-prepared and ill-founded. Mozart was equally maladroit in his dealings with publishers. When Hoffmeister commissioned three piano quartets in 1785–6—the composer was by then a mature thirty years of age—he sent Hoffmeister the recondite G minor. Upon being told that the public found the work too difficult, Mozart turned to Artaria who agreed to publish the E flat Major Quartet. This composition was less difficult technically but still too demanding for routine performances, as contemporary newspaper reviewers were quick to point out.[3] Joined to this lack of skill and strategy in accommodating patrons, publishers and the general public, was a more deep-seated dereliction. Mozart's music was no longer wholly of his own time. Haydn's art was the perfect embodiment

---

[1] 'Meine Sprache versteht man in der ganzen Welt.'
[2] Beethoven's first visit there in 1787, when he intended studying with Mozart, came to a quick end because of the illness of his mother.
[3] Cf. Abert, *Mozart*, 5th ed., vol. II, p. 193; and A. Einstein, *Mozart* (1946), pp. 263 ff.

of the late Enlightenment. Mozart's music clearly mirrored the dawn of a new era. His was the Janus-head that shed an added glow on the waning Enlightenment and at the same time heralded the coming Romanticism. Mozart's position in the evolution of style is epitomised in the fact that in the first decade of the nineteenth century, when Haydn's last works were published, Beethoven had already composed his first five symphonies. To be one or two decades ahead of his time and, inevitably, ahead of the average listener, was Mozart's personal misfortune; for he was neither a revolutionary, like Beethoven, nor unfashionable, like Sebastian Bach. Yet it was on the purse of the average listener that his career depended when he moved to Vienna in 1781.

In that year Mozart composed *Idomeneo* which, after some delays, was performed at Munich on 29 January 1782. It is the one work that separates the mature artist from the young composer and, apart from the hastily composed *Tito* of 1791, it is Mozart's single distinguished contribution to the old-fashioned style of *opera seria*. The later eighteenth century made no pretence of the fact that it found grand opera too dignified and stiff for its taste. Once more the spirit of Rousseau walked abroad and spoke through Goethe: 'what derives from grandeur cannot return to art.'[1] Mozart showed his concern for dramatic verity when he wrote to his father that the oracle in *Idomeneo*, fashioned after that in Gluck's *Alceste*, must be brief. He noted that 'if the speech of the ghost in *Hamlet* were not so long it would be far more effective'. The orchestral recitative, on the other hand, might well be lengthened, for the hovering between hope and fear would 'owing to the *chiaro e oscuro* have a capital effect'. Thus, following Gluck's example, Mozart sought to endow Metastasian opera with greater dramatic verisimilitude and with a diversity that would relieve the unbroken succession of solo arias. As a result *Idomeneo* contains some striking pieces of orchestral and choral music. The welding of these French elements into a basically Italianate structure was a necessary expedient to achieve Mozart's purpose.

The orchestral recitative, where the speaking voice alternated with expressive orchestral phrases, was one of the composer's master-strokes. The device was conceived by Rousseau, who argued that the French language was unsuitable for singing. In this vein he wrote *Pygmalion*, a new genre of musical drama in which speaking voice and orchestra were juxtaposed. The first performance took place at Lyons in 1770 and the production at the Comédie Française in 1775. (The entire text was by Rousseau, as was some of the music, though most of this was by Coignet.) The naturalistic manner in which the speaking voice was employed by Rousseau evoked widespread admiration, particularly among German poets and musicians. Goethe and Mozart each welcomed the new arrangement when the 'melodrama' was presented at Weimar and Vienna.

[1] H. Abert, *Goethe und die Musik* (1922), p. 79.

By emulating Rousseau Mozart forged works that in turn influenced Beethoven's *Fidelio* and *Egmont*, Weber's *Freischütz* and, indirectly, Schönberg's 'Sprechstimme' (song intoned in a half-singing, half-speaking voice).

The immediacy of Mozart's responses was only a prelude to his quick productiveness. He no sooner studied the works of a Schobert in Paris or a Christian Bach in London than he copied, then perfected, their style. That he wrote his three last and greatest symphonies in two months in the summer of 1788 was a prodigious feat, justly admired by posterity; nevertheless, it was only one conspicuous instance of his general habits. A study of his few sketches and many manuscripts impels the realisation that his auditory imagination and memory were *sui generis*.[1] Imitation was, invariably, Mozart's point of departure: his first string quartets (1770) are reminiscent of Sammartini's style, and the six quartets written in the summer of 1773 in Vienna are marked by Haydn's influence. The conjunction of the gallant with the strict style in Haydn's quartets of 1772 was challenging. Haydn was forty years old when he introduced an element of counterpoint in a texture that was fundamentally homophonic, with a skill on which both Mozart and Beethoven were to depend. At sixteen 'Mozart was no match for this'.[2] For the finale of his F Minor Quartet (no. 35), in fugal sonata form, Haydn used a theme, or 'tag', that had often been employed by such older masters as Pachelbel (assistant organist at St Stephen's, Vienna, 1674), Kuhnau (organist at St Thomas's, Leipzig, 1684), Handel and Sebastian Bach. The contrapuntal usefulness of this raw material was irresistible. Mozart utilized it first in the Andante of his F Minor Quartet of 1773 and later superbly in the *Requiem* of 1791. The quartet movement is stiff and laboured. Nevertheless, although his music did not reach artistic maturity until 1781, Mozart's works were in popular demand in the 1770s.

The notion of copyright, and, indeed, of originality, was much too novel to be of concern to writers and musicians. Mozart's skill in the mimicry of his predecessors was unmatched by any other composer, and his method was justified in that he consistently outstripped his models. The beautiful concerto effect in the scene of the shipwreck in *Idomeneo*, where an off-stage chorus accompanied by wind instruments is balanced by a chorus onstage with strings, may be cited as an example where his genius transcends the use of a similar device by Gluck.

The concerto as such, rather than a mere application of its effects, proved the main outlet for Mozart's talents once he had settled in Vienna. Between 1782 and 1786 he composed only two operas, *Die Entführung aus dem Serail* and *Le Nozze di Figaro*. In the same period he produced fifteen piano concertos, with which he hoped to make a fine conquest in

---

[1] *Musical Quarterly*, vol. XLIII (1957), pp. 187–200.
[2] Einstein, *Mozart* (1946), p. 176.

Vienna, the 'Clavierland'. Half a century earlier Handel, in London, had perceived the benefits of performing concerts in the Lenten season when the theatres were closed and the production of opera was forbidden. The same opportunity now presented itself to Mozart. The standard fee for an opera, Italian or German, was 450 gulden, about the equivalent of Mozart's annual rent in the 1780s. By contrast, he could earn about 1500 gulden per annum from the series of three Lenten concerts which he offered in 1784–6, not counting guest appearances in the Lenten concerts of others. In spite of these financial successes Mozart ceased, for the most part, from writing the kind of music society expected of him. 1787 seems to have been the crucial year: after the production of *Le Nozze di Figaro* and the Piano Concerto in C major in 1786 Mozart devoted himself to compositions that expressed his mature convictions regardless of popular taste. Not with Byronic *Weltschmerz* but with Apollonian calm he persisted in reminding his hearers of the ultimate ethical values within an artistic domain that encompassed the simple ditties of Rousseau and the solemn chorales of Sebastian Bach, the laughter of Arlecchino alongside the Messianic hopes of the American and French revolutions. His own belief in the brotherhood of man was fortified by the doctrines of the Freemasons to whose order both he and Haydn belonged.

Volumes have been written to prove that *Don Giovanni* (1787) is not only the perfect opera but even the perfect work of art *per se*; that *Die Zauberflöte* (1791), which brandishes Papageno's frivolity as a foil for Sarastro's magisterial tones, is profound and, at the same time, as engaging as a modern operetta. It should suffice to single out the chorale in *Die Zauberflöte* as Mozart's response to the *Zeitgeist* and the structure of *Don Giovanni* as an example of Mozart's timeless greatness. The advent of Romanticism was foreshadowed in the closing decades of the eighteenth century in the revival of the spirit and works of Sebastian Bach in Berlin and Vienna.[1] If Mozart and Schubert (born 1797) were misunderstood geniuses (and, indeed, they were favourite citations of that category throughout the nineteenth century), Bach had been a forgotten genius. His renaissance in the home of Van Swieten in Vienna was one of those private incidents which acquires significance through its historical associations, for it was there that two great composers studied and absorbed the unfashionable Sebastian. Haydn, as we have seen, proceeded gently once he had explored the new idiom in his quartets of 1772. Mozart, from 1782 until his death in 1791, was less prudent, forfeiting success by too heavy a dose of seriousness. From the minuet of the String Quartet in D minor (1783), dedicated to Haydn, the 'Qui Tollis' of the Mass in C minor (1783), and the Piano Concerto in D minor (1785) there runs a thread to the slow and solemn introduction of the overture to *Don Giovanni* and the trial scene in *Die Zauberflöte*. That the hero and

---

[1] For the development of Romanticism in musical expression see ch. VIII B of vol. IX.

heroine walk through fire, water and air to the accompaniment of a Lutheran chorale by Sebastian Bach which the Roman Catholic Mozart chose to employ is not so curious, perhaps, as the fact that the general tone of the music is quite alien to the style of Viennese magic opera, and wholly unexpected by the audience. The Ninth Symphony of Beethoven and the symphonies of Brahms and Bruckner all owe a debt to Mozart's enthusiasm for Bach.

Yet this enthusiasm was never boundless, the poignant pathos was never permitted to become the dominant (or even final) mode of expression in the manner of later works of full-blown Romanticism. The finale of *Don Giovanni* is an apt illustration of Mozart's control. Mozart termed his opera a *dramma giocoso*, that is, a comic rather than a tragic opera. True, the death-scene strains to the utmost the framework of *opera buffa*, for it is cast in the sombre key of D minor, its trombones are reminiscent of such *opere serie* as *Idomeneo* and *Alceste*, and its chromaticism of Sebastian Bach. But, having made his effect, Mozart reverts to the major mode and quick tempo as the surviving characters proclaim the creed of the living. From the time of its first performance in Prague (29 October 1787) a variety of attempts have been made to 'improve' the opera by bringing down the curtain on the death of Don Giovanni.[1] But this curtailment runs counter to the structure of Mozart's finale: musically, the finale requires the return to D major and, dramatically, the articulation of the creed of the survivors. In fact, Mozart's artistic courage in concluding with laughter, rather than tears, has had a profound influence on twentieth-century *opera*, *vide* Strauss's *Rosenkavalier* and Stravinsky's *Rake's Progress*. The fusion of the tragic and the comic has often been discussed, and rarely more dramatically than in Plato's *Symposium*. But few creators, save Shakespeare and Mozart, have succeeded in shaping a stylistic unity out of a seeming contradiction. Beethoven, who was more Puritan than Mozart, considered the subject matter of *Don Giovanni* frivolous, but he none the less followed Mozart's artistic method—the Ninth Symphony concludes, not *andante maestoso*, but *allegro energico* (and even *prestissimo*), not in the minor but in the major mode. Still, where Beethoven's last word is one of dedicated resolution, Mozart, like Prospero, dismisses us with a smile.

2. ART AND ARCHITECTURE

During the second half of the eighteenth century the dominant influence on all the arts was that form of idealism known as Neoclassicism. In France and Germany the 'excesses' of the rococo style had, by the middle of the century, produced a general reaction against exuberance and frivolity. That tendency towards classical restraint and harmony which is an essential

[1] D. J. Grout, *Short History of Opera* (1947), p. 288 f.; *Times Literary Supplement*, LXI (10 August 1962), p. 592.

part of the French tradition of Corneille and Racine, Poussin and Mansart, reasserted itself decisively under the influence of new ideals—the Enlightenment of the Encyclopaedists—and of the new aesthetic theories centred on Rome and best expounded by the expatriate German, Johann Joachim Winckelmann. Neoclassicism is, however, more than a resurgence of the eternal classic tendency in European art. The essential thing is that neoclassic theory advocated the return to classical principles by way of a strict imitation of antiquity, now made easier by the increase of archaeological knowledge and especially by the discovery of, and excavations at, Herculaneum and Pompeii. Greek art, though still almost entirely unknown in the original, was now given a leading place in theory, and the climate of nineteenth-century opinion that used the fifth century B.C. as a touchstone of all artistic excellence was prepared in the 1750s.[1] It is evident that so much enthusiasm expended on so few available examples of Greek art led to a kind of *hyperdulia*—an enthusiasm which is in itself far more romantic than classical; and indeed one of the distinguishing characteristics of Neoclassicism is precisely this romantic approach to antiquity, and especially to ruins. Piranesi's etchings of ancient Rome provide the best example of this unique combination of precise archaeology with a wild and poetic imagination.[2] The Gothic Revival in England owes something to this mixture of antiquarian fervour and romantic imaginings, and it is not difficult to see how Rousseau, Diderot, and republican virtue became equated with revolutionary art, even though most of the revolutionary artists—Ledoux, West—were conservative in politics.[3]

Rome was the capital of this international movement.[4] The reason for this is partly to be found in the Grand Tour, centred on Rome, which all patrons and *cognoscenti* now made as a matter of course; by the latter part of the century it was also becoming a matter of course for artists as well, many of whom spent years in Italy, partly learning and partly teaching. By acting as agents and guides many young artists made the acquaintance of noblemen who later became their patrons: Reynolds, Wilson and Nollekens are all, in different ways, examples of this and of the new, professional, status gradually accorded to the northern artist, who had not previously been treated with the respect traditional in Italy

---

[1] In particular by J. J. Winckelmann, *Gedanken über die Nachahmung der griechischen Werke in der Malerei und Bildhauerkunst*, 1755, and J. D. Leroy, *Les Ruines des plus beaux Monuments de la Grèce*... (Paris, 1758) and Eng. trans. (London, 1759). See below pp. 98–9.

[2] In recent years the French have employed the useful term *Préromantisme* in this connection. The phrase 'Romantic Classicism' was invented by S. Giedion in 1922 (*Spätbarocker und romantischer Klassizismus*) and anglicised by Fiske Kimball in an article in *Gazette des Beaux-Arts*, 1944, but it seems, at present, to be used too freely.

[3] Barry, Banks and Blake are obvious exceptions. Blake belonged to a later generation (1757–1827) and to a large extent his work falls outside the scope of this chapter; the other two were probably social misfits rather than conscious political revolutionaries.

[4] The great collections of antiquities, particularly the public museums in the Vatican, assume a new importance at this time.

since Michelangelo. The most notable example of the effect of a Grand Tour is to be found in France. In 1750 the future marquis de Marigny, Mme de Pompadour's brother, made a tour with the engraver C.-N. Cochin and the architect Soufflot, both of whom were strongly anti-rococo in outlook. Marigny became Surintendant des Bâtiments du Roi (in effect, Minister of Fine Arts) in 1751 and his official influence on French art in the direction of Neoclassicism was considerable.

Still more important were Piranesi and Winckelmann, both of whom spent most of their lives in Rome. Giambattista Piranesi (1720–78) was a Venetian architect who settled in Rome in 1740 and whose life was dedicated to the production of those large etchings which, distributed all over Europe, have been the most important visual factor in the formation of the European consciousness of the grandeur of ancient Rome and the splendour of its decline. It is not too much to say that the *Antichità* and the *Vedute*[1] have had an influence comparable to the *Decline and Fall*— to the genesis of which they may indeed have contributed. Piranesi's unique combination of architectural and archaeological exactitude with a towering dramatic imagination and his subtle distortions of scale give his etchings an immediacy and comprehensibility that the ruins themselves probably did not then possess and certainly do not now, stripped as they are of all romantic overtones.[2] His most original works are the etchings of imaginary prisons, the *Carceri d'Invenzione* (begun *c.* 1745, reworked 1761) which, to a generation reared on Freud, explain some of the sources of his romantic expressiveness and also some of the slight megalomania which many architects learned from him.[3] Piranesi's influence on all the visual arts was incalculable, partly because it was the herald of Romanticism; but he also endeavoured to formulate an aesthetic, and in this he was less successful. His anti-Greek bias led him into an untenable position, but the Hellenism which aroused it must first be considered in some detail.

Johann Joachim Winckelmann (1717–68) was the son of a poor German cobbler. Ancient Greece exercised a compulsive fascination on him, although he actively resisted going there while claiming it as his sole ambition; and he knew almost no original work of Greek art. Somehow, he saw beyond the Roman copies of Greek statues to the principles which lay behind them, and which he first enunciated, in limpid German prose, in a small pamphlet of 1755, *On the Imitation of Greek Painting and*

---

[1] *Antichità Romane...*, 1748 and later; *Vedute di Roma*, 1745 onwards, altogether 137 etchings of ancient and modern Rome. Piranesi published many other collections of plates of antiquarian and topographical interest, making a total of more than 1000 etchings. He was elected an Honorary Fellow of the Society of Antiquaries of London in 1757, and was also a personal friend of Robert Adam.

[2] Compare, for example, the gesticulating little figures set against the vast arches of the Basilica of Constantine (*Vedute*, H. 114) with a modern photograph of the ruins.

[3] The standard example is Newgate prison, by George Dance II, built 1770–78, and demolished in 1902.

Sculpture.[1] It is curiously typical of this strange man that this tract was published in Dresden, before he went to Rome where he was to spend almost all the rest of his life. Years later, after an intensive study of the antiquities preserved in Rome and elsewhere in Italy, he wrote a much larger *History of Ancient Art*[2] which is perhaps the first modern art history, treating ancient art as an integral part of the social and religious life of Greece and Rome. He also wrote many archaeological essays, but the pure neoclassic doctrine is already to be found, shortly and simply stated, in his first work: 'The only way for us to attain greatness, even, if it be possible, to become inimitable is by the imitation of the Ancients. ...Greek artists began to go further [beyond the observation of nature], and to form general ideas of beauty, both for individual parts of the body and for the proportions of the whole, which should rise above Nature herself.'

The most famous passage of all contains the key to the whole neoclassic movement:

The outstanding, universal, characteristic of the Greek masterpieces is thus *a noble simplicity and a calm grandeur [edle Einfalt und stille Grösse]*, both in expression and in action. Just as the depths of the ocean are eternally peaceful, no matter how fierce the tempest on the surface, so it is that the statues of the Greeks express nobility and restraint even in suffering. Such a soul is portrayed in the face of Laocöon—and not only in his face—in spite of his agony....He does not shriek out, as Virgil made his Laocöon. His mouth is not open wide enough for that—it is no more than an anguished sigh. The physical pain and the greatness of soul are expressed in equal measure by the whole of his body, and the one counterbalances the other. Laocöon suffers, but he suffers like the Philoctetes of Sophocles: his misery pierces us to the heart, yet we would wish to endure misery with the fortitude of this great man....The artist must have felt this power of the spirit in himself.

This last sentence is equally true of Winckelmann, for, as a modern critic has noted: 'Dazzled by the flash of a great revelation, he saw the distinctive qualities of Greek art as he looked at this supposedly genuine specimen. He was in fact in a trance; and like many another clairvoyant, he was uttering truths which did not apply to the object before him, but were associated with it in his mind.'[3]

There can be little doubt that the discoveries at Herculaneum and Pompeii were the immediate cause of this renewal of enthusiasm for classical antiquity; indeed, Winckelmann himself specifically mentions some of the earliest discoveries at Herculaneum as being known 'and

---

[1] *Gedanken über die Nachahmung... (op. cit.).* Two English translations appeared as early as 1765 and 1766 (the first by Fuseli, in London, the second in Glasgow). Considerable excerpts are conveniently available in E. G. Holt, *A Documentary History of Art*, vol. II (1958), pp. 335–51.

[2] *Geschichte der Kunst des Alterthums*, 2 vols. (1764). It was translated into French as early as 1766, Italian (1779 and 1783) and English (1850).

[3] E. M. Butler, *The Tyranny of Greece over Germany* (1958), p. 47. Winckelmann's main thesis was challenged as early as 1766, by Lessing in his *Laoköon*.

admired on German soil' before he went to Rome. These statues had been discovered as early as 1706, but Herculaneum was not excavated until 1738 and even then very slow progress was made. Pompeii was discovered in 1748, but systematic excavation was not begun until 1763, and in both cases the strictest secrecy was observed. Because of the attitude of the authorities little was known about the discoveries until the publication in 1755 of the first, huge, volume of engravings from the antiquities found at Herculaneum.[1] Winckelmann himself found it difficult to get precise information, but his influence was such that he was able to ascertain some facts and to publish them in his *Sendschreiben* of 1762.[2] Still more important were his last works, the *Monumenti antichi inediti*, published in 1767, but in spite of all these efforts the actual knowledge of classical art remained circumscribed by the fact that it was so difficult to obtain comparative material. For example, large numbers of Greek vases were discovered in and near Naples and two splendid collections were formed by Sir William Hamilton, British ambassador in Naples (better known as the husband of Emma, Lady Hamilton). His collections were splendidly engraved and catalogued and were thus made widely accessible—indeed his first collection was sold to the British Museum in 1772—but for long nobody realised that these were Greek vases. They were thought to be Etruscan, in spite of their Greek inscriptions, and the result was to start a fashionable craze in the 1770s, skilfully exploited by the Adam brothers, Wyatt, and Wedgwood. Wedgwood's imitations of these vases were so successful that he named his factory Etruria and to this day it bears witness to the archaeological aberrations of our forefathers.

This early phase of Neoclassicism can best be seen in the work of Anton Raffael Mengs (1728–79), whom Winckelmann called the best painter for two centuries. His *Parnassus* (1761, Rome, Villa Albani) shows the main elements of the theory which was then being elaborated by Winckelmann and by Mengs himself, who was the author of several treatises in the manner of Winckelmann. Like him, Mengs had a hard early life, became a Catholic convert, and was influenced by the same environment—Dresden (where his father was Court Painter) and Rome, where he first went in 1741, fourteen years before Winckelmann's arrival. He went to Spain twice for Charles III, as Court Painter, and most of his best work is there. In his lifetime he was regarded as the greatest painter in the world and his fame far overshadowed Tiepolo's, whose last years in Spain were embit-

---

[1] *Le Antichità di Ercolano...*, 9 vols. (1755–92). Some earlier attempts at publication were: *Descrizione delle prime scoperte* (London, 1750); *Memoirs concerning Herculaneum, translated from the Italian, with notes by W. Fordyce* (London, 1750); *Raccolta di quanto è stato pubblicato...* (Rome, 1751); *Lettres sur les Peintures d'Herculaneum...* (Brussels? 1751).

[2] *Sendschreiben von den Herculanischen Entdeckungen* (Dresden, 1762). A French translation appeared as *Lettre à M. le Comte de Brühl, sur les Découvertes...* (Dresden, 1764).

tered by the intrigues of Mengs' partisans:[1] nevertheless, Mengs' ceilings in the Spanish royal palace are markedly less neoclassic in treatment than the *Parnassus*, done under the direct influence of Winckelmann. On the whole, Mengs is probably now best remembered as a portrait painter. The academies of his own day regarded him as the saviour of painting from rococo degeneracy, although Reynolds, who shared many of his theories, realised his feebleness as a painter and refers to him only twice, and then rather disparagingly, in the *Discourses*.

The *Parnassus* was painted for Cardinal Albani, Winckelmann's employer and patron, as a ceiling-fresco in his new villa. It may have been intended as a manifesto; certainly it marks a complete break with the traditional form of baroque ceiling painting which Mengs himself had been practising only three years earlier at Sant'Eusebio in Rome. This tradition was based on illusionistic *sotto-in-sù* perspective—on the attempt to convince the spectator, looking upwards, that he was seeing through the ceiling and looking up at the figures floating above his head. The *Parnassus* breaks with this conception of illusionism in order to return to orthogonal composition; that is, the picture space is imagined as at right angles to the onlooker, without reference to the spectator's actual position or the setting in which the picture was to be placed. The composition is treated precisely as if it were a carved relief, with Apollo standing in the centre and the nine Muses grouped around him. There is practically no depth and the landscape background is merely a generalised setting. The principal figure is an almost literal copy of the *Apollo Belvedere* and the muses all derive, more or less directly, from Raphael's *Parnassus*, in the Vatican, or from antique reliefs of the type of the *Muses Sarcophagus* or the engravings in the *Antichità di Ercolano*. This was the painfully reached high-water mark of his attempt to rival both Raphael and the ancients, but his composition is too conscious, too stiff and lifeless, with entirely uninventive figures repeating poses mechanically taken over. In this he was simply the type of pseudo-classicist, but in the hands of a greater artist this copying of antique prototypes could be made the vehicle of a genuine emotion.

Early neoclassic style, then, is by no means exclusively the imitation of Greek works of art. The fact that many pictures by both Mengs and West have a faintly Poussinesque air provides the key to the stylistic problem, for the main elements at this stage are the theories of ideal beauty expounded by Bellori[2] late in the seventeenth century, and which, so far as painting is concerned, hold up the works of Raphael as models for

---

[1] Goya's early works were much influenced by both—Tiepolo in his decorative works and frescoes, and Mengs in his earlier portraits.

[2] Above all in the *Idea* which forms the introduction to his best-known work, the *Vite de' pittori, scultori et architetti moderni* (Rome, 1672).

copying rather than the unknown Greek painters. Bellori was the friend and admirer of Poussin, who was generally held to have succeeded in combining Raphael and the antique.

Rather different factors operated in sculpture and architecture. The sculptors had far more to copy, even though most of their models—the *Apollo Belvedere*, the *Belvedere Torso*, the *Laocöon*—had been known for a long time and were not Greek in the new, archaeological, sense. It is doubtful whether many people in the later eighteenth century were capable of following Winckelmann in distinguishing between Greek and Graeco-Roman: it is even more doubtful whether many sculptors cared. The greatest sculptors of the end of the century, Houdon and Canova, were more concerned with the attainment of a simple style, in reaction against the writhings of the Bernini school, than with strict antiquarianism. Houdon's *S. Bruno* (1764, Rome, Sta Maria degli Angeli) made his name because of its rapt simplicity, but his best works were his portraits, and his numerous *Voltaires*, in particular, show a pursuit of expressive realism rather than idealised form. Canova's work is more influenced by the Greek idea, but his colossal *Napoleon*, stark naked in white marble (London, Wellington Museum; a bronze in Milan) is as late as *c*. 1806–8, while his papal tombs (St Peter's, 1784–7 and 1787–92) do not seem more than superficially neoclassic. Antique Roman sculpture, however, remained a constant source of inspiration, perhaps most of all in England, where the busts and reliefs of J. M. Rysbrack (1694–1770) had shown the direct imitation of antique—but Roman—models quite early in the century. Nevertheless, his conception of relief differed fundamentally from that of the true Neoclassicists, such as Banks, preoccupied as they were with expressive contour.

In architecture the Age of Reason was marked by the first theoretical expression of a rigorous functionalism. Architecture is by definition a practical and functional art; nevertheless, the eighteenth-century theorists pushed the ideas of reason and function (and also the vaguely defined 'nature') beyond anything previously held. This doctrine was expressed by three men, all of whom were clerics and none of whom was a practising architect. It appears first as early as 1706, in the *Nouveau Traité de toute l'Architecture* by the Canon de Cordemoy (1651–1722), but here the insistence on truth and naturalness and reason in architecture is no more than the old theory of decorum in a new guise; it was taken up, however, by Lodoli and Laugier and considerably developed.

Padre Carlo Lodoli (1690–1761) never wrote a line but his teachings were widely influential and are known to us principally through his pupil Andrea Memmo, a Venetian patrician, who published his *Elementi di Architettura Lodoliana* in 1786, as well as through the earlier discussions of Lodoli's ideas in such writers as Algarotti. It is certain that his theories were widely known in his own lifetime, and his two leading ideas appear startlingly modern. First, he insists that nothing should appear as ornament, especially on façades, unless it truly represents an internal, structural feature; thus, he disapproves of Vitruvius' defence of the Greek temple, where the original timber beams gave rise to stone ornaments (metopes and triglyphs) which no longer had a 'true' function. Second, all architecture ought to conform to the nature of the materials. The first dogma, that the exterior ought to 'express' the interior, has been one of the battle-cries of modern architecture. The second is now very current among sculptors, but the plastic qualities of reinforced shell concrete have raised acute difficulties among the most advanced of twentieth-century architects. In Lodoli's day both these theories were regarded as anti-Vitruvian and, more pertinently, anti-baroque. Most of the baroque masterpieces are heavily ornamented, and façades often do not correspond in any way to the 'realities' of the building behind. Further, the plastic quality of the architecture of men like Borromini was felt to be an abuse of the essential monumentality of stone. Lodoli's functionalism was carried to the point where he demanded a new approach to furniture design, adapting it to the human shape rather than vice versa. He used the gondola as an example of an object beautiful because of its perfect adaptation to its function. Lodoli's theories were probably absorbed by the French Jesuit Marc-Antoine Laugier (1713–1770), who wrote a history of Venice (and may thus have known Lodoli) and became the populariser of the functional theory in his *Essai* of 1753 and his *Observations* of 1765.[1] His books were widely read—Soane, for example, seems to have presented his pupils with copies and there are still eleven copies of various editions in the Soane Museum. His new contribution consisted of the rejection of visual beauty in favour of character and expression—*l'architecture parlante*—while beauty was in fact to be retained by the employment of elementary geometrical forms. This theory of pure form became very popular in France, especially in the years preceding the Revolution, but English architects were less attracted by it, since the growth of the Picturesque Movement in England allowed fascinating vistas of *architecture parlante* to develop out of what had originally been a theory of landscape painting and gardening.[2]

These two factors—the persistence of seventeenth-century classicism in the Bellori sense, and the new rationalistic theory of architecture—were the principal causes of modification to the theory that 'the only way for us to attain greatness...is by the imitation of the ancients'. Two other aspects of the resistance to Greek influence may be mentioned

[1] *Essai sur l'Architecture* (Paris, 1753 and 1755); English trans. 1755 and 1786, German trans. Leipzig, 1768. *Observations sur l'Architecture* (The Hague and Paris, 1765). See also W. Herrmann, *Laugier and Eighteenth-century French Theory* (London, 1962).

[2] Even Soane, the greatest architect of the age, was a passionate believer in 'the poetry of architecture', which, as Sir John Summerson has pointed out, is 'exactly analogous to some of the landscape effects most valued at the time'. See below, pp. 106–7.

briefly. The first was the very natural revulsion from the idea that the great Roman tradition was itself merely a derivative from an earlier, purer, Greek style, and the second was the Gothic Revival. To many of the more conservative eighteenth-century artists the Greek style (if indeed the surviving examples were earlier) certainly seemed less accomplished than the Roman: immaturity, not purity, was how they described it. Naturally, this sentiment was most strongly felt in Rome, but many non-Italians subscribed to it with equal fervour, and Piranesi and Chambers may serve as examples of both types. Piranesi's theory of architecture was rather confused[1] and suffered from the impetuosity that was so marked a feature of his private life. In 1761 he published his *Della Magnificenza ed Architettura de' Romani* as a reply to the anonymous 'Investigator' (actually the Scots painter Allan Ramsay) and, even more, to Leroy's *Ruines*.[2] Piranesi asserts that the Etruscans really invented all architecture—their Grand Style being somewhat like the Egyptian. Caylus in his *Recueil d'Antiquités Égyptiennes, Étrusques, Grecques et Romaines* (1752–67) regarded the Etruscans as forerunners of the Greeks, but in fact nobody really knew very much about the Etruscans and the Italians found it convenient to invent a mythical Etruria antecedent to all Greek civilisation. The controversy was continued in the *Gazette littéraire de l'Europe* for 1764 by P. J. Mariette, to whom Piranesi replied in 1765 with his *Osservazioni sopra la Lettre de M. Mariette*, the second part of which was subtitled *Parere su l'Architettura*. Two points are worthy of note: first, he repeats his main argument by suggesting that the Tuscan Order was independent of the Doric; and, second and far more important, in the *Parere* he abandons his Vitruvian and archaeological position and argues that the genuinely creative artist may do and believe as he likes— genius justifies all in these matters. This position was precisely that adopted, a few years earlier, by Piranesi's friend Robert Adam,[3] and it is the reason for regarding both as revolutionary artists, forerunners of the romantic ideal.

In his last years Piranesi visited the Greek temples at Paestum.[4] By then he had modified his views and was able to accept them as both good

[1] But see R. Wittkower in *Journal of the Warburg Institute*, vol. II (1938–9), pp. 147–58.
[2] J. D. Leroy, *Les Ruines des plus beaux Monuments...* (1758). The first real attempt at publication of monuments on Greek soil was made in 1751–2 by Richard Dalton, later George III's librarian. This had little influence and was superseded by Leroy's book, superseded in its turn by the first volume of Stuart and Revett's *Antiquities of Athens* (1762), the fruit of their much-publicised journey to Greece in 1751–3. The important buildings were reserved for their second volume, published only in 1789, delayed by Stuart's dilatoriness and published posthumously. The full-scale Greek Revival in architecture is a nineteenth-rather than an eighteenth-century phenomenon, largely because of these delays.
[3] In a letter of 1763 to Lord Kames, author of the *Elements of Criticism*. The main statement of Adam's theories is in the preface to the *Works...*, vol. I (1773).
[4] Fifteen of the drawings he made are in the Soane Museum and are known to have been in Soane's possession by 1819: the Prince's Street vestibule at the Bank of England (1804) had heavy, baseless, Greek Doric columns.

and Greek (though this was still qualified). He was much impressed by the heavy Doric order without a base, which is their main feature, and which was so unfamiliar that it was very slow in gaining general acceptance. Conversely, it became a hallmark of the style of the most advanced architects in the latter years of the century, and particularly in France in the revolutionary era, where it was a symbol of the rejection of academic tradition.

Sir William Chambers, R.A. (1723–96), played an important part in the foundation of the Royal Academy, became its first treasurer, and was the official government architect for Somerset House, his masterpiece. He represents the Palladian and Roman tradition, brought up to date by constant reference to French and Italian work of all periods up to his own day. He rejected the idea that the Greek style was simpler and purer, and therefore better, than the Roman, which on the authority of Vitruvius he had to admit to be later than Greek work and at least partly derived from it. The crucial issue of the heavy Greek Doric, fluted but without a base and about $4\frac{1}{2}$ diameters in height (Paestum) to $5\frac{1}{2}$ (the Parthenon is 5·48), as against the Roman Doric or Tuscan orders, usually unfluted, with a base, and often 8 diameters high, gave him the opportunity to attack what seemed the graceless proportions of Greek work. He rejected the idea of Greek superiority in his *Treatise on Civil Architecture* (1759) and especially in the third, enlarged, edition of 1791, when Greek ideas were becoming much more prevalent. In the draft of a lecture he was less restrained, saying of the Greek partisans that 'they might with equal success oppose a Hottentot and a Baboon to the Apollo and the Gladiator as set up the Grecian Architecture against the Roman.... It hath afforded occasion of laughter to every intelligent Architect to see...what Encomiums have been lavished upon things that in Reality deserve little or no notice.'[1]

When Chambers died the Greek battle was nearly over, but there still remained plenty of critics of the neoclassic tendencies to be seen in Soane's Bank of England (1788 onwards); two such were the authors of an anonymous *Inscription for a Monument to the Memory of Sir William Chambers* and a piece of dreary doggerel called *The Modern Goth* (both printed in 1796).[2]

The second aspect of resistance to Greek ideals was the Gothic Revival and the associated Picturesque Movement. In the middle years of the century there were several fashions in interior decoration—Chinoiserie, Greek, Gothic, Etruscan, and, later, Hindoo. So long as these were recognised to be no more than fashions they were considered to be

---

[1] Quoted in N. Pevsner and S. Lang, 'Apollo or Baboon', *Architectural Review*, vol. CIV (1948), pp. 271–9.

[2] Both the *Modern Goth* and the *Inscription* are printed in full in A. T. Bolton, *The Portrait of Sir John Soane* (1927), pp. 62–5.

harmless trifles: Chambers was moved to intemperate language because he realised that Stuart with Greek and Adam with Etruscan were setting up potential rivals to the classical Roman style. Gothic, at first, seemed no more than Horace Walpole's new toy but, towards the end of the century, in the hands of Wyatt and as a result of the researches of the antiquaries it too became a rival style in its own right. The poet Gray was one of the first to treat Gothic architecture seriously, and the state of knowledge of the time is strikingly exemplified by the generally accepted theory that the cathedrals were built before the Danish invasions.[1]

The nationalistic appeal was easy to appreciate and the Gothic style soon became an aspect of English history. The full development of this theory came in the early nineteenth century, when the new Houses of Parliament were originally intended to be designed in Tudor, since the age of Elizabeth marked the zenith of English glory. The head-on collision between Greek and Gothic, with much moral obfuscation, occurred in the nineteenth century, but the struggle was being prepared before the French Revolution, which itself gave considerable impetus to the theory of Gothic as a national, English, glory. The precise interrelationship between the Gothic Revival and the Picturesque Movement is hard to define. Both are aspects of Romanticism and both arose from specifically English circumstances, but the Picturesque Movement was far more influential on the rest of the world than was the Gothic Revival. The Picturesque Movement was one of the most important of all English contributions to the visual arts, but because it is more fully expressed in landscape gardening than in any other medium its significance has not always been appreciated. In its original form it meant simply that a landscape had been made to look as though it were a three-dimensional realisation of a picture by Claude, or Salvator Rosa, or Gaspar Poussin. That is, its original meaning was precisely the opposite of that now current, in which a picturesque scene is one suitable to be made into a picture. Complications began to arise when Burke's *Philosophical Enquiry into the Origin of our Ideas of the Sublime and Beautiful* (1757; eleven editions by 1792) divided visual pleasures into sublime, which had overtones of awe and even terror—torrents and precipices—and beautiful, which we would now call neat or pretty—trim garden walks of a formal kind. These categories exclude such enjoyable things as the landscapes of Claude or Gaspar (but 'savage Salvator' was incontestably sublime). Hence, picturesque became a convenient middle term, with 'some strangeness in the proportion' and with the romantic pleasures of the unfinished or ruinous. Landscape gardeners could thus 'improve' the face of nature herself, and Lancelot Brown (1716–83) got his nickname 'Capability' because he could always see the capabilities inherent in his clients' parks. Humphry Repton (1752–1818) was the great exponent at the end of the

[1] Sir K. Clark, *The Gothic Revival* (2nd ed., 1950), 46 ff. and ch. iv.

century, and his Red Books still exist, showing the 'before' and 'after' of the transformations he wrought, while consulting 'the Genius of the place in all'. Extravagances soon crept in, and a long wrangle over terminology lasted well into the nineteenth century, but the *jardin anglais* was a potent factor in the spread of Romanticism, particularly when the transcription of pictures was dropped in favour of the natural beauties of the site, cunningly brought out by the gardener. The best definition of picturesque is given by Sir Uvedale Price in his *Essay on the Picturesque* (1794; final version in three volumes, 1810), where he requires intricacy of form as well as 'roughness and sudden variation, joined to irregularity'.[1] These are qualities to be found in the works of Thomas Gainsborough (1727–88), who was certainly the best English painter of the period. His landscapes and fancy pictures are models of the picturesque.

The principal centres of artistic production in the period were London and Paris, Rome being mainly important as a centre for study. Venice had three of the greatest living painters—Canaletto (1697–1768), Guardi (1712–93) and, above all, Tiepolo (1696–1770)—but all three were exponents of that rococo style which the neoclassic theorists found merely frivolous, and for that reason they may be regarded as belonging to an earlier age. The remainder of this chapter may therefore be devoted to a brief survey of the most significant trends in Britain and France.

The period covered by this volume coincides almost exactly with Reynolds' presidency of the Royal Academy, from its foundation by George III in 1768 to Reynolds' death in 1792. The first public exhibition of pictures to be held in London took place as late as 1760, and it had long been evident that the new conception of the relationship between artist and patron made it essential for painters and sculptors to have somewhere to exhibit works for sale, as had long been the case in Paris. Geoge III's own interest in the arts led him to found an academy for such a purpose, but this was regarded as less significant than the school established at the same time, since the teaching of the theory of the arts now seemed far more important than the practice, which was felt to be a mere handicraft. Reynolds was the only possible choice to head the new institution, since he was not merely a successful portrait painter, but had been to Italy, moved in literary circles, and was by birth and education a gentleman (he was the son of a clergyman, a Fellow of Balliol). During his presidency the Academy enjoyed probably its greatest prestige and effectiveness, since almost all the best artists were members.[2] Reynolds'

---

[1] At first Price and his friend Richard Payne Knight attacked Brown and Repton as not pictorial enough but they later fell out over definitions. On the whole question see N. Pevsner, 'Richard Payne Knight', in *Art Bulletin*, vol. XXXI (1949), pp. 293–320. Jane Austen's *Northanger Abbey* is the best of all comments on the extravagances of the movement.

[2] Romney and Robert Adam are the great exceptions. Adam was almost certainly excluded by Chambers, but Romney refused to exhibit and was therefore ineligible.

knighthood and his discourses, delivered from the presidential chair, gave an intellectual status to the new institution which allowed it to compare with the universities. Academicians were entitled to rank as esquires and to wear quasi-academic gowns. Reynolds himself received a D.C.L. from Oxford in 1772.

There can be no doubt that Reynolds' greatest contribution to British art lies in the character of his presidency even more than in his personal achievement as a painter. The mere fact of his friendship with such men as Dr Johnson or Edmund Burke conferred a totally new status upon all British artists. His *Discourses* were attributed to both Johnson and Burke. Burke's *Sublime and Beautiful*, of 1757, is very thin by comparison with Reynolds' *Discourses*, but contemporaries found it hard to believe that the discourses could have been written by a painter.[1]

For Reynolds as for the French Academy and all the traditional idealists, the painter's task is to express moral sentiments by ideal forms, and the best way to do this is by history painting. This was the doctrine expounded by Reynolds in the fifteen discourses read to the Academy between 1769 and 1790. He painted very few pure histories, but he did admit a judicious mixture of historical idealism into his portraits, thus ennobling portraiture itself. A good example is *Dr Beattie, or, The Triumph of Truth* (1774, University of Aberdeen) with its references to Beattie's supposed refutation of the infidels Hume, Gibbon and Voltaire. Pure history painting was being practised, in Rome, by the Scot Gavin Hamilton (1723–98) as early as 1758,[2] but Reynolds' influence on British art is more obvious in the nature of the Academy exhibitions and in the pictures produced from 1786 for Alderman Boydell's Shakespeare Gallery, as well as in the ill-fated attempts of Barry, and, later, Haydon, to make a living as history painters. James Barry (1741–1806) was a protégé of Burke, who maintained him in Italy from 1766 to 1771. Beginning in 1777 Barry spent six years on the gigantic *Progress of Human Culture* in the Great Room of the Society of Arts in London, with portraits incongruously juxtaposed to deities and personifications (Captain Cook and Father Thames). Barry was an embittered Irishman who nearly starved because of his single-minded devotion to history painting. He supported the American Revolution and it is therefore the more curious that the real revolution in history painting which took place in the 1770s was the work of two American Loyalists,[3] Benjamin West (1738–1820) and J. S. Copley (1738–1815). West was George III's favourite artist, lavishly patronised and Reynolds' successor as president of the Royal Academy. As a young man he went to

[1] F. W. Hilles, *The Literary Career of Sir Joshua Reynolds* (1936), pp. 134 ff. Hilles reproduces a page in Reynolds' writing with some verbal corrections in Johnson's hand.

[2] E. K. Waterhouse in *Proceedings of the British Academy*, vol. XL (Hertz Lecture, 1954), and *idem, Painting in Britain, 1530–1790* (1953).

[3] Both lived in London, where West was Court Painter and Copley an Academician, and neither openly espoused the revolutionary cause, but Loyalist is perhaps an exaggeration.

Italy (1760–3), where he was much influenced by the Winckelmann–Mengs–Hamilton group, and on his return to London he painted many small, Poussinesque, subjects from classical history or mythology, such as the *Departure of Regulus from Rome* (1769; Royal Collection), shown in the first exhibition of the Royal Academy, of which West was a founder-member. In the very next year he painted the *Death of Wolfe* (1770; Ottawa: other versions exist). This celebrated picture was exhibited at the Academy of 1771 and is usually regarded as marking the decisive break with neoclassical principles, since the event was contemporary (1759) and the figures wear modern dress, even recognisable uniforms. Nevertheless, the event had taken place in a strange land, which West emphasised by the introduction of a Cherokee Indian, who had not been present in fact; thus his picture represents an event 'far away' if not 'long ago'. Much of the reputation of the *Death of Wolfe* is mythical: it was certainly not the first history picture to represent modern events or even modern costume, and there had indeed been two earlier paintings of the death of Wolfe, both representing the event with some verisimilitude. Nevertheless the great reputation of West's picture is very largely due to his skilful combination of the academic Grand Style with the patriotic modernity of his subject, and his ennobling of a contemporary subject was therefore justly regarded as revolutionary. The picture was extremely successful, and even Barry exhibited a rather similar composition (R.A. 1776; New Brunswick Museum), but this was a failure—probably because it was little more than a copy of West's picture with some 'classical' gestures. The new, romantic, conception of history painting as the recording of heroic deeds performed by contemporaries and especially by compatriots was fully established by Copley in a series of highly dramatic pictures fulfilling some of the functions of modern newspaper photographs. The first, and one of the most exciting, was *Brook Watson and the Shark* (1778; Boston and Christ's Hospital). This records the adventure of a future Lord Mayor of London, who had one leg bitten off by a shark while swimming in Havana harbour and was rescued by his shipmates. The newsreel quality of this picture and its successors—the *Death of Chatham* (1779–80; Tate Gallery) and the *Death of Major Pierson* (1783; also Tate)—was something quite new in serious painting and broke decisively with the generalising principles advocated by Reynolds. David's *Marat Assassinated* (1793; Brussels), a votive picture for a hero of the Revolution, is unthinkable without the lead given by the American. Much French painting of the early nineteenth century was also influenced by another English development, the Shakespeare Gallery of Alderman Boydell. Boydell was a highly successful printseller who commissioned large paintings of Shakespearian subjects from Reynolds and all the leading academicians for his gallery in Pall Mall, the engravings being the means by which he paid for the pictures. The uncouth genius of Shakespeare was a stimulant to the latent Romanticism of men like Romney and a spur to the imagination of Fuseli. Most of the history of the Shakespeare pictures lies outside the limits of this chapter, but Romney and Fuseli were, with Barry, the main influences on the early work of Blake. The sculpture of Banks and Flaxman must also be mentioned, although Flaxman's great European reputation depended on his line-drawings rather than his sculpture, and in any case his career really begins only in 1794, after his return from Rome.

In architecture the period includes the official style of Sir William Chambers side by side with the 'Adam revolution', which reached its height in their Pompeian-inspired interiors of the 1770s; the French style of Henry Holland (1745–1806), reflecting the tastes of the Fox circle; and the beginnings of the Greek Revival, the key date being 1758, when Stuart built a temple in the grounds at Hagley which was a reduced copy of the Theseum at Athens. Thirty years later John Soane (1753–1837) was appointed architect to the Bank of England and began the rebuilding which ultimately included all the old building and a very large expansion as well. His halls and offices were in a highly personal neoclassic which owes much to both Adam and Stuart, as well as to the theories of Laugier and Lodoli, and has interesting parallels with contemporary French work.

The beginnings of Neoclassicism in France may conveniently be dated from the return of Marigny, Cochin and Soufflot from their Italian journey in 1751.[1] In the following year the comte de Caylus (1692–1765) published the first volume of his *Recueil d'antiquités* with hundreds of engravings of Egyptian, Etruscan, Greek and Roman antiquities (in that order) and with a preface explaining that he wished to make known as many models as possible, both for the historian and for the artist, to aid him in 'approaching more closely to the noble and simple style of antiquity'.[2] In 1754 Cochin published, in the *Mercure de France*, his 'Supplication aux orfèvres', which was an appeal for a return to simple forms and straight lines instead of the curlicues of rococo goldsmith's work. More important, however, was the commission given to Soufflot (1713–80) through Marigny for the church of Sainte Geneviève in Paris, better known to us as the Panthéon. This was commissioned in 1755 and completed only after Soufflot's death, in 1790–1, when it was renamed the Panthéon and several alterations were made to increase its antique austerity. In fact, the church is a combination of St Peter's in Rome as built, and even more as projected by Antonio da Sangallo and Michelangelo, with St Paul's in London. Its portico is derived directly from the Pantheon in Rome, and, at one stage, so was the dome but this was later

[1] An antecedent cause may have been La Font de Saint Yenne's *Réflexions sur quelques causes de l'état présent de la peinture en France* (Paris, 1746).

[2] 'En approchant un peu plus de la manière noble et simple du bel antique.' Caylus comes very close to Winckelmann's conception of the history of art as an integral part of the history of civilisation. The seven volumes of the *Recueil* were published 1752–67.

modified into something very close to St Paul's (Soufflot had drawings specially made in 1766). The plan, a Greek cross, could also have been derived from the great model design for St Paul's, which was well known from engravings. The Panthéon is often criticised as too light and flimsy, especially by comparison with St Peter's or St Paul's, and to some extent this is true; the criticisms stem from the building history, for cracks appeared quite early and a full-scale inquiry into its stability was held in 1778. This in turn was due to Soufflot's extraordinary combination of Gothic structural principles with what he conceived to be Greek majesty, by carrying his dome and vaulting on columns with straight entablatures, instead of on piers or buttresses. Soufflot's pupil Brebion wrote in 1780 that the main object had been to combine the lightness of Gothic construction with the purity and magnificence of Greek architecture.[1] To do this Soufflot resorted to many ingenious technical expedients, principally the use of very elaborate iron ties in the masonry.[2] This structural sophistication, added to the evident lack of knowledge of Greek architectural details, debars the Panthéon from ranking as a fully neoclassic building, even though Laugier himself greeted an early project as the 'first model of a perfect architecture'.[3] Like the contemporary work of the Adam brothers, Soufflot's Panthéon is a transitional stage towards the architecture of the years immediately preceding the Revolution.

At this time there were many admirable French architects, most of whom are now known by a single building, and the most important stages in the development of a purer neoclassic style can be followed in the church of Saint Philippe-du-Roule (before 1765 to 1784) by Jean-François Chalgrin (1739–1811) and the École de Médecine (1769–c. 1780) by Jacques Gondoin (1737–1818), both in Paris. Saint Philippe was a deliberate return to the primitive simplicity of the early Christian basilica—a type which, conveniently, could also be held to derive from antique prototypes. The École de Médecine, apart from its very skilful planning, attracted contemporaries by its façade, which was absolutely unbroken in the centre and at the ends and had a straight entablature, also completely uninterrupted and without any pediment over. Theatres were also important, and the two by Victor Louis (1731–1800), that at Bordeaux (1772–80), and the Théâtre-Français (1787–90, now Comédie Française), were contemporary with Claude-Nicolas Ledoux's theatre at Besançon (1778–84, gutted by fire 1958). Ledoux (1736–1806) and Boullée were the two major neoclassic architects, although very little of Ledoux's work survives and Boullée was almost exclusively an administrator and theorist. Ledoux was

---

[1] 'Le principal objet de M. Soufflot en bâtissant son église a été de réunir...la légèreté de la construction des édifices gothiques avec la pureté et la magnificence de l'architecture grecque', quoted by E. Kaufmann, *Architecture in the Age of Reason* (Harvard U.P., 1955).

[2] It has even been suggested that he invented reinforced concrete construction—cf. L. Hautecœur, *Histoire de l'architecture classique en France*, vol. IV (1952), p. 196.

[3] Quoted by Hautecœur, *op. cit.* p. 190.

appointed an Inspector of the Royal Salt Mines in 1771 and held the post for twenty-three years. This gave him the opportunity to build some of the works at Arc-et-Senans (near Besançon) in 1775-9, with heavy, simple shapes, fantastic rustication and 'characteristic' ornament—stone urns with pendent stalactites of salt, 'expressing' the function of the building. Much of his work there was destroyed in 1926, but Ledoux also used his opportunity to elaborate his Ideal City plan for Chaux, which was rigidly symmetrical—for geometric beauty—and the buildings of which were also conditioned by the austere beauty of such shapes as the cylinder, the pyramid, and the sphere (which would have made them difficult to inhabit) and by the expression of their function: the extreme case is the House for the Overseer of the River. It was to have been a cylinder lying on its side, with the river pouring through it, like a turbine; the unfortunate overseer lived in rooms on the perimeter, presumably deafened by the noise and with walls running with damp. Another characteristically Rousseauish idea was the *oikema*, intended as a sort of high-minded brothel, and actually a very handsome Greek temple set in a beautiful landscape.[1] In spite of his revolutionary architectural ideas Ledoux was imprisoned in 1793 and was nearly guillotined as a Royalist. His best-known works, four of which survive, were the Barrières or toll-houses of Paris, built between 1784 and 1789 and discontinued on the outbreak of the revolution. Some were Greek temples, some essays in solid geometry; but a surprising number were versions of various Italian Renaissance buildings.[2]

In 1804 he published a large, sprawling, work entitled *L'Architecture considerée sous le rapport de l'art, des mœurs et de la législation*, containing engravings of his own works and an obscure text with much Rousseauism —'The architect finds the variety of his subjects in the great Book of the Passions.'

A similar megalomania expressed in the most high-flown way may be seen in the work and theory of Étienne-Louis Boullée (1728-99), whose *Essai* has only recently been published.[3] Perhaps the most interesting of his works was a projected monument to Newton (1784) which consisted of a huge sphere, the interior of which was lit by tiny holes, giving the effect of the vault of heaven. At the bottom, inside the sphere, was a cenotaph.[4]

In spite of *architecture parlante* and Ledoux's readings in the Book of the Passions most people were inclined to attach greater importance to the subject-matter of a picture than to that of a building. The importance of the subject was stressed by Diderot, mainly in his reviews of the exhibitions

---

[1] It was thought that the sight of vice 'conduit l'homme à l'autel de l'Hymen vertueux'. This quotation, and most of the facts about Ledoux and Boullée, may be found in E. Kaufmann, *Three Revolutionary Architects* (Philadelphia, 1952).

[2] For illustrations see M. Raval and J.-C. Moreux, *Claude-Nicolas Ledoux* (Paris, 1945).

[3] By H. Rosenau (London, 1953).

[4] Several monuments to Newton were projected by French architects at this period, presumably as a symbol of Enlightenment.

at the Salon, and the 1770s saw the rise of Greuze with his tritely moral subjects of family life and his *comédies larmoyantes* very much in the manner of Diderot himself. Greuze (1725–1806) made his name at the Salon of 1755 and his popularity lasted until the stricter themes of the Neoclassics of the later 'seventies and 'eighties affected his fame and led him to counter-attack with maudlin sentiment laced with pornography. True neoclassic earnestness is to be found in a painting in which the subject was of great importance—the *Oath of the Horatii* (Louvre), by Jacques-Louis David (1748–1825). If Mengs' *Parnassus* is a typical early neoclassic picture, David's masterpiece is equally typical of revolutionary Neoclassicism in every sense. The history of the picture is well known: it was commissioned on behalf of Louis XVI in 1783, but the choice of the subject was David's own. In 1782 he had seen a performance of Corneille's *Horace* which had moved him deeply, and he therefore proposed the story from Livy on which Corneille's play was based as a subject for a grand historical work. His proposal was accepted and he spent 1784 in Rome painting the picture, which was exhibited in the salon of 1785, acclaimed and duly acquired by the Crown. The picture is important in three ways—as a stage in David's own evolution, as a political manifesto, and as a manifesto of Neoclassicism comparable with Boullée's Newton monument (1784) or Ledoux's Barrière de Reuilly (1785–9) which shares with the *Horaces* the heavy (virtuous Roman) Doric order with an arcade over it.

The subject of the *Horaces* is the most obvious aspect of its revolutionary quality. The story of the Horatii who swore to defend Rome in single combat against the Curiatii is a simple Roman moral tale of devotion to duty; but the story continues with the callous murder of his sister by the survivor of the Horatii, because she mourned her betrothed, one of the Curiatii, instead of rejoicing in the salvation of Rome. On his being tried for murder his father defended his heroic son on the grounds that devotion to the state overrides private affection. This unpleasing subject was originally selected by David, and there is a drawing of the impassioned father pleading for his surly-looking son.[1]

David, sensibly enough, abandoned this scene in favour of the more generally acceptable subject of the three sons swearing to their father that they would conquer or die. The weeping women are sufficient reminder of the conclusion of the story. The general moral of service to the state could be held to apply to Louis XVI's France as well as to a revolutionary Utopia, but what made the *Oath* a political manifesto was partly inherent in the subject and partly implicit in the actual treatment. The idea that natural affection is not to be allowed to interfere with the demands of the state—in this case, oddly, Rome in the days of the kings—was,

[1] Reproduced in F. H. Hazlehurst, 'The Artistic Evolution of David's *Oath*', in *Art Bulletin*, vol. XLII (1960), pp. 59–63.

perhaps, more current in the 1780s than nowadays. These Stoic virtues were those associated with republican Rome, and hence by an easy if illogical transition, with Republicanism. The plain brick arches on Roman Doric columns in the background, besides forming the rear plane of the stage and echoing the division of the figure into three groups, have a direct reference to Roman *gravitas* (David himself, in a letter of 1785, refers to the use of arches over columns as Etruscan; by which, of course, he meant pure, primitive, and simple). Mental substitution of Ionic or Corinthian columns will make this point clear at once, and it is also evident that such a moral overtone could not have been intended or understood even in Winckelmann's lifetime. Yet David himself is credibly reported as saying that his subject came from Corneille but he owed his picture to Poussin.[1]

Neoclassicism thus begins with the classical harmony of Raphael and Poussin and becomes a recognisable stylistic development in its concern with archaeological exactitude, fostered by the discoveries at Herculaneum and Pompeii and given a new moral force by the equivalence established between nature, sentiment, and antique simplicity by the writers who forwarded the ideals of the American and French Revolutions. It may fitly be observed that Thomas Jefferson deliberately chose the Maison Carrée at Nîmes as the model for the first public building in the new American republic, his State Capitol at Richmond, Virginia, of 1785–96.

[1] 'Si c'est à Corneille que je dois mon sujet, c'est à Poussin que je dois mon tableau', quoted by Hazlehurst, *op. cit.*, from A. Péron, *Examen du tableau des Horaces* (Paris, 1839).

CHAPTER V

SCIENCE AND TECHNOLOGY

THE brief period of thirty years from 1763 to 1793 marks an important phase in the history of science and technology, especially in the foundation of modern chemistry, and in the improvement of the steam-engine by the invention of the separate condenser, an improvement that led directly to the development of steam-power. The bases of the quantitative study of three great departments of physics, namely, heat, electricity and magnetism, were firmly established in these years; and there was much progress in geology and in biology. At the beginning of the period Newtonianism had not only permeated scientific thought but had also already passed beyond the boundaries of the world of science into general thought and literature through the writings of Henry Pemberton in England and of Voltaire and Mme du Châtelet in France. Sciences other than astronomy and mechanics were, however, not so well advanced; and chemistry still explained the material complexity of the world in terms of a small number of ultimate elementary components.

In mathematics and mechanics the researches of this period were characterised by generalisation and deduction. Joseph-Louis Lagrange (1736–1813) continued the work of the earlier half of the century on the calculus; he extended mathematical analysis and the theory of equations; and in 1788 he published his *Mécanique analytique*, a work second only to Newton's *Principia* in the history of mechanics. Adrien-Marie Legendre (1752–1833) made further studies on the calculus of variations and other branches of mathematics, as well as contributing to the study of mechanics. Gaspard Monge (1746–1818) laid the foundations of descriptive geometry, by which three-dimensional objects may be represented in two dimensions, his work being published in 1795. Of these Lagrange went furthest towards that synthesis of mathematics and mechanics that was soon to be achieved in the great dynamical system expounded by Pierre-Simon Laplace (1749–1827) in his *Mécanique céleste*. On the experimental side in the study of the resistance of fluids to the motion in them of solid bodies, the failure of previous researchers to formulate a theory that conformed to the experimental data was largely remedied by the Abbé Charles Bossut (1730–1841), the results that he obtained in experiments carried out with d'Alembert and Condorcet being published in *Nouvelles expériences sur la résistance des fluides* (1777). Many hundreds of experiments showed that the resistance varied with the square of the velocity of the moving body. Other detailed experiments of this kind were made in the 1780s by Pierre-Louis-Georges, comte du Buat (1734–1809). The con-

8-2

tinuing tradition of experiment in mechanics is seen also in the work of Charles-Augustin Coulomb (1736–1806) on elasticity, in which he studied the torsion of fibres of hair and of silk as well as that of metal wires. Valuable research was carried out in Paris in 1792 at the Observatoire by Jean-Charles de Borda (1733–99) and Jean-Dominique Cassini (1748–1845) on the measurement of an important gravitational constant, the length of a simple pendulum beating seconds.

Astronomy on the Continent was mainly mathematical and it was in this period that Laplace was formulating his nebular hypothesis and preparing the *Mécanique céleste*. In England most of the work done in astronomy was observational; under Nevil Maskelyne (1732–1811), astronomer-royal, the *Nautical Almanac* was founded in 1766 and entered upon its long history as a guide to mariners. In 1781 (Sir) William Herschel discovered a new planet, Uranus, the first planet to be discovered in historical times; and with one of his great telescopes erected at Slough he was able to catalogue many hitherto unobserved stars. In 1783 he began to measure the relative density of the distribution of the stars and in the following years he observed that the Milky Way appeared on the celestial sphere like a great circle broken at one end and with the sun not exactly at the centre; the galactic system thus seemed to be shaped like a convex lens. He observed also and studied various kinds of nebulae and he concluded that the sun was not at rest but moving towards a distant point in the heavens.

It was known that all the planets revolved about the sun in the same sense and in almost identical planes, that most satellites revolved about their primaries in that sense and nearly in the same planes and that the axial rotations of the sun and those of the planets and the satellites were likewise in that same sense. To Laplace the identity in the direction or sense of these various rotations suggested a common origin for all the component parts of the solar system and in 1796 he formulated the hypothesis that the system had been derived by the condensation and subsequent division into parts of a primordial incandescent whirling gaseous nebula that contracted as it cooled. Earlier, however, Georges-Louis Leclerc, comte de Buffon (1708–88), had propounded another theory to account for the identical sense of these rotations; he supposed that a comet had collided with the sun and torn away a limb or jet of the sun's hot incandescent matter, which had then cooled and condensed into the planets and their satellites, which naturally preserved the direction of rotation of the solar matter from which they had all originated. While Buffon's theory is more in agreement with modern views than that of Laplace, its historical importance is that Buffon in his *Époques de la nature* (1778) derived from it some general ideas about the history of the earth; he supposed that the matter drawn out from the sun slowly cooled, the sun remaining incandescent, and that the earth, as one of the parts into which that matter separated, passed through seven stages or epochs, for the length of which he gave estimates of an approximate kind, based on such data as he could obtain. In the first epoch, about 3000 years, the earth cooled from incandescence to a molten state and became spheroidal. In the second epoch, estimated at about 35,000 years, continued cooling produced further solidification with the formation in the contracting surface of primitive valleys and mountains, all surrounded by an atmosphere as yet too hot for water to condense. In the third epoch, some 2500 years, the earth and its atmosphere cooled sufficiently for water to condense on its surface and to form a universal ocean enveloping the whole planet, which, as Buffon observed, would account for the occurrence of marine fossils on the heights of mountains. In the fourth epoch, estimated at 10,000 years, land began to show above the surface of the waters, as the latter flowed down through the cracks in the cooling and contracting crust and disappeared into the interior; vegetation appeared, but much was carried away by the waters into the rents in the earth's crust, where it led to the production of volcanoes, which Buffon supposed to be the result of the violent action between water and fire. In the fifth epoch, about 5000 years, an epoch of calm in contrast with the volcanic violence of the preceding age, large animals appeared—the mastodon, the elephant, the rhinoceros, the hippopotamus—but only in the polar regions, the equatorial parts of the earth being still too hot for animal life. In the sixth epoch, also about 5000 years, the land separated into great masses or continents, the Old and the New Worlds took shape, and man appeared. In the seventh epoch, at which the earth had now arrived, man had begun to assume control of his surroundings and to use his power to aid that of nature; but the ultimate prospects were dark, since cooling of the earth would slowly but inevitably continue until it would eventually become too cold for life to persist; the early stage of this seventh or current epoch had already lasted about 5000 years; and its estimated future duration was 93,000 years, after which life on the earth would be extinct. These views are of historical significance as a coherent departure from the usually accepted figure for the earth's past history as a few thousand years since the Creation. Moreover, Buffon had tried to relate his theories to the data of geology, to the results of experiments on the cooling of hot bodies and to observations on the rate of deposition of sedimentary strata from solution. Expounded with all the clarity and charm of his unique literary style and with that gracefulness that still attracts the modern reader, Buffon's opinions were such that he felt it advisable to leave Paris at this time to put himself beyond the reach of the theologians of the Sorbonne. It is scarcely necessary to point out that modern geology and prehistory are largely developments from his theories.

The mean density of the earth was determined in this period with much greater accuracy. In 1774 Nevil Maskelyne repeated the attempt made earlier in the eighteenth century to measure the deflection from the vertical produced in a plumb-line through the gravitational attraction of the mass of a mountain near which the plumb-line was suspended; the observations, made on Schiehallion in Perthshire, showed that the mean density of the earth as compared with the density of water was about $4\frac{1}{2}$. Later, in 1797–8, shortly after the close of our period, the Honourable Henry Cavendish (1731–1810) made considerable improvements in this method and obtained a value of 5.488, which is very close to the more recently determined figure of 5.5270. Attempts at another important measurement, namely, the distance between the sun and the earth, used by astronomers as the 'yard-stick' in their measurements of the universe, were not so successful; they depended on observations of the transits of Venus in 1761 and 1769, but the results were disappointing because of the difficulty of determining accurately the times of 'contact' between Venus and the sun; the work was, however, highly significant in another sense because the astronomers of England and of France and of other countries cooperated in it on a very great scale.

There was considerable improvement in scientific instruments during this period, much too considerable and often much too technical to discuss or describe in this limited space. One of the most important was the marine chronometer of Pierre Le Roy (1717–85), constructed in 1766 and described in 1770; it enabled mariners to determine the standard time at sea and so to ascertain their longitude and therefore their position, the necessary information of their latitude being derived from astronomical observations; and it superseded the slightly earlier and almost equally famous instrument designed by John Harrison (1693–1776). The design and manufacture of scientific instruments and their improvement attracted a number of great craftsmen during this period, but again they are too many and their contributions too wide and sometimes too technical to be included here, although it is necessary to mention the high quality and originality of their work as well as the manufacturing scale on which it was in some instances conducted; in England the more eminent were elected into the fellowship of the Royal Society and in France they were honoured with a royal *brevet* for which they were nominated by the Académie Royale des Sciences; they discharged a very necessary role in the development and organisation of science.

The earliest advances in the physical sciences at this period took place in the science of heat, which was rapidly established on a quantitative basis for the first time, mainly by the work of Joseph Black (1728–99) in the early 1760s. Black's first fundamental observation on heat was that the thermometer measured the intensity and not the quantity of heat; he then devised a means of measuring the latter. Before his time, long familiarity with the use of the thermometer had led to the observation that a number of neighbouring bodies at different 'heats', as they were then described where we would now say at different temperatures, would after a time, if left to themselves, all register the same reading on a thermometer applied to them in turn; the hotter ones had cooled and the colder ones had grown warmer and, in the scientific thought of the time, it was said that they had acquired what was called 'an equilibrium of heat'. But it was well known that they differed in density, some being heavier and others lighter, and, from this observation of the so-called 'equilibrium of heat', it was concluded that heat was distributed among them, not equally, but according to their different densities, the heavier taking more and the lighter less. This conclusion, quite reasonable for its time, was thought to be in agreement with certain experiments, which had in fact been misinterpreted. However, George Martine (1702–41), a physician of St Andrews, had observed in 1739 that, when glass vessels of the same size and shape separately containing equal volumes of mercury and water at the same temperature were placed before a large fire, the mercury became hotter much more quickly than the water, while in the converse experiment it cooled more rapidly; but, according to current theory, the mercury, since it was thirteen to fourteen times as heavy as water, should have taken thirteen to fourteen times as long as the water to become hotter or colder, whereas the experiments showed that the very opposite happened. From these observations Black concluded that mercury, in comparison with water, grew hotter and colder more quickly because its 'capacity for heat', as he termed it, was much less than that of water; and he showed that different substances differed widely from one another in their 'capacity for heat', which was unrelated to their differing densities, or as was later said, 'capacity for heat' was 'specific'. About 1780 the term 'specific heat' replaced the older term 'capacity for heat'; and, in the meantime, Black showed how to measure the 'capacity for heat' of a substance in comparison with that of water by mixing known quantities of the substance at one temperature and of water at another temperature, observing the temperature of the resultant mixture and then calculating, from the fall in temperature of the one and the rise of the other, the relative quantities of heat producing the same change of temperature in equal quantities of the two substances. As water was always taken as one of the substances, it became the standard to which all 'specific heats' were referred.

Black's next research in this field led to the discovery of 'latent heat', which had the important consequence of leading James Watt to the improvement of the steam-engine by the invention of the separate condenser, the effective step towards the era of steam-power. Black began with a simple observation on the melting of snow and ice. It had been assumed until Black reconsidered the facts that, when a mass of ice was melted under the action of heat, its temperature rose steadily to the melting-point and that only a slight further rise in temperature was necessary for the whole mass to thaw into water. Black, however, was doubtful about the correctness of this commonly held opinion, because, if it were true, all the accumulated snow and ice of winter would melt almost at once in spring and pour down from the mountains in floods and torrents carrying all before it in catastrophic destruction. The very opposite happened; melting took many months and snow sometimes remained on the mountains through the summer. Moreover, he found that, when a thermometer was placed in a mixture of water and snow or ice, it continued to register the melting-point of ice as long as any ice remained unmelted, and that the temperature began to rise when and only when all the ice was melted. He remarked that, during this long period of melting, heat was steadily passing into the mixture of ice and water without any effect on the thermometer and was thus being rendered, as he said, 'latent'. In a simple way, following his analytical understanding of the change, he was able to measure this amount of heat. He took two small glass phials; he filled each of them with water; one was cooled until the water contained in it froze, and the other was cooled just to the freezing-point; they were then placed in a room at a temperature 7° Fahrenheit above the melting-point of ice. The one containing the cooled water attained the temperature of the room in a half-hour; the other, containing the ice, took ten hours and a half for the ice in it to melt and for the water thus produced to attain the temperature of the room. Therefore, said Black, since it has taken twenty-one half-hours for the ice to melt and to reach the temperature of the room and only a half-hour for the same amount of water to reach the temperature of the room, twenty-one times as much heat has entered the phial that originally contained the ice. So, as 7 degrees had entered the one phial in a half-hour, 21 times 7 must have entered the other; but from these 147 degrees it was necessary to subtract the 7 degrees that had merely raised the temperature of the water to that of the surrounding air after all the ice had melted. Thus 140 'degrees' of heat had not been recorded on the thermometer, but had been rendered 'latent'.

This discovery about the process that occurred in the melting of ice and the great amount of heat thus absorbed turned Black's inquiring mind to the similar process of boiling or evaporation. Here again the common belief was that, when water had reached its boiling-point, only a little more heat was necessary to turn it all into steam. But Black pointed out that the passage of water into steam after the water had reached its boiling-point was slow and required a further vigorous supply of heat. In some experiments similar to those that he had carried out with melting ice, he showed that a quantity of water at 50° (Fahrenheit) took 4 minutes to reach its boiling-point (212° Fahrenheit) and then a further 20 minutes before it was all converted into steam. It was, therefore, clear that in the 4 minutes in the first part of the experiment 212 minus 50, that is, 162 'degrees' of heat had passed into the water; in the second part of the experiment, in 20 minutes, five times as much must have entered the water, that is, 810 'degrees' on this system of measurement. Thus it appeared that both melting and boiling absorbed large amounts of heat that were not recorded on the thermometer as increases of temperature and so the heat thus absorbed was termed 'latent'. The quantitative study of the phenomena of heat was now widely developed; many 'specific heats' were determined, for solids and liquids and even for gases, and accurate methods and suitable instruments were devised for the measurement of thermal expansion, especially of solids, an exact knowledge of the thermal constants of which was very necessary in engineering.

The nature of heat itself appeared to be material. Since the seventeenth century heat had been considered by some as a form of internal motion and by others as a material substance. If, however, heat consisted of motion, then it should need more heat to raise equal bulks of a heavy body than a light one through the same range of temperature, since more motion would be needed to agitate the particles of the heavy body. Martine's experiments, already mentioned, had shown conclusively that this was not so: mercury, bulk for bulk, required less heat than water to raise its temperature by an equal amount. Heat seemed, therefore, to be material. Accordingly, many attempts, often ingenious, were made to discover its weight, but all of them failed or gave contradictory results. The researches carried out in 1787 by Sir Benjamin Thompson, Count Rumford (1753–1814), but not published until 1799, were the most accurate and the most decisive. He weighed in carefully controlled and elaborately devised experiments, on a very sensitive balance capable of detecting a change in weight of one part in a million, a mass of water contained in a hermetically sealed glass flask; he weighed it, first, while the water was in the liquid state and, secondly, when the water was frozen into ice. Repeated tests shows that there was no change in weight, although the amount of heat known to be necessary to melt that amount of ice and to raise the resulting water to the temperature of the room to which the apparatus was removed for melting would have raised the temperature of an equal mass of gold to a bright red heat. Rumford concluded that, if heat were material, it must be 'something so infinitely rare, even in its most condensed state, as to baffle all our attempts to discover its gravity'. He thought it more probable that heat was a form of motion.

At the middle of the eighteenth century there was little or no indication that any deep and fundamental change was imminent in chemistry. The chemist's world was still one constructed out of the four elements of earth, air, fire and water, or from the three principles of salt, sulphur and mercury. The elementary nature of air and water was unquestioned; earth too, although existing in many forms, appeared to be elementary, its different forms mere variant manifestations; and fire, although regarded a century earlier by Hooke as motion rather than matter, had received firmer experimental recognition as an element through the phlogiston theory, which dominated chemical thought for much of the eighteenth century and which, from the observations of combustion and inflammation, supposed that all combustible bodies contained in common the inflammable principle 'phlogiston', which was released from them when they burned in the form of fire and sometimes of its concomitant flame.

Nature from the chemist's point of view was, therefore, still supposed to be extraordinarily simple. In 1754-5, however, Joseph Black in studying the chemical properties of a new substance recently introduced into medicine under the name of *magnesia alba* discovered that the mild and the caustic alkalis differed in their composition in that the former contained air and the latter did not; and in continuing his experiments he found that this air differed chemically from the ordinary air of the atmosphere. This was the first time that such a difference had been noted. Black called this new air 'fixed air'. (It is now known as 'carbonic acid gas'.) He did not isolate or collect it, but he determined in exact quantitative experiments what amount of it was contained in the mild alkalis and he noted that in its properties it resembled the acids. In 1766 the Honourable Henry Cavendish (1731–1810) studied the 'air' obtained by the action of certain dilute acids on various metals; it ignited and so he called it 'inflammable air'. (It is now known as 'hydrogen'.) Cavendish thus recognised three 'airs'—the common air of the atmosphere, the 'fixed air' of Joseph Black and his own 'inflammable air'. In this field Cavendish was followed by Joseph Priestley (1733–1804), who from 1772 to 1777 isolated and recognised seven new 'airs', or gases, now more familiar under their more recent names of oxygen, ammonia, hydrogen chloride, nitric oxide, nitrous oxide, nitrogen peroxide and sulphur dioxide. About the same time, in 1772, Daniel Rutherford (1749–1819) isolated another, which he called 'noxious air'. (It is now known as nitrogen.) This rapid development of 'pneumatic chemistry', as it was called, opened a vast new field to chemical investigation.

Priestley's isolation of the gas later known as oxygen is most significant here. He obtained it in August 1774 by heating certain metallic calces. (Metals on long heating are converted into powdery substances, which were called 'calces'; and calcination was thought to be similar to combustion, the metals releasing in the process the phlogiston that was their common constituent.) Priestley found that this new 'air' greatly enhanced the burning of the flame of a candle. In March 1775 he found that it was respirable and supported respiration for a much longer period than common air did. So it was a greater supporter of combustion and of respiration than the ordinary air of the atmosphere. Now, in terms of the current chemical theory of phlogiston, the ordinary air of the atmosphere was continually being contaminated by the 'phlogiston' given off in the combustion of domestic fires and industrial furnaces, in respiration, in putrefaction and in fermentation. This new 'air', because of its higher degree of suitability for combustion and respiration, appeared to Priestley to be air freed from phlogiston, and so he called it 'dephlogisticated air', the first name by which chemists knew 'oxygen'. Since the constant corruption of common air by the phlogistic processes already named would eventually make our atmosphere unfit for both combustion and respiration, Priestley had already sought for some means by which nature restored the air thus continually rendered unfit for use; he found it in 1771 in the action of green plants, but he did not notice that this restoration of the air took place only under the influence of sunlight, an observation made later in 1779 by John Ingen-Housz (1730–99).

In the meantime Antoine-Laurent Lavoisier (1743–94) was turning from his studies in physics to some chemical problems that attracted his attention. He was much interested in tests for ascertaining the purity of the public supply of drinkable water in Paris; and he had found that for this purpose with the scientific knowledge then available and in the absence of any satisfactory chemical tests he had to rely on physical measurements of its density by means of hydrometers. But the purification of water by distillation and the subsequent measurement of its density by hydrometry appeared to be equally unsatisfactory if water, as chemists still believed, was convertible, at least in part, into earth; and the evidence collected by Lavoisier from the considerable literature on this subject did not enable him to decide about the validity of this belief. So in the autumn and winter of 1768–9 he heated a known weight of water in a weighed and sealed glass vessel for over three months; he observed the slow appearance of minute flakes of earthy matter in the water; and, when the experiment was completed, by removing the water and the earth and by weighing both the earth produced and the glass vessel, he found that the vessel had decreased in weight by an amount almost equal, within the limits of the accuracy of his experiment, to the quantity of earth formed. So the earth had been produced from the glass by the solvent or corrosive action of the water upon it, and therefore water was not even partly convertible into earth. An ancient chemical belief, held since the days of Aristotle, was thus at last refuted.

By a similar method, using sealed glass vessels, Lavoisier passed to the study of calcination and found that, when weighed amounts of metals were calcined in such vessels, there was no change in the total weight of the vessels and their contents; when, however, the sealed ends of the vessels were opened, air was heard to rush in with a whistling noise, as if some air had been consumed in the process of calcination, and the vessels with their contents gained in weight; and, further, when the calcined metals were removed from the vessels and weighed again, the gain in their weight appeared to be equal to the gain in weight of the vessels with their contents previously observed after air had been admitted on breaking the seals, or, what is the same thing, equal to the weight of air that had entered on breaking the seals to replace that consumed in the calcination. Thus, the gain in weight of metals on calcination, long a recognised fact in chemistry, appeared to be due to combination with air. About the same time Lavoisier similarly concluded from other experiments that, when sulphur and phosphorus were burned, producing the corresponding acids of sulphur and of phosphorus, the sulphur and the phosphorus combined with air to produce these acids, and that at the same time their weight was increased by the amount of air that had combined with them. These conclusions contradicted the explanations and indeed the principles of the phlogiston theory, which saw every combustion, not as a combination, but a decomposition with the release of phlogiston. After a meeting with Priestley in the autumn of 1774, when the latter was visiting Paris, Lavoisier repeated and extended Priestley's work in the light of his own new understanding of the nature of calcination and of combustion; and in 1777 he concluded that it was only a part of the air, about a sixth (more exact experiments indicated a fifth), that combined with the metals in calcination and with sulphur and with phosphorus in combustion, while the remainder of the air was inactive in these processes. In a classic experiment by heating and calcining mercury in contact with a limited amount of air in a suitably arranged apparatus, he succeeded in combining this active constituent of the air with the mercury and thus separating it from the inactive four-fifths or *mofette*, as he called it, which he found to be deadly both to life and to fire, asphyxiating small animals and extinguishing flames. Removing the calcined mercury from the vessel and heating it to collect from it the part of the air that it had combined with, Lavoisier found that this air supported both combustion and respiration. He had thus analysed air into its two components: one, as he said, 'eminently respirable' and the other 'asphyxiating'. Air could no longer be regarded as an element: it was a mixture of two very different gases.

But the rejection of the phlogiston theory was still many years away; it had proved too useful a generalisation to be given up for the limited applications of Lavoisier's discoveries to combustion and similar chemical processes; and for many years the only believer in Lavoisier's theory was its illustrious author. He was content to go no further than to offer his opinions as an alternative explanation that was more in agreement with the experimental facts. However, he continued to study these problems in a series of memoirs submitted to the Academy of Sciences, Paris, and steadily amassed evidence in his favour. He was, however, in one apparently insoluble difficulty in his theory; for, since every combustion appeared to him to be a combination with the active constituent of the atmosphere, which he had now named 'oxygen', the combustion of 'inflammable air' should give a product that was formed by combination with oxygen. All attempts to detect this compound failed. He had already shown that, when charcoal was burned, it combined with oxygen to give Black's 'fixed air', which now appeared to be 'carbonic acid'.

In June 1783 Lavoisier heard from Charles Blagden in Paris that Cavendish had found that, when 'inflammable air' was burned, water was produced. He saw at once the significance of this striking new observation and verified it in a hastily devised experiment, from which and from more elaborate experiments made later he concluded that water was a compound of 'inflammable air' and oxygen, and he confirmed this by decomposing water into these constituents by means of its chemical reaction with iron, in which the metal removed from the water its oxygen, by combining with it, and at the same time set free its 'inflammable air'. The latter was shortly afterwards renamed 'hydrogen' or 'water former' as a result of this important discovery. Cavendish did not accept these conclusions and supposed, on the contrary, that the water obtained in these experiments, the production of which he was the first to observe and to study, was originally present in both 'airs' as a constituent part of each of them and that it had been precipitated from each of them in the course of the combustion and not formed by their combination with each other. However, chemists now recognised that water had been demonstrated to be a compound. Thus two of the ancient 'elements' had been resolved into their constituents: air was a mixture of oxygen and azote (later renamed nitrogen), and water was a compound of hydrogen and oxygen. Fire had become generally accepted as 'matter of heat', an imponderable element; and 'earth' in its many forms was soon to disappear as an element through the new understanding of the chemical composition of substances that came mainly as a result of these discoveries.

Until this period there had been no satisfactory knowledge of the chemical constitution of that multifarious variety of different substances occurring in nature or prepared in the laboratories of the chemists. Their composition being unknown, no appropriate chemical nomenclature or system of names could be devised for them. Many had been called after their discoverers, as, for example, Count Palma's powder; some had been given names arising from their method of preparation, such as 'oil of sulphur by the bell'; and others preserved the ancient association of the seven known metals of antiquity with the seven celestial bodies, as, for instance, 'vitriol of Venus'. Such terms still pervaded a science that already knew the chemical composition of air and of water. It was a haphazard system, if it could be called a system at all, and it had grown up through long centuries in which nothing was known of the chemical composition of the substances thus named. As early as 1782 Louis-Bernard Guyton de Morveau (1737–1816) had embarked on a study of this problem; he was presently joined by Lavoisier together with Claude-

Louis Berthollet (1748–1822) and Antoine-François de Fourcroy (1755–1809), three French chemists who, with Laplace, were the first to accept the new chemistry of Lavoisier, the chemistry of oxygen in place of that of phlogiston. They presented proposals in 1787 under the title of *Méthode de nomenclature chimique* for naming substances according to their chemical composition. They decided to regard as simple substances all substances that could not be decomposed, although these might prove later to be compound. These were the first to be named in the new system, and most of them retained their old names. They were divided into five classes: the first included heat and light, oxygen and hydrogen; the second comprised the substances that by combination with oxygen formed the acids, and included sulphur, phosphorus, carbon and azote (nitrogen) as well as the unknown radicals of a large number of acids; the third class consisted of the metals, now for the first time regarded as simple, the phlogiston theory having taken them to be compound; the fourth class comprised the earths, silica, alumina, baryta, lime and magnesia; and the fifth consisted of the alkalis, potash, soda and ammonia. The suggestions were tentative and advanced with diffidence and it was pointed out firmly that some of these substances taken to be simple might prove later to be compound.

Proceeding to bodies composed of two simple substances, the reformers had now to deal with a very large number and variety, and they resorted to classification. One such group was the acids, which all contained, it was thought, the acidifying principle or element, oxygen; as this substance was common to all, it was decided to name each of them from its other component, and so they devised the names 'sulphuric acid', 'phosphoric acid' and so on. Where two acids were produced by the combination of greater and smaller amounts of oxygen with one and the same simple substance, as was the case with sulphur, the name 'sulphuric' was retained for the acid with the higher proportion of oxygen, while that with the smaller was named 'sulphurous acid'. The calces of metals, as they had been hitherto called, formed another group with two simple substances as components, one of these, oxygen, being common to them all; and so they were given the general name of 'oxides', being distinguished from one another by using as the other half of their names the other simple substance from which they had been formed, as, for example, zinc oxide, copper oxide and so on. Similarly, the very large range of substances, including the salts, with three simple substances in their composition, were given names derived from the acids from which they were formed and from the metal or other substance in their composition; and in this way the large group of salts derived from sulphuric acid were given the class-name of 'sulphates' and distinguished from one another as 'copper sulphate', 'zinc sulphate' and so on, with similar terms for the salts of other acids, such as 'lead carbonate', 'silver nitrate' and so on, for the salts of carbonic, nitric and other acids. The new system met with general acceptance among chemists; the soundness of the principles on which it was constructed was such that it proved to be adapted to future discovery and it is essentially that still in use today.

Two years later, in 1789, Lavoisier published his classic *Traité élémentaire de chimie*, setting forth for those beginning the study of chemistry a complete and detailed account of the new system. The *Traité* laid the foundations of modern chemistry as Newton's *Principia* had laid the foundations of modern physics almost exactly a century earlier. Although it was written for students, it contained much that was new with many illustrations. Here also was expressed for the first time what has been called the law of the indestructibility of matter. Explicit in eighteenth-century chemistry and in much of the chemistry of earlier times, this important principle was illustrated by Lavoisier from a gravimetric study of the process of vinous fermentation, in which he weighed carefully every item among the reactants and every item among the resultants and showed that the total weight of the substances produced at the end of the changes studied was equal to the total weight of the substances originally taken. His formal enunciation of the law of the indestructibility of matter was first made in these circumstances in the *Traité* and was as follows: 'Nothing is created in the operations either of art or of Nature, and it can be taken as an axiom that in every operation an equal quantity of matter exists both before and after the operation.' At the same time he introduced the 'chemical equation', now widely familiar to later generations, in pointing out that 'the whole art of making experiments in chemistry' is founded on the principle that he had just enunciated and that, 'since must of grapes gives carbonic acid gas and alcohol, I can say that must of grapes = carbonic acid gas + alcohol'. The most revolutionary feature of the *Traité* was, however, its list of elements, which was the first of its kind. Where with his colleagues in the reform of chemical nomenclature two years earlier Lavoisier had joined in the proposal to regard certain substances as 'substances not decomposed' and to name fifty-five of them, he now plainly referred to such bodies as 'elements' or, to quote his words in full, 'simple substances belonging to all the kingdoms of Nature, which may be considered as the elements of bodies'. It was a shorter list of thirty-three instead of fifty-five names, because he had (rightly) rejected the assumed elementary radicals of the organic acids; it began with light, caloric (the matter of heat), oxygen, azote (nitrogen) and hydrogen, and went on to include sulphur, phosphorus and charcoal, with the unknown radicals of muriatic, fluoric and boracic acids, followed by the metals (seventeen in number), and ending with the earths (lime, magnesia, barytes, argill and silex). The fixed alkalis, potash and soda, were omitted, although they had not been decomposed, because Lavoisier suspected from their properties that they were compounds not elements. This list was conservative and exact; early in the next century Humphry Davy decomposed potash and soda and confirmed Lavoisier's opinion about their compound nature. The new chemistry had in the *Traité* received its final and formal exposition and two years later, in 1791, Lavoisier could write: 'All young chemists adopt the theory and from that I conclude that the revolution in chemistry has come to pass.'

Before the new chemistry was complete, however, Lavoisier with Laplace had invaded the field of physiology in the quantitative study of respiration following upon his recognition of oxygen and its role in respiration. Working together in Lavoisier's laboratory at the Arsenal in Paris, they designed a calorimeter in which heat was measured by means of the quantity of ice that it melted, its latent heat of fusion (see p. 119) being known from other experiments originally made by Black. With their ice-calorimeter they showed that respiration was a kind of combustion, but the procedure was complicated, although a brief summary will be attempted here. In his earlier studies on respiration, Lavoisier had shown that the oxygen taken into the lungs in respiration was converted into 'fixed air' or carbonic acid gas; and he had concluded in a general kind of way that the temperature of the animal body, which, as was well known, remained in health at a constant level above the temperature of its surroundings, was so maintained by the release from the oxygen of 'matter of heat', as he called it, in the lungs when oxygen was there converted into 'fixed air', just as heat was given out when oxygen was converted into 'fixed air' by the combustion of charcoal in a fire.

In these new experiments carried out in 1782–4 Lavoisier and Laplace began (1) by measuring the amount of ice melted in ten hours in their calorimeter by the heat given out by a guinea-pig placed inside it; the heat given out melted 13 ounces of ice. In a separate apparatus (2) they determined the amount of 'fixed air' produced by the combustion of a weighed amount of charcoal, and in the calorimeter (3) they measured the heat produced (in terms of quantity of ice melted) by the combustion of another weighed amount of charcoal: these last two measurements gave them the measure of the heat produced in the formation of any quantity of 'fixed air'. Reverting to their first measurement, they determined (4) in another experiment the amount of 'fixed air' produced by the respiration of a guinea-pig in the period of ten hours during which the heat that it gave out had already been measured in (1); and from their second and third experiments they could now calculate the amount of heat produced by the formation of this amount of 'fixed air'. The value that they obtained in terms of the weight of ice melted was $10\frac{1}{2}$ ounces. They recognised that there must be many unavoidable errors in such difficult experiments and that the values of 13 and $10\frac{1}{2}$ ounces showed as much agreement as could be expected in the circumstances. They considered that the heat given out by the guinea-pig in the first experiment corresponded to the heat produced by its respiration during that period of ten hours, since its temperature did not fall during that time, but remained throughout very nearly the same as it was at the beginning. The animal's vital processes had during that time restored the heat that it was constantly losing to its surroundings. In that time (ten hours) 13 ounces of ice had been melted; and the corresponding amount of heat had been restored to the guinea-pig by means of its respiration and almost as much ice ($10\frac{1}{2}$ ounces) was melted by the formation of as much 'fixed air' from charcoal and oxygen as had been exhaled by the guinea-pig during that time. The heat given out in the process of respiration by the conversion of oxygen into 'fixed air' was therefore, it seemed to Lavoisier and Laplace, the principal factor in the maintenance of animal heat, that is, in the preservation of the temperature of the animal body at a constant degree above the temperature of its surroundings. They supposed that the change took place in the lungs, whereas we now know that it occurs in the muscles; but the role of oxygen in respiration had been demonstrated in these researches and the quantitative studies carried out had shown that respiration was a chemical process, not, as had long been supposed, a mere mechanical ventilation or cooling of the lungs by means of fresh air. In later experiments made on the eve of the Revolution Lavoisier found that water was also formed in the process of respiration and that this might partly account for the discrepancy in their values for the amounts of ice melted. In these later experiments Lavoisier showed that a fasting man at rest consumed more oxygen in cold than in warm conditions, that the rate of consumption of oxygen increased by about half as much again during digestion, that during exercise or movement or work the amount of oxygen consumed was increased to nearly three times that consumed by a fasting man at rest and to nearly four times when the work was done during digestion, and that the pulse-rate increased when the rate of consumption of oxygen was increased in these ways, the temperature of the subject, however, remaining practically constant. These experiments, which were interrupted by Lavoisier's execution during the Revolution, marked a great advance towards modern physiology although we now know that respiration is chemically much more complicated than these pioneering researches supposed.

Independently of Lavoisier, Carl Wilhelm Scheele (1742–86) had also studied the composition of air and had concluded that it consisted of two 'airs', 'fire air' and 'foul air', the former of which corresponded to Lavoisier's oxygen and the latter to nitrogen. Scheele was a very able experimenter and made many discoveries, including chlorine and glycerol and a number of acids, mineral as well as organic. His work on combustion was carried out in his native country of Sweden and was not known until others had carried their investigations further and published their results.

Many attempts were made to solve the problem of chemical affinity or the chemical attractions between different reacting substances. These had begun in the hope of finding some quantitative law of chemical force, possibly resembling Newton's law of gravitational attraction, but had ended merely in elaborate tables of affinity of a purely qualitative nature, mainly drawn up by the labours of Torbern Bergman (1735–84). His many thousands of experiments failed to take account of all the physical conditions that modified the action of the forces of chemical attraction; and, of course, he was working before the discovery of those fundamental chemical numbers, the atomic weights. His tables embodied, however, a very great range of highly useful qualitative chemical information. More satisfactory work was carried out by Jeremias Benjamin Richter (1762–1807) in the 1790s; although his literary style was obscure and although he tended to assume mathematical relations of a particular kind where there were none, he proceeded from his discovery that two neutral salts reacting in solution yielded compounds that were also neutral to conclude that there must be some fixed quantitative relation between the constituents of these reacting substances, and to express this principle in more general terms by asserting that there were certain fixed proportions of mass between chemical elements in their compounds. He measured these reacting quantities for a number of acids with an alkali and then with another and so on, and then for a number of alkalis with one acid and then with others and gave his results in separate tables for every acid and for every alkali, although he realised that the various weights of the different alkalis that neutralised a fixed weight of any one acid would neutralise also another fixed weight of a second and still another of a third and so on; but it remained for his successor in these researches, Ernst Gottfried Fischer (1754–1831), to embody Richter's work into one table published in 1802 exhibiting this fundamental law of chemistry, subsequently known not very appropriately as the law of reciprocal proportions, although it actually established what weights of different substances were chemically equivalent to one another.

In his *History and Present State of Electricity* (1767) Priestley surveyed the facts and theories of this developing science; he first recorded and studied the 'side-flash' and the oscillatory discharge of electricity and also in this book he suggested that the law of electrical attraction was, like that of gravitational attraction, an inverse-square law, as, in fact, was later shown by Coulomb. In unpublished experiments made at this time Henry Cavendish studied what are now called 'potential' and 'capacity' in electricity and at the same time he showed that the electrical charge on a conductor lies entirely on its surface and that the repulsive force between similar electrical charges follows an inverse-square law. This work by Cavendish was not known until his unpublished papers were edited by Clerk Maxwell in 1879. However, by means of a torsion balance Coulomb showed by careful measurements published in 1784 and later years that both electrical attraction and electrical repulsion follow the law of inverse squares. As he concluded in one of these instances, 'the repulsion between two small similarly electrified spheres varies inversely as the square of the distance apart of their centres'. About the same time he showed by similar means that the law of magnetic attraction also was an inverse-square law. Simple instruments to measure the quantity of electricity were devised. They were known as electrometers and depended for their working on the repulsion of cork or pith balls by an electrical charge or the divergence of a pair of gold-leaves mounted, as in the famous instrument of Abraham Bennet (1750–99), inside a closed cylindrical glass vessel. The most important work carried out in electricity in this period was probably that of Luigi Galvani (1737–98), professor of anatomy in the university of Bologna. In his researches, published as *De viribus electricitatis in motu musculari commentarius* (1791), Galvani noted that a frog's leg, freshly prepared for his anatomical demonstrations, exhibited convulsions when an electrical discharge occurred near to it, provided that it was connected to the earth by an electrical conductor. As is the case in so many great discoveries, this was the merest chance observation. Many experiments of various kinds led Galvani to two possible explanations of this curious effect: first, it might be the effect of what he called 'animal electricity'; or, secondly, since the convulsions could be produced by contact through two different metals, they might depend on some electrical process arising from that contact. He preferred the former explanation. His work attracted a host of investigators, among them Alessandro Volta (1745–1827), professor of physics in Como, who was already known as the inventor of the electrophorus and the electrical condenser, and also of a straw-electrometer which, with his condenser, he used for the detection of minute charges of electricity. Volta rejected the theory of animal electricity and ascribed the convulsions to metallic electricity produced by the contact of two different metals. Shortly after the end of the period here considered, Volta in applying his discoveries constructed his now famous electrical pile and so discovered current electricity (1800). While there is no important advance to record in the theory of terrestrial magnetism, many new systematic observations on magnetic declination and its variation were made; and in 1768 Wilcke published an isoclinic chart of magnetic 'dip' that was the first to cover an extensive part of the earth's surface, namely, Europe, Africa and South America with the Atlantic and Indian Oceans and part of the Pacific Ocean.

In a period characterised by increasing quantitative research in the physical sciences, meteorology was more critically studied and more systematically organised. At last breaking its long connections with astrology and freed from the ancient influence of Aristotle's *Meteorologica*, it became in this period one of the first examples of applied physics; and in the days of his early scientific researches Lavoisier could reasonably suggest that with better communications it should be possible to make daily weather-forecasts. The two most important contributors in effecting this change were Jean-André de Luc (1727–1817), a native of Geneva who settled in London in his later life, and Père Louis Cotte (1740–1815), *curé* of Montmorency near Paris. In his *Recherches sur les modifications de l'atmosphère* (1772) de Luc reported his exhaustive and critical experiments on the construction, manufacture, variety, standardisation and use of those two most necessary meteorological instruments, the barometer and the thermometer, both of which, it would not be too much to say, were perfected at his hands. He made great improvements also in the barometric determination of altitudes and he extended his work in a further study, *Nouvelles idées sur la météorologie* (1786–7). Cotte's *Traité de Météorologie* (1774) dealt with actual observations of atmospheric phenomena on a very considerable scale, including winds and rain, fog and dew, thunder and lightning, rainbows and aurorae, and so on to mock-suns and waterspouts; theories and instruments were described and discussed; and tabulated data for long periods were presented. Generalisation from these observations was difficult and the value of this work was empirical rather than scientific, but its emphasis on exact measurement was typical of the new approach to these complex problems. Cotte extended his studies in his *Mémoires sur la météorologie* (1788), which included large numbers of observations made at stations in many countries. Before the century ended, concerted meteorological data were being collected by correspondence with observers in many parts of the world, by the Société royale de médecine in Paris and more especially by the very efficient Societas meteorologica palatina founded in 1780 by the Elector Karl Theodor of Bavaria. The director of the latter society was a famous meteorologist, Johann Jacob Hemmer (1733–90), and his headquarters were located in the Elector's castle at Mannheim. At fifty-seven stations stretching from Siberia to North America observers equipped with standard instruments and directions for their use entered their detailed observations on special forms three times a day at prescribed intervals for report to Mannheim; their reports were afterwards digested and published in the society's *Ephemerides* until the 1790s when these very useful activities lapsed through the political disorganisation that followed the Revolution. Some interesting observations made at Kendal and at Keswick from 1788 to 1792 were published by John Dalton (1766–1844) in his *Meteorological Observations and Essays* (1793) before he formulated his atomic theory.

Geology was marked by much futile controversy between the Neptunists and the Vulcanists or Plutonists. The Neptunists saw all rocks as sedimentary deposits from aqueous solution. The Vulcanists allowed an important role to the internal heat of the earth, particularly in the consolidation of the sedimentary rocks; they regarded that consolidation as an important phase in the earth's geological history; and they thought that molten material from its interior had been protruded outwards into its crust, where it could be recognised, for instance, in granite. While Jean-Étienne Guettard (1715–86) had in the first half of the century identified a large number of extinct volcanoes in Auvergne in central France, he had at the same time recognised the action of water in changing the face of the earth; but he concluded that basalt was of aqueous origin. He was thus in this curious way the father of Vulcanism and at the same time of Neptunism. Nicolas Desmarest (1725–1815) detected further great areas of extinct volcanoes in central Europe; he satisfied himself, in opposition to Guettard, that basalt was volcanic in origin; and he noted the occurrence of horizontal deposits of sedimentary strata hundreds of feet in thickness above the oldest lavas. He took no part in the controversy, but advised the disputants to go into the field and look at the evidence themselves. Various attempts had already been made in the earlier half of the century to determine the temporal sequence of the principal types of strata in the earth's crust and in the second half Johann Gottlob Lehmann (died 1767) and Georg Christian Füchsel (1722–73) succeeded in establishing, the former for the Harz and the Erzgebirge and the latter for Thuringia, the geological succession of the rocks and thus laid the foundations of scientific stratigraphy. Füchsel noted also the different kinds of fossils in the different strata, some being wholly terrestrial, while others were entirely marine, indicating that some strata had formerly been beneath the sea.

The founder of Neptunism, Abraham Gottlob Werner (1749–1817), who spent most of his active life as a teacher in the school of mines at Freiberg, published little but by his teaching and through the work of his pupils he succeeded in impressing his views widely on his contemporaries. He was a good lecturer; he was simple, dogmatic and confident; he thought or rather assumed that the geological sequence that he observed in the rocks of his native Saxony was universal; he spoke contemptuously of geologists who spent time in theorising about the origin of the earth; he was concerned with fact and not with theory; and yet his system was riddled with hypotheses that had no better basis than his own belief in them. He was able, however, to propound a temporal sequence for the various geological formations in Saxony and arranged them in five groups: primitive, transitional, sedimentary, derivative and, lastly and most recently, volcanic. The earth, in Werner's view, was originally a solid nucleus covered by an ocean; the primitive rocks had been crystallised from solution in these great waters and the transitional ones were produced either by chemical reactions in solution that led to their precipitation or by simple mechanical sedimentation; the third and the fourth groups were formed when the waters receded or when the land was inundated afresh; and the fifth, the volcanic rocks, were recent and merely accidental, resulting from the combustion of the accumulated coal in the earth's crust. The sea was the great agent of geological change. James Hutton (1726–97), leader of the Plutonists, did not deny the role of water in these matters. In his *Theory of the Earth*, first read to the Royal Society of Edinburgh in 1785 and afterwards published in extended form in 1795, he held that the past history of the earth must be interpreted in terms of such natural processes as could still be seen in operation or were known to have been recently active. 'No powers', he wrote, '[are] to be employed that are not natural to the globe, no action to be admitted of except those of which we know the principle.'

While most rocks appeared to have been formed as submarine sedimentations, Hutton considered that they had afterwards been consolidated by the action of subterranean heat and that molten matter from below had been intruded into them. In such changes horizontal strata had been raised, inclined, broken, folded, and even twisted into the vertical. Change went on unceasingly; wind and weather slowly disintegrated the rocks thus formed; rain and rivers carried the detritus away to the sea; new strata were deposited beneath the oceans and in their turn raised aloft to be worn away again by wind and weather; and in this ceaseless flux of deposition and erosion there was 'no sign of a beginning, no prospect of an end'. Hutton restored a sound scientific outlook to geology. Although his literary style was obscure and difficult, his descriptions of the changes that he visualised in the surface of the earth were not lacking in grandeur. His influence on the further development of the science of geology was profound.

The theoretical study of cartography received much attention from geometers and old and new methods of projection were studied critically by Johann Heinrich Lambert (1728–77) in 1772, by Leonhard Euler (1707–83) from 1777 onwards and by Lagrange in 1779. The scientific voyages of discovery, such as those of Captain James Cook (1728–79), organised by the Royal Society of London, needed more and better charts and maps, but the greatest cartographical progress in the period here considered was made in France, where two famous maps were produced. The first of these was the well-known *Carte de Cassini* or *Carte de l'Académie*: begun seriously in 1750, but planned by Colbert nearly a century earlier, it was completed in 1789; it had numbered Jean Picard (1620–82) among its earliest contributors. César-François Cassini de Thury (1714–84), who finished the work, died of smallpox five years before publication was completed. It was published in 183 sheets and it is an enduring monument to the scientific ability and technical skill of eighteenth-century French cartographers as the first map of a whole country based on triangulation and topographical surveys.

The last few sheets were actually dealt with by Cassini's son, Jacques-Dominique (1747–1845), and 1793 is sometimes taken as the final date of production of this great map. The scale was 1 in 86,400, and the assembled 183 sheets gave a map about 11 metres by 11½ metres, that is, about 33 feet by 34 feet. The other famous French map of this period was only partly completed. It was the *Atlas et description minéralogiques de la France* (1780), compiled by Guettard and Antoine-Grimoald Monnet (1734–1817), and contained only 32 of an intended 230 sheets, but it was the first map to be compiled embodying geological or, as termed at that time, mineralogical data.

Following on the publication of Cassini's map, a joint Franco-British triangulation was made of the adjoining territories of north-western France and south-eastern England. In this project one of the objects was to measure exactly the differences in latitude and longitude between the observatories of Paris and London; and it was naturally to the Royal Society of London that Cassini addressed his proposals on this problem in 1783. In England the work was directed by Major-General William Roy (1726–1790) and the first step was the exact measurement in 1784 of a base-line, a little over five miles long, on level ground on Hounslow Heath. There were many delays, some materials and some instruments proved unsatisfactory, and the observations were not completed until 1787. Roy's ultimate object was a general survey of the British Isles and in 1791, a year after Roy's death, the Master-General of the Ordnance, the duke of Richmond, gained the support of King George III for the continuance of the survey begun by Roy and its extension to the whole country as a military task. These developments influenced the governments of other countries to survey their territories but the resultant mapping belongs to the nineteenth century.

Scientific societies increased in numbers from 1763 to 1793 and some specialist societies appeared. In Edinburgh a Philosophical Society was founded in 1739; it became by charter in 1783 the Royal Society of Edinburgh and its *Transactions* began to appear in 1788. The American Academy of Arts and Sciences was founded at Boston in 1780 and began to publish its *Memoirs* in 1785; it was the second American scientific society to be established, its forerunner being the American Philosophical Society, founded through the efforts of Benjamin Franklin at Philadelphia in 1743. The Royal Irish Academy was founded late in the eighteenth century from a society organised in Dublin about 1782 and its *Transactions* first appeared in 1788. The Reale Accademia della Scienze of Turin dates from 1783 and the Academia Real das Sciencas of Lisbon from 1779. There were also philosophical or scientific societies of professors and of students both in Glasgow and in Edinburgh in this period. In London in the 1760s an Aurelian Society for the study of insects, the second of its kind, met from 1762 to 1766; a Society of Entomologists assembled from 1780 to 1782; and another society 'for promoting natural history' began to meet in 1782. This last society is of more than usual interest because the dissatisfaction of the abler members with its methods and its work led to the foundation in 1788 of the Linnean Society by James Edward Smith (1759–1828), Samuel Goodenough (1743–1827) and Thomas Marsham (c. 1747–1819). It was Smith who acquired in 1784 the herbarium, library and manuscripts of Linnaeus, now in the possession of the society that he helped to found. On the Continent numbers of provincial academies of science were established. In England the most important provincial scientific society founded in this period was the Literary and Philosophical Society of Manchester, which was established in 1785. It had been preceded by a scientific club that met weekly. The first volume of its *Memoirs* was published in 1785. The society was founded in imitation of the practice in France of setting up provincial scientific societies and perhaps partly as a reaction against the restriction of such societies to capital cities. Opposed to anything that savoured of metropolitan parochialism, the new society considered that the promotion of the arts and sciences would be more widely extended by the formation of such societies in the principal towns of the kingdom. In Birmingham there was a rather loosely organised but very famous society, the Lunar Society, without apparently any rules or any formalities of membership. Its influence in the stimulation of scientific inquiry was considerable, as might be expected in view of the fact that among those who attended its meetings were Erasmus Darwin, Matthew Boulton, Samuel Galton, James Keir, William Withering, James Watt and Joseph Priestley.

Although these new scientific societies mostly published their work in volumes of memoirs or transactions, these additional scientific publications account for only a fraction of the new scientific periodicals that appeared in the second half of the eighteenth century. At the beginning of the century such literature included only the publications of the Royal Society of London and the Académie Royale des Sciences of Paris, Bayle's *Nouvelles de la république des lettres* and the *Acta Eruditorum* of Leipzig. By 1800 some seventy-five new scientific journals had appeared, and this figure excludes medical periodicals. Most of these originated after 1750; only five of them appeared in the first half of the century, which points clearly to the greatly increased scientific activity of the second half. Of the sixty-nine new scientific periodicals that originated in this second half, nine were published between 1750 and 1759, six between 1760 and 1769, nine between 1770 and 1779, twenty between 1780 and 1789 and twenty-five in the last decade. Thus forty-five of the sixty-nine new scientific periodicals of the eighteenth century first appeared in the last twenty years of the century. Specialised scientific journals both in physics and chemistry appeared in the 1770s, the *Observations sur la Physique* in Paris in 1771 under the editorship of the Abbé François

Rozier (1734–93) and the *Chemisches Journal* of Lorenz von Crell (1744–1816) in Lemgo in 1778. Their appearance is only partly explained by the increase in original work in physics and chemistry by increased numbers of researchers; it was to some extent due to the great delay in the publications of the academies, which were occasionally greatly in arrears, more particularly in France, while the acceleration of scientific studies towards the end of the century increasingly necessitated immediate publication, at least in the minds of many of those chiefly concerned in these matters in case their work was anticipated by others. One very interesting and very renowned English scientific periodical made its first appearance in the 1780s: this was William Curtis's *Botanical Magazine*, the first issue being published in 1787. In the 1780s also there appeared in Paris the *Annales de Chimie*, in 1789, the year of the Revolution, when the *privilège* that had been previously sought in vain was no longer necessary; among its editors were Lavoisier, Berthollet, Guyton and Fourcroy. In 1798 there appeared in London the first issue of the *Philosophical Magazine*, which soon became second only in importance to the *Philosophical Transactions* of the Royal Society of London. The *Botanical Magazine*, the *Annales de Chimie* and the *Philosophical Magazine* have all continued to the present time.

There was much interest in the practical arts in the second half of the eighteenth century, but little connection between science and technology. In a few instances scientific advances led to technical improvements. Such progress was, however, far from being in general the consequence of scientific discovery or of a better scientific understanding of the mechanism of nature. In the chemical industry, for example, practice was often either ahead of chemical theory or entirely unconnected with it. Even today technology is not merely another name for applied science. The attitude of the cultivated eighteenth-century mind towards the practical arts was derived from causes dating back to the seventeenth century. When the Royal Society of London and the Académie Royale des Sciences of Paris were founded in the 1660s, the aims of both were partly but plainly utilitarian. The Royal Society, being a numerous company of amateurs, would seem to have found the task of compiling a 'History of Trades' too onerous and the project was abandoned after some years, although the interest remained, as is evident from the society's work and correspondence. The Académie, on the other hand, was a small body, less amateur and more professional in some senses, and consisted of salaried servants of government with the duty of dealing with technical problems put to them by the minister to whom they were responsible. The duty of promoting the practical arts in England had been assumed in 1754 by the (Royal) Society of Arts, the first volume of its *Transactions* being published in 1783, and a much needed improvement was effected in the organisation of such studies and in the fostering of invention, while in the meantime John Harris (*c.* 1667–1719), secretary of the Royal Society, had produced his two-volume *Lexicon technicum* (1704, 1710) and Ephraim Chambers (died 1740) his *Cyclopaedia*, a 'universal dictionary of art and sciences', in two volumes in 1728. The Académie had, however, long had in mind the proposal made by Colbert in 1675 that a series of descriptions of the practical arts should be compiled by its own members. After much delay the series, illustrated with many engravings, at last appeared as *Descriptions des arts et métiers faites ou approuvées par messieurs de l'Académie royale des sciences*, in eighty-three folio volumes between 1761 and 1788. During this long delay the first volume of the *Encyclopédie* of Diderot and d'Alembert was published in 1751 and followed rapidly by others until it was completed in 1780 in thirty-five volumes, lavishly and magnificently illustrated. The full title was *Encyclopédie, ou dictionnaire raisonné des sciences, des arts et des métiers*, Diderot explaining that one of the intentions of the work was to praise and encourage the practical arts and those engaged in them and to lead the scientist to the workshop of the artisan. Whether Diderot succeeded in this last aim is very much to be doubted, but he did much by the great space that he gave to technology to bring science and industry together and for the moment it was probably science, having less to give, that profited more from the encounter.

The improvement by James Watt (1736–1819) of Newcomen's steam-engine by the invention of the separate condenser is one of the few instances in this period of the direct application of scientific discovery to technical advance. In 1763, when repairing a model of Newcomen's engine in the course of his duties as instrument-maker to the university of Glasgow, Watt was impressed by the great waste of heat that occurred through the practice of cooling the hot cylinder by means of a jet of cold water discharged inside it. The cold water condensed the steam to produce a partial vacuum and thereby to complete the downward stroke of the piston; at the next upward stroke a new charge of steam had to reheat the cold cylinder and much of this steam was therefore condensed and its heat wasted. In discussing his observations Watt learned from Joseph Black of the latter's discovery of latent heat and so appreciated more clearly the very great waste of heat in the working of Newcomen's engine; and in 1767 he hit upon the idea of condensing the steam outside instead of inside the cylinder, by means of a separate condenser connected with the cylinder through a tap and always kept cool. Later, he improved the working further by surrounding the cylinder with a steam-jacket to maintain its heat and by using steam, rather than the cold air of the atmosphere, to effect the downward stroke of the piston. A patent was granted in 1769, and in partnership in 1775 with Matthew Boulton (1728–1809) of the Soho works, Birmingham, Watt began to construct engines. The first models were single acting, but the double-acting engine, which developed twice the power for the same size of cylinder, was patented in 1782; the device known as the sun-and-planet gear to convert reciprocating into rotary motion was devised in association with William Murdoch (1754–1839) and patented in 1781 and the centrifugal governor was introduced in 1787. By 1788 it could be said that the rotative steam engine was standardized and had become of world-wide application. The number of engines built by the Boulton–Watt partnership, which ended in 1800, was about five hundred. Other engines were constructed during this period, but cannot be dealt with here.

The discovery by Scheele in 1774 of the bleaching action of chlorine and its use on an industrial scale by Berthollet in 1785 is another instance of the direct application of a scientific discovery. Previously fabrics were exposed in 'bleach-fields' after treatment with alkali and then with acid in a process of many stages. As a result of Berthollet's new method 'bleach-fields' were no longer necessary and the large areas so used became available for agriculture. Berthollet's attempt at a chemical explanation of the process of dyeing in terms of oxygen was ingenious but rather inspired by the inadequacy of current mechanical theories than firmly based on chemical evidence.

This was the great age for mechanical invention. The 'spinning jenny' devised in 1765 by James Hargreaves (died 1778) could, with one operator, work eight spindles and in a later model eighty spindles, in consequence of which Hargreaves had his house and his machinery destroyed by a mob through fear of starvation on account of the replacement of men by machines. (Sir) Richard Arkwright (1732–92) introduced in 1769 a new spinning machine, the 'water-frame', so called because it was driven by water-power. These machines produced firm fine threads and cotton fabrics could now be made by means of them without linen warp-threads. Samuel Crompton (1753–1827) invented in 1774 another spinning machine, Crompton's 'mule', combining the principles of the models of Hargreaves and of Arkwright, and this produced yarn as fine as the cottons of India. A steam-carriage was designed in 1763 by Nicolas-Joseph Cugnot (1725–1804), a French engineer, but it seems to have proved unstable; and Murdoch made a model steam-locomotive at Redruth in 1784. Andrew Meikle (1719–1811) of Dunbar invented the first successful threshing-machine in 1786; in a later model the chaff was blown away and the grain sieved from small corn and weed-seeds. John Fitch (1743–98) made several successful steam-boats from 1785 onwards in America, and in 1787 William Symington (1764–1831) designed an engine for use in such boats. These primitive attempts at steam-locomotion were, however, more experimental than practical. Much more spectacular success was obtained with balloons, following on the successful experiments of the Montgolfier brothers at Annonay near Lyons on 5 June 1783 in sending up large paper balloons filled with hot air to a height of 6000 feet. Two months later, on 27 August, J. A. C. Charles (1746–1823), a French physicist, sent up a balloon filled with hydrogen, a 'Charlière', from the Champ de Mars, Paris: it came down at a distance of fifteen miles. Pilâtre de Rozier (1757–85) went up in a captive Montgolfier balloon on 15 October 1783 to a height of eighty feet and on 21 November in another 'Montgolfière' and accompanied by the Marquis d'Arlandes, a major of infantry, he made the first aerial voyage from Paris, landing after twenty-five minutes in the air about six miles from his starting-point. The first human ascent in a hydrogen balloon was made on 1 December of the same year by its inventor, Charles. Many flights followed in other countries as well as in France. John Jeffries, an American physician, and J. P. Blanchard, an experienced balloonist, successfully crossed the Channel from England to France on 7 January 1785. Developments in about eighteen months had been rapid. Later, the armies of revolutionary France included a company of *aerostatiers* or balloonists under Guyton de Morveau and a balloon was successfully used for reconnaissance at the battle of Fleurus in 1794.

Engineers based their work more on empiricism and experience than on scientific principles and the relations between force, work and power were not understood. William Smeaton (1724–92), at once craftsman, engineer and scientist, studied the problem of these relations experimentally and reported his results to the Royal Society of London in 1759 and 1776, but there was still no clear understanding that the quantity of motion induced by an applied force could be considered in terms either of momentum or of *vis viva*. An age marked as no preceding one by the development of mechanical power and by the construction of heavy and powerful machinery was hampered in its study of the relevant scientific principles because it lacked a suitable system of units and a satisfactory nomenclature. At the same time the production of pig-iron was doubled between 1788 and 1796 and redoubled in the next ten years, mainly as a result of the success of the 'puddling' process divised in 1784 by Henry Cort (1740–1800) for the conversion of pig-iron into malleable iron. Iron rails replaced wooden ones, the first cast-iron bridge was erected in 1779 at Ironbridge and the first iron boat was built in 1787.

Many other ingenious devices were invented at this time, of which we mention only three. James Watt in 1779 made a simple copying-press for use with his correspondence. Aimé Argand (died 1803), a Swiss, made an improved oil-lamp in 1784; it had a tubular wick and a glass chimney to increase the supply of air, and it gave less smoke and more light. In 1792 Murdoch devised an apparatus with a retort and pipes to light his house at Redruth with coal-gas.

It was an age of discovery in the physical sciences and an age of mechanical invention. It was also the age of Lavoisier and Laplace. While English science was still the field of the wealthy amateur and while its teaching, except for mathematics, was still largely in the hands of the professors of medicine or the tutors in the Dissenting academies or the itinerant lecturers on natural philosophy, in Paris at the Jardin du Roi under the direction of Buffon the professors lecturing to public audiences included in these years Rouelle, Bernard and Antoine-Laurent de Jussieu, Desfontaines, Macquer, Fourcroy, Lamarck, and others among the leaders of French science. From the presses of Paris there came many volumes of Buffon's *Histoire naturelle* and many volumes of the *Encyclopédie*, as well as the *Descriptions des arts et métiers* and the annual volumes of *Histoire et mémoires* from the Académie des Sciences with many volumes of supplementary publications, and the new specialist scientific periodicals in physics and chemistry, the *Observations sur la physique* and the *Annales de chimie*. Besides these classic publications of eighteenth-century France, there were many text-books of physics and especially of chemistry, and it was from French authors that other nations learned their chemistry at this time. In Paris, too, in 1766 there appeared the first dictionary of chemistry by Pierre-Joseph Macquer (1718-84) and in 1781 the first dictionary of physics by Mathurin-Jacques Brisson (1723-1806). There were many scientific posts in France, in chemistry in particular and in the chemical industries, as, for instance, in the porcelain factory at Sèvres and in the dyeing industry. When the *Ferme des poudres* was abolished by Turgot in 1775 during his brief period of office as Minister of Finance to Louis XVI and when a new *Régie des poudres* was instituted to take its place for the manufacture of the national supplies of gunpowder, Lavoisier was appointed one of the four *régisseurs* because of his knowledge of chemistry and the Académie des Sciences shared in the work of reform by announcing a prize-competition for the best essay on the manufacture of gunpowder. Lavoisier in this responsible post reorganised the supply of saltpetre and gunpowder and by chemical and ballistic tests greatly improved its range and its quality as well as increasing its quantity. The range was lengthened by about two-thirds; and in a few years, instead of the former shortage, the magazines were filled with powder of excellent quality so that, during the War of Independence, France was able to export gunpowder to the American colonists. Adequate supplies of good powder of a better quality were consequently available in the Napoleonic wars and Napoleon may well have owed some part of his success to this circumstance. On another occasion shortage of supplies led the Académie to announce a prize for the best essay on the manufacture of soda. The prize was won in 1790 by Nicolas Leblanc (1742-1806) and manufacture began in 1791. Leblanc's raw materials were common salt, sulphuric acid, limestone and coal. The salt and acid were heated together and gave sodium sulphate which, when heated with a mixture of limestone and coal, gave what was called 'black ash', a mixture of soda and calcium sulphide. Extraction of this with water and crystallisation of the solution so obtained gave soda. Leblanc's 'black ash' or 'soda ash' process became and long remained one of the basic processes of the chemical industry. At the same time throughout this period the Académie made many reports on inventions, on manufactures and on problems of public importance, such as the water-supply of Paris, balloons, street-lighting, hospitals and prisons, to name only a few, and in all of these the latest scientific knowledge was applied. Moreover, French scientists had discovered the composition of air and of water, unravelled the role of oxygen in combustion and in respiration, devised a new and satisfactory system of chemical nomenclature and drawn up the first modern table of the chemical elements, besides establishing the principle of the conservation of matter in chemical change and incidentally inventing the chemical equation; they had demonstrated experimentally that the inverse-square law was the quantitative law of attraction and repulsion between electrical and between magnetic charges; they had applied the new chemistry to the manufacture of gunpowder and of soda and in bleaching; and they had shown other peoples how to map a whole country and had made the first geological maps. It was not only an age of discovery in the physical sciences and an age of mechnical invention; the thirty years before the Revolution were an age of intellectual supremacy in French science.

CHAPTER VI

EDUCATIONAL IDEAS, PRACTICE
AND INSTITUTIONS

VIRTUALLY all the changes and adjustments in educational thought
and practice during the period of the revolutions sprang from the
intellectual foundations of the Age of Reason which was just
drawing to a close. Notions about the practice and content of teaching
were highly articulate, even if they sometimes smelt more of the salon than
the schoolroom. It was during these years that the discussion of education
became conscious of its central place in all thinking about what d'Alembert
referred to as 'our minds, our customs and our achievements'. But to
hold that the developments in educational thought were linked to one or
two of the major themes of the Enlightenment would be to oversimplify
the issues. Perhaps no one was in a better position to appreciate the
range covered by the intellectual stimuli than Victor Cousin, who made
contact with the thought of the *Idéologues* in the newly opened École
Normale in Paris under the Empire, then made contact with transcen-
dentalism in the German universities, and lived on to promote the
reconstruction of French elementary education in the quite different
philosophical atmosphere in which planning was accomplished under the
Orleans monarchy. The eighteenth century, he remarked, had submitted
everything to critical examination. This was the period that 'made of
education at first a problem, then a science, finally an art; hence pedagogy'. Pedagogy, he was prepared to concede, was a ridiculous word, but
the thing itself was sacred, and its full flowering as a subject of scientific
import had been accomplished in the age of revolution.

The thinkers of the main stream of the Enlightenment endeavoured
above all to present a vision of reality which was ordered by an intelligible
set of rules. All who took part in this movement of ideas were convinced that 'human understanding is capable by its own power, and
without recourse to supernatural assistance, of comprehending the system
of the world'. So Ernst Cassirer has epitomised the spirit of the times.
This new way of understanding the world—not as new perhaps as some
thought—must lead to new ways of controlling it. The eighteenth century
was a century of optimism about man's capacity to comprehend and
master natural processes. By proper understanding of the springs of
human action he could expect to uncover the secrets of an improved
economy and a happier social order. The future of the world depended
on a great deal of close observation and comparison of factual findings,
whether by introspection in the mind or by scientific measurement

of things surveyed by the senses. And so for the educational thinker the significance of the prevailing trend of ideas was almost entirely positive.

Such a thinker was much less anxious about the arguments for disbelief in revealed religion or about the poor outlook for traditional practices than buoyed up by his confidence in the uses of reason. For, in the sense in which this word was being employed, he saw what appeared to be a fresh and invigorating technique in the use of one's mental resources to analyse without bias the evidence of facts and to generalise new truths out of them. It was a sequence to be performed in that order. To be sure, the positive yield of acceptable educational theory that could be culled from the work of the masters before the 'sixties proved to be disappointingly slight. Locke, whose influence upon the discussions of the period can hardly be overestimated, had far more success with his general argument that nothing but sense impressions presided over the growth of the child's mind than with his two essays on education. His judgements on the functions of the schoolmaster and the requirements of an improved curriculum were shrewd and practical. At the same time they were unsystematic and somewhat defeatist. His belief in the virtue of curbing the mind under intellectual discipline seemed oddly inconsistent with his startling views on the autonomy of the individual mind. Meanwhile, the contributions to the republic of free thought made by Voltaire, the master clarifier of progressive views, were not paralleled by any suggestions for the use of popular schools in the diffusion of the new culture; nor was Holbach, the last on the scene of the generation of true *philosophes*, and often regarded as the most violent critic of the old social order, able to produce any case for the redemption of the people at large by education.

Later in the century the educational implications of new doctrine came into clearer focus. Overtones once scarcely perceptible made their impression felt. When the philosophic enlightenment reached its climax in countries east of the Rhine the contrasts between old and new ways of thinking were sudden enough to throw fresh ideas and practices into very high relief.

Attitudes to education were of course influenced by the prevailing hostility of the amateur savant to traditional forms of instruction, particularly to the catechetical practices inherited from a more theocentric culture. His suspicions of the centres of academic monopoly were increased by his dislike of their religious orthodoxy. The doctrines of 'common sense', which owed so much to Locke, himself for long periods a resident student of Christ Church, had been slow in making their appeal to professional scholars. The plain fact was that the work of the older institutions of learning was almost everywhere at a low ebb. It was fashionable to hold them in contempt as anachronisms ready to give place to new ways of organising and disseminating knowledge. The idea of the university itself was on trial.

The appearance of the seventeenth and last volume of the text of the French *Encyclopaedia* in 1765 was a notable and symbolic event in the development of this protest. This great work presented knowledge in a new idiom. We see the authors themselves as a loose association of unattached specialists, some of them admittedly specialists only in the making—*une société des gens de lettres* as the title-page proclaimed—operating within a framework or organisation of subject-matter in which they not only broke all the rules associated with conventional scholarly presentation, but, with the emphasis the articles placed on empirical inquiry and on the study of manufacturing and laboratory techniques, seemed to infuse the spirit of a new *logos* into the pursuit of learning. Emasculated as much of the work was by suppressions undertaken by an anxious printer, the production was more obviously committed to a point of view than were the foreign models and imitations 'collecting all books in one'; one of which was the *Encyclopaedia Britannica*, published in three volumes in Edinburgh in 1768–71. The French *Encyclopaedia* was undeniably a manifesto of forward-looking intellectuals, dedicated to bringing about a change in the modes of thinking and teaching; at the same time it was honestly intended to provide a survey of current knowledge, of a sort never before conceived, for the guidance of a sophisticated leisured class. The Encyclopaedists were anti-scholastic in more than one sense of the word; they opened the map of knowledge to public inspection without the mediation of priest or schoolmaster. Here then was embodied a notion of adult education through the printed word bearing a message for all sophisticated readers wherever the French language was read. To be sure, the idea that poorer citizens should be furnished with epitomised knowledge through any such medium was not yet contemplated by anyone.

In these and other forms the intellectual projection of the Enlightenment, with its various messages, made an impact which was not free from disturbing features for persons concerned with education. Each one of them might find himself challenged to execute a number of tasks. A formula seemed to be needed to control the refurnishing of his curriculum around the self-sufficiency of a single principle at the heart of nature. The philosophy upon which his educational method proceeded must recognise that the laws governing both the direction of human action and the motions of inanimate particles were part of a system in which the parts were interlocked and verifiable. They afforded a chance to demonstrate to him the continuous spectrum of knowledge and to inculcate optimism. Finally theory must accommodate itself to a method of seeking knowledge which relied on the strength of observation and analytical inquiry in defiance maybe of the claims of authority. If a reading of Holbach and Diderot persuaded the educator that, by training young people to fear invisible tyrants, religious education sapped their initiative and courage in face of life's problems, then the provision of some alternative instrument for character-building fell to be considered. The whole current of thought of the age must make him conscious of a gap. And into this lacuna a satisfactory scheme for moral upbringing, freed from supernatural sanctions, had to be inserted. Perhaps the success of Rousseau's contribution was that he made a large part of his educational theory depend upon his perception of the nature of the gap. The search for a practical embodiment of novel theories implied a challenge to a world where educational institutions were ruled overwhelmingly by tradition—a consideration which incidentally explains the growing popularity all over Europe of private tutors as a substitute for school in the homes of those of the gentry who could afford them. Questions of procedure in an educational framework, of testing the integrity of one's beliefs, finally offered the most ruthless challenge to the doctrines of perfectibility and the invincibility of reason. This was one of the paradoxes of the later part of the age of reason.

Thus unexpected directions were taken by the theory of learning, often stimulated by the current psychology of the Lockian school. Knowledge was restricted to what the peripheral stimuli of the five senses could convey to their owner. It seemed to follow from the claims of the empiricists that all children have the same sort of sensations and the same needs. Therefore equality must be the common condition of those who are on the threshold of life. Further, as La Chalotais urged, unless it could be demonstrated that women have a different set of sensations, the argument would seem to demolish the superior status of the male pupil's ability.

Hume had shown that without the principles of sense experience and mental association to which his generation of thinkers pinned its faith, nothing was at hand to provide for the slightest trace of continuity in a pupil's personality development. Hence it became vital for a new generation of theorists to relate the education of both intelligence and the emotional life to a better understanding of the actual mechanism of mental growth: whereupon it became evident that, in spite of much vain talk of the value of empirical inquiry, the whole sensationalist philosophy depended upon nothing more useful than a bit of introspective imagining. The real work had yet to be done: first in discovering what were the springs of action that gave impetus and direction in the lives of people both young and old; and secondly in showing what a more life-like, perhaps more complex, model of the intellect and the passions could offer by way of guidance in the schoolroom. By the mid-century theoretical psychology, if current philosophical discussion can be so called, had drifted into a region of abstractions through excess of scruple about utilising conceptual entities beyond those already in employment. And it was at this point that the abbé de Condillac came forward with his *Traité des Sensations* and his *Traité des Animaux* to save the appearances and give promise of further development in educational theory.

The *diffusion de la lumière* knew no frontiers. In the propagation of progressive doctrine the leaders were nearly all people who had some sort of international connection. And thus in organised philanthropy or educational reform, more often the latter, ideas about human betterment crossed frontiers. A whole network of understanding, sustained by correspondence and strengthened by personal introductions, stretched from the wilderness beyond the Susquehanna river to the new waterfront in St Petersburg. These contacts were fortified by an interest in practical projects. And a score or so of individuals, among whom Benjamin Franklin was one of the more prominent, pushed and underwrote these designs. When in 1761 Johann Basedow, professor at a Danish knightly academy, moved to Altona and began to publish one of the earliest *schemas*, of the type dear to the eighteenth-century mind, for a government-directed educational system, suitable for any sizeable German state, complete with educational ladder and adjustable religious curriculum, he received intellectual support and monetary aid from all over Europe. Almost without exception these men believed in the extension of an international brotherhood of new knowledge and the growth of a more generous humanity as the outcome of this knowledge. In the world of freemasonry, to which a surprisingly large number of reformers owned attachment, education became the matter almost of a missionary enterprise. The spread of scientific notions and of ideas about 'realistic' schooling—teaching about *Realien*—owed much to visits paid between members of the lodges. The masonic movement had spread from Britain. Some of the manifestations that appeared in due course were startling enough to provoke harsh criticism; but the darker and more curious sides of the story do not belong to educational reform. Hostile to the official clerical establishment, at any rate in Latin Europe, where their antipathy was warmly reciprocated, the masons were vigorous in attempts to promote secular schooling; they came to be regarded as sworn enemies of all the teachings of traditional pedagogy.

Nowhere did their influence show itself more vigorously than in imperial Russia, where the famous educator and social reformer N. I. Novikov was the spearhead of change, especially in the newly awakened academic life of Moscow, emphasising as he did the graver and more religious side of masonic thinking against the Voltairian scepticism of the capital. Novikov was the most powerful educational innovator in Russia until he fell under the ban of Catherine's later reactionary policy.

The authentic voice of freemasonry in its special concern with educational reform was heard in Paris, where Helvétius, La Chalotais, Franklin,

Lavoisier, Fourcroy, Buffon and Dupont de Nemours were all members of the large and very influential cosmopolitan group which assumed its final organisation in 1776 as the lodge of the *Neuf sœurs* under the leadership of La Lande. The reforming spirit of this society of eminent intellectuals was powerful in the extreme. In due course every public memorandum of significance that dealt with educational reconstruction in France came from the hand of one member or another of this lodge. The missionary work culminated in the conception and creation of the *écoles centrales* of 1795.

It follows from what has been said that part of the background to educational experiment was the wider spread of scientific ideas and the growth of respect for scientific method. We notice too a swing-over of interest among the experimentally minded towards the specific uses of applied science and particularly towards biological studies. Such changes of emphasis had profound implications for chemistry, and we witness the emergence of a new attitude of mind concerning the physiological bases of human learning. New ideas developed about the processes of maturation and about the kinship between the nervous system of man and the phenomena of the animal world. Thus some transition is evident from a rather abstract mathematical ingenuity to close observation of nature as it lay about one. Children became interesting natural phenomena, to be watched, to be compared, to be made the subjects of experiment. From the work of Linnaeus, in which the foundations of modern scientific classification had been laid, both in the taxonomy of the plant and animal kingdoms and the systematic overhaul of the physician's *materia medica*, we pass to the enlarged interest in biological function. This was to be seen for example in Réaumur's work upon the chemistry of bodily activity and animal behaviour. We are impressed by the anthropological interests displayed in the monumental publications of the great naturalist Buffon, whose ideas on morphology were fundamentally hostile to the earlier methodological approach of Linnaeus, as also were his ideas on the functioning of the senses and his near-evolutionary picture of animal generation. From Buffon's hint that each individual had, as it were, a natural history of its own, came Rousseau's notion of education by natural stages. C. F. Wolff's inquiries into the metabolism of mammalian tissues and Galvani's crucial discoveries which linked muscle-nerve dynamics with physical theory were likewise concerned with the principles of bodily function. And all these pioneering studies brought the phenomena of physiological behaviour into a more convincing relationship with the phenomena of the mind. Within the world of educational thought, the change of interest was reflected in the movement from the narrower, more schoolmasterly conceptions of syllabus reform which fill the *Traité des Études* of Charles Rollin, twice rector of the university of Paris, to a concern, certainly much less technically well-informed, with larger and more general ideas about the physical and social forces which shape men's lives, both in and out of school.

In this, the heroic period of the industrial revolution in Britain, the work of all but a few of the contributors to new knowledge in the physical and human sciences lay quite outside the ancient seats of learning. The movement was autodidactic, and for that reason all the more remarkable in its precocity. Scientific invention came from the hands of relatively uneducated men beckoned on by the call for industrial improvements or by sheer curiosity. It might be said that the Scottish universities offered more encouragement to genius. Indeed, although the degrees they conferred were held elsewhere in contempt, yet the newer disciplines in medicine and natural philosophy attracted much lively talent from over the border and helped to provide personnel for the new academic centres growing up in North America. By the end of the century the fame of the Edinburgh medical school had spread throughout the world. In the encouraging atmosphere of Glasgow and Edinburgh Joseph Black, one of the greatest figures of the age in chemistry, was able to promote his investigations whilst holding academic appointments. But far more typical of the period was John Dalton, destined for greatness as a pioneer in optics and as the begetter of modern atomic theory. He came from a Cumberland weaver's cottage to work as a self-educated schoolmaster. Then, as a struggling private teacher of science, he found himself in circumstances which gave him the influential contacts that he needed. The experimental environment was provided by local philosophical societies and at length by the Royal Institution (founded 1799) of London.

In the New World, both in the Catholic world of Hispanic culture and in the mixed religious environment of the emancipated British colonies, university institutions were in somewhat better favour than in Europe. Small as were their student rolls, their services in the recruitment of the professions were indispensable, and the pressure was strong to enlarge vocational studies. At the time of their revolution the thirteen colonies, with a population of 2,500,000, had seven established colleges of university rank, or nine if one includes Dartmouth, a mission foundation in New Hampshire, and Franklin's Philadelphia Academy, later to be the University of Pennsylvania. The importance of this Philadelphia college has to be recognised. It ostentatiously flouted classical traditions, and with its scientific curriculum it served as a link between the older forms of preparation for professional careers, based on the classics, and the new-type 'realistic' academy. These small colleges and later-comers of university rank in America were important and influential, sufficiently so indeed to excite political differences when the claims of the new states to supervise their own higher education were successfully confronted by older religious controls which stood for independence of outlook and freedom from secular influences.

The principle of university leadership in the intellectual world suffered severely in Spain and Italy; whilst in France, which possessed eighteen universities having the full complement of four faculties, the almost complete obscuration of their prestige was assisted by the antics of the Sorbonne authorities, whose subservience to government policy in the condemnation of libertarian works like Helvetius' *De l'Esprit* made a mockery of their learning. In central Europe the numerous universities had been losing social influence and dignity: they were treated as provincial; they were thought to be inward-looking, clannish and wanting in civility. Despotic princes handled them with little respect; and the great current of the Enlightenment had seemed to be passing them by, even though their public contribution could not readily be dispensed with in educating the personnel of the new bureaucratic statecraft.

Yet paradoxically it was in central Europe, where ancient habits were least adaptable and most tenacious, that events brought new life and vigour into the established world of scholarship and probably saved the university idea from perishing. In both the Hanoverian and the Brandenburg-Prussian political systems were located universities of recent foundation which were not merely tolerated but encouraged to flourish by the lay authorities. Göttingen and Halle had started on new lines: they contrived to be abreast of the age. The former was still fashionable, a school for princes, an attraction to scholars from all parts, where, as professors, they were well received and by no means ill paid. The new sciences were given opportunites to spread and advertise their claims; fresh developments in the recognised academic disciplines made their appearance. Politics, law, the beginnings of historical and social sciences brought in new students. Although it had its setbacks, intellectual freedom in the lecture room was generally a reality in Göttingen. The *libertas philosophandi* of the *Gelehrte* now established itself as an example to the rest of Germany. At Halle, which as the first comer had given the needed stimulus to Göttingen, a more distinct bias in favour of theological studies was manifest. The Prussian university of Halle exhibited a similar spirit of tolerance. The central disciplines of thought were given their place, and the faculty of philosophy (that is, arts) was allowed, during the long rule of Christian Wolff, to assume the leading position. The scholarship, at the same time dignified and adventurous, of Halle made this university famous all over Germany and gave a new significance to Prussian leadership in the influential guise of a civilised state. Halle's remarkable combination of rational philosophising and Protestant pietism was an important feature of the revival of German scholarship and lent a recognisable intellectual colouring to the Teutonic *Aufklärung*. The strength of Göttingen in classical studies showed itself perhaps more significantly in the revival of humanism, which was making German learning the admiration of the world. The modern fashion of treating books as instruments of knowledge intended to be read and used as part of the discipline of the well-educated student owes much to the example of Göttingen, where an enormous university library was assembled. The fashion of independent reading and an adult attitude to higher studies came to be regular features of student life in Leipzig and Erlangen and the other universities of Germany as they began to follow the new examples. In the world of scholarship which lay to the west of the Rhine, only in Leyden and Utrecht could a similar respect for learning be found.

In Germany all the cultural and educational extremes met and by some dialectical process contributed to the creation of new forms. Here at any rate, as Paulsen has pointed out, the fashionable academies, or chartered societies of eminent men of learning, typified by the Berlin Académie Royale des Sciences et Belles-lettres, to which the efforts of Frederick the Great had given an international standing, succeeded in living in amity and a state of mutual awareness with the universities. Cross-fertilisation in ideas was possible in a manner which was probably unique. In other parts of Europe the privileged corporations of learning disregarded the universities. They knew that the scientific revolution was their business, and felt it to be theirs alone. The academies were consciously preserved as rallying points and sources of encouragement for those engaged in pioneer work; although to treat them as independent of state control, or even the whims of the royal courts, would not be correct except in Britain. Quite a number of these bodies could with good reason claim to be performing the functions of intellectual leadership, offering rewards to scholars of promise, organising lectures, demonstrations and experiments, and reporting on work in progress, stimulating new inquiries and disseminating information in print. They kept the flow of scientific publications in constant movement; they promoted new researches in the older fields of study and in new liberal fields like archaeology, history and comparative philology.

These corporations or guilds of savants were modelled on their successful prototypes, namely the Royal Society of London, the Académie Française of Paris and its sister society, the Académie des Sciences. The beneficent spirit of Leibnizian scholarship gave a measure of integrity to their functioning. On the eve of the revolutions these powerful bodies had reached the fullness of their influence in European culture. Indeed the Paris Académie des Sciences whilst under the influence of Lavoisier, who was in turn director, secretary and treasurer, became a tolerably powerful national institution comparable with the state research establishments of modern times. It was an active organiser and promoter of research in virtually permanent session. When the crisis of the revolution assailed it, further reports were still being called for by the authorities, including those on the work of formulating the new decimal system of weights and measures; but public funds were now withheld. Lavoisier, who was a most competent organiser and an authority on scientific education, as well as being the most brilliant scientific intellect of his age, kept the Académie in being with the help of his substantial private fortune until within a few months of his own journey to the guillotine.

Some academies, like the American Philosophical Society (1760), based on Philadelphia, and the Academy of Arts and Sciences (1780), based on Boston, were the sequels to spontaneous efforts of private enterprise. But the recognised model of the larger institutions became the chartered state corporation which had a prestige value for its princely patron. Thus the Swedish and Danish monarchies, like lesser principalities, imitated their greater neighbours. Here as elsewhere a practical return was expected. When reconstructing his academy in Berlin Frederick scoured Europe for scholars; and the members were expected to supply hints and research information on any subject the king proposed. Was it profitable, for example, for the people to be deceived?

Like the Prussian academy, the Académie Impériale des Sciences of St Petersburg had started in 1724 as a child of the fertile brain of Leibniz. As an organisation managed by foreigners and German Balts, it was hardly popular with Russians in the second half of the century; but it was the foremost instrument of learning, of scientific advancement and of the new educational principles in the country. Intended by its founder the Tsar Peter as the forerunner of a great university, it remained in fact the substitute for a university until Alexander's educational reforms adopted the German academic model.

These state cultural organisations were recognised as eminently suited to the requirements of a centralised despotism, which is one of the reasons why corporations of learned men were swept away in France by the Convention in 1793. But the importance of the academies can hardly be evaluated without an appreciation of the work of the less dignified but more specialised societies which often hived off from the main bodies or grew up in their beneficent shade. In London, where the Royal Society still maintained its ancient prestige, the Linnean Society and the Royal Institution came into being in this fashion. Smaller groups were found in the provincial centres. In fact Europe in the latter half of the century was generously strewn with hundreds of scientific and philosophic academies and small groups of educated men devoted to general improvement and the dissemination of culture. They formed an active if un-acknowledged part of the cultural machinery of an optimistic age. And most markedly they educated opinion in France, where some five hundred provincial societies, many of them holding the privileges of royal letters patent, were active in organising courses of lectures, making reports and working on scientific problems. Much information concerning their activities has fortunately survived; and it indicates a pronounced swing-over of interest after about 1760 among these petty seigneurs, talkative abbés and businessmen from literary inquiries to more topical concerns, such as the economy of agricultural production, trends in science and industry and the political arguments of J.-J. Rousseau. In these debates men cultivated the climate of opinion that produced the *cahiers de doléances* of 1789, and their local academies were the predecessors, if seldom in direct continuity, of the provincial political clubs that maintained the onrush of the Revolution.

The weakness of the century's thinking concerning the place of the child's development in the natural world had been evident enough in the literature of Britain and France upon which the mind of Europe was feeding. Clear and impressive as the demonstration was of the capacity of mental associations, once in mesh, to make use of material projected into the mind through the windows of sense, and so to extend their scope into the highest flights, the appeal of this psychology to its age owed less to its constructive message than to its elegant self-sufficiency. It provided the infant with an 'understanding' out of nothing, which would start up, function and expand its resources from birth onwards without any original endowment of innate ideas, without any of the tiresome implications of a soul. The senses were held to be capable without assistance of stimulating the whole apparatus of conscious life into motion; and they must obey the same rules of natural law as other physical events. All this upheld the claims of empirical observation against the Cartesian assumption of spiritual self-sufficiency. One just observed one's mind in action. One tried to remember, perhaps with indifferent success, one's earliest introspection as a child. But the rules required that the material for introspection came always from external stimuli.

The educator, flattered as he must have been by the omnipotence imputed to him as the controller of the child's environment, had little to help him towards a positive start other than the hint that motivation somehow got going in his pupil as the result of rational cogitation about the rival merits, or, as Locke would have it, the rival demerits, of alternative courses of action. Was this a useful introduction to the interior workings of his pupils' progress? What animated the will to learn? That which for the philosopher seemed a triumphant vindication of analytical method was for the schoolmaster an empty and unprofitable demonstration.

It was in Germany that the most downright distrust of the 'sensational' explanation became manifest. Newtonian and Lockian influences were here less powerful. Until Kant at length attempted a fusion of rationalism and empiricism the presiding influences over the climate of thought were Leibniz and his systematising commentator Christian Wolff. Leibniz had overthrown the geometrically inspired universe of Descartes, but he passed on much of the Frenchman's way of thinking about the powers of the mind. While adopting his mechanistic attitude towards nature at large, Leibniz was also loyal to the mind's autonomy and the efficacy of deductive logic. And it was this mental or subjective approach to problems of growth that proved to have importance in German pedagogical discussion. Leibniz's assertion that the substratum of knowledge is unchangeable and should be within the imaginative grasp of the human mind linked him with the *philosophes*. Yet he contrived to stimulate a vision of education within that quite different order of things which was implicit in the doctrine of the self-developing monads. The life of all conscious beings must germinate internally. German thought thus inherited from Leibniz a will to believe that the reasoning mind was equipped with an intuitive apprehension of truth, which demanded no support or buttressing by empirical tests; it readily believed in the mind's capacity to exploit the dynamic possibilities placed within its reach; it accepted without difficulty the power of man's reason slowly to enlarge its grasp of justice and right action as the abiding harmony of the world disclosed itself.

Thus in central Europe we find in many quarters a proneness to the belief that education is best regarded as something taking place while the personality is in process of striving towards clarity of judgement, relying all the while on its innate powers. In some sense the learner has the ability to spin knowledge out of his own consciousness. Nothing could contradict more vigorously the Lockian doctrine of the growth of the understanding. It was not without the consciousness of powerful support that Schelling preached in Jena about the restless German mind achieving itself in individual reason and self-contemplation; nor was Fichte alone in showing more interest in how pupils use their minds than in what they learn. In asserting that an intellectual élite could most properly be reared in philosophy classes he spoke for many of his university colleagues. Lessing brought clarity and a massive intelligence to the task of trying to demonstrate the powers of inborn reason at work in the stream of becoming. 'It is not the truth which a man possesses, or assumes he possesses, but the honest labour spent in the pursuit of it that determines a man's worth.' He fulfilled the grandiose task of showing that the education of all mankind, within which that of the individual is framed as a microcosm, has been accomplished by a series of stages as one phase of religious experience and morality has succeeded another. Herder generalised the experience and began to look for the morality in the bloodstream of the tribe or national group. The appeal of objective reason, already precarious in Lessing's teaching, was at an end. As the century drew to its close the question in Germany was not the willingness of the state to educate the citizen but the preservation of the citizen from indoctrination by educators imbued, like Fichte, with violent beliefs.

Since the psychology of the school of Locke with its emphasis on passive states of reception had taken strongest root in France, the attempts made in the second half of the century to recover some freedom from its insipid limitations attracted most attention there. The active will now began to come into its own. Logically the will now seemed to precede the idea. A large inarticulate element in human nature, long set aside with a sort of wry stoicism as the province of the 'passions', began to assume significance. After Hume's shattering assault on the foundations of inductive logic, the enormous respect which pure reason commanded as a moving principle of the mind, both among the admirers of Newton and in the still powerful stream of Cartesian teaching, was obviously weakening.

It was now that the psychological treatises of the abbé de Condillac, to which reference has been made, began to have enormous influence, even on minds as unsympathetic as Rousseau's. In the first place Condillac was an acknowledged pedagogical expert. He published a syllabus of studies which purported to be designed for the lessons he gave to the young Duke Ferdinand in the French court of Parma. This has some historical interest as an early example of a course of studies devised, as he says, to encourage his pupil to reflect on, rather than to amass, information; and a more important feature is that it endeavoured to put the phases of man's historical development in their natural order for the child, starting with the earliest myths of the race and finishing with modern science. Here Condillac anticipates not only modern notions about integrated courses of studies but also later doctrines of the child's recapitulation of race history in the stages of his own development.

In his endeavours to give a more realistic account of the theory of growth through the sensations, Condillac respectfully brought Locke up to date. By applying analytical method to the results of introspection he succeeded in showing that it was possible to derive all the active operations or functions of consciousness—the acts of attention, judgement, memory and so on—from the comparisons made in the mind between the data yielded by sensations. For Condillac the perception of such data constituted an activity of the soul; what is more, the 'natural history of the soul', as he termed it, could be demonstrated in terms solely of faculties which were no more than transferred sensations. Difficult as it was to explain how elementary sensations were equipped by nature to give *attention*, still, something alive and vigorous, some latent power capable of discriminating between observations, eager to learn and profit from experience, able too in a fashion to give meaning to desires and impulses, would seem to have been put back into the mind. Even if there is a hint somewhere of a piece of sleight-of-hand, we are moving into the era of modern psychology.

The many implications of these findings were not lost on Condillac's readers. They were delighted by the self-sufficiency and the neat economy of means. Was it not evident that after the first obscure explorations made in the years of infancy, mental life could properly be described as an unbroken, continuous, non-hierarchical sequence of operations conducted by the child's sensations themselves, an endless process of adjudication among ends and means, so that no one could claim any longer to distinguish between high and lower sentiments and powers, or to evaluate the work of the mind as good or bad? Moral judgement, then, was no more than the product of discrimination among needs. Later critics (and particularly Maine de Biran) were able to show that with all his subtlety of analysis Condillac had not in fact told us where to look for the data out of which the interior experience of selfhood or the generation of the will could be explained; he had been forced to neglect the education of the personality. None the less he provided the educational philosophy on which the most powerful groups of reformers during the French Revolution depended.

Condillac was not interested in the physiological proofs. It was left to others to clothe his sensations with a bodily apparatus capable of receiving and handling the stimuli which would set the model in motion. Some time before Condillac's treatises appeared David Hartley had been at work upon the physical concomitants of mental impressions in the excitation of the nerves of the body; but it was only when a translation of his theory of vibrations appeared in Germany in 1781 that Hartley became well known in Europe. The buried inconsistencies in his theories were clear even to himself, for he was a profoundly religious thinker and most unwilling to allow his physiological explanation of conscious behaviour to endanger the reality of a soul independent of nerve vibrations. Moreover, whilst laying the basis for the moral behaviourism of the utilitarian school, he was responsible for a most ingenious elaboration of associationist doctrine. In order to explain and vindicate self-interest, ambition, pain-avoidance and much discreditable human calculation, somehow he contrived to bend all of them, rather awkwardly it is true, towards the beneficent requirements of Christian perfection. In this endeavour Hartley was a true child of the Enlightenment. His psychological inquiries were to be influential in English educational thought towards the end of the century because of the strong support they received from Joseph Priestley, a tireless missionary for educational improvement and human betterment. And in due course their full implications in relation to the greatest-happiness principle were brought out by the elder Mill, who left out the now old-fashioned physiology, but so arranged his long and polemical *Encyclopaedia Britannica* article on education as to set out the steps by which a thoughtful inculcation of intelligent self-interest in the young could be made to pay fabulous benefits in democratic social welfare. Part of the significance of Mill's clever synthesis of eighteenth-century psychological notions is that he is applying them, as did the *Idéologues* in France for similar reasons, to the children of all classes.

The main line of development towards a biologically based theory of education was a Gallic one: it was promoted by men who were happy to regard themselves as Condillac's pupils. Destutt comte de Tracy and

Pierre Cabanis were both scientists, both anxious to bury the last traces of the non-corporeal soul. They translated the abbé's theory of transformed sensations into a theory of transformed nerve messages; they spoke in the language of brain tissue and nerve ganglia. To think was to use one's neural system.

De Tracy discovered an interior sense of 'movement' in the body that gave more meaning to the formation of intentions and their execution. Cabanis, physician and anatomist, said that the brain's function is to convert instincts (which he described as organic in nature) into action and to secrete thought as the liver secretes bile. His services to education, which failed to carry weight with his successors because they were too much shocked by his unblushing materialism, were in the first place that he linked the phases of mental growth and personality growth to the stages (like that of adolescence) of the body's development; and in the second place that he pursued the implications of mental behaviour into new areas where they touched abnormal psychology and social psychology. For Cabanis the emergence of mental powers in the child was affected, perhaps finally determined, by personal relationships and group pressure in early emotional life.

De Tracy, more fortunate than his friend Condorcet, escaped the vengeance of the Terror by a hair's breadth after writing down his educational theories in prison under sentence of death. Cabanis was then, as it happened, dispassionately studying the phases in which the extinction of life occurred in the bodies of the victims of the guillotine. Later, with the help of friends among the ministers, the two men were able to go into action with the educational theories of their intellectual group, known collectively as the *Idéologues*, before Napoleon Bonaparte decided to place their whole educational philosophy under a ban and to pinch these heretical notions out of teaching. In place of the *écoles centrales* he substituted new *lycées*, where teaching was to be given on conventional classical principles.

The great design for the *écoles centrales*, which was never fulfilled in any one of them during their short period of life, was one of the few national curriculum models ever to be drawn up on a single coherent pattern of educational ideas. Natural history, mathematics, applied science, the history of civilisation, were each placed, with conscious logical consistency, in an elaborate framework of alternative courses for boys who would follow a six-year régime from the thirteenth to the nineteenth year. Scientific studies were to be aided and reinforced by a new kind of 'grammar', which would provide the sort of link that Condillac would have approved between sensations and mental concepts. Ideological theory suggested that error might be avoided if words could be made to record these concepts in a kind of basic French. On this basis an intellectual integrity, purged of hypocrisy and misunderstanding, would enable the new generation to build a social utopia. The underlying notions offer a foretaste of logical positivism, whilst their psychological foundations carry more than a hint of twentieth-century behaviourism.

The role of education as an instrument of social reconstruction had already been under discussion in France for four decades. By far the most influential of the writings directly influenced by Condillac was the startling commentary upon the range and limitations of human nature which came from his contemporary Helvétius under the untranslatable title *De l'Esprit* (1758). This, perhaps the most famous work to issue from the press in furtherance of the Enlightenment, contained no fundamentally original ideas, although it might well be said that a writer who shows such ability in laying bare hidden connections has a real claim to originality of mind. The success of *De l'Esprit* was due to three things: first it vulgarised the way of thinking followed by Condillac; secondly, it so elevated the importance of ignoble motives that all lofty aspirations appeared as travesties of the demands of the passions; and thirdly, its treatment of adults and children as products of social forces had clear and inescapable levelling effects. The rough handling which religion and religious teaching received were almost incidental to the shocks administered by other parts of the analysis. There was no mistaking the argument that the welfare of the body politic depended absolutely on the kind of education received by the totality of the citizens—that is to say on the extent to which their education exposed them to infection by error or contrived to protect them against it.

If Helvétius seemed to debase ethical training by reducing it to what would contribute to the convenience of public welfare, he was at the same time raising education to a far more prominent position than that normally accorded to it; for he was in fact declaring that society and public morality were wholly dependent for their virtue upon the work performed by teachers, particularly those teachers who were responsible for the earliest years of training when the primary habits are formed. That a teacher should be instructed in his professional role Helvétius was always careful to point out. Apparent inequalities in intellectual ability and public spirit among young people were the consequence of differences in their educational history. Under the skin all healthy children were endowed with a very similar equipment: genius was not so much a natural gift as a triumph of the teacher's skill. Between them in fact the legislator and the teacher shared the responsibility for the happiness and security of the state.

Helvétius made no attempt to belittle the effects of his assertion that human motivation was nothing more than the advancement of self-love. The so-called baser passions, latent or evident in all men, might seem to threaten society. But it was useless to deplore these impulses or to try to obliterate them; it was for society to promote and utilise them to best advantage. This then seemed to point to one of the educator's functions in a reformed community. And here, incidentally, the great paradox inherent in Helvétian thought was almost brought into the open. For, if a reformed order of life in society can be made by educational policy, it first requires such a reformed order to ensure that education undertakes the task. Several decades later the men of the Mountain became acutely conscious of this problem.

Outrageous as these doctrines might seem to be to all the authorities in church, university and public office who condemned them—and over the matter of Helvétius' impiety even Jansenists and Jesuits were agreed—the author certainly harboured no intention of dishonouring the spirit of public action. To many the extremely frank discussion of motives and morals in Helvétius' works gave a sense of relief. All these monstrous suggestions were touched with benevolence and an optimistic belief in human betterment. The wide discussion of education, a process which involved the whole impact of a social environment, opened up new ways of thinking. Further, the turn taken by the argument brought it home to the educator that he was *par excellence* the creator of social values; and to emphasise this Helvétius pleaded for the specific teaching of civics and social science and for instruction in the practical knowledge which would make young people into productive workers as well as citizens.

Yet, although his tracts for the times might seem to open up exciting vistas and certainly provoked a good deal of debate, there is less evidence than we should expect of their direct influence on institutions or even on pedagogical practice until some years after his death in 1771. In that year Robert Owen was born.

Although Owen the self-made industrialist had nothing like the strong appeal of the intellectual of the Paris salons or the moral persuasiveness of William Godwin, through whom indirectly he learned his Helvétian environmentalism, he was able and willing to put the doctrine *l'éducation peut tout* to the test in the remarkable experiments in the New Lanark mills which entitle him to be called the founder of the British infant-school movement. To Owen, with his forceful, narrowly argued approach to social betterment, it was a self-evident truth that character was the product of outside forces. 'Train any population rationally, and they will be rational.'

In the event the teaching of Helvétius and his sympathisers was to stress the influence of social contacts and to direct attention to the means, predominantly practical and unimaginative, which would move the child's nature to the ends of a useful life. It is undeniable that Helvétius helped to promote utilitarian thinking in western Europe. Where this touched education, as it did at numerous points, it involved the revision of a traditional curriculum based almost wholly on language teaching and respect for received authority. Even at the level of elementary teaching the main concern of the utilitarians was for practical reading and ciphering skills, at the expense of the catechetical teaching of religion. It was in what may loosely be called secondary training that the distinctions in school organisation and method were most marked.

A 'sensation psychology' must be expected to have a practical issue in the schoolroom. The school which fitted into this pattern was based on what has sometimes been called 'sense realism', that is on kinds of instruction that rely on a matter-of-factness of approach, on the handling of materials by the pupils themselves, on activity methods and on the development of 'life situations' as part of the teaching process. These things were not all novelties; they belonged to the old Baconian tradition. A century earlier Comenius had given them some theoretical respectability. By the third quarter of the eighteenth century the ways in which this trend was socially conditioned were apparent. Occasional experiment could be seen broadening into fashion; new teaching establishments began to conform to certain demands. The particular ethos of the rising middle class, most evident in the Protestant countries, was calling for educational services in navigation, surveying, commercial accountancy, together with the mathematical skills fitted to go with these subjects. Modern languages, too, were in request from parents who saw their sons' future in trade and industry.

The *Ritterakadamien* and *académies de manège* of the nobility had familiarised generations of Germans with the idea of an alternative to the Latin schools based on vocational needs. Yet the new movement just described hardly touched the conventional schooling of the privileged classes; nor did it seem to modify the established practices of the classical teaching still largely in the hands of the religious orders and the secular clergy. We witness then in the provision of the boys' academies and *Philanthropinen* of the eighteenth century what is really the growth of an alternative form of education rather than a moderating factor in the main stream. Progressivism was canalised, and its influence to that extent was restricted.

The reasons for this characteristic inability to come to terms with tradition can best be illustrated in the English developments that provided models partly imitated elsewhere. These models were already well established by the third quarter of the century. The name so often given to these schools, 'dissenting academies', though it is not appropriate to all, indicates their original function as schools for the nonconforming parts of the population, cut off by law as these were from entry to the professions connected with public office. Neither the desire for suitable training for pastoral careers in the ministry nor the mercantile interests of the less poor of the families which supported the academies fully explains the generally high quality of teaching or the progressive interests of the tutors in science, history, politics and philosophy. In the most famous dissenting academies such as those at Daventry (1752–89) and Warrington (1757–86), the 'Athens of the North', higher studies directly challenging university standards prevailed, whilst in the private academies with a more secular bent practical and vocational elements in the curriculum provided ceaseless opportunity for experiment. The proprietors of these less famous schools, vastly interested as they were in curricular novelties, had little concern with pedagogical theory. On the outbreak of the revolution in France the independent academies of England, perhaps some two hundred in number, had probably passed the summit of their popularity. It was a limited and precarious popularity in view of the loss of some of their original religious dedication. The evangelism of the Methodist movement failed to touch the springs of dissenting scholarship, now seemingly much more easily quickened by the demands of natural theology. About the rise and fall of the smaller private schools in this group it is impossible to generalise. The larger institutions, managed by trustees, attracted most attention and were most vulnerable to public opinion. When a somewhat grandiose new adventure with obvious university pretensions was set up in the shape of Hackney College (1786–96), it soon became notorious for the Jacobin sympathies of the staff and students, this helping to enlarge the impression that dissent was tainted with disloyalty and revolution; the academies thereafter fell into decay.

But long before this the English academies had built up a network of associations across the Atlantic. Restless lecturers moved overseas to seek new experience. In the new towns of the thirteen colonies the pattern of the classical grammar schools had so far been followed almost everywhere. Franklin's *Idea of an English School* (1751) embodying his early scheme for an academy for Philadelphia attracted some interest. It was during the American Revolution, however, that a new type of modern-studies teaching began to show itself, in schools less scholarly perhaps than the English model, rather more closely linked with the vocational needs of the merchant families which gave them support, rather more secular in outlook too. A prototype is recognisable in the Phillips Academy in Andover, Massachusetts, in 1778. But already there were others. Thereafter the American academy, with its broad and experimental 'realistic' curriculum, turned its back on European tradition and prepared the way for the later state high-school.

It was in Germany that the modern school, the *Realschule*, came to earliest maturity on a foundation of child-centred theory—this even though the utilitarian curriculum provoked violent criticism from the leaders of neo-humanist scholarship. Modern-type academies which foreshadowed the possibilities were to be found in Berlin (1747) and Hamburg (1763). Johannes Basedow's *Philanthropinum*, which opened in Dessau (1774), was however the great exemplar. On to its staff the principal attracted a remarkable constellation of talent. The school was residential, co-educational. Peruques and fashionable garments were replaced by simple easy-fitting clothes. The precociously modern-sounding curriculum and the lively and imaginative ways of teaching, including languages by direct method, made a considerable sensation in the wide circles in which the founder was already well known. In Basedow's new enterprise all the progressive educational influences of his time seemed to have their opportunity, including that of Rousseau, which is sometimes credited with prompting this experiment. Basedow's genius lay in his ability to turn good ideas to account in new schoolroom techniques and in his powers as showman and advertiser; but at this point his ability ceased, for he was feckless, quarrelsome and an incompetent organiser. The real importance of his work at Dessau is that it infected others through the example of teachers who left him. His writings became universal reading among the German intelligentsia. *Realschulen* inspired by his example grew up over a wide area and were in several cases directed by men of such outstanding capacity as Campe and Salzmann and missionaries like Wolke, who under Catherine's protection opened a *philanthropin* in St Petersburg.

Part of Campe's claim on our attention is that he greatly extended the vogue of *Robinson Crusoe* and all that it stood for in educational circles. The growing popularity of Defoe's book and of its imitations is an indication of the consuming interest that the progressives were taking in practical approaches, in adaptability and self-reliance as objectives. Up to the age of fifteen Rousseau's Émile was permitted to have no other books than this; and we may see here an unconscious reflection perhaps in his creator's mind that the boy was being raised in conditions of unique isolation. Campe's own contribution as translator and adaptor of Defoe's book came from his feeling as a good progressive teacher that in the original story too many things are saved from the wreck. His own Crusoe lands with nothing to inhibit his powers of adjustment but the clothes on his back.

Learning by doing, learning by the attempted solution of life's problems, these were indeed advocated as part of the message of the new school of thought, stimulated by Rousseau, which broke away from the stereotype of the rationally directed child and set up the cult of the imagination. Rousseau had no monopoly of original ideas in the actual handling of children. Concern with practical approaches to learning had been one aspect of the Enlightenment's commitment to a progress based on common reason. But the newer views of Rousseau on the nature of children embodied an anti-intellectualism which entirely altered the attitudes adopted to the teacher's role in the business of education. The smart, up-to-date ideas of Helvétius on the function of the environment as the sole controller of habit and character were sharply challenged, as was his picture of the teacher as an illuminated and masterful moulder of children's dispositions. Rousseau substituted an internal principle of growth. Outraged by the metaphysical weaknesses of current philosophy, he turned to a new fountain-head of virtue. 'I have left reason', he wrote in 1758; 'I have consulted nature, that is to say the interior sentiment that directs my belief independently of my reason.' He brought back the heart and the will; and both his social philosophy and his educational principles recognised the primacy of the will, being founded on the belief that no ingenuity could give people, individually or collectively, what they were not in a state of readiness to accept. In propounding a new doctrine of virtue based on interior meditation, he helped to persuade the romantic movement to accept integrity of outlook as a fitter objective than intellectual agility.

It is still a matter for debate how far Rousseau, the most fertile educational philosopher of the century, influenced the mind of the schoolmasters of his own day. Certainly the maturer consideration of the possibilities latent in his writing begins to be evident in the thought of Kant and Pestalozzi a generation later, when the lesson that coercion was no key to the stimulation of learning capacity came to be fully appreciated and the implications for the schoolroom of the doctrine of interest came to be worked out. Meanwhile the immediate appeal of Rousseau's stimulating paradoxes was to the lay reader, to whom were addressed the ideas of negative education and of making haste slowly by refusing at all times to anticipate the later stages of the child's developing powers. And many were the attempts in the upper-class households of French and British and other admirers to prepare young people for life, under the conditions of freedom from conventional constraint and exposure to the influences of nature, on the model set up in *Émile* (1762). In this remarkable book Rousseau contrived to bring together a mass of reflections on life, morality and the nurture of the young and to clothe his insights and daydreams in the form of a loosely built story. Here, with variations, he followed the method he had already successfully used in his novel *La nouvelle Héloïse* (1760), where, in passages of fervid optimism, much of his philosophy of character-development had already been worked out. The adventures of Julie in this story, as well as the *Discourses* and the political writings of Rousseau, must be studied in order to discover the full effect of his message.

The fundamental considerations in all human affairs, Rousseau always claims, are the moral issues. This is as true in the dimension of individual growth and decay as among the forces which seem to direct men in their community pursuits. Thus the education of the young, when studied in virtual isolation from the social matrix—a feat accomplished as an astonishing *tour de force* in *Émile*—was as much the matter of the training of a *disposition* as was, in a different setting, the rearing of the active and committed citizen so often described or hinted at in Rousseau's political writings. Nothing could be more private than Émile's induction into life under a personal tutor. The tutor for the rich man's son is, of course, a commonplace in eighteenth-century society. Where the teaching of Émile is concerned, the tutor's responsibility is absolute; we see him accepting his charge all fresh from the state of innocence in which nature delivered him, and rearing him in sincerity and truth of outlook, almost to the age of manhood, without contamination by the immorality and corruption of ordinary life. Although Rousseau's critics have no doubt overstressed the emphasis with which he repudiated the taint of original sin on behalf of the human race, for he seems really to have seen new-born human life in a shade of neutral rather than of good, it is true that he never convincingly explained the capacity of beings, not naturally evil, to corrupt themselves so thoroughly by evil communications in their adventures in civilised life.

In this insistence on the moral degradation of realised social institutions, Rousseau turns his back upon the Enlightenment; and we must remember that the need he so often describes in his other writings for a thorough social conditioning of youth related to the conditions of an as yet unformed society, which might, by some process of particularly virtuous development, escape corruption. Here the exercise of the general will by all citizens in a collective purpose nourished by right education would have conducted the citizens of the *polis* to the stage of social beatitude. This explanation helps us to bridge the gap between the apparent individualism of *Émile*, with its extraordinary neglect of the human environment from which no ordinary child escapes, and the publicly organised training of the young insisted on elsewhere by Rousseau. When he contributed his article on *Économie Politique* for the fifth volume of the *Encyclopaedia* (1755) he was already arguing eloquently for a duty of citizenship which started at the moment of birth, and for the state's superiority as a guardian of the young over natural parents. The uncompromising institutions of Sparta were ever in the mind of this enthusiastic student of ancient history. If children are brought up in common in the bosom of equality in a realised democracy, if they are soaked in the demands which the popular will must place on everyone, surrounded as they will be by object lessons that speak to them ceaselessly of their country, their tender mother, there will be no question, he asserts, about their fitness to defend her. The courage and special qualities of virtue of the trained citizen were to receive even stricter attention when, in the *Contrat Social* (1762), Rousseau elaborated the significance of the vehicle of common purpose which he distinguished as the *volonté générale*, now greatly strengthened through the ability he gave to this communal will to draw upon the inspiration of a common civil religion. Preparation for the outlook and duties of social service are pre-eminently the task of education. Even the direction of most of the thoughts of men and women will be brought under control in participation with the general will. To make citizens of this quality there will be needed a public provision of instruction, reinforced by social rites and spectacles, and strengthened by an absorbing common purpose no less totalitarian in its character because the sense of responsibility is universally willed and shared.

In the *Contrat Social* the nature of educational agencies is implied rather than described. They emerge hardly more distinctly three years later in the projected constitution for Corsica left by Rousseau in manuscript. Imagining himself acting as the sovereign legislator for the island, he embarks on an ambitious piece of community planning. It is made clear that the inner and outer life of the individual are to be expressly dedicated at the age of twenty in a solemn and absolute act of surrender by each man. Finally in *Considérations sur le Gouvernement de Pologne*, written in 1772, Rousseau recommended without qualification the adoption of a form of state education devoted to the inculcation of public virtue in the younger citizens—the chief and most effective means towards Poland's regeneration in the face of her enemies. The recommendations are a mixture of practical shrewdness and far from practical idealism; but about one thing there can be no doubt, Catholic Poland in her new life must be equipped with a wholly secular organisation of schools, to be managed in every detail by a strong college of senior statesmen engaged in securing that the people shall be patriots, 'par inclination, par passion, par nécessité'.

We look for some reconciliation of the apparent contradiction between this picture of a state service devoted to nothing less than the wholesale indoctrination of the young, which becomes more clearly delineated as Rousseau bends his ingenious mind to constitution building, and the private encouragement of the inner forces of sentiment and intellectual independence so persuasively set out in *Émile*. Some sort of attempt to establish congruence is believed to have been made by Rousseau himself in preparation for a later edition of the book, if reports of conversations with Corancez are rightly interpreted. But a closer examination of Émile's upbringing itself shows that it is after all hardly a régime that allows the child freely to acquire experience at his own rate and of his own volition. He is constantly watched and guarded. Little surprises and new situations are always being proposed by his tutor, who follows a calculated programme of maturation. The lad's educational progress, far from being spontaneous, can be made to look like a train of carefully arranged traps. Little is left to chance in the godlike supervision of his 'natural' advance toward manhood. Kant, himself an admirer, has remarked on the expensively contrived machinery of this tutorial régime. And further, free and undisciplined as the programme may indeed look compared with the experiences designed for the young patriots of Corsica and Poland, Émile's tutor does in some ways resemble the legislator of the ideal state.

The true defence of the remaining inconsistencies is to be found in Rousseau's recognition of the disharmonies of the actual world in which he lived. Contemporary France hardly provided the right milieu for the moral training of a child like Émile, the account of whose education had to be read as an exemplary tale, an allegory, to coax and stimulate the fancies of members of French polite society and urge on them a virtual reversal of nearly all current notions about the education of the children of the gentry in 1762. Reform of social instruments of instruction could only be projected by Rousseau for a France which did not yet exist.

None the less in the real France of Rousseau's later years the traditional agencies of education did undergo changes, as did those of several other states—changes which heralded the appearance of centralised systems in which the citizen's school desired by the author of the *Social Contract* became at length a commonplace institution.

Matters were set in motion almost fortuitously when the whole educational structure of the Catholic world from Lithuania to Paraguay was profoundly shaken by the fall of the Jesuit order. The process took fourteen years to accomplish, and the apparent finality of something that closely touched both the schooling of the most powerful classes and the distribution of power in politics was sealed by Clement XIV's brief *Dominus ac Redemptor Noster* in 1773. The collapse of an educational régime conducted by some thousands of the best schoolmasters in Christendom was not without its effects upon the springs of culture; but it was an incidental casualty in a campaign covering a broader front. The Jesuit curriculum has been condemned as rigid and old-fashioned, too narrowly confined within the educational philosophy of the old *Ratio Studiorum*. Still, the colleges of the order were not lacking in scholarship or powerful instruments of intellectual training. They combined to form a major feature of the cultural map of Europe. The last census of the society's institutions had been compiled in 1749. Omitting the seminaries, the sum total of the colleges for the laity included 89 in France, 133 in Italy and 105 in Spain; while in the German province (including the Netherlands) and eastern Europe between two and three hundred colleges were in being. It has been said, with but small exaggeration, that the Society of Jesus had long been responsible for the training of the intellectual élite in the countries in which it had been permitted to teach; and it was in fact a point against the Jesuits that they knew too much rather than too little about the formative uses of education. When the fathers were expelled, it was the signal for other religious teaching orders, the Piarists, the Barnabites and the Oratorians, to move in and increase their own influence. In many cases they were encouraged to take over the school communities entire. And in France at any rate the Oratorians became significant innovators in the broadening of the curriculum; later, in the darker days of the revolution, they were singled out for favourable treatment, largely for this reason. Naturally, the schools vacated by the Jesuits came everywhere more closely under the discipline of the state. In fact the availability of large confiscated endowments and the clear field now suddenly left open for reform gave to the benevolent despots an opportunity to bring their higher education into closer conformity with the pattern of administrative centralisation which was the fashion of the day.

In France this got no farther than the transformation of some Jesuit institutions, including Descartes' old college of La Flèche, into military training centres. More important was the appearance of numerous schemes and memorials on reorganisation. Thus la Chalotais, the secularist lawyer and harrier of the Jesuits, wanted government control and a modernising of syllabuses; but he ostentatiously shrank from broadening the social basis of the schools he was asking public authority to provide, and indeed he condemned the Brothers of the Christian Schools for educating ships' boys above their station. Turgot, minuting his king with his customary clarity and vigour, sought something like a scheme of universal instruction and urged training for all in the duties of citizenship. 'In ten years, Sire, your nation will no longer be recognisable.' Diderot (if an Amsterdam pamphlet on public instruction has correctly been ascribed to him) deplored the neglect of the culture of the working population and wished to remedy it with national schools. In his well-known memorandum on scientific and modern literary studies in a university he advised the Empress Catherine that to found an academy before providing for general education was like beginning a building at the top.

In the Habsburg dominions, where Maria Theresa had been pondering reform since 1760, Kaunitz astutely avoided a situation of violence when the question of the Jesuits arose. He went on to secure their co-operation in a general reorganisation intended to affect schools at all levels. This, it was found, might be done by diverting some of the former personnel of the order to lower-grade teaching. The primary and middle schools could thus be brought into some sort of relationship with the Latin colleges of the church: they could be brought into contact with the world of higher learning. It looked on paper at least as if the Habsburg territories would possess the most highly articulated system of state control of schools known to man.

Paulsen has remarked that what characterised the impact of the Enlightenment in the Catholic states of central Europe was its suddenness. Once Joseph II had the Habsburg inheritance at his sole disposal he endeavoured to introduce compulsory schooling and curricular and linguistic uniformity and to overhaul the administration of his welfare state with an abruptness that succeeded only momentarily in paralysing the forces of opposition. For the first time in European history educational reform became a truly articulated limb in the frame of a unifying policy. The means were made available by the secularisation of religious funds and the diversion of pedagogic talent; the ends were manifest in the needs of a prospective Danubian empire on a new model, which would doubtless require thousands of trained state officials. Joseph's policy for public instruction was accordingly secular and pragmatic. It was puritannical in its aversion from the higher claims of liberal education, utilitarian in that it appeared to budget against redundancy in the production of *Gelehrten*. Whilst the speed of change caused uneasiness everywhere, an unmistakably hostile reception greeted the reforms in the distant Austrian Netherlands, where Joseph's imported toleration for all Christian denominations, with all its implications for the schools, was not even understood. The endeavour to bring the theological seminaries under public management indeed helped to goad the people of Brabant into launching the uprising of 1789.

In the German lands some of the spirit of the Josephine programme survived under the reactionary sway of Leopold II, but this far-reaching attempt to universalise education in a vast heterogeneous territory, where a powerful middle class was notably lacking, came very largely to grief through tactless planning.

It is an illustration both of the limits of Dutch toleration and of the enormous range of the scholarly influence of the University of Leyden (which was for long the schoolmaster of Europe in scientific method) that Gerhard van Swieten, the famous physiologist, was unable as a Catholic to fill a chair in his own medical faculty, but instead became the foremost physician in eastern Europe and the founder of the great clinical school of Vienna medicine. Almost incidentally he became the valued expert whose advice determined the nature of the Habsburg educational reforms and the introduction of the vernaculars in the schools.

In Prussia and Saxony too, indeed in all Protestant Germany, state regulation of popular schools began to assert itself at the expense of what had previously been confessional monopolies. How far Frederick's *Landschulreglement* of 1763 actually secured compulsory attendance in parish schools—wherever an acceptable schoolmaster could be found to teach—or how far this really affected the degrees of literacy in the people of his dispersed territories is most uncertain; but there is no doubt that the régime of Zedlitz as Frederick's Minister of Public Instruction caused the framing of a policy in which elementary and higher forms of education, together with the shadowy beginnings of organised teacher training, was thought of as a clever piece of statecraft. Both the institution of the *Abiturientenexamen* in 1788 for the boys of the classical *Gymnasien* and the edict restricting the freedom of teaching and publication of the same year were in a sense reflections of the same police-state spirit; and it is significant that the individualist element in the progressive movement that earned the support of Kant and Wilhelm von Humboldt and Goethe and at length found a working pedagogical doctrine in the teaching of

Pestalozzi was altogether out of sympathy with 'enlightenment by decree' on the Joseph II model: it was working in a spirit so different from this that it could hardly find proper expression in Prussia even in the uplifting days after Jena.

All these tendencies and a number of developments in educational thought of a far more liberal kind which were beginning to bear fruit in the Dutch Netherlands and the Swiss cantons have to be taken into account when we look for novelties and portents in what came out of the political *mêlée* in France after 1789. At what stage did the makers of the Revolution become conscious that their work had a meaning in this context? When did they realise that the overthrow of the old régime and of the financial privileges of the clergy involved them in a major work of reconstruction?

The Constitution of 1791 spoke with no finality about the future of the schools. Yet it offered hopes of a system of public instruction common to all citizens and free at least at the elementary level. By this time the system of local government had been completely overhauled and placed within a framework of departments and communes; and there was clearly an intention of utilising this structure as one to which the organisation of various grades of schooling might be attached. Talleyrand called attention to this design when he brought in an educational measure a few days after the new constitution had been decreed. He spoke of the grim facts about the country's educational destitution and called for a decision before the chamber passed on its powers to a successor. Equipped as it was with a public-education committee, the Constituent Assembly had plainly flinched from the task. The Legislative Assembly in its turn considered that the weight of the undertaking merited the appointment of a public-education committee, thus continuing a procedural device which runs right through the recorded activities of both Legislative Assembly and Convention and makes its mark as a significant new development in educational history. Education was indeed one of the deepest concerns of both bodies: these *ad hoc* committees were worked hard. The tone of debate certainly changed somewhat as the current of ideas swerved from the Brissotin conception of dispersed initiative towards the unitary-state outlook; but the feeling remained constant that, if only the emergency demands of the revolution could be abated, the need for a state system for schools would rise spontaneously to the head of the legislative agenda.

Thus numerous plans came up, some on the floor of the assemblies themselves; yet all but one of these projects came incontinently to grief. And, although the measure actually adopted by the Convention in 1793 looked viable, it dealt only with the republican principles governing the position of licensed teachers, and it failed altogether to provide the stimulus to action so badly needed by the communes. Thus the whole background of the revolutionary debates was one of apathy and neglect in the country at large. Educational agencies first lost their funds through the secularisation and confiscations of 1789, then shed most of their teachers; and they survived where they did survive without the favour of the authorities. Thus in Paris the old Jesuit college of Louis-le-Grand, once attended by Desmoulins and Robespierre, was the only survivor of the famous schools of the old congregations to remain open throughout the Revolution.

The principles of the promised reconstruction were meanwhile under examination. It became the task of Condorcet the philosopher-mathematician to report to the Legislative Assembly. The influence on educational thought of this generous-minded apostle of human progress is much greater than could be made evident from any bald statement about his career. In the last stage we see him as a political theorist putting his ideas to the test in the legislative drafts of the days of the Revolution, when all his projects came one by one tragically to nothing and the author himself fell a victim to the animosities in the Convention. In the final phase, if the *Esquisse d'un tableau historique des progrès de l'esprit humain* can be viewed as Condorcet's political testament, his thoughts on every aspect of education are displayed—except perhaps those concerning classroom techniques; they range from the promotion of the life of freedom and the coming of universal reason, to the meticulous balancing of the parts of a national system of public education which he set out in the *Rapport* itself.

Condorcets' plan for a unitary model for the education of the whole country was formally presented on behalf of the committee of public education in April 1793. It is certainly the most powerfully conceived of the various schemes of reconstruction which came before the revolutionary assemblies. Stripped of its idealistic advocacy, it can be seen to be both a practical survey of the educational requirements of a patriotic community, conscious of its ideological leadership in the world, and a collection of maxims of memorable shrewdness. It performs the marriage of a set of educational principles to a design for school planning and has a right to be regarded as the crown of the practical thinking of the French Enlightenment. The liberalism it displayed in handling political fundamentals was utterly displeasing to the philosophy of the Mountain, and caused Condorcet's ideas to be damned by Robespierre as those of a contemptible intellectual.

Brissotin influences showed themselves at every point in the scheme thus presented. They were present in the desire to keep government officials out of their own schools; in the invention of an autonomous body (*Société Nationale*)—an academy to take precedence over all academies—to assume the duties of supervising the national system and the appointment of its teachers; in the insistence that some of its members be resident provincials and that all be immune from political interferences.

Thus, if the *Rapport* had been accepted, the future of public education would have been committed into the hands of a hierarchical syndicate of *savants* and *professeurs*, among whose main tasks would have been the setting up of two kinds of primary school—the first strictly elementary in its nature, the second a kind of middle school. Here Condorcet was anticipating much of later European practice. At a higher level of instruction he planned to have 110 institutes for more advanced stages of secondary teaching; and, at the top of the pyramid, nine lyceums, doing university work. All parts of the system would interlock, and instructors of every grade would be responsible, beyond their regular teaching, for taking some part in adult education. Even the needs of the armed forces are not forgotten. As a piece of organisation, the plan seems to look forward to the foundation of the all-embracing *Université de France* which was in due course to be founded on Napoleon's educational laws of 1806 and 1808. Yet Condorcet's careful analysing of curriculum requirements provides a very different picture from that sequel. What endows his *Rapport* with its permanent significance in the history of culture is the spirit and the content of the teaching he recommends. Here we see set out for the first time the full implications of a revolutionary educational philosophy. We see him bring together, under one régime, the factual and scientific studies, in other words 'the elements of all human knowledge', and a prescription for training in progressive social improvement. It is undoubtedly a citizen-centred curriculum. Latin and ancient literature are shouldered out of the way, partly by the pressures exerted by physical and mathematical science, agriculture and the mechanical arts (amplified as these have to be by the moral and political sciences), partly by the need to substitute current social ideals for the corrupting influences of traditional errors. And at all levels of tuition Condorcet tries to persuade his readers that the new pedagogical science demands a radical change in the régime of school-teaching. Agreed that it must be beyond the capacity of a school-child to assimilate the elements of all branches of knowledge. Yet clever pupils might take several courses in parallel, while weaker pupils would follow one course at a slower pace. The *Rapport* opens up for the reformers the subject of integration of courses.

The Convention inherited Condorcet's paper formulation. It considered it, then began to move towards a more egalitarian position that took no account of the argument for an educational ladder. At length the enthusiasts of the Mountain struck out on lines of their own and produced a quite original measure in the shape of the primary-school plan of Lepeletier de Saint-Fargeau. This was the first model for the future that secured any form of endorsement from the exacting Robespierre. It is important among the documents of the Revolution neither for its pedagogical understanding nor for its practicability; yet we must take note of it because of the vigour with which it plans the use of educational instruments to produce young citizens of the right temper and mould to bring about, if anything will, that reign of eternal justice and virtue which in Robespierre's speeches and in Saint-Just's sketches of his new republican institutions is the national goal which must command the hearts of men.

The urge toward the good life, collectively willed and unselfishly forwarded by all citizens, was now, it was claimed, to be promoted in a network of new boarding schools distributed over the whole republican landscape. The schools, indeed the whole scheme of instruction, were to be something entirely new. No child's obligation to reside in one of these *maisons d'égalité* could be remitted, for this must be a *levée en masse* of the nation to be. And the lot of all French boys and girls would be sparse and simple living, much hard physical work and a combination of reading and writing, craft-instruction, military training (for the boys), spinning and laundry work (for the girls), and the learning of patriotic songs and the lessons of the deeds of free peoples. Dedicated to natural piety by this wholesome Spartan upbringing, the race of free citizens would carry foward the revolution.

This national primary-school project of Lepeletier, which seems to borrow much from Rousseau, was never decreed. It was regarded as a kind of manifesto of political faith, illuminated as it was by the incandescence of a social wish-fulfilment belonging to the men whose fall terminated in the events of Thermidor. Their feelings for equality and their desire for a democracy of *sans-culottes* made them despise the artificialities of professional training and the higher culture and indeed the need for social mobility; although the case for some biased professional preparation could not be denied where the training of artillery officers and engineers was in question. Against the background of military and social engineering, discussion was indeed already on foot concerning France's need for national institutes of advanced learning.

All that the period of the Terror achieved in the educational field was some bits of legislation of a short-sighted nature which laid the responsibility for primary training on the communes; school-keeping being left open to any private teacher who could acquire a *certificat de civisme*. All regions, whatever the local vernacular, were required to adopt the French language in the schools. There is evidence that the local Jacobin clubs scrutinised the virtue and political orthodoxy of such applicants as presented themselves for teaching posts, but little to suggest that they were concerned to bring about an improvement in the work of the schools. Indeed there is an element of paradox in the fact that part of the contemporary indictment against Robespierre and like-minded Jacobins was that they plotted to keep the oncoming generation in ignorance. Even those who took over the government in the Thermidorean reaction against the Terror appeared to be in no hurry to repair the damage done to the popular level of instruction. To be sure the duties of the inactive municipalities were now clarified by legislation, but even so the local officials secured no help or guidance from the centre. Any slight improvement that may have followed during the years of the Directory was entirely due to the recovery of esteem by private and confessional teaching, in spite of difficulties created by the anti-religious laws and such awkward features of republican society as the ten-day week. Public provision came to very little. In this field the Revolution lacked a corps of dedicated teachers for the advancement of its policies.

Thus the achievement of the heroic years in France did nothing, in spite of intense debate, to make good the gaps caused by the collapse of the schools of the old régime. Indeed the most interesting accomplishment of the early period of the Directory was the attempt, based on Lakanal's law of February 1795, to establish the *écoles centrales* in each Department as citadels of higher prevocational studies which might truly offer the opportunities of a 'career open to talent' to all French citizens. The pusillanimous retreat from this experiment in the Napoleonic reform of secondary education has already been noted. Yet even the admirers of these eighteenth-century politechnicums have had to admit the inefficiency of their organisation and staffing; the schools never measured up to the ambitious intentions of their creators.

The positive work of the revolutionary period was restricted in compass to the creation of a few specialised centres of advanced study, like the *École Normale Supérieure* and the *École Polytechnique*, together with the revival of a few temporarily suppressed scientific institutions. As a centre for all the intellectual interests of the men of learning the Thermidoriens contrived to bring into being the *Institut National* (later the *Institut de France*), which attempted to realise in turn some of the ideas of Condorcet and of the *Idéologues* and of those who wished to restore the old prestige of the revived monarchical academies of learning.

The bourgeoisie continued to secure some teaching for their children in a limited number of private schools, mostly under confessional control; but all this lay under the shadow of repression, since the Directory remained the foe of the church, and placed a ban, at least nominal, on the recruitment of public servants who had been thus educated. Thus, in all its phases, the Revolution, its resources crippled by war, inflation and the insufficiency of capital confiscations to provide welfare services as a replacement for what the religious congregations had previously offered, failed to set up schools or to train teachers. The triumph which its ideas achieved over the educational traditions of the old régime remained a paper victory. And for the populace at large the Revolution inaugurated a period of what the British were shortly to describe—in a situation of their own little better in respect of popular schools and far worse in respect of the springs of public policy—as one of 'educational destitution'.

CHAPTER VII

ARMED FORCES AND
THE ART OF WAR

I. NAVIES

THE Seven Years War and the American War of Independence were both primarily maritime struggles, but the strategic principles so successfully employed by the British in the first war were almost totally lacking in the second. The hinge of British naval strategy in the eighteenth century was the blockade of the principal fleets of France by stationing forces off Brest and Toulon. This strategy, adumbrated by Vernon and Anson, imposed by Hawke and Boscawen, and later brought to perfection by St Vincent and Cornwallis, prevented enemy fleets replenishing the French colonies overseas to any considerable degree, while at the same time it permitted the employment of conjunct operations (as they were called) for the conquest of outlying territories. When Keppel failed to force a decision off Ushant on 27 July 1778, and when Byron was dispatched too late to intercept D'Estaing's fleet from Toulon, French naval forces were not only able to co-operate with the American colonists but to appear in the Channel unopposed. Of all the leaders at that time, George Washington appears to have had the best understanding of the implications of sea-power. In his correspondence with De Grasse he frequently stresses the fact that French financial and naval aid alone enabled him to prosecute the war with success. 'You will have observed', he wrote after the brilliant combination of the French fleets with the American forces on land had ensured the surrender of Yorktown, 'that whatever efforts are made by the land armies, the navy must have the casting vote in the present contest.'[1]

Britain lost supremacy at sea during the American War not only because she was fighting without an ally to defend possessions as widely separate as India and Canada, but also because no grasp of strategic principles was displayed, which alone could atone for the inferiority in armaments to which a false sense of security prevailing between the wars had reduced her. The limited number of ships available were not concentrated on crucial occasions; instead, there was dispersal of effort and a failure to contain the enemy at vital points. The deprivation of supplies of timber and manpower in America, where a third of colonial shipping had been built and where some 2000 seamen had been available for service, was an additional difficulty. Even after the American revolt had begun

---

[1] *Washington–De Grasse Correspondence* (1931), p. 150.

to be taken seriously by Sandwich (First Lord of the Admiralty between 1771 and 1782), the Royal Navy was at a considerable disadvantage when faced by the combined fleets of France and Spain, later to be assisted by the Dutch and an Armed Neutrality of the Baltic powers.

These failings in policy and strategy were heightened by the sterility of the tactical doctrine then in vogue among all European navies. Like the military tactics of the period, it bears the stamp of extreme formalism. The preservation of the close-hauled line of battle formation was regarded as almost an end in itself. According to Bigot de Morogues, the leading theorist, whose *Tactique Navale* of 1763 was translated into English, 'there are no longer decisive battles at sea, that is to say battles on which the end of the war absolutely depends'. Since only six of the fifteen battles fought between Barfleur (1692) and the Saints (1782) can be called decisive, and since even these were chases rather than line battles, a tactical stalemate had evidently been reached. Two determined commanders employing equal forces, such as Suffren and Hughes in the Indian Ocean, could fight a series of battles without depriving each other of a single ship.

In France the *ordonnance* of 1765 summarised the teaching of Morogues that if two fleets passed in line ahead on opposite tacks and refrained from action until the lines were conterminous, neither could suffer defeat. A similar defensive procedure was laid down for the British navy in the *Fighting Instructions*, which were originally particular evolutions invented by admirals for their own use, but were now codified as the Permanent Fighting Instructions. If an admiral failed to form or preserve his line, he could be cashiered, as was Mathews in 1744; or shot, like Byng in 1757; or arraigned on a similar charge, as Keppel was in 1778. By the accumulated wisdom of experience, claimed D'Estaing, 'the course of each ship is predetermined, the ballet is designed, and if there is no sudden change of wind or other accidents, the action will pass off pretty well'.[1] So ingrained was this attitude that, when Rodney tried to concentrate a superior force against a part of the enemy line at Martinique, his captains in the van either could not (or, as he imagined, would not) understand what was intended. Similarly, when a golden opportunity of annihilating De Grasse offered in the Chesapeake on 5 September 1781, both Graves and Hood preferred to preserve the line, rather than attack in unorthodox fashion. The consequence was the fall of Yorktown in October.

Many of these failures were due to the deficiencies of a signalling system which stultified the actions of a commander-in-chief. By the 'position' method of signalling, a flag flown in a particular position denoted the relevant entry in the *Fighting Instructions*. A more flexible

[1] Quoted in Castex, *Les Idées Militaires de la Marine* (1911), p. 63. Cf. Sir J. Corbett, *Fighting Instructions* and *Signals and Instructions* (Navy Records Society).

system, by which numeral pendants were used to denote a large number of entries in a signal book, was devised by La Bourdonnais and adapted to English use in 1782 by Howe and Kempenfelt. But not until Sir Home Popham's *Marine Vocabulary* appeared in 1800, to add alphabetical flags to the numeral ones already in use, was it possible for an admiral to make an unambiguous signal to meet the needs of an unforeseen contingency.

The events of the year 1782 finally discredited such orthodox tactics. On 12 April, at the battle of the Saints, a sudden shift of wind created two gaps in the French line, thus enabling Rodney to break it in two places.[1] At the same time Suffren was practising a more offensive form of attack than was usual among the French in his fights with Sir Edward Hughes. There also appeared that year in England a contribution to tactical theory which undoubtedly influenced the minds of the younger generation, though it cannot be said (as its author claimed) to have invented the formula for breaking the line. To the question, 'why our fleets have been invariably baffled, nay worsted, without ever losing a ship or almost a man', James Clerk of Eldin replied in his *Essay on Naval Tactics* that the superiority of French tactical training could only be overcome by adopting unorthodox manœuvres. In 1804, when an expanded edition appeared, he could point to the example of Rodney and Suffren to prove his case. By 1790, when the *Fighting Instructions* ceased to remain in force, the fetters of the old doctrine had been shattered by practical example, as well as by theoretical arguments, so that (as Nelson was to show) decisive battles at sea once more became a possibility.

The peacetime establishment of the British navy varied between fourteen and twenty thousand men, to which should be added the three thousand shipwrights employed in the royal dockyards, which were the nearest equivalent to large-scale industry in the country. In wartime the fleet rapidly expanded as old ships 'laid up in ordinary' were brought into commission and new ships were laid down to meet the demands of wars fought on an ever increasing scale. Thus in 1763 there were 270 ships of all classes in sea pay, with 76,000 men, while in 1783 there were 430 ships and 107,000 men.[2]

Almost half this number of men volunteered, attracted by the bounties offered in time of war. Men and boys from the ranks of the destitute were sent to sea by Jonas Hanway's Marine Society, which founded the first training ship in 1786. The remainder were impressed from the merchant service, which was encouraged by the Navigation Acts to maintain a pool of seamen, on which the state could draw in an emergency. On the out-

[1] The credit for this manœuvre is variously claimed by Clerk (see *Mariner's Mirror*, vol. xx, for a reprint of his pamphlet of 1806); by Douglas, Rodney's flag captain (see Sir H. Douglas, *Naval Evolutions* (1832) and *Barham Papers* (Navy Records Society), vol. i, p. 279); and by Rodney himself (see Mundy's *Life of Rodney*, vol. ii, p. 229).

[2] P.R.O. Adm. 7/567.

break of war these acts were amended so that more foreigners could be employed. Until an organised impressment service came into existence towards the end of the century, press-gangs operated under warrants issued by magistrates. In the ports, gangs maintained a regular 'rendez-vous' or recruiting centre from which the men were taken on board pressing tenders or guard ships to be distributed among the ships fitting out. Captains were further empowered to press out of merchant ships at sea on their return home, to search for deserters on board foreign vessels, and even to employ foreign seamen. As the demands of the service increased, more and more sections of the civilian population obtained immunity from the gangs by 'protections' which covered watermen, fishermen, apprentices and officers on board merchant vessels, men under eighteen years of age and over fifty, and even householders, provided they did not use the sea as a profession, since only seafaring men could be conscripted. The brutality of the gangs might be attacked by novelists like Smollett or caricaturists like Rowlandson, but the legal aspect was expressed by Lord Mansfield when he stated that impressment was 'founded upon immemorial usage allowed for ages. It can have no power to stand upon, nor can it be vindicated or justified by any reason except the safety of the State.' Similar views were expressed by Blackstone and by Thurlow when, as Attorney General, his opinion was asked by the Admiralty on one of the very few appeals made against being pressed.[1] This form of conscription was certainly inhuman and inefficient, disliked equally by officers and men, but there was no alternative. When a bill was introduced in 1777 to adopt the French practice of a register of seamen from which certain classes were drawn to serve afloat, few could be found to argue that this worked any better in practice.[2] The problem of manning remained insoluble so long as the Admiralty ceased to control men as soon as a ship was paid off, and so long as pay and conditions on board made the service unattractive. The state, in fact, refused to maintain a standing navy, although its ownership of a fleet necessitated the maintenance of an officer corps. It was this, indeed, which ruled out of the question the system of purchase, such as existed in the army.

'Our fleets, which are defrauded by injustice, are first manned by violence and then maintained by cruelty', wrote Admiral Vernon.[3] The high rate of desertion which exacerbated the problem was not so much due to the severity of the discipline on board the king's ships as to the

[1] Rex. v. Tubbs, 1776. See law opinions in P.R.O. Adm. 7/299. Also J. R. Hutchinson, *The Press Gang* (1913), and Justice Hildesley, *The Press Gang* (1925). Cf. Recruiting Act, 19 George III.

[2] *Parl. Hist. XIX*, p. 81. The bill was based on a plan by Lieut. Tomlinson printed in *Tomlinson Papers* (Navy Records Society). Cf. Wood's scheme printed in *Sandwich Papers*, vol. IV, p. 389 (Navy Records Society).

[3] *A Specimen of Naked Truth from a British Sailor*. Cf. *The Vernon Papers* (Navy Records Society), p. 547.

bad food, low pay and deprivation of shore leave. The code kno vn as the Articles of War, embodied in the Naval Discipline Act of 1749, and the Admiralty Regulations limiting punishments without court martial to twelve lashes, do not compare unfavourably with the criminal code on land. The real cruelty lay in the outrageous penalties, such as a flogging round the fleet, which a court martial could impose, and in the unofficial punishments such a 'starting' or beating with a rope's end wielded by a tyrannical boatswain. A vicious circle was thus created: discipline had to be strict in view of the character of many of the pressed men; bad conditions gave the service a bad name; consequently recruiting became all the more difficult.

The scale of pay and victuals remained unchanged between the days of the Commonwealth and the mutinies of 1797. The rate of pay (19s. a month for an ordinary seaman, 22s. 6d. for an able seaman) compared unfavourably with that prevailing on board merchant ships, and there was often such delay in payment that wage tickets had to be cashed by unofficial brokers at scandalously low rates. The victualling scale appeared generous on paper, but the quality issued by the Victualling Office (commonly known as 'Old Weevil') was notoriously bad, on account of dishonest contractors, faulty methods of storage and the difficulty of preserving any food except salt meat and biscuit. The most popular issue was 'grog', so called from Vernon's nickname 'Old Grogram', since it was he who first diluted rum with water in order to check drunkenness.

Another evil consequence of impressment was the incidence of disease arising from the filthy conditions prevailing on board the tenders. Had the suggestions of Kempenfelt and others to provide a uniform instead of issuing purser's 'slops' been adopted, diseases such as typhus would not have been so common.[1] The wastage of manpower due to disease, common to all navies, was such that, on an occasion such as D'Orvillier's cruise in the Channel in 1779, a fleet could be paralysed by its incidence. There was no cure for yellow fever, so prevalent in the West Indies, where large fleets were always maintained, except cinchona bark; and though the conquest of scurvy was undoubtedly one of the medical triumphs of the century, it was over forty years before the cure was officially adopted. After Anson had lost three-quarters of his men on his voyage round the world, Dr James Lind of Haslar Naval Hospital discovered in 1753 the prophylactic value of orange and lemon juice. On Cook's second voyage not a man was lost from the disease, though he himself relied on spruce beer and pickled cabbage and actually advised against the issue of fruit juice on the grounds of expense. It was not until 1795 that Lind's disciples, Trotter and Blane, succeeded in making the issue official, so that

---

[1] *Barham Papers*, vol. I, p. 307. Cf. J. Lind's *Treatise on Scurvy*, ed. Stewart and Guthrie (1953), p. 386; and C. Lloyd and J. L. S. Coulter, *Medicine and the Navy*, vol. III (1961).

whereas in 1779 40,000 men had been sent to hospital, in 1804 the figure was only 12,000 out of a much larger navy.[1]

To officers, on the other hand, the eighteenth-century navy offered an attractive profession. After the adoption of the blue and white uniform in 1748, parity of prestige with the army was achieved. Pay could be supplemented by prize-money, so that with skill and opportunity great fortunes could be made.[2] But as there was no system of retirement, competition for the command of a ship in peacetime was fierce, and a long period on 'half pay' could strain an officer's resources—hence the popularity of service in foreign navies or in the East India Company's marine.

A boy intending to become a naval officer entered either as a volunteer-per-order (or King's Letter Boy, of whom Rodney was the last example), being nominated by the Admiralty for a place at the Naval Academy, Portsmouth; or, more commonly, as a captain's servant according to the old practice of permitting officers to carry a certain number of followers on board. Officially twelve was the minimum age, but there are many cases of a boy's name being entered on a ship's books below that age in order to gain seniority. After four years at sea, the boy was rated midshipman, a type of officer divided into the 'youngsters' waiting to take a lieutenant's examination at the age of twenty-one, and the 'oldsters' who had failed to pass it. Thenceforward promotion depended on interest and seniority. The chances of promotion from the lower deck gradually diminished, though there are examples of pressed men who became admirals and of many who rose from the warrant-officer's rank of master to be commissioned lieutenant. It was in this way that James Cook reached quarter-deck rank, having volunteered for the navy at the outbreak of the Seven Years War.

Interest depended on family or political connections, by which means official regulations could be flagrantly circumvented. Thus Rodney's son became a captain at the age of sixteen, and even Nelson, the parson's son who had gone on board his uncle's ship at twelve, was a lieutenant at eighteen (his uncle being Comptroller of the Navy) and a captain at twenty-one. Political influence and a good service record counted for more thereafter. Not only did the Admiralty control ten boroughs which were awarded to senior officers or officials, but many senior officers sat in Parliament, where they were expected to provide for the wants of others. The consequence of this admixture of politics to the fleet proved fatal when Sandwich, as First Lord, wielded his power of patronage in an unabashed way,[3] though his reputation for corruption has been grossly exaggerated.

---

[1] Barrow, *Life of Anson* (1839), p. 480. See Cook's letter to Pringle printed in Lind, *op. cit.* p. 407. An official return covering the years 1776–80 illustrates the incidence of disease and desertion: total raised, 175,990; killed, 1243; died of disease, 18,541; deserted, 42,069.

[2] For instance in 1778 Captain Finch's share in a prize was £62,000; his share in another taken three months previously was £15,000. Hist. MSS. Comm., *Rutland MSS.*, p. 14.

[3] Cf. Namier, *Structure of Politics* (1957 ed.), pp. 29, 36, 141.

12-2

THE AMERICAN AND FRENCH REVOLUTIONS

Matters came to a head after the Keppel court-martial in 1778. He was tried at the instigation of his second-in-command, Sir Hugh Palliser, who was not only a political opponent but had recently been appointed Lieutenant-General of Marines, one of the many Admiralty sinecures which Keppel coveted. On the latter's acquittal a personal grievance assumed political importance. Keppel himself refused to serve any longer under Sandwich, his example being followed by Howe and Barrington, so that no suitable commander could be found for the Channel fleet at the moment of an impending Franco-Spanish invasion. When Rodney took command of the fleet in the West Indies he found that the affair 'has almost ruined the navy', and it is typical that he himself was replaced by a nonentity soon after winning the battle of the Saints, Keppel having replaced Sandwich as First Lord.[1]

Sandwich complained that naval officers were apt to put party before public service, and that he was badly served by his admirals. But he had been warned privately by Sir Charles Middleton, Comptroller of the navy between 1778 and 1790, that his 'political system of management' was to blame for this state of affairs, and that 'the whole system of the Admiralty is rotten, and must tumble about your Lordship's ears if it is not soon altered'.[2] It was this which gave colour to the attacks made in Parliament by Fox, Keppel and Howe in 1779 when, amid scenes of prodigious uproar, Sandwich's resignation was called for. He defended himself by blaming his predecessors for the 'deplorable state' of the navy which he inherited in 1771, and undoubtedly he carried out great practical improvements during the war years, such as coppering the whole fleet, introducing the short-range carronade gun, expanding the fleet from sixty-six of the line to ninety-two, and replenishing the timber stocks. All this he adduced in his defence in 1782, when an even greater storm engulfed him in the fall of the North administration as (in Sheridan's words) 'the man born for the destruction of the British Navy'. Both Middleton, who disapproved of his private life, and Horace Walpole, who disliked his politics, testified to his superiority as an administrator to those who preceded and followed him, but the personal antagonism which he aroused, and the misfortunes of the war which he conducted, combined to ruin his reputation.[3]

What was required, and what could not be done during the war, was an inquiry into the whole state of naval administration. At that date the executive functions of the navy were directed by the Board of Admiralty,

[1] *Sandwich Papers*, vol. II, pp. 190 ff.; vol. III, p. 275; vol. IV, p. 298. *Barrington Papers*, vol. II, p. 315; *Barham Papers*, vol. I, p. 366; vol. II, p. 201. *Byam Martin Letters*, vol. III, p. 291. (All published by the Navy Records Society.)

[2] *Sandwich Papers*, vol. II, pp. 259 ff.; vol. III, p. 275. *Barham Papers*, vol. II, p. 18. *Parl. Hist. XX*, p. 174.

[3] *Sandwich Papers*, vol. IV, pp. 282 ff. *Barham Papers*, vol. II, pp. 10, 30. *Walpole Memoirs*, vol. IV, p. 170. *Parl. Hist. XXII*, pp. 878–931.

'Their Lordships', or the seven commissioners for executing the office of Lord High Admiral. Matters connected with supply were the concern of subordinate boards, of which the chief was the Navy Board, the principal officers of which were the Comptroller, Treasurer, Surveyor and Clerk of the Acts. There was also the Victualling Board, and the Sick and Wounded Board, which dealt with prisoners of war in addition to the medical department. In 1785 Middleton, as Comptroller, instigated the setting up of a commission of inquiry into fees and abuses. Its recommendations were comparatively mild—the abolition of perquisites in favour of increased salaries, the regularising of the activities of pursers and clerks, and a more careful auditing of accounts to check 'the enormous frauds which have been committed in this branch of the victualling service' by dishonest contractors. But when it became obvious that neither Pitt nor Howe, as First Lord, would act upon these recommendations, Middleton resigned in 1790. A motion that the reports should be made public was negatived in 1797, so that they did not appear in print until 18c6.[1]

The supply of timber and naval stores was a problem which affected all European navies as transport by sea increased and as larger ships were built. Colbert had warned his countrymen that France might perish from lack of wood. The forest laws which he instituted gave the crown the right of pre-emption of naval timber, but this right was not consistently exercised and the want of alternative supplies, especially in mast timber, seriously weakened the French naval effort. In England there was a similar shortage of materials for shipbuilding, in spite of the replanting which had taken place a hundred years earlier owing to Evelyn's re-afforestation propaganda. The shortage of oak was not only due to the increase in the size of the merchant marine, but also to the demands of charcoal made by the iron-smelting industry. Steps were taken early in the century to limit the amount of carved work in a ship in order to conserve supplies, hence the absence of 'gingerbread' work in eighteenth-century ships compared with their baroque predecessors. To build a third-rate man of war (the 74-gun ship was the backbone of the fleet) some 3200 loads of oak and 400 loads of elm were required. Annual dockyard consumption was about 22,000 loads, the policy being to maintain a three-year supply in order to season the wood.[2]

When Sandwich became First Lord, in 1771, a committee of inquiry was set up because 'there was scarcely any timber in any of the dockyards, and a total despondency at the Navy Office as to the means of procuring it, it being generally understood that the timber of England was

[1] House of Commons, *Sessional Papers*, 1806, vol. VII, p. 309. *Barham Papers*, vol. II, pp. 337, 347.

[2] *Sandwich Papers*, vol. IV, pp. 310, 354. See R. G. Albion, *Forests and Sea Power* (Harvard, 1926), and P. W. Bamford, *Forests and French Sea Power* (Toronto, 1956), though the former's remarks on the Sandwich period require revision.

exhausted'. Only 13,000 loads were found in stock, because 31,000 had been used annually over the past five years and because of the expansion of the East India Company's fleet at this time. Measures taken in consequence included restrictions on the latter's shipbuilding programme and the importation of more foreign timber in order to break the combination of the timber merchants. Ten years later Sandwich claimed that there were 80,000 loads in stock or on contract, but the nation had already suffered many disasters directly attributable to the shortage of seasoned oak and good masts and yards. The conservative policy of the Navy Board may have been partly responsible for this state of affairs, but it is not true to say that foreign or colonial sources had been totally neglected: extensive imports from the Baltic had been made for many years past, and, in the correspondence of the board, there is plenty of evidence of investigations of the forests of North America, where much of the timber was reserved for the crown by the marking of a broad arrow. Nor can Sandwich be blamed for the shortages prevailing at the outset of the American War, since the causes lay in the building with unseasoned timber at the height of the previous war. The *Royal George*, for example, whose bottom fell out in 1782 when she was careened because it was so rotten, was built at that time; on the other hand, the *Victory*, launched in 1765, is still preserved. Colonial yards, however, were not developed as much as they might have been and only a few small warships were built in America, the first being the *Boston* frigate of 1748. Matters improved when Middleton replaced Suckling as Comptroller, chiefly because he made more use of private yards and kept the royal yards better stocked. According to him, there were 56 ships of the line in good repair in 1766, 68 in 1783 and 101 in 1789.[1]

Most of Europe's masts, yards, planking, cordage and pitch were drawn from the Baltic. It therefore became a prime aim of British naval policy to maintain these supplies for herself and deny them to her enemies. Hence in time of war her insistence on the belligerent's right of search for contraband, which constantly brought her into conflict with the neutralist doctrine of 'free ships, free goods'. When the Baltic powers formed an Armed Neutrality to defend their attitude, as they did in 1780 and again in 1801, the British reply was armed intervention to keep the Sound open. The French Atlantic ports were far more vulnerable than the British for importation from this source, though Toulon could rely on the oak forests of Italy. What the French lacked in particular was good mast timber, so that they had to rely on masts made up of shorter pieces which proved unreliable. Nevertheless the position of their rivals was little better, as the events of the American War illustrated. In 1778 Byron failed to overtake D'Estaing partly because his fleet was dismasted in a gale and there were insufficient replacements in American yards. A

[1] *Barham Papers*, vol. III, p. 18.

similar shortage was among the reasons why Graves was too late to intercept De Grasse entering the Chesapeake in 1781. That losses by storm
were often more serious than those suffered by enemy action is shown by
the damage suffered in a gale off Newfoundland the next year, when more
ships foundered on account of their crazy condition than were lost in all
the actions of the war.

There was a remarkable revival in French naval and maritime affairs
during the decade after 1761, when the duc de Choiseul-Stainville became
Minister of Marine. His cousin Choiseul-Praslin was minister from
1766 to 1770, when both fell from power owing to the influence of the
du Barry, but their successors continued their work as far as the cleavages
in French society permitted them, until the reforms were codified by
Castries in 1786. Thus, if Colbert may be called the founder of the French
navy, Choiseul was its restorer.

The principal aim of his policy was revenge on Britain for the losses
suffered during the Seven Years War. The first field in which the rivalry
of France, Spain, and Britain occurred was the search for the fabled *Terra
Australis Incognita* in the South Pacific, for the discovery of which the
first naval-scientific expeditions were equipped under the leadership of
such circumnavigators as Bougainville, Byron, Wallis and Cook. The
latter's three voyages, between 1768 and his death at Hawaii in 1779,
overshadowed those of his predecessors by the extent of his discoveries
and by his achievements in the science of navigation. His legacy is not
only the modern map of the Pacific, but the new standards which he set
in the preservation of health at sea and in the accuracy of charts.[1] The
latter was largely achieved by his use of the first practical chronometer,
which was invented by John Harrison, whose fourth model he took with
him in his second voyage in 1772–5. This was the most important navi-
gational aid discovered during the century, since it solved the problem of
determining the longitude which had for so long defeated the French
Academy and the British Board of Longitude.

Before France could implement her policy of revenge in a European
war a reform of her navy was imperative. When Choiseul's description of
its plight and his appeal for royal aid proved fruitless, he turned to the
public, especially the merchant classes of the south and west, as a result
of which no less than fifteen ships of the line were built by subscription,
and by the date of his dismissal the navy had been increased from forty
to sixty-four of the line. A peace establishment of eighty-one of the line
was envisaged shortly before the outbreak of the Revolution, but this
figure was never actually attained. Apart from this rebuilding campaign,
Choiseul and his successors developed the chief naval ports of France and

[1] See J. C. Beaglehole's edition of *The Journals of James Cook* (Hakluyt Society, 1955,
1961).

the West Indies, new bases being built at L'Orient, Fort Royal (Martinique), Cherbourg and Dunkirk.[1]

It was in their efforts to reform the officer structure of the navy that successive Ministers of Marine were least effective. The distinction between the administrative officials of the Navy Board and the executive officers of the Admiralty which existed in England was exacerbated in France by more rigid social cleavages. The powers of the *intendants*, as laid down by Colbert, and of the administrative hierarchy known as *la plume* were greater than those of the executive, *l'épée*. By his *ordonnance* of 1765 Choiseul redressed the balance in favour of the latter, but his successor, De Boynes (1771–4), attempted to reverse this by bringing the officers into line with the army, even robbing them of their distinctive uniform. The attempt was so unpopular that De Sartines (1774–80) dismissed nearly half the administrative branch in order to create shore posts for executive officers in peacetime: hence the administrative chaos which existed when France became involved in the American War. Wider powers were therefore restored to the commissary branches of the service by Castries (1780–7), whose *ordonnances* of 1786 codified these reforms.

Even more serious than the rivalry between *la plume* and *l'épée* were the jealousies within the ranks of the executive officers. Regular officers composing the *Grand Corps* (the *rouges*, as they were called from the colour of their breeches) were drawn from a cadet entry originally known as *gardes-de-pavillon*, who were the sons of the Breton and Provençal nobility. In order to widen this entry Choiseul allowed officers of the *petite marine* (commonly called *bleus*) to serve in either the merchant or royal navies, in which, however, they could never rise higher than the rank of sub-lieutenant. Castries went further by replacing the old system of entry, under which proof of nobility had to be given, with cadets known as *élèves*, who were drawn from a wider social background. Such reforms were not to the taste of the aristocracy, who continued to regard the naval service as inferior to that of the army. But when the ranks of the *rouges* had been depleted by the Revolution it was to this Reserve that the government could turn for its officers. An equally despised class were the *intrus*—officers who had previously been in the army or some other profession. Yet it was *intrus* such as D'Estaing (once a soldier) and Bougainville (once a lawyer) who added such lustre to the naval history of the time. Even the great Suffren was looked down upon by many of his colleagues because, though a regular *rouge*, his family belonged to the *petite noblesse*, which had no tradition of service at sea.

During the American War these jealousies proved even more of a handicap than did the political differences prevailing in the British navy. If Rodney could complain that he was not properly supported by his

---

[1] G. Lacour-Gayet, *La Marine Militaire sous Louis XV* (1910), p. 420, and *idem*, *Sous Louis XVI* (1905), p. 56. Cf. M. Loir, *La Marine Royal en 1789* (1892), p. 57.

captains, how much more serious were Suffren's troubles in the Indian Ocean. 'There is no discipline in the navy', states a report of 1782, 'either among the senior or junior officers. Some captains will not obey the signals of the admiral, others do nothing on board, with the result that the greatest disorder prevails. It is not at this moment possible to abolish the detestable prejudices of the corps of officers, but when peace comes it will be necessary to remedy these abuses by reforming the vicious officer structure.'[1] The efforts of successive ministers failed to do this, so that the excessive pride of the regular officers invited attack on the part of the revolutionaries. Half of the officer corps had emigrated by 1792 and many of the remainder had been murdered or disgraced.[2] Since naval officers owed a particular allegiance to the crown the profession was identified with the Royalists, and a new navy, representing the nation in arms, had to be created to replace a professional navy which had always considered itself as something apart from the community. Between 1789 and the outbreak of war egalitarian enthusiasm had destroyed the old navy without, as yet, replacing it with a new one more in accord with the spirit of the time.

In spite of Colbert's register of seamen (*Inscription Maritime*), the problem of manning the fleet was just as intractable as in England. The system of calling up classes of the seafaring population proved as much of a hardship to the inhabitants of the maritime provinces as did the press-gang, nor was service on board any more popular. Though attempts were made to humanise a system under which some 90,000 men were liable for service, so serious was the shortage that a special corps of 'marines' had to be created. Such was Choiseul's *Corps Royal d'Infantérie et d'Artillérie*, which Castries reorganised in 1786 as a force of 6000 seamen-gunners. As these men only served on board in time of war, the force was never popular with naval commanders. Of more lasting success were Choiseul's schools of naval medicine and his corps of naval constructors (called marine engineers), whose headquarters in Paris remain to this day.

Whatever the shortcomings in personnel, the French navy was ahead of the British in two respects—its training in the art of war, and in the standard of shipbuilding. As has already been pointed out, the standard treatise on tactics was that of Morogues, which was dedicated to Choiseul. The latter returned the compliment by reforming the *Académie Royale de la Marine*, which Morogues had founded as a research establishment in 1752. Kempenfelt was not the only British officer who expressed admiration of French tactical training, but their defensive methods often stultified their efforts in actual combat.

The prestige of the navy in France was enormously enhanced by the

[1] Quoted by Lacour-Gayet, *La Marine Militaire sous Louis XV*, p. 598.
[2] Cf. N. Hampson, *La Marine de l'An II*, pp. 43, 44.

accession of Louis XVI, the only French monarch to take a personal interest in maritime affairs. This interest had been inspired by his tutor, Ozanne, the naval architect and artist. Building programmes went ahead regardless of cost, encouraged by royal visits to the dockyards. The fact that French prizes were sometimes immediately converted into British flagships, and that the draughts of English ships often have a note attached to them explaining that a particular French vessel provided the model, are the surest proofs of their superiority in this respect, though the English had a low opinion of the dirt and disorder which prevailed on board, and by the end of the century it is doubtful whether French superiority in naval architecture still remained.[1] The larger size of their ships permitted them to fire a heavier broadside, but they were never as effective in close combat because they were accustomed to fire on the up roll in order to dismast enemy rigging. This practice certainly enabled them to live to fight another day, but as Suffren complained, the improved sailing qualities of British ships consequent upon the coppering of the fleet (a practice which the French did not adopt until 1785) lessened the value of such tactics. After 1786 the line of battleships of both nations were limited to three rates—over 100 guns, 80 guns and 74 guns—though a few of the old fourth rates survived in service. At least two French three-deckers mounted as many as 118 guns.

During the American War the French navy cost about 160 million *livres* a year and during the next five years expenditure continued at a rate of about 45 million annually, so that naval expenditure may be accounted one of the principal causes of national bankruptcy.[2] The last minister before the Revolution—la Luzerne—attempted to reduce expenditure, but with his resignation and the death of Suffren in 1788 the navy of the *ancien régime* may be said to have come to an end. The excesses of the early years of the Revolution virtually destroyed the officer corps, though the ships that had been built were, of course, still available and Sané, the finest naval architect of the age, continued to serve under republican masters. In order to fill the gaps in the depleted officer corps, a law of April 1791 abolished the distinction between the merchant and military services. The new entry, known as *aspirants*, were rated ensigns after four years at sea, but continued Jacobin purges soon necessitated promotion from almost any rank. Bougainville, one of the few distinguished officers of the old navy to survive, resigned in disgust after complaining that 'military discipline, without which a navy cannot exist, had been abolished'.[3] Such was the distrust of the pride of the *grand corps* and its loyalty to the central government that the triumph of

[1] Cf. H. Chapelle, *History of American Sailing Ships* (1935), p. 78, and J. Charnock, *History of Marine Architecture* (1802), vol. III, p. 222.

[2] Malouet's figures, quoted in M. Loir, *La Marine Royale en 1789* (1892), p. 277.

[3] Quoted in E. Chevalier, *Histoire de la Marine Française sous la première république* (1886), p. 32.

the administrative officers became complete. After riots and mutinies at Brest and Toulon, naval academies were suppressed, executive officers were elected by their crews and juries served on courts martial.[1] It was ironical that the Jacobin Jeanbon Saint-André, who had been the most violent critic of the old navy, became the man chiefly responsible for the new revolutionary navy which had to be created by the Convention after the outbreak of war in 1793.

The United States navy may be said to have come into existence in October 1775, when the naval committee of Congress ordered the arming of four warships to form an American 'Continental' navy. The number was increased to thirteen frigates when a new Maritime Committee, consisting of one member from each colony, gave orders for raising two battalions of marines. By the date of the Declaration of Independence the fleet had grown to twenty-seven vessels of all types, though only six were built as warships and there were no ships of the line; at that date the British had seventy-one ships in American waters alone. The first American commander-in-chief was Esek Hopkins, who had under him five captains and five lieutenants, one of whom, Paul Jones, was first lieutenant of the 24-gun flagship *Alfred*. Apart from this Continental navy (the creation of which was viewed with distrust in some quarters), there were various state navies, notably that of Virginia, which amounted to fifty small vessels which were used for coast defence.

In matters of uniform, naval precedent, prize law, etc., the committee followed the regulations laid down by the British Admiralty. A distinction similar to that which prevailed in Britain was made between the supply functions of the navy boards, established at the principal ports, and the executive control exercised by the committee until, in 1779, it was superseded by a smaller Board of Admiralty, which may be considered the true predecessor of the modern Navy Department. At the conclusion of hostilities all the ships were sold with the exception of their one line of battleship, *America*, which was presented to the king of France in return for 'his generous exertions on behalf of the United States'. On the retirement of Robert Morris in 1784 from the office of Agent of Marine (which had in turn supplanted the Board of Admiralty), the United States navy virtually ceased to exist for the next few years.

The activities of the Continental navy were chiefly limited to co-operation with the army, though ten captures were made at sea, the most famous being that of the British frigate *Serapis* by Paul Jones in the *Bonhomme Richard* (an ex-French East Indiaman) off Flamborough Head in 1779. Jones had sailed to Europe as a commissioned officer, but as Franklin realised in his capacity of American minister at Paris whose

[1] L. Lévy-Schneider, *Le Conventionnel Jeanbon Saint-André* (1901), vol. I, pp. 299–312. Cf. N. Hampson, *op. cit.*

function it was to provide him with ships, Jones' importance was primarily that of a commerce raider and his crew were of the heterogeneous type common on board privateers. It was due to the traditional popularity of privateering among the inhabitants of New England that the personnel of the navy never exceeded 3000 men and 170 officers, most of whom had begun life as privateersmen. Hence whereas the number of privateers increased from 186 to 327 between 1776 and 1782, that of the navy decreased from 25 to 7. The total number of American privateers commissioned during the war was 1151, the losses of British merchant ships amounting to 3386.[1]

Privateering was an essential part of maritime warfare at that date, because it was the principal means of commerce destruction. In European waters its importance was on the decline, though it continued to be far from negligible, on account of the growth of convoy protection and official disapproval on the grounds that it denuded navies of thousands of prime seamen. But in an age when smuggling flourished, such excellent seamen easily turned themselves into privateersmen. Saint-Malo and Dunkirk continued their historic activity in this respect, and in one year alone 120 Liverpool privateers employed 8754 men. Altogether some 2150 letters of marque were issued in Britain during the war. On the American seaboard privateering flourished as never before, the New England colonies being particularly well placed to intercept the West Indies trade returning with the Gulf Stream to the latitude of the westerlies. However, Nova Scotia was equally well placed to prey on American coastal shipping, with the result that 319 prizes were condemned at the Vice-Admiralty court at Halifax. Many of these were captured by warships, but it is probable that one of the reasons why the colony did not join the American revolt was the chance of wealth to be gained by privateering.[2]

Commerce destruction was carried out, apart from naval cruisers, by two types of vessel which are easily confused. The privateer proper was a private ship of war, carrying no cargo but armed and commissioned by a letter of marque. The term 'letter of marque' had, however, come to be used to denote a trading vessel as well as the document she carried (which was supplemented with official instructions on prize procedure, forbidding private ransom or sale, and directing the captor to take the prize into the nearest Vice-Admiralty court for condemnation). The purchase of such a letter was, indeed, essential if a charge of piracy was to be avoided, and if an owner's crew was to be protected against the press-gang. If the for-

[1] C. O. Paullin, *The Navy of the American Revolution* (New York, 1906), p. 157; E. S. Maclay, *History of American Privateers* (New York, 1899), p. 113.

[2] Records of Halifax court printed by Essex Inst., Salem, 1911, and Nova Scotia Hist. Soc., vol. XII. Cf. G. Williams, *History of Liverpool Privateers* (1897); *Law and Custom of the Sea* (Navy Records Society, 1916); Register of letters of marque, 1778–83, P.R.O. Adm. 7/325. R. Davis, *Rise of the English Shipping Industry* (1962).

tunes made by privateers were not as great as formerly, the losses suffered by British merchants from American and French cruisers certainly helped to make the war unpopular in England.

Another new naval power which appeared at this time was that of Russia. When he made his country a Baltic power, Peter the Great had largely founded the first Russian navy with English and Dutch assistance. This navy fell into neglect after his death, until it was revived by Catherine II for her Turkish and Swedish wars. A large proportion of its officers were still of foreign extraction, but the Russians were by this date building more of their own ships, often under the supervision of foreign technicians. Of the British contingent of officers Sir Charles Knowles, John Elphinston and Samuel Greig were the most distinguished. On the conclusion of the American war, many half-pay officers entered the Russian service, though when it was proposed to employ Paul Jones as their commander in the Baltic they threatened to resign rather than serve under a man whom they regarded as a renegade; Jones was consequently employed for a short time in the Black Sea. Samuel Bentham, originally a colonel in the Russian army and later Inspector General of the Royal Navy, played an important part in fitting out a galley fleet against the Turks in the Crimea, and in 1787 a gun foundry was established near Lake Ladoga where British engineers introduced the carronade and other new forms of artillery.[1]

In 1769 Russian ships first appeared in the Mediterranean, where the fleet was commanded by Admiral Orlov, though it was Greig's conduct of the fireships which defeated the Turks at Tchesma. By the outbreak of the second Turkish war in 1787 Russia had acquired bases in the Crimea, so that a Black Sea fleet, first under Voinovitch and then under Ushakov, was now a possibility. This fleet increased from seven to twenty-one of the line in four years. The larger Baltic fleet of fifty-four of the line (though only a quarter of these were in commission) was used at the same date for the war against Sweden. Its commander, Greig, was killed in the only outstanding victory at Hogland, the success at Viborg in 1790 being due rather to the inefficiency of the enemy than the energy of Tchitchagov, the new commander-in-chief. At the conclusion of the war Russia became the dominant Baltic power, and therefore the chief threat to the supply of vital naval stores to the West in the event of an Armed Neutrality.[2]

It is impossible to contrast the chief European navies on the eve of the revolutionary wars with any precision because the number of ships listed often bore little relation to their effectiveness at sea. The lesser naval powers could seldom commission all their ships at the same time, nor did

---

[1] M. S. Anderson, 'Great Britain and the Growth of the Russian Navy', in *Mariner's Mirror*, May 1956.
[2] See R. C. Anderson, *Naval Wars in the Baltic* (1910), and *Naval Wars in the Levant* (1952). Cf. *Memoir of James Trevenen* (1959; Navy Records Society).

their officers have sufficient experience at sea to achieve a reasonable standard of efficiency. Thus the numerous ships composing the Spanish navy (which included the 114-gun four-decker *Santissima Trinidada*, the largest warship afloat after the destruction of the French 118-gun *Commerce de Marseilles*) had little practical value on account of poor manning and worse supplies; and when the Jacobins claimed that the French navy was the strongest in Europe they omitted to point out that most of its experienced officers were no longer in command. However, the number of capital ships, excluding frigates and smaller vessels, does give a reasonable basis for comparison. In 1792 the British had 115 of the line, the French 76 and the Spanish 76. The Dutch listed 49, their ships being of peculiar construction owing to the shallowness of coastal waters; the great East India fleets occupied the main part of Dutch maritime activity. At the battle of the Dogger Bank in 1781 Dutch ships fought with great spirit, as they were to do again at Camperdown in 1797, but in the interval they were not accounted a formidable force, and when the French invaded the country they were easily captured by a squadron of cavalry which caught them in the ice. There was a rapid increase in the size of the Baltic navies between 1780 and 1790—the Danish fleet increasing from 14 to 40, the Swedish from 15 to 27 and the Russian from 22 to over 50—on account of the alarms aroused by the Armed Neutrality and by the Spanish (or Nootka Sound) and Russian crises.[1] Nevertheless, on 17 February 1792 the situation was such that Pitt could advise a reduction of the naval estimates on the ground that 'unquestionably there never was a time in the history of this country when, from the situation in Europe, we might more reasonably expect fifteen years of peace than we may at the present time'.[2]

2. ARMIES

By the end of its existence the *ancien régime* had reached the limit of its powers in military no less than in other spheres. The size of armies and the scale of warfare had greatly increased,[3] but there was a fatal clumsiness in the means by which this was achieved and the uses to which the expanded resources were put. The rigid line formation adopted to get the best out of mediocre weapons and troops made it hard to concentrate force for a telling blow at key points on the front. The large armies with their ponderous supply-trains could only move slowly and were not readily able to force an engagement on an inferior opponent. Consequently battles were either evaded by the weaker side or failed to be decisive. Wars dragged on without result until the huge expense which

[1] For comparative figures see Charnock, *History of Marine Architecture*, and W. James, *Naval History of Britain* (1837 ed.), vol. 1. The estimates of French and Spanish ships are probably too high: only 67 French ships were in commission in 1793.

[2] *The War Speeches of William Pitt the Younger*, selected by R. Coupland (3rd ed., 1940), p. 16.　　　[3] M. Roberts, *The Military Revolution, 1560–1660* (1956), pp. 14–15.

their expanded scale involved led the combatants to desist. From this impasse only an occasional stroke of luck or genius afforded escape.

Between 1763 and 1792 there was little fighting on land between the major European powers. In this breathing space, means were devised of making decisive victory the normal, instead of the exceptional, outcome of a major war. The new military thinking was an integral part of the general movement of criticism of established institutions; inspired by the same ideas, it triumphed only when the general cause of reform did so. This was inevitably the case in the all-important matter of improving the quality of the troops and their commanders. This could only be done by altering the composition of the armies, which can never happen save as the cause or result of a political upheaval. But even in questions of tactics, strategy and the improvement of weapons the rule still applied. Vested interests stood in the way, not least that of departmentalism. Specialists of the different arms, often men of real brilliance in their chosen line, were unable to see war as a whole and make their own special activities a contribution to a general scheme rather than an end in themselves. This departmentalism was part of the essential clumsiness of the old régime. Only those accustomed to thinking in the new way *en philosophe*, testing the adequacy of all organisations by reference to certain general principles, could rise above it. Only a powerful reforming government, the sworn enemy of vested interests, could overcome it.

Military reformers had the special difficulty that their civil counterparts, though in general sympathy with them, viewed part of their plans with suspicion. At first the soldiers, like the civilians, hoped for reform from above; but they generally felt that only a ruler who was himself an experienced soldier and personally commanded his forces could succeed. Increasingly they had to look to revolutionaries and parliamentarians; but only under pressure of necessity would these give the soldiers what they wanted. Thus it was only with the French Revolution that the adoption of the new methods began in real earnest. Till then the military system remained very much as it has been described in the previous volume. But the work of preparation which had been done was so extensive as to enable the transformation, when it came, to be violent and rapid. It is with these indispensable preliminaries that this chapter deals.[1]

The first essential was to find a way of fighting battles that rewarded the victor with the total rout, not the mere discomfiture, of his opponent. A revolution in tactics normally requires the invention of new weapons. The eighteenth century saw much improvement but little outright innovation in this field. Consequently the new tactics were rather

[1] See in general S. Wilkinson, *The French Army before Napoleon* (1915); C. von der Goltz, *Von Rossbach bis Jena* (French trans., 1896); L. C. Hatch, *The Administration of the American Revolutionary Army* (1904).

an improved version of the old than a complete repudiation of them. The Industrial Revolution came just too late to have a really profound influence on even the Napoleonic wars.[1] Individual inventions made their mark but a host of complementary inventions were required before they could have their full effect. Small arms changed little, though they were made more efficient by minor inventions and by a tendency, especially in France, to allow the individual to aim and fire in his own time instead of at the word of command. A line only two ranks deep now had sufficient fire-power for battle purposes, but in no country did the authorities dare to depart from the customary three. The superior accuracy of rifled weapons was recognised and attempts were made to introduce them. European rifles were clumsy and inaccurate but by 1750 the British American colonists had developed a light, long weapon with which a good shot could hit a man at 300 yards. (With a musket he had only a 40 per cent chance at 100 yards.) In 1775 many Americans hoped by this technological achievement to win their war for independence. They received an early warning not to put their trust in technology. The rifles were muzzle-loaders and the tight-fitting bullets and grooved barrels which made them accurate also made them hard to load: they could only fire one shot to the musket's three. They were not strong enough to carry a bayonet and in battle the riflemen, after a first devastating volley, were liable to be bayoneted before they could reload. A British officer, Ferguson, invented a rifle fitted with a bayonet and loaded at the breech through an aperture which could be opened or shut by a single revolution of a handle. It could fire at least as fast as a musket and, perhaps its chief advantage, could be loaded by a man lying down under cover. But there were further difficulties. The dense smoke then usual on battlefields tended in any case to make accurate fire impossible and preliminary long-range firing resulted in shortages of powder. Smokeless and more portable ammunition was needed before the rifle could really come into its own. For sniping in broken country it was ideal, but it was of little use otherwise and even the Americans soon greatly restricted its use. As an American authority wrote in 1811: 'where the musket ends, the rifle begins.'[2]

By contrast there was almost a revolution in the artillery. Its activity in battle had hitherto been much restricted by the weight and slowness of the guns. A great effort was now made to achieve mobility, helped on by several important discoveries. Jean de Maritz (1680–1743), a Swiss employed in the French arsenal at Strasbourg, developed a method of making cannon by first casting a solid cylinder of metal of the required shape and size and then hollowing it out by boring with a drill. Hitherto cannon

---

[1] J. U. Nef, *War and Human Progress* (1950), pp. 330–1.
[2] J. W. Wright, 'The Rifle in the American Revolution', *American Historical Review*, vol. XXIX (1923–4), pp. 293–9.

had been cast hollow, by means of a central core in the mould. Drilling produced a weapon that was stronger and more accurately made, so that the windage—the gap between the ball and the sides of the barrel—could be reduced. This meant that the explosive force of the charge was more fully utilised. Maritz's son took his invention to Holland and from there it was brought to Britain. There Benjamin Robins (1707–51) had discovered how to measure the velocity of projectiles and made possible the scientific study of the power of particular weapons. It was found that the velocity of the ball did not necessarily increase with the size of the charge and that the quantity of powder then used for each shot was excessive. Again the result was that a ball of a given weight could be propelled the same distance by a smaller charge, and so by a lighter gun.

All this was the work of civilians. It was in Germany that soldiers first became really interested in lighter guns. In 1744 Prince Liechtenstein was put in charge of the Austrian artillery, then much inferior to the Prussian. He collected experts from all over Europe and their work resulted in radical improvements in the Austrian guns, especially from 1753. Among his subordinates was Gribeauval who, after distinguishing himself in the Austrian service, was placed by Choiseul in charge of the artillery of his native France. From 1765 the new principles were introduced there. Without lessening their effectiveness, the guns were made much lighter by shortening the barrels. They could be more easily and accurately aimed. The carriages were made much more smooth-running and ceased to resemble clumsy farm carts. Bullocks were no longer used for traction and the lighter pieces could be moved about the battlefield by men. The artillery could now keep pace with the infantry. By mounting the crews on horseback, a portion of it could even be made to follow the cavalry and skirmishers. Horse artillery seems to have been used first by Frederick the Great in 1762. The French introduced it in 1791 as specially suited to the *élan* of a revolutionary army.

Because the guns were now more useful, their numbers greatly increased from the mid-century onwards. The advances in metallurgy now beginning in Britain promised to facilitate this. Guns for the land service had hitherto been made of bronze, which was relatively scarce and expensive. Iron was not strong enough: the guns made from it had to be so thick and heavy that they could only be used at sea. Coke smelting not only increased the supply of iron but made it stronger, so that it could be used for army guns, thus removing an impediment to expansion.

Thus although the fire-power of the infantry had increased only moderately, the fire of heavier weapons was now much more readily available to them for softening-up the enemy line before an assault. Du Teil in his pamphlet *Sur L'Usage de L'Artillerie Nouvelle* (1778) envisaged troops and guns working as one unit, each protecting the other. In an attack, the guns were to get within 1000 yards of the enemy before opening fire, trusting to their mobility for their safety. They were to seek to place themselves on the prolongation of the enemy's line and bombard him from the flank. This had always been the ideal, for a ball passing along a line of troops hit more men than one passing across it. But the old artillery took such a time to reach the prolongation that one impatient commander exclaimed 'il prolonge toujours'. The close and deadly fire of the new guns was to make them a force hard to resist, and it is fitting that Du Teil's elder brother should have been the chief military instructor of the greatest of all artillerymen, Napoleon.

Yet the power of the artillery remained severely limited. Despite improved construction (and better roads) it remained a heavy burden to transport. A balance had to be struck between fire-power and mobility and remarkable technical achievements could be a military weakness if they upset it. Gribeauval's work was almost ruined because his more conservative colleagues, who for a time succeeded in discrediting him, could not see this. They urged for instance that the old, long guns could fire further and straighter than the new short ones. For the most part this was untrue, but not invariably. In those instances, performance at long range had been sacrificed to save a little weight because experience had shown that it was of little use in battle. Gribeauval took a broad military, his opponents a narrow technical, view. The innovators themselves were not free from departmentalism. Proud of their work in increasing mobility, they too complacently allowed the number of guns and attendant ammunition wagons to increase. Many of the small guns in particular may have been more trouble to transport than they were worth. All this threatened once again to slow down the movements of the armies. It was perhaps Gribeauval's system that came nearest to a perfect balance and it remained in force in France till 1825. It was only with the building of the railways that the full potentialities of the artillery now first revealed could be realised.[1]

The dubious outcome of the attempt to improve weapons made it difficult to decide how to go about the improvement of tactics. Increasing fire-power suggested the adoption of irregular formations in place of the perfectly ordered line. This would produce both greater mobility and the more effective exploitation of the terrain. 'Light troops' who fought in this way were everywhere much in vogue by the 1780s. Britain had learnt their value in America and the War of Independence made this the preoccupation of most of her more intelligent officers. The wildness of their terrain made the Russians also pioneers in irregular warfare. The irregular formations of Peter the Great interested Saxe and his disposition at Fontenoy was inspired by the chain of fortified posts which had broken the Swedish line at Poltava. It was the Austrians, however, who first

---

[1] G. Ffoulkes, *The Gunmakers of England* (1937); *L'Encyclopédie*, s.v. 'artillerie de campagne'; A. Dolleczek, *Geschichte der oesterreichischen Artillerie* (1887).

used light troops extensively in western Europe, bringing to Germany the native irregulars raised in Hungary and Croatia to serve against the Turks. The French needed them as a corollary of the use of the column described below and did so much to develop the training and tactics of light troops that they probably had little left to learn from participation in the American War of Independence.[1] The experience of that war was, however, of great importance for the Prussians. In the mid-century they had sought to oppose the Austrian light troops by hasty levies, mainly of foreigners, at the start of each war. In the 1780s permanent formations of light troops were set up and were joined by many German officers returning from service in America, including the young Gneisenau and such experts as Ochs and Ewald. The Prussian light infantry was no less master of its craft at Valmy than in the campaigns of 1813–15.[2]

But although fighting in irregular formation was henceforth of great importance it was, until weapons had improved still further, essentially something subsidiary. What was needed above all to break the deadlock on the battlefield was an easy means of concentrating superior force against an enemy's weak points: for this the close formations of the old school were still required. The good shooting of the American revolutionary army was largely nullified at first by the looseness of their formation consequent on bad drill. They lost the battles of Brandywine and Germantown partly because, as they marched in single file, their full strength was not on the field as soon as that of the British. Thereafter they gladly learned from Baron Steuben the parade-ground formations of the Old World.[3] An army that put exclusive trust in light troops would be lost and both David Dundas in England and Guibert in France strove against the fashion that was leading military opinion that way. The former considered that it was only the absence of good cavalry that had allowed light infantry to become so important in America. The latter thought that the whole craze was simply an evading of the essential problem of how to give more flexibility to the main forces at the centre of the battle.

Here the vital inspiration came from those who had sought improvement in an entirely opposite direction and by putting the emphasis not on the potentialities of fire-arms but on their limitations. To Folard (1669–1752) 'shock' rather than 'fire' was the decisive element in battle. He almost regretted the introduction of fire-arms and was nostalgic for cold steel. He proposed that the bulk of an army should be arranged in columns at intervals along the front, able by their mass to puncture and then roll up an enemy deployed in line and relying on fire. The ill-aimed volleys of a line he thought of no more effect than a few men firing accurately and therefore the spaces between his columns were to be held by

---

[1] J. Colin, *L'Infanterie au 18e Siècle: La Tactique* (1907), p. 275.
[2] C. Jany, *Geschichte der königlich preussichen Armee* (1929–33), vol. III, pp. 130–1, 165–8. [3] J. M. Palmer, *General von Steuben* (1937), pp. 144–66.

13-2

small detachments of what were, in fact, light infantry. These ideas found much support in the French army, where the column of attack had occasionally been used and was thought especially suited to the national temperament. French soldiers always drilled badly and did not excel at standing firm in line under fire but performed prodigies when stimulated by the excitement of a mass charge. In the 1750s columns of attack were prescribed in the official French drill-books.

These early columns were clumsy affairs. Their inventors were far too contemptuous of fire-arms and their conception of 'shock' was far too crude. A mass of men was expected to have the properties of a solid object—a battering ram. In practice their dense formation resulted in either disorder or slowness of movement. Either way, the 'shock' effect was dissipated. Fighting in column prevented most of the troops using their guns and gave no certain advantage in return. As fire-power increased, so did the idea lose credit. After facing the Prussians in the Seven Years War, the French largely lost faith in columns.

Nevertheless the column was the expedient which the situation called for. It was the only means of combining mobility with close formation. A line could only move slowly and virtually could not change direction. A column, if not too dense, could move quickly in any direction and was not impeded by natural obstacles. It was the obvious means of concentrating men at a given point on the front for a telling blow. French and Prussians alike investigated the possibilities of using it, not for fighting, but for movement on the battlefield. After 1763 the French adopted a new style of column, smaller, less dense and more suited to rapid movement. The great problem now was to find a means of changing really quickly from column into line and back, so that maximum mobility could be combined with maximum fire-power. This was done by the Guiberts, father and son, using a manœuvre invented, but seldom used by, the Prussians.[1] The younger Guibert's *Essai Général de Tactique* (1772) attempted a synthesis of the divergent branches of new military thought and managed to produce something like a formula for the winning of decisive battles.

The object of Guibert's system was to enable troops to manœuvre freely in the presence of the enemy instead of being tied to a prepared position. His methods were, firstly, to make all evolutions natural, simple and easily learnt—in this he was a true child of his age. Four basic movements had to be practised. Every other movement was a combination of simpler ones and the evolutions of large bodies of men were essentially large-scale reproductions of what was done by small units. Secondly, he advanced as far as he dared towards an irregular formation. Lines no longer had to be more than roughly straight and the units of which they consisted might be deployed in the reverse of the usual order when this was quicker.

[1] Colin, *op. cit.* pp. 135–50.

The result was that an army marching in parallel columns could form at the double a line parallel to or at any angle with (and either astride or to one side of) the line of march. Further, troops posted at, or on their way to, one part of the line could be as rapidly moved to another part. A general could take very full advantage of the terrain in placing his troops and he did not have to place them anywhere irrevocably until they actually came under enemy fire. By reinforcing certain sections of his line at the last minute and by varying the formations of the different columns, so as to make them look stronger or weaker than they were, he could intensify the effect of surprise. An old-style army, which had to form line before the battle began and could only change its position slowly, would be overwhelmed. If the new system were in use on both sides, the more cunning of the two generals might still hope to gain a victory that was decisive.

Guibert envisaged the decisive attack as an overwhelming concentration of fire on a portion of the enemy's line, followed by a charge merely to administer the *coup de grâce*. He favoured a charge by the infantry still formed in line, but left his general free to use two other methods. Frederick the Great relied largely on cavalry charges as the means of dispersing an enemy shattered by his fire-power. He trained his horses to charge at high speed and the Prussian cavalry was probably even more ahead of the rest than the infantry. Guibert desired cavalry formed on this model and thought cavalry charges the proper weapon against a thoroughly disorganised opponent.

Infantry charges in column were recommended by Guibert when an attack was made on a narrow front, when the attacking troops could approach under cover and when a salient was being attacked. In this last case, the front of the salient was to be engaged by sharp-shooters and the column was to charge at the side, where the fire was less. For two reasons the charge in column was to play a larger part in the new system than Guibert foresaw. Firstly, its morale-building qualities made it especially useful when, during the Revolution, the French army was augmented by a mass of inexperienced citizen soldiers. Secondly, there was the tendency, inherent in Guibert's system, and accentuated by the increase of light troops, to fight in a more irregular formation. This implied that the defence would form a line curving about to take advantage of natural obstacles—in other words a series of salients—and that the attackers would seek to approach under cover. On Guibert's own principles it followed that the attacks would be made in column. To this extent the central principle of Folard and his school triumphed—namely that there should be a specialisation of function between light troops supplying 'fire' and columns to give 'shock', in place of a formation in line vainly intended to combine both functions. It was Guibert and his generation, on the other hand, who provided the practical means of applying the principle and they had the added merit of being free from monomania and insisting on the need for a free choice among several different formations designed for different circumstances.

Even in France the triumph of the new formula was long delayed by the last efforts of the old schools. New methods had been devised by the Prussians to enable a line to advance more rapidly. Brought to France by a soldier of fortune named Pirch, they led to some loss of interest in the column, which had little place in the 'Prussianised' drill-book of 1776. Du Mesnil Durand, an old partisan of the column, thereupon produced a new version of his ideas, incorporating a means for columns to form line when fire-power was required. In 1778 manœuvres were held at Vaussieux in Normandy at which the two systems were tested against one another. Du Mesnil's methods of conversion from column into line proved hopelessly clumsy, but the columns as such seem to have re-established their reputation for superior mobility. The result was a desire for compromise and a general rallying to the eclectic system of Guibert. From it the drill-book of 1791 was mainly derived although the research on which it was based had been done (mainly in 1788) by outright partisans of the column. This drill-book was the basis of French tactics and training right through the great wars and was not superseded until 1830.[1]

Ways had thus been found of making battles more decisive. This would have been unavailing without the development of a new strategy which would enable the army taking the offensive to force its opponent to fight. Paradoxically, the key to this problem was found in a strengthening of the defensive, which initially had been among the factors making for stalemate. The fire-power of infantry and artillery was now sufficient to allow detachments of an army to defend themselves for a time against greatly superior numbers. It was therefore possible to divide an army into a number of sections each of which, if attacked, could engage the enemy until the rest could reach the spot and join to overwhelm him. A sort of net of advancing detachments could be spread round an inferior opponent, making escape impossible without a fight. The system could not work, however, unless the attacking troops could move quickly and here the economic advance of western Europe made a vital contribution. A great improvement in roads and inland waterways facilitated the movement not only of men and material but of orders and intelligence. Until well after 1700 troops on campaign as often as not did not use the roads at all, partly because they were so bad, partly because the old system of drill had required the men to stand so far apart that a marching column was too broad for a road. The troops had further been slowed down by the difficulty of supplying them with provisions. The growth of wealth and pro-

[1] Colin, *op. cit.*; J. F. C. Fuller, *British Light Infantry in the Eighteenth Century* (1925): E. M. Lloyd, *History of Infantry* (1908), is less reliable.

ductivity that was in progress meant, however, that there was more food and forage in each area and more carts to carry it. An army was therefore more likely to be able to live off the country by requisitions and less obliged to carry everything with it. Already, in the brief war of 1778-9 between Austria and Prussia, the opposing armies subsisted extensively on the potatoes grown by the peasants in the theatre of war. The conflict has been known as the *Kartoffelkrieg* (potato war) ever since.[1] The division of an army into detachments also made it easier to move and feed than an army jammed on to one road.

Such a division, however, did not readily commend itself to the reformers as a solution to their strategic problem. To Guibert, it seemed at first a characteristic vice of the old school. Concentration of force was the key to success and he therefore wanted less division of an army, not more. It was only later that he concluded that the enemy's main force might be engaged by a detachment, the skilful disposition of the other detachments and the alertness of their commanders being relied on to make them march to the sound of the guns. There was one case, however, where the nature of the terrain obliged the strategist to think in terms of detachments, namely mountain warfare in which the fighting was confined to a number of separated passes. Now in 1764 Bourcet, who like Guibert's father had been on Broglie's staff during the Seven Years War, became director of the staff college at Grenoble. His attention was naturally drawn to the problems of Alpine warfare and for the instruction of his students he wrote *Principes de la Guerre des Montagnes*. His natural preference seems to have been for an army divided into three columns, with not more than a day's march between the centre and either flank to allow for quick concentration. In the mountains he was obliged to allow more numerous detachments, to win the advantage of surprise by operating simultaneously on all the routes running through the range. The detachments of an advancing army were to make all the use they could of the lateral passes connecting those along which they were marching. Each stage of the march was to end as near as possible to the entrance of one, so that if a detachment was attacked the others could quickly march across the front to its help. A column unable for a time to avoid isolation had to move with great circumspection. The columns were to keep in touch as far as they could by means of signals and couriers and the great object was that they should converge together on the enemy force to be attacked and debouch simultaneously on to the battlefield.

An army advancing in this way had the same advantage as that given by the new formation on the field of battle—it could oblige the enemy to watch the whole of a front while the attacker remained able to concentrate at any point on it. Bourcet advised a 'many branched' plan of operations

---

[1] H. Delbrück, *Geschichte der Kriegskunst*, vol. IV (1920), p. 479, cited by Nef, *War and Human Progress*, p. 323.

with one 'branch' as the main attack and a number of subsidiary attacks elsewhere which could be expanded if the main attack went wrong. He argued that the attacker, by being able to make the first move unknown to the defence, had an advantage equivalent to that of working on interior lines: as he put it, the defence had to hold the arc of a circle while the attacker need only hold the chord. The best that the defence could do was not to try and hold a line but retire to a point where all the passes through the mountain range could be covered. The attacking army was bound to become more dispersed as it advanced, owing to the need to defend its line of communications and besiege fortresses. The defending army, if kept together, might then hope to defeat it in detail. If the attackers were bold enough to leave their communications unguarded, a counter-attack could be made on their own country. The victory, argued Bourcet, would go to the army which showed itself cleverest in manœuvre. The clever choice of a defensive position occupied a large place in his system but it had ceased to be the essential thing. Guibert went much further. Few positions, he said, were impregnable everywhere. If the defending army was found in a strong position, the attacker should simply march round it, however hard the going. The defenders would be bound to give battle in the end and a battle, even on disadvantageous terms, was better for the stronger side than none.

The new strategy that was just beginning to emerge had important implications for the character and organisation of the defensive forces. During the period of relatively static warfare, the states of Europe had striven to protect their frontiers by lines of fortresses. The utility of these was now called in question. Bourcet thought them valuable, but he was concerned with the special conditions of the mountains. Guibert thought them useless: an enterprising army would simply march past them and make for the capital; fortifications were only needed for the protection of arsenals. He criticised the engineers for failing to apply their special knowledge in a militarily useful way, as when they built fortifications so huge that there was no hope of sufficient troops ever being available to defend them. To all this the work of Montalembert afforded some answer. His 'perpendicular' system of fortification was a sort of outgrowth of the rise in quality and quantity of the artillery. Fortresses were not to be defended by earthworks but by fire-power, by large numbers of guns mounted in 'casemates'. These were vault-like buildings with very thick roofs and walls, the guns firing through openings at the sides. Fortresses were thus to become less like castles and more like modern pillboxes. These ideas were received sceptically as yet, especially because the smoke and fumes of gunpowder tended to make the casemates uninhabitable.[1] But it is interesting to see the first glimmerings of modern ideas of defence appear at the same time as modern doctrines of attack.

[1] M. Reinhard, *Le Grand Carnot* (1950), vol. I, chap. VIII; M. R. Montalembert, *L'Art Défensif supérieur à L'Offensif...ou La Fortification Perpendiculaire* (1793).

That a new method of provisioning the army would be needed has already been indicated. Bourcet was anxious not only that the carriage of supplies should not impede movement but that the preparation of magazines in advance of the troops should not give away the direction of the march. His remedy was the establishment of magazines along all possible lines of march. In 1760 he had proposed the setting up of depots at specific points on the circumference of the German theatre of war to allow Broglie's army to execute a turning movement by moving from one supply line to another. But the multiplication of depots involved great expense and effort. Guibert recognised the value of well-placed magazines on the lines that Bourcet suggested, but he was more anxious that the army should be able to live off the country for fairly long intervals while executing forced marches out of range of them. He especially complained of the influence of contractors on strategy. Their interest was simply to maximise their profit and they therefore desired that the army should march at the times and by the routes which would allow provisions to be bought and disposed of on the best terms. If a plan of campaign was proposed that conflicted with their interests, they declared that the difficulties of supply were insuperable and the generals, ignorant of supply problems, acquiesced. Guibert wished to entrust the supply of provisions to a *régie*.

If an army was to operate mainly in separate detachments, much closer co-operation between the different arms of the service would be required. Many subordinate commanders, instead of just one or two at the top, would find troops of all arms under their command and would need to know the proper use and problems of each. Guibert in consequence proposed that the drill of the cavalry should be as far as possible identical with that of the infantry, so that it would be easier for an officer of either arm to command the other. Gribeauval made the study of infantry tactics an integral part of the training of artillery officers. The amount and complexity of staff work would be much greater. The command of an army scattered in detachments involved a great multiplication of written orders and reports. The movements of the detachments had to be planned in some detail, to ensure that they all moved quickly in the right direction and were always so placed that they could be rapidly concentrated. Extensive reconnaissance of the terrain was required. A basis for all this had to be laid in peacetime by the preparation of accurate maps and by travelling in territories likely to be fought over. The making of maps had been attracting attention since the beginning of the century but it was now that accurate and thorough surveying really began.

Stimulated by these needs, the armies of Europe took the first steps towards the creation of the modern General Staff. Usually the initial move was the establishment of a cartographical section in the Quartermaster General's department. This department was concerned with the supply and so with the movement of troops. The cartographers were well placed to give advice both on this and on the choice of positions. They thus developed into planners of military operations. In map-making the Austrian army took the lead. Under Joseph II they produced a survey of the whole Habsburg empire in 5400 sheets. In Britain the national survey was entrusted to the Ordnance (1784) which alone had the necessary technical resources. This was one reason for British backwardness in staff organisation for many years thereafter. The first great survey of France (begun in 1744) was done by civilians, but it was the French who advanced furthest in the direction of staff planning. Their great desire, after 1763, was for a workable plan for the invasion of Britain. The work done on this under Bourcet's direction resulted in the only eighteenth-century military scheme at all resembling the time-table planning made necessary and possible by the invention of railways. The organisation established by Bourcet in 1766 was officially in abeyance in the years 1771–83 and again abolished in 1790; but continuity seems in fact to have been maintained. Prussian staff organisation was almost non-existent under Frederick the Great. Only under his successor was a formal structure given to the Quartermaster General's department. In 1796 it was entrusted with the work of surveying. It was only after 1800 that Prussian staff organisation drew ahead of French. For this, Napoleon's phenomenal capacity to do much of his own staff work seems to have been largely responsible.

Not much had been achieved anywhere by 1793. Staff officers were few and their special knowledge was not always well applied. Mainly topographical, it led them to think that positions were more important than combinations of force and made them, as often as not, the opponents of the new strategy to which they were so necessary. In strategy as elsewhere, specialism was as big a hindrance as simple conservatism. It is no accident that two brilliant and important pioneers in the field of staff organisation—Mack in Austria and Massenbach in Prussia—should have been among the most catastrophically unsuccessful generals in the ensuing great wars.[1]

Strong as were the technical obstacles to reform, they were slight when compared with the obstacles that were wholly political. The real basis and justification of the old style of warfare was the belief that officers and men alike were lazy and stupid and that the lower ranks would run away whenever they dared. The new methods called for intelligence and initiative in all ranks—even the simplification of the drill seems to stem from a confidence that men were sensible enough not to need to learn every single

[1] J. Colin, *L'Éducation Militaire de Napoléon* (1901); D. D. Irvine, 'The Origin of Capital Staffs', *Journal of Modern History*, vol. x (1938), pp. 161–79; J. Paldus, 'Die militärischen Aufnahmen im Bereiche der Habsburgischen Länder aus der Zeit Kaiser Josephs II', *K. Akademie der Wissenschaft in Wien, Philosoph. hist. Klasse, Denkschriften*, Bd. 63, II (1919).

step of a movement by rote. A strong devotion to duty was also required: an army scattered in detachments and living frugally and uncomfortably on whatever local produce it might find could not be kept together by anything else.

The regeneration of the army was believed by intelligent soldiers to depend on the regeneration of the state. Guibert attributed the military weakness of the European governments to their oppressiveness, which made them unable to excite loyalty and unwilling to excite martial ardour for fear that a warlike people would also be rebellious. His first demand was for government in the interests of the people, even for parliamentary institutions. Patriotism would then revive, the people would willingly take up arms in defence of their country and the army would henceforth contain an abundance of able and respectable citizens.

Several factors led the military thinkers to sympathise in an astonishing way with the reformist and even the anti-authoritarian ideas that were spreading among civilians. Many belonged to the world of the *philosophes*. Guibert was a friend of Mlle de Lespinasse and the publication of his *Essai* made him a figure of some importance in the salons. In Germany, intellectual soldiers contributed to literary journals and even held university posts. War and the progress of ideas were closely linked for officers of the technical arms like Carnot, an engineer, who was a member of the academy of Arras and won a prize from that of Dijon. They were necessarily interested in the scientific investigations of their day—at a time when scientists usually concerned themselves with social problems as well—and as they had few or no men under their command they were readily drawn into Utopian ideas on the subject of discipline.[1] The admiration of ancient Greece and Rome characteristic of the age led to a widespread belief that a republic defended by its citizens in arms was the military ideal, to be approached as far as circumstances would permit. The American War of Independence seemed to confirm this view. 'It takes citizens', declared Lafayette, 'to support hunger, nakedness, toil, and the total want of pay, which constitute the condition of our soldiers, the hardiest and most patient that are to be found in the world.'[2] The soldiers were right in thinking that there were unique military possibilities in political and social advance. Unfortunately these possibilities tended to appear in forms not according easily with the soldiers' plans and disfigured by military errors. In particular, military thinking in parliamentary countries was vitiated by imperishable and not always unjustified fears that the army coveted political power. Until the means of utilising it had been found, the progress of a state could not regenerate its army.

For improving the quality of the officers, continental military opinion long favoured methods inspired very largely by narrow class-interests.

---

[1] Reinhard, *Le Grand Carnot*, pp. 205–6.
[2] Quoted in E. Robson, *The American Revolution* (1955), p. 166.

The lesser nobility, finding it increasingly hard to live off their estates, were turning increasingly to the army as an alternative means of support. They provided the bulk of the commissioned officers in most armies, including many of the ablest. Their position was not, however, a happy one. Usually the higher and more lucrative posts were monopolised by the wealthy court nobility. Sometimes wealthy *bourgeois* also forced their way into the charmed circle. In France there were even cases of colonels heavily in debt turning poor noblemen out of their regiments in order to sell their commissions to wealthy plebeians. Continental states usually had rules reserving most military commissions for members of the nobility. The law, however, was extensively evaded.

The lesser nobility fought hard to preserve their declining stake in the army. With growing bitterness they asserted that military virtue was a characteristic of their own class and that the *bourgeoisie* could never provide good officers because they had no sense of honour. The marquis de Crénoiles wrote in 1764 that officers should come from 'the purest part of the nation', which he explained by saying that they should be such that 'If one of them had not been born with honour in his blood, the fear of losing caste, the shame which would result for his family, would act as a check on him and to some extent replace what he may lack in courage. Certainly it is only the nobility who are like that.'[1] They urged also that industry and frugality were needed in a good officer and on these grounds they could oppose the giving of the best jobs to idle courtiers. It was here that their cause was linked with that of military reform. Army officers had hitherto regarded themselves less as a profession than as government servants assigned to particular duties but available for others of different kinds. Military reformers were now in effect demanding high professional qualifications and this was a good battle-cry for poor noble officers seeking to preserve their interests and the social standing of their class.

It was the Prussian army which first showed what military reform could do for the lesser nobility. The kings took a keen personal interest in their forces and they deliberately ordained that military officers should be regarded as the first class in the state and have precedence over civil officials. The lesser nobility were the dominant element among those officers. After the Seven Years War, most of the *bourgeois* who had perforce been admitted as a result of wartime expansion were turned out again; more important and unusual, promotion was not reserved for courtiers and princes—there was equality among the nobility and the poorest could rise to the top. The army afforded a very ample provision for the nobility—it had a much greater number of officers in proportion to the number of men than the Austrian army and this was a reason for its success. In return, the officers were obliged to give of their best. Dis-

[1] E. G. Léonard, *L'Armée et ses Problèmes au XVIIIe siècle* (1958), p. 175.

cipline was as severe for them as for the men—another unique feature which probably explains why the discipline of the Prussian army was considered unusually harsh.[1]

What was a reality in Prussia appears elsewhere as a set of principles for general application. The chevalier d'Arc, a bastard grandson of Louis XIV, wrote *La Noblesse Militaire* (1756) to refute the view that the nobility should abandon their prejudice against earning a living by trade. Thinking that poor noblemen made the best officers, he was actually opposed to their ceasing to be poor. Luxury would corrupt them and make them unfit for service. Commercial expansion might therefore be a bad thing for the state. If it raised the price of necessities too much, everyone would be forced to go into trade and try to get rich; the same thing would happen if luxury increased so much that everyone who was not rich was despised.

D'Arc wanted a campaign against luxury, led by the king himself. The people were to be taught to despise it; the nobility to renounce it and live an austere life of devotion to the public service, retaining thereby the supremacy in the nation which must otherwise go to the plutocrats. However, 'it is important for the state that a noble family' should have 'an assured income, so as to augment the defenders of the nation by its own increase'.[2] The army was therefore to provide sustenance for the whole nobility. Noblemen not required as officers would be accommodated as ordinary soldiers in special cadet companies. The army was to be the visible embodiment of the nobility as a superior caste. Significantly, d'Arc wished officers always to appear at court in uniform, which was the reverse of established French practice. True he believed, logically enough, that military merit should be rewarded by ennoblement and that commissions should be given to deserving men from the ranks. But this would serve only to close the gap between the officers and their subordinates and associate the army with the privileges of its commanders. Well might Carnot speak in 1792 of 'cette dernière et terrible corporation qu'on nomme armée de ligne'.[3]

Such ideas were open to serious objections on military grounds. The opinion that an officer ought to be a 'gentleman' was defensible. It was reported in 1775 that the discipline of the new American army suffered from the fact that officers and men were social equals, 'for men cannot bear to be commanded by others that are their superiors in nothing but in having had the good fortune to get a superior commission, for which perhaps they stood equally fair'.[4] Officers, moreover, needed to be educated men. But outside eastern Europe these considerations did not point to a monopoly of commissions for persons of noble birth. The game was given

---

[1] Jany, *op. cit.* pp. 35–8; Mirabeau, *De la Monarchie Prussienne* (1788), Book VII.
[2] Léonard, *op. cit.* p. 184. [3] Reinhard, *op. cit.* p. 230.
[4] *Historical MSS. Comm., MSS. of Mrs Stopford-Sackville*, vol. II, p. 17.

away by the fact that non-nobles were not normally excluded from the artillery, engineers or light troops. When exceptional resourcefulness or a high level of education were needed, the nobles could not be relied on. They were indeed—especially the poorer ones—not at all well educated. Hence the attempts to create a system of cadet schools, reserved in the main for nobility. They were not very successful. Those established in France by Saint Germain failed because he could not get the award of commissions made conditional on the passing of an examination. The Prussian Académie des Nobles was too ambitious in its curriculum and better adapted for training diplomats than soldiers. Gribeauval's artillery schools did good work but attempts to train French nobles as engineers seem to have failed.[1] Another suspicious thing was the demand by the military reformers for promotion according to seniority—certainly no guarantee that efficient officers would be promoted. It must be said, however, that the officers of the new American army were as much sticklers for seniority as any European aristocrats and the Continental Congress had a hard fight to preserve the right to promote whom they pleased. Even in revolutionary France the Constituent Assembly accepted promotion by seniority within regiments, though higher up a mixture of seniority and royal favour was to apply.

It should have followed that states able to recruit their officers from a numerous educated *bourgeoisie* had a military advantage. But the political consequences of that class growing strong made the outcome rather different. Parliamentary assemblies, with their fears of military usurpation, were primarily concerned to ensure that the officers were always drawn from, and in sympathy with, whatever body of the citizens possessed political power. The resulting policies were no improvement on the reservation of commissions for the nobility and often made it hard to reward merit or attract it into the service. In Britain the purchase of commissions survived, to the detriment of able men without money, because it was believed to ensure that control of the army remained in the hands of the propertied classes. The American authorities, more drastically inclined, were reluctant to grant half-pay on retirement to the officers of the Continental army. Army pressure eventually forced them to promise it but few of the officers ever got any money. The Americans hated the thought of placemen living at public expense, even if they were disabled ex-service men. They wished to regard officers as simple citizens who would return to their jobs or their land at the war's end. There was no encouragement here for professional soldiers.

In the auxiliary forces these principles were more explicitly applied. From 1757 a scale of property qualifications existed for officers in the English militia and they were obliged to retire after five years' service if (an unlikely occurrence) properly qualified persons then offered to serve

[1] Reinhard, *op. cit.* p. 149.

in their stead. American militia officers were elected by their men, who were assumed to be ordinary citizens in arms: it followed that the officers would be the same. When constitutional government was established in France, the same principles were adopted there too. In the army, new officers, if they had not risen from the ranks, had to be either *citoyens actifs* or their sons—that is, they had to have a property qualification. The officers of the National Guard and of the regiments of volunteers raised from them for service at the front were elected by their men. Neither wealth nor popularity were good criteria in the choice of officers and service suffered accordingly.

France finally achieved a fairly sane policy, but only after experiencing the last agonies of the privileged classes, the effects of which on the army were very bad. Saint Germain, war minister in 1775–7, espoused the cause of the lesser nobles. He opposed the power of wealth in the army. A scheme was brought in for the gradual extinction of the purchase of commissions. They were to lose a quarter of their original value at each sale until they changed hands for nothing. The promotion of non-commissioned officers to commissioned rank on the recommendation of their fellows was introduced. These ideas were accepted by the Constituent Assembly and applied more thoroughly. Purchase was abolished outright with payment of compensation (1791) and a quarter of the vacancies in the lowest commissioned rank were reserved for men rising from below (1790). They were to be chosen half by seniority, half by vote of all the officers. At long last also, a pass examination was instituted for first commissions not given to rankers.

It was otherwise with the rest of Saint Germain's programme, carried through by the efforts of his friends after his retirement. In 1781 a royal *ordonnance* obliged most new officers to prove four generations of purely noble ancestry on the father's side. This order has been much misunderstood. It was not a novelty but a reinforcement of earlier measures of the same sort; it was itself amended by later and stricter orders. It did not make it impossible for *roturiers* to become officers: promotion from the ranks was still allowed, though admittedly it was made less easy. What was reserved to the nobles—and not in all cases—was the right to become officers without first passing through the ranks. This was again a blow against the power of wealth. Poor men would not mind a spell in the ranks; middle-class men would.[1]

If after 1781 the situation of the army officers rapidly became intolerable, it was not because of restrictions on entry but because of those on promotion. To gain support for their schemes the reformers had to do a deal with the court nobility. The higher ranks became more than ever the courtiers' preserve and in compensation it was necessary to confine

---

[1] G. Six, 'Fallait-il quatre quartiers de noblesse pour être officier à la fin de l'ancien régime?', *Revue d'Histoire Moderne*, vol. IV (1929), pp. 47–56.

roturiers and semi-nobles to the lowest.[1] Moreover the nobility were now seeking to invade the technical arms which, as explained above, had not hitherto been reserved for them. The army seethed with discontent. The lesser nobility hotly demanded equality—within their own order. The *bourgeois* officers gloomily watched the worsening of their own position. On the eve of the Revolution the bulk of the officers were little inclined to defend the old order and this was an important reason for its fall.

After 1789 retribution descended on the noble officers, rich and poor alike, for what were mainly the sins of the former. The Constituent Assembly abolished all their special privileges in the army and harried them with oaths of loyalty and finally with outright dismissals. Most of them remained in the army until the flight to Varennes but then there was a mass exodus. Of the 6633 noble officers serving in 1789 (and comprising two-thirds of the total number of officers) 5500 had emigrated by the end of 1794.[2] But then under the auspices of Condé a little band of these formed just such an army as d'Arc had envisaged, austere in its life and devoted to its cause. The nobility had not said its last word.

For filling the ranks of the armies, thoughtful soldiers were increasingly attracted by universal military training. This would give the army a better type of recruit: sturdy, honest peasants, full of patriotic loyalty. It would lessen the financial burden of armies which was generally thought to have risen so much that the European states were threatened with bankruptcy and the collapse of their governments. A short spell in the army for everyone would create a massive reserve of trained manpower, immediately available in an emergency but costing the state almost nothing at other times.

The system of 'conscription limited to the criminal and pauper classes'[3] which existed in most countries could not supply men of the quality required and the numbers it yielded tended to diminish. It was too unpopular. Its administration was often arbitrary and unjust. Men of democratic sympathies like Rousseau condemned it as an intolerable burden on the poor. The economists and their political disciples objected to the diminution of the number of productive workers. Unfortunately conscription could not be made more popular by making it universal. Its extension to the middle class and skilled artisans intensified the economic objection. It was held also that universal service would discriminate unfairly against certain regions. Some areas were short of manpower, while others had persistent under-employment; the latter were the natural source of recruits.[4] In England and France the mass of the people showed their

[1] See *ante*, vol. VII, pp. 181–2.
[2] L. Hartmann, *Les Officiers de l'Armée Royale et la Révolution* (1910).
[3] C. M. Clode, *The Military Forces of the Crown* (1869), vol. II, p. 10.
[4] C. Poisson, *L'Armée et La Garde Nationale, 1789–92* (1858), pp. 186–93; A. Depréaux, 'Les Régiments provinciaux et l'ordonnance du 19 Octobre 1773', *Revue d'Histoire Moderne*, vol. XIII (1938), pp. 267–86.

hostility to compulsory levies by numerous riots. To the illiterate and immobile country folk of those days, it was a terrible thing to be taken from the settled community which was their whole world. For military doctors nostalgia was a recognised disease and there were little epidemics of it when men seem actually to have died of homesickness, or at least to have become excessively prone to die of other diseases because of it. There were good reasons why soldiers should be recruited among the vagabonds.[1]

After 1763 the trend was consequently away from, not towards, conscription. The French militia ceased to be used as an instrument for pressing men for the army and was moribund for many years before its abolition in 1790. Pressing for the army ceased in Britain after the American War. In Prussia the regimental authorities had naturally been very exacting in their levies of men during the Seven Years War. A more effective system of supervision was established to prevent abuses and the intake of men declined. The law of 1792 (which remained in force till 1813) reiterated the principle of universal service but retained the massive schedule of exemptions.[2]

Far from aiming at 'citizen armies' most governments were reluctant even to eliminate foreign mercenaries from their service. It seemed so reasonable that barren countries with surplus manpower—Switzerland and Hesse for instance—should supply the defenders of prosperous states short of labour. Saint Germain was able to initiate a 'nationalising' policy in Denmark, where he was war minister before holding that position in France. He sought to replace the many German troops by native conscripts. Danish replaced German as the army's language of command in 1773. But the exclusion of foreigners was only complete in 1804. The French Constituent Assembly sanctioned an establishment of 26,000 foreign troops. After Varennes all but the Swiss were deprived of their quasi-autonomous organisation. In 1792 the Swiss Guards fought for Louis XVI against his subjects, who were then obliged to send the remaining Swiss troops home. Prussia continued to aim at an army about one-third foreign until obliged by the treaty of Lunéville (1801) to desist from foreign recruiting. In both France and Prussia, however, foreign regiments seem to have fraudulently enlisted large numbers of natives to avoid the expense of transporting real foreigners from their distant homes.

Conscription might have had little future had not the politicians of the constitutional states been attracted by its cheapness and the hope that a conscript force—'the people in arms'—would show more loyalty to the constitution than could be expected of professional soldiers. They tried

---

[1] M. Reinhard, 'Nostalgie et service militaire pendant la révolution', *Annales Historiques de la Révolution Française*, vol. XXX (1958), pp. 1–15.
[2] J. Gebelin, *Histoire des Milices Provinciales* (1882); W. O. Shanahan, *Prussian Military Reform, 1786–1813* (1945).

to create by compulsion forces more congenial for civilians to enter than the regular army. By slow degrees these were made to satisfy military requirements. Each of the United States had a militia for local defence. Service in them was compulsory for all male citizens, but they were embodied for training only for a few days each year and seldom expected or willing to serve far from home. They could, however, do valuable service against an invading army provided that they were acting in conjunction with regular formations which could prevent the attacker from concentrating his main force against them. They could then prevent his occupying effectively the country through which he passed, deny him all local supplies and repeatedly interrupt his communications. In this way they contributed notably to, for instance, the surrender of Burgoyne at Saratoga. But they were no substitute for a standing army.

More able to be this was the English militia after the reform of 1757. Its purpose was essentially to take over the defence of Britain in wartime, freeing the army for offensive action abroad. It was embodied for the duration of each war and obliged to serve anywhere in Britain. In peacetime it met only for occasional training: from 1786, two-thirds were assembled for a month each year. In theory all fit men had to serve: a contingent was chosen by lot to serve for a term of years and was successively replaced by other contingents until all had passed through. In practice almost everyone served by substitute. Yet a good many countrymen who would not have volunteered for the army willingly entered the militia because they were not then liable to be sent abroad and served with their neighbours under the protection of the local gentry. The militia rather disappointed its political friends, who had intended it to be embodied for shorter spells and to be more like its American counterpart. But although it seemed to them very like the regular army, its spirit was not quite the same and it did provide a net addition to the country's military manpower.

In France the Constituent Assembly replaced the militia by an Army of Reserve which was recruited by voluntary enlistment and intended to contain much the same sort of men as entered the army. It was not meant to be a levy on each district in proportion to its population: the poorer districts which sent their surplus manpower into the army were expected to contribute more than their share.[1] The men received a little training in peacetime and in wartime were to be incorporated in the army. Meanwhile the National Guard had been formed, mainly for police purposes, by voluntary action among the revolutionaries throughout the country. The Constituent Assembly made membership of it compulsory for all citoyens actifs and it was then much like the American militia. When the flight to Varennes led the Assembly to fear attack both from foreign foes

[1] C. L. Chassin and L. Hennet, Les Volontaires Nationaux pendant la Révolution (1899–1906), vol. I, pp. 4–8.

and its own regular army, it was naturally to the National Guard that they turned. The whole force was alerted for a short time and a standing force of 97,000 men was raised from it by calling for a quota of volunteers from each unit. Subsequently it was decided, to the great detriment of their efficiency, that these men were to be given an opportunity each December to resign from the service. When war broke out in the spring of 1792 another 74,000 volunteers were called for. The volunteers seem mostly to have been not actual members of the (middle-class) National Guard but substitutes hired by them; however, they did include many respectable *bourgeois* entering from patriotic motives and destined to provide many distinguished officers. Like the English militia, this system was an indirect approach to conscription and brought in a number of men who would never have joined the ordinary army. In July 1792 the Legislative Assembly ventured a step nearer to compulsion by ordering the National Guards in each canton to choose some of their number to complete the quotas that had previously been asked for.

Semi-conscript armies of reserve thus began to emerge in England and France but as yet they were small and their discipline was inferior. This inefficiency was not inevitable. Warfare was still a simple business and soldiers could be quickly taught the rudiments. Napoleon's conscripts seem to have been trained, like the original volunteers, on the march to the frontier.[1] If the English militia drilled only a month a year in peacetime, the Prussian conscripts drilled only two. But good results were entirely conditional on a far closer connection with the regular army than was acceptable to civilian opinion. A cadre of experienced officers and N.C.O.'s was essential. They could produce remarkable results with raw men in a very short time;[2] amateur officers could not. The English militia was well drilled because the adjutants and some of the sergeants were regular soldiers, but it was not well led. The French volunteers, though good material, were at first in great confusion. Progress was slow until dire military peril obliged the politicians to sanction amalgamation with the regular army. This took place in France in 1793. In England it came gradually and imperfectly through the service of more regular officers in the militia and the passing of trained militia-men into the regular regiments by voluntary transfer, which first occurred in 1799.[3]

Of course if the character of the regular army could be changed there might be less objection to incorporating conscripts in it and in addition a better type of man might be induced to enter the army voluntarily. Short-term enlistments were advocated for the latter purpose and with the hope of building up a large reserve without conscription. When war broke out in 1792 the French invited men to enlist for the duration *or* either two or four years. The American Continental army was at first

[1] G. Lefebvre, *Napoléon* (1935), p. 191.   [2] See Shanahan, *op. cit.*
[3] For France, see C. Rousset, *Les Volontaires, 1791–4* (2nd ed. 1870).

211   14-2

enlisted for one year only. Later, enlistment for three years or the duration was introduced in both the American and the British service. In each case there was a troublesome misunderstanding over whether the men were entitled to discharge on the expiry of whichever term was the shorter. This caused a mutiny among the Americans in 1781 and something near to it among the British in 1783. The experiment was not a success.

As for discipline, the whole new doctrine of war implied that the soldier was no longer to be driven but intelligently led. 'We do not reason enough with the soldier' was Guibert's view. Even Saldern, the great exponent of Prussian orthodoxy, came to think that 'severity towards recruits is inappropriate and inhumane....One must never cease to think of a soldier as a man; most can be got to do everything by good treatment and a soldier will do more for an officer who treats him well and whom he trusts than for one who terrorises him.'[1] He and others stressed the need for officers to have a close personal knowledge of the men under their command. Training was better planned and the recruit was to be taught the meaning of what he did. The Prussian drill-books of Frederick's day were a confused compilation of heterogeneous rules. The French drill-book of 1791 was a well-designed course of instruction, divided into lessons.

Brutal punishments were tending to diminish. The Anglo-Saxons, it is true, stuck to the lash. The Americans who had taunted the British troops with cries of 'bloody back' soon saw flogging introduced into their own army: Congress limited the number of strokes that could be inflicted but ways were found of making that limited number more painful.[2] In Prussia, on the other hand, flogging declined somewhat after 1787. In France Saint Germain replaced the lash by the flat of the sword but this reform was ill-judged because the new instrument was looked on as even more degrading than the old. The Constituent Assembly abolished corporal punishment and greatly liberalised the whole system of military justice. Courts martial were henceforth to have juries on which all ranks were represented.

There were various attempts to make the soldiers' living-conditions less demoralising. It was thought desirable that they should marry: family life was expected to encourage responsible behaviour. The Prussians encouraged their foreign recruits to marry native wives, finding that this discouraged desertion. There were many demands for simpler uniforms, more warm clothing, better food and healthier living-quarters. Two objectives striven for in France were pure bread and a maximum of two to a bed in barracks. There were even increases in pay, despite the financial obstacles so generally felt. That of the French soldier was virtually doubled

---

[1] Pp. 3–4 of the French translation of his manual, *Élemens de la Tactique de l'Infanterie* (1783).

[2] B. Knollenberg, *Washington and the Revolution, a Reappraisal* (1941), pp. 216–19, cited in Robson, *The American Revolution* (1955), p. 158.

in 1790. In Britain the pay of the soldiers was entirely consumed by stoppages for food and clothing and was not really sufficient to supply these. A tiny increase in 1792 left them with a cash surplus, after stoppages, of 18s. 10½d. a year.[1] The American Continental army was very well paid—according to its congressional employers—at 6⅔ dollars a man a month. But the men thought it insufficient and its real value fell as the currency rapidly depreciated.

In France and Britain some provision had long existed for pensioning old soldiers. In Prussia, on the other hand, pensions both for officers and men were a matter of favour and a rarity. Financial stringency hindered improvement, with the sad result that unfit men could not afford to retire. Everywhere the system of subjecting pay to stoppages to pay for various of the soldiers' requirements was conducive to fraud. In Britain the system of accounting was improved after 1780 and in France (where something had already been done by Choiseul) the auditing of the accounts for six years past was entrusted by the Constituent Assembly to a committee in each regiment representative of all ranks. The soldiers thus stood more chance of getting their financial due and this meant more likelihood of loyalty and good discipline.[2]

Such reforms made the army a shade fitter for the respectable citizen to enter. They did not abate the political hostility to it. Parliamentary politicians often sympathised with humanising measures: they sometimes thought that if the troops were less brutalised they would be less servile and more likely to refuse to be the instrument of tyranny. But the danger was that relations between officers and men would become too good for the health of the state. A patriot army, tried in the adversities of the new and more drastic school of war—as the Americans were by the terrible winter at Valley Forge—might well emerge with a strong feeling of solidarity and a belief that they had earned the right to political influence. Revolutionary politicians were rightly afraid of the power which might accrue to a victorious general. Expedients were devised to minimise the danger. The constitution of the United States made the president commander-in-chief of the armed forces. The Constituent Assembly gave the legislature a veto on the declaration of war and renounced wars of conquest for ever in the name of the nation. This was not the idealistic effusion it has commonly been thought. Rather did it provide a legal basis of action against a military clique starting a war of conquest for its own political aggrandisement. In the ensuing Legislative Assembly the Left sought vainly to devise means of distinguishing 'rational' from 'passive' obedience, so that soldiers would only obey orders that were legal. Unfortunately there arose from all this a standing temptation to sow

---

[1] J. Fortescue, *History of the British Army*, vol. III (1902), p. 522.
[2] See Shanahan, *Prussian Military Reform*; L. Mention, *L'Armée de l'Ancien Régime* (1900).

discord between officers and men. The French assemblies nullified much of their good work for the army by taking up the cause of mutinous troops against their superiors, to the serious prejudice of good order.

How far had the different powers advanced in military reform by 1793? It will have been seen that France was the country which made most progress. For some time she had lagged behind the German states. Now she caught up and passed them. Social factors had much to do with this. Prussia was weak in the technical arms, at a time when these not only made important progress but provided more than their share of thinkers and leaders for the service at large. This was because the middle class from which the technicians came was less respected in Germany than in France. Technicians were despised in the Prussian army, which consequently failed to attract able men.[1] The ideal of a citizen army likewise was more easily applicable in France than in Germany. But too much should not be made of this: it was the French equivalent of the *Junkers* who provided much of the impulse behind reform, while the *Junkers* themselves proved able to assimilate new ideas later on. The progress of Austria in several fields has been noted. She did not have the social advantages of France but her army was fostered by an able prince, Joseph II. Under the Archduke Charles' care it was destined for a time to draw ahead of Prussia and stand up manfully to the regenerate French.

It was because France had earlier suffered defeat that she was goaded into an effort that now gave her the lead. It was not that reforming activity was lacking in Germany. A surprising number of periodicals devoted to military matters was published in various German cities. In Prussia victory had not brought complacency and existing institutions were criticised with the greatest freedom. The trouble was that all this activity was devoted to refining existing ideas or to the elaboration of extravagant novelties. French defeat had been salutary not least for the French reformers: their pet theories had suffered the challenge of the rival and victorious Prussian system. They had had to discard their prejudices and learn from their enemies. It was on a fruitful synthesis of French and Prussian thought that future French triumphs were to rest. Prussian victory gave full rein to the German craving for the abstract: her academic warriors rode their hobby-horses undisturbed. The brilliant specialist without a sense of military relevance was everywhere in evidence. Professor Meinart published a work on the *Study of Military Mathematical Sciences in the Universities* (1788) and Lindenau complained (1790) that the tactics of Frederick the Great were not based 'on the exact rules of geometry'.[2]

But for the moment France's technical superiority was nullified by political embarrassment. The important reforms of Choiseul were en-

---

[1] Mirabeau, *De la Monarchie Prussienne* (1788), book VII.
[2] Shanahan, *op. cit.* ch. III; Goltz, *Von Rossbach bis Jena*, pp. 253–5, 286–90.

dangered when he fell (1770); the great work of Saint Germain, a ministerial colleague of Turgot, was halted by their dismissal. In 1788-9 a military council controlled by Guibert and other reformers initiated important changes and the work of improvement was henceforth continuous. But the purging of officers and decay of discipline which resulted from the revolution seemed for a time to make the whole valueless. In the relative size of her forces France had long been falling behind, due to the political impossibility of all measures for enlarging them. The Constituent Assembly in 1791 sanctioned an army and reserves totalling about 250,000. Prussia, with a much smaller population, could now muster almost 200,000 men, Austria almost, and Russia more than, double this. France under Louis XIV had taken on almost all Europe. Now several individual powers could match her.

British and Russian progress in tactics was slowed by conflict between the 'native' tradition of irregular war and the ideas imported by the admirers of Prussia. British strength was kept down by political factors as in France, and by the needs of the navy. The peacetime establishment of army and militia was under 100,000 and could at most be doubled in war. The army was very unprofessional in spirit and was hard put to it to maintain, let alone increase, its standard of efficiency. By contrast the Russians started with the advantage of differing greatly from their neighbours in religion and customs. This meant that their wars commonly had something of a 'national' character and excited a measure of enthusiasm among the troops. This facilitated the development of a flexible system of tactics similar to that emerging in France. Soviet historians have claimed that in such matters as the development of the column the Russians were the true pioneers. This does not in fact seem to be the case; but Russia appears to have kept up with the west remarkably well.

What really held Russia back—and Britain no less—was the transport problem. Between the British and the various theatres in which they fought was the sea. The Russians were similarly isolated by huge expanses of territory in which roads and local supplies were scarce. In each case the whole new scheme of highly mobile armies living off requisitioned local supplies was hard to apply except on a small scale. British strength at sea should in their case have provided compensation. But the army's shipping needs were constantly increasing: as much was required at the start of the American as at the height of the Seven Years War. Furthermore, the administrative machine was not equal to the speedy assembling of ships, escorts, men and supplies—mainly because the work was shared among a number of independent ministers and high officials, often on bad terms with each other and without a superior to direct them. An expedition planned in October 1775 and intended to sail before Christmas did not leave until early February 1776 and then met headwinds which delayed its arrival in the New World until May. Command of the sea should have given the British in America the advantage of interior lines but they could never move fast enough to make this a reality. Sir Charles Middleton (following the elder Pitt) urged the establishment of a permanent reserve of transports with bottoms coppered to make them swift.[1] His advice was not taken and the British army remained becalmed.

There was thus roughly a military equilibrium in Europe. It was upset when the progress of her revolution removed the obstacles to France's military advance. France had long been growing increasingly pacific. The views of moralists, who had long condemned most wars as a manifestation of princely egoism, had been powerfully reinforced by the teaching of the free-trade schools of economists. To them aggressive war, like tariffs, was a foolish attempt to increase the wealth of a nation at the expense of its neighbours and could only result in impoverishment all round. War was not only wrong but inexpedient. Not only the Constituent Assembly but the leading ministers of Louis XVI—Turgot, Necker, Vergennes—were deeply influenced by this view. A military reformer like Guibert did not think otherwise. His ideal state was to be peaceably disposed towards its neighbours. 'It will not be jealous of their wealth. It will not be so of their conquests. It will not disturb their possession of distant territories. It knows that too much territory means weakness; that distant colonies feeding the luxury trades nourish the vices of the home country....It will not attack their commerce....It knows that commodities call for exchange; that provided outlets are left open, they will circulate of their own accord without need of encouragement.'[2] Only a defensive war, he thought, could arouse the patriotic ardour so urgently required among the soldiers.

Now from 1792 France was engaged in just such a war—for the defence of the Revolution. If its fruits were not to perish, the army had to be given all the moral and material support it had so long craved. Perforce the revolutionaries became as bellicose as they had been pacific—indeed the more pacific they had been the more bellicose they became. Military historians sometimes play down the military importance of the Revolution, pointing out that the methods used in the ensuing wars were evolved —the commanders trained, even—under the old régime. But the *progrès des lumières* which produced the advance in military science also produced its antidote, a distaste for war and armies. Only the Revolution could resolve this dilemma and nothing less than the ideological heat which it aroused could have given the necessary driving force to the new system of war. Without this, it might have remained an intellectual exercise; the two in combination both transformed European society and frightened the remaining European states into an equal enthusiasm for military reform.

[1] E. Robson, 'The Expedition to the Southern Colonies, 1775–6', *English Historical Review*, vol. LXVI (1951), pp. 535–60; Navy Records Society: *Sandwich Papers*, vol. I, p. 97, and *Barham Papers*, vol. II, p. 45.   [2] *Œuvres Militaires* (1804), tome I, pp. 47–8.

Guibert had already imagined the course that events now took: 'Suppose that there arose in Europe a vigorous people with talents, resources and organisation; a people who joined to austere virtues and a national militia a fixed plan of aggrandisement never lost sight of; who, knowing how to make war cheaply and live on the spoils of victory, was not obliged to lay down its arms for reasons of finance. This people would subjugate its neighbours and overturn our feeble constitutions as the north wind bends the frail reeds.'[1] Yet perhaps his words on the general spirit of future wars were more prophetic still. His ideal state was to fight only when 'injured in its subjects, territory or prosperity'. But

When it does so, it will be with all its might and with the firm resolution not to lay down its arms until it has received reparation proportionate to the offence. Its method of war will not be that of the states of today. It will not wish to conquer for the sake of conquest. It will send out expeditions rather than garrisons. Terrible in its anger, it will carry fire and sword to the enemy's land. It will terrify by its vengeance all peoples who might be tempted to disturb its repose. Let no one call barbarism or violation of the pretended laws of war these reprisals founded on the laws of nature. This contented and peaceful people has been visited with insult. It arises and leaves its hearths. It will perish to the last man if need be, but will win satisfaction, avenge itself, and by the magnitude of its revenge assure its future tranquillity. It is thus that a temperate jurisprudence, active in the prevention of crime, knows when the crime is committed how to become inexorable, pursue the criminal, chastise him with the rigour of the law and by making an example remove from the evilly inclined the temptation to become criminals.[2]

Absent since the wars of religion, passion returned to the battlefield—the passion for justice. The moral foundation of 'total war' was laid.

[1] *Ibid.* p. 16.   [2] *Ibid.* pp. 51–2.

CHAPTER VIII

EUROPEAN RELATIONS WITH ASIA AND AFRICA

I. RELATIONS WITH ASIA

THREE main developments may be seen in Europe's relations with Asia during this period—the rise of the English East India Company as one of the strongest governments in India, the expansion of English trade further east, and the widening and deepening of European knowledge of Asia. In the struggle for power that followed the disintegration of the Mughal empire the English company emerged as the ruler of the rich and fertile provinces of Bengal and Bihar and succeeded not only in excluding the French from effective participation in Indian politics but also in meeting the challenge of its chief rivals, the Marathas and Mysore. The company was now an Indian power, ruling those provinces on behalf of the Mughal emperor and reforming the administrative system that it found there. If its reforms had the effect of excluding Indians from high office, they also gave rise to a class of Indian landholders endowed with property rights and loyal to its rule. Indian investors were among the purchasers of its bonds to finance its campaigns against Tipu Sultan of Mysore. Indian goods were exported not only to Europe but also in the expansion of British trade to the eastern seas, past Dutch opposition, and to China, thus helping to pay for its rapidly growing tea exports to Europe. Although it was disappointed in its expectations of the profits of empire in India and had to seek the home government's help and submit to a measure of control, the profits of its China trade came to overshadow its losses elsewhere and it was saved from extinction. The Dutch company, on the other hand, was weakened by the interruption of its European trade during the American war and by growing competition in Asia, and did not long survive the establishment of an unsympathetic government at home. Meanwhile, the European interest in Chinese civilisation which had been fostered by the Jesuit missionaries was taken up by the *philosophes*, and the rococo taste for the exotic and grotesque in Chinese art was supplemented by the fashion for Chinese landscape-gardening with its feeling for nature. India came to attract more attention, as the English company's concern for her administrative problems stimulated an interest in her civilisation, and some of the company's servants became distinguished Orientalists. Just as they were prepared as officials to govern India by Indian methods, so as scholars they could assert that Indian literature and philosophy were worthy of consideration on their own terms, which were not necessarily those of Europe.

When Clive secured from the Emperor Shah Alam, in 1765, the grant of the *diwani*, or civil administration, of Bengal, Bihar and Orissa,[1] in return for an annual payment of tribute, he thought that the company would find it advantageous to rule under Mughal authority. The emperor might lack power, but he could still command respect and confer respectability. His approval might well be of value both in India and in Europe, for it could help not only to secure the loyalty of the company's Indian subjects but also to ward off the jealousy of its European rivals. Even Parliament might feel reluctant to take over for the Crown territories that lay under the emperor's authority, however nominal. To collect the revenues of Bengal and administer justice, which comprised its duties as diwan, the company appointed an Indian deputy, Muhammad Reza Khan, whom the nawab also appointed as his deputy to administer the executive government, which included the administration of criminal justice. As the company's government in Bengal remarked with some satisfaction in 1767: 'we may in our present circumstances be regarded as the spring which, concealed under the Shadow of the Nabob's name, secretly gives motion to this vast Machine of Government'.[2] Clive himself forecast great profits from what seemed such an economical arrangement. He predicted a 'clear gain' of '£1,650,000 Sterling, which will defray all the Expense of the Investment, furnish the whole of the China Treasure, answer the demands of all your other Settlements in India, and leave a considerable Ballance in your Treasury besides'.[3] But the costs of administration proved greater and the revenue smaller than was expected, while in 1767 the ministry in England decided to exact an annual payment of £400,000 from the company. Speculators who had bought the company's shares in the expectation of a continued rise in value used their influence to keep up the rate of dividend in spite of a financial crisis in 1772. When the company was finally forced to appeal to the government for help, there was little doubt that some form of political control would follow.[4]

Although the company was in such difficulties, its servants seemed rich enough. The nabobs who returned with the spoils of the East were already disliked as upstarts. Now they were denounced as tyrants, and it was even said that their private trading activities had helped to promote famine

[1] Orissa signified merely the district of Midnapur.

[2] Despatch from Bengal, 24 January 1767, para. 4, N. K. Sinha (ed.), *Fort William–India House Correspondence*, vol. v (1949), p. 277.

[3] Clive to Court, 30 September 1765, para. 12, India Office Records, Letters from Bengal, vol. vii, pp. 29 ff.

[4] Part of the assistance given by the government was the passing of the Tea Act of 1773 allowing the company to sell tea direct to the American colonies without putting it up for public sale in England. This measure did much to alienate powerful colonial interests at a crucial stage of the constitutional conflict; see below, ch. xvi, p. 458.

in Bengal. Besides lending the company £1,400,000 to tide it over its immediate distresses, the government tried to remedy the abuses to which its attention was being loudly called both in pamphlets and in Parliament. But its remedies made no fundamental change in the company's administrative system, and produced conflict rather than reform. A governor-general and four councillors were appointed by name in the Regulating Act of 1773, but subsequent appointments were left to the company. Three of the councillors were sent out from England in the spirit of reformers, but the governor-general, Warren Hastings, was an old servant of the company, and had no power to override them. He was soon involved in conflict with them. A supreme court was established for the purpose of hearing complaints against the company's servants and British subjects generally. But the extent of its jurisdiction was not clearly defined, and it was soon involved in conflict with the company's Bengal government. The Madras and Bombay governments were forbidden to declare war or make treaties without the consent of the governor-general and council, but an exception was allowed for 'cases of imminent necessity', and this too left scope for controversy.

Meanwhile, the company itself had been modifying the 'dual system' established by Clive. The Court of Directors soon came to suspect that a substantial amount of revenue was being intercepted by an 'immense number of Idle Sycophants' before it could reach the public treasury.[1] Some of the company's European officials were sent into the districts as Supervisors, in 1769, to investigate. But in spite of the Bengal famine of 1770, which was thought to have carried off one-third of the inhabitants, the revenue for 1771 was, in the government's words, 'violently kept up to its Former Standard'.[2] However, the court had decided that the company must take more part in the administration, and in 1771 ordered the Bengal government to 'stand forth as dewan'. Muhammad Reza Khan was dismissed from his post as the company's deputy, and there followed a period of experiment and argument. The Supervisors were turned into Collectors, but the court did not trust them, and they were soon withdrawn. Provincial councils of revenue were established, but without success. The Collectors had in the end to be restored to their districts. The problem before the government was how to ascertain the capacity of the land, but serious social consequences followed its decision to replace the annual revenue settlements with the zamindars by five-yearly leases which were put up to public auction. In the speculative bidding which the auctions encouraged many of the old zamindars were either outbid or forced to bid too high in their anxiety to retain their lands. The new policy

<hr />

[1] Despatch to Bengal, 30 June 1769, para. 13, N. K. Sinha (ed.), *Fort William–India House Correspondence*, vol. V (1949), p. 212.

[2] Despatch from Bengal, 3 November 1772, para. 7, India Office Records, Letters from Bengal, vol. XI, p. 84.

thus produced both economic distress and social dislocation, and the rights of the zamindars provoked controversy for the next two decades. It was argued on the one side that they were merely revenue farmers and on the other that they were hereditary landlords. Underlying the arguments about revenue policy was the assumption that the company's task was to follow Mughal practice. In fact, the term 'zamindar' was applied to a variety of persons ranging from recently appointed revenue farmers to rajas of ancient family. But during the decline of Mughal authority there was a general tendency for office to become hereditary, and the Court of Directors had some historical justification for their decision to prohibit the holding of further auctions, after the expiry of the five-year leases, on the ground that they were prejudicial to hereditary rights.

The zamindars were also affected by the changes in the judicial system which followed the company's decision to stand forth as diwan. In the decline of Mughal authority many of them had become the virtual rulers of their districts, for the nawab's justice did not run far beyond the chief towns. Now regular civil and criminal courts were set up. Again, there was much experiment and alteration. At first the Collectors were given charge of the civil courts, then the provincial councils of revenue, and in 1781 separate judges were appointed. Again, the assumption was, as Warren Hastings told Lord Mansfield, that 'no essential change was made in the ancient constitution of the province. It was only brought back to its original principles.'[1] In accordance with the theory of the *diwani*, which included only civil justice, the criminal courts were left in the charge of Indian judges responsible to Muhammad Reza Khan, who still remained the nawab's deputy. Muslim law was administered in the criminal courts, and the personal law of the suitors, whether Hindu or Muslim, in the civil courts. How to ascertain that law was at first a problem. Collections and translations were made by scholars like Sir William Jones, and Hindu and Muslim legal advisers were appointed to the courts. This made the laws more rigid, even if their administration became less arbitrary. The zamindars themselves were made subject to the courts, and the new civil judges, acting as magistrates, were empowered to supervise their police administration. Local customs and immunities were already giving way to system and uniformity in the administration of justice.

However much the company professed its intention of restoring the true principles of Mughal administration, its connection with the emperor was sharply interrupted in 1771. Attempting a heroic recovery after their disaster at Panipat ten years before, the Marathas had sent a large force to northern India and persuaded the emperor to return to Delhi under their protection. Hastings stopped payment of the company's tribute and made light of the affair: the emperor's grant of the *diwani* was merely

[1] Hastings to Mansfield, 21 March 1774, G. R. Gleig, *Warren Hastings*, vol. I (1841), p. 401.

'a piece of paper', 'a very flimzy argument, not intrinsically worth three half pence': the company held its territories by 'the best of all Titles, power'.[1] The Marathas set more value on the emperor's prestige, but they were soon preoccupied with the struggle for power at Poona that followed the murder of the young Peshwa Narayan Rao in 1773.

The Bombay government was soon involved. In return for a promise of territory it rashly agreed to support the dead peshwa's uncle, Raghunath Rao, who claimed the succession but was suspected of complicity in the murder and was opposed by a council of regency under Nana Phadnis, who continued to administer the state on behalf of the peshwa's post-humous son, Sawai Madhav Rao. To support the claims of a rival to the throne was an established method of gaining influence, but the Bombay government overestimated both its own strength and Raghunath Rao's statesmanship. The result was a series of exhausting and fruitless campaigns, in which the Bengal government had to send help to Bombay. Haidar Ali, the vigorous soldier who had usurped power in Mysore, would have been a useful ally against the Marathas, but the Madras government provoked his hostility, and in 1780 he swept through the Carnatic to the walls of Madras.[2] This was at a time when England was at war with the French and the Dutch, and the French were offering help both to the Maratha government and to Haidar Ali. The company's position seemed grave. But besides sending Sir Eyre Coote to Madras, Hastings succeeded in establishing peace with the Marathas by striking at Mahadji Sindia, the most powerful and ambitious of the peshwa's overmighty subjects. After the fall of his fortress at Gwalior and his own defeat at Sipri, Sindia agreed to use his influence with the Poona government. By the Treaty of Salbai (1782) the company promised not to support Raghunath Rao and the peshwa promised not to ally with other European nations, while Sindia stood as guarantor for the proper observance of the treaty by both sides. This encouraged the disintegration of Maratha power. Sindia, who had been growing impatient of control from Poona, was now treated as an independent prince by the company, which established a resident at his court. When the Mughal emperor asked for help to suppress local disorder, Hastings declined to intervene, and Sindia was left free to devote his energies to establishing his influence at Delhi. Meanwhile, after Haidar's death, the company made peace with his son Tipu on the basis of a mutual restoration of conquests, and declined to join the Poona government in a fresh war against Mysore. But the growth of Sindia's power in the north had given rise to alarm and resentment at Poona, and Nana Phadnis was soon asking the company to appoint a resident

---

[1] Hastings to Sir G. Colebrooke, 23 February 1772, British Museum Add. MSS. 29127, 15b.

[2] Contrary to legend, he did not ravage the whole of the Carnatic, which he wanted to occupy himself. See C. C. Davies (ed.), *Private Correspondence of Lord Macartney* (Royal Historical Society, Camden third series, vol. LXXVII, 1950), p. ix.

at the peshwa's court as well. With the energies of its old enemies thus engaged, and with its residents in such strategic posts, the company was in a stronger position than ever before.

In England, however, the energetic policies of Warren Hastings had been watched with concern. He was represented as a warmonger impatient of restraint. Dundas likened him to 'an Alexander or an Aurungzebe'.[1] The Regulating Act had merely hampered the company's government but provided no means of controlling it. The ministry had the right to see despatches from India, and in 1781 it also gained the right to veto the replies from the Court of Directors. But to carry through a policy of its own it had to rely on informal methods of influencing the court, and this was not always effective. On two occasions, after the ministry had persuaded the Court of Directors to recall Warren Hastings, the Court of Proprietors—the general body of shareholders—reversed the Directors' decision. In 1784 Pitt's India Act therefore established a permanent Board of Control, with the right of approving or amending the despatches to India. But the company still retained some power and much influence. The Court of Directors remained the governing body. The despatches from India were still addressed to the court, and its replies were still composed at the East-India House and signed by the Directors. But once a despatch had been approved by the Board of Control, it could not be altered by the Court of Proprietors. The Court of Directors still had the right of nomination to the coveted writerships in the company's service. But in practice a share of this patronage was conceded to the President of the Board of Control. Governors-general and governors were still to be appointed by the Court of Directors, and were liable to recall by the Crown as well as by the court. But in practice the ministry chose, subject to the court's approval.

This was, in short, a system of checks, and it encouraged deliberation at the expense of speed. But the slowness of communication with India had already left a large measure of discretion to the company's governments there, and speed was therefore of less importance to the home government than it was to them. Warren Hastings, indeed, felt greatly hampered by the failure of the Regulating Act to enable him to override the obstacles to his authority. When the historian Ghulam Husain Khan, who wrote at this time, compared the company's administration with that of an Indian ruler, he thought that one of its main defects was the slowness of decision that resulted from the council system of government. But an act of 1781 set limits between the jurisdiction of the Supreme Court and the company's administration; in 1784 Pitt's India Act strengthened the authority of the Bengal government over the foreign relations of the subordinate presidencies; in 1784 also the governor-general's councillors

[1] Quoted in L. S. Sutherland, *The East India Company in Eighteenth Century Politics* (Oxford, 1952), p. 384.

were reduced in number from four to three, and two years later he was empowered to override them in exceptional circumstances. Parliament was thus quite willing to strengthen the company's Indian government once it had secured a firm voice in the company's home government. The impeachment of Warren Hastings may have been evidence of Parliament's intention to apply moral standards to Indian politics, but it arose out of a situation which was now ended. Philip Francis had been one of the councillors sent out under the Regulating Act, and as one of the chief organisers of the impeachment he was in effect trying to punish Hastings in England for what he had failed to prevent him from doing in India. There seems to be no positive evidence for the view that Dundas persuaded Pitt to support the impeachment because he was jealous of Hastings as a possible rival at the Board of Control. On the other hand, Hastings had allowed himself to be associated with interests that were opposing various Indian policies of the ministry.[1] But whatever the motives of those most responsible for the impeachment, the proceedings provided an outlet for the jealousies and suspicions that had been excited against the company since the days of Plassey, and an occasion for many eloquent speeches to the effect that the rights of the governed were worthy of great consideration. Meanwhile, Pitt's India Act had provided some security for the future. Henceforth, the company would be left to administer its territories in uneasy union with a Board of Control which could check any reckless impulse towards an empire which it could not support and any disposition towards corruption which it could not afford.

The loss of the American colonies and the dangers which had recently threatened the company in India seemed proof of the need for stability and caution. Besides the establishment of the Board of Control, some statutory restraints upon the company's policies were attempted. Its dividend had already been fixed by statute. Pitt's India Act warned it that 'to pursue Schemes of Conquest and Extension of Dominion in India' was 'repugnant to the Wish, the Honour, and Policy of this Nation', and prohibited aggressive policies.[2] Reports had reached England of the social consequences of the recent revenue policies in Bengal, and the company was directed by the same act to inquire into the grievances of the zamindars and establish 'permanent rules' for the payment of their rents.[3] Similarly, the Court of Directors concluded that the zamindars were 'discontented, many of them deprived of their Lands, overwhelmed by Debts, or reduced to beggary'. In general, the court condemned the Bengal government's 'disposition to experiment, without

---

[1] Dr S. Weitzman, *Warren Hastings and Philip Francis* (Manchester, 1929), pp. 186–7, questions the assumption that Pitt suddenly changed his mind, or that he had ever intended to support Hastings. Dr C. C. Davies, 'Warren Hastings and the Younger Pitt', *English Historical Review*, vol. LXX, pp. 609 ff., suggests that Pitt had for some time held an unfavourable opinion of Hastings, perhaps as a result of the propaganda of Burke and Francis.

[2] 24 Geo. III, c. 25, xxxiv.   [3] *Ibid.* xxxix.

urgent necessity or apparent cause'. The people might well think that there was 'no steadiness in our Government'.[1]

The appointment of Lord Cornwallis as governor-general in 1786 indicated that the reforms desired by the home authorities would be carried out and that steadiness was likely to be a characteristic feature of the reformed administration. In spite of Yorktown, Cornwallis had a reputation for competence as well as integrity. Unlike his predecessors, he was not a servant of the company and was therefore involved neither in its traditions nor in its corruptions. Clive had forced the company's servants to sign covenants that they would not accept presents, but they were still engaged in private trade, although Hastings had ended that exemption of their goods from duty which had given them such an advantage over other merchants and which had so annoyed Mir Kasim as nawab. What particularly vexed the Directors was that the company's exports from India seemed of inferior quality to the goods which its servants sent home on their own account or sold to foreign companies. What particularly troubled Cornwallis was the discovery that nearly all the Collectors were engaged in private trade to the detriment of their administrative duties. They could hardly have been prevented from supplementing their meagre wages in this way unless those wages were increased. Cornwallis persuaded the Directors to sanction substantial increases and strictly prohibited private trade. Those who managed the company's commercial business were formed into an entirely separate branch of the service, and private trade was permitted them because of the practical difficulty of preventing it. Even so, they were henceforth to provide the company's investment not by lucrative contracts but as agents required to supervise production and render accounts. But if Cornwallis effected the separation of the covenanted civil service from commerce he also began its separation from Indian society. His other reforms had the effect of restricting high office to the members of that service, who were all Europeans. Once Indians had been excluded from responsibility they were soon thought to be unworthy of it, and the highly paid civilian who now had no Indian colleagues soon came to have few Indian friends.

Recoiling from the complicated and costly experiments of the Hastings period, the Court of Directors had decided that it would 'tend more to Simplicity, Energy, Justice and Economy' if the Collectors were given the powers of civil justice and the magisterial functions which had then been entrusted to separate judges.[2] This change was welcomed by many of the company's servants as in closer accordance with Indian traditions. But the arrears of suits which soon accumulated led Cornwallis to the con-

---

[1] Despatch to Bengal, 12 April 1786, paras. 6, 23, India Office Records, Bengal Despatches, vol. xv, pp. 330 ff.

[2] Despatch to Bengal, 12 April 1786, para. 85, India Office Records, Bengal Despatches, vol. xv, pp. 373 f.

clusion that the Collectors lacked the time for judicial work; he also thought it dangerous to give them so much power. Only a system of checks could ensure an impartial administration of justice, especially in revenue cases. He therefore established a complete separation of powers between the executive in the person of the collector and the judicature in the person of a district judge who also acted as magistrate. Criminal justice had hitherto been administered by Indian judges responsible to Muhammad Reza Khan. Cornwallis thought that they would never consent to the changes that he proposed to make in the Muslim criminal law, and he replaced them by courts of circuit under English judges. The company was now openly encroaching upon the jurisdiction that Clive had left to the nawab. There was no question of introducing the English criminal law with its many capital offences. The execution of the Brahman Nanda Kumar for forgery, under sentence of the Supreme Court, had seemed a savage punishment in Indian eyes. But there were aspects of the Muslim criminal law that seemed equally unjust or inhuman to the English. Hastings had tried without success to persuade the Muslim judges to assess the degree of a murderer's guilt by considering his motives rather than the type of weapon he had used. The Court of Directors had cautiously suggested that the judges might be persuaded 'to refrain from ordering punishments of a cruel nature'—in other words mutilation.[1] Cornwallis also objected strongly to the practice of allowing the next of kin to pardon a murderer, on the ground that it enabled Brahmans to escape punishment by virtue of their caste, since no Hindu would be a party to the execution of a Brahman. In these and other respects the criminal law was amended in accordance with English ideas. Imprisonment took the place of mutilation; murderers were to be judged by their motives not their methods, and the victim's next of kin lost the right of pardon. In general, the judicial system became more rigid and detailed, but also more systematic and uniform. There were no distinctions of persons: Brahmans and non-Brahmans, Muslims and non-Muslims, zamindars and peasants, were equal before the courts. Cornwallis did not try to justify his reforms as a return to the best days of the Mughal government. On the contrary, he claimed that 'even during the vigour of the ancient Constitution' there was room for many abuses of power.[2] Nor did he propose the wholesale introduction of English institutions. When he could find a precedent for a reform in Muslim law, he appealed to it. What he intended was the correction of 'such parts of the Mahomedan Law, as are most evidently Contrary to natural Justice and the good of Society'.[3] This was no doubt partly a matter of expediency, of

---

[1] Despatch to Bengal, 12 April 1786, para. 88, India Office Records, Bengal Despatches, vol. xv, p. 375.
[2] Minute, n.d., India Office Records, Bengal Revenue Consultations, 3 December 1790, pp. 191 ff.   [3] *Ibid.*

attending to the state of public opinion. He himself may well have thought that natural justice was more manifest in the institutions of England than in those of other countries. But one result of his reforms, at least, was a system of punishments less cruel than those of either English or Muslim criminal law. Nevertheless, in its separation of powers, in its reliance upon the written law, and in its undiscriminating but cumbrous procedure, the judicial system established by Cornwallis was more akin to English than to Indian ideas.

He also valued it as a necessary background to his revenue policy. Pitt's India Act had called for 'permanent rules' to govern the amount of revenue payable by the zamindars. Cornwallis found them in 'a general state of poverty and depression', and decided that a fundamental change of system was essential. In 1793, he declared the government's revenue demand to be unalterable. He thought that the zamindars would improve their lands if they knew that an increase in productivity would not be followed by an increase in the revenue demand. The zamindars, however diverse in status, would henceforth be regarded as a homogeneous class, endowed with property rights in their land, which they could sell to anyone without the government's permission, and which the government itself could distrain and sell for non-payment of revenue. Whether the old zamindars survived seemed immaterial to Cornwallis: if they could not pay the revenue demanded, their lands would be sold to those who could. Possible buyers included those Indians, probably merchants, whom he knew to be investing in the company's bonds and who, he thought, would have no other outlet for their savings once the public debt was discharged. Improvidence and incompetence would thus give way to thrift and efficiency. The rights of landed property would be protected by the judges from unjust encroachments even at the hands of the Collectors. Prompted by self-interest, a regenerated landowning aristocracy would develop the resources of the country and prove a loyal support to the government. Less protection was, however, provided for the rights of the peasants. The zamindars were supposed to give them decennial rental certificates (*pattas*), as a defence against unjust demands. But the peasants proved reluctant to confine to a decennial certificate rights the validity of which they considered everlasting and lands the extent and capacity of which they preferred to leave indefinite. The zamindars were also empowered to distrain and sell their tenants' property for non-payment of rent. Cornwallis assumed that the zamindars would consider it to be in their own interests to have a prosperous and contented tenantry. But that was at a time when Bengal had not fully recovered from the effects of the famine of 1770, and tenants were none too easy to find. With the rise in population the zamindars had less reason for moderation. Besides, the strict enforcement of the sale laws tended to break the traditional bonds between zamindars and peasants by dispossessing some of the old zamindars and forcing others to be equally strict with their tenants. At the same time, the zamindars as a class were required to disband their own local police and were deprived of their responsibilities for the preservation of law and order. Their function in the districts was to be merely an economic one, and economic self-interest was to be the only link between them and their tenants. As productivity increased, the revenue paid by the zamindars came to form a decreasing proportion of the country's wealth. Cornwallis had foreseen this, and assumed that the state would be able to meet its needs from the increased yield of commercial tariffs, but this proved to be an optimistic assumption. However, the growing wealth of the zamindars encouraged subletting, and layers of absentee landlords had eventually to be supported by the peasantry of Bengal. Just as an impersonal relationship between the officials and the people was to facilitate the rule of law, so an impersonal relationship between the zamindars and their tenants was to facilitate the working of economic laws. The permanent settlement did in fact provide some stability in rural Bengal, in which the country's resources could be developed, but the social cost was high. It was not until the second half of the nineteenth century that tenancy legislation was instituted there.

After the adventurous and erratic policies that the company's governments of the Hastings period had pursued towards the other Indian powers with so much danger and such little apparent profit, the home government had called for an end to schemes of war and conquest. When the Emperor Shah Alam was deposed and blinded by the Rohilla chief Ghulam Qadir in 1788, during the temporary weakness of Sindia, Cornwallis declined to intervene. On the other hand, he considered that a further war with Mysore could hardly be avoided, and determined that the company must not again be isolated in such circumstances. When the nizam proposed a fresh agreement with the company he explained that he was prevented by Parliament from concluding a new treaty but promised the help of the company's troops when required, provided that they were not to be used against any of its allies. When specifying who those allies were, he pointedly excluded Tipu Sultan of Mysore. This has been criticised both as an evasion of the spirit of the act of 1784 and as a provocative gesture, although it may be doubted whether the warlike Tipu needed much provoking. The result of the ensuing war, in which the company was joined by the Marathas as well as the nizam, was that Tipu was deprived of half his territories, and Cornwallis could claim that 'we have effectually crippled our enemy without making our friends too formidable'.[1] Maratha power, indeed, seemed to be disintegrating from within. Sindia soon recovered his position at Delhi, restored Shah Alam in spite of his blindness and inflicted a grim revenge upon Ghulam Qadir. But as he

[1] Cornwallis to H. Dundas, 4 March 1792, C. Ross (ed.), *Correspondence of Charles, First Marquis Cornwallis*, vol. II (London, 1859), p. 154.

extended his power over northern India, Nana Phadnis at Poona became all the more suspicious of his ultimate aims, and encouraged the ambitions of his chief rival, Holkar, as a counterpoise. Nana's suspicions seemed justified when Sindia moved south to Poona in 1792 and proceeded to establish his influence over the Peshwa. Holkar duly challenged his influence in the north, but was defeated at Lakheri. However, Mahadji Sindia's triumph was only temporary, for he died in 1794, leaving a much less capable successor, and the main result of these struggles was merely to weaken the power of the Maratha confederacy and the authority of the Poona government. Meanwhile, the English company prospered.

The French company, on the other hand, did not long survive the Peace of Paris. France was then restored to the Indian possessions that she had held in 1749. But the English now had the mastery of Bengal, and Chandranagar could no longer be fortified. Even for the provision of its exports the company was dependent on English good will. But it lacked sufficient capital, and soon had to appeal to the government for help. The revelation of its financial position provoked such criticism that its privileges were suspended in 1769, and its territories were taken over by the Crown in 1770. But the government took little further interest in India, and when war broke out with England in 1778 the English found little difficulty in capturing the French possessions there. The arrival of a French fleet in Indian waters in 1782 and the landing of 3000 French troops in support of Haidar Ali caused consternation at Madras. The French troops failed to co-operate effectively with Haidar, but the French admiral de Suffren proved more than a match for the English admiral Hughes, and quickly took Negapatam and Trincomali, which the English had only recently taken from the Dutch. This put the English in a weak position, for they had no harbour on the Coromandel coast and had to go to Bombay both to refit and to shelter from the north-east monsoon between October and January. The French, on the other hand, were able to threaten the Bay of Bengal both from Trincomali, which had a good harbour that could be used all the year round, and also from Achin, in Sumatra, where Suffren decided to winter. But in the peace negotiations the English refused to countenance any revival of French political power in India. They agreed to restore the French possessions there but again refused to allow the fortification of Chandranagar. They would concede the French only a free, sure and independent commerce. But if the French could not revive the past they were determined not to surrender the future by allowing the English to hold Trincomali, which was therefore restored to the Dutch. The English had to be content with Negapatam, which, as Vergennes remarked, was 'bien plus innocent' in their hands than Trincomali.[1] In their subsequent relations with Indian powers the French

[1] Vergennes to Rayneval, 18 January 1783, quoted in V. T. Harlow, *The Founding of the Second British Empire*, vol. I (London, 1952), p. 392 n.

continued to hint at expeditions that would one day drive the English out of India. But when Tipu's ambassadors arrived in Paris in 1788 the government had nothing but compliments to offer them, and the ship in which they returned carried, unknown to them, the orders for the evacuation of French troops from India. The National Assembly decided in 1791 to send some troops to reinforce Pondicherry, but less than 400 in fact arrived, and on the outbreak of war in 1793 the English again had little difficulty in taking possession of the French settlements in India. The East India Company established by Calonne in 1785 made a promising start by concentrating on the India trade, but lost its monopoly in 1790 and was subsequently dissolved by the Convention. Only the French military adventurers survived to trouble the English. During this period many of them rendered good service to Indian powers, raising and training cavalry, infantry and artillery by European methods. Men like Madec under the emperor, Gentil under the nawab of Oudh, Raymond under the nizam and de Boigne under Sindia were only the most famous.[1] Soldiers like these remained, to be distrusted by the English as much for the strength which they imparted to potential enemies as for any loyalty that they might retain for France.

While political and administrative considerations were thus determining the course of English power in India, its expansion beyond was determined more by economic considerations.[2] Just as the *philosophes* welcomed France's expulsion from Canada as diverting the country's energies into more profitable channels, so the unrest in the American colonies seemed to many Englishmen to point to the advantages of an empire based on commerce rather than colonisation. Such considerations were more acceptable in English than in French governing circles. Even the younger Pitt declared that the main purpose of his India Act was to facilitate the progress of the company's commerce. From the 1760s onwards Alexander Dalrymple, that restive servant of the company, had taken the lead in campaigning for voyages of discovery in Asia as a preliminary to the expansion of England's trade. Such arguments were reinforced by the difficulties which the company experienced in paying for its growing exports of tea from China, especially when the supply of Spanish silver was interrupted by the outbreak of war with Spain in 1762, and it proved impossible to fill the gap from India.

The company had ceased to import silver into India after Plassey enabled it to pay for its exports with the public and private profits of empire, and the hoarding that accompanied political instability accentuated the shortage. Ghulam Husain Khan, among others, suspected that Bengal

[1] De Boigne was in fact a Savoyard. Even after he had left India the governor-general, Wellesley, mistakenly feared his influence as 'the chief confidant of Bonaparte'. See S. P. Sen, *The French in India, 1763–1816* (Calcutta, 1958), p. 542 n.

[2] This expansion increased the strategic importance of control of the Cape in the Anglo-French struggles, see below p. 238.

was being drained of its treasure by Englishmen returning home with their fortunes, and the idea that the Industrial Revolution had been financed by 'Plassey plunder' was later developed by nationalist writers.[1] In fact, the returning nabobs found it simpler and more profitable to remit their fortunes by buying bills of exchange from the European companies, which used the money in the purchase of goods to export from India. During this period, the chief exports to Europe remained cotton piece-goods, silk, saltpetre and pepper. But towards the end of it the European market was being invaded by English machine-made cottons, and the English company tried without much success to encourage other exports. Indigo, however, was successfully developed by private enterprise into a profitable export. The company realised that economic problems might be created by the export of goods without an equivalent in imports. In 1785 the Court of Directors wrote to Bengal: 'We conceive that there is a danger, lest by bringing to Europe too large an amount of the Revenues of those Countries in Goods for which no return is made, we should occasion a drain which our Territories may be unable to support.' But they decided none the less to increase their 'investment', or purchase of goods for Europe, consoling themselves with the thought that the Indian artisans who produced those goods would have been injured if the company bought less than usual. This idea subsequently re-emerged in the writings of those who defended British rule against nationalist criticisms. In general, whenever silver could be exported from Bengal, it was sent either to the other presidency governments in India or to China. The Court of Directors still hoped that some means could 'be found of supplying our China purchases from Bengal, without draining that Country of its circulating Specie, which should on no consideration be admitted of'.[2] This problem was intensified by the stimulus which Pitt's Commutation Act of 1784 gave to the company's tea trade.

There was still a European market for Chinese silk, porcelain and exotic luxuries, but tea was the most important commodity during this period. England was the chief consumer, although the costs of war forced up the tea duties to a height that made smuggling very profitable. When the Commutation Act reduced the duties from 119 to $12\frac{1}{2}$ per cent, the dominance of the English company over the trade was assured. The trade of the Danish and Swedish companies quickly declined, and the less reputable upstart companies suffered even more. The Dutch company, however, which had developed its own European markets, had never been so dependent on smugglers for its customers. Its extensive trade within Asia also enabled it to import large quantities of pepper, sandalwood,

[1] And by writers in sympathy with them, like Brooks Adams (*Law of Civilization and Decay*, 1895) and William Digby ('*Prosperous' British India*, 1901). Brooks Adams' statement was accepted without question by Pandit Jawaharlal Nehru (*Discovery of India*, 1946).

[2] Despatch to Bengal, 15 September 1785, India Office Records, Bengal Despatches, vol. XIV, pp. 111 ff.

spices and tin at Canton. But the English company was hard put to it to find means of paying for the great increase in its exports from China after 1784.[1] In addition to sending large amounts of silver it increased its imports of English woollens and lead, and even experimented with consignments of English tin and copper. The company's Indian governments did what they could, but a more important contribution to the closing of the gap in the balance of payments was made by the private merchants engaged in the 'country' or Asian trade. The company encouraged them to bring Indian goods—especially Bihar opium and Bombay cotton—to Canton, provided that they deposited the proceeds in its treasury there in return for its bills. This money it used to pay for its exports of tea. At the same time expansion of English trade with China imposed strains upon the Co-hong merchants' monopoly established by the Chinese authorities at Canton, while the company's monopoly was criticised by English manufacturers as preventing them from securing their fair share in that expansion. The two main objects of Macartney's mission to Peking in 1793 were to increase the facilities for English trade with China and to seek out fresh markets for British manufactures elsewhere in Asia. Secondary objects were to collect information about China and the Far East generally, to remedy the grievances of the English at Canton and to raise the English reputation in China. All that Macartney achieved, however, was the collection of information. It has been suggested that he would have been more successful if he had conformed to Chinese custom and kowtowed to the emperor, but it has also been argued that the Dutch mission which did perform the kowtow in the following year received worse treatment than Macartney. On the other hand, it has been pointed out that the discourtesy endured by the Dutch on their journey to Peking resulted from the boorishness of local officials and was no part of imperial policy, and that on their return they were accorded particularly favourable treatment. But the Chinese government regarded all such missions as tribute-bearers, and saw no reason to change its system of trade.

When an English settlement was established at Balambangan off the north-east coast of Borneo in 1773 it was with the aim of attracting Chinese junks and of generally forwarding English trade with China and with what the Court of Directors called 'the unfrequented Parts of Asia'.[2] But the settlement was mismanaged and undefended, and two years later it was abandoned to Sulu plunderers. Again, when Francis Light, trader and ship's captain, urged the company to establish a settlement at Penang he stressed its usefulness not only as a harbour but also as a trading

---

[1] The quantity of tea sold at the company's sales increased from 5,857,882 lb. in 1783 to 20,750,994 lb. in 1796. These and other figures are analysed in E. H. Pritchard, *Crucial Years of Early Anglo-Chinese Relations, 1750–1800* (Research Studies of the State College of Washington, vol. IV, nos. 3–4, Pullman, Washington, 1936), p. 150.

[2] Court of Directors to Lord Weymouth, 28 October 1768, quoted in V. T. Harlow, *op. cit.* p. 86.

station between India and China. This was a more successful enterprise, although the Bengal government was determined to refrain from political adventure in the neighbourhood. The sultan of Kedah indeed made the grant in the expectation of the company's help against Siamese attack, but after establishing a settlement there in 1786 the government refused to conclude any sort of defensive alliance with him, and he continued to believe that he had been tricked. Penang did not entirely fulfil its early promise. But in the expansion of the China trade 'country' merchants from India were already forcing their way past Dutch opposition into the markets of Indonesia with Indian products to exchange for silver and local commodities to take to Canton, and in the peace treaty of 1784 the Dutch finally conceded freedom of navigation to British shipping in the eastern seas.

In spite of its economic difficulties during this period, the Dutch company was able to maintain its political power in Asia against local opposition. In Ceylon, the Dutch took the offensive against the king of Kandy because they thought that he had been encouraging opposition to their authority in the Colombo district. A Dutch force plundered Kandy in 1765, although it could not maintain itself there for long, and the treaty which was signed in the following year gave the Dutch sovereignty over the whole coastline of Ceylon. The Kandyan kingdom was now isolated from the outside world, and the king promised not to enter into any agreement with a foreign power, while the Dutch promised to defend him from foreign attack. But the British had no difficulty in capturing Trincomali in 1782, although they did not leave a strong enough garrison to defend it against Suffren. It was only restored to the Dutch because neither the English nor the French were prepared to see it in each other's hands. The war also interrupted the company's trade with Europe, and it had to turn to the home government for financial help. By sending a squadron under Van Braam the government enabled the company to repel the rising power of the Bugis who had seized control of Johore and were raiding Dutch posts in the Malacca straits. To counter a similar threat to their interests in Borneo, the Dutch established their influence in both the west and the south of the island by supporting rivals to the established rulers. But they were unable to sustain this effort, and in 1791 decided to withdraw. When Holland came under French control and the Batavian republic was founded, William V from his exile in England ordered the company's officials in the East to hand over its territories to the English in order to save them from the French. Whatever the effect of these orders, the English in fact had no difficulty in taking control of the Cape, Ceylon, and the Dutch possessions in India, on the west coast of Sumatra, and in Malacca. Java they left for the time. In Holland, the company's governing body was replaced by a government-controlled committee in 1795, and the company itself came to an end on 31 December 1799. Its financial condition had been a matter of concern to the home government for some years past, while its servants were still making their fortunes at its expense. The English company had only recently been saved by Cornwallis from the corruption of its own officials, and now that the profits of its growing China trade were overshadowing its losses elsewhere its charter could be renewed for another twenty years in 1793. The Dutch company was less fortunate, after the collapse of the state with which it had been so closely linked.

However, both in England and in Holland it was widely assumed that a career in the East was the quickest road to fortune and that those who went there had no other interest. Such an assumption was strengthened by the revelations of successive parliamentary inquiries in the Clive and Hastings era and by radical writings, especially those of the abbé Raynal which were extensively circulated in Europe. Indeed, the very appearance of cities like Calcutta, with its classical columns and porticoes, or Batavia, with its canals and Dutch-style brick houses, must have suggested that the Europeans living there were not much concerned with oriental notions of beauty. There almost seemed to be more appreciation of such things in Europe, when a Chinese pagoda was to be found at Kew, or in the English Garden at Munich, or when the Jesuit Attiret's praise of Chinese landscape gardening, with its use of art to imitate nature, was taken up by Sir William Chambers, and the taste for Chinese gardens spread from England to France and Germany. But it could be argued that all this was far from being a genuine appreciation of oriental ideas for their own sake. A taste for irregularity, for the 'beautiful disorder' and 'anti-symmetry' which Attiret had praised, happened to coincide with the reaction against classicism.[1] Both in gardens and in houses Chinese and Gothic objects and motifs were equally acceptable, and were sometimes to be found side by side.

Again, when Europeans studied the civilisations of China and India they tended to study them not so much for their intrinsic interest as for their relationship to Christian Europe, often looking with particular attention for traces of the primitive language of mankind, or for traces of the religion that must, they thought, have prevailed before the Flood. The Jesuits were emphatic in their praise of Chinese civilisation in the face of accusations that they had compromised with paganism, while the Figurists among them professed to find references to Abraham or Noah in ancient Chinese texts. In India, when Francis Wilford's pandits realised what he was looking for they forged a sacred text for him which contained the story of Shem, Ham and Japhet under the names of Sharma, Charma and Jyapeti, and even the great Sir William Jones was deceived. But such arguments were double-edged. If it could be suggested that Brahma was a corruption of Abraham it could also be suggested that Abraham was a

[1] Ch'en Shou-Yi, 'The Chinese Garden in Eighteenth Century England', *T'ien Hsia*, vol. II, no. 4, pp. 321 ff.

corruption of Brahma.[1] Thus Voltaire emphasised the antiquity as well as the enlightenment of what he considered to be the teachings of uncorrupted Hinduism. Perhaps India was the cradle of civilisation and Vedic Hinduism the primitive religion of mankind? What he took for an ancient Vedic text seems to have been in fact the work of a Christian missionary or convert, setting forth Hindu doctrines that seemed compatible with Christianity. When he praised the merits of Chinese civilisation and portrayed Confucianism as an enlightened Deism he placed much reliance on Jesuit sources. But his implication was that both China and India had had civilisations that were older and often more enlightened than those of Christian Europe, and Frederick the Great suggested that he was following the example of Tacitus, who praised the Germans in order to improve the Romans. To criticise one's own country by portraying the surprise or indignation of an enlightened oriental visitor was by now a favourite literary device, but the *philosophes* found in China a factual basis for their theories. Here was a truly benevolent despotism, where competitive examinations ensured that the administrators were as intelligent as *philosophes*, and the emperor governed according to natural law without the help—or hindrance—of revealed religion. Poivre exhorted the rulers of Europe to imitate the emperor of China, who so realised the importance of agriculture that he himself turned the first furrow of spring—a theme which was developed by Quesnay. The Physiocrats were not wholly uncritical, however, and there were some others—like Anson, or Grimm—who strongly dissented from the chorus of praise. But in general China was presented as a model for Europe.

Although Europeans still tended to look at Europe when they wrote about Asia, there was nevertheless a widening of interest during this period, and Voltaire had some right to criticise Bossuet for the limited scope of his *Universal History*. India, too, was attracting more attention, and service there awakened the interest of a select few in the civilisation, and especially the religion, of that country. Dow and Holwell, from whom Voltaire derived so much of his knowledge of Hinduism, had both served the English company there, and were anxious to stress the depth and subtlety that could be found in Hindu doctrines. Warren Hastings himself recommended the publication under official auspices of the English translation of the *Bhagavad Gita* that had been made by Charles Wilkins, another of the company's servants. As the company assumed greater administrative responsibilities it called forth the services of linguists and translators of Hindu and Muslim laws. A tradition of oriental scholarship was thus beginning, marked by the foundation of the Asiatic Society

[1] For the comparable tendency of Chinese scholars to argue that Christianity had its origins in Chinese beliefs, see C. S. Ch'ien, in *Philobiblon*, vol. I, no. I, pp. 13 ff., where he also suggests that the spreading of western knowledge by the missionaries was hampered by its association with Christian teaching, though it remains a question whether anyone else would have attempted to spread it.

of Bengal in 1784. The Society of Arts and Sciences had also been founded at Batavia in 1778, though with at first a less pronounced leaning to oriental studies. There also developed a realisation that European standards of taste were not the only ones to be considered. When Thomas Percy published some translations from Chinese literature in 1761 he thought it necessary to state apologetically that 'examined by the laws of European criticism' they were 'liable to many objections'.[1] But Wilkins's *Bhagavad Gita* was published under the authority of the Court of Directors in 1785 with a prefatory letter from Warren Hastings to the effect that it should not be judged by 'rules derived from the ancient or modern literature of Europe' but on its own merits as a profound philosophical and theological work.[2] Similarly, when Sir William Jones published his translation of *Shakuntala*, he praised Kalidasa as 'the SHAKSPEAR of India'.[3] Hastings and Jones even hoped to encourage the study of oriental literature in England. On the one hand, oriental literature had its own artistic and intellectual merits. On the other hand, Hastings hoped that a knowledge of works like the *Gita* would eradicate the tendency of his countrymen to despise Indians as uncivilised. Soon afterwards William Robertson was citing Wilkins's *Gita* and Jones's *Shakuntala* as evidence of the high standard of civilisation that India had attained, and drawing the moral that Europeans should improve their behaviour towards Indians.[4] Again, when Marsden wrote his *History of Sumatra* he tried to show how offensive European manners must appear in that country: even in dancing, while Europeans often found the oriental style 'ludicrous', Sumatrans found the European style equally 'ridiculous'.[5] But these were exciting years of discovery. They were followed soon enough by an age in which oriental ways were dismissed as inefficient or despised as ungodly.

2. RELATIONS WITH AFRICA, 1763–93

By the later eighteenth century, Europeans were looking at Africa with new expectations and hopes. Malachy Postlethwayt, citing Leo Africanus, claimed that the continent and its peoples could produce not merely precious metals but 'all the richest articles of the East and West India commerce'; 'if once a turn for industry and the arts was introduced among them, a greater quantity of the European produce and manufactures might be exported thither than to any other country in the whole

[1] Thomas Percy, *Hau Kiou Chooan or The Pleasing History*, vol. I (London, 1761), p. xii.
[2] Hastings to Nathaniel Smith, 4 October 1784, in Wilkins (trans.), *Bhăgvăt-Gēētā* (London, 1785), p. 7.
[3] Jones (trans.), *Sacontala* (Calcutta, 1789), p. v.
[4] Robertson, *Historical Disquisition Concerning the Knowledge which the Ancients had of India* (London, 1791), pp. 288 ff.
[5] W. Marsden, *History of Sumatra* (London, 1783), p. 230.

world'.[1] Merchants and manufacturers seeking new markets, statesmen whose colonial systems had been damaged in war, dreamed similar dreams; and, in this period, some took tentative steps to discover what substance might lie behind them.

The primary need, if speculations based on Leo Africanus were to give way to credit-worthy enterprises, was for precise geographical knowledge. The aspiration to extend trade powerfully reinforced the interest which students of the developing natural sciences showed in Africa, as in other unexplored regions. Inspired by Linnaeus, many Swedish botanists made modest journeys into unfamiliar country, noting, like Sparrmann at the Cape, what economic potentialities the land seemed to hold, together with much miscellaneous sociological detail. Sir Joseph Banks, President of the Royal Society and sponsor of botanical studies at Kew, also encouraged botanical collectors in Africa; among his correspondents was James Bruce, whose observations during his journeys in Abyssinia (1768–73) were inspired by a widely ranging scientific curiosity. In 1788 Banks was instrumental in founding the Association for Promoting the Discovery of the interior Parts of Africa. This dining-club of gentlemen prominent in scholarship and public life, though primarily concerned to advance knowledge, interested itself quite naturally in possible commercial developments; it deliberately concentrated its modest resources on the region believed to be the richest and most populous of Africa—the western Sudan.

The north-west received priority, even though considerable European settlement in Africa was found only in the extreme south. Here the European population numbered about 20,000 by the century's end, with an advancing frontier of settlement. Capetown alone had about 15,000 inhabitants, one-third Europeans; the owners of its more substantial and elegant houses enjoyed some of the urban amenities of contemporary Europe. The eighteenth century had brought little new immigration from Europe and until 1795 distinctions based on national origin tended to decrease, as the South African environment produced a distinctively colonial culture, unified by the Afrikaans language and by the widespread influence of the Dutch Reformed Church.

Economically, however, the future of the colony remained uncertain. The Netherlands East India Company did not greatly encourage production for export, regarding the Cape as a strategic base and a supplier of grain, meat and wine to its merchantmen rather than as a colony. Nor was it easy to suggest a staple for expanding commerce; this temperate region, not especially fertile, could offer little that Europe could not produce more efficiently at home. Abundant land allowed the colonists, as

[1] M. Postlethwayt, *The Universal Dictionary of Trade and Commerce* (London, 2nd ed. 1757), Articles: Africa (vol. I, pp. 24–5), Guinea (vol. I, pp. 923–8); *The Importance of the African Expedition Considered...* (London, 1758).

a whole, to attain a comfortable standard of life, but the role assigned to them in the Dutch economy, as regulated by fiscal and commercial restrictions of the company, held little promise of growth. By 1779 a patriot movement at the Cape was beginning to cite Locke, Grotius and Adam Smith in its demands for administrative reform and freer trade, wider civil rights and broader representation.

But from about the same time international rivalries were becoming the decisive influence in the fortunes of the region. Anglo-French conflicts in India, and the subsequent consolidation of British power there, made authorities in London anxious both to secure their own 'half-way house' to India, and to deny the use of Capetown to France. Dutch intervention in the American War; Admiral de Suffren's occupation of the Cape, forestalling a British expedition, in 1781; the patronage later extended by the French to the 'patriot' opposition in the United Provinces —all indicated southern Africa as a growing area of imperial rivalries. Hence the invasion of the Netherlands by revolutionary France was liable to threaten Britain's eastern, as well as her continental interests; it provided her with the opportunity to seize the Cape in 1795.[1]

The restless elements in South African society were Afrikaner frontiersmen of the eastern districts; patriarchal herdsmen and hunters, tougher, cruder in taste, even more resistant to government and restraint than the settled slave-owning farmers to the west.[2] To secure the indivisible loanfarm of 6000 acres, which each member of each new generation came to regard as a birth-right, the *trek-boers* pushed on the frontiers of settlement until they met the Xosa, vanguard of the Bantu-speaking peoples who were moving gradually southwards, also seeking new pasturelands. The company's government tried to separate the two peoples by defining a boundary line, but neither side would voluntarily limit its expansion. Gradually the Boers, strengthened by fire-arms and by a determination compounded of Calvinism, cupidity, fear, and hardening racial arrogance, pushed the frontier eastwards. In 1779 Xosa raids on Afrikaner cattle, not unprovoked, opened the 'first Kaffir war': after the successes of Boer commandos in 1781 the frontier was advanced to the Fish river. But this represented only an uneasy truce in the relations of the two peoples; many Xosa remained west of the Fish river (some trading with the Boers, or in their employment), while some Afrikaners crossed to the east of the river. During the drought of 1793 fighting was resumed, immediate responsibility at least lying with the Boer farmer Lindeque; Maynier, the government's agent, made peace without driving the Xosa across the Fish river or recovering all stolen cattle. Conflicts continued; in 1795 the frontiersmen, angered by what they judged sentimental negrophilia on the part of

---

[1] V. T. Harlow, *The Founding of the Second British Empire*, vol. 1 (London, 1952), pp. 125–35.

[2] I. D. MacCrone, *Race Attitudes in South Africa* (Johannesburg, 1937), chs. VI and VII.

government, rebelled, and proclaimed the independent frontier republic of Graaf Reinet.[1] Although the aims of these Afrikaners were parochial, within their territorial limits they were being rigorously pursued; and they ran contrary to Postlethwayt's dream of developing the economic potentialities of the native Africans.

North of the Fish river, European influence on the east coast was represented primarily by the declining Portuguese settlements in Mozambique; and here most of the colonists were Goanese or mulattoes. A few slaves were shipped to the Cape, and the Americas; but though traders occasionally talked of 'new sources of traffick' in these waters, few ever touched there on their journeys east. The French, with their thriving plantation colonies in the Mascarenes, had the strongest interest in obtaining slaves and supplies from East Africa or Madagascar, but their half-hearted attempt to re-establish political footholds on the latter island after 1768 petered out almost farcically in the hands of the Magyar adventurer Benyowski.[2] In 1777 a French trader proposed that the government should establish a new colony at Kilwa, whence a new privileged company was to trade along the coasts for slaves and ivory, selling French fire-arms and brandy, and Indian cloth. This plan was intended primarily to give French merchants a share of the trade between East Africa and West Asia, hitherto controlled by the Omani Arabs; but the French authorities were unwilling to risk a conflict with Muscat, and left this relatively minor commerce under Arab protection.[3] France was more interested in exercising political influence in the western approaches to India than in speculative plans for East African trade.

Similar considerations governed the powers' relations with Egypt. A few Europeans appreciated the country's commercial possibilities, both as an entrepôt for trade with Asia and as a terminal for African caravans: but actual trade remained small. This was partly because the resistance of the Mameluke Beys to the sultan's authority produced political uncertainty and disorder, partly because of opposition from established interests. The British East India Company was anxious to protect its privileges in the oceanic trade-route; the Turks prohibited Christian commerce in the Red Sea, and were supported by the British Levant Company. When the beys, between 1766 and 1779, encouraged British ships from India to sail to Suez, both companies successfully urged the government to oppose such development. French traders did rather more business in Egypt;[4] and some Frenchmen understood Egypt's potential importance as a base for a new attack on British interests in Asia. Choiseul-Gouffier's appointment as ambassador in Constantinople in 1784 initiated new attempts,

[1] J. S. Marais, *Maynier and the First Boer Republic* (Cape Town, 1944).
[2] H. Deschamps, *Histoire de Madagascar* (Paris, 1961), pp. 79–91.
[3] R. Coupland, *East Africa and Its Invaders* (2nd ed., Oxford, 1956), pp. 76–83.
[4] G. Rambert (ed.), *Histoire du Commerce de Marseille*, tome v, *Le Levant de 1660 à 1789*, by Robert Paris (Paris, 1957), pp. 367–92.

not yet successful, to cultivate French influence in Egypt. The British responded only erratically, although Egypt's strategic importance had been convincingly demonstrated during the American War, when urgent despatches to India first went by Suez. Their consulate in Cairo, re-established in 1786 to secure communications and counter French activities, was abolished in 1793 to save money—precisely when France revived hers.[1]

European relations with the rest of the North African littoral are more relevant to Mediterranean than to African affairs. Commercially the regencies of Tripoli, Tunis and Algiers were most closely connected with the Levant, although the extent and stability of their commercial relations with southern Europe are often underrated. Resident European communities imported manufactured goods, some of which fed the trans-Saharan caravans, and exported grains, and other local produce, notably to Leghorn and Marseille. In Morocco also, strong rulers like Moulay Mohammed (1757–90) encouraged European merchants, while controlling the places and conditions of their trade. Interested Europeans occasionally proposed military operations in these North African states; Spain retained five small territorial footholds between Ceuta and Oran, and Portugal held Mazagan until 1769; but generally, Europe was satisfied with the protection afforded to existing trade, and sought no major transformation of political or economic relations with the Maghreb.[2]

It was however increasingly appreciated that the Maghreb had a hinterland; that the Saharan caravan routes (by which several thousand slaves, with gold, ivory and other produce, reached the Mediterranean every year) might facilitate the opening of broader commerce with the western Sudan.[3] The African Association at first favoured this approach to its work of exploration. In 1788 its first emissaries, Ledyard and Lucas, started respectively from Cairo and Tripoli; and though the former died and the latter turned back, the association was able to give substantially more precision to the African map by the unspectacular method of interrogating Sahara traders. But physical difficulties, combined with the resistance offered to foreign intrusion by those interested in the established pattern of trade, made the Sahara formidable to explorers and unpromising for mercantile enterprise. In 1790 the association's new agent, Houghton, began his exploration from the Gambia, as did Mungo Park in 1795. The west coast, where European influence was already most intense, was also the crucial area for its future development.

---

[1] F. Charles-Roux, L'Angleterre, L'Isthme de Suez et l'Égypte au XVIIIe siècle (Paris, 1922); Les Origines de l'Expédition d'Égypte (Paris, 1910). H. L. Hoskins, British Routes to India (New York and London, 1928).

[2] Cf. F. Charles-Roux, France et Afrique du Nord avant 1830 (Paris, 1932), especially pp. 305–7.

[3] For example, Saugnier, Relation de plusieurs Voyages à la Côte d'Afrique (Paris, 1791); P. Masson, Histoire des Établissements et du Commerce Français dans l'Afrique Barbaresque, 1560–1793 (Paris, 1903), pp. 642–4.

In 1763 the economy of most of western Africa was dominated by the export of slaves across the Atlantic. The demand for plantation-labour was still expanding, and was checked only temporarily by the American War. The British led the way, often supplying French and Spanish colonies besides their own. French slave-dealers quickly recovered from the complete stoppage of the trade after the Seven Years War; after 1784, supported by government subsidies, they largely displaced the British in Angola. Portuguese slavers apparently continued to flourish; North American traders were shipping slaves even before independence; Spain claimed Fernando Po in 1778 in the hope of entering the trade; only the Dutch, and possibly the Danes, seem to have lost ground. No research has yet produced reliable figures of the scale, distribution and fluctuations of the slave-trade, but contemporary estimates converge sufficiently to suggest that during this period the average number of persons exported from western Africa was of the order of 80,000 annually. Probably over half of these sailed in English ships; the French carried perhaps a quarter.[1]

Although slaves were by far West Africa's most important export, they were not the only one. Gold and ivory were profitable to purchase as opportunity offered; but quantities were small. The elephant population of coastal regions declined; and men gradually learned to treat with prudent scepticism the alluring stories of rich African mines. The trade in dye-woods, carried directly home to Europe, employed a dozen British ships by 1788.[2] Gum from forests near the Senegal, essential in certain textile finishing processes, was a major object of international rivalry. Britain and France in turn, while established at St Louis, sought to direct the gum-trading Braknas and Trarzas exclusively towards Podor and river-ports, while the rival power tried to trade on the Atlantic coast, at Arguin or Portendic. But nowhere else was any African product sufficiently important to provide a staple for direct trade between Europe and Africa. The value of cargoes entering British ports direct from Africa in these thirty years remained only one-ninth that of British exports to Africa.[3] Hides and wax, palm-oil and indigo, might be bought in small quantities to make up the cargo, and carried to Europe by way of the Americas; but labour remained the only commodity of major importance to the Atlantic economy which Africa could provide in bulk.

It was not then any peculiarly cruel twist of character which made Europeans concentrate upon the slave-trade—nor even, primarily, the desire of governments for tidily planned imperial economies. One feature of this period is the continual recurrence of projects, more or less vague and ill-informed, for the development of new crops and new markets

---

[1] The most detailed and authoritative of these estimates is probably that by Robert Norris, *Accounts and Papers*, 1789 (xxvi), *Report...of the Committee of Council*. Its figure of 74,200 seems rather too low.   [2] *Ibid.*, part I, evidence of Teaste, Deane.

[3] Calculated from *Accounts and Papers*, 1789 (xxvi), and D. Macpherson, *Annals of Commerce* (London, 1805).

in western Africa. In 1766 Governor O'Hara of British Senegambia cherished wild hopes of European settlement in gold-bearing Galam, of supplies of cotton, rice, tobacco and indigo from the neighbouring countries, of a vast market for British manufactures still further east to be explored by agents attached to caravans on the Mediterranean coast.[1] Meanwhile in Angola Pombal's energetic governor, Sousa Coutinho, was struggling to develop white settlement, commercial agriculture, even iron-founding; and Abbé Demanet (later a promoter of the Senegal Company) was seeing in the Saloum and Casamance rivers, not only roads towards the gold mines, but sources of timber, indigo and other wild products. Demanet's notion that cotton and sugar might be cultivated on Bulama island was taken up by the governor whom he served as chaplain.[2] In 1777 it was Britain's turn to seek substitutes for American colonies; Temple Luttrell, M.P., while attacking the existing organisation of British African interests, held out fantastic prospects of reaching the Nile by way of the Gambia river, thus opening great new markets for British goods, and rich sources of 'every valuable production we receive from America'.[3] In 1785 the British government contemplated colonizing the upper Gambia with transported convicts. But hopes of using the Old World to redress the changing balance of the New were still based on inadequate geographical and agricultural knowledge.

In both Britain and France, the later eighteenth century saw a tendency towards the 'freeing' of African trade, in the limited sense that monopolies were ended, and that legislation sought to assure commercial opportunities to individual traders under the national flag. The corollary of this process was that governments, assuming administrative and military responsibilities formerly supported by the profits of privileged companies, themselves had to play more active roles. The British Company of Merchants trading to Africa, established in 1750 on the ruins of the Royal Africa Company's monopoly, was prohibited from corporate trading; it existed to elect an administrative committee which Parliament subsidised and charged with the management of existing forts in the interests of all British traders to Africa. Such a body might satisfy established merchants on the Gold Coast, though critics alleged inertia and profiteering; it was hardly qualified to administer conquered Senegal, with its inland trade and more complex frontier problems, nor to resist the continued rivalry of the French in that region.[4] So in 1765 the Senegal

[1] Public Record Office, London: C.O. 267/13, O'Hara to Conway, 28 May, 25 July, 7 September 1766.
[2] J. Duffy, *Portuguese Africa* (Cambridge, Mass., 1959), pp. 71–3, 143; Demanet, *Nouvelle Histoire de l'Afrique Françoise* (Paris, 1767), vol. I, pp. xiv, 213 ff., 226 ff.; C. Schefer, *Instructions Générales...* (Paris, 1927), vol. I, p. 20, Mémoire du Roi pour Mesnager, 22 December 1764.
[3] *Parliamentary History*, vol. XIX, pp. 311–15.
[4] P.R.O.: C.O. 389/31, Board of Trade to the king, 21 February 1765; E. C. Martin, *The British West African Settlements 1750–1821* (London, 1927), chs. V–VII.

conquests were united with the older Gambian settlements in the colony of Senegambia, with a constitution constructed, 'as far as differences of circumstances will permit', on American models. But the British government did not command adequate machinery to administer such a colony, still less to realise O'Hara's dreams; it reconciled itself without difficulty to the loss of the Senegal during the American War and handed back the Gambia fort to mercantile control.

In 1763 the French Compagnie des Indes gave up to the Crown the remains of their African establishments (retaining the fort at Whydah until 1767). Goree was placed under royal governors, who did their best to revive French fortunes on the mainland, leasing land around Dakar, re-establishing posts at Joal, Portudal and Albreda, and trying to divert interior trade away from the British in the Gambia. But they were weakly supported from Paris, and the colony served chiefly as a port of call for French slavers sailing further south. As usual in African settlements, conflicts arose within the colonial community; merchants complained that governors were abusing their position to their private profit, while governors and private traders joined in denouncing a new company which, under successive titles in the 'seventies and 'eighties, began to use influence in Paris to secure new privileges in Africa. It was the change in Atlantic naval power during the American War, not any superiority of African policy, which enabled France to reconquer St Louis in 1779. This gain was confirmed by the Treaty of Versailles, the British negotiators concentrating on securing access to the gum-trade at Portendic. Further south the balance of military operations had been more even, and the treaty contained no provision directly prejudicial to British leadership in the slave-trade.

But victory permitted the French government to undertake a deliberate extension of the range of its African policy. In the Senegal river itself the Senegal Company gradually obtained control; between 1786 and 1791 it held a monopoly of all trade between capes Blanco and Verde, and assumed responsibility for the colonial budget. But further south encouragement was given to private traders by subsidies for the carriage of slaves, and by annual naval cruises. Treaties were made with such coastal kingdoms as Saloum, in hope of diverting inland trade from the Gambia; in the Sierra Leone estuary Gambia Island, where Frenchmen had traded for some years, was acquired in January 1785. Instructions to Governor de Boufflers (November 1785) for the first time contained general information about French merchants even further south.[1] In 1786 a French post was established at Amoku on the Gold Coast, and placed under the supervision of the governor of Whydah, who was also assigned a more active role in the protection and extension of French commerce from Cape Lahou to Ardra.[2] Captain Landolphe, on behalf of a St Malo house,

---

[1] Schefer, vol. I, pp. 128 ff., *Mémoire du Roi*, 18 November 1785.
[2] *Ibid.* Instructions to Gourg, 23 November 1786.

established a factory in Warri, although without securing exclusive privileges for French commerce.[1] A forward movement of some significance was cut short by the fall of the régime which initiated it.

Despite the increasing interest of 'projectors', and even of governments, in the interior, the direct impact of European trade on the peoples of West Africa remained restricted, in significance and in geographical extent. Europeans seldom moved more than a mile or two beyond the coasts and navigable estuaries; on the 'Grain Coast' it was customary for commerce to take place actually aboard the vessels as they lay off shore. Only in the north of the slaving area were attempts made to establish trading posts any distance up-river, and with very mixed success. In the Gambia, traders regularly went above the island later known as MacCarthy's, and several voyages progressed beyond the Barrakunda falls. Up the Senegal, Podor was an important trading-centre, weakly garrisoned by the British and French in turn; and annual trading journeys were made as far as the ruined Fort St Joseph above the confluence with the Faleme. An agent of the Senegal Company travelled overland to this fort in 1786, but was killed after trading for a year. These conditions were quite exceptional; no other region yet contained waterways free from the worst obstacles to navigation, an economy not entirely dominated by the aspect of slaves, and inland states willing and able to protect European trade in return for stipulated benefits to themselves.

For elsewhere the most serious obstacles to inland penetration were not caused by difficult terrain, nor even by the prevalence of disease. African rulers, favourably established near the littoral, were reluctant to allow Europeans to pass into the territory of their neighbours lest their commercial monopoly should be endangered; even on the Senegal the Galam convoy had to run a gauntlet of hostile peoples on the middle stretches. Resolute Europeans could doubtless have overcome even this opposition, given sufficient incentive; but so long as slaves formed the staple of West African trade, little was to be gained by inland penetration. Without maintaining considerable military forces in Africa—which the profits of the trade could hardly support, and which nobody contemplated —Europeans could not go and capture their own slaves, still less transport them safely to the coast; they preferred delivery close to the ships. Hence, where the littoral peoples could provide ordered institutions and ensure a regular supply of slaves, the merchant's interest was to co-operate with them, paying the customary duties, observing local commercial practice, and accepting most of the restraints on movement which his customers prescribed. Such relationships could be far more stable than is commonly appreciated; not only did many isolated Europeans live for years in Africa in perfect personal security, but they commonly found it safe and

[1] *Mémoires du Capitaine Landolphe*, ed. J. S. Quesne (Paris, 1823), vol. II, pp. 44 ff., 90 ff.

profitable to give very substantial credits, in the form of trade goods, to African brokers and middlemen.

And yet the cultural impact of Europe remained superficial. The dependence of Europeans on local suppliers might induce a certain interested respect for African institutions; racial arrogance was not an invariable characteristic of slave-traders, and the worst examples of European lawlessness or fraud were not the work of regular traders, who had reputations to keep up. But intimate social contacts rarely developed. Even where permanent trading establishments were formed on the mainland, Europeans often found it prudent to reduce their dealings with their neighbours to a minimum, and to conduct them according to more or less formalised procedures. Christian missions on any scale existed only in Angola and the Congo, where some attempts were made to develop the work of earlier generations; their influence appears rarely to have penetrated deeply.

Of course, African society responded in its own terms to changes in economic relationships. Sometimes, as in Ashanti and Dahomey, foreign trade increased the economic and military resources of an adaptable local dynasty, assisting it to fortify and extend its power. At Old Calabar, on the other hand, Efiks who had prospered by supplying European ships with slaves came to exercise extended political authority, especially in commercial matters, within the framework of traditional political institutions. These traders lived in imported wooden houses of two stories, corresponded in English with Liverpool merchants and are said to have founded their own English schools; Efik society was clearly being transformed by trade.[1] Yet they, like most African peoples, had as yet taken little directly from Europe except a shrewd knowledge of commercial practice, and a taste for certain types of consumer goods.

The nearest approach to a genuine European colony in West Africa was St Louis, a town created by Frenchmen on an island in the Senegal river. The population restored to France in 1779 numbered 3018, including 383 Europeans and 777 mulattoes or free negroes; in about ten years the total was doubled, largely by voluntary immigration from the interior. Many Africans and mulattoes were artisans or petty traders, but others had made substantial fortunes on the trading voyage to Galam, which most Europeans preferred to avoid. The majority were Catholics, some Muslims; after 1779 French governors nominated a mayor from their number, charging him with local police duties.[2] The Portuguese settlements of Bissao, Loanda, and Benguela, once impressive, now showed evidence of decline. Still, at Bissao many Africans and mulattoes were at least nominal Catholics, and rosaries and crucifixes figured among the

---

[1] D. Forde (ed.), *Efik Traders of Old Calabar* (London, 1957).
[2] P. Labarthe, *Voyage au Sénégal...* (Paris, An X), pp. 22–3; S.M.X. Golberry, *Travels in Africa...* (trans. F. Blagdon; London, 1802), vol. I, pp. 112 ff.; P. Cultru, *Histoire du Sénégal* (Paris, 1910), pp. 241, 258–9, 262.

merchandise of slave-dealers; and substantial African traders, literate in Portuguese, navigated their own vessels as far as Lisbon.[1] But at the Gold Coast settlements (hopefully called 'forts'), only a few African traders or servants, within the walls or in dependent villages, learned European skills or ideas. In 1780, 211 Africans were on the strength of the French fort at Whydah; this number was officially regarded as excessive, and five to six hundred served for ten British forts.

There was indeed some demand from coastal Africans for European education, often for a reason frankly stated: 'Read book, and learn to be rogue as well as white man.'[2] A few reached Europe in search of it. Prince Boudakon of Warri learned court dances in Paris and played martial airs on the clarinet; and there were estimated to be fifty negro or mulatto school-children each year in Liverpool alone. Philip Quaque, after being educated and ordained in London, returned to Cape Coast in 1765 with an English wife, and opened a small school, chiefly for children in the forts.[3] But in general, European footholds in West Africa remained self-contained enclaves of an alien culture, rather than bridgeheads for the diffusion of that culture through the continent.

In some regions, frontiers might be less rigidly drawn. Between the Gambia and Cape Mount, where Portuguese and British traders settled on the coast in relative isolation, a sort of Eurafrican commercial class came into being. Native Africans and mulattoes played important roles as principals or middlemen, trading on credit in inland areas which foreign merchants could not reach themselves. Wage-labourers, or 'grumettas', sometimes learned European skills; some British factories built substantial coasting vessels with local labour, slave-ships sometimes employed African seamen. In the Bight of Benin, where Portuguese mulattoes were being joined by negroes returned from slavery in Brazil, Captain Adams noted the growth of an export-trade in Yoruba cloth.[4] Members of these commercial classes might speak a Portuguese or English patois, send their children to Europe for education, even profess Catholicism, repeating the *Pater Noster* and having their children baptised by the occasional visiting priest. Yet on the whole, the effects on African society of even the most intimate commercial contacts were surprisingly few and superficial. It is difficult to sustain the contemporary claim that contacts born of the slave-trade were gradually 'civilising' Africa.

Nor was such an effect being produced indirectly, by means of the actual goods imported in exchange for slaves. The great majority of these were textiles (many of Indian manufacture) and hardware; the ruling factor

---

[1] P. Beaver, *African Memoranda...* (London, 1805), pp. 40 ff., 275, 320 ff., 405. D. Rinchon, *Les Armements Négriers au XVIIIe Siècle* (Brussels, 1956), p. 30.

[2] A. M. Falconbridge, *Two Voyages to Sierra Leone* (2nd ed., London, 1802), p. 37.

[3] *Accounts and Papers*, 1789 (XXVI), part I, apps. 4 and 5; F. L. Bartels, 'Philip Quaque, 1741–1816', *Transactions, G[old] C[oast] and T[ogoland] H[istorical] S[ociety]*, vol. I (1955).

[4] J. Adams, *Sketches taken during Ten Voyages to Africa...* (London, n.d. [1821]), p. 25.

was the local consumer. In parts of the Gold Coast, Brazilian tobacco was an essential item of trade; rum, brandy and other intoxicants were finding an expanding market, but remained merely subsidiary items.[1] But even if few of Africa's imports served to demoralise its people, neither were the goods received in return for men calculated to assist economic growth—productive implements are conspicuously lacking from the list. The most significant imports from an African point of view were fire-arms, powder and ammunition, which by 1775 had become essential and commanding articles in the trade. Despite the inferior quality of the guns used in trade, their possession often gave decisive power to the peoples possessing them. This was well understood by the kings of Dahomey, who fought several wars during the eighteenth century to ensure that the region's imports were concentrated under their control at Whydah, and maintained the purchase of arms there as a royal monopoly.

The precise manner and degree in which the external slave-trade caused the degradation of African society remains a subject for debate. Many wars may have been started for the purpose of procuring slaves, but slaving was by no means the sole cause of African wars; in the nineteenth century 'legitimate trade' was likewise to produce many occasions of conflict. Nor were wars the only source of slaves; a few were kidnapped, some sold for debt; many were transported for witchcraft, murder or adultery. But even if compassion sometimes caused enemies of the trade to exaggerate its evil effects, one fundamental criticism may summarise the rest. The apparently insatiable demand for slaves at the coast made it extremely difficult for peoples whose economies were based on the export of men to adapt themselves and use their labour to increase the production of agricultural or forest crops. Even Postlethwayt, the apologist of the Royal Africa Company, had seen that the slave-trade 'will ever obstruct the civilising of these people, and extending of the trade into the bowels of Africa'.[2]

Clearly there was economic reason behind the philanthropic demand for the abolition of the slave-trade; but suggestions that abolition had become an economic necessity are another matter. By the 1780s economic changes in Europe were making the interests dependent on the slave-trade relatively less important. But since Africa produced no commodity of major importance to the new industries, and had not been proved capable of producing any, there was no evident necessity for the positive step of legislative abolition. In many undeveloped regions of the Americas there remained great demands for unskilled labour; indeed, the rising need for cotton by British spinners was likely to make such demands increase. As the nineteenth century would show, there was still an ample

---

[1] Details of British exports to Africa, 1783–7, are in *Accounts and Papers*, 1789 (xxvi), part IV, Table A.

[2] *Universal Dictionary*, vol. I, p. 25.

economic basis, not merely for continuing the Atlantic slave-trade, but for considerable expansion.

Given the mercantilist assumptions, however, this was not necessarily true for every nation. The Danes had found that the demands for labour of their West Indian plantations—roughly 1200 new slaves annually—were too small to support a profitable slave-trade, whether by private merchants or privileged companies. In the 1780s they tried to encourage plantations of coffee and cotton on the eastern Gold Coast, but with small success.[1] In 1783 the governor of Christianborg tried to strengthen the Danish base by a forward military policy on the Volta, leading to the establishment of three new forts. But this merely increased the overhead costs of trade without altering the economic problem, and in 1792 the monarchy adopted a new policy. The Danish West Indies were to rely for labour on natural reproduction instead of foreign imports; for ten years the slave population of the islands, and the proportion of females, were to be built up, but from 1803 the African slave-trade would be forbidden to Danish subjects.[2]

Other states found it less simple to reconcile humanitarianism with sound policy. The French West Indies, notably Saint-Domingue, still required large importations of labour; and the eminent French opponents of the slave-trade became important only when class and racial conflicts in the Antilles forced such questions to the notice of the revolutionary assemblies. The Société des Amis des Noirs, founded in 1788, commanded intellectual respect by the distinction of its members—Brissot, Condorcet, Mirabeau, Lafayette, Sieyès among them—but the conditions for an effective movement of anti-slavery opinion hardly existed in France. Only forty-nine of the general *cahiers* submitted to the Estates General commented adversely on the institution of slavery and few of these were prepared to advocate more than the eventual abolition of the slave-trade.[3]

In Great Britain economic developments gradually pointed the path towards a new relationship with Africa. While the loss of America suggested a need for new sources of tropical produce, the growing manufacturing interests sought expanding markets. The West Indian plantations were relatively losing their importance in the imperial economy; their privileged position seemed less essential to national prosperity, and so became more vulnerable. Later, the far-sighted understood that declining fertility of the soil made fresh imports of labour less essential to the

[1] H. Debrunner, 'Notable Danish Chaplains on the Gold Coast,' *Transactions, G.C. and T.H.S.*, vol. II (1956), p. 15; C. D. Adams, 'Activities of Danish Botanists in Guinea, 1783–1850,' *Transactions, Historical Society of Ghana*, vol. III (1957), esp. pp. 35–8; C. B. Wadstrom, *An Essay on Colonization*... (London, 1794), pp. 175–8, 316–17.

[2] E. Donnan, *Documents Illustrative of the Slave Trade to America* (Washington, 1931), vol. II, pp. 616–17, Royal Ordinance, 16 March 1792.

[3] G. Gaston-Martin, *Histoire de l'Esclavage dans les Colonies françaises* (Paris, 1948), pp. 169–71; B. F. Hyslop, *French Nationalism in 1789 according to the General Cahiers* (New York, 1934), pp. 276–7.

British islands than to their rivals. The abolitionist movement was not due solely to a sudden access of national virtue; but neither is it wholly explicable in economic terms. Economic changes do not become universally apparent overnight; and many powerful people long believed that their own and the national fortunes depended on a continuance of the slave-trade. A parliament predominantly representing landed proprietors was strongly biased in favour of the rights of property, mercantilist economic doctrines, and West Indian privileges: even though economic change was allowing members to enjoy the luxury of a conscience, legislative action might have been long delayed had not humane and religious men deliberately challenged those consciences.[1]

After the broadening in 1787 of a committee formed by Quakers four years earlier, the abolitionist campaign developed with surprising speed. Thomas Clarkson, its leading agent, used significantly new methods in his field investigations; he toured the country, measuring ships, inspecting documents, and interrogating innumerable seamen in order to bring exact information before the Privy Council, successive parliamentary committees and the articulate public. Much attention was given to testimony about African products which might, the slave-trade once abolished, feed a growing trade with Europe. Tracts and pamphlets, containing evidence as well as exhortation, were circulated in thousands; pious men and women in provincial towns organised petitions against the trade. Abolition was first debated in the Commons in 1788; Dolben's Act, regulating the number of slaves a ship might carry, was passed that year; by 1792 the defenders had resorted to delaying-tactics, and the Commons approved in principle of abolition within four years. The battle was not won, and wartime developments further delayed the final decision; but progress had been surprisingly rapid.

The abolitionists did not limit their African policy to the prohibition of the export of slaves; many sought also a new economic basis for relations between Europe and Africa. Some supported the exploring projects of the African Association, and some promoted colonisation, notably at Sierra Leone. The settlement there originated when Granville Sharp and other philanthropists concerned for 'the relief of the Black Poor' in England took up the plan of Henry Smeathman, a naturalist, for an anti-slavery colony to develop the resources of that area. The government gave some assistance, and 411 settlers, black and white, left Plymouth in April 1787. Despite Sharp's warm-hearted concern for details, the colony's problems had not been realistically foreseen, and by 1791 only sixty-four of the original settlers could be reassembled. But meanwhile the project

---

[1] For the abolitionist movement, compare R. Coupland, *Wilberforce* (1923), and *The British Anti-Slavery Movement* (1933), and G. R. Mellor, *British Imperial Trusteeship, 1783–1850* (London, 1951), ch. I, with Eric Williams, *Capitalism and Slavery* (Chapel Hill, 1944). See also T. Clarkson, *The History...of the Abolition of the African Slave Trade* (London, 2 vols., 1808).

had secured broader support through the Sierra Leone Company, incorporated by Parliament in 1791; the appointment as chairman of Henry Thornton, M.P., banker and evangelical churchman, promised a more business-like approach. It was now proposed to rely for the main body of colonists on Negro Loyalists, domiciled in Nova Scotia since the American war; 1196 of them sailed for Africa in January 1792.[1]

The dual aims of the new sponsors are reflected in their original instructions; the colony was to establish 'a Trade with Africa on the true principles of Commerce, carrying out British Manufactures and other articles of Traffick and bringing back African Produce in exchange', with the ultimate purpose of 'introducing to a vast country long detained in barbarism the blessings of Industry and Civilization'. Efforts were to be made to cultivate sugar and other crops within the settlement, and to open commerce with the far interior.[2] The Directors did not recognise any conflict between humanitarian ideals and business sense. Though profits were not their chief aim, profits were ultimately expected, if only as a proof that the design was well-conceived. It is later writers who have alleged mercenary motives; one disgruntled contemporary judged the Directors 'a parcel of hypocritical puritans' whose methods were not commercial enough, and their own reports devote far more space to describing the progress of the settlers and denouncing the slave-trade than to defending the unhealthy balance sheet.[3]

It is unsatisfactory to regard Sierra Leone as an isolated venture by an uneasy alliance of covetous bankers and cranks. The economic aims were a direct development of the earlier projects for African development; the philanthropic purposes also were now shared by others. In 1779 a group of Swedenborgians had planned a Utopian colony in West Africa, which for a time attracted the less disinterested attention of Gustavus III.[4] In 1792 a party of 275 settlers, the great majority British, embarked on an ill-planned and ill-fated attempt to develop plantations of sugar, cotton and indigo on the island of Bulama, using free African labour.[5] Soon after the Nova Scotians reached Sierra Leone, neighbouring slave-dealers resumed attempts to grow plantation crops on Tasso Island.[6] When considering the many errors of its sponsors, it is well to recall that Sierra

[1] R. R. Kuczynski, *Demographic Survey of the British Colonial Empire*, vol. I (London, 1948), ch. 2, II.

[2] L. E. C. Evans, 'An Early Constitution of Sierra Leone', *Sierra Leone Studies*, vol. XVIII (1932).

[3] Falconbridge, *Two Voyages to Sierra Leone*, p. 186; *Substance of the Report...by...the Sierra Leone Company* (London, 1794).

[4] C. B. Wadstrom, *An Essay on Colonization...* (London, 1794), part II, pp. 179–96; Sten Lindroth, 'Adam Afzelius', *Sierra Leone Studies*, n.s. 4 (1955).

[5] P. Beaver, *African Memoranda...* (London, 1805); Wadstrom, *op. cit.* part II, pp. 130–74.

[6] Falconbridge, *op. cit.* p. 48 n.; Wadstrom, *op. cit.* part II, p. 116; *Accounts and Papers*, 1789 (xxv), pp. 288 ff. (evidence of Anderson).

Leone represents the best financed, most boldly conceived and most successful of many attempts to develop cultivation on the African coast and commerce with the far interior.

All the same, its success was only moderate. Disease killed many settlers in the early months, before proper buildings were erected; the peninsula proved disappointing agriculturally; the persistence of the slave-trade in the neighbourhood raised many difficulties. With weaker financial backing, the settlement might have collapsed. Yet the community which survived did transplant to Africa such various features of contemporary British culture as evangelical Christianity and juries: indeed, the previous colonial experience of the Nova Scotians made them too insistent on their political rights, too zealous in certain religious observances, to suit even the pious Directors. Surrounding districts were also influenced. Neighbouring cultivators sent foodstuffs for sale in Freetown; Mandinka traders from the Sudan brought gold, ivory and hides for sale; some local people sought schooling, or work at wages, in the settlement; settlers began to move out to trade in rivers from the Pongos to the Sherbro, and in 1794 two European servants of the company reached Futa Jallon.[1] Within narrow limits, the new colony was beginning to change African society.

When war commenced in Europe, the possibilities of an expanding commerce in African produce were thus becoming more widely recognised and some small experiments had been made, with mixed success. But entrenched interests in the slave-trade, European and African, remained liable to prejudice any new departure; and the revolutionary war retarded and distorted the efforts of the abolitionists.

[1] C. H. Fyfe, *A History of Sierra Leone* (London, 1962), ch. II.

CHAPTER IX

EUROPEAN DIPLOMATIC RELATIONS, 1763–90

THE settlement of 1763, which ended the Seven Years War in Europe and overseas, was in many ways the most important of the eighteenth century. The Peace of Paris established Britain as, with the exception of Spain, the greatest colonial power in the world. She was now clearly dominant in North America and had at least the possibility of dominating much of India. Simultaneously the Treaty of Hubertusburg saw the consolidation of Prussia's position as one of the major powers of Europe, if not yet as a great power in the fullest sense of the term. Her retention of Silesia appeared to many contemporaries the greatest military achievement of the age; and the leadership of Frederick II seemed sufficient to counterbalance many of her material weaknesses.

A long period of peace, however, could hardly be expected, and indeed was not expected by most observers, after 1763. Neither Britain's colonial and maritime predominance over France nor Prussian security against the Habsburgs was as yet beyond challenge. France's pride had been deeply wounded by her failures during the war. Humiliation and anger were little reduced, desire for revenge on Britain little weakened, by the reflection that much of commercial value—most of her West Indian islands and her trading-posts in Africa and India—had been salvaged from the wreck of her overseas empire. Moreover Britain's successes had aroused everywhere in western Europe a real fear that her sea-power might now be used to give her a monopoly of Europe's overseas trade, and of possibilities of overseas expansion. Frederick II also found that his successes had, inevitably, earned him increased resentment as well as respect from his unsuccessful opponent. Maria Theresa was now tired and disillusioned by her experiences during the war, by the huge costs of the struggle which the Habsburg provinces were still poorly equipped to meet, and by the disappointment of victories which led nowhere. Henceforth her outlook on international affairs was to be cautious and pacific. But she never lost her intense personal dislike and distrust of the king of Prussia; while the traditional determination to assert Habsburg leadership in Germany was effectively represented in Vienna by the chancellor, Prince Kaunitz-Rittberg, and above all by the empress's eldest son, the Archduke Joseph, whose influence was certain to grow as time went on.

It was clear therefore that Anglo-French jealousies and Austro-Prussian (or more accurately Habsburg–Hohenzollern) rivalries would influence international relations for many years to come. Side by side with these by now well-established antagonisms, however, can be found a third factor, in some ways more important than either, which threatened the peace of Europe throughout the generation after 1763. This was the tragic and potentially dangerous situation in Poland. The weakness and misgovernment of the country, already great when the eighteenth century began, had been increasing for decades, and the Seven Years War saw Poland's effectiveness as a political and military force fall to a very low ebb indeed. In 1763 the plans for a partition of the country between her more powerful neighbours which had been appearing for over a century were still merely plans; but the likelihood of their eventual realisation was visibly increasing. The approaching death of Augustus III fore-shadowed another election to the Polish throne, with all the possibilities of internal disorder and international strife which this involved: when he died, early in October, the choice of his successor became at once the most pressing problem of European politics.

The fate of Poland, moreover, was likely to have repercussions on those of two other once-great and now declining states. These were Sweden and the Ottoman empire. The former had never recovered the international status lost as a result of her defeat in the Great Northern War, while her nobility was almost as factious and unpatriotic as that of Poland. The Turkish empire was declining hopelessly in military and political efficiency, mainly because of a religious conservatism, inspired by the learned and priestly class (*ulema*) and defended by the Janissaries, which was stronger than anything of the kind to be found elsewhere in Europe.

The history of European diplomacy during this period can therefore be written largely in terms of these three problems—Anglo-French rivalry at sea and overseas; Habsburg–Hohenzollern antagonism in Germany; and the Polish question. To them was added, from the end of the 1760s on-wards, a fourth, that of Russo-Turkish relations. All, and especially the second and third, were interconnected; but each can be treated to a con-siderable extent in isolation. The fact that three of the four arose in central and eastern Europe meant that after 1763 the centre of interest and activity in European politics moved noticeably to the east. In the Rhineland, in the Low Countries, in the Italian peninsula, all for generations the scene of fierce international rivalry, the territorial position was now relatively stable. This was a marked contrast with the state of affairs in Poland or the Balkans. None of the west European powers, with the partial exception of France, could hope to have much direct influence on events in the eastern half of the continent; and none except France (and she only intermittently) really wished for such influence. The Anglo-French colonial rivalries of this period, whatever their long-term significance for the world, had little direct importance to the majority of Europeans. Many of the greatest European questions of this period did not originate in western Europe, and in their solution the western states played in general only minor roles.

In the West the most important development of the 1760s was a marked recovery of strength and self-confidence by France. This recovery owed a good deal to the leadership of Étienne de Choiseul-Stainville, duc de Choiseul, a minister of energy though not of the highest abilities, and by the end of the decade it had placed the country in a position from which she might hope to regain in the near future some of the territory and prestige lost in the Seven Years War. This resurgence of French power and ambition can be seen in efforts during the 1760s to reorganise the army, and still more in the reconstruction of the French navy. More important still, Choiseul attempted systematically and successfully to consolidate and strengthen France's wartime alliance with Spain, an alliance embodied in the Family Compact of August 1761. Throughout the period between the Peace of Paris and the French Revolution it was her Spanish alliance, far more than that of 1756 with Austria, which was the real pivot of French foreign policy. Choiseul himself in 1765 referred to the Austrian alliance as 'precarious, very different from the fundamental alliance with Spain', and told Louis XV that if Charles III of Spain became involved in a war with Britain he must be supported by France 'in whatever condition your kingdom might find itself'.[1] The maintenance of good relations between Paris and Madrid was in some ways easier than might have been expected. In spite of its total lack of military or naval success the Franco-Spanish alliance survived the last years of the Seven Years War unshaken, in striking contrast to the *de facto* Anglo-Prussian alliance which had emerged in 1758 and broken up so disastrously and irrevocably in 1762. Charles III and his ministers were as alarmed and angered as the French by Britain's maritime and colonial victories; while Britain's possession of Gibraltar and recovery of Minorca produced a nagging sense of grievance in Madrid and led to endless petty Anglo-Spanish disputes. The ambitions of the French and Spanish governments were by no means always identical. But France and Spain had a certain fundamental unity in their mutual hostility to Britain, and the 1760s saw the alliance between them consolidated, most noticeably by a commercial treaty of 1768.

The war of revenge against Britain for which Choiseul began to plan at least as early as September 1765 was to be essentially maritime and colonial. He was determined not to be drawn into expensive and distracting military commitments in Europe, as his predecessors had been in 1756. Britain might be forced to disperse her energies and resources by threatening concentrations of troops in Flanders, Brittany or northern Spain, or by a Spanish attack on Portugal; but the war was not to become a European one. Hanover could be left untouched, and France's energies must be concentrated on seizing British colonies, on helping the British colonists in North America if they should rebel against the mother-

[1] *Mémoires du Duc de Choiseul* (Paris, 1904), pp. 389–90.

country, and above all on carrying out a successful invasion of Britain herself.[1]

These ideas were sensible; and they were to be applied with some effect by Choiseul's successor, the comte de Vergennes, in the War of the American Revolution. But the British cabinets of the 1760s completely failed to understand the direction which French strategic thinking was now taking. Continental allies, they assumed, were still needed by Britain to divert to land warfare in Europe as much as possible of the strength of the Bourbon powers and to protect Hanover, which continued to be thought of as a hostage which history and geography had conspired to place at the mercy of France. To find such allies, however, was very difficult. Austria was still thought of by a good many Englishmen (not least by George III himself) as in some way the natural ally of Great Britain; but she was now bound to France by ties which she had clearly no intention of breaking. Frederick II, apart from the memory of the bitter Anglo-Prussian recriminations of 1762, rightly believed that an alliance with Britain was likely to draw him into a new Anglo-French war which he was determined to avoid. Moreover from 1764 onwards the international position of Prussia was secured by his alliance with Catherine II;[2] henceforth he had nothing to gain from a combination with Britain. Thus Russia was left as the only great European power with which Britain might hope to ally. Negotiations for an Anglo-Russian treaty began in 1762 and went on intermittently for over a decade before they petered out. They failed because successive British governments, though they undoubtedly wished for Russia's alliance, refused to pay the price which Catherine II set upon it. They refused to provide money on the scale which she demanded in order to bribe the Swedish Council and Senate, and thus keep them subject to Russian influence and immune to that of France. They refused to help her in securing the election of a Russian-sponsored candidate to the Polish throne after the death of Augustus III. Above all they refused to promise her support in case of a Turkish attack on her southern frontiers. In support of this refusal they pleaded the damage which might be done to Britain's Levant trade by what would be taken in Constantinople as a demonstration of hostility; more probably it was inspired by a justified belief that a Russo-Turkish war was likely in the fairly near future and that Britain had nothing to gain by supporting the empress's Near Eastern ambitions.

It was above all upon the 'Turkish clause' that the alliance negotiations broke down. But they several times appeared to be upon the point of success and aided the conclusion, in 1766, of an important Anglo-Russian commercial treaty. If they had succeeded the Anglo-Russian alliance

[1] Choiseul's strategic plans, and their development in the later 1760s, are conveniently summarised in J. F. Ramsey, *Anglo-French Relations, 1763–1770* (Berkeley, 1939), ch. III.
[2] See below, p. 258.

would have become one of the main elements in the 'Northern System' which the Russian Foreign Minister, Count N. I. Panin, attempted to construct in the middle and later 1760s. This ambitious scheme, which seems to have been originated early in 1764 by Baron Korf, the Russian minister in Copenhagen, envisaged a great combination of Russia, Prussia, Britain, Sweden, Denmark and Poland against the Bourbon powers, and above all against France. Such an alliance, Panin hoped, would 'draw Russia away from her continual dependence on others and place her...in such a position that she will be able to play an important role in the affairs of Europe, and also to preserve quiet and stability in the North'.[1] His schemes were not completely without result. They led him to think of a strengthened and rejuvenated Poland under Russian influence as Russia's main future ally, in place of Austria, against the Ottoman empire; and this attitude had for a number of years some influence on Russia's Polish policies. They also led to the conclusion in 1765 of a Russo-Danish alliance which helped to pave the way for the final settlement, two years later, of the long-standing dispute between the two states over Holstein.[2] But the Northern System projected by Panin, like so many schemes for extensive new combinations of states during the eighteenth century, was impossibly grandiose and unwieldy. Britain and Russia, as has been seen, failed to reach political as distinct from economic agreement. Frederick II, moreover, felt no enthusiasm for such a system. He wished to remain Catherine II's only important ally, and therefore threw his influence at St Petersburg against the conclusion of a treaty with Britain; he disliked any strengthening of Poland, which might well check his own expansionist ambitions in that direction; and he was profoundly cynical about the real value of such a far-reaching political combination. With the outbreak of war between Russia and the Ottoman empire in September 1768 the Northern System rapidly faded into the background of European politics.

It is true that an alliance with Russia, even if it had been made, would have been of little use to Britain in an essentially maritime and colonial war with France such as Choiseul envisaged. Nevertheless her diplomatic isolation during the 1760s, combined with the spectacle of her internal political conflicts and the growth of unrest in America, did much to reduce her influence and prestige in Europe. France, by contrast, was clearly growing in strength and self-confidence. In 1766, on the death of Stanislaus Leszczynski, the Duchy of Lorraine at last became formally French territory under the terms of the Treaty of Vienna of 1735. More important from the standpoint of international relations, in 1768–9 the island of Corsica was conquered and annexed. Unable to repress the revolt against her rule there which had been in progress for many years,

---

[1] *Sbornik Imperatorskogo Russkogo Istoricheskogo Obshchestva*, vol. LXVII (St Petersburg, 1889), p. 25.   [2] See vol. VII, p. 350.

the republic of Genoa had agreed, in August 1764, to allow French troops to garrison five towns in the island. In May 1768 it signed with the French government a treaty by which, in effect, Corsica was sold to France in return for a payment of two million livres and a French guarantee of Genoa's mainland territory. It took the French a year to break the resistance of Pasquale Paoli, the Corsican insurgent leader, and his followers; but by June 1769 the island was completely in their hands. British protests, inspired partly by fear that the conquest might strengthen French naval power in the Mediterranean, proved completely ineffective. The cabinet was weak and divided, and by the autumn of 1768 had drifted into a sulky acquiescence in France's action. Its supineness did much to reduce Britain's prestige in Europe, and in particular to confirm Catherine II's growing feeling that Britain was unlikely to prove an active or energetic ally.

Little more than a year later it seemed that the new Anglo-French struggle which the Corsican episode had failed to produce was about to break out. In June 1770 a Spanish expedition, despatched by the governor of Buenos Aires, took possession of the tiny British settlement of Port Egmont in the Falkland Islands. In London there was a burst of indignation, while in Madrid, where the Falkland Islands had always been regarded as Spanish territory, there was no willingness to make concessions or listen to British protests. An Anglo-Spanish war, for which both sides were making energetic preparations, seemed very near; and in such a war France would certainly be involved. If Choiseul had remained in power the war of revenge against Britain for which he had prepared might well have taken place, though he himself worked hard to achieve a peaceful settlement of the dispute. But his position at court had for some time been increasingly threatened by rival ministers, by the hostility of Madame du Barry, the king's mistress, and by extreme Catholic influences which disliked his internal policies. The result was that he was suddenly dismissed by the king in December 1770. Deprived of any immediate prospect of French help, the Spanish government had to give way. In January 1771 it agreed to restore Port Egmont to Britain, though it avoided any explicit renunciation of its claim to the Falkland Islands. The crisis had thus resulted in a British victory. But it was an incomplete victory, one which Britain owed to the weakness of Louis XV as much as to her own strength, and it did little to halt the steady decline of her prestige in Europe. 'In fact', wrote a sarcastic pamphleteer two years later, 'so magnanimous, so manly, so consistent have of late years been the measures of the British government, that notwithstanding our laurels and conquests we have contrived to draw upon ourselves contempt and indignity from every European potentate.'[1]

More important than the questions of Corsica and the Falkland Islands, however, were the crises of the 1760s and early 1770s in eastern Europe.

[1] *A Sketch of the Secret History of Europe since the Peace of Paris* (London, 1772), p. 37.

As early as February 1763 a council of Russian statesmen and military leaders had decided that the next king of Poland must be a *piast* (Polish noble) and not a foreigner. In the months which followed Catherine II concentrated considerable bodies of troops on the Polish frontier, and also made arrangements for the bribing of influential Poles and the strengthening of the pro-Russian forces, led by the Czartoryski family, in Poland. It was known in St Petersburg that France would try to influence the next royal election, probably in favour of some member of the Saxon ruling house, which had provided the last two kings of Poland, and there was also a more serious fear of possible Turkish intervention. Catherine was therefore anxious to secure if possible British, Austrian or Prussian support for her Polish ambitions. It soon became clear that there was little to be hoped for from Britain; and the Austrian government, though it had no particular desire to oppose Russia in Poland, was the ally of France and therefore bound to some extent to share her anti-Russian attitude. Moreover Saxony would be a very useful ally for the Habsburgs in any future war in Germany; this in itself was a considerable argument for favouring a Saxon candidate for the Polish throne. There remained only Prussia. In February 1763 Frederick II began that long and insincere correspondence with Catherine which was to last almost until his death; by August he was able to send her a draft Russo-Prussian treaty of alliance. By October (Augustus III died on the fifth of that month) the empress regarded an alliance with Prussia as imminent; at the end of January 1764 a Russian draft sent to Frederick was accepted by him with only minor modifications; on 11 April the alliance was signed. It was to last for eight years, and each power promised military help to the other if it were attacked.[1] Each pledged itself to maintain the Swedish constitution of 1720 and, most important of all, guaranteed the existing Polish constitution (in other words the continuance of political chaos in Poland) and the elective character of the Polish monarchy. By a secret additional convention it was agreed that the two powers should support Stanislaus Poniatowski, Catherine's former lover, as their candidate for the Polish throne. In September he was duly elected.

The events of 1763–4 made it clear that France, which regarded herself as the traditional protector of the Poles, could no longer exert much real influence in Poland. This was partly because of the disunity and disorganisation of French diplomacy there. Side by side with the official representative of France, the marquis de Paulmy, and often in conflict with him, worked members of Louis XV's futile *Secret*, the network of agents which he had built up since the 1740s for the conduct of a secret personal diplomacy. Indeed the position was even more complicated than this, for sometimes these secret agents worked against each other,

---

[1] Except in case of a Turkish attack on Russia, or any attack on Prussian territory west of the Weser, when merely financial help was called for.

or in ignorance of each other's existence. Above all, few French statesmen now really cared deeply about what happened in Poland. Their
attention was focused on colonial and maritime affairs, on relations with
Britain and Spain. The more necessary a reassertion of France's position
against Britain, the greater the incentive to avoid being drawn deeply
into the affairs of eastern Europe. In May 1763 the duc de Choiseul-
Praslin, the French Foreign Minister and cousin of the great Choiseul,
argued forcibly in a memorandum on French policy that France had now
only a vague and indirect interest in the affairs of Sweden, Poland and the
Ottoman empire, her former protégés, and that even a partition of Poland
would probably be of little significance to her.

Nevertheless the French government could not see without anger the
placing of a Russian puppet on the Polish throne. Not until a year after
his election was Poniatowski recognised as king by France; and even then
no French diplomatic representative was sent to Warsaw. It was humiliating to feel that French power and prestige were waning in eastern
Europe, and both Choiseul and Louis XV were intensely anti-Russian.
'Everything that may plunge Russia into chaos and make her return to
obscurity', wrote the king in September 1763, 'is favourable to our interests.'[1] France by herself could do little to achieve this objective, and
could expect little help in achieving it from her ally Austria. But the
Turks, it seemed to many French statesmen, might well provide an effective weapon with which to halt and even reverse the growth of Russian
power. In 1763–4 the French ambassador at Constantinople, the Chevalier
de Vergennes, made strenuous efforts, on instructions from Paris, to persuade the Porte to support the Saxon candidate for the Polish throne and
to oppose by force the entry of Russian troops into Poland. He had no
success; and in July 1765 the Turkish government decided to recognise
Poniatowski. Nevertheless French efforts to embroil the Turks with
Russia continued, and Choiseul, with remarkable irresponsibility and
lack of foresight, repeatedly urged upon Vergennes the need to provoke
a Russo-Turkish war.[2]

That war, however, when it broke out in September 1768, was the
outcome not of French diplomacy in Constantinople but of events in
Poland. As resistance to Russian influence increased there, and as Russian
military control of the country began to be exerted more and more openly,
fear and resentment rapidly grew at the Porte. The formation of the Confederation of Bar early in 1768 helped to bring matters to a head. In July
Ukrainian irregulars (*haidamaki*) in pursuit of fleeing Confederates burnt
the small town of Balta in Podolia, a clear violation of Turkish territory.

---

[1] P. Rain, *La Diplomatie française d'Henri IV à Vergennes* (Paris, 1945), p. 265.
[2] See his despatches of 21 April and 19 June 1766 in L. A. de Bonneville de Marsagny, *Le
Chevalier de Vergennes, son ambassade en Constantinople* (Paris, 1894), vol. II, pp. 304–8,
317–19.

The culprits were not strictly Russian soldiers, and the Russian government attempted to disclaim responsibility for their action, but in vain. On 6 October Obreskov, the Russian minister in Constantinople, was imprisoned in the castle of the Seven Towers and war between Russia and the Ottoman empire had begun.

The war was most unwelcome to Catherine II and her ministers. It involved new and very heavy commitments on Russia's southern frontier. It complicated the Russian position in Poland. Above all it might lead to anti-Russian intervention in the Near East by one of the great European powers, most probably by Austria. Nevertheless they decided at once to wring all the advantage they could from the struggle with the Turks. In November 1768 a council at St Petersburg decided that Russia must obtain, when peace was made, freedom of navigation for her ships on the Black Sea (an objective of Russian policy since the reign of Peter I) and possession of a port there. She should also secure some extension of her territory at the expense of Poland. To these war-aims was soon added a third—that of establishing the khanate of the Crimea, whose territories embraced a huge area of the Black Sea steppe, as an independent state. This also was to some extent a traditional objective of Russian policy, and the idea of an eventual Russian annexation of the Crimea had already begun to take shape.[1] But the khanate had been for almost three centuries a Turkish satellite-state whose rulers were appointed by the sultan; and its continued subjection to Turkish control was regarded by the Porte as an indispensable protection against the growth of Russian power in the Black Sea area. The demand for its independence, therefore, was certain to be violently opposed in Constantinople. Nor did this demand complete the growing list of Russian war-aims. By 1770 it was generally agreed in St Petersburg that Russia must also annex the fortresses of Kerch and Yenikalé and thus control the Straits of Kerch leading from the Sea of Azov to the Black Sea proper. Without this, possession of Azov itself, which had been achieved early in 1769, would be of little value. By the end of 1770, moreover, the Russian government was demanding that the Danubian principalities of Moldavia and Wallachia be placed under its control for twenty-five years as an indemnity for Russia's war expenses, and that the Kabardas, a large and ill-defined area east of the Sea of Azov, be annexed by Russia.

Russian war-aims were therefore very ambitious. Yet the brilliant successes won by the Russian army and navy in 1769–71[2] showed that there was a good chance of achieving many of them if there were no outside intervention in the struggle. By 1771, however, it had become clear that the powers of Europe were not willing to give Catherine II a completely free hand in the Near East. From the outbreak of the war

[1] H. Uebersberger, *Russlands Orientpolitik in den letzten zwei Jahrhunderten*, vol. I (Stuttgart, 1913), pp. 265, 269.   [2] See below, ch. XI, p. 324.

Frederick II had been urging her to make peace as soon as possible, perhaps through joint mediation by Austria and Prussia. There were also offers of mediation by Britain (which Catherine might have been willing to accept) and by France (which she was determined to refuse). Above all the danger of some action by Austria to protect the Turks and prevent Russia exploiting her victories to the full could not be ignored. It was the possibility of an Austrian initiative of this kind, and of a resulting Austro-Russian war which would certainly involve Prussia, which so worried Frederick II.

His fears had some justification, for in the early months of the Russo-Turkish struggle Kaunitz was urging strongly in Vienna the need for active opposition to Russia in Poland and the Near East. He even suggested a possible *rapprochement* between Austria and Prussia based on the recovery of part of Silesia by the former and the compensation of the latter with the Russian-dominated duchy of Courland, which was formally still part of the Polish republic. His arguments had no result. Maria Theresa was determined to remain at peace. Joseph, who had succeeded his father as Holy Roman Emperor in 1765, had personal meetings with Frederick II at Neisse in Silesia in August 1769 and at Neustadt in Moravia in September 1770. But these, though they aroused much interest and speculation, had no significant results. Until early in 1771 Austria remained remarkably quiescent in face of the brilliant victories won by Russia. By early February of that year, however, Maria Theresa had decided that any further expansion of Russia must be resisted; and when in June the full extent of the Russian demands on Turkey became known in Vienna there was an explosion of alarm and indignation there. By then the Russian government had amended its terms so that only the independence of the Principalities, not their temporary transfer to Russian control, was demanded. But even this was too much for Kaunitz and Joseph II to stomach. Such a drastic truncation of the Ottoman empire, it was argued, would overthrow the European balance; and early in July, in great secrecy, an Austro-Turkish convention was signed in Constantinople. By this agreement (which was never ratified) Austria promised the Porte diplomatic support for the maintenance of the Ottoman empire's territorial integrity. In return she was to be paid a large annual subsidy, which would be used for the strengthening of her army, and would also receive some territory in the western part of Wallachia. In July–September 1771 Austro-Russian relations remained very critical. Catherine II showed no disposition to give way over the Principalities, while the Austrian government began military preparations and negotiated in Paris for French help in the war with Russia which seemed certain to break out in the following spring.

But there was little real desire for war in Vienna and none in St Petersburg. On 5 September Maria Theresa assured Rohde, the Prussian representative in Vienna, that she wished to maintain peace and if possible persuade the Turks to come to terms with Russia. This independent action by the empress, which was bound to weaken the effect produced in Berlin and St Petersburg by Austria's belligerent attitude of the preceding months, intensely annoyed Kaunitz. But both he and Joseph II now saw that many of Catherine's demands on the Turks could not be effectively resisted, and in particular that the creation of an independent state in the Crimea was inevitable. By October a kind of *de facto* compromise had been reached. It was now fairly clear that Austria would not oppose Russia's creation of such a state, and that Russia would not object to the return of the Principalities to Turkish overlordship.

Quite apart from this, however, it had become likely several months earlier that territorial ambitions denied full expression in the Near East might find a safer and more convenient outlet in helpless and anarchic Poland. At the end of 1770 Prince Henry of Prussia, a younger brother of Frederick II, visited St Petersburg. He had already shown himself much more optimistic than his brother about the prospects of annexing West Prussia in the near future; and in October he had drawn up a scheme by which Austria, Russia and Prussia would jointly supervise Polish affairs. He made a good impression on Catherine II, and the visit had unexpected and most important results. On 8 January 1771 the empress suggested to him, in half-jocular fashion, a partition of Poland. Austria, she pointed out, had already occupied the two *starosties* of Zips,[1] and 'why should not all of us take some?' The Russian War Minister, Count Z. G. Chernyshev drove home the point by urging that Prussia should take the bishopric of Warmia (Ermeland) which formed a large Polish salient in East Prussia.[2]

Prince Henry eagerly welcomed the idea of a partition, and on his return to Berlin some weeks later he overcame his brother's fears that Russia might benefit unduly from one. The result was that from early in 1771 Frederick II began to urge the Austrian government to accept a division of Poland as the best means of preserving international peace. In May he attempted to force the hands of Kaunitz and Maria Theresa by concluding a preliminary partition agreement with Russia. By the end of October Vienna had been brought to agree in principle to a partition. Though many questions of detail remained to be settled and Maria Theresa accepted the partition treaty, with much heart-searching, only in August 1772, the fate of the Republic was decided. The Russo-Turkish war and the Austro-Russian antagonism in the Balkans which sprang from it were not in any fundamental sense the causes of the first partition of Poland; but they undoubtedly did much to accelerate it and perhaps to determine the form it took.

[1] See below, ch. XII, p. 338.
[2] *Politische Correspondenz Friedrichs des Grossen*, vol. XXX (Berlin, 1905), pp. 406-7.

Even after a partition of Poland had been agreed upon and the danger of active opposition from Austria had disappeared, Catherine II still found herself faced with the task of forcing the Turks to make peace on her terms. It proved a very difficult one. In August–September 1772 Russian and Turkish plenipotentiaries met at the little town of Foksiany in Moldavia; but negotiations quickly broke down over the insistence of the Turks that the sultan should retain at least the right of confirming the khan of the Crimea in the exercise of his powers, if not that of appointing him. When a new peace congress opened at Bucharest late in November the Russians gave way on this point, but fresh difficulties arose over the resistance of the Turks to the Russian annexation of Kerch and Yenikalé and over their wish to deny freedom of navigation on the Black Sea to Russian warships. The discussions dragged on fruitlessly till March 1773. To the Russian government this long delay in making peace was serious. The war had cost Russia great sacrifices which could not be indefinitely prolonged. From September 1773 onwards a considerable part of the country was convulsed by the great peasant revolt led by Pugachev.[1] Above all Sweden, paralysed for decades by factional struggles and political corruption, seemed suddenly to have regained much of her unity and strength and become once more an active opponent of Russia in the Baltic.

For a number of years French policy in Stockholm had been directed not, as formerly, towards taking advantage of the struggles of the Swedish parties, but rather towards the strengthening of the Swedish monarchy. King Adolphus Frederick, who died in February 1771, was not the man to overthrow the Swedish constitution and unite the country behind a revived monarchy; but his son and successor, Gustavus III, young, energetic and physically brave, promised better things. He was visiting Paris when his father died, and was at once given promises of French financial help in a restoration of the power of the monarchy. His position during the first few months of his reign was very difficult, but in August 1772 he was able, by an almost bloodless *coup d'état*, to overthrow the Swedish constitution of 1720 and recover much of the position which the monarchy had formerly held.

The Swedish revolution was a great international event. To contemporaries it seemed a striking political victory for France, whose influence might now become dominant in Stockholm, and a severe setback for Russia, who might soon find herself at war with the triumphant Gustavus III. Neither of these impressions was completely justified. French proposals for a defensive alliance with Sweden had no result; partly because under the new constitution Gustavus could not make agreements with foreign powers without the approval of the Senate, and partly because Louis XV showed no wish to involve France in any new obligations to

[1] See below, ch. XI, p. 313.

other states. The expected Russo-Swedish war did not break out, though for several months at the end of 1772 and early in 1773 the likelihood of one seemed very great. Catherine II was infuriated by events in Sweden; and in a struggle with Gustavus III she could rely on the active support of Denmark, where the fall of Struensee[1] had brought pro-Russian forces back into power. Peace in the north was maintained, however, partly by the refusal of the British government to give Russia any support if she attacked Sweden and above all by the fact that Catherine II was still at grips with the Porte and had much of her military strength absorbed by the struggle. It was the break-up of the congress at Bucharest, and the resulting necessity for at least one more campaign against the Turks, which put paid to any effort by Russia to undo the effects of the *coup d'état* of August 1772. The empress was thus compelled to pay a considerable price in the Baltic for the successes she had won in the Balkans and the Black Sea littoral.

By the autumn of 1773 pessimism about the outcome of the war with Turkey was growing in Russian ruling circles. In September Count Chernyshev urged that the demand for Kerch and Yenikalé be given up to facilitate the making of peace, and there were even doubts whether the independence of the Crimea could be obtained. Catherine II now displayed the courage and energy which were to distinguish her in more than one crisis of her reign. In April 1774 Field-Marshal P. A. Rumyantsev, the Russian commander-in-chief, crossed the Danube on orders from St Petersburg. By the beginning of July the main Turkish army, under the Grand Vizier Muhsinzadé Pasha, was in grave danger of being cut off and surrounded by the Russian advance. Early in that month, therefore, Muhsinzadé suggested to Rumyantsev that peace negotiations be opened: on the 21st the peace treaty was signed in the Bulgarian village of Kutchuk-Kainardji. It was, as the delighted Catherine told Rumyantsev, 'one such as Russia had never had before'.[2] It gave Russia the Kabardas, Kerch and Yenikalé, and a small area of territory between the lower courses of the rivers Bug and Dnieper with the mouth of the latter—in other words a secure though as yet limited foothold on the Black Sea. It gave her freedom of navigation on that sea and permitted her merchantmen to pass through the straits, closed for two centuries to all non-Turkish ships. It granted her the right to build an Orthodox church in Constantinople and, in a vague and potentially dangerous phrase, to make representations

---

[1] John Frederick Struensee, a German doctor who acquired great influence over the half-insane Christian VII of Denmark from 1768 onwards. He became the lover of the queen, Caroline Matilda, the younger sister of George III of England, and dominated the Danish government from the latter months of 1770 till he was overthrown by a conspiracy in January 1772. His brief rule was marked by very rapid and extensive, though sometimes ill-conceived, reforms in most aspects of Danish life, and by a temporary decline in Russian influence over the country's foreign policy.

[2] *Sbornik*, vol. XIII (St Petersburg, 1874), p. 429.

to the Turkish government on behalf of it 'and those who serve it'. By a secret article the Porte agreed to pay a war indemnity of four and a half million roubles. Above all the Crimean khanate was to become an independent state: the sultan was to retain the right of investing the khan with his office, but this was to be a purely religious ceremony conveying no suggestion of political control.

From the Turkish point of view these terms, especially the independence of the Crimea, were disastrous. Not until January 1775 was the treaty very reluctantly ratified by the sultan. Even after this strenuous efforts were made to avoid compliance with its terms. In May 1775 the province known as the Bukovina, in northern Moldavia, was surrendered to the Austrians in the hope that this would buy off possible Habsburg hostility to the Ottoman empire and free the latter for more effective resistance to Russia. Above all Turkish intrigues and the threat of Turkish military action helped to keep the Crimea in constant turmoil. In March 1779, by the Convention of Ainali-Kavak, the main provisions of the Treaty of Kutchuk-Kainardji were repeated and the independence of the Crimea once more proclaimed, but even this was far from being a final settlement of the question.

The peace settlement of 1774 alarmed not merely the Turks but also some of the great powers of Europe. It seemed to foreshadow the creation of a great Russian fleet on the Black Sea, followed by a new and irresistible Russian onslaught on the tottering Ottoman empire. The collapse of that empire, which now seemed imminent, would mean an enormous accession of strength to Russia and raise immensely difficult problems. To France, which was the traditional ally of the Turks and did far more trade with the Levant than any other state, this prospect was especially unwelcome. But one of the main lessons of the events of 1768–74 had been that there was very little she (or any other west European power) could do to protect the victim-states, Poland and the Ottoman empire, which were now threatened by the advance of Russian power. France was geographically distant from these states and herself suffering from severe internal divisions. Her government, as has already been seen, was preoccupied after 1763 mainly with colonial and naval rivalry with Britain and thus unwilling to commit the country to quixotic adventures in eastern Europe. Moreover the few suggestions which were made during this period for French action, however limited, on behalf of the Poles or Turks were stultified by British hostility and distrust. Thus a suggestion in March 1772 by the French Foreign Minister, the duc d'Aiguillon, of Anglo-French diplomatic co-operation on behalf of the Poles aroused no response in London. In the spring of the following year a proposal to send a French squadron to the Levant as a gesture of support for the Turks had to be abandoned in face of British opposition. The Russo-Turkish war and the first partition of Poland emphasized a fact which had been made visible by the Polish crisis of 1763-4—that western Europe on the one hand and eastern and central Europe on the other were, at least for the time being, separate political worlds, and that members of one were likely to have little influence on events in the other.

The War of American Independence is another illustration of this point. A great Anglo-French-Spanish struggle was waged, great changes in the colonial balance of power were achieved, without the states of eastern and central Europe having any important influence on the march of events. In the late summer and autumn of 1775 the British government had high hopes of hiring from Russia a corps of 20,000 infantry for use against the rebellious colonists; but by October it was clear that nothing would come of the idea. During the war there were several proposals for the restoration of peace through the good offices or mediation of Joseph II and Catherine II; but these again had no result. A suggestion by the British government in January 1781 that Russia might acquire Minorca in return for making peace between Britain, France and Spain on the terms agreed in 1762 also proved fruitless. It is true that the League of Armed Neutrality which Catherine II began to create early in 1780 proved a serious nuisance to Britain. In a declaration of 10 March to the belligerent governments the empress proclaimed a series of doctrines highly distasteful to Britain, though for the most part not new. (The declaration was largely copied from proposals made in September 1778 by the Danish statesman Bernstorff.) Neutral ships were to be free to navigate between the ports of the belligerents. Property belonging to the citizens of a belligerent state could not be seized on board a neutral vessel unless it were contraband. A blockade of any belligerent port, to be legal, must be effective. The Armed Neutrality, which was eventually joined by almost all the maritime states of Europe, was thus directed against British interference with neutral shipping and against the 'maritime rights' which the British government, like its predecessors, claimed to exercise in time of war. It seriously hampered the full exertion of British sea-power in the last years of the war. But it had no decisive influence on the outcome of the struggle; and before the end of the war in America the attention of Catherine II and her ministers was once more focused mainly on the Near East.

The French government was thus able to devote its energies to the struggle with Britain from 1778 onwards without the need, as in 1744-8 and 1756-63, to maintain large armies in Germany, Italy and the Netherlands. Yet the comte de Vergennes, who had become Foreign Minister in 1774 and was to retain the post till his death in 1787, had serious difficulties to face during both the war and the peace negotiations. Effective political co-operation between France and Spain was always very difficult. This was partly because Charles III, feeling that he had been abandoned by France in 1770 during the Falkland Islands crisis, was now unwilling to follow a French lead. It was still more because the two states regarded the war from radically differing standpoints. The French government showed no unwillingness to recognise the independence of Britain's American colonies or to receive American diplomatic missions, as her recognition of the colonies in February 1778 and the subsequent enormous popularity of Franklin in Paris showed. Charles III of Spain, on the other hand, like almost all other European rulers, deeply disliked the idea of colonial rebellion, and as the ruler of a great empire in central and south America had every reason to fear the triumph of the colonists in the north. They might follow up victory over Britain by attacking the Spanish colony of Louisiana; or, more serious, their example in achieving independence might find imitators in the Spanish dominions. American envoys were not officially received in Madrid. Not until the end of the war was American independence recognised by the Spanish government. Moreover Vergennes and his colleagues were not aiming primarily at the acquisition of territory. They wished to reduce the prestige and the dangerous maritime predominance of Great Britain; but the French empire of the future which they envisaged was to be essentially a commercial one based on relatively small gains in Newfoundland, the West Indies and India. To the Spanish government, on the other hand, substantial territorial gains at the expense of Britain—Florida, Minorca, possibly Jamaica, above all Gibraltar—were of supreme importance. It was not the urgings of Vergennes but the refusal of Britain to cede Gibraltar, and her rejection in March 1779 of Spanish mediation proposals inspired by the hope of recovering the fortress, which led to Spain's entry into the war.

Nor did the events of the war do much to unite France and Spain more effectively. There was little military or naval co-operation between them except in the unsuccessful siege of Gibraltar; and there were even Anglo-Spanish peace negotiations, though never very serious ones, for several months from the summer of 1780 onwards. France's other European ally in the struggle, the United Provinces, was little more reliable than Spain. Britain declared war on the Dutch in December 1780 because of the trade they persisted in carrying on with the American rebels, and above all because of their acceptance of Catherine II's invitation to join the Armed Neutrality. Her action inflicted great damage on Dutch trade. But it did not destroy the pro-British sympathies still felt by a good many people in the republic, not least by the Stadtholder William V himself. In 1781 there were fears in Paris that the Dutch (who also had not yet recognised the American colonies as independent) might make a separate peace with Britain.

Thus Britain, in spite of the military failures of the war,[1] was in a fairly strong position *vis-à-vis* her European opponents when peace negotiations began in Paris and London in April 1782. She was facing not a real

[1] See ch. XVII, pp. 503-5.

alliance but rather four separate antagonists—France, Spain, the Dutch and the Americans—whose interests were dissimilar and even conflicting. Lord Shelburne, the British Prime Minister, was able to exploit this position skilfully by signing a separate treaty with the colonists, much to Vergennes' annoyance, on 28 November 1782. Moreover the shakiness of France's financial position made the French minister anxious not to prolong the war, while Rodney's victory at The Saints in April and the defeat of the great Franco-Spanish attack on Gibraltar in September placed new and strong cards in the hands of the British negotiators.

Britain's losses to her European adversaries, when the terms of the Treaty of Versailles were finally agreed in January 1783, were thus a good deal less than had sometimes seemed probable. Vergennes, in spite of great efforts, could not secure for France the gains in India, producing a large territorial revenue, which he much desired. An extension of France's fishing-rights in Newfoundland, the acquisition of St Lucia and Tobago in the West Indies and of Senegal and Gorée in West Africa, were considerable gains from the point of view of French trade but not otherwise of great importance. Spain recovered Florida, and also Minorca which had been captured from Britain by a French expedition in February 1782. But the supreme prize, Gibraltar, eluded her. The efforts of the Spanish government to obtain it very nearly wrecked the negotiations, and both George III and Shelburne would have been willing to part with it in return for adequate compensation elsewhere—Puerto Rico or some combination of French islands in the West Indies were suggested. But public opinion in Britain refused to contemplate the cession of a fortress which had now, after its successful defence in the great siege of 1779–82, become what a contemporary called 'the Golden Image of English Idolatry'.[1] With the utmost reluctance, therefore, Spain made peace without recovering it. The treaty with the Dutch, the terms of which were agreed in September 1783, was signed in its definitive form only in May 1784. It provided for the cession to Britain of the trading-post of Negapatam in Ceylon and the grant to her of the right to navigate freely among the Dutch possessions in the East Indies.

Britain had been forced to recognise the independence of her former colonies; but apart from this great admission of defeat she lost little of real value in the negotiations of 1782–3. 'I thank Providence', wrote George III in January 1783, 'for having through so many difficulties, among which the want of Union and Zeal at home is not to be omitted, enabled so good a peace with France, Spain, and I trust soon the Dutch, to be concluded.'[2] This was a fair summary, from the British point of view, of the European and Asiatic aspects of the settlement.

[1] V. T. Harlow, *The Founding of the Second British Empire*, vol. I (London, 1952), p. 361.
[2] *The Correspondence of George III, 1760–1783*, ed. Sir J. Fortescue (London, 1927–8), vol. VI, p. 222.

The political as well as geographical separation which now existed between events in America and those in Germany is well illustrated by the fact that the serious Austro-Prussian friction, culminating in war, which arose in the later 1770's, had hardly any effect on the War of the American Revolution.

The idea of acquiring the electorate of Bavaria, or at least part of it, had for nearly a century attracted statesmen in Vienna. In particular there had been, since the 1680's, several suggestions that the Spanish or Austrian Netherlands might be exchanged for the electorate. The benefits which the acquisition of Bavaria would confer on the Habsburg monarchy, by giving it a more compact block of territories centred on the Danube and by increasing its influence in Germany, were obvious. But for this very reason any effort by the Habsburgs to strengthen themselves in this way was certain to be bitterly opposed by Frederick II, who realised very well that Joseph II was anxious to acquire territory wherever it could be had and resentful of the restraining influence of his mother. At the beginning of 1778 it seemed that events had played into Austria's hands and that she was to acquire, by peaceful means, a large part of Bavaria. The Elector Maximilian-Joseph died on 30 December 1777. His successor was the Elector Palatine, Karl-Theodor of Sulzbach, who had no legitimate children but a considerable number of illegitimate ones for whom he was anxious to provide. The result was that in January 1778, within a few days of his succession, he agreed to recognise Habsburg claims to about a third of Bavaria (the territory in question was alleged in Vienna to be composed of lapsed Austrian, Bohemian and imperial fiefs). In return Karl-Theodor received the Order of the Golden Fleece for himself and relatively lavish provision for his illegitimate children.

This agreement displayed a remarkable disregard for legal rights, for even Maria Theresa admitted that the Habsburg claims in Bavaria were 'outdated and poorly based'.[1] In particular it ignored the claims of the heir-presumptive to the electorate, the duke of Zweibrücken-Birkenfeld, while the Elector of Saxony also had claims to Maximilian-Joseph's allodial lands in Bavaria. Yet Kaunitz and Joseph II believed that they would encounter no very serious opposition to their plans. They hoped for diplomatic and if necessary military support from France, the ally of the Habsburgs since 1756, while Russia, the ally of Frederick II, seemed still too preoccupied in the Near East to be a serious opponent. Protests from Berlin were taken for granted, but Frederick II was now an old man unwilling to face a new war. Moreover he had dynastic ambitions of his own. The Franconian principalities of Ansbach and Bayreuth were ruled by a junior branch of the Hohenzollern family. If it died out, as seemed likely, the king wished the right of succession of the senior, Brandenburg,

---

[1] *Maria Theresia und Joseph II. Ihr Briefwechsel*, ed. A. von Arneth (Vienna, 1867–8), vol. II, pp. 171–2.

branch to be recognised by the powers. Recognition of Frederick's claims to Ansbach and Bayreuth might thus be bartered against his recognition of the Habsburg claims in Bavaria.

Events were soon to show that a great miscalculation had been made in Vienna. The duke of Zweibrücken, under Prussian influence, violently opposed the sacrifice of his rights and the absorption of part of his inheritance into the Habsburg dominions. His attitude won a good deal of sympathy from the smaller German princes, to whom the aggressive and overbearing policies of Joseph seemed increasingly menacing. More serious, the attitudes of both France and Russia were much less favourable to Austria than had been expected. Catherine II (herself by birth a member of a minor German ruling family) disliked the idea of radical change in the political structure of Germany, though she was unlikely to act decisively there while Russo-Turkish tension remained as acute as it was in 1777–8. Above all the French government was quite unwilling to give Austria any support. Vergennes wished to continue the alliance of 1756 with the Habsburgs; but like Choiseul he refused to make it the foundation of France's foreign policy. Already in April 1777 he had told Louis XVI, in a long memorandum, that Austria derived far greater advantages from the alliance than France, and that the only real reason for continuing it was to preserve peace on the Continent and thus allow France to concentrate on her maritime and colonial rivalry with Britain. No extension of France's obligations under it should be considered, and in particular it was in France's interest to preserve the power of Prussia as a counterweight to that of the Habsburgs in central Europe. Even the acquisition of the Austrian Netherlands, he concluded, could not compensate France for a large growth of Austrian power.[1] This attitude was maintained throughout the crisis of the following year. On 10 March 1778 the Baron de Breteuil, the French ambassador in Vienna, was told that the French government could not recognise an Austro-Prussian struggle over Bavaria as a *casus foederis* under the alliance of 1756 and that 'circumstances did not permit His Majesty to take any part but that of neutrality in the war which might break out in Germany'.[2]

By the time this despatch was written Austro-Prussian tension was becoming acute. Neither power wanted war, and on 20 May the Prussian government put forward a complicated plan for a compromise settlement. This proposed that the Habsburgs should retain only two districts of Bavaria. In return they should cede to the Elector Palatine the duchies of Limburg and Gelders in the Netherlands, as well as the imperial fiefs which still remained dotted about Bavaria. The Elector of Saxony, as compensation for his allodial rights in Bavaria, would receive part of the Upper Palatinate and the imperial fiefs in Suabia. Austria would not oppose

[1] G. de R. de Flassan, *Histoire…de la diplomatie française* (Paris, 1811), vol. VII, pp. 132–40.
[2] *Ibid.* vol. VII, pp. 195–7.

the eventual union of Ansbach and Bayreuth with the electorate of Branden-burg or (an important provision from Frederick's point of view) the exchange of these territories for Lusatia if the rulers of Prussia and Saxony agreed on this. The refusal of Joseph II and Kaunitz to accept these terms made war in-evitable, and early in July Prussian forces crossed the Bohemian frontier.

The struggle which followed, in which Prussia was joined by Saxony, was of little military interest. There was hardly any fighting of significance and both armies suffered far heavier losses from desertion and disease than from battle casualties. Nor did the half-hearted fighting mean the end of negotiations between Berlin and Vienna. Only a few days after the outbreak of war Maria Theresa, without the knowledge of Joseph, sent Baron Thugut, a leading Austrian diplomat, to discuss a compromise settlement with the Prussian government. In August she offered, without success, to abandon the agreement made in January with the Elector Palatine if in return Frederick II would renounce the idea of uniting Ansbach and Bayreuth with Brandenburg. By the middle of that month the negotiations had been broken off. By mid-September the attitude of Catherine II, who, as Russo-Turkish tension relaxed, was increasingly stressing her determination to defend the rights of the German states, was causing growing concern in Vienna. Early in November the French government agreed, in spite of its preoccupation with the war against Britain, to act as joint mediator with Russia, and by the end of the year talks were in progress for a Russo-Prussian military convention which would provide for the despatch of a force of Russian auxiliaries to help in the struggle with Austria. Frederick was dissatisfied with what he con-sidered the inadequate help offered him by Catherine; but it was now clear that Austria, which had won no military victories and could call on no effective support from any other power, would have to give way. On 16 February 1779 the government in Vienna accepted preliminaries which gave it only a small part of Bavaria and on 13 March the peace congress opened at Teschen in Austrian Silesia. Prince N. I. Repnin for Russia and Breteuil for France acted as mediators. The settlement which had emerged by 13 May, when the congress broke up, was embodied in a series of agreements between Austria, Prussia, the Elector Palatine and the Elector of Saxony. Austria received the part of Bavaria bounded by the Inn, the Danube and the Salza, and abandoned her other claims in the electorate. She also agreed not to oppose the eventual union of Ansbach and Bayreuth with Brandenburg. The Elector of Saxony received a money compensation for his allodial claims in Bavaria.

Frederick II was thus justified in claiming that the war had ended in a victory, though by no means an overwhelming one, for Prussia, and that 'in the Empire we shall in future be thought of as a useful counterweight to the despotism of Austria'.[1] More important, the struggle over the

---

[1] *Politische Correspondenz*, vol. XLII (Leipzig, 1931), p. 420.

Bavarian succession had brought Russia into the affairs of Germany more clearly and explicitly than ever before. As a guarantor, with France, of the agreements of 1779, she obtained a position in German politics comparable to that enjoyed by France, as a guarantor of the Westphalian settlement, for the last four generations.

However, the check of 1778–9 had done nothing to reduce Joseph's hunger for territorial expansion. The death of his mother at the end of 1780 freed him from her moderating influence and aroused widespread fears that he might embark upon a series of aggressive adventures. Even before the death of Maria Theresa he had been envisaging an alliance with Russia which would isolate Prussia and link Austria with the strongest military power in Europe. Within six months of his assuming sole control of the Habsburg dominions the alliance had been made, in fact if not in form. It was embodied in an exchange of letters between the emperor and Catherine II in May 1781 by which each guaranteed the other's territories and the existing position in Poland. To this were soon added vague but alluring schemes for joint action against the Ottoman empire and a possible partition of its European territories. To Catherine the possibility of Austrian aid against the Turks had been the main reason for making the alliance; and it was to prove its value to her when, in April 1783, she ended the incessant confusion and upheavals in the Crimea by annexing the khanate to Russia. The efforts of the French government to resist the annexation by diplomatic means were hamstrung by the refusal of Joseph and Kaunitz to support them, and in January 1784, on French advice, the Porte recognised formally that the Crimea and the Kuban were now part of the Russian empire. Catherine, with some exaggeration, told the emperor that her success was 'due solely to the good offices which Your Imperial Majesty employed in favour of His ally'.[1]

Joseph, to the surprise of some observers, did not take advantage of the Crimean crisis to seize Turkish territory for himself; but even before it ended his restless ambitions had begun to show themselves in the Netherlands. He had always objected to the closure of the river Scheldt to non-Dutch shipping laid down by the Treaty of Münster in 1648. To him it appeared not merely a humiliating check on the trade of his Netherlands dominions but also a clear infringement of the natural right of his subjects to use the river—and the idea of natural rights was already beginning to have considerable influence on thinking about international affairs. By 1781 he had determined to open the river to shipping. He began by forcing the Dutch, at the end of that year and in the early months of 1782, to withdraw their garrisons from the now useless barrier fortresses. This was followed, in October–November 1783, by a number

---

[1] *Joseph II und Katharina von Russland. Ihr Briefwechsel*, ed. A. von Arneth (Vienna, 1869), pp. 218, 223.

of deliberately engineered frontier incidents and the seizure of three small Dutch forts, while the Austrian government made for the first time an open protest against the existing régime of the Scheldt. Early in April 1784 an attempt was made to send a merchantman down the river from Antwerp past the Dutch fort of Lillo; the ship was fired on by the guns of the fort. On 23 August Count Belgiojoso, the governor of the Austrian Netherlands, made a final demand for the opening of the Scheldt; in return the Austrian government would give up its territorial claims against the Dutch, of which the most important was to the territory of Maestricht. This proposal, which seemed to threaten gravely the commercial life of the United Provinces, stimulated a violently hostile reaction there, and on 8 October an Austrian ship which had left Antwerp for Ostend was captured by the Dutch near Sanftingen. The Austrian minister to the Hague was at once recalled, and war seemed on the point of breaking out.

That the crisis was settled peacefully, and once more in a way unsatisfactory to Joseph, was due partly to the attitude of France. Vergennes was disillusioned by the attitude of Austria to the Russian annexation of the Crimea and anxious to avoid any action which might throw the Dutch into the arms of Britain; as early as 21 May 1784 he had promised them French good offices in their dispute with the emperor. In spite of all the efforts of Marie-Antoinette and the Austrian ambassador in Paris, Mercy-Argenteau, Franco-Austrian relations deteriorated badly towards the end of 1784, and a French note to Vienna of 17 November made it clear that France would support the States-General, if necessary by force. Catherine II, the emperor's new ally, did not oppose his ambitions; but she gave him no help beyond a note to the States-General in which she said that she recognised the justice of his demands and hoped that a settlement satisfactory to both sides would be found. Joseph's willingness to come to terms with the Dutch was being increased, however, by another and quite different factor in the last months of 1784. He was now hoping to exchange the whole of the Austrian Netherlands for Bavaria, for in August his representative in Munich, Lehrbach, had opened negotiations with the Elector Karl-Theodor in the hope of realising this long-cherished Habsburg dream. By making concessions over the Scheldt, an issue of relatively minor importance, the emperor hoped to secure the consent of France to the exchange. French support on this issue would be particularly valuable to him because, though Karl-Theodor was quite willing to exchange Bavaria for the more valuable Netherlands, the duke of Zweibrücken, still the heir-presumptive to the electorate, was not, and the French government was thought to have considerable influence over him.

In the event Joseph secured neither the opening of the Scheldt nor the Bavaria–Netherlands exchange. At a meeting of the royal council at Versailles on 2 January 1785 it was decided that the acquisition of Bavaria might make Austria a threat to the French possession of Alsace, besides dangerously increasing her influence in Italy and overthrowing the balance of power in Germany. French consent to it must therefore be dependent on that of Frederick II. This decision destroyed any possibility of the exchange being carried out; on 13 February Karl-Theodor issued a denial that it had ever been contemplated. In July Frederick II succeeded in forming in Berlin a union of Prussia, Saxony and Hanover, which was later joined by many of the smaller German states, Catholic as well as Protestant. This *Fürstenbund* (League of Princes) was designed to maintain the *status quo* in the Empire. By a secret article of the treaty which united them its members promised to support each other in resisting any invasion or seizure of Bavaria. The blow to Joseph's prestige was considerable and the check to his German ambitions complete.

The negotiations for a settlement between the emperor and the Dutch, which were carried on in Paris under French auspices, dragged on for months like all those in which the States-General was concerned. Not until 8 November 1785 was the Treaty of Fontainebleau signed. It gave Joseph a little territory in Brabant and Limburg, complete possession of the Scheldt above Sanftingen, and the sum of ten million florins in return for the surrender of his claims to Maestricht. But the Scheldt remained closed; in essence the treaty was a defeat for the emperor.

The effective separation of the politics of eastern Europe from those of the west which became visible after 1762–3 began to disappear in the later 1780s. The outbreak of a new war between Russia and the Ottoman empire in August 1787 began a sequence of events which had produced by 1789–90, for the first time for a quarter of a century, a crisis of European as distinct from merely regional dimensions. Russia's Near Eastern ambitions were far from being satisfied by the annexation of the Crimea, and in the early 1780's Catherine II and her advisers were playing with grandiose schemes for further expansion. A 'Greek Empire' embracing not merely Constantinople and Greece proper but also Bulgaria, Thrace and Macedonia might be created, perhaps with her grandson the Grand Duke Constantine as ruler. Moldavia and Wallachia might be united to form an autonomous state under Russian influence, a 'Kingdom of Dacia' which might be ruled by the empress's favourite, Prince G. A. Potemkin. These schemes, however, were always dreams or aspirations rather than plans; the war of 1787 had more limited and specific causes. It sprang above all from Turkish resentment of the growth of Russian power in the Caucasus (where most of Georgia had become a Russian protectorate in the summer of 1783), from the efforts of the Porte to limit the activities of Russian consuls in the Ottoman empire and from its deposition of the pro-Russian hospodar of Wallachia.

The Russian government, as in 1768, was taken by surprise by the outbreak of the war, and in the early stages of the conflict its forces failed to win any very striking victory. Nor was its international position very happy. Joseph II could not deny that the *casus foederis* under his alliance of 1781 with Catherine had arisen. But he entered the war, in February 1788, with extreme reluctance, and soon found that its demands were increasing the already great unpopularity of his régime in Hungary. More important, in July 1788 Gustavus III of Sweden, hoping to recover the Finnish territory lost at Åbo in 1743 and the Baltic provinces surrendered at Nystad in 1721, suddenly attacked Russia. For a moment he seemed to threaten St Petersburg, for the defence of which only a few thousand men were available. Above all the death of Frederick II in August 1786, and the new direction this had given to Prussian policy, meant that a powerful Anglo-Prussian combination had now emerged as a factor in European affairs for the first time since 1761 and seemed likely to take a hand in the affairs of the Near East.

In September 1787 a Prussian army, with British support, destroyed the power of the pro-French 'Patriot' party in the United Provinces and restored the former authority of the *stadtholder*, whose wife was the sister of Frederick William II. This was followed by the signature of an Anglo-Prussian convention at the beginning of October, of Anglo-Dutch and Prusso-Dutch treaties of alliance on 15 April 1788, and, much more important, of a defensive alliance between Britain and Prussia on 13 August 1788. This provided for mutual help in case of outside attack and a guarantee by both signatories of the integrity and constitution of the United Provinces. By the end of the summer of 1788 Joseph II, surrounded by difficulties, was acutely anxious at the prospect of having to face a Prussian attack on Bohemia and Moravia as well as a difficult struggle with the Turks in Bosnia and Serbia. By December Catherine had decided that the hope of creating a kingdom of Dacia must be abandoned. Moreover the virtual paralysis of France as a factor in international relations, as a result of her internal troubles from 1787 onwards, did a great deal to free the hands of Britain and Prussia for possible action against Russia and Austria. Negotiations which dragged on throughout 1788–90 for a combination of Russia, Austria, France and Spain, a grouping which would, under normal conditions, have done much to strengthen the position of Joseph and Catherine, eventually collapsed, largely because of the obvious worthlessness of France as an ally.

In fact Catherine's difficulties were less serious than appeared on the surface. Gustavus III was facing serious discontent within Sweden (the hope of strengthening his domestic position by a successful war was one reason for his sudden attack on Russia) and within a few weeks of his declaration of war his military operations were temporarily paralysed by a serious mutiny in the Swedish army. Neither Britain nor Prussia approved of his attack on Catherine II and in September Denmark entered the fray against him in fulfilment of her alliance obligations to Russia.

Within a matter of days a Danish army seemed on the point of capturing Göteborg. Only the intervention (without instructions from London) of Hugh Elliot, the British minister at Copenhagen, forced the Danes to agree on 9 October to a temporary armistice. Prussian threats to invade Jutland if they continued the struggle with Sweden forced them first to prolong the armistice and then to make peace with Gustavus III, but Sweden had been placed, by the rashness of her king, in greater danger than at any time since the end of the Great Northern War.

Against these setbacks Gustavus could set nothing but a rather ineffective alliance and subsidy treaty made with the Porte in July 1789 and some financial help from Britain and Prussia. His forces achieved little against the Russians apart from an important naval victory at Svensksund in July 1790. On 14 August of that year, therefore, he made peace with Catherine II at Verela in Finland. His attack on Russia had undoubtedly been of considerable value to the Turks, and it gave him for a time a key position in European politics; but Sweden gained nothing by it. By agreeing to the Treaty of Verela he broke his promise to the Porte to make no separate peace; and Turkey and her interests did not figure at all in the text. Almost as soon as it had been signed Gustavus, with typical inconsistency, opened negotiations for a Russo-Swedish-Danish alliance.

Even more helpful from the Russian point of view than the weakness of Sweden was the essential disunity of Great Britain and Prussia. Pitt had made the alliance of 1788 only after long hesitation and regarded it as an instrument for the maintenance of peace and stability in Europe, while the fate of the Ottoman empire still seemed to most British statesmen of minor importance. In Berlin, by contrast, the alliance was seen as a stepping-stone to important territorial gains and events in the Near East now dominated the political horizon, as they were to do until well into 1791. In return for large gains in the Balkans, it was hoped, Joseph II might be compelled by the armed mediation of Prussia to cede Galicia to the Poles. They, in exchange, would hand over to Prussia Danzig and Thorn, thus rounding off and greatly strengthening the eastern borders of the Prussian monarchy. This scheme, so typical in many ways of the international relations of the age, had been drawn up by Hertzberg, the Prussian Foreign Minister, in November 1787. It aroused no enthusiasm in London and from the beginning the members of the Anglo-Prussian alliance were at cross-purposes. Moreover the progress of the anti-Austrian revolution in the southern Netherlands led to the rise in 1789 of another source of Anglo-Prussian disagreement, since Prussian proposals that the independence of these provinces be recognised were totally unacceptable to the British government, which still hankered after some alliance with Austria.

Nevertheless by the early months of 1790 the position of Catherine II was becoming increasingly difficult. On 31 January Dietz, the Prussian minister at Constantinople, signed with the Porte a treaty which provided for Prussia's entry into the war in the spring of the following year and for the return to the Turks of the Crimea and all the territory they had lost since 1787. Two months later the Prussian government made with Poland, where anti-Russian forces were becoming increasingly strong, a treaty by which the two states guaranteed each other's territories and promised each other aid in case of attack by some third power. In Berlin the military party was urging that Prussia should disregard the warnings and hesitations of Britain and launch an attack on Bohemia; after the collapse of Austria, which it was assumed must soon follow such an attack, terms could be imposed on Russia. The British government also was slowly and reluctantly moving into opposition to Catherine II. Increasingly the ministers in London were thinking of developing Poland as a source of the essential naval stores which had hitherto come from Russia;[1] by the spring of 1790 the idea of a commercial treaty with the Poles and the ensuring for Polish trade of free access to the Black Sea as well as the Baltic was becoming central to British policy.

Above all the death of Joseph II on 20 February 1790 deprived Catherine of the help of her Austrian ally. His brother and successor, Leopold II, perhaps the most intelligent ruler of the age, was well aware of the dangerous international position of the Habsburg dominions. The threat which Prussia now offered to them must be averted, and Leopold at once wrote a personal letter to Frederick William II expressing his desire for better relations between the two states. Though Kaunitz was bitterly opposed to anything which looked like a surrender to Prussia, by April negotiations for a settlement of Austro-Prussian differences were under way. The continued insistence of Hertzberg on the cession of at least part of Galicia to Poland (and therefore, it was hoped, of Danzig and Thorn to Prussia) made agreement seem very unlikely; but a conference between representatives of the two powers opened at Reichenbach in Silesia on 26 June. On 11 July the weak and changeable Frederick William II, realising that the exchange plan was strongly opposed by Turkey and Poland as well as by Great Britain, suddenly decided to make an agreement with the Austrians on the basis of the *status quo*. Hertzberg's schemes were jettisoned, and by the Convention of Reichenbach of 27 July Leopold II retained Galicia and agreed to make peace with the Porte through the mediation of Britain, Prussia and the Dutch. Prussia had won a superficial diplomatic victory at the price of temporarily sacrificing her expansionist ambitions; but Leopold had secured his essential objective—peace on reasonable and honourable terms.

The Convention of Reichenbach did not, of course, end the Russo-Turkish war. Not until January 1792 did Catherine II make peace with the Porte on terms which allowed her to push her south-western frontier

[1] D. Gerhard, *England und der Aufstieg Russlands* (Munich–Berlin, 1933), pp. 292 ff.

forward to the Dniester. The events which followed the Austro-Prussian settlement of July 1790 are, however, outside the scope of this chapter. By the time of the Reichenbach agreement the structure of international relations which had existed in 1763 had undergone at least two radical changes. Russia, in 1763 powerful but still remote and half-despised by western statesmen and diplomats, had shown a greater capacity for territorial expansion than any other European state and was now the greatest power on the continent. France, in 1763 still in most respects the greatest European state, now appeared to be doomed for many years to relative impotence in international affairs; the real nature of the change she was undergoing was still misunderstood by nearly all observers. The weaknesses of the Habsburg dominions, already clear under Charles VI and Maria Theresa, had been illuminated and in some ways increased by the career of Joseph II; those of Prussia were rapidly becoming more visible, and obviously Germany would remain, as in the past, an area of weakness and instability in European politics. Britain, her prestige and resources recovered from the defeats of the American Revolution, was still, in spite of Pitt's new-found interest in the Near East, essentially isolationist—more so in many ways in 1790 than she had been in the 1760s.

Above all, the foundations were now laid for a great change in the questions around which European diplomatic activity revolved. Near Eastern issues, even to some extent Anglo-French colonial rivalries and the Habsburg–Hohenzollern feud in Germany, were soon to be pushed into the background. In their place would arise the problems posed by the existence of a new régime in France and by the destruction of Poland.

CHAPTER X

THE HABSBURG POSSESSIONS AND GERMANY

I

THE conclusion of the Seven Years War inaugurated a period of recovery and reform in many German states. Large areas of central Europe—Prussia, Saxony, Bohemia, the Rhinelands—had suffered severely through devastations, looting, requisitions and heavy impositions. Everywhere extraordinary war-taxation had brought about a state of economic exhaustion. For many states reconstruction and reform were a condition of survival.

In Vienna, the exigencies of the war clearly revealed the inadequacy of Haugwitz' work of reform.[1] The effects of the loss of Silesia had indeed been overcome, and a most remarkable increase in revenue had been achieved. Nevertheless, after four years of war, the finances of the Habsburg monarchy were utterly exhausted, the administration had become chaotic, and the brilliant diplomatic perspectives of 1756 were displaced by the fear that Austria would sink to the status of a second-rate power.

The lesson was clear: the reform work of Haugwitz would have to be extended. The initiative for further changes came from the Chancellor of State, Kaunitz, who felt that his foreign policy had been robbed of the success it deserved because of the breakdown in the internal administration. At this stage, Kaunitz confined himself to purely administrative proposals. To promote a greater measure of unity among the diverse Habsburg provinces, more administrative coherence and continuity of policy, he proposed an advisory Council of State (*Staatsrat*), competent to consider 'from the centre' all internal affairs. The Council of State began its work in 1761. Kaunitz, who was himself one of its most influential members, seized the opportunity to strengthen the financial administration. This was now made autonomous and, in 1765, was put under the supreme direction of Hatzfeld.

Hatzfeld's financial administration, supplemented by the work of his rival Ludwig Zinzendorf at the *Hofrechenkammer*, was eminently successful. For the first time since the accession of Maria Theresa, the government gained a reasonably exact idea of its resources and expenditure, outlined a budget for the coming year, and checked the accounts for the preceding one. The crushing burden of the national debt incurred during

---

[1] Cf. vol. VII, pp. 412–14.

the Seven Years War was alleviated in 1766, when the new emperor Joseph II used the considerable fortune left by his father to secure a reduction of the average interest rate from 6 per cent to 4 per cent. A balanced budget was in sight.

The underlying problem of the Habsburg monarchy, however, had not thereby been solved. Unless special measures were adopted to avert the danger, war might once again involve the same sort of financial embarrassment and administrative confusion as had followed the outbreak of the Seven Years War. The government therefore planned not only to strengthen the defences of the monarchy, but to prevent a financial collapse in a future war. This could not be achieved on the basis of purely administrative reform. It was necessary to secure a substantial increase in revenues.

The experience of the Seven Years War had shown that the non-privileged classes, who bore the main burden of direct and indirect taxes, could not under existing circumstances be expected to pay any more. Indeed they were in obvious need of some relief. Maria Theresa's aim, therefore, was to tap the wealth of the undertaxed privileged orders. With this purpose in mind, she convoked the Hungarian diet in the summer of 1764.

The Hungarian 'nation'—that is, the magnates, gentry and clergy who alone were represented in the diet—had succeeded by virtue of their constitution and their special position within the Habsburg monarchy in keeping Hungary's contribution to the revenue at a very low level as compared with that of other provinces. Maria Theresa and her advisers realised how difficult it would be to get any concessions out of the diet. They prepared for the coming struggle in a manner which was characteristic not only of Habsburg policy, but of enlightened despotism in general. A Hungarian scholar, Adam Kollar, was encouraged to research into Hungarian law and history in order to provide legal and historical justification for the demands which the queen of Hungary intended to put to the diet. Just before the opening of the diet, Kollar published the results of his research, apparently on his own initiative.[1]

The queen's message to the diet contained two demands: an increase in the Hungarian contribution, and the conversion of the personal obligation of the nobility to serve in the feudal levy (*Insurrektion*) in time of war into a cash subsidy payable by lay and clerical nobility alike. The diet, infuriated by the publication of Kollar's book, refused to consider the demands until the book had been prohibited and its author punished. Though Maria Theresa's pride was deeply hurt by the diet's attitude, she was prevailed on to prohibit the book formally to clear the way for the discussion of her demands. Even so, the diet remained obstinate. The

---

[1] F. Maass, *Der Josephinismus—Quellen zu seiner Geschichte in Österreich 1760–1790*, I, *Fontes Rerum Austriacarum*, 2. Abt., LXXI, pp. 206–8.

demand for the commutation of the feudal levy was rejected outright. The demand for an increased contribution was countered by the argument that the Hungarian peasants were already in a state of the most extreme poverty and in no position to pay more taxes. In its reply the government foreshadowed the next great step in the reform programme: 'If the diet applied the appropriate means [thus ran the royal reply] to further the welfare of the tax-paying population, Her Majesty does not doubt for one moment that the latter will...soon be in a position to discharge the increased tax-obligation which has been demanded.'[1]

The diet did not take the hint. Prompted by the more pliable magnates, it voted a small increase in the contribution, but it allowed itself to be dissolved rather than discuss the government's proposals for lightening the feudal burdens on the peasantry.

Maria Theresa was nevertheless determined to secure a reduction of feudal burdens on the peasantry despite the opposition of the Estates. Her determination was strengthened by reports about the condition of the peasants, which seems to have shocked her deeply and to have outraged her humanitarian feelings. From 1766 onwards royal commissioners were sent to all the counties of Hungary to determine and regulate the obligations of the peasants *iure regio*. The decree of regulation for Hungary as a whole (*Urbarium*) was published in 1767. It turned the Hungarian peasant into an hereditary leaseholder with the freedom to leave his holding. Peasants occupying a holding of standard size were obliged to do one day's labour-service a week with draught cattle, or two days' without (twice this amount when urgent work was needed on the lord's fields), and to attend the lord on the hunt on three days in the year. The general tendency of the decree has been aptly summarised as that of converting the 'existing minimum into a maximum'.[2] The task of enforcement lay in the hands of royal officials and not in those of the county authorities. Maria Theresa's government was thus establishing its first direct contact with the lords' subjects. The consequent increase in royal power at the expense of the constitution filled the nobility with anxiety about the future.

The principles thus enforced in Hungary were no less applicable to other parts of the Habsburg dominions. In the very year in which the Hungarian *Urbarium* was published, the government demanded proposals from the Estates of Styria[3] on ways and means of reducing the peasants' feudal burdens. The rescript left no doubt as to the ruler's determination to secure such a reduction. Traditional burdens were probably heaviest

---

[1] F. Krones, *Ungarn unter Maria Theresia und Joseph II.* (Graz, 1871), pp. 17–18.

[2] H. Marczali, *Hungary in the Eighteenth Century* (Cambridge, 1910), p. 193.

[3] In most hereditary provinces the Estates consisted of the three 'benches' of clergy, lords and knights. The royal boroughs were the official 'fourth estate'; their representation had in most cases been reduced to an ineffective formality. The peasants were represented in the Estates only in the province of Tirol.

in Styria, at any rate until 1772, when Galicia brought a new record of feudal oppression into the monarchy. The Styrian Estates organised a series of obstructions which delayed regulation for more than ten years.

Meanwhile, peasant rebellions and famine in Austrian Silesia and Bohemia focused the government's attention on the lands of the Bohemian crown. During the preparatory negotiations with the particular Estates, explicit formulation was given to the principles on which the government now insisted. It was laid down that 'the peasantry, as the most numerous class which constituted the basis of the state's power, must be maintained in a satisfactory condition; that the peasant must be able to support his family and in addition defray the public expenses incurred in times of peace and war'. No established customs would in future be allowed to infringe this principle.

The first regulating decree outside Hungary was published in Austrian Silesia in 1771, and fixed a maximum of three days' labour services a week. The new provincial governments controlled from the centre and independent of the Estates provided the necessary means of enforcement.[1] Despite the widespread distress caused by the famine and the impatience of the co-regent Joseph, the Estates of Bohemia resorted to delaying tactics. The next decree, therefore, followed in the more docile Lower Austria in 1772. In this province traditional burdens had been comparatively light, and the decree fixed a maximum of two days' labour service with draught cattle. The overdue decrees for Bohemia and Moravia were finally published in 1775, after Councillor Kressel had reported that further delay would lead to serious disturbances. The maximum service was fixed at three days a week. This rather generous allowance was also secured by the Estates of Styria in 1778.

State regulation of feudal burdens benefited the peasantry wherever it was enforced. All the regulating decrees stipulated that dues traditionally lighter than the new legal maximum were not to be increased. Moreover, the peasants' security of tenure improved, as the government used its new executive organs in the provinces to enforce the old decrees against eviction and thus to prevent a reduction in the number of tax-payers.

The detailed knowledge which Maria Theresa now had of peasant conditions gave her an uneasy conscience, particularly since peasant unrest continued in Bohemia after 1775. She was aware that her legislation had not put an end to all feudal malpractices, and she condemned in no uncertain terms the lords' continued exploitation of their serfs. 'The lords fleece the peasant dreadfully', she wrote to her son Ferdinand in January 1777; and a fortnight later she wrote: 'We know and we have proof of the tyrannical oppression under which the poor people suffer.'[2] In this frame of mind, she was prepared to accept the advice of radical and

[1] Vol. VII, pp. 156–7.
[2] Quoted by F. Fejtö, *Un Habsbourg révolutionnaire—Joseph II* (Paris, 1953), p. 140.

enlightened councillors, such as Raab and Blanc, who had taken a leading part in drafting the regulating decrees, when they recommended further reforms for Bohemia. From the pen of the co-regent Joseph we have the following account of her intentions: '...she wanted to abolish serfdom, to fix arbitrarily all contracts and all payments which peasants have rendered to their lords for the lease of their land for centuries, to change the whole system of rural economy, and finally to lighten all her subjects' dues and obligations without the slightest consideration for the lord...'.[1]

Joseph was clearly of the opinion that for a ruler of a feudal state his mother had allowed her conscience and her fears to take her too far. He calculated that most lords would lose half their revenues and go bankrupt if the new programme were put into practice. He therefore made common cause with the aristocratic ministers who opposed Maria Theresa to a man, and the great project was dropped.[2] Blanc was exiled to Swabia, and Raab had to content himself with applying his principles to the crown lands and the estates of the dissolved Jesuit Order.

Thus the consistent determination to tap more of the wealth of the nobility led Maria Theresa and her government a long way along the road of social reform, and turned out to be the starting point of important social changes. When the government turned its attention to the great wealth of the Church, the consequences were no less momentous.

The government's demands on the clergy were precisely the same as those on the nobility—a greater contribution to public revenues. They also wished to ensure that no more wealth should escape the full impact of impositions by being transferred to ecclesiastical ownership. The partner with whom the government had to negotiate in this case was not a provincial diet, but the papal Curia. The question was, whether the latter would be more amenable to the government's demands than the Hungarian diet had been, or whether here too Maria Theresa would have to proceed *iure regio*.

The indications are that no serious opposition was expected. Kaunitz repeatedly emphasised that the empress had made it a rule not to act without the agreement of the papal Curia in these matters. Moreover, there is no evidence to suggest that any effort was made, in 1762, at the beginning of the negotiations, to reinforce the government's case by the findings of 'committed' historical research into the question of secular and ecclesiastical powers.

Soon, however, it became abundantly clear that the new pope Clement XIII and his secretary of state Torrigiani were most reluctant to make any further concessions to the secular power. On the contrary, their policy of asserting to the full the right of papal provision in the duchy of

---

[1] Joseph II to Leopold of Tuscany, quoted by Fejtö, *op. cit.* pp. 139–40.
[2] E. Guglia, *Maria Theresia, ihr Leben und ihre Regierung* (Munich, 1917), vol. II, pp. 355–6; Fejtö, *op. cit.* pp. 141–5.

Milan seemed to indicate that the papacy had gone over to the offensive. A papal *breve* of October 1762 refused permission for an additional tax on the Milanese clergy. Negotiations to obtain a renewal of existing dispensations for clerical taxation were cleverly obstructed by Torrigiani by making agreement conditional on an extension of papal influence over the Austrian clergy which was unacceptable to Kaunitz.

Maria Theresa's reaction to papal opposition was identical with her reaction to the opposition of the Hungarian diet. When Kaunitz submitted a report of the lengthy negotiations with the Curia early in 1768, she added the following resolution: 'If the papal Curia should refuse to give its consent to the renewal of the dispensation, there are to be no further negotiations; for I have decided to make use of my legitimate rights, and to proceed in this matter *propria authoritate*.'[1]

In the matter of preventing more wealth falling into ecclesiastical hands, Maria Theresa's government could point to numerous decrees published under her predecessors which had been consistently ignored. Her own decree of 1753 was equally ineffective. The papal Curia showed itself unmistakably hostile. The great administrative reorganisation which took place after 1760, therefore, included provisions for the enforcement of state regulations dealing with ecclesiastical matters. A *Giunta Economale* was set up in 1765 in the duchy of Milan, and this was followed in 1769 by the *Concessus in Publico-Ecclesiasticis* for the Austrian and Bohemian Lands. The Secret Instruction for the *Giunta*, dated 2 June 1768, laid down the principle that every ecclesiastical concern which had not been specifically entrusted by Christ to the Apostles came within the competence of the secular authority; it contained a very short list of the spiritual tasks entrusted to the Apostles; and it asserted that every right and privilege granted freely by the sovereign to the clergy could be amended or revoked like any other decree.[2] In 1769 the principles contained in the Secret Instruction were given general application.[3] The foundations of 'Josephinism' had been laid.

The task of providing theoretical and historical justification for the new policy, which was bound to meet with powerful clerical opposition, fell on the shoulders of Councillor Heinke. Kaunitz also wrote voluminously on this subject, but we have no evidence to show what use was made of his numerous drafts.[4]

Maria Theresa's government had thus fashioned for itself practical and theoretical weapons with which it could not only enforce its original rather limited aims, but also put the entire wealth and organisation of the Church at the disposal of the State. Joseph II later used these weapons to the full. Meanwhile, however, Maria Theresa, despite her Catholic piety, was determined to make wide use of them herself. The year 1767 saw the first

[1] Maass, *op. cit.* p. 266.
[2] *Ibid.* pp. 289–90.
[3] *Ibid.* pp. 105, 386.
[4] *Ibid.* pp. 335–84.

effective decree against the acquisition of property by the Church enforced in the duchy of Milan. From 1768 onwards the clergy were taxed without papal dispensation. In 1769 the first monasteries were dissolved and their endowments transferred to poor parishes. Decrees published in 1771 fixed a minimum age of twenty-four years for people taking monastic vows, and a maximum value of 1500 florins for the property they could bring with them into the monastery.

The dissolution of the Jesuit Order fitted logically into this pattern. The government was unwilling and unable to pay for the new educational system which was urgently needed if the work of reform was to be a lasting one. The sequestrated property of the Jesuits was used to endow an educational fund (*Studienfond*), with the help of which state elementary schools were established in every province of the Habsburg monarchy. The syllabus, drawn up by the Silesian Abbé Felbiger in 1774, was designed to produce 'useful, obedient and Christian citizens'. The new fund also made possible a reform of the secondary schools, designed to enhance their value as preparatory schools for the universities. Last, but not least, the fund provided for new Chairs at the universities, whose holders instructed the future civil servants in the principles put forward in defence of the government by Kollar and Heinke.

During all these years of change and reform, Joseph was in charge of military affairs. It was his principal concern that the growing financial and administrative strength of the monarchy should be fully reflected in its army and its defences. To this end he worked with unflagging energy in co-operation with his mentor, Field-Marshal Lacy, who was a first-rate organiser. He raised the number and quality of his soldiers by introducing a system of partial conscription in place of the old press-gang. The troops were constantly exercised on parade and in manœuvres. Their morale was raised by improved provisions for their families and for invalids. Equipment was brought up to date and fortifications were strengthened along the Bohemian and Hungarian frontiers. The vast quantities of new artillery astonished contemporary observers.

It is undoubtedly true that Maria Theresa had undertaken the work of reform after the Seven Years War 'with no immediate objective of war'.[1] The experiences of the war had inspired her with a genuine passion for peace. This passion was not, however, shared by Kaunitz or Joseph. The chancellor was still intent on schemes of aggrandisement to restore the lost supremacy in relation to Prussia. Joseph was burning to see his new army in action and to prove himself a great general. Both assumed that under the eighteenth-century international law of the jungle a state would have to expand if it were to survive.

Thus there could be no question of Austria declining to participate in the first partition of Poland. The empress wept—but Kaunitz and Joseph

[1] Vol. VII, p. 415.

took. So did Prussia, and the balance of power between the two countries remained unchanged.

To upset it decisively was the purpose of the Austrian aggression of 1778. Charles Theodore, the new ruler of Bavaria, was willing to sell the country to Joseph in return for a pension and empty honours. Austria was firmly allied to France. Prussia's alliance with Russia was weakening. Kaunitz was not willing to let such an opportunity go by unused. The Austrian army crossed the frontier and occupied Lower Bavaria, enabling the Chancellor to negotiate from a position of strength. He did not really expect that Frederick would risk war. But Frederick had little to gain from partition in this case. He was therefore determined to secure a reduction of the Austrian claims even if it meant war. As Joseph remained adamant, a Prussian army crossed the frontier into Bohemia in July 1778. Though few shots were fired, Joseph lost his confidence in the ensuing campaign. He had put himself at the head of his army, but lacked the essential ability to make decisions. The coveted military glory eluded him.

Joseph's lack of success, his mother's opposition to the war, and Frederick's ability to conjure up the threat of Russian intervention on his side, made the surrender of Austria's claims inescapable. At the Treaty of Teschen in 1779 the *Innviertel*, a little district north of Salzburg, was given to Austria 'to satisfy her pride'. Considering the enormous cost of the war, it was a meagre result.

II

Maria Theresa died in November 1780, and Joseph succeeded as sole ruler of the Habsburg dominions. The new reign marked no fundamental change in policy. The basic principles underlying all the acts of government between 1780 and 1790 had already been laid down. Only the political tact and cautious hesitation, such a marked feature of the late reign, were lacking in the new. Joseph had not inherited all his mother's strength of character, and made up for the deficiency by being outwardly harsh, sarcastic, and impatient of opposition.

The new ruler regarded the work of reform as unfinished. He was deeply dissatisfied with the level of military power which had been attained. The War of the Bavarian Succession had revealed unsuspected military weaknesses. Only further reforms could remedy this situation: 'I recognise above all that our situation has greatly deteriorated after the last war through the excessive burden of debt, that our provinces are impoverished, and cannot afford to maintain the present military establishment, and that only the improvement of our agriculture, industry, trade and finance will make possible the upkeep and expansion of our military forces to meet future eventualities.'[1]

[1] 'Bemerkungen zu einem Memoire von Kaunitz, 1779', in E. Benedikt, *Kaiser Joseph II. 1741–1790* (Vienna, 1936), pp. 263–4.

As Joseph saw the situation at the outset of his reign, even a purely defensive programme, designed to make the monarchy safe against possible attacks by its neighbours, would require a considerable improvement in the finances of the state. But before very long he set himself and his civil servants a more ambitious target: he must have sufficient resources to embark on offensive operations with a solid prospect of territorial gains. To create the financial basis for such a military machine, it was necessary to practise the strictest economy in government expenditure, to secure a much greater contribution from the wealthy classes, and to facilitate the greatest possible expansion of every branch of the country's economy. This was the political programme of Joseph II. With the experience of the last reign in mind, the new ruler avoided coronation, so as to prevent the traditional formulas and promises being used against him as weapons of obstruction by those whose wealth and privileges would be affected by his projected reforms.

Immediately after his accession Joseph began to enforce rigid economies. The court as a whole had to adopt the emperor's own simple and frugal way of life. His normal dress was an ordinary army uniform, and his palace seemed to contemporaries to resemble a military headquarters rather than the residence of Europe's pre-eminent sovereign. The aim and result of Joseph's administrative reorganisation was greater economy at least as much as greater centralisation. The department of finance (*Hofkammer*) was merged with the Bohemian-Austrian Chancellery, the Chancellery of Transylvania with that of Hungary, the provincial governments of Austrian Silesia, Görz and Carinthia with those of Moravia, Trieste and Styria respectively. In this way the number of officials drawing salaries from the state could be drastically reduced.

A typical 'Josephinian' economy was enforced in the field of higher education. By means of an appropriate manipulation of tuition fees and scholarships, the yearly admission of students was precisely limited to the number of anticipated vacancies in the civil service. Universities were allowed to continue as such only in Vienna, Pest, Louvain and Pavia. The others were down-graded to the status of *Lyzeen*. It is clear that Joseph II did not wish to have to patronise scholars and writers dedicated to 'pure' science and the arts. He invited none from other countries to come to Vienna, and he made as sure as he could that no native ones should develop. Even Mozart, whose music the emperor played and appreciated, suffered severely under this resolute economy drive.

On taxation, Joseph II had already put his views on record as co-regent: 'It is the task of the financial administration to collect the taxes as cheaply, exactly and correctly as possible, without imposing excessive burdens on the lower classes. Burdens should be evenly distributed, and nobles, peasants and burghers should pay according to their means. If there are some individuals who enjoy certain privileges, they should be treated like the others; and the same is due in justice to those who bear a disproportionate burden.'[1]

The taxation system inherited by Joseph II in 1780 did not correspond to these requirements at all. The burden was unfairly distributed both as between provinces and classes. Much noble land was not entered in the existing land-register, and registered noble land was taxed less heavily than peasant land. The Hungarian nobles considered themselves altogether exempt. And when Leopold of Tuscany examined the accounts for 1782, he commented on the 'enormous' sum of 21,000,000 florins entered as expenses incurred in the collection of taxes.[2]

The emperor's simple remedy for all these shortcomings was a project for a uniform land-tax based on a complete land-register. The finances of the state were expected to benefit in a number of ways: the higher yield of the land-tax would make possible the abolition of uneconomic taxes; the adjustment of burden to means would remove an important obstacle to the development of industrial activities; and the increased burden on land would help bring about, according to the prevailing physiocratic theories, a much more intense utilisation of land.

Joseph embarked with enthusiasm on the vast amount of preparatory work which was needed, if the project was to materialise. What he needed was an eighteenth-century Habsburg Domesday Book. In the Austrian and Bohemian provinces a census of population had already been made as a basis for the system of conscription introduced in 1771. In 1784 Joseph ordered that a census should be taken in Hungary. The reaction of the proud and independent Magyars was not unlike that of the Anglo-Saxon chronicler to the Domesday survey, partly no doubt because they suspected the purpose behind the count. The county assemblies recorded solemn protests, the officials encountered a good deal of active resistance, and the autonomous administration of the kingdom showed clearly where its sympathies lay by refusing to carry out its instructions.

In the course of his visit to Hungary in 1783 Joseph had discovered that his mother's ordinances were dead letters in many areas, where the county authorities did not dream of interfering in the unrestricted feudal tyranny of the magnates. He therefore regarded the execution of the census as a crucial test case. If he gave way, 'it would be the end of royal authority in all future issues'.[3] To secure compliance, he dispatched a battalion of infantry into the country with orders to arrest and send to Vienna any recalcitrant, whatever his rank. The census was carried out.

The year 1785 saw a start made with the work of compiling a complete land-register in the Austrian and Bohemian provinces. In Hungary Joseph

[1] Quoted by P. v. Mitrofanov, *Joseph II.—Seine politische und kulturelle Tätigkeit* (Vienna, 1910), p. 411.
[2] A. v. Arneth, *Joseph II. und Leopold von Toskana—Ihr Briefwechsel von 1781 bis 1790* (Vienna, 1872), vol. I, p. 159.   [3] *Ibid.* p. 240.

put an end to the constitutional authorities who would have obstructed this work indefinitely. In their place he introduced the Theresian administrative system. 'I have replaced fifty-four individuals who do nothing by eight who will see to the execution of my orders'—thus Joseph's brief account of the reform to his brother.[1] In 1786 the land-surveyors commenced work in Hungary.

It was the work on the land-tax which made Joseph reconsider his mother's proposals concerning further peasant legislation. At the time of these proposals and since, Joseph had shown concern at the increasing amount of evidence that the peasants, especially in Bohemia, were using the method of political agitation to secure further reductions in their feudal burdens. The peasant legislation of 1781 was designed largely to secure governmental control over all the efforts of the peasants to improve their condition. After 1785, however, Joseph was mainly concerned to achieve a simple and satisfactory method of calculating the peasants' resources for the purpose of land-tax assessment. He decided that the peasants were to pay their lords a fixed percentage (approximately $17\frac{7}{9}$ per cent) of their gross yearly income in money in place of all their former feudal obligations. Everyone, lord and peasant alike, could thus be assessed for the land-tax on the basis of the estimated gross income from his land.[2]

Census and land-register were complete by 1789. In February of that year a patent was published fixing the land-tax uniformly at $12\frac{2}{9}$ per cent of the gross yearly income from noble and peasant land alike. Added to the $17\frac{7}{9}$ per cent in respect of the commutation of his feudal dues, this left the peasant 70 per cent of his gross income for his own and his family's maintenance, his seed requirements, and for the contributions he had to pay to his parish, his priest, and the village schoolmaster. As the administrative machinery of the Estates had meanwhile been absorbed by the provincial governments, the collection of the tax became entirely a government responsibility. To counteract the belief of many peasants that they were, or ought to be, entirely freed from feudal obligations, a paragraph was inserted threatening severe penalties for refusal to pay the rents due to the lords. To refute the legal and historical arguments advanced by the nobility, the patent included some propositions taken from the historical theories of the Enlightenment. Thus we may read in the patent: 'Is it not nonsense to maintain that the nobles possessed their land before there were peasants, and that they gave their land to the latter under certain conditions? Surely they would perish of starvation immediately if no one cultivated the soil?'[3]

Despite these precautions, the patent aroused the unanimous opposition of the Estates and widespread unrest among the peasants. It must be

---

[1] *Ibid.* p. 269.
[2] Cottiers and landless labourers were excluded from this legislation.
[3] R. Raithel, *Maria Theresia und Joseph II. ohne Purpur* (Vienna, 1954), p. 105.

regarded as doubtful whether even Joseph II, had he lived longer, would have been able to enforce its implementation.

Considering the relative economic backwardness of the Habsburg dominions, a reorganisation of taxes was not likely to result in any considerable increase of state revenues, unless it was linked to a policy of economic expansion. Joseph, it has been noted,[1] pressed for the new land-tax partly because he saw in it a means of furthering economic expansion. Maria Theresa and her ministers had realised the importance of economic expansion for the revenues and strength of the state, but little real progress had been made in this direction during her reign. Joseph II pursued this aim with such single-mindedness that he allowed neither vested interests nor his own inclinations to stand in the way of its attainment. He judged all existing traditions and institutions by the simple criterion of whether they impeded or promoted agricultural and industrial production in his dominions.

We may see this most clearly illustrated by Joseph's policy concerning religious toleration. As so often, he found occasion to expound his attitude during his co-regency. It presents a sharp contrast to that of his mother, who hesitated to interfere in any way with the paramountcy of the Catholic religion in her dominions. 'I stand for freedom of belief', he wrote, 'in so far as I am prepared to accept everyone's services in secular matters, regardless of denomination. Let everyone who is qualified occupy himself in agriculture or industry; I am prepared to grant the right of citizenship to anyone who is qualified, who can be of use to us, and who can further industrial activity in our country.'[2]

Joseph put this principle into practice immediately after his accession, and ordered the reversal of precedents set down in the previous reign. His original intention was to confine the matter to the purely practical level: existing discriminations were to be removed as a matter of fact, but quietly, without any public pronouncements which might undermine the prestige and authority of the Catholic church.[3] In an age of rapidly awakening public opinion, however, this was not a practicable procedure. Information about the new *de facto* toleration soon leaked out, and gave rise to feverish speculation about the character of the new policy. Joseph was therefore compelled to proceed with the publication of a Patent of Toleration (October 1781), so that there should be no mistake about the limits of his toleration policy.[4] He was seriously concerned at the large

---

[1] Above, p. 288.

[2] Mitrofanov, *Joseph II*, p. 712.

[3] C. Hock and H. I. Bidermann, *Der österreichische Staatsrat* (Vienna, 1879), pp. 335–9. The fact that Kaunitz, too, for a time opposed the promulgation of a Patent of Toleration (*ibid.* p. 338) would seem to invalidate F. Maass' new thesis that the chancellor's religious policy was motivated by hostility to the Catholic church; cf. also Mitrofanov, *op. cit.* p. 713.

[4] Hock–Bidermann, *op. cit.* p. 340; Mitrofanov, *op. cit.* pp. 713–14.

number of his subjects who registered their adherence to one of the tolerated Protestant creeds, and before long issued instructions which rendered such registration much more difficult.

If creed was not to prevent 'qualified' men taking up the trade of their choice and putting their skill at the service of the state, neither was the institution of serfdom which still tied men to the estate of their lord in many Habsburg provinces. The decrees of November 1781 to July 1782 which abolished serfdom stated that the new freedom would benefit agriculture and industry, but warned the peasants that they still owed obedience to their lords. The realisation that raising the status of the peasantry meant raising also the level of agriculture could lead to far-reaching conclusions. Joseph followed the advice of enlightened 'Cameralists' like Joseph von Sonnenfels who had championed the cause of the peasants since the 1760s, and concluded his peasant legislation by extending to all the security of hereditary tenure.

Of great importance for economic expansion was Joseph II's legislation concerning the guilds. Though not suppressed outright, these essentially restrictive organisations lost all their power to impede productive or commercial activities in any way. It was but another aspect of the policy of letting everyone who was qualified carry out the trade of his choice without hindrance of any kind.

The coping-stone of Joseph II's economic legislation was the protectionist system established in 1784. This rigidly excluded all foreign-produced goods, materials and foodstuffs which could be produced in the Habsburg dominions, or for which home-produced substitutes were available. Naturally this system affected adversely the interests of all those whose livelihood depended on trade with the countries whose goods were now being excluded. But it provided a powerful stimulus to increase production for the well-protected home market. Moreover, Joseph was able to conclude a number of advantageous trade agreements which did not conflict with his import prohibitions—with Morocco, Turkey, Russia and the new United States of America.

If we may believe Joseph's own testimony, the desired results of his policy were not long delayed. In what was perhaps the most confident and optimistic letter to his brother Leopold he wrote: 'Shipping on the Danube heading for the Levant and the Crimea is daily increasing.... Industry and manufactures are prospering in the absence of the prohibited goods. A large number of people from Nuremberg, Swabia and even from England, who used to make their living by producing in their own country, have recently settled here to carry on manufacture.'[1]

Joseph II's ecclesiastical policy must be considered in relation to the general policy just outlined. The desire to raise the level of agricultural and industrial production, and to press all available institutions into the

[1] Arneth, *Joseph II. und Leopold von Toscana*, vol. II, p. 17, letter dated 14 May 1786.

service of the state was of fundamental importance in this as in all other departments of the Josephinian government.

The basis for a state-sponsored reformation of the church had been laid by Maria Theresa and Kaunitz in the 1768 instructions for the *Giunta Economale*.[1] Most of what Joseph II intended to do could be justified by reference to the principles embodied in these instructions.

With his urgent concern for the economic development of his territories, Joseph was bound to regard monasticism as a most undesirable phenomenon. It deprived the economy of much badly needed capital and withheld from the state the service of many potentially useful citizens. It was a state of affairs which the emperor was unwilling to tolerate. By a series of decrees issued in the first months of his reign, he made himself the sole master of the monasteries' human and economic resources. In November 1781 a governmental investigation into the malpractices of the Carthusian monastery in Mauerbach (Lower Austria) gave him the welcome opportunity of decreeing the dissolution of all monasteries belonging to the contemplative orders. The government justified its action by referring to 'the long-established proof that those orders which are absolutely useless to their fellow men cannot be pleasing to God'.[2]

Numerous monastic buildings were now converted into factories and warehouses, granaries and residences. A good deal of land came on to the market. And it was decided, on the basis of a report submitted by the Josephinian theologian Rautenstrauch, that the monks could apply to the bishop of their diocese for dispensation from their vows.[3] They could then enter the ranks of the secular clergy and carry out the many 'useful' functions which the emperor expected the latter to perform.

The secularised property of the suppressed monasteries constituted the basis of the *Religionsfond* with which the government financed a wholesale diocesan and parochial reorganisation. Bishops residing outside the Habsburg dominions lost their ancient jurisdiction. Energetic 'Josephinians' were promoted to the newly created sees. Old parishes were reorganised and many new ones created on the basis of the principle that no one should be more than one hour's walk away from his parish church. Clearly, Joseph considered that the clergy had a most important function to fulfil among the people. He had, in fact, cast them for the role of highly trained and specialised civil servants. Their instructions were to wean the people from old superstitions which wasted their time and money; to teach them the value of practical Christianity; to impress on them the supreme importance of obeying the laws and regulations; to encourage them in adversity; and, where possible, to be of practical help as well.

The strong resistance among the clergy encountered by Joseph convinced him that it was necessary to bring the education and training of the

---

[1] Above, p. 284.   [2] Quoted by Hock–Bidermann, *op. cit.* p. 395.
[3] Maass, III, *Fontes Rerum Austriacarum*, 2. Abt., LXXIII, p. 74.

clergy under state control. To this end he ordered the establishment of a 'General Seminary' in each provincial capital (1783). Rautenstrauch worked out the curriculum to which all had to conform. By 1786 the new seminaries had a monopoly of education for secular and regular clergy alike.

Like his mother, Joseph was concerned to obtain the pope's sanction for his ecclesiastical measures, but quite prepared to act on his own authority, if this sanction should be refused. In 1782 Pope Pius VI set out on an unprecedented journey to Vienna with the aim of securing some modification to the emperor's ecclesiastical legislation. The course of the negotiations convinced him that he must either accept what had been done, or see his rejection contemptuously ignored as of no consequence. He chose the former course, which saved appearances, but opened the door to further demands. In 1783 Joseph reasserted the lapsed right to appoint the bishops in the duchy of Milan. Once again, the pope could only save appearances in the 'friendly convention' of January 1784, by which he 'granted' to the emperor what had already been seized.[1] An open breach between pope and emperor seemed imminent in 1787: Pius refused canonical investiture to one of the archbishops newly appointed under the diocesan reorganisation. Joseph, prompted by Kaunitz, threatened 'to fall back upon what was customary regarding the confirmation of bishops in the entire Catholic church through thirteen centuries'.[2] The death of the controversial candidate, however, forestalled the implementation of this threat.

The facts and figures, in so far as we know them, indicate that the great programme of reforms fulfilled its authors' expectations. The textile and metal industries were expanding in Bohemia, Lower Austria, Styria, Tirol and Vorarlberg. In Bohemia the number of factories had increased by 150 per cent. The industrial suburbs of Vienna were growing rapidly, and the city's population was passing the 200,000 mark. Austria was assuming the dominant position in the Balkan trade. The success achieved in economic expansion was reflected in the increased revenues of the state. From 65,777,780 florins in 1781, they had risen to 87,403,740 florins in 1788. The normal establishment of the army, fixed at 108,000 after the Haugwitz reforms, was now 300,000. Conditions, status and equipment of the soldiers were much improved. Joseph had achieved a truly remarkable success in a very short time.

The tragedy of his reign lies in the emperor's inability to translate this success, as he intended, into an effective foreign policy. Indeed, the failure of his foreign policy may be said to have undermined the successes he had already achieved.

[1] L. Pastor, *The History of the Popes*, vol. XXXIX (London, 1952), p. 473, describes the convention as 'a victory for the Emperor', and there seems to be no basis for Maass' new interpretation of it as 'a serious reverse for...Kaunitz' (*op. cit.* II, F.R.A., 2. Abt., LXXII, p. 108).

[2] Maass, *op.cit.*, II, pp. 516–17.

The cornerstone of Joseph's foreign policy was the alliance with Catherine II of Russia, concluded in 1781. Joseph and Kaunitz congratulated themselves on having detached Russia from the Prussian alliance. If France observed a benevolent neutrality, the two partners had every hope of securing territorial advantages. Turkish territory was the object of Catherine's ambition. She coveted the Crimean peninsula and dreamt of a satellite Greek empire. Joseph still looked for territorial gains in Germany, which would serve to restore the old supremacy over Prussia.

Catherine made the opening move in 1783 by presenting her territorial claims to Turkey. Joseph gave full support to his ally, and brought effective pressure to bear on Turkey to yield. He eventually succeeded and astonished the diplomatic world by not making any claim for himself. The reason is clear. Having helped Catherine to acquire the Crimea without firing a shot, he reckoned that he had now imposed an inescapable obligation on her to give him effective support in Germany. For his plans of territorial acquisitions in Germany were about to mature.

Bavaria was once more the object of Joseph's ambition. Outright annexation as envisaged in 1777 was now out of the question, but Joseph was quite prepared to offer the Austrian Netherlands in exchange, notwithstanding his conclusion that he would suffer a net reduction in his revenues. The military and political advantages which the occupation of Bavaria would bring him *vis-à-vis* Prussia far outweighed the small financial loss.

Joseph and Kaunitz were confident of strong Russian support. Russian influence thrown on the side of Prussia had been decisive in frustrating Austrian ambitions in 1779. Why should it not be equally decisive now in securing their realisation? Vergennes, who had been hostile in 1779, was to be bullied into acquiescence by the threat of war against the United Provinces over the Scheldt dispute, and coaxed into a positive attitude by the offer of Luxembourg. Prussia was to be pacified by the offer of commercial privileges on the Vistula.

The design failed above all because Catherine's support for the ally to whom she owed the painless acquisition of the Crimea was ludicrously formal. This astute German princess had not the slightest desire to satisfy the German ambitions of an ally whose services could still be of vital importance in the attainment of her own Balkan ambitions. An emperor busy with the digestion of Bavaria could not be expected to take a very active interest in adventurous Balkan schemes for some time.

Catherine's obvious lukewarmness towards the exchange project confirmed Vergennes in his policy of opposition, and provided Frederick II with the opportunity of inflicting a most humiliating political defeat on the emperor with the organisation of the League of Princes (*Fürstenbund*). Joseph had tried to restore Habsburg supremacy in Germany only to find himself confronted by an organisation in which Catholic and Protestant princes alike acknowledged Prussian leadership.

After this experience, Joseph was prepared to question the usefulness of the Russian alliance. The alternative of a *rapprochement* with Prussia, however, was rejected out of hand by Kaunitz. Catherine was therefore able to go ahead with her plans for further aggrandisement in the Balkans. To make sure of Austrian co-operation, it was necessary to give Joseph the impression that she was strong enough and fully determined to embark on war against Turkey on her own, in case such co-operation was not forthcoming. Hence the invitation to Joseph to visit the Crimea. This invitation was so clearly addressed to the junior partner that the proud emperor was strongly inclined to refuse it. Again it was Kaunitz who prevailed on him to swallow his pride and stick to the alliance.

Despite the elaborate spectacle organised by Catherine and Potemkin, Joseph remained sceptical about Russia's striking-power. He was certain that his own was not yet adequate for a full-scale offensive against the Turks, and therefore strongly favoured delay. The pace of events was set by Catherine and the Porte. The former was merely concerned to secure Austrian co-operation and not at all anxious that the balance of power within the alliance should change in favour of Austria. The Porte knew that an attack was coming and was not prepared to wait until the aggressors were at full strength. Thus Catherine's presentation of her new demands in Constantinople, and the Turks' violent reaction to these, put the reluctant Joseph in the *casus foederis* before the end of 1787. If there was any chance of Joseph declining the role of Russian auxiliary for which Catherine had so subtly cast him, it was quickly destroyed by the Austrian ambassador to St Petersburg, Ludwig Cobenzl. This mediocre diplomat obligingly believed everything the Russian ministers told him concerning Russian military strength and Catherine's firm determination to act alone if necessary.[1] Joseph accepted his ambassador's information, and declared war on the Porte in February 1788, having twice failed to take possession of Belgrade.

According to the jubilant tsarina, Joseph's decision 'revealed the great prince, the man of outstanding genius'.[2] In reality it was a colossal blunder and an important cause of his failures. The emperor's eastern preoccupations gave the Belgians the chance to rise in rebellion against his administrative and ecclesiastical reforms. The enormous requirements of the army gave the recalcitrant Hungarian nobility the chance to revert to open opposition, and provided them with a mass following among their peasants. The dislocation of trade, the unprecedented rise in prices, and the new war-tax aroused bitter opposition among all classes in all provinces, and therefore helped to make the aristocratic opposition irresistible.

[1] A. Beer, *Die orientalische Politik Österreichs seit 1774* (Prague, 1883), pp. 86–7.
[2] *Ibid.* p. 89.

There were no gains to be set against these losses. Extraordinary war expenditure quickly ruined the finances which had been so carefully put in order by Count Charles Zinzendorf, president of the *Hofrechenkammer*. The campaign of 1788 was a total and costly failure. As in 1778, Joseph II failed as a general. He was compelled to witness some humiliating reverses. The military strength of Russia proved to be far below the estimates made by the credulous Ludwig Cobenzl. Bad health compelled Joseph to refrain from leading his army in person for the campaign of 1789. This campaign culminated in the capture of Belgrade under the direction of the veteran field-marshal Laudon, and thus restored in some measure the honour of Austrian arms. Even then, there was no prospect of a successful conclusion to the war. Prussia, Poland and Saxony were massing their troops along the Austrian frontiers, and encouraged the rebels in Belgium and Hungary. Joseph had to prepare for a war on two fronts. Anxiously he inquired whether Catherine would give him adequate support against the threatened Prussian attack. If not, he would have to consider a separate peace with Turkey.

In fact Joseph II had led the monarchy into its most serious crisis since 1740. Fully aware of this fact and tormented by the sense of failure, he died on 20 February 1790, leaving his brother, Leopold of Tuscany, to face the consequences.

III

As a programme of reforms representative of what is called 'enlightened despotism', the work of Maria Theresa and Joseph II is unique. No other ruler within the Holy Roman Empire attempted half so much. Many of them, of course, rulers of a few square miles, simply lacked the scope, even if they had the intention, to be effective reformers. Of the rulers of medium-sized states, only three can be mentioned in this context. Emmerich, Elector of Mainz till 1774, subjected the ecclesiastical organisation of his territory so thoroughly to his own exclusive control that Kaunitz was able to use his decrees as precedents and models for his own plans of ecclesiastical reform in the Habsburg dominions.[1] Frederick Augustus IV, Elector of Saxony since 1768, helped his country by means of his administrative and economic reforms to recover from the devastation and requisitions of the Seven Years War, and to become economically one of the most advanced regions of Germany. Charles Frederick, margrave of Baden, imposed a land-tax, abolished serfdom, reduced the feudal burdens of the peasantry, and practised religious toleration. One must not conclude that the other rulers renounced the prospect of increasing their revenues. But it seems that methods other than those of enlightened despotism were preferred if they were available. Thus a number of them made large fortunes by hiring out their subjects for military

[1] Maass, *op.cit.* III, *Fontes Rerum Austriacarum*, 2. Abt., LXXIII, p. 33.

service to Great Britain and the United Provinces. By this method Charles of Brunswick-Wolfenbüttel made a net profit of five million taler during the War of American Independence.

It used to be fashionable to refer to Frederick II of Prussia as the foremost representative of enlightened despotism. Now it is difficult to resist the conclusion that such a judgement is a relic of the era of Bismarck, when German historians were expected to pay homage to Prussia if they wanted promotion or permission to use the archives. The Prussian king's political writings may contain an unrivalled theoretical exposition of enlightened despotism. His practice, however, fell far short of his theory, and resembles that of the unenlightened petty tyrant more often than that of the enlightened despot. Like Joseph II, Frederick was a protectionist and welcomed foreign settlers to bring waste lands under cultivation, thus fostering industry and agriculture. But he scrupulously refrained from interfering, however slightly, with the wealth and privileges of the Prussian nobility. The direct tax on land remained at its original low level throughout his reign, while the indirect taxes were steadily raised. So far from undertaking a reform of taxation, Frederick imported the most regressive aspects of the French system of tax-farming. No considerations of commercial or financial advantage induced him to give the peasants freedom of movement or to insist on a reduction of their excessive feudal burdens. His vigorous opposition to anything which impaired the feudal divisions of society is perhaps the most thoroughly medieval feature one can find in eighteenth-century Germany.

The judicial reform in Prussia is the only one which allows a valid comparison with Austria to be made. In the nature of things the details of the reform had to be left to the jurists who, in Prussia no less than in Austria, were inspired by the legal ideals of the Enlightenment. Cocceji, Carmer and Suarez in Prussia shared a common outlook with Martini and Keess in Austria. Frederick and Joseph, on the other hand, resembled each other in their frequent disregard of legal principles, and their arbitrary interference in the process of the law.

Frederick II's freedom from any religious bigotry is largely responsible for his contemporary reputation as an enlightened despot. The resulting freedom of religious discussion which prevailed in Berlin greatly impressed the intellectuals and writers who helped to form public opinion. More penetrating minds, however, realised the limitations of 'Berlinese freedom'. Lessing was stifled in Berlin. When he decided to leave in 1769 he wrote to Nicolai, who was evidently satisfied with conditions in the Prussian capital, to explain his decision:

Don't talk to me about your Berlinese freedom of thought and writing. It only consists of the freedom to make as much fun as you like of religion. . . . Let someone try to write about other things in Berlin as freely as Sonnenfels has written in Vienna; let him try to tell the mob at court the truth in the way he has done; let someone in Berlin stand up for the rights of the peasants, or protest against despotism and exploitation as they now do even in France and Denmark, and you will soon know by experience which country is to this day the most slavish in Europe.[1]

IV

The reforms of enlightened despotism were accompanied by a great political awakening among the non-privileged classes. The original stimulus came from above, especially in the Habsburg dominions, where the government of both Maria Theresa and Joseph II frequently tried to mobilise the support of public opinion against aristocratic and clerical opponents. Kollar's work on Hungarian law, mentioned earlier in this chapter, Sonnenfels' articles in *Der Mann ohne Vorurteil* depicting the condition of the peasants,[2] the flood of anti-papal and anti-clerical pamphlets published at the time of the pope's visit to Vienna—these and many similar ventures were unobtrusively encouraged by the government in order to facilitate the implementation of controversial legislation.

The consequences of this appeal to public opinion were greater than the government foresaw. Political ideas and principles originally put forward to justify governmental policies were elaborated by the publicists and eventually used to question the fundamental assumptions of aristocratic privilege, of Christianity, and of absolutism itself.

In this 'age of the democratic revolution', as it has now been called, the influence of radical political literature on the general climate of opinion was very great; and it was not restricted by political boundaries. Throughout Germany and the Habsburg dominions middle-class intellectuals and civil servants, frequenting the new semi-public reading rooms (*Lesekabinette*), and peasants gathering round those who could read the newspapers to them, were airing opinions and aspirations which profoundly alarmed the governing class, enlightened and unenlightened alike.

Enlightened despotism restricted aristocratic privileges which impeded the full unfolding of the power of the state. Public opinion was beginning to deny the justification of aristocratic privilege as such. To find the characteristic expression of the new attitude in the countryside, we must look not at the peasant riots and *jacqueries* which preceded the feudal reforms of enlightened despotism,[3] but at the agitation which followed them. The peasants were gaining enough prosperity to desire more. The apparent conflict between the sovereign and the feudal lord was taken to herald the speedy end of the feudal system. Solemn proclamations concerning

[1] Quoted by F. Mehring, *Die Lessinglegende* (new edition, Berlin, 1953), p. 379.
[2] Cf. E. Murr Link, *The Emancipation of the Austrian Peasant 1740-1798* (New York, 1949), pp. 98–102.
[3] This category includes the Horia rising of 1784 in Transylvania, because the reforms of the preceding years had not been properly implemented in this province.

the continued obligations to the lords were dismissed as tricks perpetrated by the latter. The peasants could not but be confirmed in their attitude by the events of July 1789 in France, about which they kept themselves well informed through their newspapers. Hence the period 1789–91 saw vigorous and widespread efforts by peasants to rid themselves of all remaining feudal obligations in the Habsburg provinces, in Saxony, Silesia, and many other parts of Germany.

If we may judge by the literature of the period, the middle classes were at one with the peasantry in their opposition to feudal privileges, and were advancing their own claim for economic and social equality. Despite the relative backwardness of their own political environment, the writers, theoretical, creative and journalistic, fully participated in the intellectual ferment which helped to prepare the way for the French Revolution. The creative artists could no longer endure dependence on the aristocracy of birth. Many of them felt this to be a humiliation so intolerable that they preferred the life of poverty which, under the conditions existing in Germany and the Habsburg dominions, was the inevitable alternative. From their position of independence, they could stake their claim to full equality, proclaiming the true nobility of the heart, and taunting those who sought or accepted empty titles.[1] Everything that could be said in condemnation of feudal privilege thus found its way into the German literature of the period in whatever form could best express the writers' embittered and passionate feelings in this matter. The summons to a final reckoning is unmistakable in the short, savage verses of Bürger's 'The Peasant—to his Most Gracious Tyrant',[2] while Lessing's tragedy *Emilia Galotti* and Schiller's *Kabale und Liebe* announce the doom of the privileged orders as clearly as Beaumarchais's comedy *Le Mariage de Figaro*.[3]

Turning to the religious and ecclesiastical policies of enlightened despotism, we find a similar discrepancy between the motivation of these policies and the result of their impact on public opinion. Frederick II and Joseph II practised toleration only to the extent to which it served the interests of the state as they conceived them. Immigrants whose skill or energy was required could practice their own religion. But Frederick summarily executed Jesuits who taught that desertion from his army was not a mortal sin, and Joseph tried ruthlessly to stamp out heresy among the Bohemian peasants. Nevertheless, even the limited extent of official toleration stimulated public opinion, and helped the principle of toleration to take root. The development, again, is reflected in the literature of the time. A poetic definition of toleration by the Austrian poet Alxinger was

---

[1] Cf. Mozart's celebrated phrase, 'Das Herz adelt den Menschen' (*Briefe Mozarts und seiner Familie*, ed. Schiedermair, Munich, 1914, vol. II, p. 91), and Gottfried August Bürger's poem 'Auf das Adeln der Gelehrten' (1789).

[2] 'Der Bauer—an seinen durchlauchtigen Tyrannen' (1773).

[3] G. Lukács, *Skizze einer Geschichte der neueren deutschen Literatur* (Berlin, 1955), pp. 24–5, suggests the comparison.

banned by Joseph II's censorship; and Lessing in his *Nathan der Weise* has given us the greatest drama ever written in this cause.

The new attitude to toleration prepared the way for religious speculation on a large scale. Lessing was himself a pioneer of German biblical criticism, and was approaching the conception of Christianity as a stage in the 'education of humanity'. In educated circles everywhere the 'great debate' on religion was carried on, and scepticism became in varying degrees the fashion of the day. Joseph II's religious innovations brought the entire population into the controversy. By the time of the French Revolution, cobblers and tailors in the suburbs of Vienna were discussing the theological books of Lessing, pondered Genesis and the New Testament, and concluded that outside nature there was no God.[1]

When one considers this offensive against traditional beliefs and authorities, one can only regard it as inevitable that the validity of absolutism itself should have been called into question. The enlightened despots admitted in theory that they were 'servants of the state', whose duty was the promotion of their subjects' welfare. Their subjects, however, lacked any kind of guarantee securing the constant application of policies conducive to this welfare.

The most interesting journalistic venture in Germany during this period, Schlözer's *Staatsanzeigen*, was in part an attempt to supply a substitute for such a guarantee. So long as his sovereign, George III, granted him the required freedom of the press, Schlözer undertook to discourage acts of tyranny by the threat of unfavourable publicity.

At the same time, we find in Austria the first traces of the demand for constitutional and representative government in its modern form. The idea was canvassed that the aims of government, the rather nebulous 'general welfare' to which the enlightened despot paid lip-service, should be concretely defined in the form of fundamental laws binding on the sovereign and his successors. Sonnenfels, who combined the functions of a professor of political science with those of a high-ranking civil servant, actually submitted a project to this effect to Maria Theresa and her successors. The absolute monarchy was to limit itself by promulgating as fundamental laws such principles as would secure the rights of the citizen and the needs of an expanding capitalist economy.[2] Under the influence of the French Revolution, Sonnenfels developed his project in the direction of representative government. The emperor was to consult truly representative diets about important legislation and about the application of the principles of government in the various provinces.

In the Habsburg dominions the new political awareness was further

---

[1] E. Wangermann, *From Joseph II to the Jacobin Trials* (London, 1959), pp. 16–19.

[2] S. Adler, 'Die politische Gesetzgebung in ihren geschichtlichen Beziehungen zum Allgemeinen Bürgerlichen Gesetzbuche', in *Festschrift zur Jahrhundertfeier des Allgemeinen Bürgerlichen Gesetzbuches* (Vienna, 1911), pp. 94–104.

enhanced by the dissatisfaction resulting from so many of Joseph II's policies. The peasants resisted interference in their religious practices, feared the new land-tax, and resented the continuation of feudal burdens. The townspeople objected to the prohibition of their favourite imports and the abolition of price control. The emperor's arbitrary aggravation of court sentences aroused indignation among all classes. The war against the Turks was very unpopular, since the old antagonism against the eastern neighbour had largely disappeared, and the enormous needs of the army were causing an unprecedented rise in prices. In a period of widespread newspaper reading, new political aspirations, speculation and discussion, the intense public discontent expressed itself in a type of articulate criticism which was a new phenomenon in the political scene. Public opinion throughout the monarchy became a factor to be reckoned with by the government. In Belgium and Hungary, where nationalism provided a powerful unifying force, the people actually followed the banner of rebellion raised by the privileged classes.

V

The social and political ferment, unintentionally stimulated by enlightened despotism, soon provoked a wave of repressive legislation in the Habsburg dominions and throughout Germany, which blurred the distinction between enlightened and unenlightened despots. The new emphasis on repression was general and by no means confined to states in which a new ruler succeeded at about this time. Moreover, it was fully in evidence some years before the outbreak of the French Revolution which has often been regarded as its cause.

The first indication of the new policy appeared in the Habsburg dominions as early as December 1785 with the patent concerning freemasons, which introduced the police to the new job of keeping a watchful eye on the trends of public opinion. In the following years the police was reorganised under an autonomous ministry headed by Pergen. It was furnished with secret instructions in which the supervision of public opinion figured as the principal task. The use of paid secret agents was specifically prescribed, and these were occasionally employed as *agents provocateurs*. Joseph II used the police to impose precautionary arrest, to inflict punishments which could not be secured at law, and to deport 'undesirable' foreign residents.[1]

The limited freedom of speech and of the press which all rulers who laid some claim to enlightenment had allowed was an early victim of the new policy. Here Bavaria led the way with the suppression of the *Illuminati* in 1785 and the clerical reign of terror unloosed by Charles Theodore's ex-Jesuit confessor Franck. Protestant Prussia followed suit after the

[1] Wangermann, *op. cit.* pp. 37–44.

accession of Frederick William II. The important ecclesiastical department fell into the hands of the obscurantist Wöllner. He was the author of the *Religionsedikt* of 1788, which enforced the narrowest orthodoxy on all teachers of the Lutheran religion. The widespread and bitter criticism levelled against the edict failed to secure any amendments, and indeed helped to bring about a considerable tightening of the censorship regulations (December 1788). A new censorship commission headed by Wöllner's protégé Hillmer was set up in May 1791. This was speedily followed by the exile of Berlin's best-known literary periodicals—Nicolai's *Allgemeine Deutsche Bibliothek*, and Gedike's *Berliner Monatsschrift*. Having perfected the machinery of repression in Prussia, Wöllner exerted pressure on the rulers of the neighbouring German states to take similar action.[1]

Habsburg policy on religion and censorship closely followed these precedents. Joseph II no longer ignored the representations of the Austrian primate, Cardinal Migazzi, and in 1788 took steps to enforce strict Catholic orthodoxy on university professors. A few days before his death he issued a decree which reveals the intention of securing orthodoxy in the schools as well. The censorship patent of January 1790 revoked some of the liberal provisions of 1782, substituting those of Wöllner's edict of December 1788. Continuing this policy, Leopold II took further measures to restore the weakened authority of the Catholic faith at the universities, and to suppress publications likely to impair the prestige of the Church and of religion.

The problem in Prussia was comparatively simple. Having no other active opponents to deal with, Frederick William and his ministers could concentrate their fire on the 'neologues and self-styled Enlighteners'. Joseph II, on the other hand, was compelled to fight on two fronts. For the privileged orders did not make common cause with him against the new menace from below. On the contrary, they did not hesitate to exploit the emperor's difficulties and universal unpopularity for the purpose of organising mass support for their rebellion. Hungarian nobles resisting the new land-tax, and Belgian clerics battling against the state-controlled General Seminary, raised the cry of 'liberty' and put themselves at the head of a mass movement embracing all classes, each conscious of its own grievances and aspirations, and becoming accustomed to independent political action. If the Estates of other provinces had taken similar action, they would have met a similar response.

Coinciding with the disastrous failure of his foreign policy, this state of affairs compelled Joseph II to make the far-reaching concessions to the privileged orders which mark the end of his reign. The complete loss of

---

[1] J. Droz, *L'Allemagne et la Révolution française* (Paris, 1949), pp. 29–30; H. Brunschwig, *La Crise de l'État prussien à la Fin du XVIIIe Siècle* (Paris, 1947), pp. 201–2: the date of the censorship edict is here wrongly given as 1789.

Belgium early in 1790 revealed the inescapable alternative to such concessions. To avoid more disasters of this kind, Joseph revoked all but three of his decrees for Hungary; only peasant emancipation, toleration, and the parochial reorganisation were salvaged from the wreckage. After Joseph II's death in February 1790, Leopold II had to continue for some time along the same road. He revoked the February Patent on the land-tax and commutation of labour services, and discontinued the General Seminaries. The Estates of all provinces were convoked for the consideration of further grievances.

Had Leopold II allowed the monarchy to remain in the perilous external and internal isolation into which his predecessor had brought it, the Estates (representing almost exclusively the privileged orders) would have been able to wrest from him any other concessions they fancied. There can be little doubt that such freedom of action would have meant the destruction of the work of enlightened despotism in the Habsburg dominions. Leopold II, however, succeeded in rescuing the monarchy from its isolation, and thus restored his own freedom of action to save and develop the work of his predecessors.

By his consummate diplomacy and willingness to give up the recently conquered fortress of Belgrade, Leopold extricated his country from the disastrous war against Turkey, and dispelled the growing threat of war on his Bohemian and Galician borders. The negotiations with Prussia, culminating in the Convention of Reichenbach in June 1790, deprived the Hungarian and Belgian rebels of the foreign support on which they had been relying. Thereafter, Leopold consistently refused to be stampeded or tempted into any other foreign adventures either in France or in Poland. Lacking reliable allies and adequate financial resources, he wisely confined himself to a 'passive' foreign policy. In this he was fully supported by the ageing Kaunitz who now abandoned his earlier aggressive policies.[1] During his short reign, good relations were restored with Prussia, Great Britain and Poland, while a breach with Russia or France was avoided.

To end the monarchy's internal isolation, Leopold II decided to exploit the conflicts dividing the opposition. He was aware of the disappointment of the non-privileged orders with the purely feudal ambitions voiced in the diets. He was no less aware of the nobility's anxiety concerning the rapidly developing social and political aspirations of the middle classes and the peasantry. And he profited from both.

When the peasants took steps to resist the reimposition of labour services, Leopold welcomed and encouraged this development, and exploited it to secure a moderation of the lords' demands. In Hungary he encour-

---

[1] Cf. *Haus-, Hof- u. Staatsarchiv (Wien), Staatenabteilungen, Polen, Weisungen,* 1791, F. 82, fols. 14–15: 'Da unsere Verhältnisse so bescheiden sind, dass wir uns sorgfältig von aller Theilnehmung an den pohlnischen Angelegenheiten ferner enthalten müssen....'

aged all nationalities and classes whose interests and aspirations conflicted with those of the dominant Magyar nobility. To this end he commissioned and financed pamphlets designed to frighten the diet away from its extreme demands by drawing attention to the growing desire of the burghers and peasants for political and social equality. He admitted representatives of the cities to the Commission on Grievances, and he encouraged their and the peasants' campaign for real representation in the diets. In this way Leopold succeeded in wresting the initiative from the diets, and induced them to embody some important reforms of the previous reigns in their own legislation. By the end of his reign the Hungarian diet had adopted the Theresian decree on limitation of labour services, the abolition of serfdom, and the principle of freedom of worship for Protestants. The Bohemian Estates were ready to accept the Josephinian land-register as the basis of taxation, as well as the principle of equality of assessment as between peasants' and lords' land. Plans were ready for the compulsory enforcement of commutation of labour services in Styria, Bohemia and Lower Austria.

The encouragement which Leopold was thereby giving to the non-privileged orders naturally stimulated their ambitions and raised their expectations. If he wanted to win and retain their confidence in the monarchy, to detach them once and for all from the opposition, he would have to fulfil at least some of these expectations.

Leopold II's effort to satisfy the political aspirations of the non-privileged orders in the period of the French Revolution constitutes the most interesting aspect of his unexpectedly short reign. It is almost the only attempt in Europe to meet the challenge of the Revolution with something more than mere repression.

The restoration and maintenance of peace made possible the alleviation of some of the hardships which had resulted from the Turkish War. Leopold rescinded the most cruel provisions of the Josephinian criminal code which had outraged contemporary enlightened opinion. He allowed the Supreme Judiciary to investigate the extra-legal actions of Pergen's unpopular Ministry of Police. This resulted not only in the release and rehabilitation of its victims, but also in the publication of a *habeas corpus* decree prohibiting precautionary arrest and establishing a measure of judicial control over the police (February 1791). Pergen refused to accept the implied criticism of his actions during the previous reign and resigned (March 1791). Leopold did not appoint a successor to Pergen; instead he undertook the reform of the police on the basis of a plan submitted by Sonnenfels, the declared opponent of arbitrary rule. The 'secret' police hardly survived the abolition of the autonomous Ministry of Police; the public functions of the police were increased, notably through the establishment of a free public health service which was attached to the police organisation of Vienna set up by the decree of November 1791.

Having encouraged the efforts of the non-privileged classes to secure better representation in the diets, Leopold had to face the problem of constitutional reform. Rumours of the lines on which the emperor was thinking reached the British ambassador who reported that 'His Imperial Majesty is supposed to have adopted the idea that the dangerous contagion of French Reform can hardly be averted, or at least that the fatal progress of that levelling spirit cannot be so effectually circumscribed as by new modelling the Constitution of several of the countries which belong to his dominions by voluntary concessions on the part of the Sovereign'.[1]

In May 1791 the Styrian cities were granted the right to send ten deputies to the diet and one to the standing committee of the Estates. In the autumn of that year Leopold was in Prague for the coronation, and raised the question of constitutional reform in Bohemia. According to the British ambassador, it was the emperor's intention to sanction 'regular meetings of citizens and peasants'. In December a majority of councillors at the Court Chancellery recommended a favourable decision on the petition of the Styrian peasants for representation in the diet. In February 1792 deputies from the Bohemian estates came to Vienna to hear, among other things, Leopold's proposals concerning the representation of the non-privileged classes in the diet. At the same time the ground was being prepared for similar changes in Hungary. Then, unexpectedly, on the first of March, Leopold died after an attack of colic.[2]

Few of his policies survived him, and some were reversed by his successor. Nevertheless, he had done much in the course of his brief reign to ensure that some at least of the achievements of the Enlightenment survived in the period of reaction which followed.

[1] *Public Record Office*, Foreign Office, 7/28, no. 109, report dated 15 October 1791.
[2] For a fuller discussion of Leopold's reforms and possible intentions, cf. Wangermann, *From Joseph II to the Jacobin Trials*, pp. 82–105, and A. Wandruszka, *Leopold II.*, 2 vols. (Vienna, 1963–4).

CHAPTER XI

RUSSIA

I N the fifty years between the founding of St Petersburg and the end of the Seven Years War, the river fortress and business capital planned by Peter the Great had been transformed into a rambling showplace of luxury and leisure. The Russian nobility, conscripted by Peter into life-time service in the armed forces or the administration, had since 1735 evaded more and more of their responsibilities. In February 1762 they had been relieved of their obligation to serve the state at all: and, while many of them were content to slip backward into the unimaginable idleness of provincial life, families which remained at court and in the capital seemed determined to spend their way into extinction. The modest buildings erected by Peter's architects had been surrounded and outnumbered by new palaces for monarch and members of the court alike, designed on more expansive lines by Rastrelli and his compatriots from Venice. Thrift was not highly regarded as a virtue in a period when unspent fortunes might be confiscated overnight after a palace revolution.

But St Petersburg was only the shop-window of the new empire. For the trappers scattered in settlements along the northern rivers, for the peasants who struggled to win a livelihood from the unyielding soil of central Russia, life had changed little from the days of Muscovy, except that taxes were higher and each village had to surrender more of its men-folk for the army. Peter's plans to create a new system of local government, new law-courts and a country-wide network of elementary schools had all been abandoned through indifference or lack of funds. Even in Moscow, where a new university had been founded in 1755, 'the streets still lay three arsheens deep in ignorance'. The new freedom acquired by the landowners was not matched by any corresponding concessions to their serfs, though the landowners' obligation to serve the tsar had long been regarded as a moral justification for serfdom. On the contrary, most landowners were demanding higher rentals or more labour from their serfs. The College of Mines had been unable to make a profit from the state iron-foundries in the Urals, and by 1740 nearly all of them had been let out to private operators. For a short period during the 1750s Russia had been producing and exporting more iron than any other country in Europe, but by 1763 output was already declining. Prospectors were unable to find coal and iron-ore in reasonable proximity in Russia and, as the Russian operators could not change over from charcoal to coke smelting, they were soon to lose their predominating position to

Britain.[1] While Peter the Great had taken pride in his feat of keeping the budget balanced throughout the Great Northern War, none of his successors even attempted to follow his example. In spite of new and ingenious forms of indirect taxation, and though state revenue had been swelled by the appropriation of income from church lands since 1757, the treasury was exhausted when Russia withdrew from the Seven Years War. For eight months in 1762 Russian soldiers in Pomerania had not received a single copeck of their pay.

Nothing then would have served the Russian people better than four or five decades of peace in which to revive and consolidate Peter's efforts to create the sinews of a modern state: but for some time to come peace at least was not vouchsafed to them. In 1762 providence instead provided Russia with the most civilised, but at the same time the most ambitious and most prodigal ruler she had ever had. At the time of Catherine's accession no one in Russia or abroad foresaw that she was to reign longer than any of her predecessors since Peter the Great. In London and Paris it was thought that Peter III's abdication was merely the beginning of a new series of palace revolutions, like those of 1740–1. The new empress herself was most sanguine about her chances of survival. There was not a single ground on which she could pretend that her accession was legitimate. Her husband had been placed in confinement after his abdication but, as long as he was still alive, his claims to the throne were indisputable. The same could be said of Ivan Antonovich, who had reigned as an infant in 1740, had been overthrown by Elizabeth in 1741 and had spent the intervening years in a monastery. In addition to possible rivals for the throne she had usurped, Catherine had to make up her mind how to deal with an ambitious section of the nobility, led by Nikita Panin, which was ready to accept her as empress provided that she would put an end to absolute monarchy in Russia and turn over the most important of her royal functions to a privileged oligarchy. To meet these many-sided threats, Catherine found no counsel from her book-learning about monarchy. Montesquieu and Voltaire might offer their precepts for the conduct of a well-established monarch, but they had no advice to give an empress who was still struggling to consolidate her power. She had no choice, therefore, but to fall back on the practice of her immediate predecessors, the ruthless elimination of rivals and the generous bestowal of privilege on the nobility. A week after her accession, her husband was strangled in the fortress of Ropcha. The murderer, it seems, was Aleksey Orlov. Whether Catherine gave the order for Peter's death is not known, but she connived at it at least. Six months later, a group of officers in the

---

[1] Geographical and technical, as opposed to organisational, reasons for the failure of Russian iron producers to meet the challenge of their competitors in western Europe are discussed in Alexander Baykov, 'The Economic Development of Russia', *Economic History Review*, second series, VII (1954), no. 2, pp. 137–49.

Izmailovsky regiment tried to emulate the good fortune of the Orlovs by releasing Ivan Antonovich from his guards and restoring him to the throne. They failed; but, when a second attempt was made in 1764, Ivan Antonovich was done to death on the empress's express orders, and for some years she had no serious rival to the throne except her son Paul (though his claim that he was entitled by birth to succeed his father was, under Peter the Great's succession law, invalid).

Those who had hoped that Catherine would delegate her powers to a council of nobles were equally disappointed. In 1762 Panin presented for her consideration the draft of an *ukaz* providing for 'the transfer of a reasonable exercise of legislative power to a small number of persons chosen for the purpose'. Catherine signed the *ukaz*, and even went so far as to appoint six members of the council; but, as soon as Panin's designs became apparent to her, the project was shelved without explanation. Thenceforward she refused even to consider the possibility of delegating her authority but, to retain the good will of the nobility, she did satisfy nearly every demand they made for additional privileges in law and local government.

The first sign of her deference to the nobility in matters of privilege was her decision on the final disposal of the estates formerly owned by the church as a whole and by individual monasteries. The income from these estates had been diverted to the treasury as a temporary wartime measure in 1757 but in April 1762, more than three months after Russia had withdrawn from the Seven Years War, Catherine's husband had ruled that control over church lands was to be retained by the treasury in perpetuity. A fixed sum would be allotted to the Holy Synod and the monasteries each year; the surplus would be retained by the state. Immediately after Peter's abdication the church leaders appealed to Catherine to reverse his decision. The attitude of the empress towards the religion of her adopted country was, to say the least, disingenuous. Protestant by birth, freethinker by education, she was unlikely to emulate the simple devoutness of her predecessor Elizabeth, and in private she was known to utter ribaldries about the rites of the Russian church. But in public she was keenly aware of what was expected of her as empress and, when occasion demanded, she would intone a prayer with the rest. At the beginning of her reign, too, she welcomed support from whatever quarter it might come, and in the hope of obtaining the church's approval of her accession she agreed to rescind Peter's *ukaz* and return the management of the church lands to the Synod. But this decision, too, was to be countermanded, after some of the wealthier nobility had protested that church ownership of land was an infringement of their own monopoly. At the end of 1762 the question was reopened and laid before a commission in which the lay members were in a distinct majority; and in March 1764 Catherine adopted the commission's proposal to transfer all church estates (and church serfs as well) back to the treasury. On this occasion no effort was made to represent the change as a temporary one, and in consequence nearly 500 of the existing 900 monasteries were closed. It was not possible, either, to maintain all the diocesan seminaries which had been the backbone of the educational system since the 1720's and, contrary to the declared purposes of Peter the Great, the educational standard of the clergy sharply declined. The only churchman to raise his voice in protest was Arseny Matseyevich, bishop of Rostov. Matseyevich was condemned by the Synod itself, dispatched to a distant monastery in the north and later placed in solitary confinement in the fortress of Reval, where hunger and cold killed him.

After 1764 the ownership of all land in Russia, apart from crown and state land, was confined to the nobility, though the noblemen's monopoly of land ownership was not recognised in law for another twenty years. But other privileges were conferred at once. In 1765 noblemen were permitted to sentence their serfs to forced labour without reference to the public courts and, to help them dispose of their grain surplus, they were granted a monopoly in the distillation and marketing of vodka. Catherine was pressed to extend the privileges of this class still further but, before doing so, she was to conduct a much wider inquiry into the ambitions and requirements of every social group in the country.

Her reputation as the living embodiment of Voltaire's ideal of the enlightened monarch rests above all on her decision to convene a commission for the codification of the law in 1767. The commission was never intended to be a permanent legislative assembly, though Diderot on his visit to St Petersburg urged Catherine to transform it into one. Its sole function was to prepare a new code of law to replace the code drawn up by Aleksey Mikhailovich in 1649 and the mass of confused and often contradictory legislation which had since been enacted. The idea of convening a commission for this purpose had been fathered by Peter the Great, and separate commissions had indeed tackled the task, without notable success, in the reigns of Peter himself, Catherine I, Peter II, Anna Ivanovna and Elizabeth. Further, both Peter II and Anna Ivanovna had invited the provincial nobility to elect 'good and knowledgeable men' to take part in the work. Catherine was not therefore breaking any fresh ground either in convening a commission or in arranging for it to include elected members: but the commission of 1767 was unique because of the *Instruction* which Catherine issued for its guidance, because every social group except the serfs was represented in it and because each group was asked to prepare a statement of its needs and aspirations.

When the commission assembled for the first time in August 1767, it contained over 560 members, only 28 from the administration (including the sole representative of the clergy) and 536 from the population at large. This proportion was strikingly different from that of earlier commissions, where the representatives of officialdom had been in the majority, and the predominance in the new commission of men who were totally inexperienced in legal matters made the work of preparing a fresh code of law infinitely more difficult. Between them the 536 elected representatives presented 1441 petitions, of which more than 1000 were submitted by the free peasants. On some points, all the petitions were in agreement. None of them contained any protest against absolute monarchy. Every class, on the other hand, called for some decentralisation not only of authority but also of education, legal procedure and other benefits which as yet only St Petersburg and Moscow enjoyed. This demand was coupled with a complaint about the burden of taxation, for it was asserted with some justification that taxes levied in the countryside were used exclusively for the welfare of St Petersburg. Each class, too, desired a stricter definition of its status and an extension of its privileges. Nearly every petition presented by the landowners insisted that they be granted exclusive rights in the possession of land and serfs, and even greater powers over their serfs. They claimed exemption from torture and corporal punishment (branding and slitting of the nostrils were the commonest punishments in this category): some even demanded exemption from imprisonment. They insisted on the right to engage in commerce and industry, if they wished. The latter demand was most vehemently opposed by the merchant class, though the merchants themselves wished to share with the noblemen the right to own serfs. The petitions of the free peasants ran counter to those of the merchants and noblemen alike, for the free peasants claimed the right both to engage in commerce and to own serfs.

The serfs themselves, who comprised more than half the entire population, were not invited to send any representatives to the commission, nor was any one appointed to be their official spokesman. But, even before the commission was convened, the empress had made her attitude to serfdom fairly clear. She had asked the Imperial Free Economic Society, founded under her patronage in 1765, to organise an essay competition on the theme of serfdom. Participation was international and the prize-winner, a doctor of law in the University of Aachen, submitted a work strongly condemning serfdom both on humanitarian and economic grounds. Catherine was not prepared to consider emancipation of the serfs, since this would deprive her at a single stroke of the goodwill of the nobility, but she believed that the arbitrary character of existing landowner/serf relationships should be mitigated by legislation or some other type of control, to ensure that plots of land allocated to serfs were adequate in size, and that dues exacted from the serfs in the form of money or labour were not immoderate. Some of the enlightened landowners in the commission, such as Peter Panin and the freemason Elagin, called for legislation along these lines as the best means of avoiding social disturbances and accelerating economic progress.

At the commission's opening session the essentially practical demands put forward by the various social groups in Russia were overshadowed by Catherine's own *Instruction*. She had started work on this early in 1764; in July 1765 she had told Voltaire of her plans to endow her country with a new set of laws, and she enjoyed his advice and encouragement right up to the publication of the *Instruction*. The document itself, however, was not based on any of Voltaire's writings, but almost exclusively on Montesquieu's *De l'Esprit des Lois* and Beccaria's *Dei delitti e delle Pene*, which only came into her hands in 1766. Catherine made no effort to disguise her indebtedness to these two authors. In fact, she tended to stress the points of similarity between her own work and theirs, and to pass over in silence passages in the *Instruction* where she had revised Montesquieu to suit her own purposes. The extent of the Russian dominion, she wrote, required absolute power to be vested in its ruler. The true end of monarchy was to correct the actions of the people in order to attain the supreme good. The equality of citizens consisted in the fact that they should all be subject to the same laws. The use of torture was contrary to all the dictates of nature and reason. The law of nature commanded the ruler to shun all occasions of reducing people to a state of slavery, but 'a great number of slaves ought not to be enfranchised all at once, nor by a general law'.[1] Nikita Panin, after perusing an early draft of the *Instruction*, remarked that 'these principles are strong enough to shatter walls'; but he need not have been concerned. The very language in which the *Instruction* was couched was so unfamiliar to a representative Russian audience that it provoked open-mouthed curiosity rather than iconoclastic passion.

The proceedings of the commission are of minor interest. In most of the seventy-seven sessions, deputies from each class made set speeches reiterating the views already set forth in their petitions. There was no close debate and no effort was made, by reconciling the views of different classes, to draft the text of any new law. Both the commission in plenary session and the nineteen committees into which it was divided passed inconclusively from topic to topic, and little positive progress had been made by December 1768, when Catherine announced that plenary meetings of the commission were to be suspended, though some of the individual committees were to continue working. The reason for the suspension, she asserted, was to allow representatives to rejoin their regiments for the campaign against Turkey, but few have believed that this was her only motive. The empress's critics have assumed that her 'liberalism' was never founded on sincere conviction, and that the commission was assembled merely to impress the western world. Others, remembering Catherine's description of herself as a 'commenceuse de profession', have

---

[1] A complete text of the *Instruction*, in the English translation of 1768, appears in W. F. Reddaway, *Documents of Catherine the Great* (Cambridge, 1931), pp. 215–309.

assumed that, because a new code of law could not be drafted in a few months, she lost interest in the project. The truth, judging from Catherine's correspondence, seems to differ from either of these versions. Until 1767 she was under a curious, but fashionable, misunderstanding about her people. She had been convinced (Leibniz had expressed the same view to Peter the Great) that, as a backward country, Russia was a virgin stone upon which an original mind could carve any imprint it desired, and it was the commission which first opened her eyes to the fact that Russia had traditions which could not be overlooked, that noblemen, merchants and peasants had conflicting aspirations which they would not easily abandon and that the Russians in fact were no more malleable than, say, the French or the Austrians. At all events, the sudden end to the commission's work did not mean that it was altogether without effect. The *Instruction*, the petitions and the debates together represented a legalised beginning of national self-examination, and the issues raised for the first time in 1767 remained before the national conscience until they had been settled to popular satisfaction. Beccaria's reflections on the form of criminal courts, reproduced in chapter x of the *Instruction*, were the basis of the court reform law of 1864, and regulation of landowner/serf relationships was discussed again and again in the early nineteenth century before it was formally commended to landowners during the 1840s and legally imposed on them in a two-year transitional period after the Emancipation Act of 1861.

Before the end of the 1760s Catherine was to test, and abandon, two other methods of achieving a radical alteration in the character of the Russian people. In her studies of Russia as a young woman she had been particularly struck by the fact that Peter the Great's initiative in founding a country-wide network of secular schools had been abandoned by his successors, and after her accession she aimed not only to bring Peter's plan to fulfilment but also to refashion the educational system in such a way as to create 'a new breed of people'. In this project she was supported by Ivan Betsky who, as President of the Academy of Arts and Director of Public Works and Gardens, was also responsible for the embellishment of St Petersburg. Betsky was convinced that bad morals were merely the result of bad family upbringing and bad schooling, and that 'noble citizens' could be produced without difficulty by removing young children altogether from parental influence and educating them by special methods in conditions which precluded any contact with the outside world. After experiments with a school for foundlings in Moscow, both the *gymnasium* attached to the Academy of Sciences in St Petersburg and the Cadet Corps of the Nobility were opened to children aged 4–5 years, who followed a special curriculum designed by Betsky to inculcate moral virtues rather than learning. At the same time Catherine founded a society for the education of young noblewomen (later known as the Smolny Institute) which was to be run on identical lines.

For a short time, too, Catherine herself assumed the role of preceptor by offering moral guidance to the educated society of St Petersburg in the pages of a satirical journal. At the time social satire was a relatively new feature of Russian journalism. Its first exponent was the dramatist Sumarokov, whose *Busy Bee* (1759) had tilted at the arrogance and ignorance of the country nobility. Catherine, in her *Omnium Gatherum* (*Vsyakaya Vsyachina*) which first appeared in 1769, tried to improve the manners of her readers. She complained, for instance, that women spoke too loud in society, that they discussed unsuitable topics in front of their children. In one issue an imaginary correspondent, probably Catherine herself, asked the editors to distinguish between 'inborn and Russian' and 'evil and Tartar' habits. The editors replied that it was a Tartar habit to break promises, an ancient Russian custom to observe them. Impoliteness, greed and envy were all Tartar habits. Five or six other journals of this type appeared during 1769. Some of them played the role of admiring pupil to Catherine's *Omnium Gatherum*, trying to show how well her lessons had been learnt: but one, *The Drone*, had stronger meat to offer. Its editor, Nikolay Novikov, had been secretary of one of the committees in the commission of 1767, and in *The Drone* he criticised the nobility for their attitude to the merchants and their treatment of the serfs. Catherine's journal reproved him for striking too serious a note. Their first literary skirmish lasted barely a year, but it was to be resumed in earnest before the end of the reign.

The empress's abandonment of her venture into journalism marked the end of her preoccupation with good principles as the best recipe for good living and good government. In 1770 her energy was still unimpaired and she was still determined to leave her special imprint on the administrative structure: but henceforward she tended to adopt a more pragmatic and utilitarian approach, and she allowed events in Russia, rather than her own initiative, to set the pace for change. Of the three major statutes she enacted in the following fifteen years, all were designed to meet specific requests which had been put forward in petitions to the 1767 commission, and one was drafted almost in panic as rebellion swept across the eastern provinces of European Russia.

The rebellion of 1773 was not confined to a single group of malcontents. Its leader, Emelyan Pugachev, united under his banner without discrimination members of every social and religious group which complained of the indifference St Petersburg had shown to the aspirations of the common man in Russia since the days of Peter the Great. The rising began among the Cossacks of the Yaik (Ural), where the hatred of the rank-and-file Cossack for his 'elders' (most of them nominees of St Petersburg) had been intensified by Catherine's decision to put an end to the autonomous status of the Cossack hosts in 1772. Defeated in their first encounter with government troops, the rebels were reorganised by Pugachev, himself a

Don Cossack and a deserter from the Russian army. In the autumn of 1773 Pugachev proclaimed that the report of Peter III's death was an official fabrication, and that he himself was the former emperor. By this ruse he gained thousands of new supporters to his cause, the Cossacks now being joined by peasants working in the factories of the southern Urals, by non-Russian elements in the local population, such as the Kirghiz and Bashkirs, and by groups of Old Believers. The fate of the Old Believers had varied greatly since the beginning of the eighteenth century. Peter the Great's policy of conditional tolerance had been abandoned by his immediate successors, and under Elizabeth the authorities had organized military expeditions to convert dissenters to the official faith. Peter III, on the other hand, shocked the Synod by condemning persecution on religious grounds: and, though Catherine imposed no penalties on the Old Believers, it was her husband's name that they associated with religious freedom.

By the end of October 1773 Pugachev's motley army was at the gates of Orenburg, and the surrounding countryside was entirely in his hands. A force of 1500 government troops from Moscow failed to dislodge him, and it needed a full-size army under Prince Bibikov to raise the siege of Orenburg. Defeated here, Pugachev moved north into the Bashkir region, promising the inhabitants he would drive the Petersburgers out for ever. Defeated again, he outflanked the government force, moved westward towards the Volga, captured the stronghold of Kazan and thereby turned his Cossack revolt into a peasant war. In the countryside around Kazan serfs rose up against their masters and plundered their estates, and it was expected that the rebel army was about to march on Moscow. Defences were erected around the ancient capital and Alexander Suvorov, fresh from his victories in Poland and Turkey, was dispatched to engage the rebels in battle. But Pugachev had overreached himself, and, instead of making for Moscow, he turned southward to his home country, the valley of the Don. On the march his army was decimated by desertions; the Don Cossacks refused to give him any further support; and by January 1775 he had been betrayed to Suvorov's forces, tried and hanged.

In the final stages of the campaign Catherine had moved to Moscow to form a clearer picture of the military situation, to discover how it was that the rebellion had spread so far and so fast, and to decide how a recurrence could be prevented. In the first place, she felt it necessary to make clear where her own sympathies lay in the conflict between serf and landowner, and issued a public statement that the welfare and security of the nobility were inseparable from those of the empire as a whole. Secondly, the rebellion had revealed the shortcomings of the existing system of local government. The haphazard methods which had prevailed since the reign of Peter II, and by which each provincial governor was permitted to administer his province virtually as he wished, led to evasion of responsibility, difficulties in obtaining reliable information and delay in organising countermeasures; and Catherine decided to lay the foundations of a more stable and reliable system as soon as possible. Some work on drafting a new local government statute had already been done by one of the surviving committees of the 1767 commission. The empress took over the incompleted draft from the committee and, with the help of Jacob Sievers, Governor General of Novgorod, she composed most of the final text herself. Inspiration for the new statute, she said, came from Blackstone's *Commentaries on the Laws of England*, which she had read in a French translation early in 1774. Her purpose, she alleged, was to allow the Russian nobility to play the same role in local government as the gentry in England. But for the greater part of the statute the true source was to be found much nearer home. In their petitions of 1767 the nobility had asked for properly established administrative councils and law-courts in the provinces, and had suggested that some posts in the new system of local government be filled by their own elected representatives. Catherine decided to accede to this request by extending over the whole of European Russia the system of administration which already existed in the Baltic provinces acquired from Sweden in 1721.

Under the local government statute of 1775 the country was divided into fifty provinces (*gubernii*), each with a population of 300,000–400,000. The province in turn was subdivided into districts (*uyezdy*), each with a population of 20,000–30,000. The administrative head of each district (*kapitan-ispravnik*) was to be elected by the district nobility. In each provincial and district capital there were to be separate law-courts for the nobility, merchants and free peasants respectively, members of each court being elected by the class concerned. In each provincial capital the three elected courts combined together to form a public welfare board (*prikaz obshchestvennogo prizreniya*) which dealt with public health, education and distribution of charitable funds. The nobility of each province and each district elected their own provincial or district marshal (*predvoditel'*). This office was much sought after for reasons of prestige, though the duties of the holder were confined to the care of widows and orphans of noble birth. But, while many posts were now to be filled by election, the long arm of St Petersburg still stretched right down through the administrative apparatus to the capital towns of districts. Police supervision in every town remained in the hands of a *gorodnichy*, who was appointed by the central government. The decisions of the elected justices were subject to review by civil and criminal law-courts in the provincial capital, all of whose members were nominated by St Petersburg. Tax collection and the allocation of funds for road building and other public works were entrusted to a provincial treasury (*kazennaya palata*), likewise staffed by government officials; and final responsibility for all provincial affairs rested with the governor and members of his council (*pravlenie*), all of whom were appointed by the empress on the nomination of the Senate.

The new statute was to a certain extent complemented by the charter of the nobility (*zhalovannaya gramota dvoryanstvu*) and the city statute, both of which were enacted in 1785. The charter conferred permanent and official status on the provincial and district assemblies of the nobility which, under the local government statute, had merely been called upon to meet triennially and fill the elective posts in the administration. The assemblies were permitted to make submissions to the provincial governor, and in some cases to the monarch herself. For the rest, the charter granted without exception all the requests which the nobility had made in their petitions of 1767. Henceforward, the nobility alone were to have the right to own or acquire 'populated land' (that is, land with serfs). They were permitted to build factories, and to retail the produce of their land. They were to pay no taxes. They were to be exempt from corporal punishment, and could only be deprived of their rank, their property or their lives after trial by their peers. The privileges of the Russian nobility had never been so extensive before; and never, in the last century of tsardom, were they to be increased again.

As the local government statute of 1775 had been based largely on the system already existing in the Baltic provinces, so the city statute for the whole of Russia was modelled on the charter of Riga. In 1767 the merchant class had asked for some stricter definition of social grades within the city population; and city dwellers were now divided into six categories, ranging from merchants of the three guilds established by Peter the Great to the *posadskie*, persons permanently established within the city boundaries who 'earned their daily bread by manual labour'. All city dwellers without discrimination were entitled to participate in elections to the common council (*obshchaya gorodskaya duma*), as well as to the city bench referred to in the local government statute. The common council selected one person from each category of city dwellers to serve for three years on the council of six, the executive authority which was to meet once a week under the chairmanship of the mayor (*gorodskoy golova*).

The system of local government devised by Catherine was to operate without substantial change until 1864. Her city statute remained in force until 1875. The long-term effects of these administrative changes could not be assessed during her lifetime, since it took between thirty and forty years to convert the whole of European Russia to the new system. The only consequence immediately visible was the huge drain on the national resources caused by the recruitment and payment of hundreds of new officials for provincial government. Catherine justified the expense on the grounds that the new system would lead to more efficient and more responsible administration throughout the country. She was not to foresee that the venality, the pomposity and the interminable dilatoriness of petty officials in the provinces would become a favourite target for the satire of Gogol and other mid-nineteenth-century authors. The elected administrators were hardly more zealous than the government officials. Though the nobility as a class had clamoured for the right to elect administrators, the persons elected had little taste for the work. To many of them it seemed like a renewal of compulsory service, which had been abolished in 1762; and, to make matters worse, service in local government did not carry with it an automatic right to promotion in Peter the Great's table of ranks, as did service in the armed forces or the central administration. The provincial assemblies of the nobility were for the most part indifferent to the course of provincial affairs; and it was not until 1857, when the economic security of the nobility was at stake, that they became genuinely interested in a national issue.

Both before and after 1785 Catherine spoke of her intention to 'crown' her work of local government reform by reorganising the central administration; but, apart from the establishment of an advisory state council at the beginning of the Turkish War in 1768, this intention was never fulfilled. By 1785 the empress was nearing the age of sixty. If her confidence in the efficacy of good principles had been replaced in the early 1770s by a belief in the value of good institutions, this in turn had given way by 1785 to a conviction that the main requirement for good government was good people. Years of unwholesome flattery had caused her to overrate the abilities she undoubtedly possessed and, in domestic affairs at least, she had come to think that the best of all good people was herself. Khrapovitsky, her personal secretary in the later years of her reign, has described how she managed her 'little estate'. Each morning those who desired audience with her assembled in her ante-room. From ten o'clock onwards they would be summoned, one at a time, into her bedroom which was furnished with two tables, one for the empress herself and one for the visitor. Normally a few minutes' discussion would be enough for her to make up her mind on matters which might range from the punishment of a court servant to the partition of Poland. The reception of visitors never lasted more than three hours each morning, the rest of Catherine's day being devoted to personal distraction. She was often ill-informed about the matters she decided so rapidly, but she relied upon the tact of her visitors not to reveal this ignorance, and was content to base her decisions mainly upon instinct, which served her uncommonly well.

Before the end of the 1780s, however, she did turn her attention once again to the educational system. The results of Betsky's efforts to produce 'noble citizens' rather than well-trained officers at the Cadet Corps had been unimpressive, and had increased Catherine's respect for more conventional methods of education. For a time she considered founding a new university in the south, but was dissuaded on the grounds that the existing university in Moscow had so far failed to attract a reasonable number of students. She asked the Moscow professors if they could account for the university's slow development, and they replied that it was due to the shortage of funds, which made it impossible to appoint teachers in all subjects of interest to students. They also asked that a pass in the final university examination should be made an essential qualification for entry into government service. But the empress was not convinced by these arguments. She believed that there would never be any considerable demand for higher education until proper opportunities existed for schooling at lower levels, and in 1786 she announced her intention of opening national schools, for the education of children of all classes, in every provincial and district capital town. The person responsible for the new programme was a Serb named Jankovic, who had already supervised the establishment of a network of schools in Hungary and had been commended to Catherine by the Emperor Joseph II. Besides reading and writing, the new schools were to teach mathematics, history and geography, and in the higher classes natural history, physics and mechanics. For this purpose Jankovic had selected and translated a number of Austrian textbooks, and had also produced a guide to the principles of teaching, based on the Austrian *Methodenbuch*. But, in spite of all these careful preparations, serious difficulties were encountered in putting the new programme into effect. In the first place, funds for the new schools had to be found by the provincial public welfare boards. As the funds available to the boards for all purposes were not large, school budgets were generally kept to a minimum. Secondly, there was no eager rush of young children to attend the new schools. In some provinces children were press-ganged into school by the police. In others the authorities closed all previously existing *pensions* and offered inducements for their pupils to transfer to the new schools. Children of noble families showed most reluctance to attend, for schools to which the sons of merchants were admitted had little attraction compared with the Cadet Corps in the capital or a course of study with a private tutor. Even where children were willing to attend, there might be a shortage of teachers. The first draft of teachers was recruited from the diocesan seminaries and, when this source had been exhausted, a special teachers' training establishment was opened belatedly in St Petersburg. These difficulties are reflected in the educational statistics for the last ten years of Catherine's reign. Between 1786 and 1791 the number of children attending all types of schools in Russia rose from just over 4000 to nearly 18,000. Between 1791 and 1796 there was no further expansion at all.[1]

Catherine was particularly concerned about the success of her new educational programme, for reasons connected with her own personal

[1] P. N. Milyukov, *Ocherki po istorii russkoi kul'tury* (Paris, Jubilee ed., 1931), vol. II, 2, p. 763, based on the records of the Ministry of Education in St Petersburg.

prestige. In her later years she was unable to tolerate the initiative of private persons in activities in which she herself was interested, and by 1786 education was the central issue in a conflict between Catherine and several of the more active masonic lodges in Russia. The first Russian freemasons, during the 1730s, had been attracted mainly by the ritual of masonry. In the 1760s the martinist element had predominated in the lodges of St Petersburg and Moscow (the majority of members were students of the Cadet Corps or Moscow University), but towards the end of the 1770s Nikolay Novikov began to devote himself to the practical application of the masonic ideals of brotherhood among men and moral regeneration by trying to promote the welfare and the education of the common man in Russia. Novikov had first become interested in masonry as an alternative for what passed in St Petersburg of the 1770s as Voltaireanism. When Catherine described herself as a Voltairean, she had at least attempted to understand the essence of Voltaire's teaching, but lesser members of St Petersburg society styled themselves *volteryantsy* on more slender grounds. For them Voltaireanism meant simply the rejection of religious beliefs, of social obligations and of all the commonly accepted virtues. It was an attitude of total cynicism, a pose which they adopted as the hallmark of an expensive foreign education, as a symbol which distinguished them from the vulgar and ill-born. Novikov, too, was prepared to surrender his attachment to the church, but the fashionable cynicism of his contemporaries did not appeal to him, and in the ideals of masonry he found a more acceptable foundation for belief and action.

In 1777, with fellow members of a masonic lodge he had joined two years earlier, he founded two schools in St Petersburg for the city poor. Funds for the maintenance of the schools were to be raised by the sale of a new journal, *Morning Light*, whose innocuous articles on moral themes were popular with the public and did not excite the suspicions of the authorities. Catherine refused to give official support to the schools, and declined an invitation to subscribe to the journal. In 1779 Novikov moved to Moscow, founded a new masonic lodge, leased the printing-press of Moscow University and extended the range of his publications. Here, too, he joined forces with a German named Johann Schwartz, who had recently been appointed professor of philosophy in the university. Mystic and martinist himself, Schwartz believed at the outset that Novikov was perverting the true aims of masonry, but by 1782 he had been induced to part with his whole fortune to pay for a teachers' training school in Moscow. In 1783, when private individuals were for the first time allowed to own and operate printing-presses, Novikov and Schwartz together founded a printing company which was to produce more than 400 books in eight years.

Some of the books were educational; others, such as *The Town and Country Library*, were designed to appeal to the reading public at large;

none of them contained any serious political or social comment. But the more Novikov's activities expanded, the more resentful the empress became. At first, in the hope of turning public opinion against the freemasons, she wrote and circulated a pamphlet ridiculing their ideals. When Novikov had published a history of religious dissent in Russia, she tried to have him convicted of religious heresy; but the archbishop of Moscow, who was instructed to peruse the publications of Novikov's printing company, could find no cause for complaint. In 1787, when the central provinces of Russia were struck by famine, Novikov launched an appeal for funds, collected thousands of roubles from the wealthy merchants of Moscow and bought grain for distribution among the victims. Catherine accused him of 'trying to gain the sympathy of the lower classes' (a similar charge was made against the *zemstvo* liberals who organised famine relief in 1891), but Novikov disregarded the sinister implications of this latest attack. He continued his publishing activities in Moscow until 1791, when the empress placed his case in the hands of Stepan Sheshkovsky, her chief of secret police.

It was unfortunate for Novikov that the outbreak of revolution in France coincided with the advent of a new favourite in St Petersburg. In 1789 the sixty-year-old empress had fallen in love with Platon Zubov, an officer of the Imperial Guard who was more than thirty years her junior. Narrow-minded and impetuous by temperament, Zubov had a rooted dislike of compromise or tolerance. He was prone to quick and cut-and-dried decisions. He was inordinately suspicious of any activities which seemed likely to impair Catherine's security; and, as his hold over her grew, his outlook came to colour her own. Catherine herself had watched the collapse of the French monarchy with deep concern. She was 'shocked' by the storming of the Bastille, 'indignant' at the abolition of titles, 'amazed' by the extent of the power which was placed in the hands of the 'savetiers et cordonniers' of the *Assemblée nationale*; and she warmly commended the efforts of her ambassador in France to help the royal family to escape from Paris. But at the same time she believed that developments in France were due solely to the weakness and incompetence of Louis XVI and his advisers, and that an able and forceful ruler need have no fear of revolution. Zubov, on the other hand, was continually warning Catherine of dangers at home. He recalled that the Illuminati had been unmasked in western Europe as a political organisation, and argued that the Russian freemasons also must have political aspirations. It was on a political charge, in fact, that Novikov was arrested in 1791. Sheshkovsky alleged that he had tried to induce the Grand Duke Paul to join the masonic movement, and planned to place Paul on the throne in place of his mother. While there was some substance in the first charge, Novikov firmly rebutted the second; but Catherine still suspected that he had been engaged in a conspiracy against her, and he was sentenced to imprisonment in the fortress of Schlüsselburg for fifteen years, 'that there may be time for him to repent of his misdeeds'.

The severity of Novikov's punishment has been explained on the grounds that he was the leader of a movement with a considerable following, and that he had been a thorn in Catherine's flesh since the earliest years of her reign. But at the same time a solitary figure, who had incurred the empress's displeasure by the publication of a single book, was overtaken by the same fate. The book, entitled *Journey from St Petersburg to Moscow*, appeared early in 1790, and Catherine read it in June of the same year. In form, it appeared to be an imitation of Sterne's *Sentimental Journey through France and Italy*, but its author Alexander Radishchev, impassioned disciple of Rousseau and Raynal, had filled his twenty-five chapters with reflections on the injustices of Russian life, the plight of the serfs and the inhumanity of local officials; and he had concluded with a proposal for the emancipation of the serfs. Catherine described him as 'tainted with the French madness' and 'a rebel worse than Pugachev', and ordered Sheshkovsky to investigate his activities. He was sentenced to exile in Siberia for life. Zubov urged Catherine to prevent the French madness from spreading more widely among Russian youth, and all Russian students attending universities in western Europe were ordered to come home. The purchase of French books and journals was prohibited entirely. After the death of Louis XVI, all French citizens in Russia were required to take an oath of loyalty to the new king, or leave the country. The quarantine, as Catherine called it, was maintained and intensified by her son, and only relaxed after his death in 1801.

If the projects of Catherine the administrator became less ambitious and more practical as she grew older, the reverse is true of Catherine the diplomat, for in her conduct of foreign affairs she progressed from cautious empiricism to extreme audacity. When she came to the throne, there was no clear-cut policy for her to follow. In spite of all the funds expended and all the casualties suffered, Russia had gained no material advantages from her participation in the Seven Years War. The most she had gained was a reputation for the fighting qualities of her troops, but even this had been impaired by Peter III's sudden decision to make peace with Prussia in January 1762. The new alliance with Prussia was unpopular in the country, and frowned upon by a majority in the college of foreign affairs, which wished to revert to Peter the Great's system of permanent alliance with Austria. But the college had had no official president since the dismissal of Bestuzhev-Ryumin in 1757 and, without a responsible minister to guide her, Catherine had to frame a policy herself. In her accession manifesto, she satisfied nationalist feeling in St Petersburg by criticising her husband for delivering the country into the hands of its former enemies, but she did not seek to revive the old connection with Austria. She believed that she could best advance the interests of Russia by standing apart from each of the two major coalitions. She wished to keep her hands free of any commitments to other powers; to profit by the preoccupations and the weakness of her European neighbours in order to pursue her own aims in Poland and the Black Sea without foreign aid and foreign interference; and to enhance her personal prestige and increase the influence and weight of Russia in European politics by acting, when the opportunity arose, as peace-maker and arbiter of international disputes. This was the underlying principle of her foreign policy throughout her reign. Three times she decided to depart from it under temporary pressure or to secure a temporary advantage, but on each occasion she regretted her decision afterwards.

The first two years of this experiment in isolation brought Catherine one major disappointment and one initial success. She had hoped that, as a neutral, she would be asked to preside over the peace conference at Hubertusburg in 1763, but she was not even invited to take part in the deliberations which brought the Seven Years War to an end. In the same year she expelled Prince Charles of Saxony from Courland and reinstated Bühren in the dukedom; and after the death of Augustus III she secured the election of her former lover, Stanislav Poniatowski, as the king of Poland. But by 1764 advice from home and pressure from abroad had induced Catherine to surrender her independence of action. A few days before the death of Augustus III Catherine had appointed Nikita Panin as president of the college of foreign affairs. He was an educated man, but an idler and a dreamer, a weaver of diplomatic patterns which had little connection either with Russia's traditional aspirations or with existing possibilities; and he urged Catherine to abandon her position of neutrality and to try to link together the northern states of Europe in a system of alliances, under Russian leadership, against France and Austria. All the states involved, except Russia herself and Poland, were Protestant states, and Panin believed that they would willingly range themselves together against the two great Catholic powers. All, except Russia, were territorially small states, and Panin had planned his system of alliances as a kind of union of the weak against the strong. But, in reality, the Northern Accord had poor prospects of success. Genuine co-operation between Russia and Poland was unlikely, so long as Catherine herself wished to settle the question of the 'western lands' on her own terms. Panin had hoped that Britain would be induced to join the system, and would assume the role formerly played by France in the domestic politics of Sweden and Denmark; but prolonged negotiations with Britain failed to produce agreement on terms for a full-scale alliance, though the British ambassador did sign a commercial treaty with Russia in 1766. Liberal distribution of Russian funds in Stockholm during the 1760s failed to prevent the restoration of absolute monarchy in Sweden, with French encouragement, in 1772: and, though Panin tried to gain the support of

Denmark for his project by inducing Catherine to surrender her son's claims to the duchy of Holstein, he received little gratitude for this handsome gesture. As to Prussia, Frederick did not relish the prospect of a military alliance embracing Russia, Britain, Denmark and Saxony, nor did he wish to join any coalition in which Russian influence predominated. But he did believe that, by concluding an alliance with Russia alone, he might be able to curb Catherine's ambitions in Poland and further his own. Panin welcomed the proposal for a Russo-Prussian alliance as the foundation of his Northern Accord system and, by the treaty concluded on 11 April 1764, the two powers exchanged mutual assurances of support in the event of attack by a third party; and they undertook to pursue a common policy in Sweden and Poland, to prevent any amendment of the Polish constitution and to make joint efforts to secure full civil and political rights for the Polish dissenters, both Orthodox and Protestant.

The treaty was twice renewed, and remained in force until 1781. In later years Catherine was to describe its consequences as 'tout ce qu'il y a de plus ignominieux et de plus insupportable au monde'. From the moment of its signature, every move she made in Poland or the Black Sea was followed by complaints and admonishments, threats and warnings from Berlin. At the end of 1764, when the Russian representative in Warsaw had forced the Diet to extend the political rights of the Orthodox and Protestants in Poland, Frederick observed that this issue was of lesser importance, compared with the maintenance of the *liberum veto* in the Diet. In 1768, when Prince Repnin had induced the Diet to endorse a Russo-Polish agreement naming Catherine as protector of the Polish constitution, Frederick complained that she was being too high-handed. When the sultan declared war on Russia in the same year, Frederick immediately sought, and obtained, a renewal of his treaty with Russia. When Rumyantsev had captured Bucharest and was waiting for reinforcements to advance beyond the Danube, Frederick warned the empress that Austria would not tolerate the permanent occupation of Moldavia and Wallachia by Russian troops. The only means of avoiding a new conflict in central Europe, he said, was for both Russia and Austria to satisfy their requirements at the expense of Poland.

But, if Catherine complained of Frederick's interference, her freedom of action was restricted to an equal extent by the number of troops she could afford to mobilize. She had expected fighting in Poland, where an army of more than 30,000 Russians had been deployed almost without interruption since the end of the Seven Years War. What she had been most anxious to avoid was that Russia should be involved in war with Turkey at the same time; but in October 1768 a regiment of pro-Russian Ukrainian troops crossed the Turkish frontier at Balta in pursuit of a detachment of Polish nationalists, and the sultan, encouraged by promises of support from Austria and France, decided to regard the frontier incident as a *casus belli*. On the outbreak of war Catherine summoned a special council to advise her, just as Elizabeth had done on the eve of the Seven Years War. The council decided, first, that no large-scale action should be undertaken against Turkey until the last stronghold of the Polish nationalists had been reduced. When the Polish campaign had been completed, one Russian corps was to hold the line of frontier outposts in the south against the Crimean Tartars, while the main force was to advance towards the Danube to prevent the Turkish army from moving northwards towards Polish territory. Further, to startle western Europe with the power of Russia's navy and to incite the Christian peoples of the Balkans to rebel against the sultan, the reigning favourite, Grigory Orlov, proposed to send the Baltic fleet around the coast of France and Spain and into the eastern Mediterranean. The military and naval campaigns both started successfully, but soon came to a halt owing to lack of reinforcements and shortage of funds. By 1770 Rumyantsev had captured, lost and recaptured Bucharest, but complained that he had insufficient troops to continue his advance (contrary to the expectations of the council, fighting still continued in Poland). By February 1770 three squadrons from the Baltic fleet, commanded by Orlov's brother but fitted out at British expense and with the assistance of British naval officers, had made a landing on the west coast of Greece. For months beforehand the Greeks had talked boldly of their preparations for the uprising but, now the time had come, they lost heart and complained they were not ready. Orlov was disgusted, and after ten days ashore he recalled his men aboard and changed his plans. A fourth squadron under Admiral Elphinstone was on its way to Greece, and when it arrived Orlov decided to join battle with the Turkish fleet. In a four-hour engagement in the bay of Chesme the Russians sank or put out of action all the vessels the Turks could muster to oppose them, but it was a prestige victory above all. The destruction of the Turkish fleet in the Mediterranean had little bearing on the main theatre of war, and Orlov was not strong enough to consider forcing a passage through the Straits.

It was at this stage that Frederick pressed his proposal for the partition of Poland. Catherine was not at first receptive. As early as 1763 she had approved a plan to advance the western frontier of Russia as far as the Dvina and the Dnieper,[1] but it was no part of this plan that the central powers should receive a compensatory share of Polish territory, and she wished them to pay a high price for it. Panin declared that the empress would not consent to the annexation of any part of Poland by Austria and Prussia, unless they in turn agreed to the acquisition of Azov and Taganrog by Russia, the creation of an independent Crimea and the permanent occupation of Moldavia and Wallachia by Russian troops. But it was impossible to strike a bargain on these terms. When the Austrian chan-

[1] *Sbornik imperatorskogo russkogo istoricheskogo obshchestva*, vol. LI, pp. 9–11.

cellor made clear that his country would not tolerate the presence of Russian troops on the Danube, Panin changed his tune. Of the two alternatives before him—either to face war with Austria or 'to realise what we all desire' by annexing Polish Lithuania—there could be no doubt which was the more attractive. He waived the Russian claims to Moldavia and Wallachia, and agreed to discuss with Austria and Prussia how large a portion of Poland each of them should take.

He was bitterly criticised at home for this decision, particularly by Grigory Orlov, who complained that Panin had allowed Frederick and the Austrian empress to profit by the victories of Russian arms in Poland: but he argued that the advance to the Dvina on any other terms might have been impossible and that, without agreement on partition, the Turkish war could not have been brought to a satisfactory conclusion. Negotiations for peace were started at the Turkish request in June 1772, but were broken off some months later owing to the sultan's refusal to grant independence to the Crimea. But by the spring of 1774 Alexander Suvorov, the most brilliant of Catherine's younger generals, had been transferred from Poland to the Danube front; he and his commander Rumyantsev had each won a demonstrative victory over the Turks; the empress was anxious to recall a portion of Rumyantsev's army back to Russia to deal with the Pugachev rebellion; and fresh overtures for peace from Constantinople were immediately accepted. The terms agreed at Kutchuk Kainardji on 21 June 1774 would have warmed the heart of Peter the Great. The Crimea was declared independent. Russia acquired the northern coastline of the Sea of Azov, with the ports of Azov and Taganrog, and a foothold on the Black Sea between the Dnieper and the Bug. Russian merchant vessels were assured freedom of navigation on the Black Sea and free passage of the Straits; and on Catherine's insistence, the sultan agreed to recognise her and her successors as protectors of the religious freedom of his Christian subjects. With the new frontier, there was easy access to the sea from the most fertile areas of southern Russia. There was a sea route, at least in times of peace, connecting Russia to the rest of Europe by the warm waters of the Mediterranean; and by recognising the ethnic and religious connection between the Russians and his Christian subjects, the sultan had provided St Petersburg with grounds for interfering at will in the domestic politics of the northern sector of the Ottoman empire.

With peace restored, Panin still remained faithful to the Prussian alliance, but the empress had other plans. For her Kutchuk Kainardji was not an end, but only the beginning. In 1772 she had been forced in an emergency to purchase the approval of Austria and Prussia before imposing her conditions on the sultan. The experience of bargaining under pressure had not appealed to her; and, to prevent the need arising again, she planned to obtain advance consent for further expansion in the south from both the central powers by creating a triple alliance. Another lesson she had learnt from the first Turkish War was the need to conserve and concentrate her forces. Between 1768 and 1774 the number of troops at her disposal had been inadequate to conduct simultaneous campaigns in Poland and Turkey. If she could not maintain an army sufficient for her own needs, it was unthinkable that Russian forces should be committed in the interests of other powers. Twice in the five years after Kutchuk Kainardji she was asked to give military assistance in disputes which were of no direct concern to Russia, and twice she refused. In one instance she used her position as a neutral to mediate between the contestants; in the other she emerged as the champion of the rights of neutrals. In the conflict between Austria and Prussia over the Bavarian succession, Frederick was confident that under the terms of the 1764 treaty he could count on military support from Catherine. After reflection the empress decided that Frederick did have the stronger case, but she was not prepared to go to war to help him. Instead she tried to persuade the two parties to come to terms, and the settlement reached under her guidance at Teschen in 1779 increased her conviction that she was marked out to be the arbiter of Europe. Panin's successor was to boast that 'after Teschen not a gun was fired in Europe without the approval of Russia'.

In the American War of Independence, too, her political sympathies lay genuinely and wholeheartedly with Britain, but she did not regard that as a sufficient reason for supplying a Russian force to fight the colonists, and was surprised that the British felt slighted by her refusal to assist them. Once more she was to add lustre to her name by declining to commit herself. The declaration of Armed Neutrality was hurriedly composed, and the decision to form a league of neutrals hurriedly taken, to convince the belligerents that Russia's strength and standing were in no way inferior to their own. Towards the end of the war, Lord North promised to cede Minorca to Russia if Catherine could induce France and Spain to make peace on his terms, and she came near to accepting the offer. But she was convinced that there were some conditions attached to it, and in the end decided that to retain her freedom of action was safer even than to acquire a foothold in the western Mediterranean.

With the formation of the league of neutrals, Panin's career at the college of foreign affairs came to an end. He himself had never enjoyed Catherine's undivided confidence. She had already decided to sever her attachment with Prussia. By the end of 1781 she had signed a new treaty of alliance with the Emperor Joseph II, and the direction of foreign affairs in St Petersburg had passed into the hands of two men who came into prominence during the first Turkish War. Grigory Potemkin had started his career in the administration but, having volunteered for service in the south under Rumyantsev in 1768, he was rapidly promoted to the rank of general, commended by Rumyantsev to the empress and summoned to

St Petersburg at the end of the war. For two years after 1774 this moody and vainglorious man was Catherine's lover; from 1776 until the advent of Platon Zubov in 1789 he continued to advise and guide her. He shared her taste for the flamboyant and the sensational. In intellect and education he was her equal, but he lacked her thoroughness and concentration, and in this respect he found the perfect complement in Alexander Bezborodko, who became Panin's official successor. Ukrainian by birth, a former student of the Kiev academy, a polyglot and a historian, Bezborodko was gifted with an extraordinary memory and a great capacity for hard work. Under Potemkin's influence Catherine gave up her plans for a triple alliance on the grounds that, when the time was ripe for a further advancement of the southern frontier, the assent of Austria alone would be enough. Contact with Vienna had been renewed by the correspondence between Catherine and Maria Theresa prior to the Teschen agreement. The Austrian chancellor was in any case seeking some additional security in anticipation of a further conflict with Prussia. The first overtures were made when Joseph II visited Russia in 1780, and a formal alliance was concluded in May 1781. But, while Kaunitz believed it was directed primarily against Prussia, for Catherine it was merely the preliminary for a new offensive against Turkey.

By 1781 Bezborodko had prepared a plan for a political reorganisation of the entire Balkan peninsula, known as the 'Greek project'. According to this, Russia was first to acquire the Black Sea coastline between the Bug and the Dniester, including the fortress of Ochakov which commanded the mouths of both rivers, and would then renounce all claims for additional territory in this area. The next stage would be to free Bessarabia, Moldavia and Wallachia from the Turks, and combine them into a single principality of Dacia, independent of Russia but governed by a prince of the Orthodox faith (it was believed outside Russia that Potemkin had reserved this title for himself). Finally, when the Turks had been driven out of Europe altogether, it was planned to revive the Byzantine empire, with the Russian Grand Duke Constantine (born in 1779) as the emperor. At the same time Bezborodko proposed that Austria should receive part of Serbia, including Belgrade, while Egypt or some other part of the Ottoman empire in Africa might be offered to France. There was mention, too, of some compensation for Britain and Spain.

For two years Catherine discussed the 'project' with the Emperor Joseph, but even her new ally was dismayed by its implications. He complained that the Austrian share of the spoils was too small and demanded Moldavia and Wallachia as well. But Catherine would not be discouraged or dissuaded. In the spring of 1787, in the company of the Austrian emperor, she made a demonstrative journey to the Crimea, which had declared its allegiance to Russia four years earlier. The sultan replied by demanding the restoration of Crimean independence. On 1 September the Turks opened fire on two Russian vessels off Ochakov, and Catherine declared war. In 1788 new plans were made to sail the Baltic fleet into the Mediterranean, but the British Admiralty declined to provide the same assistance as in 1770. Moreover, before the fleet could set sail from St Petersburg, the king of Sweden with encouragement from Pitt recalled an ancient treaty of alliance with Turkey, declared war on Russia and mounted a land offensive only a few tens of miles from the capital. Austria entered the war late, fought with half an eye on events in western Europe and, when revolution spread to Belgium, hastened to make peace with Turkey. The king of Prussia sided openly with the Turks, promised military aid to Sweden and made a demonstration of force along the frontier of Courland. In March 1791 Pitt prepared an ultimatum calling upon Catherine to abandon her designs on Ochakov and to make peace on reasonable terms. Worst of all, in May of the same year, the Poles took advantage of Russia's preoccupations in the south to proclaim a new constitution.

While Potemkin took charge of the campaign on the Black Sea, Bezborodko decided to give way before the almost unanimous opposition. In the summer of 1790 the king of Sweden was anxious to prepare for war with France, and Bezborodko eagerly accepted his offer of peace on the basis of the *status quo* before the war. He even agreed to abandon Russia's claims to Finland and to renounce Catherine's rights as protector of the Swedish constitution. He ignored Pitt's protest at the capture of Ochakov (the ultimatum was in any case never presented), but decided not to proceed further with his project for the conquest of the Balkans, and to transfer part of Potemkin's army to Poland. Potemkin died in October 1791 and, though Suvorov had captured the fortress of Izmail and Prince Repnin had defeated the Turks in pitched battle south of the Danube, the peace terms negotiated at Jassy in January 1792 by Bezborodko himself were relatively mild. The sultan was obliged finally to accept the loss of the Crimea to Russia. He ceded the coastline between the Bug and the Dniester (the city of Odessa was founded here, on the site of a ruined Turkish fortress, in 1793). For the rest the Treaty of Jassy merely confirmed the terms agreed at Kutchuk Kainardji eighteen years earlier.

Six weeks after the end of the war in Turkey Catherine informed the ambassadors of Austria and Prussia that she proposed to annul the Polish constitution of May 1791 and compel the Poles to honour their former undertakings to her; and a Russian army, 65,000 strong, entered Poland 'to restore its freedom'. This announcement was not intended as a challenge to Frederick William, who had concluded a defensive alliance with Poland two years earlier, but Catherine could not have imagined that the central powers would allow her to settle the fate of Poland on her own.

Potemkin had long insisted that Russia should try to seize the rich Ukrainian provinces of Poland, by partition or otherwise, and the empress had made clear in a memorandum addressed to him in 1791 that she would not be adverse to another partition.[1] By the second partition of Poland, in fact, Russia acquired not only the whole of Polish Ukraine, but the areas of Minsk and Vilna as well. With Poland reduced to half its former size, Bezborodko complained that it was too small to act as a buffer state between Russia and the central powers, and that it needed a whole army for the maintenance of order: and on these grounds, after Kosciuszko's rising in 1794, he justified his country's participation in the final dismemberment. By the three partitions Catherine had liberated all 'those of the same faith and blood as ourselves'. She had recovered all the 'western lands' and acquired in addition a considerable expanse of Polish territory which not even the most extravagant historical arguments could assign by right to Russia. But for her the future was more important than the past, and she was more interested in the potential wealth of the land she had seized in southern Poland, and more gratified to reflect that with the new frontier along the Niemen and the western Bug the limits of her empire had been carried 400 miles forward into central Europe.

The size of the Russian share in the second and third partitions was due mainly to the fact that the brunt of the fighting in Poland was borne by Russian troops, Austria and Prussia being simultaneously engaged in war with France. With this end in view Catherine had repeatedly urged them both to intensify their efforts against France and leave her to deal with the 'Jacobins' in Poland. With equal insistence she promised that she would provide military support for the coalition as soon as the campaign in Poland was ended. But after the fall of Warsaw she was reluctant to honour her promise. She complained that the conclusion of peace between Prussia and France made it unsafe to withdraw her troops from Poland, but there were other reasons for delay as well. Zubov, her newest favourite, had tried to outdo Bezborodko by devising his own project for the conquest of Constantinople. One Russian army was to resume the traditional offensive through the Balkans, while a second was to enter Asia Minor through the Caucasus and Persia. As the two armies converged, the Black Sea fleet under the command of Catherine herself was to enter the Bosporus and invest the Turkish capital from the sea. In February 1796 an expedition left St Petersburg for Persia, and it was not until November that Catherine at last agreed to send some of her picked troops under Suvorov's command to the relief of Austria. But she died before Suvorov left Poland, and her orders were countermanded by her successor.

The cost of the campaigns in Poland and Turkey was immense, and its

---

[1] The memorandum is reproduced in full in X. Liske, 'Zur polnischen Politik Katharina II 1791', *Historische Zeitschrift*, vol. xxx, pp. 295–301.

impact on the national economy was intensified by the empress's indifference to budgetary problems. In the early 1760s she had borrowed money from banking houses in Amsterdam,[1] but from the beginning of the first Turkish War she issued paper money to cover her expenses. The first issue in 1769 amounted to no more than two and a half million roubles, and for some years the paper rouble (*assignatsiya*) held its value against silver coin both inside and outside Russia. But by 1787 the amount of paper money in circulation was approaching 100 million roubles, and Catherine made a formal declaration that the issue would not be increased. The promise was not kept, a further fifty million roubles were printed in the early 1790s, and by 1796 the value of the paper rouble stood at seventy silver copecks inside Russia, and at 2s. 6d. in the London exchange market compared with 3s. 5d. ten years earlier. Russia's foreign trade balance did not change appreciably under Catherine, the value of imports varying between two-thirds and three-quarters of the value of goods exported, but there had been a marked change in the character of the export trade. Iron accounted for only 5 per cent by value of total exports in 1796, compared with 25–30 per cent during the 1750s. Naval stores were now the main export, amounting to more than 40 per cent of the total. The export of grain from ports on the sea of Azov had already begun, but as yet it was an insignificant item in the total trade turnover. It has been estimated that of all the grain produced in Russia at the end of the century only 20 per cent was sold by the producers and only about one per cent exported.[2] At home, there was a steep rise in the number of manufactures, most of the new ones being cotton-mills. With the rise of the cotton industry, a new phase began in the development of industrial organisation, since the cotton-mills were not owned by the state, by rich merchants or noblemen, but by a new class of entrepreneurs including wealthy serfs; and, whereas the labour force in the iron-foundries and linen manufactures consisted mainly of serfs, ascribed peasants or convicts, the cotton-mills employed a considerable percentage of hired labour from the outset and soon free hired labour exclusively. Some of the mills employed as many as 1000 workers and, though the first report of a mechanical loom in St Petersburg dates from 1793, production was almost entirely by hand. But the growth of industry was still too small to affect population distribution. Since Catherine's accession, the population of Russia had increased from 19 millions to 29 millions (or, including the population of the newly annexed territories, to 36 millions). At the end of the century, less than a twenty-fifth of the total lived in towns. Moscow and St Petersburg each had a population approaching a quarter of a million but, apart from them,

---

[1] J. von Bloch, *Les Finances de la Russie au XIX siècle*, vol. I, p. 73.

[2] D. Protopopov, 'O khlebnoi torgovle v Rossii', *Zhurnal ministerstva gosudarstvennykh imushchestv*, vol. v, no. 3 (1842), quoted in P. A. Khromov, *Ekonomicheskoe razvitie Rossii v XIX–XX vekakh*, p. 95. I have been unable to consult Protopopov's article in the original.

there were only three towns—Riga, Astrakhan and Kazan—with as many as 30,000 inhabitants.

In a mock epitaph written for herself, Catherine claimed that 'when she ascended the throne of Russia, she wished to do good and tried to bring happiness, freedom and well-being to her subjects', and the claim should not lightly be rejected. The sincerity of her motives in the early stages of her reign cannot be impugned by reference to the political atmosphere in St Petersburg during her last years. There are no grounds for doubting that before 1767 she earnestly hoped it would be possible to translate the principles of the Enlightenment into reality in Russia by inspired legislation. Even in the 1770s, after she had lowered her sights, she still made unremitting efforts to put an end to the haphazard methods of government employed by Peter the Great's successors. Even in the 1790s, when her capacity for self-criticism had been dulled by flattery, her conscience was still troubled from time to time by thoughts of unsolved problems and uncompleted work. As it was, she had taken Russia a stage further towards modern statehood by establishing institutions which, for all their defects, were to survive for nearly ninety years; and, apart from the practical attainments of her lifetime, the ideas which she had publicly propagated from the throne during the 1760s were to a large extent fulfilled in the social legislation of the nineteenth century. In her foreign policy, too, assisted by brilliant generalship and the domestic weakness of France, she had done far more than Peter the Great to bring Russia right into the heart of Europe. Apart from the acquisition of Finland in 1809, Bessarabia in 1812 and 'congress Poland' in 1815, the frontiers of European Russia were to remain unchanged from 1796 until the collapse of the monarchy; and, in almost every sphere of national activity, the tempo of change was negligibly slow in the sixty years after her death compared with what it had been during the thirty-four years of her administration.

Of all the charges that may be levelled against her, the most serious is not that on occasion she regarded her personal reputation as more important than the public good; not that, under pressure from the nobility, she turned a blind eye to a progressive deterioration in the condition of the serfs; not that, under the influence of Platon Zubov, she framed an anti-revolutionary policy which was refined to the point of absurdity by her son Paul and expanded into a doctrine of international conduct by her grandson Alexander I. It is that, unlike Peter the Great, she did not attempt to develop the material resources without which Russia could never confidently play the role of great power; and that her campaigns in Poland and Turkey left the country crippled with an intolerable burden of national debt and a critically depreciated currency. But, if Catherine was unmoved by the financial consequences of her foreign policy, so for the most part were her people. In their eyes, Catherine was the first

Russian ruler to arbitrate between the powers of Europe and impose her will on them, and she was given part at least of the credit for the unbroken series of victories which Rumyantsev and Suvorov had won over the traditional enemies of Russia. For a people already sensitive about its standing *vis-à-vis* the rest of the world, and traditionally prodigal in its private and public spending, national bankruptcy for three or four decades was a small price to pay for so invigorating a tonic.

CHAPTER XII

THE PARTITIONS OF POLAND

Voyez ce qu'ont fait les encyclopédistes; de francs ignorants les rois sont devenus des menteurs moraux. On partage savamment les royaumes, comme autrefois on divisait les sermons, et l'on massacre le peuple avec autant de sang-froid qu'on les ennuyait. Voilà un siècle de lumières!

HORACE WALPOLE to Madame du Deffand, 13 April 1773

No sooner were the partitions of Poland accomplished than political thinkers and historians began to investigate the circumstances that had brought them about. The accounts and aspersions of eye-witnesses and contemporaries were followed in the next generation by rue-ful tales of misgovernment and, after the failure of the uprising of 1830–1, the whole question of national existence was sublimated and poeticised. The messianic hopes of the romantic poets were dashed by a series of setbacks beginning with the Galician massacre of 1846 and ending with the disastrous uprising of 1863. Thereafter, as Romanticism finally ceased to be the stuff of poetry, history became the object of serious academic study. Already in 1862 a chair of Polish history had been established in Warsaw, the universities of Cracow and of Lvov followed suit in 1869 and 1882. In 1880 Szujski, who occupied the chair at Cracow, expressed the opinion that if a nation failed to maintain law and order within its frontiers and to defend itself from external aggression, it was bound to become incapable of further evolution and to lose its independence. Poland's downfall had been caused by the Poles' own guilt of several centuries' standing. Szujski was apparently influenced by Darwin, though by no means exclusively so, since this thesis—a theological rather than a zoological concept—had first been adumbrated by the precursor of the 'Cracow school', Kalinka. Having set out to estimate the moral worth of Poland in the reign of its last king, Kalinka reached the conclusion (in 1868) that it was the Poles themselves who caused their country's down-fall and that the misfortunes that had since afflicted them were a well-deserved penance. Like Szujski, Bobrzyński, writing in 1879, deplored Poland's eastward expansion and attributed her decline and fall to her failure to create a modern state. Poland perished because she had refused to sacrifice political freedom for the sake of strong government. The reac-tion against the 'Cracow school' set in in the 1880s. Smoleński, in 1886, pointed out the unsoundness of many of the pessimists' conclusions, while Korzon, in his study (1881–6) of the era of the partitions, found many signs of the country's organic strength despite serious external lesions. Askenazy, who devoted himself to the investigation of Poland's position against the background of European diplomacy, was able to state that the cause of the partitions was not inherent in the republic itself but resided in contemporary Europe. In 1915 O. Balzer asserted that the defects of Poland's institutions were common to most countries in central Europe and that the *causa efficiens* of the partitions was, therefore, not misgovernment but the unchecked rapaciousness of her neighbours. The somewhat confusing methodological suggestions made by T. Brzeski in 1918[1] do not appear to have been followed. In 1927 the economic historian Rutkowski[2] found the reason for the partitions in a combination of factors—economic, political and moral. In 1935 O. Górka pointed out the inverted logic of the traditional 'optimistic' and 'pessimistic' views of Poland's past and future. Considered objectively, the 'pessimists' were optimists since the harm resulting from a nation's own faults could be remedied by its own efforts, while the 'optimists' were in fact pessimists since a conspiracy between Poland's neighbours was ever capable of depriving her of national independence, no matter how high the degree of her development. While the rest of Górka's argument makes pathetic reading today, the validity of the revaluation must be recognised.

Partition was a major political fashion of the eighteenth century, a rational way for monarchs to settle their differences and adjust one another's potentials in the name of the balance of power. The absolute monarch was considered the owner of the territories over which he ruled, nationalities had no recognised rights and the acquisition of land, no matter by whom it was inhabited, was regarded as an unmixed blessing. The territory of any state, and of a composite state in particular, was liable to become the object of a piratical conspiracy between its neighbours who found a promise of impunity in their complicity. Thus the Great Northern War originated in a scheme to share out the Swedish possessions on the southern shore of the Baltic and the Spanish succession was divided in 1713–14, a fate which the Austrian inheritance narrowly escaped in 1741. In the west, at various times, Prussia, Austria, France and England in different dual combinations, when not compelled to exchange the role of the wolf for that of the lamb, showed an appetite for such morsels as Bavaria, parts of the Rhineland, the Netherlands, Austrian Italy, Hanover and the English, French and Dutch colonies. In the east, Russia and Austria were preparing to reduce the size of Turkey with the possible help of England and France. In eastern and central Europe especially the choice seemed increasingly to lie between partitioning or being partitioned. It was in order to weaken Prussia that Russia entered the Seven Years War. According to a plan drawn up by Bestuzhev, in the event of victory, Austria was to be rewarded with Silesia, Poland was to

---

[1] *Kwartalnik Historyczny* (1918), pp. 173–240.

[2] 'Les bases économiques des partages de l'ancienne Pologne', *Revue d'histoire moderne*, vol. VII (1932), pp. 363–89.

receive East Prussia, but in return to yield her suzerainty over Courland to Russia and to accept a rectification of the Russo-Polish frontier in White Russia. The reason for Poland finding herself in such sharp company was not the astuteness of her diplomats—for she had none to speak of—but the fact that Augustus III, as well as being the elective king of Poland was also elector of Saxony and consequently had a direct interest in checking the growth of Prussia. Finally, in the case of Poland, dismemberment—an operation by which territorial limbs were severed from the trunk—gave way to partition pure and simple. By August 1769, within less than twelve months, both Russia and Austria had been prepared to pay with Polish territory for an alliance with Prussia, while France had suggested partition first to Austria and then to Prussia in order to forestall a Germanic partnership.

This perversion of the principle of the balance of power was noted and described by Vergennes soon after the first partition of Poland: 'For two centuries the great powers have concentrated their entire attention, often to the point of exhausting all their resources, on preventing any one of them from becoming preponderant. Now a new combination has replaced the system of general balance; three powers have set up one of their own. It is based on the equality of their usurpations and thus the balance of power is made to tip heavily in their favour.'[1] This is in fact what Sorel calls the 'système copartageant' with its attendant casuistry which confuses the equitability of the action with the equality of shares. It is characteristic of the disingenuous mental habits of the period that each of the monarchs concerned in the first partition of Poland should have invoked the principle of the balance of power. Frederick II informs posterity that the principal reason for the partitions was the desire to avoid the general war which was on the point of breaking out. 'What is more', he continues, 'the balance of power between such close neighbours [that is, Prussia and Russia] had to be maintained';[2] Catherine II called the determination of the partitioning powers to keep the balance between them by means of equal acquisitions—a formal arrangement on which Maria Theresa had insisted—'a truly noble and impressive [imposante] idea to set before Europe'.[3]

Poland was carved up and the various portions of her territory were thrown into the scales of the balance of power because she was weak, a backward area notable for the absence of absolutism and capitalism, illuminated by only a glimmer of the new learning. Her 18,500 officers

[1] F. Piggott and G. W. T. Ormond, A Documentary History of the Armed Neutralities (London, 1919), p. 45.

[2] Mémoires, 1763–1775, Œuvres, vol. VI (Berlin, 1847), pp. 35, 37.

[3] A. von Arneth, ed., Joseph II. und Katharina von Russland...Briefwechsel (Vienna, 1869), pp. 3, 4. G. Zeller in 'Le principe de l'équilibre dans la politique internationale avant 1789', Revue historique (1956), p. 36, wrongly maintains that the partitioners did not invoke the balance of power in 1772.

and men could not hope to defend her against Russia's 350,000, Prussia's 200,000 and Austria's 250,000. For this sorry state of affairs contemporaries blamed principally the political system untouched by reform since the fiscal and administrative modifications made in 1717, still, in Bobrzyński's phrase, an 'anarchical oligarchy', presided over by an elective king who could only aspire to governing. The throne was a weak bargaining position, enabling its occupier, by distributing offices and beneficed sinecures, merely to bid for the oligarchs' co-operation in the Senate and the support of their henchmen in the sovereign Seym. The magnates thus favoured were better able to give armed protection, employment and tenancies to *szlachta* of various denominations. These in turn expressed their gratitude by electing their patron's nominees to the Seym, where each of the two-hundred-odd deputies, by exercising the free veto, could nullify the work of a whole session. The electorate's dissatisfaction with the executive found constitutional expression in a confederacy formed more frequently against the king than round his person. Only a confederate parliament was exempt from the rule of unanimity and free to legislate by a majority of votes. The further east a palatinate or a 'land' lay, the greater was the power of the local oligarch, the more devoted and numerous were his retainers, officials and tenants and the greater the degree of economic and political dependence upon him also of the intermediate *szlachta*. The *szlachta* or gentry as a whole, often poor and illiterate but always proud of its birth and jealous of its privileges, touchy on a point of honour, pugnacious, unruly, devoutly Catholic, backward-looking and contemptuous of foreigners, heretics and traders, formed the apex of the social pyramid, at least three-quarters of which consisted of peasants (*villani, subditi*), tied to the soil and obliged to till it. Only here and there was exemption granted from labour and service in return for a money rent, an exceptional arrangement in a period when both enclosure and increasing claims by the landlord on the peasants' time were the rule. This retrograde neo-feudal society was productive of *aurea libertas* but not of material wealth. Agricultural production was inadequate; as late as 1787 it was calculated that, whereas further west the crop from one seed-corn was between fifteen and eighteen, in Poland fifteen was the maximum; manufactures were lacking, communications were slow, taxation fell heavily on the merchant and crippled trade but favoured the *szlachcic* by exempting from duty goods imported for his own use, and consequently stinted the exchequer. Money was in short supply and seldom to be seen in the hands of the peasantry. In addition the coinage was debased, largely owing to the fraudulent operations carried out on behalf of Frederick II during the Seven Years War and again in 1770.

In the seventeenth century perhaps the most alarming early symptom of Poland's growing weakness had been the recession of her eastern frontier, in striking contrast with the growing area and population of

Prussia and Russia. By 1667, as a result of the peace treaty concluded between the republic and Muscovy at Andrusovo, the length of Poland's frontiers lying beyond main rivers and therefore strategically advantageous fell from 70 per cent to 37 per cent, the length of her frontiers lying on the near-side of main rivers—a strategic liability—rose from 30 per cent to 63 per cent, while only the length of her border actually running along main rivers remained unchanged. In the reign of Augustus III (1733–63), or even earlier, Poland had ceased to be an active force in Europe. Her size alone prevented her from becoming a negligible quantity rather than an object of policy.

All her kings elected in the eighteenth century were placemen of a foreign power—Stanislas Leszczyński of Sweden and of France, Augustus III of Russia, and now, in 1764, Stanislas Poniatowski (1732–98) occupied the throne[1] by the grace of his former mistress, Catherine II of Russia, as the *sujet convenable* acceptable to Russia and Prussia and, incidentally, to the Polish electorate. He differed from his immediate predecessor in realising that he could not hope to reign effectively over unreformed Sarmatia, a conviction which he shared with the other leaders of the party of reform and members of his mother's family, the Czartoryskis. Poniatowski—since his coronation Stanislas Augustus—was ambitious, endowed with great natural gifts developed by a good education and travel in Germany, France, England and Russia. He had charm, good looks and a great capacity for work, but at the same time was vain, extravagant and pleasure-loving in the extreme. Having taken 'Courage et patience' for his motto, he never showed any lack of either, but his conception of kingship was different from the national ideal and posterity never forgave him for having, in 1792, sided with the traitors, in order to save what could still be saved, instead of dying a hero's death. His knowledge of Poland's limitations was taken for weakness, his pliability for pusillanimity. Being to the fingertips an intellectual, steeped in the cosmopolitan culture of the eighteenth century, he sought grandeur not on the battlefield but in gradual reform and *virtú*. Did he find it? His co-authorship of the 1791 constitution and his brave efforts to promote industry are often overlooked and his moral stature is much reduced by his endorsement of two ignominious treaties of dismemberment. But while the political events of his reign go under the melancholy name of 'the period of the partitions', the spectacular artistic and intellectual revival stimulated and tended by the king himself bears his own name—*epoka Stanisławowska*, a fitting if somewhat oblique tribute to his efforts.

Stanislas and Catherine were soon to realise that they had been acting at cross-purposes. The empress was expecting docility and inertia while the king was hoping, at the very least, for non-interference with his programme of reform—a permanent Seym bound by the will of the majority.

[1] See S. Askenazy, *Die letzte polnische Königswahl* (Göttingen, 1894).

He did not suspect the lengths to which Catherine was prepared to go in order to preserve what she liked to term Poland's 'happy anarchy'—armed intervention in concert with Prussia, implementing a secret clause in the Russo-Prussian alliance concluded in 1764 and extended to 1780 in 1769. Such a course of action was bound to lead to partition. The word, however, was still taboo in St Petersburg. A 'rectification' of Russia's western frontier was advocated by the Chernyshev brothers, but partition was opposed by Panin as running counter, not only to the principles of his Northern System,[1] but to the entire tradition of Russia's policy towards Poland since Peter the Great: undivided influence rather than a share-out of territory. But even Panin was more than once inclined to yield to Prussian temptation.

While Catherine herself, with her dislike of ready-made systems, was prepared to change the objectives of Russian foreign policy according to 'circumstance, conjuncture and conjecture', Frederick II never lost sight of his aim to join together the *disjecta membra* of Pomerania and East Prussia through the acquisition of Polish Prussia, not to be conquered by force of arms but, according to his political testament of 1752, 'consumed in peace after the manner of an artichoke, leaf by leaf'.

As for Maria Theresa, Frederick's sarcastic *mot*, 'elle pleure mais elle prend toujours', sums up her behaviour as an unwilling partitioner torn by her duties as a ruler and a Christian. But in 1769, even before the queen's confessor[2] had resolved this *casus conscientiae*, the *Hofkriegsrath* ordered the occupation of Zips, a Polish enclave to which Hungary could lay but a spurious legal claim; in 1770 three more districts were occupied. It was this latter action that showed Austria's readiness to join in a partition and provoked Catherine II's historic utterance directed at Prince Henry of Prussia 'Why don't we all help ourselves?', announcing the success of his self-imposed mission to St Petersburg. Only recently had Frederick II confessed in a letter to his brother that the idea of partition still appealed to him, but that he did not feel equal to the task. But by January 1771 many important events had taken place and strengthened Prussia's hand. Catherine had created a situation which she could no longer master alone: the conflict over the rights of the religious dissenters had led to civil war and foreign intervention.

There were two kinds of dissenters in Poland: just over 200,000 Protestants, living mostly in the north-western part of the country, and some 600,000 Orthodox in present-day White Russia and the Ukraine. Poland, known in the sixteenth century as *asylum haereticorum*, had long since abandoned her tradition of religious toleration. The Protestant *szlachta*, mostly Calvinist, was excluded from the Seym and the judiciary

---

[1] See above, ch. XI, p. 322.
[2] See O. Forst Battaglia, 'Maria Teresa i pierwszy rozbiór Polski', *Kwart. Hist.* (1926), pp. 411–16, with appendix in German.

and debarred from civil office; the community at large was prevented from building new conventicles and deprived of its old-established schools and places of worship. The Orthodox community had been some four million stronger, but had lost to Rome the majority of its members and virtually its entire privileged class, including its bishops, through conversion to the Uniate rite. What had begun as a more or less voluntary process finally became a systematic coercion of monasteries, flocks and churches. For Frederick, as for his predecessors, the religious minorities were merely another lever for the subversion of whatever law and order was still left in the republic. His aim was not to 'écraser l'infâme' by obtaining a re-dress of the wrongs suffered by the dissenters but, together with Catherine, to continue protecting their interests and to strengthen the Russo-Prussian alliance by the joint action provided for in a secret clause figuring in every treaty between the two countries since 1720. Not so the empress: she had staked her reputation on coercing the Poles into granting the dissenters toleration on a scale that even the British Secretary of State for the Northern Department, Conway, considered 'unreasonable' and likely to cause 'danger' and 'envy'.[1] Directed from abroad, the dissenters formed two confederacies early in 1767, the Orthodox at Słuck and the Protestants at Thorn. Hoodwinked by the Russians, the discontented Roman Catho-lics did likewise (at Radom) only to be compelled to negotiate a political and religious settlement under the aegis of the Russian ambassador. This was accomplished by the confederate Seym of 1767–8. Its 'delegation'— a representative committee—granted the Orthodox, the Lutherans and the Calvinists complete freedom of worship, the right to build and rebuild churches and schools, and admission to public offices. For the rest, the laws of the republic were divided into three classes: fundamental laws, including the free royal election, the free veto and the privileges of the *szlachta*; *materiae status* (taxation, coinage, the size of the army, foreign affairs, etc.); and, thirdly, current economic matters for the approval of which a simple majority was to be enough from now on. Religious free-dom was thus associated with political licence.

The movement known from its place of origin as the confederacy of Bar (in Podolia), formed for the defence of the faith and of liberty, was a guerrilla organisation, formed by independent raiding parties given to looting as much as to fighting. Of the political leaders, perpetually in-triguing against one another, some were working for a restoration of the Saxon dynasty, others principally thwarting the Czartoryskis; all were anti-Russian. A single political programme was therefore lacking but there seems to have been a fairly general desire for a diminution of royal

---

[1] P.R.O., S. P. Poland, 94, Conway to Wroughton, 8 December 1767. For Anglo-Polish relations see W. Konopczyński, 'England and the First Partition of Poland', *Journal of Central European Affairs* (1948), W. F. Reddaway, 'Great Britain and Poland 1762–72', *Cambridge Historical Journal* (1934), and D. B. Horn, *British Public Opinion and the First Partition of Poland* (Edinburgh, 1945).

patronage, in return for the abolition of the free veto. Not all the confederates were bigoted Sarmatians; their ranks included Protestants, freemasons and admirers of the West who sought the advice of J.-J. Rousseau, Mably and Mercier de la Rivière. In travel and negotiation some of the confederate leaders learnt political wisdom; their final declaration issued in 1773 abstains from recrimination and launches the new watchword of national independence—*niepodległość.*

The progress of the confederacy of Bar in south-eastern Poland was checked by a revolt of the Ukrainian populace against the Polish landlords, their Jewish agents and the proselytising ways of the Uniate clergy. The *haydamaki*—'restless, discontented men'—in the belief that their social and economic grievances would receive as much support from Russia as their religious zeal had received encouragement, attacked manor houses, parsonages and townships 'with consecrated knives'. The Russians soon felt obliged to repress this would-be fifth column, especially since the rebels had set fire to the Turkish town of Balta. The Turks, however, instigated by France, were implacable and in October 1768 declared war on Russia.

The other local confederacies formed meanwhile in Poland in sympathy with the confederacy of Bar, were finally at the end of 1769 united in a General Confederacy. Its headquarters were situated in Hungary and it was thither that Choiseul sent a military mission under Colonel Dumouriez, at whose instigation the confederate chiefs announced a state of interregnum, branding Poniatowski as a tyrant and usurper. But the attempt made in the autumn of that year to kidnap the king discredited the confederates in Poland and abroad. Whatever chance there might still have been since the summer of a reconciliation between the confederacy and the Czartoryskis through the good offices of France, and with the help of Austrian action against Russia, was now lost. In the spring of the following year the confederate parties began, one by one, to surrender to the Russian and Prussian armies. By that time the Russo-Prussian convention regarding partition had already been signed with the knowledge that Austria would not implement the secret promise made to Turkey in July to safeguard her integrity and Poland's independence by taking the field against Russia, but would join in a partition. This was carried out in accordance with the treaties signed in August 1772.

Poland lost to Prussia the area lying between Pomerania and East Prussia in the west and, further to the east, Ermeland; to Austria a large triangle based on the Carpathians, its northern side running just south of Cracow, its eastern side well to the north-east of Lvov; to Russia the regions east of the Dvina, the Druć and the Dnieper; in all, more than a quarter of her territory, about 50,000 square miles with four million inhabitants out of a total population of about eleven and a half million.

Despite this crippling amputation the period that followed saw the execution of a programme of political reform and a burst of intense intellectual activity unequalled since the sixteenth century. Before the early 1780s the ideas of the Enlightenment were absorbed at the top of the social scale and thence diffused for the benefit of those who could not afford to travel or engage foreign tutors for their sons. Later, under the impact of educational reform, political events and changing social condition, 'les lumières' came to be generated locally.[1]

Travel abroad was once again the rage. According to a contemporary poet one of the attitudes struck by a young gentleman returned from his grand tour was religious indifference:

> Voltaire does not say 'Go to Mass on Sundays',
> Helvétius said divorce was not a sin,
> Rousseau is an enemy of holy water,
> Locke said the tithe was simply a trick,
> Newton hated the forty days of Lent,
> Diderot thinks it a pity to listen to sermons,
> D'Alembert has written against confirmation....

The ideas of these and other western authors were popularised by the periodical press, notably by *Monitor*, a Polish version of *The Spectator*. Religious observance was on the wane and for many the humanitarian precepts of freemasons, united in 1784 in the Grand Orient of Poland and Lithuania, proved more attractive than the catechism. But no rift developed between faith and reason, indeed religion was often united with politics or literature or science in the person of an *abbé* or a learned Jesuit. The Jesuits were in fact among the pioneers of astronomy and experimental physics in Poland, though they did not find it easy to square their observations with the doctrine of the church.

The secularisation of life and thought was most of all assisted by the agency set up in 1773 for the purpose of taking over the endowments and educational duties of the newly dissolved Jesuit Order. The National Education Commission,[2] as reorganised in 1783, directed an autonomous body responsible for the whole of higher and secondary education, including the training of teachers, in Poland and Lithuania. The newly reformed academies of Cracow and Vilno constituted the headquarters of the two provinces, in turn divided into departments and subdepartments. At the time of the second partition some seventy schools supervised by the commission were teaching between 14,000 and 15,000 pupils. The course in a departmental school lasted seven years, the curriculum was uniform and comprised Latin, Polish, ethics, law, ancient history and geography, Polish history, mathematics, geometry, logic, natural history

[1] See J. Fabre, *Stanislas-Auguste Poniatowski et l'Europe des lumières* (Paris, 1952). B. Leśnodorski, 'Le siècle des Lumières en Pologne. L'État des recherches dans le domaine de l'histoire politique, des institutions et des idées', *Acta Poloniae Historica*, vol. IV (1961), pp. 147–74.
[2] See A. Jobert, *La Commission d'Éducation Nationale en Pologne* (Dijon, 1941).

(botany, mineralogy, and hygiene), physics, agriculture, horticulture and calligraphy. Even though many of these subjects, literary and scientific alike, were studied in conjunction with Latin or Latin authors, this syllabus was still a substantial advance on the half medieval, half human-istic and entirely Latin education formerly provided by the Jesuits. If the work of the commission was only a partial success it was because it did not have at its disposal the necessary cadres of secular teachers or the in-dispensable textbooks and educational aids and because it all too seldom received the backing of public opinion.

Nevertheless the language of the commission's textbooks became the foundation of Polish scientific terminology while its Latin-and-Polish grammar not only systematised spelling but also formed the language of many future writers. Modernised and pruned of excessive Latinity, Polish was once more a pliable literary medium. Without producing any great masterpiece, the literature of the period met and stimulated the demands of the public. Poetry, especially satire and the sentimental lyric, was of the highest quality, the imitations or adaptations of foreign plays were moderately successful, and the debates of the Great Seym were often pro-voked and extended in print.

Most of the luminaries in literature and the arts, in education and in learning, made up a minor solar system revolving round the king, a planet-arium constructed and driven by himself. One of the many subjects to attract his versatile mind was historical research. In order to satisfy his own inclination as much as to demonstrate to his countrymen the advan-tages of a strong monarchy, he commissioned Naruszewicz, an ex-Jesuit, to rewrite the history of Poland. Archives and copyists were put at his disposal but the task proved too heavy for the historiographer *malgré lui*: the six volumes written between 1775 and 1779[1] cover the period up to 1385. In accordance with the practice of the age, Naruszewicz's method aims at being critical, 'for criticism teaches to tell good from evil and appearance from truth, to weigh human affairs in the scales of reason, to trace their causes, to study their ways and judge their results'.

In the teeth of Russia's ill-will and thanks to an enlightened minority, the legislation passed by the various Seyms between 1764 and 1768 and again in 1775 imperceptibly prepared the ground for the work of the Great Seym of 1788–92. Slowly something like a centralised government could be seen replacing the former stalemate or open war between the conflicting interests of individuals, provinces and the state. The inviol-ability of the fundamental laws and the unanimity governing *materiae status* delayed reform and hampered the executive but 'economic matters' provided an avenue of escape from the veto and, together with the device

---

[1] See M. Neomisia Rutkowska, *Bishop A. Naruszewicz and his 'History of the Polish Nation'* (Washington, 1941). The publication of volume I of the *History* was prohibited by the Russian envoy.

of confederacy and new regulations for parliamentary procedure, made some progress possible. As a first step the provincial diets had their fiscal powers restricted and were to be bound by the will of the majority when electing deputies to the Seym. In accordance with the view now beginning to form that birth makes a gentleman but only property makes him a citizen, their membership was reduced by the exclusion of a section of the landless *szlachta*, and the influence of the magnates dwindled with that of their clients. The administrative system was made more expert and more uniform; the new army and treasury commissions of the kingdom of Poland and the grand-duchy of Lithuania circumscribed the hitherto all too wide authority of the treasurers and *hetmans*; the education commission formed in 1773 was common to both kingdom and duchy. The transfer of many of the crown's prerogatives to a permanent council of senators and deputies was not without its administrative advantages, although the institution of that unpopular body was ordained by one of the additional fundamental laws, dictated by the Russian ambassador, adopted in 1775 by a 'delegation' of the Seym, and guaranteed by Russia.

The cost of these improvements had to be met out of increased and reliable revenue. Estimates resembling a budget were approved in 1768 and again in 1775 and 1776; the right of mintage was restored to the king, a new currency was issued in 1766 and important changes were made in the system of taxation. In 1764, for instance, the tax paid by the Jewish community was put on a *per capita* basis; in 1768 the excise duty on alcohol was turned into a purchase tax; in 1775 more permanent and far-reaching changes were made. The chimney money, which had been abolished together with the general poll-tax in 1764, was now reintroduced. In its new form it became the main source of state revenue and with a 50 per cent surtax also replaced the *hiberna*, formerly due to the army from the tenants of royal estates. The duty payable on imported or exported merchandise was reintroduced for good; the *subsidium charitativum* contributed by the clergy was raised to 700,000 zlotys[1] per annum; the *kwarta*, a fee of 25 per cent on the income from benefices and tenements allotted from the royal demesne, was almost doubled; new imposts were introduced, such as taxes on salt and on tobacco and stamp duty. The result was a steady rise in revenue, from 12 million in 1776–7 to 15·4 million in 1789.

The Great Seym (1788–92)[2] continued with increased intensity the work accomplished in the two preceding decades. No budget was voted but the Seym exercised constant control over public expenditure. One of its most urgent tasks was rearmament. In 1789 it approved for this purpose a 'perpetual offering' in the shape of a tax on income from land at the rate

[1] Forty zlotys equalled £1.
[2] W. Kalinka's *Der vierjährige polnische Reichstag* (Berlin, 1896–8) is obsolete but still useful. I have not seen J. Klotz, *L'Œuvre législative de la Diète de quatre ans* (Paris, 1913).

of 10 per cent from the *szlachta* and 20 per cent from the clergy. The Jewish poll-tax, chimney money in towns, and the *kwarta* were all increased and a tax was imposed on hides and slaughter. Poland's state revenue was thus more than doubled; from 15·5 million in 1788–9 it rose to 43·5 million in 1789–90 and then fell to about 30 million in 1790–1. In Lithuania the rate of increase was similar. The establishment, in 1789, of commissions for the maintenance of good order, elected by the *szlachta*, brought further improvement in public administration.

Nor were the rights of the unprivileged individual overlooked in an effort to ease the restraints and mitigate the inequalities characteristic of a medieval society. In 1768 the landlord forfeited the *ius vitae ac necis* over the peasants on his estate without, however, becoming liable to pay with his life for murdering a villein. The death penalty for witchcraft was abolished in 1776, and so was judicial torture. From 1775 the *szlachcic* who engaged in trade no longer did so under pain of derogation. The townsman remained 'not fully a human being, half-way between the *szlachcic* and the peasant', but the 'liberties' or extra-territorial rights, as it were (*jurydyki, serwitoriaty*), of the gentry and clergy in the towns were reduced in 1764 and 1768.

The constitution of 3 May 1791 is generally regarded as the crowning achievement not only of the Great Seym but of the whole reign of Stanislas Augustus, since it bore witness to Poland's viability as an independent state. The preservation of national sovereignty and territorial integrity were in fact the aims of the authors of the constitution, who declare in its preamble that they value the nation's political existence more highly than life and personal happiness. The eleven articles of the act itself may be summarized as follows:

I. The holy Roman Catholic faith remained the dominant religion but freedom of worship was guaranteed to adherents of other religions.

II. The rights and privileges of the *szlachta* were confirmed and declared inalterable.

III. The earlier act of the same year regulating the status of the municipalities was confirmed and incorporated in the constitution. In consequence all boroughs created by the crown received self-government. A new judicial system was set up for the towns and all town-dwellers whether *szlachta* or townsmen were to be judged according to municipal law. The cardinal law of *neminem captivabimus nisi iure victum* (hitherto a privilege of the *szlachta*) now applied to all town-dwellers. Cities in which the new municipal courts of appeal were located were to be represented by their plenipotentiaries in the police and treasury commissions and in the municipal high-court. The municipalities were likewise to be represented on the regional commissions *boni ordinis* and in the Seym. A townsman might obtain ennoblement by serving as a plenipotentiary, or upon promotion to the rank of captain or to certain corresponding legal or administrative offices, or through the purchase of land, or by special act of parliament under a quota system. The *jurydyki* were now finally abolished.

IV. The peasants were taken into the custody of the law in that any agreement concluded between a landowner and a peasant on his land was mutually binding and subject to the supervision of the government. Complete freedom was granted to all newcomers and returned emigrants.

V. The government was to consist of three powers: the legislative, the executive and the judiciary.

VI. The Seym was to consist of the chamber of deputies and of the chamber of senators, the latter under the presidency of the king, who had a casting vote. The deputies could discuss all proposals concerning general laws and resolutions as to policy and in the first place those put forward by the king. The Senate's suspensive veto was to relate to law-making only; resolutions affecting policy must be voted upon by the whole Seym. The Senate was to be composed of the bishops, palatines, castellans and some ministers. The Seym, ready to be convened at short notice, was to be renewed every two years. 'Everything, everywhere' was to be decided by a majority of votes; the free veto, confederacies and confederate parliaments were abolished. The constitution would be revised every twenty-five years. The earlier law regulating the function of the *sejmiki* was confirmed; their membership was further restricted to landowners and certain categories of life-tenants and mortgagees. A separate law relating to the Seym was also passed in 1791. The 204 deputies were no longer bound hand and foot by the instructions received from the *sejmiki*, the twenty-four representatives of the towns were voteless and almost voiceless: they could only speak on municipal matters; the standing orders were revised.

VII. The supreme executive power was vested in the king in council. The duty of the executive was to guard the laws and ensure their observance. The throne became hereditary, within the house of the Elector of Saxony. The king's person was declared sacred and inviolate. Unable to do anything of his own accord, he could not answer for any of his actions. The king's council was to consist of the primate, five ministers appointed by himself but removable by the Seym, and of two non-voting secretaries. Each resolution of the council had to be signed by the king and countersigned by a minister. For the proper functioning of the executive four commissions were established to deal with matters concerning education, police, the army and the treasury. Their members were elected by the Seym; the regional commissions *boni ordinis* were to act on their instructions.

VIII. The judicial power could be exercised only by a court of law. The landowners, the towns and the peasantry each received their judicial hierarchy.

Article IX provided for the establishment of a council of regency, Article X dealt with the education of the royal children, Article XI with the armed force of the nation. The relationship between Poland and Lithuania was redefined later in 1791; the kingdom and the duchy were to have one exchequer, one army and a common government but the ministries outside the council were duplicated.

To what models the authors of the constitution (of whom the king was one) were most indebted, the student of comparative constitutional law must decide for himself.[1] He will do well, however, to take with a large grain of salt the statement made by Stanislas Augustus in his open letter to the *Assemblée Nationale* that the Poles had followed the great example set by France. Writing in confidence to one of his diplomatic representatives he puts the Polish constitution 'in antipodo' of the French, and with good reason: an act of sweeping political reform, it left intact the existing order of society and thus won the approbation of Burke. A constitutional monarchy replaced the self-styled republic but the division into estates was preserved and confirmed. Only the design of the upper tiers of the social pyramid was modified. First, the process of restratification already perceptible within the *szlachta* was legalised and accelerated. The landless, some 407,000 out of the estimated total of 725,000, lost their political rights and the former oligarchs had to be satisfied with seats in the Senate while the middle *szlachta* rose to the top. Secondly, in the division separating the townspeople from the *szlachta* a passage was cut in order, in the words of the constitution, 'to give new and effective strength' to the *szlachta* through the promotion of the most successful members of the *bourgeoisie*, only about 400,000 strong. The constitution then, however far-reaching the plans of some of its authors may have been,[2] was not a blue-print for the future but rather a sum of the social changes and a culmination of the political reforms dating from 1764.

What was accomplished in the way of legislation was highly creditable but must be judged by practical results and may therefore, in some instances, have to be entered on the debit side of the balance sheet. The silver currency which had been bad was now too good; undervalued in relation to gold, it was being driven out by inferior foreign silver. There was no munitions industry to equip an army of 100,000 men; the tax approved by parliament to pay for the new army fell short of its promoters' estimates. Ambiguous drafting led to under-assessment, the lack of trained collectors did the rest and in 1789 the tax brought in nine million zlotys instead of the expected sixteen.

But the Poles had not only themselves to blame for their failure to achieve a higher degree of economic development; they were labouring under the handicap of the consequences of the first partition. To the irre-

[1] Cf. C. E. L. Konic, *Comparaison des constitutions de la Pologne et de la France de 1791* (Lausanne, 1918). W. Kula, 'L'histoire économique de la Pologne au dix-huitième siècle', *Acta Poloniae Historica*, vol. IV (1961), pp. 133–46.

[2] See J. Dihm, *Sprawa konstytucji ekonomicznej z 1791r.* (Wrocław, 1959; English summary).

parable losses of territory sustained in 1772 must be added the impoverishment brought about by the depredations of the military, suffered at the time of the confederacy of Bar and the disastrous treaty of commerce with Prussia concluded under duress in 1775.[1]

Its terms amounted to the erection by Prussia of a customs system designed in such a way as to obtain from Poland primary commodities at minimum prices and to secure in Poland a market for Prussian manufactured goods. As well as preventing the development of a Polish industry, the operation of this turnpike brought in a handsome profit of nearly nineteen million zlotys per annum. On goods crossing the frontier in either direction an ordinary duty of 2 per cent was paid on either side. The transit duty on goods travelling through Prussian territory was 12 per cent but in the case of articles considered indispensable to Prussian industry it was 30 per cent. Moreover the vital traffic between Danzig, still in Polish hands, and Poland via formerly Polish Royal Prussia was treated as transit trade. In practice the duty of 12 per cent, as calculated by Prussian customs officials, worked out at between 30 and 50 per cent, and the duty of 30 per cent in some cases, for example on dyestuffs, at over 300 per cent.

The effects of this economic blockade became apparent almost at once. In 1776 the commercial traffic between Poland and Danzig on the Vistula fell to two-thirds, and the number of ships calling at Danzig harbour to nearly half of the figures for 1770, the amount of agricultural produce exported via Danzig fell to 37 per cent of the figure for 1769. Poland's adverse trade balance now rose to twenty-six million zlotys on a total of seventy million; the volume of her trade both with and via Prussia shrank to such an extent that even Frederick grew alarmed and, in 1781, instructed his customs officers not to impose duties higher than the statutory 12 per cent and ordered an investigation into the effects of the tariff on Prusso-Polish trade. The Prussian stranglehold was eased but the improvement that followed was also due to the rising prices of grain and the new export routes to the Black Sea. Polish exports increased and in 1784 balanced the imports. In 1781 it was estimated that apart from Hungarian wines Poland was importing nine million zlotys' worth of luxury goods. A large proportion of these was supplied by Prussia. Under the terms of the 1775 treaty, Poles buying silk and high-grade cloth in specified Prussian towns paid a transit duty of only 4 per cent while artisans settled along the Polish frontier and subsidised by the Prussian government supplied western Poland with other manufactured goods. The combination of the Prussian blockade with a trade offensive had a stifling effect on the nascent Polish industry. The exorbitant duty raised on dyestuffs caused the ruin of the textile workshops in Wielkopolska (*Polonia Major*). By 1785, within a decade, the workers engaged in this cottage industry were reduced

[1] J. A. Wilder, *Traktat handlowy polsko-pruski z r. 1775* (Warsaw, 1937; appendix in French and summary in English).

to penury, and their numbers dropped by 15 per cent since the entrepreneurs found it more economical to send the cloth and linen produced
for them to be finished over the border.

The fate of the various industrial ventures promoted by Stanislas
Augustus on his private estates or on crown lands, as well as their diversity,
may serve to illustrate the position of manufactures in his reign.[1] Of the
two blast-furnaces put up by the king one, established near Brest in 1768,
did not pay and had to be leased, the other, near Sambor, active between
1766 and 1775, produced iron of poor quality for which in any case there
was no demand. A cloth-factory in south-east Poland built in 1765 was
lost in the first partition, the Belvedere pottery started in Warsaw in 1768
had to be closed down in 1780, in all probability because of excessive production costs, due in turn to insufficient division of labour and standardisation of the products. The complex of manufactures for the production
of luxury goods established and run on the king's behalf by Tyzenhaus,
the treasurer of Lithuania, on the crown estates near Grodno between
1765 and 1780, also failed to prosper, with the exception of the cloth-mill.
A contemporary observer attributes the failure of Tyzenhaus' system
(based on the *corvée*) to bad internal organisation, the comparatively high
cost of skilled labour and imported materials and, in consequence, of un-
competitive prices, and also to the lack of capital and credit. Like the
other potentates, the king could afford to put up a manufacture but could
not always afford to run it owing to the lack of adequate working capital.
The hopes of a quick return were seldom fulfilled, borrowing at the prevalent
rate of 12 per cent was expensive and the services of an established distribu-
tive trade could not be called upon. The results of the king's other industrial
ventures were equally disappointing. A copper-mine operating between
1782 and 1795 proved uneconomical and had to be leased, a marble quarry
supplied the court between 1782 and 1794, but an early attempt at surface
coal-mining had to be given up because of the high cost of transport.

The largest and most successful manufacture of the period was the
linen-mill at Łowicz, west of Warsaw, located on a benefice appertaining
to the primate, Michał Poniatowski, and owned by a company whose
board consisted of an equal number of *szlachta* and townsmen. The six
magnates assumed their directorships in order to encourage the development of home industries, the six townsmen to sell their goods or services
to the company. The work was put out to women in the villages of the
district and also to the female inmates of the prison and the workhouse
(not an uncommon practice in those days, especially in Warsaw); the
yarn spun by them was woven and finished in the central works. Raw
linen was also bought from outside suppliers and finishing was undertaken for other producers.

[1] See W. Kula, *Szkice o manufakturach w Polsce w XVIII w.* (Warsaw, 1956). The
English summary is not altogether reliable.

The activities of these and other manufactures, some (though not all) short-lived, some hardly more highly organised than workshops, resulted only in a slight increase of the national product. The virtual absence of a pool of free labour, of demand on a national scale and of any appreciable accumulation of capital made capitalism as yet a distant prospect. The country's methods of production had undergone as little change as the composition of society and Poland's backwardness in these respects forms a glaring contrast with the intellectual revolution.

Cut off from Danzig, deprived of large tracts of territory in the north and south, and consequently of a large proportion of her Polish-speaking population, Poland began perforce to gravitate politically towards the east and economically towards the south. The two canals planned so as to connect the Baltic with the Black Sea and completed in 1784, the Royal and Ogiński's, linked the Vistula and the Niemen with the Dnieper. The Turks, however, were still unwilling to allow shipments of Polish grain by way of the Dniester and the Russians had forbidden the restoration of the disused harbour at Połąga (Polangen) in Samogitia. Catherine frowned upon the prospect of Poland's economic emancipation and in 1782 would not go beyond making a small reduction in the tariff on Polish goods exported by land to Kherson, where Prot Potocki, a magnate turned merchant, had established his Black Sea Trading Company. But Stanislas Augustus was aspiring to much more than that—permission to carry out political reform in return for help in the conquest of the Crimea. His offer to this effect, refused in 1783, was renewed in 1787 in a modified form. Given the chance, the king would not have scrupled to join Russia and Austria in their projected partition of the Ottoman empire. The ethics of such a policy were despicable but its economics were sound; Bessarabia alone would have provided Poland with a good seaboard and the Dniester would have eked out the Vistula. The possibility of joint action was discussed by Stanislas and Catherine at Kaniów (on the Dnieper) in the spring of 1787; in September, after the outbreak of the Russo-Turkish war, the king submitted his detailed proposals for an alliance. After a silence of nine months, Catherine accepted the military aid offered and was prepared to subsidise it but refused to allow political reform or territorial acquisitions.

The Russian rebuff made nonsense of the programme of the new Seym, whose members had formed a loyalist confederacy for the purpose of augmenting the state revenue and the army. As Russia and Austria had kept secret their determination to defend an unreformed Poland in the event of a Prussian attack, the Prussian envoy was able to make his counter-bid. On behalf of his master he disclaimed any right to meddle in Poland's domestic affairs and made the unreserved offer of an alliance, thus obliging the king to withdraw his proposal for an alliance with Russia. On 20 October the Seym resolved to raise an army of 100,000 men (a target subsequently reduced to 65,000); in November the military department of the Permanent Council was suppressed and replaced by a parliamentary commission in violation, as the Russian ambassador was quick to point out, of the fundamental laws and the guarantee treaty of 1775. But Catherine being at war with both Sweden and Turkey, Poland could for once ignore the threat of Russian reprisals and prosecute a programme of reform. In February 1789 the Permanent Council was abolished and its functions were taken over by parliamentary commissions, in the spring Russia and Austria complied with Poland's request for the withdrawal of their troops from Podolia, an event unprecedented since 1719. In May an envoy was sent to London to explore the possibility of developing Anglo-Polish trade and by-passing the Prussian customs barrier. Pitt showed interest in securing naval stores in the event of a war with Russia but considered Prussia's friendly participation in a trade agreement essential.

Meanwhile the alliance with Prussia was slow to materialise. Prussia's original intention had been simply to seize Danzig and Thorn in the course of intervening in Poland on behalf of the anti-Russian faction. She was consequently, despite protestations to the contrary and her offer of an alliance, unfavourably disposed towards the Polish programme of rearmament and political reform. Once, however, late in 1789, she had decided to attack Austria in the spring of the coming year, the Polish alliance became a necessity and negotiations to this end began, but the vexed question of Poland's trade with Danzig impeded agreement. The *quid pro quo* visualised by the Prussians—the cession of Danzig and Thorn in return for a reduction in the customs tariff—was totally unacceptable to Polish public opinion; even the pro-Prussian patriots would only have been satisfied with a vicarious promise of Galicia into the bargain. In the end, for the sake of compromise, the question of trade was deferred for further discussion. Under the terms of the Prusso-Polish treaty concluded on 29 March 1790 the two countries guaranteed the integrity of one another's territory. In the event of one party being attacked the other was bound to undertake mediation, to be followed, if necessary, by military action. The same conditions applied should any foreign power, in virtue of any previous agreement, interfere in the domestic affairs of the republic. If hostilities could not be prevented the king of Prussia was to intervene with 30,000 men. The Poles little knew that this latter article was from the outset looked upon in Berlin as extremely onerous and the whole treaty as useful only in case of war with Austria. Because, among other reasons, of the unprepared state of the Polish army, it was agreed in June that the terms of the treaty notwithstanding, Poland's attitude in the war with Austria, eagerly expected by both allies, should be one of friendly neutrality. By midsummer Austrian and Prussian troops were poised for action in Silesia, but the negotiations opened by Prussia in order to provoke war unexpectedly led to a settlement. By the convention of Reichenbach, Austria accepted the harsh conditions laid down by Prussia: an armistice with the Porte prior to a pacification based on the *status quo*. Having thus cut her own losses, Austria precluded any Prussian gains even by negotiation and Hertzberg's cherished exchange scheme dating back to 1778, by which Austria gave up Galicia to Poland in return for acquisitions in Turkey while Poland rewarded Prussia with Danzig and Thorn, was ruled out for good.

In the interval Poland had advanced further on the road to reform. In September 1789 a parliamentary commission for the improvement of the government was formed, in November 269 deputies from the royal boroughs arrived in Warsaw and petitioned the king for the renewal and extension of their ancient privileges, a request satisfied by the municipal law passed in April of the following year and later incorporated in the constitution. After the debates on the Prussian alliance in 1790, the Seym, which was nearing the end of its statutory tenure, decided to double the strength of the existing chamber by the election of a new set of deputies. The voters, besides being given the chance of pronouncing on the principle of reform, were asked to express their views on the question of the succession which the Seym and the king were proposing to offer to the elector of Saxony. At the election, held in November, the cause of reform carried the day; out of the 180 new deputies 120 were 'patriots'. When the augmented parliament opened in December, the commission for constitutional reform put forward a number of proposals, some of which, for example government by the king in council, were soon to be embodied in the Government Act of 3 May.

In September, before the prorogation, the Seym had already approved a new set of fundamental laws drafted by the same commission, together with two important amendments: the territory of the republic was declared indivisible and Russia's guarantee of 1775 was renounced. After the fiasco of the plans for war against Austria and the peace recently concluded between Russia and Sweden a gesture of this kind could only provoke Russia and offend Prussia. It offered no encouragement to the Prussian king to work *pour le roi de Pologne* and ill accorded with the plans, then being canvassed, for offering the Polish succession to a Prussian prince. Still, no disastrous consequences followed upon the amendments, the first of which Hertzberg ominously described as 'perfidious'—at any rate not immediately. The forces that had been marshalled against Austria could yet be used against Russia. In January 1791 Britain and Prussia demanded from Russia a return to the *status quo* in Turkey, in the same month Britain expressed her readiness to enter into a commercial and political agreement with Poland but only with the participation of Prussia. This implied the cession of Danzig and Thorn, the prime objective of Prussian policy and one to be achieved at all costs, either with or without

Poland's consent. If such consent were given, Prussia would feel obliged to defend Poland against Russia but otherwise she could be expected to combine with Russia against Poland. So cruel was the dilemma that was staring the Polish leaders in the face that they preferred to shut their eyes to it. Nor could there be any hope of converting the Seym, flushed with patriotic zeal, to such a policy and the maximum that the British envoy, Hailes, and his Polish friends were able to obtain was a directive authorising the foreign affairs committee to continue the negotiations. Hailes, however, felt that there was no basis for further discussion.

In Poland, in the absence of a proper government, public and parliamentary opinion were supreme; in Britain, the essential constitutional differences notwithstanding, the situation was not dissimilar. On 28 March George III announced to Parliament that he felt obliged to augment his navy so as to add weight to the Prusso-British demand for the restoration of the *status quo strict* on the Black Sea. The royal message was inspired by Pitt's conviction that Russia must not be allowed to keep Ochakov and the coastal area between the Bug and the Dniester lest she become the great maritime power of the south. But neither Parliament nor the public had any clear idea of where Ochakov lay or why it should be handed back to the traditional enemies of Christendom by Britain's old friends and good customers. The northern export trade was in danger and the cry went up in London, Norwich, Wakefield, Leeds and Manchester: 'No war with Russia!' This mood was echoed in the House of Commons and in the government; the Tory majority was shrinking and the Cabinet was divided. Pitt weakened and yielded; it was 'the greatest mortification he had ever experienced'.[1]

The failure of the Russian Armament[2] spelt the collapse of the projected coalition against Russia. In Poland the king and the patriots who had been brought together a few months earlier by a common desire to provide the country with an effective and stable government felt compelled to act while they could. On 3 May the new constitution, a product of much secret discussion, was sprung on a more than half-empty chamber and approved by the majority of those present. The throne made hereditary ceased to be a counter in international politics and a government headed by the king would, it was hoped, be able to conduct a long-term foreign policy. But it was too late for diplomacy.

Prussia's attitude[3] towards the constitution was ambiguous. While her diplomatic representative had warned the 'patriots' that his government

[1] J. H. Rose, *William Pitt and National Revival* (London, 1911), p. 617.
[2] See M. S. Anderson, *Britain's Discovery of Russia 1553–1815* (London, 1958), chapter VI, and D. Gerhard, *England und der Aufstieg Russlands* (Munich, 1933), chapter VI.
[3] The complex and controversial question of Prusso-Polish relations between 1788 and 1792 has been most recently investigated by J. Dutkiewicz in 'Prusy a Polska w dobie Sejmu Czteroletniego', *Przegląd Historyczny* (1935), and 'Sprawa Gdańska...', *Zapiski Tow. Nauk. w Toruniu* (1954).

would refuse to implement the treaty of alliance if important changes were made in Poland's system of government without Prussia's consent, Frederick William officially expressed his approval of 'this decisive step'. The truth was that the Prussian government did consider itself released from its obligations but left the Poles to infer this from unofficial intimations. Nevertheless, in the convention concluded between Prussia and Austria in July 1791 (after the peace between Austria and Turkey) a clause guaranteeing the inviolability and integrity of Poland's territory and her constitution was inserted at the instance of Leopold II. Early in 1792, however, when the peace between Russia and Turkey was followed by a renewal of the Austro-Prussian alliance, the Prussians, taking advantage of the situation in France, were able to enforce an amendment in the clause relating to Poland: the two powers merely undertook to respect a free constitution. The Prussian government now considered that the re-establishment of Russian influence in Poland would not be harmful and by mid-February was already contemplating partition. The death of Leopold on 1 March 1792 brought this prospect nearer still. In April the Prussian envoy declared in a verbal statement that his government did not consider itself obliged to defend the new constitution. Poland now had to face alone the wrath of Catherine, determined to fight and defeat Jacobinism in Poland, to teach the Poles not to make light of Russia and to punish their king for his ingratitude. On 14 May 1792 under her auspices, the Polish conservatives formed a confederacy (ostensibly at Targowica but in fact at St Petersburg) against what they called the revolutionary conspiracy of 3 May 1791; four days later the Russian armies invaded Poland. When the Poles ingenuously invoking the treaty of alliance turned for help to Prussia they were advised to defeat the Russians. The Polish army offered the invaders what little resistance it could while the king resorted to negotiation. In July, giving in to Catherine's demands, and his innate preference for compromise, he acceded to the confederacy of Targowica. After the renewal of her treaties of alliance with Austria and Prussia, Catherine's position was strong enough to enable her to deal with Poland single-handed but she chose the more prudent course of dividing the spoils with Prussia while Austria forwent her share in exchange for a promise of Russo-Prussian help in acquiring Bavaria. The treaty between Russia and Prussia signed on 23 January 1793 presents the partition as an operation conducted against revolution: at one blow sedition was crushed in Poland and strength gained for doing likewise in France. Prussia seized Danzig and the area to the west of a line drawn from Częstochowa through Sochaczew to Działdowo with a population of about 1,100,000 and Russia the region east of the line running from Druja to Pińsk and thence to the river Zbrucz with three million inhabitants.

A Seym summoned to Grodno in June to endorse the act of partition proved unexpectedly recalcitrant and submitted only to brute force—

cordons of troops, incarceration, confiscation of property—and threats of further reprisals. All that remained of Poland was a small Russian protectorate, about 80,000 square miles with some 4,000,000 inhabitants and a retrograde constitution.[1]

The Polish army, though defeated in 1792, was not routed. Many of its generals were waiting to resume the fight at the earliest opportunity, while in Warsaw and elsewhere a number of prominent civilians, impressed with the success of the French Revolution, were contemplating a mass revolt. The network of masonic lodges provided a meeting-ground for the leaders of both groups, soon united in a single conspiracy, remaining in close touch with some of the promoters of the May constitution who had taken refuge at Dresden. With them was general Kosciuszko[2] who had given a good account of himself in the recent war and was regarded as the future leader of the uprising. Its outbreak was precipitated by the impending reduction in the size of the army from about 37,000 to 15,000 and by the arrests carried out among the Warsaw conspirators. At the end of March 1794 Kosciuszko arrived in Warsaw and assumed command of the insurrection. The programme of the movement was summed up in the motto 'liberty, [territorial] integrity, independence'. The powers taken by Kosciuszko were those of a dictator but were to end with the emergency.

His army was from the start outnumbered by two to one, and the addition of local militias, though a feat in itself, did not make up for the lack of trained troops and especially of equipment. The vertically fixed scythes, deadly in the hands of peasant auxiliaries, were no substitute for guns, rifles and ammunition, and strategic considerations apart, the insurgents would still have been obliged to lay down their fire-arms, empty, worn-out and irreplaceable, at the end of eight months.

The scythemen first covered themselves with glory on 4 April in the battle of Racławice near Cracow, Kosciuszko's first victory. Having thus gained prestige and momentum, the insurrection spread to the south-east as far as Volhynia and northwards to Lithuania. In mid-April the inhabitants of Warsaw attacked the Russian garrison and scored the greatest Polish victory in the war and in the whole century. By the end of April the insurgents were in control of almost the entire territory left in Poland's possession after the second partition. The irruption of the Prussians in May and their junction with the Russians in June increased the odds against Kosciuszko. After two defeats suffered early in June, and the loss of Cracow, the Poles, some 28,000 men, retired to Warsaw where they joined the 9000-strong metropolitan militia. The 25,000 Prussians did not attack the capital until late August but were thrown back and soon after-

---

[1] See B. Dembiński, ed., *Documents relatifs à l'histoire du deuxième et troisième partage de la Pologne*, vol. I (Léopol, 1902; no more publ.), and R. H. Lord, *The Second Partition of Poland* (Cambridge (Harvard), 1915).

[2] See M. Haiman, *Kosciuszko, Leader and Exile* (New York, 1946).

wards withdrew westwards in order to suppress a local insurrection in western Poland; the 14,000 Russians after lingering before the entrenchments retreated towards the south. Wilno, however, was less fortunate and fell to the Russians earlier in August. With the arrival of the formidable Suvorov from the southern Ukraine, the Russians' sheer numerical superiority became overwhelming. On 10 October, a small corps under A. Poniński having failed to join forces with Kosciuszko at Maciejowice, his small army was destroyed and he himself wounded and captured. Less than a month later, after the suburb of Praga had been stormed by Suvorov's troops and, contrary to his instructions, its defenceless population slaughtered, Warsaw surrendered. Thomas Campbell bewept the failure of the insurgents:

> Oh, bloodiest picture in the book of Time,
> Sarmatia fell, unwept, without a crime;
> Found not a generous friend, a pitying foe,
> Strength in her arms, nor mercy in her woe!

The reactions of Catherine in St Petersburg and Igelström, her plenipotentiary in the Polish capital, to the outbreak in Warsaw had been identical: to enlist Prussian aid. It would appear that Russia lacked the money and the men required for single-handed action. So eager was Prussia to secure her reward that she anticipated the Russian request with a spontaneous offer of help brought to St Petersburg by the prince of Nassau. The Russian statesmen were divided in their view of the Polish question but Bezborodko, Osterman and probably Catherine herself advocated partition. By the end of June at any rate her mind was made up and Austria had been consulted as to the principle. Thugut's acceptance gave the cue for Catherine's announcement that the time had come for the three courts to take measures, not only to extinguish the last spark of the fire that had burst forth in Poland, but also to prevent it from ever flaring up again from the ashes.

If the operation did not proceed smoothly from now on it was because the spark proved to be a blaze and the firemen squabbled among themselves. Austria and Prussia laid conflicting claims to Cracow and other territories and Catherine's indignation at Frederick William's retreat from Warsaw knew no bounds. Suvorov's victories enabled Catherine to arbitrate in the even fiercer tussle that followed the suppression of the uprising. In November Austria accepted the terms laid down by the empress but Prussia insisted on pushing her frontiers as far as the line made up of the rivers Windawa, Niemen, Vistula and Narew. Since the negotiations with Prussia had ended in deadlock, Russia and Austria exchanged three ministerial declarations regulating and seeking to justify the new dismemberment. According to the first, in view of the republic's absolute incapacity to live peaceably under law and to produce a firm and vigorous government capable of preventing the recurrence of such troubles as the recent insurrection, the three powers felt obliged to enforce a final partition of Poland among her neighbours. The second provided for Austria's accession to the partition of 1793, the third revived the secret plans for a partition of Turkey. Contrary to all expectation and, indeed, to the intentions of an influential group of statesmen and generals, Prussia, after signing a separate peace with the French at Basle on 5 April 1795, did not turn against her abandoned partner Austria and her ally, Russia, with the aim of making good her claims in Poland. She lacked the resources to wage such a war alone, and since no suitable ally presented himself, peace was preserved. In August 1795 Prussia at last accepted Russia's territorial demands but reserved the right to negotiate further with Austria. The relevant treaties between Prussia and the two other powers were signed in October 1795. The Russo-Austrian frontier was now extended along the river Bug beyond Brest and the Russo-Prussian border ran from that point to Grodno and along the Niemen. The frontier between Prussia and Austria followed roughly the river Pilica, the section of the Vistula between Czersk and Warsaw and most of the lower Bug. Prussia absorbed about 900,000 Polish subjects and Warsaw, Austria about 1,000,000 and Cracow, Russia increased her population by 2,000,000. The republic's affairs were wound up in a convention concluded at St Petersburg in January 1797 and recording the recent abdication of Stanislas Augustus. In a separate and secret article the signatories agreed never to introduce into their titles the term of 'the Kingdom of Poland' which would thenceforth be suppressed for all time.[1]

As the first commoner to take over the leadership of his captive nation, Kosciuszko (1764–1817) marks the beginning of a new epoch. Nearly everything about him is typical of the new age or announces the nineteenth century—his middling birth, his education in Poland and in Paris as a protégé of the Czartoryskis, his participation in the American War of Independence, his Rousseauist trust in the common man and his romantic inclination to gauge his strength by his intentions. A veteran of two wars, he found his vocation as leader of the insurrection. He rated morale more highly than numbers and put as much faith in side-arms as in conventional weapons. To Kosciuszko's mind the Polish scythe was as good a weapon as the French pike or bayonet, especially when wielded by the deep infantry column recommended in the writings of the chevalier de Folard and General H. Lloyd. If ananimous, Kosciuszko argued, Poland could defend herself against Russia and Prussia and the best way of obtaining unanimity was to give the peasants what they had not obtained on 3 May. The declaration issued by him at Połaniec on 7 May 1794 did precisely that. The peasants were freed from bondage and received the right to bring a legal action against their landlords, who were

[1] See R. H. Lord, 'The Third Partition of Poland', *The Slavonic Review* (1925).

prohibited from seizing peasant holdings at will. The *corvée* was reduced in inverse proportion to the number of weekdays worked hitherto and consequently to the size and working capacity of a holding: from 5 or 6 days to 3 or 4, from between 2 and 4 to between 1 and 3, from 1 to ½ a day. In return for this relief the peasants were put under an obligation to work as hired labourers for a reasonable wage and also to help in the cultivation of holdings belonging to those called up for military service. But the landlords, impelled by self-interest, hindered the execution of the regulations of Połaniec. Had they been observed, they would have created in Poland social and economic conditions more favourable to the peasant and more advanced than those prevailing in Austria and Prussia. As it turned out, the *szlachta* was alienated from the uprising and the peasantry, for all the ruthless exactions and ill-treatment practised by the Russian troops, was not won over.

Yet for all his sympathy with the peasant's lot, Kosciuszko did not long for a Polish version of the French Revolution. The greatest number of its devotees were to be found among the 100,000 or more inhabitants of Warsaw, but neither the discontented mob nor its vanguard of erstwhile political pamphleteers idle since 1792, and craftsmen apt to turn their guilds into political clubs, were numerous or powerful enough to make another Paris of the Polish capital. The riots and demonstrations crowned by the public hanging of notable collaborationists, summarily on 9 May and without trial on 28 June, were brought under control by the authorities. Nearly a thousand 'Jacobins' were arrested; the paroles and countersigns used by the Warsaw militia in June 1794 record their political programme: 'Serfdom—Ignominy, Birth—An accident, Freedom—Happiness, The People—Power'. The reaction of the population at large to the French Revolution amounted to an expectation that it would bring liberation not so much from internal as from external enemies. This hope was also cherished by Kosciuszko and underlay his strategic plan for the insurrectionary war on two fronts.

The revolution was already in Poland's debt since 1792 when France was saved not so much by her own strength as by the weakness of her enemies divided by the events in Poland. The Prussians, even more anxious to secure Danzig, Thorn and the maximum share of Polish territory than to crush the revolution, were content to let the Austrians bear the brunt of the French campaign and the French played on this desire by allowing their armies to withdraw intact. In the autumn of 1793, the Seym at Grodno, secretly egged on by the Russian and Austrian envoys, refused to cede any territory to Prussia, whereupon Frederick William, feeling himself unable to sacrifice 'the primary' to 'the secondary', hastened to Poland from the confines of Lorraine and Alsace, thereby saving the French armies from certain disaster. Contrary to the Convention's readiness, declared on 19 November 1792, to lend gratuitous assistance to all peoples wanting to regain their freedom, this debt was never repaid. Encouraged by the Convention's foreign policy, the patriots in Dresden dispatched Kosciuszko, recently elected an honorary citizen of the republic, to represent them in Paris.[1] The memorandum submitted by him to the Girondin leaders shows that he expected the example about to be set by Poland to be followed by the oppressed peoples of Austria (in Hungary, Bohemia and Galicia), of Prussia (in Silesia), and even of Russia, obliging the three partitioners to withdraw their troops from Poland. The recipients of the memorandum deluded Kosciuszko with fantastic schemes for naval expeditions to the Baltic and the archipelago, having already decided tacitly to sanction a further partition in exchange for peace with Prussia, should the occasion arise. In any event, even if they had been willing to keep the Convention's promise, they would have been unable to do so for in the spring of 1793 France was fully engaged in defending her own territory. Kosciuszko returned to Dresden having achieved nothing. The next envoy, who arrived in Paris at the end of the year, fared no better. The outbreak of the insurrection did nothing to shake the Montagnard government's determination to defend the French Revolution to the exclusion of all others. Only after the fall of Robespierre was the Polish envoy admitted to the bar of the Convention whose chairman, Collot d'Herbois, lectured him on the ill-effects of insufficiently strong measures in a great revolution. When in the late autumn the *Comité de Salut public* resolved, with a view to mounting a co-ordinated diversion by the Poles, the Swedes and the Turks, to send to Poland an agent armed with a sum of money, the Russians had already entered Warsaw. The cost of this cautious and belated gesture was out of all proportion to the advantage that France derived from the collapse of Polish resistance. By the Peace of Basle the Polish insurrection was sacrificed to the French Revolution.

At the time of the revolution of 1830 Poland was again to render the same vital service to France by performing the part of decoy. On neither occasion had Poland any allies and in 1794 she was surrounded by neighbours seeking outlets for colonial expansion on the continent of Europe. These adverse circumstances notwithstanding, Kosciuszko's uprising should be regarded as an ill-calculated risk rather than a reckless gamble. There was much to be gained and very little to be lost; the partition that followed the insurrection might have occurred in any event, and before it came the Poles had at least shown that they knew not only how to set their house in order but also how to defend it. The uprising was a logical consequence of the May constitution.

The mistaken belief that Poland did have an ally contributed much to the second partition. In the events leading up to it the Poles displayed

[1] See J. Grossbart, 'La Politique polonaise de la Révolution Francaise jusqu'aux traités de Bâle', *Annales Historiques de la Révolution Française* (1929, 1930).

rashness and gullibility, the Prussians duplicity, the English insularity and Catherine of Russia vindictiveness. Poland was now punished with partition for wanting to govern herself well, just as in 1772 she had been punished for governing herself badly. The first partition was brought about by Polish anarchy which invited Russia's and Prussia's self-seeking interference. The basis of the transaction effected in 1772 was compensation: to Russia for the limited success of the war against Turkey, to Austria for her failure to obtain a cession of Turkish territory, to Prussia for her work as go-between and also for good measure, lest she should lose where others had gained. Although in this instance as in 1793, and to a large extent in 1795, the impulse came from Prussia, she received from public opinion and posterity much less than her proper share of censure.

As to the 'causes' of the partitions, these may be seen in the attendant circumstances, domestic as well as external, but the fact remains that if Poland's institutions had been stable and her economy better developed, she would not have laid herself open to dismemberment. The partitions therefore do not make up a tragedy in three acts but are the last act of a drama whose beginnings go back to the sixteenth century.

Poland's disappearance from the map of Europe brought certain benefits to the partitioners, some relative, some absolute, but none lasting. Prussia achieved territorial unity; Austria acquired an uneasy conscience and yet another nationality to keep in subjection, Russia had driven a territorial wedge into central Europe and was brought face to face with Prussia. The removal of the geographical barrier between these two powers delayed the renewal of the conflict between them but did not in the long run prevent it. On the whole, by presenting the nineteenth century with the Polish Question, the partitions created more problems than they solved.

The period between 1772 and 1794 also saw the appearance of new phenomena in Polish public life. Warsaw assumed the undue political importance of a modern capital and everywhere, as if to counterpoise the conservative and collaborationist outlook of the men of Targowica and their followers, the reformed schools were producing a new class of Poles, radically minded and democratically inclined, of urban or landed origins but often without private means, later to be known as the *inteligencja*. But the suppression of the Polish state put back the clock of progress and compelled the members of this composite élite to divert their energies from political, social and economic reform to the noble but restricted task of recovering national independence.

CHAPTER XIII

THE IBERIAN STATES AND THE ITALIAN STATES, 1763–93

I. THE IBERIAN STATES

IN 1763 Spain emerged from the Seven Years War a weaker and a wiser power. It was now clear to Charles III and his ministers that there was no short-cut to strength and security, and that the survival of Spain as a colonial power and her recovery of status in Europe depended on her own political and economic resources, the decline of which the earlier Bourbons had done something to arrest but little to reverse. Already before his accession to the throne of Spain in 1759 Charles III had displayed his reforming ideas as duke of Parma and king of Naples and had declared his intention of leading Spain back to greatness. He had considerable qualifications for the task. In spite of his own limited intelligence— seen perhaps in his childish obsession with hunting—he impressed foreign observers and his own subjects with his seriousness and application to business. His religious devotion was accompanied by a sober personal life and a chaste loyalty to the memory of his wife, María Amalia of Saxony, who died soon after their accession to the Spanish throne. He was highly conscious of his own sovereignty, and his absolutist views can be seen in the advice which he gave to his son: 'Anyone who criticises the actions of the government, even though they are not good, commits a crime.'[1] Above all, however, he showed his talent for government in his ministerial appointments: he chose his advisers not from the aristocracy, who were politically inept, nor, as is sometimes alleged, from the middle classes, who were not yet a recognisable force in Spain, but from a group of university-trained lawyers among the lower ranks of the nobility, who were devoted to absolute monarchy and whose minds were open to the practical applications of the Enlightenment. His early appointments, however, revealed a penchant for foreigners, particularly Italians—such as the marquis of Squillace, Minister of Finance, and the marquis of Grimaldi, Secretary of State for Foreign Affairs—which provoked some unpopularity among his new subjects. But he learned by experience to replace these by Spaniards and gradually to improve his government by introducing men of higher quality like the efficient lawyer Manuel de Roda, Minister of Justice; the reforming economist Pedro Rodríguez de Campomanes, fiscal of the Council of Castile from 1762; the soldier-

---

[1] Quoted in A. Domínguez Ortiz, *La sociedad española en el siglo XVIII* (Madrid, 1955), p. 27.

administrator, count of Aranda, president of the Council of Castile from 1766 to 1773; and above all, the ideal servant of enlightened absolutism, José Moñino, count of Floridablanca, who was fiscal of the Council of Castile from 1766 and who replaced Grimaldi as First Secretary of State in 1776.

In spite of the encyclopaedic influences which some of these men absorbed there was little ideology in their policies and no overt attack on religion. The philosophy of the Enlightenment had no place in Charles III's own formation and little influence among his subjects. The literature of the French *philosophes* was known to only a small minority of educated Spaniards who did not accept it indiscriminately. French criticism of contemporary social, political and religious institutions found little response in Spain, and this was due, not to the Inquisition, which could be evaded, but to the fact that both the administration and the Spanish people remained Catholic in conviction and devoted to absolute monarchy. They were looking in fact not for a new philosophy but for practical answers to administrative, economic and educational problems. The spirit of reform in Charles III's government was animated by no other desire than to increase the strength and prosperity of the state. Scientific discoveries were valued, not for their own sake, but as ways to improve manufactures and agriculture. This can be seen in the work of the quasi-official Economic Societies which spread in the course of the reign from the Basque country to the main towns of the rest of Spain, and whose aim was simply to encourage agriculture, commerce and industry by study and experiment. Although they met with some hostility from conservatives, they were by no means anti-clerical in outlook and numbered some of the clergy among their members. The whole movement of reforming speculation had been aptly described as 'culture utilitaire et culture dirigée'.[1] Its object was to promote technical skill and practical knowledge.

The impulse to reform came from above and at first it was too abrupt to be acceptable to the conservative elements in Spanish society. The presence of foreigners in the government and the existence of genuine grievances gave these early protests a patriotic and popular appeal. Spain's failure in the Seven Years War, a rise in the price of foodstuffs caused by inflation and a series of bad harvests, and the higher taxes demanded by Squillace to pay for his reforms caused widespread resentment which could be exploited by those who were alarmed at the new direction the government was taking. Finally, Squillace's attempt to enforce an old law forbidding men to wear in Madrid their broad-brimmed slouch hats and long capes on the ground that it provided camouflage for criminals, sparked off violent riots in Madrid in March 1766 which spread to many other towns in central Spain. In the capital a determined mob attacked the houses of the Italian ministers, and the king himself fled to

[1] J. Sarrailh, *L'Espagne éclairée de la seconde moitié du XVIIIe siècle* (Paris, 1954), p. 165.

Aranjuez where he accepted the terms of the insurgents in humiliating circumstances: exile of Squillace, the revocation of the dress order, and a lowering of the price of foodstuffs. In the official view the riots of 1766 were not merely a reaction against a foreign minister who was trying to change the national dress, nor even the result of popular grievances, but were an attempt to alter the personnel and the policy of the government by force and implied resistance to reforms or projects of reform, particularly in economic and ecclesiastical affairs, on the part of those whose interests were threatened. It was reported that the riots were planned by groups of nobles and clergy who wished to evict Squillace and discourage Charles from further reforms. The truth of these reports is still an open question.[1] There is no evidence that the Jesuits were involved as an order, but there is little doubt that some individual Jesuits were implicated and subsequently attempted to justify the riots. This provided the government with material to incriminate the entire order and gave it an opportunity to eliminate an institution whose previous record had caused it to be regarded as a threat to absolute monarchy.

Charles III had inherited a strong position with regard to the Spanish church, a position which had been legalised by the Concordat of 1753 confirming the Spanish crown in extensive rights of appointment, jurisdiction and revenue, and which he proceeded to consolidate and extend. The church itself was hardly in a position to offer any resistance to absolutism. With 200,000 ecclesiastics out of a population of ten million, and about 3000 religious houses, it probably contained more clergy than the country could support. Economically it was a powerful institution with immense wealth in land and revenue, much of which was spent on charity, education and donations to the state but which was also criticised by reformers as unproductive. In spite of its material strength, however, the church could not present a united front to the encroachments of the state. The bishops were crown appointees, and while they were usually worthy of their office most of them were also convinced regalists. The difference of wealth and education between the higher and lower clergy, the maldistribution of clergy between places like Toledo and rural parishes without priests, the divisions between the monastic orders and their rivalry with the secular clergy weakened the Spanish church and left it open to attack. Moreover, royal authority in ecclesiastical affairs had its supporters in Spain, even in the church itself. These supporters of regalism were called Jansenists by their opponents, and although their Jansenism had little to do with the problems of grace posed by the early French Jansenists, it was recognisable in the way in which it criticised papal

---

[1] See V. Rodríguez Casado, *Política interior de Carlos III* (Valladolid, 1950), and 'Iglesia y Estado en el reinado de Carlos III', *Estudios Americanos*, vol. I (1948), pp. 5–57, who argues that the riots were planned with Jesuit connivance, and C. Eguía Ruiz, S.J., *Los Jesuitas y el Motín de Esquilache* (Madrid, 1947), who maintains that they were spontaneous.

jurisdiction, the religious orders and various kinds of popular devotion which were regarded as superstitious. Those who wished to fashion a more national church in Spain also drew support and encouragement from the anti-papal bias of other foreign influences such as Gallicanism and Febronianism.[1]

The record of the Spanish Jesuits in the eighteenth century was not an ultramontane exception to the regalist spirit of the rest of the Spanish church: many Jesuits, particularly the royal confessors, had defended regalism as firmly as its other adherents. Nevertheless, the Jesuits still retained their special vow of obedience to the pope and their reputation of papal agents, while their loyalty to the crown in the American colonies was also suspect. An order with an international organisation whose headquarters were outside Spain was regarded as an obstacle to royal sovereignty, and in seeking to implement the Concordat of 1753 Charles III believed he had to reckon with its resistance in Spain and in Rome. A few years after his accession he showed his hand when he prohibited the publication of a papal brief condemning a French catechism which denied papal infallibility and contained views hostile to the Jesuits. When the inquisitor-general published the papal prohibition he was banished from Madrid and detained in a monastery until he begged royal pardon. Moreover, by a decree of 18 January 1762 Charles III ordered that henceforth royal permission—the *exequatur*—must be given to all papal documents before they could be published in Spain, and although this decree was suspended in July 1763 it was revived in 1768.

Jesuit opposition in this and other incidents confirmed Charles III in his determination to remove what he regarded as a challenge to his absolute power. Such a decision had the resolute support of his ministers, some of whom, like Campomanes and Moñino, came from a class which resented the influence of the Jesuits in education and their affiliation with the higher aristocracy. Consequently, although there were obvious social and economic reasons for the discontent which led to the riots of 1766, the government preferred to believe that they had been instigated by the Jesuits and their allies who wished to change the government and block further reform. The papacy protested that the actions of individuals did not compromise the entire order, but it soon became clear that the institution itself was at stake. The official inquiry was in the hands of Aranda, who had been appointed president of the Council of Castile in 1766 with the task of restoring order after the fall of Squillace and who was assisted by Campomanes and Moñino. The charges against the Jesuits had all the violence and passion of propaganda and showed that they were being condemned, not merely or even mainly for alleged intervention in the Madrid riots, but for what their enemies in the government called their 'spirit of fanaticism and sedition, false doctrine and intolerable pride',

[1] On Febronianism see vol. VII, pp. 121–2.

and for constituting 'an open faction which disturbs the state with interests directly opposed to the public welfare'.[1] A royal commission, which included members of the hierarchy, found the Jesuits guilty of provoking the riots and this was followed by a royal decree of 27 February 1767 expelling the Jesuits from Spain and its dominions, as they had already been expelled from Portugal in 1759 and from France in 1762. The decree, which also imposed public silence on the affair, was carried out with a ruthless and military efficiency by Aranda, although there was in fact no opposition either from the 8000 Jesuits involved or from the rest of the Spanish church. The measure was supported not only by rival orders like the Augustinians but also by the majority of the regalist-minded episcopate. When in 1769 the pope asked the Spanish hierarchy for its opinion on the measure, forty-two bishops approved, six opposed and eight declined to answer.

Not content with expelling the Jesuits, the Spanish government was also determined to suppress the order everywhere. For this it needed the co-operation of the papacy. The Jesuits who left Spain settled in the papal states and other parts of Europe. Pope Clement XIII, for political and financial reasons, had not wanted them in his states, but he resisted pressure from the Bourbon powers for their suppression. Therefore Charles III and his allies had to work for a more amenable successor, and the election of Cardinal Ganganelli as Clement XIV was a victory for the anti-Jesuit powers, who eventually procured a papal brief suppressing the Society of Jesus on 21 July 1773. The principal agent working for the Spanish government in Rome was José Moñino, assisted by Fathers Vázquez and Boixadors, generals respectively of the Augustinians and Dominicans. Moñino was influential even in drawing up the papal brief and he was rewarded for his efforts by Charles III with the title of count of Floridablanca.

There remained the question of Jesuit doctrines and Jesuit property. The former were proscribed and the latter was sequestered by the state, which now entered the field of public education for the first time. The government tried to ensure that the property of the Jesuits was used for establishing new teaching centres, colleges of medicine and university residences for poor students, while Jesuit revenue was to be assigned to hospitals and other social services. Royal decrees confined primary education to secular teachers, made school attendance obligatory and regulated the chairs in the universities. Not all of these projects came to fruition and it was the state rather than society that gained from the dissolution.

The subordination of the church to the state in Spain was completed by the curtailment of the jurisdiction of the Inquisition. Potentially the

[1] Consulta del Consejo extraordinario, 30 April 1767, in M. Danvila y Collado, *El reinado de Carlos III* (6 vols., Madrid, 1890-6), vol. III, pp. 628-33.

atter was already a royal tool, but in the eyes of the government it was compromised by its past association with the Jesuits and was regarded as ultramontane by the reformers in Charles III's administration. The Council of Castile reasserted the sovereignty of the crown over the Inquisition, and Charles III began to use this sovereignty more effectively than his predecessors had done. By decrees of 1768 and 1770 the procedure for censoring books was regulated and the inquisitors were advised to confine themselves to matters of heresy and apostasy and to imprison only when guilt was established. The significance of royal action in restricting the jurisdiction of the Inquisition should not be exaggerated, for the latter still preserved intact its traditional powers in spiritual matters. But even the Inquisition could not ignore the spirit of the government, and the appointment of more moderate inquisitors combined with its own lethargy to temper its actions.

The suppression of the riots of 1766 and the expulsion of the Jesuits were victories for the reforming ministers of Charles III who were thenceforth sustained by the prestige and authority of the new president of the Council of Castile, the count of Aranda. As an aristocrat, soldier and moderate reformer, Aranda was useful to Charles III in restoring order and confidence, but he was not the author of any policy. This role was filled by Campomanes, the government's chief economic adviser, and by Floridablanca who in 1776 replaced Grimaldi as Secretary of State. In the hands of this group royal policy changed not its objectives but its methods and it now proceeded with more caution.

Reform depended not only on legislation but also on agencies of government to implement it. The local immunities of Aragon, Catalonia and Valencia had been destroyed earlier in the century, and gradually a centrally controlled bureaucracy subjecting all Spaniards to a common régime had been applied. Charles III continued this policy of centralisation and absolutism, and under him the cortes—*one* cortes for the whole kingdom—played no more part in the national life than it had done under the earlier Bourbons. But the crown also sought to make itself more absolute by making itself more efficient. The conciliar system of government, typical of the Habsburgs, a system of administration by committees in which political, administrative and judicial functions were combined and confounded, had already been modified by the earlier Bourbons who, drawing on the experience of the French monarchy, had begun to experiment with individual ministers. The latter, anxious to resolve policy themselves, preferred to reduce the authority of the councils, which were gradually confined to routine administration. This decline of conciliar government was halted somewhat under Charles III, and the Council of Castile enjoyed a new lease of life when he appointed Campomanes and Floridablanca its fiscals and Aranda its president. But the slowness of its procedure was an obstacle to efficient government and the council itself was anxious to confine itself to judicial work. In fact the royal secretaries, now also called ministers, were the mainsprings of government under Charles III. He inherited five such ministries—State, War, Finance, Justice, and Marine and the Indies. The concentration of power in the hands of a small number of men and the continual contact they maintained with the king gave policy a vigour and direction which had previously been lacking. Leaving administrative and judicial detail to the councils, these ministers could prepare and promote policy, extend the central power to the length and breadth of Spain, and inaugurate reforms in the collection of revenue, national defence, local government and other fields. Moreover, to co-ordinate the work of the departments there began a more frequent and more systematic use of the *Junta*, or committee, where ministers could meet and discuss policy. At first the practice was to appoint *ad hoc* juntas for specific purposes, but gradually a *Junta de Estado* began to meet, though irregularly, and was found to be a useful way of resolving differences between departments and of devising a concerted policy. Floridablanca encouraged his ministerial colleagues to assemble more frequently and was eventually responsible, by decree of 8 July 1787, for giving permanence and organisation to this cabinet, which was an instrument of collective responsibility and continuity long needed in Spanish government.

The ministers in turn had their agents, and the most important of these were the intendants, whose introduction into Spain in 1718, but more effectively in 1749, was probably the most characteristic of the Bourbon administrative reforms. The intendants were responsible for the general administration and the economic progress of their provinces, as well as for military conscription and supplies, and under Charles III it was their reports that provided the local information on which the government hoped to base its policy. The task assigned to them was probably unmanageable, and there was always the danger that they would clash with the jurisdiction of the more familiar and more traditional *corregidores*, who in the smaller divisions of the provinces mirrored the activities of the intendants. Less tyrannical in the eighteenth century than they had been in the seventeenth, the *corregidores* were still badly recruited. The decisive reform came in 1783 when these posts, previously granted by favour and arbitrarily revoked, were reorganised and graded according to their importance and income into three categories, thus becoming a career open to talent with a regulated system of promotion.

In such a régime there was little room for municipal independence. Moreover, the revenues of the municipalities were too considerable to be ignored by the central government, and from 1760 they were closely supervised by a committee of the Council of Castile and its agents the intendants. Yet while he strengthened the authority of his officials, Charles III also attempted to widen the franchise of local government and to make it more representative. In 1766, possibly as a result of the disturbances in the towns of Castile, a reform devised by Campomanes was imposed, introducing into the town councils representatives of the commons elected annually, four in the larger towns and two in those with less than two thousand inhabitants. Theoretically this was one of the most striking reforms of the period, since it gave the people a place in municipal government and promised to remove the town councils from the exclusive control of the hereditary and life councillors. In practice, however, the result was quite different. Amidst the hostility of the hereditary councillors and the indifference of the people the new representatives were too weak to make their influence felt and simply aspired to join the local oligarchy by making themselves life appointees. Yet the reform indicated the desire of the government to attract the collaboration of Spanish society in its own revival.

The most urgent problem facing the government was the economic condition of the country. Agriculture was suffering from past neglect and a contemporary crisis. The immediate cause of the crisis was inflation; prices rose by about 35 per cent between 1750 and 1790. Rents were rising even higher than prices, and this was due to the shortage of cultivated land in the centre and the south of Spain. At the root of the bigger demand for land was the notable rise in population—from about six million to over ten million in the course of the century—but the situation was aggravated by the traditional pasture privileges of the powerful sheep-owners' organisation, the *Mesta*, which removed large tracts of land from arable agriculture, and by the unjust distribution of land in Spain where the aristocracy and the church owned vast and largely unexploited estates in rigid entail and mortmain. In central Spain a system of short-term leases with risk of eviction weighted the scales heavily against the peasant. In the south, and especially in Andalusia, the predominance of aristocratic latifundia, cultivated by a force of day-labourers, created a rural proletariat that lived in very precarious conditions. For the peasant, therefore, common lands were essential to his very subsistence. Yet it was difficult to procure them against the encroachments of the *Mesta*, the great proprietors, and the towns themselves which, administered by a local oligarchy in alliance with the aristocracy, preferred to let most of the town lands to private individuals, reserving only a small portion for common use. Finally, to make matters worse, there existed extensive seigneurial jurisdiction in the hands of the aristocracy which enabled them to name judges and local officials as well as to collect revenue in thousands of towns and villages.[1] It was clear, therefore, that some basic remedies were needed to remove the many obstacles to agricultural progress and the welfare of the rural masses.

[1] For figures see G. Desdevises du Dezert, *L'Espagne de l'ancien régime* (3 vols., Paris, 1897–1904), vol. III, pp. 130–1.

The agrarian programme of Charles III's government began with an attempt to plan a more rational policy. In 1762 Campomanes was appointed fiscal of the Council of Castile with a wide commission in economic affairs. Three years later he published his *Tratado de la regalía de amortización* in which he argued that the prosperity of the state and its subjects could only be increased by attracting the peasant to the soil that he worked, and in which he advocated state intervention to modify the conditions of land distribution in the interests of society. He also conducted an extensive inquiry into the agrarian situation through intendants and local authorities, whose reports were edited and published in 1771 and 1784. Meanwhile a small measure of reform had begun. In 1763 the government ordered the suspension of evictions in the case of short-term leases. In April 1766 on the initiative of the intendant of Badajoz town lands there were distributed to local citizens at low fixed rents; the Council of Castile sanctioned this practice and ordered its extension to other towns of Extremadura, and in 1767-8 to Andalusia and La Mancha, with preference to landless labourers and farmers. In 1770 all Spanish localities were ordered to enclose and allot their town lands not then under cultivation. But except in Catalonia and Asturias this was ineffective, for without capital labourers could not be expected to make barren land fruitful, while the municipalities either ignored the decrees or favoured the local oligarchy. An attempt to distribute private waste land was also unsuccessful. As far as seigneurial jurisdiction was concerned, although Campomanes would have liked to abolish it, the crown hesitated to touch seigneurial dues and property rights, and was content to extend its intervention in the appointment of officials. The colonisation of desert land in the Sierra Morena seemed to offer greater prospects. In 1767 Campomanes drew up a plan for the creation of colonies in the deserted regions of royal land in the Sierra Morena and Andalusia. Supervision of the project was given to Pablo de Olavide, and after a faltering start communities of German and French Catholic immigrants, followed later by Spaniards, promoted agriculture and industries in a hitherto barren region. But it was only a small part of Spain.

The *Mesta* was not abolished by the government, though something was done to weaken its authority. In 1786 its right to use in perpetuity and at fixed rents any land that it had once used as pasture was abolished, and in 1788 landowners were given the right to enclose their lands and plant whatever they wanted. But these measures came at the end of the reign and merely acknowledged existing conditions. The lag of wool prices behind those of grain on the international market, the desperate need to cultivate more land to feed an increasing population, the anxiety of the great proprietors to profit from higher agricultural prices, these were the factors that helped to redress the balance against the sheep-owners in favour of agricultural interests, because 'for once the objectives of the crown coincided with the desire of landowners to get more farm-land under their control'.[1] The same coincidence of interests can be seen in the corn laws of 1765 which abolished price ceilings on grain, permitted free trade within Spain and allowed exports except in time of dearth: these laws provided yet another stimulus to agriculture until their repeal in 1790. But at a time when the agricultural boom was making farming more profitable the profit was not going to the peasant. Consequently, in spite of its promising start, it must be concluded that it was never the intention of Charles III's government to impose a fundamental agrarian reform and that its policy contained no threat to conservative interests.

The tendency of the government to follow prevailing economic forces was also seen, but with better results, in its commercial policy. In fact the main concern of Charles III's administration was not agriculture but colonial commerce and domestic manufacture. It was its policy to open all major ports to colonial trade and to protect Spanish manufactures from competition. In opening the colonial trade to most Spanish and American ports and to all Spanish nationals by the decrees of 1765 and 1778,[2] the state helped to release an industrial and commercial expansion that had already begun. Either via Cadiz or directly through contraband, other Spanish ports than Seville and Cadiz were trading with America. In particular Barcelona was heavily engaged in the colonial trade before the legal concession, and the basis of her exports was an industrial revival which had begun about 1730.

The government of Charles III, unlike that of the earlier Bourbons, based its industrial policy not on state manufactures—though royal factories producing luxury goods were extended and remodelled—but on improving the conditions in which private enterprise could operate. Royal edicts hopefully tried to make manual work respectable for hidalgos. The more restrictive practices of the guilds with regard to industrial recruitment and methods were removed. Under the pressure of Spanish manufacturers a customs policy was imposed which aimed at protecting domestic production either by taxing or prohibiting the import of foreign goods such as cotton, in the interests of the Catalan product, and of hardware, in the interests of the Basque iron industry. In 1778 many small cloth articles were kept out, and in 1788 all cloths and other products of linen, wool and cotton were excluded. An inefficient customs service could not prevent smuggling, yet the policy did have some effect. A similar attempt to improve the conditions in which industry could operate is to be seen in the internal fiscal policy of the crown. Castile paid more and heavier taxes than Aragon, Catalonia, Navarre and the Basque provinces, which partly accounted for the industrial backwardness of Castile compared with the rest of the peninsula, for the incidence of taxation discouraged

[1] R. Herr, *The Eighteenth-century Revolution in Spain* (Princeton, N.J., 1958), p. 117.
[2] See below, ch. XIV, p. 401.

manufacturers from founding industries. The crown appeared ready to sacrifice revenue in order to promote Castilian manufactures. In 1779 the *alcabala*, or sales tax, was removed on wholesale transactions in domestic woollens, including exports to America, and it was reduced from 14 per cent to 2 per cent on retail sales. In 1785 there was a general reduction of the *alcabala* on all objects, and in 1786 it was abolished entirely on domestic linen and hemp cloth sold in Spain. At the same time, in an attempt to cut the delays and the costs of transport between central Spain and the periphery, new highways and canals were begun which were intended to enable Castile to compete with foreign imports in the other areas of Spain. While none of these measures restored the balance for Castile they did improve her prospects.

The other areas of Spain, however, were advancing much more rapidly. Valencia, which already exported its high quality raw silk, now began to produce the manufactured article, and while it could still not compete abroad with the French product, it was at least challenging it for the domestic market. The ironware of the Basque provinces, produced in local forges and factories, was given an added impetus by the prohibition of foreign hardware imports in 1775. Catalonia had begun to industrialise even more intensely. Among its various industries a new one, cotton, was making spectacular progress, absorbing capital from other merchant ventures and being assisted in its formative years by the tariff policy of the early Bourbons which at first Charles III discontinued. In 1760 the prohibition of foreign cotton cloths was replaced by a heavy duty, but, following the complaints of the Barcelona cotton manufacturers, the prohibition was reimposed on foreign printed cottons in 1768, and in 1771 on all cotton cloths. Rapid growth followed, more factories appeared and foreign methods and machines were copied. Spain's participation in the War of American Independence and the consequent cutting of communications with the overseas markets put a break on this expansion, but the decade after the peace of 1783 saw the industry at its zenith. With at least eighty factories, 2500 looms and 80,000 workers, Catalonia ranked second only to England in the production of cotton cloth.

The freedom given to the export trade, backed by a higher industrial output, enabled Spain to challenge foreign competitors for the supply of her own markets. There was nothing amounting to an industrial revolution and Spain was still unable to compete with France and Britain in the world market, but she could challenge them for her domestic and colonial markets and her share in these noticeably increased throughout the 1780s. As in the case of the agricultural boom, the Spanish working classes did not share in the new prosperity. The lag of wages behind prices, while it created large profits for manufacturers and capital for industrial investment, was unaccompanied by any social welfare legislation on the part of the state. The mass of the people were left in poverty and ignorance with only the charity of the church to look to. Strength, not welfare, was the aim of Charles III's régime. And the question still remains, did Spain have strength enough to improve her prospects abroad?

Commercial objectives were closely connected with imperial defence. Spain was anxious to defend her possessions from the attacks of rivals as well as to protect her trade from foreign interlopers.[1] Her most powerful rival was Great Britain, and Charles III's anxiety to maintain a colonial balance of power was one of the main features of his foreign policy. This was the reason why in August 1761 he entered the Family Compact with France which created an offensive and defensive alliance between the two Bourbon powers and which took Spain into the colonial war which France was waging with Britain when the latter declared war on Spain in January 1762. Charles III's miscalculation lay in underrating Britain's war potential and in entering a colonial conflict with inadequate naval resources. Britain was equal to the united forces of both France and Spain, and the Seven Years War was a disaster for Spain as well as for her ally. By the Peace of Paris (February 1763) not only had Spain to allow Britain's wood-cutting claims in Honduras and renounce any rights to the Newfoundland fisheries, but she also had to return Sacramento—her only conquest of the war—to Portugal, and cede Florida and all Spanish territory in North America east of the Mississippi to Britain. The latter returned her conquests, Havana and Manila, while from France Spain procured Louisiana—and a new frontier to be defended against her rival. If Spain was defeated, however, she was not crushed, and the Bourbon allies worked to strengthen the alliance and its resources. For Spain this was the only alliance available, and although the Family Compact faltered once again in 1771 when France refused to co-operate with Spain in an attempt to eject Britain from the Falkland Islands, the opportunity to settle accounts was not long delayed.

The revolt of Britain's North American colonies removed the danger of British expansion southwards at the expense of the Spanish empire and gave Spain a chance to recover her losses. Profiting from her rival's preoccupation she sent an expedition from Cadiz which in 1777 occupied the island of Santa Catalina off the coast of Brazil and captured the Portuguese outpost of Sacramento at the mouth of the River Plate. The War of American Independence, however, was not an easy field for intervention. Charles III was caught between the desire to embarrass his colonial rival, which accounts for his undercover aid to the rebels from 1776, and fear for his own American possessions, which led him to offer his mediation in June 1779. A victory for the rebels might set an example to her own colonies that Spain would later regret. The temptation to do damage to Britain, however, was irresistible, and Charles III followed France into war in 1779, attempting to solve the dilemma by pursuing

[1] See below, ch. xiv, pp. 398 and 400.

Spanish interests without giving much direct support to the British colonies and without recognising American independence. Before entering the conflict the Spanish government had signed a secret treaty with France (April 1779) which defined objectives and stipulated for the return of Gibraltar to Spain under the pèace treaty.[1] American independence was only mentioned incidentally and was merely an opportunity for Spain to promote her national interests. She reconquered Florida, occupied the British outposts in the Bahamas and expelled the enemy from their logging bases in Belize. In Europe, after the failure of an attempted invasion of England by a joint Franco-Spanish fleet, Spain turned her attention to Gibraltar and laid siege with an army of 8000. The siege was long and unsuccessful: unable to blockade it by sea Spain was powerless to prevent relief reaching the garrison. On the other hand, a successful expedition to Minorca recovered the island for Spain in February 1782. By the Peace of Versailles (3 September 1783) Spain regained Florida and Minorca, but restored the Bahamas to Britain and gave the English certain rights in Belize.

In view of the defeats she had suffered, Spain emerged from the war with moderate success. Economically, however, it had been harmful to her. Far from striking a blow at her major colonial and commercial rival, Spain had not the naval strength to maintain communications with her own colonies. The effects of the free trade regulations of 1778 were delayed and the Spanish export trade was hit. The government was also deprived of what income it received from America. American treasure was still an item in government revenue, and whether it arrived or not depended on whether Spain was at peace or war with Britain, the major seapower. War meant blockade, and the non-arrival of its American income would force the Spanish government to adopt other financial expedients either in the form of new taxes or by the issue of paper money with consequent inflation. Charles III, who was so well served in other departments, had no good financial administration and never balanced his budgets; he had recourse to foreign loans, always in worse conditions and with increasing debt. Eventually his government succumbed to the temptation to issue paper money. The war with Britain from 1779 meant the stopping of American treasure. When an increase in taxes failed to supply enough money for the war, interest-bearing royal bonds were issued to circulate as legal tender. To restore royal credit, a French-born financier, Francisco Cabarrús, was authorised in June 1782 to found the first national bank of Spain, the Banco de San Carlos, with the object of redeeming the bonds. Peace with Britain was followed by the arrival of the accumulated treasure from America and the bank began to retire the bonds, which now recovered their value, and retained it for the next decade.

With peace Spanish foreign trade was released once more and industry

[1] See below, ch. XVII, p. 501.

responded to the post-war consumer demand at home and in the colonies. The effects of freer trade and the industrial boom were now being felt and Spain began to enjoy some of the fruits of her empire which had long been the preserve of her commercial rivals in northern Europe. The government of Charles III had provided the conditions in which landowners, merchants and manufacturers could promote their interests, which were also regarded as the interests of the state. When he died in 1788 it was clear that Charles III had led his country in a political, economic and cultural revival, and had left Spain a much better place for some classes to live in than it had been thirty years previously.

The political inheritance left to Charles IV, therefore, was not without promise, if only he could continue the policy and the administration of his father. Two things, however, made this impossible—the personality of the new king and the impact of events in France. The success of absolute monarchy depended among other things on the quality of the monarch. Badly educated, intellectually feeble and lacking the will-power of his father, Charles IV showed little aptitude for affairs of state to which indeed he devoted scarcely any time. The weak and stupid benevolence depicted by Goya was also characteristic of his political attitudes, and Godoy recalled how each night the king used to ask him, 'What have my subjects been doing today?'[1] He was not incapable of political decisions, and the notion that his wife was responsible for all his actions is a mistaken one. Yet the failure of Charles IV's government to command respect and confidence was due in no small part to the political influence of the strong-willed and unscrupulous María Luisa of Parma whose libidinous inclinations were reputed to have shown themselves even before she discovered the young guardsman Manuel Godoy about 1786 and started his astonishing promotion.

Charles IV did, in fact, begin his reign by continuing the policy and the ministers he inherited. He retained Floridablanca as First Secretary of State and his government seemed to show liberal tendencies by attempting to prevent the accumulation of property in entail and by measures to promote commerce and marine. But nothing came of these schemes, and in any case events outside Spain quickly shattered the government's complacency.

The outbreak of the French Revolution horrified Floridablanca and thenceforth conditioned all his policy. Yet it would be a mistake to regard his subsequent conduct as a reversal of all he had previously stood for. His reaction to the French Revolution was a natural one for a Spanish royal minister. However much he had believed in progress and enlightenment Floridablanca was also devoted to absolute monarchy of which he was the servant. His political views had no place for disobedience to

[1] Príncipe de la Paz, *Memorias* (*Biblioteca de autores españoles*, 2 vols., Madrid, 1956), vol. I, p. 409.

legitimate authority. In a letter to Fernán Núñez, the Spanish ambassador in Paris, he declared his anxiety at events in France: 'It is said that the century of enlightenment has taught man his rights. But it has deprived him of true happiness and content and of his personal and family security. In Spain we do not want so much enlightenment nor the consequences it brings—insolence in deeds, words and writings against legitimate powers.'[1] He believed that at all costs Spain must be preserved from contagion, and he quickly took steps to keep Spaniards ignorant of events in France. By a rigid press censorship he tried to suppress news from France. To check the entry of French newspapers he ordered in September 1789 stricter vigilance in the ports and on the frontier and in December he authorised the post-office to inspect and seize suspect packets. A decree of 1 January 1790 forbad the entry or publication of any material referring to the revolution in France. When the revolutionary literature continued to enter Spain during 1791 he mobilised the Inquisition in his service and even placed a cordon of troops on the French frontier. On 24 February 1791 a royal edict ordered the suspension of all private Spanish periodicals, and only the official press with its heavily censored news was allowed to continue. In this way fear of propaganda caused the government to suppress political speculation in Spain itself and to encourage the Inquisition to proceed with more vigour against the exponents of enlightenment. The reaction was also seen in changes in the personnel of the government. In 1790 Cabarrús was denounced to the Inquisition and imprisoned. Jovellanos was banished to Asturias. Campomanes himself was relieved of his position as governor of the Council of Castile in 1791.

The object of this campaign was to preserve the Spanish régime from subversion. But such fears were imaginary. Although there was much discontent in Spain it was economic in content and not ideological—bread riots in Barcelona in February 1789, tax riots in Galicia in the winter of 1790–1—while the existence of a few Encyclopaedists and even of some admiration for the French constitution of 1791 in government and intellectual circles was quite unrepresentative of the opinions of the mass of the Spanish people who knew little about events in France and showed even less concern. On 28 February 1792 Floridablanca himself was dismissed. The reason for his fall is not clear. Was it aristocratic resentment of his power and humble origin? Was it the result of the interference of the queen who resented his urging Charles IV to banish Godoy, suspected of being her lover? It is more likely that the minister's intransigent policy towards France, and in particular Spain's refusal to recognise Louis XVI's oath to the French constitution as valid, was thought to endanger the French royal family, and that Charles IV sacrificed his minister for the sake of his relations. Floridablanca was replaced as First Secretary by

[1] Quoted in C. Alcázar Molina, 'Ideas políticas de Floridablanca', *Revista de Estudios Políticos*, vol. LIII (1955), p. 53.

Aranda who set about reversing his predecessor's policies. The *Junta de Estado* was abolished and its place taken by a purely advisory Council of State, long moribund and now irrelevant. Aranda also relaxed the official Spanish attitude towards the French Revolution and moderated the stringent press laws with which the government had sought to protect itself.

It was soon decided, however, that moderation was premature. The deposition of Louis XVI and the imprisonment of the French royal family in August 1792 together with the military victories of the new republic and its policy of revolutionary expansion caused Spain to close its ranks once more. On 15 November 1792 Aranda was dismissed and replaced by Manuel Godoy whose rapid rise via the royal guards to the rank of grandee and the office of First Secretary at the age of twenty-five was reputed to be due to the favour of the queen. With the appointment of Godoy Spanish government reverted to the improvisation typical of the later Habsburgs. Godoy was a classical *privado*, or favourite, owing his position not to his qualifications—he was inexperienced and untalented— but to his personal relations with the monarch. He was expected to deal firmly with France, but his attempt to save the life of Louis XVI without involving Spain in war with France failed. The Convention resented Spanish interference and rejected it with contempt. Godoy in turn rejected the French demands—mutual disarmament except that France was to keep troops near Bayonne—and France declared war on Spain on 7 March 1793. In accepting the inevitability of war Godoy had the Spanish people behind him. Yet the important factor was not what Spain wanted but what France wanted and that too was war, a war to remove another Bourbon from his throne and to carry the Revolution to the Spanish people.

The Spanish people, however, did not want the Revolution, and the war of 1793–5 produced one of the most spontaneous war-efforts in Spanish history. Priests preached it from their pulpits. Gifts of money poured into the government. The rush of volunteers made it unnecessary to conscript for the army. The Spanish people's traditional passion for their religion and their monarchy reasserted itself and they rejected the Revolution and all its implications with a militant fervour that caused a revolutionary agent writing at the beginning of 1793 to declare, 'The religious fanaticism of the Spaniards is higher than ever.... The people regard the war as a war of religion.'[1] To the surprise of the Revolutionaries a Spanish army invaded Roussillon in April, a premature success to be sure, but during the rest of 1793 the French Army of the Eastern Pyrenees was occupied in repulsing the Spanish invasion.

While the Spanish régime in this period might aptly be described as one of enlightened absolutism, the term has little justification when applied to Portugal. It is true that in Portugal, as well as in Spain, there was an

[1] In P. Vidal, *Histoire de la Révolution française dans le département des Pyrénées-Orientales* (2 vols., Perpignan, 1885), vol. II, pp. 100–1.

attempt to reform society through the action of the state. But in Portugal this attempt owed nothing to the thought of the Enlightenment, while the state itself was much weaker and society even more immovable than in Spain. The monarchs themselves—José I (1750–77) and Maria I (1777–1816)—took little part in affairs of state. There was no tradition of administration, no agencies by which reforms could be sustained, and no fundamental remedies applied to these defects. There was abundant legislation, most of it inspired by the royal minister, the marquis of Pombal, but most of it was ineffective. Pombal himself was not a man of the Enlightenment. His policies and methods of government, declining as they did into terrorism and senseless brutality, were grotesque distortions of the reforming ideas of the time and earned the contempt of the French Encyclopaedists. Pombal's distinctive feature was that he could react effectively to an emergency situation, as he did to the earthquake of 1755, and his subsequent reconstruction of Lisbon made the most lasting monument to his rule a successful piece of town planning.[1]

Absolutism in Portugal, based ultimately on the gold from Brazil which gave the government an independent supply of money, was not without its opponents, political and ecclesiastical, and one of the earliest tasks of Pombal was the removal of all possible centres of opposition. As a member of the lower nobility himself Pombal was not anti-aristocratic in principle, but he was concerned to remove the higher nobility from sources of power. After the attack on José I in 1758 he implicated the great house of Aveiro and his other enemies, the Távoras, and brought them down on a charge of attempted regicide.

As in Spain, state control of the church was intensified in the second half of the eighteenth century and there was a similar attack on the Jesuits. Having evicted them from court and forbidden them to engage in business, Pombal then implicated them in the regicide plot of 1758, confiscated their property and expelled them from Portugal in 1759. After their expulsion from France and Spain, Pombal also supported the Bourbon courts when they approached the papacy to request the dissolution of the society. Pombal's attack on the Jesuits was only part of a wider ecclesiastical policy which he pursued in the interests of the state. He limited religious bequests, attempted to secularise education, and placed the jurisdiction of the bishops in all save spiritual matters under the crown. There was no liberalism in his religious policy. He was concerned not to abolish the Inquisition but to place it more securely at the service of the state, as can be seen in his requirement that all Inquisition sentences were to receive royal assent before they could be carried out. On the other hand Pombal attempted to curb the anti-Semitic bias in the Inquisition's activities by abolishing the distinction between New and Old Christian in 1769.

[1] For a different interpretation of Pombal and his policies see vol. VII, ch. XII, pp. 290–1.

In spite of the attempts of some historians to reduce Pombal's economic legislation to a carefully thought-out plan, it is clear that he himself had no coherent programme and simply worked from day to day. He believed that Portugal suffered from Britian's pre-eminence in the Portuguese domestic and colonial trade, and so he wished to revive the Portuguese economy by protecting it against the commercial privileges of Britain. His mistake lay in attributing Britain's predominance to treaty privileges instead of to superior capital resources and the quality of her goods. He thought he could redress the situation by legislation and the founding of commercial institutions. Like Spain, Portugal suffered from a balance-of-payments problem: she was importing—particularly in the way of English manufactures—more than she was exporting—mostly wine—and the balance had to be paid in gold from Brazil. Pombal prohibited the export of gold and imposed restrictions on trade, confining its benefits to privileged groups by creating large companies with a monopoly in certain regions, like the General Wines of the Upper Douro Company established in 1756. In the same year he also established a *Junta do Comercio* with control over all matters relating to commerce, and the new agency began to restrict English imports. However, in the absence of capital resources and a strong middle class, legislation could achieve little. His industrial policy attempted to combine direct state action in royal factories with support to private manufactures in wool, linen, glass and paper, but it was too derivative and theoretical to succeed. Pombal in no way initiated an industrial revolution.[1]

In education too there were many paper plans, like the founding of public schools in 1759 without, however, the staff to teach in them. In 1761 Pombal founded a College of Nobles with detailed regulations for the curriculum of a hundred boys of noble birth, but the programme was too overloaded to be practicable. In 1768 the Royal Board of Censorship was established with the right to approve all books and papers in Portugal; in 1771 it was granted direction of primary education. In 1772 Pombal personally overhauled the courses of study at Coimbra University in an attempt to bring them up to date. Yet he was no Encyclopaedist, and the works of Hobbes, Locke, Voltaire and Rousseau, among others, were still proscribed. On the other hand in 1773 he abolished slavery in the new generation born of slave parents in Portugal.

In February 1777 José I died and was succeeded by his eldest daughter, Maria I, who like her father was uninterested in and incapable of government. Lacking the confidence of the new monarch, whom he had tried to exclude from the succession, Pombal offered his resignation in March 1777. This was accepted and at the age of seventy-eight he retired to the small town from which he took his title. Various charges of peculation and despotism were brought against him and he was found guilty though

[1] See J. de Macedo, *A situação económica no tempo de Pombal* (Porto, 1951), p. 263.

pardoned. He died in 1782. Meanwhile the new reign had begun with the sensational re-emergence from prisons and convents of hundreds of the victims of Pombal's terrorism. The queen also reversed Pombal's policy towards the Távoras and the other aristocratic malcontents of the previous reign; between 1777 and 1780 they were declared innocent of regicide, released from prison and rehabilitated. Under the influence of her consort, Pedro III, who was also her uncle, she provided pensions to deported Jesuits and individual Jesuits were allowed to return. Owing to her insanity, however, Maria I ceased to govern in 1792 and her son, the prince of Brazil, ruled in her name, assuming the title of Prince Regent in 1799.

The re-emergence of the aristocracy was also seen in the appointment to the government of two prominent nobles, Angeja and Cerveira. The most urgent problems facing them were the government's financial deficit and the adverse balance of trade. But before these problems were solved they were overshadowed by events abroad. The French Revolution struck similar terror in the Portuguese government as it did in absolutist régimes elsewhere in Europe. After the failure of a French attempt to secure Portugal's neutrality, a provisional treaty was signed with Spain in July 1793 for mutual aid against France, while in September a treaty of mutual aid and protection of commerce was arranged with Britain. With these reassuring provisions, Portugal sent a force to assist Spain on the Catalan front.

2. THE ITALIAN STATES

Superficially, the peninsula of Italy is a unity, bounded by sea and mountain. A closer look at the map reveals an agglomeration of regions, rather than a geographic whole; its structure is dominated by the Apennine chain and the great contrast between north and south. In the eighteenth century, its diversity was very great. Italy contained societies almost isolated one from another and shaped by climate and topography into startlingly different forms. The rich Po valley had little in common with the semi-desert of the Apulian Capitanata; the Legations were rich while the papal territories west of the Apennines were poor. Potenza is sixty miles from Salerno but has one of the coldest climates in Italy. The lives of Italians varied as much as their landscape and climate; at a time when Arthur Young found the farms around Lodi fat and prosperous, men were living in caves near Otranto. Even language helped to divide the peninsula. Twenty-odd dialects made it uncertain that a man speaking Italian—the speech of Tuscany—would be understood in the countryside. Nor were these differences blurred by eighteenth-century communications. The one good road in the kingdom of Naples led out of it, to Rome. In some parts, the towns were barely linked to one another; they often represented yet other divisions, historical and political, which had broken up the peninsula still more. There were more great cities than in other countries but no metropolis drew the cultural life of Italy to a focus. The big cities provided, at best, provincial capitals and most of the small towns of Italy slumbered in *campanilismo*.

In such a setting, a few might think of themselves as culturally Italian, but most men knew only that they were Bolognese, Venetian, or, if their sense of group membership went beyond the walls of their town, Piedmontese or Calabrians. They knew that (in many different senses) they were the subjects of certain rulers; the political framework which enclosed Italy's provincialism had been settled since 1748. There were two kingdoms, Sardinia and the Two Sicilies, the grand-duchy of Tuscany, the smaller duchies of Parma and Modena, and the little principality of Piombino. There were three ossified republics: Venice, Genoa, Lucca (San Marino was so tiny that it barely merits consideration in the same scale, yet it has outlived its sister-republics). Austria ruled the former duchies of Milan and Mantua in the Lombard plain. And finally there were the Papal States.

Such a list hides important structural differences. In most of these states, it is true, the principle of sovereignty was becoming clearer and most of them were to be touched by the techniques of 'enlightened despotism'. But resemblances did not go much further than this. In the first place, in spite of governmental and legal rationalisation, most of these states were not solid units. The very name of the Legations emphasised the difference between them and the patrimony of St Peter, while the formal tie between the components of Tuscany was little more than a common allegiance to the person of the grand-duke. Although in the Venetian provinces the administrative system was reasonably coherent, there was a big difference between the government of Treviso, proverbially loyal, and that of the fiercely independent nobles of Friuli. Feudal immunity, privilege, legal diversification and practical isolation puzzle the historian who is looking for an Austinian sovereign in these states, and the same facts continuously emphasised to Italians the local and provincial nature of their public life. They also explain great variations of power and stamina among the states. Although, for example, the three republics were all governed by tight oligarchies, they faced very different problems. Venice was unable to adapt her political structure to the decline of her commerce; few statesmen believed she could long endure. The Genoese still commanded some of the resources of a great entrepôt but faced grave political problems in Corsica; moreover, the oligarchs had been regarded with suspicion since the republic's capitulation to Austria in 1746. Only Lucca seemed stable. The big monarchies were more powerful than the republics and could compete in European struggles. Yet Sardinia, formally feudal but with a highly centralised administration, was a far more formidable power than the Two Sicilies, the deployment of whose resources was encumbered by privileges and the particularism of the island. Tuscany was a special case; Pietro Leopoldo was to provide a model for 'enlightened' administration which only Austrian Lombardy could rival. The Papal States, on the other hand, were a byword for administrative confusion and suffered from the imponderable disadvantage of being ruled by a priest in an age of enlightenment. Distinctions could be multiplied, but to do so would be pointless. It is sufficient to repeat that the first great strategic factor shaping the lives of eighteenth-century Italians was, as it had long been, political, social and topographical diversity. It is, therefore, not easy to discern general historical trends. For the most part, Italians lived in 1763 in small societies which imposed an intense local pressure on their consciousness. There is little point in ferreting in this diversity for the seeds of Italian nationalism.

Nor is there any point in searching for the seeds of liberty. Italians had few guarantees either of civic or political freedom. Where estates or parliaments existed—as, for instance, in Sicily or the island of Sardinia—their functions were rigidly circumscribed or they merely sheltered the privileges of small cliques. In the republics and monarchies alike, legislative control was concentrated in the hands of a few persons. Neither existing institutions nor the class-structure made the development of truly representative bodies likely. What the Italians possessed instead of political liberty was the insulation from centralised authority provided by the incoherence of the state-structures. The undergrowth of corporate and local privilege and the little clots of power in the municipal and corporate oligarchies were effective restraints on government. Beyond this, Italians enjoyed precarious freedoms which, though sometimes extensive, hung on the goodwill or the indifference of their rulers. In 1763, political Italy was a mass of old-fashioned 'liberties' and the modern state had still to establish itself.

Nearly a half-century of peace (from 1748 to 1796) made possible a great number of experiments in economics and administration within the states, and also preserved Italy's fragmented political system. The peace rested, fundamentally, on the ending of Habsburg–Bourbon rivalry at the Diplomatic Revolution. When the two great patrons of Italian troublemakers, France and Austria, ceased to compete for Italian satellites, an expanding Sardinia lost her chance of auctioning herself as an ally. No Italian ruler was powerful enough to shake the Italian settlement of 1748 and, except for the transfer of Corsica to France by Genoa in 1768, no important territorial changes took place in Italy until 1796. This stability was not troubled by the newness of the ruling dynasties. Although the Bourbons had only recently arrived in Naples and Parma, and the Habsburgs in Tuscany and Lombardy, they quickly assimilated themselves to their new settings and were soon firmly settled. Minor changes in the balance of influence might be attributed to the marriage of Maria Carolina (the daughter of Maria Theresa) to Ferdinand of Naples in 1768 and the bequeathing of Modena to the Habsburgs on the extinction of the house of Este, but they are not important. Nor did the impact of French cultural influences in Parma or of British commerce and diplomacy in Sicily and Naples disturb the peninsula. Its unchanging political structure has no history, therefore; the significance of these years has to be sought elsewhere.

Italy shared one great change with the rest of Europe: her population rose rapidly in the eighteenth century. Precise figures are hard to establish but it seems that the increase in Italy added about seven millions to a population of eleven millions at the beginning of the century. This rise in numbers must have pressed hard upon resources because Italian economic life was backward. Although agriculture was immeasurably its most important component, the economy was dominated by the institutions of an earlier age, when the cities had been the basic units of the economic structure. The '*economia cittadina*' of the city-states had continued to dominate economic thinking and legislation long after Italian industry had collapsed and world trade had shifted away from the Italian ports. Italy's share of international trade was never lower than in the eighteenth century. Her industries have little importance, therefore, in the history of this period. They were mainly north of the Po, and did little to provide a livelihood for a rising population. Arms were still made at Brescia and the silks of Piedmont or the woollens of Lombardy and the Veneto had importance for their regions. The beginnings of modern factory organisation can be seen in some textile enterprises which brought together hundreds, and, in one or two cases, even more than a thousand workers. Yet these nuclei seem insignificant beside the flourishing export industries of earlier centuries. The ports, of course, were important as employers of labour. (Four of them, Genoa, Palermo, Naples and Venice, had more than 100,000 inhabitants by 1800 and Rome and Milan were the only other two Italian cities in this class.) Yet only Leghorn seems to have known the prosperity of earlier ages. And what is known of Italian exports simply emphasises the predominance of agriculture in the whole economy.

That agriculture was as varied as the regions themselves. The main products were grain, oil, rice, wine, silk, hemp and flax, and their relative importance varied from area to area. Silk-growing was mainly a supplementary activity of the northern peasants: it was very important to them and the export of raw silk to France rose spectacularly during the century. In her food crops Italy was always supposed by foreigners to be a land blessed by nature and it is likely that the peninsula as a whole was self-supporting, or nearly so, in foodstuffs. Yet although the population rose, there was famine from time to time. The major grain-growing areas were in Lombardy, Lucca, Venice, Naples and Sicily and they hoped to export their surplus. Genoa, Parma and Modena always expected to import grain and the Papal States could only avoid doing so in the rare event of all their territories having good harvests in the same year. Cattle had to be imported into north Italy from central Europe; livestock was even scarcer in the rest of the peninsula, except for the sheep-runs of the south. The diversity of conditions could be helpful: it was said in Naples that the crops never failed on both sides of the mountains in the same year. All in all, it seems that Italian agriculture was a successful industry in that it was able to feed a growing population.

Nevertheless, this global picture is an artificial one. A mass of the period's agronomical writing draws attention to backwardnesses. Production did not stagnate, but it remained dismally low for a country envied by foreigners. Natural factors were sometimes to blame. The period opened badly in Sicily, for example, where the crops were diseased in 1763. Many people died in the resulting famine and in 1764 the same thing happened at Naples. This threw the supply of grain into confusion all over Italy, but the damage was not so great as in 1766 when about two-thirds of the crops were destroyed almost everywhere. Because of the low level of the peasant's diet a grain shortage was not by itself overwhelming, but it could mean death for many thousands. These bad years were exceptional, perhaps, but scarcity was something that often recurred. A distinguished Tuscan agronomist said that he expected the grand-duchy to be short of grain one year in every three. Besides disease, frost, drought, flood and earthquake also took their toll. Even in the prosperous setting of Lombard agriculture the imperial tax commissioners allowed abatements in the land-tax to compensate for calamity. Variations of soil and climate meant that natural disasters of this sort struck unevenly. The wide spread of harvesting dates—from May to mid-July—indicates the variety of Italian agriculture. While five crops of hay in a year were taken from some parts of the Milanese, cattle feed was eked out with leaves elsewhere and sometimes leaves made up the whole of it. Although its farming was technically more backward, Sicily produced better corn than the Neapolitan mainland, thanks to better soil. Marshes afflicted some regions; there were 40,000 acres of Pontine marshes and others almost as bad on the lower Po and Reno and around Lake Commacchio. Besides wasting land, they bred malaria. Some areas were often flooded; this could mean not merely the loss of a year's production but also the ruin of the land for long periods. Sometimes flooding was combined, ironically, with a lack of good water or a short rainy season of heavy downpour, as it was near Ferrara. One of the consequences of decades of failure to solve these problems had been the stripping of the hillsides of their vegetation and the appearance of deforested and eroded wastes.

These natural handicaps, unevenly distributed and unpredictable, were not always offset by technical advances. Knowledge and skill were available;[1] some Tuscan landlords were experimenting with drainage and

---

[1] The *Accademia dei Georgofili*, one of the most famous of Italian learned societies was founded in 1753 at Florence and devoted itself to agricultural improvement.

rotation long before their government took a hand. In some places good farming was the rule. Careful tending made ungrateful land fruitful in Piedmont and the hydraulic achievements of the highly organised Po valley were the fundamental explanation of its rich crops. Yet the general impression is of technical backwardness in a land of potential wealth. The Lombard irrigation system might be good, but the Roman one had all but collapsed. Bad rotations were common. Good stock was rare. Even the simple use of obvious resources was sometimes surprisingly neglected; only in these years did peat begin to be used as fuel. The explanation of this backwardness must be an elaborate and complicated one and has yet to be made. Besides simple conservatism and superstition it must take account of the attractiveness or unattractiveness of improvement schemes to capital. But it must also take account of the basic vice of the Italian economy, the fragmentation which was the legacy of the domination of the cities. Italian agriculture cannot, as a practical fact, be treated as a single food-producing industry.

The consequences of fragmentation were small markets and artificial prices. These kept production at little more than subsistence level. Poor communications were another result; it is significant that prosperity was highest in an area with good water communications, the Lombard plain. Local boundaries prevented regional action on regional problems; the Reno was of concern to both Ferrara and Bologna but they quarrelled bitterly with one another over it. A chaos of currencies and separate systems of weights and measures exhausted the businessman whose transactions cut across political frontiers. Civic privilege and selfishness also interfered deliberately with the free flow of trade; Genoa would allow no corn to be landed at Spezia, Verona forbade the importation of wine from the Vicentino, and all Istria's foreign imports had to come through the port of Venice. Everywhere, the natural interests of an agricultural economy were sacrificed to the petrified relics of the town-centered economics of the Middle Ages. The most serious hindrances to trade were the tolls and customs-barriers, which were only gradually and partially removed during these years. Their incidence varied; light in Piedmont, they were heavy in Genoa. In Naples, there were hundreds of them and their rates varied capriciously. The decline of the Lombard provinces of Venice seems to have been at least in part attributable to her customs policy. Grain had special restraints placed upon it. Most governments approached the grain trade with their eyes on public order and state finance, rather than on commercial prosperity. Regulations against export were common and most states had officers charged to procure an adequate supply. Yet although growers were compelled to take their grain to public granaries, and the grinding and baking processes were minutely regulated, governments rarely succeeded in obtaining an assured supply. Recourse to compulsory purchase in Naples in the shortage of 1764 only drove what little grain was available into hiding. The sale of export permits and of baking rights at Rome led to corrupt administration and higher bread prices. All that can be said in mitigation of such regulations is that they were tempered in practice by evasion and violation. The customs-barriers, for example, made smuggling almost a separate industry. None the less, in spite of poor administration, such over-regulation was a heavy burden on an economy whose outstanding characteristic was near-immobility.

In spite of regional differences, this economy supported a similar population structure all over Italy. At the top was a small dominant élite. Not enough work has yet been done to describe it but its general characteristics were, usually, that its members were formally noble and that their power was mainly based on landed wealth, buttressed by high office in church and state. The origins of the noble families differed widely: they might lie in feudal tenures, in an urban patriciate, or in recent creation. In 1763 they still sometimes possessed corporate institutions with which to defend their status and privileges. Some nobles and members of the traditional élite did not exercise political power, while others provided a true ruling class; there were many local variations in their status and behaviour. In some parts of Naples and in Friuli nobles enjoyed an almost medieval independence; four out of five Neapolitans were said to live under feudal jurisdiction and many were liable to personal labour services. Yet in Lombardy feudalism had practically disappeared. In Venice, many of the patricians farmed out their estates in the *terraferma* and had the usual privileges and disadvantages of absentee landlords. Lombard nobles, on the other hand, lived among their tenants and labourers and often enjoyed cordial relationships with them. In Piedmont, large estates were the exception; in the Neapolitan hinterland they were the rule.

One general characteristic of this élite must be noted. It showed no willingness to share its powers. It really had no rivals. There was no middle class generally aspiring to power. The low level of economic activity held back the development of a commercial and industrial bourgeoisie; such rich bourgeois as appeared became landowners. There was usually little danger from the professional and administrative men as a class (the threat they presented as the servants of monarchs was a different matter) although the lawyers were important at Naples. The result of this was that so far as political life existed, it was a matter of faction-fighting and rivalries within a ruling class, or of nobles opposing acts of government which were not in accordance with their class interest. The only other possible rival for power was the church and here, too, the noble class was firmly entrenched among the higher clergy.

What was left outside this class was a comparatively small urban population and the great mass of peasants. In the towns lived many thousands of near-proletarians in many occupations. Comparatively few worked in big factories; those who had industrial occupations were more likely to be found working as masters or journeymen, whether for themselves or for a big entrepreneur who supplied their materials. A large proportion of the town-dwellers were servants or in other ways clients of the nobility. Others were beggars: the restraints of the guilds kept down opportunities of employment. But the demographic base of Italy was its peasantry. Different tenures and different legal systems meant that they varied from the wretched settlers of the Pontine marshes to the comparatively affluent farmers of the Alpine foothills. In Sicily, the peasants were mainly town-dwellers, in Lombardy they lived in the countryside. Some were for practical purposes completely dependent on their feudal overlords, while others were migrant labourers. *Mezzadria* (share-cropping) was common in Lombardy and Tuscany; under it the landlord often took a close and encouraging interest in his tenants' cultivation. Some peasants were still formally serfs. The one thing which was true of most of them was that they were poor. Moreover, they seemed to be getting poorer. The number of landless labourers (*braccianti*) grew during the eighteenth century. In the countryside there was much violence, rural insurrection and brigandage, although some areas were more turbulent than others. The peasant's standard of living was low; he seems to have lived usually on a diet of maize or millet, oil, beans and salt. (The potato was slow to establish itself in Italy.) The occasional hints of a 'rural bourgeoisie' rising out of the common herd do not dispute the general prevalence of rural poverty outside a few lucky areas. And there was nowhere for the peasant to go; the towns could offer him nothing except the chance to beg.

The second great conditioning fact of Italian society in these years was, therefore, the economic and social immobility which pervaded its fragmented political structure. Not surprisingly, this immobility was questioned. Changes were demanded by the economists whose demands were part of the history of the Enlightenment in Italy. The movement of thought to which they contributed was the most dynamic force in the general history of Italy in these years. Economics was by no means the only interest of the Italian thinkers.

The *settecento* was one of the great creative periods of Italian intellectual history; certainly the ideas of the age are its most interesting feature. This chapter must confine itself to considering the instrumental importance of ideas in changing Italian society but they must be placed in their historical context. The setting, in the first place, was especially favourable. The long period of peace left Italy easily accessible to foreign books and foreign travellers; Italians, for their part, travelled abroad. The foreign dynasties, too, brought servants with them; the court of Parma was especially well stocked with French artists and savants. Moreover a wide tolerance existed for the circulation of advanced ideas. The press was censored and the Inquisition still exercised its waning powers in some states, but the persecution of ideas was unusual. The formal catholicism of the socially

powerful was tempered by scepticism. The very subdivision of the peninsula may have had the fortunate result that governments rarely co-
operated to restrict the circulation of ideas. The cultural élite was, perhaps,
the only group outside the Church with a sense of community transcend-
ing locality. Although visitors from France might find Italian *salons* somewhat provincial, the existence of a real Italian cultural élite was important.
Its weakness was that it was likely to follow fashion (and could be taken
in by a Cagliostro); it was also true that *Il Caffè*, the most important journalistic enterprise of the Italian Enlightenment, survived only for two years.
Yet, however immature it might be, an audience existed for the speculations of the Italian equivalents of the *philosophes*. Important social resources were available to the cause of Enlightenment. Education was, on
the whole, well-endowed in Italy and many of the most prominent Italian
thinkers held university chairs at a time when the Italian universities were
full of vigour. Beside the universities were libraries and academies which
helped in the circulation of ideas. But the most important single fact in
obtaining support for the ideas of the Enlightenment was that governments wished to employ men of ideas. There were many posts available
in public administration. Some men passed from the service of one ruler
to that of another; Pompeo Neri[1] began his administrative career in
Tuscany, then helped to reform Lombard local government for Maria
Theresa, and finally went back to Tuscany to work for her son.

The men of the Enlightenment therefore worked in a favourable climate.
There were a great many of them and they are difficult to characterise as
a group. They owed much to the literary and historiographical work of
their predecessors, above all to Muratori,[2] but their own achievements
were usually either in the natural sciences or in administration and jurisprudence. Of science, where the work of Galvani,[3] Volta[4] and Spallanzani[5] was of European distinction, no more need be said here; its
immediate impact on Italian life was small, although its scientific import-

[1] Pompeo Neri, born Florence, 1706, was professor of public law at Pisa before entering
the service of the grand-duke in 1735. He went to Milan in 1748 and was president of the
Tuscan Council of State in 1770. He died in 1776.

[2] Ludovico Antonio Muratori, born Vignola, 1672; the greatest Italian scholar of the
century. From 1695 to 1700 he worked in the Ambrosiana, at Milan; thereafter he was
employed in the royal library at Modena until his death in 1752. Of his very large number
of publications, the most famous are the *Rerum italicarum scriptores* (1723–38), the *Anti-
quitates italicae medii aevi* (1738–43), and the *Annali d'Italia* (1744–9).

[3] Luigi Galvani, born Bologna, 1737, taught anatomy at the university and made observations of the physiological effects of electricity which led to an important controversy with
Volta, q.v. He died in 1798.

[4] Alessandro Volta, born Como, 1745, the most famous Italian physicist of his day, made
important discoveries in many fields. He taught at Pavia and conducted a long series of
important experiments during his controversy with Galvani; among his inventions were the
condenser and the voltaic pile. He died in 1827.

[5] Lazzaro Spallanzani, born Scandiano, 1729. A biologist who made important contributions to embryology and the study of the circulatory system and of digestion; he taught
at Reggio, Modena and Pavia. He died in 1799.

ance was great. But the work done in jurisprudence, penology, economics and history by men like Palmieri,[1] Filangieri,[2] Pietro Verri[3] and Beccaria[4] (to mention only a handful) was immediately effective. With the exception of Beccaria's book *Dei delitti e delle pene* (1764) the impact of these men was Italian rather than European. One phrase may be thought to have made history: *maggior felicità divisa nel maggior numero*. But the Italian Enlightenment was before all else Italian, the eyes of its writers focused on Italian problems. Their work is stamped by a sense of immediate context. Utilitarian and relativist in its assumptions, its aim was usually to achieve *felicità pubblica* and it was undogmatic about the means to the end. Institutions were to be judged by their effects: Verri and Galiani[5] took into other fields Beccaria's penological principle of judging by results. This made them willing to work through existing governments and to take employment with them. They had no worries about the potential dangers of this until the reforms of Joseph II reached their climax. Meanwhile they took service with the monarchs in order to carry out their programme. This is a misleading term in that the precise aims of the reformers varied from state to state. Yet they were based on common assumptions. The *felicità pubblica* to which the reformers aspired was largely a matter of economic improvement. Furthermore, this improvement was believed to be attainable by freeing property and labour from restraints on their free employment. Free trade was tempered by pragmatism; both Carli[6] and Galiani insisted that circumstances should alter cases. But most of the reformers found *laisser-faire* arguments persuasive. It is not a paradox that the reformers also wanted to strengthen the powers of their states. Confident of the success of the policies they wanted governments to carry out, they everywhere sought to concentrate state power and improve its machinery. Obstacles to the sovereignty of the prince were to be weeded out.

---

[1] Giuseppe Palmieri, born Martignano, 1721. A professional soldier who became in later life a civil servant and from 1791 the director of the Neapolitan Council of Finance. He died in 1793.

[2] Gaetano Filangieri, born Naples, 1752. His *Scienza della legislazione* (1780–9) is his claim to remembrance. Most of his life was spent in study and he died in 1788, shortly after joining the Council of Finance at Naples.

[3] Pietro Verri, born Milan, 1728. Engaged in work for the Austrian administration 1766–86, he also produced an important body of publications on economics and finance. His major administrative achievement was the abolition of the Lombard farm of taxes (1770) and his most famous publication was the *Storia di Milano*, the second volume of which appeared two years after his death in 1797.

[4] Cesare Beccaria, born Milan, 1738. Besides his most famous book, he wrote on economic subjects and lectured on political economy as a professor at the Palatine School in Milan. He also served in the Austrian administration. He died in 1794.

[5] Ferdinando Galiani, born Chieti, 1728. Abbé, diplomatic agent, civil servant and man of letters. His most famous book is the *Dialogues sur le commerce des blés* (1770), published just after his return to Naples from Paris, where he had been secretary to the Neapolitan embassy. He afterwards held several important administrative posts and died in 1787.

[6] Gian Rinaldo Carli, born Capodistria, 1720. Writer on economic subjects and employed in the Austrian administration at Milan, where he died 1795.

In practice, few states closely fitted the model of enlightened despotism believed in by the reformers, except, perhaps, Tuscany. Elsewhere, the pace and success of reform greatly varied. The concentration of governmental power which was achieved by the Austrian in Lombardy can be contrasted with Tanucci's[1] failure to uproot the abuses of feudal privilege in Naples. Moreover, reform was not exclusively a matter of 'enlightened' influences; almost everywhere, reform followed the need for revenue. Sometimes it occurred in very conservative states like Sardinia or Venice and it was certainly not unknown before 1763. Nor were rulers always in close harmony with their reforming advisers, as the reaction to Joseph II's reforms in Lombardy showed. Nevertheless, much that was done in these years is attributable only to the influence direct and indirect of the Enlightenment. It was the great dynamic of Italian life.

The strengthening of central government in the states went furthest in Lombardy and Tuscany. New representative bodies for local government were created there, but with strictly limited and revocable powers. Leopold wished his people to be self-governing, but he was unique; elsewhere governments were too anxious to cut down local autonomy to give it a new lodgement. The centralisation of the judicial system took place in many states and the Neapolitan government abolished a number of privileged courts. In Lombardy, the attack on the local magistracies was connected with fiscal reforms; elsewhere it was municipal rather than noble privilege which was the obstacle to fiscal reform. Sometimes economic policy pressed governments in the same direction. A right to levy tolls, for example, was not compatible with the removal of restraints on trade.

In economic matters, the governments of the states had their own customs systems to reform. Tuscany was their leader. In 1766 grain was freed from all internal restrictions. Then, in 1775 its export was allowed and the *abbondanza* or office of public supply was wound up, and, finally, in 1781, all the internal customs-barriers were abolished. Other states followed—Lombardy in 1785, Naples in 1791, and even the Papal States carried out a partial abolition. Another target was the mass of corporations and guilds which hampered trade; Tuscany abolished hers in 1770, and Sicily and Lombardy followed suit. This was another side of the liberation of the economy from the stranglehold of the cities. There were also reforms of such legal institutions as mortmain, primogeniture and *fideicommessi* (entails), although the last two had, in most instances, to wait for reform by the revolutionary governments. When the positive work done by governments in promoting economic improvement by drainage, cultivation and improvement schemes is added to this, the total

---

[1] Reonardo Tanucci, born Stia, 1698, taught law at Pisa before going to Naples where he served first Charles IV and then in the Council of Regency and as minister until 1776. His policy was strongly anti-curialist. He died in 1783.

achievement, though it varied in its effectiveness, is impressive. It undoubtedly accelerated the transition to the regional economy.

Not surprisingly, education greatly interested the reformers. The appearance of administrators as able as those who filled the cadres of government during these years is in itself eloquent evidence of the fundamental soundness of the universities. Several of these men had either taught or studied at Pisa or Padua. The University of Pavia, the subject of special reforms between 1771 and 1773 and later the centre of the reform of theological studies, was of even greater importance. It was in their educational work that the concern of some of the rulers for moral improvement appeared most clearly. It also had more banal embodiments—in Leopold's priggish attitude toward gambling, for instance, or Joseph's concern over the dangers of wearing stays in convents—but no account of the Italian Enlightenment and its expressions would be balanced if it did not take account of its pervading concern for moral improvement. This, oddly enough, was one of the features which brought the reformers most decisively into conflict with traditional and conservative forces. Self-interest determined such resistance as that of the Senate of Bologna to the papal *catasto*,[1] or of the patricians of Milan to the reforms of Joseph II, and led the barons of Sicily to stir up popular disorders against their reforming governors. But the ideas which animated many of the clerical opponents of the reformers had much more to them and raised more fundamental questions than those of utility and self-interest.

The problem of church and state is the nearest equivalent available in this period to a thread of conventional political narrative. It was a general influence in Italy, although its particular embodiments might vary, and as such deserves consideration as a shaping factor of the same order as economic structure or Enlightenment. It is much more complex than can be suggested by a simple antithesis. The papacy and the episcopate were by no means in principle hostile to all the aims of the reformers or their monarchical patrons. If only for financial reasons, the Papal States could not afford to be; their poverty demanded economic improvement. Of the three popes of this period, Clement XIII (1758–69), Clement XIV (1769–74) and Pius VI (1775–99), the last, at least, was anxious to be remembered as a reformer and builder, who devoted much attention to economic matters and public works. (He had good precedents in the pontificate of Benedict XIV.) The main factors hampering economic advance in the Papal States were clerical privilege—which the pope could hardly do anything to curb—and the persistence of local divisions and privileges, above all in the Legations. This reinforced the intricate customs system, which, through the grant of exceptions, tended to work in favour of a few individuals and corporations. Pius reacted to this in much the same way as any temporal ruler would have done. In 1777 he abolished all internal

[1] A cadastral survey of land, undertaken for tax purposes.

customs except in the Legations and he poured money into public works, above all into draining the Pontine marshes and into building highways. He also set up industrial schools. Even though the achievements of his pontificate were not outstanding they at least demonstrate that there was no necessary opposition between papacy and governmental reform.

Nor was there anything new in the existence of quarrels between church and state in Italy. A long regalist tradition at Naples had nourished a school of polemicists of whom Giannone had been the greatest figure and had forced important concessions from the papacy long before 1763. In Venice, too, there were long-standing quarrels; *In coena domini*[1] could not be published there. It is important, therefore, to distinguish what is new in the violence of church and state rivalry in this period.

Something must be attributed to the whole climate of enlightened thought. However many thinkers and writers might remain good Catholics, the European background of their age was secular and rationalist. The papacy was in the unhappy position of appearing to some of its critics to offend *de natura* against the standards of reason and common sense. It was against this background of a generalised lay spirit that specific controversies arose. Clerical landholding, for example, was disliked by the economists; they believed that it held down productivity and that mortmain restricted a free market in land. The theoreticians of population regarded celibacy with alarm: one of them spoke of the *pestifero celibato* and almost all of them wished to limit the numbers of the clergy, especially the regulars. But legal questions aroused the fiercest polemic. The tendency towards the assertion of unchecked sovereign power was cut across by an institution such as sanctuary, by the existence of canon law and its operation over the laity in such matters as marriage and testamentary questions, by the extra-territorial jurisdiction over their members of the orders, and by the predominance of clerics in education.

On these questions quarrels erupted all over Italy. At Naples, Tanucci was always personally irreconcilable, but so his successors proved to be, too; many Neapolitan sees were vacant at the end of this period because no appointments were made to them. Joseph II made Pius swallow his choice of archbishop in Milan. In Tuscany Francis had even left parishes vacant as a way of rearranging them. His successor, Leopold, limited the right of sanctuary. Venice sequestered church land, attacked mortmain and limited the numbers of religious festivals. Modena legislated against mortmain and imposed clerical taxation. In Parma the economic danger of clerical landholding was met by forbidding mortmain in 1764. Moreover, royal permission was now required for the publication of papal letters and bulls. It was this which helped to bring to a head the first great

---

[1] A papal bull published annually on Maundy Thursday (hence its name) which contained a collection of censures of excommunication against those committing certain offences, absolution from which was reserved to the pope. It was last published in 1768.

crisis of church and state relations in these years, that over the order of the Jesuits.

Most of the story of the dissolution of the Jesuits belongs properly to European history. Their unpopularity with European rulers had been growing and they had been suppressed in Portugal and France before the Bourbon governments of Naples and Parma turned on them in 1767. Clement XIII had already shown sympathy to the society. Now, in 1768, he decided to reply to the reforming legislation by excommunicating the duke of Parma and by publishing a *monitorio* forbidding the faithful to obey the Parmesan laws on mortmain and clerical taxation. The Bourbon courts promptly closed ranks. Naples matched the French seizure of Avignon and the Venaissin by occupying Benevento and Pontecorvo, two papal enclaves in Neapolitan territory. All the Bourbon courts together then demanded the abolition of the Society of Jesus. The death of Clement XIII (1769) was followed by the election of Clement XIV, in the choice of whom Bourbon influence was supposed to have been decisive. In 1773 he issued the bull *Dominus ac redemptor* which dissolved the society; the enclaves were then returned.

The significance of this episode lies in the effectiveness of the united front shown by the Bourbon monarchies and the demonstration it gave of the new sharpness in church and state relations. It was supposed that Clement XIV would have been a pope willing to make concessions to the new temper, but he died in 1774 (perhaps it is not surprising that he was believed to have been poisoned by the Jesuits). Pius, his successor, was less ready to make concessions and under his pontificate new quarrels of church and state arose. In Tuscany Leopold had already followed up his attacks on sanctuary by limiting money payments to Rome. In 1788 relations with Naples deteriorated so far that the papal nuncio was expelled. In Lombardy, Joseph abolished sanctuary, the Inquisition, clerical judicial immunity, and mortmain; all these things could be paralleled elsewhere in Italy, but they were carried through in the Austrian provinces with great drive and thoroughness and were accompanied by the suppression of convents and seminaries, the annulment of *In coena domini* and the appointment of Joseph's archbishop in Milan. Even a visit by Pius to Vienna did not shake Joseph's determination.

After 1775, then, in spite of the concession over the Jesuits, things did not go better for the papacy—and its troubles were not confined to Italy. Yet this did not lead to a weakening of Pius' stand. What seems to have taken place may be described as a crystallising of the church-and-state quarrel: both sides became more resistant and intransigent. Some who had previously been anti-curial now became supporters of the papacy because they feared that Catholicism itself might be in danger. On the other hand, many of those who had previously only been opponents of the Jesuits now became anti-papal, especially when Pius was believed to be influenced by former Jesuits behind the curtain. It is at this point that it is necessary to say something about the Italian Jansenists, if only because of the amount of attention and ink that has been spent on them by Italian historians in the last thirty years.

There are times when the words 'Jansenism' and 'Jansenist' seem to be extended by some contemporary and later writers to include adherence to almost every shade of progressive opinion. Though this is only over-enthusiasm for a general explanation, its excuse is the confused nature of Italian Jansenism and it is misleading. Jansenism was ambiguous from the start; it had many aspects and not all Jansenists felt equally concerned over all of them. It was from one aspect a theological movement, concerned to reassert and purify Augustinian doctrines. It was also a moral movement, seeking to reform clerical discipline and lay manners. It was liturgical and ecclesiastical in deploring the cult of saints and vindicating the authority of bishops. It was also often political, first in an anti-Jesuit and then an anti-curial sense. These aspects are inseparable, though distinguishable. It is also worth remembering that Italian Jansenism never produced a memorable book or a great reformer; it had no heroic figure of the stature of the great French leaders. Too much has been claimed for its influence. The true importance of Jansenism in Italy was twofold: as an influence inside the Italian church and as an anti-papal force in alliance with the reforming monarchies.

Jansenist influence inside the church had been important at Rome itself. Identifications are hard to make. Cardinal Marefoschi, for example, was the centre of an important group, although it is uncertain whether he should be called a Jansenist. He was, it is true, closely connected with the leaders of the anti-Jesuit party at Rome and himself organised the supression of the society. He appointed Jansenist theologians like Zola[1] and Tamburini[2] to important teaching posts, and he had taken part in conferences with representatives of the schismatic Church of Utrecht with which many Jansenists were in communication. Under Clement XIV such activities might even be considered to have papal approval; he was sympathetic to many of the causes advocated by the Jansenists. In 1765 Clement had been a member of the Congregation of Rites which opposed the concession of an office of the Sacred Heart and it was under his pontificate that the representative of Utrecht came to Rome. While he fitted an earlier eighteenth-century tradition of papal encouragement of intellectual and speculative endeavour, such a tradition had certainly lapsed under Clement XIII, who, to the Jansenists, appeared a desert between the two oases of Benedict XIV and Clement XIV.

[1] Giuseppe Zola, born Concesio, 1739, theologian, rector of seminary at Pavia 1788–99. He died at Pavia in 1806.

[2] Pietro Tamburini, born Brescia, 1737. Called to the Irish College at Rome, he taught later at Pavia (1778–92). In 1794 he published his *Lettere teologico-politiche* and he worked later for the Napoleonic kingdom of Italy. He died at Pavia in 1827.

With such important sympathy available to them, it is surprising that the Jansenists achieved so little. But this perhaps reveals something important about their movement. Their greatest victory was the dissolution of the Jesuits, yet this was not won by their pressure but by that of the Bourbon monarchs on a pope who was at least no friend to the Jesuits. The Italian Jansenists were too diverse to be effective, because they were predominantly scholars and theologians, interested in intellectual and critical questions and going little beyond this until the pontificate of Pius VI. Then their anti-curial views gave them some cohesion.

In the late 1770s, although there was in no sense a sharp break, there was a change of atmosphere at Rome which testified to the ebbing of Jansenist influence there. Many Jansenists actually left the city. One result of this was the accentuation of a tendency they had shown to look to the civil power for sympathetic support for their essentially ecclesiastical and doctrinal interests. This was made easier because of the tendency of Jansenist doctrines of grace always to minimise the influence of the visible church. The attacks of the reforming monarchs on papal claims did not therefore greatly disturb the Jansenists; some of them could even regard the monarchs as God's instruments against Rome. Their sympathy for the independence of bishops and local churches in their dealings with Rome also harmonised with the reforming states. They were little worried by the state's threat to religious independence; practically Erastian, they read in a different sense from the curialists the injunction that 'My kingdom is not of this world'. Finally, to some of them, the patronage of the monarchs may in itself have been flattering.

In practice the results were varied. Not all monarchs supported Jansenists; the kings of Sardinia were actively hostile. Although there was plenty of anticurialism at Venice, Jansenism left few traces there. The great patrons of the Jansenists were really two: Leopold of Tuscany and Joseph II. Under the patronage of Joseph the University of Pavia became the main Italian centre of Jansenist study and teaching. In Tuscany the results were more spectacular. Leopold's wishes for the reform of the Tuscan church were abetted there by the bishop of Pistoia, Scipione De' Ricci, who had belonged, a few years earlier, to a prominent Jansenist group at Rome. De' Ricci summoned a synod of the clergy of his diocese at Pistoia in 1786. It sat for ten days (18–28 September) and produced a number of propositions enunciating Augustinian doctrinal views, denying papal supremacy in matters of discipline and church organisation, declaring the pope only *primus inter pares*, and attributing to bishops the discipline of regular clergy and the supervision of their ordination and study. The synod also approved the Gallican Articles of 1682. This did not content Leopold, who urged De' Ricci, against the bishop's misgivings, to summon an assembly of Tuscan bishops in the following year. It was done, with unfortunate results; the bishops roundly condemned the synod and its Jansenist propositions.

This was a good indication of the minority nature of Jansenism inside the church. Nor did it have popular support outside. There were violent disturbances at Prato over Jansenist liturgical changes there. In 1790 popular tumult drove De' Ricci from Pistoia and in 1791 he resigned his see. The synod had, in fact, been the climax of Italian Jansenism. It was in 1791 that the *Annali ecclesiastici*, the Jansenist publication, removed from Tuscany to Lugano. But it was only in 1794 that the bull *Auctorem fidei* condemned the synod and its works.

The decline in the fortunes of the Jansenists did not quite end their influence in Italian affairs. Nevertheless, their period of importance was over. A minority, their concern had been mainly with theology and the internal ordering of the church, even though many Jansenists were devoted pastors of their flocks. Once the common focus of enmity in the Jesuits had been removed, Jansenists and near-Jansenists were distinguished by too many fine shades of opinion to be an effective force. Their success had always been local and intellectual, or, where it was more lasting, had been obtained by leaning on a powerful patron, whether a Clement XIV or a Leopold. This showed their essentially non-political nature: later some of them were to take up with the revolutionary republics. For some of them, it is true, sympathy for revolution was more than opportunistic. De' Ricci was a correspondent of Grégoire,[1] and there were many Italian Jansenists who watched with interest the development of events in France towards the Civil Constitution of the Clergy, where it seemed that Gallicanism had at last come into its own. But such sympathies lost the Jansenists the support of their Italian patrons and soon they had to defend themselves against charges of democratic sympathies. Their position was transformed as was that of many Italians in the years after 1789.

Italian history was eventually changed by the revival of European intervention in the peninsula, although, for the moment, this consequence of the French Revolution was not apparent. Down to the end of 1792 its effects were much more limited. Immediate reactions to the news of the fall of the Bastille had varied. Alfieri[2] was enthusiastic, but *émigrés* soon began to arrive to spread their version of what had happened. The Bourbon courts remembered their family ties. When Joseph II died and Leopold moved to Vienna in 1790, the major exponents of enlightened reform in the peninsula had gone. Already, the pace of reform had slack-

---

[1] Baptiste-Henri Grégoire, born Vého, 1750, active in the French National Assembly of 1789, constitutional bishop of Blois and administrator of Loir-et-Cher 1791–1807. Sympathetic to Gallican, Jansenist and republican views, his election to the French chamber in 1819 caused a scandal and was annulled. He died in Paris, 1831.

[2] Vittorio Alfieri, born Asti, 1749. Poet and tragedian, he lived in Paris from 1787 to 1792, when he left for Florence, where he died in 1803.

ened. The Lombard reformers had begun to turn against Joseph, alarmed by the radicalism and the speed of his innovations, and by the loss of local autonomy which followed. It was fortunate that so much had been done, for most of the Italian states now reacted strongly against the danger of innovation, although such new and reformed institutions as existed were usually left intact. So, although the government of Naples went on quarrelling briskly with Rome, it vented its fears of revolution by burning the works of Filangieri and by banning French newspapers. In Venice, the Inquisitors of State began rummaging for dissidence inspired by French ideas. Soon the word *giacobini* was applied to the mildly liberal nobles of Lombardy who attempted to interest themselves in the progress of events in France. The Papal States banned the publication of Alfieri's tragedies (the playwright himself left Paris in 1792, disenchanted with the revolution) and began to hunt for freemasons. A stir was caused by the discovery of a 'club' at Ferrara in 1792.

None of this was very important. Nor was the diplomatic response of the Italian states. They expressed their sympathies after Pillnitz only in words. When the Papal States and Sardinia became the first victims of French aggression, Ferdinand of Naples toyed with the idea of an Italian league. But Genoa, Venice, Modena, Parma and Tuscany all remained obstinately neutral and the papacy still distrusted him too much. (This was known in Paris and in 1792 the Neapolitan government was receiving French encouragement to help itself to papal territory.) By the end of this period, French influence had penetrated far into the peninsula. In spite of British pressure a French ambassador was received at Naples in December 1792. It was true that he was accepted only after an ultimatum from a French admiral, but this in itself was a testimony to French power in the Mediterranean. Rome soon became more accommodating. Her ports were ordered to victual French ships and in December the new French *chargé d'affaires*, de Bassville, arrived there. His uncomplimentary remarks about purple geese in the Capitol and peremptory demands for the expulsion of the *émigrés* did not promise well for future relations, but for the moment the papacy, like all the other Italian states except Sardinia, was willing to try to preserve relations with France.

At the end of 1792, therefore, no useful line can be drawn in Italian history. It falls half-way in a transformation scene between two phases of Italian history. The insulation of peace which had protected the peninsula's political and economic structure while permitting the experiments of the Enlightenment was now disappearing. Yet the conditions in which it was to end were to show again how misleading the term 'Italy' can be; all the states and regions were to react differently to the French Revolution. There was no *Italian* response to the Revolution by 1792. For this very reason it is hard to discern how the lives of Italians had changed between 1763 and 1792. It is made harder, too, by many gaps in the ascertained knowledge: close study is still needed to elucidate the part played by the Italian newspapers in Enlightenment, the role of the masonic lodges, the social composition and activity of the clergy, the economic consequence of the reformers' legislation, the detailed structure of Italian agriculture. The *settecento*, in fact, now requires the sort of attention which in the last three or four decades has been given to the pre-revolutionary history of France.

CHAPTER XIV

THE DEVELOPMENT OF THE AMERICAN COMMUNITIES OUTSIDE BRITISH RULE

W HEN the last of her Habsburg rulers died in 1700, Spain, in the words of José de Gálvez, was 'hardly less defunct than its dead master'.[1] 'With dominions more extensive and more opulent than any European state',[2] the country lacked roads, industry and commerce. The population had declined by a million and a half in the last hundred years. Agriculture was in decay. The administrative system was chaotic, the currency in confusion, and the treasury bankrupt. And if, in the New World, it might almost be said that there was 'no peaceful desart yet unclaimed by Spain', the Spanish American empire seemed to survive more by the forces of habit and inertia, and by the mutual jealousies of the European powers, than by any internal strength of its own. If it was not, as was sometimes thought, ripe for plucking or on the brink of collapse, nevertheless there is abundant testimony to its political, social and economic ills. The devastating report written for the information of the crown in 1749 by the two young naval officers Jorge Juan and Antonio de Ulloa, though dealing, it is true, with but a part of the colonial world, is a classical example.[3]

Yet in the years between the War of the Spanish Succession and the Napoleonic invasions of the Iberian peninsula Spain herself rose with remarkable resilience from the decrepitude into which she had fallen in the seventeenth century. Her economic decline was first arrested and then reversed. Her administrative system was overhauled, centralised and modernised, on French and absolutist lines. Her population again increased—it almost doubled during the century. The royal revenues expanded, though so also did the royal expenditures. And if the course of economic change, the revival of agriculture, the development of industry, the growth of commerce, failed to fulfil the hopes of the economists and reformers, under Charles III and during the early years of Charles IV the country enjoyed what seems in retrospect to have been an Indian summer of prosperity. The Pyrenees had not ceased to exist. But Spain, in the later eighteenth century, no longer lived in a purely Spanish world.

The growth and expansion of Spain's American dominions were still

[1] John Lynch, *Spanish Colonial Administration, 1782–1810. The Intendant System in the Viceroyalty of the Rio de la Plata* (London, 1958), p. 1.

[2] William Robertson, *History of America* (5th and definitive edition, 3 vols., London, 1788), Book VIII.

[3] *Noticias Secretas de América* (London, 1826). Though the work is ascribed to both men, Ulloa was the principal, if not the sole, author.

more striking. Immense in 1700, the empire was far larger in 1763 and larger again twenty years later. For though at the end of the Seven Years War Spain lost Florida, she acquired instead New Orleans and the vast but ill-defined area of Louisiana. And in 1783, with Florida restored as the price of her aid to the revolt of the mainland colonies of England, she was left in complete control of the Gulf of Mexico as well. Louisiana, it is true, was a troublesome gift, and Spain returned it to France in 1800 without reluctance, Napoleon, three years later, selling it to the United States. But even without Louisiana the empire, at the beginning of the nineteenth century, still stretched in unbroken line, and through nearly a hundred degrees of latitude, from California to Cape Horn; and while, in the far north, Spain had been compelled (at the time of the Nootka Sound Convention in 1790) to retreat from her exclusive claims to the north-west coast of North America, in the far south she had begun, in the 1770s, the colonisation of Patagonia.[1]

Defence was the motive which lay behind this expansion of the empire's frontiers. Fear of Portugal impelled Spain to undertake the occupation of the Banda Oriental,[2] now the Republic of Uruguay—an occupation begun with the foundation of Montevideo in 1724–6 and carried to conclusion only when the little port of Colônia do Sacramento was finally wrested from Portuguese hands in 1777. Fear of England—had she not occupied the Falkland Islands in 1766, though agreeing to withdraw from them in 1774?—dictated the southern drive to the coast of Patagonia. And on the northern frontiers of New Spain similar motives operated. Louisiana, it was hoped, would serve as a barrier against Anglo-American penetration into the trans-Mississippi west. And it was to counter Russian advance in the Pacific that Spain began in 1769 the colonisation of California. When, on 4 July 1776, the Liberty Bell in Philadelphia sounded the death-knell of the first British empire, the defensive expansion of the far older empire of Spain was still continuing. It was at this time that the Spaniards were founding San Francisco.

As the empire attained to its greatest territorial extent in the late eighteenth century, so also it attained to its greatest prosperity. The relative importance of its several provinces indeed changed. In South America, Peru, the traditional seat of Spanish wealth and power, lost its old pre-eminence. The provinces of the Río de la Plata, in the south, on the other hand, and Venezuela, in the north, awoke to a new existence. The rise of these hitherto peripheral and neglected regions was paralleled, among the island colonies, by that of Cuba, and, north of the isthmus of Panama, by the economic revival of New Spain, recovered now from its long years of population decline and providing from its mines a half of the world's out-

---

[1] Carmen de Patagones, on the Río Negro, was founded in 1779.

[2] The name given to the territory to the north of the Río de la Plata and east of the Uruguay.

put of the precious metals. It is no accident that the eighteenth century in New Spain was an age of building. Though the streets of Mexico City— on nearly every count the leading city in the western hemisphere— swarmed with beggars, the public revenues had increased more than six-fold in the course of the century and so also had the produce of the mines.

The primacy of New Spain in the economic structure of the empire in the later years of the century was beyond dispute. But the volume of shipping at Havana and in the Río de la Plata, the customs receipts at Buenos Aires, the exports of sugar from Cuba, of cacao from Venezuela, and of hides from the provinces of the Río de la Plata, as well as the general increase in trade between Spain and Spanish America, all told the same expansionist tale. It is true that not all parts of the empire or all segments of the economy reaped equal benefits from the growth of trade. Local and regional stagnation, even indeed local and regional decline, were also evident, and as Spaniards criticised conditions in Spain, so some Spanish Americans, and some Spaniards also, lamented the economic back-wardness of Spanish America. But however justified their complaints, the fact remained that with an expanding trade and a rising population—half as large again as that of Spain in 1800 (though no greater than that of England, Wales and Scotland at the time of the first Reform Bill)—the empire as a whole was never more prosperous than on the eve of its collapse.

The most obvious stimulus to this economic, and indeed political, re-habilitation of the empire was provided by the Bourbon administrative, commercial and economic reforms. Spanish rather than Spanish Ameri-can problems had occupied the attention of the early Bourbons. But to them was due one major administrative change. The vast area now com-prised in the republics of Colombia, Ecuador and Venezuela hitherto subordinate to Lima, and, as to a part, to Santo Domingo, was erected in 1717 into the viceroyalty of New Granada, temporarily suppressed in 1723–4 but re-established in 1739, though Venezuela itself became a sep-arate captaincy-general three years later. They were responsible also for two important innovations in the imperial commercial system. After a vain attempt to reanimate the flotas and galleons, the convoyed fleets in-tended to supply the trades respectively of New Spain and South America but now long since fallen into decay, Philip V in 1740 suspended them altogether. Thereafter specially licensed vessels were permitted to sail alone to one or another port of the Indies and round Cape Horn directly to Peru. The flota was indeed revived in 1754, sailed again to New Spain in 1757 and dragged on a fitful existence till 1778. But the galleons totally disappeared and with their demise there expired also the famous Porto-bello fair and the prosperity of the kingdom of Panama. The second in-novation (though earlier in date) was the establishment of privileged trading companies, of which one at least, the Caracas or Guipuscoan Company, granted in 1728 a near-monopoly of the trade of the coasts of

Venezuela, enjoyed a long and relatively successful life, much to the benefit, incidentally, of Venezuela, though not wholly to the satisfaction of its inhabitants.

Under the early Bourbons a beginning had thus been made in opening up the natural trade-routes of the Indies; within the theoretical monopoly of the trade of Spanish America by Spain the practical monopoly of the merchants of Cadiz and Seville had been partially infringed, though only by the creation of rival monopolies elsewhere; and for northern South America, at least, a more realistic administrative organisation had been tried out and found indispensable. In Spain itself, moreover, the creation in 1714 of a Ministry of the Indies—along with other Ministries of State, Justice, and War—foreshadowed the decline of the once all-powerful Council of the Indies and the replacement of conciliar government by a new and more efficient agency of imperial control.

Not till after the close of the Seven Years War, however, did Spain undertake, as Britain also undertook, though on a far narrower scale than did her greatest colonial rival, the task of imperial reorganisation and reform. And for Charles III, the ablest monarch of the Bourbon line, who had succeeded to the throne in 1759, the disastrous experience of his late and rash entry into that European and colonial conflict—Havana was occupied, Florida lost—was decisive. The striking changes in the imperial administrative and economic systems now cautiously introduced owed something to French precept abroad, and something also to Spanish opinion at home. But their aim was severely practical. If the crown now sought to introduce a new efficiency into colonial government, if it sought to rehabilitate colonial trade, these were not so much ends in themselves as means to an end; and the end was imperial defence, the protection of the empire against aggression, particularly English aggression, the elimination of foreign economic competition, and the restoration of Spanish maritime and military power in Europe. And as in British colonial policy after 1763, so in Spanish, the financial problem was paramount. Defence demanded revenue; revenue meant reform.

Already at the end of 1763 an inter-ministerial committee had been instituted in Madrid, meeting every Thursday, 'to discuss matters relative to the future security of the Spanish Indies and the augmentation of His Catholic Majesty's revenues in America', as also the restoration of the navy.[1] And this was supplemented in 1764 by the appointment of a *Junta Técnica*, a committee of five, to consider the problem of trade. Meanwhile, a visitor-general, Alejandro O'Reilly, had been dispatched to the Antilles to inquire into the defences of Cuba and Puerto Rico and in 1765 José de Gálvez, the future Minister of the Indies, was appointed Inspector-General of the finances of Mexico and Visitor-General of New Spain.

[1] A. S. Aiton, 'Spanish Colonial Reorganization under the Family Compact', *Hispanic American Historical Review*, vol. XII (1932), p. 274.

The report of the *Junta Técnica* was made in February, 1765, a week before the appointment of Gálvez. No royal commission could have been expected to propose a complete abandonment of the policy of colonial monopoly, and certainly the junta did not do so. But it had before it an impressive object-lesson of the disastrous consequences of the old restrictive system: Havana, normally visited by two ships a year, produced an annual revenue from import and export duties of 30,000 pesos; in British hands, in 1762, the trade yielded a revenue of 400,000 pesos. As for the ravages made upon the volume and value of imperial trade by the illicit trade of Spain's colonial rivals, these were plain for all to read. Dionisio de Alcedo, writing in 1761, estimated the extent of the contraband at 6,000,000 pesos a year,[1] though this was merely to echo earlier writers,[2] and the figure was probably well below the reality. One obvious move was to institute more vigorous measures against the contraband trader himself, and this was done. But defence of the Spanish monopoly against pressure from without must also, it was clear, be accompanied by a revision of the conditions of that monopoly within. Freer, though not free trade, the liberalisation of the old commercial system, was the remedy proposed and one which informed Spanish opinion supported. So, by a striking paradox, the results which Britain in part proposed to effect in her own empire after 1763 by tightening up the acts of trade, Spain proposed to effect by their relaxation.

A preliminary step, the institution of a monthly mail service between Coruña and Havana, with connections to New Spain, the islands and Tierra Firme, was taken in 1764, later supplemented by a maritime post to Buenos Aires. Now, however, by a decree of 16 October 1765, the West Indian islands—Cuba, Santo Domingo, Puerto Rico, Trinidad and Margarita—were thrown open to trade with nine of the principal ports of Spain, ranging from Santander in the north to Barcelona in the east. At a stroke the limitation of transatlantic commerce to the Andalusian ports of Seville and Cadiz was ended, and while ships could now sail without special licence from the crown, tonnage and other dues were simplified and reduced. The experiment was so successful that the freer trade area was enlarged to include Louisiana in 1768, Campeche and Yucatán in 1770, Santa Marta and Río de la Hacha on the South American mainland in 1776–7, and Buenos Aires in February 1778. Finally, by the so-called Decree of Free Trade of 12 October 1778, all the more important ports of Spain and of South and Central America, except (in the interests of the Caracas Company) those of Venezuela, were allowed to trade, if not freely, at least directly, one with another. The formal exception of Venezuela

---

[1] Octavio Gil Munilla, *El Río de la Plata en la Política Internacional. Génesis del Virreinato* (Seville, 1949), p. 103.

[2] It is the figure of Gerónimo de Ustáriz, based on an English pamphlet of 1704. See John Kippax, trans., *The Theory and Practice of Commerce and Maritime Affairs* (2 vols., London, 1751), vol. I, p. 137.

lasted till 1789, by which time the Caracas Company had disappeared, and in the same year the privileges given to the rest of the empire were granted also to New Spain. While, moreover, step by step the ports of America and the ports of Spain were opened and the tariffs and duties hampering trade revised, the age-old restrictions on inter-colonial trade were lightened or removed. New Spain, Guatemala, New Granada, Peru, Chile and Buenos Aires, all, by 1777, enjoyed a relative freedom to trade between themselves in their own products. To foreigners and foreign trade the empire, of course, still remained closed, though, for quite special reasons, trade between Louisiana and France was permitted to Spanish subjects and Spanish shipping in 1782, and in 1789 foreigners were allowed to supply slaves to the West Indies. For the rest the principle of imperial monopoly remained intact. But, when, in 1790, two years after the death of Charles III, the Casa de Contratación, or Spanish India House, was itself abolished, the event was symbolic of the almost complete liquidation of the practices which had governed the conduct of imperial trade for more than two and a half centuries.

Relaxation of imperial control formed no part of the political and administrative reforms of Charles III, which moved, indeed, in an exactly opposite direction. Territorial readjustments were carried out and the status of certain areas was raised. The captaincy-general of Venezuela was enlarged in 1777 and provided, nine years later, with an *audiencia*, or high court of justice, of its own. The captaincy-general of Chile achieved independence of the viceroyalty of Peru. The frontier provinces of northern New Spain were organized, in 1776, into the Provincias Internas under a commandant-general largely independent of the viceroy of New Spain. And in the same year also, for political and strategic reasons—fear of Britain on the one hand and of Portuguese aggression from Brazil on the other—a fourth American viceroyalty, the viceroyalty of the Río de la Plata, was created to embrace not only the old provinces of the Río de la Plata, but those of Upper Peru (the modern Bolivia) as well. As a 'bastion of South America'[1] the viceroyalty was made permanent in 1777, and its foundation was as much a landmark in the political history of the later empire as was the Decree of Free Trade of 1778 in its economic history.

These and other changes reflected a growing awareness in Spain of geographical problems and regional conditions in America: the main outlines of the future Spanish American states were already drawn in the territorial arrangements which existed at the end of the eighteenth century. But territorial decentralisation of this kind, if such it may be termed, left untouched the central principle of colonial rule. Habsburg

[1] G. Céspedes del Castillo, 'Lima y Buenos Aires. Repercusiones Económicas y Políticas de la creación del virreinato del Plata', *Anuario de Estudios Americanos*, vol. III (1946), p. 791.

or Bourbon, the empire was an absolutism, a paternal absolutism it is true, but an absolutism none the less. Its principle was the principle of authority, and as the Bourbons had extended the reach of royal authority in Spain, so also they sought to tighten its grasp in America. In the interests of better and more efficient government—and the increase of the royal revenues—Charles III revived the well-worn institution of the *visita*, the general inspection of a colony by a royal commissioner: the general inspection of New Spain by José de Gálvez from 1765 to 1771 is the most notable instance. Enlightened despotism in Spain, moreover, was reflected in the appointment of abler civil servants in America. The second conde de Revillagigedo in New Spain was an outstanding example. But to 'unify', as Charles wished to unify, 'the government of the great empires which God had intrusted to me, and set in good order, make happy and defend my extensive dominions in America',[1] more was needed. The answer which the most far-reaching of the Bourbon administrative reforms attempted to supply was to systematise and centralise colonial government by the division of the colonies into intendancies, to invigorate authority, and control it, at the level where authority was least responsible and most ineffective, at the level, that is, of local and provincial administration.

French in origin, Spanish by adoption, the intendancy system was first tried out in limited form in Cuba in 1764. Gálvez, appalled by the conditions which he had found, strongly advocated its full extension to New Spain in 1768. But fourteen more years of experiment and debate were required before the system began to be adopted in its entirety, first in the new viceroyalty of the Río de la Plata in 1782, then in Peru two years later, and in New Spain itself in 1786. By 1790 it had been applied to most parts of the empire. Everywhere, or almost everywhere, *gobernadores intendentes* appointed from Spain supplanted the *corregidores* and *alcaldes mayores*, the former district officers, whose tyranny and corruption form a melancholy page in the annals of Spanish colonial administration and whose malpractices in Peru, roundly denounced by Juan and Ulloa[2] in 1749, directly precipitated the great Indian rebellion of Tupac Amaru three decades later. The new officials, with their attendant *subdelegados* and other assistants, took their place in the colonial hierarchy as maids-of-all-work in their intendancies, charged particularly with the four departments of justice, general administration, finance and war, and dividing, uneasily enough, the exercise of power with viceroys and captains-general themselves. There was room for conflict, and conflict ensued. But no reform reflected more clearly the ideas of enlightened despotism at its most enlightened. It was designed to achieve good government as well as efficient government, and if it looked

---

[1] L. E. Fisher, *The Intendant System in Spanish America* (Berkeley, 1929), p. 97.
[2] See above, p. 397, n. 3.

to the welfare of the crown, and particularly to its financial welfare, it followed a great Spanish tradition in looking also to the welfare of the subject.

Three further aspects of Bourbon policy deserve attention. One, the strengthening of the overseas military establishments by the formation or reformation of a colonial militia supplementary to the now increased force of regular troops from Spain and dangerously endowed with specific legal immunities and privileges, was, of course, merely a part of the larger plans of imperial defence which resulted in the general overhaul of the old colonial system. It opened, however, a new field to the ambitions of the Spanish American creoles. A second, the contraction of ecclesiastical privilege and the extension of the royal *patronato*, continued what had been begun in the earlier eighteenth century and formed a parallel, in ecclesiastical affairs, to the tightening up of royal authority in civil government. The nature of that authority and the extent of Bourbon regalism were abundantly illustrated by the sudden and dramatic expulsion of the Jesuit Order from the Spanish dominions in 1767: absolutism could brook no rival, real or imaginary. The third aspect, and in some respects the most remarkable, was the encouragement given by the crown to scientific investigations in the New World and its attempts to stimulate production, particularly mineral production. Mining experts—the Eluyher brothers and Baron von Nordenflicht—were sent to New Spain, New Granada and Peru in the 1780s. In Mexico the Royal College of Mines was opened in 1792. It was this institution, together with the Botanical Garden and the Academy of Fine Arts, that led Humboldt to observe that 'No city of the new continent, without excepting those of the United States, can show scientific establishments as fine or as well established as the capital of Mexico'.[1] Botanical expeditions—the expeditions of Ruiz, Pavón and Dombey and of Martín Sessé—left for Peru and New Spain in 1777 and 1787 respectively. The crown supported in New Granada the botanical work of José Celestino Mutis, and at the end of the century it afforded every facility to the great expedition through northern South America, Cuba and Mexico of Alexander von Humboldt and his companion, the French naturalist Aimé Bonpland.

Charles III died in 1788. The reforms which he had initiated were not yet complete. But the empire which he left to the hands of his well-meaning but incompetent successor was not only larger and stronger than the empire which he had inherited: it was more opulent and better governed. The royal revenues had substantially increased, though so also had the costs of collecting them and the expenses of the colonial establishments in general. The imperial defences, both on the mainland and in the islands, had been strengthened. The fortifications of Port Royal in

[1] Alexander von Humboldt, *Essai Politique sur le Royaume de la Nouvelle-Espagne* (5 vols., Paris, 1811), vol. II, p. 11.

Jamaica could ill compare with those of San Juan in Puerto Rico. The imperial administrative system had been overhauled, the personnel of royal government, at least in the higher reaches of the civil service, much improved, and the control of central over local government made more effective and more pervasive. Imperial trade had been rehabilitated. Its value is estimated to have multiplied sevenfold in the ten years between 1778 and 1788 alone, and, a sure sign of the industrial renaissance now taking place in Spain in the Basque provinces and in Catalonia and Valencia, the proportion of Spanish as opposed to foreign goods shipped in this trade had also increased. Colonial manufactures suffered. The textile industry of Quito and the wine industry of the western provinces of the Río de la Plata were hard hit by the competition of lower-priced imported goods. On the other hand the output of the mines in New Spain reached unprecedented heights. And with a rising population in Spanish America and a growing demand in Europe for the drugs and dyewoods, the hides and skins, the sugar and tobacco, as well as the gold and silver, which Spanish America supplied, it was not only mineral production that was expanding. So also was pastoral and agricultural production. Buenos Aires, shipping 150,000 hides in 1778, shipped 1,500,000 in 1783. And it was Humboldt's opinion, at the end of the century, that while, in Cuba and Venezuela, agriculture had founded more considerable fortunes than had been accumulated by the working of the mines in Peru, in New Spain the value of the gold and silver of the Mexican mines was less 'by almost a fourth' than that of the agricultural produce.[1]

In America as in Spain the great reforms of Charles' reign roused little open opposition. Even the expulsion of the Jesuit Order occasioned no more than local tumults, and tumults were nothing new in the colonial world. These riots of 1767 paled into insignificance at the side of the great rebellions of the 1780s, the Indian rising in Peru under Tupac Amaru in 1780–1 and the revolt of the Comuneros in New Granada. But these movements were the product of local circumstances and particular conditions. The one was directed against the oppression, more vicious in Peru than in any other part of the empire, of the local *corregidores*, and the *corregidores* were thereafter replaced by intendants. The other was a protest against high taxation, essentially the result of Spain's entry into the War of American Independence. Both were suppressed with alarmed brutality. They cast a sudden and vivid light on the condition of the Indian and mestizo masses. But they indicated no general or widespread spirit of disaffection to the king or to the crown. And though the revolt of the English colonies in North America might indeed have been read as a warning to Spain and an example to Spanish America, it was not so much disruption from within that the Spanish authorities feared as the 'powers of Europe' and disruption from without.

[1] *Ibid.* vol. II, p. 25; vol. III, p. 286.

Yet though, for a time, new life had been breathed into the imperial system, it was the paradoxical result of the Bourbon reforms in general that the measures designed to strengthen that system led in the end to its weakening. The tide of creole self-consciousness was mounting steadily in the eighteenth century with the mounting prosperity of the colonies, and the cleavage between creoles and *peninsulares*, between Spaniards born in America and Spaniards born in Spain, was widening and deepening. Humboldt noted, in a famous sentence, that 'the most miserable European without education, and without intellectual cultivation, thinks himself superior to the whites born in the new continent'.[1] He noted also that after 1783 (the Treaty of Versailles), but more particularly after 1789, creoles began to refer to themselves as Americans.[2] And while the reforms of Charles III, offending against custom and tradition, were too 'enlightened' and too 'liberal' to suit those members of the governing bureaucracy and of the commercial oligarchy whose powers and privileges they eliminated or curtailed, they were not liberal enough for the liking of the creole landed gentry and of the rising creole bourgeoisie. Masters of the land, merchants and mine-owners as well as landowners forming at their apex a native aristocracy, and even at their base far removed from the classes that served them, the Spanish Americans native-born sought to reinforce economic power with political power. But the reforms which held out the promise of better and more efficient government denied to Americans a share in it. In the reorganised system of provincial administration the newly appointed intendants were almost invariably Spaniards. On grounds of principle reinforced by prejudice, creoles were only admitted to inferior posts—it was no part of Bourbon policy to create a creole administrative class—and the affront to creole pride was intolerable. Nor was it only the political ambitions of the creoles which the reforms of Charles III helped at once to stimulate and to frustrate. The commercial system had been liberalised. New and more enterprising merchants entered trade. The volume of business increased. But 'freedom of trade within the empire only engendered a desire for freedom to trade with the world at large'.[3] If the Spanish economy, during the later years of Charles' reign, flourished 'in a way that had been unknown for centuries',[4] nevertheless the economic recovery of Spain had failed to keep pace with the economic needs of the colonies. Not for long, amidst the swelling volume of international trade, would the creoles rest content with an imperial economic system in which Spain herself was cast for a role which her financial and industrial capacities, her facilities and skills, forbade her adequately to fulfil.

The closing decades of the eighteenth century witnessed an efflorescence

---

[1] *Ibid.* vol. II, p. 2.   [2] *Ibid.* vol. II, p. 3.
[3] C. H. Haring, *The Spanish Empire in America* (New York, 1947), p. 345.
[4] Richard Herr, *The Eighteenth-century Revolution in Spain* (Princeton, 1958), pp. 146–7.

of colonial society, reflected in civic adornment and urban improvement
—themselves an indication of increased material wealth—in the growth
of local patriotisms, in a heightened intellectual activity, in the rise of a
periodical press, and in the foundation of societies and clubs. Not till
1801 did Buenos Aires acquire a newspaper, and Caracas and Santiago
de Chile had still longer to wait. But in Mexico the *Gaceta de Literatura*
of José Antonio de Alzate (not the first of his literary ventures) ran from
1788 to 1795, its pages crowded with articles on natural and applied
science, on medicine and philosophy, and on geography and history. The
still more celebrated *Mercurio Peruano* appeared in 1791, and, issued
every three days, survived till 1795. The *Gaceta de Guatemala* was revived,
after more than sixty years, in 1794. The *Papel Periódico* of Havana began
publication in 1790 and the *Papel Periódico* of Santa Fe de Bogotá in
1791. And there were many other *gazetas* and *semanarios*, part newspapers, part reviews, most of them relatively short-lived, but multiplying
rapidly in the early years of the nineteenth century. In the 'eighties and
'nineties also *Sociedades Económicos de Amigos del País* made their
appearance, nine of them before 1795 and six thereafter. Founded on
the model of similar societies in Spain, these American societies were
primarily interested in the improvement of local economic conditions
and the development of local economic resources. But they were interested also in the promotion of useful knowledge in general. Thus the
Havana Society, inaugurated in 1793, established a public library and
superintended a girls' school; and the Guatemala Society, dating from
1794, not only founded schools for spinning, drawing and mathematics, it offered a prize for a dissertation in favour of American
literature.

The economic societies were a direct illustration of the penetration into
Spanish America of the eighteenth-century 'enlightenment' in Spain.
The revival of the colonial universities, now engaged in emancipating
themselves from the authority of Aristotle and the schoolmen, was a
further sign of the transmission to Spanish America of the philosophical
and scientific ideas, stemming from England, France and Germany, prevalent in Europe. Despite the censorship of the Inquisition the continent
was not closed to ideas. They entered from Spain in the writings of
Spaniards. They came in the train of Charles III's 'enlightened' administrators. They were brought in the intellectual baggage of returning
travellers—wealthy creoles increasingly visited Europe. They were fostered by the scientific expeditions which the Spanish crown promoted in
the New World. And they penetrated also by contraband routes in the
form of prohibited books. The study of the physical sciences, as Humboldt
pointed out, made its greatest progress in Mexico. But in philosophy as
in science the cultural time-lag between America and Europe was steadily
diminishing. The 'enlightenment', though it affected only a small minority,

was well on its way in Spanish America by the time of the death of Charles III.[1]

The new spirit in colonial government, on the other hand, did not long survive the accession of Charles IV. By the end of 1792 the great ministers of Charles III's reign were dead or fallen, and the increasing weakness of Spanish government was soon reflected in America. Many of the abuses of the old order reappeared. The crown had never been able to bring itself to pay its lesser servants adequately, even when it could bring itself to pay them at all: under the new system of provincial government, as under the old, their lethargy was only equalled by their venality. As for the operation of the intendancy system at its highest level, in the viceroyalty of the Río de la Plata, at least, the vigour of the intendants had a wholly salutary if unexpected effect in galvanising into a new activity the local *cabildos* or town councils. But the wide powers given to the intendants offended vested interests, public and private. They led to conflicts of jurisdiction between newer and older officials, between intendants and viceroys, and between intendants and judges of the royal *audiencias*. In Upper Peru—an extreme example—the intendants and the *audiencia* of Charcas were constantly at war: colonial government was divided against itself, and there, certainly, a reform intended to strengthen the royal hand merely succeeded in weakening it.

If the empire reached its greatest height in the closing years of Charles III's reign, its decline—and the decline of Spain—proceeded rapidly after 1792. Already in 1789 the outbreak of the French Revolution had set on foot a process which was to lead to the division and disintegration of Spanish society and to have profound repercussions, eventually, upon Spanish America also. In 1790 a dispute with England over rival claims to Nootka Sound on the western shores of Vancouver Island—a dispute in which Spain was forced to give way—marked the end of the empire's defensive expansion and the beginning of territorial retreat. War with France three years later resulted in the surrender, under the Treaty of Basle (1795), of the eastern two-thirds of the island of Hispaniola—the Spanish colony of Santo Domingo—and in 1796 war with England led to the loss of Trinidad in 1797. Finally, in return for an enlargement of the duchy of Parma, Louisiana in 1800 was retroceded to France—to be bought three years later by the United States.

But the entry of Spain into the French revolutionary wars, first as an enemy and then as an ally of France, had other and more important consequences than the loss of two comparatively unimportant West Indian colonies or even than the voluntary surrender of the territory of Louisiana.

---

[1] Compare, on the above paragraphs, R. J. Shafer, *The Economic Societies in the Spanish World (1763–1821)* (Syracuse, N.Y., 1958); J. T. Lanning, *The Eighteenth-century Enlightenment in the University of San Carlos de Guatemala* (Ithaca, N.Y., 1956), and A. P. Whitaker, ed., *Latin America and the Enlightenment* (New York, 1942).

The war with England, which began in October 1796, lasted, with an interval of only two and a half years, till 1808; and its results were fatal. England was mistress of the seas. Spain and her colonies were severed, or almost severed. The Spanish economy was seriously deranged. The Spanish navy was almost destroyed. And the colonies were thrown upon their own and foreign resources. So severe was the economic crisis—the value of the exports at Buenos Aires fell from $5,000,000 in 1796 to less than $335,000 in 1797—that the crown by royal order of 18 November 1797 opened the ports of Spanish America, though under stringent limitations, to neutral shipping. This was a measure of desperation, and the order was revoked in 1799 because it had 'redounded entirely', as the decree of revocation complained,[1] to the injury of the state and of the interests of its subjects. But what the law forbade, local regulations continued to tolerate and the crown itself to license; and though the restoration of peace in 1802 restored the old restrictive system also, with the renewal of the war in 1804 once again the ports were opened.

The result, or partial result, was the rapid growth of United States shipping and United States trade from Cuba to Buenos Aires and from Buenos Aires to Chile. But it was not only United States trade, legitimate and illegitimate, that flourished. So also did British trade. The Spanish coast-guard ships and the commercial reforms of Charles III had done something to check the growth of the contraband trade. But they had certainly not eliminated it. To tap the trade of the Gulf of Mexico and the Spanish Main (as well as that of the French West Indian islands) Britain, in 1766, had established free ports in Dominica and Jamaica, and the system was extended after 1787 to other strategic points in the West Indies. The trade from the free ports with the Spanish colonies—a smuggling trade from the Spanish point of view, a legalised trade from the British—was encouraged in time of peace and specially licensed in time of war, and, despite temporary vicissitudes, it met, on the whole, with mounting success. Jamaica was the hub of the system, but Nassau and Trinidad, as well as other of the islands, all played their part: Trinidad alone, at the end of the eighteenth century, was alleged, probably with exaggeration, to supply the Spanish colonies with goods to the value of one million pounds a year.[2] It was not only in the Caribbean, however, that the contraband trade flourished during the revolutionary and Napoleonic wars. British traders, like United States traders, made their way to the Río de la Plata. And even on the Pacific coast, thanks in part to the South Sea whalers, the contraband extended and strengthened its hold. In the years after 1796 external economic pressure upon the walls of empire was steadily increasing. The crown, in 1802, could theoretically re-establish the old system of imperial monopoly. But already, by 1802,

---

[1] *Documentos para la Historia Argentina*, vol. VII (Buenos Aires, 1916), p. 157.
[2] Memorandum on Trinidad, Public Record Office, C.O. 318/2.

that system had been almost irretrievably undermined. After Trafalgar its ruin was completed.

How far did events in Europe after 1789 assist in preparing the political as well as the economic emancipation of Spanish America? If the 'enlightenment' was well on its way in the Spanish American empire by the death of Charles III, of the literature commonly associated with the political doctrines of the French Revolution the writings of Rousseau in particular had long been familiar to educated creoles. All of Rousseau's works published before 1764 had entered the colonies freely, and they continued to enter. Simón Rodríguez, the eccentric tutor of the future liberator of northern South America, Simón Bolívar, brought up his pupil according to the best principles of *Émile*. Francisco Xavier Espejo of Quito, imprisoned in 1795 on account of his alleged subversive activities, had also fallen under *Émile's* spell. In Buenos Aires Mariano Moreno produced a Spanish edition of the *Contrat Social*, with the chapter on religion omitted, in 1810. It is probable, indeed, that no other European author exercised quite so profound an influence as did Rousseau.[1] Yet whatever the influence of Rousseau in the Spanish American world, the French Revolution itself startled and shocked Spanish Americans. At the outset some of the younger creoles, such, for example, as Manuel Belgrano of Buenos Aires, who was then in Spain, were moved by the same generous surge of emotion which moved Wordsworth and Southey in England. Antonio Nariño, in New Granada, printed on his own press in 1794 a Spanish translation of the Declaration of the Rights of Man, for which he suffered imprisonment and exile; and a conspiracy at La Guaira in Venezuela three years later, the conspiracy of Manuel Gual and José Maria España, clearly reflected the influence of French revolutionary doctrines. But the example of the French Revolution was not one which most creoles wished to see imitated in Spanish America. Subversive political ideas were not widespread. They were confined to a small minority of the creole intellectuals, and of these the most tireless in revolutionary activity, Francisco de Miranda, who had seen the French Revolution at first hand, had left his native Venezuela in 1771 and did not return to it again till 1806.

If, however, the pure milk of French revolutionary doctrine made little headway in Spanish America, the Anglo-Spanish wars and the severance of communications between Spain and Spanish America brought the American Revolution, or the force of its example, nearer home. During the late wars, as a British observer remarked in 1804, Spanish Americans had seen with regret and indignation that, while their ships could not venture far from their shores, the Americans of the north navigated every sea

---

[1] Among the intellectual influences of the late eighteenth century, however, much—probably too much—has also been made of the revival of the doctrines of Spanish Catholic thought of the sixteenth century and of those of Francisco Suárez in particular.

and entered every port;[1] and more than one United States trader, perhaps, like the young Richard Cleveland of Massachusetts on a voyage to Chile, carried in his cargo a copy of the Federal Constitution and of the Declaration of Independence conveniently translated into Spanish. Humboldt similarly noted that since the island of Trinidad had fallen into English hands the near-by mainland had changed its appearance, and here, at Cariaco, 'for the first time in these climates', he heard the names of Franklin and Washington 'pronounced with enthusiasm'.[2]

The empire, moreover, was now exposed to direct attack, and as Britain formerly had wavered between plundering the Spanish colonies and trading with them, so now she hesitated between their conquest and their emancipation. In 1797 the governor of Trinidad, two months after the island had been captured, was instructed to encourage revolution on the mainland, and an invasion of the Río de la Plata was prepared, and cancelled, in the same year. Fundamentally, however, Britain was more interested in trade than in territory. Her designs were commercial and strategic rather than imperial; and when, in 1806, Buenos Aires fell to an expedition undertaken from the Cape of Good Hope by Commodore Sir Home Popham and Brigadier-General Beresford, the responsibility for the attack lay with Popham, and his plans were wholly unauthorised. Like the filibustering expedition which Miranda led to Venezuela, also in 1806, the filibustering invasion of the Río de la Plata failed. An initial success was followed by a resounding defeat, the recapture of Buenos Aires, the capitulation of the army which attempted to reconquer it, and the evacuation of Montevideo. These events left a permanent mark upon the history of the Río de la Plata. The viceroy had fled. It was the creoles who defeated the British. The 'Americans' native-born had tasted power and felt their strength. But it was in Europe, not in America, that the decisive page in the history of the Spanish empire was about to be written. Napoleon in 1807 invaded the Iberian peninsula, and under the tremendous impact of 'the French Revolution in its Napoleonic expression'[3] the Spanish empire in America, and the Portuguese empire also, were to be shaken to their foundations.

The expansion and growth of the Spanish empire in America in the eighteenth century had been matched by the expansion and growth of the great Portuguese colony of Brazil. By the Treaty of Tordesillas in 1494 the dividing line between the Portuguese and Spanish dominions had been defined as a line running north and south 370 degrees west of the Cape Verde islands, a line which, in Spanish eyes at least, crossed the continent

[1] W. Jacob, Plan for Occupying Spanish America, with observations on the character and views of its inhabitants, 26 October 1804. P.R.O., Chatham Papers, G.D. 8/345.
[2] *Personal Narrative of Travels to the Equinoctial Regions of the New Continent, during the years 1799–1804* (trans. Helen Maria Williams, 7 vols., London, 1814–29), vol. III, pp. 196–7.
[3] Sir Charles K. Webster, ed., *Britain and the Independence of Latin America, 1812–1830. Select Documents from the Foreign Office Archives* (2 vols., London, 1938), vol. I, p. 8.

of South America from a point slightly to the east of the mouth of the Amazon to a point on the coast of São Paulo slightly to the west of the present town of Santos. Yet, already in the seventeenth century, explorers, traders and missionaries from the state of Maranhão in the north, and gold-seekers and slave-hunters, the famous *bandeirantes* of São Paulo, in the south, had penetrated far to the west and far to the south of the old imaginary treaty-line; and this westward movement of the Portuguese colonists was confirmed and strengthened by the great gold discoveries at the end of the century in the region thereafter known as Minas Gerais,[1] followed by further discoveries in the 1720s of diamonds in Minas Gerais and of gold in Goiás and Mato Grosso.

The resulting gold rushes from Bahia, Rio de Janeiro and São Paulo affected not only all the settled parts of Brazil but Portugal also. Immigrants in their thousands, Brazilian, Portuguese, whites, Negroes, mulattoes, poured into the mining areas. New towns were founded, new captaincies created. Minas Gerais, Goiás and Mato Grosso all came into existence as separate captaincies between 1720 and 1748. And while Brazil found a new source of wealth to bolster up the declining fortunes of the sugar plantations of the north-east, already suffering from West Indian competition, João V in Portugal was enabled to live in lavish and unexpected splendour, and Brazilian gold in immense quantities flowed from Portugal to Britain.

But Portuguese power had not only been pushed westwards to the Tordesillas line and beyond it, it had also been pressed southwards to the Río de la Plata. There in 1680, on the northern bank of the river, the crown had established the settlement of Colônia do Sacramento—a Portuguese base directly opposite to Buenos Aires and a centre from which contraband goods, mostly English goods transported from Lisbon to Rio de Janeiro in the Brazil fleets, could be smuggled to the heart of Peru. What Jamaica was to the Spanish Main, Colônia was to the Río de la Plata. Its foundation—the town was immediately destroyed by the Spaniards but was soon re-established—was followed four years later by that of Laguna, in what was to become the captaincy of Santa Catarina. Thereafter Brazilian colonisation turned to the rich pasture lands of the south, to Santa Catarina and Rio Grande do Sul, as well as to the inland provinces of Minas Gerais, Goiás and Mato Grosso. Colônia itself, repeatedly falling into and out of Spanish hands, was ceded to Spain by the Treaty of Madrid in 1750, Portugal obtaining in return the territory occupied by the famous Jesuit missions east of the Uruguay river, together with the recognition also of her claims to a large part of the Amazon basin. But the mission Indians resisted the transfer; Colônia remained in Portuguese hands; and the treaty itself was annulled in 1761. Not, indeed, till 1777 was the clash of imperial ambitions in the border

[1] General Mines.

lands north of the Río de la Plata temporarily resolved when the newly arrived viceroy of the new viceroyalty of the Río de la Plata, in command of an expedition of some ten thousand men, captured Colônia and the island of Santa Catarina, and Spain and Portugal, by the Treaty of San Ildefonso, again attempted to define the boundaries of their American possessions. This time Spain retained both Colônia and the territory of the old Jesuit missions. But Portugal made good her claim to the vast inland world of Amazonia. She retained Santa Catarina and the cattle ranges of Rio Grande do Sul, and in 1801 she occupied also the territory of the former Jesuit missions east of the Uruguay River. The elevation of Rio Grande de São Pedro to the status of a captaincy followed in 1807.

These territorial and economic changes were accompanied by administrative change. Till 1762 the seat of the governors-general of Brazil, sometimes styled viceroys, had been at Bahia. And it was a recognition both of Portugal's forward policy in the debatable lands north of the Río de la Plata and also of the rising importance of southern and central Brazil, especially of the captaincies of Rio de Janeiro and Minas Gerais, that the capital of the colony, now officially erected into a viceroyalty, was transferred in 1763 from Bahia to Rio de Janeiro. This was the work of Sebastião José de Carvalho e Melo, marquis of Pombal and virtual dictator of Portugal during the long reign of José I (1750–77). 'The great and laudable object of his ambition', wrote Southey, who found him 'without conscience and without humanity', 'was to benefit his country, and restore Portugal, if not to the foreign empire she had once possessed, at least to her former state of plenty and prosperity at home.'[1] Tireless in activity, expelling the Jesuits from Portugal and the Portuguese dominions eight years before Charles III expelled them from Spain and Spanish America, curbing the power of the nobility, reorganising the national finances, and revolutionising the internal administration of the state, Pombal also turned his attention to Brazil; and though the Pombaline reforms in the Portuguese empire were less far-reaching than the Caroline reforms in the Spanish empire, they served a similar purpose— to strengthen the royal hand and to increase the royal revenues.

The Portuguese imperial administrative system had always been less systematic than its Spanish counterpart, and it remained less systematic. But Pombal did much to promote the unification of Brazil and to consolidate royal authority. The administration of justice was improved. A new High Court, similar to the court already existing at Bahia, was established at Rio de Janeiro in 1751. The laws were codified—in thirty-nine volumes—between 1754 and 1757. *Juntas de Justiça* were erected in the several provinces in 1765. The remaining private *capitanias-donatárias*— semi-feudal hereditary captaincies—were extinguished by purchase or confiscation. The state of Maranhão, hitherto directly dependent on

[1] Robert Southey, *History of Brazil* (3 vols., London, 1810–19), vol. III, pp. 505–6.

Lisbon, was dissolved, and the captaincies formed out of it—Pará and Maranhão—were finally to be incorporated with Brazil. Indian slavery was, in law, abolished, and the persecution of the Jews was brought to an end. The militia system was extended, colonial regiments were raised, more regular troops brought from Portugal. In 1765 the convoyed fleets sailing from Lisbon were replaced by a patrol system, though, in quite special circumstances, the fleets were temporarily re-established between 1797 and 1801; and, partly to introduce fresh capital into Brazil, partly to undermine England's command of the Brazil trade through Lisbon, monopolistic trading companies, the *Companhia Geral do Grão Pará e Maranhão* and the *Companhia de Pernambuco e Paraíba*, the second less successful than the first, were organised in 1755 and 1759, though neither of them long survived the fall of Pombal in 1777.

By this time a further change was evident in Brazil. The mineral cycle had run its course. Gold exports steadily declined after 1760, and by the end of the century the mining settlements of Minas Gerais, including the famous Vila Rica (Ouro Preto), were falling or had fallen into decay. Agriculture, on the other hand, experienced in the second half of the eighteenth century a notable revival. Partly this was due to the growing European demand for such agricultural staples as sugar and cotton—the latter, like the coffee grown in the southern captaincies, a relatively new export crop. In the 1780s it was no longer Brazilian gold that flowed from Portugal to Britain but Brazilian cotton. And while in the middle of the century gold and diamonds had led to the rise of Rio de Janeiro, at its end sugar and cotton had restored to Bahia and Pernambuco something of their old pre-eminence.

Despite the decay of the mining areas, and despite also the restrictive policy of the mother-country—the crown, in 1785, did its best to put an end to colonial manufactures—Brazil was steadily increasing in wealth and population. The country's population, indeed, had multiplied some ten or eleven times in the eighteenth century, and in 1800 already equalled, and was soon to surpass, the population of Portugal. Half-slave, half-free, and embracing an infinite gradation of race and colour, its island settlements stretched in a great coastal arc from the cotton and cacao plantations of Pará to the cattle ranges of Rio Grande do Sul. Far into the interior, Tabatinga, 1400 miles up the Amazon, and Corumbá, upon the upper waters of the Paraguay, were outposts of empire. The inland province of Minas Gerais was the most populous of the captaincies. But the greater part of the population still lived on or near the Atlantic seaboard. The plantation system, based on a single crop and slave labour, dominated Brazil; and north and south the possession of land had formed the entry into a native aristocracy which already considered itself to be, not Portuguese, but Brazilian. As in the Spanish colonies, so also in Brazil, the jealousy between Americans and Europeans was a factor to be reckoned with. The landed gentry—the *senhores de engenhos* (lords of the sugar-mills), the great cotton and provision planters, the ranchers and cattle-owners—great men on their own estates and in their own provinces and often dominating also the municipal *câmaras*, or town councils, despised the Portuguese merchants and immigrants who in general controlled the colony's commercial life; and the antipathy was returned. It was to become the more important when, in 1807–8, the Portuguese royal family, fleeing the tide of Napoleon's invasion of the Iberian peninsula, sought refuge in Brazil, and Rio de Janeiro, which barely half a century earlier had become the capital of Brazil and the residence of the viceroy, became the capital of Portugal and the seat of the sovereign.

Brazilian society was rural rather than urban, and educationally it was backward. The colony possessed no printing press; it had no university—wealthy Brazilians of the professional classes were educated abroad at Coimbra or Montpellier; and schools were not numerous. Much of the teaching had been in the hands of the Jesuits: their expulsion did little to improve the educational scene. A scientific society, the *Sociedade Científica do Rio de Janeiro*, was founded in 1772, transformed into the *Sociedade Literária* in 1779, and disbanded in the 1790s, its members, or some of them, being arrested on account of their alleged political activities. Of the arts the most notable was architecture, and among architects and sculptors one name in particular stands out, that of Aleijadinho, the 'little cripple', whose real name was António Francisco Lisboa (1730–1814), and who evolved in his delightful baroque churches in Minas Gerais a style of his own—the *Estilo Aleijadinho*.

But though the intellectual life of Brazil was less well developed than that of some of the Spanish American colonies, it was not negligible. It was nourished from Portugal and Coimbra, from Montpellier and France. Brazilians travelled abroad. The young José Bonifácio de Andrada e Silva, later to play a dominant part in the establishment of Brazilian independence, was sent to Coimbra at the age of seventeen and became a professor there in 1800. European books, French, Portuguese and English, were read. Cláudio Manuel da Costa, later implicated in the famous *Inconfidência Mineira*, and one of the leading literary figures of the day, attempted to translate the *Wealth of Nations*; and the library of his friend, Canon Luís Vieira da Silva, also in Vila Rica, contained works in Latin, French, Portuguese, English, Italian and Spanish, including those of Montesquieu, Mably, Condillac and Voltaire.

The importance of the *Inconfidência Mineira* itself, which led to Cláudio's suicide, has perhaps been exaggerated. A conspiracy organised in 1788 by a second-lieutenant in the army, Joaquim José da Silva Xavier, popularly known as Tiradentes—he had practised as a dentist—with the support of a number of other residents in Minas Gerais, aimed at the destruction of Portuguese rule, the proclamation of a republic and the

415

removal of the capital to São João del Rei. The conspirators, however, were denounced to the government; Tiradentes was executed at Rio de Janeiro in 1792, and his fellow-conspirators were banished to Africa. Reflecting in some degree the influence of the American Revolution among the intellectuals of Minas Gerais, and, far more clearly, the political ideas of the 'age of the enlightenment' in France, the movement drew its inspiration mainly, perhaps, from dissatisfaction with local conditions in Minas Gerais, and, above all, from the personal discontent of Tiradentes. An isolated phenomenon, it left little permanent mark upon the history of Brazil. Neither in 1788, nor twenty years later when the Portuguese court arrived in Rio de Janeiro, were revolutionary ideas in Brazil widely diffused.

To the north-west of Brazil two other European powers besides Spain and Portugal possessed colonies on the South American mainland. These were the colonies of French and Dutch Guiana. French Guiana (Cayenne), after a century and a half of intermittent colonisation, had fallen ever deeper into stagnation and was the home, in the middle of the eighteenth century, of about five hundred Europeans and some fifty thousand slaves. In an ambitious scheme designed to compensate France for the loss of Canada Choiseul, in 1763, attempted to found a large white settlement on the Kourou river, with no other effect than the loss of 14,000 lives and 30 million livres. Victor Pierre Malouet, who arrived as governor in 1776, tried to induce the planters to grow more sugar and drink less rum. He tried also to drain the coastal lowlands and generally to put the colony on its feet. The planters, however, opposed him bitterly, and he retired in disgust in 1778. To such improvements as had been begun the disorders which resulted from the French Revolution effectually put a stop, and when, in 1794, the Convention abolished slavery—Napoleon re-established it in 1803—most of the slaves left the plantations. Vigorously defended by Victor Hugues during the Napoleonic wars, the colony was compelled to surrender to an Anglo-Portuguese force in 1809, and was not restored to France till eight years later.

While French Guiana stagnated, the Dutch settlement of Surinam gave, by contrast, an impression not only of wealth but even of luxury. Governed by the Dutch West India Company and its associates (forming the Chartered Society of Surinam) it enjoyed in fact a moderate prosperity, producing not only sugar and cacao but coffee and cotton also. It lived, however, in constant fear of slave insurrections and suffered greatly from the depredations of rebel Negroes. Essequibo and Demerara, under the direct control of the Dutch West India Company, owed much to the work of Laurens Storm van's Gravesande, the greatest of Dutch Guiana administrators, who arrived in Essequibo in 1738, became its *commandeur* in 1742, and from 1750 to 1772, after the foundation of Demerara, held the post of Director-General of the Two Rivers. The rivers had been opened to settlers of all nationalities, with the promise of ten years' freedom from head-tax, and with Storm's encouragement British planters from Barbados and other West Indian islands were quick to take advantage. By the end of the century the greater part of the white population was British and all the cotton and most of the sugar and coffee plantations were in British hands. Berbice, governed under a charter granted in 1732 to the directors of the Berbice Association, was less prosperous. It suffered severely from a slave insurrection in 1763 and did not recover till many years later.

For all the Guiana colonies the closing years of the eighteenth century were a time of crisis. When Holland joined the Armed Neutrality in 1780, Essequibo, Demerara and Berbice were promptly captured by British privateers, to be 'liberated' by France a year later. The restoration of Dutch rule was followed, in Essequibo and Demerara, by a fierce struggle between the colonists and the Dutch East India Company over the question of taxation, only terminating with the expiry of the company's charter in 1791. The Two Rivers (like Surinam) then came under the direct control of the Estates General. But the flight of the stadtholder in 1795, and the transformation of the United Netherlands into the Batavian Republic and the close ally of France, again exposed the Guiana colonies to capture. Essequibo, Demerara and Berbice were all occupied in 1796, and Surinam was captured in 1799. Restored to the Batavian Republic in 1802, they were again occupied in 1803–4. This time only Surinam, originally colonised by England, was returned to Holland, Essequibo, Berbice and Demerara becoming, in due course, the colony of British Guiana.

The Guianas remained colonies, though some of them changed hands. So, also, despite the revolt of England's North American colonies, did the European possessions not only in Central and South America but in the West Indies. There was one exception—the old French colony of Saint Domingue, occupying the western end of the island of Hispaniola.

The rise of Saint Domingue in the eighteenth century had been meteoric. By the eve of the French Revolution the colony had become one of the richest and most productive areas in the world, ruthlessly and efficiently organised for the production of sugar, coffee and cotton, and employing in its trade with France more than a thousand ships a year. Its government, even more authoritarian than that of the Spanish colonies, lay in the hands of a military governor-general and a civilian intendant. Representative institutions there were none. Its social structure was extraordinarily complex. A handful of whites, numbering about 35,000, was divided into the *grands blancs* and the *petits blancs*: the *grands blancs* comprising the great planters, the rich merchants, and the higher civil servants, the *petits blancs* including all the rest. But the whites were also divided into creoles and Europeans, the natives and the foreign-born, each class bitterly resenting the other. Below them, and despised by all whites, whatever their status, were the *gens de couleur*, known also as the *affranchis* or freedmen. There were some 28,000 of these. All free persons who possessed any tincture of negro blood were *gens de couleur*. A few of them were pure Negroes, a few were almost pure white, the majority were plainly mulattoes. The material prosperity of the *gens de couleur* had been steadily increasing. Many of them were both slave-owners and landowners. But they were subjected to intense social humiliation, more particularly from the *petits blancs*; they were excluded by law from the learned professions; and they were even hindered by sumptuary legislation from adopting European fashions, such as the carrying of swords or side-arms. Finally, at the bottom of the social scale and, indeed, outside the class structure proper, was an enormous force of slave-labour. The slaves numbered nearly half a million. More than half of them were relatively recent importations, African-born rather than bred in the island. A few, like the rebel Negroes of Surinam and the 'maroons' of Jamaica, had escaped from slavery and lived a wild and marauding life deep in the forests and mountains. The rest, often subjected to great brutality at the hands of whites and *gens de couleur* alike, were kept down by fear and themselves inspired fear.

At the outset of the French Revolution an aggressive minority among the *grands blancs* insisted, despite the opposition of the governor-general, on sending delegates to the Estates General in the hope of winning a measure of self-government for the colony, with themselves as the governors. Appalled by the Declaration of the Rights of Man, and realising too late the danger of attracting revolutionary attention to the affairs of Saint Domingue, they hurriedly obtained royal authority to convoke a colonial assembly, responsible solely to the crown. But the damage had been done. Henceforth the fate of the colony was linked to the fate of France. The French abolition society, the *Amis des Noirs*, vigorously championed the cause of the *gens de couleur*; and the National Assembly, at first issuing a series of inconsistent and ambiguous decrees (each of which had violent repercussions in the colony) upon the political rights of the freedmen, finally, in April 1792, not only decreed the enfranchisement of the *gens de couleur* but dispatched three Jacobin commissioners with six thousand troops to ensure that the decree should be observed. These, in August 1793, proclaimed the emancipation of the slaves, and their action was ratified in February 1794 by the French Convention.

Terrible scenes, meanwhile, had been enacted in Saint Domingue. The *grands blancs* had been the first to challenge the constituted authorities. But the revolutionary infection rapidly spread, first to the *petits blancs*, then to the *gens de couleur*—the first mulatto risings occurred in the spring and autumn of 1790—and finally to the Negro slaves. The great Negro insurrection in the north of the colony began in August 1791, its horrors soon to be paralleled by the horrors of racial war—the rising of the *gens de couleur*—in the west and in the south. The arrival of the Jacobin commissioners from France, superseding in September 1792 an earlier group of commissioners, merely added fuel to the flames. Assuming dictatorial powers, the commissioners first exacerbated the divisions between the *grands* and the *petits blancs*; they then exalted the *gens de couleur* at the expense of *grands* and *petits blancs* alike; and finally they alienated the *gens de couleur* by transferring their support to the blacks and by decreeing the emancipation of the slaves. By the end of 1793 the colony of Saint Domingue lay in ruins, its prosperity destroyed, its social order overthrown. In the north the whites in their thousands had emigrated or been massacred. In the east invasion threatened from the Spanish part of the island—war between France and Spain had been declared in March 1793; while in the south, and soon in the north and west also, British troops had been landed in response to the petitions of despairing planters and of white *émigrés*, and an intervention had been begun which was to last, with great loss of life and at great expense, till 1798.

The next seven years witnessed a triangular struggle between the blacks, the mulattoes, and the British forces of occupation. The Negroes were led by François-Dominique Toussaint, who adopted also the name of Louverture. An ex-slave, Toussaint had joined the Negro insurrection of 1791. On the outbreak of war between France and Spain he entered the Spanish service in the eastern part of the island, rose rapidly, and in 1794, massacring the Spanish soldiers under his orders, deserted with his black troops to the French. His services were invaluable, and he was rewarded in 1796 with the post of lieutenant-governor. He arranged in 1798 for the evacuation of the British forces, and he also contrived, with much skill, to ensure the departure of the last official French representatives to France. In his struggle with the British he had been aided by the mulatto leader, André Rigaud, who controlled the south (where he virtually re-enslaved the Negroes) as Toussaint controlled the north. But the alliance had always been uneasy, and with the departure of the British troops Toussaint and the blacks were free to turn upon Rigaud and the mulattoes in a war of the castes which left the south devastated and depopulated. All that remained was to occupy Spanish Santo Domingo, ceded to France at the Treaty of Basle in 1795, but still, with French agreement, held by the Spaniards. It was overrun in 1801, and in the same year a constitution was promulgated for the whole island designating Toussaint governor-general for life with the power to nominate his successor. The *émigré* whites were invited to return; the Negroes were set to work; and a semblance of prosperity returned to Saint Domingue.

The end came a year later, when Napoleon, temporarily freed by the Peace of Amiens to turn his attention to the New World, sent his brother-in-law, General Leclerc, to reassert French authority. Toussaint was forced to submit. Treacherously seized and sent to France, he died in a

French prison in April 1803. Leclerc had died before him of the yellow fever which ravaged the French army. Blacks and mulattoes, driven to desperation by the news that the social disabilities of mulattoes had been renewed and the slave trade restored, had again risen, this time in a war of independence. It was waged on both sides with appalling ferocity. But the renewal of the war in Europe sounded the death-knell of French Saint Domingue. In November 1803 the French capitulated to the British naval forces off-shore; on 1 January 1804 the Negro leader, Jean-Jacques Dessalines, proclaimed the independence of Haiti; and within little more than a year hardly a white man was left alive.

CHAPTER XV

SOCIAL AND PSYCHOLOGICAL FOUNDATIONS OF THE REVOLUTIONARY ERA

THERE was a revolutionary era at the close of the eighteenth century somewhat as there had been an era of the Protestant Reformation in the sixteenth. In neither period did the same things happen in all countries. Everywhere, in the sixteenth century, there had been dissatisfaction at conditions in the church, but only certain places turned Protestant, each in its own way, Lutheran, Anglican or Calvinist, with no acceptance even of the common designation of Protestant until long after the event; some Protestant regions went back to Catholicism, and in the end most Europeans remained in the Roman church. Similarly, in the revolutionary era, by which the last third of the eighteenth century is to be understood, there was a widespread dissatisfaction at conditions in government and society. There were similar ideas in many countries on the direction of desirable change. The same vocabulary of political key words appeared in all European languages: 'aristocracy' and 'feudalism' acquired a bad sense for those who favoured a new order, for whom 'sovereignty of the people', 'equality' and 'natural rights' had a good sense, with a few terms, such as 'constitution', 'law' and 'liberty' favoured by all, though with different meanings. But only in two countries, the British American colonies and France, did revolution reach the point of permanently destroying the older authorities. Only in France did the revolution make social changes of the deepest kind. Only the French made a successful revolution entirely by their own efforts, since even the American Revolution owed its decisive outcome to French intervention. Other revolutionary movements there were in abundance, both before and after 1789, in Ireland, the United Provinces, the Austrian Netherlands, Geneva, Poland and the Italian states. In England and Hungary there were men whose views would have been hardly less than revolutionary if successfully carried out. A monarchist revolution against the privileged class was attempted by Joseph II in the Habsburg countries, and carried out with more success, in a more limited way, by Gustavus III in Sweden. The corresponding phenomenon in Germany, as various Germans said in the 1790s, was a 'revolution of the mind'. Latin America became independent after 1810. In the end—though 1815 was hardly an end—most Europeans lived again under their older authorities. But all Europe and the world of European or Western civilisation had been shaken to its foundations.

There is nothing new in such an observation. To Tocqueville it seemed that the French Revolution had had no territorial boundary. Burke saw it as a civil war of all Christendom. To repeat the excited outcries of French and other revolutionaries in 1792, who hoped for a war of all peoples against all kings, would nowadays be unconvincing; it is better to turn to the conservative young Dutch patrician, G. K. van Hogendorp. Writing in 1791 at Rotterdam, he saw two great parties forming 'in all nations'. One, he said, the party of church and state, believed in 'a right of government to be exercised by one or several persons over the mass of the people, of divine origin and supported by the church'. The other, which he called the party of the sovereignty of the people or democracy, denied any right of government 'except that arising from the free consent of those who submit to it', and held 'all persons who take part in government accountable for their actions'.[1] So far as the conflicts of the revolutionary era may be reduced to only two sides, no better statement of their difference can be found.

The strength, the composition, the development, the aims and the fate of the two parties, to use Hogendorp's word, varied a great deal from country to country. The European world, at this time as at all times in its history, was a blend of unity and diversity. Its most active centre, in the eighteenth century, was an area within which a horse might in a few days take a man to London or Paris. It extended eastward into Russia, and westward into those parts of the Americas where persons of European descent had now for several generations been established. The problem set for the present chapter is to survey this region, so far as possible, with a view to explaining those features of society, and of thought and feeling, by which the presence or absence of revolution, or of revolutionary agitation, or of sympathy for revolution, may be understood. It is to draw a general map on which differences, resemblances and interrelationships may be seen. On such a map much must be sacrificed, with complex mountain chains appearing only as a few lines and great cities as mere dots. Obviously such a map cannot replace larger-scale and more accurate treatments; yet it may have its uses.

We have learned, especially from Professor Georges Lefebvre, to think of the French Revolution of 1789 as a coming together of four discernible movements: an aristocratic revolution, a bourgeois revolution, a peasant revolution and a revolution of the urban working class. It was the concurrence of all four that made the great Revolution, and it was their divergence, since they had different objectives, that made the Revolution complicated and prolonged. A rebellious aristocracy, momentarily supported by the bourgeoisie, forced Louis XVI to call the Estates General in 1788; but it had been the differences between nobles and bourgeois, or the failure of Louis XV and Louis XVI to impose the necessary reforms, that

[1] *Brieven en Gedenkschriften* (The Hague, 1876), vol. III, pp. 60–1.

had caused the breakdown of government before 1788; and it was the difference between nobles and bourgeois, or refusal of the bourgeois to accept the aims of an aristocratic revolution, that transformed the Estates General into a National Assembly in June 1789. It was the rising of the peasantry against the manorial system, and the acceptance of peasant demands by the bourgeois leaders, that enabled the Assembly to remain in being. It was the insurrection of the small people of Paris—market women, artisans, shopkeepers and journeymen—that gave strength to the advanced parties in the Assembly. The drift of the nobility toward counter-revolution, and even to the soliciting of foreign aid, inflamed and in a measure consolidated the various revolutionary groups. Bourgeois, peasant and working-man disagreed on much; but none, as a class, could be won to a programme of counter-revolution. Their ability to work together, such as it was, made the French Revolution successful to the degree that the old régime was never restored. The French Revolution saw the arousal of all classes to political action. Had any one of the four classes named been apathetic, or merely conservative, events would have taken a different turn. We may say, at some risk of dogmatism, that without the aristocratic revolt there would have been no Estates General, without the bourgeois revolt no National Assembly, without the peasant revolt no abolition of 'feudalism', without the popular restlessness in the cities no firm stand against reaction, and without the peasant and popular upheavals no citizen army to withstand the First Coalition.

On the other hand, and at the same level of generality, it may be seen why certain other revolutionary movements were abortive. In Hungary in 1790 the aristocracy in the Diet was in open rebellion against Leopold II; but the bourgeoisie was weak, and the peasantry hostile. The peasants were also rebellious, as much so in places as in France the year before. Their uprising has been called the worst Hungarian jacquerie since 1514; but, stirred by the attempted reforms of the late Joseph II, the peasants fought for his brother Leopold, and against their own Magyar lords. Hungary was quieted by the dispatch of troops from other parts of the empire. In Poland, between 1788 and 1792, the king and the gentry made a kind of revolution against the magnates and the Russian influence; the weakness of the town class, and passivity of the peasants, left the reformers helpless against counter-revolution. Events in Holland, the Austrian Netherlands and Ireland made apparent the limitations of a movement confined to the middle classes of the towns. The Dutch Patriots brought about a kind of revolution between 1784 and 1787, but the rural population remained quiet, and the urban lower classes favoured the prince of Orange. The Belgian Democrats of 1789–90 were suppressed by the Estates party, and terrorised by fanaticised peasants. The Irish Volunteers, and even the United Irishmen of 1798, had no adequate base in the rural Catholic mass. The same weakness afflicted the various short-lived republics set up by native revolutionaries in collaboration with the French armies during the wars of the First and Second Coalitions—the Batavian, Helvetic, Cisalpine, Ligurian, Roman and Parthenopean republics. In none was the agricultural population won over to the new order. All were essentially middle-class régimes, in which handfuls of more advanced radicals played a part; revolution here rose from native causes to meet local needs, but its strength depended on the French armies. The case of these middle-class and urban revolutionary movements may be contrasted with the establishment of the United States of America. Here, too, it was the action of the French army and navy that made possible a clean-cut military and diplomatic settlement. But the American revolt against Britain enlisted strong support among the farm population, especially in New England and Virginia, as well as among the lesser townspeople, and among some of what passed in America for an aristocracy; it was a true revolution, and, without French support, would probably have maintained an irregular resistance for an indefinite period of time.

These remarks are made at this point to suggest that, if one wishes to look into the social and psychological foundations of the revolutionary era, as promised in the title of this chapter, it is necessary to examine the aristocracy, bourgeoisie, peasantry and town labouring class of various countries, to see to what extent such classes existed at all, to get an idea of their numbers and strength, take note of their attitudes to each other and to government, and observe the conditions that might draw them together or hold them apart. 'Aristocrat', 'bourgeois', 'peasant', 'working-man' are the names of abstract categories, not so much empty as over-full. The French nobility was very composite, the French peasantry made up of various sub-classes. Applied to a dozen countries, the same words cover an even wider range of concrete meanings. The lordliness of Bohemia was not the lordliness of England; the burgher of Warsaw was a different animal from the *bourgeois* of Toulouse or the 'bourgeois' of Liverpool or Philadelphia; and the difference between the 'peasants' of eastern Europe, France, Kent and Connecticut was, if anything, even greater. It is important to see these differences without reducing everything to the unique or the merely local, to find how the four social categories were concretely represented in different countries.

In social structure there was a great difference between western and eastern Europe, with the line of division running in general along the Elbe river and the western border of Bohemia to the Adriatic Sea. Towns east of this line were small and far apart, and it was common enough, in the Baltic provinces of Russia, in Poland, in Bohemia and in Hungary, for the town populations to be German, or in places Jewish, and in either case ethnically distinct from the surrounding country. In Poland all the inhabitants of the fifty largest towns, taken together, were only a little more than half as numerous as the nobles—a ratio that may be contrasted with that in France, where the population of the fifty largest towns was five times as large as the nobility, or in England, where the combined population of Manchester, Liverpool and Birmingham alone about equalled, in 1801, the number of all those whom Patrick Colquhoun classified as peers, baronets, knights, esquires, and ladies and gentlemen living on incomes. In eastern Europe, the relatively low state of commercial development, and of monarchical government, had impeded the growth of a bourgeoisie either of the commercial or of the civil-service type as found in the West. Towns enjoyed less political stature than in the Middle Ages. In the diets of Poland and Bohemia they had virtually ceased to be represented, and in the lower house of the Hungarian diet they cast together a single vote, the same as one gentleman from the country.

It was the landlords who predominated in this eastern zone. The Prussian, the Habsburg and the tsarist states had been built on conciliation of their wishes, and in Poland they had prevented the growth of any effective state at all. Their chief wish was to maintain local control of their agricultural work force. The peasant was unfree. Called a serf by historians, he was generally known in the language of the day as a 'subject', a lord's subject rather than the king's. The serf performed uncompensated labour services for the lord, from three days a week where the laws of Maria Theresa were observed, to as many as six days of the week where they were evaded, or where, as in Poland and Russia, there was less attention to the relief of serfdom than in the Habsburg dominions. Without the lord's permission the serf could not leave the manor, nor marry off it, nor learn a trade. Labour mobility for the agrarian mass stood near zero, or rather it depended purely on direction by the lord, who could either run his estate in a routine manner, or develop it in capitalistic fashion by selling agricultural or forest products in distant markets, or divert some of his labour force to industrial or mining activities. Capitalism in eastern Europe, such as it was, grew up in large measure as a noble enterprise in association with servile labour. The serf, so to speak, stood outside both the economic and the political systems, insensitive to either economic or political motivations; he might starve or eat, according to a season's crop, but fluctuations of wages, of opportunities for employment, of prices of goods to be bought and sold, such as might excite a French peasant, meant much less in eastern Europe; and political authorities or courts of law, beyond the lord himself, were remote things known by hearsay from another world.

Separation and mutual strangeness of classes were the result. We hear of antipathies of a kind associated in the twentieth century only with racial difference. In the Four Years' Diet in Poland some members were so incensed at the thought of burghers as deputies that they threatened to leave the assembly. The diet, in connection with the revolutionary constitution of 1791, did allow admission of burgher representatives, but it refused to call them deputies, a term reserved for nobles sent by the provincial assemblies, and called them plenipotentiaries instead, as if the towns were an alien element in the country. Peasants seemed a race apart, as indeed they were, given the conditions in which they lived. After Joseph II, by his reforms, had attempted in effect to convert the peasantry of his empire to something like the French peasantry before the Revolution, free from compulsory labour and physical punishment, working for wages, or on land held in return for stated dues, the noble landowners in all the diets of the empire raised choruses of warning and disapproval. The common people, they said, were too childish to respond to monetary incentives, too irresponsible to keep from squandering wages in taverns if paid in wages at all, too lazy to work unless driven, too poor and ignorant to carry on cultivation except under overseers, too 'vulgar in spirit' and lacking in honour to be deterred by threats of jail, in short, too primitive to get along without 'the wholesome effects of corporal punishment'.[1] The Diet of Bohemia expressed amazement that Czech peasants should be referred to as 'part of the nation'. The 'nation' in eastern Europe did usually mean a political nation of nobles and gentry; burghers were outsiders, peasants barely human; the idea of the nation as a community of all classes—an essential idea of the revolutionary era—could with difficulty obtain any currency east of the Elbe. Class difference more than ethnic difference stood in the way.

The harsh juxtaposition of a landed gentry and a servile labour force made parts of America resemble eastern Europe, notably parts of Latin America, the West Indies and the English-speaking regions from Virginia to the south. Burke compared the Virginians to the Poles, and he might have compared them to the Hungarians also, believing that in both cases a certain high sense of liberty was made more acute by the slavery that surrounded it. In their busy political life in county meetings, their suspicion of cities, their dislike of central government and joy in resisting it, their aristocratic self-consciousness, and bland assumption of incorrigible inferiority in their own workers, the American slave-owners and east European serf-owners were unknowingly akin. From an opposite point of view the resemblance was evident to Hugo Kołłątaj, the most radically minded of the Polish reformers, who even favoured the immediate abolition of serfdom. He remarked, in 1790, that slaves black or white (that is, in America or in Europe) were men, equals, and citizens of the earth. The American plantations undoubtedly resembled the latifundia of eastern Europe. Still there was a difference. Even in South Carolina over half the population was white and free. Not only were there many smaller landowning farmers who owned no slaves, but there were many, especially

---

[1] P. von Mitrofanov, *Joseph II: seine politische und kulturelle Tätigkeit, aus dem Russischen übersetzt* (Vienna and Leipzig, 1910), p. 632.

in the western part of these southern provinces, who, having recently moved in from Pennsylvania or Ireland or Germany, had not yet accepted a view of life in which slavery seemed essential. In the eighteenth century, before the rise of the Cotton Kingdom, the merits of slavery were doubted by many slave-owners themselves. Above all, for present purposes, the landed aristocrats of Virginia and the Carolinas could and did mix easily with merchants of Charleston and the northern towns. They could rally lesser farmers as political followers. There could be sporadic class conflict, but in so new a country there was no sense of immemorial class separation, and except for Negroes no feeling of insuperable hereditary apartness.

Western Europe can be understood in contrast to eastern Europe. West of the Elbe, in Germany, the Netherlands and France, lay the land of what the Germans call *Grundherrschaft* as distinguished from *Gutsherrschaft*. The lord lived, not by managing his own estate, selling its product and directing a dependent work force either in person or through overseers, as in the East; he drew his income from seigneurial or manorial dues, quit-rents, tolls, heriots, fees for the use of ovens and winepresses, and the like, paid to him by peasants who were legally free to come and go, to buy and sell, to take employment for wages, and to till their own plots of ground within the limits of village rights or custom. The lord possessed a vestigial jurisdiction, subject to royal or other territorial courts; but, essentially, 'feudalism' had become a form of property and income. Characteristically it was the nobleman who received such income, but, especially in France, the ownership of manors was legally open to anyone, and there were many bourgeois, church bodies, colleges, hospitals and even peasants who received revenues of this kind. The recipients, however, no longer performed any economic service, managerial or other, of any social utility. Such income therefore could be, and was, abolished in France and adjoining countries during the revolutionary era, with or without compensation, and in any case without violent disturbance to the economic system. The revolutionary era was to see great changes in politics and society, but in the economic system, as a system, it saw continuity.

The peasantry had become differentiated according to wealth and income. Some were owners of property, in that their holdings of land, though subject to manorial payments, were secure, heritable and defensible in courts of law. Others rented parcels of land for terms of years, or worked it on shares. There was in most places a large agricultural proletariat, hired for daily wages by other peasants, nobles, bourgeois or other owners of land. A good many peasants sold some of their own produce in the towns, and there were few places in western Europe, unlike eastern Europe and America, that were more than a day's journey from a town of at least some regional importance. In the East a peasant might be the

427

victim of natural calamities; in the West he might be the victim or beneficiary of economic forces also. The rise and fall of prices and wages could
directly affect him. The middle of the eighteenth century was a period of
relative well-being for the agricultural population. A slow gradual rise
of farm prices benefited those who owned or rented enough land to offer
goods for sale. The cessation of this rise, after about 1770, at least in
France, where the work of Professor Labrousse has made the situation
known, was of great disadvantage to the peasants, since with declining
incomes the burden of seigneurial dues, rents and taxes, even when it remained fixed, was felt as more heavy. In fact the burden itself tended to
rise; governments needed more taxes, and the rising standard of living
of the upper class induced many owners to exact a stricter collection of
seigneurial dues, in what is known as the 'feudal reaction' at the close of
the old régime. Meanwhile, the purely wage-earning class, both agricultural and urban, suffered from the fact that wages rose much less than
prices of food and shelter.

The region west of the Elbe, and including most of Italy, was the land
also of the bourgeoisie. Estimates of numbers cannot be given, since the
term itself is hard to define. Size of cities is an uncertain indication, for
the bourgeois, especially in France, might be mainly an owner of rural
land. Given the nature of eighteenth-century capitalism and technology,
urbanisation was no index to industrial growth. Naples appears to have
been the largest city in Europe except London and Paris, without being
any great centre of bourgeois life.

Institutions rather than persons made a 'bourgeois' type of society, and
in such a society the landed aristocracy itself, and even some of the
peasantry, might be *embourgeoisé*. A country was 'bourgeois', rather
than 'feudal', to the extent that property in land was distinguished from
personal jurisdiction, that an owner was not a *seigneur*, that land could
be bought and sold in a market open to anyone possessing the money,
that the landowner was not content to receive customary income but developed his property by calculated methods to increase the yield, or held
it for a rise in value, like the owners of London real estate or land speculators in America, or used it as collateral on which to raise capital for
commercial or industrial undertakings, or for agricultural improvements.
Development of this kind had gone farthest in England, where it gave a
common outlook to members of the aristocracy and the middle class, and
so contributed, along with the absence of legal class-distinctions, to soli-
difying at least all property-owners against the seductions of revolution.
If there was a revolution in France, it was in part because so many of the
nobility continued to rely on seigneurial forms of income, without having
the actual power of landlords in the East; and because at the same time
various of the bourgeoisie, the peasants and wealthy liberal noblemen
were able to envisage property rights of more modern kind, dissociated

from manorial custom and from personal status, and allowing more free-dom to the owner in the use of his possessions.

Of the northern provinces of British America, from Pennsylvania to New England, it may be observed, for the present comparative purpose, that they were already 'bourgeois' without having much of a bourgeoisie. The United States at the time of its foundation was overwhelmingly rural. Less than three Americans in a hundred lived in any town as large as Boston, which had only 16,000 people. The corresponding figure for England and Wales in 1801 was about seventeen in a hundred; for France, in 1787, it was about eleven. British America, numerically at least, was a world of farmers, and except for the great plantations in the South, and the forms of a manorial system in the Hudson valley, it was a world of small farmers who were not even farmers in the British or French sense of the word, since they were owners rather than tenants. They held by clear and unencumbered property right, tracing their titles back, not to somebody's manor house, but to royal grant within remembered times under conditions of modern law. They looked neither up to a gentry, nor down on a fixed pool of hired labour. Each family worked its own land, without being emotionally bound to it like a European peasant. The farm was used as a source of income; it could be readily abandoned, in the search for a better farm and better opportunity farther west. A sense of ownership, enterprise, mobility and independence infected the whole population, by contrast, at least, with corresponding lower classes of Britain or Europe.

Nevertheless, in both Europe and America, there were persons as well as institutions that may be usefully thought of as bourgeois. They were persons of a certain degree of education, carefulness of upbringing, regularity of income and habits of work, who sensed themselves as being above the popular mass, but as not belonging to the social élite. Though new members might join it, the class itself was about as hereditary as the aristocracy or the peasantry. Since we are engaging in generalisations, it may be said that bourgeois families had arisen since the Middle Ages in two ways: in association either with government or with trade. In central Europe the official bourgeoisie was stronger than the commercial. Lack of access to the sea, multiplicity of small political units, the strength of guild systems and of autonomous towns, had inhibited the growth of trade and banking and capital formation on the largest scale. The burgher here was either an administrator in the service of a prince, or the employee of a manufacturing enterprise planned and financed by the state, as in Prussia. Or he might carry on a business as modest in its capitalisation as in its market; the richest banker in the Austrian Netherlands, for example, Edouard de Walckiers of Brussels, had an income of £6000 a year, which may be contrasted with the £100,000 a year of William Beckford, reputedly the richest man in the city of London. In small places that were essentially republics, as in the German free cities and in the Swiss cantons, certain burgher families might in themselves constitute the permanent personnel of government, and draw their incomes from the perquisites of rule, like the twenty patrician families who governed Nuremberg, or the corresponding patricians of Bern or Milan. A Milan patrician, like a nobleman of Germany or France, 'derogated' or lost his status if he went into trade.

A bourgeoisie of commercial origin was most important in England and Holland, where it owed its strength and its independence to the private ownership of capital, to the profits of trans-ocean trade, and to the habits of bearing risks and managing affairs under only a general supervision and protection by government. Nowhere else did the commercial class bulk so large; it is estimated that out of a total national income of £228,000,000 in England about 1800 some £40,000,000 came from foreign and internal trade, as against £35,000,000 from landed rents, and the predominance of commercial income in Holland must have been much greater. In the Dutch provinces, however, certain families of burgher and commercial origin had turned into 'regents', occupied more with government than with trade. The wealthy Dutch had come to live in large measure from foreign investments. In 1777 they owned 40 per cent of the British national debt, and, with the French, they financed the American Revolution.

In France both the official and the commercial bourgeoisie were numerous and important. The old and elaborate monarchy, the complex networks of law-courts, the rapid growth in the eighteenth century of the War Office, the postal system, the administration of roads and bridges, all added to the number of lawyers, office-holders, engineers and various experts associated with government. There were seventy-eight towns on the eve of the Revolution with populations of over 10,000; each had not only its trading class, but its established and often privileged body of municipal oligarchs. A bourgeoisie of more purely economic origin was represented by the bankers and tax-farmers of Paris, and by merchants and shipowners of the ports who had grown rich on trade with the West Indies and Asia. In addition, more vocal in France than elsewhere, because of the development of the sciences, the academies, the press and the reading public, was the great number of writers and intellectuals. They were more dissatisfied with prevailing conditions than corresponding groups in Germany or England, and in general had less habitual connection with either government or business. Some, like Voltaire, were by origin true bourgeois who made a good deal of money; more, perhaps, were financially in the plight of Rousseau; some, like Montesquieu, were noblemen of old stock; most, like Dupont de Nemours or the marquis de Condorcet, whatever their own social standing, favoured a form of society in which privilege and aristocracy should be abolished, and the way opened for persons who were not noble to play a larger role in affairs.

It was against 'aristocracy' that the revolutionary and radical movements were mainly directed. The term sometimes had a relative sense, varying according to the social position of him who used it. Thus the blue-blooded French country nobleman might complain of the aristocracy of the court in 1788, and the English squire might detest the aristocracy of great lords and ladies. At the other extreme, in the Paris of 1795, a city of some 600,000, an infuriated working-man could cry that 'all the rich are scoundrels, there are a million of them in Paris to be punished!'[1] Yet it is possible to give the word some definition for the present purpose.

Aristocracy was not the same as nobility. On the one hand, in certain monarchies, some quite ordinary people might acquire noble status by royal action, like the Jewish father of Sonnenfels ennobled by Maria Theresa, or like Dupont de Nemours, who obtained a patent of nobility for his service as inspector of manufactures. They did not thereby become aristocrats. On the other hand, countries lacking a nobility undoubtedly possessed an aristocracy. There was an aristocracy in British America before 1776, composed of certain intermarried families that had held seats on the governors' councils for three or four generations, played a continuing role in public affairs, and enjoyed marked advantages in obtaining grants of land. There was an aristocracy at republican Geneva, where the established patricians of the Small Council were opposed by burgher democrats in the revolution of 1768. The patricians of Milan were certainly aristocrats, as were the highly un-feudal 'nobles' of Venice, or the governing families at Nuremberg, who allowed themselves, but no one else, to carry swords and wear hats with plumes. At the free city of Frankfurt on the Main a law of 1731 classified the population into five estates, or *Stände*. The top estate was for persons who had sat on the town council 'for a hundred years', and who also had obtained patents of hereditary nobility from the Holy Roman Empire. In Holland the nobles were insignificant; indeed all the nobles in the province had only one vote in the estates, with the eighteen towns having eighteen votes. The Dutch aristocracy was composed of the regents, mainly of burgher origin if one went far enough back, but who now kept control in the hands of certain families generation after generation. In England there were only two hundred actual noblemen, and all others were legally commoners; but there was a landed aristocracy that in effect governed the country through Parliament. Its size was estimated both by Gregory King and by Patrick Colquhoun at less than one and a half per cent of the population, a figure exactly corresponding to estimates for the *noblesse* of France. The less refined nobility of eastern Europe was larger

---

[1] Quoted by G. E. Rudé, 'The Motives of Popular Insurrection in Paris during the French Revolution', in *Bulletin of the Institute of Historical Research*, University of London, vol. XXVI (1953), p. 71.

and less exclusive, being estimated at eight per cent for Poland and at six for Hungary.

An aristocracy, in the eighteenth-century sense, may be thought of as a set of people enjoying an inherited superior position, looked up to by others, known personally to each other or expecting to be accepted as equals when introduced, generally intermarried, receiving income from dignified sources, such as landed rents, old investments or the emoluments of office in church or state, habitually taking part in public affairs, believing, at the best, in a duty of looking out for the welfare of others. In countries of mixed religion, even where toleration existed, it was necessary by law or in fact for the ruling group to belong to an established church. Thus in England under the Test Act only Anglicans could hold important office, and in the United Provinces only members of the Dutch Reformed Church; at Frankfurt only Lutherans could sit in the town council. Everywhere church membership was necessary to full political participation. In an age of subdued religious feeling it would be too much to say that religious dissent was a political force, and indeed those who felt the most zeal in religion, like the Methodists in England and Pietists in Germany, were as a rule uninterested in public affairs. But dissent, in the sense of non-membership in the established church, was in some places a ground of dissatisfaction; it produced a feeling of exclusion or discrimination, and was in fact usually a badge of middle-class status. Dissenters in England, Presbyterians in Ireland, Catholics and Protestant sectaries in the United Provinces, were among the most inclined to favour change. Jansenism had a similar significance in France and Italy. In France the Protestant minority reacted much like the bulk of the population, but the appearance of fifteen Protestants in the Estates General of 1789, and of about thirty in the Convention, was in itself, for Protestants, a revolution. To attribute the French Revolution to the action of Protestants, as of *philosophes* and *illuminati*, was, however, a vagary of a later counter-revolutionary philosophy.

The aristocrat saw it as his business to govern, to give direction to other men, on his own estates or in a more public sphere, in the higher reaches of the church, the army and the government. An aristocrat deprived of authority felt more frustrated than a bourgeois in the same position. Everywhere there were institutions through which an aristocracy could play some public role: in Great Britain and Ireland, the parliaments; in British America, the councils appointed by the governors and recruited from the leading local men; in the Dutch and Belgian Netherlands and in the small states of Germany, Switzerland and Italy, complex systems of town councils and estate assemblies; in France, the several law-courts called *parlements*, and such provincial estates as still remained; in Prussia, the army and civil service; in Poland, the provincial and central diets; in Sweden, the diet where the nobility formed one of four houses; in the

Habsburg countries, the diets and county assemblies where landed magnates and gentry enjoyed a monopoly. Even in Russia, by the statute of nobility of 1785, the aristocracy was set up with certain individual and corporate liberties of the western type. From the anarchy of Poland to the parliamentary régime of Britain, from the small states of central Europe to the great and so-called absolute monarchies, government involved the action or at least the collaboration of corporate bodies of this kind. It was a general feature of such bodies either to name their own members, or to be self-recruiting within a limited class. It is well known that membership of the House of Commons was mostly determined by Parliamentary politicians, or by ministers of the crown who were themselves members of Parliament. Real election, in either a medieval or a modern sense, was a rarity in the world of the eighteenth century. It may be that the lower houses of the colonial assemblies in British America were the most truly elective bodies in the European world, even before the American Revolution, and elective in many of the colonies by a very wide suffrage; over 90 per cent of all adult males are known to have actually cast a vote at Watertown, Massachusetts, in 1757. Political bodies generally insisted on their 'independence', against either a king or a populace outside. 'It is our business...to maintain the independency of Parliament', said the young Charles James Fox in 1771; 'whether it is attacked by the people or by the crown is a matter of little consequence.' Spokesmen for the *Parlement* of Paris, the Dutch or Belgian estates and various other bodies felt the same way.

The picture drawn so far has been static. It remains to indicate such changes or trends as may be distinguished for Europe as a whole. It is well to remind the reader again that for events in any particular country he should look to other pages of this volume. The remainder of the present chapter attempts a sketch of developments that may be found on more than one national scene. One may single out the following as characteristic of the twenty-five years before 1789: an apparent tendency for society to become, so to speak, both more aristocratic and more bourgeois at the same time, or for both aristocracy and bourgeoisie to make increasing claims to recognition, with resulting conflict; a rapid growth of population, especially in the younger age-groups, which made life more difficult for the working classes in town and country, and which produced a crisis for the bourgeoisie, for whom satisfactory careers for young men were more difficult to find, with resulting frustration; a general effort by governments after the Seven Years War to increase their revenues, with resulting constitutional crises, by which various ideas of the Enlightenment were brought into the arena of practical politics; the outbreak, as the result of one such constitutional crisis, of the American Revolution, and the excitement caused in Europe by this event, which also gave many ideas of the Enlightenment a more immediate and practical application; the remarkable growth, meanwhile, of the press, of communications in general, and an increasingly effective public opinion, one of whose characteristics was a great expectancy of desirable change in the near future, and belief that such change, in 'an age so enlightened as ours', might be made with relative ease.

That the bourgeoisie was rapidly growing is evident; everything in the economic as well as the literary history of the period goes to prove it. The aristocracy was by no means correspondingly declining; in fact, the very growth of the bourgeoisie, the appearance beside them of persons like them except in birth, seems to have made the upper classes more self-consciously aristocratic. Many evidences suggest a growing exclusiveness. Entrance into the ruling group was rarest in certain small republics: at Bern the number of families qualified to hold office dropped between 1651 and 1787 from 80 to 68, and at Venice, a city of 140,000 people, there were only 111 such families in 1796, where there had been 240 in the smaller city of 1367. In Prussia the long reign of Frederick II was favourable to the Junker nobility, who obtained increased advantages in the government and the army, with families like the Bismarcks now for the first time becoming warm supporters of the new Hohenzollern state. The proportion of burghers to nobles in the chief civilian offices of the Prussian government was higher in the 1730s than at any time thereafter until the Weimar republic. Members of the French *parlements* became more consciously aristocratic. With each generation the date of their ultimate bourgeois origin receded farther into the past, and in the 1760s various of the *parlements* began to require four generations of nobility in their new members. The *parlements* blocked attempts of the French government to create a *noblesse militaire* and a *noblesse commerçante*— that is, proposals to use elevation to the nobility as an incentive to bourgeois army officers and to notable merchants. By the 1780s there were no longer any French bishops of bourgeois birth, and young men seeking commissions in the army without passing through the ranks were required by the ordinance of 1781 to prove four generations of noble descent.

In a society setting high value on ancestry the mere passage of time added to the number of knowable ancestors and hence of family connections among the living. In the Virginia governor's council, in 1775, ten of the twelve members were sons or grandsons of former members, and ten were related to at least one other of the twelve. Well over half the members of the British House of Commons in the century from 1734 to 1832 were sons, nephews or grandsons of earlier members. In the House elected in 1761, the first to have trouble with America, there were 113 who were baronets, or Irish peers, or the eldest sons of English peers expecting some day to sit in the House of Lords. In the House of 1790, which went to war with revolutionary France, there were 134 in these categories. There was also, throughout the period, an increasing proportion of members who had been to the public schools and to Oxford or Cambridge, where they had absorbed the group spirit of a governing class. At the same time, beginning with the parliament of 1761, the number of members drawing all or part of their incomes from commercial operations began perceptibly to rise. This was mainly because the economic institutions of England allowed persons of the landed and mercantile classes to invest capital in the same enterprises, though the number of actual business-men in the House, as distinguished from gentry, seems to have been slowly increasing. Class difference remained, and may even have been accentuated. City men bought rural acres without turning into gentry, as they would have in an earlier day. Gentlemen's sons were less commonly apprenticed in towns. By 1760, according to Sir George Clark, 'the stratification was not like a system of caste, but it roughly blocked out the difference of functions between different groups of the community'. Holdsworth found a growing exclusiveness in the selection of justices of the peace, with increasing objection 'to anyone engaged in trade or manufacture'.[1]

The aristocrat was content to be, the bourgeois had to become. The true gentleman seemed easily to possess what the middle-class man had to make an effort to obtain—education, position, prestige, a suitable marriage, a career, the right tone in conversation, or correct manners on entering a drawing-room. Deep in the attitude of the bourgeois toward the aristocrat was a mixture of envy and contempt, a kind of moral class-consciousness, a contrasting of solid qualities of character against the idleness and superficiality of one's social superiors. Such sentiments, penetrating even to the lesser ranks of society, were to make 'virtue' a watchword of the French Republic in 1793, but they were evident everywhere at all levels of the bourgeois class in many countries. Prussian burghers were known for their moral earnestness; much of Kant's philosophy was based upon it. An Austrian, von Kees, high in the counsels of the Emperor Joseph II, revealed his feelings toward the arrogant young noblemen of the Bohemian estates: 'I wish that young men of distinguished families would devote themselves to the study of law and science, and set an example of zeal and industry by their mode of life....I would then be the first to support their claims. But! I know from many years of experience in government service where the nobly born young gentlemen find their pleasures!'[2]

Young men of the upper and middle classes competed for many of the same positions. With the growth of population both aristocratic and bourgeois families had more sons surviving to adult age; and the growth of schools, and in Germany of the universities, meant that more young

[1] G. N. Clark, *Wealth of England to 1760* (London, 1946), p. 160; W. S. Holdsworth, 'The House of Lords, 1689–1783', in *Law Quarterly Review*, vol. XLV (1929), p. 438; for statistics on the House of Commons, see G. P. Judd, *Members of Parliament, 1734–1832* (New Haven, 1955).

[2] Mitrofanov, *Joseph II*, p. 627.

men, of various social backgrounds, were led to expect careers corresponding to their education. Places in the government, the army and the church were the more in demand since other professions were only slightly developed, and salaried positions involving large management of private affairs were very few. For the British, the continuing expansion of the empire, even after the loss of the thirteen colonies, and the rapid commercial and industrial growth, made suitable employments available for young men of various classes. Elsewhere it is likely that commercial, governmental, military and ecclesiastical organisations, if expanding at all, did so much less than the number of men at the youthful ages in the last half of the century. In France, in the 1780s, middle-aged officers of bourgeois birth could still become generals, at a time when young bourgeois could in principle not receive commissions unless they had previously served in the ranks. In Prussia at the same time the ratio of nobles to burghers in the civilian government was increasing, especially, by an understandable paradox, in the most bourgeois or western parts of the monarchy, since in the East the nobles were more content to remain on their own estates.

It was generally easier for the young man of aristocratic family to obtain the desired positions. In Silesia the average age of noblemen upon appointment to the governing boards was twenty-seven, of commoners forty-two. In the House of Commons the average age of country gentlemen on first sitting was thirty-two, of commercial men forty; and those whose fathers or grandfathers had been in the House entered on the average nine years younger than others. In the French *parlements*, where tenure was for life, average age was surprisingly low, since family influence made for very early ages at admission. In the *Parlement* of Grenoble half the members had entered, by special dispensation, before the statutory age of twenty-five; and half of all the members of the *Parlement* of Paris on the eve of the Revolution were under thirty-five. It is well known that revolutionaries of the period were generally young men. It is less often realised that the same is true of many of their opponents.

The Seven Years War left governments more heavily indebted and in need of money. They resorted to a variety of measures to increase revenues. They devised new taxes. Or they sought by stimulating trade and production to raise the total of taxable wealth; such policies led to conflict over guild regulations and local liberties by which customary economic activities were protected. The continental monarchies made many attempts to draw up new rolls or cadasters in which the assessed value of land should be brought into line with true income. In England, where the value of land for taxation remained fixed as at the year 1692, the power of landowners in Parliament prevented such attempts from being made, and the British government increasingly used stamp duties and other indirect taxes. On the Continent, landowners resisted reassessment by all means at their disposal; it was largely over this question that the French monarchy came to a crisis with the *Parlement* of Paris and the other *parlements* between 1763 and 1774. Governments also sought to tax classes and provinces hitherto exempted. Thus in Hungary, which paid less in taxes than Austria, Maria Theresa in 1764 tried to increase revenues by a million florins, and to do so by putting more of the burden on the nobles and prelates who had hitherto escaped it. The Hungarian diet blocked her efforts, insisting on its constitutional liberties. She thereafter did without it, and it never met again until 1790, under the quasi-revolutionary conditions of the last days of Joseph II. Similar threats of the Habsburg central government to guild, municipal and fiscal privileges produced constitutional resistance in the Belgian provinces and in the Milanese. There ensued the Belgian revolution of 1789, and the state of mind at Milan which welcomed Bonaparte in 1796.

In France disputes of the same kind gave rise in the 1760s to a revolutionary vocabulary, if not yet to a revolutionary psychology. Ministers tried to increase the tax yields and otherwise to exert the royal authority. The *parlements* undertook to combine against them, under the leadership of the *Parlement* of Paris, and to assert, not merely their customary right to 'verify' royal legislation or remonstrate against it, but to take part in legislation itself. They claimed to act *en citoyen*, to voice the 'cry of the nation', to defend the constitution, natural rights and fundamental laws. Collectively, in their view, the *parlements* were the 'universal, capital, metropolitan and sovereign court of France'.[1] Louis XV in 1766, at the Session of the Flagellation in the *Parlement* of Paris, responded with the most dramatic affirmation of absolute royal sovereignty ever made by a French king. It would seem to be these disputes arising from actual politics, more than the ideas of men called philosophers, that brought into question the nature and locus of sovereignty, the nature of the constitution, of true political representation, of law, and of citizenship. From 1771 to 1774 the old *parlements* were abrogated entirely. It was a royalist pamphleteer that denounced them as a 'monstrous hereditary aristocracy'. It was a nobleman, in their defence, who declared that France must be 'de-Bourbonised'. Louis XVI restored the old *parlements* at his accession. They rejoiced in a liberty which they used consistently in the defence of privilege. In the year 1776 it was not only the American Congress, but also the Estates of Brittany, as privileged a body as any in Europe, that vaunted its 'imprescriptible and inalienable rights'.

In the same year the *Parlement* of Paris made clear what it meant by the constitution. It protested against the mildly equalitarian programme of Turgot, which involved certain incidental tax reforms, abolition of guild privileges and conversion of the royal *corvée*, or peasant road work,

[1] R. Bickart, *Les parlements et la notion de souveraineté nationale au 18e siècle* (Paris, 1932), p. 173.

into a tax payable by all classes. Such 'an equality of duties', warned the *parlement*, would 'overturn civil society'. Such 'efforts of the human mind' were a vain defiance of the 'law of the Universe' which maintained all in its due place. The *Parlement* of Paris thus anticipated Edmund Burke. 'The French monarchy, by its constitution', it also declared, 'is composed of several distinct and separate estates. This distinction of conditions and persons originated with the nation; it was born with our customs and way of life.'[1]

Meanwhile the British government had attempted to raise revenue in its American colonies. These, seen in any comparative light, had been virtually tax exempt. Taxes in British America in the 1760s did not average more than a shilling *per capita*; they stood at twenty-six shillings *per capita* in Great Britain. The Americans resisted the Stamp Act and the levying of effective tariff duties. They denied even the right of the British Parliament to tax them. Parliament countered with a sweeping statement of its sovereignty in the Declaratory Act of 1766, while for a time refraining from using it, and forgoing taxation. Events soon brought the full meaning of this sovereignty into view. To relieve the East India Company Parliament authorised it to make direct sales of tea in America, against the wishes of colonial merchants, and of political leaders generally, who feared taxation in surreptitious form. When the company's property was destroyed in Boston harbour, and considering that the famous tea-party came as the last of a series of disorderly episodes, the British authorities concluded that government could no longer be carried on under the Massachusetts charter of 1691. Parliament, by its sovereign power, passed an Act for Better Regulating the Government of Massachusetts Bay. This made essential changes in the constitution of Massachusetts without consultation of the inhabitants. It reduced the powers of the democratically elected assembly, and it strengthened those of the royally appointed governor. Americans in all provinces sensed an illimitable menace to their political liberties, and sent delegates to a Continental Congress to uphold Massachusetts.

Formally, the American Revolution thus began as a conservative movement, to preserve a fiscally and politically privileged autonomy within a larger political system. To this degree it resembled agitations in Belgium or Hungary, and even the French Revolution itself, so far as the French Revolution began with a reassertion of corporate privileges and tax immunities against the crown. Americans, like Hungarians, Belgians and Bretons, or like the *Parlement* of Paris, defended their historic constitutional liberties, their 'imprescriptible and inalienable rights', their 'customs and way of life'. The difference was in the substance. History, custom, constitutions, rights, and liberties had a different sense in America. In Europe these terms covered hierarchic, feudal, aristocratic

[1] J. Flammermont, *Remontrances du Parlement de Paris* (Paris, 1898), vol. III, pp. 278–87.

and ecclesiastical forms of society. It was not so in America. The assembly of Massachusetts, the lower house of legislation, was actually elected, and elected by a population of small and relatively equal independent farmers. In this respect it was as different as possible from the Diet of Hungary, the Estates of Brabant or Brittany, the *Parlement* of Paris, or, for that matter, the Parliament of Great Britain. What was conservative or customary in America was radical innovation for Europe.

Events in any case soon drove the Americans beyond the mere conservation of an outraged *status quo*. Fighting with the British army began in April 1775. Many Americans, shrinking from armed rebellion, now remained loyal to king and Parliament. This was especially true of many, though by no means all, of the provincial aristocrats who had for generations been close to the British authorities and who had reason to admire the contemporary British style of life. The effect was to discredit them in the eyes of the patriots. Leaders of the rebellion needed popular support to strengthen themselves against restoration of British authority. Men of standing, compromised and in danger, made themselves agreeable to the lower classes. Defying Parliament, repudiated by the king, declared outside the protection of the British crown, with all lawful forms of government and courts of law falling to pieces, the insurgents needed a new principle of authority, a new sovereign in whose name their actions could be considered legitimate. They found it by proclaiming the sovereignty of the people. To emerge from anarchy, to clear the ground for the creation of new governments, to gain access for their shipping in the ports of Europe, and to obtain French aid, the American insurgents, in July 1776, after more than a year of hostilities, declared the existence of an independent United States.

How far these new United States were merely the old colonies separated from Britain, and how far they were internally revolutionised at the same time, has always been a matter of debate in America. To the refugees who flocked back to England, or into Canada, it was a true revolution. Their property was confiscated, and found its way into the hands of new owners, great and small. In some states the suffrage was enlarged. Governors were now chosen by the assemblies in most states; in Massachusetts the governor was elected by a popular vote. The old appointive governors' councils were replaced by elective upper houses. The Anglican clergy having proved sympathetic to England, the Anglican church was disestablished in most of the states where it had been established at all. In New England, where the Congregationalist clergy had been anti-British, their church retained certain special advantages. Nowhere after the Revolution, however, did any group feel excluded from political rights on religious grounds. In general, the Revolution seems to have added to the exaltation of popular virtues, the scepticism toward aristocratic pretensions, and a certain suspicion toward all forms of individual superiority, that had appeared in America since the earliest settlements, and have characterised American attitudes ever since. If the United States has been the land of the frustrated aristocrat, whereas in Europe it has been the democrats who have been frustrated—in the words of Louis Hartz— it is to the American Revolution and its subsequent glorification that this state of affairs can be ascribed.

In any case the impact of the American Revolution in Europe was immediate and very great. The war itself had wide repercussions. It overwhelmed the French treasury, this time fatally. By involving the Dutch, it brought on the abortive Patriot revolution of the 1780s. Adversity in America persuaded Britain to grant autonomy to the Irish Parliament in 1782. Psychological influences are more difficult to gauge. The Irish Volunteers and the Dutch Patriots formed armed companies with American precedents in their minds. In England those who had begun to urge parliamentary reform, men like Wilkes, Cartwright, Price and the earl of Abingdon, remained more sympathetic to the Americans, even after their overt rebellion, than parliamentary Whigs of the Burke persuasion. Radicals in England shared with Americans a disbelief in the sovereignty of Parliament as a corporate institution, and a theory that it should truly represent and be answerable to the 'people'. The Westminster Committee of 1780 went even beyond the Americans in its proposals for a modern democratic type of representation. Henry Flood, the firebrand in turn of both the Irish and the British House of Commons, pointed to the Americans in 1790. 'This secret of inadequate representation was told to the people in the thunders of the American war,' he said in the British Commons, and he proceeded to review the fallacies of 'virtual' representation, which he said the British would no more stand for than the Americans had. English reformers were largely Dissenters, and so felt a bond with New England. Seeking repeal of the Test and Corporation Acts, they tried to strengthen their argument by observing that in the American state and federal constitutions members of various religious bodies were treated politically alike. Pitt replied that the constitutions of the two countries followed very different conceptions of church and state.[1]

'We talked of nothing but America', said Talleyrand many years later, recalling the years before the revolution in France.[2] Excitement was greatest in France, but hardly limited to it. In Finland certain noblemen conspiring against the Swedish king talked of George Washington. In Russia Alexander Radishchev incurred the displeasure of Catherine, who said that he was worse than Pugachev because he read Benjamin Franklin. In Poland the reforming King Stanislas put a bust of Washington in his study, and in Tuscany Leopold drew on the constitution of Virginia in

---

[1] *Parliamentary History*, vol. XXVIII (1790), pp. 413, 457.
[2] Talleyrand, *Mémoires* (Paris, 1953–5), vol. I, p. 83.

preparing a constitution for his duchy. At Budapest the freemasons called themselves the American lodge, and in Italy a secret society of Philadelphians preceded the Carbonari. In Germany opinion was more divided, with a British view of the American war emanating from Hanover; but a great many Germans expressed enthusiasm for the Americans in poems, essays, histories and learned tracts; and resentment at the action of the landgrave of Hesse, when he leased troops to Britain for use against the Americans, is said to have been the earliest occasion on which public opinion became critical of the small absolutist state.

In France, in addition to incredible effusions on the state of nature in which the Americans were supposed to have been living, there was a good deal of serious discussion of the new American governments, to which such notables as Turgot, Mably, Condorcet, Morellet and Mirabeau gave close attention before 1789. What impressed them the most was that the Americans had created new governments by rational and deliberate planning. In each state delegates had met in an assembly or convention which exercised the sovereignty of the people. This assembly had prepared a written constitution for the state; it created government, calling it into being and issuing authority to it by explicit grant; it set up and defined various offices and functions, which it artfully balanced one against the other to prevent the abuse of power. In short, the Americans seemed to have acted out and thereby proved the idea of the social contract. Quarrels of king and *parlements* had made the constitution a live issue in France. Praise of the British constitution since the days of Montesquieu had the same effect. The American constitutions, which were repeatedly published in France beginning in 1776, were different from the constitutions described by the *Parlement* of Paris or by Montesquieu. In origin they seemed to represent an act of free and rational self-determination. In content, they knew nothing of inherited position, royal, magisterial or lordly; no one possessed any but a delegated authority; there were no governing classes, no legal orders, no estates of society, no one privileged in taxation, and no one with any special or personal right to govern because of birth. All were citizens, all were equal, and all were free. The French, dissatisfied at home, idealised the Americans. Some saw that they had carried over a good deal from their English and colonial past. Others, and it was an intimation of a growing revolutionary psychology, magnified and exulted in the extent of change which the Americans had undergone. They thought of the Americans as having no past, unencumbered by history, free of prejudice, superstition and Gothic night—specimens of man in the abstract. J. B. Brissot in 1780 confided to a friend his preference for 'radical and entire reform', and added, 'O hundred times happy America where this reform can be executed to the foundations in every part!'[1]

[1] Brissot, *Correspondance et papiers* (Paris, 1912), p. 18.

The emancipation of the New World had an especial appeal to a generation conscious of its philosophical breadth of view, and the feelings aroused by this dramatic spectacle merged with others produced by conditions nearer home. The whole tenor of the Enlightenment had been to spread a strong confidence in social progress. With American independence, this became more definitely a sense of a new era already dawning. The American Revolution, except for the most complacent, seemed but the first in a series of great liberating changes that had now begun. The air became charged with expectation, conditions that had existed for centuries seemed easy to dispense with, ideas of humane but theoretical writers seemed more capable of realisation, and what the Americans had done could presumably be done by others also. Feeling for the necessity of existing arrangements was undermined. Impatience grew. 'In a little while', wrote a Toulouse lawyer, eulogising America—a man who was to sit in the Convention and vote for the death of Louis XVI ten years later—'in a little while there will be nothing to which man cannot attain.'[1]

In particular, there was growing impatience for aristocratic manners and privileges on the part of persons belonging mainly to the bourgeoisie. It was produced by conditions in Europe, and made acute by the sight of America. The middle-class European saw with satisfaction a land where no one stood higher than himself. He saw a country where people like himself were appreciated, where true merit obtained its reward, where no class was frivolous or ornamental, and men were judged by their abilities and their usefulness. An employee of the French foreign office, in a poetic flight, longed for a land, like America,

> Où sans distinction de naissance et de rang
> L'homme le plus honnête et le plus respectable,
> Le plus utile enfin, soit toujours le plus grand.[2]

And the anonymous author of a poem in the *Berlinische Monatschrift*, in 1783, yearned for the country 'where sweet equality dwells, and no spawn of nobles, the plague of Europe, pollutes simple customs despite better men'.[3] In such remarks, as in others not relating to America, we can sense a profound alienation from the society in which such men lived, an estrangement from its prevailing values, a repudiation or spiritual flight. Mme Roland had daydreams of herself and her husband living happily in Pennsylvania, a German was surprised that half of Europe had not crossed the Atlantic, and in England even men as well established as James Watt and Matthew Boulton, annoyed by the violence done to their

[1] J. B. Mailhe, *Discours qui a remporté le prix à l'Académie des Jeux Floraux en 1784, sur la grandeur et l'importance de la révolution qui vient de s'opérer dans l'Amérique septentrionale* (Toulouse, 1784).
[2] L. G. Bourdon, *Voyage d'Amérique: dialogue entre l'auteur et l'abbé* (Paris, 1786), p. 23.
[3] Quoted by H. P. Gallinger, *Die Haltung der deutschen Publizistik zu dem amerikanischen Unabhängigkeitskrieg* (Leipzig, 1900), p. 65.

friend Priestley by the church and king mob at Birmingham in 1791, let their minds dwell on the thought of moving to the United States. A surprising number of restless spirits did in fact emigrate. The Dutch Adrian van der Kemp, after the collapse of the Patriot movement, went to New York; a young Swiss imprisoned for subversive agitation by the Bern authorities escaped and fled to America; a German, Schmohl, having written a pamphlet on *Nordamerika und Demokratie*, made off in the same direction. The Pole Niemcewicz, after Kosciuszko's defeat in 1794, settled and married in New Jersey, returning to Poland only at the time of Napoleon's grand-duchy. Of Englishmen the most famous to emigrate was Joseph Priestley, but there were many others, such as Thomas Cooper and John Binns, who took the same course upon suppression of the reform movement in England. Among the Irish, Hamilton Rowan, Wolfe Tone and Napper Tandy all went to America in 1795, the last two returning to Europe when the French war gave new promise to their cause. The political annals of the United States in the 1790s abound with names of men newly arrived from England, Scotland and Ireland, who had left home for political reasons, and usually became pillars of the rising Jeffersonian party. 'Vile organs of a foreign democracy' the conservative Federalists called them.[1] It was chiefly against British and Irish radicals that the American alien and sedition laws of 1798 were directed, since despite all the talk about French Jacobinism few Jacobins or Frenchmen actually emigrated. It is noteworthy, however, that Edmond Genêt, the fiery Girondist who stirred up the country as minister to Philadelphia in 1793, not only settled in America but married into good New York society. Tocqueville, years later, discovered an old Jacobin of the Terror living in the American West, where he had turned into a solid and satisfied citizen in the receptive atmosphere of the new country.

The excitement over the American Revolution coincided with another development, of at least equal magnitude, without which the revolutionary era can hardly be understood. The second half of the eighteenth century was a time of extraordinary improvement in communications. There was much activity in the building of roads, in postal services, in stagecoaches and inns that brought travellers of different places and classes together. When A. R. Thibaudeau first went from Poitiers to Paris about 1760 he rode on horseback and took a week; when he went as a deputy of the Third Estate of Poitiers in 1789 he went in a stage-coach, a *turgotine*, and reached Versailles in three days. When the duke of Orléans, in 1788, wished to circulate his views in the provinces, he simply put his propaganda in the mail. No previous duke of Orléans could have stirred up trouble so easily. There was phenomenal growth in the press, in the number of books, magazines and newspapers, in their popular character, and

[1] Quoted by John C. Miller, *Crisis in Freedom: the Alien and Sedition Acts* (Boston, 1951), p. 32.

in the size of the reading public. In England there were ninety news-papers and magazines published in 1750, 158 in 1780 and 264 in 1800. Growth in Germany was even more rapid. In America, in a state that was not expanding geographically, namely New Jersey, one new paper was launched in the 1760s, five in the 1770s, ten in the 1780s, and nine-teen in the 1790s. In France the greatest outburst came with the revolu-tion, which was among other things a revolution in journalism, with no less than 1350 new papers known to have been launched in Paris alone between 1789 and 1800, many of them of course very short-lived.

The very term 'public opinion' seems to have come into use at this time in a number of European languages. Not only were more people reading and talking, but they were reading and talking more frequently on political questions. There was a mounting sense of public interest; a feeling that improvements were to be expected, that they need not be left to the closed operations of government, but were legitimately matters of general concern. In Germany twenty-nine journals before 1790 called themselves *Der Patriot* with various distinguishing adjectives. People dis-covered that there were many others with ideas like their own, that there were great common questions, of more than local or private import, which hosts of unknown and distant persons were also aware of. Reading clubs and discussion groups grew up everywhere, or at least one finds signs of them wherever one looks, in what Cochin called the *sociétés de pensée* in France, in the *sociétés de lecture* at Liége, in the reading rooms described by Peter Ochs at Basel in 1787, in the Literary and Philosophical Society at Manchester, or at Mainz, Amsterdam, and other cities. Such groups, subscribing collectively to books, newspapers and magazines, usually interested themselves in all matters to which men of education then attended, scientific, literary and philosophical, but with more thought given to politics as time went on. They probably had more real importance than the better-known masonic lodges, whose taste for secrecy and mysti-fication had a restrictive effect on their influence.

In stimulating and increasing the significance of public opinion the news of the American Revolution was of great importance. The Britain that emerged from the Seven Years War was for many Europeans the modern Carthage, the ruthless tyrant of the sea. That a band of far-away patriots should defy this colossus seemed indescribably thrilling. The public documents of the insurgents were full of ideas made common by the Enlightenment. Casual readers could thus absorb general principles in a context of recent dispatches, exciting events and interesting person-alities, such as George Washington. In countries of significant censorship, France to a degree, or the Austrian Netherlands and the German states, the discussion of the pros and cons of the American revolt, and of the merits of the new American governments, allowed a vicarious airing of political ideas where the structure and conduct of one's own government could not be publicly debated. For simple readers the issues were conveniently simplified. The British represented despotism, exploitation and pride. The Americans stood for liberty and equality, and for courage, resourcefulness and self-sacrifice. It was not only Thomas Paine who called the cause of America the cause of the human race. So prudent a journalist and philosopher as the Swiss Isaac Iselin thought that oppression of America was oppression of all mankind.

Of the lower classes, without habits of reading or writing, less can be known, especially for the years before 1789. Yet their role in determining events of the revolutionary era was decisive. Even in France the agricultural and urban labouring classes were the last to be politically aroused. Elsewhere, they generally remained apathetic, or were indeed easily inflamed against new ideas. The Dutch populace favoured the prince of Orange, and the Breton peasants their gentry. James Watt, the engineer (whose son became a notorious 'Jacobin'), was indignant at the paradox in the Birmingham riots of 1791: that it was the aristocrats who could rally the common herd, and the 'democrats', among whom he included himself, who really believed in law and order and in giving authority to competent men.[1]

Nevertheless, there are signs of serious discontent, even in England, at least as far down as the ranks of skilled and self-respecting working men to which Thomas Hardy or the youthful Francis Place belonged. Indeed, there may have been more real working-class consciousness in England in the 1790s than in France. The London Corresponding Society, in the words of its organiser, Thomas Hardy, was composed of tradesmen, shopkeepers and mechanics. It discussed the 'low and miserable conditions of the people of this nation'. But men of this social level, like middle and even upper-class reformers, thought their troubles due to evils of government, to the profits drawn from government by a ruling class, to defects in the representation and in the constitution. There was an almost revolutionary bitterness at being excluded from the community. 'What is the constitution to us, if we are nothing to it?' asked a group of Sheffield workmen in 1794.[2] The enemy was seen as aristocracy. Thomas Hardy, in the somewhat rambling language of a private letter penned by a self-taught man, attributed the sufferings of honest workmen to 'the avaricious extortions of that haughty and voluptuous and luxurious class of beings who wanted us to possess no more knowledge than to believe all things were created for the use of that small group of worthless individuals'.[3] One is reminded of the strong moral disapproval of aristocrats that characterised the French *sans-culottes* at this same time.

[1] Eric Robinson, 'An English Jacobin: James Watt, Junior', in *Cambridge Historical Journal*, vol. XI (1955), p. 351.
[2] 'An Address to the British Nation', printed with *Proceedings of a public meeting at Sheffield...7 April, 1794* (Sheffield, 1794), p. 41.
[3] Manuscripts of Francis Place, British Museum, Additional MSS. 27814, fol. 178.

Men of both the labouring and the business class in England could thus demand parliamentary reform. It was the reaction of the British government to the French Revolution that drove them apart, beginning in 1792. The British business class might be discontented, but it hardly had enough grievances to persist very far. At Manchester, a few years before, far more signatures had been gathered for a petition against liberalisation of the Irish trade laws than for a petition for representation in Parliament. In 1792 the government, which is to say the aristocracy, began to take measures against political clubs and meetings. Men like James Watt, or Thomas Walker at Manchester, simply had too much to lose by continued opposition, especially in time of war. Serious working-class agitation went on for years, but the reform movement, decapitated, died out for a generation.

For France the best study in the social psychology of the small people of the Revolution is provided by Professor Lefebvre's account of revolutionary crowds and mobs.[1] The problem is to explain how casual strollers in the Palais Royal on 14 July 1789, or swarms of peasants, or angry men and women suffering from the scarcity and high price of bread, could be suddenly transformed by some incident into a collective force, recognising momentary leaders, feeling hostility to an agreed-upon enemy, sharing in a realisable objective, willing to run risks, to sacrifice calculations of prudence, to court danger, and to act. Mobs and bread riots were common enough in France and other countries in the eighteenth century. In the Revolution something new was added. The embarrassment and collapse of accepted authority as early as 1788 made a great difference. The king's summoning of the Estates General, and the ensuing elections held in forty thousand local assemblies, aroused even the poorest people to a state of tense expectation of great things to come. Small episodes served as sparks. Something seen or heard in a moment might bring deeply latent attitudes into play, precipitating into action what Lefebvre calls an anterior collective state of mind, which had been building up for decades. Conversation, reading, listening to newspapers read aloud by more literate friends, life in taverns, in church, in the market place, the proximity of town and country, the moving from job to job, the passing of travellers, the scandals whispered about great personages, news of the king's war in America, references to daring books or pamphlets which may or may not have been seen or read, the impression that the existing state of affairs was commonly criticised by persons whose names one might not even know, the feeling that much that existed was neither just, necessary or permanent—all went into the making of a potentially revo-

---

[1] Georges Lefebvre, 'Foules révolutionnaires', in *Études sur la Révolution française* (Paris, 1954), pp. 271–87. For the revolutionary psychology of the French lower classes see also the recent articles by G. E. Rudé, already cited, and by Richard Cobb, 'The Revolutionary Mentality in France, 1793–94', in *History*, vol. XLII (1957), pp. 181–96.

lutionary psychology before 1789. Each man had his own grievances, his own private tale of woe; no one suffered all grievances, and some did not suffer very many. What happened was that grievances were somehow pooled into the indictment of a system. The peasant, reflecting on his troubles, did not attribute them to personal misfortune, or to having a bad man or unfair individual as his lord. He attributed them to the type-figure of the *seigneur* as such. The creation of such a type-figure, or common target, made possible the peasant revolution of 1789, in which, with amazing spontaneity in many parts of the country, masses of peasants with no prior leadership or organisation invaded the manor houses and destroyed the legal papers on which their obligations and their status rested.

For working people in the towns the type-enemy became the 'aristocrat', and hence the lesser people could for a time make common cause with the bourgeoisie, until, as the Revolution continued, the bourgeois himself seemed an aristocrat to the common man. When the king favoured the aristocracy, the country turned against him also; and if a great wave of destructive popular agitation engulfed the church, it was because, as Tocqueville observed, the church did not distinguish its interests from those of an aristocratic or feudal order, so that the ideas of actual unbelievers were well received. The small people who made demonstrations in Paris, though pressed by the elemental need for daily food, had ideas of larger scope. A cook, arrested for signing the republican petition of 1791, testified that she understood it to call for 'a new organisation of the executive power'. Above all, there was a general aspiration to work for *bonheur universel*, a feeling that only evil and designing men opposed it, a sense that the critical moment had come to obtain it, that if lost it might never return. This is enough to explain what is called revolutionary fanaticism. And considering the struggle that the Revolution produced, the opposition it aroused, the war, the array of aristocratic forces of the old order on an international scale against those of the new, taking into account the stakes, the issues and the alternatives, and reducing *bonheur universel* to the more tepid English general welfare, it is hard to say that these feelings aroused by the Revolution were subjective delusions, or entirely mistaken.

CHAPTER XVI

THE AMERICAN REVOLUTION, 1763–93:
CONSTITUTIONAL ASPECTS

FOR the political historian the period in North American history between the end of the Seven Years War, or 'French and Indian War',
and the outbreak of the wars of the French Revolution is divided
into two parts by the successful establishment of a new nation—the
United States of America. The constitutional historian may concern himself rather less with this break in continuity. The constitutional problem
before the American Revolution was that of providing an acceptable
framework of common institutions within which the individual colonies
could continue to exercise their characteristic inheritance of internal self-
government; after it, it became a question of whether the several states
into which the colonies had been transmuted could supply themselves
with such organs for common action as their new situation in the world
seemed to require. The new national government had to find solutions
that had eluded the advisers of George III. From this admittedly limited
point of view, the story has an underlying unity which it is the object of
this chapter to present.

By the middle of the eighteenth century, the thirteen British colonies
that were to form the nucleus of the new United States all enjoyed some
form of representative institutions, as did indeed eight other island
colonies in the western Atlantic and Caribbean sea. Despite the important
differences in situation and in the economic and social make-up of the
colonies, their institutions had a family likeness. They were indeed the
product of two features that distinguished British colonisation in North
America from the comparable activity of rival European powers. It had
been largely the product of individual enterprise, often though not always
taking a corporate form; and it had been carried through in part by
groups in opposition to the prevailing political and religious temper at
home.

In all the colonies the English were the politically dominant element,
and they had come from a country singularly rich in the tradition of free
association, in which, indeed, most work of a public kind was normally a
concomitant of social leadership rather than the affair of a professional
bureaucracy. And this characteristic feature of the scene at home was
closely paralleled in the local institutions of the colonies, whether of the
New England township variety or of the county pattern of the colonies
further south.

The familiar structure of central government as it came to exist in most of the New England colonies on the model of Massachusetts—an elected Assembly acting as a legislature, together with the governor and his assistants or council—was the fruit of the transfer across the Atlantic of the institutions of the great chartered companies. Virginia, after the failure of company rule from London, acquired what were to be the normal institutions of royal colonies: a nominated governor and council and an elected Assembly. Maryland represented the prototype of the proprietary colony which was in essence an attempt to transplant the notions of feudalism to a New World setting. But the New World proprietorships, while retaining some economic and social significance, were politically limited; the proprietors' nomination of a governor required royal approval, and the settlers' demand for a representative assembly could not well be gainsaid. By the eighteenth century the presumption was indeed in favour of representative institutions in all colonies of settlement, and in 1774 Lord Mansfield laid down the principle that once an assembly had been granted the crown's prerogative right of taxation had lapsed.

Although each colony was a separate entity from the imperial point of view, the general tendency was towards an assimilation of colonial governments to a single pattern. In Pennsylvania and Delaware, and in Maryland, the proprietorships, though interrupted in the late seventeenth century, lasted until the Revolution. But New York became a royal colony in 1685, New Jersey in 1702 and the Carolinas in 1728. The powers and tenure of the Georgia trustees were limited from the first; and that colony too came directly under the crown in 1751. The new charter of Massachusetts of 1691, which largely assimilated its institutions to those of the royal colonies, meant a lessening of autonomy for the colony's government; though by extending the franchise beyond the select circle of church membership it ended the rule of the hitherto dominant oligarchical puritan theocracy. Despite this liberalisation in Massachusetts, established tax-supported churches were preserved in nine of the colonies until the Revolution itself: the Congregational church in all New England except Rhode Island, and Anglicanism in most of the remainder. Political discrimination based upon religious adherence was universal although in different degrees. With the changes in the composition of the population, particularly in the Anglican colonies, religious divergences added their quota to the elements of discontent.

The executive branch of government in the colonies was represented by the governors and their councils. The governor's functions were important and derived from those of the sovereign. He was commander-in-chief and head of the civil administration; he could summon, adjourn and dissolve the Assemblies, veto their acts or reserve them for consideration by the imperial government. With his council he acted as the colony's court of appeal. The assemblies themselves were elected upon a variety of franchises which on the whole gave the greater weight to the more substantial elements in the population, and to the older settled areas as against the interior. Their legislative functions were subordinate to those of the imperial parliament and their main importance lay in their control of the purse.

In all but three of the colonies, the governor and council were crown nominees. In Massachusetts, the crown nominated the governor though not the council, and in Connecticut and Rhode Island both were elected by the Assembly. The executive branch thus normally claimed a different source of authority from that of the Assembly and this reinforced the principle of the separation of powers which characterised the whole system. The courts were set up by the executive and assimilated their own position as far as possible to that of the English judiciary.

The institutions of the colonies on the eve of the decisive conflict with the mother-country reproduced in miniature, then, not so much the institutions of contemporary Britain as those of England in the times of the first two Stuarts. The executive branch of government was not responsible to the legislature but was largely dependent upon it for supply. In so far as there was a contemporary analogy it was to be found in Ireland; and the Dependency of Ireland Act of 1719 had made it clear that the existence of an Irish Parliament did not affect the powers of the British Parliament to legislate for that country. No such general statute governed the relations between the imperial government and the American colonies, and there was ample room for misunderstanding as to the significance of the institutions through which imperial control was actually exerted.

The colonists held that their right to be represented through Assemblies of their own choosing was inherent in their being Englishmen, and that the royal instructions to the governors to summon Assemblies were declarative and not creative of their rights. The veto power was also disputed; although the legislatures could act through votes and orders not subject to reservation. Uppermost was however the question of supply; the governors tried to secure a permanent support while the colonists held that if this were done, they would have no opportunity of guarding against misappropriations. From the crown's point of view the practice of annual appropriations meant that salaries could be withheld from governors, judges or other officials of whose nomination or conduct the colonists disapproved, and that revenues were controlled not by an appointed official, but by the treasurer elected by the Assembly itself.

In dealing with legislation submitted from the colonies, the imperial government had four main concerns: to prevent discrepancies arising between English and colonial laws and to defend the Constitution; to guard the interests of citizens of the home-country in their dealings with the colonists; to prevent what was regarded as hasty or ill-considered legislation, under which heading came the various efforts to provide the colonies with a more flexible medium of exchange; and finally, to avoid technically defective laws. In the royal and proprietary colonies these objects could be achieved by direct disallowance of the offending laws, and in this respect the Privy Council acted as a kind of second chamber. In the charter and corporate colonies direct disallowance was not possible; but appeals from their courts lay to the Privy Council, which exercised what was in effect a power of judicial review; and this procedure came to be applied to all the colonies. Only about 5 per cent of colonial laws were directly disallowed; but review on appeal was more important. Between 1695 and 1783, 795 cases were carried from colonial courts to the Privy Council; 157 judgements were affirmed, and 336 reversed; 147 cases were dismissed. Privy Council judicial business from the mainland colonies alone, in the decade before the Revolution, was only slightly less than that dispatched by the Supreme Court of the United States in the first ten years of its existence. No attempt was made to introduce English law as such into the colonies and English statutes did not extend to them unless the colonies were specifically mentioned in them. But English law was the standard applied; above all the prerogatives of the crown and the laws of trade must be safeguarded against any possible encroachments. The colonists took the view that all the rights of Englishmen, including their right to enjoy the benefits of the common law, were theirs by inheritance, and the eighteenth century witnessed a steady assimilation of common law procedures and of its substantive doctrine by the colonial courts.

The particular attention given to the enforcement of the laws of trade, which were administered by the imperial customs system extended to the colonies by an act of 1673 and subsequent legislation, was shown by the creation of vice-admiralty courts in the colonies from 1697 onwards. Cases under these laws could be tried either in these courts or in the ordinary courts of the jurisdiction whence the case arose. The committee of the Privy Council, which was the formal source of authority for the colonial governments, was advised on their affairs by the Board of Trade and its president—an institution and office dating from 1696; and it was the board that carried on routine administration. But the really important decisions on appointments, on military and naval questions, on finance and on Indian policy were in the first half of the eighteenth century the affair of the Secretary of State for the Southern Department.

In 1748 Lord Halifax became President of the Board of Trade and began an attempt to revitalise it with the intention of making it in effect an American department of the imperial government. An Order in Council in 1752 brought about changes which went a good way towards fulfilling his objective. But when Halifax left the board in 1761, colonial patronage was returned to the Southern Secretaryship now held by Pitt, and in 1766 the remainder of the order of 1752 was revoked. But with the growing importance of American questions, a further experiment was made. In 1768 Lord Hillsborough was made Secretary of State for the Colonies or 'American Secretary', combining this office as did his successor, Lord Dartmouth, with the presidency of the Board of Trade.

But no single department could deal with all the matters in which colonial activities impinged upon the interests or policies of the home-country. The Treasury had direct contacts through the Surveyor and Auditor General of the colonies, and through the Commissioners of Customs. The work of the office of the Secretary at War and of the more important Admiralty touched upon colonial concerns at every turn; and there were specialised imperial officials such as the surveyor general of the king's woods.

A colony interested in any case before the Privy Council or in any administrative or political issue needed to know what was going on in most of the major departments of state and to be in a position to make its own voice heard. By the eighteenth century each colony retained someone to act as its agent in London—the list of agents includes the names of Benjamin Franklin and Edmund Burke. But the most important development of the period after the Glorious Revolution was the increasing role of Parliament in colonial affairs. Not only was there more legislation, but, with the development of the cabinet system, the persons chiefly responsible for American matters—the Secretary of State, the President of the Board of Trade, the Chancellor of the Exchequer—were increasingly and ever more closely involved in the shifting bargaining world of parliamentary politics. The agents did not merely require contacts with the able and experienced officials of the Board of Trade; they also needed to know their way about Westminster. In the language of a later day, they needed to become 'parliamentary lobbyists'. Nor was it simply a question of policy. We are unlikely nowadays to overlook the importance of patronage in eighteenth-century politics; and American patronage, which was considerable, was a happy hunting-ground for politicians with needy relatives and clients. Indeed the resentment caused by the low quality of some of the men jobbed into civil or military posts in the colonies has been considered one of the underlying causes of the growing friction between the imperial government and the Americans.

The principal difference between the imperial government and the Americans was that the former took it for granted that the large and flourishing communities that the colonies had come to be could continue to be subject to a sovereign assembly in which they were not represented, and which had greatly increased its powers and claims as a result of events in which they had had no share. It was easier for people in Britain than in America to accept without question the view that what suited the interests of the empire as a whole was best conducive to the interests of the individual colonies. The colonists themselves were not only unwilling to discuss their interests from an imperial viewpoint, they were for the most part unwilling to take a wider view than that of each separate colony. Schemes of colonial unification had been mooted in London at different times between 1686 and 1721; the only one tried, James II's 'Dominion of New England', had collapsed with his fall. The French challenge in the middle of the eighteenth century revived ideas of colonial unity. Benjamin Franklin's plan presented to the inter-colonial Albany Congress in 1754 would have delegated some colonial powers to a confederal government, while reserving others for the imperial government. But it made no headway in either Britain or America.

Furthermore there was on the Americans' side an element of archaism in their approach to British constitutional doctrine. The British had accepted the idea of parliamentary sovereignty, while the Americans still thought in terms of its being limited by the common law and natural equity. Such at any rate was the argument of the Massachusetts lawyer James Otis when the colony's administration asked the courts for new writs of assistance after the accession of George III, so as to permit the searches and seizures required to enforce the anti-smuggling campaign.

The colonists further held to the view that the colonial charters were a species of fundamental law and that their political rights and privileges derived directly from the crown. Parliament was not competent to alter the imperial constitutional structure as it pleased; from the colonists' point of view the empire was a quasi-federal one. There were local legislatures under a common crown with the British Parliament exercising certain powers on behalf of the whole empire. The full revelation of how far these differences could lead was to take some time, but although one can write of the argument as having developed from one about the rights of Englishmen to the appeal to universal rights in the Declaration of Independence, almost all the elements which made up the final case for separation can be found in the earliest documents of the dispute; and they would probably have been even more clearly set out in them, if counsels of caution had not prevailed. In a pamphlet written in 1762, Otis argued that money in the colonies could be raised solely by their legislatures, and that the executive had no right to incur unauthorised expenditure, even in an emergency. Otherwise how could one say that the colonists enjoyed the full rights of British subjects to which they were entitled 'by the law of God and nature, by the common law, and by Act of Parliament (exclusive of all charters from the crown)'?

Even without the crisis brought about by the financial requirements of the British government after the Seven Years War, and by the new freedom of action acquired by the colonists through the removal of the French threat, the constitutional situation was unlikely to have remained stable. Certainly, the colonists' attitude to it could hardly provide a permanently acceptable basis. It was not easy to decide what the imperial functions of government actually were, nor whether an admittedly imperial function, such as defence, could be made the source of further powers. Did the crown's responsibility for the defence of the whole empire entitle it to raise revenue through imperial legislation, or to make regulations governing land-settlement, relations with the Indian tribes and so on? The latter question was brought to a head by the proclamation of 1763 putting a temporary ban on further land-settlement until an imperial policy for North America should be worked out.

Again, as we have seen, the powers of the crown were in fact exercised by ministers whose attitude could be affected by pressures in Parliament. The colonists' prolonged effort to make out that their quarrel was really with Parliament and not with George III was meaningless. When the imperial government acted, how were the colonists to be assured that it was acting for the good of the whole empire and not merely for the benefit of some powerful pressure-group? If it claimed the right to tax the whole, would it not be certain to make the major burdens fall on the unrepresented? What redress did the distant colonies have against malpractices by imperial officials—racketeering in the customs for instance? Did not this demand a maximum authority for their own courts of law? Finally, was it not unreal to believe that the imperial government and Parliament could act without affecting the internal situation in the colonies? Imperial influence had been thrown against attempts to make the colonial assemblies more representative; economic regulations had directed production into certain channels and blocked it from others; it had affected debtor–creditor relationships, always the key-factor in a new community; it had consolidated social and political hierarchies. The traditional leaders in the colonies who formed these hierarchies might have been prepared to give at least partial support to the imperial power; but they feared being outstripped by more radical elements. In the same way, the clash over American policy at home became associated with the radical challenge to the existing political system. The leaders on both sides found compromise increasingly difficult. The constitutional debate was carried on by contestants who did not enjoy the political freedom necessary to find a more lasting foundation for compromise.

Furthermore the possibilities of compromise were obscured by misunderstandings on both sides as to the grounds upon which their opponents stood. Not for the last time in British politics, a parliamentary opposition, partly wilfully and partly no doubt unconsciously, managed to distort the real demands of a movement in opposition to colonial rule by identifying it with their own cause, and by exploiting it for party purposes. Chatham's intermittent vision of a united empire resting upon local self-government had its grandeur; but it was not a vision that appealed to the parochially minded in America. They wanted both less and more.

The British effort to tighten the machinery of imperial control had begun in the 1750s but had been interrupted by the war. The main objective had been to stop the widespread evasion of the regulations concerning trade. To this purpose was now added that of providing standing forces for frontier defence combined with the control of western trade and of relations with the Indians. The policies of George Grenville's administration between 1763 and 1765 had all these ends in view.

The colonists could not directly object to the Sugar Act of 1764 since the right of the imperial Parliament to regulate trade was still admitted; but the new provisions for the trial of offenders against the customs regulations, and in particular the proposed increased use of vice-admiralty courts, were much less conducive to evasion. A new Quartering Act of 1765, designed to facilitate the maintenance of standing military forces, also encountered colonial opposition. But the main offence was caused by the Stamp Act of 1765 which raised in the most direct fashion the issue of the right of the imperial Parliament to tax the colonies. Whereas the colonists universally held that they could not be taxed by a body in which they were not represented, and whereas most of them believed that representation in it was technically impossible, British opinion was, almost without exception, aligned against the Americans on the point of principle. Since so small a proportion of Englishmen themselves were represented, the right to tax had nothing to do with representation as such but was inherent in the House of Commons, as 'part of the supreme power of the nation'. 'They say', reported one of the colonies' agents, 'that a power to tax is a necessary part of every supreme legislative authority and if they have not that power over America, they have none, and then America is at once a kingdom of itself.' And there were precedents for such taxation.

The colonists were still prepared to accept duties whose prime purpose was to regulate trade and not to produce revenue. Some of their friends in Parliament argued that this meant that they drew a distinction between 'internal' and 'external' taxes which was not the same thing; but some of their agents were willing to allow the misunderstanding to remain uncorrected so as not to dissipate the sympathies they needed in order to secure the repeal of the Stamp Act itself. On the other side of the Atlantic, the resolutions of private groups and the language of newspapers, and even the declarations of the colonial Assemblies, and of the Stamp Act Congress in which their delegates met at New York in October 1765, almost universally denied to the British Parliament any power of taxation at all. Sir Francis Bernard, the percipient governor of Massachusetts, clearly perceived that behind this dispute over the location of the taxing power lay the even wider claim of the Americans that their governments were in no way subordinate to the government of Great Britain but rather co-ordinate with it, so that their only connection with Great Britain was through the crown common to both. His suggestion was that Parliament should be temporarily afforced by representatives of the colonies, and should then establish a general and uniform system of imperial government which would both establish the rights of the American governments and the proper limitations upon them. But this idea of a kind of imperial constitutional convention was altogether too bold for its time.

Two more immediate questions required an answer. Was the new tax meant merely to pay for the common defence or was it a way of undermining the colonial Assemblies by providing funds which would render their administrations independent of local grants? And if Grenville was right in standing by the language of the act which referred only to defence, was there any other means by which the money could be raised? The agents of the colonies argued that the colonies should be allowed to raise the money themselves; but it was not hard to show that their past record of bickering and disagreement made it most improbable that they could agree upon the proportions to be levied by each.

More convincing than the constitutional arguments advanced by the Stamp Act Congress was the practical nullification of the offending Stamp Act by extra-legal associations such as the 'Sons of Liberty'. The possibility of a widespread boycott of British goods moved commercial circles in England to petition against the act. The Rockingham ministry which succeeded the Grenville administration was too weak to resist the campaign at home, and moved towards repeal. But the repeal of the Stamp Act in 1766 was not an indication that Parliament had been won over to the American view of the nature of the constitution. It was accompanied by a Declaratory Act setting out the right of Parliament to 'make laws and statutes of sufficient force and validity to bind the colonies and peoples of America, subjects of the crown of Great Britain in all cases whatsoever'. It may be that any specific reference to taxation was omitted in the hope of satisfying both sides. The colonists would note that the act was modelled on that for Ireland and that Ireland was not in fact taxed from London; the die-hards in Parliament could rest assured that nothing important had been given away.

The financial problem was partially solved by the Revenue Act of 1766 which reduced the duty on molasses and applied it to imports from British as well as from foreign possessions; the reduction made smuggling unprofitable, and the amount collected rose steeply. But the Americans persistently opposed all attempts to strengthen the enforcements of the customs, and refused to carry out the provisions of the Quartering Act. The legislatures of Massachusetts and New York also incurred anger in Britain by their refusal to compensate the victims of the Stamp Act riots. The constitutional question was raised again by the programme of Charles Townshend, Chancellor of the Exchequer in the Pitt–Grafton ministry. A reduction in the land-tax at home was to be met by duties on certain commodities brought into colonial ports. The proceeds of this act were to be set aside to pay for the salaries of governors, judges and other royal officials in the colonies. The customs administration was to be further strengthened by setting up a special Board of Commissioners to operate at Boston; and in 1768 a series of new courts of vice-admiralty was set up. Another act suspended the New York Assembly, one of those that had resisted the Quartering Act. Only on the territorial side was there a retreat from imperial control with the abandonment of the policy of the proclamation of 1763.

In February 1768 the Massachusetts legislature sent a circular letter to the legislatures of the other colonies, urging united action against the Townshend policies, and basing its opposition on a clearly enunciated view that the king's American subjects had 'an equitable right to the full enjoyment of the fundamental rules of the British constitution', which included the right not to be taxed except by representatives of one's own choosing. Furthermore they could not be said to enjoy freedom if their governors, judges and other civil officers were wholly dependent upon the crown for their maintenance. Lord Hillsborough wrote that the Assembly was to rescind their resolution on pain of dissolution and that other legislatures taking it under consideration were to be dissolved too. New colonial elections only succeeded, however, in strengthening the opposition. Violent action on the model of the Stamp Act riots was undertaken against the new Commissioners of Customs in Boston, and there were cautious moves towards a general boycott of British goods.

Already men were beginning to wonder whether the middle ground still advocated by such American moderates as John Dickinson would do. It was all very well to say that Parliament had some powers—to control trade for instance—but could it be kept within such bounds? Must it not be the case that either Parliament had full legislative authority or none at all; and Americans like Franklin were beginning to regard the latter view as the more plausible one. On its side, Parliament itself had no hesitation in plumping for the former alternative. In February 1769 a series of resolutions were passed denouncing the views expressed in Massachusetts, and claiming that the provincial convention called at Boston after the dissolution of the Assembly was evidence of a design 'to set up a new and unconstitutional authority independent of the crown of Great Britain'. If there were treasonable individuals they should be brought to England for trial. This threat further inflamed colonial opinion, and the agitation now spread to the southern colonies.

The new crisis also passed without the constitutional conflict being resolved. The Townshend duties were a financial failure and were repealed in 1770 except for the tea duty which was retained to save the principle, though evaded in practice by large-scale smuggling. For their part, the American leaders, alarmed by the growing radicalism of colonial opinion, were prepared to acquiesce. As a result there was an uneasy truce for the next few years during which the historian's interest naturally shifts from the disputes with the mother-country to the colonists' perfection of their own organisation for inter-colonial co-operation, the lack of which had handicapped resistance in the past. But there were in fact a whole series of disputes which served to keep the central issues alive: friction in Massachusetts about the payment of officials out of the customs revenues and over the tendency of the town-meetings to turn themselves from organs of local government into political forums; the question of the continued presence of British troops brought to the fore by the so-called 'Boston massacre' of 1770 and the acquittal of the troops who had fired on the hostile and aggressive mob; the appointment of a special commission to look into the destruction of the revenue vessel *Gaspee* off Rhode Island and its failure to discover the perpetrators. We find no difficulty in recognising a situation in which individual law-breakers cannot be located or punished because the community in which they live repudiates the constitutional and moral sanction of the law under which officialdom acts. But the immediate result was the setting up in March 1773 of the Virginia Committee of Correspondence with instructions to look into the authority by which a court of inquiry had been entrusted with the power 'to transmit persons accused of offences committed in America to places beyond the sea to be tried'.

The situation had thus developed to a point at which there was a powerful party in America which looked at events from the point of view of Americans as such and of their alleged rights; it had the makings of a national revolutionary movement at a time when Britain was still thinking in terms of individual colonies. It was at this point that the Tea Act of 1773 provided the colonial leaders with the issue they required in order to turn their movement into an embryonic rival government. The Tea Act which permitted the East India Company to sell by retail in the American colonies was a challenge in three respects: it threatened the livelihood of merchants who had hitherto been a class reluctant to hazard business prosperity for the sake of abstract constitutional doctrine; it would make tea cheaper and thus take much of the profit out of smuggling, and the smuggling interest was an important one and unlikely to balk at direct action; finally it seemed to show that Parliament was likely always to subordinate colonial policy to powerful corporate interests at home.

Once again the legislatures protested and once again force was used—the 'Boston Tea Party'. This direct and public defiance helped to alienate what sympathies for the colonists remained in Parliament. Chatham was almost alone in clinging to the view that Parliament had no right to tax America, though Burke was convinced that such action, although constitutional, was inexpedient. Most public men supported the government in its appointment of the commander of the British forces in North America as governor of Massachusetts with the clear object of restoring authority in the colony by force, and in passing through Parliament what the Americans were to term the 'four intolerable acts' of 1774. These were the Boston Port Act closing the port until compensation was paid for the tea destroyed by the rioters; the Massachusetts Government Act revising the colony's charter so as to lessen the authority of the Assembly and increase that of the governor; a new Quartering Act and, finally, an Administration of Justice Act by which officials in Massachusetts accused of capital crimes in the performance of their duties could be sent for trial to other colonies or to England. In the same year, another measure, the Quebec Act, by attaching the 'Old North West' to Canada at Virginia's expense, and by sanctioning the perpetuation of French law and the privileged position of the Roman Catholic religion in Canada, challenged colonial opinion at two highly sensitive points.

By now the American leaders had come round to the view expressed in James Wilson's *Considerations on the Authority of Parliament* published that August, that Parliament's powers derived wholly from those it represented and that it was therefore, in Jefferson's phrase 'a body of men foreign to our constitutions, and unacknowledged by our laws'. Such was the background to the first Continental Congress which was called for September in Philadelphia and whose purpose was to co-ordinate such economic sanctions against Britain as might bring about a wholesale repeal of the offending measures, and the redress of all other grievances that it might define. Although the Virginia Convention which authorised such a boycott and elected delegates to the congress referred to itself as made up of 'His Majesty's dutiful and loyal subjects', the distance between their view of duty and the British one was too great to be bridged.

The coming together of the first Continental Congress marks a new stage in the constitutional history of the period. Attempts at finding a formula for reconciliation with the mother-country were not abandoned; but since Congress took over the conduct of relations between the colonies and the imperial government, it was obliged to function as an embryonic governmental structure for the colonies as a whole. Since this involved preparing for measures of resistance its activity in this respect obviously hampered the chances of a settlement.

Within the congress there was both a radical and a conservative party. The popular leaders by now denied the right of Parliament to pass legislation affecting the colonies as regards any subject at all. The conservatives still held that the empire must have a common legislature and that this must be Parliament, but wished to limit its powers—the task that had already proved so difficult. In discussing the way in which the colonists should present their grievances, there were fairly sharp differences of opinion. Some wished to take the broadest possible ground—the law of nature, and to argue that all government rested upon consent and nothing else. 'Our ancestors found here no government,' declared R. H. Lee. Others still wished to restrain the argument within the framework of the

British constitution. The emigrants had not alienated their allegiance; and if consent was the only test, on what grounds could they protest against the Canada Act?

In the upshot the Declaration of Grievances was a conservative document admitting the royal veto over colonial acts and the right of Parliament to legislate for the control of trade. Both the 'immutable laws of nature' and the 'principles of the English constitution and the several charters or compacts' were referred to as foundations for the colonists' rights.

But all this was by now academic, since Congress approved the Suffolk County Resolves which denied that the recent acts of Parliament with regard to Massachusetts need be obeyed, and which advocated the building up of a rival government within the colony which should retain all the taxes and create a militia. Congress also prepared for far-reaching measures of boycott and embargo with regard to trade with Britain. Such measures were to be enforced until all offending acts of Parliament were repealed, and there were implied threats against any colony refusing to co-operate in this programme of resistance.

Popular opinion, as revealed in contemporary newspapers and pamphlets was also ahead of Congress's formal position, with talk of the desirability of independence, the depravity of kings and the principles that should govern constitution-making for a free America.

The conservatives were now forced to try for a more constructive solution of the problem than a mere return to the situation before 1763, the year which the colonists treated as marking the beginning of the policies of which they complained. This took the form of a fully fledged plan of imperial federation put forward by Joseph Galloway. Galloway was prepared to reduce the rights claimed by the colonists to one only: exemption from all laws made by the British Parliament since the ancestors of the Americans had left Britain. On the other hand, there must be some common institutions to look after the general interests of the empire. For this purpose there should be (in addition to the existing British Parliament) a federal legislature in America consisting of a president-general appointed by the crown, and of a council elected by the different colonial assemblies. Acts of general concern to the colonies should require the assent both of this body and of the British Parliament. Thus the colonies would recognise their need for protection and, in return, continue to give their allegiance to the crown.

Galloway's plan had little chance of acceptance at a time when people's minds were increasingly fixed upon the goal of total independence; but the debate upon it is interesting in that the arguments of such opponents as Patrick Henry of Virginia foreshadow in many respects the later 'states-rights' attitude towards the problem of finding common institutions after independence. Galloway's defence of it foreshadows, too, the later arguments for federation, particularly in his emphasis that apart from the imperial tie, there was no link between the several colonies, and that they were totally independent of each other, whereas there must be some common regulation of commerce.

In Britain also, attempts were still being made to preserve the imperial tie. Chatham, who had been in touch with Franklin, suggested in a bill introduced on 1 February 1775 that the American Congress should be invited to acknowledge the legislative supremacy of Parliament exclusive of the right to use military force 'to violate and destroy the just rights of the people' and the right to tax the Americans other than through their own assemblies. In return for this, the congress should take into consideration the question of a financial contribution towards the burdens of the imperial government. North's resolutions of 20 February did not go so far. While each individual colony would have been able to free itself from imperial taxation by making a contribution towards imperial defence and the cost of its own civil government (which would free the latter from Assembly control), there was no recognition of the possibility of any general authority in America.

All this was however far behind events. In the winter of 1774–5, conventions elected in the various colonies put them on a war-footing; the clash at Lexington on 19 April 1775 was an inevitable outcome of the growing tension between the arming colonists and the royal garrisons. But in the fighting which became serious in the Boston area in June the Americans were still without a defined political purpose. On its side, the British government took measures, including measures against the colonists' trade, that showed it to have every intention of reducing them to obedience.

The ground upon which the Americans would have to stand had to be provided by the Second Continental Congress which met on 10 May. Its declaration on 6 July of the causes for taking up arms was still a conservative document; British policy was blamed both for the political breach, and for the need to resort to arms in self-defence. The Americans still did not wish to establish independent states; they would lay down their arms when the dangers they were faced with had been removed.

On 8 July a new petition to the king was approved. It was suggested that a solemn agreement be drawn up setting out the rights of the king's American subjects, a sort of American Magna Carta. If Britain would yield the right to levy taxes upon them, the colonies would submit to the regulation of their trade; or if they could trade freely with the world they would bind themselves to raise their share of the revenues required by the empire, provided that Britain should tax itself at a rate no lower than that they imposed on themselves. It has been suggested that the rejection of this overture marked the end of the last possibility that the Americans would be content with anything short of total independence. In any event we do not need seriously to concern ourselves with the various suggestions of some kind of imperial federal settlement that were made at different junctures in the ensuing struggle. North's conciliation resolutions of 1778, largely dictated by the wish to forestall the American-French alliance, would have given up the claim to direct taxation, retaining only the regulation of trade; the instructions to the Carlisle peace commissioners, who arrived in America in June 1778, would have given the colonies virtual autonomy within the empire, and representation in the imperial Parliament. Galloway, who had left for England in October 1778, produced a new plan in 1779 which involved the creation of an American branch of the British legislature, complete with an aristocratic upper house. As late as 1782 Franklin was allowing the unofficial peace envoys from Britain to carry away the illusion that a satisfactory peace-settlement might lead to some form of federal union between Britain and her former colonies. Lord Shelburne certainly seems to have cherished the hope that there might be agreement upon allegiance to a common crown with separate parliaments—'dominion status' in the parlance of a later period. The unsuccessful attempt in 1783 to bring about a close commercial relationship between Great Britain and a now independent United States—an attempt that broke on the rock of the Navigation Acts—may be regarded as the last echo of such federal notions. But in fact there had been little in them for a long time past; from the summer of 1775 those men who controlled America politically had set their course towards total independence.

North's proposals of February 1778 were rejected by Congress on 31 July as hypocritical, and as having for their real purpose the creating of divisions between the colonies. It concentrated now upon its military task; but the conservative elements were still strong enough to block resolutions looking towards independence—abolishing customs houses, setting up independent governments in the colonies and opening American ports to the trade of the world. But the British attitude helped to undermine their position. John Adams declared that the American Prohibitory Act of 22 December 1775 should be called the 'act of independency', and its receipt was followed by a defeat in Congress of a motion denying that the colonies were indeed seeking independence. On 6 April 1776 Congress opened the American ports to all countries, and on 15 May it took the decisive step of recommending to the individual colonies that they provide themselves with independent constitutions. Here Congress had been outstripped by the more radical colonies; on 4 May Rhode Island had declared its own independence of Great Britain.

On the same day as Congress acted the Virginia Convention resolved that Congress should be recommended to declare the colonies free and independent states and that it should form a confederation out of them while leaving to each colony the framing of its form of government and

the regulation of its internal concerns. This resolution is important because it marks a new source of radical–conservative conflict within Congress. Some of the conservatives had become or would become 'tories'
—that is, supporters of retaining the British connection by whatever means
were necessary. Those who accepted in principle the idea of independence,
and continued to take part in American political life, wanted to get the
problem of the central government settled first, and all inter-colonial disputes cleared up before the assumption of an independent status; the
radicals wanted to get independence worked out at the level of the separate colonies, and to postpone confederation until this was done. These
differences were explicable in terms of party advantage; but they helped
to hold up the completion of the moves towards independence.

There had been some discussion in the winter of 1775–6 of a plan
for confederation put forward by the indefatigable Franklin, though this
was still nominally a scheme under which the British connection might
be restored. As compared with his 'Albany Plan' of 1754 the proposed
union was to be stronger, though the taxing power was now withheld
from the central authority, no doubt in deference to the recent arguments
adduced against Parliament's claims in this respect. But the colonies
were to be represented according to population, not as units; Congress
would have full powers over external affairs and the control over western
expansion, as well as legislative powers extending to all matters 'necessary
to the general welfare'. But the radical elements now generally in the
saddle did not wish to exchange one central authority for another.

The argument that independence should wait upon an agreed form of
confederation was overridden because the situation of the colonies demanded independence if they were successfully to prosecute the war. The
Americans could not offer the compensations that foreign powers, notably
France, would require of them in return for their aid, unless they could
give the kind of guarantees only possible for an independent nation. That
Americans had the right to consider themselves an independent nation
was now generally accepted and the success of Tom Paine's *Common
Sense* is perhaps the best evidence of the new mood.

On 7 June R. H. Lee proposed and John Adams seconded three resolutions: the first declaring that the 'United Colonies' were, and of right
ought to be 'free and independent states'; the second that it was expedient
to take the most effectual measures for 'forming foreign alliances', and the
third 'that a plan of confederation be prepared and transmitted to the
respective colonies for their consideration and approbation'. The conservative delegates from the middle colonies managed to get a decision
postponed until 1 July; but a committee was appointed to prepare a
declaration of independence when this should be agreed upon. The
committee's draft, the work mainly of Jefferson with some assistance
from Adams and Franklin, was presented on 28 June and its arguments

bore a strong resemblance to those advanced by Jefferson in his pamphlet *A Summary View of the Rights of British America*, published two
years earlier.

On 2 July the resolution for independence was carried in Congress and
the draft declaration taken up; after certain amendments in the text it
was adopted on 4 July, and possibly signed on the same day.

The form of the document, whose later fame owes much to its purely
literary qualities, was a simple one: the statement of a political philosophy,
its application to the American colonies, an enumeration of the steps by
which their rights had been invaded with the idea (so it was alleged) of
placing them under a despotism, and as the conclusion—independence.

Jefferson was no doubt right when he claimed long afterwards that the
declaration was not original but rather 'an expression of the American
mind' and even such striking ideas as the right to 'the pursuit of happiness'
can be found in earlier documents. But what was important was the
essence of the doctrine, that governments were set up to secure certain
rights and that their just powers could be derived only from the consent
of the governed. The Americans were thus launched upon their independent constitutional existence on the basis of a purely contractual theory
of the state, and without the buttressing of prescription. In the several
states, indeed, the process of creating governments resting on the consent
of the governed (not forgetting the use of force to coerce the support of
the still strong loyalist elements) had been in process for some time
already.

The various conventions and committees through which the revolutionary governments took over state powers in 1775 early devoted
themselves to securing more permanent institutions. It was presumably
the Americans' familiarity with colonial charters that made them draw
up formal written constitutions—the first to be created *de novo* in the
English-speaking world since the Cromwellian interregnum. The early
ones were drawn up by the conventions sitting as legislatures and were
not submitted for popular ratification. But after objections to this
procedure in Massachusetts a special constitutional convention met in
1779–80 and made some show of submitting the document to the people.
New Hampshire's first convention actually had its work disapproved by
the electorate and a new constitution was produced in 1783 and ratified
in 1784. Through these tentative essays was worked out what became the
typically American method of constitution-making; a special convention
followed by a referendum. The difference between this procedure and that
followed in ordinary legislation was to pave the way for the idea of the
superiority of constitutions to laws, and so for judicial review in its
American form.

The new constitutions were similar to each other in many respects,
being mainly patterned on the colonial model, with elected governors

and upper houses replacing the nominees of the crown or the proprietors. They thus included provision for legislatures, normally of two houses, a single executive head—the governor—elected by the legislature or by the voters directly and a suffrage limited to property-owners or taxpayers. The question of the suffrage was one of the issues fought over between conservatives and radicals and they also differed over the provisions regarding religion, over qualifications for office-holding, over legislative apportionment and over the extent of the powers of the governor as against the legislature. The radicals stood for legislative supremacy, the conservatives for the principle of the separation of powers. On the whole the radicals achieved notable success both as regards a wider franchise and as regards a better representation of the interior. Again, authority was on the whole concentrated in the legislatures and especially in the lower houses. Only in Massachusetts was the governor given a veto, and elsewhere his powers were often very restricted. The radicals also distrusted the idea of an independent judiciary, and in several states the judges were to be chosen by the legislatures and for very short terms only. In contrast however to the more democratic provisions of the new constitutions in states such as Pennsylvania, Virginia and North Carolina, some states like Maryland which remained under conservative control showed less radical influence in their constitutional documents.

The clash over constitutional provisions was, of course, only a reflection of the clash over the uses to which independence was to be put; where the radicals gained control they proceeded to act against such matters as the privileges of established religions, the slave-trade, entail and primogeniture, and to press for law reform and for the extension of education. It is the importance attached to this background in the states that has coloured recent interpretations of constitutional development at the centre. The inspiration of this school of thought comes primarily from Charles Beard's book, *The Economic Interpretation of the Constitution of the United States*, in which he advanced the thesis that the ultimate constitution of 1787 was forced upon the nation by a group of conservatively minded property-owners, in particular owners of government paper, who feared the kind of democracy established in the states and wished to provide a central check upon its alleged excesses. The weakness of the American government under the Articles of Confederation was, in his view, exaggerated for propaganda purposes, and those who wished for change thereby took in not only their own contemporaries but later historians as well.

Beard's thesis was taken up and developed by Merrill Jensen in his two books on the period, *The Articles of Confederation* and *The New Nation*. Jensen maintains that the struggle against Britain was part only of the internal struggle between radicals and conservatives in the colonies, and that the conservatives opposed independence because they relied upon

British protection against radical demands. Those conservatives who did not swing over to the loyalist camp now threw their weight in favour of giving the greatest possible power to the new confederal or federal government so that it could perform the same restraining role. Originally they failed and the Articles of Confederation gave the minimum of powers needed to constitute a central authority, little more than Congress was already exercising in order to wage the war.

It was only afterwards that a successful conservative reaction brought about the acceptance of the new federal constitution as described by Beard.

It should be noted that Beard's historical methods and the validity of his conclusions have come under considerable criticism from American historians; it is for the social and political historian to say what has been left standing and unassailable. From the point of view of constitutional development, Jensen's elaboration of the Beard point of view seems to have two weaknesses. In the first place, he seems to make too little of the continuity between pre- and post-revolutionary attempts to provide common institutions for the American political communities. In the second place, he tends to play down overmuch the effects of the country's international position and requirements upon the shape of its institutions. The problems of defence, of policy in regard to the expansion of the area of settlement, and of commercial relations figure too prominently in the documents of both periods for one to feel justified in decrying their importance for the constitution-makers.

It should be remembered that, in many important respects, the Continental Congress acted as a government even before its position was validated by the Articles of Confederation; the raising and officering of armies, the negotiation of treaties, the issuing of currency and the borrowing of money—none of these could wait upon the slow process of constitution-making. The delegates to the congress found themselves not only legislators for the embryonic nation, but as members of its committees, also engaged in executive functions, and even in some judicial activities. This experience, and their experience of the colonial governments, together with their knowledge of the methods of the imperial government, formed the basis upon which they worked to create a more permanent system; nor, of course, at this time could they be aware of the attention which later generations would pay to each recorded word of theirs in the attempt to answer the perhaps metaphysical question as to which was temporally and logically prior, the independence of the states or the formation of a national American government.

On 12 June 1776 Congress appointed a Committee of Thirteen (one from each state) to draft a constitution. A month later it presented its conclusions, which were based upon a draft by John Dickinson. This draft allotted very considerable powers to Congress which was to continue as a unicameral body of delegates voting by states. Although authority to tax was reserved to the states, as in the abortive Franklin project, they were to contribute to the common expenses according to their populations, and Congress was to have the right to settle their boundary disputes, limit their westward frontiers, and set up new states. Although Congress was not given the specific right of regulating trade, the states were prohibited from levying duties in conflict with treaties made by Congress. Indeed although the 'United States of America', as the proposed confederacy was described, would have guaranteed to each state the exclusive control of its internal affairs, this was only to be in such matters as did not interfere with the powers allotted to the centre.

The Dickinson draft was the subject of vehement debate in Congress. The large states which would pay the most towards the expenses of the general government objected to having only an equal voice in its decisions; the question of the enumeration of slaves in calculating their taxable capacity was also strongly canvassed; but the most important objection was that of those states which had large claims to unsettled lands in the West, and objected to the proposed grant of authority to Congress in this field.

The fortunes of war interrupted the constitutional debate which only began again in September 1777. By 15 November the Articles of Confederation were finished. Generally speaking they followed the Dickinson draft, but their language made the retention of sovereignty by the states much clearer and, to this extent, they can be regarded as a victory for the radical element. On the main points of controversy between the states, it was decided that financial contributions to the centre should be based on the value of improved lands in the different states; and the attempt to fix western boundaries for the claimant states was abandoned. This retreat was to bring about a considerable delay. After the rejection by Congress of various proposed amendments, eight states acceded to the articles on 18 July 1778 and two more during the winter. But Maryland stood out against the land proposals, and in September 1780 Congress agreed that all western land-claims should be ceded to Congress; they should then 'be settled and formed into distinct republican states' which should 'become members of the federal union, and have the same rights of sovereignty, freedom and independence, as the other states'. With this impediment removed, it was possible for Congress to announce acceptance of the articles on 1 March 1781.

The position of Congress under the Articles was undoubtedly a weak one in spite of its control over all aspects of external relations and its right to act as an arbiter between the states. For this there were two principal sets of reasons. In the first place, it had hardly any authority over the actions of the states themselves; for instance, they had full freedom to issue paper money. In the second place, various devices limited its own prestige. No one could be a Congressman for more than three years out of every six, nor its president for more than one year in three. The delegates were subject to recall by their state legislatures to whom they were thus effectively subordinated. It is understandable that many leaders preferred the wider scope offered by the state governments. One consequence was inadequate representation of the states in Congress itself, partly because they grudged the expense. Seven delegations were the minimum required for the transaction of business and this was often hard to attain; and for important matters the votes of nine states were needed. Major decisions required unanimity. The representatives of the larger states blamed this deficiency upon the nature of the body itself. It would be different if states were represented in proportion to wealth or population and if Congress could act by a majority.

While Congress was empowered to appoint civil officers as well as committees for the management of executive matters, thus laying the foundation of the subsequent executive departments, it was significantly determined that members of Congress were not to be eligible for paid office—after a period of undifferentiated government, the principle of the separation of powers was again coming uppermost. Its immediate effect was to further inhibit the chances of congressional leadership.

The principal weakness in the system, as might have been foreseen, was in its financial provisions—it depended upon the states and the states could not be depended upon to pay up. There were early proposals that this state of affairs should be remedied by granting Congress the right to levy import duties, but inter-state rivalries prevented their coming to fruition. Another gap that soon revealed itself was that Congress's lack of control over the states hampered its discharge of its external responsibilities, notably the conclusion of commercial treaties. In 1784–5 Congress discussed the possibility of amending the Articles by giving it powers to regulate trade. But although it was suggested that any revenues that accrued might simply be apportioned out among the states, this concession proved insufficient to disarm the objectors.

In other respects also the states impeded the use of the treaty-making power. In March 1787 Congress resolved, with two dissentients, that constitutionally made treaties were 'part of the law of the land', called upon states to repeal any acts contrary to treaties, and to direct their courts to act upon this principle notwithstanding anything in state laws to the contrary.

In the summer of the previous year Congress's awareness of its own deficiencies had led to the setting up of a committee to consider the whole position, and on 7 August it proposed seven additional articles. Congress was to be empowered (with the assent of nine states) to regulate foreign and interstate commerce, and to levy additional requisitions on defaulting states by way of punishment. As a last resort it was to be empowered to lay and collect taxes itself, compelling state officials to act on its behalf. States were to be obliged to send representatives to Congress; all powers of coercion other than the use of military force were to be used against states that defied its jurisdiction; a federal judiciary was to be set up; and as an ultimate sanction there could be a declaration that a state had violated the federal compact.

Given the existing state of opinion such proposals were an admission of defeat; had an attempt been made to put them into effect, the Confederation would have been shattered. But it is clear that the deficiencies of the governmental system set up by the Articles were fully recognised before Shays's rebellion in Massachusetts in the late summer of 1786 and the successful agitation for laws favouring debtors in Rhode Island—the two aspects of the situation usually regarded as having sparked off the conservative 'reaction'. It is also clear that most of the remedies later taken under consideration had been fairly fully canvassed before the movement for full-scale revision got under way.

Before its demise the congress acted to fulfil the responsibilities imposed upon it by the decision in the matter of the western lands. An ordinance of 1784 based upon a report by Jefferson laid down the method by which the new areas should graduate into states as their population grew; but it was superseded by the famous North-West Ordinance of 13 July 1787, which (as re-enacted in 1789) became the basis for the later government of the region between the Ohio and the Mississippi and the model for similar developments in other areas. The ordinance provided for what was to be the typically American device of providing for a stage of limited self-government of a settled type, as a preparation for full participation in the federal union on the basis of equality. The passage of the ordinance suggested that in some respects Congress regarded itself as having certain powers not wholly ascribable to a contract between the original states; and an even more far-reaching and ultimately more controversial assertion of its claims to quasi-sovereign powers was to be found in the provision which permanently excluded slavery from the area affected by the ordinance.

An opportunity for those concerned to promote constitutional revision arose almost accidentally. After a meeting between commissioners from Virginia and Maryland to settle problems arising out of the navigation of the Potomac held in March 1785, it was suggested that Pennsylvania and Delaware be asked to accede to the agreement. When this proposal came before the Virginia legislature, Madison put forward a plan for a meeting of commissioners from all the states 'for the purpose of digesting and supporting the requisite augmentation of the power of Congress over trade'. This was agreed upon in January 1786 and the meeting was subsequently fixed for September, at Annapolis.

Many of those concerned with the nation's future believed this attempt at constitutional reform to be the crisis of its existence; if it failed, it was doubtful if the Union could survive. But could it succeed when the states had to agree to send deputies, the deputies to agree on a plan, and the states be prepared to ratify it? Some indeed suspected that the object was in fact to prevent an enlargement of the powers of Congress, and wondered whether the northern and eastern states would not do better to cut their connection with the South and form a more stable confederacy on their own.

The Annapolis Convention turned out to be incomplete; only New York, New Jersey, Pennsylvania, Delaware and Virginia sent delegates; the New Jersey delegation suggested that a convention with wider scope be called, and on 14 September a resolution drafted by Hamilton was agreed to and signed by the chairman, John Dickinson. The delegates suggested that the states represented 'use their endeavours to procure the concurrence of other States, in the appointment of Commissioners to meet at Philadelphia on the Second Monday in May next [1787], to take into consideration the situation of the United States, to devise such other provisions as shall appear to them necessary to render the constitution of the Federal Government adequate to the exigencies of the Union; and to report such an Act for that purpose to the United States in Congress assembled, as when agreed to by them, and afterwards confirmed by the Legislatures of every State, will effectually provide for the same'.

From 'motives of respect' a copy of the resolution was sent to Congress and laid before it on 20 September 1786. At first its reception was rather cold; some would have preferred Congress itself to take the initiative, others that a start should be made with conventions in the separate states. But the alarm created by Shays's rebellion had its effect particularly in Massachusetts; and in Congress, which had been in recess from 3 November to 17 January, support for the proposed convention became more pronounced. By the beginning of March attempts at delaying action had been fought off, and Congress agreed to let the proposed convention try its hand.

Even so, there was much scepticism about; but this moderated a little when it was known that all states (except the very democratically-minded Rhode Island) would be represented and that their delegates would be given liberal instructions, and not be confined to considering commercial subjects only.

At the first working session of the Convention on 28 May 1787, twenty-nine delegates were present representing seven states. In all, seventy-four delegates were chosen and fifty-five actually attended, the average number present at each session being around thirty. The quality of the delegates was impressive; a large majority of them had had public service, thirty-nine of them in Congress, and many were known throughout the country. Washington had been chosen chairman on 25 May; and this was not a nominal position, particularly since his own views on most important issues were already known. Franklin, now eighty-one years old, was too frail to take part in debate, but his influence was important behind the scenes. His presence provided a direct link with the first major attempt at inter-colonial union at the Albany Congress thirty-three years earlier.

The delegates decided to meet in private and the secrecy of their discussions was well preserved; it is hard to see how compromises could otherwise have been reached. On the other hand, this has placed historians at some disadvantage and it was only with the publication of Madison's notes in 1840 that the course of the discussions could be followed in any detail. It has recently been alleged by an American legal historian (Professor W. W. Crosskey) that Madison's notes are unreliable, and that he had tampered with them in order to make his record at the Convention more consistent with his later stand in favour of states-rights; but this view has not been generally accepted, and there seems no good reason for altering the accepted view of what took place. Such partial notes as other delegates took bear out the essential accuracy of Madison's record.

The proceedings of the Convention must have been preceded before 28 May by informal discussions; otherwise it is difficult to see how there could have been agreement so swiftly on an approach that went beyond anything that could be called revision of the Articles, and that amounted to the drafting of a constitution upon a new plan. Some delegates would probably have preferred to go still further and to surrender state sovereignty altogether to a new consolidated government; but the majority foresaw that the only practicable course was to confer wide powers upon a strong federal government deriving its authority directly from the people and to give it the controls necessary to prevent the states impinging upon its sphere of action. Such was the basic position of the two men who did most to shape the outcome of the convention, Madison and James Wilson. Hamilton, the most prominent advocate of further centralisation, presented a plan of his own on 18 June, but without expecting it to be accepted. He was indeed absent during much of the time that the Convention was sitting.

Madison was probably largely responsible for the plan presented to the Convention by Randolph of Virginia on 29 May. This plan, which represented the views of the larger states, was debated in committee of the whole until 14 June, when the smaller states asked for an adjournment in order to enable them to present their own views. An alternative scheme giving less authority to the centre was presented by William Paterson of New Jersey on 15 June and discussed for three days more. A vote on 19 June showed that the Virginia plan was backed by seven states and it was thereupon reported to the Convention in a modified form. This report was discussed by the Convention from 19 June to 26 July; this was the crucial period during which the great compromises were reached. The results of these discussions were handed over to a Committee on Detail which met between 26 July and 6 August, on which day the full Convention reassembled. A Committee on Style put the document into shape between 8 and 12 September and the final touches were given by the Convention between 13 and 17 September.

The Randolph plan, though altered in some fundamental respects, was the foundation upon which the subsequent constitutional structure was built and its proposals followed directly from a consideration of those aspects of government under the Articles which had seemed most unsatisfactory. The three branches of government, legislative, executive and judicial, were to be separate. The legislature was to consist of two houses, the first branch directly elected, and the second chosen by the first from persons nominated by the state legislatures. In both, voting was to be proportional, to either the wealth or the population of the states. The legislature was to have all the powers of the existing congress with additional ones to cover all cases where the separate states would be incompetent to act. In addition it was to have a veto upon state legislation infringing the constitution, and the right to use force to coerce any state violating its obligations. The executive was to be chosen by the legislature and to be ineligible for a second term. The executive together with 'a convenient number of the national judiciary' was to constitute a council of revision with a suspensive veto over legislation. Far-reaching powers in matters affecting the whole country were to be conferred upon a national judiciary. State officers were to be bound by oath to support the Constitution.

The debate on the Randolph proposals as reported from the Committee of the Whole on 19 June revealed the essential dilemma: was it necessary to swallow up the sovereignty of the states and did the new constitution in fact do this? Wilson denied that the states were sovereign in that they had none of the external functions of sovereignty. A union of the states would be a confederation in some respects, but a consolidated government in others, since within the limits of its allotted powers the union was one of the citizens themselves and could act directly upon them. The whole discussion showed how vague and ill-defined were such notions as sovereignty, union, federation and confederation. The definitions were worked out for American purposes in the course of handling the particular issues that required settlement.

The Paterson plan showed the limitations of any scheme which should amount to no more than a revision of the Articles of Confederation. It would have conferred more powers upon Congress and provided a plural executive at the centre, and a national judiciary. The Confederation would have had, with regard to the states, roughly the powers that the British government claimed with respect to the colonies after 1763. But it retained the congenital weakness of government under the Articles; against a state refusing to comply with requisitions or acting in defiance of treaties its only recourse would have been to coercion. And as Madison pointed out in a long speech against it, nothing in the plan would help to 'secure good internal legislation and administration in the particular states'. Such guarantees would have been obtained had the Convention adopted something like the plan presented by Hamilton on 18 June. This scheme copied from imperial practice the idea of state governors appointed by the federal government, and with a veto over state laws contrary to the federal constitution or legislation.

But the extreme nationalism of Hamilton had even less chance of acceptance than the limited proposals of the 'Small State' group. Nor did Madison get his way in any direct fashion. The ultimate solution was found in a series of prohibitions upon particular exercises of state sovereignty, and the insistence that the lawful commands of the federal government were binding upon individuals rather than on the states. They could thus be enforced in the first instance by judicial process.

The actual making of the Constitution did not consist of a series of decisions on major questions of principle, but of the hammering out of compromises on questions raised by the Randolph plan. The divisions that mainly arose were not those over the form of the federation, but those between the larger and the smaller states, and to a less extent between the slave-holding and the non-slave-holding communities.

The most serious clash was that over the form of the new congress. The large states wanted two houses with proportional representation in each; the smaller states wished to continue as under the Articles—one house, with each state having an equal voice. The rejection of their minimum demand of equality in one house nearly broke up the Convention; but on this they got their way. In the lower house (where money bills were to originate) there would be proportional representation.

A related question was that of the reckoning of slaves in this proportion. The Southern states wished to include the slaves when their population was reckoned for the purpose of allotting congressional seats, but not when it was a matter of apportioning direct taxes. The Northern states naturally demanded the reverse. The compromise, that for both purposes five slaves should be reckoned as the equivalent of three free citizens, had appeared in the Paterson plan. Another related compromise was that Congress should have the contested power of trade regulation on condition that it was prevented from prohibiting the external slave-trade before 1808, and from giving preference to the ports of one state over those of any other.

The question of the future of the interior of the continent had not been settled finally by the adoption of the Articles of Confederation and the passage of the ordinances; and the conservative elements did what they could to limit the creation of new states or the splitting up of existing ones. On the latter point they were successful in that no new states could be formed out of the territories of existing ones without their own consent; but the West was to pass through the territorial stage on the way to full statehood as already provided. It is likely however that the constitution-makers were thinking only of land already within the political boundaries of the United States; for there were no constitutional provisions governing the acquisition of more territory.

On the question of the composition of the new federal government the main novelty was in the constitution of the executive branch, and the decision to entrust it to a single person. Fears that such an arrangement might 'squint towards monarchy' were partly allayed by the provision that the Senate should be associated with the President in making important appointments and in the negotiation of treaties. The Senate was thus expected to act like the old councils in the colonies rather than as a mere upper house of the legislature.

Fears were also expressed about the potential authority that the veto power might confer upon the President, and it was only after long debate that it was agreed not to associate the judiciary with him in the exercise of this function. It was, however, limited by the provision that it could be overridden by a two-thirds vote in both houses—a significant departure from colonial precedent.

The most curious aspect of the constitution-making debates and their outcome is the failure to take account of the development by which, in Britain, the executive was increasingly coming under parliamentary control. Instead of enforcing political responsibility, the constitution confined itself to providing for the legal sanction of impeachment which extended to other federal officers besides the President, despite the fact that British experience had already proved the clumsiness of impeachment as a political device. Nevertheless neither this fact nor the total exclusion of placemen from Congress can be used to prove that the idea of some kind of responsible ministry was altogether absent.

The question of the role of the proposed national judiciary was one frequently considered at different stages of the constitution-making process. The Randolph plan had dealt with it, by listing the type of case (admiralty, affecting foreigners, or revenue) in which the national judiciary should have jurisdiction. But on 18 July the Convention resolved that it should extend more widely to 'cases arising under laws passed by the general legislature, and to such others as involve the National peace and harmony'. The final version combined specific and general powers. On the constitution of the judiciary itself agreement was also hard to obtain. In the end the Convention confined itself to providing for the nomination of justices to the Supreme Court by the President with the approval of the Senate, and left it to Congress to settle the organisation of the inferior courts.

On the future role of the American judiciary in its most characteristic aspect the Constitution provided no conclusive answer. There was no specific reference to judicial review either as concerned state legislation or with reference to acts of Congress itself. Some later commentators have been able to argue that only the former can have been intended. The argument that review of state acts at least was intended is indeed overwhelming, and it can be shown that the provision that the federal courts should have the right to judge of the constitutionality of state laws was a deliberate substitute for Madison's original proposal to give Congress a veto over them. The claim that the phrase in the Constitution making 'The Constitution, and the laws of the United States *which shall be made in pursuance thereof*' as well as treaties 'the Supreme Law of the land' was a proper basis for the judicial review of national legislation is a little harder to sustain on the basis of the evidence of the debates themselves though the prospect was used as an argument against the proposed association of the judiciary with the President in a Council of Revision. But the warrant for it can clearly be deduced from the nature of the constitutional settlement itself, and it was so argued by contemporary commentators such as the authors of the *Federalist* papers.

It is not unlikely that here and elsewhere in the Constitution deliberate ambiguities were accepted in order to make it more likely that it would be ratified. The ratification struggle was in several states a very intensive one; in the first place each state had to elect a special convention, and both sides sought to secure the election of as many as possible of their own supporters; then there were the debates in the conventions themselves. The states fought out the issue separately; but news of what was going on in one state obviously had its effect in the others. In New York, for instance, where Hamilton despite his personal reservations about the Constitution took the lead in its support, which included lending his powerful pen to the composition of the *Federalist*, the supporters of the Constitution were defeated in the elections but carried their way in the end, partly because of the news that ratification had been secured in other states, notably Virginia, and partly because of the threat that New York City might secede from the state and make its own terms with the Union.

Generally speaking, the opponents of the Constitution could be divided into two sections: those who had taken part in or approved of the Convention but disliked the actual document, and those who had been against the constitutional movement from the beginning. But another division can be made from the point of view of the arguments they produced. One group stood on the ground of antique republicanism: no republican government could work successfully over an area as great as that of the

United States; local interests would be ignored; compact urban areas would be more influential than the country districts; elected officials would be too remote from their voters for proper control to be exercised; they would misuse, to their own or to some sectional advantage, their control over elections or the treaty-making power; finally, the Constitution lacked a Bill of Rights. On the whole this line of attack was mainly a Southern one.

On the other side there were those who feared that the arrangements at the centre gave too much power to individuals or institutions, who wanted still more checks and balances, who wanted the President to have some formal body of advisers when the Senate was in recess, and who thought that there were too few provisions for rotation in office, and for preventing the President and Senate making themselves perpetual. Their basic attitude was one of mistrust of all government, and in particular of democratic government.

Nothing was said about judicial review in the ratification debates, and little attention was paid to the restrictions upon the powers of the states—a telling argument against Beard's view that the essential issue was a social one. As the chronology of ratification shows, the small states were those where the contest was easier: it is likely that, although their own scheme had been rejected by the Convention, they had been placated by the grant of equal representation in the Senate. Delaware was the first to ratify, on 7 December 1787 by a unanimous vote of its convention; Pennsylvania followed on 12 December (46 votes to 23) and New Jersey (unanimously) on the 18th. Georgia ratified (unanimously) on 2 January 1788, Connecticut on 9 January (128–40), Massachusetts on 6 February (187–168), Maryland on 26 April (63–11), South Carolina on 23 May (149–73), New Hampshire on 21 June (57–47), Virginia on 25 June (89–74) and New York on 26 July (30–27). Nine had been decided upon as the minimum number for ratification (for those states only which had done so). The Constitution was now in effect. North Carolina refused on 2 August (by 184 votes to 83) to ratify until a Bill of Rights and other amendments had been accepted. It eventually ratified on 21 November 1789 (195–77). Rhode Island held out until 29 May 1790 (34–32). The convention had also contemplated the adhesion of Vermont, which had regarded itself as an independent state since 1775, although New York, which had contested with New Hampshire for its possession, had held up its admission to the Union. Vermont adopted the Constitution on 10 January 1791 and was admitted by Congress on 4 March—the first addition to the original thirteen.

North Carolina was not the only state where the omission of a Bill of Rights had been objected to, and in some states undertakings had been given that there would be amendments once the Constitution was passed; although it was pointed out on the other side that a Bill of Rights was in fact superfluous since the new government, unlike the British government, had no prerogative powers and could not act except within the powers conferred upon it. A series of amendments was proposed by Madison in the first congress, and the ten that were accepted were subsequently termed the Bill of Rights. The first eight of these went over historic ground in the struggles between kings and their subjects: provision for religious liberty (with a prohibition upon any establishment) and freedom of speech and press, assembly and petition. Americans were to have the right to bear arms and were protected against seizures and searches, double jeopardy and self-incrimination, and to have other procedural guarantees of fair treatment by the courts. The other two amendments dealt with the interpretation of the constitutional structure itself; the enumeration of popular rights was not to be regarded as exhaustive; and powers neither delegated to the United States, nor prohibited to individual states, were to be regarded as 'reserved to the states respectively, or to the people'. But an attempt to limit the powers of the federal government to those expressly delegated to it was significantly opposed (and successfully) by Madison and other moderates, as well as by the out-and-out nationalists. The majority agreed that in any effective government 'powers must necessarily be admitted by implication'.

The last act of the old congress had been to set the new machinery of government in motion. In September 1788, after eleven states had ratified the Constitution, it designated the first Wednesday of the following November for selecting presidential electors, the first Wednesday in February for the casting of their votes and 4 March 1789 for the inauguration of the new President.

The states arranged for the choice of presidential electors in a variety of ways by popular election, or by the state legislatures. Washington was elected President unanimously; and John Adams was top of the six next candidates and thus became the first Vice-President. The states also elected their representatives to the lower house of Congress and their legislatures chose the first senators. The new congress, like the executive branch which was much under Hamilton's influence, was nationalist in temper and when unresolved issues came up for settlement it tended to handle them with a nationalist bias. Its first main tasks were the working out of its own procedures and the creation by legislation of the executive departments. In the latter function it built on the work of the Continental Congress. For after the early success of the radicals in getting everything done through committees of Congress itself, conservative elements had taken control and secured the handling of affairs by single executive officers. No new officer took over the equivalent of Charles Thomson's role as Secretary to the Congress which he had held ever since the First Continental Congress. The new office of Secretary of State, created in 1789 after the proposal to have a Home Department had been turned down, combined the responsibility of the former Secretary of Congress for communications between the federal government and the states, with the conduct of foreign affairs for which there had been a separate secretary since 1781. In creating a War Department, Congress merely took over what had been a going concern since 1781; and the Post Office was still older, having been set up under Franklin in 1775. The Judiciary Act of 1789 created the office of Attorney-General. The Attorney-General became an important executive officer and presidential adviser though without a department of his own.

The question of the organisation of the treasury was the most controversial, since the future of the federal union would so largely depend upon the financial policies adopted in the early years and their effects upon relations with the states. Congress under the Articles had made a number of changes in the organisation of this side of the government. The powers exercised by Robert Morris as Superintendent of Finance between 1781 and 1784 had been so powerful that the office had been put into commission after his fall. It was suggested that a board of commissioners should again be appointed but it was decided to go back to a single departmental head. On the other hand, the act creating the Secretary of the Treasury gave him special responsibilities for informing and advising Congress that his colleagues did not share; and if Hamilton, the first incumbent of the new office, had retained his position and predominant influence for longer, he might have built on this to turn the headship of the treasury into something like the British premiership, relegating the President to a more formal position.

But several decisions taken during the first months and years of the new constitution helped to ensure that the federal government should be what came to be called 'presidential' in form. Although the President required senatorial approval for his appointments, an attempt to make its consent necessary for removals also was fought off in the debate on the bill setting up the Secretaryship of State; it was further decided that the heads of departments would not be allowed to take part in debates on the floor, so that their contacts with Congress were limited to written communications and subsequently to appearances before committees; finally there was the rapid development of the President's cabinet, an institution nowhere provided for in the Constitution itself.

The cabinet arose partly to fill the gap created by the failure of Washington's attempt to use the Senate as a council; his one appearance before it for consultation was not a success, and it became the rule that where treaties were concerned 'the advice and consent of the Senate' would be deemed to mean *post facto* ratification of the executive's action. The President's formal contacts with Congress were through annual or special messages—both devices were elaborated by Washington. In these circumstances, the provision in the Constitution authorising the President to seek the opinions of departmental heads in writing was insufficient, and by 1793 regular meetings of these officers with the President had become the rule and the word 'cabinet' was coming into use.

The tendency of Congress to seek the Treasury's advice on matters that came before it made the Department the effective source of much early legislation, but the further extension of the Secretary's powers was hindered by the opposition that developed to the financial programme that Hamilton put forward in a series of reports in 1790 and 1791, calling for the refunding of the confederal debt at face value, the assumption and refunding of state debts, the chartering of a national bank and the establishment of a protective tariff. The probable economic and social consequences of such proposals were not congenial to upholders of an agrarian outlook, and their objections were reinforced by constitutional doubts. The bank bill in particular could only rest on implied powers, since the right to set up such a bank was nowhere conferred upon the federal government. When the bill was passed in 1791, Washington asked for the opinions of Hamilton and Jefferson upon its constitutionality; and in their conflicting views were set out the main principles upon which the first political parties of the new system were to be founded

Hamilton, having failed to get powers for the national government as wide as he had asked for at Philadelphia, now argued that every sovereign government must have the right to extend its powers in any necessary direction unless barred by an express prohibition. Jefferson (supported in Congress by the great authority of Madison himself) argued that such breadth of interpretation would mean sweeping away all the restrictions of the Constitution, and would turn Congress into a body exercising plenary powers at its own discretion. Hamilton in the course of this controversy upheld the view that the President's cabinet must be unanimous on policy, and that heads of departments could not with propriety attack each other's policies. This object was to be achieved with the retirement from office of Jefferson at the end of 1793 and of Hamilton himself early in 1795. The Washington administration remained in the hands of what was now the federalist party; with the emergence of the anti-federalists (a states-rights party) as an active opposition, the shape of the American constitutional system and of American political life had received its decisive imprint.

CHAPTER XVII

THE AMERICAN REVOLUTION IN ITS IMPERIAL, STRATEGIC AND DIPLOMATIC ASPECTS

GREAT Britain's vast territorial gains from the Seven Years War made it necessary for her to tackle in earnest the task of imperial reorganisation, tentatively begun a decade earlier. The acquisition of French Canada, the Floridas, and virtually all the territory between the Alleghenies and the Mississippi river not only doubled the size of the British possessions in North America, but created new and complex problems of organisation, administration and defence. The empire was called upon, firstly, to assimilate some 80,000 French-Canadians, alien in language and religion, and unfamiliar with British law and forms of government. The acquisition of the vast trans-Allegheny wilderness demanded a coherent western policy, which took into account the conflicting needs of land settlement, the fur trade and the Indians. Above all, the sudden transformation of Britain's American possessions from a commercial into a territorial empire necessitated a reformed system of internal and external defence.

British efforts to solve these problems led directly to the break-up of the empire. The reformation of the old colonial system, and the attempt to force the colonists to contribute directly to the upkeep of the enlarged empire, compelled colonial leaders to re-examine their position in the imperial structure and to question the constitutional basis of British demands. Such a reaction was, perhaps, inevitable. Because of their remoteness from England and because of British preoccupation and neglect, the American communities had long enjoyed a substantial measure of political and economic freedom. This they had come to regard as their inalienable right. But that American opposition culminated in independence was due to the radically changed position of the colonies after the expulsion of the French from North America. Relieved after 1763 of a long-standing threat to their security, the colonists became increasingly unwilling to accept even the existing restraints upon their freedom, far less to countenance the imposition of new ones.

With regard to the West the ministry of George Grenville, which succeeded that of Bute in April 1763, was able to temporise. The royal proclamation of 7 October prohibiting settlement beyond the Alleghenies was simply a provisional measure, designed to afford time for a comprehensive western policy to be worked out.[1] But in its military aspects the imperial problem admitted of no such postponement. Though the French menace had been removed, there seemed every likelihood of its early revival, while the need for continued protection against the Indians was graphically illustrated by Pontiac's rising of 1763. The decision to station permanently in the colonies an army of 10,000 men had already been taken during the war. Past experience had seemed to prove that no system of colonial defence was feasible save one depending upon British regulars. The failure to achieve voluntary union at the Albany Congress of 1754, the belated and niggardly colonial contributions to the struggle to expel the French, and the lack of response to Amherst's appeal for assistance to suppress the Pontiac conspiracy—these circumstances argued that inter-colonial jealousies were too deep-seated for Americans to unite in their own defence. That the colonists should nevertheless assume part of the increased burden of colonial administration and defence seemed to the ministry both necessary and just. The cost of the American civil and military establishment had risen from £70,000 in 1748 to £350,000 in 1763. According to British opinion the Seven Years War had been undertaken largely to safeguard colonial interests, and the colonists had been the greatest beneficiaries of British victory. Yet while the war had doubled the British national debt and while taxation at home remained at the high wartime level, the colonists were lightly taxed and made little direct contribution to the imperial exchequer.

The raising of a colonial revenue thus became the principal aim of Grenville's policy. His first measure, the Revenue Act of 1764, commonly known as the Sugar Act, replaced the Molasses Act of 1733 which had provided, *inter alia*, for a duty of sixpence a gallon on colonial imports of foreign molasses, but which had been largely a dead letter. Grenville's new measure, while imposing heavy duties on wines, coffee, lawns and cambrics, reduced the duty on foreign molasses to threepence a gallon, but was intended to be strictly enforced. To ensure its effectiveness, the machinery for enforcing the Acts of Trade and Navigation was overhauled. The American customs officers, many of whom had remained in England, were ordered either to carry out their duties or to resign; to check smuggling, additional certificates were required of vessels requesting clearance, and writs of assistance were authorised; to counter the notorious reluctance of colonial juries to convict smugglers, jurisdiction

---

[1] British frontier policy in the decade after the Treaty of Paris is analysed in C. W. Alvord, *The Mississippi Valley in British Politics* (2 vols., Cleveland, Ohio, 1917). Alvord's account is substantially amended at certain points, however, by T. P. Abernethy, *Western Lands and the American Revolution* (New York, 1937), and by R. A. Humphreys, 'Lord Shelburne and the Proclamation of 1763', *English Historical Review*, vol. XLIX (1934), pp. 241–64, and 'Lord Shelburne and British Colonial Policy, 1766–68', *ibid.* vol. L (1935), pp. 257–77. The whole question is re-examined in Vincent T. Harlow, *The Founding of the Second British Empire, 1763–1793* (London, 1952), pp. 162–98.

in revenue cases was given to vice-admiralty courts with greatly enlarged powers; and Pitt's wartime policy of using the navy to suppress illicit commerce was revived. By these means it was hoped to reform the inefficient and venal colonial customs service, which had hitherto brought in only a quarter of the amount it had cost to run.

The Sugar Act, and still more the prospect of its enforcement, thoroughly alarmed the colonial merchants, particularly in New England. There it had long been the practice, despite the Molasses Act of 1733, to import the bulk of the molasses required in distilling from the French West Indies. This trade, New Englanders contended, could never bear such a duty as the Sugar Act imposed. The measure, they argued, would deprive them of the only customer with whom they enjoyed a favourable balance of trade, and would thus cut off their greatest single source of specie. But colonial protest was not long confined to the sphere of economics. Since it differed from previous trade laws in that its avowed purpose was to raise a revenue rather than to regulate commerce, the Sugar Act was soon challenged on constitutional grounds.

Colonial opposition remained localised, however, until the passage of the Stamp Act of 1765. This measure, adopted because the Sugar Act would bring in only a fraction of the amount the colonists were required to contribute, extended to the colonies a tax which had been in force in England since 1694. Passed with little parliamentary opposition, the act required revenue stamps to be affixed to newspapers, commercial bills, and legal and other documents. Affecting as it did the most vocal and influential classes of the community, the Stamp Act produced a widespread and violent colonial reaction.[1] Denounced as an unjustified innovation, the measure was nullified by mob action; stamp distributors were terrorised into resigning and supplies of stamps were destroyed wherever they could be reached. Colonial merchants, moreover, turned to non-importation as a means of bringing pressure on the British government, while the representatives of nine colonies, meeting at New York in the Stamp Act Congress of October 1765, drew up a Declaration of Rights and Grievances which condemned the Stamp Act as having a 'manifest tendency to subvert the rights and liberties of the colonies'. Nevertheless, the repeal of the Stamp Act in 1766 was not attributable to colonial pressure. The paralysis of colonial trade as a result of non-importation brought a flood of protest from the British commercial interest, and the Rockingham ministry, shunning the alternative of compelling obedience by force, was glad of an excuse to abandon Grenville's measure.

Colonial rejoicing at the repeal of the Stamp Act was based upon the misconception that there had been a change of heart in London. As the Declaratory Act should have made plain, Parliament had not retreated an

[1] Colonial protests are described in E. S. and H. M. Morgan, *The Stamp Act Crisis: Prologue to Revolution* (Chapel Hill, North Carolina, 1953).

inch on the constitutional issue; nor was there any weakening of the ministry's determination to raise a colonial revenue. This was soon evident, indeed, from the continued attempts to enforce the Mutiny Act of 1765. This measure, designed to remedy the shortage of military accommodation in colonial seaports, amounted in reality to a direct tax for it required colonial assemblies to provide barracks and vote supplies for British troops. Though most of the colonies complied, at least in part, they did so grudgingly and with qualifications designed to preserve their future freedom of action. The New York Assembly at first refused point-blank to obey the act, and did so ultimately only when threatened with suspension.

Following the repeal of the Stamp Act, the Rockingham administration sought still further to appease the colonists by the Revenue Act of 1766 which reduced the duty on molasses from threepence a gallon to one penny, though extending the tax to British as well as to foreign molasses. While the measure increased the yield from the colonial customs, the financial problem remained. It had, indeed, been aggravated by Parliament's decision early in 1767 to relieve the burden on the landed interest at home by a reduction of the land-tax. To cover the loss of revenue involved, Charles Townshend, Chancellor of the Exchequer in the Chatham ministry, introduced new duties in 1767 upon colonial imports of glass, lead, paint, paper and tea, the proceeds of which were to be used to defray the cost not only of colonial defence but of the colonial civil administrations, which would thus be freed from dependence upon the assemblies. To tighten still further the machinery of trade enforcement, Townshend also established an American Board of Customs Commissioners, to be stationed at Boston.

Townshend's measures revived the uproar in America. Denounced on constitutional grounds in John Dickinson's *Letters of a Pennsylvania Farmer* (1768) and in even stronger terms in the Massachusetts Circular Letter, the new programme persuaded the colonists to revert to the retaliatory measures which had apparently proved so effective against the Stamp Act. In March 1768 non-importation was adopted by Boston and after varying intervals by the other colonial seaports. At Boston serious disorders developed out of the efforts of the new Board of Customs to enforce the revenue laws and the Acts of Trade.[1] Owing to the open hostility of the townsfolk the commissioners found their task increasingly difficult, and in June their authority collapsed altogether after their abortive attempt to seize the sloop *Liberty*, belonging to the prominent radical John Hancock. The dispatch of troops to restore order led only to further friction which culminated, in March 1770, in the so-called 'Boston

---

[1] The role of the American Board of Customs Commissioners in provoking colonial hostility is emphasised in Oliver M. Dickerson, *The Navigation Acts and the American Revolution* (Philadelphia, 1951).

Massacre', in which five Bostonians were killed in a clash with British soldiers.

But by this time colonial unity had begun to dissolve. Conservative opinion had become alarmed at the threat to the social order which it detected in radicalism and mob action. It was also apparent that the commercial boycott was not being uniformly observed; some ports were taking advantage of the situation to profit at the expense of their rivals.[1] Hence many were ready to welcome the olive branch held out by the newly formed ministry of Lord North. North had concluded that the Townshend duties were unprofitable, and on the day of the Boston massacre all were repealed save that on tea which was retained 'as a mark of the supremacy of Parliament, and an efficient declaration of their right to govern the colonies'. At this, New York abandoned non-importation and, notwithstanding radical protest, the remaining ports followed suit.

Apart from the burning of the British revenue cutter *Gaspee* off Rhode Island in 1772, the years following the repeal of the Townshend duties were a period of comparative calm. Prosperity had returned to the colonies after a long post-war depression, the colonists seemed weary of contention, and radicalism went into eclipse. Smuggling, though by no means eradicated, was at least reduced and parliamentary taxation was an established fact. But the lull was broken by the passage of the Tea Act of 1773, which attempted to help the East India Company out of its financial difficulties by permitting it to export tea to the colonies direct and to sell it there by retail. The act would have made tea cheaper to the consumer but, by threatening colonial merchants with monopoly and the smuggling rings with extinction, it united both those powerful interests with the radicals whose opposition was based on constitutional grounds. The consignment of tea sent to Charleston was landed but not offered for sale; those sent to New York and Philadelphia were rejected and returned to England; while at Boston, on 16 December 1773, the tea-ships were boarded by a group of men disguised as Indians and their cargo was thrown into the harbour.

The Boston Tea Party brought to a head the dispute which had gone on intermittently since 1763. The British government, confronted with colonial defiance for the third time, abandoned appeasement and turned to coercion. The series of laws passed in 1774 and known as the Coercive or Intolerable Acts closed the port of Boston until compensation was paid for the destroyed tea, revised the Massachusetts charter so as to increase the powers of the executive at the expense of those of the assembly, provided for the removal of certain offenders to England for trial, and attempted to check evasions of the requirement to provide suitable quarters for troops.

[1] A. M. Schlesinger, *The Colonial Merchants and the American Revolution, 1763–1776* (New York, 1918), chs. IV and V.

Far from isolating Massachusetts as had been intended, these measures united the other colonies in her defence. Thanks to the skilful propaganda of the radicals and to the work of committees of correspondence, the colonists were fully alive to the necessity of common action. In May 1774 the Virginia assembly sent out a call for an inter-colonial meeting, and on 5 September twelve colonies sent delegates to the first Continental Congress at Philadelphia. By now colonial opinion had been further inflamed by the passage of the Quebec Act. This measure, nowadays regarded as a statesmanlike attempt to solve the problem of governing Canada,[1] was believed by the inhabitants of the older colonies to pose a fresh threat to their liberties. The recognition of the privileged position of the Roman Catholic church in Canada and the continuance there of the French legal system seemed to American opinion to 'smell strong of popery' and to presage the establishment of an autocracy, while the extension of the Canadian boundary to the Ohio appeared designed to check westward expansion. Convinced of the need for concerted resistance, though at first divided as to the form it should take, the Continental Congress drew up a declaration formulating the constitutional argument, petitioned the king for redress, and subscribed to an association consisting of non-importation, non-exportation and non-consumption agreements, to go into force on 1 November 1774.

The appearance of committees of inspection to ensure the strict observance of the association gave to colonial protest an unmistakable air of illegality which, in the winter of 1774–5, developed into open, if still unavowed, rebellion. The provincial congresses, which had sprung into existence to elect delegates to Philadelphia, continued to meet in defiance of the royal governors. In places assuming the functions of government, they everywhere placed the colonies upon a war footing, supervising the organisation and drilling of militia and the collection of military stores. These defensive preparations should have warned the ministry that only substantial concessions could bring about a peaceable end to the dispute. But Lord North's Conciliatory Resolution of 20 February 1775 yielded nothing of substance; it was in fact designed to sow dissension rather than to conciliate. North's offer, which was to suspend parliamentary taxation in any colony paying the cost of its own civil administration and making a satisfactory contribution to imperial defence, was in any case too late. By the time it reached America hostilities had already begun.

They had been precipitated by a British attempt to interrupt American military preparations. In the autumn of 1774 General Thomas Gage, the commander-in-chief of the army in North America, had been appointed governor of Massachusetts with orders to enforce the Coercive Acts. Six months later, on receiving instructions from London criticising his inactivity and ordering the arrest of the colonial leaders, Gage sent a force

[1] See R. M. Coupland, *The Quebec Act: A Study in Statesmanship* (Oxford, 1925).

of 700 men from Boston to seize the guns and powder the colonists had been amassing at Concord, sixteen miles away. But the countryside had been aroused, and at Lexington on 19 April the British found their path barred by a body of Massachusetts militia. Shots were fired and a skirmish developed, while at Concord itself, where a larger militia force had gathered, there was a heavy exchange of fire. After destroying what remained of the military stores the British turned for Boston, being continuously attacked along the line of march. Regaining the town with difficulty, they then found themselves closely besieged by an ill-organised but formidable New England army.[1]

The news of Lexington and Concord, skilfully embroidered by radical propagandists, went far to heal colonial divisions and to strengthen determination to defend colonial rights. The majority of delegates to the Second Continental Congress, which assembled at Philadelphia on 10 May 1775, was still hopeful of preserving those rights within the framework of the empire. But there was no hesitation in resolving that the colonies 'be immediately put into a state of defence'. In response to a plea from Massachusetts, Congress agreed to assume responsibility for the army besieging Boston; a Continental army of 20,000 men was authorised, and the colonies were called upon for specified quotas. On 15 June George Washington was appointed 'general and commander-in-chief of the army of the United Colonies'. Washington's appointment owed more to expediency than to his military experience, which was slight. It was felt that to place a Virginian in command of a predominantly New England army would be to promote colonial unity; the choice of a wealthy, conservative planter satisfied those who feared the spread of radicalism; and that Washington had been a member of the Continental Congress seemed a safeguard against military rule. Political and sectional considerations also played a part in the selection of Washington's immediate subordinates. Major-generalships were granted to Artemas Ward, who commanded the troops around Boston; Israel Putnam, another New Englander; Philip Schuyler, a Hudson valley landowner; and Charles Lee, a former British regular officer who had settled in Virginia. Another product of the British army, Horatio Gates, became adjutant-general.

On assuming command at Cambridge in early July, Washington found the Continental army recovering from the effects of the sanguinary engagement known, inaccurately, as Bunker Hill. At the end of May Generals Howe, Clinton and Burgoyne had arrived at Boston to assist Gage and to bestir him to take the initiative. But despite the arrival of reinforcements which brought up his numbers to 6000, Gage would agree only to ensure against attack by seizing Bunker Hill, which dominated Boston from the Charlestown peninsula. Before he could actually do so,

---

[1] The controversial aspects of Lexington and Concord are ably treated in Allen M. French, *The First Year of the American Revolution* (Boston, 1934).

however, he was forestalled by an American force which, though sent to occupy Bunker Hill, established itself on the still more dominating Breed's Hill. Howe, who led the attempt to dislodge the Americans on 17 June, was confident that colonial militia would prove no match for British regulars. But his slowness allowed time to the Americans to improve an already strong position, while Howe also erred in neglecting to use the navy to cut off the American retreat to the mainland. Three frontal assaults were necessary before Breed's Hill was taken and the Americans were driven off the peninsula. Of Howe's attacking force of 2500 more than a thousand became casualties; the defenders lost less than half that number.

Gage, chastened by his army's heavy losses, made no further offensive moves after Breed's Hill. Howe, who succeeded him in October, shared his predecessor's caution and was anxious moreover to withdraw from Boston to a more promising base of operations. Nor were the Americans in any condition to attack. Washington was obliged, indeed, to devote all his energies during the next few months to remedying the glaring weaknesses that Breed's Hill had exposed in the Continental army. Thoroughly undisciplined and disorganised, the forces of the united colonies were also poorly officered and woefully deficient in arms and powder. Even worse was the steady decline of strength as soldiers refused to serve beyond the term of their enlistments; 'such a dearth of public spirit and want of virtue' Washington had not foreseen.

By the early spring of 1776 these difficulties had been partly overcome; re-enlistments had filled the ranks of the Continental army and fresh supplies of ammunition had been obtained. Having also received a large train of artillery captured at Ticonderoga and brought down to Boston during the winter by prodigies of effort, Washington was at last in a position to take the offensive. Early in March his army seized Dorchester Heights, which commanded the town of Boston and which the British had been too weak to occupy. Realising that Boston would shortly become untenable, Howe momentarily contemplated an attempt to oust the enemy, but after a heavy storm had disrupted his preparations for an assault, he decided upon evacuation. Washington, anxious to spare the city, made no effort to hinder the British withdrawal. On 17 March 1776 Howe's army, together with more than a thousand loyalists, sailed off to Halifax, thus relinquishing for a time the last British foothold in the thirteen rebellious colonies.

An American invasion of Canada had meanwhile been repulsed. Its objects had been to induce Canada to become the fourteenth member of the nascent colonial union, and to forestall a British attempt to use the province as a springboard for punitive action. When the Continental Congress sanctioned the Canadian enterprise, in June 1775, it appeared to have a good prospect of success. Only a few hundred British regulars were available for the defence of Canada, while the seizure in May of Ticonderoga and Crown Point by a New England force under the joint command of Ethan Allen and Benedict Arnold had exposed the province to a thrust from Lake Champlain. The Americans were also confident of French-Canadian assistance.

This hope proved ill-founded. The Quebec Act had largely assuaged Canadian discontent, while the outburst of anti-Catholicism it had provoked in New England had had an adverse effect upon Canadian opinion, especially upon the *seigneurs* and the Catholic hierarchy. Thus the invaders found the *habitants* unhelpful, if not openly hostile.[1] Owing moreover to dilatoriness in its preparation, the Canadian expedition did not get under way until September. While Benedict Arnold led an assault on Quebec across the wilderness of Maine, the bulk of the invading force under Richard Montgomery advanced up the Champlain waterway. Montgomery was held up for two months by the stubborn British defence of Fort St John's on the Richelieu river, and Montreal did not fall to him until 13 November. Winter had thus already set in before his army, weakened by desertion and sickness, joined Arnold's forces before Quebec. The governor of Canada, Sir Guy Carleton, had taken advantage of the respite to strengthen the defences of the fortress, and the besiegers lacked the heavy artillery needed to breach its massive walls. Nevertheless, with a large part of his army due for disbandment at the end of the year, Montgomery was obliged to try to take Quebec by storm. The attempt, made in a heavy snowstorm on the night of 30 December, was an American disaster: Montgomery was killed, Arnold wounded and heavy losses sustained. Though Arnold continued to besiege the fortress for several months longer, success was now beyond him. Smallpox decimated his army, and, with the arrival of strong British reinforcements in the spring of 1776, he was obliged to raise the siege. By the end of June the Americans had also abandoned Montreal and were retreating from Canada in disorder.

More than a year elapsed between the first fighting at Lexington and the Declaration of Independence. For several months the Continental Congress continued to protest its loyalty to the crown. Most delegates, like the majority of the colonists, still clung to the hope that separation might prove unnecessary. They affected to believe that coercion was the policy not of the king but of 'a venal ministry', and were in constant expectation of a conciliatory answer to their petitions for redress. But during the winter of 1775–6 it became increasingly apparent that George III, no less than his ministers, was bent on subjugation. No answer was made to the Olive Branch Petition sent in July, while the king's speech at the opening of Parliament in October ridiculed colonial professions of loyalty

[1] Canadian attitudes are analysed in G. M. Wrong, *Canada and the American Revolution* (New York, 1935).

and reiterated a previously announced intention of waging war. The Prohibitory Act of 22 December, declaring the rebellious colonies to be outside the protection of the crown and laying an embargo upon colonial trade, convinced many waverers in the colonies of the necessity of separation. So did the news that German mercenaries were to be employed to suppress the rebellion. Thomas Paine's pamphlet *Common Sense*, which was published in January 1776, expressed the developing mood. By a direct and vehement attack on monarchy, Paine disabused Americans of the notion that they might rely upon George III for protection, and showed that the only alternatives were submission or independence. Events themselves were suggesting the same conclusion. The colonists had come to realise that foreign aid, essential if they were not to be overwhelmed, would continue to be unobtainable as long as they remained within the empire. A year's fighting had, moreover, produced considerable bitterness and had greatly weakened attachment to the mother-country. Hence in the spring of 1776 colony after colony instructed its delegates to the Continental Congress to vote for separation. On 6 April Congress opened American ports to the vessels of all nations save Britain; on 10 May the formation of independent state-governments was advised; on 2 July Richard Henry Lee's resolution asserting American independence was adopted, and two days later Congress voted approval of the great declaration.

For all the inspiration it afforded the patriot cause both then and later, the Declaration of Independence divided rather than united American opinion. Enthusiastically greeted by those who deemed the time ripe for separation, it alienated others who could not bring themselves to abandon traditional loyalties. What proportion of the colonial population remained loyalist is not known. The commonest estimate is that one-third supported the Revolution, one-third opposed, and one-third were indifferent. But this division, however neat, seems incorrect.[1] It is more likely that by the summer of 1776 at least half the American population favoured independence, while of the remainder those of loyalist sympathies were probably outnumbered by the neutrals. Nevertheless the number of active loyalists was not inconsiderable. They were to be found in every colony and in all classes of society. In New York and New Jersey they were probably in the majority; in Pennsylvania and Georgia they were not much less numerous; and the Carolinas, too, had substantial numbers. Only in New England, Virginia and Maryland—the oldest colonies—were loyalists insignificant. Proportionately, loyalism was strongest among the well-to-do, largely because of their innate conservatism and fear of anarchy. Royal officials and the Anglican clergy tended especially to remain loyal; and, except in Virginia and New England, so did lawyers, merchants and large planters. But such attempts to analyse loyalism in

[1] J. R. Alden, *The American Revolution, 1775–1783* (London, 1954), p. 87 n.

terms of class or occupation break down in face of the fact that the Revolution was essentially a civil war, in which social groups and even families were divided against themselves. Possibly 30,000 Americans served in the armed forces of the crown during the conflict, and when it was over perhaps as many as 80,000 people took part in the loyalist exodus to Canada, Nova Scotia and other parts of the empire.

In Britain, too, opinion was divided on the American war, though not perhaps to the extent that was once believed. In Parliament the policy of force was loudly criticised. Burke consistently preached conciliation; Fox displayed his American sympathies by appearing in the buff and blue colours of the Continental Army; David Hartley and John Wilkes argued the impossibility of military reconquest. But much of this criticism was simply factious.[1] Even Chatham was not above exploiting the American issue for party advantage; and while he and other opposition leaders were genuinely anxious for conciliation, they were just as unwilling as was the government to yield Parliament's right to legislate for the colonies. Once the issue had been clearly drawn between surrender or coercion, only a small minority continued to make common cause with the rebels. The revival of a levelling spirit at home added further to the hostility of churchmen and squires towards the rebels, thus ensuring for the ministry comfortable majorities for its war measures. True, a number of army and naval officers resigned their commissions rather than fight the Americans; but these cases, so emphasised in older accounts, were not numerous in the aggregate, and the loyalty of the armed forces as a whole was never in question. And while there was certainly some mercantile opposition to a war which threatened to derange trade and hinder the collection of American debts, it was neither whole-hearted nor lasting.[2] The bulk of British opinion, indeed, firmly supported George III and Lord North and continued to do so, though with declining enthusiasm, until the final disaster at Yorktown.

At first sight the task of reconquest seemed well within British capabilities. Outnumbering the Americans in population by more than three to one, Great Britain possessed infinitely greater war-making resources and overwhelming military and naval supremacy. But the odds were not as heavily in her favour as they appeared to be. Formidable problems of logistics were involved in carrying the war to the rebels. To transport and maintain an army across three thousand miles of ocean was an immense undertaking. Communications with America were slow and undepend-

---

[1] Harlow, *The Founding of the Second British Empire, 1763–1793*, pp. 150 ff.

[2] L. B. Namier, *England in the Age of the American Revolution* (London, 1930), shows (p. 296) that some at least of the merchants' protests against coercion were not sincerely meant. The Glasgow merchants, for example, while sending a strong petition in favour of the colonists early in 1775, assured North through their Members of Parliament that they did not mean opposition, but merely wished to gain credit in America with a view to an easier collection of their debts.

able; supplies, which in previous American campaigns had been obtainable locally, had now to be ferried in all their huge quantity from Britain. America, with its forests, mountains and swamps, its harsh climate and vast distances, was ill-suited to European methods of warfare. Movement of any kind was difficult because of poor communications; swift advances by heavily equipped armies impossible. Moreover, the outbreak of war found Britain as usual unprepared. British naval strength had suffered a startling decline since 1763, chiefly because of Parliament's passion for economy, though in some degree also owing to corruption in the royal dockyards under Sandwich's administration. The army, too, had been allowed to fall below strength, and when additional troops were hastily required for operations in America they could be obtained only from the rulers of petty German states. During the war almost 30,000 mercenaries were so obtained, about half of them from the landgrave of Hesse-Kassel.

Responsibility for the direction of the war lay with Lord George Germain, who joined North's ministry in November 1775 as Secretary of State for the Colonies. As a war minister Germain was by no means as incompetent as has been alleged.[1] His was the energy which overcame the confusion at first surrounding the British war effort; his too the credit for the timely reinforcement of Canada and the building up of Howe's powerful expeditionary force at Halifax. Nor was Germain guilty of the absurdity frequently charged against him of trying to run the war from London. His instructions for the campaign of 1776, for example—to seize New York and move against New England—were neither positive nor binding on Howe, who was given full discretionary authority to suppress the rebellion. Yet Howe's appointment both as commander-in-chief and as peace commissioner betrayed a certain confusion of purpose, reflecting as it did the ministry's inability to decide whether to conciliate or to repress. This indecision, coupled with Germain's excessive reliance on loyalist support, led to that dispersal of effort which characterised British military operations in America.

Germain's faith in loyalism induced him to launch an early expedition against the southern colonies. Confident that the southern loyalists needed only the help of British regulars to overthrow the rebel governments, he ordered Clinton early in 1776 to lead an assault on the Carolinas in cooperation with Sir Peter Parker's fleet. But by the time that Clinton's expedition assembled off the Cape Fear river in May, the southern loyalists had suffered two severe reverses which left them disinclined for further adventures. In Virginia the capture of Norfolk by rebel militia on 1 January 1776 deprived loyalism of its last foothold in that colony. In North Carolina a force of sixteen hundred Scottish Highlanders who had

---

[1] Alden, *op. cit.* p. 68. For a more recent defence of Germain see P. Mackesy, *The War for America, 1775–1783* (London, 1964), which appeared when this chapter was already in proof.

rallied to the crown in the back-country was intercepted *en route* to Wilmington and routed at the battle of Moore's Creek Bridge (28 February 1776). His plans disarranged by this setback, Clinton resolved to attack Charleston, the largest city and seaport in the south. But the enterprise was a failure. Congress had reinforced Charleston, and formidable defences had been erected there. After failing to reduce the harbour forts by naval bombardment on 28 June, Clinton and Parker realised the futility of their efforts and sailed off to join Howe at New York, thus leaving the southern colonies to enjoy two years' freedom from attack.

Following his withdrawal from Boston to Halifax, Howe's first objective was the seizure of New York, which commanded the Hudson–Champlain route to Canada, possessed the best harbour on the Atlantic coast and was the leading centre of loyalism. The attack on the city began with a landing on Staten Island on 2 July 1776, the day Congress voted for independence. The British expeditionary force of 34,000 was powerfully supported by a fleet under the command of the general's elder brother, Admiral Lord Howe. Washington, appreciating New York's strategic importance, had transferred the bulk of his army there in April and had built a fortified line on Brooklyn Heights. But his forces were badly disposed and in the battle of Long Island (27 August 1776) they were outflanked and heavily defeated. Only Howe's dilatoriness in following up his victory enabled Washington to withdraw across the East River to Manhattan.

After a brief interval in which the Howe brothers attempted, in vain, to end hostilities by negotiation, the British offensive was resumed in mid-September and New York was easily captured. Washington, with an army greatly inferior to Howe's, was anxious at all costs to avoid a general engagement, and in face of the British advance withdrew to the northward, first to Harlem Heights and then to White Plains and North Castle. Howe's slowness in pursuit lost him several opportunities to trap his adversary against the Hudson but, suddenly changing front, he overran Fort Washington at the northern tip of Manhattan, capturing 3000 men and large quantities of equipment (16 November). This opened the way to the invasion of New Jersey, and by the beginning of December Cornwallis had advanced to the Delaware, pushing Washington's dispirited army before him. A quick thrust would then almost certainly have given the British Philadelphia. The city was virtually defenceless and so imminent did its fall appear that the Continental Congress fled to Baltimore. But Howe, cautious by nature and wedded to European notions of warfare, had no stomach for fresh operations so late in the campaigning season. The ease with which New Jersey had been overrun had persuaded him that American resistance was disintegrating, and that the *coup de grâce* might safely be postponed until the spring. He therefore ordered Cornwallis into winter quarters, thus squandering the last and best opportunity afforded a British general of crushing American resistance at a single stroke.

This unexpected respite gave Washington the opportunity, which he was quick to seize, of striking back at the over-extended British lines. On Christmas night 1776 he recrossed the Delaware and fell on the Hessian garrison of Trenton, capturing 1000 prisoners. A few days later he slipped round Cornwallis's relieving army and defeated another British force at Princeton. Withdrawing to Morristown, where his army was to remain for the next six months, Washington could look back with satisfaction upon the results of his brief winter campaign. With an army one-sixth the size of Howe's he had forced the British to relinquish most of their gains in the 1776 campaign. By so doing he both revived his own declining reputation and breathed new life into the American cause.

Only comparatively recently has historical research exploded the myths surrounding British strategy in the fighting of 1777.[1] It was formerly believed that, in an ill-considered attempt to co-ordinate from London the movements of two widely separated armies, Germain planned a concentration of force in the Hudson valley; that Howe was required by the plan to move northward in strength to meet Burgoyne's army advancing south from Canada; and that disaster resulted from Germain's failure to inform Howe of what was expected of him. But in fact there was no such attempt to direct overall strategy from London. The only plan devised there was that for the descent from Canada, agreed between Burgoyne and Germain during the former's visit home in the winter of 1776–7. Burgoyne's expedition was planned as an independent venture; its success was not thought to require Howe's close co-operation. Howe continued to be free to make his own plans and, with Germain's approval, decided that his principal business in 1777 would be the invasion of Pennsylvania. He also decided, however, to leave 3000 men on the lower Hudson to 'facilitate in some degree the approach from Canada'.

With a characteristic lack of urgency Howe waited until midsummer 1777 before resuming operations. Not until 23 July did he sail from New York for the Delaware with 260 ships and 15,000 men, with Philadelphia as his objective. Finding the Delaware river heavily fortified, the expedition put about for Chesapeake Bay, where it disembarked on 25 August, fifty miles to the south of the rebel capital. Washington tried to halt the British advance at Brandywine Creek (11 September), but as at Long Island was outflanked and forced to retreat. He could do nothing to prevent the British capture of Philadelphia (25 September), but a surprise attack on Howe's unprepared army at Germantown (4 October) achieved initial success and failed only when fog brought confusion to the battlefield and Cornwallis arrived with reinforcements. A month later, having

---

[1] The authoritative work is that by Troyer S. Anderson, *The Command of the Howe Brothers during the American Revolution* (New York, 1936).

reduced the defences of the lower Delaware, Howe had opened the river to British shipping. While he prepared to spend the winter in comfort at Philadelphia, Washington withdrew his army to the desolate plateau of Valley Forge, twenty miles to the north-west. But the occupation of Philadelphia was a less impressive victory than it appeared. Washington's army, whose destruction should have been Howe's main purpose, was still in being. And while Howe sparred ineffectually with his adversary in Pennsylvania, disaster overtook British arms in the woods of the far north.

Though he was later to assert the contrary, Burgoyne knew when he began his southward advance from Canada that he could expect no major assistance from Howe. He was nevertheless confident of success when, in mid-June 1777, he set off with an army of 9500, chiefly British and German, but with Canadian, loyalist and Indian auxiliaries. But he had underestimated the difficulties of a wilderness campaign, and although on 6 July he captured Ticonderoga, only seventy miles from Albany, his subsequent progress was slow. Encumbered by an enormous baggage train, his army found movement increasingly difficult because of destroyed bridges and blocked roads. On 15 August part of Burgoyne's forces suffered a severe check at Bennington at the hands of the New Hampshire militia, and by early autumn lack of supplies and increasing American opposition had halted the advance. Simultaneously an attempt by British and Indian forces under Lieutenant-Colonel St Leger to reach Albany from Lake Ontario had ended in failure. Checked by the stubborn resistance of the American garrison at Fort Stanwix, St Leger repelled only with difficulty a militia attack at Oriskany (6 August). And when, at the approach of a second American army under Arnold, his Indian allies deserted him, he was obliged to retreat to Oswego and Montreal. Burgoyne's situation thereafter deteriorated rapidly. His army, weakened by Canadian and Indian desertions, now numbered only 5000; his long supply line, stretching back to Canada, grew daily more vulnerable as the New England militia gathered to the eastward; before him stood Gates' army, numbering ultimately 12,000 militia and 5000 Continental troops. Only a swift retreat could now have saved the invaders. But Burgoyne chose to gamble on breaking through to Albany, now only twenty miles away. He made two attempts to hack his way through the American lines, at Freeman's Farm (18 September) and Bemis Heights (7 October); after each had been repulsed with heavy loss, Burgoyne found himself surrounded. On 17 October at Saratoga his exhausted men laid down their arms. There was, however, no surrender. Gates, fearing Clinton's approach from the south with a relieving force, agreed to Burgoyne's proposal of a convention, whereby the defeated army would be allowed to return to England on condition that its members did not again serve in America during the war. But the agreement was kept by neither side, and the 'Convention Army' eventually became prisoners of war.

Saratoga was the war's turning-point. It brought France into the struggle, thus transforming a localised rebellion into a world war and one in which the scales were weighted increasingly against Britain. But the Franco-American alliance took time to mature and in the winter of 1777-8, while the diplomats were at work in Paris, the American cause went through a period of tribulation and dissension. While Gates' victorious army disintegrated after the return home of its militiamen, Washington's Continentals endured great privations in their wretched encampment at Valley Forge. The surrounding countryside had been stripped of provisions in the preceding campaign; speculation and profiteering made supplies difficult to obtain elsewhere; and as there was also a transport breakdown, food and clothing reached Valley Forge only irregularly and in insufficient quantities. Indeed, had it not been for the comparatively mild winter and the absence of epidemics, complete disaster must have overtaken the ragged half-starved Continentals.

Like that of his army, Washington's own position was in jeopardy during these grim months at Valley Forge. That there was an organised conspiracy against him now seems improbable; no evidence has been found to prove the existence of a 'Conway cabal' such as Washington and his military family believed in.[1] But both in and out of Congress there was undoubtedly an undercurrent of dissatisfaction with the commander-in-chief. In some quarters there were fears that a military dictatorship would result from what John Adams had earlier called 'the superstitious veneration that is sometimes paid to General Washington' by those around him. There was also criticism of Washington's defensive strategy, which was blamed for his repeated failure to defeat Howe. Moreover, in their chagrin at the fall of Philadelphia, some Americans began to question Washington's military ability and to contrast his record with that of Gates, the victor of Saratoga. Matters came to a head in November 1777, when the contents were made public of a private letter written to Gates by General Thomas Conway, an Irish-born French officer serving in the Continental army; in it Conway had expressed the hope that Gates would supersede 'the weak General'. But criticism was no sooner brought out into the open than it expired. The bulk of the army had already given Washington its devotion; Congress, forced to take sides, hastened to express its confidence in him. Conway resigned, while Gates, though innocent of conspiracy if not of ambition, retired to an obscurity broken only by a brief and unhappy appearance in the southern campaign of 1780. Henceforth, despite the fact that success continued for long to elude him, Washington's authority was unquestioned.

From an early stage in the struggle, Congressional leaders had realised

---

[1] This is the conclusion reached both by Bernhard Knollenberg, *Washington and the Revolution...* (New York, 1940), pp. 65-7, and by L. H. Butterfield in his edition of the *Letters of Benjamin Rush* (2 vols., Princeton, 1951), vol. II, appendix I, pp. 1197-1208.

that the foreign aid they deemed essential could be obtained only from the maritime powers of France and Spain. Towards both these countries, and particularly towards France, Americans had traditional antipathies, and it was a measure of their necessity that they decided to approach the Bourbons for aid. This they did even before independence was declared. In November 1775 the Continental Congress set up a Committee of Secret Correspondence to make contact with 'our friends in Great Britain, Ireland, and other parts of the world'. The committee immediately authorised Arthur Lee, a Virginian resident in London, to sound out foreign powers; and in March 1776 authorised a Connecticut merchant, Silas Deane, to go to France to seek military and financial assistance. But before Deane could even reach Paris the government of Louis XVI had decided, for reasons of self-interest, to grant secret aid to the rebellious colonists. To Vergennes, the French Minister for Foreign Affairs, the American rebellion was 'a singular and unexpected piece of fortune for France', affording her a long-sought opportunity to avenge the humiliations of the Seven Years War. But in seeking to separate Britain from her colonies Vergennes was not aiming at the recovery of France's lost possessions in North America. His ambitions were not territorial but commercial. American independence, he believed, would cripple the commerce of Britain while benefiting that of France. Louis XVI was nevertheless unwilling at first to run the risk of war involved in the policy of secret aid; so was Turgot, the Comptroller-General of Finance, who saw in Vergennes' policy a threat to his own efforts to avert national bankruptcy. But Vergennes' arguments prevailed, and on 2 May 1776 Louis XVI authorised the expenditure of one million livres for secret shipments of arms and supplies to the Americans; shortly afterwards Spain contributed a similar sum for the same purpose. The war material this money purchased was sent for the sake of secrecy through a fictitious concern, Roderigue Hortalez et Compagnie, headed by the playwright Beaumarchais, who worked in close association with Vergennes and who has sometimes been credited with the authorship of the secret aid policy. The value of Bourbon assistance to the American cause can scarcely be exaggerated. Ninety per cent of the powder the Americans used during the early years of the war came from Europe, most of it through Beaumarchais' bogus company. In particular, the guns and ammunition which wrought the defeat of Burgoyne at Saratoga came largely from French arsenals. In addition, the facilities granted to the Americans in the ports of France and of the French West Indies were responsible for the success of their privateers against British shipping.

Nevertheless, the peril facing the United States after Howe's victories in the autumn of 1776 impelled Congress to make fresh approaches to France. Ignorant as yet of the French decision to help, Congressmen on 26 September nominated Silas Deane, Benjamin Franklin and Thomas

Jefferson (later replaced by Arthur Lee) as commissioners to the court of Versailles, with instructions to obtain munitions and to press for an immediate and explicit recognition of American independence. A proposal in Congress that an alliance should be offered to France was finally rejected after long debate owing to fears of any commitment tending to involve the United States in the affairs of Europe. Thus early was American foreign policy influenced by the isolationism which was to become its guiding principle for the next century and a half.

From the moment that he landed in France in December 1776, Franklin assumed the leadership of the American commission, as indeed his superior abilities and long political experience entitled him to do. In Paris he enjoyed extraordinary popularity. His fame as a philosopher and a scientist had already preceded him; his charm and simplicity of manner captivated intellectual circles. But for all the sympathy he aroused for the American cause, Franklin's efforts to make France a belligerent in the war were for long unavailing. That he ultimately achieved his object was due, perhaps, less to his own astute diplomacy than to the transformed situation resulting from Saratoga. Burgoyne's defeat at last convinced Vergennes that France could safely intervene without fear of an American collapse. That she must not delay her intervention seemed to him equally evident in view of the imminence of British efforts at reconciliation. Compelled, however, by the Family Compact of 1761 to consult Spain before committing France to hostilities, Vergennes first attempted to secure joint Franco-Spanish intervention; but, his efforts meeting only with Spanish procrastination, he then persuaded Louis XVI to act independently. To the American commissioners Vergennes offered not only the commercial treaty they had been authorised to conclude, but also a formal alliance. The offer being promptly accepted, two Franco-American treaties were signed in Paris on 6 February 1778. A treaty of amity and commerce granted reciprocal privileges to the commerce of the United States and France, while a second treaty provided for an alliance to become effective when Britain and France went to war. By the terms of the alliance France and the United States guaranteed each other's possessions in the New World, agreed to wage war until American independence was 'formally or tacitly assured', and bound themselves not to make peace separately.

As Vergennes had anticipated, Lord North's reaction to the news of Saratoga was to offer concessions in the hope of bringing the Americans back into the empire. North's Conciliatory Propositions of February 1778 yielded everything Americans had demanded three years earlier; in particular, the claim that Parliament had the right to tax the colonists was explicitly relinquished. The plan received the grudging assent of Parliament, which was also persuaded to repeal the Tea Act and the Coercive Acts of 1774, and to authorise the sending of a negotiating commission to America. But although the Conciliatory Propositions reached the United States before the news of the French alliance, they were unanimously rejected by Congress as being inadequate and insincere. Ignorant of this rebuff, North dispatched a royal commission headed by the earl of Carlisle to offer Congress any terms short of independence. But when the Carlisle commission reached Philadelphia in June the hopelessness of its mission was at once apparent. Not only had Congress already ratified the treaties with France, but the military situation had been suddenly transformed. The commissioners had confidently expected that their peace offer would be backed by armed force, but found Clinton in the midst of preparations to evacuate Philadelphia, in accordance with royal instructions of which North had deliberately kept them in ignorance. Their approach to Congress meeting with a refusal to negotiate except upon a recognition of American independence or a withdrawal of British military forces, there was no alternative but to retire with the army to New York.

The withdrawal from Philadelphia was the first consequence of a modification of British strategy made necessary by news of the Franco-American alliance. In March 1778 instructions were sent from London to Clinton, Howe's successor as commander-in-chief, requiring him to assume the defensive in the north, to prepare an expedition against Georgia and to supply troops for operations in the West Indies. On abandoning the American capital the British fleet and army were to be concentrated at New York; the naval base of Newport, Rhode Island, captured by Clinton in December 1776 was also to be held if possible.

Sending part of his force from Philadelphia to New York by sea, Clinton set off overland with the main body in mid-June 1778. He was closely pursued by Washington, whose troops had not only survived the hardships of Valley Forge but had emerged from their ordeal with new vitality. Through the vigour of its newly appointed quartermaster-general, Nathanael Greene, the Continental Army had been largely re-equipped, while its organisation, discipline and training had greatly improved, thanks in part to the work of 'Baron' von Steuben as adjutant-general. At Monmouth Court House on 28 June Washington ordered an assault on the British rearguard by a force under the command of Charles Lee. Through Lee's incompetence the attack failed and a serious American reverse might have resulted but for Washington's timely arrival with his main army. Monmouth exploded Lee's inflated reputation and brought about his retirement from command. Court-martialled after a verbal clash with Washington on the battlefield, he was found guilty of disobedience of orders, needless and shameful retreat and disrespect to the commander-in-chief. The engagement itself was indecisive, and Clinton reached New York without further hindrance.

Monmouth was the last major battle of the war to be fought in the north, where British military effort was thereafter limited to frontier raids and seaborne descents. The frontier war was waged with unparalleled ferocity, notably by Colonel Walter Butler, whose Tory Rangers and Indian auxiliaries were responsible for the Wyoming and Cherry Valley massacres of 1778 on the frontiers of Pennsylvania and New York respectively. Butler's operations, though conducted with unnecessary savagery, had at least a definite military purpose, that of diverting Washington's attention from the movements of the main British army. This was also the object of the plundering coastal raids of 1779–81, in the course of which New England towns like New Haven and New London were put to the torch. Virginia was to suffer similar treatment, but the principal British objective in the south in 1778 was Georgia, the most isolated and thinly settled, and thus the weakest state in the union. The Creeks and Cherokees along her frontier were known to be well disposed towards Britain and, notwithstanding the hitherto disappointing response to the appearance of British arms, great hopes were placed in the strength of Georgia loyalism. That these hopes were not entirely illusory was proved by the great numbers flocking to the royal standard after Savannah had fallen to a British army under General Prevost (29 December 1778). The capture of Augusta a month later and the repulse of General Benjamin Lincoln's relieving army at Briar's Creek, fifty miles above Savannah (3 March 1779) completed the reconquest of Georgia and enabled civil government to be partially re-established.

The French entry into the war in June 1778 posed a major threat to British command of the sea. Until then Britain had been able to blockade American ports, attack any part of the coastline at will and ferry supplies across the Atlantic without serious interference. The Americans possessed no navy capable of fighting as a fleet, far less of challenging Howe's squadron. The naval committee established by Congress in the autumn of 1775 put in all more than fifty vessels into service in the Continental navy, while there were almost as many more in the navies of the individual states. But these vessels were not ships-of-the-line but converted merchantmen or, at best, small frigates; though occasionally involved in single-ship actions, their function was mainly that of commerce-destroying. The outstanding figure in the American navy was the Scots-born ex-slaver John Paul Jones, who from his base at Brest raided British shipping in the Channel, spiked the guns of Whitehaven and, in September 1779, captured the British fifty-gun frigate *Serapis* in a hard-fought action off Flamborough Head. But Jones' exploits, however striking, had only slight military significance. The most successful American activity at sea, indeed, was privateering, which at times employed more men than were enrolled in the Continental army. More than two thousand American privateers were commissioned during the war, the great majority of them in New England. Privateering was not only a patriotic activity but a lucrative, if risky, business; its profits founded the fortunes, for example, of such New England families as the Cabots of Beverly and the Derbys of Salem. The amount of damage inflicted upon British merchant shipping by privateers has been variously estimated, but was unquestionably formidable. Yet privateering was of little direct benefit to the American cause; it did little to sustain Washington's army, while the threat it offered to British transatlantic supply lines had by 1778 been effectively countered by an efficient convoy system.

Britain's strength at sea was, however, inadequate to deal with the powerful French navy which had come into being since 1763, largely through the exertions of Choiseul. In July 1778 Keppel could fight only an indecisive action against a superior French naval force off Ushant, an engagement which, according to some historians, implied the ultimate loss of America. When Spain entered the war in 1779 Britain's naval power was strained still further. Invasion, which was constantly threatened from 1778 onwards, was averted in the following year only when a Franco-Spanish armada was dispersed by a gale in the Channel. Gibraltar was besieged, a French squadron was active in the Indian Ocean, the West Indian sugar islands of Dominica, St Vincent and Grenada fell to the French, and even Jamaica was in grave danger.

But although, as we have seen, loss of command of the sea forced Britain on to the defensive, the presence of a French fleet in American waters did not at once produce the results which might have been expected. As early as March 1778, three months before war was formally declared, the comte d'Estaing left Toulon for the United States with twelve ships-of-the-line and five frigates. But d'Estaing's operations were a succession of lost opportunities. Owing to his exceptional slowness in crossing the Atlantic the French admiral reached the Capes of the Delaware only on 8 July, just too late to intercept the British contingent evacuating Philadelphia. Even then a successful blow might have been struck at New York, for Lord Howe's fleet at Sandy Hook was both outnumbered and outgunned by the French. Yet d'Estaing refused the attempt, fearing that his vessels drew too much water to enable them to pass the bar with safety. A projected Franco-American assault on Newport, Rhode Island, met with no better fortune, d'Estaing's fleet being damaged in a storm and having to put back to Boston to refit. This left the Americans feeling they had been deserted, and their disillusion at the fruits of the French alliance deepened when in November d'Estaing departed for the West Indies. Apart from a brief reappearance in the autumn of 1779, when d'Estaing took part in yet another unsuccessful operation, the siege of Savannah, the French navy did not return to the American mainland in strength for almost three years. Nor was this surprising, for France had entered the war not so much to achieve American independence as to weaken Great Britain. Accordingly, she concentrated her naval effort in the Caribbean with the object of acquiring British sugar islands.

If France was indifferent to American interests, Spain was openly hostile. Though Spain entered the war against Britain in June 1779, she did so as the ally not of the United States but of France. In Madrid the birth of the American republic was from the first viewed as a threat to Spanish imperial interests. Spain feared, justifiably as it proved, that American republicanism and expansion would encourage rebellion in her colonial empire and undermine her position in the Mississippi valley. Owing to these fears and to the offence caused by France's decision to declare war unilaterally, the Spanish court did not respond for more than a year to Vergennes' continued pressure upon it to intervene. Throughout the American War Spanish policy looked to the expulsion of Britain not only from the Mediterranean but also from the Caribbean, which had become a base for British commercial infiltration into Spanish America. But Spain's overriding obsession was the recovery of Gibraltar, by diplomacy if possible, by war if necessary.[1] She at first tried to obtain the fortress from Britain as the price of her continued neutrality, this being her motive in making tentative offers of mediation to Britain in 1778. This failing, Charles III and Floridablanca were ready to come to terms with France. By the Franco-Spanish Convention of Aranjuez (12 April 1779), Spain secured substantial concessions in return for an undertaking to enter the war. France agreed to aid in the recovery of Minorca, Mobile, Pensacola, the bay of Honduras and the coast of Campeche, and promised that no peace would be concluded which did not return Gibraltar to Spain.

The Dutch, too, eventually joined Britain's enemies, though taking little active part in the conflict. From the beginning of the war there was friction between Britain and the Netherlands over the maritime rights of neutrals, and over the huge arms traffic with the Americans centring in the Dutch West Indian island of St Eustatius. The supply of naval stores to France and Spain by Dutch merchants was, for Britain, the final straw and an ultimatum to the Netherlands in November 1780 was shortly followed by a British declaration of war.

A further stage in the diplomatic isolation of Britain was marked by the formation of the League of Armed Neutrality. Encouraged by Vergennes, Catherine II of Russia brought together in February 1780 the Baltic states, which resented the British practice of searching neutral vessels for contraband. As a means of protecting neutral commerce the league was ineffective—Catherine herself referred to it as an 'armed nullity'—but by 1783 it had been joined by nearly every state in Europe.

The growing difficulties which Britain faced in Europe could not for some time be turned to advantage by the Americans. Far from being able to take the offensive against Clinton, Washington experienced continued difficulty in 1779–80 in keeping an army together. The French entry into the war had persuaded many Continental soldiers that fighting could

[1] Samuel F. Bemis, *The Diplomacy of the American Revolution* (New York, 1935), ch. VI.

safely be left to their allies. Moreover, the hardships of military life, which increased as the war went on, became doubly difficult to endure when contrasted with the profits to be made in civilian pursuits. Many of the troops either deserted or refused to re-enlist; even high-ranking officers like Schuyler and Sullivan, and men of prominence like Hamilton and Monroe, felt they could honourably resign their commissions. But a far graver menace to the American cause than this combination of complacency and selfishness was the appearance, first of treason, and then of mutiny. Benedict Arnold's offer to Clinton to hand over the fortress of West Point for the sum of £20,000 may have been due in part to his being heavily in debt and to his loss of faith in an American victory. But a more compelling reason for his change of allegiance was the resentment Arnold felt at failing to receive from Congress the recognition he believed to be due to his military services, and at being reprimanded by court-martial for misappropriation of public property. Washington's view that the loss of West Point 'must have given the American cause a deadly wound if not a fatal stab' was probably an exaggeration, though it would certainly have given Clinton command of the Hudson and enabled him to isolate New England. But the plot miscarried. The capture of Clinton's emissary, Major John André, while returning from a final rendezvous with Arnold in September 1780, revealed to the Americans what was afoot. André, having been taken in civilian clothes within the American lines, was executed as a spy, but Arnold escaped to become a British general, to lead a raid on his native New London and to participate in the final southern campaigns.[1]

The mutinies of the Pennsylvania and New Jersey Lines early in 1781 were in a different category from Arnold's treason. They were manifestations not of disloyalty but of long-smouldering discontent with conditions of service in the Continental army. Despite Greene's reform of the commissary department, supplies of food and clothing had remained inadequate, partly owing to the neglect of state authorities, partly to the financial chaos resulting from the collapse of Continental and state paper as a medium of exchange. The depreciation of the currency also hit the soldiers more directly, by diminishing the value of their pay, which was meagre to begin with and usually several months in arrears. But while these hardships were those of the army as a whole, the Pennsylvania Line had a special sense of grievance arising out of a dispute with the civil authorities over terms of enlistment. Though they spurned Clinton's invitation to desert, the mutineers refused in January 1781 to obey their officers until they were promised redress. The success of the Pennsylvanians in writing their own terms for a return to duty prompted the New Jersey Line to follow its example. But Washington felt that negotia-

---

[1] Carl Van Doren, *The Secret History of the American Revolution* (New York, 1941), deals principally with the Arnold conspiracy.

tion with mutineers had gone on long enough, and insisted upon using force to suppress this second rising.

The failure of the allied siege of Savannah in the autumn of 1779 and the return of d'Estaing's fleet to France paved the way for the large-scale British offensive against the Southern states which opened the war's last phase. Repeatedly unsuccessful in her endeavours to induce Washington to fight a decisive battle in the north, Britain resolved to transfer her major effort to a region in which the Continental army would find supplies, transport and reinforcements difficult to obtain, and whose large Negro population, Indian neighbours and reputed loyalism invited attack. In December 1779, with Georgia already recovered and with his communications no longer threatened by the French, Clinton sailed southward from New York with a large fleet and army which, after a four-month siege, captured Charleston and its garrison of 5000 (12 May 1780). Under Cornwallis' command the southern expeditionary force rapidly completed the pacification of South Carolina, and in the battle of Camden (16 August) heavily defeated a hastily gathered American army under Gates, whose precipitate retreat into North Carolina led to his being dismissed, perhaps unjustly, from his command. But although in three months the invaders had eliminated two American armies each the size of that defeated at Saratoga, the tide now began to turn against them. Cornwallis' southern campaign was to illustrate the basic difficulty confronting Britain in her attempts to recover America, namely, that of holding and consolidating her conquests. With inadequate forces to garrison such an immense region, British outposts were always vulnerable to attack as soon as the main army had moved on elsewhere.

Despite many appearances to the contrary, the subjugation of South Carolina had been far from complete. Resistance had merely gone underground, and guerrilla bands led by Marion, Sumter and Pickens had remained in being in the swamps. Moreover, many South Carolinians who had been prepared to submit to British rule when Charleston fell had subsequently been alienated by the savage vengeance wrought by the loyalists upon their former oppressors. Thus, as soon as Cornwallis advanced northwards from Camden into North Carolina to crush, as he thought, the last vestiges of Southern resistance, the countryside rose behind him to threaten his communications and raid his frontier outposts. Simultaneously the British invasion of North Carolina suffered an unexpected reverse. Though Cornwallis' main army reached Charlotte unopposed, a loyalist auxiliary force was surrounded and wiped out at King's Mountain (7 October 1780). The British position became still more difficult as a new American army was formed by General Nathanael Greene, who succeeded Gates as commander of the southern theatre. The first fruits of Greene's efforts was the rout by General Daniel Morgan of a British detachment under Banastre Tarleton at Cowpens (16 January

1781). Shortly afterwards Cornwallis inflicted on Greene the first of a series of defeats at Guilford Court House (15 March), but suffered such losses in the engagement that he was obliged to withdraw from the interior of North Carolina and make for the coast at Wilmington. And when, in April, Cornwallis marched northward to link up with British forces operating in Virginia, Greene seized the opportunity to take the offensive in the Carolinas. Though repulsed at Hobkirk's Hill (25 April) and again at Eutaw Springs (8 September) Greene, with the aid of South Carolina guerrillas, reduced one by one the scattered British outposts in the backcountry. By the end of the summer, Cornwallis' conquests had entirely vanished, and all that remained in British occupation south of Virginia were Charleston and Savannah.

Cornwallis' unauthorised march into Virginia exposed his army to the danger of being cut off by a French fleet in Chesapeake Bay, and was thus the original cause of the disaster which subsequently overtook him at Yorktown. But part of the blame for that defeat must rest with Clinton who, though appreciating his subordinate's peril, neither insisted upon evacuation while time remained nor did anything to save him until it was too late.[1] Resentful though he was of Cornwallis' attempt to dictate strategy, Clinton's slowness in preparing a relief expedition was due rather to his belief that a Franco-American assault upon New York City was imminent. New York had indeed been Washington's original objective upon learning early in 1781 that a French fleet under Admiral de Grasse was on its way to co-operate with him and with the French army under Rochambeau's command at Newport. Only later was Washington persuaded by Rochambeau to transfer their joint operation to Virginia so as to make Cornwallis' army their quarry. That the French fleet was able to leave the West Indies unchallenged was due to Admiral Rodney's failure to obey his instructions, which were to follow De Grasse, if necessary, to the American mainland. But though he knew of De Grasse's departure and correctly guessed his intentions, Rodney merely ordered Hood to pursue and, after sending a warning to Graves at New York, departed for England upon the plea of ill health. Rodney's precautions miscarrying, De Grasse was able to arrive in the Chesapeake unopposed at the end of August, bringing with him 4000 troops to assist Lafayette in preventing Cornwallis' escape. Shortly afterwards, the armies of Washington and Rochambeau reached Virginia, thus confronting Cornwallis with an army twice as large as his own, and effectively trapping him on the Yorktown peninsula. The chances of escape by sea, already slim because of Rodney's shortcomings, were still further diminished by the repulse of Graves' fleet by De Grasse in an action at the mouth of the Chesapeake

---

[1] For a defence of Clinton and a reassessment of responsibility for the Yorktown disaster see William B. Willcox, 'The British Road to Yorktown: a Study in Divided Command', *American Historical Review*, vol. LII (1946), pp. 1–35.

(5 September). But what finally sealed Cornwallis' doom was the protracted delay in the despatch of a relief expedition from New York. Not until 17 October did Clinton and Graves set forth in their rescue attempt, and by the time they reached the Chesapeake Cornwallis had already surrendered. Completely surrounded and driven within their inner fortifications at Yorktown, Cornwallis and his army of 7000 laid down their arms on 19 October.

The surrender at Yorktown brought the war in America virtually to an end. Washington's hopes of further French co-operation disappeared with De Grasse's return to the West Indies, which left the Continental army too weak to attack alone. Britain, too, was content to remain on the defensive in America, though she still had 30,000 troops at New York. The naval war continued, however, and the last months of fighting brought about a marked revival of British fortunes. Though Minorca was lost to Spain, the siege of Gibraltar was finally raised in September 1782 by the arrival of a relief squadron under Howe. British command of the sea had already been restored by Rodney's victory off the Saintes islands near Dominica (12 April 1782), when De Grasse's fleet was destroyed.

But the huge expense of the American war and its continued lack of success had by now convinced British opinion of the futility of further effort. Yorktown produced a swelling demand for peace, reflected in the ministry's dwindling parliamentary majorities. In March 1782, after the Commons had adopted a motion to abandon all attempts at coercion, North resigned, to be succeeded first by Rockingham and then by Shelburne. George III, chagrined at the turn of events, spoke momentarily of abdication but nevertheless acquiesced in April in sending Richard Oswald, a retired Scottish merchant, to Paris to discuss terms with Franklin.

The peace negotiations revealed deep fissures in the Franco-American alliance. Despite her efforts to achieve American independence, France was anxious to deny the United States every accession of strength, an aim which became increasingly apparent to the American peace commissioners, Franklin, Adams and Jay. With good reason the commissioners suspected that Vergennes meant to exclude the United States from the Newfoundland fisheries, and to support the Spanish claim to territory between the Alleghenies and the Mississippi. The French themselves, in fact, had designs upon the fisheries, while Vergennes felt obliged to offer Spain compensation in America for his failure to restore Gibraltar to her. Though they had been instructed by Congress to make peace in close consultation with France, the American commissioners decided that their country's interests demanded the opening of separate negotiations with Britain. But while Shelburne was anxious to exploit the disagreements which had arisen between the allies, and by a generous peace wean the United States away from France, he found Franklin's demand for Canada unacceptable. Nevertheless, though negotiations were protracted, the terms eventually agreed upon in the preliminary treaty of 30 November 1782, and confirmed in the definitive agreement of the following September, were extremely favourable to the United States.[1] American independence was formally recognised by Great Britain, while the boundaries of the United States were defined as follows: the northern boundary was to be a line following the St Croix river and the height of land between the St Lawrence and Maine as far as the forty-fifth parallel, thence to the St Lawrence and along that river and the Great Lakes to the Lake of the Woods and the source of the Mississippi; the Mississippi itself was to be the western boundary; in the south it was to be the Apalachicola and St Mary's rivers. Thanks largely to John Adams' spirited defence of New England interests, the Americans were granted the 'liberty', though not the right, to fish off Newfoundland and to dry and cure fish in the unsettled parts of Nova Scotia and Labrador. The treaty also dealt, unsatisfactorily as it proved, with two matters over which there had been much wrangling during the negotiations. It was agreed that British merchants should 'meet with no lawful impediment' in seeking to recover their *bona fide* pre-war American debts, and that Congress should 'earnestly recommend' to the states the restoration of confiscated loyalist property.

Successful in concluding a separate peace with the United States, and buoyed up by a revival of naval strength, Britain was able to make peace with her other adversaries at less cost than had at one time seemed possible. The peace treaty with France and Spain (20 January 1783) changed only in detail the settlement of 1763. It awarded Senegal and Tobago to the French, who also recovered the forts and factories they had possessed in India in 1763, and slightly enlarged their fishing rights in Newfoundland; Spain recovered Minorca and received an acknowledgement of her right to the whole of the Floridas. These terms, together with those agreed separately between Britain and the United States, as well as those of an Anglo-Dutch treaty, were confirmed by the definitive Peace of Versailles (3 September 1783) which formally ended the war.

Shelburne's object in the peace settlement with America had been to restore Anglo-American friendship and to lay the 'Foundations of a new Connection better adapted to the present Temper and Interest of both countries'. The generous peace terms granted the Americans were designed as the first step towards such a *rapprochement*; they were to be followed immediately, so Shelburne hoped, by a commercial alliance and eventually by some form of political reunion. But Shelburne's vision was shared by only a handful of his contemporaries, and his hopes were speedily shattered. Parliamentary dissatisfaction with the terms of the preliminary American treaty, and particularly with its failure to secure

[1] See Bemis, *op. cit.* chs. xiv–xvii for details of the negotiations.

reparation for the loyalists, led in February 1783 to Shelburne's overthrow. Parliament was equally unsympathetic to Pitt's bill placing American ships and products on practically the same footing as those of British ownership and origin. The British commercial interest was in favour of these concessions, but opinion generally was greatly influenced by Lord Sheffield's pamphlet, *Observations on the Commerce of the American States*, which appeared during the parliamentary debate on the bill. Sheffield argued that the measure would cripple British merchant shipping, and thus deprive the navy of its reserve of seamen. Concessions, he asserted, were in any case unnecessary to capture the trade of the United States since that country was too weak to retaliate against British discrimination. These arguments prevailing, Pitt's bill was lost and, by a series of Orders in Council, American vessels were in 1783 excluded from the British West Indies and from all but the direct trade in American products. The fears expressed in Sheffield's pamphlet were also responsible, together with the American fear of entangling alliances, for the failure of the attempt, initiated by Shelburne and continued by Fox, to conclude a commercial treaty with the United States.[1]

The adoption of Sheffield's policy brought immediate, though short-lived, gains to British shipping. So largely triangular was Anglo-American trade that the exclusion of American vessels from the West Indies diverted the bulk of the traffic to British bottoms. As Sheffield had forecast, the United States proved unable, under the Articles of Confederation, to take effective counter-measures against Britain; the central government had no jurisdiction over commerce, and state efforts to retaliate failed because of inability to agree on a common policy. But there was a different story to tell after 1789, when the federal constitution went into force. Using the wider powers granted to the federal government, Congress hastened to pass laws discriminating in favour of American shipping. Especially successful was a law regulating tonnage duties (20 July 1789) which, by restricting the American coastal trade to American shipping, effectively debarred British vessels from the developing triangular trade in cotton.

Britain's commercial exclusiveness, particularly when contrasted with the privileges that American vessels and products were accorded by other European powers, could not fail to rouse resentment in the United States. Equally serious obstacles to Anglo-American understanding arose out of the peace treaty of 1783, of which practically every clause contained ambiguities which were fruitful of later controversy. Boundary disputes and friction over fishing rights were both postponed until the nineteenth century, but there were immediate quarrels over treaty violations. The requirement that British creditors should not be impeded in their efforts to recover pre-war debts was openly flouted by many states, particularly in the south, where the planters owed large sums to Scottish merchants.

[1] Harlow, *The Founding of the Second British Empire*, chs. VI–IX.

Even more flagrantly disregarded were the loyalist clauses; practically every state ignored the recommendation of Congress to restore confiscated loyalist property. These violations gave Britain a pretext for refusing to carry out her treaty obligation to evacuate American soil 'with all convenient speed'; British garrisons remained in occupation of seven military posts on the American side of the new boundary with Canada. Though prior American treaty violations were pleaded as an excuse, the real British motive for the retention of these north-west posts was to afford time for Canadian fur-traders in the region to reorganise their businesses and withdraw their property. Not until 1796 were the posts finally handed over.

The ambiguities of the peace settlement led also to friction between the United States and Spain. While the definitive Anglo-American treaty of 1783 had recognised the thirty-first parallel as the south-western boundary of the United States, Spain claimed the line of the Yazoo River, 100 miles to the north, and retained possession of Natchez on the left bank of the Mississippi. In addition, controversy developed over the navigation of the Mississippi, which Spain denied to the Americans in 1784. Neither on this question nor on the boundary dispute had agreement been reached in 1793.

American independence was still at that date incomplete. With British and Spanish garrisons on her soil, the United States had still to gain undisputed control of the territory she had been granted by treaty a decade earlier. That she was hemmed in by the empires of two great European powers both threatened her security and appeared to rule out her further expansion. The lack of an outlet to the sea from the heart of the continent bred western dissension to such a degree as to menace the permanence of the Union. The desire for isolation, which had done much to foster the movement for independence, would remain unfulfilled while the obligations of the French alliance continued in force; so long as the United States was committed to the defence of the French West Indies in case of war, it would be impossible for Americans to dissociate themselves from European affairs. At the opening of an era of almost continuous European warfare, which was to add greatly to the security, prosperity and possessions of the United States, her future and even her continued existence seemed uncertain.

CHAPTER XVIII

AMERICAN INDEPENDENCE
IN ITS AMERICAN CONTEXT, SOCIAL AND
POLITICAL ASPECTS, WESTERN
EXPANSION

B Y the terms of the Treaty of Paris of 1763 the North American mainland was shared between Britain and Spain. France retained only
two small islands, St Pierre and Miquelon, off the coast of Newfoundland, at which her fishermen could dry their fish. By 1793 Britain
had lost her colonies south of Canada: to the original thirteen, which
became independent in 1783 and, hesitantly, united in 1787, two new
states had been added (Vermont, 1791, and Kentucky, 1792); and the
Floridas, East and West, had been returned to Spain in 1783.

In 1763 the British colonies of the North American mainland extended
for sixteen hundred miles along the seaboard, from stormy Cape Breton
Island to the humid Okefinokee swamps. At either extremity there was
a military outpost. Nova Scotia, which had been captured by Britain in
1710, had been for fifty years a weak imperial base against the French in
Cape Breton. Halifax was founded in 1749 as a counterpoise to Louis-
bourg, and 3000 colonists were sent out. In 1755 the French were expelled from the Acadian settlements on the Bay of Fundy and the Annapolis river. Helped by immigrants from New England, the British numbers
grew to 11,000 in 1766 and 20,000 in 1775. A representative assembly was
granted to Nova Scotia in 1758. In 1769 Prince Edward Island (formerly
Isle St Jean) was given a separate government, and its assembly first met
in 1773. There were only a few settlers at St John (originally Parrtown) in
1784 when an influx of 3000 American Loyalists led to the erection of New
Brunswick into a separate colony. Behind these maritime colonies, with
their undetermined frontiers, lay the province of Quebec, unripe as yet
for representative government, French in character, with, Governor
James Murray calculated in 1766, only nineteen Protestant families living
outside Quebec and Montreal—as a group, 'the most immoral collection
of men I ever knew'. And in the remote Illinois country, at Vincennes,
Kaskaskia and St Louis lived some 1500 French people—in 1763 people
without a country.

In the years after 1763 several military posts were established in the
Floridas, the latest of the buffer colonies against Spain, and particularly
in West Florida, that part of old Spanish Florida that lay beyond the
Chattahoochee and Apalachicola rivers. It included most of the province

of Louisiana to the south of the thirty-first parallel of north latitude and east of the Mississippi, and the towns of Pensacola, Biloxi and Mobile. It did not include New Orleans, ceded by France to Spain. In 1764 the northern boundary of West Florida was moved from the thirty-first parallel to a line running east from the confluence of the Yazoo and the Mississippi, bringing in the fertile country around Natchez. British garrisons were established at Mobile and at Manchac on the Iberville, although the latter did not last; Pensacola became the headquarters of the Southern Indian superintendency and the seat of government, and an elected assembly for West Florida came into being in 1766. Progress in East Florida was slower and, remote from the Mississippi, was a more deliberate matter. There was a regular parliamentary grant to encourage 'silk, vines and other articles of beneficial produce'. Experiments in colonisation were begun—in 1767 a curious and ill-fated colony of 1500 Greeks, Italians and Minorcans under the leadership of Dr Andrew Turnbull was settled at New Smyrna, sixty miles south of St Augustine, to raise indigo and sugar cane. In 1781, two years before it ceased to be a British colony, East Florida acquired an assembly. The pattern set by the Carolinas and by Georgia was being followed.

The colonies that lay between the Everglades of Florida and the high tides of the Bay of Fundy differed widely in their governments, in their economies and in their populations. Despite their various origins, the crown had gradually established direct rule over one colony after another. By 1763 only the proprietorships of Pennsylvania, Delaware and Maryland, and the self-governing or corporate provinces of Connecticut and Rhode Island, remained outside royal control. Even Penn's liberalism availed him little: in 1765 Benjamin Franklin was sent to England to ask that the proprietorship be cancelled and that George III assume direct control of Pennsylvania—without result.

With the exception of Rhode Island and Connecticut, whose governors and legislatures were fully elective, and of Massachusetts, where the council was elective, all the colonies had approximately the same form of government. The governor was appointed by the king or the proprietor, and he in turn appointed the council—almost always from the wealthiest citizens; and with their interests he normally identified his own. He was normally but not always English, and frequently an absentee, whose duties were carried out for him by a lieutenant-governor—sometimes mistakenly described as 'governor'—himself often a Scot. All the colonies had elective assemblies, which by 1763 had established their right to initiate legislation, to levy taxes and to make appropriations—provided these were consistent with the colonial charters and the laws of England.

In America the long tradition of political argument took varied forms: the struggle for control of the assemblies between great and small landholders or between eastern and western counties, the struggle over quit-rents, the struggle to win religious freedom for minorities, or the struggle —everywhere in evidence in the decade before 1763—between assemblies and governors for control of the public purse. In most colonies, the governor's salary had become dependent on an annual appropriation; hardly ever could he for long resist legislative pressure. And the curb on him, if rarely thought of as a check on 'royal' authority, was at least seen as a curb on the overmighty subjects on whom he often leaned. Whatever the situation in Britain in 1763, the issues of 1688 were kept alive in the colonies, and many local situations, before as well as after the French and Indian wars, were seen in terms of the stereotypes of the Glorious Revolution. For king read governor, and for Parliament, assembly; and invoke appeals not only to the Bill of Rights but to the written charters, as guarantees of colonial liberties: and one sees how close was the parallel between 1688 and 1776. It is true that the suffrage was limited, as in Britain, by property qualifications, and that an office-holding class monopolised the most desirable posts; but elections were fought openly and often violently, and voting was oral. There is controversy on the question of the relation of voting rights to property. Recent views have emphasised the extent of voting, and the ease with which property restrictions were overcome. Moreover, through the parish vestries, the county courts, the town meetings and assemblies, there was abundant opportunity for participation in public affairs. The pattern of government might appear to be royal; in some provinces, like New York, it was oligarchic, and in others, like Rhode Island, exclusive; and many of the statutes, though thus far laxly enforced, were imperialist in intention; there was, nevertheless, a vitality in public controversy and in the election of representatives and selectmen in the colonies that belied, and was in the end to challenge, the authority of Whitehall.[1]

Generalisation is more difficult about the colonial economies and societies. Although the social, like the political, implications of the settlement of America might be democratic, democracy came late on the scene. The mass of the colonists were far from being aristocratic, there was considerable social mobility and the widespread ownership of property weakened the sense of class division. Yet the social structure was as aristocratic as that in contemporary Britain—which it reflected. By 1763 there was a distinct upper class, composed of the large landowners, the wealthy merchants and lawyers, the governors and lieutenant-governors, the revenue officers and 'the friends of government'. In some colonies those groups were seeking to be exclusive—though they never were completely

---

[1] Cf. C. S. Sydnor, *Gentlemen Freeholders: Political Practices in Washington's Virginia* (1952), Robert E. Brown, *Middle-class Democracy and the Revolution in Massachusetts, 1691–1780* (1955), Philip S. Klein, *Pennsylvania Politics, 1817–1832* (Philadelphia, 1940), J. R. Pole, 'Suffrage and Representation in Massachusetts: a Statistical Note', in *William and Mary Quarterly*, vol. xiv, no. 4 (October 1957). Cf. Leonard W. Labaree, *Royal Government in America* (1930).

so. They could include an enterprising privateer like John MacPherson of Philadelphia, or an enterprising painter like J. S. Copley. Below them was a large and fluid middle class, of clergymen, teachers, lesser merchants and lawyers, landowning farmers, town craftsmen and shopkeepers, minor officials in government, plantation overseers, ship-captains, 'the middling sort'. Below them in turn was a labouring force of mainly property-less and therefore voteless workers, artisans, yeomen farmers or poor frontiersmen, many of them German or Scots-Irish. Originally many of these had been indentured servants working under a labour contract for a term of years, or convicts. Maryland alone received over 9000 convict servants between 1748 and 1775.[1] In the eighteenth century a new type of indentured servant appeared: the redemptioner. In the South, artisan and craftsman were harder to discover. By 1763 the Negro slave had almost entirely replaced the indentured servant as the South's labour force, although elsewhere white workers under contract continued to arrive. George Washington's first schoolmaster came under this system, and one of the most interesting diaries of the revolutionary period was that kept by an indentured servant, John Harrower.[2] According to tradition, at least one signer of the Declaration of Independence, Matthew Thornton of New Hampshire, was an indentured servant; so were William Buckland who built Gunston Hall, and Charles Thomson, Secretary of the Continental Congress. 'You may depend upon it', said William Allen, 'that this is one of the best Poor Man's Country's in the World.'[3]

By the mid-eighteenth century, there was a further labour force, owning no man master, coming into being in the high valleys of the Alleghenies and on the western fringe of society, from the Mohawk valley to the pine barrens of Georgia. This was largely recruited from Germany, from Scotland and from Ulster. But recruits for the West came from tidewater America also. Native and immigrant alike sought in land ownership, and to a lesser degree in physical remoteness, a security and a freedom that they had not enjoyed in the older societies, in Europe or in tidewater. In America itself, this western migration not only settled the frontier but released productive forces generally, and kept wages high. The Mohawk, Hudson, Susquehanna and Shenandoah valleys, the Indian trails and wilderness roads, became channels of traffic and of trade, and of economic optimism.[4] They were channels of variety, too, for frontiersmen were of many types: in the lush canebrakes of the Western Carolinas they tended cattle, in the Cumberland Gap they were trappers and traders, from the Kennebec and Penobscot they went out to the Grand Banks for cod and mackerel, or cut oak and white pine.

---

[1] Cf. A. E. Smith, *Colonists in Bondage* (1947).
[2] Published in the *American Historical Review*, vol. VI (1900–1), pp. 65–107.
[3] Bridenbaugh, *Cities in Revolt*, p. 148. Cf. T. J. Wertenbaker, *Planters in Colonial Virginia* (1922); R. B. Morris, *Government and Labour in Colonial America* (1941); Bridenbaugh, *The Colonial Craftsman* (1950), ch. 1.
[4] Cf. Merrill Jensen, *The New Nation* (1950), p. 424.

It was this force on the frontier that had precipitated clashes with French outposts and with Indians. Once its western enemies had been removed, it proved less amenable than ever to British—or tidewater—control. It was hostile to all taxes to maintain others in an ease it did not share, or to support institutions with which it had no sympathy; though its 'democratic' character has probably been overstated, it challenged the Establishment, whether aristocracy, monarchy or church, whether French, British or American. By 1776 well over a quarter of a million people were in the backcountry—and in South Carolina four out of every five of its white population were on the frontier or in the piedmont. Hard though tidewater planters or Quaker merchants or Hudson valley patroons might seek to maintain the culture of and the links with Europe, their influence waned with every step of westward advance: there was utility, and symbolism also, in the deerskin of Daniel Morgan's riflemen and the coonskins of Daniel Boone. Behind the political challenge presented to Britain by colonial nationalism was the deeper and less tractable challenge of frontier protests to eastern merchants and planters. Culture on the moving frontier might be basically English, as Louis B. Wright has recently claimed,[1] but it was unsophisticated and austere, a culture remote from Philadelphia or Charleston. This was a land of log cabins and small-scale subsistence farming, of a diet of 'hog'n hominy', and of linsey-woolsey home-spun; a land of opportunity, poverty and revivalism.

This colonial society was increasing its numbers by its own fertility as well as by immigration: high birth-rates and large families were the rule—the average number of children per colonial family was 7·5, and wives were exhausted by the constant child-bearing. The population was in fact doubling every generation, although more slowly in New England than elsewhere. In 1763 it was almost two millions, of whom approximately one-quarter were Germans and Scots-Irish, and approximately one-sixth Negro. By 1775 it was two and a half millions: by 1790, at the first census, it was 3,929,214, of whom 757,208 were Negroes.[2]

The most striking characteristics of this colonial society were its diversity and its sectionalism. In the decade before 1763, and in the three decades after it, eastern Connecticut quarrelled with western, and in 1771 there was an ugly civil war between western and eastern North Carolina. New England was contemptuous of minute and lawless Rhode Island; Newport and Providence were mutually contemptuous of each

---

[1] Louis B. Wright, *The Atlantic Frontier: Colonial American Civilization* (1947), *Culture on the Moving Frontier* (1955). In his *Intercolonial Aspects of American Culture on the Eve of the Revolution* (1928) Michael Kraus shows how uniform through all the colonies was the cultural pattern.

[2] Evarts B. Greene and Virginia D. Harrington, *American Population before the Federal Census of 1790* (New York, 1932), and Stella H. Sutherland, *Population Distribution in Colonial America* (New York, 1936).

other; to Gage, as early as 1765, Rhode Island was 'the little turbulent colony'.[1] There was much suspicion, then as later, of New York. Almost all colonies had boundary disputes with each other; all were as slow to help each other against Indians as they had been against the French—and as New York and Philadelphia were to be to help all the rest against Britain. 'Were these colonies left to themselves tomorrow', James Otis gloomily forecast in 1765, 'America would be a mere shambles of blood and confusion.'

The sectionalism was even more deeply rooted, product of rock and soil, race and religion. From early days the indented coastline and numerous harbours of New England encouraged maritime industries, the short but rapid rivers were a source of water-power, timber for ships was abundant. Though agriculture was primary here as elsewhere, it was diversified and small in scale, and free from the price fluctuations and overproduction that beset the South. There was a ready market for surplus fish in the West Indies and in southern Europe; and the triangular trade between the West Indies, New England and Africa flourished. Behind this vigorous if ugly traffic in rum, molasses and slaves was an unusual homogeneity in race and religion and a dominance of the English and the puritan strains in church and state. Here as elsewhere fundamentalism and deism were making inroads, but as yet they had not got far. To a South Carolinian like Edward Rutledge, New England was peopled by men of 'low cunning and levelling principles'. It was nourished by a strong current of democracy in congregation and in town meeting. The Yankee virtues of industry and thrift, caution and esteem for learning moved west with the New England settlers into the Ohio and upper Mississippi valleys. There, as well as in New Haven and Boston, rose the little red school-houses and the tall white spires.

The middle colonies—New York, Pennsylvania, New Jersey and Delaware—were very different. In the three great river-valleys, the Hudson, the Susquehanna and the Delaware, there was abundant and fertile soil; and the middle colonies were the granaries of the rest. Navigation inland was much easier than to north or south, and the West was first reached along the Mohawk and the Susquehanna. Population was unusually mixed: to the first Swedes on the Delaware or the Dutch in New York were added the layers of Rhineland Germans—by 1776 at least one-third of the population of Pennsylvania was German—of combative Scots-Irish, of peaceful Quakers and other pietist groups. If Quakers and Germans were both good husbandmen, the Germans were among the leaders in glass, brick and iron production, and the Scots-Irish the most venturous frontiersmen. Dutch influence had left its mark on the Hudson valley in a distinguished upper class of 'Vans' and 'velts': government was distinctly less democratic here than elsewhere in the colonies;

[1] Gage to Conway, 23 September 1765. C.O. 5/83.

the Van Rensselaer manor covered an area two-thirds the size of Rhode Island. Philadelphia, New York and Baltimore were the most active ports in the colonies; the first, with its 23,000 population in 1763, was in fact the largest city in North America, with the first circulating library, the first medical school, the first fire company and the first legal journal in the country, with no less than 77 bookshops, and 117 public houses.

The South was still more distinct, settled early, by English traders or landowners, and developing, along its slow-moving, wide-mouthed tidal rivers, along novel lines.[1] John Rolfe's 'discovery' of tobacco had made it, despite the fulminations of James VI and I, the staple crop of the Chesapeake Bay region; in South Carolina the basis was rice and indigo; in both, the plantation developed early. A plantation economy demanded a large labour force—four-fifths of the Negro population were south of the Mason–Dixon line; it promoted self-sufficiency and executive ability among its masters—Washington had a larger staff to direct at Mount Vernon than he had when he assumed the presidency in 1789; it preserved the class distinctions, the Episcopalian church, the parish government and the *mores* of an older England. From Britain it was largely recruited; to Britain it sent its crops and from it it bought its goods; and to it also came its sons for education—although as often to Edinburgh and the Inns of Court, incidentally, as to the older universities. The South was rural; the big house of the plantation was a manufactory and hotel as well as a home, and could occasionally be a cultural centre, like 'Westover' on the James, Robert Carter's 'Nomini Hall' or Jefferson's 'Monticello'. The traditions of the Tidewater South were as well-established as those of New England or Philadelphia, but very different. This was a society warm and convivial, quick to anger, sensitive to injury, open, unshrewd and feckless. Yankees found it not to their taste: South Carolina was, to Josiah Quincy, a land of 'opulent and lordly planters, poor and spiritless peasants and vile slaves'.[2] And tied to the land there was an inefficient coloured labour force, almost completely without initiative, and a tobacco economy that was ruining the soil. The indebtedness of the South to England was not only social but economic. Jefferson bluntly described his fellow planters as 'a species of property annexed to certain mercantile houses in London'.[3] Virginians owed British creditors some £2,000,000 sterling in 1775.

If there was, then, a certain political and social uniformity about each

---

[1] There were, however, at least three 'souths'. Carl Bridenbaugh distinguishes between Chesapeake society, Carolina society and the back settlements. Cf. *Myths and Realities* (1952).
[2] 'Journal of Josiah Quincy, Junr.', *Massachusetts History Society Proceedings*, vol. XLIX (1916), p. 454.
[3] *The Writings of Thomas Jefferson*, edited by Paul Leicester Ford (New York, 1894), vol. IV, p. 155. Cf. B.M. Add. MSS. 33030, fols. 160–2.

of the thirteen colonies in 1763, there was very little unity between them, even between those sharing a common sectional character. Colonial prides and jealousies were notorious. They were as much geographic as psychological. Communications were still difficult: as late as 1801, Jefferson, as president, lamented that of eight rivers between Monticello and Washington, five had neither bridges nor boats. Franklin's labours to produce a plan of union at the Albany Congress in 1754 were less successful—and less important—than his role as postmaster and builder of postal roads.

Sectionalism makes difficult any simple description of the colonial reaction to British measures after 1763, even though many general causes impelling towards separation were at work. One of these was the growing awareness in America, though not at home, of the differences between the colonies and the mother-country. This truth has often been presented in patriotic terms, by contemporary pamphleteers like Tom Paine to justify the Revolution, by nineteenth-century nationalist historians like Bancroft and by many an American school text: those who first went to America were pilgrims seeking religious or political toleration; those who fled from the tyranny of Charles I were levellers and democrats before their time; those who fled from Cromwell's tyranny were Cavaliers and aristocrats; Bacon's rebellion of 1676 in Virginia and the struggle against Governor Andros in New England, along with the heritage of Locke and the English Revolution, inspirited the men of '76. There has been much extravagance in this *simpliste* view: half the 'Pilgrims' were convicts; few Puritans sought or practised toleration; Professor Wertenbaker has punctured the inflations of the Cavalier thesis in Virginia.[1] Nevertheless, recent research has produced a significant revival of the arguments that the Revolution was the triumph of a principle, notably by Clinton Rossiter, Max Savelle, Edmund S. Morgan, and Irving Brant in the first volume of his life of Madison.[2] A distinct, almost nationalist, attitude was growing in the colonies, not least in those areas stocked by Germans and Scots-Irish, Dutch and French, who had no natural reason to venerate the British connection. The fifty-six signers of the Declaration of Independence included eighteen men who were not of English descent; the great and affluent Dutch estates on the Hudson produced revolutionary leaders like General Schuyler. The colonies had been peopled for a century and a half by groups which, if they had fewer sprigs of the nobility among them than

[1] *Patrician and Plebeian in Virginia* (1910). Louis B. Wright has in turn qualified Wertenbaker's excesses: *The First Gentlemen of Virginia* (1940).

[2] Clinton Rossiter, *Seed-time of the Republic* (1953); Max Savelle, *Seeds of Liberty* (1948); Edmund S. Morgan, *The Birth of the Republic, 1763–89* (1956); Irving Brant, *James Madison: The Virginia Revolutionist* (1941). Cf. the similar views a generation ago of C. H. Van Tyne, *The Causes of the War of Independence* (1922), and Charles Warren, *The Making of the Constitution* (1929).

the Daughters of the American Revolution would like to claim, at least had more than their share of men of courage and adventure, and of dissenting principles. America provided a new environment that emphasised closeness to nature, simplicity, enterprise and adaptability. Behind the viewpoint of Hector St John de Crevecoeur in his *Letters from an American Farmer* (1782) ranged a whole school of thinkers led by Jefferson, interested in American flora and fauna and in the geological and scientific as well as the political differences between the Old World and the New.[1] So, whether the frontier produced democrats or natural aristocrats, it can be agreed that America's polyglot population and its remoteness from Europe brought a new point of view into the political situation—just as within the next generation the frontier communities themselves would present these old issues in a still more novel and baffling context.

Moreover, as we have seen, the issues of 1688 were still alive in the colonies. Although Jefferson described his declaration as 'an expression of the American mind' and said that he 'turned to neither book nor pamphlet while writing it', the phrases are those of Locke. And, again as Jefferson said, the ideas were familiar to Americans. There had long been unwillingness to tolerate a high degree of imperial control. Until 1765 the only area in which Britain had intervened was commercial—the Navigation Acts remained a dead letter, colonial governors were regularly browbeaten by colonial legislatives, much imperial legislation was quietly ignored. This policy, or lack of policy, has been praised as salutary neglect or as 'statesmanlike obliquity' (Professor Pollard's phrase). It represented in fact the usual easy triumph of administration over statesmanship; it piled up a series of constitutional problems which brought catastrophe to George Grenville, the keen, rash and pedantic minister who first sought a clear legislative solution for them. British authorities regarded the colonial assemblies as no better than municipal corporations or county councils, existing by the grant of a charter—their position in law, as Lord Mansfield said. To the colonists they were the equivalent of the British Parliament—'perfect states', said Governor Bernard, 'not otherwise dependent on Great Britain than by having the same King'.[2] When they sought a justification for their protests, they found it in the seventeenth century, in the supremacy of law and no taxation without representation, which, they had read, were the motives of the struggles in England. The American Revolution arose out of a sense of constitutional loyalty to seventeenth-century ideas. There was no 'republican' sentiment before 1774.

If recent research has therefore given some support to this, the earliest

---

[1] Cf. Thomas Jefferson, *Notes on Virginia* (1784); D. J. Boorstin, *The Lost World of Thomas Jefferson* (1948).

[2] Bernard to Barrington, 23 November 1765, *The Barrington–Bernard Correspondence*, ed. Channing and Coolidge (1912), p. 98.

of the American revolutionary myths, it has completely overthrown the most persistent of them; the Americans might have been fighting for liberty and the rights of Englishmen, but they were not fighting against a tyranny. Bancroft's view of the wickedness of George III has been disproved by the research of Sir Lewis Namier and the late Richard Pares. The keynote of British policy was its vacillation and its weakness, not its assertion of authority. Apart from the constitutional ambiguities, the administration of the colonies was haphazard. To Newcastle, as Secretary of State for the Southern Department, the colonies had furnished not opportunities for policy-making but for patronage. Until 1768 there was no Colonial Department where a consistent, or even well-informed, policy could be shaped. There was no political agency for all the colonies, and no administrative centre in the colonies themselves. Their inability to combine had compelled Britain to act for them, and to take the risk of their displeasure. Thus far it had been a safe gamble; and Grenville at least gave warning of his proposals in 1764, without any black cones being hoisted from Cape Cod or Old Point Comfort. Like many an American storm, the squall arose suddenly, and without warning.

The emphasis in the scholarship of the last decade on the extent of the colonial concern with liberty has tended to discredit one fashionable thesis that has been prevalent for forty years, since Charles Beard produced his *Economic Interpretation of the Constitution* in 1913. In this, he argued that the Founding Fathers were the richest Americans of their day, seeking to conserve the interests of property against the menace of democracy; forty of the fifty-five delegates at Philadelphia in 1787 had interests in government securities, in slaves or in land; the document they drafted was designed to curb, not to promote, social change. The American Revolution—to use Burke's phrase for the English Revolution—was 'a revolution not made, but prevented'. Beard was not the first to stress the importance of class conflict and social antagonism,[1] but he pushed it further than most others, and stimulated a most valuable series of monographs examining the social and economic tensions behind the Revolution,[2] tensions not only between rising colonial capitalism and restrictive Whitehall but between colonists and colonists. This thesis, though it has given a new dimension and depth to the study of revolutionary problems, has never found universal approval. It was questioned by C. M. Andrews

---

[1] J. A. Smith, *The Spirit of American Government* (1907), and Carl Becker, *History of Political Parties in the Province of New York* (1909), in which he used the now famous phrase that he was examining a contest not merely about home rule but also about who should rule at home.

[2] Arthur M. Schlesinger, Senior, *Colonial Merchants and the American Revolution* (1918); J. Franklin Jameson, *The American Revolution Considered as a Social Movement* (1926); Carl Bridenbaugh, *Cities in the Wilderness* (1938), *Cities in Revolt* (1955); Merrill Jensen, *The Articles of Confederation* (1940), *The New Nation* (1950); L. M. Hacker, *The Triumph of American Capitalism* (1940); Elisha P. Douglass, *Rebels and Democrats* (1955). Support for Beard's thesis can be found in a large number of studies of particular states.

in the fourth volume of his *The Colonial Period of American History* ('clever, ingenious and seemingly plausible but really superficial manipulations of fact and logic in the interest of a preconceived theory'), by a number of students of the revolutionary period in Massachusetts[1] and, in 1956, by Robert E. Brown in a full-scale criticism of Beard, *Charles Beard and the Constitution*. There is by this time a sufficient body of research available on each individual state to make any single interpretation of this sort unsatisfactory, and certainly enough to qualify Beard's central argument.

Nor is the thesis easier to substantiate in the years 1763–76. The alignment in the colonies varied from state to state in a bewildering and almost patternless way. The radicalism of New England was rooted in proud and pious Boston, and not in the levelling frontier; the Virginia plantations, like the Dutch estates, provided revolutionary leaders, though no doubt of a conservative cast of mind once the break with Britain was made; some Scots-Irish frontiersmen, notably the highlanders in North Carolina, who had fought against the duke of Cumberland at Culloden in 1746, were illogically fighting for his nephew, George III, at Moore's Creek Bridge thirty years later. If the South Carolina frontier was loyalist, Virginia's and Maryland's were on the whole patriot. Maryland's and Virginia's merchants tended to be Tories; so did Charleston's, but two of the wealthiest in Charleston—Henry Laurens and Gabriel Manigault—were patriots. In Pennsylvania and New York the merchant groups shifted their allegiance with the shifts of fortune; in Massachusetts at least two hundred left Boston with the British in March 1776. The economic and social forces operated in a local rather than a national framework: although they might push some groups in a revolutionary direction, they did not generate the same vehemence as did the issues of constitutional or political principle. It is impossible to believe that Washington's little army was held together over eight grim winters merely by concern over economic issues.[2]

Two new emphases have been offered by recent scholars. Philip Davidson and Arthur M. Schlesinger have shown that the coming of the Revolution was no spontaneous outbreak but a triumph of skilful propaganda. There was not only Samuel Adams but a whole team of patriots—or agitators. Josiah Warren could caution the children who visited the scene of their fathers' 'martyrdom' after the Boston 'massacre' to take heed, lest 'your feet slide on the stones bespattered with your fathers' brains'; he did not emphasise that the soldiery were defended by John

---

[1] Robert E. Brown, *Middle-class Democracy and the Revolution in Massachusetts 1691–1780* (1955); Oscar and Mary Handlin, 'Radicals and Conservatives in Massachusetts after Independence', in *New England Quarterly*, vol. XVII, p. 343; Robert Taylor, *Western Massachusetts in the Revolution* (1954).

[2] For a generation, however, Boston had suffered acutely from war, taxes and inflation. Cf. Bridenbaugh, *Cities in Revolt* (1955), p. 48 and *passim*.

Adams and were exonerated at their trial by a Boston jury, nor that the martyrs numbered only five. Nor did Otis, Josiah Quincy, Joseph Hawley, Francis Hopkinson, Isaac Sears, Alexander McDougall and Tom Paine counsel moderation. Behind these men were the machines of persuasion —the local committees of correspondence, the clubs and workingmen's societies and merchants' groups in every colony, the Sons of Liberty, the Mohawk River Indians, the Sons of Neptune, the Philadelphia Patriotic Society and other groups. Their festivals, said John Adams, tinge the minds of the people and 'impregnate them with the sentiments of liberty'.[1] And behind these in turn were the forty-two newspapers published in America in 1775—almost all of them Whig—and the countless pamphlets and broadsides. The press was hit by the Stamp Act, and then by the Townshend duties on paper, and saw itself as the first victim of tyranny. The Congregational and Presbyterian clergy repeated the themes from their pulpits. It was natural for General Gage and Governor Hutchinson to believe that the movement for independence was a deeply laid plot of wicked men. Their views were greedily accepted at home.[2]

In recent research, the other major contribution has been that of L. H. Gipson, that the Revolution was in essence an ironical aftermath of the 'Great War for the Empire'. The nine years' fighting, in which the colonists had not carried anything like the load borne by Britain, left them in 1763 in a highly favoured position, and they resented Grenville's policy, considerate and intelligent in intention though it was. The Revolution, whether or not it was in the minds of the people, as John Adams claimed, was in some measure inevitable once the French threat was removed. The new imperialism that, in Burke's words, made Britain appear 'like a porcupine armed all over with Acts of Parliament, oppressive to trade and America', was resented by a people free now from French curbs, even though the imperialism was in itself vacillating and hesitant. The colonists were not willing to submit to any controls, or in the end to any taxes, imposed from outside. What John Adams said in 1780 was equally true in 1770—'America is not used to great taxes, and the people there are not yet disciplined to such enormous taxation as in England.' Peter Kalm, the Swedish traveller, in the 1750s saw the same force—'exceeding freedom and prosperity nurse an untamable spirit'. And other historians have proved that it was in the details rather than in the intent that the new vigour in London was found vexing in America; the regulatory methods —and the rapacity—of British customs commissioners, revenue collectors and vice-admiralty courts after 1764 were bitterly resented. So, too, was

[1] J. Adams, Diary, 14 August 1769. *The Adams Papers, The Diary and Autobiography of John Adams* (ed. L. H. Butterfield, 1961), vol. I, p. 341.

[2] P. Davidson, *Propaganda and the American Revolution* (1941); A. M. Schlesinger, Senior, *Prelude to Independence, the Newspaper War on Britain, 1764–1776* (1958).

the idea of a standing army in peacetime: the presence of the 'lobster-backs' even more alarming than their cost.[1]

Recent research has, then, established the potential diversity of interests between colonies and mother-country. It has not demonstrated any general discontent with the mercantile system as such.[2] As Professors Harper and Dickerson have shown, the Navigation Acts in themselves were no great impediment to colonial trade, less so indeed than the similar measures of France and Spain. Colonial tobacco, sugar and coffee enjoyed a monopoly of the British market; there were bounties on the production of naval stores; thanks to the Navigation Acts, there was a flourishing colonial merchant marine; there was—though it was little esteemed—protection for the colonies on the seas and on the western frontier. Many unpopular mercantile statutes had not been enforced. It was less the colonial system than its reinvigoration and reformation after 1763 that caused trouble.

Yet, by nature rather than by any error of policy, one section of British America found it hard to fit itself into the imperial system. New England produced none of the staple crops, the tobacco, the cotton, the wool, the rice, that the home government sought from the colonies—although ship-building flourished. It presented few opportunities for the investment of British capital. Like Old England before it, it took to trade and to the sea: its commerce, it was said, smelled as strongly of fish as its theology did of brimstone. Having no commodities to exchange for the manufactured goods it needed, it tried to encourage local industry and it developed its trade with Spain, Portugal and Madeira, and with the West Indies—French and British—exchanging its timber, its shoes, its flour and vast quantities of inferior fish for specie, but still more for sugar and molasses for conversion into rum. There were some sixty-three distilleries in Massachusetts in 1750 and perhaps half that number in Rhode Island.[3] Despite the Molasses Act of 1733, significantly unenforced, the illicit trade with the French islands developed apace, even during the Seven Years War. New England merchants in 1763, as ten years later, made most of their profits from illegal trade or from smuggling: they showed anger when they were requested to obey the law, by denying the law's validity. As John

---

[1] L. H. Gipson, *The British Empire before the American Revolution* (in progress); L. A. Harper, *The English Navigation Laws* (1939); O. M. Dickerson, *The Navigation Acts and the American Revolution* (1951), especially pp. 208–65; C. E. Carter, 'The Office of Commander-in-Chief', in R. B. Morris (ed.), *The Era of the American Revolution* (1939), and 'The Significance of the Military Office in America 1763–1775', in *American Historical Review*, vol. XXVIII (1923), pp. 475–88.

[2] But cf., however, L. M. Hacker, who argues that the Revolution was as much a struggle against the curbs on free enterprise as it was for political independence: *The Shaping of the American Tradition* (1947), ch. XVII.

[3] L. M. Hacker, 'The First American Revolution', in *Columbia University Quarterly*, vol. XXVII, no. 3 (1935), part I. Newport alone had sixteen distilleries; New York and Philadelphia were not far behind (C. Bridenbaugh, *Cities in Revolt*, p. 74).

Adams said, rum was an essential ingredient in the American Revolution. It was the check on his tea smuggling by Lord North's act of 1773 that made profiteer John Hancock a patriot. The merchants of New England are Beard's best—though still not unanimous—witnesses.[1]

The South, for whom the mercantile system seemed in large measure designed, had by 1763 its own grievances, though, again, they were less against policy-makers than against nature itself. Concentration on tobacco was ruining the soil and reducing the value of the crop; over-production was producing a slump in prices while freight and insurance costs remained high; Scots factors at the Chesapeake Bay ports and in commercial houses in Glasgow and London appeared to fleece the planter. 'Scotchmen' were as unpopular in America in 1763 as in London. Of the loyalist property confiscated by Virginians during the Revolutionary War, one-third belonged to the Scots merchants of Norfolk. The planter was perennially short of ready cash and badly hit by the Currency Act of 1764. Only if, like Washington, he acquired big estates (by skill, by inherited wealth or by marriage with a widow) and then diversified his crops or indulged in land speculation, could he live at ease. But even Washington resented his dependence on the factor three thousand miles away or at the ports, and the sense of being the victim of injustice.

One further problem in the South—and to a lesser extent in the middle colonies—was that of western land. It was indeed closely related to the southern economy, which was in constant need of fresh land. Under the royal proclamation of October 1763 French Canada to the east of the Great Lakes was organised as the province of Quebec, Spanish Florida became the province of East Florida, and the area between the Apalachicola and New Orleans the province of West Florida. The territory across the Appalachians, however, was proclaimed as an Indian reserve, into which white men could not move except by special permission of the crown. Indian trade was limited to specified posts. This has frequently been held both to have been a psychological blunder and an offence to existing colonial rights, the sea-to-sea clauses of the colonial charters. It was, in fact, an honest attempt to fulfil undertakings made with the Indians during the war (for example the treaties of Easton 1758, of Lancaster 1760, and of Detroit 1762 with the Ohio Valley Indians, and the settlement of 1761 with the Cherokee) and to pacify—too late—the Seneca whom Pontiac was leading in revolt. Its intentions were liberal, not least as seen by Egremont and Shelburne. The settlements in the Illinois country needed defence and in the end civil government.[2] It was a matter of justice—and of furs. It is true that it ran counter to the

---

[1] A. M. Schlesinger, *The Colonial Merchants and the American Revolution, 1763–1776* (New York, 1918).

[2] Cf. Bouquet MSS., B.M. Add. MSS. 21638 *et seq.*; Illinois Historical Collections, vol. x: *The Critical Period 1763–1765* (ed. Alvord and Carter, 1915); Gipson, *The British Empire before the American Revolution*, vol. ix, p. 226.

interests of some frontiersmen, who ignored it, and of some companies of speculators, like the Ohio Company in Virginia and the Richard Henderson Company in North Carolina. But it was not intended as a permanent barrier and it had very little influence. In 1767–8 the Board of Trade considered a number of new projects for the West without overmuch enthusiasm—largely because of their effect on the fur-trade. Of these, the most important was the Vandalia scheme or the Indiana Company, which had originated in the complaints of 'the suffering traders' of Pennsylvania. Among its supporters were Franklin and Sir William Johnson. After considerable dissensions—not least with their rivals, the Ohio Company of Virginia—a patent was made out for Vandalia in 1773, which would have given it most of what is now West Virginia and eastern Kentucky. But in February 1774 North's government restricted all land grants. With the coming of the Revolution these projects—like Judge Henderson's in Kentucky—lapsed.

Nor had the restrictions much influence on individual speculators, the entrepreneurs of the American Revolution. Practically all the colonial governors were speculators, successive governors in New York like Moore, Dunmore and Tryon, William Franklin in New Jersey, Dobbs in North Carolina. Washington in 1767, urging his friend William Crawford, living on the Youghiogheny, to buy up land for him, said that he had never seen the proclamation but as 'a temporary expedient to quiet the minds of the Indians'. By 1768 the home government had to acquiesce in the breakdown of the Proclamation Line. The Treaty of Fort Stanwix with the Iroquois and the treaties of Hard Labour (1768) and of Lochaber (1770) with the Cherokees pushed the line farther west. After the failure of the Pontiac rising in 1763–5 the Indians were kept at their uneasy peace with the columns of incoming settlers not by statutes drawn in Westminster but, first, by the defence measures of 1763–8, and the British garrisons that Grenville felt the colonies should help pay for, and second, by the skills of the Indian superintendents, John Stuart in the South (superintendent 1762–79) and that half-legendary figure in the Mohawk country, Sir William Johnson, reigning Indian-fashion at Johnson Hall (superintendent 1755–74). Britain was well served by her frontier administrators, better served than she deserved to be. They knew well enough that they could not hold back the flood of uitlanders, who resented the Quebec Act, and North's restrictions on land sales of February 1774. By 1775, Pittsburgh and Wheeling were important centres of trade. Americans were not to be stopped by laws that ran counter to what was now appearing as their western destiny.[1]

[1] Destiny pointed south as well as west. Cf. Israel Putnam's Company of Military Adventurers in West Florida in 1773; A. Pound, *Johnson of the Mohawks* (1930), especially for its appendices; J. R. Alden, *John Stuart and the Southern Colonial Frontier* (1944); A. F. C. Wallace, *Teedyuscung, King of the Delawares* (1949); J. W. Lydekker, *The Faithful Mohawks* (1938).

By 1775, then, a new nation had proclaimed itself, under the impact of a history of repeated injuries and usurpations. Protests against Britain had already produced passionate outbursts of nationalism. At the Stamp Act Congress of 1765, Christopher Gadsden had declared, 'There ought to be no New England man; no New Yorker, known on the continent, but all of us Americans'. Nine years later, Patrick Henry orated, 'The distinctions between Virginians, Pennsylvanians, New Yorkers and New Englanders are no more. I am not a Virginian, but an American.... All distinctions are thrown down. All America is thrown into one mass.' Despite these paeans of patriotism, sectionalism and particularism were as much in evidence in 1776 as they were still to be in 1861. The thirteen colonies were very precariously united against Britain. They were, in Professor Van Tyne's phrase, thirteen independent states 'temporarily acting together in the business of acquiring their individual independence'.[1] The struggle against Britain by the Continental army was accompanied by a struggle for power, for influence—and for land—between each state and section, and between social groups inside each state and section— a struggle, that is, over who should rule at home.

Among the states there were boundary disputes that threatened conflict. There was the twenty-year-old dispute over Fort Pitt between Pennsylvania and Virginia. Connecticut had claims on the Wyoming valley along the Susquehanna and was attempting to settle it with armed men. New York and New Hampshire were wrangling over the possession of the Green Mountains. There was suspicion—still a reality in Maryland until 1781—over the sea-to-sea claims of the Old Dominion. Many besides Otis, Galloway and Braxton believed that only British power prevented the outbreak of a number of civil wars between the colonies.

More alarming were the social tensions, of which there had been significant indications in the years between 1763 and 1776. They were found particularly in Pennsylvania, New York, and the Carolinas; Virginia and Maryland had a happier record. In 1763 the Scots-Irish on the Pennsylvanian frontier, alarmed by the Pontiac rising, murdered twenty friendly Conestoga Indians near Lancaster. Frontier justices and juries proved indifferent to Governor Penn's proclamations ordering the culprits to be tried. Out of this grew an ugly frontier challenge, and the march on Philadelphia in 1764 of 600 Paxton Boys, named after one of their townships, who were angry at the indifference of the eastern Quakers to their plight, and at their inadequate representation in the Assembly. Sixteen thousand voters in the three eastern counties had twice as many members in the Assembly as the fifteen thousand voters in the five western counties. The Paxton Boys were placated by Franklin; their leader, Lazarus Stewart, moved out into the further frontier of the Wyoming valley, where he was killed in 1778. They made a common front with the mech-

[1] C. H. Van Tyne, *The American Revolution* (1905), p. 182.

anics and their popular leader in Philadelphia in the revolution, and most of their demands found expression in the Pennsylvania constitution of 1776.[1]

In 1766 the New York assembly took a more sympathetic view of the Quartering Act than it had a year before. It requested the help of royal troops when it faced a series of riots over land tenantry and high rents in Westchester and Dutchess counties. Threatened with eviction, the farmers who called themselves Sons of Liberty sought to apply it literally; they broke open Poughkeepsie gaol and organised a march on New York to burn the homes of Pierre Van Cortlandt and Lambert Moore. The Whigs, liberal enough towards authority in London, were less happy when rebellion was pointed so directly against themselves; John Morin Scott and Robert Livingston handed down severe sentences on the 'levellers', out of the conviction, as a cynic put it, that 'no one is entitled to Riot but themselves'.[2]

From 1764 to 1771 there was persistent trouble in North Carolina. The settlers in the backcountry, many of them recent immigrants from the North via the Great Valley of Virginia, were fighting over land claims in Mecklenburg County in 1765. By 1767 they were campaigning against the corruption of treasurers and sheriffs, and the exorbitant fees of lawyers. In 1768 they organised 'The Regulation', a vigilance society in intention, and were curbed only by Governor Tryon's calling out the militia and promising reforms. In 1769 they captured control of the assembly, but Tryon dissolved it because of its attitude to Britain; no reforms were forthcoming. In 1770, at Hillsboro', they demanded unprejudiced juries and public accounting. As in New York and Pennsylvania, there was fear of a march on the capital. Tryon led a colonial militia against the all-but-leaderless Regulators, defeated them at the battle of the Alamance, 1771, and executed some of them. Again, there was a frontier evacuation, this time into Tennessee, and a legacy of bitterness. For this struggle conditioned the state's attitude to the Revolution. When their enemies of 1771 became revolutionaries in 1776 and when Governor Martin showed a sympathy for them that Tryon had not, the Regulators remained loyalist. They fought for Britain at Moore's Creek Bridge and continued an ugly but tiring civil war on her behalf and their own for five more years. Those who shouted in the low country for Home Rule from Britain were reluctant to grant it to their own countrymen in the western hills.[3]

The South Carolina backcountry was similarly disturbed, due again to the lack of law-courts, of magistrates and—embarrassingly—of clergy in

---

[1] J. P. Selsam, *The Pennsylvania Constitution of 1776* (1936); A. Nevins, *The American States during and after the Revolution* (1924); Elisha P. Douglass, *Rebels and Democrats* (1955), pp. 214–86; R. L. Brunhouse, *The Counter-revolution in Pennsylvania 1776–1790* (1942).

[2] Irving Mark, *Agrarian Conflicts in Colonial New York, 1711–1775* (1940), pp. 134–45.

[3] *Colonial Records of North Carolina* (ed. Saunders), vol. IX (1890), pp. 329–33.

the interior, and to the sense of being the victims of tidewater—and of Episcopalian—domination. The gracious planter-merchant aristocracy of Charleston was Janus-like: liberal and Whig as it looked across the Atlantic, hard-faced and Tory as it looked west across the pine-barrens.[1]

Behind these examples there were forces in the West that were to continue throughout the revolutionary period, and were to come again to the surface in Shays's rebellion in Massachusetts in 1786, and in the Whisky Rebellion of 1794.[2] Courts of law were too few, and justice remote, unpredictable and expensive. In Pennsylvania there was fear of Indians, and in the Carolinas still more fear of other whites. 'We live not as under a British government... but as if we were in Hungary, or Germany, and in a state of war, continually exposed to the incursions of hussars and pandours....'[3] Prophetic demands were being voiced: for a paper currency; for more adequate roads; for the replacement of a poll-tax by a tax levied in accordance with capacity to pay, and to pay in kind; for election by ballot; for a curbing of the speculators, who had acquired their vast and empty estates through their influence 'back east'; and for a fairer representation of the West in eastern assemblies, a common cry from the Mohawk to the Smokies. If Woodmason's diatribes against 'vexatious pettifoggers or litigious miscreants', 'Rogues and Whores', have been thought fevered by later historians, there can be no querying the less eloquent but more moving petition of the 260 inhabitants of Anson County, North Carolina (October 1769), ending with the request 'that Doct^r Benjamin Franklin or some other known patriot be appointed Agent, to represent the unhappy state of this Province to his Majesty, and to solicit the several boards in England'.[4]

They did not once mention the Proclamation Line or the wickedness of Britain; they wanted justice, good order, religious freedom and democracy; their enemies were mercenary attorneys and little bureaucrats in the tidewater, doing the harm here that Britain's agents were doing at the ports. This was the country for whom Patrick Henry spoke; and it was in Waxhaws that Andrew Jackson spent his formative years. South of Virginia the frontier tended to Loyalism throughout the Revolution. In Pennsylvania, in New England and not least in Vermont, it was avidly patriot.

As the Second Continental Congress moved slowly towards independence, these social forces were erupting. The Virginian planters had long been aware of them and for that reason among others had hesitated

---

[1] *The Carolina Backcountry on the Eve of the Revolution. The Journal and other writings of Charles Woodmason, Anglican Itinerant* (ed. R. J. Hooker, 1953).

[2] Herman Husband, the Regulator leader, escaped at the Alamance in 1771 and, oddly, later became involved in the Whisky rebellion. Douglass, *Rebels and Democrats*, p. 99.

[3] Woodmason, *op. cit.* p. 213.

[4] *The Colonial Records of North Carolina*, vol. VIII, p. 78. Cf. the cautious judgements on the regulators by Carl Bridenbaugh, however, in *Myths and Realities*, p. 160.

over independence—'namby pambys', Charles Lee called them, whose 'little blood has been suck'd out by musketoes'. The planters' hesitations were in part overcome by their governor's seizure of arms and his proclamation of emancipation to those Negroes who would rise in revolt. Whatever their views about the mountain men, they were useful allies if Britain called on slaves and Indians to make war; but they were still uncongenial bedfellows.

The revolutionary leaders showed considerable skill in enlisting support from the frontier for their cause. But skill in method did not necessarily mean political sympathy nor did it produce a clear programme of social or political reform. Sam Adams distrusted the farmers in western Massachusetts; John Morin Scott sat in judgement on them in New York; there was no love lost between New Bern or Charleston and the Regulator leaders. Only in Pennsylvania did backcountry and town make common cause; and this largely because of the abdication of leadership by the Whigs in Philadelphia.

The Revolution was carried through as an exercise in moderation, both against Britain and against this social unrest. The colonies, as John Adams said, were groping after the middle way. The unrest drove some moderates into loyalism, especially in New York and among Philadelphia aristocrats. But fear of it was evident from the beginning among revolutionary leaders. Southern planters, like Carter Braxton in Virginia, or Rawlins Lowndes in South Carolina, scorned the 'darling Democracy' of New England without in the end doubting the value of independence. Gouverneur Morris opposed independence because he thought that after it New York would be ruled by a 'riotous mob'—'believe me, Sir', he wrote to John Penn, 'freedom and religion are only watchwords'. Throughout his life, not least when he toyed with rescuing Marie Antoinette sixteen years later, he scorned the 'Jack Cades of the day...the bellwethers of the flock'. But he too became a patriot in the end. John Adams of Massachusetts and Thomas Wharton of Philadelphia echoed these fears. When wealthy James Allen joined a battalion for the defence of Philadelphia in October 1775 he gave as his reasons that 'a man is suspected who does not, and I choose to have a musket on my shoulder to be on a par with them; and I believe discreet people mixing with them may keep them in order'. In March, 'the madness of the multitude', he thought, 'is but one degree better than submission to the Tea Act'. In nothing was British handling of the colonies so culpable as in the driving of men with these doubts not only into independence but into the leadership of the Revolution.

The middle way and what John Adams called the 'skilful steerage' were evident in the political and the social reforms of the war years. Despite the fears of the aristos, there was no anarchy—except perhaps in

North Carolina, where it was not a novelty. No royal governor lost his life. Congress declared in May 1776 that all royal government was to be suppressed, and that new state governments should be set up. This was smoothly done. Each state produced a constitution—sometimes, as in Connecticut and Rhode Island, by altering existing charters. Except for Massachusetts they were all drafted within a few months. All were written documents, and the work of lawyers; all contained declarations of rights; all emphasised separation of powers and the primacy of the elected legislature—elected by those people with some—though now a smaller—stake in the community. In Georgia and the Carolinas, in Massachusetts and New Jersey, only Protestants could hold office. There were normally property qualifications imposed on members of legislatures or state officials. The legislature usually elected the governor, who held office for only one year, and who lost his veto power in practically all states. In Pennsylvania, where the franchise was unusually wide and all taxpayers had the suffrage, and in Georgia's first constitution, there was only one house; elsewhere, there were two, the second, sometimes chosen by an electoral college, designed to act as a check on the 'Mobility' that James Allen and John Adams and many other revolutionaries feared. The western areas in the states south of the Potomac gained some seats but not their fair share, least of all in South Carolina. Only in Massachusetts, Pennsylvania, North Carolina and Georgia could the new constitutions be said to be democratic documents.

Nor was the social revolution much more pronounced than the political. There was the striking disappearance of the Loyalists, and the confiscation of crown and proprietary lands. The estates of Sir John Wentworth in New Hampshire, of Sir William Pepperrell in Maine, of Sir John Johnson in the Mohawk Valley, of the Phillipses in New York, Lord Fairfax in Virginia, Sir James Wright in Georgia were destroyed. But when loyalist land was sold the motive was punitive or fiscal rather than egalitarian. Except in New York, where there was unusual break-up of the fifty-nine estates that were confiscated, the land was usually sold as a unit to wealthy men or to speculators; practically all the state governors were interested in real estate. The prices and terms of sale were in fact much less favourable to 'little men' than the British had been. In the end, however, at inflated prices, land percolated down to smaller holders, and carried voting rights with it as it came. The right to acquire and possess property without restriction was indeed as important a civil right as free speech—and to most people in the eighteenth century it meant more. Property was largely real estate and was widely dispersed; it was esteemed as the reward of effort and success rather than of inheritance. The disappearance of its feudal aspects was strength rather than weakness. Quit-rents were abolished in every state between 1775 and 1789. Entail and primogeniture disappeared also from New York and the South: but entail had not been a universal custom, even in tidewater, docking had been a common practice, and primogeniture had applied only in cases of intestacy. Their removal, egalitarian though it seemed, in no way weakened the plantation economy or the long-tailed families; rather did it indicate a right to do what one liked with one's own in an ever-expanding society in which there was more than enough for all. Religious freedom was strengthened, partly by the separation from parent churches, partly by the disestablishment of the Anglican (but not of the Congregational) church, partly by the spread of rationalism and deism.

There were some trends that can be described as liberal without qualification. The colonial criminal codes were always much less harsh than Britain's, and in the northern states at least they were now made even more liberal. In the Pennsylvanian constitution of 1776 capital punishment was restricted to four offences. Jefferson's code for Virginia would have limited it to murder and treason—defeated by one vote, it was not enacted until the 1790s. Congress similarly limited capital punishment in the Northwest Territory in 1788. The anti-slavery movement developed: by the end of the century the majority of states had forbidden the importation of slaves, and all New England, New York and Pennsylvania had provided for abolition or gradual emancipation. Most Southerners thought it an evil and manumitted slaves by deed or will—as did Robert Carter and George Washington. It was, optimistically, expected to die a natural death. Freedom for the person was a real thing: it was, however, tightly confined to one sex, and it brought little native blossoming of the arts.

Behind the political tensions, it was an age of unusual stability. One reason was the unusual one, lack of immigrants: in the years from 1776 to 1825 only a quarter of a million immigrants entered the United States. This allowed the mould of the country to become fixed; western land was acquired before the human flood poured in. The republic was in happy equipoise. Liberal forces were at work but they were of a traditional and largely an inherited kind. In almost all the new states, frontier and tidewater, the men of substance were in control; and the idealists sometimes proved themselves incompetent executives. Not the least striking feature of the years of construction from 1776 to 1787 was the minor role played by the propagandists and pamphleteers of the decade of agitation.[1]

Yet in three respects the war for independence was productive of major social and political change: farmers to some degree and financiers to a major degree profited from it; Loyalists lost completely by it; and at the centre liberty and order were in the end reconciled in the federal constitutions of 1777 and 1787.

If the merchant class suffered in the war, and if some tidewater planta-

---

[1] Cf. Daniel Boorstin, *The Genius of American Politics* (1953); Elisha P. Douglass, *Rebels and Democrats* (1955), esp. ch. XVI; A. Nevins, *The American States During and After the Revolution* (1924); and *The Papers of Thomas Jefferson* (in progress, 1950-) (ed. Boyd).

tions, unable to export their products, never regained their old prosperity, many small farmers flourished. The number of men in the army was always small, and agriculture was little affected by the war—except in the South towards the end. In New England military operations almost ceased after 1776. Farmers were helped by the high prices paid for their produce—by both armies, and by the inflation of the currency—which allowed them to pay off their debts. In Rhode Island debtors pursued creditors in their eagerness to force depreciated currency upon them. The farmer prospered, as long as the war lasted.

Moreover the ties with Britain that were broken by 1783 were social and psychological as well as political. Although the new state constitutions might reflect a British caution, for seven years Britain was the enemy, and hostility to her was visited upon the Loyalists. The size and fate of this loyalist element has been minimised by American historians—as their military possibilities were ignored by contemporary British leaders. Their disappearance was immensely important: not only because of the estates they left behind. It marked the disappearance of most of the colonial aristocracy. There was now for a generation room at the top, even though it was not yet for poor men. Today's old families of Boston are for the most part derived from the *nouveaux riches* of the Revolution: Hancock, like the Browns of Rhode Island, came up in the smuggling trade. This was not presumably quite what Jefferson had in mind when he spoke of 'the aristocracy of talent and virtue, which nature has wisely provided'. But he probably had not any Bostonians in mind. Self-made men were numerous, of course, in colonial America, but there was in this sense a real shift in power by 1783.

The transition to independence was a great deal easier at the local than at the 'national' level. Indeed many radical leaders, in revolting against Britain, were revolting against government at any level beyond their own local boundaries. And both locally and at the centre that government was best, said Jefferson, which governed least. It was in this spirit, and because of the primacy in their reckoning of these social issues, that the Continental Congress accepted the Articles of Confederation in 1777, and submitted them to the states. The articles were not ratified until 1781 since several states, especially Maryland and New Jersey, thought it unfair that those states with sea-to-sea charters (Virginia, Massachusetts, Georgia, Connecticut and the Carolinas) should obtain all the land between the Alleghenies and the Mississippi or even the Pacific. Maryland was not herself utterly virtuous: some of her citizens, interested in the Illinois-Wabash and Indiana companies, hoped for better terms from Congress than from the other states. None of these land claims was clear: New York's, based on the surrender of their property-rights by the Iroquois, perhaps least of all; Virginia's was the largest and strongest, and had been reinforced during the war by George Rogers Clark's successes against the

Illinois towns in 1778–9. But if maintained, these claims would give vast areas of land, won by a common effort, to particular states—and would allow them to pay off their war veterans and their debts, and thus keep their taxes low. When these states agreed to surrender their claims (though before they had all done so), Maryland gave her assent to the articles; Virginia's surrender was particularly noble, and in Jefferson's and Richard Henry Lee's case was made for genuinely republican reasons. It was not until 1802, however, that Georgia, the last of them, agreed to surrender. The United States, when they won their independence in 1783, inherited a great public domain in the West of some hundred million acres—as a common possession.

This concession to emergent federalism was a remarkable step for states not thus far noticeable for their unselfishness. It has been all too little appreciated by historians. Indeed, until recently, it has been the fashion to condemn the articles, under which the country was governed for a decade (1777–87), and to give to these years, after John Fiske, the name of the Critical Period.[1] Merrill Jensen has in recent years offered a salutary corrective.[2] He has stressed, first, that the articles were an expression of colonial experience, a statement of democratic theory far clearer than that of the individual states: a powerless executive, the taxing power in local hands, the importance of the legislature. If there was a failure of government in these years, it was due rather to the reluctance of the states to honour requisitions by Congress than to the constitutional limitations of the document. When Congress requested authority to raise money by taxing imports—shades of 1768—Rhode Island refused. Congress could neither tax nor persuade the states to tax. She was driven to issue a paper currency that rapidly depreciated, and soon 'not worth a Continental' became a cliché. The states issued their own paper, and when creditors refused to accept it and began to foreclose on the farmer, Captain Shays and some 2000 farmers in Massachusetts rose in rebellion. These troubles were hardly attributable to Congress.

Secondly, Professor Jensen has demonstrated that it is inaccurate to attribute to the articles themselves the acute problems that arose in the years from 1783 to 1787. There was a severe depression and deflation. The war stimulus to home industry and agriculture ceased. British forces disappeared, and farmers everywhere lost a market. Secession from the empire deprived New England of her West Indian trade, and the South lost its bounties—though not always it markets—in Britain. When Massachusetts tried to prevent the dumping of British goods New Hampshire eagerly absorbed them. The frontier clashes and tariff disputes of state with state continued. The Green Mountains, contested between New York and New Hampshire, were dominated by the colourful and

[1] J. Fiske, *The Critical Period* (1888).
[2] *The Articles of Confederation* (1940); *The New Nation* (1950).

34-2

unreliable brothers Allen, and, not yet a state, contemplated union with Canada. Rhode Island, the last of the original thirteen states to join the Union in 1790, did so only because it was threatened with tariff discrimination by all the rest. It was indeed in the attempts by Washington, at the Mount Vernon Conference in 1785, to settle disputes of this sort along the Potomac that the discussions began that led to the Constitutional Convention of 1787. Nor were the articles responsible for Britain's retaining the north-western fur posts, nor for the intrigues of Spain with Indians and whites in the Mississippi country. The difficulties of the new nation were real enough, and they were economic and diplomatic as much as constitutional. But by 1787 prosperity was returning, especially to the South.

One achievement of the confederation it would be impossible to question: the settlement of the territories surrendered by the states to Congress in 1781. This north-west, stretching from the northern edges of the Kentucky country to Canada, was little known, and for this reason was of great appeal to Jefferson in his character as naturalist and scientist, as well as politician. Congress drew up three ordinances (1784, 1785 and 1787) for the north-west, although the first of them was repealed later. They provided for a survey of the territory before settlement and the creation of townships on New England lines—to minimise friction with other settlers and with the Indians. Sections were to be reserved for schools, and as bounty land for veterans (out of which arose Virginia's Military District and Connecticut's Western Reserve); the rest was to be sold at a dollar an acre, but the minimum sale was to be of 640 acres. This gave opportunity not to the little man but, once more, to the land speculator. The law of 1787, based on the earlier plan of Jefferson's of 1784, provided for three stages of government for a territory: first, under a governor and judges provided by Congress; second, when it had five thousand free adult males it could elect its own legislature; when the population reached sixty thousand, it could be admitted to statehood on complete equality of status with existing states. Out of the whole area not less than three and not more than five states were to be formed: they became Ohio (a state in 1802), Indiana, Illinois, Michigan and Wisconsin. Had Jefferson's draft of 1784 been followed—he had proposed fourteen new states—the names would have been more romantic still: he had shown his interest in Old World as well as New World culture by suggesting, in addition to these familiar titles, Metropotamia (Northern Ohio), Saratoga (southern Ohio), Assenisipia (Chicago), Sylvania (Minnesota), Pelisipia (eastern Kentucky) and Chersonesus (Michigan).[1]

The north-west ordinances are fully as important as the Constitution. They guaranteed freedom of religion, trial by jury, and education to these,

[1] *The Papers of Thomas Jefferson*, vol. VI, p. 581, and map, p. 591. Cf. Dumas Malone, *Jefferson the Virginian* (1948), p. 413.

and thus to subsequent, new territories; they permanently prohibited slavery in the entire area, north and west, that is, of the Ohio—its first national limitation, and one that, by encouraging the entry of the free white settler, gave the area its free character. It took at least one more generation, however, before lower prices and laxer credit laws gave the smallholder his chance. And speculators, meantime, especially the Reverend Manasseh Cutler, General Rufus Putnam and the Ohio company, had a field day, abetted by corrupt Congressmen. Nevertheless, more than any other feature in the years after 1770, the ordinances extended the principles of the Declaration of Independence and applied them successfully to a vast and virgin land. They set a precedent that was followed by the next thirty-six states as they came into being. They were non-colonial in spirit: the original thirteen states enjoyed the primacy that came with early settlement, but exercised no imperial control over other states. As a result the new territories naturally looked to the new national government for authority: these areas became and remained areas of national interest rather than of states' rights, and the appeal to states' rights has never had quite the same magic in these territories as in some of the original thirteen colonies. The ordinances quickened settlement too at Marietta and Cincinnati—although it was not until 1795 at the Treaty of Greenville that a peace with the Ohio Indians was won. However unsatisfactory the articles might be, the provisions of 1785 and 1787 were remarkably far-sighted and mature.

The old south-west presented very different problems. There were three major obstacles to settlement there, but all were being overcome before 1785: they were the Proclamation Line of 1763, ineffective before 1776 and automatically abrogated by the Revolution; the Indians; and the mountain barrier of the Alleghenies itself, quite the most substantial obstacle of all. And there were four main routes of penetration: the Hudson–Mohawk route to the Great Lakes and the upper reaches of the Ohio; the difficult road to Pittsburgh followed by Washington and Forbes in 1758; the Great Philadelphia Wagon Road via Lancaster, York, the Valley of Virginia and the Cumberland Gap, where it met the Wilderness Road and crossed 'the Warrior Path' of the Shawnees; and the route to the east and south of the mountain chain, the Fall Line Road. The Mohawk was held by the Iroquois, who under the influence of the Johnsons stayed loyal to Britain, and whose chief, Joseph Brant (Thayendanegea), had fought with his braves alongside St Leger in 1777. With the support of General Haldimand, the Iroquois were 'rewarded' after 1783 with lands in Ontario. The Creeks held the south, and in the years after 1783 they attempted under a half-breed leader of talent and duplicity, Alexander McGillivray, to play off British, Spanish and Americans in the south-west. McGillivray was trader as well as warrior—a member of the firm of Panton and Leslie that had monopoly rights in the Indian trade in the Floridas. Creeks, Spaniards, ex-Loyalists and adventurers like William Augustus Bowles made the Alabama country intractable to govern. It was in any case heavily forested, hardwood country, difficult to clear—but its black soil looked tempting.

The central pass through the mountains was the Cumberland Gap on the present Virginia–Kentucky–Tennessee divide. It has the romantic interest in the history of the American frontier, says a Southern historian, 'that the pass of Thermopylae had in ancient Greece'.[1] It was at the Cumberland Gap that F. J. Turner, in his famous essay, had his mythical watcher stand in 1793, and through which 'impelled by an irresistible attraction' passed 'the procession of civilisation, marching single file—the buffalo following the trail to the salt springs, the Indian, the fur-trader and hunter, the cattle-raiser, the pioneer farmer...'.[2] From the gap access was easy to the Kentucky bluegrass, to the Nashville basin, or to the fertile bottom-land of the Cumberland Great Kanawha and Tennessee rivers. The gap had been discovered or rediscovered in 1750 by Dr Thomas Walker of Virginia and a number of settlements near it or beyond it came into being. In 1769 a Virginian settlement was begun at Watauga, reinforced in 1771 by 'Regulators' led by James Robertson and John Sevier. In the same year the survey of the Virginia–North Carolina boundary revealed that Watauga was in North Carolina—although the nearest North Carolina settlement was over a hundred miles away. The Wataugans had learnt independence and valued it: they formed the Watauga Association, based on manhood suffrage and representative government, which survived until 1776, when they became Washington County, North Carolina. After the Revolution, when North Carolina ceded her western lands to the United States, Sevier led them in forming the 'lost' state of Franklin, which provided a government, but never won recognition from Congress.

Beyond Watauga, Daniel Boone and the Long Hunters were active between 1769 and 1775, tracing the Wilderness Road through the gap to Boonesboro on the Kentucky. To these efforts, the Shawnees offered resistance, but they were defeated in Dunmore's war of 1774 by General Andrew Lewis at Point Pleasant, fought near the mouth of the Kanawha. Cornstalk, the Shawnee chief, signed a treaty surrendering all title to lands south and east of the Ohio. Judge Richard Henderson of North Carolina attempted to organise a company for this area similar to the Ohio and

[1] Clement Eaton, *A History of the Old South* (1949), p. 115.
[2] F. J. Turner, *The Frontier in American History* (New York, 1920), p. 12. Turner's major omission from his list was the land-speculator, who, if not in the 'procession', was its chief organiser in the east. For a revisionary estimate of Turner, cf. George W. Pierson, 'The Frontier and Frontiersmen of Turner's Essays', *Pennsylvania Magazine of History and Biography*, vol. LXIV (October 1940), pp. 449–78, and 'The Frontier and American Institutions', in *New England Quarterly*, vol. XV (June 1942), pp. 224–55; cf. also M. Kane, 'Some Considerations of the Frontier Concept of Frederick Jackson Turner, in *Mississippi Valley Historical Review*, vol. XXVII (December 1940), pp. 379–400.

Vandalia companies; by buying up the further titles of the Cherokees ('Treaty of Sycamore Shoals', 1775), he claimed mastery over an area stretching from the gap westwards to the junction of the Tennessee and Ohio: he called his domain Transylvania. His hopes of royal support came to a premature end with the Revolution, and the Continental Congress rejected his petition to recognise his colony, because of Virginia's sea-to-sea claims. In 1777 Virginia, acting at the request of the settlers in Harrodsburg, marshalled by George Rogers Clark, took the area under its—all too inadequate and entirely self-interested—protection as the County of Kentucky. By 1783 there were perhaps twenty thousand settlers in Kentucky, and a similar number in the Nashville area of Tennessee, where another isolated group had signed another romantic treaty, the Cumberland Compact. Of its 284 signers only ten survived ten years: and of the 274 who died, 273 died violent deaths. Yet, despite the ravages of Creeks and Cherokees, numbers increased fast in the southwest; they were encouraged by speculators like William Blount who persuaded North Carolina in 1783 to open up for sale its Tennessee lands. In 1785 more than one thousand boats, each containing several families, were counted on the Ohio. The first census of 1790 estimated that Kentucky had 74,000 people and the Tennessee settlements some 40,000: there might well have been a quarter of a million people in the south-west as a whole by 1793.

The problems presented to the new Union here were not those of encouraging settlement but of curbing premature government and mediating between many claimants to land and to political authority. In neither South nor North was it a case of a conservative federal government restraining a democratic frontier. The transmontane frontier was established almost entirely by land-speculators—as were the earliest colonies themselves—and until its numbers were considerable it generated opportunism and proprietaries rather than democracy. To propriety it was never sympathetic. Democracy and communication alike made slow progress across the mountains between 1763 and 1796.[1]

The future of the West, and the intrigues of Spain with many westerners, posed awkward problems for the first president. Washington's first brush with the Senate was over an Indian treaty. In 1790 he invited McGillivray to smoke the pipe of peace at Philadelphia—though without appreciable result except to strengthen the bargaining power of the Creeks. But the south-west, with its vast quantities of game, its rich soil and its long growing seasons, was developing fast. Kentucky, prospering with the Ohio trade, was admitted to statehood in 1792. Its constitution was the first in the South to provide for manhood suffrage and office-holding without property qualifications; but slavery was preserved and

---

[1] Cf. T. P. Abernethy, *From Frontier to Plantation in Tennessee* (1932); *Western Lands and the American Revolution* (1937).

until 1799 the governor and senators were elected via an electoral college. Tennessee, formed by a merger of the Watauga and Cumberland settlements, became the 'Territory South of the River Ohio' in 1790 and a state in 1796, though still less democratic than Kentucky. The honour of being the first new state, however, went to Vermont in 1791. If the war unified the country and the new constitution gave it a federal government, it was the frontier north and south that was the greatest nationalising factor of all. If, in Professor Morgan's phrase, the American nation was the child, not the father, of the Revolution,[1] it may be said that it was also the offspring of the western frontier.

[1] Edmund S. Morgan, *The Birth of the Republic, 1763–89* (1956), p. 101. Cf. Hans Kohn, *American Nationalism* (New York, 1957).

CHAPTER XIX

THE BEGINNINGS OF REFORM IN GREAT BRITAIN, IMPERIAL PROBLEMS, POLITICS AND ADMINISTRATION, ECONOMIC GROWTH

THE Peace of Paris of 1763 brought the first British empire to the summit of its power and glory, and set the problems of diplomacy and imperial organisation which in the next generation became the chief substance of English politics. In America the power of France was broken, but the problem of imperial defence remained, for as the Pontiac rebellion showed, Indian power could still be a menace, and perhaps a stalking-horse for renewed French ambitions. By the proclamation of 1763 the British government sought to keep white settlers out of the Indian hunting grounds where they had aroused great hostility, and in attempting to restrict expansion set themselves in opposition to some of the most powerful forces of American life. A standing army was also to be maintained, controlled from England but paid for by the colonists. To men of influence on both sides of the Atlantic the time also seemed ripe for a reorganisation of the constitutional machinery of the colonies, which had frequently obstructed the efficient conduct of the last war. Hitherto the British government had concentrated upon the control of the maritime and commercial links of empire, and under its system of imperial autarky the American colonies had flourished, rapidly increasing in population, extent and prosperity. To a very late date few Americans openly opposed imperial regulation of this sort, but they distinguished sharply between legislation which sought primarily to regulate trade, and that which sought primarily to raise revenue. The extensive control of the Commons over the latter appeared to them evidence that the granting of revenue was a function of local representatives, not to be usurped by an imperial parliament in which they had no part; this view seemed to be confirmed by the status of the highly dependent, but financially autonomous, parliament of Ireland, a colony whose history was to be linked ever more closely with that of America. Rumours of constitutional reorganisation made resistance to imperial taxation more urgent. Grenville's Sugar Act in 1764 aroused opposition, and his maladroit efforts to circumvent American opposition to the Stamp Act of 1765 exposed him to charges of deception. In this crisis the Americans and the imperial parliament adopted the constitutional principles which eventually led to war. The Americans admitted an imperial right of legislation but denied that of taxation; the

Rockingham Whigs repealed the Stamp Act, but in the Declaratory Act went beyond Grenville's claim that the Americans were 'virtually' represented at Westminster, to a statement of the full parliamentary sovereignty on which king and politicians came more and more to take their stand. The one side came to harbour dark suspicions of English plots to undermine their liberties, the other to suspect that Americans would stick at nothing short of independence and the overthrow of parliamentary authority.

The negotiations for peace in India caused immediate trouble nearer home, for a final breach between Clive and Lawrence Sulivan[1] was occasioned by misunderstandings which arose from consultations between the East India Company and the government as to the terms to be sought in the peace treaty. Clive sought the support of the Pelham connection, now in opposition; Sulivan was supported by the ministry, and for the first time since the end of the previous century, political factions entered the contest at India House, with speedily disastrous results to the company. In India too the destruction both of France and the native powers contributed greatly to the disintegration of the company's administrative standards.

The immediate signing of peace in 1763, as in 1783, occasioned acute financial tension on an international scale. The Bank of England was mainly concerned with giving assistance to continental houses in much worse trouble, but its stock of coin fell dangerously low, and there was a sharp drop in the prices of Bank stock and Consols. However, there is some reason to believe that the Seven Years War increased rather than diminished the real wealth of the country; after the initial crisis a period of cheap money set in from 1764 to 1769, and the steady rise in public stocks had its usual eighteenth-century effect of encouraging investment in more profitable private channels. There was a convulsive increase in canal, turnpike and enclosure schemes. Exports of copper and iron increased, and though prosperity was not universal, these years mark a favourable eddy in a wider tide of economic advance from which both England and France benefited.

The negotiation of the peace had also given George III the opportunities which war denied him at his accession, of putting affairs in the hands of his favourite, Bute. Pitt, unable to carry his demand for immediate war against Spain, had resigned in October 1761; subsequently converted to the Spanish war, Newcastle and Hardwicke resigned the following May, when they found Bute rigidly supporting the king's insistence upon a peace, and gaining steadily in influence in the ministry. George Grenville (now politically separated from his brother Lord Temple) and

---

[1] Of obscure Irish origin; was in India for some years before 1740 when he entered the company's service: rose steadily after 1748; returned to England December 1752; director of the company 1755; deputy chairman 1757; chairman 1758–64.

the duke of Bedford came in to fill the gaps, and in October 1762 Fox was brought into the ministry to get the peace terms through the Commons. Newcastle had encouraged many of his friends and protégés to remain in office, hoping that, as in 1756, he would make a speedy return, but during the Christmas recess Fox gave a decisive demonstration of the tenor of royal favour by a wholesale dismissal of the duke's parliamentary associates. Amidst great outcry this purge extended even to his creatures in the civil service; for many of these, alternative provision was made, but no such upheaval had been seen for a generation, and many civil servants already assumed that they had a life interest in offices which they held technically during royal pleasure. Vacancies were filled by friends of the king, Bedford and Fox.

The king had thus established his favourite not only in office but in power, but already with results very different from his expectation. George had been reared on the patriot programme worked out by his father with the opposition leaders, and had acquired a pathological distaste for all politicians from what he regarded as the 'desertion' of Pitt and other friends. Immature as they were, Bute and he grossly exaggerated the present cohesion of the leading politicians of the late reign, but they began with platitudinous intentions of introducing a reign of virtue, accompanied by interested promptings to break party from Leicester House and Tory quarters which recalled the commencement of the two previous reigns. Lacking roots of his own in English politics, Bute found that as Pitt would not serve, he must co-operate with one of the parties, and consequently his reign of virtue was introduced by Henry Fox, who of all politicians most equated politics with patronage.

Unlike his master, Bute never learned to battle with the storms of politics. He carried the peace terms by great majorities, but was viciously attacked by Wilkes in the press, and, as a business recession set in, personally experienced the mob violence which the City Radicals could command; his efforts to court support in Tory and independent quarters were frustrated, and Pitt was temporarily reunited with the Pelhams by the Cider Bill promoted by the Chancellor of the Exchequer, Dashwood. On 8 April 1763 Bute resigned. Fox also retired from the leadership of the Commons and, keeping his lucrative office of paymaster-general, ended his active career by taking the title of Lord Holland. Little as he liked him, Fox could see no alternative to a government led by Grenville. Narrowly based upon Grenville's few followers and the Bedford connection, the new government seemed too weak to endure, but in fact it lasted for two years, and united two of the political groupings which eventually formed part of the strong court party created in the 'seventies.

Grenville had grown up in politics with Pitt, Temple and his family and had only lately revealed a pronounced streak of stubbornness. Breaking from his old moorings in favour of peace, he had been repudiated by

Temple when he took the lead in the Commons in 1761. Nor would he yield in approaching the two great issues of the day, Wilkes and America; a similar degree of consistency was forced upon his Pelhamite opponents and thus contributed to the rebirth of party. At first stubbornness formed a bond between the king and Grenville, and when no. 45 of Wilkes' *North Briton* was published on 23 April 1763 containing a vicious attack upon the king, the secretaries of state issued a general warrant for Wilkes' arrest. This procedure, followed only after the law officers of the crown had been consulted, had hitherto been confined to times of national emergency. Wilkes was cleared by the courts, began retaliatory proceedings, and though expelled from the House without difficulty, presented the opposition with a promising issue. Early in 1764 Meredith and Savile, supported by the wilder young men of the Pelham connection, began a series of motions on the legal issues raised by Wilkes, and on 14 February reduced the ministerial majority to ten votes. It was at this point that the king and Grenville were most determined to resist. A year later the opposition again pressed the government hard on general warrants, but once more failed to hold their forces together.

While the political world could raise a frenzy on the subject of Wilkes, Grenville's measures for raising a revenue in America slipped through quietly with no anticipation of the violent opposition they speedily aroused across the Atlantic. Nor did his dismissal owe anything to such fundamental issues. George III came to detest Grenville's manner, and his opposition to the influence of Bute behind the scenes. It was doubtless suspicion of Bute which led the ministry to attempt to exclude the Princess Mother (with whom Bute was popularly associated) from the list of possible regents, an episode which the king came to regard as deception, and which made him more determined than ever to change his administration. In the present weak state of the opposition such a change could not be construed as royal weakness. The opposition of Newcastle and his friends suffered from the duke's initial distaste for opposition, his inability to organise and his tendency to submit against his judgement to the promptings of the younger men; it was hampered by the ambition nursed by Hardwicke's sons, and weakened worst of all by the aloofness of Pitt, who would never forgive their opposition to the Spanish war in 1761. Much as he despised Newcastle and his friends, however, the king had no option but to turn to them now. The cabinet held together, and in their desire to exclude the influence of Bute, the Grenville clan sank their differences, and made a working alliance with the Bedford connection; Pitt also, though fearing nothing from Bute, resolved not to enter office. With the Grenvilles, Bedfords and Pitt standing together, the king had to admit Newcastle's friends *en bloc*.

At the age of seventy-two Newcastle resolved to put into force the plan he had attempted in 1762, to exercise influence in the ministry without taking office; to the surprise of the general public therefore, Rockingham, hitherto known only for his passion for horse-racing, became First Lord of the Treasury. Few ministries have ever begun less prosperously. The king was annoyed by extensive dismissals designed to compensate the whig innocents massacred in 1763, Newcastle because dismissals were too few. The duke of Cumberland, the chief advocate of the ministry in the closet, died before Parliament met. Above all the ministry was formed on the assumption that Pitt would join later, and provide much needed leadership in the Commons, but Pitt knew he had only to wait to receive power on his own terms. The ministry began by serving the causes they had adopted in opposition; they repealed the cider tax and humoured the City Radicals by protecting the Spitalfields silk industry, and declaring general warrants illegal. In the hope that pursuing Pitt's policy might bring him in, they repealed the Stamp Act, but passed another 'declaratory' of the full sovereignty of Parliament. Pitt, however, was not to be won, and not only did the Grenville and Bedford connections stand by their Stamp Act, but many Tories and King's Friends urged the folly of yielding to American resistance. Lacking all confidence in themselves the ministry seemed likely to break up at any time after January 1766, the final blow being delivered by a hostile Pitt who ostentatiously dissociated himself from party, and offered the king the prospect of forming a ministry independent of the Grenvilles.

The Rockinghams ascribed their fall to the subversive activities of Bute's party, directed against them by the king. Certainly the Rockinghams were so short of parliamentary talent that they had to employ some of Bute's men of business, and the king not only wished to strengthen their government by taking in more, but actually consulted Bute when finally convinced that the ministry was breaking up. But much else is obscure. Bute's party, doubtless more accurately known as the King's Friends, formed only at the end of Grenville's ministry, when a group of men of business, Scots members, and others who had formed connections with Bute before 1763 found themselves threatened by the Prime Minister's violence against 'the Favourite' and his determination to monopolise the Scottish patronage. They had still less to hope for from Rockingham, and on his appointment some, such as Jenkinson, resigned while others were turned out to compensate the martyrs of '63. At Rockingham's insistence the king warned the group to support the new ministers, but conformity could not be secured to measures as controversial as the repeal of the Stamp Act, nor to a government with such precarious prospects of survival. The evidence concerning Bute's relations with the king and the King's Friends in these years is tenuous and contradictory; the other parties probably harboured exaggerated suspicions, for in January 1766 the King's Friends regarded themselves as the basis for a ministry only if some fresh leader could be found, and when in the following summer the king became estranged from Bute, they began individually to seek security in other ways.

In July 1766 George III gave Pitt plenary authority to form an administration, and at last there seemed a prospect of a stable ministry which could commend itself to both crown and Parliament. Pitt himself had been the great disrupting force since his resignation. Neither government nor opposition had been able to neglect or rely upon him, but now he enjoyed the supreme authority he had refused to share, and a degree of royal confidence denied to both Grenville and Rockingham. Yet Pitt's efforts to break party speedily drove the three parties into opposition, and before his resignation they had hardened into the form which they were to assume during the American Revolution. Pitt himself took the privy seal and a peerage, brought with him his personal following, and proposed to exercise the superintending authority himself; Northington was the only intimate of the king in the cabinet; Conway and Grafton came in from the Rockingham group. Rockingham nevertheless strove to get Conway out of office, and others of his friends resigned as a result of dismissals in the household. After much hesitation the Bedfords also stood firm, and Chatham was driven back upon Bute's men of business who were themselves uncertain which way to go. To complete the ruin of his bold imperial policies and projected Russian alliance, Chatham succumbed to acute mental illness early in 1767, and shut himself up unwilling to see anyone.

At any time Chatham would have found it difficult to hold together a ministry composed on the one side of his discordant friends Grafton and Shelburne, and on the other of the insubordinate Conway and Charles Townshend; but now contentious issues in India and America cut across both government and opposition. Encouraged by the triumph of the 'bulls' who had secured the raising of the East India Company's dividend against the advice of the directors, Chatham threatened the company with a parliamentary intervention designed to exact cash for the relief of an embarrassed budget, a plan which Townshend and Conway opposed in favour of negotiations with the directors. At once the factions within the company linked up with the factions in Parliament, and the government might have split had not Chatham's withdrawal from politics enabled Shelburne to secure a compromise; the company should pay the state £400,000 per annum, without any relief from its territorial responsibilities, and its dividends should be limited. This settlement paid scant regard to the fundamental problems of empire which had been raised, and augured further political intervention both by its temporary nature and by the provisions to regulate dividends and split voting which had been incidentally introduced. Meanwhile, almost unnoticed, the erratic Townshend laid up fresh trouble by giving an unauthorised promise in the House to extract a revenue from America to support the garrisons there.

Weak as the government was, the divided opposition seemed still weaker, but by the summer of 1767 it was clear that there could be no stability without a coalition, either a coalition of opposition factions as some of the opposition men of business hoped, or a coalition between the government and a section of the opposition. In July 1767 Grafton was empowered by the king to buy off part of the opposition, and favoured an approach to the Bedfords. Conway, on the other hand, favoured the Rockinghams, whose hostility to Grenville might endear them to the king. Rockingham, however, would only consider reconstructing the entire government on the basis of a coalition so wide as to deprive the king of any alternative choice, a coalition beyond his power to construct. Fruitless as they seemed, these negotiations marked an important moment in constitutional development. Rockingham acknowledged the king's right to choose his minister, yet refused office under the leadership of Grafton, and sought to confine the king's choice to himself. Even the support of the Grenvilles and Bedfords he would accept only on the terms of his own supremacy. Moreover with the Rockinghams refusing office, and the king still hostile to Grenville, it was inevitable that the ministry should turn to the Bedford group, and it was almost certain that the latter, led by the ageing duke and the grasping Rigby, would accept subordination to Grafton in office rather than subordination to Rockingham in opposition. In December 1767 the bargaining was complete, and, as an unwitting consequence, the balance in the cabinet was tilted against a policy of conciliation in America.

At the general election of 1768 the opposition somewhat increased their strength, but the court was in a much stronger position at the end than at the beginning of this Parliament. The first victim of the new circumstances was Shelburne. Faithful to Chatham's imperial policies, he was alone in opposing the use of strong measures in America and the expulsion of Wilkes; Grafton, faithful to Chatham's hopes of conciliating the Bedfords, dismissed him in October 1768, and found that Chatham resigned with him.

The issues raised by John Wilkes not only drove the Chathamites from the government, but finally brought down Grafton himself. Wilkes returned to England in 1768 and was elected M.P. for Middlesex. After provoking both king and ministers he was again expelled in 1769 for publishing a libel, and, three times re-elected, was declared ineligible by the House, and his seat awarded to his defeated opponent. Two years' imprisonment made Wilkes an unrivalled hero with the democracy of the metropolis, and an important political figure in his own right. Although it was normal in the eighteenth century for ministries to create majorities, it was commoner for oppositions to appeal to opinion outside the House than to conspire at court, and to appeal especially to the independent gentry, and to two corporations totally dissimilar except in their love of opposition, the University of Oxford and the City of London. 'City

Radicalism' was unique in English politics; it thrived upon the bourgeois pride of the London tradesmen and their sense of exclusion from a political system contrived mainly for the benefit of the landed classes and the great monied men. That Wilkes was now able to mobilise the force of London with peculiar success was due to two chief factors. In the past his cause had been taken up by the opposition factions of Chatham and Rockingham for their own ends. Urgently in need of some fresh impulse, they now began to seek an interest in the City, and Wilkes used the competition between them to exploit the City's resentment at subordination to either opposition or government, aristocracy or crown. Then, secondly, unlike Beckford and Barnard, the earlier prophets of City Radicalism, Wilkes took advantage of his persecutions, of the pecuniary support of those who regarded him as a martyr, and of the appalling condition of local government in Westminster and other parts of the metropolis, to become a master of mob politics; indeed it was difficult to find opponents to him in the Middlesex elections. By these means for a few years Wilkes drove the official opposition connections out of the City, and compelled them to advocate radical measures which they disliked and which injured their parliamentary interests.

The Wilkes question provided common ground for the opposition factions in 1769, and as disturbances grew worse, the prospects of the cabinet became increasingly precarious. Sensing the opportunity, Chatham came back to the Lords in January 1770, made common cause with Rockingham, and used all his influence to bring Camden and Granby out of the ministry. Charles Yorke was pressed into the chancellorship by the king, but died immediately, perhaps by his own hand. Deserted by these colleagues, abandoned by many independents in the Commons, mortified by the vicious pamphleteering of Junius, Grafton himself resigned, as did the timorous Conway.

Once again the king must press into service whom he could, and his choice fell upon Lord North, a non-party politician of remotely Tory origin and conservative instincts. Lord North's merits as a minister in the Commons were immediately to be tested, for a crumbling government afforded the maximum encouragement to the opposition who sank their differences in an onslaught on the ministry. On one important issue— Grenville's Election Act, which transferred the trial of election petitions from the whole House to a select committee—North was defeated, but on the questions thrown up by Wilkes and the City Radicals on which the opposition took their stand, he triumphed by moderate but decisive margins. Already the cause of Wilkes had begun to stale; it had driven independent opinion towards the ministry, and was a source of ill-concealed differences among the opposition factions. The Rockinghams thought little of the 'bill of rights men' whose cause was being vehemently championed by Chatham.

As the next session opened on 13 November 1770 the opposition was weakened further by the death of Grenville, whose adherents followed their old Bedford allies into the new court connection. An attempt to exploit an international crisis arising from the occupation of the Falkland Isles revealed the real weakness of the opposition, and with the ministry strengthened early in 1771 by the adhesion of Wedderburn, opposition declined. On major issues Chatham and Rockingham could rarely agree; the routine labour of maintaining a connection was despicable to the one, and irksome to the other. When war broke out in America Chatham was no longer of consequence, and the Rockingham connection was dying by slow degrees. As in 1765, so now, a recrudescence of imperial issues and sorry failures on the part of government were necessary to revive their fortunes.

Thus favoured by the disillusionment of the opposition, North's system held firm for almost a decade. Cordially supported by the king, whose hour seemed now to have struck, the ministry was sustained by the labours of professional administrators among the King's Friends—John Robinson, Jeremiah Dyson, Charles Jenkinson—men of ability, though accused of all manner of villainy by the Rockinghams. North's solid if unspectacular parliamentary talents made the best of a favourable situation. Wilkes, the disturbances in America, and a militant liberal agitation for the repeal of clerical subscription to the Thirty-Nine Articles, were all driving independents of conservative inclinations towards the court, and North, all things to all men, seized this opportunity both within the House and without. Too sensitive to parliamentary opinion to be an adamant defender of the religious establishment, North was nevertheless elected Chancellor of the University of Oxford in 1772, and virtually ended the career of that venerable body as an organ of opposition. Imperial issues, however, presaged fresh distress.

After 1767 ministerial concern with the affairs of the East India Company was prolonged by the need to arrange a permanent settlement. By the middle of 1769 an agreement was reached by which the state, without assuming any responsibility for the government of the Indian territories, limited the dividend of the company to $12\frac{1}{2}$ per cent, and imposed severe financial burdens whenever the dividend exceeded 6 per cent. While the internal factions pursued their feuds by borrowing Dutch stock for voting on highly speculative terms, the weaknesses of the company were exposed and the settlement of 1769 rendered obsolete by two great crises. In May 1769 the boom in East India stock was drastically broken by bad news from India, and with the company facing ruin, ministry and opposition went to unparalleled lengths to end the contest at India House. Warren Hastings was chosen as Governor of Bengal with increased powers, but hopes of reform at home were set back by the severest credit crisis yet seen, which hit London in June 1772. With business houses tumbling by the dozen, the company was in a critical position, for it borrowed heavily from the Bank of England twice a year while waiting for the receipts of its twice-yearly sales. Now the company was dunned for payments which would normally have been delayed, while its own receipts came in abnormally slowly. To complete the disaster, the company's dividends and payments to the state had been based on an over-optimistic assessment of its revenues from Bengal, and its purchases there had been financed on a wild scale by bills on London which in any case could not have been met. All palliatives were now swept aside by the need to rescue the company and secure better rule from it in return. Legislation was framed, the most important item of which was North's Regulating Act, which sought to check the worst abuses of the company's operations at home and abroad by the minimum of reform and governmental supervision, and looked to a more radical reorganisation when the charter came up for renewal in 1780. The Rockinghams did their best to exploit the crisis by violent demagogy among the East India proprietors, but made little impression, for the company was now thoroughly discredited.

On subsequent imperial issues, and first of all the Quebec Act of 1774, the opposition connections displayed greater cohesion, and found that the weaknesses of the North ministry, already revealed in the crisis of 1772–3, offered serious grounds for criticism. The machinery of eighteenth-century government was at no time well fitted for the energetic execution of policy, but Lord North's administration was inert and loosely knit beyond the average. Stout and somnolent in person, lacking a political following of his own, North was unusually dependent on avoiding giving offence, and the eclectic East India legislation of 1772–3 was the best settlement negotiable by his able men of business in the absence of genuine political leadership. For such a system, however, the turmoil brewing in America was to prove altogether too stern a test.

Not only the king but the majority of the cabinet had recently favoured firm measures in America, but North's characteristic yielding both to the demands of the opposition leaders in America and to the rallying forces of conservatism at home seemed to justify the worst fears of the Americans without securing any English advantage. There was a similar lack of determination and co-ordination in the conduct of operations once war had broken out. North's indecisiveness discouraged some of the ministers; Dartmouth and Suffolk were ineffective secretaries of state, while the two men of action, Sandwich and Germain, were both unpopular. North himself soon longed for retirement, but he was now the object of the king's possessive affection, somewhat as Bute had been earlier: the king generously paid North's debts, and secured a promise that he would not desert as long as his service was required. As disasters in America mounted, North became less a war leader than a martyr, complaining miserably of being 'tied to the stake'. So incapable did he become that for a year after Suffolk's death one secretaryship of state remained unfilled, while Weymouth, on whom the duties of the office devolved, was suspected of flirting with the opposition.

Much therefore depended upon the king and the men of business in the lower ranks of government. This was in many ways the king's finest hour; staunch when all about him seemed to fail, he yet cost the country dear by his lack of imagination, while his resolute determination gradually undermined his precarious mental balance with startling results when once political tension eased. Chief among the men of business was Charles Jenkinson who in 1778 succeeded Barrington as Secretary at War. Barrington had established good general rules for purchase and promotion in the army, but lacked administrative drive and the parliamentary talents now needed; moreover he disapproved of the war and had worked halfheartedly for some time. Jenkinson admirably enforced efficiency and economy in that small sphere of the war effort for which he was responsible: though not a member of the cabinet, by virtue of office he enjoyed frequent access to the king, the head of the armed forces, and the confidence he enjoyed occasioned a legend that he was one of George's tools in a supposed struggle to break ministerial despotism. John Robinson, Secretary to the Treasury, and an archetype of the government servant, was North's perpetual staff, stiffening his resistance to Eden's and Wedderburn's bullying intrigues for promotion, prodding Jenkinson to prod the king to prod the premier; although by 1780 Robinson had become exasperated by North's indifference, a word from the king sufficed to keep him at his post.

The American War not only produced an odd distribution of responsibility in the ministry, but vastly altered the aspect of British politics and administration. In itself the conflict raised urgent issues which inevitably bore fruit in sharper political divisions. Conservative sentiment which had been drifting towards the government for some years, now rallied more strongly. Church, universities and many of the gentry were roused as a century earlier to the defence of the sovereignty of Parliament, and many independents came permanently within the orbit of the court; but the opposition as well as the ministry received new life. For the first time since Wilkes and Middlesex the Rockinghams found themselves in possession of a cause; they were anti-court and anti-war, and were the likeliest beneficiaries from the succession of disasters.

In 1779 and 1780, indeed, the circumstances of Walpole's downfall seemed about to recur on a far more tragic scale. Military defeat and naval peril came to pass in a measure then undreamt of, the more bitter for being unexpected. The hatred between North and Thurlow was common knowledge, cabinet divisions as in Walpole's day encouraged the opposition. Once again France joined the struggle, and now raised the imperial problem in its acutest form. Lord North's Regulating Act gave not even the temporary respite hoped for in India; by the time circumstances were becoming serious for North's ministry at home, troubles in Bengal and at Madras were complicated by the Mahratta War and the attacks of Hyder Ali, and early in 1781 a French fleet was reported off the Coromandel coast. The operation of the system created in 1773 had been left mainly to the overworked Jenkinson and Robinson, but they could not be expected to shape the new Indian settlement promised for 1779 and 1780; before the attacks of a rejuvenated opposition plied with material by Philip Francis, North with his 'distressing fits' was in no condition for statesmanship, and the existing position was prolonged by annual acts until 1781, when further stop-gap legislation was introduced.

Imperial difficulties were felt even more urgently and much nearer home in Ireland also. In 1768, in return for additional troops and money to safeguard the American frontier, the life of the Irish Parliament had been restricted to eight years and a ministry unused to electoral management had had to conduct a general election. The Lord Lieutenant now resigned, and in 1776 was succeeded by Lord Buckinghamshire who hoped to make Ireland useful in the struggle against America by a policy of improvement. Nevertheless serious social problems remained, and the financial position of the Irish government was unhealthy. The American war aggravated every problem. Ireland responded to the example of rebellious dependencies; the threat of French intervention was as real in Ireland as in America. Moreover the war destroyed an important clandestine trade, as well as the French commerce, and led the government to put an embargo upon the export of Irish provisions. It was the more tempting to blame the distress of the country upon the British government as North was known to be not unsympathetic towards Irish demands, and in his pliant way had made concessions both religious and commercial. On 8 April 1778 with North's support five resolutions were carried in the House of Commons removing most of the burden imposed on Ireland by the Navigation System. At once there was a violent reaction from the manufacturing towns of England and Scotland; again the government yielded, and the commercial concessions were whittled almost completely away.

This open sacrifice of Irish prosperity to British vested interests was the more hazardous because it coincided with the growth of the Volunteer movement in Ireland; beginning as a defence against France, the Volunteer movement soon threatened the whole English connection. Just before the storm aroused by the Irish trade bills, North had prepared to concede all American demands short of independence. The moral for Ireland was obvious; non-importation agreements began and control passed to the Volunteers, who rallied both dissenting and Roman Catholic support. In 1779 and 1780, to the accompaniment of provocative speeches from the English opposition, greater economic concessions were finally made than even the Irish leaders hoped for. To complete North's misery legislative independence was now demanded.

With empire tottering both in east and west, the constitution in church and state which had seemed so glorious at the close of the Seven Years War bore a very different aspect, and a legion of critics arose to point out its weaknesses. For some years before the outbreak of war in America the liberal dissenters had given a new lead in controversy, attacking Blackstone's view that by the law of England dissent was a crime of which only the penalties had been removed by the Toleration Act, or ferociously supporting the Anglican liberals in their demand for a less narrow subscription. Now they not only wished prosperity to their brethren in America, but could derive from their notion of the church as a federation of gathered congregations the analogy of a constitutional system providing American Home Rule. The political issues thrown up by the war revived the hopes of the dissenting underworld which had never ceased to publish editions of civil-war tracts; dissenting leaders such as Price came out openly in favour of America and reform; concessions made to Roman Catholics to encourage recruiting during the war could not in justice be denied to Protestant Dissenters; and as Lord North, Chancellor of the University of Oxford, gradually chiselled away the bulwarks of church and state he had been elected to defend, an important movement for parliamentary reform and the repeal of the Test and Corporation Acts gathered force among the Dissenters.

There were critics of economic orthodoxy too, even though in wartime when the Navigation System was partially suspended there was always evidence of the benefit which it normally conferred upon English shipping; the proportion of foreign tonnage entering British ports rose from 13 per cent in 1775 to 36 per cent in 1782. The shock of rebellion extended the influence of those such as Josiah Tucker and Adam Smith who were already critical of the system of economic regulation by which the 'dependency' of the colonies had been ensured. The Irish tariff disputes showed that British industry had not yet outgrown the desire for protected markets for its products, but the ideas were already in circulation which underlay the foundation of the second British empire.

The most immediate problem posed by the war, however, was budgetary rather than commercial. The English tax structure was relatively inelastic, and in consequence, a very high proportion of the cost of the Seven Years War had been met by borrowing.[1] The increased cost of the national debt reduced the scope for tax relief when peace returned; it took a surprise by the opposition to reduce the land-tax from its full rate of

---

[1] 43·4 per cent of all government receipts from 1756 to 1763 were raised by net borrowing; how far war expenditure in particular was met from this source may be illustrated by comparing the first with the last great year of the war—total expenditure in 1762 exceeded that of 1756 by £9·79m.; net borrowing in 1762 exceeded that of 1756 by £7·34m.

four shillings to three shillings in the pound in 1767. Chancellors cast about for a revenue from America or India, and a section of the gentry who rallied to the Rockinghams during the American War concluded gloomily that the tax system was so inelastic that another war must bring disaster, and hence that peace must be preserved at any price.

The alliance of the United Provinces with the enemy in 1780 created a new embarrassment by cutting off an important source of credit; fortunately for the government, English estimates of Dutch holdings in the national debt had generally been exaggerated, and the American War was financed by borrowing to almost the same extent as the Seven Years War. Of necessity North added to the duties on articles of popular consumption to service the debt, and, regarding an income tax as an administrative impossibility, sought to tap the increasing total of personal incomes by taxes on expenditure—house rents, servants, horses, carriages, dogs and the like. The new work fell mainly upon the window-tax administration, and especially upon the surveyors whose duty was to keep up the assessments. Under pressure from his civil servants, North introduced reforms into this branch of the administration, and appointed inspectors to supervise the surveyors.

The tax yield increased little, however, until the later years of the war, but the burden contributed to the political crisis as the general election of 1780 approached. Dislike of taxation, and fear lest the land-tax be reassessed, entered into the Yorkshire, and still more the Middlesex reforming movement. Wyvill conceived that with the general election near, his association might bring about a reduction in civil-list expenditure. He hoped to unite the reformers of various counties with the object of strengthening the independent elements of the constitution, if need be to impose sanctions by refusing to pay taxes, or by supporting only parliamentary candidates who would uphold their objects, and cast a friendly eye upon the techniques of resistance evolved in Ireland and America. The Rockinghams sought to turn the reform movement to their own purposes, but they were outmanœuvred by Wyvill who turned the General Meeting of Deputies, the London committee on which the county associations were represented, into a vehicle of his personal authority. Rockingham, however, taunted the Yorkshire men with the fact that the comparatively heavy parliamentary representation of their county had helped to shield them from taxation, an embarrassment which did not trouble the reformers from the heavily taxed urban areas of Middlesex; and the reform movement finally split when Wyvill concluded that if they were to accomplish anything at all they must compromise with the Rockinghams, and demand triennial instead of annual parliaments.

The Rockinghams meanwhile had sought to profit from the crisis by demanding economical reform. To prune the administration, it was alleged, would both ease the budgetary problem, and redress the balance of the constitution against the crown. From 1777 Barré was moving resolutions for inquiries into the land-tax administration, and in 1780 Burke moved his Economical Reform Bill which was designed to reduce expenditure in the king's household. It was not North's way to oppose the principle of the bill outright, but he defeated it in detail. Moreover the debates on the bill consumed time needed for the discussion of the numerous petitions for reform which had come in from the country. These were finally discussed together on 6 April 1780, the very day on which the Westminster Association, to the accompaniment of banners and an inflammatory speech from Charles James Fox, met for its second assembly. In the House Dunning surprised the ministry by moving two resolutions which epitomised the pleas of the petitioners, the first of which declared 'that the influence of the Crown has increased, is increasing and ought to be diminished'.

This claim, stimulated no doubt by the furious closet activity of the last couple of years, had been implicit throughout Burke's campaign, and underlay Crewe's bill for the disfranchisement of revenue officers: it was however in important respects untrue, and the wild allegations with which the debates of this period abound illustrate the ignorance of the technicalities of administration which prevailed in parliamentary circles. The number of revenue officers entitled to vote in elections, and of government pensioners in the House of Commons were both greatly exaggerated by Dunning and his friends, and by 1780 the numbers both of placemen in the House of Commons and of parliamentary seats at the disposal of the Treasury had declined significantly since the beginning of the reign. However, Dunning sounded a traditional chord in the ears of the independent members too loudly to be disregarded; his famous motion was carried by 233 votes to 215, his second without opposition. But he was incapable of exploiting his success. Crewe's bill was defeated in the Commons, the Contractors' bill in the Lords; a recess during Newmarket week gave time for the spirit of battle to subside; Dunning's efforts to turn the present House into a Long Parliament until royal influence should be diminished alienated independent support; and before the general election the Gordon Riots had once more rallied conservative opinion to the government.

Thus the concurrence of crises in the cabinet, in the country, and in Irish, American and East Indian affairs failed to uproot the government, but the ministers gained nothing from the premature dissolution of 1780, and there was no fundamental improvement in the political situation. An East India settlement had been merely postponed. In 1780 very extensive commercial concessions, access to the colonial trade, and relief to Dissenters from the sacramental test were granted to the Irish, but agitation continued. In 1781 an Irish Habeas Corpus Bill was granted and in the following year Grattan won legislative independence. In England the petitioning movement became divided, and the energies of the county committees were diverted into less spectacular channels. Majorities against economical reform increased, but Parliament still called for papers, and the Commissioners on the Public Accounts whom North was driven to appoint in 1780 proved to be the forerunners of many more independent commissions of inquiry. Their reports spread over the next six years dispelled much of the ignorance of politicians in matters administrative; they set forth a plan of improvement by which the performance of ministries might be judged; and both by their reports and by their individual labours the members of the commission set a pattern for reform in the machinery of government.

Constant too was North's desire to withdraw from office and the tide of military disaster. In America, the West Indies and Minorca there were defeats, and the French fleet threatened both in home and Indian waters. In February and March 1782 independent supporters of the ministry began to ebb away and to swell the minority demanding peace. On 19 March a group of country gentlemen gave North notice that they could support him no longer and on the following day the ministry resigned. All attempts to secure support for the ministry failed, as did the king's endeavours to exclude Fox from office, and at last Rockingham received the opportunity of forming a ministry.

The tactics which Rockingham had pursued in 1767 implied a marked diminution of what most politicians considered to be the king's legitimate powers; the king's influence in the constitution, and the stubbornness of his character were now to be fully tested. The king had identified himself with the American War for which a parliamentary majority could no longer be maintained; Rockingham furthermore insisted that the king agree to legislation permanently impairing royal patronage. The second Rockingham ministry, a coalition of the Prime Minister's followers with Shelburne and the Chathamites, proved even more brief and inglorious than the first. Ireland could not be denied the legislative independence which the Rockinghams claimed for America, and Burke passed his Civil Establishment Bill; but this succeeded neither in abolishing permanently the third Secretary of State, nor in stopping overspending on the Civil List. Crewe's bill at last reached the statute book, but proved of no immediate effect; Clarke's act excluded government contractors from the House without reforming the system of government contracting. The king behaved more icily towards Rockingham than to any other Prime Minister he ever had, and the ancient grudge which the Rockinghams had borne Chatham exacerbated their relations with their Chathamite colleagues. The end came barely three months after the beginning with the death of Rockingham. To keep Shelburne from office Fox audaciously claimed that the cabinet had the right to elect its own head, and proposed the duke of Portland. This claim, not even favoured by all of his own followers, was rejected and brought about his resignation.

Shelburne's new ministry contained Chathamites of two generations. Of the older generation were the Prime Minister himself, Grafton and Camden; the young William Pitt, to procure whom Shelburne had pressed Rockingham in vain, became Chancellor of the Exchequer, and with him came his later henchman, Dundas (already prominent in the Commons and in Scottish politics), and his relatives, Lord Temple and William Grenville. The strength of the new ministry in the Commons was reckoned at between 130 and 140, North's group at 120, and Fox's at almost 90, the remaining members being unclassified. To pass the peace terms with America the ministry must at all costs prevent an alliance of the two other parties. Shelburne, however, devoted no great pains to managing his cabinet, much less the Commons; the political descendants of Rockingham were still thirsting for any means to overcome those of Chatham, even at the price of an alliance with North. On his side North must improve his prospects of a return to office if his following was to hold together, and deprive Shelburne of the credit of ending the war which he himself had waged so ineffectively. Shelburne acted too late to prevent the coalition between Fox and North and was forced from office before the end of February 1783.

Fox's friends now refused to serve except under Portland, who was inspired by Fox to eliminate the personal power of the king by demanding a free hand, particularly in the appointment of junior ministers. The king held out as long as he could in the hope that Pitt might save him, but Pitt, emulating his father's contempt for aristocratic faction, made no move, and even in November 1783 Fox had hopes of winning him. The king, given to moodiness from his youth, sulked continuously, and displayed his hostility to his ministers by refusing to create peerages. Nevertheless the ministers began the session with an overwhelming majority, and the king's preparations came as a surprise.

By the second week in December John Robinson had concluded from a careful parliamentary survey that there was no hope of a majority for another ministry in this parliament, but that a substantial majority could be obtained after a general election. By this time also Fox had already presented the king with an issue in the shape of his East India Bill. As early as 1778 John Robinson had drafted a scheme for an East India settlement which underlay the legislation of the next decade, but nothing of consequence was achieved owing to the growing disintegration of the North ministry, the breakdown of their system of management in the company, and the emergence of the disorders in the company into a bitter political issue. The ministries of Rockingham and Shelburne had succumbed before accomplishing anything. So precarious were the company's finances, and so vociferous its critics, that a settlement could no longer be deferred. Fox's bill proposed radically to reduce the powers of the company and to transfer them to a body of Commissioners appointed in the act for a term of years. By this means Fox hoped to act consistently with the past declarations of his party and to secure reform in India without increasing the power of either governor-general or crown. Fox's enemies in the company resisted bitterly, they beat the drum of respect for charters, they insisted that Fox was seizing the patronage of a continent whether he could hold his ground in office or not. Moreover the furor drew to the king and to one another a number of enterprising and able men, Dundas, Pitt, Jenkinson, Thurlow and some of North's friends, including John Robinson. Robinson's intimate familiarity with the mechanism of the Commons and India House was of the greatest immediate importance; of more ultimate significance was the young Pitt, and, having secured the rejection of the East India Bill in the House of Lords, the king turned to him to form a government on 18 December.

Pitt's motives at this stage of his career have always been a matter of dispute. He could hardly have played his cards better had he, as Fox believed, been animated mainly by ambition. But Pitt had the self-conscious purity of his father, the same assurance of his mission to rule, and as English politics settled down after the war, perhaps concluded that now was the time to fulfil in alliance with the king the bent for administrative and fiscal reform which he derived from his Grenville ancestors. At any rate with the king's backing he refused to withdraw before the ferocious onslaughts of a numerically superior opposition in the House of Commons.

Not till March, by which time Fox's majority had crumbled away, did Pitt dissolve the House. This delay enabled Robinson to turn his election forecasts of December into firm agreements with the borough patrons, and as independent members flowed in after the Christmas recess, and Fox committed mistakes, the opposition appeared increasingly as a spent force. The election when finally held proved to be the foundation of Pitt's whole system, for about seventy of the opposition members, including some of the leaders, lost their seats. The election, however, was not different in kind from those of earlier years. Robinson organised furiously, but his forecasts were more accurate in general than in detail, and although the East India Company campaigned vigorously for the ministry, they could hardly do more than they had done in the past. In some places too there was a genuine public reaction in favour of the ministry.

The new cabinet included Thurlow and Gower, two old Bedford whigs who had abandoned North; two of Pitt's friends, Leeds and Rutland; Sydney, a Shelburne Whig; Howe at the Admiralty, and the radical Richmond. This cabinet and an electoral victory were not enough to keep Pitt safe. No Prime Minister could avoid becoming a party leader in the sense that he was bound to collect followers who formed a favourable estimate of his chances of retaining office; but no one ever gave himself to party leadership with less enthusiasm than Pitt, and in 1788 his following was computed at only fifty-two, of whom only twenty would keep their places if he lost office, as compared with a Fox–North group of over 150. Since Shelburne's political reputation made him an impossible ally Pitt depended therefore on 'the party of the crown', and (like his father) on the support he could win amongst the independent members. The parliamentary situation influenced both the composition and the policies of the ministry. Retrenchment and reform were policies congenial not merely to Pitt's temperament and brief political record, but also to the independent members, and in Pitt's hands the 'country' traditions of the past were turned to the wholesale transformation of the machinery of government. Such a policy required able men of business. John Robinson now retired to comparative obscurity, but in 1786 Charles Jenkinson returned at the head of the recently revived Board of Trade with a peerage, and the ambitious William Eden obtained a place and a commercial mission to France.

The ruling influence in the government was in the hands of men not dissimilar in type. Henry Dundas, too fond of office, women and money, was yet of vast capacity for work, and not without idealism, as is shown by his plan for an East India settlement which Pitt passed into law in 1784 and in subsequent amending acts. Of similar capacity was Pitt's cousin, William Wyndham Grenville, joint paymaster-general, vice-president of the Board of Trade, and Speaker in 1789, who with Pitt made up the active triumvirate in the ministry. As the years passed the narrow basis of the ministry as a personal, almost family, affair became more pronounced. The real weakness of the government should the ministers give offence to independent members or some of their own supporters was spectacularly revealed more than once. In 1785 Pitt's efforts to introduce a low reciprocal tariff with Ireland were defeated, and his proposals for parliamentary reform revealed a further weakness. Pitt had taken office as the saviour of the king, but George III had left the question of reform open and claimed to have done his duty by allowing the measure to come forward and by not influencing anyone against it. The cabinet, however, was divided, the fact that the king was known to be hostile also influenced the court party, and some even of the gentry who would have gained most from the bill were deterred by fear that land-tax reform might follow parliamentary reform; all these factors contributed to the defeat of the bill, and of a cause which Pitt never resumed.

The question of royal support was acutely raised again by the king's insanity in 1788. With the king no longer capable of exercising his powers, Pitt's parliamentary majority began to ebb away, and a party in the cabinet recommended a coalition with the opposition. Pitt, however, successfully played for time. During the crisis he profited from a wave of sentimental middle-class royalism, and gained permanently from the king's gradual withdrawal from politics of which his mental breakdown was only one of many causes.

In subsequent years the minister went warily as well as the king. In 1788 Pitt, who had ordered an inquiry by the Board of Trade, gave notice that he would take action against the slave-trade in the next session, against the abuses of which he was disposed both by personal conviction and by his friendship with Wilberforce. But the cabinet was divided on the question; the vested interests in the great ports which had so often supported Pitt in the past now turned against him; there were Tories who thought the anti-slavery agitation a dissenting manœuvre (despite the support given to it by the University of Oxford); in the end Pitt refused to take the initiative, and only a minor measure promoted by Dolben, to improve the treatment of slaves during their ocean passage, was obtained. Similarly on the questions of the repeal of the Test and Corporation Acts and of parliamentary reform Pitt abandoned the initiative. Doubtless his experience of power and his sense that it was now dangerous, let alone ungrateful, to press the king to distasteful policies, blunted the edge of his youthful appetite for reform. Doubtless also he was unwilling to risk his still precarious majority in controversial causes. But most of all the serious business of government consisted not in legislation, but in the conduct of foreign affairs, and in enlightened administration.

The permanent achievement of Pitt's peacetime government was, indeed, its fiscal and administrative policy. In this sphere Pitt appeared at his weakest in his approach to the budgetary problem. North had attempted to pay for the American war by taxes on luxuries and by loans serviced largely by duties on articles of popular consumption; as the cost of servicing the national debt had increased during the war by about 60 per cent there was no prospect of peacetime relief from the land-tax. The urgent need was to increase the elasticity of the tax system by a tax on income, the most popularly canvassed form of which was a reassessed land-tax. Pitt, however, was prolific in the nostrums favoured by North, and poured forth taxes on horses of all varieties, on male and female servants, and stiffened the window duties; even after war broke in 1793 he still clung to duties on hair powder, dogs, clocks and watches, caustically described by Lord Sheffield as 'calculated to please elderly ladies, or men who merit that description'. Not until 1797–8, by which time only a third of the cost of the war was being met by taxation and Consols had dropped to 50, was Pitt driven to introduce the taxation which had so long been necessary.

The reason for Pitt's ineffectiveness in this matter was no doubt that he was under strong public pressure to provide against calamity in another way. On the eve of the formation of his government the Commissioners on the Public Accounts had sought to alarm the nation into paying off the debt by voluntary contributions. By 1785 Pitt was hoping for a million-pound surplus annually in Walpole's old sinking fund, and sought advice in various quarters to remedy so apparently overwhelming an evil as the national debt. The new sinking fund established in 1786 bore the marks of the report of the Commissioners on the Public Accounts, for the most stringent precautions were taken not only to guarantee an annual surplus of one million pounds, but to consecrate it inviolably to debt redemption. These surpluses were increased by fresh legislation in 1792, the last year of peace. Thus the revenue surpluses which might have enabled Pitt to gild the pill of an overhauled tax structure were diverted to what influential voices urged as the most pressing need, the reduction of the national debt. This scruple proved doubly unfortunate on the outbreak of the revolutionary wars; on the one hand Pitt could screw no appreciable extra yield from the existing tax system, and on the other he was driven by the prime merit of the sinking fund—its inviolability—to consume revenue in unprofitable debt redemption.

There were great advances, however, in many branches of fiscal administration, though some major tasks remained unperformed when war broke out. One of the causes to which the Commissioners on the Public Accounts returned most insistently was the need for improved auditing. The object of the Exchequer system was to stop peculation, and it neither informed the government of its overall financial standing, nor kept public accountants up to date with their accounting. Already opinion was turning against a system by which Henry Fox after eight years as Paymaster-General (1757–65) had made an average unofficial profit on balances remaining in his hands of £23,657 annually for the rest of his life; that his profits were enormous was generally inferred from the vast sums he laid out in purchases of lands, and in payment of his sons' debts. He was further suspected of using information and money derived from official sources for purposes of stock-market speculations. Fox's successor, Rigby, was known also to have profited greatly during the American War. For the offices of both the Treasurer of the Navy and the Paymaster-General the commissioners recommended that private holdings of public funds should cease, and cash should be deposited at the Bank of England in the name of the Treasurer in his official capacity, not as an individual. This principle was adopted in an act promoted by Dundas in 1785 and was afterwards extended to all the departments of revenue and expenditure. The provision that balances should pass automatically from a Treasurer to his successor was more than an administrative convenience, it effected a revolution in the status of public office by creating the notion of an impersonal Treasurership executed by a succession of individuals. The act failed to prevent a notorious evasion by Dundas himself but it represented legislative affirmation of the objects to be attained. Furthermore, the creation of official accounts at the Bank facilitated an important reform introduced by Pitt in 1787, the establishment of the Consolidated

Fund into which all public receipts were paid, and from which all expenses were met.

In the revenue departments there were important changes both in method and personnel. Under Pitt senior civil-service appointments went less frequently than in the past to members of families with electoral influence in the boroughs, and more often to professional administrators of ability, who also contributed to the cause of reform. The commutation tax, designed to check smuggling by substituting an extra window tax for most of the tea duties, was based on a plan which had been discussed in the Customs Board for some years; another scheme, championed by the Commissioners on the Public Accounts, the consolidation of the customs duties, was also hatched in the department, and worked out in detail by two distinguished customs officials, William Stiles and Richard Frewin. In the sphere of direct taxation, Pitt introduced important changes among the surveyors, the local officials appointed to keep up the rating to the assessed taxes. They were to treat their duties as full-time employment, they were to be appointed only after examination and a period of instruction, and were to be encouraged by the prospect of promotion as inspectors. Inspectors had been first appointed to supervise the surveyors by Lord North; the grade was now reformed, enlarged and put to good use against defaulting taxpayers. The inspectors were the lineal ancestors of the modern inland-revenue inspectors, and the whole machinery of local rating to the assessed taxes was now ready to be adopted for the income tax. Furthermore, despite a substantial increase in the total yield of the assessed taxes, Pitt brought about a marked reduction in balances of public cash in the hands of the receivers.

Some progress was made in accordance with other principles enunciated by the Commissioners on the Public Accounts. They condemned the payment of civil servants by fees and gratuities, and recommended that a salary be annexed to every office. Hopes of retrenchment damped the enthusiasm of the ministers for this policy, but the issue was crucial in the case of the Auditors of Imprests, whose fees had multiplied greatly with the increase of the budget. After further pressure Pitt replaced them in 1785 by five salaried commissioners under whom the work of other auditors was gradually concentrated. In reporting on the Ordnance Office, the commissioners recommended that the government ought to pay cash for goods and services rather than work on credit, and that they should stimulate competition for their contracts. Pitt now sought competitive tenders for military stores and loans. Certain officials had the exclusive right of supplying the Secretary of State's and other offices with stationery, but in 1787 Pitt established a government stationery office in New Palace Yard which expanded rapidly.

Finally the Commissioners on the Public Accounts very strongly condemned the existence of sinecure and useless offices executed by deputy.

These were particularly numerous in the Customs Office and Exchequer, and suffered savage inroads from the movement for economical reform. Burke's Establishment Act abolished 134 offices in the household and ministry, Shelburne dealt even severer execution both by Treasury regulation and act of parliament, Pitt was estimated to have abolished 765 useless revenue offices in 1789 alone. At this point as at many others the introduction of modern principles of administration had direct political consequences by diminishing the 'influence' of the crown. The waning of that influence, which had begun before 1780, gathered speed steadily thereafter, and contributed to the slow process by which the crown withdrew from the personal exercise of its rights, the cabinet gained in cohesion, and party organisation gained ground in the House of Commons.

Party distinctions were sharpened and the whole temper of politics eventually embittered by the French Revolution. The early stages of the Revolution were widely approved in England, not simply by the convivial Revolution Societies which revived in 1788 to celebrate the glories of the English Revolution, but by those who were glad to see the diplomatic power of France crippled. Nevertheless fresh reforming societies took inspiration from events across the Channel, supported especially by a number of liberal dissenters whose unitarian theology was subject to even severer legal discrimination than their political ambitions. One of them, Dr Price, preached a sermon demanding the repeal of the Test and Corporation Acts which provided a text for Burke's famous *Reflections on the Revolution in France*. The London Revolution Society before which he preached also initiated friendly correspondence with the French revolutionary societies which lasted till February 1792, and encouraged panicky conservatives to identify the society with the excesses committed in France. By this time, however, men much further down the social scale in the London Corresponding Society and other bodies were in the van of the reforming movement, and noble and clerical *émigrés* had awakened the upper classes to the threat which the Revolution carried to both church and aristocracy. In England and still more in Scotland, the wilder reformers entered into equivocal relations with France; Paine and the unitarian Priestley were elected deputies to the National Convention; loyalist and anti-leveller associations sprang up, and in London and the provinces reformers and unitarians were threatened with violence. By November 1792 war with France was plainly imminent. In January 1793 Louis XVI was executed, and the following month France declared war on Great Britain and Holland.

By this time reformers and conservatives had found a gospel in the respective works of Paine and Burke, and the political cleavage had come home directly to members of Parliament with the formation in April 1792 of the Association of the Friends of the People, a society containing Philip Francis and a group of Fox's wilder young adherents, though not Fox himself. Members were subject to a fiery press campaign, and in 1793 Grey's motion for reform, branded by Pitt as revolutionary, was overwhelmed by 281 votes to 41. The political situation altered in two important respects: most of Pitt's repressive measures were carried by overwhelming margins and the days of his unreliable majority were gone; gone also was the one issue, that of parliamentary reform, which had separated him from the king. Pitt's increasing hold on royal favour had been evident in the ministerial changes since the regency crisis, and in 1792 he finally induced the king to dismiss Thurlow. With the Whigs divided openly by Grey's notice of a reform motion, Pitt resolved to offer terms to the conservative group of Whigs and pursued negotiations with them from May 1792 till June 1794.

Pitt afterwards admitted that he had overestimated the divisions among the Whigs created by the formation of the Friends of the People. Pitt and Fox were not far apart in desiring such a measure of parliamentary reform as would secure the people in their liberties, and in regarding the French Revolution as irrelevant to the issue; Fox indeed could see no threat to liberty except from the king, and was embarrassed both by the group of Portland, Fitzwilliam and former followers of North who were terrified of revolution and openly or secretly wished to join the government, and by the noisy group of admirers of things French who had appointed themselves Friends of the People. However, Fox held the party together by urging that they had a good opportunity to displace the government altogether, so weakened had it been by the dismissal of Thurlow, while Pitt kept the door open by supporting the duke of Portland in his election as Chancellor for the University of Oxford and offering him the Garter. By the beginning of 1793, however, none of Fox's gambits against Pitt could disguise the divisions in the Whig party any longer. Secessions began, and it was only Fox's hold on Portland's affections which kept the duke out of office till 1794. Yet Pitt like Fox was still far less influenced by the extremity of politics in France than were the Portland Whigs, who greatly altered the radical character of Pitt's ministry and formed the nucleus of a new conservatism. The French Revolution had accomplished indeed what Wilkes, religious liberalism, and the American War had accomplished only in part; it had created for the first time in English politics a party of order.

At the same time there were important changes of view among the rulers of the church. The rationalism of the enlightenment had deeply eroded respect for the old high church tradition and for the Thirty-Nine Articles as an exposition of the biblical revelation; in 1773 even the University of Oxford maintained subscription to the articles as a university test only from inability to agree on an alternative such as approved itself to the sister university. The efforts of the Feathers Tavern Association and the liberal dissenters in the 'seventies to dispose of clerical subscriptions on rationalist grounds had revealed how hard it was to defend the existing order on the same assumptions; meanwhile the evangelicals, who were steadily gaining influence and numbers both inside and outside the Church of England, and were passionately opposed to the unitarian tendencies of the liberals, reproached the rulers of the church for their lukewarmness towards the full gospel of the articles, especially in the matter of pre-destination. The discomfort of the ruling Arminian party in the church was increased by the fact that Warburton's apologetic for the establish-ment had been based on the utilitarian grounds that the Anglican church held the loyalty of the overwhelming majority of the nation, but now the strength of the Dissenters (including the Methodists) was multiplying at a stupendous rate, especially in Wales and certain parts of the midlands and north. The grant of full civil toleration in Ireland without apparent harm to monarchy and government was a great inspiration to the English Dissenters, who demanded repeal both of the Test and Corporation Acts and of the subscription required under the Toleration Act. In view of the nonconformist revival of the last quarter of the century, such concessions could only strengthen dissent and weaken the establishment.

The bishops therefore almost unanimously opposed further concessions to the Dissenters, and in their charges and sermons counselled the clergy to oppose evangelical enthusiasm by stressing the unity of faith and works, insisting on the authority of the ordained clergy, and improving their own professional standards. The bishops carried Pitt reluctantly with them in their opposition to the Dissenters' claims, and came noisily into the fray upon the downfall of Louis XVI. The attacks upon the church in France turned the war into a crusade in the view of the bishops. In a way then almost forgotten, the bench now took their stand upon revelation, from which both the authority of the state and the principles of Christian con-duct were derived. In this strenuous assault upon the forces of rationalism, attacks upon Methodism died away. Not till the turn of the century, when Napoleon made peace with the French church, did the hierarchy go back to a totally defensive position. Its differing rivals, rational and evangelical dissent, continued to gain ground, with the result, when the threat to the church was renewed in the next age of reform, that a far more violent reassertion of church authority was provoked. Meanwhile evangelicals and bishops had contributed in their respective ways to the growth of romantic thought and sentiment which was to challenge the reign of enlightenment.

The evangelical revival had begun in the 'thirties and 'forties with many independent cases of conviction of sin and assurance of salvation of a pattern which eventually became familiar, and always grew faster than the authority of Wesley, Whitfield or any other of the great leaders. Thus a movement originally Anglican achieved its most resounding successes outside the church, and sharp theological differences separated evangelicals on questions both of faith and order. At first the movement won adherents in all classes, and at the end of the century Wilberforce was far from the only representative of Anglican evangelicalism in Parliament: the countess of Huntingdon's Connection, however, and the followers of Wesley, found that they could secure protection for their property only by registering as Dissenters under the Toleration Act, could maintain a succession to the ministry only by abandoning episcopal ordination, and drifted gradually into nonconformity. Methodist participation in Anglican rites fell finally victim much later to Anglo-Catholic notions of churchmanship, but before the end of the eighteenth century the Methodist body included many who had severed themselves from the church, and many more who had never had any active connection with it. Since the end of the seventeenth century dissent had been losing ground among the upper classes, ground which evangelical dissent, strong among the middle and lower classes, did little to recover. Nevertheless, among the Dissenters, even more than in the church, evangelicalism exercised a potent influence; numerous new congregations were gathered opposed to the fashionable unitarianism and the liberal politics which went with it. In matters liturgical the writing and use of hymns increased enormously, and there was a renewed enthusiasm for eucharistic worship. Methodist toryism probably exercised little restraint upon the radicalism of the working classes, but the existence of a Tory dissent created a novel situation in a few boroughs.

Beneath the changes in church and state were economic developments of fundamental importance. The end of the war in 1783 had seen the usual economic difficulties, but had been followed by a boom even more impressive than that which followed the Seven Years War. This tide of economic prosperity underlay the optimism of politicians of all shades in 1792. To Pitt and those of conservative disposition economic progress appeared to derive from sound finances, from the spirit of enterprise, and not least from 'the natural effects of a free but well-regulated government'. On the other hand to the opposition and to the liberal Dissenters it appeared that the best way to give full scope to a beneficial spiral which the government had not created was to widen the circle of free institutions. By the end of 1792 the credit facilities of the country were under strain, and rising rates of interest and bankruptcy figures seemed to presage a crisis not unlike that of 1772–3, when the outbreak of war precipitated a sudden panic, and a general effort to keep assets liquid. War expenditure financed by credit and reviving exports soon softened the effects of the blow, but the crisis of 1793 was accompanied by a great spread of radical politics.

The recovery which began in 1784 seems to have been stimulated first by the expansion of foreign trade. Between 1784 and 1792 exports increased by almost 70 per cent and the United States proved to be a splendid and growing market. British exports to the U.S.A. increased two and a half times between 1788 and 1792, and included some 87 per cent of American imports of manufactured goods; expanding markets were also found in the West Indies, Asia and Germany. A boom in investment followed the expansion in exports. Enclosure bills, turnpike bills and expenditure on canals multiplied, while brick production almost doubled, and there was a steady increase in the output of shipping to sustain the new volume of overseas trade. Macpherson noted in 1793 that 'of the wealth accumulated in nine peaceful years of successful commerce a very considerable proportion was invested in machinery and inland navigation' and, indeed, these years saw not only a great canal boom, but new developments in iron, textiles and power which make up much of the traditional story of the Industrial Revolution. Although machine-spinning was still uncommon in all the textile industries, the factory system made great headway both in the north of England and Scotland, and efforts were made to introduce it not only in Wales, but in the textile counties of the south and west of England. Raw cotton imports and exports of cotton manufactures increased steadily, though the latter did not yet equal woollen exports in importance. The woollen industry was technically more conservative than the cotton industry, but its output expanded rapidly, almost doubling in the West Riding between 1783 and 1792. Even the iron industry, which was depressed until 1786, began to prosper.

Between 1784 and 1792 Bank stock rose from 111 to 200, Consols from 54 to 90, and high prices for public stocks encouraged investment in private enterprise; additional credit was now made available by the rapid expansion of country banking. At the height of the boom, however, even these resources were fully extended, and the bullion reserves at the Bank began to feel the strain. This bubble was bursting when war broke out in 1793, and precipitated a crisis which proved fatal to many of the country banks, especially those which issued notes payable on demand. For a time the entire financial structure was shaken, and after pressure from the City the government prepared to issue Exchequer bills to ease houses of repute in temporary straits.

The question of the real wages of labour continues in dispute. Though agricultural prices were volatile, other prices were relatively stable until the outbreak of war in 1793 opened the way both to war expenditure financed by credit, and to rising prices on the sharpest scale of the whole century. Some wages, especially in the building industry, were equally stable, but this was uncommon. In the decade separating the American from the French wars, wage rates for skilled men in both agriculture and industry appear to have risen, and although this does not itself establish that their standard of living rose, such an inference is suggested by the increased consumption of tea, sugar, beer and cheaper textiles, and the proliferation of institutions supported by artisans, such as chapels, friendly societies, and trade unions. For the less skilled, and those engaged in declining trades, the outlook was less rosy, especially in those areas where the struggle for employment was aggravated by Irish immigration.

Thus the generation between 1763 and 1793 witnessed the birth of many institutions which not only sustained the nation in the great struggle against France, but became characteristic of nineteenth-century England. An empire designed to guarantee supplies of raw materials was lost, but was absorbing vast quantities of British manufactures, and suggesting a pattern for an empire designed to guarantee markets; in the special case of India a longstanding division of authority between the crown and the company was established. Ireland also fitted awkwardly into the scheme. When American independence had at last to be recognised Shelburne and Fox had sought to minimise their losses by a treaty of commerce and defence; they failed, but sought similar guarantees when granting autonomy to Ireland, and failed again. Pitt too hoped to bind Ireland closer by a generous commercial treaty in return for an Irish contribution to the cost of imperial defence, and hoped to secure the Protestant ascendancy by means of parliamentary reform. All these hopes were dashed. Fox wrecked Pitt's proposals by an agitation whipped up among manufacturers who had not yet the self-assurance to dispense with their old defences. Hopes of parliamentary reform in Ireland were frustrated by the defeat of reform in England, but, reluctant as Pitt was to recognise the fact, successive crises showed that English security could no longer be safely purchased by Castle influence in the Irish parliament. The commercial resolutions of 1785 were pressed through the House by a majority so narrow as to make it impracticable to proceed. Early in 1789 when the prince seemed likely to become regent, the leading borough-mongers and Grattan both sought terms from Fox, and for a time overwhelmed the remnant of the court party. To re-establish the power of the Lord Lieutenant required more corruption than ever before, but still offered no assurance of salvation to the government should some fresh crisis arise as the French Revolution made its impact upon Ireland. By 1793 the union which transformed Ireland into a domestic problem could be foreseen.

In domestic politics, by 1793 party was being reborn, the personal power of the king had passed its peak, modern machinery of government was being constructed. Pitt had already developed the machinery for the new fiscal system he was soon to be compelled to introduce, and the quantitative scale of the most recent developments in coal, iron, cotton and steam, on which Britain's future rested, were sufficient to justify the term 'Industrial Revolution'. Liberal rationalism had already made its mark on both the theology and the politics of the English churches, while the evangelical revival was creating attitudes which were to become influential in the next century, and had given an impulse to the first great British missions overseas. But for the revolutionary and Napoleonic wars the old order must surely have ended much sooner than it did.

CHAPTER XX

FRENCH ADMINISTRATION AND PUBLIC FINANCE IN THEIR EUROPEAN SETTING

DURING the late eighteenth century there was a movement common to many European countries towards powerful and efficient central government. This movement was the counterpart of the more spectacular endeavour to increase the liberty of the individual. Thus, the era of the American Declaration of Independence, of the Declaration of the Rights of Man, and of Adam Smith's *The Wealth of Nations*, the charter of economic liberalism, was also the time when the modern state began to consolidate its forces. Just as the thinkers of the Enlightenment[1] attempted to define the nature of the state as well as the nature of man, so their ideas were reflected during the ensuing years in a clearer identity of both. The growth of central authority and individual liberty hand in hand is shown by events such as the destruction of Jesuit power in Spain, Portugal, Austria and France, and the destruction of the power of the church and the nobility in the French Revolution. In France and England, the great social, political and constitutional changes which eventually gave the middle classes control over the central government tended to obscure the growth of bureaucratic power; and the liberal tradition has sometimes led to the belief that during the great age of revolution the state increased in strength only in countries where 'enlightened despots' flourished: the Prussia of Frederick II, the Austria of Joseph II, the Spain of Charles III, and the rest. But Henri Pirenne, by his definition of enlightened despotism as 'la rationalisation de l'État',[2] diverted attention from the enlightened despots themselves to the nature of their work of reforming the state, which was remarkably similar in its intentions and results to contemporary reform programmes being carried out in England and France. In those two countries there was state-building which, though less spectacular, lost nothing in quality and permanence through being authorised by assemblies and their committees rather than imposed by despotic monarchs. Profound changes began to take place in public finance and administration. In England a number of bodies, of which the chief was the Commission for Examining the Public Accounts (1780–7), submitted reports to Parliament which furnished a basis for reforming legislation so different in kind from what had gone before that

[1] Above, vol. VII, ch. v, 'The Enlightenment', by A. B. C. Cobban.
[2] Quoted in 'Histoire du despotisme éclairé', *Bulletin of the International Committee of Historical Sciences*, vol. IX (1937), p. 193.

the decade beginning in 1780, it has been said, 'seems to represent the dividing line between the ancient and the modern'.[1] In France similar reforms were begun during the last years of the *ancien régime* and carried further by revolutionary governments. A veritable administrative revolution, brought to completion in both countries during the first half of the nineteenth century, sprang from the reform programmes of the late eighteenth.

It will be useful to discuss the general nature of these changes as a background for a more detailed treatment of the French reform movement. Their total effect was to render the machinery of state more efficient and powerful by improvements of a quasi-technical character. Indeed, the basis of the transformation appears to have been a new view of the administration as a machine with various parts to be organised in a complex relationship, each with its special function but subordinated to the whole. It was seen that, if men were organised in teams, they would be more effective for practical purposes than if they worked independently of one another. Servants of the crown had acquired a highly individual status, their relationship with each other and the public being thoroughly personal. Many were paid fees by members of the public whom they served; many were entitled to a proportion of the public moneys which they handled; some were even expected to draw revenue from their own private investment of public funds. Those who bought venal offices received interest on their investment. From the late eighteenth century, these various means of payment tended more and more to be replaced by fixed salaries paid from a central treasury which could therefore serve to control and co-ordinate the activities of public servants. Public servants had hitherto often regarded their own records and other documents as personal property which concerned no one but themselves. It had therefore been difficult to compile accurate statistics and other official information. Now there was a movement to gather records together in central depots as public property. Again, most officials had employed their own clerks and office boys, just like private employers, but the state began to engage personnel at all levels as public servants with specific duties. Duties, like salaries, began to be defined and apportioned among employees in an orderly way, so that sinecures became fewer and the government might know how each official was supposed to be employing his time. The shift away from independent officials with personal importance and towards impersonal teams is clearly seen in the evolution of accounting practices. Whereas auditing the accounts of officials had once been only a judicial review, to test the honesty of the individual accountant, it now became also an administrative survey, to discover the state of public business. And finally, for the personal bond of allegiance to the king,

[1] J. E. D. Binney, *British Public Finance and Administration, 1774–1792* (Oxford, 1958), p. 282.

whom the official might once have known in person, was now substituted a more impersonal tie of loyalty to the crown or the state.

As the individual public servant became more and more part of a group, the nature of the group changed. The administration became not only more impersonal, but more functional. Indeed, the concept of function in France brought with it the term *fonctionnaire public* for the civil servant. Administrative bodies began to be systematically organised in the now-familiar pyramid structure, with chains of responsibility rising from the broad base of junior employees up to the under-secretary or deputy minister at the apex. The pyramid structure represents a system of sub-ordinating personnel and delegating duties in such a way that one man can direct and control the work of hundreds in an economical and efficient manner. In this system a distinction is drawn between the employees and their duties, and the organisation is based on the needs of the work to be done, rather than on the needs of the men employed to do it. In the words of the comte de Saint Germain, prominent in the reform movements in Denmark and France, 'Les emplois ne sont pas faits pour les hommes, mais les hommes pour les emplois'. It was only with the application of this principle of utility that work of a similar nature began to be gathered together and consolidated in the same ministry or service. Each administrative organisation began to have a fundamental purpose, such as the collection of revenue or the control of internal administration. Matters relating to finance or justice, once dealt with in a confused way by many different agencies, were now destined to come under the administration of a ministry of finance or a ministry of justice. This systematic concentration of duties resulted in a demand for men with special knowledge and training which could be acquired either before or during service. Thus the amateur public servant tended to give way to the professional, for if the public administration was to become more like a machine, its parts had to be prepared with greater care. At the same time the civil and military services came to have a certain professional coherence and *esprit de corps*. Even though human beings do not function with the same precision as the parts of a machine, the systematic organisation of men and work enormously increased the power of government.

Sociological theories of the organisation or 'housekeeping' (*Wirtschaft*) of the state were being developed in German countries by the Cameralists, of whom J. H. G. von Justi (1720–71) and J. von Sonnenfels (1733–1817) were perhaps the most influential, and in France by the Physiocrats led by François Quesnay (1694–1774) and the marquis de Mirabeau (1715–89). The two groups held radically different views of the relation of the state to nature, the Physiocrats believing that the state existed to restore and maintain a 'Natural Order' and not to interfere with its operation, and the Cameralists tending to regard the state as part of the natural order and its organisation as a natural science. Yet both schools taught a gospel of systematic utilitarian reform to be put into practice by powerful despotic monarchs. Although these intellectuals influenced public opinion and were therefore politically important, especially in the case of the French group, they were probably less important as a cause than as a symptom of the administrative revolution of their time, for the reforming impulse seems to have come largely from within government circles.

The general features of European administrative development may nowhere be seen more clearly than in the history of France. At the highest level there was a tendency to unify the king's councils and to confine their attention to the most important matters of state, leaving the continuum of administration to officials. In practice it was difficult for the councils to learn to use their time to best advantage, and they were often to be found discussing some questions in too great detail while leaving others entirely to their permanent officials. This was partly because they continuously suffered from lack of leadership, for Louis XV took little hand in government towards the end of his reign; the dauphin, who attended the councils from 1757, died in 1765; and his son had had no experience in them when he ascended the throne in 1774 as Louis XVI. No strong figure emerged from the struggles of court factions to take matters in hand. It is surprising therefore that the conciliar system evolved even so far as it did. According to the *Almanach royal*, Louis XV presided over four main councils: the *Conseil d'État d'En-haut*, concerned with foreign relations, the *Conseil des Dépêches*, which dealt with certain matters of internal administration, the *Conseil royal de Commerce*, and the *Conseil royal des Finances*. In addition, the king was in principle at the head of the *Conseil d'Etat privé Finances et Direction*, but in practice the Chancellor or the Keeper of the Seals presided over it. This was a larger council which included many of the thirty *Conseillers d'État*, the six Intendants of Finances and the eighty *Maîtres des Requêtes*, and it dealt with current matters of judicial and financial administration. This conciliar structure, although apparently much the same in 1763 as it had been under Louis XIV, had radically changed underneath the official façade. The *Conseil royal de Commerce* had not met for over twenty years and was not to meet again, except fleetingly after an attempt to revive it in June 1787. Some important commercial matters were dealt with by the *Conseil royal des Finances*, but many others were decided instead by the *Bureau du Commerce* which was an administrative council composed largely of officials. Within the four working councils, the senior administrators— the Chancellor or his deputy the Keeper of the Seals, the Controller General of Finances, and the four Secretaries of State for War, Marine, Foreign Affairs and the Royal Household—were extremely influential. The Controller General of Finances, for example, dominated the *Conseil royal des Finances* because he and his ministry prepared questions for the council meetings. Furthermore, although the council delegated its less important work to two commissions, the *Grande Direction* and the *Petite Direction*, reserving for itself only subjects requiring a definition of principle or an interpretation of law, yet it still found itself overburdened with duties and obliged to leave more and more of them for the Controller General to decide together with the king, or even alone with his senior officials, the Intendants of Finances. In consequence, many of the laws published as *arrêts de Conseil* were in fact not made by the king-in-council at all but by administrators. This state of affairs received official sanction in an edict of June 1777 which created an administrative *Comité contentieux des Finances* to deal with all except policy matters. The creation of this committee was an important step towards a proper distribution of responsibilities. Composed mainly of certain Intendants of Finances, the *Comité contentieux* freed the *Conseil royal des Finances* and the Controller General from routine matters and allowed them to devote more attention to questions of policy. The *Conseil royal* might then have commenced firm and vigorous action to resolve the financial problems of the state, but instead it soon began to meet no more than seven or eight times a year, leaving the direction of affairs virtually in the hands of the Controller General and the *Comité contentieux*, which the Keeper of the Seals described in 1788 as 'the real *Conseil des Finances*'.[1] Meanwhile, a similar tendency in the other councils to sift out policy matters and leave administration to the officials culminated in a law of 9 August 1789 by which a *Comité contentieux des Départements* was charged with the routine work of the *Conseil des Dépêches*. The same law completed the integration of the councils by fusing the *Conseil d'En-haut*, the *Conseil des Dépêches* and the *Conseil royal des Finances* into a single *Conseil d'État*. This unified council had no opportunity to prove itself more effective than its predecessors for within a few weeks the National Assembly had assumed the direction of the state.

The council members who were responsible for the execution of policy —the Secretaries of State and the Controller General of Finances—were by the mid-eighteenth century already heads of large ministries. But the efficiency of these ministries was impaired by the haphazard way in which the various governmental functions were divided among them. The idea of grouping services logically under headings like Justice, Public Works, and the Interior had never been rigorously applied to the administration, which was confused as a result of its empirical development. Even such apparently unified ministries as those for War and Marine were cluttered up with much of the internal administration of the country and with financial and judicial duties irrelevant to their primary functions. As a result there was a wasteful duplication of many services and senior officials were extremely dependent on their subordinates, whose various and un-

[1] Michel Antoine, 'Les conseils des finances sous le règne de Louis XV', *Revue d'Histoire moderne et contemporaine*, vol. v (1958), p. 183.

related duties they could not hope to understand. This disunity was increased by the independence of most senior officials who, having bought their offices, were able to ignore both their colleagues and their superiors. An administrative career being difficult in most ministries because of these defects of organisation, it is surprising that many employees were keen and capable. Such critical analysis would be irrelevant except that men at the time were beginning to grasp the importance of administrative organisation. In this, as in so many matters, royal officials were writing books and making plans which appear to have sprung from a growing desire for order, simplicity and efficiency. One of the most influential was the Director General of Finances, Jacques Necker, who showed in his work and in his books that he realised how important it was for a ministry to function in a logical and integrated manner if the minister was to control it with all the limitations of one man's time, attention and understanding.

The Ministry for Foreign Affairs had been given its secretariat, archives and *Académie politique* to train young diplomats by the Secretary of State, de Torcy (1699–1716). The financial services were consolidated in the *Bureau des Fonds* in 1775. From 1767 accounts and records were systematically kept, and Choiseul, who had ordered this reform, discovered that an intelligence service relying on careful studies of newspaper cuttings and reports was in many ways more useful than a spy service. By a regulation of 1767 Choiseul fixed hours of work and consolidated the coding service which had hitherto been distributed through the branches of the ministry in a haphazard way. Coding was not to be seriously and effectively treated until the nineteenth century, but at this time it was organised separately under its own chief in order to promote efficiency and secrecy. In 1775 a topographical bureau was set up, to concern itself with national frontiers and geographical questions, and in 1780 a bureau for the conservation of maps. When, after the War of American Independence, Vergennes grouped these services in two *bureaux politiques*, each under a *premier commis*, it only remained to combine the two, which Dumouriez accomplished in 1792, and to assign the irrelevant duties concerning provincial administration to the new Ministry of the Interior.

Although it began later, the reform of the Ministries of War and Marine was just as thorough and perhaps more important because far greater sums were spent on war than on diplomacy. After the Seven Years War Choiseul attempted, with only indifferent success, to improve the methods of military recruiting, supply and manoeuvre. This work was carried further to permanent effect by the comte de Saint Germain, Secretary of State for War from 1775 to 1780, who laid the foundations of the French army which was to prove so effective during the revolutionary and Napoleonic wars. He worked towards a flexible hierarchical structure by attacking venality, by reducing the number of ranks of officer and the number of officers in each rank, and favouring a system of promotion. He took recruiting from the companies which had procured men for a price (100 livres for an infantryman; 120 livres for a cavalryman) and put it in the hands of the army itself, not allowing officers to press men into service as hitherto, but setting up recruiting depots under the supervision of administrative councils. The administrative council of a regiment was composed of five officers of various ranks who met regularly to decide on the spending of regimental funds, to keep records and accounts, and to report to the Commissioners for War. The latter had hitherto been civilian officers, powerful, venal, and continuously in conflict with their military counterparts. Saint Germain made them an integral part of the army and, abolishing their venal posts, organised them in a hierarchy as a career service. The work of Saint Germain was carried on by the comte de Ségur who made such useful contributions as establishing a permanent General Staff. Parallel reforms were carried out in the Marine Department by two able Secretaries of State, Sartine (1774–80) and Castries (1780–7). The ordinances of 31 October and 1 November 1784 and 1 January 1786 became the bible of the Royal French Navy. Improvements in naval and military organisation benefited greatly in the 1770s, and the navy again in 1788–9, from the expectation of war with Britain, for the reforming ministers were permitted to spend vast sums of money.

The Ministries for War and Diplomacy developed before the others because the urgency of their functions caused them to be concentrated very early in the hands of the royal government. A unified control of them, essential for the very existence of the state, had resulted in a specialisation of the Secretaries of State for War, Marine, Foreign Affairs and the Royal Household by the end of the sixteenth century when internal administration was still divided among a variety of provincial, private, judicial and royal authorities. It was not until 25 May 1791 that the national government set up the ministries of Justice, Taxation (*Contributions Publiques*) and the Interior, thereby asserting its authority over the courts, the nobility and the provinces. But the process of centralisation had begun in the seventeenth century when the *Conseil d'État* began to send out its permanent representatives to the provinces, the *commissaires départis* or Intendants of Justice, Police and Finances, as they were usually called. During the later eighteenth century, there were from thirty-two to thirty-four intendants, some appointed to the frontier provinces by the Secretary of State for War and the rest to the internal provinces by the Controller General of Finance. The intendants were not controlled so closely as to prevent them from exercising any initiative, as were the administrative boards in the provincial departments of Prussia. Being commissioned and not venal, and appointed more often for their ability than their relations at court, they came to be, as Necker observed, the best administrators which the *ancien régime* produced. However, their effectiveness was limited by three less disciplined groups of authorities: the provincial Estates, the sovereign courts, and the administration in Paris.

The three estates had survived in the thirteen *pays d'États*, comprising a total area of about half the kingdom, only by a staunch defence of ancient rights and privileges against the encroachments of the royal administration. Their extensive powers of justice, police and finance, which they reviewed in regular meetings, gave them a vested interest in a provincial loyalty that sustained them until it was swept away by a national enthusiasm for the Estates General in 1789. In addition, the provincial governors, even though they had lost much of their power, could still give the intendants much trouble. But a more satisfactory relationship between the intendants and the provincial assemblies, set up in 1787-8, foreshadowed the truce between the central and the provincial powers which, after the struggles of the Revolution, was to last uneasily throughout the nineteenth century. Intractable though they were, the provincial Estates and governors were not so formidable an obstacle to a growing national administration as the sovereign courts. The thirteen *parlements*, with their administrative as well as judicial functions, were powerful enemies of the royal bureaucracy, and so were many of the financial courts: the *Bureaux des Finances*, the *Cours des Aides*, the *Chambres des Comptes* and the *Cours des Monnaies*.

If it was hampered by the opposition of the courts and Estates, the royal administration was weakened by the disorder in the ministries and other services in Paris. The intendants had to correspond with a great number of uncoordinated agencies. In the *Contrôle général*, with which they had probably the closest relations, there was an absence of organisation, as in most ministries, as well as such a variety of duties that little real control was possible. Much was left to the discretion of the individual bureaux, which tended to work according to the ideas of their directors or of some faction rather than the policy of the government. Many of these bureaux were extremely useful and were later incorporated into the ministries of Public Contributions and the Interior set up in 1791, but the *ancien régime* was haunted by the problem of organising them into an effective government department. In 1763 these bureaux had long been grouped haphazardly under the direction of six Intendants of Finances. An outstanding Intendant of Finances like Daniel Trudaine could supervise all the manifold activities of his group of services and improve the quality of many of them. Trudaine was virtually the creator of the Bureau of Mines, which encouraged and directed the exploitation of coal, iron and other mineral deposits, and of the *Ponts et Chaussées* which built the magnificent French highways praised by Arthur Young and other travellers.[1] But the less able ones had to depend on their *commis*, who

[1] Jean Petot, *Histoire de l'Administration des Ponts et Chaussées, 1599-1815* (Paris, 1958), pp. 138 and 157.

sometimes exploited that dependence for their own profit. In any case, as venal officers the Intendants of Finances were virtually independent of the Controller General. Therefore Necker, who wished to create an integrated ministry, abolished their offices in June 1777. When the Intendants of Finances reappeared after Necker's fall, it was as specialised Intendants of Mines and Minerals, of Tax Farms, or of *Ponts et Chaussées*. Meanwhile the Intendants of Commerce responsible for the direction of trade and industry had been more successfully integrated into the department. Beginning in 1764 their venal offices were abolished as they fell vacant and *Maîtres des requêtes* simply commissioned as Intendants of Commerce. In June 1787 their bureaux were combined under the direction of one of them, de Tolozan. The eventual removal of all these purely administrative functions of the *Contrôle général des Finances* was heralded in 1764 by the establishment of a fifth secretariat of state to which the former Controller General, Henri Bertin, was appointed to take over some of the duties of the future Ministry of the Interior: agriculture, mines, canals, archives and others. But it disappeared in 1781 without ever having relieved the *Contrôle général* of its most important non-financial function, the administration of trade and industry.

Trade and industry had long been administered together with finance mainly because of the prevalent view that state revenues would only increase with the total national wealth, which in turn depended upon a prosperous foreign trade. For well over a century, but especially since the time of Colbert, the government had been sponsoring an exports-drive in the belief that this was the most direct means of increasing its own gold and silver reserves. To encourage the sale abroad of textiles, hardware, leather and metal products, and luxury goods, official standards of quality and size were maintained by an able corps of from forty to fifty Inspectors of Manufactures and nearly as many *commis de la marque*. Agricultural products and anything that might serve as industrial raw materials were not to be exported because profit on the sale of goods was thought to be received in payment for the labour and skill which had gone into their manufacture. The export of manufactures, however, was favoured by subsidies and low customs duties. In order to gauge the effect of these measures the customs registers were used to compile statistics of imports and exports in the *Bureau de la Balance du Commerce*. The administration of internal trade, on the other hand, was seen as a matter of keeping a just 'balance' among conflicting interests. The crown felt responsible for harmonising the claims of provinces, cities, guilds and individuals who were forever petitioning for monopoly rights, exemption from taxes or other privileges. Petitions and official matters requiring a decision from Paris were usually received in the office of one of the Intendants of Commerce who might submit them to the Controller General or bring them before a meeting of the *Bureau du Commerce*, composed of Councillors of State, the Secretaries of State, the Controller General, the Lieutenant-General of Police, the Intendant of the Generality of Paris, a number of *Maîtres des requêtes*, and the Intendants of Commerce. But in most cases, the Intendants of Commerce would first refer a controversial question to the representatives of the Farmers General of taxes and to the Deputies of Commerce from the chief commercial cities. There was frequently a clash of views between the two. This characteristic procedure reveals that the basic function of the *Contrôle général* was to harmonise the financial needs of the state with the welfare of national trade and industry. The Controller General was supposed to collect the golden eggs while caring for the goose that laid them. Unfortunately, owing to the desperate financial difficulties of the government which made it increasingly dependent on the Farmers General, decisions tended to go against the merchants and manufacturers and in favour of the financiers. This tendency was reinforced by the dislike of the readiness of merchants, manufacturers and municipal and provincial authorities to use government aid as a weapon against one another and by the conviction that every decision in their favour would be a concession to private interests at variance with the needs of the state for revenue. Worst of all, until the Revolution the government tended to sacrifice even general administrative reform to its hunger for cash.

During the middle years of the century, however, a new surge of interest in the general economic welfare of the country led many officials in the administration of commerce to take up the cause of trade, industry and agriculture. The Intendants of Commerce, Vincent de Gournay, Isaac de Bacalan and Clicquot-Blervache, the Intendants of Finance, Trudaine and Montaran, the Inspector General of Manufactures, François Brisson, and many others devoured books on economic subjects, which were appearing in increasing numbers. The defeat of France in the Seven Years War and the poverty of the state which contributed to it called for a change and made this new study of political economy seem timely. Though economic theory varied a good deal it was undoubtedly led by the sensational gospel of the Physiocrats that regulations, customs duties, monopolies and all other restraints on trade and industry should be done away with in order that France might enjoy the benefits of the 'Natural Order'. The actions and writings of most officials, however, reveal only a growing conviction that national wealth and prosperity could best be encouraged, not by regulating trade and industry, but by creating favourable conditions for their growth. The question at issue was not, except for the Physiocrats, whether the government should intervene in economic affairs, but how it should intervene and where it should bend its efforts to increase the general prosperity. How could steady supplies of grain best be ensured? Should 'free fairs' be encouraged or not? Should the domestic consumption of luxury goods be permitted? Under what conlitions should the government allow the manufacture and sale of printed calico (*toiles peintes*)? How could government financial needs be harmonised with the welfare of the national economy? These were some of he questions preoccupying officials in the administration of commerce. As a practical consequence there was a tendency to rely less on regulation, to give greater encouragement to economic enterprise, and to gather more information—especially statistical information—about trade, industry and agriculture. Earlier Controllers General, such as Orry, had already made use of statistics, and through the second half of the century the Chambers of Commerce, the Intendants of the provinces, the Deputies of Commerce (who were becoming royal officials), the Inspectors of Manufactures and other officials were burdened with the preparation of more and more economic records and reports. C. E. Labrousse writes: 'Le Contrôle général, qui réglemente au XVIIIe siècle de moins en moins observe de plus en plus.'[1] As for assistance, occasional loans and grants were already being made, especially to the textile industries, from the funds of the tax farms and of the *Caisse du Commerce*, supported by a tax on colonial goods. Now an attempt was made to provide a ready source of cheap short-term credit, and by doing so to lower the prevailing interest rates, through the establishment in 1776 of a discount bank, the *caisse d'escompte*, to discount short-term commercial bills at the low interest rate of 4 per cent. The desire to encourage credit also led to the creation of the *mont de piété* the following year. Yet all in all trade and industry probably gained more from government technical assistance. Stipends, grants and prizes were awarded to inventors, technicians, designers, and writers of technical books. Members of the Academy of Sciences were commissioned to do research: Bertholet on dyeing techniques, Vandemonde on machines, Daubenton on sheep-rearing. John Holker, Manchester manufacturer and Jacobite refugee, made successful efforts to procure English machines and to attract English inventors and skilled workmen, this in his capacity as Inspector General of Foreign Manufactures (1755–86). The other four posts of Inspector General of Manufactures and Commerce often came to be used as sinecures for men like Vaucanson who was experimenting with new machines, and Dupont de Nemours who worked on various economic projects such as (in 1785–6) compiling information on foreign tariffs and trade and advising the French representatives who were negotiating the Commercial Treaty with England. In 1791 the National Assembly abolished these posts, but it increased certain types of direct encouragement to enterprise. For example, by a law of 27 September 1791 a committee of experts was set up to make recommendations for the spending of two million livres set aside during that year for the encouragement of inventors of machines and new industrial processes.

[1] C. E. Labrousse, *La Crise de l'économie française à la fin de l'ancien régime et au début de la Révolution* (Paris, 1944), p. 7.

Far more effective and fundamental than financial and technical assistance was the integration of the national economy through the establishment of a uniform system of weights and measures and more especially a single uniform customs barrier on the national frontiers. Since the Middle Ages kings had tried in vain to have standard weights and measures adopted, and even Colbert, who succeeded in unifying the coinage system, was baffled by this difficult task. The adoption of the metric system by a series of decrees in 1791 was therefore a proof of the national government's new-found authority over the kingdom as well as a precious convenience in economic life. But the unification of the customs system by a series of laws from 30 November 1790 was much more than that, for it put in the hands of the government an administrative engine of unprecedented force for controlling the national economy as a whole. Internal customs barriers which had hitherto obstructed trade between provinces were abolished and the customs on the national frontiers strengthened in order to make them really effective against smugglers. Instead of more than a thousand bureaux scattered over the country, slowing up traffic by their inspections and bureaucratic controls, there were now some 750 concentrated on the frontiers alone. By collecting duties of not more than 15 per cent or 20 per cent on the importation of foreign manufactures and on the exportation of valuable raw materials, the government could give national industry a modest though real protection against English competition while at the same time encouraging French exports.

This reform completed a task begun by Colbert in 1664 when he gathered the provinces of the northern half of the kingdom into a customs union known as the *Cinq Grosses Fermes* after the amalgamated company of tax farmers which governed it. As the other provinces refused to give up their provincial tariffs and join this customs union, Colbert endeavoured instead to protect the French economy by encircling the kingdom with his tariff of 1667, imposing high duties on a range of manufactured imports and raw exports. This system remained substantially the same until the Revolution. It was not very effective in excluding undesirable foreign manufactures, partly because by paying the duties of the tariff of 1667 they were thereby exempted from all internal duties whatsoever and thus could sometimes undersell French products which were subject to internal duties that often raised their price by 15 per cent or more. Furthermore, to offset the extra cost of French goods due to the internal duties, foreign manufactures sent to France had to be charged high duties of perhaps 30 per cent or higher at the frontiers, or excluded outright. But prohibition and high duties encouraged large-scale contraband trading; in fact, so weak were the frontier customs barriers that there were *assureurs* in most ports, especially the free-ports of Bayonne, Marseille, Dunkirk and l'Orient, who made fortunes by smuggling goods into France for as little as 12 per cent or 15 per cent *ad valorem*. These customs barriers were weak mainly because the Farmers General who administered them regarded them not as an economic control but as a tax that must be made to yield as much revenue as possible. They and their employees were not therefore concerned with freeing trade within and eliminating smuggling from without, and indeed, they even profited from the fines on merchants and smugglers and the proceeds from the sale of confiscated goods.

Together with this half-reformed system Colbert bequeathed to the eighteenth century the inspiration of his policy of reform. And it was this, rather than the writings of economic theorists, which led nearly four generations of reformers to endeavour to put into effect what they called 'le projet du droit unique'. Most of the reformers, like Colbert himself, were government officials with a knowledge of the practical problems involved. From 1700 to 1710 the Deputies of Commerce, led by Jean Anisson from Lyon, championed reform and in 1720 their project was revived and nearly carried by Michel Amelot, the de facto chief of the Council of Commerce. From 1726 until about 1745 the movement was led by a Farmer General, Lallemant de Betz. But it was not until after the Seven Years War, when the Controller General Bertin had fresh plans drawn up by a team of Intendants of Finances, Intendants of Commerce, Deputies of Commerce and Farmers General, that the government began to make serious efforts. The final project, which was urged at the Assembly of Notables in 1787 and adopted with only minor changes by the National Assembly in 1790, was planned and championed for ten years by a special government Customs Reform Bureau headed by a salaried official, Mahy de Cormeré.

The reasons why the reform project was not put into practice until the revolution throw light on the character of finance and administration during the *ancien régime*. Strong opposition arose in Brittany, Alsace, Lorraine, the Three Bishoprics, Flanders, Guyenne and other frontier provinces where it was felt that a customs union with the rest of the kingdom would damage provincial trade. Further opposition came from trading, manufacturing and municipal interests which had secured the privilege of exemption from internal duties and did not want to lose their own special 'freedoms' in a general freedom of internal trade. Worse still —for resistance in these quarters might have been overcome by a strong central government, as it eventually was in 1790—after the Seven Years War the Farmers General came to oppose reform. Until then they had been willing to support unification of the customs system in the hope that it might be followed by a similar unification of the more lucrative salt and tobacco monopolies, the *gabelle* and *tabac*. The sale price of royal salt and tobacco varied from province to province according to ancient agreements, some provinces like Brittany being exempt altogether from the *gabelle*, and others like Alsace being exempt from the *tabac*, and the barriers needed to separate the different price zones coincided more or

37   577

less with the internal customs barriers. Excise revenue could have been enormously increased if all these barriers had been abolished at the same time and the entire country subjected to a uniform *gabelle* and *tabac* as well as a single customs tariff. Many government officials and tax farmers, such as Lavoisier, pointed this out. However, the resistance of the privileged provinces to the introduction of the *gabelle* and the *tabac* had always been powerful, and after 1763 it became part of a nationwide movement to abolish these monopolies altogether. In growing fear of this, the Farmers General became opposed to customs reform, especially after 1783 when the salt and tobacco monopolies were virtually all that remained to them, the other taxes having been placed under government commissions on which they were not so strongly represented. In view of its financial dependence on the Farmers General, the royal government was unable to unify the customs unless it also unified the *gabelle* and the *tabac*, but it could not extend these monopolies equally over the whole kingdom in the face of overwhelming popular opposition. During the year 1790 the Constituent Assembly broke out of this dilemma by ignoring the Farmers General, abolishing the *gabelle* and *tabac*, and placing the reformed customs system under the control of an administrative commission (*régie*). In doing so it sacrificed the entire revenue from the first two and most of that from the second, which became no longer justifiable as a tax, only as an economic control. It is evident that these changes were only made in the course of a reform of the entire fiscal system.

The trends in tax reform show the growth of central government power. The inequality of the taxes, by general admission their principal defect, survived because of the weakness of the crown in the face of the resistance of privileged cities, provinces and social classes. Unequal taxes meant injustice to the citizen, but to the central government they meant tenuous control, administrative confusion, and a lower yield of revenue. During the Revolution, the citizen won equality of taxation at the price of submission to a stronger national government. 'What is striking about the financial organisation of the *ancien régime*', writes a student of the tax system, 'is the great care taken of private interests even to the detriment of the superior interests of the king.'[1] With the suppression of privilege during the years of revolution, private interests in matters of taxation were defined and limited, albeit protected, and the state arrogated the supreme privilege of collecting whatever revenue it required in the national interest. For when the National Assembly laid down the principle that the citizen should contribute one-fifth of his revenue to the state, it meant not only that it would take no more but that it had every intention of taking that much.

Superficially tax reform was characterised by a shift away from 'indirect' to 'direct' taxation. These terms, which rapidly became current in

[1] Jean Villain, *Le Recouvrement des impôts directs sous l'ancien régime* (Paris, 1952), p. 8.

the eighteenth century, were adopted by the Physiocrats[1] to distinguish between taxes imposed directly on land, or revenue from land, which they regarded as the only source of wealth, and taxes imposed only indirectly on land, as for example duties on the manufacture, transport or sale of goods. In accordance with their doctrine, the Physiocrats approved of the 'direct' taxes and condemned the 'indirect'. This doctrinal distinction coincided with a real difference in methods of collection, and as it happened the collection of the 'indirect' taxes aroused such popular fury that the Constituent Assembly found it politically expedient to abolish most of them in 1790–1. The principal ones were the *gabelle*, the *tabac*, the customs, the *aides* or duties on the sale of wine and other alcoholic beverages, the *droits de marque* imposed at different times on products of leather, iron, paper and cloth, certain *octrois* collected for the central government on goods entering towns, and the *domaine* including, on the one hand, feudal dues on crown lands, and, on the other, a stamp-tax and a duty on the compulsory registration of transfers of property. They were collected at different rates in different parts of the country, according to ancient contracts between the crown and the provincial authorities; and to prevent the smuggling of wine, salt, tobacco, etc., from a province where the duty was low or non-existent to a neighbouring province where the duty was much higher, brigades of guards moved on a constant patrol. These internal tax-frontiers were so long and difficult to guard that thousands of men, women and children thought the profit of smuggling worth the risk of fines, imprisonment or branding and the galleys, and with popular opinion very much in their favour carried on a kind of civil war with the tax officials. Nearly all the indirect taxes were collected by the Farmers General, and as Necker remarked, the crown was thankful that it was the Farmers General who drew the fire of popular resentment. The real opponents of tax reform, however, were the privileged provinces like Brittany and Alsace; for if the Farmers General, Necker, Calonne and other reforming administrators had been able to overcome the resistance of provincial privilege, all these variegated taxes could have been unified throughout the kingdom, so that no internal barriers and few controls would have been necessary. But the inequalities and absurdities of the system, though defended by the privileged, were emphasised by the efficiency of the General Farm in exploiting the taxes. Popular anger was roused to such a pitch that taxes and tax farms were both swept away in the years of the Revolution. Only the customs, the stamp-tax, and the registration duties survived. But there were many doubts about this sacrifice of revenue. The Constituent Assembly abolished the *tabac*, for instance, by a vote of only 372 to 360. Under the Directory and later régimes most of the 'indirect' taxes were revived, but in unified form and under the direct supervision of the national government.

[1] Ferdinand Brunot, *Histoire de la langue française* (Paris, 1930), vol. VI, p. 484.

37-2

The principal 'direct' taxes were the *taille*, imposed on non-noble and non-privileged landowners by the crown in the *pays d'élection* and in the *pays d'État* by the Estates, who paid the crown a regular indemnity (*don gratuit*) for the privilege; the *capitation*, originally a poll-tax but, by 1763, recognised as a surtax on the *taille*; and the *vingtième*, which was a tax of 5 per cent of the revenue from land and other property, public offices and industry. Although they were as irregular as the 'indirect' taxes these were less hated, partly because their irregularities were not so obtrusive, partly because they were collected with less violence, and partly because the Physiocrats regarded the 5 per cent land-tax of the *vingtième* as the prototype of the single tax they advocated, and believed that the *taille* would be satisfactory if it were similarly imposed as a proportion of land values. To so reform the *taille* it was first necessary to compile a land-register and this was prevented by the opposition of the privileged. Thus the inequalities of the *taille* and its low yield went hand in hand with the weakness of the central government. Governments in other countries were facing the same problem at this time. In Spain Charles III attempted without success to implement a proportional land-tax. Joseph II actually completed a land-register for his Austrian empire but the revolutionary tax reform that was based on it went into effect in November 1789 and died with Joseph II three months later. Only in France did the central government, as the beneficiary of a social revolution, have enough power to carry out this reform. Local land-registers had been drawn up, as for example by Turgot in the Limousin during the 1770s, and a national one had been thought of and even planned in the administration. The land-register was no novelty to the team of officials, under de Prony, an engineer of the *Ponts et Chaussées*, who were commissioned by the Constituent Assembly to compile it. But such difficulties were encountered during those disturbed years that no satisfactory land-register appeared until the First Empire. The new property tax, most important of the four new direct taxes, had at first to be based on the crude assessments of the *ancien régime*. Yet the trend was clearly towards taxation according to an exact knowledge of the assets of the individual for whom, therefore, the price of equality was to be helplessness before an inquisitorial state.

The yield of a tax depends primarily upon the efficiency of the collecting organisation and of those under the *ancien régime* the General Farm was the most efficient. As a semi-private profit-making firm of tax collectors it stood condemned by almost the entire nation. But regarded purely as an administrative system, by 1763 it had become remarkably competent. Frederick II paid tribute to it by calling upon many of its officials to assist in the reform of his own financial system and engaging a Director of the Farms, de la Haye de Launay, to be his chief financial adviser. The General Farm was directed by forty Farmers General (raised to sixty from

1756–80) of whom the richest and most experienced made all the fundamental decisions for the company as members of the *Assemblée des Caisses*, which was also the only legal link with the government. Other Farmers General worked in the directing boards of the company or in the correspondence bureaux which supervised the work of the provincial Directors. A Director (there were 123 of them in 1763) was in charge of collecting one of the five main groups of taxes—*domaines, aides, gabelles, tabac*, or customs—for a specific geographical area. In each Direction was a number of operating units such as tobacco stores, salt granaries and brigade headquarters for the guards, each managed by a small group of Receivers, Controllers, clerks and guards officers. Resident and travelling inspectors were always testing operations and examining records and accounts. Being paid employees, from the Director downwards, all of them were organised in a strict hierarchy of subordination like a modern firm or government department. There was a continuous flow of circulars and orders downwards; records were kept at every level; and the Directors and Farmers General were informed by regular reports on every aspect of the work. To facilitate all this paper work there was a wide range of printed forms. Personnel records show that, on the whole, employees were required to maintain a high standard of conduct and efficiency, even though the records usually took note of employees' patrons and protectors. There was a constant movement of personnel from one bureau and Direction to another to prevent their striking up relations with smugglers. A move sometimes brought promotion, for up to certain levels the General Farm was a career service. Conditions of service were attractive enough to make long service the general rule. As early as 1739 officers in the guards were granted an annual fortnight's leave with pay. By a *Délibération* of 21 February 1768 a superannuation fund, to which both employees and the company contributed, was established in certain branches of the Farm. Salaries, graded according to rank, were established in each district according to an estimate of the cost of living. When in 1781 the employees in the Paris headquarters wanted a rise in pay they wrote to their employers 'that successive increases in rents and in the price of food and all essential commodities have long ago destroyed the proportion established twenty years ago between the wages of [our] labour and the price of the necessities of life'.[1] Salaries were frequently raised in response to such demands, especially during the 1780s, but they remained so low that, unlike those of most crown officials, they were hardly reduced at all when the committees of the Constituent Assembly came to organise the civil service in 1790–1. The efficiency of this organisation was maintained by the Farmers General for their own private profit. They invested large sums in it and drew large revenues from it. The part they paid to the crown, according to agreements signed every six years, rose from an

[1] Archives nationales, Paris, carton G¹ 63, MS.

annual 124 million livres in 1763 to 150 millions in 1788, even though by the latter date little remained to them except the *gabelle* and the *tabac*. But profits taken by the Farmers General and others who invested in the company also ran into millions. Had the Farmers General been salaried officials serving the crown as their own Directors served them, the increase in crown revenues would have been considerable. During the Revolution, such parts of the General Farm as survived were nationalised and integrated into the civil service.

The royal financial officials who collected the direct taxes in the *pays d'élection*, being venal and therefore independent, had a contractual relationship with the crown somewhat like that of the Farmers General. But they were neither combined in any practical way nor served by an administrative organisation. Each of forty-eight or more Receivers General signed a *traité* by which he undertook to pay the crown a certain part of the *taille*. Each of them in his turn, by a similar contract, was supposed to receive the sum for which he was responsible from a number of Receivers of whom there were normally 408. Finally, each Receiver was bound by a contract with a number of parish Collectors. A similar body collected the *vingtième*, while the *capitation* was collected as a surtax on the *taille*. These officials were not paid salaries but received a proportion of the revenue which passed through their hands, as a commission, and 5 per cent interest on the price which they had paid for their offices. Their only tie with their superiors was a legal obligation to pay a fixed amount of money. Legal action against a dishonest or inefficient Receiver was slow and altogether a poor substitute for continuous administrative control. The only accounts they rendered were to the *Chambre des Comptes* and were so late as to be useless for administrative purposes. And as the Receivers and Receivers General were not required simply to hand over their takings to the Royal Treasury but were used to make payments on behalf of the crown, there was virtually no check on their operations. When the Receivers General were finally brought to account in 1792 it was found that out of a total of fifty-six, thirty-six were in arrears to the extent of about twenty million livres. If much revenue was lost in the process of collection, much was also wasted by the spending machinery, and for identical reasons. A great number of independent, venal Treasurers and Controllers managed the funds granted to the civil and military services. In 1787 the *Chambre des Comptes* reported that in less than twenty years fifty of them had gone bankrupt causing a loss to the crown of forty million livres. The officers of the Mint, *payeurs des rentes* and many others had a similar independent command of funds and the results were the same.

In addition to the price of their dishonesty and inefficiency, the state paid the cost of the services of all these officials and of the General Farm in making payments. The French government, like any other, needed constant supplies of money in all parts of the country to pay for the goods and services it used. Partly because the transportation of coins was slow, expensive and risky, and partly because an articulated system of public finance required a sustained effort of planning and reform that was not forthcoming until the late eighteenth century, payments had come to be made with whatever funds were closest to hand. Thus government employees or supply merchants would receive salaries or settlement of accounts from a nearby Receiver or other financial officer. When that officer had not enough cash to meet the demands upon him—and the government increasingly overdrew its accounts—he would use his own money and charge the government interest on the use of it. The government was always so badly in need of money that it accepted these advances, even at 6 per cent to 10 per cent interest. The Treasurers, Receivers General and Farmers General became bankers of the state, and they were accustomed to borrowing from private sources at 5 per cent interest in order to lend to the crown at 6 per cent or more and pocketing the difference. The system became pernicious when the departmental Treasurers began to take funds which they had been granted to keep in hand for a year's departmental expenses and lent these funds back to the crown. It was estimated that through such operations a single Treasurer could cost the state 1,150,000 livres a year of which he would himself gain 400,000 livres.[1] These officers received for their advances promissory notes of various kinds—*rescriptions, assignations*, etc.—most of them discounting future revenue. As it became increasingly impoverished, the crown could not always honour them so that in some cases it contributed to the bankruptcy of its own officials. On the eve of the Revolution it owed the General Farm nearly seventy million livres, much of it contracted in this manner.

The use of such expensive short-term credit is a measure of the government's distress. Rarely able to find revenues to meet more than four-fifths of current expenditure, the Controller General was forced to borrow to cover the annual deficit. By 1788 this had risen to 125 million livres. Loans were hard to place because the government was saddled with its own past record of bad faith. Louis XV himself shared public mistrust and preferred to invest his personal fortune in the Estates of Languedoc and the General Farm. So bad was its credit that while the provincial Estates, the clergy and reputable financiers could borrow at 4 per cent interest and the British government at even less, the French government was obliged to pay up to 10 per cent not only on its short-term loans but also on its bonds (*rentes perpétuelles*), annuities (*rentes viagères*), tontines, and other loans. Whenever it could, the crown borrowed through the provincial Estates in order to have the benefit of their better credit. But by

[1] *Eclaircissements sur l'organisation actuelle du Trésor public* (1790), British Museum, FR Tracts, F.R. 502.

1763 the debt charges had already cumulated to the point where the government could no longer pay them. By compounding the interest with the principal, deferring and repudiating whenever possible, and resorting to other expedients, successive Controllers General kept the ship of state steady enough to induce other investors to place their money in her. The credit of the crown was not exhausted until 1788 in which year half the total expenditure of the state or nearly 320 million livres was required to service a capital debt estimated to have been about five billion livres.[1] In August, Loménie de Brienne, president of the *Conseil royal des Finances et de Commerce*, declared a suspension of all payments of interest charges on the debt. Necker, who immediately replaced him as chief minister of finances, kept up these payments to the *rentiers* mainly with notes borrowed from an embryo state bank, the *caisse d'escompte*. Necker intended this to be an expedient to bridge the gap until the Estates General met in June 1789, but it became a new way of financing the state.

A central bank had already been found to be an indispensable adjunct to the Treasury in the United Provinces (1609), Sweden (1656), England (1694), Denmark (1736), Prussia (1765), Russia (1770), and other countries. Two of its main uses were to manage the public debt, thereby saving the profits and commissions which would otherwise be lost to officials and financiers, and to discount government bills at a low rate of interest with bank notes which served the government as a form of cheap credit. A central bank seemed to be the best agency for handling government finances in a businesslike manner. Whether it was because the catastrophic failure of John Law's bank (1720) aroused a profound mistrust of such institutions or because the laws against usury (not abolished until 12 October 1789), the influence of interested financiers and the inertia of the royal government combined to prevent it, no central bank was created in France until 13 February 1800. But long before then the writings of Law, Petty, Child, Culpeper and especially Richard Cantillon, together with the example of English banking practice, convinced many of the necessity for doing so. At first they were mainly interested in an institution which, by providing cheap credit, would lower the general interest rates and stimulate economic development.[2] After several false starts, a group of financiers led by Panchaud persuaded Turgot in 1776 to sponsor the *Caisse d'escompte* for this purpose. But it was involved in government finance from the first because Turgot issued its charter on the understanding that two-thirds of its subscribed capital of fifteen million livres would be deposited with the Royal Treasury. In 1783, 1787 and 1789–90 the government induced its directors to make loans through issues of its notes which were given forced circulation as legal tender in

---

[1] Frédéric Braesch, *Finances et monnaies révolutionnaires*, fasc. II, part 3 (1934).
[2] Robert Bigo, *La Caisse d'Escompte et les origines de la Banque de France* (Paris, 1927), p. 25.

Paris from 18 August 1788 and throughout the kingdom from 17 April 1790. It issued notes to the value of 100 million livres in 1789, 200 millions in 1790, and escaped ruin only because the Constituent Assembly began to meet its commitments with paper notes from another source: the *Caisse de l'Extraordinaire*.

The new notes, the ill-fated *assignats*, were issued as a result of two important decisions: to accept responsibility for all the debts of the *ancien régime*, as well as for new debts incurred in the process of reform, and to repay them with the proceeds from the sale of the property of the church. The expropriation of church lands—a classic expedient of central governments asserting their authority—was followed by a revolutionary way of turning the potential wealth to account. The government would not contract with a private company of financiers to liquidate the property but kept the operation in its own hands. The land could not be simply offered for sale all at once because its price would drop. In any case, cash was needed far more quickly than these sales could be negotiated. Therefore the *Caisse de l'Extraordinaire* was created to issue bonds representing the value of the expropriated land. These *assignats* were to be paid out by the *Administration de la Liquidation* in settlement of claims and as the church lands were sold an equivalent value in *assignats* was to be taken out of circulation and destroyed. In this shift of capital from government debt to real estate, this burying of the past in the lands of the church, the only loser was to be the church, for the clergy were to be put on the state payroll. As it turned out, the *assignats* proved so useful as ready cash that the government eventually gave them forced currency as legal tender and issued far too many of them. It did so mainly to meet an annual deficit even larger than it had been under the *ancien régime*; during the years 1790–1 the government could meet barely two-fifths of its expenditure from regular receipts. In 1790 nearly 125 million livres in paper *assignats* were issued and in 1791 over 600 millions. Yet during 1791 only 37½ million livres were recovered in payment for church property. By the end of that year the *assignats* had depreciated by nearly a quarter of their value. Thus, whatever the intentions of the new régime, the national debt, like the value of the currency in which it was measured, had already been reduced by nearly 25 per cent. Obviously tax revenue, too, had lost nearly a quarter of its purchasing power so that more *assignats* would be needed to meet the deficit. But worse was to follow. In 1792 France went to war and the *Caisse de l'Extraordinaire* was called on to assist in financing it. Inflation continued at an ever increasing rate and although the Committee of Public Safety had some success in controlling it by fixing prices in 1793–4 there was no serious attempt to establish a stable or normal monetary system until 1796.

The concept of normal finance (*l'ordinaire*) as opposed to abnormal (*l'extraordinaire*), widespread in eighteenth-century France, implied a regular balancing of receipts and expenditure which the governments of the *ancien régime* and the Revolution never achieved. In a constant state of emergency, they used whatever funds were available for whatever obligations were most pressing. Yet it was during the last quarter of the century that the modern state budget, with all the control which it implies, began to take shape in France along the lines of the English budget, which had been developing since the Glorious Revolution. The budget is a complete financial plan, drawn up at the beginning of the year, for the purpose of governing all receipts and expenditure for that year alone. Any sudden emergency may, of course, call for extraordinary measures. For a budget to be effective the government must be able to predict and control state expenditure and to find adequate ways and means to meet it. Most Controllers General were able to do neither and attempted only to take soundings, as it were, of the financial system, and to draw up rough balance sheets for the years during which they were in office. Necker, in his *Compte rendu*, published the fruit of his endeavour to discover the *normal* receipts and expenditure for the year 1781, excluding, that is, the extraordinary sums spent on the War of American Independence. The ensuing controversy over Necker's figures proved his contention that radical reform would be necessary merely to get an accurate picture of the state finances. The *ancien régime* increased in self-knowledge during its last years, not least as a result of Calonne's careful preparation of reform projects for the Assembly of Notables, and in 1788 Loménie de Brienne was able to publish the first (and last) serious budget before the Revolution. He had no opportunity to put it into effect, and events in the ensuing years foiled all attempts at normal financing with a budgetary control. Nevertheless, beneath the surface of political events, a state budget was rapidly becoming possible through an increase in the central control of finances by the Royal Treasury. By the end of 1791, if not before, probably no funds were being paid unless authorised by decrees of the legislature. And the summary tables which the Treasury prepared to control its own operations for periods of a few months at a time came increasingly to resemble a budget of the state.

Under the *ancien régime*, the Royal Treasury was only one among many *caisses* (an independent account or fund for collecting and disbursing money) which received and paid out royal revenues. The various *trésoriers*, the Receivers General, the Farmers General, the *Payeurs des rentes* and a great many other officials or groups of officials who performed financial duties managed their own funds entirely beyond the control of the Treasury. The receiving *caisses* often fed the paying *caisses*, and paid the interest on government bonds and annuities, without the money passing through the Treasury at all. The surplus after all these payments had been made was supposed to be sent to the Treasury, but the government often overdrew its accounts so that nothing remained to be sent. Most of the time vast sums lay frozen in the various *caisses* beyond even the knowledge of the Treasury. In 1788 the Treasury received and paid scarcely more than half of the funds in the total budget of the state.[1] But long before then the work of consolidation had begun with the suppression of financial posts for the sake of control as well as economy. In 1772 Terray abolished the offices of *payeur* and *contrôleur* of most of the high courts whose stipends were henceforth to be paid by the Receivers General. In pursuit of the same policy Turgot planned to cut and unify until he had welded a single *caisse* which was to be that of the Royal Treasury. Turgot called this 'mon plan',[2] but it was in fact the common plan of several Controllers General. He watched with interest while his principal successor, Necker, carried it much further than he himself had been able to do.

Two chief Ministers of Finance, Jacques Necker (1777–81) and Loménie de Brienne (1787–8), contributed most towards the growth of Treasury control before the Revolution. Necker began by asserting in an *arrêt* of 18 October 1778 that all the *caisses* were emanations of the Royal Treasury and therefore accountable to it as well as to the *Chambres des Comptes*. Then, in a great series of laws, he abolished the posts of an army of Treasurers in all government services, replacing them by one for each of the Secretariats of State, one each for certain separate services such as the *Ponts et Chaussées*, and one *Trésorier payeur des dépenses diverses* for all the rest. Finally, he ordered the replacement of the forty-eight Receivers General by a twelve-man commission. These reforms were expensive, for the price of each suppressed post had to be repaid to the incumbent and until it was repaid it bore 5 per cent interest. Moreover the remaining Treasurers would require staffs of subordinate employees. Thus, although there would ultimately be a saving, the principal aim of these measures, as Necker stated in more than one preamble, was to organise the financial system in such a way as to increase the powers of control of the Minister of Finance and the Royal Treasury. He passed other measures to this end, such as a law ordering that all pensions and gratifications not due to people actually working in the paying departments should be paid by the Royal Treasury. When Necker fell, much of his work was undone, but it was taken up again in 1787 when Loménie de Brienne became president of the Council of Finances. Edicts of November 1787 and January 1788 suppressed nearly three hundred financial offices. Most vital of all, an edict of March 1788 replaced the offices of the departmental *trésoriers* and those of the two *Gardes du Trésor royal* by a five-man commission responsible for the control of all the receipts and expenditure of the Treasury. An advisory committee set up on 15 March 1788 reorganised the Treasury so that it controlled departmental expenditure more closely. Depart-

---

[1] Braesch, *op. cit.* fasc. II, part 3, p. 205.
[2] Turgot, *Œuvres* (ed. Schelle), vol. V, pp. 573, 593, 312.

mental funds were no longer to be left in the hands of the minister or financial officer of the department. But many *caisses* were still independent.

During the revolutionary period, the consolidation of national finances under the control of a unified Treasury was due mainly to the work of the marquis de Montesquiou, member of the Committee of Finances of the Constituent Assembly, of Théodore Vernier, member of the Constituent Assembly and the Convention, of Étienne Clavière, Minister of Public Contributions in 1792–3, and of Pierre Cambon, member of the Convention and the Committee of Public Safety. In December 1790 the Treasurers and Receivers General of the *Pays d'État*, and the Receivers General who had been restored to office after Necker's fall in 1781, were suppressed and ordered to turn their accounts and receipts over to the Director of the Royal Treasury. The Treasury was henceforth to deal directly with the new District Receivers who had replaced the old Receivers the previous month. The financial independence of the General Farm, too, came to an end in December 1790 when the Receivers of the Farm were ordered to pay directly to the Treasury. One by one the separate *caisses* were abolished and the control of their funds turned over to the Treasury until at last even the *Caisse de l'Extraordinaire* for the issue of *assignats* was abolished on 4 January 1793. This consolidation was completed by a series of laws which unified the scattered parts of the national debt, beginning on 15 August 1793 with the creation of the *Grand Livre de la Dette publique* on which government debts of more than fifty livres were to be recorded. In the meantime, the committees of the Constituent Assembly had found it convenient to work directly with the Director of the Treasury, Bertrand Dufresne, in matters of financial reform. The Treasury had grown more powerful with use, and in the ministerial reorganisation of 1791 it became the principal heir of the defunct *Contrôle général*. The decrees of 10 and 18 March 1791, which ordered a reorganisation of the Treasury as an independent body under six commissioners, concealed a victory of the Left Centre of the Assembly in their struggle for legislative control of the Treasury against the Right Centre supporters of executive control. When the Treasury was eventually handed over to the executive after the revolution, it had gained something from the work of its early commissioners. Their first task was to make a thorough study of the expanded Treasury organisation. Of the few changes which they recommended in the organisation left by Loménie de Brienne, probably the most important was the general introduction of double-entry book-keeping to facilitate the task of preparing accounts for the legislature. Well might the legislature scrutinise the Treasury accounts, for they were beginning to give a reasonably complete picture of government revenue and expenditure.

One of the reasons often given in the eighteenth century for the existence of separate and independent *caisses* was that they made accounting easier. The financial officer in charge of each *caisse* kept accounts for which he was responsible to one of the thirteen *Chambres des comptes*. The accounts which he was supposed to submit annually were a record of his dealings in royal funds for which he was *personally* responsible. He was only freed from his responsibility when the *Chambre des comptes* had audited his accounts, made good any errors, and finally acquitted him. The price he paid for his office was regarded as a deposit or guarantee which could be confiscated if he defaulted. Although it checked the accuracy of his accounts, the *Chambre des comptes* was not interested in how much money had been spent. It was, in short, a kind of financial court which carried out a judicial audit. So long as accounts were of this personal, judicial nature, accounting was certainly made easier by permitting each officer or service to enjoy an independent management of funds.

But during the period 1763–93 a fundamental change began in the use and character of official accounts. The change stemmed from the desire of the Controller General and others to have a complete picture of national finances. They wanted to determine the financial position of each *caisse*, not so much in order to check the honesty of the officials as to compile statistics of revenue, expenditure and cash-in-hand. They found this to be impossible for two reasons: the accounts were always so far in arrears as to be useless for current practical purposes, and in any case the officers resented this interference in their personal affairs for which they felt responsible only to the *Chambre des comptes*. The lag in accounting, which did not matter for purposes of judicial audit, was from two to four years for the General Farm and other efficient services, and only became a matter of serious concern when it reached ten or fifteen years. This delay was partly because funds were always designated either for collection or expenditure during a certain year, and the accounts for that year (*exercice*) could not be closed until the allotted sums had been spent, collected, or written off in some appropriate way. So slow was the movement of funds that officers were obliged to run accounts for several years concurrently. Many Controllers General attempted to have accounts submitted sooner so that they could discover through the *Chambres des comptes* the financial state of the realm. But the first to make a serious attempt to discover the real financial situation, and not just the state of the Royal Treasury, was Necker. Grasping the importance of control in this as in so many other spheres, Necker ordered all financial officers to send monthly summaries of their accounts to the Treasury. Loménie de Brienne carried this even further and eliminated some of the worst delays and confusions. Most important of all, under Brienne changes began to be made in the techniques of book-keeping which were the principal reason for the delays. The French administration, like most others at the time (the British Treasury and revenue departments were exceptions), used a cumbersome system of book-keeping which made it extremely difficult to balance the books until the end of the fiscal year (*exercice*). And balancing and closing the books of one year was so arduous and long that it was one of the reasons why senior financial posts were held by two different officers alternately year by year, each one balancing his accounts during the year when he was out of office. The technique of double-entry book-keeping makes it possible to balance books at any time and to have a constant check against the amounts of money actually in hand. It can thus provide a current check on operations as well as a post-check. This technique had been in use in many private firms since the sixteenth century; and attempts had been made to introduce it into the General Farm and the *caisses* of the Receivers General early in the eighteenth century. It was introduced into the section for naval accounts in the Royal Treasury just before the revolution, at a time when increasingly large sums were being spent on the navy. In 1791 the Committee of Finances of the Constituent Assembly insisted that it be used throughout the reorganised National Treasury, but had great difficulty in finding personnel trained in its use. Nevertheless it gradually replaced other methods because accounts were henceforth needed constantly for administrative and statistical purposes.

The books of the Royal Treasury accounted for only a fraction of the revenues of the state, and the delays in accounting together with the resistance of the financial officers prevented any accurate picture of the remainder. Ignorance of its own financial position was one of the main problems facing the royal government. For the year 1781 Necker announced a surplus of ten million livres, whereas Calonne argued that there was a deficit of over forty-six millions, and although this difference was partly due to a misunderstanding, it still indicates how vague were the accounts available to the Controller General. The National Assembly and all the régimes which followed were determined to know the true financial situation and also to discover and to settle all outstanding accounts. After abolishing the *Chambres des comptes* (6 December 1790) they established a system whereby all accounts were sent in turn to the Treasury for administrative purposes, to a Bureau of Accounting for the final audit, to the legislature for approval of the audit, and finally to the District Tribunals for any necessary action arising out of the accounts. The Treasury played its part satisfactorily, but the Bureau of Accounting was for many years understaffed and overburdened with thousands of national accounts going back to 1759 and by over two thousand municipal accounts going back to 1781. By 1795 its fifteen commissioners had completed the audit of hardly more than four hundred of them because they were afraid of making a mistake which the legislature might discover. But the Convention, for its part, had not found time to approve a single one. The laws of 16 February and 9 December 1795 rectified the situation, chiefly by restoring the former independent judicial character of the accounting authority. Established once more as a *Cour des comptes*, it settled by 1800 nearly half of the accounts-in-arrears of the *ancien régime*, although its report for 1810 still spoke of seeing accounts from the Seven Years War.[1] The adaptation of accounting to administrative purposes had been vital, but it had been found equally essential to leave the final audit in the hands of an authority not unlike the old *Chambres des comptes*. The most essential change had been the replacement of thirteen independent *chambres* by a single national *cour*.

The royal government was never able to account for either its funds or its employees. In practice the difference between royal and private moneys was so obscure that officials and financiers were able to enrich themselves by speculating in semi-public assets in a twilight of semi-private finance. But by the year 1793 when the Committees of Public Safety and General Security began to persecute financiers, supply merchants, and war profiteers,[2] a measure of order and control had given public funds a clearer identity. The goal of efficient organisation of the state, pursued by this great generation of reformers and revolutionaries, was not to be fairly won until after the Restoration, but by 1793 it was possible to speak of *public* finance. By that time, too, the public service had a new coherence and status, the growth of which was reflected in the coining of the word 'bureaucratie' during the late eighteenth century. The government had always been badly informed about its own administrative processes. For example, Necker was able to make only approximate guesses as to how many employees there were in the various government services. But his desire to find out was in tune with the administrative revolution of his time. The Constituent Assembly decreed on 5 July 1790 that the Committee of Finance should print in detail the composition of all the various ministries and services as they were then, as they had been in 1788, and as they had been at two previous times at least ten years apart. Although this was found to be an impossible task, it was a sign of a strong urge for knowledge and control of the public service. And the bureaucracy could now be called a public service, for it was national rather than royal and its life and property were distinguishable from the private lives and property of its members. What Frenchmen called 'la chose publique' had come into being.

[1] Victor Marcé, *La Comptabilité publique pendant la Révolution* (Paris, 1893), p. 48.
[2] Jean Bouchary, *Les Manieurs d'argent à Paris à la fin du XVIII siècle* (three vols., Paris, 1939–40), vol. I, introduction.

CHAPTER XXI

THE BREAKDOWN OF THE OLD
RÉGIME IN FRANCE

THE old régime in France—a monarchical bureaucracy working amid the survivals of a medieval society and a welter of prescriptive powers—had often displayed signs of weakness and instability. But these shortcomings in no way signified to contemporaries that the old régime was on the verge of disruption. The monarchy was taken for granted both by conservative and by revolutionary thinkers, and both, in their different ways, endowed the monarchy with an idyllic past. Conservatives, opposing the innovations of the growing bureaucracy, claimed to have discovered evidence of an old constitution under which the monarchy had worked in harmony with other powers of the realm. The revolutionary thinkers—that is to say those who wished to bring about radical changes in administration—thought in terms of absolute monarchy. They had in mind the royal power served by an enlightened bureaucracy, which would govern for the common good, unimpeded by medieval institutions and vested interests. The despotic state was merely to collect taxes (in moderation), maintain an army and a navy, and provide for police and justice. It was to be truly despotic in restricted functions and it was to maintain conditions under which natural laws would prevail, unhindered by medieval prejudice and unnecessary regulation. This idea of a powerful government which would reduce and simplify the tasks of government runs through all French eighteenth-century liberal thought; and it is here that even Rousseau finds some common ground with the Encyclopaedists and the Physiocrats.

During the reign of Louis XV many attempts were made by enlightened officials serving the French monarchy to improve the state finances and to remove restrictive practices which impeded the progress of commerce, industry and agriculture. Throughout this period the bureaucratic machine steadily improved. Not only did it enlist the services of enlightened and able men, but the number of hard-working officials (as distinct from the multiplicity of useless office holders) substantially increased without, however, assuming those proportions that render a governmental machine a costly and cumbersome contrivance. The *contrôle général* and the central *intendances* came to have a number of able chiefs of divisions and competent subordinates.[1] In the provinces the intendants of the *généralités* became, as Ardascheff[2] in his general study and others in studies of

[1] See above, ch. xx, pp. 572–3.
[2] P. Ardascheff, *Les Intendants sous le règne de Louis XVI*, trans. Jousserandot (three volumes, 1909).

592

individual intendants have shown, a body of enlightened and able administrators, who were assisted by a service of subdelegates. Indeed, Louis XV bequeathed to his successor a much more efficient bureaucracy than he inherited from *le roi soleil*.

Nevertheless the achievements of this bureaucracy were exceedingly moderate. The problems to be dealt with were many and difficult, and the king, a prisoner of the society which surrounded him, rarely gave to his ministers the continued support they needed. All attempted reforms—even those which were moderate and which efficiency and common sense demanded—met with opposition from vested interests. There are times, indeed, when vested interests control government, giving it vigour and purpose; but in France under the old régime the vested interests were, for the most part, ranged against the administration of the royal bureaucracy. Represented by important persons at the court and supported by moral and philosophical concepts, these interests frequently prevailed over the royal will. Time and time again reforms were attempted, only to be dropped; ministers were dismissed at frequent intervals and no one was sure of office from one day to the next.

Attempts to introduce reforms in France had been made intermittently ever since the days of Colbert and many of the projected reforms in the eighteenth century (for example, the attempt to abolish internal customs barriers[1]) were largely a repetition of or a continuation of Colbert's efforts. As a result of the increased interest in political economy and of the need to maintain French influence in Europe, the urge and the necessity to introduce reforms became greater and the reforms envisaged became wider in scope. It was not, however, until the end of the Seven Years War or even later that reform became at all urgent; and even then reform was hardly a matter of life and death for the old régime. For the most part the society of old France was satisfied with its traditional arrangements; and even the advocates of reform, despite their revolutionary thinking, pressed only for moderate reforms which common sense demanded. More moderate still and almost timid were the enlightened members of the royal bureaucracy, who sought merely to increase the national revenue, to effect a few economies, to give some encouragement to industry and agriculture and perhaps to abolish a few of the more glaring abuses of the fiscal system. Such reforming zeal did not extend to the king's ministers in general. Most of those who served Louis XV and Louis XVI, if they bothered to bestir themselves, merely endeavoured by fiscal expedients to raise sufficient funds for the improvement of army and navy. For of the need to maintain the fighting services in good trim most Frenchmen were painfully aware. Like Louis XV (or Louis XVI) himself they sensed that France was menaced by Russia and Prussia and constantly thwarted in Asia and America by Great Britain. They also realised that

[1] See above, ch. xx, pp. 576 ff.

disciplined troops were necessary to deal with disturbances within the country; but it never occurred to them—and there was no reason why it should—that they were in danger of revolutionary upheaval.

Typical of the ministers of the old régime (though in many ways he was outstanding) was the duke of Choiseul, who in December 1758 had succeeded Cardinal Bernis as secretary of foreign affairs. Of an old noble family and married to the daughter of the financier Crozat, after service in the army he had become ambassador, first in Rome and then in Vienna. His entry to the ministry he owed to Madame de Pompadour and to certain connections at the court. At the time, French policy both at home and abroad was chaotic. The war was going badly, the finances were precarious and the monarchy was assailed by the *parlements*.[1] Choiseul hung on grimly and then in February 1763 concluded the Treaty of Paris, by which France lost nearly the whole of her colonial empire. But in the France of the old régime a government which lost an empire was in no greater danger than one which tried to make the privileged classes pay a little more taxation. Choiseul remained in office and faced with his colleagues the task of paying for the war and of rebuilding the much-depleted fighting services.[2] Fruitful in expedients and courageous, he hit upon the plan of appeasing the magistrates by expelling their enemies, the Jesuits; and he succeeded in persuading Louis XV to reverse the religious policy of earlier years. In November 1764 Louis dissolved the Jesuit organisation and in the years that followed Choiseul prevailed upon other Bourbon rulers to follow the example of Louis XV. He was also largely responsible for the pressure that the Bourbon Family Compact put upon the Papacy to dissolve, in July 1773, the Society of Jesus. By means of this same Family Compact, which was welded to Austria by no less than six Bourbon-Habsburg marriages, he then planned for revenge on England.

In many ways Choiseul served the monarchy well, and Louis XV appreciated his services—so much indeed that Choiseul was one of the few servants of the crown who could threaten resignation as a means of scotching the many intrigues to remove him. But on the whole Choiseul did the monarchy much harm. His foreign policy, though vigorous, was not far-sighted. It ignored Russia's growing influence in Europe and her alignment with Prussia, which combination was dangerous for Poland, a client state of France. Here Louis XV was perhaps wiser than his minister; and he carried on independently his own foreign policy, known as *le secret du roi*, a policy of maintaining alliances with Poland, Turkey, Sweden and Prussia. This policy, however, never went much beyond a series of paper transactions. The king had insufficient funds to influence events in Poland itself, and, in any case, the agents conducting his policy were by no means geniuses. Poland was eventually partitioned by the three north-

[1] On the earlier conflicts between crown and *parlements*, see vol. VII, pp. 220–1, 230–6.
[2] See above, ch. VII, p. 183.

ern courts, Austria having deserted France to patch up an entente with Prussia. By that time Choiseul was out of office. Had he remained in power it is possible that, even though he set little store by Poland, he could have prevented the partition; but what is more likely is that he would have found a diplomatic situation unfavourable to France. In many ways France's position in Europe in the eighteenth century resembled her position in the nineteenth century. Her geographical situation encouraged her in maritime enterprise in the New World, the Far East and the Levant; but it also involved her in continental struggles, so that even her defensive measures often had the semblance of aggressive intention. Not only was her dual position a great strain on her finances, but she acquired the reputation of being the public enemy of Europe. In the pursuit of even reasonable national interests or even of the European equilibrium, France was highly suspect and constantly thwarted by unfavourable combinations. There were moments, indeed, when the diplomatic situation produced a relaxation of the restraining grip of Europe, but the age of Choiseul was not one of these. We might therefore say of Choiseul that as a diplomat he had ability and tenacity; and would have undoubtedly done better in more favourable times.

Of greater importance than his failure in foreign policy was his omission to uphold the royal authority in France. Though he improved the army and the navy, his expenditure impaired the state's finances. His policy of placating the *parlements* did not secure for him, or for the king, their unqualified support. Indeed, their pretensions were now greater and Choiseul, having staked all on his alignment with the magistrates, could not finance the bold foreign policy he stood for. In December 1770 he fell from power, his dreams of revenge on Great Britain unfulfilled. Just before his dismissal he had arranged the marriage of the king's grandson (the future Louis XVI) with Marie Antoinette. By this he had fondly hoped, not only to strengthen the Austrian alliance, but also to ensure his own position should Louis XV die.

Choiseul's fall—like that of most ministers in eighteenth-century France —was the result of a conflict between crown and *parlements*. This particular struggle had begun when La Chalotais, Attorney-General of the *Parlement* of Rennes, aroused his fellow magistrates to denounce the able administration of the duc d'Aiguillon, the *Commandant* of Brittany. Not that Choiseul himself was in open conflict with the magistracy: at the time he was still trying to appease the *parlements* and was encouraging them to bring about the dismissal of his fellow-ministers, Maupeou, the Chancellor, and Abbé Terray, the Comptroller-General. In April 1770 Maupeou had advised Louis to annul proceedings in the *Parlement* of Paris against d'Aiguillon. To this move Choiseul was opposed. But the immediate cause of his downfall was his policy of encouraging Spain to resist Great Britain in a dispute over the Falkland Islands, a policy likely to lead to war. On this occasion Louis came down on the side of Terray, who convinced the king and his other ministers of the inability of the Treasury to finance hostilities. Choiseul was banished to his estates at Chanteloup near Amboise. The remarkable thing about him is not that he fell from power, but that he had remained so long in office.

Following a series of court intrigues, d'Aiguillon was at length appointed Foreign Minister, and so began the rule of the Triumvirate which held office to the end of Louis XV's long reign. At no time in the eighteenth century was the French monarchy apparently so strong and yet so unpopular. On the night of 19 January 1771, following further conflicts during which the magistrates had defied a *lit de justice* and had gone on strike, musketeers delivered to each magistrate *lettres de cachet*[1] ordering him to say whether or not he was prepared to return to his judicial duties. Nearly all refused to give this assurance. The next night 130 of them were exiled to remote places and deprived, without compensation, of their venal offices. The following month, by a decree, the preamble of which denounced the abuses of the judicial system, Maupeou established six superior councils to exercise in their respective areas the judicial authority formerly exercised by the *Parlement* of Paris. But a part of the *Parlement*, the *Grand Conseil* (which became known as the *Parlement Maupeou*), was retained to act as a special tribunal for crown affairs and as a Court of Peers. It was also to act as a registry for the laws of the state, and to it was given the right of making legitimate remonstrances, that is to say remonstrances against the form and not the substance of royal legislation. Soon afterwards Maupeou abolished both the *Cour des aides* (a court dealing with fiscal cases) and the *Châtelet* (the central criminal court). He hoped also to suppress the provincial *parlements* and to establish superior councils throughout the country, but for this plan he could not win the king's approval. Nevertheless he had broken the power of the high magistracy; and there were many who believed that his timely action had frustrated a republican plot to abase the monarchy and to transfer sovereignty to an aristocracy—a relatively new aristocracy which had wealth and office (itself a kind of property) and which in varying degrees had absorbed, replaced or outmoded the old aristocracy of the sword. There were others, however, who believed that the balance of the constitution had been too violently disturbed in favour of absolutism and who feared that a monarchy which was too despotic would provoke opposition. Indeed, the greater part of France deplored the fall of the *parlementaires*. Jansenists and Gallicans discerned in Maupeou's *coup d'état* the hand of the Jesuits; the provincial nobility feared a loss of privileges and local liberties; and even the *philosophes* (Voltaire is an exception) were highly suspicious of Maupeou, little as they loved the *parlements*. To the *philo-*

[1] Sealed orders (emanating from the sovereign and countersigned by a Secretary of State) delivered to an individual.

596

sophes Maupeou's despotism was not enlightened despotism; and they therefore feared that the masses would be abandoned by the government to the leadership of the exiled magistrates. For, although the masses received Maupeou's new magistracy with some enthusiasm, Maupeou himself, and above all his colleague Terray, were most unpopular. But Maupeou was never so vicious as his unpopularity and the many libels (the *Maupeouana*) would suggest: he was always prepared to give employment to those exiled magistrates who would promise to mend their ways; and there is no doubt that his new organisation of justice, which soon began to work smoothly, was preferable to the old. Moreover it was Maupeou's intention, besides extending the system of superior councils, to reform thoroughly and humanise the whole judicial procedure. Much of the preparatory work was begun. But Maupeou fell from power before he could carry his plans into effect. His secretary Lebrun, however, was to draw extensively upon Maupeou's work when, under the consulate of Bonaparte, he codified laws and reformed procedure.

Of greater urgency than judicial reform was the need, if only to avoid bankruptcy, to reform the finances. Throughout Louis XV's reign, successive Comptrollers-General, Orry, Machault d'Arnouville, Bertin and d'Invau, had made attempts to improve the fiscal system and to impose a small amount of taxation on the privileged classes, only to find themselves thwarted either by the magistracy or by persons with influence at the court.[1] The Abbé Terray, however, although in a stronger position than his predecessors, made no frontal attack on privilege. But he tried hard to make ends meet. He put into effect Machault's improved method of assessment of the *vingtième*; he reformed the *capitation* in Paris, nearly doubling its yield; he levied additional amounts on various tolls and taxes; and in a new tax-lease that he made with the Farmers-General[2] he hauled in an additional twenty million livres. What is more, he suspended payment on the Treasury bonds; he converted with profit the *tontines* or perpetual annuities into annuities on single lives; he reduced arrears payable to holders of various *rentes*; he postponed the repayment of capital where loans had expired; and he suspended debt redemption. He also borrowed lavishly by creating further life and perpetual annuities. He did not, however, carry out his promise made to Louis XV on taking office—his promise to economise on the Household, the army and the navy. Instead he squandered money freely among the friends of Madame du Barry to keep himself in office. This he was able to do because, being a successful and courageous extortioner, he had warded off bankruptcy and had found sufficient ready cash. A sinister figure, tall, stooping and ungracious, he gave the impression of being an able financial administrator. But the truth is that Terray knew very little about the finances; and

---

[1] See volume VII, pp. 225, 231, 234.
[2] On the administration on the Farmers-General, see above, ch. xx, pp. 580–1.

the statements he drew up for the king did not reveal the exact position. Terray had got over immediate difficulties by a series of expedients, which, for the most part, were heavy mortgages, ruinous in the long run to the government's credit. When in 1774 Turgot became Comptroller-General, he estimated that the annual deficit was 37 million livres and the total debt 235 millions.

If those figures are somewhere near the truth (the system of accounting was so chaotic that the Comptroller-General could never tell exactly where he stood[1]) the government was by no means at the end of its tether. What was alarming was not the amount of debt and annual deficit, but the apparent difficulty of dealing with the problem while it was still of a manageable size. The total debt and annual deficit were to increase considerably during the reign of Louis XVI. French participation in the American War of Independence was to cost about 2000 million livres, a sum equal in figures (though not in real value, for there was a general rise in prices) to French expenditure on the Polish Succession War, the Austrian Succession War, and the Seven Years War. By the end of the American War the annual deficit was 80 millions and by 1787 it had risen to 112 millions. The exact amount of the public debt is not known, but the annual cost of handling it was well over 300 millions, or about half of the annual state expenditure. Of this annual state expenditure of just over 600 millions, just over a quarter was absorbed by the army, the navy and the diplomatic service. Just under a quarter went on civil expenditure. The cost of the court (that is the cost of the several royal establishments, of pensions and gifts to courtiers) was not at all crippling: at the most it amounted to about 35 millions.

One simple but striking fact stands out in the history of the old régime in France: the monarchy was unable to finance efficiently its wars. It did indeed manage for one hundred years to avoid bankruptcy, but during that time (roughly from the fall of Colbert to the eve of the Revolution) the public debt grew, its cost causing the annual deficit to increase. Neither occasional measures of economy, nor the growing yield of indirect taxes arising from the increase in consumption and in prices, was sufficient to meet the expense of the public debt and the rising cost of the services. More and more the monarchy came to depend on loans, which took various forms. In so doing it created a powerful class of financiers and rentiers, which was closely linked with other interests.

But great as were the costs of the wars and the armed services, they were not fundamentally too great for the country to bear. After all, France had fertile land, a population of about twenty-six millions and a quite considerable industrial and commercial development. State taxation, direct and indirect, amounted on an average only to fifty or sixty livres per family. Had the indirect taxation only been levied on articles

[1] See above, ch. xx, p. 589.

of luxury and had the direct impositions been assessed entirely in proportion to income, then the burden of taxation would have fallen on classes well able to bear it and indeed well able to shoulder a much heavier one. As it was, direct taxation fell chiefly on the peasantry and the poorer classes in the towns. From the *taille* (a 'cut' or proportion of productions) the nobles, the clergy, the numerous office-holders, and many towns were exempt. The same is true of the *capitation* (which was not strictly a poll-tax, but a tax on income reckoned not as clear profit but in terms of production) and in some measure of the *vingtième*, which was levied on the nobles at extremely moderate rates.

Indirect taxation, although somewhat more equitable since it was paid according to consumption, also constituted a heavier burden for the poorer than for the richer classes, since much of it fell on consumable goods in general demand. The *gabelle*, a tax on salt, a commodity which was essential to the rural economy, was, in certain districts, particularly onerous, its total yield at the end of the old régime being about fifty million livres. Another great burden was the *marque de cuir*, which was levied on shoe leather. This tax was one of the *aides*, or excise taxes, which were levied on drink, tobacco, iron, precious metals and numerous other commodities. Also levied on commodities were the *traites*, or customs dues. These dues were collected at the frontier, at the ports and at many customs barriers within the country (a relic of the time when certain provinces lay outside the French kingdom). On French industry and commerce the *traites* levied in the interior had a very adverse effect. For example, goods from England could often be sold more cheaply than similar French commodities, which might have to pass several customs barriers and in addition pay various tolls (*péages*). From the time of Colbert onward many plans were made to abolish the internal customs barriers, but although these plans were admirable in scope and carefully prepared, the government would never risk the temporary loss of revenue or delay in its realisation which might arise from the execution of such reform.[1]

Although the national revenue increased throughout the eighteenth century (partly as a result of increased consumption and partly as a result of heavier assessments of indirect and direct taxation), the prevailing fiscal system did not permit of an increase of revenue appropriate to the growing needs of the state. There was always a limit to the amount the poorer classes could pay; and, in any case, the state was not alone in the field when it came to mulcting the taxpayers. The French peasant bore a triple burden, for besides paying taxes to the government, he had to pay a tithe to the church and numerous feudal dues to his landlord. The tithe (though rarely levied at one-tenth but more usually at one-twelfth or one-fifteenth) was, like the *taille*, a most pernicious imposition, since it was levied on

[1] *Ibid.* p. 577.

productions and not on clear profit. The feudal dues were indeed less onerous than in earlier times, for, having been usually commuted into money rents, they had declined in real value as prices rose. In the three decades before the Revolution, however, the landlords, themselves often in need, or wanting capital for investment, employed lawyers (*feudistes*) to search the charters (*terriers*) in order to revive claims that had fallen into desuetude. The resulting increase of the financial burden on the peasantry probably caused more annoyance than real hardship. *Jacqueries* or peasant disturbances were not unknown, and, though in normal times they quickly fizzled out, when in 1789 a revolutionary situation developed, the peasants rose in a mass against their landlords, burned the feudal charters and began to slaughter game, which hitherto had been protected by the game laws.

Of the threefold burden shouldered by the peasantry—royal taxation, tithes, and feudal dues—it is impossible to give a generalised assessment. Like all social classes in France, the peasants were not homogeneous: they ranged from substantial farmers employing labour to *métayers* (share-croppers) and day-labourers, who sometimes, though not always, had small plots of land. As a general rule, the poorer the peasant, the higher relatively was the burden of taxation. In the regions where *métayage* and very small farms predominated (*la petite culture*), the tithe, the first charge on production, could often absorb forty or more per cent of profit. Feudal dues and *rentes foncières* might often take one-twelfth of what was left. Of the remainder up to one-half might disappear in state taxation. According to calculations made in 1766 by Turgot,[1] in a poor region like the Limousin (where at the time he was intendant), a family would often be left with only 125 to 150 livres (or six English pounds). Nor was this all the tale of woe. The peasants were required to perform *corvées* (or labour services), the most onerous of which was forced labour on the roads. Although most of the peasantry were under-employed and could usually afford the time, they greatly resented having to work for nothing.

A country in which some four and one-half million poorer families paid the bulk of taxation and in which about half a million enjoyed varying degrees of immunity from state impositions was bound to be lacking in well-balanced development. The taxation system indeed created a fund of wealth among the privileged classes from which the monarchy could borrow; yet, at the same time, it restricted the flow of capital into productive enterprises; and caused commercial, industrial and agrarian development to be much less than it might have been. Had the peasants been less down-trodden, many more among them would have become substantial farmers. Such farmers were, indeed, to be found in places

[1] *Mémoire sur la surcharge* (published in vol. II, pp. 445–77, of G. Schelle, *Œuvres de Turgot...*, five vols., 1913–23).

where the towns provided a market sufficient to offset the retarding effect of heavy taxation. Elsewhere, however, the sheer weight of impositions preserved *la petite culture*—an agrarian régime of tiny farms, some held in a form of ownership and others as *métairies*. In preserving this somewhat primitive agrarian order, the habits of the nobility also played an important part. Enjoying exemption from taxation and an income from feudal rents, they rarely bothered to farm their own lands: when they spoke of doing so, they usually meant that they employed bailiffs who let out the land, sometimes to tenant farmers, but more usually to *métayers*.

The poverty of the peasantry in turn restricted the industrial development of France in that the peasantry provided a very limited market for industrial productions. On the other hand, under-employment among the peasantry made available a labour force for rural industry which was expanding outside the towns, where the restrictive régimes of the guilds retarded industrial development. There was certainly a steady flow of capital into the newer and freer industries and into commercial ventures, much of this capital being provided by those who escaped heavy taxation. Towards the end of the old régime even members of the nobility invested in industrial and commercial enterprise. But although the growth of capital was sufficient to bring about an expansion of French industry and commerce, the general conditions in which that growth of capital took place prevented the adequate exploitation of the riches of France in population, technical skill and natural products. There were certain developments like those more widely to be found in England, but over the greater part of the country large pools of economic stagnation predominated.

All the same, the economic development of eighteenth-century France had modified considerably the class structure of the old régime. This class structure can be viewed either from the legal or the economic standpoint. From the latter there are changes to be observed. Although, as of old, France was divided into three legal classes—the clergy, the nobles and the Third Estate—the persons within those classes had undergone changes. The higher clergy, recruited almost entirely from the court nobility, had, on account of their lands (one-sixth of the kingdom), of their tithes and exemption from taxation, become relatively richer. The lower clergy (the parish priests and priests without parishes) had, owing to the rise in prices, grown relatively poorer. A similar variation in wealth was to be found in the ranks of the nobles (who held 50 per cent of the land in some areas and only 10 per cent in others). The higher nobility, augmented by ennobled recruits from the world of finance and often intermarried with merchant and financier families, displayed greater variations of wealth than hitherto; and some of the nobility were very prosperous. At the other end of the scale, many of the *hobereaux* or provincial nobles were outwardly distinguishable from the peasantry only by their arrogance and the rusty swords they carried. Poor as they often were, they considered themselves a race apart. This exclusiveness of the nobility became more pronounced in the closing decades of the old régime, above all among the new nobility, that is to say among the nobles who held judicial or municipal office or who had become by purchase one of the very numerous king's secretaries.

The Third Estate, or all those outside the ranks of the clergy and nobility, ranged from rich merchants and industrialists on the one hand to an industrial and agrarian proletariat on the other. Its structure was ably analysed by Turgot,[1] who saw clearly the effects of the development of capital upon the France of his day. He noticed in particular the affinity between the day-workers in industry who had no capital and the agricultural wage-earners who had little or no land. He also saw that the *métayers* bore some resemblance to the agricultural day-workers and he thought that, as time went on, most *métayers* (except for a few who might become tenant farmers) would join the ranks of those who worked for daily wages, as indeed would ultimately the small peasant owners. For, owing to the growth of capital, *la grande culture* would gradually replace everywhere *la petite culture*, the very small peasants being forced to sell their land, which would be bought either by richer peasants or by those who had obtained capital from industry and trade. At the end of the old régime the peasants still owned nearly one-half of the cultivated soil of France. Although we can speak of them as owners (since they were free to sell their land and farm it as they pleased) their lands were nevertheless subject to various feudal impositions. Only a few of the peasants' tenures were allodial. This is true even of much of the soil held by the bourgeoisie who had bought land from the peasants or poorer nobles. In all probability the bourgeoisie held about one-sixth of the cultivated area of France. It was usually on this land that tenant farmers were to be found, but it was not uncommon for the bourgeois owners to farm their own lands, employing managers and day-workers, or even to let it out to *métayers*.

As Turgot realised, the number of landless men was increasing. This in part was due to the rise of population from 18 millions in 1726 to 26 millions in 1780. True, during this period the cultivated area of France was increased, but the soil won from moors, marshes and woodlands was insufficient to meet all needs; and, in any case, the newly cultivated land was usually acquired by those who already had capital to reclaim it. Again, although in France there was no enclosure movement comparable to that which took place in England, the loss of the commons here and there increased the number of peasants who found it hard to gain a livelihood from their holdings. More important, however, in this respect were the laws of inheritance which, combined with the growing population, meant that a given amount of land came to be divided among more and

---

[1] In his *Réflexions sur la formation et la distribution des richesses* (G. Schelle, *op. cit.* vol. II, pp. 533–601) and in his official correspondence (*passim*).

more inheritors. Hence, besides the growth of landless men, there was a steady increase in the number of peasants whose holdings were insufficient to support a family. Some of these found employment in rural industry or as day-workers; but the general progress of agriculture and rural industry was never sufficient to produce full employment. The consequence was that the numbers of vagabonds and beggars (some doing seasonal or casual work) increased considerably in the closing decades of the old régime. The plight of these unfortunate people and indeed that of the wage earners was made worse by the frequent crop failures, which caused the price of bread to rise, and by a general increase, throughout the greater part of the century, in the prices of consumers' goods, which prices rose much more rapidly than wages.[1] A detailed study of prices reveals that the poorer classes consuming the inferior quality grains were the hardest hit and that the purchasing power of day-wages had fallen by about a quarter. But although consumers' prices had risen, the peasant farmers did not, as one might expect, benefit from rising profits: indeed, agricultural prices (at least from 1776 onwards) definitely declined. Needless to say, the majority of the nobles also felt the pinch, their only consolation being that they could exploit their feudal rights and pass some of their losses on to the unfortunate peasants.

The inescapable conclusion is that, in the closing decades of the old régime, wealth was being concentrated in fewer hands, but under such conditions as not to afford a general rise in the standard of living. No wonder then that the nobility clung to their privileges more tenaciously than ever. No wonder that there was occasional unrest in the countryside and towns. No wonder, too, that the nobles of the robe found considerable support among the masses whenever they defied the crown. In the course of the Revolution the masses were to find other leaders; but already, under the old régime, there existed all those discontents which, given a breakdown in authority, might lead to a social upheaval. Just as there were revolutionary ideas in existence before there were revolutionaries, so also there were dissatisfied and potentially subversive elements, which, when leaders appeared, would easily be led. All this was not apparent at the time. To all appearances the peasants, for example, were docile; and it was not until the parish *cahiers* of grievances were drawn up in 1789 that we have any definite evidence of the intensity of their discontent, and not till the August of that year, when the peasants rose to destroy the feudal régime, that we have proof of the bitterness with which they looked upon their landlords. There is no reason to suppose that their behaviour in 1789 was the result of a sudden transformation of their thoughts: what was new was a political situation which intensified their feelings and enabled them to translate thought into action. Their leaders were the

[1] See C. E. Labrousse, *La Crise de l'économie française à la fin de l'ancien régime et au début de la Révolution* (Paris, 1944).

bolder spirits among them. The men of the National Assembly had always tended to ignore them. Hence their revolution was spontaneous, the insurrection spreading by imitation and not organisation.

The leaders of the political revolution in Paris did not come from the down-trodden masses of the old régime, but from the upper strata of the Third Estate—from among those who had failed to pass into the ranks of the nobility. They found kindred souls among the lower clergy, who greatly resented the idleness, ostentation and exclusiveness of the higher clerical orders. They were joined even by certain nobles (a very small minority, to be sure) who accepted the humanitarian and equalitarian ideals of the Enlightenment. All these leaders were men of substance, owning property and believing in the right of everyone to the property he acquired. Not very mindful of the poorer classes, their conception of equality was limited to their desire to abolish rank. Above all they hated the privileges and arrogance of the nobility, whose exclusiveness was not confined to Versailles but was paraded in the Paris salons and in the salons of provincial towns. They had read and taken to heart Rousseau's attacks on the nobility, the writings of the elder Mirabeau and Boncerf's denunciation of the feudal order, a work which Turgot, himself a noble, but an enemy of privilege, had caused to be published.

In these and numerous other writings, the whole basis of the old régime was being questioned; and the system of thought employed was as old as the ancient régime itself, for its antecedents lay in the scientific revolution of the seventeenth century and beyond in the Renaissance.[1] The new fashion in thought was to be found even among the higher clergy and at the court itself. Throughout the second half of the century scepticism, criticism and profanity became more widespread, and all the efforts upon the part of the authorities to impose censorship were of little avail, for the police system of the old régime was not adequate to suppress all clandestine writings and meetings, or to prevent the importation of subversive publications from abroad. In the course of time several of the more important schools began to teach Newtonian physics and to depart, almost completely, from the older educational system; and, with the suppression of the Jesuits, there was removed one of the strongest bastions of the old order. All the same, orthodox thought found staunch defenders who, by their writings, endeavoured to prevent the flow of converts to the new ideas. The Age of Reason, therefore, was a time when old doctrines, formerly taken much for granted, were strongly and eloquently reasserted. It was also a time of religious revival among a declining but still substantial body of the faithful (sometimes in the form of strange and emotional cults) and of an intellectual revolt against the materialism of the Enlightenment—a movement which was one of the antecedents of the great

[1] See A. Cobban, *In Search of Humanity. The Role of the Enlightenment in Modern History* (London, 1960), pp. 29, 40.

Catholic revival of the nineteenth century. At the court, despite the levity and free thinking of several factions, was to be found a strong religious party (the *dévots*) with which both Louis XV and Louis XVI had the profoundest sympathy. Nevertheless, those who defended the religious way of life were divided. The Jansenist magistrates (no longer doctrinal Jansenists as in the seventeenth century) disputed the crown's control of the church, claiming for themselves the right to persecute and claiming for the state a more extreme Gallican authority than the crown itself was prepared to accept. Needless to say these disputes served only to discredit still more the old organised religion, and the attempts to defend orthodox belief only led to an even more vociferous expression of anticlerical ideas and materialism.

Attempts have been made to assess (in a quantitative fashion) the prevalence of the new ideas during the old régime. These attempts were prompted largely by the fierce disputes of historians over the question whether the Revolution was a revolt against economic oppression or whether it was the result of new ideas. Taine[1] had contended that France of the old régime was a perfectly healthy body politic which drank the poison of materialistic and atheistic philosophy; and Roustan,[2] too, explained the origins of the revolution in terms of the influence of a few philosophical writings. Mornet, who spent a lifetime on his great work,[3] asked the question whether the writings of the philosophers were widely read and, if so, by whom. He also set himself the task of discovering at what level of thought the new ideas passed into more general currency. He therefore studied the lesser-known literature, the local journals, the records of lesser salons and literary gatherings, library catalogues and private letters. He came to the conclusion that the new ideas were widely held and that the great writers (even Voltaire in his earlier days) had a public before they wrote; but he also found that the ideas which were widely held were not charged with revolutionary fervour. His verdict was that if old France had only ideas to fear, then she had no reason to be afraid. Lest he might be thought to favour, therefore, an economic interpretation of the collapse of the old régime, he removed all doubt by stating that he was not competent to discuss that problem.

What Mornet found was that everywhere in France, among the literate classes—in Paris, in the provincial towns both large and small and even in the countryside—most people were very much aware of practical problems—problems of taxation, industrial restrictions, farming, feudal dues, the corn trade, and so forth. As for the peasant masses, there was very little to go on, except for certain parish *cahiers* of 1789, which unlike the common ones based on circulating patterns, show signs of having origi-

---

[1] H. A. Taine, *The Ancient Régime*, trans. J. Durand (1876).
[2] M. Roustan, *Les Philosophes et la société française au XVIIIe siècle* (1906).
[3] D. Mornet, *Les Origines intellectuelles de la Révolution française* (1933).

nated in a parish assembly. These (as do the *cahiers* in general) display great moderation and a narrowly practical purpose. Indeed, the main feature of eighteenth-century French liberal thought was utilitarian; and, though the metaphysical conception of a natural order underlies it, its presentation, for the most part, was simple, direct and practical. But to say that French liberal thought was practical and utilitarian is not to deny that it was revolutionary. It was revolutionary because of its basic attitude, because it established new criteria and because, in demanding changes and improvements, it denounced most of the arrangements of the old régime. The very practical forms in which this thought existed meant that it became widely diffused at different levels among a great part of the population. But being practical (albeit revolutionary) it did not dwell in fervent and politically conscious minds; and even the high priests of the new religion lacked any truly subversive design—any ideal of political upheaval or organised revolt. Revolutions that lead to violence, said Rousseau, must be avoided; and the thought of suddenly overturning the mighty structure of the French monarchy appalled him. Mably, too, one of the fiercest critics of feudal privilege, and other more extreme thinkers, the priest Meslier, Linguet and Brissot, Abbé Morelly and Rétif de la Bretonne, were totally devoid of any political design for overthrowing the monopoly of power and wealth enjoyed by the privileged classes. Content merely to denounce existing institutions and to formulate ends, the most extreme revolutionary thinkers had nothing revolutionary to offer by way of means. All they could do was to hope for revolution from above. And to an age which believed that reason was bound to triumph and that the masses were incapable of speedy enlightenment, this faith in revolution from above is only to be expected. So many ministers and officials had already shown enlightenment that it was not outrageous to suppose that the monarchy could be quickly enlightened and set to work for enlightened ends. Yet the strange thing is that though people thought in terms of a quick and easy route to perfection, they had—at least in the last years of Louis XV's reign—no sense of urgency.

In the closing years of Louis XV's reign, as at the end of Louis XIV's, everyone waited for the old king to die and prepared themselves, in terms of the politics of the old régime, for an uncertain future. The court factions made ready to renew the party conflict and the philosophers fondly hoped that the new reign would bring enlightenment to the king's counsels. At length, on 10 May 1774, rather sooner than expected, Louis, formerly the well-beloved, passed away, unregretted by his subjects. He was succeeded by his grandson Louis, the duc de Berry. The new king, however, seemed to promise little. Although his religious convictions disposed him to work for the welfare of his people, he lacked intelligence and strength of will; and he preferred fierce bouts of manual labour and hunting to the drudgery of administration. His queen, Marie-Antoinette, was likewise unfitted for the position she held. Irresponsible, with no ideals of government and certainly no desire for power, impulsive, often generous and therefore easy game to the intriguers, she was for ever soliciting favours for her friends and passing on to Louis the slanders of the court. All the same (as the Austrians realised) she was unlikely to exert any predictable influence upon the policy of France and even Choiseul (whose protégé, the Abbé Vermond, was close to the queen) was soon to realise that he was unable to turn the tables on Maupeou, D'Aiguillon and the Abbé Terray for the simple reason that his enemies, the *dévots*, had the ear of the king. It was this party which persuaded Louis to send for Maurepas, an elder statesman who, it was hoped, would steer the new king through the labyrinths of court intrigue. The king's mentor did not, however, assume the title of first minister; and he was much too indolent to become a Fleury; but he occupied a position of great importance and he made a serious attempt at the outset to encourage the king to make his own decisions. It was not long before changes in the ministry came about. Much to the delight of the masses, the Triumvirate was dismissed; Vergennes became Minister of Foreign Affairs; Miromesnil became Chancellor and Turgot, after a brief period at the Marine, became Comptroller-General. Strange to say he owed his promotion to high office largely to the influence of Abbé Vermond, much to the annoyance of the *dévots*, who knew that Turgot never went to mass.

For thirteen years Turgot had occupied the post of intendant at Limoges, where he had carried out a number of reforms. His entry to the government was therefore hailed by the philosophers (Voltaire included) as the dawn of a new age; and the Physiocrats were hoping that he would carry into effect their economic doctrines. Turgot himself was not a Physiocrat (he did not accept the theory that land was the sole source of wealth), but he did accept many of their views on taxation. Like the Physiocrats he held that all taxation fell ultimately upon the land and that to tax industry and commerce was to ignore a natural law. He also held that taxation should be levied only on sheer profit and then only at a moderate rate, so that there would be accumulated a fund of agricultural capital, without which there could be no progress. Finally he believed in complete free trade and in the necessity to remove all restrictions on industry. Such, in brief, were Turgot's theories. As Minister of State, however, he took a considerably lower flight, working only for minor reforms which, given the support of the king, were certainly feasible. He clearly wished not to arouse political storms by introducing at once extensive changes but only to meet the immediate fiscal difficulties of the state and to mitigate here and there abuses which oppressed the poorer classes. From the outset, however, reactionary opinion feared he would make a frontal attack on privilege; and, much to his embarrassment, many of his supporters announced prematurely a wide range of reform.

Though not a politician in the sense that Choiseul and Maurepas were politicians (they had a thorough knowledge of people and factions), Turgot was not devoid of political wisdom. He saw that he must keep in with Maurepas, who with Abbé Vermond would speak to the king and queen in his favour. He also realised that reforms must be gradual, knowing only too well that, though moderate reforms might survive the attacks of isolated vested interests, any truly radical programme would arouse concerted opposition. He further saw that every financial reform must be so arranged as not to cause any temporary loss of revenue, and it was for this reason that he decided against any immediate attempt to suppress the internal customs barriers—a reform which, though already planned in the *contrôle général*, might lead to temporary financial loss.

Turgot was by no means an inflexible theorist. Although by tradition and conviction he was an *anti-parlementaire*, he nevertheless thought it expedient to restore the high magistrates, but with their powers curtailed. He probably hoped that the government would have wider support if the old magistrates were allowed to return, and in any case he knew that Maurepas and Miromesnil would eventually bring about a return of the old courts, perhaps without conditions. The whole problem was thoroughly discussed in a committee of four—Turgot, Maurepas, Miromesnil and Sartine—which met secretly with the king. As Maurepas refused to take the lead, it was left to Turgot to suggest the compromise and it was his idea that a *Grand Conseil*, composed chiefly of the Maupeou magistracy, should be retained to take over the administration should ever the magistrates be suspended or refuse to carry on. Turgot's decision was probably wise, and he himself cannot be held responsible for the sequel— the reassertion of the magisterial claims—for neither the king, Miromesnil, nor Maupeou gave him the support required. The result was, nevertheless, that his reforms were jeopardised from the outset. What is more, Turgot had incurred the resentment of the *dévots*, who, already fearful of his philosophy, now denounced him for restoring the Gallican *parlements*.

Turgot was already committed to some measure of reform and indeed there would have been no point in retaining office if he had not attempted to put some order into the finances. On accepting appointment as Comptroller-General he had written (24 August 1774) to the king giving the outline of his programme and translating the language of reason into that of sentiment, which was more likely to appeal to Louis.[1] In brief his programme was: 'No bankruptcy; no increase of impositions; no borrowing;...reduction of expenditure below receipts...with a view to redemption of long-standing debt.' Accordingly, throughout the remainder of the year he carried out a number of minor economies and minor reforms of indirect taxes, including a small reform in the *gabelle*. He also abolished the *contrainte solidaire*, an outrageous practice, by which the receivers of

[1] G. Schelle, *Œuvres de Turgot*, vol. IV, pp. 109–13.

the *taille* could force the higher-taxed members of a parish to pay the sums owed by parochial defaulters. Other minor reforms and economies followed. By the end of 1775 Turgot had reduced expenditure by 66,200,000 livres. He had also (and it was this that gave the greatest hope of financial recovery) reduced the interest upon loans from 8,700,000 to just over 3,000,000 livres. His credit abroad was good, and it was now possible to borrow money cheaply in Holland to carry out a debt conversion from 7 per cent to 4 per cent. The new loan (sixty millions) could not have been raised in Paris, for the financiers, who were thoroughly suspicious of Turgot's intentions, were known to be about to engineer a shortage of money. Turgot hoped, however, to raise ten millions direct from the investors by establishing a *caisse d'escompte* but this project raised an outcry from the clergy, who denounced it as usury and prevented it from being carried out while Turgot was in office.[1]

Already Turgot had made other enemies by his decree of September 1774 which re-enacted Bertin's measure of May 1763 establishing free trade in grain. This measure freed the internal grain trade outside Paris. The feeding of the capital always presented a special problem and Turgot thought it unwise to establish a free grain trade there until a large and free commerce was flourishing in the provinces. Moreover, he knew that, though the magistrates were in favour of a provincial free grain trade (in their exile they had learned that a considerable body of provincial opinion supported it), they were not likely to approve the abolition of the Paris corn laws. Turgot was, therefore, content with a restricted measure of reform which seemed likely to raise little difficulty. It was not long, however, before a fierce pamphlet war arose between the mercantilist and free-trade schools. The physiocrat journalists, in supporting Turgot, aggravated the controversy and gave the false impression that Turgot would soon carry out a whole series of reforms in accordance with his academic theories. Of even greater importance than this pamphlet warfare were the grain riots which began in March 1775 and which, by the beginning of May, had spread to the environs of Paris and to Paris itself. Here a mob some five hundred strong, having pillaged certain supplies, swarmed around the *contrôle général*. Lenoir, the chief of police, was inexperienced, and it fell to Turgot himself to organise military measures for the protection of property in Paris and the surrounding countryside. Quite soon the situation was in hand. But already the affair had given rise to yet another conflict with the *Parlement*. Nevertheless, Turgot survived the upheaval; the king remained firm; and Turgot went on to issue twenty-three further regulations increasing the liberty of the grain trade. But his victory led to renewed attempts to undermine his position. Already there was talk of replacing him by Necker, the Swiss financier, who, assisted by his talented wife, had found favour with many persons at the

[1] See above, ch. xx, p. 584.

court and who already enjoyed the reputation of being capable of putting the finances in order without delving into the pockets of the privileged classes; and Necker himself was paying the inferior poet, the marquis de Pezay, who maintained a secret correspondence with the king, to criticise Turgot and to sing the praises of his paymaster. All this time the Choiseulistes at the *salon* Guéménée, which was frequented by the queen, renewed their efforts to bring back their leader in place of Maurepas; and yet another attack came from the higher clergy and the *dévots*, who knew that Turgot had tried to change the coronation oath and that he was hoping to relieve the disabilities of the Protestants.

All these attacks which Turgot's policy brought upon the ministry were much resented and feared by Maurepas; and Turgot, on his side, became more and more impatient of the delays caused by Maurepas, of his petty intrigues, of his haste to protect himself even when his position was not seriously threatened. Turgot, who wished to convince Louis of his worth, therefore decided to press on with his reforms and in January 1776 he began to submit to the council, where they were discussed in Louis's presence, a series of reforms, usually called the Six Edicts. These reforms were relatively moderate, for Turgot still believed that he must postpone major changes until the king was older. One of the edicts suppressed most of the dues on the grain trade in Paris; a second abolished certain useless offices on the quays, halls and markets in Paris; a third suppressed the *Caisse de Poissy*, a useless and extravagant institution which levied impositions on the Paris meat trade; a fourth reorganised the administration of impositions on suet. Much more important were the two remaining edicts. One of these (it was carefully prepared by Albert, former intendant of commerce) suppressed most of the guilds of Paris. The other abolished the royal *corvées*—a measure carefully prepared after consultation with the provincial intendants. To replace the labour services of the peasantry on the roads, there was to be levied on all landowners a tax— a very moderate one—which was to supply funds out of which those labouring on the roads were to be paid. The preamble to the edict, which like the other edicts prepared by Turgot were read out in the churches, contained a general condemnation of privilege; and it was for this reason that the magistrates, assured of the support of the clergy, concentrated their attack on this measure rather than upon that suppressing the guilds —which reform found some favour among the clergy since it transferred the guild charities to their control. Even before the edict had been submitted for registration, the magistrates denounced it: Miromesnil had informed them that this and other measures were in preparation and that there were differences of opinion about them in the council. In order to save his edicts, Turgot had reluctantly conceded that the clergy should be exempt from the tax replacing the *corvées*.

The edicts were at length submitted to the *Parlement* on 7 February.

The magistrates protested and at the same time condemned Boncerf's *Inconvénients des droits féodaux*, till then quite an obscure work, which tried to show that it was really in the interest of the seigneurs that feudal dues should be abolished. Both in condemning Boncerf and in remonstrating against the Six Edicts the magistrates denounced what they described as a new, theoretical system which was being insidiously unveiled by degrees. But Louis, despite opposition from Maurepas, held on 12 March 1776 a *lit de justice*. That night Paris was illuminated and there were great rejoicings among the working population. And when the news spread to the provinces the peasantry celebrated the abolition of the *corvées*. Such scenes, however, only led to more determined efforts to remove Turgot from office; and Maurepas, under this pressure, now turned decidedly against his colleague. A forged correspondence between Turgot and a friend—letters which purported to incriminate Turgot— was brought to Louis's attention; and this, combined with other manœuvres and with the influence of Marie Antoinette (who was now hostile towards the minister) led to Turgot's dismissal. Only a few days previously he had warned the king that it was weakness that had brought Charles I of England to his tragic end.

And so fell—as Calonne was later to fall—a minister who, if given adequate support, might perhaps have overcome the fiscal difficulties of the monarchy and who, given time, would have established a régime favourable to a more rapid economic development of the kingdom. But, as Turgot himself realised, the chances of continued political support for any extensive plan of reform were indeed very slender. 'The root of the evil, sire'—so he told the king on one occasion—'is that your nation has no constitution.' He went on to formulate his political ideas. But the constitution he envisaged consisted merely of a hierarchy of administrative assemblies and it hardly occurred to him that the privileged classes would refuse to co-operate in a scheme which obliterated social distinctions. Any conception he had of calling upon popular forces to overcome the aristocracy was, like Rousseau's, vague and unrealistic—as indeed it was bound to be with anyone who lived before the Revolution. He had fondly hoped that the popularity of reform would prevent the privileged from persisting in their opposition and would cause all classes ultimately to co-operate in carrying out an administrative policy determined from above.

Turgot's work was rapidly destroyed in the summer of 1776. Clugny, his successor, reimposed the *corvées*; free trade in grain was suspended; and the guilds were given again legal existence. Early in 1778 the king took the decision to assist the Americans in their War of Independence— a move which Turgot had earlier opposed because of the cost and because of the danger that the British would compensate themselves for losses in America at the expense of France. It was to Necker that the task of financing this war fell. On the death of Clugny in October 1776 he had been appointed counsellor to a nominal Comptroller-General, Taboureau des Réaux, and in June 1777 he had become Director General of Finances. Believing in the miraculous power of credit, he resorted to borrowing in all its forms (loans, lotteries and life annuities), thus piling up the debt and increasing the annual deficit. He did, however, attempt to make a few economies and to increase the control of the Royal Treasury over the finances. He continued Turgot's policy of reorganising and thus saving on the administration of certain taxes of the general tax-farm; he tried to improve the system of public accounting; he suppressed numerous offices; and he made minor economies in the royal household, which saving, however, was offset by an increase in pensions. In his commercial policy he was a moderate *Colbertiste*: though maintaining for the most part a restrictive régime, here and there he freed certain goods and certain trades and even allowed some freedom to the grain trade. In August 1779 he abolished *mainmorte* on the royal domains, but was not prepared to risk the application of this reform to the lands of the seigneurs. It was, moreover, his intention to proceed, after the war, to extensive administrative reforms in the collection of taxation; and in view of these plans in February 1778 he took up but modified considerably Turgot's idea of local administrative assemblies. By way of experiment he established in the summer of that year a provincial administration at Bourges in Berry, a body consisting of twelve clergy, twelve nobles, and twenty-four commoners, who were to vote by head and not by orders. This assembly was to allocate taxation, administer the *corvées* and arrange works for the employment of the poor. Its decisions were to be submitted to the intendant and to the council. From its inception, this assembly was denounced by the nobility and magistrates and even by the *économistes* (who much preferred Turgot's plan), but these last soon changed their tune when the provincial assembly itself proposed that it should be transformed into an elective body and should be empowered to reform the *taille* and the *corvées*. The government, however, refused to adopt these suggestions. All the same it decided to establish three further assemblies in the *généralités* of Moulins, Grenoble and Montauban; but, owing to local opposition, the first two never functioned.

Despite the attacks on his plan for administrative assemblies, Necker enjoyed widespread popularity; for, apart from his reputation of being able to wage war without increasing taxation, he had been careful not to attack the nobility or clergy or to work for the removal of the political disabilities of his fellow Protestants.[1] Nevertheless, there were many persons hostile to him, and as time went on some of the higher clergy and the magistrates began to intrigue against him. Like Turgot he never

[1] An edict of November 1787 removed most of the disabilities of the Protestants, but complete equality was not established until September 1791.

enjoyed the full support of Maurepas and the other ministers. Although in October 1780 he was able to replace Sartine by his personal friend Castries, and although in December Ségur (a pro-Necker Choiseuliste) entered the ministry, Maurepas, returning after a period of illness, was keener than ever to get rid of Necker. In self-defence Necker obtained from the king permission to publish in February 1781 his famous *Compte rendu*. Hoping to revive his waning popularity, he claimed a surplus of 10,000,000 livres instead of confessing to a deficit of 46,000,000. His story was widely accepted and his publication had an enormous sale, the result being that a new loan was easily raised. But at the same time the *Compte rendu*, because of its erroneous information and because it vaguely announced reforms, gave rise to many attacks on his administration. His enemies even pirated and published his memorandum to the king on the provincial assemblies, a memorandum hitherto kept secret. Quite soon the *Parlement* entered the fray and drew up remonstrances against the edict setting up the provincial assembly of Bourbonnais; and Calonne, one of Necker's most powerful critics, came out with a pamphlet ridiculing Necker and his projects. Necker now demanded of Louis the title of Minister of State, control of the finances of the Ministries of War and Marine, and the establishment of provincial assemblies throughout the whole of France. But Maurepas won the day and, knowing the game was up, Necker resigned on 19 May 1781. Six months later the aged Maurepas died. Louis, determined to dispense with a mentor, refused demands that he should appoint Cardinal de Bernis, or Choiseul, or Archbishop Brienne to take the place that Maurepas had occupied. But he made Vergennes, Minister of Foreign Affairs, the president of the Council of Finance. Vergennes was thus a kind of principal minister, but he did not have the title, nor indeed the ability for such a role.

The new Comptroller-General was Joly de Fleury, who had close ties with the high magistracy. He took charge of the finances only on the understanding that he would soon succeed Miromesnil as Keeper of the Seals. Levying a third *vingtième* and increasing indirect impositions instead of depending entirely on borrowing, it was not long before he provoked a general opposition and in March 1783 he was dismissed. His successor, d'Ormesson, paid the same penalty in November for his attempt to squeeze the Farmers-General. He was succeeded by Calonne, intendant of Lille, who like his colleague in the ministry, Breteuil, owed office chiefly to the influence of the duchesse de Polignac and the queen. On taking the oath the new Comptroller-General vaguely intimated that he would reduce the public debt and redistribute the burden of taxation. At first he seems not to have realised the appalling conditions of the finances and for two years he liberally rewarded those to whom he owed office. Saint-Cloud was bought for the queen; the debts of the king's brothers were paid; and large sums went to help the bankrupt family of

Guéménée. But Calonne did realise that, owing to the failure of his predecessors to pay interest on loans, the credit of the government was very poor. To restore confidence he spent lavishly on public works. As time went on he began to see that the finances were fundamentally unsound; and in 1786, assisted by Turgot's old confederates, Dupont de Nemours, Trudaine, Le Noir and Fourqueux, he began to formulate thorough-going reforms. He also saw that fiscal reforms, to be successful, must be accompanied by political and administrative changes. Therefore, when he designed a new land-tax in kind to replace the *vingtièmes*—a tax to be levied uniformly and without exemptions—he planned for it to be administered by a hierarchy of local assemblies, which were to be composed of persons drawn from all orders. At the same time, he planned the commutation of the *corvées* and the abolition of *gabelles* and internal customs barriers. He also hoped to extend the stamp duty, so that, like the new land-tax, it would fall principally on the privileged and wealthy classes. Finally, to ease the burden on the lower orders, he proposed to restrict the *taille* to one-twentieth of income.

To wipe out the annual deficit of 112,000,000 livres, he designed to increase revenue by 70,000,000 and decrease expenditure by 45,000,000; and to ease the burden of the public debt he planned to spread the redemption of short-term loans over a period of twenty instead of only ten years. To meet redemption payments he intended to raise new loans. In time, as the yield of taxation increased, he hoped to reduce the public debt. This increased yield from taxation—so he reckoned—would derive from the increased prosperity which would result from the abolition of internal customs barriers, the removal of major restrictions on the grain trade and the leasing of the royal domain on leasehold tenures.

Calonne's proposed reforms were revolutionary for they meant, besides the abolition of privilege, a demolition of much of the structure of the old régime. To facilitate these extensive changes, he advised the king to call an assembly composed of Notables, who were to be nominated by the crown. He had hopes that this procedure would enable the government to avoid a conflict with the magistracy and would silence the demands already being made for the convention of the old Estates General. He imagined that the Notables, who would form a kind of enlarged king's council, would be flattered by the honour conferred upon them and, therefore, tractable. Above all he wanted the whole business carried out speedily so that excessive dispute might be avoided. But Louis, as usual, procrastinated; for he little cared for an attack on privilege and he had no wish to make any inroad into the corporate existence of the clergy. Advised by Miromesnil and Vergennes, he was inclined to a policy of reform in stages. Calonne, however, rejected piecemeal reform and half-measures; he wished to marshal opinion against the privileged classes; and he wanted to employ the royal authority in one supreme effort to break the stranglehold of the public debt and annual deficit. At length the king gave way and, at the end of November 1786, agreed to assemble the Notables on 29 January. But by gaining this victory Calonne had made implacable enemies of Vergennes and Miromesnil, who began to plot his downfall, knowing that he was not likely to find the Notables so tractable as he imagined. This body (which Calonne made no attempt to pack) consisted of 144 members, among whom were thirty-seven high magistrates, forty-three great nobles and princes of the blood, twelve councillors and intendants, twelve representatives of the provincial estates and twenty-six municipal officers. The clerical members were only fourteen.

In calling on the assistance of a body of this kind (which had been last summoned in 1626) Calonne was certainly optimistic. Although the members were to vote by head and not by orders they were all privileged persons. But then Calonne was not in a position to ignore the privileged classes and it was not within the scope of his political vision to do so, any more than it was within that of Turgot or of Necker. Like all reformers who served enlightened despotism, Calonne, Turgot and Necker were revolutionaries only in the sense that they rejected many of the assumptions of the old régime, seeing clearly that the fiscal and economic problems of the age could be solved only by abolition of privilege and restrictive practices. In a general way they saw the need for marshalling a wider public opinion to overcome vested interest and ancient prejudice; but thinking always of government in terms of administrative perfection, they could think only of revolution from above and it was not within their range of thought to think of calling to action the upper strata of the Third Estate. Indeed, it is doubtful whether this could have been done, even had they let their thoughts stray outside the realm of their traditional ideas; for the higher bourgeoisie did not form a homogeneous, still less an organised interest, except perhaps in those provinces which had provincial estates, and even there the representatives of the Third Estate more often than not followed the lead of the other two orders.

Calonne's expedient of summoning the Notables may to us seem utterly futile; but to him it was perhaps the only political means at his disposal, as he had ruled out all ideas of calling the Estates General, which had last met in 1614. Those who belonged to the bureaucratic traditions of the old régime regarded the Estates General as a medieval and antiquated institution which was embarrassing to the royal bureaucracy; and they tolerated the provincial Estates only because it had never been expedient to abolish them. In pronouncing for the Notables, Calonne could at least hope that patriotic sentiments might prevail over the sectional interests of classes and of the different areas of France. But in this he was quickly disappointed. The fourteen clergy, ably led by de Dillon, archbishop of Narbonne, and by Calonne's rival for power, Loménie de Brienne, archbishop of Toulouse, were to dominate the assembly, in which were to be found many persons who were hostile to Calonne. The assembly's first meeting had been postponed until 22 February and during the delay Calonne's enemies had got together and had prepared their case. When at length the assembly met they were in no mood to accept Calonne's revolutionary programme which he introduced in what must to them have seemed highly revolutionary language. They challenged him to produce detailed accounts—the very thing he wanted to avoid. Their general tactics were not openly to defend privilege but to attack Calonne's plans in detail and to forecast difficulties. But it was privilege they defended and it was soon quite clear that they would not accept the new land-tax. In vain did Calonne attempt to turn the tables on them by appealing to public opinion in a memorandum entitled *Avertissement*, written by a lawyer Gerbier and circulated free of charge mainly through the agency of the lower clergy. But this pamphlet found little sympathy with the Third Estate. In so far as public opinion counted, Calonne came off worse than the Notables, for it had been given out and it was generally held that he had been guilty of peculation. There is no doubt that he laid himself open to charges of this kind. At length, on 8 April, he was dismissed from office, falling from favour much in the same way as Turgot had fallen a decade earlier. It is just possible that Calonne might have fared better if, instead of calling the Notables, he had prevailed upon Louis to reduce the power of the magistracy. Under his successor, Brienne, the attempt was indeed made, for on 8 May 1788 the king held a *lit de justice* to enforce the edicts designed by Lamoignon, the Keeper of the Seals, to destroy the political power of the *parlements*. These edicts established a plenary court (somewhat on the lines of the *Parlement Maupeou*) for the registration of royal legislation, and forty-seven bailiwicks to take over much of the judicial work of the *parlements*. But this attempted *coup d'état* came too late. The monarchy was soon to be committed to calling the Estates General, which action had been recommended by the Notables and was now demanded by the magistracy, the Assembly of the Clergy and by public opinion. What is more, Lamoignon's attempted reforms had prompted the magistrates to stir up revolts in several provinces. Brienne gave way and Lamoignon's reforms were suspended.

These events had demonstrated once again the failure to inaugurate revolutionary changes from above. They had also demonstrated the conflict within the monarchy itself—the conflict between the monarchy as a bureaucratic organisation and the monarchy as an aristocratic institution. That conflict had never been resolved one way or the other. Had the Estates General continued to meet, there might possibly have evolved a monarchy on the English pattern. As it was, however, the monarchy as a bureaucracy had managed, at the price of concessions to prescriptive powers, to avoid control by representative institutions, except to some extent in those regions where there were provincial estates. In the absence of the Estates General, the *parlements* had claimed to represent the nation and in the closing phases of their struggle with the crown had come, despite their innate conservatism, to use revolutionary language and to hold up for admiration the ideas of the American Revolution. By the middle of 1788 it was clear that the monarchy could not find within the context of the old régime a new basis for its authority. Gone were the days when the French body politic could pass through a period of *déréglement* without upheaval—without radical changes in the legal and social structure of society. Although the principle of monarchy was not immediately assailed, the implication was that the monarchy must radically transform itself. Such a transformation was not outside the realm of possibility; but, as events were to show, neither Louis XVI nor those who tried to save the monarchy were capable or strong enough to lead the Revolution, which was left to develop in its cataclysmic fashion.

CHAPTER XXII

THE HISTORIOGRAPHY OF THE FRENCH REVOLUTION

'Go calmly and look English.' Bagehot's formula for immunity in Parisian insurrections might well serve as a guide to his countrymen who study the historiography of the French Revolution, for party strife and inherited prejudices have branded their mark upon most French histories of the Revolution, so that the Anglo-Saxon student automatically enjoys the advantage of comparative detachment. Yet it is dangerous to presume upon this immunity and overemphasise the relationship between the disagreements of French historians and their particular political prejudices. A good deal depends on what we choose to include in our definition of 'historical writing'. If, on the one hand, we consider all the journalism which offers interpretations of the Revolution, or, on the other, confine ourselves to comparing the broad conclusions of general histories[1] a close correlation with contemporary politics is bound to emerge, as surely as the cup from Benjamin's sack. By either of these methods, and indeed, by the mere concentration upon developing interpretations (which are the necessary themes of any historiographical study), a mass of research, opinion on details, and narrative slips through our net.[2] The main corpus of real historical writing is useful to everybody. 'Progressive' historians remain indebted to the vast collections of information made by 'reactionaries' like Mortimer-Ternaux, Wallon and Lenôtre; Gaxotte's attack on the Revolution leans heavily on Mathiez's labyrinthine investigation of the underworld of corruption.

But the problem is still not solved by admitting that there exists a wide no-man's-land of 'fact'. The strong personal opinions of an historian are not just his 'bias', to be discounted; very often they also constitute the essential groundwork of his originality and insight. Continually, new aspects of the Revolution must unfold as the world changes. Serious works on religious history, by both clericals and anti-clericals, were written against the background of the break-down of the relations of

---

[1] Two works which are particularly interesting to students of the historiography of the Revolution may be cited: as an example of the first method, S. Mellon, *The Political Uses of History: a Study of Historians in the French Restoration* (1958); and of the second, P. Farmer, *France Reviews Its Revolutionary Origins* (1944).

[2] For example, to quote the first older works that come to mind, no reference is made in this essay to indispensable studies like Droz, *Histoire du règne de Louis XVI* (1839–42); Sciout, *Histoire de la Constitution civile du clergé* (1872–81); Chuquet, *Les guerres de la Révolution* (1886–96); Brette, *Recueil des documents relatifs à la convocation des États Généraux* (1894–1904); Mellié, *Les Sections de Paris* (1898).

church and state under the Third Republic. The rise of socialism drew the attention of historians to neglected aspects of their studies, just as rationing and inflation from 1914–18 encouraged a new appreciation of the economic background of the Terror. To be sure, broadly speaking, we can detect a 'Right' interpretation of the Revolution, a 'republican' one and a 'socialist' one. Yet, within the 'Right', why does one choose to praise Louis XVI, another the émigrés, or Napoleon, or even the Committee of Public Safety? Why do 'Republican' historians regard the Terror as a disgrace to their ideals—or as a necessity? Why do 'Socialists' choose Robespierre or Hébert, or show sympathy or hatred towards the role of the bourgeoisie? Politics cannot account for all these choices, and in so far as it can, the sentimental side of political allegiance does not always square with the logical one. Among French historians, psychological predispositions on the issue of violence and its legitimacy have been as crucial a dividing line as party affiliations, and patriotism has been a unifying 'bias' to a greater extent than politics has been a divisive one. Influences are manifold: what appears to come straight from Karl Marx may well go back to a tough legitimist like Balzac. There is a complexity in human affairs and motives which baffles historians, and a similar complexity in the work and motives of historians which baffles historiographers. The history of history, like history itself, must be 'a debate without end'.

Though to some extent it is true that the modern historian's term 'French Revolution' partakes of the nature of Max Weber's *Idealtypus*, a nominalist concept to facilitate discussion, it is important to remember that, from the very first, the events of 1789 were a 'revolution' to contemporaries. Believing that they were involved in a pattern of circumstance which had its own coherence, they naturally attempted to write its history. In approach and method, their publications reflect the influence of the models of historical writing and research which had been available to educated readers at the end of the old régime. The vast repertories of lay and canonical jurisprudence of Guyot and Durand de Maillaine have their counterpart in Baudouin and Rondonneau's seven-volume dictionary of revolutionary legislation (Years VIII–IX); the chronologies of the Benedictines of Saint-Maur are recalled by Rondonneau's *L'Art de vérifier les dates de la Révolution* (Year XII). From Voltaire, Montesquieu, and classical antiquity, and, on a lower plane, from Daniel, Mézeray and the Abbé Vertot, the compilers of general histories derived an emphasis upon style and literary form and an inclination towards 'philosophical' presentation which were dangerous ideals for writers of ordinary ability. By the end of 1792 two works had been published which could reasonably be called 'histories' of the Revolution, one by 'Deux Amis de la Liberté' and one by Rabaut Saint-Etienne, both of which provided patterns of interpretation which were taken up by later historians. The 'two friends of liberty', bourgeois, afraid of the populace as well as of the court, anti-clerical but not irreligious, writing an account limited to political events and movements of public opinion in Paris, foreshadow Thiers; Rabaut, glorifying the Revolution as the crown of French history and of human reason, defining it as a clash between privilege and the nation, and emphasising the role of the people, 'exalted in its passions, penetrating in its conjectures, brusque in its movements, prompt and sometimes cruel in its vengeances', anticipates Michelet in his enthusiasms and 'philosophical' historians like Mme de Staël and Quinet in his method. Between 1796–7 and 1800–1 new attempts were made to write a coherent history of the Revolution; these were years when press restrictions were relaxed, when events marched more slowly and when the accumulation of memoirs put more information at the disposal of publicists. With one exception, these histories are of little value, though they occasionally transmit fragments of unusual information about incidents within the range of their authors' personal experience. 'I claim the authority, not of an impartial observer (Great Heavens, who could have been?) but of an eye-witness', said Lacretelle disarmingly in defence of his condemnation of the Revolution —a literary work in the style of Tacitus put together from the *Moniteur* and a few memoirs. Of these post-Thermidorian histories only one was well documented and politically liberal, that of the vicomte de Toulongeon, a nobleman who had rallied to the Third Estate and the Republic. He garnered materials from private archives, making a clear distinction between his sources and his recollections, and, a professional soldier himself, produced an intelligent study of the revolutionary wars which prepared the way for Jomini and Thiers. Though not an apologist for any faction, he admitted that he favoured whatever administration had ruled his country's destinies—he was 'un peu gouverniste'. It was a confession which could appropriately be made by many subsequent French historians of the Revolution.

Tocqueville somewhere argues that contemporaries should write the broad interpretative history of their own age and leave later generations to establish the detailed narrative. A measure of support for this theory may be found in a consideration of the quasi-historical literature produced by the Emigration. It was amid the psychological tensions of exile, and to meet propaganda ends, that the 'plot theory' of the Revolution, already hinted at in many a pamphlet, was codified. Barruel's voluminous *Mémoires pour servir à l'histoire du Jacobinisme* (1798–9) provided the key to the labyrinth; there had been an inner plot and an outer one, an alliance of philosophers and masons with adventurers of the Jacobin Clubs, with behind it all, a brooding Providence using the wickedness of men as a scourge of blasphemy. For the Right, this explanation was a partial absolution. Whatever they had done, the crimes which took place were unavoidable: in the words of the Abbé Proyart's title-page (1800), Louis XVI was 'dethroned before he was crowned'.

The conspiracy theory, however, had one great virtue, for it drew attention to the fundamental and most fascinating problem in revolutionary studies, that of the relation between ideas and events. For Barruel the link was achieved by deliberate organisation. Chateaubriand and Sénac de Meilhan, who refused to disavow the Enlightenment, and the comte de Provence, the future Louis XVIII, saw the connection more realistically and more subtly; a process of selection had operated upon ideas, either through ambitious interest or by the tyranny of 'fashion', or a distortion had taken place, thanks to the *esprit de système* of the century. A minority remained sceptical about the role of ideas, believing, with Mallet du Pan, that passions rule the world; or preferring to regard philosophy as a symptom of the general malady, rather than its cause. Certainly the arguments of the Right showed an awareness of nuances. They manœuvred, reluctant to abandon the chief glories of eighteenth-century literature to a crew of conspirators. Following the clues offered by the Emigration, many subsequent writers, especially conservatives, were to seek for the origin of the Revolution in ideas and in the machinery by which ideas are disseminated, an approach which Taine was to free from conspiratorial fancy-dress and which Cochin exempted from Taine's over-systematisation. One might observe of this, as indeed of many other general views, that there is no logical necessity appropriating such a thesis to right-wing historiography, unless it be crudely argued that the guillotine lurks behind the humanitarian externals of all radicalism, or proofs be sought of the obvious proposition that revolutions are staged by minorities. Too much weight has been given to the role of special pleading in historiography, and too little to the persistence of patterns of traditional interpretation, religiously preserved like sacred white elephants in certain intellectual *milieux*. The standard right-wing interpretation of the Revolution was born in the Emigration, and its continuance probably owes as much to sentimental inheritance as to the necessities of polemical logic.

In other ways the intelligent and resentful theorising of the émigrés added to the common stock of ideas about the Revolution and provided future historians with preliminary hypotheses. An ex-intendant himself, Sénac de Meilhan was quick to detect the waning power of the old centralisation; Bonald fancifully drew attention to the corporative nature of the *ancien régime*, where privilege and the sale of office had created the equivalent of a free constitution; Chateaubriand, Maistre and Sénac de Meilhan, each in his own way, ascribed the beginnings of the Revolution to an aristocratic Fronde; Montlosier acutely described the Revolution as a vested interest created by the opening of careers to talent and the putting of vast landed property under the auctioneer's hammer. And, oddly enough, it was from the Right, from the Emigration, that the most cogent explanations of the Terror originate. To both Maistre and Chateaubriand, this is the heart of the Revolution. In spite of personal losses, the one is prepared to contemplate calmly Providence pruning the tree, the other to recognise the despotism that is necessary for ages of decadence. These Jacobins, says Chateaubriand, came up from Hell, but brought all the talents with them. They overcame foreign armies, civil war, inflation, famine, corruption. Robespierre, the greatest of them, saw, with terrible clarity, the logical results of his principles, and tried to put through by force that moral revolution which is the prerequisite of democracy. Patriotic zeal for the country of his intellectual adoption compelled Maistre, the Savoyard, to go further. He condemned the Emigration as a crime, and praised the bloodstained Jacobins and the usurper Napoleon, who had repelled the foreigner and saved national unity. Thus, in the Emigration, we see in its earliest and acutest form the dilemma which the right wing of French historiography could never evade, and which was to form a bridge between it and the history of the left. The principles of '93 could be condemned, but not the achievements. It was France which marched to victory under the tricolour. *La patrie*, the plot of land, the tomb under the trees in the place where you were born, is not really exportable into the Austrian and Prussian baggage trains.

Just as patriotism provided common ground between the émigrés and their expropriators, so too did historical determinism. The exiles were haunted by the idea that the Revolution was a work of Providence, or of Fate—call it what you will so long as eternity is invoked to provide miscalculation with its alibi. They were not, however, the only ones who had miscalculated, nor was a mystical conservative fatalism the only kind of determinism. As the Revolution went on, it assumed unforeseen and terrifying forms, yet all the while continued to interweave itself with the belief in progress; it shed layer after layer of its supporters, while making its cause more and more inseparable from the whole national interest. It thus encouraged men to hypostasise events which they failed to understand or which they did not know how to resist, until confusion appeared an organic unity, an ineluctable process. Given certain data, said Toulongeon, revolutions, like physical changes in the material of the universe, are inevitable. Napoleon, with that unfailing realism by which he measured everything except his own ambitions, saw this tendency as the historical formula to reconcile all Frenchmen. In his now notorious historiographical instructions to the Abbé Halma (1808) he recommended an unemotional approach to the horrors of recent years—'the blame attaches neither to those who have perished nor to those who have survived. There was no individual force capable of changing the elements or of foreseeing the events which were born from circumstances and the very nature of things.' Had the emperor written revolutionary history instead of regarding it as a prelude to his legend, he would have spoken with the accents of Thiers and Mignet. These two historians were to be accused of 'fatalism'. It was not their invention. The victor was glad to have 'the very nature of things' legitimising his rule, as it had necessitated the Terror: the defeated were glad to have succumbed to no lesser foe than destiny.

Of the generation which reached manhood in 1789, brilliant representatives survived to interpret the Revolution to the period of the Restoration. The greatest of these had been banished, and spoke from St Helena. By himself, Napoleon constituted a new Emigration. Comfortable in Ruritanian Elba, he might have dwindled to life-size: on a rock in mid-Atlantic the aureole of a new mystique encircled him. From thence, a gospel of the Revolution emanated, a Revolution which found in the emperor its son and heir, the hero who continued its tasks and carried its standard of national self-defence to the pinnacles of glory. The myth and reality of Bonaparte stood between nineteenth-century historiography and 1789. His career was either the supreme example of determinism or its *reductio ad absurdum*. With him, the Revolution came to its logical conclusion—or its betrayal. Yet, challenging and divisive as it was to historians, Bonapartism was also a patriotic unifying theme. Frenchmen resented their final defeat and were reluctant to abandon their hero. Detestation of the Empire did not prevent Quinet's mother from weeping when the Hungarian cavalry went through, or relieve the sadness of Mme de Staël at seeing troops from the boundaries of Asia mounting sentry on the steps of the Opera. Patriotic allegiance, evident in literature with Stendhal, Balzac and Hugo, was equally reflected in the historiography of the first half of the nineteenth century. There was, it has been said, 'a conspiracy of glory' which united the victories of the Convention with those of the Empire and with those of earlier feudal and monarchical ages. The culmination of the eighteenth century in Napoleon's superhuman adventure helped to give the historiography of the Revolution a more acute sense of its paradoxes—and its chief bias, something more subtle and more honourable than Right or Left distortions: the bias of patriotism.

Like Bonaparte, Chateaubriand, Mme de Staël and Saint-Simon had been in their twenties in the year of the Estates General; Maistre, Bonald, Montlosier and Roederer had been rather older. Now, twenty-five years later, they reviewed the handiwork of their generation. Theirs was the intensity of complicity, yet they had a certain detachment, for all were either 'foreigners' or émigrés—except Saint-Simon and Roederer, and the one was too fantastic and the other too judicious to subscribe to partisan prejudices. These writers lived for ideas, and with them the great debate on the role of ideas in causing the Revolution continued. Maistre and Bonald continued to insist that freedom of thought, initiated by the Reformation, had been the original disaster, so that beneath the glitter of eighteenth-century literature revolution lurked, like plague amidst precious cargoes in a vessel from the Levant. 'From the Gospels to the

Contrat social', said Bonald, 'it is books that have made revolutions.' On the other side, Mme de Staël, faithful to Necker's memory, to English constitutionalism and to progress, defended the liberal ideas of '89 by separating their eternal principles from the passions of those who had applied them; vanity had made Frenchmen attack privilege rather than despotism, pride had prevented them from imitating England, they had wooed abstractions and missed realities. *Amour-propre* was an inadequate formula, but to emphasise the onslaught upon privilege—'Le principe moteur de la Révolution était l'égalité'—was to strike a main highway of interpretation. From Mme de Staël and from Bonald, Chateaubriand and Royer Collard went on to develop the theme of a dialectic between liberty and equality, of a revolutionary egalitarianism which had reduced society 'to a mere dust of isolated individuals', lacking the cohesion to resist either anarchy or despotism. This antithesis of liberty and equality was to have an illustrious course, which led finally to Tocqueville.

If equality had been the driving force, it might be inferred that social tensions had been more important in the genesis of the Revolution than movements of ideas. Saint-Simon and Roederer thought so, the one because he believed that the constructive principle of science was only now emerging from the ruins of the past, the other because he assessed ideas with the cynicism of an intellectual turned administrator. For both these thinkers, a particular social force, gaining momentum for at least six centuries, had been the agent of revolutionary change. For Saint-Simon, it was the *légistes* who had created the monarchy and then, like Janissaries, had destroyed it; for Roederer it was the bourgeoisie demanding equality before the law and careers open to talent—and, as an epiphenomenon, liberty. This theme of a rising middle class was to be the ground where the most acute theorisings of the generation of 1789 blended with the historiography of the young generation of 1820. Augustin Thierry and, more particularly, Guizot took it as their clue to interpret the whole movement of French history. Oddly enough, they arrived here, not as a result of Roederer's analysis—for he long delayed to publish—but by way of a dusty eighteenth-century controversy resurrected by an injudicious work of another representative of the old generation, Montlosier, who argued that the Frankish conquest of Gaul provided title-deeds of the nobility's right to pre-eminence. In 1820 Thierry and Guizot made sardonic replies. Like Sièyes in 1789, they accepted this racial hypothesis, but reversed the deductions to be drawn from it. Jacques Bonhomme, in Thierry's famous parable, was entitled to his revenge, and his cruelty in victory was a result of his miseries and his unfamiliarity with the disciplines of liberty. 'For more than thirteen centuries', wrote Guizot, 'the defeated race fought to shake off the yoke of the conquerors. Our history is the history of this struggle. In our day, a decisive battle has been fought; it is called the

Revolution.' There was a tragic fallacy here, for Third Estate and *bourgeoisie* are not identical; the middle class is not the people.

The generation which had savoured the *douceur de vivre* of the old régime and felt the impact of revolutionary chaos was obsessed with a search for causes and with the mysterious workings of fate. Those who were born half a generation later, the schoolboys of 1789, were tempted to see the Revolution as essentially materialistic—an opening of the gates to careerists, and a vast transfer of property. The realism of Stendhal and P.-L. Courier prepared the way for Balzac. To him, they transmitted the harsh flavour of the material interests that had been building steadily behind the façade of proscriptions and victories. The first histories, properly so-called, of the Revolution, those of Thiers and Mignet, were to be progressive, complacent and—with their recitals of battles, orations and *journées*—essentially political. But alongside them, another history was to be written in the margins of historiography, a chronicle of the new society which had been created by inflation and the sale of *biens nationaux*. Ultimately, the *Comédie humaine*, that labyrinthine masterpiece of insight and pessimism, was to be a more important document for interpreting the Revolution than the narratives of its first historians.

Thiers, whose volumes began to appear in 1823, and Mignet, who published in the following year, both belonged to Balzac's generation. They had been educated under the Consulate and Empire, when France had been too busy making history to teach it, when text-books were crude skeletons of facts, and the Université had made history a mere accessory of literature courses. Thus, in contrast to their great German contemporary Ranke, who moved in a professional academic world, Thiers and Mignet were self-taught, ambitious young men who came to study the Revolution by way of political journalism. Yet their writings form part of a genuine revival of historical studies in France. Scott's novels and Chateaubriand's return to the Middle Ages played their part in this orientation, but essentially, Frenchmen were now confronting history because history, in the form of the Revolution, had confronted them. There is no one among us, said Thierry, who does not know more even than Voltaire of the fall of empires. Thiers and Mignet had avowed political aims in writing; they proposed to justify the revolutionary epoch and demonstrate that its sequel, the overthrow of the Bourbons, had yet to come, as 1688 had followed 1640 in England. But Mignet's future career was to show that he wished to be an historian, not a politician, while Thiers, whose career shows the opposite, would hardly have written ten volumes if his aims were merely those of a pamphleteer. In 1823 it was almost inevitable that young men desirous of literary fame would turn to history, and being journalists with liberal political views, it was as probable that they would choose the history of the Revolution.

There is poetic justice in the application of 'inevitability' to these writers, for they lavishly invoked the forces of determinism upon the characters in their histories. They sighed for Louis XVI, admired Mirabeau's ideas, idolised La Fayette, revered the Girondins as heroic, intelligent and magnanimous—and dismissed all possibility that any of them could have succeeded. With Thiers, this determinism is unsystematic: with Mignet, it is the iron framework of his interpretation. Apart from a mysterious reference to 'an immense and fanatical sect' which carried on the doctrines of Rousseau, he gives little place to the movement of ideas—it was but a reflection of more permanent driving forces. The Revolution was the inevitable outcome of a process by which the Third Estate had risen in wealth and intelligence; that was why 'the States General only decreed a Revolution already formed', why despotism had to end and equality oust privilege. However, while some events arose from this basic necessity, others arose from a proximate determining factor, the resistance of the privileged. But for the Emigration and religious schism there would have been no republicanism, but for the foreign war there would have been no Terror. These patterns of argument, explicit in Mignet, are implicit in Thiers. Both historians divide the Revolution at 10 August, 'the insurrection of the multitude against the middle classes and the constitutional throne', 'the beginning of the system of absolute equality'. Before that date the Revolution was directed by long-term necessity, and assured victory to the middle class; afterwards Mignet's 'multitude', Thiers' 'vile populace', which 'has not changed since Tacitus saw them applaud the crimes of the emperor', must rule, because the war had to be won. Thus came about 'the gloomy and ragged administration of the people', and the uncultured masses are cruel. In 1789 the people were where they ought to be—under the leadership of an educated bourgeoisie; in 1792–3 they were called in as the last grim resort to save France, because reaction had made a liberal bourgeois solution impossible.

The predestined rise of the middle class is a basic concept which Mignet and Thiers shared with Guizot and Thierry, Roederer and Saint-Simon, while the proximate necessity which made Terror and popular rule the result of reaction and war is a bourgeois adaptation of the patriotic admissions which the Revolution had wrung from aristocrats like Maistre and Chateaubriand. It is the second of these deterministic factors which accounts for the tragedies which took place between 1789 (when, Mignet admits, Louis XVI could have avoided disaster by making sacrifices) and 1799 (when Bonaparte had a choice between preserving liberty and destroying it). The crucial mistakes, in fact, were made by despots, and the horrors between were perpetrated by the populace. This absolves the enlightened middle classes, who remain available to take over control when a next instalment of revolution—free from the distortions of violence—ultimately arrives. Thus, while contemporaries saw Thiers and Mignet as 'fatalist' historians, we see them rather as 'bourgeois', and their fatalism as none other than the 'thesis of circumstances' of later republican historiography. Fate and Chance are, after all, but different names for the same thing.

Contemporaries, friends and political allies as they were, Thiers and Mignet are naturally considered together, the Siamese twins of revolutionary studies. This joint treatment of their work can, however, be misleading. With his usual flair, Sainte-Beuve discerned how two very different temperaments were engaged beneath the surface of an apparently identical interpretation. Mignet, from his early essay on medieval institutions to the end of his career, was deliberately in search of those necessities which 'use men as means', for history's inner framework, its 'osteology', while Thiers' determinism is linked with his genius for clear exposition, with a narrative style which is always more lucid than events as they happened. One might add, that, while Mignet, both as historian and propagandist, was austere and uncompromising, Thiers was a natural exhibitionist, whose ebullient omniscience was to be the delight of anecdotists, an intellectual entrepreneur who was anxious to please. Massacres and cruelty in the Revolution are coldly noted by Mignet and accounted for by his central thesis; Thiers gives full, even apocryphal details, and advances subsidiary circumstantial and psychological explanations—all too briskly, it must be admitted—'Mens immota manet, lacrymae volvuntur inanes'. Both historians are anti-clerical and unsympathetic towards the aristocracy; but, while the one simply refers to the Vendée as uncivilised, the other describes it as a primitive paradise, ruled by a devoted clergy and patriarchal squirearchy, at once a menace to France and a quaint world apart, which was tragically crushed by the Revolution's imposition of uniformity. Both historians are patriotic; but where the one sees only the cruel necessity of survival, culminating in the crowning of a soldier who understood no more of the Revolution than its material side, the other revelled in details of campaigns, rallied to the flag whatever hands held it, and finished in the cult of Napoleon. Mignet's was a single-minded analysis. Thiers, insensitive to tragedy as he was, yet had wider sympathies and greater tolerance. Already he was a politician, with a programme he believed in, but on whose margins he was willing to flatter and compromise. Like the republic which he sponsored half a century later, his was the form of history 'which divides us least'.

The peaceful revolution which Thiers and Mignet had hoped for occurred in July 1830. Then came disillusionment. The great Revolution was already the dominating theme of the past, as the wars of Greeks and barbarians had been to Herodotus: the failure of the July Monarchy compelled a generation, whose philosophy of history was a single-minded belief in progress, to postulate an unfinished revolution, still driving on towards its logical goal. But why was it unfinished, what had been missed in the decade following 1789 and again in 1830? In social terms, the reply could be sinister—'the Revolution', said Victor Considérant, was but 'a quarrel between the upper classes'. Liberal historians praised '89 and the bourgeoisie; what if a man should exalt '93 and the proletariat, make Robespierre the embodiment of revolutionary ideals, justify Terror as an instrument of regeneration and regret the untimely cessation of social progress at Thermidor? There was, in fact, an unbroken memory which did all these terrible things. Babeuf had risen against the Directory in 1796 in the name of Robespierre's ideal, Buonarroti had kept faith with his leader by publishing, in 1828, an account of their conspiracy for equality. This tradition carried on—in Laurent, Laponneraye and Cabet, and true historical scholarship took up the theme in Louis Blanc's history, where regrets for Robespierre's cruelty mingled with respect for him as the embodiment of the principle of the future against bourgeois Constituents and Girondins. From Babeuf, an analysis of the Revolution thus descends to Jaurès (who called him 'great and good', 'our master'), to Mathiez and to socialist historians generally; from Babeuf too stems a theory of revolutionary dictatorship which passed through Buonarroti to Blanqui and to Marx and finally to Lenin, who put it into practice. Socialist interpretations of the significance of 1789 are ambivalent, for they judge the Revolution in the context of a theoretical pattern which was partly, in origin, its own creation.

The Left's heritage from Babeuf was dictatorial, sentimental and egalitarian; from Saint-Simon and Comte a different pattern of ideas descended, organising, scientific, hierarchical. The first tradition claimed Rousseau and Robespierre as its prophets, and believed that the Revolution had lighted upon its true inspiration only to be brutally arrested in mid-course; the second claimed Diderot as its theorist and Danton as its first practitioner, and considered that the Revolution had achieved necessary demolitions without discovering its true goal. Comte, born in the year before Napoleon's *coup* of Brumaire, had no personal experience of these years, and did little reading which could have kept him abreast of historical knowledge. Even so, he contrived to theorise about the Revolution in an intelligent fashion. Eighteenth-century philosophy had been, he considered, essentially negative; one eighteenth-century thinker, however, foresaw the recomposition which must follow destruction—Diderot, whose *Encyclopédie* epitomised science, synthesis and order, and one hero in the Revolution applied these principles—Danton. Comte liked enlightened dictatorships. With him, for the first time the Convention was praised with non-Robespierrist arguments, as an admirably conceived and self-consciously temporary dictatorial experiment. Under the illusion that Danton had instituted the religion of reason and had ruled France from 10 August 1792 to his execution, Comte awarded him the distinction due to a Richelieu or a Cromwell. This rehabilitation of Danton coincided —within a few years—with Michelet's favourable intuitive appreciation and with Villiaumé's rejection of the charges of venality which, even after Thermidor, had remained unrefuted. By the mid-century then, there were two schools of thought which made the Convention period the great age of the Revolution. The Robespierrists had an unbroken tradition: the Dantonist school was a new creation.

Interpretations which went too far to the Left were a threat to national unity. That, perhaps, was one of the reasons why Esquiros, Cabet and Laponneraye attempted to argue that the Revolution had a providential and Christian origin, and why Buchez, who differed from them in being as fanatical a Catholic as he was a socialist, declared that the Revolution was 'Catholic in essence' and embarrassingly defended the Terror on an equal footing with the massacre of Saint Bartholomew.[1] Certainly, one of the deepest instincts of Frenchmen was the desire for patriotic unity and internal peace. Louis Blanc's admiration for Robespierre and dislike of bourgeois individualism did not diminish his revulsion against the idea of an open class-struggle. Of the terrorists he wrote, 'their violence has bequeathed a peaceful destiny for us...the Terror by its very excesses has forever become impossible'. It was to emphasise precisely this lesson that Lamartine wrote his vividly inaccurate *Histoire des Girondins*. 'Don't read it', he wrote to a friend, 'It is written for the people. The people are about to play the principal part. They must be prepared; they must be given a distaste for executions in order that the coming revolution may be exempt from the excesses of the first.' His bland indifference to truth was such that Levites of historiographical studies are tempted to pass by on the other side and leave the wreck of the *Girondins* to expire peacefully under the weight of its own errors; it had, however, 'raised history to the level of the novel', and as a novel, the book is brilliant and generous. Lamartine's picture of the Revolution is a great harmonising myth, in which all oppositions reach their final conciliation. All who died, died for posterity—'let us be reconciled over their graves'. The *Girondins* is an epic based upon the dark romantic tension between pity and necessity. Far from 'gilding the guillotine', Lamartine repudiated all cruelties, even when demonstrating their inevitability. Social democracy must come but let it come without further violence, as a peaceful revolution that will conquer the world.

The year 1847 saw the appearance of Lamartine's *Girondins* and the early volumes of the histories of Louis Blanc and Michelet. These three writers belonged to the same generation as Thiers and Mignet, only they were publishing one revolution behind them, and looking forward, not to a constitutional bourgeois monarchy, but to a republic, to the advent

---

[1] There is not space here to deal with Quinet's unique position in the debate concerning a 'religious' interpretation of the Revolution. The arguments of this 'Protestant de Maistre' stand at a fascinating point in the history of ideas, but may, perhaps, be fairly omitted in a brief essay.

on the political stage of 'the people'. By 1847, *le peuple* had become a mystical concept, indefinite, but infinitely emotive. From 1830, Romanticism in literature, which had been linked with right-wing political views under the Restoration, moved left and evidenced social preoccupations. 'Autrefois le poète disait, *le public*; aujourd'hui le poète dit, *le peuple*.' From various points of the political compass, literature reflected this movement towards the masses; it is found in Balzac's preface to *Le dernier Chouan* (1829), his most important work referring directly to the Revolution, and in Hugo's preface to *Angelo* (1835), in Ozanam's 'Passons aux Barbares', in Lamennais's intuition that universal suffrage would be a conservative stabilising factor, as well as in more direct and Rousseauistic challenges from the furthest left. Michelet's *Le Peuple*, published in 1846, was an appeal to the bourgeoisie to forget its fears—fears of Communism, impossible in a land of small proprietors, fears of Terror, a bloody institution which had been run by individuals of the middle classes—and to cast in its lot with, to renew its strength in, the people. This was to be the central idea of his great history of the Revolution. Spontaneous and generous emotion, not reason, was the glorious passion of the revolutionary years; so-called 'leaders' had been but 'ambitious marionettes'. 'From the first page to the last', Michelet wrote of his own book, 'there is but a single hero—the people.'

Michelet's concept of the people squares so neatly with the dominant political and literary trends of the mid-century, with the Revolution of 1848 and the Romantic Movement, that it is easy to underestimate his originality. His thought, like his style, is intensely personal, the inner creation of his private lonely world. 'Né peuple, nous allions au peuple.' The Parisian populace of his history is seen in the image of his adored father, the printer working his presses during the Revolution in the nave of an abandoned church; the revolutionary masses are exasperated by the grinding poverty he himself had known as a boy. This sentimental inheritance was refined and reinforced by early studies of the philosophy of history, undertaken by a young man whose ambition was to be a philosopher. From Quinet, who introduced him to German thought, particularly to Herder, from Cousin, that strange Hoffmanesque philosopher and administrator who flits in and out of so many intellectual biographies, and, more especially, from his own discovery of Vico and study of songs and sagas, Michelet developed the essential ideas of his philosophy of history—the eternal warfare of liberty and necessity, the divinity of humankind, the great ideas which manifest themselves in the people. To these he added a conviction which came to him from Rousseau and the Revolution itself: a faith in the inherent goodness of man. The concept of the people which emerged from this philosophy of history was essentially sentimental and collective. It was not based upon an analysis of economic structure: it had no internal tensions or hierarchies. Moulded by geography, myth and language, bearer of the idea of justice, the people was the spontaneous force behind historical development, instinctively seeking, not individual liberty, but a Rousseauistic collective freedom. Michelet began on medieval history, accepting monarchy and church as instruments in the battle of liberty against necessity, but from 1843 he became an anti-clerical, partly because his tremendous imagination instinctively took the dominant colour of the period he was studying. He thus came to the Revolution with his remarkable powers of style and historical evocation at their fullest, but with his mind constricted and intolerant. He 'resurrected' the Revolution (to use his favourite word), in the sense that he recaptured and succumbed to its fanaticism. Having condemned Christianity, Michelet's dialectic lost its universality, and in his hands the 'People', that vast collectivity, became a nationalist phenomenon, a mythical creation of the most patriotic of French historians.

In his *Introduction à l'histoire universelle* (1831) Michelet had described his country as the crowning glory of civilisation, so that when he came to the Revolution and found there the quintessence of France, he felt himself at the crucial point of all world progress. 'Here is my blood,' said France to the nations, 'drink.' He adopted the sacramental parallel deliberately, for to him the Revolution was nothing less than a new religion, the religion of justice. The Declaration of the Rights of Man, which Thiers had dismissed as a philosophical commonplace and which Mignet had patronised in a few respectful lines, now became a subject for lyrical praise, 'the *Credo* of the new age'. It arose from the work of two great prophets: Rousseau who taught the people their divine mission to make a new world, and Voltaire (unjustly described as 'bourgeois' by Louis Blanc and Buchez) who was heir to Rabelais, Molière and the humane and satirical genius of France. Under their inspiration, the Revolution was 'a church in itself', which ought never to have resorted to the Civil Constitution of the clergy, a futile compromise with outworn Christianity.

A nation spiritually unanimous in 1789, a Third Estate unfissured by social hatreds even up to the shootings of the Champ de Mars, a 'people' abominating cruelty and generous to the very end: on the other side, court, nobility and church, fundamentally vicious, and a criminal conspiracy of foreign powers led by pharisaical England, against which France drew the sword in a 'sublime war'—this is the essence of Michelet's interpretation of the Revolution. Beneath his generous emotions lurks the fanaticism of a revolutionary imperialist, putting enormous powers of poetry, sympathy and erudition at the service of two superb myths, 'France' and the 'Peuple'. Without them, our understanding of the dynamic forces of the Revolution would be poorer: with them, the historiography of the Revolution is in perpetual danger. The greatest of its historians was also the greatest of illusionists. Yet Michelet's writings have retained a sort of biblical status in French historiography, for however much higher criticism may devastate their literal interpretation, they remain a source of inspiration and refreshment. They gave hope to republicans under Napoleon III, and when the Republic triumphed, they were a resort against the drabness of shoddy official politics. Lucien Febvre turned to them under the German occupation during the second World War, just as Monod had done under the Second Empire. Republican, but anti-socialist, anti-clerical, but devoted to a religion of humanity, patriotic, yet avoiding the spell of Napoleon, interpreting the Revolution by its ideals rather than by its events, and by its place in mankind's future progress rather than by its roots in the past, Michelet wrote a gospel, which, under the Third Republic, was to harden into an orthodoxy. As is the way with creeds, this was more moderate, logical and intelligent than the myth from which it sprang: on the other hand, no subsequent formulation ever recaptured the magic of the original enthusiasm.

To protect his sanity against such necromancy the reader cannot do better than turn to Carlyle, and set enchanter against enchanter. Ten years before Michelet applied his technique of 'resurrection' to the Revolution, Carlyle had evoked revolutionary Paris in an incomparable series of tableaux, vivid with lightning flashes and black with thunder wrack. Both writers had an astonishing power of recalling the past to life—the one in a delirium of enthusiasm, the other through a sort of nightmare hallucination. To both, the protagonist in the drama was the people; they agreed in admiring Danton at the expense of Robespierre, and were at one in blaming revolutionary violence upon European encirclement, 'plotting Aristocrats' and 'excommunicating Dissident priests'. Yet, though there are resemblances, it would be hard to find two interpreters of the Revolution who differ more. Patriotism and progress mean nothing to Carlyle. He defines the Revolution by what it destroyed, by the past, not the future. It was 'the open violent Rebellion, and Victory of disimprisoned Anarchy against corrupt worn-out authority'. We begin at Louis XV's death-bed to give us time to review the 'lies' and 'imposture' that must be swept away. Nothing replaces them. Crowds surge, soldiers die on the frontier, constitutions prove but 'ropes of sand', the people are betrayed, until the bronze lips of a young artillery officer give orders for a whiff of grapeshot and 'the thing we specifically call *French Revolution* is blown into space by it, and becomes a thing that was'. Carlyle ends when Bonaparte appears. He had not yet entered his hero-worshipping stage, and his *French Revolution* remains the great and only triumph of his theory that history is the essence of innumerable biographies. Like a God, indifferent to human ideals, seeing them as futile *sub specie aeternitatis*, he broods over chaos, expending his concern on poor humans trapped in events beyond their control. He urges us to forgive the most despicable characters, like Robespierre, whose landlord at least loved him and whose brother died for him—'may God be merciful to him and to us', and he is haunted by the fate even of minor figures—'Mrs Momoro' at supper with her bookseller husband after playing the goddess of reason, the Swiss who kept their plighted word for 6*d.* a day to the king who forsook them, the baby girl named 'Pétion-National-Pique'—'Universal History is not indifferent'. To Michelet the true reality is the collectivity, the people: to Carlyle only individuals are real, and the collectivities of the Revolution are mobs, united, not by patriotic social bonds, but by frenzy. The elemental duel between light and darkness which fills Michelet's canvas is fought out, for Carlyle, not in public causes, but secretly, in each individual soul. 'There are depths in men that go the lengths of lowest Hell, as there are heights that reach highest Heaven.' The Revolution which others defined and hypostasised was to him a sulphurous conflagration barely susceptible of historical explanation. It was a stage setting for the moral struggles of innumerable individuals. Thus Carlyle at once fails to understand the Revolution and at the same time adds to its study a dimension lacking in many other historians, the dimension of tragedy. The evening sun of July sets on ships far out on the silent main and on dancers in the Orangerie, while heads go aloft on pikes at the Hôtel-de-Ville; there are reapers in the fields while the September butcheries proceed; Chateaubriand wanders in the virgin forests of the New World as his family go to the guillotine. These things happen, but outside the soul of the individual they have no meaning. The Revolution was incoherent and destructive, its vision of the millennium an illusion.

As a comparison with Carlyle reveals, Michelet exercised a powerful and distorting influence on the interpretation of the French Revolution. In technical approach, too, his work marks a decisive change for, though he scorned scholarly references, his history was the first to show a systematic knowledge of the archives. In France, 1830, a year of political and literary revolution, also proved to be the beginning of a new era in historical scholarship, when Guizot inspired the great work of locating, inventorying and publishing the documentary sources of national history, and Michelet himself became head of the historical section of the National Archives. The impact of the new spirit of erudition was first evident in revolutionary studies in 1833, when Buchez, in the interests of his peculiar Christian Socialism, began to publish his volumes of speeches, debates, budgets and the proceedings of clubs and assemblies, a vast collection of materials which is still invaluable to scholars. The historians of the Restoration period had leaned heavily on memoirs (not all of them authentic), oral reminiscences, and a limited range of newspapers. Aided by such facile sources, interpretation, brilliant, lucid and partial, had far outrun research, while the principal sources for the history of the Revolution lay undisturbed. The inefficient centralisation of the old monarchy had revelled in bureaucratic paper-work; the Revolution with its petitions, legislation, inventories, requisitions, its confiscation of ecclesiastical and private archives, had produced even more, so that municipal libraries and departmental and central archives were now silted up with a mass of documents, unsorted treasure left behind by a receding tide. Historians may never again have access to such primary materials for the study of a revolution, for this was the last great revolution of the age of bureaucracy before the practice of manipulating the record for posterity was established. Michelet, however, was the first to plunge into the uncalendared morass of the archives, and with him, the serious documentation of the Revolution began. Logically, one would have expected that the first result of archival research would have been a series of definitive monographs—which might have preserved for us more of those records of Paris Sections and of the Cordeliers which have since been destroyed. What happened, however, was that erudition was immediately placed at the service of sweeping syntheses. Michelet came to the Revolution from philosophy and universal history, Tocqueville came from his comprehensive sociological analysis of democracy. It was, after all, an age of *Comédies humaines* and *Légendes des siècles*.

In 1850 it seemed to Baudrillart that memories of 1848 were likely to be disastrous to the historiography of the French Revolution, encouraging controversy between demagogic pamphleteers and absolutist chroniclers, and preventing the emergence of a 'liberal and parliamentary' interpretation. Within another year, however, his prediction was falsified, for the first volume of a history of the Convention appeared, written by Prosper de Barante, an academician of Orleanist views. This work has little significance except as a voice crying in the wilderness to herald Alexis de Tocqueville. Barante's praise of the men of '89 and his denial of all worth-while achievement, save in national defence, to the Convention, was standard doctrine with the brilliant group of liberals of varying persuasions who were left high and dry in their salons and the Academy when the popular tide swept away towards the Empire. The duc de Broglie (who had married a daughter of Mme de Staël), his son Albert, and his son-in-law the comte de Haussonville, Barante and Tocqueville, finding their hopes of parliamentary government and administrative decentralisation overtaken by despotism, sought refuge in history. Barante found his theme in the Convention, Haussonville joined in the attack upon the Napoleonic legend which the Second Empire provoked, Tocqueville produced a study of France on the eve of the Revolution which was at once a statement of the liberal case against Napoleon III and a supreme work of analytical history.

The lucid argument of *L'Ancien régime et la révolution* has the deceptive simplicity of a great work of art. Viewed from one angle, it is a political pamphlet: in eighteenth-century France had lived a spirit of proud independence unknown under Napoleon III—a haughty aristocracy, a clergy glorying in its landed possessions and right to vote taxation, *pays d'état* retaining powers of local administration, magistrates and holders of venal offices secure in their abusive tenure, a whole multitude of classes and corporations each determined to defend its own privileges. Kings then were obeyed out of loyalty; the bourgeois passion for comfort, the smooth egalitarian surface of society which facilitates the exercise of power, the universal servility of a nation of isolated individuals to a dictator, were unknown. From another point of view, the book is an essay in sociology and political theory. Twenty years before, in *La Démocratie en Amérique*, Tocqueville had used the United States as an example of the working of the laws behind modern civilisation—the inevitable advance of democracy, the eternal dialectic between liberty and equality, the constitutional devices, social arrangements and religious beliefs which are necessary to maintain some sort of freedom in the Gaderene rush down to absolute equality. Now, from his own country, he illustrated a pathological variant of the process; how the desire for liberty was born later than the desire for equality and how it was the first to die, so that Frenchmen, who had wanted to be free, ended up by strengthening their centralised administrative machinery and being willing to live equal under a master. As a work of history—and that is its essential title to fame—*L'Ancien Régime* is richly ambivalent beneath its flawless crystal surface. In some respects, its ideas are a synthesis of brilliant generalities left lying on the margins of historiography by the Emigration and liberals of the Restoration period—Chateaubriand's awareness that the Revolution began with an aristocratic Fronde, Bonald's peculiar insistence on the abuses of the old régime as the equivalent of a free constitution, Royer Collard's liberty-equality dialectic, Mme de Staël's insight into the egalitarian nature of the revolutionary spirit. In other respects, Tocqueville's interpretation springs from his own direct observations of the society of his time and his flair for framing historical hypotheses to explain what he saw. In an article published twenty years before his book, he had already clearly stated some of his main conclusions. 'Il a commencé à penser avant d'avoir rien appris', said Sainte-Beuve critically, meaning that he had gone to America with preconceived ideas. But this was characteristic. Tocqueville is a standing example to historians of the value of preliminary hypotheses, and of the devastating truth that there is no substitute for intelligence. Yet, when all this is said, the most significant feature of his method is his direct resort to archival sources—the Archives Nationales, the departmental archives of Indre-et-Loire, registers of communes, terriers, *cahiers*—used, not to insert picturesque details into a narrative structure already existing, but to serve a planned design in a new historical field, the study of the administrative and class structure of the France from which the Revolution emerged.

'History', says Robert Graves through the mouth of Claudius, 'is an old man's game.' Born in 1805, in the last year of a decade which had seen the birth of Mignet, Thiers and Michelet, Tocqueville did not publish his great work until 1856, long after these near-contemporaries of his had made their names as historians of the Revolution. A patriot, he had had time to become disillusioned; an aristocrat, he had come to see that the day of his own class was gone forever; his religious beliefs had mellowed into a deism designed for social utility; 1848 had proved the existence of a threat to property, but he had enjoyed a breathing-space to forget his panic and to reflect on this spectacle of class warfare; he had gained that unique insight into practical affairs which only a political career, especially an unsuccessful one, can afford to an intelligent observer. Everything had conspired to give him an impartiality lacking in his predecessors. Believing, with Montesquieu, that his own class was the ideal barrier against despotism, he had a ready-made hero in the French aristocracy. But the nobles, separated by their privileges from the nation, had become a caste; unlike their English counterparts, they no longer ruled or shaped opinion. Having made this clear-sighted appraisal of their decadence, Tocqueville was left with his affections disengaged. A little contemptuous of the bourgeoisie, a little too partial to the Gallican church, whose internal divisions he passed over, comprehensive and just in his treatment of peasant grievances, but, like a benevolent *grand seigneur*, too aloof to differentiate between the various lower strata of rural France, he remains, nevertheless, the most serene and impartial of the historians of the Revolution.

Previous histories (Quinet's excepted) had been narratives: *L'Ancien régime* is an analysis. Others had seen the Revolution as beginning in 1789 under the impulse of the bourgeoisie or 'the people': for Tocqueville, 1787 is the starting date, and had he lived to publish his second volume, he would have devoted a section to the *révolte nobiliare*. Most of his predecessors wrote in hope, their faces turned towards a dawning new era: Tocqueville, pessimistic about the future, interpreted the Revolution by the past—'c'est dans les temps qui la précèdent qu'il faut chercher la seule lumière qui puisse l'éclairer'. Where others had used sweeping and imprecise deterministic phraseology, Tocqueville, committed to a large-scale historical movement towards equality and to an admission that the old social edifice would have fallen sooner or later, weighed more nicely the possibilities open to men within the circle Providence had traced out for them. Individuals, however, do not play a decisive role in his interpretation, nor does he deal in politics, court life and war, those happy hunting-grounds for exponents of stirring narrative and psychological portraiture. He wrote administrative, social and economic history. The impact of the centralising policy of the monarchy, of the sale of office, the rise of the middle classes, the impoverishment of the nobility, peasants buying land, the growth of an industrial proletariat in Paris, the bad harvest of 1788—these are the essential stuff of his analysis. Revolutionary tensions are described within the framework of the class structure. It is true that, with Marx, his contemporary, Tocqueville made the error of making his historical groups too homogeneous—bishops versus *curés*, robe versus sword; richer peasant versus poorer peasant are not emphasised, just as his *philosophes* show a unity of doctrine that would be incredible among thinkers of any age. Even so, he had made a decisive step forward in methodology. 'Je parle des classes,' he said, 'elles seules doivent occuper l'histoire.'

The over-simplification of social units in *L'Ancien Régime* is offset by Tocqueville's genius for detecting nuances of motivation within classes. Contemptuous of those who invoked vast portmanteau explanations like 'race' and 'climate' on one hand, and those who wallowed in a 'dung heap' of facts on the other, he was determined to lay bare precise and logical linkages. When possible, he sought comparisons—between English aristocrats who paid taxes and ruled and French nobles who evaded taxes and didn't; between the Church of England immune to attacks of scepticism and the vulnerable Church of France; between progressive land-owning peasants in the Rhineland and around Paris who welcomed the Revolution and backward peasants of the Vendée who defied it, between enlightened despotism or feudalism as they existed in France and in the rest of Europe. An obvious answer did not satisfy: the evidence had to be subjected to a further turn of the interrogatory screw. Where Michelet saw a crisis of famine, Tocqueville considered that increasing prosperity was a more potent revolutionary force; feudal dues were hated, not because they were oppressive, but because they had lost their *raison d'être*; the peasant brooded, not just because he was in misery, but because he was isolated from all other classes; the people revolted, not when their condition deteriorated, but when they saw an opportunity for making it better; the most dangerous moment for a bad government was when it tried to reform. Formulae like these, now common coin of historical trading, were originally struck in the mind of Alexis de Tocqueville.

L'Ancien Régime et la Révolution has had an enormous and continuing influence on revolutionary studies. It has encouraged both synthesis and research. The Left adopted its method, the study of class tensions, the Right followed up its clues towards a rehabilitation of pre-revolutionary France. Oddly enough, however, the greatest single achievement which it directly inspired was in diplomatic history, a genre which Tocqueville had avoided. 'The French Revolution', wrote Sorel, summarising his *L'Europe et la Révolution française* (1885–1904), 'which appeared to many as the subversion, and to others as the regeneration of the old European world, was the natural and necessary result of the history of Europe.' The continuity of French history, which Tocqueville had detected in the administration and the countryside, Sorel found in embassies and on battlefields. Absolutism, national unity and natural frontiers, these were keys to an understanding of foreign policy under the old monarchy—and under the revolutionary governments. Sorel, son of a Norman industrialist, and Tocqueville, son of a Norman nobleman, had much in common. Rich, cultured, cosmopolitan (both made unconventional foreign marriages), experienced in affairs of state and authorship, they came to the study of the Revolution mature, poised and tolerant. They detested Terror and regretted war, but they insisted that the Revolution, through deep-rooted causes and lasting achievements, was an integral part of French history. In doing so, each drove his thesis of continuity too far. *L'Europe et la Révolution française* ends in fatalistic justification of Napoleon: in *L'Ancien Régime* there is an unproven assumption that the centralised administrations of the old régime, Revolution and nineteenth century are one continuous phenomenon. Had Tocqueville completed his second volume, it seems certain that he would have connected Terror and revolutionary dictatorship with levelling egalitarianism rather than with war. The supposition that the horrors of the Revolution were a result of its general causes rather than of accidental circumstances was one which had been welcome to the extreme reactionaries of the Emigration, and which was shortly to be taken up by the systematic and reckless ingenuity of Taine.

Tocqueville had the insight of pessimism, Taine its frenzy. According to Paul Bourget, history appeared to Taine as 'a vast experiment set up by Chance for the benefit of the psychologists'—if so, he might have come to the study of the Revolution, that revealing phase of the national mind, in any case.[1] As it was, however, the defeat of 1870 and the Commune drove him to the duty of pathological consultant to his nation, looking back for the origins of the obscene disease which had caused the loss of Alsace-Lorraine, like the gangrenous fall of two fingers. That Taine became a reactionary in 1871 out of panic is a legend which his earlier correspondence disproves; the essential effect of Sedan and civil war was to make his Darwinian pessimism radical and total. There were other intellectuals, like Renan, Émile Montégut and Courcelle-Seneuil, who saw in the Revolution the beginnings of that brittle patriotism and creeping paralysis of centralisation and *mandarinisme* which had ruined France. But Taine wrote his *Origines de la France contemporaine* (1876–93) in a mood far surpassing that of his contemporaries in bitterness. His sole remaining belief—a belief in science, was crumbling, and he was desperately anxious to distinguish it from the corrosive 'reason' of eighteenth-century *philosophes*. A determinist, he was incapable of a mellow acceptance of necessity, for his determinism was intensely moral,

[1] Perhaps in the spirit of his remark of 1860 (censuring Carlyle's too sombre picture of the Revolution)—'la générosité et l'enthousiasme ont abondé ici'.

like the predestinationism of Jansenists and Calvinists with which he loved to compare it. 'Virtue and vice are products like sugar and vitriol', men and nations are formed by race and milieu—none the less, they are subjects for trenchant moral judgements. Such a judgement had to be made on France, and it was impossible to avoid wishing that things had been otherwise. Taine's correspondence shows him haunted by his own thesis of inevitability—'we missed our natural evolution in 1789', 'there were two roads open', 'just a little more common sense...'. This internal tension sharpened the edge of criticism, and as volume after volume of the *Origines* appeared, it became evident that it implied a global condemnation of the historical ideals of all parties—of the Monarchy, of the Revolution, and of the Empire. It was not a work of propaganda, at least it supported no cause and advocated no remedy. History provided a bitter intellectual satisfaction. It is better, as Spengler was to say, 'to go down-hill, *seeing*'.

Commentators on Taine agree in finding in him a peculiar blend of two contrasting inspirations, poetical and logical, and a revealing personal confession suggests that in 1862 he was conscious of a sort of conversion in which the second tendency gained the upper hand, rhetorical talent and the logical alignment of ideas becoming subject to lightning flashes and violent sensations. Taine's 'method' was, in his own view, 'scientific'. It was founded on detailed research like the German historical scholarship he so greatly admired, it sought laws, in the sense of Comte's positivist sociology, it classified into types in the manner of zoologists and geologists, it followed Cuvier in deducing the secret of living wholes from detailed study of a particular organ. Yet, Taine cherished his infinitude of 'little facts' with a love exceeding that of zoologists and geologists, with the love, indeed, of his essential masters, Stendhal and Balzac, and he visualised them with an intensity that approaches the 'resurrections' of Carlyle and Michelet. His scientific realism was, more than anything, an artistic phenomenon. Taine was to historiography what Flaubert, Zola and Maupassant were to literature. Each acutely observed and carefully recorded detail is silhouetted against the phosphorescent luminosity of despair.

'De tout petits faits bien choisis... voilà aujourd'hui la matière de tout science'—they too were the basic stuff of contemporary naturalistic literature and of a prose style based on the military tactics of 'charging in masses'. Amidst his facts Taine sought for clues which would lead him to sweeping interpretative formulae; the *faculté maîtresse* which was the secret of a personality, the *milieu* which governed an historical period. Once the formula was detected, an explanation which embodied all the facts could begin. This famous 'method' rolled forward relentlessly over nuances of explanation. As Sainte-Beuve remarked, between great historical factors and individuals there is room for a multitude of causes, 'et tant qu'on ne les a pas saisies, on n'a rien expliqué'. Instead of being set at different levels in contrasting social environments, events moved forward in a single national *milieu*. Historical interpretation became monolithic; the court under the Regency, Louis XV and Louis XVI became a single static tableau; an insurrectionary geography of patches of light and shadow became universal confusion, an 'anarchy' established by 'eighteen' examples; bodies like the Committee of Public Safety or the Revolutionary Tribunal, and individuals like Napoleon were described, brilliantly frozen into a single unchanging attitude.

No one before Taine had illustrated the revolutionary situation with such vivid complexity: few before or since have dared to reduce all this complexity to a single formula. The revolutionary spirit is described as consisting of an explosive mixture of *l'esprit scientifique* (wholly good) and *l'esprit classique*, the destructive spirit of abstract argument from pure reason—'la raison raisonnante'. From it came the dogma of the sovereignty of the people, epitomised in Rousseau's *Contrat social*, which passed down from literature, through café politicians, to the savages of the streets. This was the 'morbid germ', which, entering the blood of a diseased society, caused delirium and convulsions. The assumptions here—that seventeenth- and eighteenth-century literature contain a unified ideology, and that ideas are the primary motive forces (rather than the results or the outward garb of other factors)—are unproven, and a mere list of thinkers, from Descartes to Rousseau, who served 'la raison raisonnante', is a confutation in itself. In formulating his *esprit classique*, Taine had been a victim, not only of his method, but also of his temperament. Methodology had excluded movement from his description of the eighteenth century (he omits the struggle between crown and *parlement*) and had predisposed him to a vast psychological generalisation. By temperament, he was unwilling to justify disorder, so that the miseries of the old régime, of which he draws so sombre a picture, had to take a secondary place as an explanation of the Revolution. Coming to general history from the history of literature (willing, he said, to exchange a hundred volumes of diplomatic documents for the memoirs of Cellini), he tended to seek a central theme in the field which was most familiar to him. Intellectuals can too easily convince themselves that the camp of ideas where they bivouac contains the armies that march out to the conquest of the world.

The revolutionary spirit had its instruments—the Jacobins. A minority in the nation, drawn from lower bourgeoisie and upper people, inflamed by those revolutionary abstractions which may temporarily affect young men but can become a permanent mania only in a society in decomposition, they are the men who leagued together under the banner of the *Contrat social* to confiscate property, destroy family life and religion, and to use for their ends the dregs of a society that had lost all traditional restraints, the 'epileptic and scrofulous multitude'. With *l'esprit classique*, its Jacobin devotees, and the rising of the scum, Taine's explanation of revolutionary horrors is complete. The Bastille falls without reference to royal troop concentrations, the émigrés are driven out as Louis XIV drove out the Protestants, the risings of 20 June and 10 August and the September massacres take place with only incidental reference to the war and national defence. It is as if, says Aulard, one were to describe the inhabitants of Paris in December 1870 crouching in cellars and eating cats and dogs, and conceal the fact that German forces were besieging the city. Taine's revolutionaries are not just fanatics. By omitting their struggle for survival, he reduces their actions to meaningless hysteria.

The argument of the *Origines* is monomaniacal, like its author's Jacobins, and its lush documentation has wilted under hostile critical scrutiny. Yet both by his prejudices and his 'science', Taine has had an enormous influence on historiography. Though he was partial to memoirs and prejudiced witnesses, by casting his net far beyond newspapers and official reports, and by working across the grain of his sources, he indicated possibilities of a vast new documentation. France for him consisted of the provinces as well as Paris, and her history was economic and social, as well as political. If he did not entirely achieve the ideal set out in his history of English literature—to see humble citizens in workshop, office and field—he at least contrived to see them terrifyingly closely in mobs and rural jacqueries. Other historians had concentrated on official 'indispensable' violence in the capital: Taine, with that eye for mean motive and macabre incident which had characterised his favourite novelists, added to the chronicle the anarchical violence of the provinces. The 'Peuple', that glorious myth of Michelet, disintegrated under his pessimistic scrutiny into its constituent elements, and the Revolution, in so far as it was coherent, appeared as the work of a minority. It is, perhaps, significant that Taine had come to see England as superior in government, Germany in philosophy and the northern countries in literature; he had served an intellectual apprenticeship which freed him from the bias of patriotism. His condemnation of the Revolution was in the interest neither of Bonapartism nor legitimacy. The monarchy had dug its own grave, theoreticians smashed the last barriers of civilisation, the gutter wreaked its will and a tyrant seized his opportunity. This was the French Revolution.

The first volume of the *Origines* appeared in 1875, at a time when historical studies in France were undergoing transformation. Diverse influences had prepared this change—German scholarship, the École des Chartes, Renan and Fustel de Coulanges, Duruy's educational policy in the latter years of the Empire. In 1876 Monod, who had followed Taine's advice to study in Germany, founded the *Revue historique*, modelled on the *Historische Zeitschrift*; a dozen major historical journals, including *La*

Révolution francaise, arose in the next three decades, and in 1894 technical historiographical training won its place in higher education. The crucial change in revolutionary studies had come about eight years earlier, when the municipality of Paris endowed a course on the Revolution at the Faculty of Letters of Paris, and Aulard became first professor. In the next thirty-six years he published, in addition to numerous original works, thirty volumes of documents—an amazing achievement, which was only possible, as Cochin and Mathiez pointed out with relish, by some sacrifice of critical method and the employment of 'ghosts'. Aulard also inspired others to undertake extensive researches in his field, Renouvin, Cahen, Braesch, Miss Söderhjelm, Pariset and Mathiez (the disciple who deserted his master and outshone him) being his pupils. A sort of 'industrial revolution' was taking place in French historiography, characterised by detailed researches, division of labour, technical expertise and vastly increased production.

A corresponding change took place in the *milieu* within which scholarly inquiries were conducted. The Academy, where Barante, Guizot, Broglie, Tocqueville, Haussonville and (after discreditable delays) Taine had been enthroned, still crowned its historians—Sorel, La Gorce[1] and Madelin— but the centre of gravity had shifted to the Université. Here was a world of scholarly introversion, where documentation was strict and accurate and where the atmosphere was republican and *dreyfusard*. Historians like Sée, Hauser, Seignobos, Aulard and Mathiez were members of the *Ligue des Droits de l'Homme*, which perpetuated the ideals it had invoked to free Dreyfus and brought together republicans of varying persuasions who were willing to meet 'on the common ground of the Revolution'. Aulard's confession of allegiance was frank: 'I am a respectful and grateful son of the Revolution, which has emancipated humanity and science.'[2] The Third Republic, embattled but triumphant in the 'affair' and in the struggle to smash the Concordat, found in the events of 1789 to 1794 its ancestry and inspiration, a cult of the past which affected scholarship as well as politics. It was, said Pierre Laserre sardonically, 'the official doctrine of the Université'. The gibe was justified—but unjust; though Aulard himself did a great deal of political journalism for Radical-Socialist newspapers, and, believing that the *école laïque* had converted Thiers' conservative republic into a democratic and irreligious one, wrote unashamedly anti-clerical and republican text-books for schools, he still believed that his professional researches remained strictly impartial. 'The more you determine to keep politics out of your scientific work', he observed, 'the greater the obligation to indulge in political activity else-

[1] P. de la Gorce, *Histoire religieuse de la Révolution*, 5 vols. (1909–23); Catholic in sentiment.
[2] In his journal, *La Révolution française*, Aulard published a series of essays on the historians of the Revolution which have been invaluable for the subject of this essay.

where.' The pontifical self-assurance of Aulard and Mathiez's bellicose certainties are so out of fashion today that it is important to remember that these writers achieved a mastery of their sources which would not have been believed possible before and which few have achieved since. They lacked humility, but not sincerity. Their deficiencies, like Taine's, though in a very different sense, resulted from excessive reliance upon a 'scientific' method. This method, as summarised by Langlois and Seignobos in a famous manual, began from the premise that 'l'histoire n'est que la mise en œuvre de documents'. History is considered, not as a reply to a question which we put to the past, but as isolated 'facts' established by evidence and put together again in their original pattern like a mosaic disturbed by an earthquake. 'Scientific' history as developed in France by the end of the nineteenth century was masterly in critical erudition, but marred by the illusion that all that was necessary for impartiality was to overcome the personal factor, the astigmatism of the observer. Few saw the need for sympathy in dealing with religion or clashes of ideals. History was identified with a method: little consideration had been given to what might be termed its 'epistemology', the problem of the nature of historical knowledge and certainty.

'Pour la comprendre il faut l'aimer', said Aulard of the Revolution, a sympathetic approach which he was not willing to adopt towards rival themes. He refused to regard his subject as an ordinary period of French history, or to include in its essence every grim contemporary event. On the contrary, the Revolution was 'the Declaration of the Rights of Man of 1789 and the attempts to realise it', a continuing process which was the unique flowering of French history. Confronted by a reference to a unique period of history two thousand years ago and a definition of Christianity as 'the Gospels and the attempts to realise them', Aulard would have been the first to allege the scandal of particularity and expose this facile repudiation of superstitious and intolerant incidents. A religious parallel of this kind is revealing, for Aulard, like Michelet, believed that 1789 had founded a new lay and humanitarian religion which was the origin of modern progress. Until the recent victory of the lay republic over the 'theocratic principle', he declared in 1906, attempts to write scientific history in France had necessarily been premature. It was a strange impartiality which needed Combes and Clemenceau as its promoters. The voice that popularised the conclusions of the historian not infrequently spoke with the accents of the chairman of the propaganda committee of the *Mission laïque*.

What Michelet said in poetry, Aulard said in prose, with scholarly references. The spirit of the Federations, of the armies of Year II, is the spirit of the Revolution, and Danton, pragmatic, yet dreaming of progress through education, pacific, yet flamboyant in patriotic resistance, is its hero. Comte and Michelet were (with Voltaire) the chief influences that shaped Aulard's mind; he combined their admiration, positivist and lyrical, with arguments drawn from more recent research on subjects like Danton's 'corruption', or his responsibility for the September Massacres. Michelet's concept of 'the people' is revived, but with a realistic quali-fication—'on condition of seeing the French people, not in the form of a multitude, but in the form of organised groups'. The people, coming together spontaneously in patriot municipalities, the National Guard and the armies, are the motive force of the Revolution. Aulard, who accused Taine of establishing a 'general anarchy' from seventeen examples, com-mitted something like the same error on a vaster canvas. He did not sufficiently discount the propaganda element in sources like newspapers or the correspondence of *représentants en mission*; he wrote political history inattentive to its seamy side and to personal idiosyncrasies of motive; he concentrated on 'official groups', legislative assemblies, clubs, municipalities, the vast revolutionary bureaucracy, the army battalions which 'voted with their feet', and said little of social groups and the economic questions which divided them; he postulated a unity, and a loyalty to the Revolution in the minds of anonymous millions whose un-recorded opinions must always be a subject for conjecture. His reasons for declaring the Revolution (in its strictest sense) ended at Napoleon's coronation are illuminating. The Concordat and the ceremony in Notre-Dame were the essential 'counter-revolutionary' acts, the betrayal of the new belief in humanity, while the mainspring of action was broken when the Parisian workers, hungry for bread and for glory, welcomed their master and left the republican bourgeoisie in impotence. 'It is from that moment that the breach between liberals and people dates; for long democracy and universal suffrage were to appear incompatible with liberty.' The Revolution ends when the lay principle is betrayed and the unity of 'the people' is decisively broken.

Since Thiers and Mignet, something resembling a 'thesis of circum-stances' had become accepted doctrine with apologists for the Revolution. Avenel's *Lundis révolutionnaires* in Gambetta's newspaper, *La République française* (1871–4), offered a standard version; there was no republican movement in 1789, no 'communist' theory then or later—extreme courses had been a simple reaction to the resistance of privilege. Aulard adopted this thesis of circumstances and supported it with monumental docu-mentation. Republicanism was not a serious force until Varennes, and it was the Prussian invasion that brought ruin upon the monarchy. Revo-lutionary parties, unlike nineteenth-century ones, had no programmes, and revolutionary constitutions were not based upon systematic theory. The Declaration of Rights borrowed its ideas from certain American states, the Constitution of 1791 was a compromise, that of 1793 an ex-pedient, that of Year III a reflection of accumulated fears. Terror was a reply to civil and foreign war and the resistance of privilege, the last resort of 'an average generation of liberal and pacific intentions, which was driven on by exceptional circumstances'. Though these conclusions were not new, and some of them were too simple to do full justice to the complexity of history, Aulard's exposition was masterly. Fantastic essays in condemnation, like Taine's, were henceforth impossible. All future studies of the Revolution would be obliged to pay deference to the chronology of circumstance and crisis.

Aulard, as a republican moderate, was on the defensive against socialism, admitting that the principles of '89 gave some support to the extreme Left, but insisting that change must be gradual. What socialists admired in the Revolution he dismissed as emergency expedients. Such a lukewarm tradition was not likely to satisfy the descendants of Babeuf. Violence, however, has the quality of imposing its own divisions upon those created by theory, so that memories of the Terror, then of the Commune, helped to divide French socialists into reformist Possibilists and intransigent Guesdists. Thus, left-wing interpreters of the Revolution inherited no single ready-made formula. They would have to decide upon the degree of economic determinism that was appropriate to their theme, they would have to choose between Robespierre and Hébert, between the bourgeoisie as playing a role in progress and the bourgeoisie as opposed to the proletariat, and finally, they would have to choose between doctrines of violent and non-violent change. The great virtue of Jaurès *Histoire socialiste* (1901–5) consists in the fact that in each of these choices, its author took the most civilised alternative. 'It is from the socialist point of view', he begins, 'that we mean to recount to the people, the workers and peasants, the events which took place from 1789 to the end of the nineteenth century.' Few historians have been so frank in avowing bias and so fair in avoiding it. A politician, Jaurès was also an intellectual who had graduated from the École Normale one place below Bergson; a passionate socialist, he always remained a man of peace, anxious to 'save the proletarian revolution from the sickening odour of blood and hatred which had remained attached to the bourgeois Revolution'. Ideas were not subordinated to economic determinism; he simply insisted that they were dependent on the advent of a new social class, created by capitalism, to achieve decisive change. The French Revolution had been, in essence, the accession to political power of the bourgeoisie, but the idea of class warfare between bourgeois and proletariat was then undeveloped—the *loi Le Chapelier*, for example, passed unnoticed—the middle classes made property the foundation of liberty as a result of honest conviction, and 'in the circumstances of that day, they spoke for all humanity'. Both in home and foreign policy, Jaurès was a pacifist. With a clarity undimmed by patriotic illusions, he saw that the 'despots' of Europe would have preferred to avoid war with revolutionary France, and he regretted that the opportunity to convert the world by a spectacle of peaceful reform had been lost. With all its passion and irony, the *Histoire socialiste* has something of the serenity of the *Ancien Régime et la Révolution*. Both Tocqueville and Jaurès interpreted history in terms of social groups, and to this study they brought the sensitivity of cultured minds and the realism of politicians who had learnt the limits of the possible in human affairs. They brought too, the impartiality of a relative detachment: their personal allegiances were bound up with classes whose interests they regarded as peripheral in the Revolution—an aristocracy whose day was over, and a proletariat whose day was yet to come.

While Jaurès' researches, though extensive, had been episodic and unprofessional, his disciple, Mathiez, brought to the socialist side of revolutionary studies all the weight of the new scientific erudition of the Université. The interpretation which emerges from his extensive writings is not 'Marxist'—no more than Jaurès' was. Mathiez emphasised the role of ideas and individuals in history, indeed, so far as we know the true story of his breach with Aulard (1908), it began with a disagreement about intellectual movements and was consumated by a dispute about personalities. His doctoral thesis argued that the religious experiments of the Revolution were profoundly related to movements of thought, not, as Aulard contended, expedients of national defence,[1] and after this preliminary difference of opinion, the two historians diverged decisively in their interpretations of the characters of Danton and Robespierre. Robespierre was Mathiez's idol—'we love him for the teaching of his life and for the symbol of his death'. Danton was sunk in corruption, while Robespierre's decrees of *ventôse*, aimed at redistributing property for the benefit of the poor, were the high-water mark of revolutionary idealism. Mathiez interprets the Revolution in terms of classes and of economic forces (sometimes too crudely—in a simple antithesis he equates the Girondins with property and commerce and the Montagnards with artisans and consumers), but for him, the real Revolution consists, in the end, of a few idealists, isolated, misunderstood even by the disinherited multitude they served, wrestling hopelessly with corrupt humanity in an attempt to force on the reign of social justice.

The ideals of Jaurès live again in Mathiez's powerful and learned history, but not his serenity. The bourgeoisie 'duped' the people, and its so-called National Guard was principally an organisation to prevent pillage. The declaration of war, which Robespierre had opposed, is censured, but the Terror is defended—it was no worse than the shooting of deserters in the World War, and it finally became, in the hands of Robespierre, Couthon and Saint-Just, a 'red crucible where future democracy was

---

[1] Though in a subsequent study of the Civil Constitution of the Clergy (1911) Mathiez put great weight upon the economic causes of the breach between the Constituents and the church.

being forged'. Mathiez's verdicts on individuals were trenchant, utilising an elementary psychology, and based on a subjective principle of loyalty to the Revolution, a sort of artificial knife-edge which sheared through reputations as crudely as the guillotine itself. He sat in judgement, says Lucien Febvre, 'draped in his civic virtues...like the public prosecutor in a judicial film, or a Fouquier-Tinville of melodrama'. Yet it is difficult to regret Mathiez's ruthlessness, for his contribution towards an interpretation of the Revolution was thereby made all the more decisive. Though in one book (and its date of publication, 1916, is sufficient explanation) he speaks of the patriot and sovereign people in lyrical terms, the whole trend of his work is destructive of the myth of 'the People' which Michelet had popularised and which Aulard had smuggled into scholarship. In another respect also, Mathiez appears as a Taine of the Left, for just as Taine resurrected the world of the *jacquerie*, Mathiez plunged into the Parisian underworld—spies, company promoters, venal journalists, army contractors, police intrigues. From the Right, observers had long peered down into chaos hoping to detect an elaborate formal conspiracy; it was now revealed that, from the heights of the Left, it was possible to glimpse the actual and multifarious conspiracies of selfishness which thrive like fungus in the dark shadows of periods of disorder.

This insight, partial and lurid, together with the influence of socialist principles and experience of an economy geared to total war, were to draw Mathiez's genius towards economic history. For long Proudhon's gibe against the historians—'they have written the scenario of the French Revolution'—had retained its force. There had been Tocqueville of course, and Levasseur's pioneer history of the working classes (1859-67), and the continual subconscious pressure of Balzac's novels, but a decisive change came only towards the end of the nineteenth century, when Loutchitsky, predisposed to study peasant economies by Russian experience, published a study of small rural properties and the sale of *biens nationaux* (1897), and Jaurès, six years later, persuaded the government to set up a committee to publish documents on the economic history of the Revolution. Mathiez never found opportunity for close study of peasant France, feudal dues and the structure of landholding, subjects which are lightly treated in his general history (1922-7), but towards the end of his life he concentrated on the economic background of war and Terror. *La vie chère et le mouvement social sous la Terreur* is a study of inflation and a series of crises in food supply, with an accompanying movement of ideas—the old régime's theories of economic regulation surviving among the lower classes, and the bourgeois desire for free trade. The first Maximum is seen as the price paid by the Mountain for the support of the Enragés against the Girondins, the Terror as an instrument to enforce the general Maximum, and Thermidor as sealing a victory

THE AMERICAN AND FRENCH REVOLUTIONS

which the bourgeoisie had won by dealings in cheap land and by inflation. *La vie chère* was published in 1927. Three years before this, M. Lefebvre's superb masterpiece *Les Paysans du Nord pendant la Révolution* had appeared. Revolutionary historiography had entered the most significant of its phases—the detailed study of the economic structure and forces which lay behind social change.[1]

Aulard had considered the Revolution as his fief, a private demesne where he levied tribute. So said Mathiez, who himself gave short shrift to trespassers. Conservative intruders, unable to compete with the professionals of the Université, found consolation in the favour of the Academy, which awarded its Grand Prix Gobert to Madelin's[2] history of the Revolution (1911), and welcomed Gaxotte and Bainville. After the first World War, there was an enormous demand for 'vulgarised' history. Mass education in a drab milieu and an uneasy sense of involvement in tragic processes of change had created a nostalgia for a picturesque past and a yearning for facile explanations, impulses which historians of the Right appealed to in brilliantly written manuals—Funck-Brentano on the old régime (1926), Gaxotte on the Revolution (1928), and Bainville on Napoleon (1931). All are patriotic, though in different fashions. Gaxotte is not seduced by military victories, but he does what he can to put the blame for the social overturn on German literary influences and 'foreigners' like Grimm, Rousseau, Benjamin Franklin and Necker. On the other hand, Madelin burns incense before the heroes of nationalist war—Danton, 'a Frenchman to the marrow of his bones', Carnot plotting strategy among his green portfolios, Bonaparte and his marshals waiting in the wings to begin the second act of glory. By contrast, Louis XVI is damned with pale sympathy, a pathetic king with none of the blood of Henry IV in his veins, a worthy grandson of that Stanislas who spent his life in abdication. Though its patriotism had variants, the Right showed a common front in portraying the France of the old régime. Tocqueville had provided clues towards a rehabilitation of the old society, and since then the ideal of a state organised in functional groups and organic regions had been propagated—by La Tour du Pin's Social Catholicism, by Le Play's studies of 'the unstable family' created by the testamentary legislation of the Revolution, by Durkheim's *solidarisme* and Duguit's pluralism, and by the traditionalist regionalism of Mistral. Local antiquaries had published a great deal of fascinating bric-à-brac, which enabled Babeau to write his sketches of rural life and the Abbé Sicard to evoke the colourful independent days of the Gallican church. The rich diversity of the old régime was attractive. Jaurès and Mathiez had helped by emphasising a revolution of prosperity, created by

[1] In 1933–4 Schnerb, Braesch and Harris began to publish studies in taxation, finance and the assignats—Marion's work (1919–21) had laid the foundations.
[2] In 1900 Madelin had published a scholarly biography of Fouché.

a rising bourgeoisie. The Right was glad to appropriate this evidence, extending it to rural life (on the ground that peasants concealed their real wealth from the tax-gatherer), adding to it anecdotes about the comforts of the Bastille and the patriarchal nature of *lettres de cachet*, and heightening its force by comparisons with the over-centralised inglorious France of the twentieth century.

How then, from these halcyon days of the old monarchy, did bloody Revolution arise? Presumably, an answer could be found in the tradition of a fermentation of perverse ideologies among a reckless minority, though since the rise of socialism, the Left also showed an embarrassing interest in this very explanation—shorn of pejorative adjectives.[1] It was a conservative, Faguet, who in 1904 declared that the *cahiers* proved that the 'principles of '89 never existed', and it was Mathiez who confuted him. Once the myth of the united spontaneous 'People' had collapsed and it was accepted that the work of the Revolution had been carried on by minorities, the thesis of intellectual conspiracy began to lose its strategic value as a right-wing argument. Why blame fascinating, though wayward, intelligences, when the turn could be served by Orleanist and foreign intrigues, and a multitude of climbers who kept passions seething for personal gain long after all reasonable reform had been achieved? Such, at least, was Madelin's interpretation, and in 1911 it might have seemed that right-wing historiography was on its way towards a cynical Bonapartist view of a revolution of disparate interests and manœuvre, in which ideas were just a pretext. That this did not happen and that the right swung back to the traditions of the émigrés and Taine was the result of the genius of Cochin, a brilliant pupil of the École des Chartres whose mastery of the archives made him a match for the great historians of the Université. Aulard had spent two years of his life in detective work to unmask Taine; in an ingenious reply (1909) Cochin turned the tables, and coined the famous phrases which henceforward were to summarise the two sides of the argument on revolutionary origins—'the thesis of circumstances' and 'the thesis of conspiracy'. A 'thesis of conspiracy' sounds melodramatic, and Cochin's researches to support and define it were never completed, but his two chief works, a study of the elections to the Estates General in Burgundy (1904) and the posthumously published *Les sociétés de pensée et la Révolution en Bretagne* (1925) reveal that he was engaged upon an investigation which was more subtle and less melodramatic than might be supposed. He was contemptuous of cloak-and-dagger masonic or Orleanist conspiracy theories; the 'ingenious system and mysterious entente' which he told Maurras he was seeking was a network in a sociological analysis, not a web with a single sinister spider

---

[1] The Bolshevik revolution showed how revolutionaries could glory in the educative role of a minority, as did Trotsky. It was left to Kerensky to argue that the revolution was 'born in the chaos of the collapse of Tsardom'—the thesis of circumstances.

at its centre. To defend Taine, he abandoned Taine's elemental fear of the mob, and went back to Tocqueville's ideas about the inherent danger of tyranny in democratic movements, and utilised Ostrogorski's revelations of the working of political 'machines' behind the electoral façade. In masonic lodges, literary societies, in thousands of local groups and associations, he detected the propagation of revolutionary doctrines and the rudiments of the organisations which shepherded voters in the elections to the Estates General. Many volumes had been written on the revolutionary doctrines of the eighteenth century, while in other books, in a separate compartment of historical studies, the *révolte nobiliaire* and the rising bourgeoisie were being studied—Cochin's work comes at the crucial point between, where ideas actuate social classes and events. At a time when the study of the class structure at the end of the old régime is disintegrating simple categories like 'bourgeoisie', 'nobility' and 'peasantry' into conflicting interest groups, it is all the more necessary to account for the apparent unanimity of 1789. Cochin's *sociétés de pensée* provide a formula towards an understanding of this remarkable coalition of ambitions and ideals.

Cochin was killed in the first World War, Aulard died in 1928 and Mathiez four years later, the primacy in revolutionary studies subsequently passing to M. Lefebvre, a master of economic history who also brought courtesy into controversy and nuances of argument into synthesis. The study of the Revolution is now a massive intellectual industry, with its own journals, institutions and experts. Foreign scholars are joining in the great investigation, and French intervention in the War of American Independence is being repaid in historiographical coin. Critical method is bearing its full fruit. One has only to compare M. Lefebvre and Mlle Terroine's edition of documents on the Estates General with Aulard's collections, or Caron's sifting of evidence on the September massacres with earlier studies of the subject, or Camille Bloch, Sée and Lesort's method of publishing interrelated *cahiers* with that of previous editors, to see what great progress has been made. Statistical studies have replaced generalisation from fragmentary evidence; Crane Brinton has analysed the social strata from which members of the Jacobin Clubs were drawn (1930), Greer has shown the incidence, social and chronological, of the Terror and of the Emigration (1935, 1951), and work is in progress on the social composition of Parisian insurrections. Study of the intellectual origins of the Revolution is now aided by precise knowledge concerning the circulation of printed literature which Mornet has provided (1933), supplemented by information concerning the diffusion of clandestine manuscripts, and though Mornet stopped short of 1789, others are now following his themes into the revolutionary years. The works of M. Labrousse (1933, 1944) have brought statistical precision into economic history, so that we can now combine Michelet's 'revolution of hunger' and Tocqueville's 'revolution of prosperity' into a single pattern based on the curve of prices in the eighteenth century.

Historians still have sharply contrasted opinions. It is obvious that M. Leflon is a Catholic and that M. Soboul is a Marxist—yet the one is no more a partisan supporter of the church than the other is of the proletariat. A polemicist like Guérin, who accused even Jaurès and Mathiez of being sewn up in the 'cocoon of bourgeois democracy', is rare. The Left admits that peasants and workers had no programme or class-consciousness, while two total wars have made all parties recognise the barbarous necessities which crisis can impose. The sort of synthesis which holds the field, exemplified in M. Lefebvre's work, is greatly indebted to Aulard and Mathiez, but more complex and many-sided. Within a cadre of class conflict, the interdependence of the action of social groups and their internal divisions are emphasised; the bourgeoisie, for example, make the Revolution, but they follow in the wake of the aristocratic revolt and have various degrees of alliance with the *sans-culottes*; they emerge victorious, but neither collectively nor as individuals are they identical with the class which began the struggle. In a brief essay, M. Lefebvre quelled the war between the adherents of Danton and of Robespierre, not by producing new evidence, but simply by examining the presuppositions of the two schools. Though the thesis of circumstances remains central, it is modified by many refinements; the Terror was a class war, a clash of personal hatreds, a substitute for disorganised violence, an epiphenomenon of de-Christianisation and the sanction of the war economy as well as an expedient of national defence, and was bound up with fears of a *complot aristocratique* which existed from the very first days of the Revolution.

This heightened subtlety in explanation is not entirely explained by the progress of research in new directions, but in part arises from a changed attitude to the problem of the nature of historical knowledge, which first showed itself in France when M. Aron, from the side of philosophy, challenged historians to forsake the 'fatality' implicit in positivism and study 'retrospective probability'. Such a method implies the necessity of escaping from the single homogeneous 'revolution' which hypnotised contemporaries and from their partisan procedure of adding up points for and against this great totality. It also implies the abandonment of the idea of a main pattern of respectable events upon which 'circumstances' descended like evil hobgoblins. There were many revolutions within the one Revolution, each with its own 'causes', and there were also 'causes' which explain why all these interlocked. Each of these processes of change has its own 'for' and 'against', if one chooses to argue them, and each is a causal chain which runs athwart the others. These clashes, at once logical and unpredictable, are the very stuff of tragedy, and each cancels a series of possibilities, tragedies of what might have been. But it is not the task of this chapter to suggest how a fresh synthesis could arise from the mass of new materials and methods of approach which are now available—that is for the real historians, the 'princes and legislators' of their subject, not for mere historians of historical writing. 'Si j'étois prince ou législateur', observed Rousseau at the beginning of his *Contrat social,* 'je ne perdrois pas mon tems à dire ce qu'il faut faire; je le ferois, ou je me tairois.'

CHAPTER XXIII

THE OUTBREAK OF THE FRENCH
REVOLUTION

To the nineteenth-century historian the French Revolution was largely a battle of ideas and its outbreak the more or less fortuitous climax to a series of political crises—the rejection of Calonne's proposals for tax reform by the Assembly of Notables of 1787, the convocation of the Estates General, and the king's dismissal of Necker on 11 July 1789; while, in the background of events, an undifferentiated mass of peasants and turbulent town-dwellers, prompted by age-old grievances or hopes of easy spoils, waited to settle accounts with *seigneurs*, tax-collectors and city authorities. During the past half-century, however, this general thesis has been largely modified by the work of such writers as Jaurès, Mathiez, Lefebvre and Labrousse, all of whom have been more or less influenced by Marx's historical methods. As the field of research into the origins of the Revolution has widened, it has been found necessary to pay more attention to social and economic factors in general and, above all, to the particular grievances and social claims of an extremely heterogeneous peasantry and urban *menu peuple*, whose intervention, therefore, no longer appears as a mere echo or reflection of the actions or speeches of aristocrats, lawyers and journalists at Versailles and in Paris. More attention has also been paid to the 'feudal reaction' of the last twenty-five years of the old régime in France and to the aims of the *parlements* and provincial *noblesse*, who staged the famous *révolte nobiliaire*, or aristocratic revolt, of 1787–8; in fact, it has even been claimed that this episode was not merely a curtain-raiser to the events of 1789, but marked the opening shot of the Revolution itself.[1] This view is, of course, not a new one: it was held by Robespierre, and Chateaubriand wrote: 'Les patriciens commencèrent la Révolution; les plébéiens l'achevèrent.' More generally, however, the result of recent research has been to shift the point of emphasis somewhat from Versailles and Paris to the provinces and to present the outbreak of the Revolution as the point at which a whole complex of social forces came into violent collision in the summer of 1789.

It is, of course, a commonplace that the origins of these various conflicts can be traced to the reign of Louis XV, if not to that of the 'grand monarque' himself. Yet, between the death of Louis XIV and the great financial crisis of 1787, it was neither substantial peasant proprietors, nor

---

[1] A. Mathiez, *La Révolution française* (3 vols., 1922–7).

dissident bourgeois, nor even *frondeur* nobles—all of whom proved eventually to have their own particular score to settle with the old régime —that challenged the existing order. This challenge came, on the one hand, from the recalcitrant magistrates of the Paris and provincial *parlements*; on the other, it came from the small consumers of town and countryside—above all, the purchasers of wheat and bread—who, throughout the century, found themselves in frequent, and often violent conflict, with the authorities. The urban wage-earners, it is true, often engaged in strikes over wages and hours of work: wages tended to lag behind the price of food, particularly in the latter years of the old régime; and there were extensive strikes of Paris stocking-frame weavers, bookbinders, building workers and porters in 1724, 1737, 1776, 1785 and 1786 and of Lyons silk-weavers in 1744, 1774 and 1788 (the latter attaining almost insurrectionary proportions). But, at a time when there was as yet no factory system and no national trade-union organisation, the wage-earners, like other small consumers, were more concerned with the provision of cheap and plentiful bread than with the size of their pay-packet and resorted more readily to the food riot than to the strike as a form of social protest. Yet the urban wage-earners, though numerous in Paris and in the centres of the textile industry (Lille, Lyons, Troyes, Sedan, Rouen and Rheims), were in a small minority in the small provincial towns and homes of the traditional crafts; in any case, they were greatly outnumbered by the professional *manouvriers*, or agricultural labourers, and far more so by the host of small peasant proprietors, petty strip-farmers, *métayers* (share-croppers) and wine-growers, who formed the bulk of the peasant population and yet depended on the purchase of bread or grain for the greater part of their subsistence—particularly in times of cyclical depression.[1] To all these millions bread was the staple diet and, even in normal times, accounted for something like 50 per cent of their budget. In times of sharply rising prices—as in the famine year of 1709–10 and in less spectacular years of *hausse*, such as 1725, 1740, 1752, 1766–8, 1770 and 1775—they would be obliged to spend 60, 70, or even 80 per cent of their earnings on bread; or more likely, they would be compelled to go hungry. It is therefore not surprising that such years witnessed violent outbursts of rioting, often accompanied by popular price-control (or *taxation populaire*), by urban workers, shopkeepers and craftsmen and small peasants in different parts of the country. Though never constituting in themselves a serious threat to the existing order, they are important as marking both the most prevalent type of economic unrest of the period and a form of disturbance which the Revolution inherited, with so much else, from the old régime.

---

[1] C.-E. Labrousse, *Esquisse du mouvement des prix et des revenus en France au XVIIIe siècle* (2 vols., 1933), vol. ii, p. 637; *La Crise de l'économie française à la fin de l'ancien régime et au début de la Révolution* (1944), pp. xiii–xiv, 625.

Among the more widespread of these disturbances, the nearest to the point of revolutionary outbreak and that bearing the closest resemblance to many of the popular movements of the Revolution itself was the so-called *guerre des farines*, which swept through Paris, the Île de France and neighbouring provinces in April–May 1775.[1] Yet, despite their magnitude and the concern that they aroused among authorities and propertied classes, the riots yielded no immediate results. This was, in part, because the food crisis itself, although severe and widely felt, was comparatively short-lived: prices began to fall again in October. Secondly, Turgot managed to crush the movement with the aid of both the pulpit and the army, which as yet remained entirely loyal to the government. More important still, only a small part of the peasantry was involved; the question of tithes, feudal dues and game laws did not arise. Lastly, and perhaps most important of all, the bourgeoisie had not yet begun to challenge the existing order and, in any case, were bound to be hostile to a movement against members of their own class and against a minister whose advent they had hailed with enthusiasm and whose reforms—including free trade in grain—they actively supported: in several towns, in fact, the *milice bourgeoise* was mustered in order to crush the riots. The main lesson of the *guerre des farines* was, in short, that, in the conditions of eighteenth-century France, no isolated movement of wage-earners, artisans and village poor could hope to yield revolutionary results. It was to be quite different, of course, when such outbreaks were to be supplemented and strengthened by the activities and ideas of other social classes.

The twelve years that followed, though years of falling profits and business recession,[2] were years of low or stable grain prices. For the whole of France, the average price of the *setier* of corn ranged between 20 and 24 livres and, in Paris, the price of bread remained remarkably steady: from the manuscript journal of the Paris bookseller Hardy we learn that, whereas in the period 1767–75 the price of the 4 lb. loaf rarely fell below 11 sous, between 1776 and 1789, the normal price was 8 or 9 sous and it only rose to 10½ or 11 sous for very brief spells in 1784. Therefore, although a crisis of considerable proportions was already maturing, it was not visible to contemporaries and this was a period of comparative social calm. Such popular movements as took place were scattered and sporadic, arising over a variety of issues: there were bread riots at Toulouse and Grenoble in 1778, at Bayeux in 1784 and at Rennes in 1785. Paris witnessed in 1784 and 1786 the first of a series of protests directed against the *barrières*, or ring of customs posts, recently erected by the Farmers-General to tax livestock, meat, wine, firewood and other consumers' goods entering the capital. In Paris, too, there appears to have been a resurgence of anti-clerical feeling among the people: Hardy records a

---

[1] See above, ch. XXI, p. 609. [2] See page 659 below.

number of incidents between 1783 and 1789 that are reminiscent of the hostility to Jesuits in the 1720s and to the archbishop of Paris over the *billets de confession* in 1752–3.

The year 1787 saw the opening of the *révolte nobiliaire* which served as a curtain-raiser to the revolutionary crisis of 1788–9. It grew out of the financial crisis arising from France's entry into the War of American Independence. To meet the mounting deficit, Calonne, as Controller-General, proposed a series of new and drastic remedies—of which the extension of the stamp-duty and the levying of a general land-tax upon the annual production of the soil were to rouse the deepest controversy—and which, had they been brought into operation, would have revolutionised the whole fiscal system and assured the Crown of a permanent and expanding income from direct taxation.[1] To avoid running into the certain opposition and obstruction of the Paris *Parlement*, to whom the scheme would normally have been submitted, it was decided to convene a special assembly of Notables, a body hand-picked by the king, which met on 22 February 1787.

But the plan miscarried—both because of a clash of interest and because of the minister's general unpopularity. The die-hard minority naturally resented the threat to their cherished immunities; the spokesmen of the cities objected to the stamp-duty, whose burden would mainly fall on the business community; and the liberal aristocracy, though not opposed to the measures in principle, objected both to their inadequacy and the abuse to which they might be put, for lack of effective guarantees, by an unscrupulous minister. To break the deadlock, the king dismissed Calonne on 8 April. He was replaced, at the queen's instance, by Loménie de Brienne, archbishop of Toulouse. Though enjoying the confidence of the Notables, and one of Calonne's sternest critics, his success was, in practice, not much greater. Having made some concessions in detail, he was driven to fall back on the substance of his predecessor's programme. Up to a point, the Notables were co-operative: they agreed to all the proposals but, smitten with a sudden sense of their own incompetence (possibly due to the flood of pamphlet literature which their meeting had called forth), they insisted that they be referred before enactment to the *Parlement* of Paris—or, better still (the suggestion was Lafayette's), to the Estates General, which had not met since 1614. Having given this grudging verdict, the Notables were dismissed on 25 May.

Once more, it was the judicial oligarchy rather than the higher clergy, provincial nobility or princes of the blood that most resolutely challenged the king and his ministers and fired the opening shot in the 'aristocratic revolt'. Yet the *parlement*, at this time, was by no means a solidly reactionary body. Apart from a sprinkling of princes, dukes and bishops, its main deliberative assembly—the cour des pairs—was largely composed

---

[1] See above, ch. XXI, pp. 613–14.

of young *conseillers* (of seventy-two whose ages are known fifty-nine were under thirty-five years of age[1]), who fell into two main political groups: those who were willing to use every opportunity to assert their privileges —both ancient and usurped—against the claims of government; and a minority led by Adrien Duport, the future Constituent, who, fired by the *philosophes* and the American Revolution, were eager for far-reaching constitutional reform. It was the circumstances of the moment that brought these groups together: though divided as to their ultimate aims, they were both distrustful of ministerial 'despotism' and both, for differing reasons, looked to the Estates General to solve their problems. So, when faced with Brienne's proposals, they readily consented to relax controls on the sale and export of grain and welcome the provincial assemblies; but they protested against the stamp-duty, categorically rejected the land-tax, and demanded that the Estates General be summoned to deal with the financial crisis. Though the decrees were promulgated, none the less, in a *lit de justice* in August, and the Paris magistrates were exiled to Troyes a few days later, it was the *parlement* rather than the minister that won the first round in the contest. The provincial *parlements*, following recent practice, rallied to the support of Paris; and the ministry, being further embarrassed by its inept handling of the Dutch crisis, hastily withdrew the decrees on the land-tax and stamp-duty, and reinstated the Paris *parlement* in late September, in return for its agreement to a prolongation of the *vingtièmes* until 1792.

The return of the *parlement* to Paris was the occasion of remarkable scenes of jubilation in the Place Dauphine, the Rue du Harlay and other approaches to the Palace of Justice. The magistrates were experienced demagogues: in the course of previous disputes, they had begun to popularise such terms as 'nation' and 'citoyen', and they enjoyed considerable support among both bourgeois and *menu peuple* as the proclaimed custodians of traditional liberties. On this occasion, the celebrations were relatively restrained; yet they marked the first recurrence of large-scale popular disturbance in the capital since the grain riots of 1775. Calonne and the comtesse de Polignac, governess of the royal children, were burned in effigy, bonfires were lit on the Pont Neuf and fireworks were let off at the Guards. From Hardy's description and from the arrests made on 28 September (the climax to a week's celebrations), it appears that the riots were started by the clerks of the Law Courts and supported by the apprentices and journeymen of the luxury trades of the Cité. The people of the *faubourgs* and markets, the main support of future demonstrations, took little part; and, of the bourgeoisie, none but the lawyers were as yet involved.

Yet the crisis deepened. At first, the Paris *parlement* agreed to register further loans in return for a firm promise that the Estates General should meet—in 1792. But negotiations broke down again in November; the

[1] J. Egret, *La Pré-Révolution française* (Paris, 1962), p. 154.

duke of Orleans and two leading magistrates, who had been particularly outspoken in the debates, were exiled; and, in May 1788, the *parlement* won further popularity by issuing a declaration condemning the whole system of arbitrary government, including the obnoxious *lettres de cachet*. The government's reply was to ring the Law Courts with troops, to force the *parlementaires* to surrender their leaders to royal justice and to issue six edicts drafted by Lamoignon, the Keeper of the Seals. These suspended the *parlements*, vested the greater part of their appellate jurisdiction in forty-seven new tribunals and transferred their powers of registering royal edicts to a so-called 'plenary court'.

By these measures, the government had hoped to drive a wedge between the fractious *parlements* and the nation at large—particularly the host of middle-class *avocats* and lawyers, whose hopes of preferment were blocked by the monopoly of the privileged 'sovereign courts'. It was a serious miscalculation and the ministerial *coup d'état*, far from winning allies, provoked a nationwide rebellion against its authors. First, the clerical assembly, having been invited to vote a *don gratuit*, protested against the suspension of the *parlements* and reasserted clerical immunity from taxation. The dukes and peers, too, associated themselves with the protests of the *parlements*. Finally, the *noblesse*, though long rivals of the judicial oligarchy, found the occasion auspicious for declaring their support: they hoped thereby to defend their financial privileges from further attack and to extend their political authority through the newly created provincial assemblies. And, most significant: the 'patriots'—the champions of 'the nation' against both privilege and 'despotism'—who had been inclined, like Mirabeau and Lafayette (but unlike Duport and Barnave), to pin their hopes on ministerial reform, now tended to line up behind the *parlements* instead: only thus, they believed, could there be any guarantee that the Estates General would be called together. Riots broke out during the summer at Bordeaux, Dijon, Grenoble, Pau, Rennes and Toulouse—all cities with a tradition of provincial separatism and aristocratic self-government. In Dauphiné, *noblesse* and Third Estate co-operated in illegally reviving the ancient Estates of the province; in Brittany, they united in common protest against ministerial 'despotism'. At Grenoble, massive riots, launched by the lawyers' clerks and supported by the townsfolk and visiting peasantry, prevented the suspended magistrates from leaving the city for five days. At Rennes, where the nobility demagogically exploited the people's anger over the high prices resulting from the free trade in grain, the intendant and commandant were attacked in the street and besieged in their houses.

Faced with such a united opposition, the government was once more compelled to retreat: the Estates General were promised for May 1789, Brienne was replaced by Necker, Lamoignon's judicial reforms were suspended and the *parlements* were recalled soon after. In Paris, the news was greeted with another outburst of celebrations in the Place Dauphine and the approaches to the Palais de Justice. Bonfires were lit and the occupants of coaches crossing the Pont Neuf were compelled to bow low to the statue of Henri IV and to shout, 'à bas Lamoignon!' A new factor, however, was to extend these disturbances beyond the scope and limits of the previous year. The harvest had been disastrous and, on 17 August, the price of the 4 lb. loaf, after long remaining at 9 sous, rose to $9\frac{1}{2}$ sous, on the 20th to 10 sous, on 2 September to $10\frac{1}{2}$ sous, and on 7 September to 11 sous. Under this stimulus, the people of the *faubourgs* joined the riots started two days earlier by the Palais clerks, and changed their whole character: they spread to the markets and university quarter, continued, with short lulls, until the end of September and took a heavy toll in casualties and arrests, mainly of wage-earners and craftsmen of widely scattered districts. The Parisian *sans-culottes*, like the peasants of Brittany and Dauphiné, had entered the movement; but it was yet as a junior partner of the privileged orders. The real revolutionary crisis was still to come.

This developed in the winter of 1788–9 and brought about a radical realignment of forces. In this process, the decisive elements were the deepening economic crisis and the preparations for the meeting of the Estates General. One of the great merits of Professor Labrousse's researches is to have illustrated so graphically the particular, as well as the general, causes of the dissatisfaction of different social classes in France on the eve of the Revolution. For many, including peasant proprietors, industrialists, merchants and tenant farmers, the greater part of the century had been a period of economic expansion and prosperity: from 1733 to 1778 industrial and agrarian prices were advancing steadily and, as we saw, explosions of economic discontent were largely confined to wage-earners and small consumers—and refractory magistrates. After 1778, partly as the result of the American War, there followed a decade of falling prices—gradual in most industrial and farm products, though reaching crisis proportions in wines and textiles. During this period the net profits of small tenant farmers, peasant proprietors, wine-growers and other *métayers*, because of the heavy and sustained toll of tax, tithe and seigneurial exaction, tended to drop out of all proportion to the fall in prices, while large landed proprietors were able to cushion themselves against loss by means of their feudal revenues. On top of this 'malaise pré-révolutionnaire' came the more sudden catastrophe of 1787–9, which took the form of a succession of bad harvests and consequent shortage of grain, aggravated by the government's free-trade policy, with the price of wheat doubling within two years in the main productive regions of the north and reaching record levels in twenty-seven out of thirty-two *généralités* in mid-summer 1789.[1] In the Paris region, crops were further

[1] Labrousse, *La Crise de l'économie française*, pp. ix–xli; *Esquisse du mouvement des prix et des revenus*, vol. II, pp. 640–1.

reduced by a freak hailstorm in July 1788. The price of the 4 lb. loaf in the Paris markets rose to 12 sous on 8 November, to 13 sous on the 28th, to 14 sous on 11 December and, finally, to 14½ sous on 1 February 1789; it was to remain at this level until after the fall of the Bastille. Meanwhile, an industrial crisis, already developing since the American War, had been aggravated by the sharp rise in agricultural prices and the competition from England resulting from the Anglo-French commercial treaty of 1786. Consequently, many thousands were out of work that winter in every textile centre: according to the reports of the industrial inspectors for September 1788 to January 1789, there were 46,000 unemployed in Amiens, 10,000 in Rouen, 8000 in Falaise, 30,000 in the neighbourhood of Carcassonne, 25,000 in Lyons; while at Troyes and Sedan half the looms were idle. In Paris itself there were 80,000 unemployed reported in December, and more thousands were flocking in from the impoverished countryside. Thus an accumulation of economic ills and social grievances most ominously attended the preparations that now began to be made for the meeting of the Estates General.

It was against this background that the propertied classes of the Third Estate, having hitherto abstained from participation in events or merely played second fiddle to the dissident privileged orders, made their entry on the revolutionary stage. The general cause of conflict had its roots deep in the old régime: while colonial trade, land-values and luxury-spending had enormously increased in the course of the century, capital investment and expansion of manufacture had, even in periods of prosperity, been impeded at every turn by the restrictions imposed by privileged corporations, feudal landowners and absolute monarchy on the elementary capitalist freedoms—the freedom to hire labour, the freedom to produce and the freedom to sell. Yet, while the ensuing conflict owed its eventual sharpness and finality to these deeper antagonisms, the clash between the bourgeoisie and the privileged orders which now followed arose, in the first instance, over representation and voting in the Estates General. On 25 September the Paris *parlement* had already begun to lose its reputation as the spokesman for popular liberties by demanding that the Estates General should be constituted as in 1614—namely that each order should have equal representation and vote separately. Though it retracted this pronouncement later, the damage had been done. An even more forthright insistence on the maintenance of privilege was voiced by the princes of the blood who, in December, denounced the claims of the Third Estate as a danger to the safety of the state. To the professional men and property-owners, who formed the politically vocal element within the *tiers*, the purpose of such manœuvres was obvious enough—to preserve the ascendancy of the privileged orders inside the Estates General, to confine the role of the Third Estate to one of voting taxes approved by the other orders and, above all, to safeguard the cherished immunities of the clergy and nobility. The Paris *parlement*'s declaration released a flood of pamphlets of unprecedented proportions, which continued, almost without a lapse, until the spring of the following year. The most famous was the Abbé Sieyès's pamphlet, *Qu'est-ce que le tiers état?*, published at the end of January 1789, which boldly claimed that the Third Estate alone constituted the 'nation' and denied that the other orders had any useful part to play within it. But most writers limited their arguments to contesting the claims of the *privilégiés* and to insisting that the Third Estate should have double representation within the Estates General, and that voting should be in common ('par tête') and not by each order separately assembled. A first victory for this view was won on 27 December 1788, when Necker, having first consulted a second Assembly of Notables (who gave him the contrary advice), persuaded the royal council to allow the Third Estate double representation; the form of voting, however, was still left in abeyance.[1]

But even this partial victory had remarkable results. In January, Mallet du Pan noted that there was no longer any question of a constitutional conflict between the king and the *privilégiés*, but of 'a war between the Third Estate and the two other orders'. Simultaneously the Third Estate emerged as the recognised leader of the 'nation' and the privileged orders lost all semblance of popular support. In Dauphiné, it is true, the *parlement* continued to espouse popular causes and to command popular favour until the summer of 1789; and in Brittany, where *noblesse* and *tiers* came into armed conflict over Necker's declaration, the nobility was still able to find support among the common people of Rennes who, in late January, rioted for bread to accompanying shouts of 'Vive le Roi! Vive la noblesse!' But such manifestations were exceptional, and were becoming more so. Even more startling was the reappearance of the monarchy as the champion of popular liberties. By the declaration of 27 December, Louis XVI had appeared to identify himself with the nationwide demand for reform and economic relief. From this grew the great hope—'la grande espérance'—that the Estates General were being summoned by the king in person in order to find effective remedies for age-old grievances. As a peasant-woman of Les Islettes in Champagne told Arthur Young in July 1789: 'It was said, at present, that *something was to be done by some great folks for such poor ones, but she did not know who nor how*, but God send us better, *car les tailles et les droits nous écrasent.*'[2] Such hopes, which were often accompanied by the contrary conviction that the privileged classes would do all in their power to prevent their realisation ('le complot aristocratique'), were to play their part in stimulating the small proprietors and poor of town and country-

---

[1] Necker's secret report, however, made it clear that, legally, voting by order was still the rule. G. Lefebvre, *Quatre-Vingt-Neuf* (Paris, 1939), p. 67.
[2] *Travels in France during the years 1787, 1788 and 1789* (Cambridge, 1929), p. 173.

side to remarkable displays of revolutionary energy during the coming spring and summer.

Meanwhile, regulations had been issued on 24 January 1789 to govern the election of deputies to the Estates General and, as an earnest of the government's sincerity, to invite the people to prepare their own *cahiers de doléances*, or lists of grievances, to guide their deliberations. The electoral arrangements were highly complicated, though liberal in scope; and as the government, inspired by Necker, refused to give any guidance as to candidates or programmes, considerable initiative was left to corporate oligarchies and professional bourgeoisie to influence proceedings as they might; this greatly affected the final outcome. In general, electoral districts were formed out of the ancient subdivisions used for administering justice, the so-called *bailliages* and *sénéchaussées*; but Paris was treated as a separate electoral division and the revived Estates of Dauphiné were accorded the right to appoint their own deputies. Deputies were to be elected in separate orders. The privileged orders enjoyed direct male adult suffrage: all lay nobles, aged twenty-five and above, had the vote in their electoral assemblies, either in person or by proxy; the same right was enjoyed by bishops and parish clergy, though canons and monks were only entitled to send representatives. Deputies of the Third Estate, on the other hand, were chosen by a rather more restricted franchise and by a more complicated system of indirect election. Except in Paris, where the suffrage was limited to those paying six livres per annum in *capitation*, Frenchmen of twenty-five years of age, whose names were inscribed on the taxation rolls (for however small an amount), were eligible to vote in their primary assembly—that is, either in that of their parish or in that of their urban guild. In brief, all male adult commoners had the vote, with the exception of domestic servants, non-householders (*non-domiciliés*), sons living in the parental home, the poorest labourers and downright paupers. But the finally elected representatives of their Estate only emerged after two, three or four stages of the electoral process, depending on whether the constituency was urban or rural and whether it was a principal or secondary *bailliage* (or *sénéchaussée*).

Whatever had been the government's intention, the system most definitely favoured the urban and professional bourgeoisie, who dominated discussions and voting in the assemblies of the Third Estate, took full advantage of their practical monopoly of literacy and vocal expression, and enjoyed the means and the leisure to concert common action among 'patriots', to print circulars and pamphlets and to conduct electoral campaigns denied to the rural craftsmen and peasantry, let alone to the labourers and village poor. It was therefore no accident that the urban bourgeoisie captured the great bulk of the seats among the deputies of the Third Estate: of the 610 that went to represent their order at Versailles, some 25 per cent were lawyers, 5 per cent were other professional men,

13 per cent were industrialists, merchants and bankers; at most, 7–9 per cent were agriculturalists—but, even of these, only a handful were peasants.[1]

It was during this campaign that the so-called 'patriot' party emerged among the promoters of constitutional reform. Though mainly voicing the aims of the Third Estate, it included such wealthy aristocrats as La Fayette, the duc de Larochefoucauld-Liancourt and the marquis de Condorcet, and distinguished *parlementaires* such as Adrien Duport, Hérault de Séychelles and Lepelletier de Saint-Fargeau: many of these were to play a prominent part in the Revolution. Some belonged to masonic lodges; others to the famous Committee of Thirty, which met at Duport's house and was composed of a medley of lawyers, liberal aristocrats and clerics (Talleyrand and Sieyès were of their number); others again, such as Sieyès and Mirabeau, acted as a link between the Committee of Thirty and the duke of Orleans, who carried on his own independent campaign. Such facts have led historians to lay too much stress on the existence of a central direction of all revolutionary agitation and to exaggerate the part played by freemasons and the Committee of Thirty alike, whose operations have been seen as evidence of a concerted 'plot' to undermine the institutions of the old régime. There is little factual basis for this view: the masonic lodges recruited men of every shade of opinion and communications were as yet not sufficiently developed to allow of a highly organised direction by comparatively unknown men. Yet such evidence as there is suggests that leaders were already beginning to emerge from among both bourgeois and liberal aristocrats, who were able to give some guidance to the nationwide discussions and to impress their personalities and ideas on the spontaneous actions of many thousands that broadly shared their views in every part of the country.

Meanwhile, the electors had drawn up their *cahiers de doléances*. They were of two main kinds: those drafted in the preliminary assemblies of the parishes and guilds for submission to the assemblies of the *bailliage*; and those drafted in the assemblies of the *bailliage* for direct submission to the Estates General. Of these general *cahiers*, some 522 of an original 615 have survived and are fairly evenly divided between the three orders.[2] As might be expected, the *cahiers* of the clergy and nobility (with the notable exception of that of the *noblesse* of Paris *intra muros*) stress their attachment to their traditional privileges and immunities, though they concede the principle of fiscal equality. At the same time, they join with those of the Third Estate in demanding the removal of many of the more oppressive and wasteful practices of the absolute monarchy. They roundly condemn fiscal abuse and extravagance, the arbitrary acts of

[1] A Cobban, *A History of Modern France*, vol. 1 (1957), p. 140.
[2] B. Hyslop, *French Nationalism in 1789 according to the General Cahiers* (New York, 1934), p. 8.

ministers, the system of *lettres de cachet*, the anomalies and vexations of the internal customs and the prevailing system of weights and measures. More positively, they demand freedom of the press and of the individual (though not that of conscience) and a constitution that, while upholding the traditional power and authority of the monarch, will invest a periodically convened Estates General with the right to frame laws and vote taxes, whose assessment and collection will be entrusted to elective provincial and municipal assemblies. In brief, on matters affecting political and administrative reform there was a considerable measure of agreement among the three Estates.

But the general *cahiers* of the Third Estate, drawn up in nearly every case by the bourgeoisie, go very much further. They not only demand liberty of speech, writing and assembly, freedom of trade and freedom from arbitrary arrest; but they generally insist on the complete civil equality of all three Estates—that is, that the clergy and nobility must surrender not only such utterly discredited relics as serfdom, but they must give up such age-old privileges as tithe, *banalités*, *champart*, hunting rights and seigneurial jurisdiction. So much the bourgeoisie had learnt, if not from their own experience, at least from a study of peasant grievances; but the most urgent peasant demand of all—for land—is seldom, if ever, voiced in these *cahiers*.

For the particular demands of the peasants and the less frequently voiced demands of the craftsmen and wage-earners we must turn to the numerous parish *cahiers* and occasional *cahiers* of the guilds. Some of these, like the general *cahiers* of the Third Estate, are (either wholly or in part) set pieces based on circulated models; and often wage-earners and poorer peasants, even when entitled to attend the assemblies, were kept away or silenced by intimidation, the pressing needs of labour, or by deep-grained servility to employers or social superiors. Yet a sufficient number of genuine parish *cahiers*, at least, have survived to illustrate two truths—the one, that these classes wholeheartedly supported the criticisms levelled by the bourgeoisie against the absolute monarchy and the feudal survivals in land-tenure and justice; and the other, that they had social claims of their own that, in other respects, often sharply divided them from the urban property-owners (or landowners) within the Third Estate.

The voice of the urban wage-earners is as rarely heard in the *cahiers* as it is in the whole pamphlet-literature of the period. In Paris, the guilds were not invited, as elsewhere, to put forward preliminary *cahiers* at their own specially convened meetings; and, even where this was the case, the *compagnons*, or journeymen, were generally excluded from the assemblies of the master-craftsmen. By local circumstance or accident, however, wage-earners' grievances were, in fact, heard at Rheims, Troyes, Marseilles and Lyons; and here they express more often the workers' concern at high prices rather than at low wages. Most frequently, they follow the lead given by their employers in political, social and industrial matters. The peasant *cahiers* are far more downright. In addition to the general grievances of the whole rural community, we hear the particular *doléances* of *laboureur*, *métayer*, petty strip-farmer and *manouvrier*. In the Rouen district, where the price of the bushel of wheat had risen to 8 livres and that of the 4 lb. loaf to 16 sous, villagers demand that the price be reduced to a half in both cases. In Brittany small peasants around Rennes complain that such are the burdens of taxation and seigneurial exaction that a strip of land with a gross yield of 40 livres per annum scarcely brings its owner a net income of 10 livres, once the demands of tax-collector and landlord have been met. In the parish of Pierreville (Cotentin), the *laboureurs* are so downright in their condemnation of royal officials and of tithe and gaming rights that the *bailli* refuses to accept their grievances and dictates a *cahier* of his own! In Lorraine and Hainault landless peasants and small *laboureurs* join forces in opposing enclosure edicts and land-clearance schemes promoted by the more prosperous members of their community. And, in the Vosges, a parish *cahier* protests that the allocation of land to landless *manouvriers*, following the division of the commons, has disturbed the harmonious relations hitherto existing between *manouvriers* and *laboureurs*! In short, the parish *cahiers* reflect both the common bonds of interest linking all members of the peasant community in opposition to royal tax-gatherer, tithe-owner and landlord, and those further divisions separating small consumer from large producer and landless labourer from tenant farmer or proprietor. Both factors were profoundly to influence the course and outcome of the Revolution in the village in the years that lay ahead.

Meanwhile, the small consumers had not limited their protests to such verbal expressions as are found in the *cahiers*. In response to the bad harvest of 1788 and to sharply rising grain prices, the first prolonged consumers' movement since that of 1775 opened up in December. This time it was not only to be continuous until the autumn of the following year, but it soon began to merge with that of small peasant proprietors against feudal game laws, tithes and seigneurial dues. Both movements were, in turn, to merge with the political action of bourgeois and townsmen and reach a common climax in the summer of 1789.

The revolt against shortage and rising prices is recorded in the reports of the intendants and their *sub-délégués*; it was largely from this source that Taine constructed his one-sided picture of 'spontaneous anarchy'. It took traditional forms—varying from pillaging of grain-boats and granaries, enforcing price-control of bread, flour and wheat (sometimes with the co-operation of compliant authorities), rioting in bakers' shops and at markets and town-halls, to assaulting customs officers, merchants, millers and farmers, and the widespread, though rarely indiscriminate, destruction of property. In December and January such reports came in from Brittany, Normandy and Touraine; in March and April from Burgundy, Dauphiné, Île de France, Languedoc, Nivernais, Orléanais, Picardy, Poitou, Provence and Touraine; in May and June from Cambrésis, Limousin and Lyonnais; in July from Champagne and Normandy. The most sensational of these disturbances was that which broke out in the Faubourg Saint-Antoine in Paris at the end of April. The houses of two prominent manufacturers and respected members of the Paris Third Estate, Réveillon and Henriot, were ransacked and burned down. The Royal Cravate regiment was ordered to fire and many rioters and on-lookers—including mainly craftsmen, apprentices and labourers of the Saint-Antoine and neighbouring districts—were killed and wounded. Though the immediate cause of disturbance was that the two manufacturers were believed to have called for a reduction of wages, the underlying reason was the prevailing scarcity and high price of bread. A remarkable feature was that, though abbés and other reputed supporters of the privileged orders were suspected of having incited the disturbances, in order to discredit the Third Estate on the eve of the Estates General, the rioters were reported to have chanted the 'patriot' slogans of the hour: 'Long live the king! Long live M. Necker! Long live the Third Estate!'

In the Paris region poaching and attacks on gamekeepers had become frequent in the latter months of 1788; these developed, in the spring, into a more general movement against the game laws and hunting rights of the crown and the nobility. On the estates of the prince de Conti at Cergy, Pontoise, L'Île-Adam and Beaumont—all scenes of the grain riots of 1775—peasants and landworkers, having reaped no harvest owing to the ravages of hail, set out in December to trap and destroy the rabbits that infested their fields. The movement spread in the spring to Conflans Sainte-Honorine and adjoining villages, and led to clashes with the mounted police. Violent collisions occurred at Corbeil and Chatou; and, in June, whole villages to the south and west of the capital, goaded to action after years of depredation from royal warrens, were disarmed for trespassing on the king's forests and aristocratic preserves. In February peasants in Dauphiné had refused to pay their traditional quit-rents to their landlords; the next month they rioted against clergy and nobility accused of hoarding grain. The same charge was made at Manosque in March against the bishop of Senez; and in Brittany peasants invaded the markets, shouting 'The nobles and high magistrates are corn merchants in disguise'. Meanwhile, at Oisy, in Artois, peasants of a dozen villages banded together to exterminate the count of Oisy's game and refused in future to pay him the traditional *soyeté*, or *terrage*; while other peasant revolts against royal taxes, tithe and seigneurial dues were reported in Provence in March, at Gap in April, in Picardy, Brittany and Cambrésis in May, and in Flanders in July. This movement led, in turn, into that far greater movement of late July and August which, spreading over regions as widely apart as Alsace, Normandy, Hainault, Mâconnais and Franche-Comté, left in its trail the widespread destruction of châteaux and manorial rolls.

It is therefore perhaps not surprising that the Estates General, which were formally opened by the king at Versailles on 5 May 1789, should be rent by crisis and discord. It was natural enough that the *tiers* should exploit its advantages to the full: it had already won the important concession of the doubling of its traditional representation; in its further demand for voting in common it was known to have the support of a large minority of the clergy (two hundred of the deputies of the First Estate were parish priests) and a smaller minority of some fifty liberal aristocrats among the nobility. Besides, the proximity of Paris, where the party of 'patriots' had redoubtable strength, lent it something more than moral support in its tussle with the other orders.

At Versailles nothing was done to spare the commoners' susceptibilities or to realise their high hopes of early reform: they were ordered to wear the traditional black, to enter the hall of assembly by a side door and in every respect made mindful of their inferiority of status. Once more, the council, divided between the conflicting policies of Necker and Barentin, the Keeper of the Seals, gave no firm lead: while Necker, in the course of a three-hour speech, recommended the privileged orders to renounce voluntarily their fiscal immunities, he equally advised the Third Estate to show forbearance and not to press its demand for common voting by all three orders, who should decide separately which subjects might be discussed and voted in common. It was evident to the *tiers* that, on the crucial issue, the king had come down on the side of the privileged orders: without a union of the orders, the double representation of the Third Estate would prove a useless concession; without the support of like-minded deputies of the other Estates, they could always be outvoted by the combined strength of their opponents. It was such considerations that underlay the long wrangle that now ensued over the procedural matter of the verification of powers. The Third Estate insisted on a joint session to consider the validity of the mandates of each deputy, as a first step to holding common sessions on more fundamental matters. The leaders of the first two orders equally saw that to surrender on this point would be to go some way towards accepting the principle of a single assembly, which would effectively destroy the ascendancy and voting strength of the nobility and clergy.

The first five weeks of the Estates General were taken up with the attempt to solve this seemingly insoluble problem. On 7 May the Third Estate refused to verify its powers or to constitute itself as a separate chamber. The nobility, on the other hand, on 11 May, adopted the exactly opposite course and, a fortnight later, solemnly declared that voting by order was a fundamental principle of the monarchical constitution. The clergy, however, was rent by internal divisions and, on 8 May, although it consented to verify its powers, it refrained from declaring itself a separate chamber; and, on 27 May, the conservative bishops only succeeded by a narrow majority in preventing their order from accepting the *tiers'* invitation to a joint discussion of the issues in dispute. Ministerial attempts to find a compromise solution also ended in failure.

On 10 June the Third Estate, encouraged by popular support, decided to take the bit between its teeth. It invited the other orders to a common verification of powers: if they refused to attend, it would proceed without them. Joined by a few parish priests, it completed a check of the election returns on the 14th; elected a president (Bailly) and two secretaries; and, on the 17th, by a majority of 491 to 89, arrogated to itself the title of National Assembly. This first revolutionary action of the Third Estate was followed by the issue of two decrees, one of which provided that a dissolution of the Assembly, for whatever cause, would invalidate all existing taxes; and the other that, as soon as a new constitution had been determined, the public debt should be consolidated and underwritten by the nation as a whole. On 20 June a further challenge was thrown down when the new Assembly found itself—accidentally, it seems—locked out of its usual meeting-hall: following President Bailly into an adjoining tennis court, every deputy except one solemnly swore that the National Assembly should not disperse until the constitution had been firmly established. The previous day the clergy had by a narrow majority decided to throw in its lot with the Third Estate, and most of them joined it a few days later.

Even before this last act of defiance, Necker had urged the king to assert his authority, break the deadlock between the orders and take the initiative in legislative reform. To this end, he suggested that a royal session (*séance royale*) be held, where it should be announced that such matters as the future constitution of the Estates General should be discussed in common sessions, whereas matters involving the vested interests of individual Estates should continue to be separately examined. After bitter arguments within the council, a first decision was taken on 19 June to hold a *séance royale* on the 22nd—presumably on the basis of Necker's proposals. But meanwhile the king, indecisive as ever, had let himself be prevailed upon by other counsels: surrounded at Marly (where the court had retired on the death of the young dauphin in early June) by a group of courtiers led by his younger brother, the comte d'Artois, whose arguments were supported by the queen and the leaders of the privileged orders, he was persuaded to agree to quash the self-styled Assembly's decrees of 17 June, to refer discussion on the future organisation of the Estates General to each of the separate orders, and to overawe the Third

Estate by a display of force. The session was deferred until 23 June; Necker, whose removal had been secretly agreed upon, decided to stay away. Once more, nothing was done to spare the feelings of the Third Estate: they were kept waiting in the rain while the privileged orders took their seats; the hall was ringed with troops; and the proceedings had all the arbitrary atmosphere of a *lit de justice*. The main business was devoted to the reading of two royal declarations by Barentin. The first pronounced the National Assembly's resolutions null and void and, while recommending the acceptance of the principle of common sessions for matters of common concern, expressly reserved for separate deliberation all questions relating to the special privileges and immunities of the first two Estates. The second declaration outlined the royal council's legislative programme. It provided, broadly, for a reform of the institutions of the old régime along lines already advocated by all three Estates in their respective *cahiers*; but the social fabric of the old order was to remain intact: it was categorically stated that tithes, feudal and manorial dues were to be treated as proprietary rights and that no surrender of fiscal privilege would be called for without the consent of the parties concerned. Finally, the Estates were ordered to disperse and to resume discussion in their separate chambers on the morrow.

Yet the plans of the court party miscarried. Thousands of Parisians invaded the courtyard of the palace to demand that Necker be retained in office; soldiers under the command of the prince de Conti refused to obey the order to fire; the deputies of the Third Estate, having declined to disperse after the termination of the *séance*, were rallied by Mirabeau in an historic speech. The king was compelled to yield: Necker remained in office and not only was the National Assembly (now consisting of 830 deputies) left in possession of its chamber, but, on 27 June, the remnants of the other orders were expressly commanded to fuse with it.

Meanwhile, a revolutionary leadership was emerging in Paris and was soon, with the aid of a popular rising, to give decisive support to the Assembly at Versailles. Up to now, the professional and commercial classes of the capital had viewed the insurrectionary simmerings in the *faubourgs* and markets—the product of the food crisis—without sympathy; but, with the latest news from Versailles, they began to give a direction to affairs without which the July revolution could hardly have been carried through. About this time the pamphleteers and journalists in the entourage of the duke of Orleans (who had joined the new National Assembly) began to establish a permanent headquarters at the Palais Royal; here thousands congregated nightly and acquired the slogans and directives—if not the funds—of what Hardy called 'the extreme revolutionary party'. Also at this time the 407 electors of the Paris Third Estate, whose original task it had been to appoint the Parisian deputies to the Third Estate at Versailles, began to meet regularly at the Hôtel de

Ville in the heart of the capital. These two bodies were to play distinctive, yet complementary, parts in the events of July. In the early days, however, it was the Palais Royal alone that gave a positive direction to the popular movement. Whereas the Hôtel de Ville contented itself with drafting paper schemes for the creation of a citizens' militia, or *milice bourgeoise*, the Palais Royal took effective measures, by public agitation and liberal expenditure, to win over the Gardes Françaises, the main body of troops stationed in the capital, from their loyalty to the court. On 30 June crowds directed from the Palais Royal released from the Abbaye prison eleven guardsmen who had been jailed for refusing to fire on the people at Versailles on 23 June. Tracts supporting the standpoint of the Third Estate were distributed among the Paris garrison: on 8 July a news-vendor was arrested for trying to sell such materials to officers and men encamped at the Champ de Mars. On 10 July eighty artillerymen, who had broken out of their barracks in the Hôtel des Invalides, were publicly fêted in the Palais Royal and the Champs-Élysées.

Yet the disaffection of the army, which was a vital factor in the events that followed, could not have been achieved by such means alone and had its origins in the deeper social conflicts and divisions of the old régime itself. The great efforts made since the Seven Years War to improve the efficiency and morale of the troops were fatally compromised by bitter conflicts over the appointment and promotion of officers. For the lesser provincial nobility a military career was the only avenue to public distinction and often the only means of livelihood. Their interests were injured by the claims of the court aristocracy (princes of the blood, the landed magnates and the so-called *présentés*) to a virtual monopoly of all posts of command. Governments were continuously faced with the impossible task of satisfying both sections of the nobility and reconciling their demands with the pressing need to replenish the exchequer by the sale of commissions to the wealthy bourgeoisie. As in other fields, the 'feudal reaction' of the latter years of the old régime sought to redress the balance in favour of the nobility as a whole, thus deepening the resentment of the *roturiers* and *anoblis* against them. But it also deepened the cleavage within the nobility. Its benefits went largely to the court aristocracy, and the provincial *noblesse* saw with resentful disgust that in the higher military posts the share of their courtly rivals was larger than ever.[1] This trend was given formal sanction by the *ordonnances* of March 1788, which virtually debarred the lesser nobles from promotion to full colonelcies and the officers of fortune (bourgeois risen from the ranks) from holding commissions higher than that of lieutenant. Nor were the discontents aroused by these and other measures confined to lesser nobles and *roturiers*. The loyalty of the court nobility itself had been strained by the interference of reforming ministers from Turgot to Brienne; and a

---

[1] See above, vol. VII, pp. 179, 181–2; and ch. VII, §2, of the present volume.

part of the military aristocracy—men like La Fayette, Noailles, Laroche-foucauld-Liancourt and Louis de Narbonne—had become convinced, either by service in America or the reading of the *philosophes*, of the need for far-reaching constitutional reforms. To this general state of disquiet and confused loyalties among the officers must be added the unrest among the soldiers themselves, brought about by the introduction of new-fangled drill and discipline, imported from Prussia by Frederick the Great's admirers, and the seemingly endless stream of new regulations emanating from the cabinets of reforming ministers.[1]

These elements combined to make the army on the eve of the Revolution an unreliable instrument for the suppression of civil disorder. During the *révolte nobiliaire* it was officers mainly drawn from the dissident provincial nobility that, in Brittany, Dauphiné and elsewhere, ordered their troops not to fire on demonstrators, refused to arrest rebellious magistrates, and generally set their soldiers an example of disobedience to the higher command which they were soon to follow. The events that followed the 'résultat du Conseil' of December 1788, which doubled the representation of the Third Estate in the Estates General, undoubtedly swung back a large and growing proportion of the officers to loyalty to the court; but, by this time, the troops themselves had begun to voice their own grievances against their officers and the harshness of the disciplinary code, and the ideas and slogans of the 'patriots' were gaining support among them. In February Necker told Malouet that a cause of his own reluctance to urge firmer measures was the disaffection of the army; and in mid-April (so Madame de Staël reports) he advised the king not to bring troops to Versailles to overawe the Estates General, as a public display of their sympathies for the deputies would be a sign of weakness rather than of strength. In June these fears were realised when the prince de Conti's troops at Versailles refused to fire on Parisians protesting at Necker's dismissal; and, a few days later, the Gardes Françaises, who had been loyal to the court in the Saint-Antoine riots in April, paraded the streets of Paris to shouts of 'Long live the Third Estate! We are the nation's soldiers', fraternised with revolutionary crowds and played a decisive part in the assault on the Bastille. This disaffection was to spread to frontier regiments and even to some foreign units (comprising one-quarter of the nation's military forces); and it has been claimed that three regiments alone—two-thirds of them Protestants from the Cevennes and Languedoc—remained completely untouched by the contagion of 'patriot' ideas and consistently loyal to the throne up to the final debacle of August 1792.[2]

[1] For the foregoing, see H. Carré, *Histoire de France*, ed. E. Lavisse, vol. IX (1910), pp. 53–60; L. Hartmann, 'Les officiers de l'armée royale à la veille de la Révolution', *Revue Historique*, vol. C (1909), pp. 241–68; vol. CI (1909), pp. 37–79; also E. G. Léonard, *L'Armée et ses problèmes au XVIII siècle* (1958), chs. XII and XIV (though these add little to the previously cited works).   [2] Léonard, *op. cit.* p. 293, n. 1.

Meanwhile, to counter the agitation of the 'patriots' in Paris, the court party attempted a final assertion of royal authority. On 26 June six provincial regiments had been ordered to Versailles and, on 1 July, ten further regiments, mainly composed of Swiss and Germans, were summoned from the provinces to ring the capital. Marshal de Broglie was placed in supreme command at Versailles with Besenval, a Swiss, directing operations in and around Paris. Finally, on 11 July, the king was once more persuaded to dismiss Necker, who was sent into exile, and to reconstitute his ministry under the baron de Breteuil, a favourite of the queen's. The news reached Paris at noon on the 12th and had startling consequences. During the afternoon Parisians flocked into the Palais Royal, where orators—Camille Desmoulins among them—gave the call to arms. Groups of marchers quickly formed; the busts of Necker and the duke of Orleans, the heroes of the hour, were paraded on the boulevards; theatres were compelled to close as a sign of mourning; in the Place Louis XV, demonstrators clashed with cavalry commanded by the prince de Lambesc, who had been ordered to clear the Tuileries gardens. Besenval withdrew to the Champ de Mars. The capital was in the hands of the people.

As the tocsin pealed, bands of insurgents joined those who, two days earlier, had already begun to burn down the hated *barrières*, whose exactions were bitterly resented by shopkeepers, wine-merchants and small consumers and which had already been the scene of frequent disturbance and attempted smuggling. Forty of the fifty-four customs posts were systematically demolished in the course of four days' rioting: documents, registers and receipts were burned, iron railings were pulled down, offices and furniture were fired and customs officers expelled from their lodgings. The Palais Royal had a hand in the affair; it is also no doubt significant that two posts said to belong to the duke of Orleans were spared. While the incendiaries generally were most interested in settling accounts with an institution that added materially to the price of food and wine, the organisers appear to have been more concerned to destroy the monopoly of the Farmers-General and to control the entry and exit of arms and persons to and from the capital. The same night a similar operation was carried out on the northern fringe of the city, when armed civilians and Gardes Françaises, once more directed from the Palais Royal, broke into the monastery of the Saint-Lazare brotherhood, searched it for arms, released prisoners and removed fifty-two cartloads of grain and flour to the central markets. This part of the proceedings was followed by a large-scale invasion of local poor and unemployed, who stripped the building of money, food, silver and hidden treasure.

But the main feature of the night of 12–13 July was the search for arms. Religious houses were visited and gunsmiths', armourers' and harness-makers' were raided in different parts of the capital. Numerous eyewitness accounts of these proceedings have come down to us and the Parisian gunsmiths eventually submitted to the National Assembly a statement of their losses, amounting to a total of 115,118 livres. They do not appear to have been paid and must be counted among the minor victims of the Revolution.

On the morning of the 13th the Paris electors made a firm bid to gain control of the situation. They formed a permanent committee to act as a provisional government of the city and determined to put a stop to the indiscriminate arming of the whole population. To them the bands of unemployed and homeless, some of whom had played a part in the raids on the *barrières* and the Saint-Lazare monastery, were as great a menace to the security and properties of the citizens as the privileged orders conspiring at Versailles. It was with both threats in mind that they now seriously set about organising a citizens' militia; and it goes without saying that it was on the former score alone that the king was persuaded to give his consent to the undertaking the next day. Householders were summoned to attend meetings in the sixty electoral districts into which Paris had been divided; each district was to provide 200 (later 800) men; and, the same evening, Barnave wrote that there were 13,200 citizens registered and equipped. From this body all vagrants, *gens sans aveu*, and even a large part of the settled wage-earning population, were specifically excluded; and the disarming of 'irregulars' began forthwith. Yet arms continued to fall into unauthorised hands as long as the insurrection lasted. Crowds besieged the Hôtel de Ville, demanding arms and powder. Jacques de Flesselles, *prévôt des marchands* and acting head of the provisional government, being anxious to limit their distribution, sent parties off on fruitless quests to the Arsenal and the Carthusian monastery: this 'treachery' was to cost him his life on the morrow. Meanwhile, the electors had deputed one of their number, the Abbé Lefevre, to guard the stocks assembled in the vaults of the Hôtel de Ville; but so great was the pressure of the half-armed crowds surging round the building that he was compelled to hand out his powder with more speed and less discrimination than he would have wished.

The search for arms continued on the morning of the 14th, when a spectacular raid was made on the Hôtel des Invalides across the river. Here some 30,000 muskets were removed by the 7000–8000 citizens taking part. It was they who raised the cry, 'To the Bastille!' The object was not to release prisoners (there were only seven of them), but to seize the powder that had lately been sent there from the Arsenal. Besides, the fortress was widely hated as a symbol of past tyrannies. It was believed to be heavily armed and its guns, which that morning were trained on the Rue Saint-Antoine, could play havoc among the crowded tenements. In the night, too, it had been rumoured that 30,000 royalist troops had marched into the Faubourg Saint-Antoine and had begun to slaughter its inhabitants. Yet there was no serious intention, at the outset, of taking the

Bastille by storm, least of all on the part of the committee of electors, who had thrust on them the task of directing operations from the Hôtel de Ville. From their own account of the event, we learn that they proposed to negotiate with the governor, de Launay, for the surrender of the gunpowder in his keeping and for the withdrawal of the guns from his battlements. De Launay received their deputations and promised not to fire unless attacked. Nevertheless, the besieging crowds, already filling the outer courtyard, managed to lower the drawbridge leading into the inner Cour du Gouvernement; and the governor, believing a frontal attack to be imminent, ordered his men to fire. In the ensuing affray, the besiegers lost ninety-eight dead and seventy-three wounded. Their blood was up and the electors lost control of operations. The decisive blow was struck by two detachments of Gardes Françaises who, responding to the summons of Hulin, a former regular N.C.O., marched to the fortress with five cannon removed that morning from the Invalides. Supported by a few hundred armed civilians—master-craftsmen, journeymen and labourers of the Saint-Antoine and neighbouring districts[1]—they trained their cannon on the main gate. De Launay first threatened to blow up the fortress, but after being dissuaded by his own garrison, lowered the main drawbridge and surrendered to the besiegers. He himself and six of the hundred defenders were massacred; de Flesselles met a similar fate. So the Bastille fell.

Though of little importance in itself, its fall had far-reaching consequences. Besenval withdrew his troops to Saint-Cloud. The National Assembly, for the time being at least, was saved and received royal recognition. The court party began to disintegrate and Condé, Breteuil and the Polignacs went into exile. In the capital power passed firmly into the hands of the electors, who set up a city council with Bailly as mayor and La Fayette as commander of the National Guard. On 17 July the king himself made the journey to Paris, escorted by fifty deputies (Robespierre among them), was received by the victors at the Hôtel de Ville and, in token of acquiescence in the turn of events, donned the red, white and blue cockade of the Revolution. It seemed as if now the National Assembly might proceed quietly with its work.

But the provinces had yet to have their say. Peasant revolt, provoked by hunger and the sudden hope of the redress of age-old grievances, had been endemic since the spring. The news from Paris, reaching the villages and market-towns by word of mouth and by deputies' letters during the third week in July, intensified it and spread it. It also had given further impetus to a series of minor municipal revolutions. Unlike the peasantry

---

[1] Archives Nationales, T 514, *Noms des vainqueurs de la Bastille* (662 names). Although incomplete, this list of active participants in the capture of the fortress is important as being the only one of its kind which records the addresses, occupations, and even militia units, of the great majority of the persons concerned.

and small urban consumers, the provincial bourgeoisie had mainly waited on events in Paris and Versailles. When the news of Necker's dismissal reached Nancy on 15 July, Arthur Young was told, 'We are a provincial town; we must wait to see what is done in Paris'. The 'municipal revolution' took different forms. Sometimes, as in maritime Flanders, the old town corporation broadened its base, adopted the tricolour cockade and carried on. Sometimes, as at Bordeaux, it followed the example of Paris and gave way to the local assembly of electors. More often—as at Lille, Rouen, Cherbourg, Dijon, Rennes and Lyons—the old authorities were overthrown and replaced by entirely new bodies, often pledged to reduce the price of bread. In nearly every case, the transfer of power was accompanied by the creation of a National Guard formed, as in Paris, to meet the double danger of aristocratic reaction and popular revolt. Meanwhile, the intendants were either expelled or quietly disappeared; in either event, the royal authority was weakened.

The food riots and peasant revolts of these weeks were accompanied by the strange phenomenon known as 'la Grande Peur' (the Great Fear), itself the product of economic crisis and the Paris revolution. The crisis had both increased the number of vagrants and stimulated the peasants' dissatisfaction with the exactions of the *seigneurs*. The plots of the aristocratic faction at Versailles, genuine enough in themselves, had been magnified out of all proportion; its defeat in Paris on 14 July, accompanied by the emigration of its leaders and the dispersal of the Paris military forces to country districts, lent colour to the belief that the aristocrats were preparing to wreak summary vengeance with the help of armed vagrants, or 'brigands', who were being let loose on the countryside. During the latter half of July no less than six main currents of the 'Great Fear', each one nourished by local incidents and panic, covered the greater part of the country: only Alsace, Brittany and Lorraine were free of them. In many cases, they reacted upon and further stimulated the movements of peasant proprietors against their *seigneurs*; as at Virieu in Dauphiné, where the peasants, having armed to meet imaginary 'brigands', turned their arms against the châteaux. At all events, in July and August they left a trail of razed châteaux and burning manorial registers in every part of the country. Often, they were led by persons bearing orders purporting to come from the king himself ('de par le Roi'); and there seems little doubt that the peasants believed that, in settling accounts with their *seigneurs*, they were carrying out the king's wishes, if not his specific instructions.[1]

The news from the provinces compelled the Assembly to pay immediate attention to feudal privilege and peasant demands. It was bound to make concessions and these took the spectacular form of the surrender of their feudal rights and fiscal immunities by the deputies of the liberal aristo-

[1] G. Lefebvre, *La grande peur de 1789* (1932).

cracy and clergy on the famous night of 4 August. But the Assembly's claim that 'the feudal régime had been entirely destroyed' was misleading: while the remnants of serfdom, the *corvée* and ecclesiastical tithes were abolished outright, some of the more onerous privileges and obligations—*champart, lods et ventes* among them—were later made redeemable by individual purchase. The fact that the landlords never got their money (the total compensation has been estimated at 4000 million livres) was due less to the foresight or generosity of the legislators than to the continued militancy of the peasantry. Eventually, the Jacobin Convention faced the accomplished fact and, by an act of July 1793, declared the outstanding debt null and void.

The Assembly had, already on 11 July, been given a first draft of a Declaration of the Rights of Man and the Citizen, submitted by La Fayette. Once the provincial riots had subsided, discussion of the project was resumed; and, on 27 August, after heated argument, the final Declaration, embodying seventeen articles, was adopted. Like the American Declaration of Independence, it was intended to be a statement of the general principles underlying a revolution that was still in progress. It also laid down, in sober and practical form, those rights which the Third Estate had demanded in its general *cahiers* and which Frenchmen might now be expected to enjoy—the protection of property, freedom of conscience, equality before the law, equal taxation and equal eligibility to office; to these the Constituent Assembly would in due course give separate legislative expression. The king, however, alleging that the declaration would encourage further unrest, refused his assent, as he had already refused to assent to the decrees issued after the night of 4 August.

The king's action could not fail to encourage that minority among the deputies who, in alliance with the court, still hoped to arrest the Revolution's course, if not to undo what it had already achieved. The conflict between this group (the 'English party', as it became called) and the majority was fought out over the constitutional issues of the Second Chamber and the royal veto; it was only resolved by the transfer of the king and Assembly to Paris after a further uprising in the capital. The moderates, led by Mounier among the commons and Lally Tollendal among the nobility, urged that the king be given an absolute veto over legislation and that an elective Second Chamber be established. The second proposal had little chance of success, as not only were Left and Centre within the Assembly ranged against it, but it was strongly opposed by the provincial nobility who feared their own exclusion from an upper Chamber. The veto proposal, however, was more tenaciously upheld and created sharper divisions, which extended beyond the confines of the Assembly itself. The Parisian 'patriots', established at the Palais Royal, called for its outright rejection; but Barnave, who spoke for the 'patriot' deputies at Versailles, was prepared to negotiate with the help of the

Centre, who favoured a compromise. When negotiations broke down on 29 August, the hands of the Parisians were strengthened and a first result was an attempt, promoted by the marquis de Saint-Huruge and a group of Palais Royal journalists, to induce Parisians to march to Versailles to fetch the king back to his ancestral home in the capital. This first attempt failed, not only because Barnave and his colleagues opposed it, but because the project still lacked that degree of support among the Parisian *menu peuple* that alone could give it reality.

This objective was, however, realised five weeks later by a combination of factors—the indoctrination of the common people with the political ideas of the 'patriots', the sharpening of the food crisis, and the provocative measures of the court. That ordinary Parisians were deeply influenced by the currents of advanced opinion had already been evident during the electoral campaign, when rioters in the Faubourg Saint-Antoine and others had freely championed the claims of the Third Estate against its opponents. The debates at Versailles were relayed with amazing speed to crowds in the Palais Royal and the Place de Grève. Already on 24 August, before the Declaration of the Rights of Man had been adopted, a journeyman gunsmith, when cross-examined at the Châtelet after arrest, insisted that 'le droit de l'homme' entitled him to a fair hearing. A week later, according to Malouet, 'Sedan-chair porters could be seen outside the Assembly greatly excited about the veto'; and, during September, as the political crisis deepened, wage-earners in the Place de Grève and unemployed workers in the *ateliers de charité* are reported as expressing their readiness to go to Versailles to fetch the royal family to the capital.

Yet, once more, it was the food crisis that lent a particular insistence and intensity to popular agitation. The price of the 4 lb. loaf had been reduced, on 22 July, from 14½ to 13½ sous; and, on 8 August, after demonstrations at the Hôtel de Ville, it was further reduced, with the aid of subsidies, to 12 sous. But the periods of calm that followed were shortlived. The harvest had been good, but, owing to a prolonged drought, millers were unable to grind sufficient corn. The shortage of flour and bread that resulted was a boon to speculators but a matter of deep concern to bakers, who were the most ready target of popular vengeance. During August and September there were constant bread riots in Paris, Versailles and Saint Denis, in the course of which a baker and a municipal officer were killed by angry crowds and many others were threatened with 'la lanterne'. It was noted by Hardy that, from mid-September, a leading part in this agitation was played by the women of the markets and *faubourgs*; and it was they who took the initiative and gave a lead to their menfolk in the great march to Versailles on 5 October.

But, as in July, it was developments at Versailles that gave the final impetus to the uprising of 'patriots' and *menu peuple* of the capital. On 11 September Barnave had persuaded the Assembly to urge the king to agree to the compromise solution of a suspensive veto; in return, it was intended that the king should withdraw his objection to the August decrees. It was the Assembly's insistence on this latter point that determined the court to attempt to break the deadlock by a new display of military force. On 15 September Louis, having rejected the moderates' advice to transfer the Assembly to a provincial town, ordered the Flanders regiment, stationed at Douai, to march on Versailles. It arrived on 29 September and was welcomed by a banquet given by the royal Gardes du Corps on 2 October. On this occasion the national cockade was trampled underfoot and the queen and her children were received with almost mystical fervour. The incident was widely reported in Paris the next day and the 'patriot' press called for vengeance. This time Barnave withdrew his objection to a resort to force; so, at least, it would appear from his comments after the event. Danton carried a resolution in the Cordeliers Club, urging La Fayette to go to Versailles with an ultimatum; and Desmoulins repeated his call to Parisians to fetch the king to the capital. The call was echoed at meetings in the Palais Royal on Sunday, 4 October. Early next morning women of the central markets and the Faubourg Saint-Antoine invaded the Hôtel de Ville, calling for bread and searching for arms. They were joined outside by Stanislas Maillard, an usher who had distinguished himself at the Bastille, who was induced to lead them to Versailles and to present their demands to the National Assembly. So they set out in two great columns, in the rain, chanting as they marched (or so tradition has it), 'let's fetch the baker, the baker's wife and the baker's apprentice'; they were followed, a few hours later, by 20,000 National Guardsmen of the Paris districts, who had compelled the reluctant La Fayette to put himself at their head, and a motley band of civilians armed with muskets, sticks and pikes. Faced with this impressive array, the king needed little further persuasion to give orders for the provisioning of the capital and to sanction the August decrees and the Declaration of Rights. But these concessions no longer satisfied the insurgents; and, the next day, the king and his family, having thrown away their last chance to seek refuge in flight, were compelled to accompany the marchers back to Paris, where they were joined, ten days later, by the National Assembly. Thus the French monarchy, after an absence of over a hundred years, returned for a brief sojourn to its ancestral home.

For the second time Paris had saved the Assembly—indeed, as Barnave wrote, it had saved 'la liberté publique'. The gains of the July revolution, made precarious by the continued presence of a court party at Versailles, were now consolidated. By placing the king under the watchful eye of the majority in the Assembly, the Paris city government and districts and by destroying the influence of the 'English party', whose leaders followed Artois and Breteuil into exile, the October insurrection established the ascendancy of the constitutional monarchists which, in Paris, was reflected in the long rule of Bailly as mayor and of La Fayette as commander-in-chief of the National Guard. Shortly, by firm measures, the bread crisis was brought under control and the insurrectionary energies of the Parisian *menu peuple*, having served their purpose, were restrained by the institution of martial law, the death sentence for 'rebellion' and a censorship of the radical press; already on 21 October a Bastille labourer, Michel Adrien, was hanged for attempting to provoke a 'sedition' in the Faubourg Saint-Antoine. So, at last, it seemed as if, after the protracted violence of the revolutionary outbreak, the professional and commercial bourgeoisie and their allies among the liberal aristocracy—the men of 1789—might proceed undisturbed with their task of legislating and creating a constitution in their own image.

But, although the eighteen months that followed were a period of remarkable calm and social concord, it was to prove an illusion. The Revolution was not half completed. Not only would the monarchy, in peace as in war, prove itself treacherous and incapable of regeneration; but the peasants remained obstinately unsatisfied; the small property-owners would not long accept their exclusion from the ranks of 'active' citizens; and the mass of small consumers would challenge even more forcibly the 'freedom of the market' as conceived by merchants, bankers and large producers. The great social convulsions to which these issues gave rise lay in the future and would carry the Revolution far beyond the point of October 1789; but the Revolution was all of one piece and their seeds had already been sown by the events, the conflicts and ideas which attended its outbreak.

CHAPTER XXIV

REFORM AND REVOLUTION IN FRANCE: OCTOBER 1789–FEBRUARY 1793

WHEN, after the October crisis, the National Assembly followed the French court from Versailles to Paris, it was able quickly to come to grips with the task of devising a new constitution. The danger of counter-revolution had once more receded and by November the food shortage in the capital was over.[1] The timely surrenders of feudal privileges made in the August decrees, officially promulgated on 3 November, allayed peasant discontents at least temporarily and bought time for the lawyers of the feudal committee to consider how total the alleged 'destruction' of the feudal régime was to be in fact. A hiatus in the administration of justice and in the conduct of local government was averted by the provisional continuation of existing office-holders. The suspension, on 3 November, of the activities of the *parlements* removed a possible spring-board for counter-revolutionary resistance in the provinces. Though the October crisis prompted Louis XVI to send a secret and solemn protest against the restrictions forcibly imposed on the crown's authority to Charles IV of Spain,[2] and though, by contrast, it encouraged the Belgian democrats to launch a revolt against the Austrian government in the Netherlands, neither of these repercussions involved much danger of European intervention in France. Most European governments were content to feel that France's political influence on the continent had been extinguished for some time to come. The first serious difficulties in France's foreign relations were in fact delayed till May 1790 and culminated in a solemn renunciation by the National Assembly of aggressive warfare and territorial conquest. Above all, when on 2 November the Assembly nationalised the landed estates of the Gallican church, it removed the impending danger of national bankruptcy.

The immediate measures taken to undermine further the powers of the executive and to safeguard the independence and legal supremacy of the legislature indicated, however, how deeply the Assembly had resented the king's stubborn defence of the feudal privileges of church and aristocracy and how suspicious it still was of his potential disloyalty. Louis had already been deprived of the right to prorogue or dissolve the legislature and of the power to initiate legislation. His suspensive veto applied only to ordinary and not to 'constitutional' decrees. Though preserved as the

---

[1] J. Godechot, *La Contre-Révolution, 1789–1804* (Paris, 1961), ch. II.

[2] J. Chaumié, *Les relations diplomatiques entre l'Espagne et la France, de Varennes à la mort de Louis XVI* (Bordeaux, 1957), p. 8.

hereditary and inviolable sovereign, he now held his crown on terms specified in the constitution and not as a matter of divine right. No longer 'king of France and of Navarre' but 'king of the French', he was soon to be given a civil list and described as 'first functionary'. Even more serious in its political consequences was the assembly's rejection of a motion of Mirabeau which would have allowed ministers to take part in its deliberations, though not to vote. The decree of 7 November 1789, excluding deputies from the ministry for the existing session, was never reversed and it was in this way that revolutionary France was deprived of the benefits of ministerial responsibility and parliamentary government.[1] Ever since the October days Mirabeau had cast himself for the role of saviour of the monarchy as a minister sitting in the assembly; henceforth, in the collapse of these ministerial ambitions, he could only aspire to become the king's secret and paid adviser, seeking to countermine not the revolution but the evolving constitution.

The pre-eminent authority now given to the future Legislative Assembly owed as much, however, to the influence exerted, from inside the reconstituted constitutional committee, by the Abbé Sieyès, as to the assembly's fears of the executive or its deference to the doctrine of the separation of powers.[2] Sieyès, who had already done much to formulate the political pretensions of the Constituent Assembly, now assumed the mantle of Mounier as the chief prophet of revolutionary constitutional theory. An enemy of privilege before the revolution, but aggrieved by the abolition of clerical tithes, Sieyès revealed his suspicions of direct democracy and gave his support, along with the liberal aristocracy, to the physiocratic idea that the constitution should provide for government by an élite. His distinction between 'political' and 'civil' rights and between 'active' and 'passive' citizenship was used as the basis for the restriction of the electoral franchise. His emphasis on the 'representative' character of the constitution reinforced the assembly's decision to confine popular political rights to the mere exercise of the franchise. The importance he attached to the revolutionary concept of national unity was reflected in the dogma which he formulated and which was enshrined in so many modern French constitutions that the deputy represented, not his own local constituency, but the nation as a whole.

Sieyès's influence was immediately apparent in the new electoral process devised for the Legislative Assembly. The indirect election of deputies and the fiscal qualifications required for candidates, electors and voters in the primary assemblies, however, restricted the exercise of the electoral function within narrower social limits than even Sieyès had originally

---

[1] R. K. Gooch, *Parliamentary Government in France, Revolutionary Origins, 1789–1791* (Ithaca, New York, 1960), p. 127.

[2] See in this connection the illuminating article by P. Bastid, 'Sieyès et la pensée politique de la Révolution', in *La Révolution Française* (1939), pp. 142–65.

contemplated. Despite the protests of the Abbé Grégoire and of Robespierre, the assembly decided, on 22 October 1789, to confine eligibility for election as deputy to those paying direct taxes to the value of a silver mark (about fifty francs) and, on 22 December, required voters in the primary assemblies and electoral colleges to pay respectively the value of three and of ten days' labour in such taxes. Even so, the franchise thus determined was more liberal than it subsequently became at the time of the Restoration and of the July Monarchy, since it created about 4,300,000 'active' citizens as against two million 'passive' citizens. The system of indirect election of deputies, so often criticised as anti-democratic, survived in France till 1817 and the fiscal qualification for electors was only temporarily removed in 1792, and did not disappear till 1848.[1]

The future legislative assembly was given an independence and sphere of authority which were meant to ensure its virtual monopoly of political power. The deputies were released from the control or supervision of their constituents by the abolition of 'imperative mandates', and they were also given the right of parliamentary immunity. Annual sessions, the unfettered control over their own meetings and procedure, freedom from dissolution, the right to initiate legislation and to elude even the restricted operation of the suspensive royal veto by the issue of proclamations, gave the legislature a hitherto unheard-of independence from interference on the part of the executive. Full control over the national finances, an annual check on military expenditure, the power to create or abolish all public offices, the right to enforce the legal responsibility of ministers and a close control of foreign policy endowed the Legislative Assembly with an omnicompetent and sovereign authority reminiscent of that of the British parliament.

Though this concentration of authority at the centre seemed to critics like Mirabeau to involve the danger of a new type of despotism on the part of a single-chamber legislature, it was, to some extent, offset by a very considerable decentralisation of administrative responsibility to a wide range of elected local authorities.[2] In the replanning of the institutions of local government the urgent need was not so much to fill a vacuum created by the collapse of the authority of the intendants, as to regularise the position of the elected revolutionary municipalities which had sprung into existence earlier in the year. It was also necessary, if the chaotic administration of the *ancien régime* was to be rationalised, for a unified and coherent framework to be established to which new units of ecclesiastical and judicial administration could later be assimilated. The way for reform had been cleared by the overthrow of many of the old municipal oligarchies, by the rejection of Necker's timid proposals for

[1] P. Campbell, *French Electoral Systems and Elections, 1789–1957* (London, 1958), p. 19.
[2] The administrative reforms of the Constituent Assembly are studied in detail in ch. III of J. Godechot's *Les Institutions de la France sous la Révolution et l'Empire* (Paris, 1951).

the reform of the provincial estates, but above all by the sacrifices made on 4 August of the financial and corporate privileges of the *pays d'états*. The issue of administrative decentralisation had first been raised at the end of July 1789 by Dupont de Nemours, Turgot's former collaborator. Draft proposals for the division of France into departments, communes and cantons and for the establishment of a hierarchical system of elected local authorities had been reported to the assembly on 29 September by Thouret, in the name of the constitutional committee. The idea of the geometric dissection of the historic provinces into eighty-three departments emanated from Sieyès and the organisation of the new local authorities was copied by Thouret from the provincial assemblies of 1787. As there was general agreement that the unit for town government should be the parish, and as the need for speedy action in this sphere was obvious, discussion was concentrated initially on the problem of municipal organisation and the new system was approved by a decree of 14 December 1789. This provided all the towns and village communities throughout France with small executive corporations (*corps municipaux*), consisting of a mayor and a variable number of officials and with deliberative assemblies (*conseils généraux*), formed from the corporations, and a more numerous body of notables. Representing the king in the general assembly and with the right to be consulted on all local affairs was a *procureur*, who carried out functions analogous to those of an English town-clerk. All these officials and councils were to be directly elected by the 'active' citizens of the commune from those who paid the value of ten-day's labour in direct taxes. Though the consent of the general council of the commune was required for the transaction of the most important local business, the effective agents of the communal administration were the municipal corporations. In addition to their routine responsibilities for local affairs these bodies were given wide police powers, including the duty of enforcing martial law when necessary, and were later entrusted with the assessment and collection of the new direct taxes.

The organisation of the new departments, districts and cantons, outlined in a decree of 22 December 1789, was not, however, completed till 26 February 1790. This was because the original plans of the constitutional committee were considerably modified by the assembly and because the delimitation of the departmental boundaries was settled in relation to historical circumstances and geographical conditions by those best qualified to arbitrate on local differences—the deputies from the areas concerned. The administrative structure of the departmental and district authorities was analogous to that of the communes, but the system of election, like that prescribed for the National Assembly, involved not one but two stages—the departmental electoral colleges being elected by primary assemblies of 'active' citizens in the cantons. Departments and districts (but not cantons) were now endowed with deliberative general councils, the former composed of thirty-six and the latter of twelve members, elected for four years and renewable, as regards half their membership, every two years. Half the numbers of the departmental and one-third of the district general councils were to be elected to departmental and district 'directories', which were to exercise executive functions. The departmental authorities were to assess direct taxes, organise hospitals, prisons and *ateliers de charité* and to supervise schemes for agricultural or commercial development. The districts were called on to draw up lists of 'active' citizens and the new taxation rolls, to control the organisation of the national guards and later to organise the sale of nationalised property. Some form of liaison with the central government was provided by the election of a *procureur-général-syndic* in the departments and of a *procureur-syndic* in the districts. The essential function of these important officials was to ensure the local application of laws passed by the National Assembly. At the time of the revision of the constitution in March 1791 the king was given power to annul acts of the departmental authorities contrary to law or ministerial order and also to suspend them from their functions. Similar disciplinary authority over the districts was also entrusted to the departments. In either case, however, suspension of these local assemblies had to be confirmed, and could be quashed, by the Legislative Assembly, which alone had the power to dissolve them.

By February 1790 the whole country had been divided into 83 departments, 547 districts, 4732 cantons and 43,360 communes and the new local assemblies were elected between February and the end of June. The new administrative machinery had its weaknesses—the municipal organisation, especially in the capital and the larger towns, was unnecessarily complex, the disparity between the social composition of the communal, district and departmental councils led to friction, while the lack of effective control from the centre meant that little or no check could be imposed on the progress of direct democracy in the communes.[1] The effective decentralisation, imposed on the Assembly by popular demand, did, however, give France a new consciousness of national unity, which was signalised by the regional federal unions of the spring of 1790 and by the Festival of Federation in Paris on the first anniversary of the fall of the Bastille. The provincial separatism, which had defeated all attempts under the *ancien régime* to endow France with administrative unity, and which was still vigorous in 1789, had now been extinguished. The framework of local government thus devised has lasted, with modifications, till our own day.

The next piece of unfinished business to occupy the Assembly was the vast and complicated issue of agrarian feudalism. The practical contra-

---

[1] A balanced assessment of the strength and weaknesses of the new local authorities is given in A. Cobban's article, 'Local Government during the French Revolution', in *English Historical Review*, vol. LVIII (1943), pp. 13–31.

diction between the 'total destruction of the feudal régime', announced in the August decrees, and the provisional preservation of certain feudal rent-charges pending their redemption, required explanation, if not justification. Interim solutions hurriedly drafted under the pressure of the agrarian revolts needed to be given final legislative form. Since 9 October 1789 these problems had been remitted to the feudal committee of the Assembly, and subcommittees, presided over respectively by the eminent lawyers Merlin de Douai and Tronchet, had been entrusted with the task of classifying the feudal dues and of determining the method of their proposed extinction. The decrees of 15 March and 3 May 1790 which disposed of these questions made it clear, however, that though feudalism in a legal sense was now extinct, the radical and immediate destruction of economic feudalism was still to be withheld. This refusal to concede what the peasants were determined at all costs to bring about was to have grave social and political consequences and can only be attributed to middle-class respect for property rights, the short-sighted conservatism of the lawyers and the desire of interested parties to restrict, and if possible to recoup, their earlier financial sacrifices.

In the week immediately following the night of 4 August when the surrender of feudal rights had been given more detailed formulation, self-interest had reasserted itself and even those who had precipitated what Rivarol had called the 'Saint Bartholomew of property' had had second thoughts about the wisdom of their actions. At that time it was still possible for the nobles who had surrendered to the infectious enthusiasm of the famous night session to doubt whether their impulsive action would secure the approval of their constituents; some who had acted from prudential motives thought that the salvage of feudal property rights could easily be compromised if radical solutions were allowed to prevail, and others, who had been absent on 4 August, were critical of the 'snap' voting in the Assembly, which had been engineered by the liberal 'cave' in the Breton club.[1] These attitudes explain the attempts made between 5 and 11 August 1789 to contest the abolition of feudal hunting rights and of private jurisdictions, the postponement, till 20 July 1790, of the extinction of the honorific distinctions of the nobility, and the various restrictive clauses in the August decrees. Though it was realised that nothing should be done to question the abolition of the few surviving traces of serfdom, and that little could be done to recall or qualify the sacrifice of dues deriving from servile status, many owners of feudal rent-charges became convinced that such dues ought to be preserved as long as was consistent with the maintenance of public order. This pointed to a system of redemption which would make it difficult, rather than easy, for the poorer peasants to free themselves from these charges. The intrusion of capitalistic methods into agriculture in the later stages of the *ancien régime* had

[1] G. Lefebvre, *Quatre-Vingt-Neuf* (Paris, 1939), pp. 183–6.

also resulted in an increased financial yield from this type of feudal due and the problem of profitably reinvesting any capital from their redemption, at a time when interest rates were tending to decline, was a real one.[1]

The principle governing the detailed classification of feudal dues in the decree of 15 March 1790 was the legal distinction derived from Roman Law between *féodalité dominante* and *féodalité contractante*. On this basis feudal and manorial dues were divided into two categories—on the one hand, personal dues, which were regarded as having been usurped or exacted illegally by feudal lords and, on the other, dues which were in effect contractual rent-charges, whose payment represented the concession of land either on a free or servile tenure. In reinterpreting and giving effect to the August decrees, the Assembly now explained that the abolition of the feudal régime meant that what had hitherto been feudal property would henceforth become freehold and that the feudal rent-charges, which were to be maintained until redeemed, would be converted into economic land-rents.[2] The distinction between personal and contractual dues, though satisfactory to the lawyers, could not, however, be applied with consistency to the vast complex of feudal obligations and in so far as it was understood by the peasantry was rejected as mere legal sophistry.[3]

The decree of 3 May 1790, by stipulating that annual money dues of a contractual nature should be redeemed at twenty years' purchase and dues in kind at twenty-five times their annual yield, established redemption rates which were, in themselves, not unreasonable. The conditions attached to the actual process of repayment, however, often made redemption a practical impossibility. Redemption was, in any case, only permissive and not mandatory: when it occurred it was to result from agreement between the owner and his individual tenants and no form of collective bargaining was permitted. Before the annual dues could be redeemed all arrears had to be paid up and all casual dues extinguished, even though the majority of tenants could normally expect not to be subject to these heavy contingent exactions at all. Dues which in the past had been paid collectively had also to be redeemed simultaneously, so that the inability of some tenants to raise the necessary capital prevented others, who could have afforded to do so, from acquiring the unrestricted ownership which all desired.

The consequent disillusionment of the peasants was increased still further by the repercussions on them of the Assembly's fiscal and economic reforms. Although it had been decided in principle, in August 1789,

---

[1] G. Lefebvre, 'La révolution française et les paysans', in *Études sur la Révolution Française* (Paris, 1954), p. 256.

[2] M. Garaud, *Histoire Générale du droit privé français, La Révolution et la Propriété Foncière* (Paris, 1959), p. 186.

[3] *Ibid.* p. 196. The distinction was also unsatisfactory since, in the case of *féodalité contractante*, most of the title-deeds containing the contract for the transference of land had been lost or destroyed. Sometimes these landed dues rested not on contracts but on immemorial custom.

that ecclesiastical tithe should be abolished without compensation, it had also been stipulated that it should continue to be levied until such time as the expropriated clergy should be paid salaries by the state. By a decree of 20 April 1790, these clerical salaries were to commence as from 1 January 1791, so that until then the collection of tithe was still legal and was in fact enforced. Even after that date the benefit resulting from the abolition of tithe was confined to the actual owners of land. Similarly the decision of the Assembly, on 14 May 1790, that the nationalised church lands should be sold by auction to the highest bidder deprived the poorer peasants of the chance of extending their holdings, even though they would have preferred to use their scanty capital resources in that way, rather than in the redemption of the contractual dues on their existing tenures. Finally the measures taken to free agriculture and trade from restrictions and monopolies in accordance with physiocratic ideas alienated the majority of peasants, who were profoundly attached to the collective methods of pre-capitalistic agriculture and to the state regulation of the corn trade. The only concessions made by the Assembly to the interest of the smaller agriculturalists were the retention of the embargo on the export of grain, the abolition of most of the indirect taxes on food and the maintenance of the right of common pasturage. These measures totally failed to protect the peasants from the economic distress caused by the new facilities accorded to the larger proprietors for the extension of enclosures and other forms of capitalistic production. Such were the origins of that endemic rural unrest which was only dissipated by the more drastic reforms of the Legislative Assembly on the eve of its dissolution.[1]

Even more tragic in its consequences was the prolonged and embittered religious schism which resulted from the Assembly's efforts to remodel the organisation of the Gallican church in the civil constitution of the clergy.[2] This redefinition of the position of the Roman Catholic church in France in its relationship to the secular authority and to the papacy was consequential partly upon the demands for reform expressed in the clerical *cahiers*, partly upon the destruction of the corporate organisation of the Gallican church on 4 August 1789, and also upon the subsequent nationalisation of the clerical estates. The immediate need for this reform of ecclesiastical institutions arose, however, from the assembly's obligation in the spring of 1790 to provide for the future cost of public worship and for the redemption of the pre-revolutionary clerical debt. The Assembly's essential objective was the creation of a national church, free of the political abuses and social inequalities of the *ancien régime*, independent of any kind of foreign ecclesiastical control, democratic in its forms and

---

[1] See below, p. 706.
[2] One of the most informed and balanced accounts of this controversial topic is to be found in ch. xiv of J. M. McManners' recent study, *French Ecclesiastical Society under the Ancien Régime. A Study of Angers in the Eighteenth Century* (Manchester, 1960).

geared to the new system of local administration. Reform of this kind, so it was argued, would affect the civil, but not the spiritual, affairs of the clergy and no attempt would be made to interfere with either dogma or ecclesiastical discipline. Since the reforms would be part of the secular constitution, they would not be subject to the royal veto and it was generally assumed that, if necessary, the papacy could be either persuaded or forced to acquiesce. It was well known also that a substantial majority of the clerical deputation in the assembly, including a number of liberal prelates, led by de Boisgelin, the influential archbishop of Aix, would lend its support to the plans. The mood in which the Assembly and its ecclesiastical committee approached the problem of church-state relations was, therefore, confident, though far from intentionally provocative. The proposals of the ecclesiastical committee came before the Assembly at the end of May 1790, were approved by a large majority on 12 July and were 'accepted' by the king on 22 July, on the recommendation of his clerical advisers in the council of ministers—Champion de Cicé, archbishop of Bordeaux, Keeper of the Seals, and Lefranc de Pompignan, archbishop of Vienne.

The main features of the new settlement were the adjustment of the boundaries of the dioceses to those of the departments, the abrogation of the Concordat of 1516 by provision for the election of bishops and *curés* by all those on the roll of 'active' citizens, irrespective of their religious beliefs, the payment by the state of reasonable salaries to both upper and lower clergy and the canonical institution of bishops, by French metropolitans instead of by the pope. There was much in the civil constitution that appealed to the lower clergy—it offered them a chance of rising in the hierarchy of the church, whose upper ranges had, in the eighteenth century, been confined to those of noble status; it doubled their incomes; it enabled them to nominate their own vicars; it gave them complete security of tenure; and it satisfied those who had supported Richerist arguments for the establishment of diocesan and metropolitan synods.[1] On the other hand, under the new régime, the former prestige and authority of the bishops were diminished. The bishops were now deprived of all except their purely spiritual or ecclesiastical functions, they were held strictly to the duty of residence and their jurisdictional powers within their dioceses were to be exercised in consultation with a permanent council of vicars-episcopal. Nevertheless freedom from the necessity of seeking papal confirmation for their election was undoubtedly considered by many bishops as an important compensation for their sacrifices and as a welcome concession to episcopal Gallicanism.[2]

[1] For the influence of Richerist doctrines on the eighteenth-century lower clergy in France see E. Préclin, *Les Jansénistes du XVIIIe siècle et la constitution civile du clergé* (Paris, 1929).

[2] The important article by Lévy-Schneider, 'L'Autonomie administrative de l'épiscopat français à la fin de l'ancien régime', *Revue Historique*, vol. CLI (1926), pp. 1–33, perhaps exaggerates this point.

In fact, however, though clerical opposition was slow to declare itself, the provisions of the civil constitution were bound to prove unacceptable not only to the French episcopate but also to the papacy. The reduction of the number of dioceses from 135 to 83 meant that some bishops would be deprived of their sees, while others would have their jurisdictions extended over larger areas. The decisions of the Council of Trent, however, and the formalities of canonical institution—whereby bishops were empowered to exercise their jurisdiction only over their own strictly defined dioceses—excluded the possibility of such transfers of authority, unless permission were given by the observance of regular canonical procedure.[1] The Assembly had also gone beyond the wishes expressed in the clerical *cahiers*, when it provided for the participation of laymen, who might be Protestants, Jews or even atheists, in the election of the 'constitutional' clergy.

The actual conflict between church and state which broke out in the autumn of 1790 was due mainly, however, to the Assembly's uncompromising rejection of de Boisgelin's suggestion that the reforms should be submitted for approval to a national synod of the French church. Such procedure might have paved the way for an acceptable compromise, but only at the cost of infringing the sovereignty of the National Assembly and it might also have involved the risk that the church would attempt to bargain for the restoration of its status as a corporation within the state.[2] Consequently the Assembly presented the church with a virtual ultimatum and left the ministers with the difficult task of negotiating its acceptance by the papacy. This alternative method of securing the canonical 'baptism' of the civil constitution was accepted with equanimity even by the radical reformers in the Assembly, because they considered that the consent of the pope, Pius VI, could, in the last resort, be enforced by threats to annex the papal enclaves in French territory—Avignon and the Venaissin. Before the results of these negotiations could be known, the Assembly took a further, and this time an irretrievable, step in the direction of religious schism when, on 20 November 1790, it imposed on all beneficed clergy in France an oath requiring them to uphold with all their power the constitution decreed by itself, on pain of deprivation. The clergy were thus compelled to choose between accepting the civil constitution, which had by then been condemned by many of the French bishops, and the loss of their clerical offices. In this crisis of conscience there was a striking and significant contrast between the behaviour of the bishops and that of the lower clergy—for whereas all except seven bishops refused, almost half the *curés* took the oath. The religious schism in the church

---

[1] See G. Pioro, 'Institution canonique et consécration des premiers évêques constitutionnels', *Annales Historiques de la Révolution Française*, vol. XXVIII (1956), pp. 346–55.

[2] J. Leflon, *La crise révolutionnaire, 1759–1846*, vol. XX of *Histoire de l'Église*, ed. A. Fliche and V. Martin (Paris, 1949), p. 63; K. D. Erdmann, *Volks-Souveränität und Kirche* (Cologne, 1949), ch. IV.

was thus precipitated, even before the pope, at long last, condemned the civil constitution and the political and social reforms of the revolution in briefs addressed to the French bishops on 10 March and 13 April 1791. The main results of Pius' action were to provoke a number of retractions among the clergy who had taken the oath, to cause the majority of the French bishops to emigrate in the course of 1791 and finally to persuade Louis XVI, torn by his religious scruples, of the necessity to break with the Revolution by seeking safety in escape from Paris.

Parallel with the religious schism an important cleavage developed in the political leadership of the Constituent Assembly. This was the consequence of a conservative reaction among that section of the liberal aristocracy, led by the Triumvirate of Barnave, Duport and Alexandre Lameth, which in September 1789 had wrested the control of the *parti patriote* from Mounier and the Moderates, by forcing the pace of social and political change. By the spring of 1791, however, this group had convinced itself that the time had come to halt the Revolution and to consolidate the conquests made by the propertied and enfranchised notables before these could be endangered by the opposite extremes of counter-revolution and radical egalitarianism. In one sense the Triumvirs merely assumed the policy, ambitions and secret commitments of Mirabeau after his death early in April 1791. They too wished to revise the constitution so as to strengthen the monarchy and to pave their way to ministerial office by abolishing the decree of 7 November 1789. In the altered circumstances of 1791, however, when new social and economic conflicts were emerging in the capital, when the government had hardly recovered from the serious military and naval mutinies at Nancy and Brest of the previous autumn and when large areas in the south of France were convulsed by outbreaks of religious fanaticism and aristocratic counter-revolution, the new moderate or 'constitutional' group cast itself for the role of a party of 'order'.

The fears and anxieties underlying this conservative trend had been inspired by the rapid proliferation of new political clubs and fraternal societies in the capital in the winter of 1790 and by the emergence, in the spring of 1791, of an organised working-class movement. Originally designed to promote the civic and political education of the unenfranchised proletariat, these societies, with the encouragement of Marat, soon became active political pressure groups.[1] Composed largely of 'passive' citizens and admitting women to their membership, the clubs gave expression to the rising popular dissatisfaction with the restricted electoral régime imposed by the Assembly and put forward claims that not only the constitution but even ordinary legislation should be submitted for popular ratification. They also became vigorous critics of the bourgeois

[1] For these clubs see Isabelle Bourdin, *Les Sociétés Populaires à Paris pendant la Révolution* (Paris, 1937).

establishment of the Parisian municipal administration and of the social exclusiveness of La Fayette's National Guard. It was in these clubs that the Parisian *sans-culottes* first emerged as a recognisable revolutionary element, whose political and economic demands represented a new and more formidable challenge to the predominance of the middle-class élite.[1] Though the first popular clubs had sought and received the patronage of the Jacobin club, the later societies, established in the spring of 1791, were virtual offshoots of the radical Cordelier club. As such they were the first practical exponents of Rousseauite theories of direct democracy.

The working-class movement of the spring of 1791 in the capital was marked by the intense indignation of large numbers of unemployed at the news of the impending closure of the public workshops maintained by the municipality and by a widespread campaign of journeymen carpenters, hatters, typographers and master-farriers in support of minimum daily wages. For the middle-class legislators of the national assembly the disquieting features of these developments were, first, that the working-class claims were championed by the radicals of the Cordelier club and its affiliates in threatening petitions to the legislature, and secondly, that in early June a 'coalition générale' of 80,000 Paris workers was threatening to secure wage demands by direct pressure, picketing and general strikes, at a time when the former trade guilds dominated by the masters had recently been abolished in the name of economic liberalism.[2]

In response to these developments the Assembly carried a series of decrees in the spring of 1791 which clearly demonstrated its growing fears of radicalism. At the end of April it excluded 'passive' citizens from the Parisian National Guard; on 7 May, in the name of religious liberty and moderation, it allowed refractory priests to celebrate mass in the parish churches; on 9 May a decree forbidding collective petitioning struck at the popular clubs and finally, on 14 June, on the motion of Le Chapelier, a law was passed forbidding, under severe penalties, the formation of trade unions and employees' associations, any form of collective bargaining for the raising of wages, as well as picketing and strikes.[3] Meanwhile an open breach between the Triumvirs and Robespierre had resulted from Barnave's defence of the vested interests of the West Indian planters in the important colonial debates between 11 and 15 May and from Robespierre's self-denying decree of 16 May, which excluded members of the Constituent Assembly from election to the following legislature.[4] The

---

[1] Much new light is thrown on the social and political attitudes of the *sans-culottes* by R. Cobb's study, 'Revolutionary Mentality in France 1793–1794', in *History*, vol. XLII, no. 146 (October, 1957), pp. 181–96.

[2] G. Rudé, *The Crowd in the French Revolution* (Oxford, 1959), p. 84.

[3] Strikes remained illegal in France till 1864 and trade unions till 1884.

[4] For the colonial debates see J. Bruhat, 'Maximilien Robespierre und die Kolonialprobleme', in *Maximilien Robespierre 1758–1794. Beiträge zu seinem 200. Geburtstag*, ed. W. Markov (Berlin, 1958), pp. 115–58.

44-2

Triumvirs had now clearly emerged as Moderates, whose political ambitions would only be realised if direct democracy in Paris were stamped out and if the assembly could be persuaded to revise the constitution, so as to allow a strengthened executive to act as an effective bulwark against class conflict in the capital and the danger of civil war in the provinces.

The flight of the royal family to Varennes on 20 June 1791 and its return in captivity to Paris on the 25th have always been regarded, and rightly so, as marking a turning-point in the history of the Revolution. These events forced the issue of republicanism for the first time to the forefront of public attention in France: they perpetuated the breach between the moderate and democratic leaders of the Jacobin club; they sowed fresh and ineradicable suspicions of royal duplicity in the mind of the people; demonstrated that even so large a country as France could be governed effectively at a period of national emergency without a king; and provoked the European great powers—particularly Austria and Prussia—into a heightened awareness of the solidarity of their monarchical interests against the revolutionary new order.

The immediate response of the general public to the royal flight was a curious mixture of anger and indifference in the capital and panic fears in the provinces of counter-revolution and foreign invasion. Popular demonstrations in favour of a republic followed quickly. The campaign was launched in Paris by the Cordelier club and the fraternal societies and the example was imitated by some of the affiliated societies of the Jacobin club in the provinces. In the capital republicanism received the 'philosophic' blessing of Condorcet and was prominently canvassed in the radical journals of Brissot, de Bonneville and Camille Desmoulins. Before the movement had time to gain real impetus, however, it ran into difficulties. Not all the radicals declared for a republic—Marat called, as usual, for a popular dictatorship. Danton appeared to favour an Orleanist regency, while Robespierre reserved his views and seemed to prevaricate. A republican manifesto, drafted by Thomas Paine, was countered by Sieyès and fizzled out like a damp squib.[1] The return of the king to Paris, the declared hostility of the Constituent Assembly to any form of republicanism and the prevalent feeling that the deposition of Louis XVI might involve the country in war with Austria, quickly robbed the republicans of the initiative.

As soon as the king was safely back in Paris the Assembly suspended his powers until such time as final decisions could be taken as to his fate and future status. The legislature then calmly absorbed the powers of the executive, took immediate steps to provide for national defence by calling for a hundred thousand volunteers to man the frontiers, suspended the

---

[1] For evidence that Sieyès's defence of monarchical institutions was collusively arranged with Paine and Condorcet see A. O. Alridge, *Man of Reason, The Life of Thomas Paine* (London, 1960), p. 148.

elections for the new legislature and gave Louis the benefit of the doubt by instituting its own inquiry into the circumstances of his alleged 'abduction'. In this crisis the initiative in the determination of policy was seized by the small group of Moderates headed by the Triumvirate. As part of a secret compact with Marie Antoinette, Barnave and his associates were able to secure the exculpation of the king and queen by the Assembly (15 July). With the backing of the Assembly and the support of La Fayette as Commander of the National Guard, the Moderates were able to uphold this decision by the use of force against the republican petitions of the popular clubs on the Champ de Mars (17 July).

After the flight to Varennes Barnave was able to play even more successfully than hitherto on the Assembly's fears of radicalism and of foreign intervention. In this sense his main opponents—the Parisian radicals and the militant émigrés proved to be his most effective allies. It was easy to persuade the Assembly to take a short way with the republicans when the Cordelier and popular clubs flouted its authority by pressing for the fate of the monarchy to be determined, not by the deputies, but by their constituents. To this open defiance of the sovereignty of the Assembly there seemed to be but one effective answer—the resort to martial law against the Champ de Mars demonstrators, the suppression of the popular clubs and the persecution of the radical leaders. Even though Robespierre and the democratic minority of the Jacobin club had dissociated themselves from the republican demonstration on the Champ de Mars, the Moderates broke away from the Jacobin club, which they themselves had originally organised, to found a new society of their own —the *Feuillant* club.[1] It was only the loyalty of its affiliated societies in the provinces and the exertions of Robespierre which preserved the Jacobin club from complete extinction as a result of this schism.

Nor, at this juncture, did the Assembly need to be reminded by Barnave that the trial or deposition of the king, in accordance with the wishes of the radicals, might involve the country in the danger of civil war and foreign intervention. Events spoke more loudly than arguments. The Emperor Leopold II, brother of the queen, who had so far been reluctant to promise Louis XVI any form of active assistance until the royal family was safely out of Paris, now suggested joint action by the powers to safeguard the interests of the French monarchy. In the so-called Padua circular of 6 July 1791, forwarded to the empress of Russia and the kings of England, Prussia, Spain, Naples and Sardinia, he urged the need for concerted action 'to vindicate the liberty and honour of the most Christian King and his family and to limit the dangerous extremes of the French revolution'. He recommended that the powers should sponsor a strongly worded protest to be handed over in Paris by their ambassadors. In this

[1] For the *Feuillant* club see ch. XII of G. Michon's *Essai sur l'histoire du parti Feuillant. Adrien Duport* (Paris, 1924).

693

they were to demand that Louis should be set at liberty without delay and declare that they would refuse to recognise any French law or constitution that had not been freely accepted by the king. If the extremists at Paris were not intimidated by this joint *démarche*, more vigorous measures would follow. Though Spain, Naples and Sardinia welcomed this proposed concert, the reply of Catherine II was guarded and the British government refused to commit itself. Nevertheless the essential basis of a future anti-French coalition was formed when, on 25 July, Prussia and Austria, hitherto jealous rivals, concluded a preliminary defensive alliance in which they agreed to take united action to bring about a European concert for the settlement of French affairs. Shortly afterwards, on 4 August, Leopold freed himself from his commitments in eastern Europe by making peace with the Turks at Sistova.

Meanwhile Louis's brother, the comte de Provence, who had escaped to Belgium, had early in July joined the comte d'Artois and Gustavus III of Sweden at Aix-la-Chapelle. Here the émigrés made noisy and threatening preparations for an early restoration of the *ancien régime* in France by force of arms. With Provence claiming to be regent of France as of right, with Condé's forces at Worms swollen by mass desertions of officers from the frontier regiments, these threats no doubt seemed more serious to the French Assembly than they were in fact.

To save Louis from trial and deposition and to scotch the immediate danger of 'red' republicanism was, however, much easier than to arrest the Revolution by a policy of reconciliation and constitutional revision. As the Constituent Assembly drew towards its close the Triumvirate pinned its hopes of a speedy termination of social and political conflict to a programme which, if statesmanlike in conception, was yet unrealistic in its presuppositions. This policy was, first, to heal the deep political and social schisms which the Revolution had opened up by appealing to the émigrés to return to France before their estates were confiscated and also by modifying the civil constitution of the clergy. Secondly, the Triumvirate wished to revise the constitution, so that its acceptance by the king could be made the basis for the restoration of the royal authority. Thirdly they hoped, by using Marie Antoinette as their secret intermediary, to persuade the emperor to refrain from further threats of intervention in French affairs.[1] The corner-stone of the Triumvirate's entente with the court was its attempt to revise the constitution so as to strengthen the executive. In this way they hoped to facilitate the achievement of their own ministerial ambitions, and to convince the emperor that a stable political régime would be created in France which would render superfluous any attempt to restore the *ancien régime* at the dictation of the émigrés. All their efforts, however, in the course of August and September

[1] *Marie Antoinette et Barnave. Correspondance secrète (Juillet 1791–Janvier 1792)*, ed. A. Söderhjelm (Paris, 1934), pp. 54–61.

1791 to abrogate the decrees excluding deputies from ministerial office and from the succeeding legislature failed, their hopes of providing the king with an absolute veto and of instituting a second chamber foundered, and the modifications of the existing constitutional provisions were on a minor scale and largely illusory.[1] This failure was due partly to the deep-seated suspicions in the Assembly of the political ambitions of the Triumvirate and partly to the refusal of the right-wing deputies to co-operate.

Though neither Marie Antoinette nor the emperor wished to truckle to the émigrés, each had their own reasons for not wholly accepting the policy of compromise and co-existence advocated by Barnave. The queen repudiated all contact with La Fayette, she regarded the constitution, even after its revision, as a 'monstrosity', and had no compunction in deceiving the Triumvirs by continuing to plead with the emperor for the restoration of the monarchical authority by means of an armed congress of the powers. Leopold, though recognising that the personal safety of the French royal family had been ensured by the *Feuillants*, was convinced that the political situation in Paris had been re-established mainly by his own initiative in issuing the Padua circular. Cautious by temperament and suspicious of the aggressive designs of Catherine II in Poland, the emperor thought it wise not to repudiate the Triumvirs. He decided, nevertheless, to maintain the policy of intimidation and bluff which he thought would discipline the French extremists, without committing him to the armed intervention recommended by the émigrés. It was this temporising attitude which led him, on 20 August 1791, to assure the *Feuillants* that he would recognise the revised French constitution if it was freely accepted by Louis and, on 27 August, in close concert with the king of Prussia, to issue the famous declaration of Pillnitz. In this document the emperor and king, recognising that the restoration of order in France was a matter of common concern to all European sovereigns, invited the powers to join them in helping Louis to establish a monarchical system compatible both with the rights of sovereigns and with the welfare of the French nation. If the powers jointly agreed on this policy, the contracting powers would take prompt measures to implement it. Since Leopold already knew, from the replies to the Padua circular, that this condition would not be realised, the declaration in no way committed him to armed intervention. Nevertheless the presence at Pillnitz of both

---

[1] The two main modifications were the removal of the civil constitution of the clergy from the constitution and the changes in the electoral régime. The former was intended to facilitate the revision of the ecclesiastical settlement by the new Legislative Assembly, so as to heal the religious settlement. This possibility was removed, however, by the fresh wave of anti-clericalism in the new Assembly, see below, pp. 697–8. The increase in the qualifications for electors did not help the Moderates, for the elections to the Legislative Assembly were conducted on the original franchise arrangements devised by the Constituent Assembly in 1789.

the comte d'Artois and of his political adviser, Calonne, and the emphasis subsequently placed on the counter-revolutionary significance of the declaration by the émigrés only deepened French fears of the warlike intentions of the emperor.

In these circumstances the acceptance of the revised constitution by Louis XVI on 13 September 1791 and the issue of a political amnesty liberating the Parisian radicals and republicans did nothing to bolster up the waning popularity of the Constituent Assembly. Despite its great achievements in constructive reform, the Assembly had long forfeited popular support by the exclusiveness of its concern for the narrow interests of the middle-class notables and by its subservience to the political guidance of the *Feuillants*. It was a tired and discredited Assembly which closed its doors at the end of September.

The tasks awaiting the new Legislative Assembly, when it met on 1 October 1791, were serious enough to daunt even the most experienced of politicians. For the most part its problems were the legacy of the Constituent Assembly and were concerned with internal administration and the practical working of an untried constitution. From the outset its members were confronted with a deteriorating financial situation, a deepening religious schism, growing disorders in the provinces and Negro revolts in San Domingo, and by the problem of strained relations with a suspect executive. Even more urgent and perplexing, however, was a fresh problem—that of France's relations with the European autocracies in the tense situation created by the declaration of Pillnitz. In the circumstances it was perhaps inevitable that these issues, which in normal times might have been dealt with separately, should have been regarded as inseparable, since they were all affected by, if they did not actually arise from, the threatened counter-revolution at home and abroad. The attitude of the new generation of revolutionary legislators to these problems was indicated by the Brissotin orator Isnard. 'Our predecessors', he said, 'achieved liberty by means of the doctrines of philosophy and popular revolts; our duty is to consolidate it by means of diplomacy and the sword.'[1]

Elected on a more restricted franchise than the Constituents, the members of the Legislative Assembly were nevertheless less distinguished intellectually and less wealthy than their predecessors. Predominantly they came from the professional classes and were mostly lawyers, journalists, doctors, soldiers and merchants, though a few liberal nobles and a small group of 'constitutional' clergy helped to diversify the social structure of the Assembly. The great majority of the members—about 350 out of a total of 745—formed a centre group, originally independent of a right wing consisting of 264 associates of the *Feuillant* club and a left wing of 136 members of the Jacobin and Cordelier clubs. The centre held

[1] *Archives Parlementaires*, 1st series, vol. XXXVII, p. 545.

moderate views and was mainly concerned to uphold the constitution both against the *Feuillants*, some of whom would not have been averse to the kind of constitutional revision contemplated by Barnave, and also against the left-wing Jacobin extremists, who in time began to veer towards a cautious republicanism. The Assembly, however, soon showed a tendency, both on the right and on the left, to split into factions. When in December 1791 a secret alliance of convenience was contracted between the 'liberal' faction of the *Feuillant* group, which took its instructions from La Fayette, and the Brissotin faction, the residual elements of the *Feuillant* and Jacobin groupings were reduced to political impotence. This was one of the developments which explain the bellicose tendencies displayed by the Assembly, for both the factions which had been outmanœuvred were critics of the war policy to which the neutralist centre party was eventually converted. Both the defeated groups were led from outside the Assembly by ex-Constituents—the more reactionary group of the *Feuillants* by the Triumvirs and the Jacobin minority by Robespierre. The group which eventually gained political predominance was, by contrast, strongly led from within the Assembly by Brissot. The latter was the faction known to contemporaries as Brissotins and to posterity as the Girondins.[1]

Within a few weeks of its first meeting, the assembly turned its attention to the dual aspects of the counter-revolution—the seditious activities of the non-juring priests in La Vendée and the Auvergne and the hostile demonstrations of the émigrés in the Rhineland and the Netherlands. Largely at the instigation of the group of Jacobin politicians led by Brissot, repressive measures were decreed against the émigrés on the 9th and against the refractory priests on 29 November. Though it was recognised that the émigrés congregated at Worms and Coblenz offered only a potential military threat to the country's security, it was against these enemies rather than against émigrés in general that action was directed. Other reasons, however, lay behind the decree. There was, for example, the practical problem of filling the twelve hundred commissions in the army vacated by the emigration of royalist officers. Nor could the Assembly ignore the need to check the flight of émigré revenues from France at a time when the assignats were beginning to depreciate. The decree of 9 November imposed on all émigrés who had joined the armed concentrations outside French frontiers and who failed to repatriate themselves by 1 January 1792 the penalties of treason—confiscation of their property and capital punishment if caught. Much time was devoted to the legislation against the refractory priests. The original draft, suggested by Gensonné and moved by François de Neufchâteau, provided a well-conceived compromise which might well have allayed the bitterness of

[1] M. J. Sydenham's *The Girondins* (London, 1961) provides a valuable reinterpretation of the origins, character and political significance of this group.

the religious schism.[1] Unfortunately, in its final form, the decree of 29 November was almost completely repressive in its provisions. The new civil oath, however, now exacted from clerics who had refused to take the oath of 27 November 1790, was intended not to impose a burden on religious consciences and the penalties imposed on all who demonstrated their disloyalty by refusing it were correspondingly severe. The decree declared such persons 'suspect' of treasonable intentions, deprived them of the ecclesiastical pensions which had been granted by the Constituent Assembly, made them liable to eviction from their homes and, if convicted of having provoked civil disturbances, to two years' imprisonment.

When both these decrees were vetoed by the king on the advice of the Triumvirs, the tension between the executive and the legislature became acute and a ministerial crisis inevitably followed. Hitherto the existing ministry had consisted of nonentities who had been content to follow the guidance of Barnave and his collaborators, but in late November and early December, under sharp attacks from the legislature, its composition was changed in a way that was to compromise the influence of the Triumvirs and to strengthen the Brissotin faction in the Assembly. The main change was the inclusion in the ministry of a newcomer to the political scene, Count Louis de Narbonne, who replaced Duportail as War Minister on 7 December.[2] Although lacking the royal confidence, Narbonne, by his energetic measures to place the army on a proper war footing, by the harmonious relations he established with the legislature, and by the strength of his personality, soon gained an ascendancy in the government indistinguishable from that of a leading minister.

In the second half of December Narbonne and his supporters concluded their secret agreement with Brissot in order to unite the forces which were then pressing for war with Austria. The close relations between the War Minister and the Assembly facilitated the granting of the necessary credits to finance the formation of three armies, totalling 150,000 men, which were placed under the command of Rochambeau, Lückner and La Fayette. The union had come about because La Fayette had once more broken with the Triumvirs and because a rift had appeared in the ranks of the Jacobins, as a result of Robespierre's opposition to Brissot's war policy. The understanding was based on Narbonne's conversion to the Brissotin thesis that France's real enemy was not the elector of Trèves but the emperor and that in preparation for war, an alliance should be sought with Prussia and, if possible, with Great Britain. The ulterior

[1] Gensonné's draft would have modified the system for the election of the clergy and the form of the clerical oath: it would also have deprived the clergy of the responsibility of keeping the registers of civil status. J. Leflon, *La crise révolutionnaire, 1789–1846*, vol. XX in the *Histoire de l'église*, ed. A. Fliche and V. Martin (Paris, 1949), p. 91.

[2] E. Dard, *Le Comte de Narbonne 1755–1813* (Paris, 1943), and J. Poperen and G. Lefebvre, 'Études sur le ministère de Narbonne', *Annales historiques de la Révolution française*, vol. XIX (1947), pp. 1–36, 193–217, 292–321.

motives of Narbonne and Brissot were, however, diametrically opposed. Whereas Brissot favoured war partly because he thought it would expose the secret relations of the court with the emperor and thus undermine the king's influence, Narbonne was thinking in terms of a military dictatorship to bring the revolution to an end and to restore the authority of Louis XVI. The alliance could not have survived long, but for the moment it check-mated the moderating counsels of the Triumvirs and helped to smother the warnings of Robespierre.[1]

Up to this point the case made out by the Brissotin orators for war with Austria was not impressive. Their arguments were contradictory, they mistook the real direction from which the external danger was to come, and they contented themselves with fiery eloquence, popular slogans and misplaced illusions as to the duration and character of the impending conflict. It took Robespierre—the virtuoso of suspicion—to reveal to them the dangers of military dictatorship implicit in their deal with Narbonne and the unreality of their hopes of assistance from the 'enslaved' peoples of the Austrian dominions. They allowed themselves to be deluded by potential profiteers such as the war contractors and financial speculators and they took at their face value the assurances of the ill-assorted bands of Belgian, Genevan and Dutch exiles, who were anxious to return to their homes in the wake of the French armies. Yet they accurately reflected provincial impatience with the counter-revolutionary intrigues of the refractory priests, they made a true assessment of the treasonable designs of Marie Antoinette and their chauvinistic grandiloquence was attuned to the rapidly rising spirit of French nationalism.

It was, nevertheless, not until late December 1791 that serious provocation seemed to come from Vienna. After Louis XVI had accepted the constitution in mid-September and had been restored to his kingly office, the emperor had been content, not only to allow the plans for a European concert to stagnate, but had even ridiculed suggestions reaching him from Marie Antoinette that an armed congress of the powers should be held at Aix-la-Chapelle.[2] On 24 December, however, Lessert, the French Foreign Minister, communicated to the Legislative Assembly a note from the emperor demanding the restoration of the feudal rights of the German princes in Alsace infringed by the decrees of 4 August 1789. A week later an Austrian diplomatic instrument or 'office', drafted by Kaunitz, and dated 21 December, also reached the French Assembly. In this, after announcing the dispersal of the émigrés by the emperor and the elector of Trêves, the Chancellor warned that, if the elector was threatened by

<hr>

[1] For Robespierre's criticisms of the war policy see G. Michon, *Robespierre et la Guerre révolutionnaire, 1791–1792* (Paris, 1937).

[2] Leopold's view of this project was that it was 'useless and even harmful' (J. Arnaud-Bouteloup, *Le rôle politique de Marie Antoinette* (Paris, 1924), p. 101).

undisciplined French troops, military assistance would be given by Marshal Bender, the imperial general in the Low Countries. In thus championing the rights of the German princes in Alsace based on the strict interpretation of the terms of the peace of Münster (1648), and in responding to the elector's appeals for protection, Leopold was merely fulfilling his elementary duty as head of the Empire. His intention was certainly not to precipitate war. Nevertheless, the Austrian note gravely provoked the French Assembly. The suggestion that the French government was not able to restrain its forces from infringing imperial territory was a gratuitous reflection on its lack of authority. An allusion to 'sovereigns united in concert for the maintenance of public tranquillity and for the safety and honour of crowns' signified Kaunitz's belief that he could give orders to the French Assembly. The December 'office' thus played directly into the hands of the Brissotin connection and gave their arguments a force which they had hitherto lacked. It initiated a fresh phase in the public debates in the assembly on the issue of war and peace in which all the advantages were with the war party. Henceforth the descent to the edge of the abyss was precipitous, and though it is best to interpret the subsequent notes of Kaunitz as exercises in 'brinkmanship', there can be no doubt that majority opinion in the Legislative Assembly was hardening all the time in favour of hostilities.

After the implications of Kaunitz's message had been considered by the diplomatic committee, its reporter Gensonné moved, on 14 January 1792, a draft decree that the king should be asked to seek specific undertakings from the emperor that he would not commit himself to any action against the French constitution 'or the full and complete independence of the French nation in the control of its own government'. Leopold was also asked to confirm that, if France were attacked, he would honour his obligations under the Franco-Austrian treaty of alliance of May 1756. If these guarantees were not given before 10 February 1792, the emperor's refusal would be regarded as an act of hostility. These proposals were intended to prepare the way for a preventive war—this being the purpose of the short-dated ultimatum. Leopold was charged with having already infringed the French alliance by his preliminary defensive treaty with Prussia of the previous July, though what was being demanded of him, above all, was a public repudiation of the project of a European concert.[1] The only modifications made in these proposals between 18 and 25 January was the extension of the period of the expiry of the ultimatum to 1 March and the demand that the treaty of 1756 should be regarded as one contracted not with the French king but the French nation.

Kaunitz's reply to this ultimatum, in a dispatch of 17 February, was an attempt to redeploy the tactics of intimidation which he mistakenly

[1] H. Glagau, *Die Französiche Legislative und der Ursprung der Revolutionskriege, 1791–1792*, p. 116.

thought had been so successful when used against the Constituent Assembly in the previous summer. The move was intended as a frank appeal to the uncommitted centre of the Assembly to repudiate the ascendancy of the Brissotin minority and to adopt the policy advocated by the Triumvirs. It had, in fact, precisely the opposite result, for after the Lameths had won a short-lived triumph by inducing Louis to dismiss Narbonne on 9 March, it enabled the Brissotins to impeach Lessart for his policy of appeasement on the following day, and to bring about the collapse of the whole *Feuillant* ministry. This was replaced by a new administration headed by Dumouriez as Minister for Foreign Affairs, with the Brissotin nominee, Roland, at the Interior, and Clavière, the Genevan inventor of the *assignats*, in control of finance. The other ministers, de Grave at the War Office, in place of Narbonne, and Lacoste at the Admiralty, as successor to de Molleville, represented the royal interest. Though the government was not, therefore, politically homogeneous, the dominating influence of Dumouriez, and the purge of the permanent officials in the Ministries of Foreign Affairs and the Interior, meant that it was effectively controlled by the Brissotin faction.

With the extinction of the political influence of Lameth and Duport, the death, on 1 March 1792, of the Emperor Leopold II and the advent to power of Dumouriez, the chances of preserving the precarious peace dwindled to vanishing point. Leopold's successor, as Austrian ruler, Francis II, was young, impetuous and more under the influence of the Austrian war party, headed by Baron von Spielmann, than of the ageing and calculating Kaunitz. Dumouriez, after thirty years in the secret diplomacy of the *ancien régime*, at last saw his chance to reshape the diplomatic structure of Europe. A disciple of Favier—the leading French critic of the Austrian alliance before the revolution—Dumouriez was determined on war and was the advocate of a military assault on the Netherlands. He adopted from Narbonne the scheme to continue diplomatic approaches to both Prussia and Great Britain with the idea of isolating Austria, and like Narbonne secretly hoped to restore the authority of Louis XVI by means of a *coup de force*. The corner-stone of his foreign policy was the creation of an independent and neutral Belgian republic, a solution which he thought would ensure the neutrality of Britain. Sanguine of success, even when the negotiations with the British and Prussian governments made no progress, Dumouriez during March contented himself with merely exchanging ultimatums with Kaunitz. On 20 April, with only seven dissentient votes, the Legislative Assembly voted for war on 'the king of Bohemia and Hungary', hoping thereby that neither Prussia nor the Empire would be involved.

Hopes of a successful military promenade in the Netherlands were quickly dispelled; the diplomatic negotiations designed to isolate Austria collapsed: counter-revolutionary movements broke out in south-eastern

France and the Assembly's authority was challenged by recalcitrant generals in the field and by the king's veto on urgent measures of national defence. Under these strains and stresses the constitution of 1791 crumbled and on 10 August 1792 the Bourbon monarchy was overthrown by a popular insurrection in the capital. Four main factors exercised a decisive influence upon the evolution of this internal crisis. These were, firstly, the efforts of La Fayette to impose on the Assembly constitutional revision by means of military force; secondly, the conspicuous failure of both executive and legislature to grapple with the problems of internal security and national defence; thirdly, the intervention in the political struggle between executive and legislature of the extra-parliamentary forces represented by the Paris sections and the provincial *fédérés*; and lastly, the political leadership of these democratic forces by Robespierre.

Louis XVI had secretly forecast that war with Austria would result in military defeat for the French armies: Robespierre had prophesied that it would expose the country to the danger of a military dictatorship. Both these predictions were promptly fulfilled, for in the first few weeks of hostilities the French forces, which had advanced into the Netherlands, retreated in confusion before the Austrians, massacring some of their own leaders, while General La Fayette resolved to recapture the dominating position in the capital which he had forfeited as a result of the 'massacre' of the Champ de Mars. The military reverses were partly the result of Brissotin inefficiency in not preparing adequately for war. Partly, however, they were due to the insistence of Dumouriez on offensive operations in the Netherlands, against the advice of the generals who were wedded to the formalised defensive strategy of the *ancien régime*. Hardly had the campaign opened when the French commander-in-chief —Rochambeau—tendered his resignation, while La Fayette initiated secret negotiations for an armistice with the Austrians. La Fayette had now broken with his Brissotin allies and had finally committed himself to the political views of the *Feuillants*. The purpose of the projected armistice was to allow the general to divert his forces to the capital in order to enforce the kind of constitutional revision advocated by the Triumvirate. La Fayette was now convinced that the chief dangers to France came, not from the émigrés, nor from the Austrians, but from the affiliated Jacobin clubs and the popular societies. Having recovered from the 'tricolour terror' of 1791 the latter would need to be crushed by force. Though his overtures to the Austrian government were repelled and though his troops showed no disposition to further his political ambitions, La Fayette held himself in readiness throughout the summer months of 1792 for intervention in Paris in the interest of the party of order. He had, in fact, already cast himself for the role of a military dictator.

Meanwhile, neither the Brissotin ministry nor the Legislative Assembly had displayed the energy or resource which the accumulating internal problems and the deteriorating military situation so clearly required. In January and February 1792 the economic troubles caused by the over-issue of *assignats* and sugar shortages resulting from the West Indian revolts of the previous autumn had led to the looting of grocers' shops in the Paris faubourgs of Saint Antoine and Saint Marcel and to the forced sale of consumers' commodities at popularly determined prices. These riots were rigorously repressed and popular demands for the official regulation of food prices had been ignored.

Aristocratic conspiracies in the south-east of France were checked, not by the tardy measures of the central government, but by the vigorous local action of 'patriotic' forces from Marseille against Arles and Avignon. Even more serious was the recrudescence of châteaux-burning and agrarian outrage which was allowed to spread over large areas in the departments of Lot, Cantal and Aveyron. By this time the king, by re-fusing his sanction to further legislation directed against the refractory priests and to the formation of a camp of 20,000 provincial national guards at Paris, had produced a political deadlock. Acting on the advice of Théodore Lameth and Duport, he dismissed the majority of his Girondin ministry on 13 June and vetoed its recent security measures. Dumouriez resigned shortly afterwards and was given a military command in the army of the north.

Against the court dominated by the so-called 'Austrian committee', and the new *Feuillant* ministry, consisting of political nonentities, the Parisian *sans-culottes* of the democratic faubourgs quickly reacted by invading the Tuileries palace on 20 June in an illegally armed mass-demonstration designed to extort from the king the restoration of the Girondin ministers and the sanction of the Assembly's decrees. This demonstration not only failed to intimidate the king, it also provided the opportunity for which La Fayette had been waiting. Fortunately for the Assembly, when the general appeared before it on 28 June to demand the dissolution of the Jacobin and popular clubs, he was not accompanied by his troops. He also failed on the following day to persuade the Parisian national guards to march on the clubs. Isolated and rebuffed the general had no alternative but to return to the military post he had deserted, without, however, abandoning his ultimate objectives.

As the external danger came closer and no decisive action was taken by the Assembly, the way became clearer for a fresh intervention of the extra-parliamentary forces, so soon as these could be organised, armed and reinforced by an accession of strength from the provinces. The latter was provided by the armed and resolute battalions of national guards from the departments, some of whom had been invited by the Girondin leaders to attend the festival of federation on 14 July as one way of circumventing the royal veto on the armed camp at Paris. Others had volunteered for service in a camp which the new *Feuillant* ministry had, out of prudence, located at Soissons. On 2 July the Assembly had authorised the latter to pass through the city *en route* for their destination, provided that they moved on three days after the festival. These *fédérés* began to arrive in the capital a week later. In contrast with the Parisian national guard, whose staff-officers were conservative or royalist in their political sympathies, most of the provincial *fédérés* were militant revo-lutionaries or éven republicans. It was the *fédérés* who, on 17 July, first raised the demand for the suspension of the powers of Louis XVI, in a petition to the Legislative Assembly. Although they arrived in Paris in small detachments during the course of July and although their total numbers never exceeded 5000, the *fédérés* acted as a powerful pressure-group for the extension of the political powers of their hosts in the radical sections, or electoral wards, of the capital. Under this combined pressure the Assembly allowed the sectional assemblies to meet in daily session as from 25 July, while the municipality made provision on 27 July for the establishment of a central committee of correspondence, consisting of delegates from the forty-eight sections at the Hôtel de Ville. By so doing it transformed the Commune of Paris itself, at least by contagion, into a centre of insurrection.

One initiative taken by the Assembly on 11 July—the proclamation that the 'fatherland was in danger'—also helped to crystallise the situation and had an immediate effect in tilting the balance of forces in the capital in favour of the democrats.[1] Politically it led to the demand on the part of the sections and the *fédérés* for the deposition of the king, rather than for the mere suspension of his powers, and it also clinched the case for the admission of 'passive' citizens into the sectional assemblies and the battalions of the National Guard. The effect of this decree in heightening the political tension in the capital and in electrifying the general population was further enhanced at the end of the month by the publication of the duke of Brunswick's threatening manifesto and the arrival in Paris, to the strains of its famous marching song, of the battalion of *fédérés* from Marseille.

Finally it remains to stress the importance of the part played by Robespierre in determining the tactical methods and political objectives of the insurgents. It was he who persuaded the *fédérés*, once a national emergency had been declared, that they should, even in defiance of the legislature, remain in the capital, after the festival of federation, until the constitutional crisis had been resolved. As vice-president of the Jacobin club, he had concerted plans of action with the central committee of the *fédérés* and had drafted their petitions to the Legislative Assembly and their addresses to the departments. Above all, in a great speech before the Jacobin club on 29 July, he had clarified and reformulated the political plans that were to be achieved by insurrection. In this, Robespierre re-

---

[1] F. Braesch, *La Commune du Dix Août 1792* (Paris, 1911), pp. 105, 125 and 139.

nounced his previous role as 'defender' of the constitution of 1791 and delivered a frontal attack on both the executive and the legislature. In a four-point radical programme, he argued for the overthrow of the monarchy, the displacement of the Legislative Assembly by a National Convention elected by universal suffrage, the frequent summons of the primary assemblies to exercise surveillance over the deputies and a purge of the departmental authorities, tribunals and public officials. Some of these demands had been initially expressed by the Cordelier club, by leaders of the Paris Commune, such as Manuel and Danton, and by the sections, but not until they had been approved and reformulated by Robespierre did they become the agreed formula of revolt. Hitherto he had warned both the *fédérés* and the sections against precipitate action; now he had realised that the moment to strike had arrived.

Under the impression created by the issue of Brunswick's manifesto, which was known to have been provoked by the king, all except one of the forty-eight Parisian sections united on 3 August to petition the assembly for the deposition of Louis XVI. By refusing on the 8th to sanction proceedings against La Fayette and by ignoring the demand of the Commune for Louis's deposition, the assembly did nothing to avert the rising, which it was aware had been planned for the 10th. Nevertheless, though it was now no more than a rump, the Legislative Assembly exercised a considerable influence on the character and consequences of the new democratic revolution which accompanied the capture and partial destruction of the Tuileries. Inevitably it was compelled to recognise the emergency powers of the new insurrectionary Commune which had given the orders for the final assault on the palace. It had to surrender the custody of the king to this body and agree that he and his family should be imprisoned in the Temple. At the behest of the Commune it fixed a term to its own existence by summoning a National Convention to be elected by universal manhood suffrage. By its control over the sections, the police and the National Guard the new Parisian municipality was indeed master of the political situation in the capital. By recognising this new rival the Assembly was able to preserve its own existence for the time being. If its prestige in the capital had been sadly diminished, the Assembly was still the only constitutional authority whose powers were generally accepted in the country as a whole.

Once the moderate elements in the Assembly had seceded, effective decisions were monopolised by the Girondin deputies. They now found themselves the unexpected beneficiaries of the popular revolt which, from the middle of July, they had sought to circumvent. The result was that the Assembly did not formally depose the king but merely suspended his powers and established in his stead a provisional Executive Council of six elected ministers. The former Girondin ministers—Roland, Clavière and Servan—returned to power and were joined by Monge at the

Admiralty, Lebrun at the Foreign Office and Danton at the Ministry of Justice. The latter was the effective, though not formal, head of the new administration and, until his resignation in late September, acted as the driving force in the conduct of national defence. The eligibility of ex-members of the Constituent and Legislative Assemblies for election to the National Convention and the indirect system of election (designed to offset the probable effects of universal suffrage) also resulted from Girondin initiatives.

Between 10 August and 20 September, when it held its final session, the dying Legislative Assembly hurried through a spate of legislation which refashioned the French state on the principle of equality. The most fundamental changes were the virtual extinction of the surviving traces of feudalism, the transformation of the laws of inheritance, the decision to alienate the sequestrated estates of the émigrés in small lots, and the provision for civil marriage and divorce.[1] A fresh stage of anti-clerical terrorism was initiated by decrees imposing voluntary exile or compulsory deportation on the non-juring clergy and extending the new oath of liberty and equality to all clergy without exception.[2]

Hardly less important were the diplomatic and military consequences of the fall of the monarchy. The suspension of Louis XVI's executive powers automatically terminated the missions of foreign ambassadors who had been accredited to him and deprived French diplomatists abroad of their official status. On 13 August a general exodus of foreign representatives began with the departure of the Swedish minister. On the 17th the British ambassador, Lord Gower, was recalled, and, before the end of the month, all France's normal diplomatic connections with the Dutch republic, Spain, Denmark, Poland, Russia, the Swiss Confederation and the majority of the Italian states had been severed. Though the British government emphasised that the withdrawal of its ambassador was not meant to infringe its policy of neutrality, the prospect of an eventual rupture between the two countries loomed sensibly nearer. Meanwhile on 19 August Prussian armies under the command of Brunswick had crossed the French frontier and Lafayette had deserted to the Austrians. A purge of French aristocratic commanders in the field became necessary and was effected by the dispatch of special commissioners to the French armies. Lafayette's command was transferred to Dumouriez and

---

[1] A decree of 25 August 1792 virtually extinguished all annual feudal dues hitherto subject to redemption, which could not be supported by the production of the original title-deeds showing a transfer of land. The decree concerning the sale of émigré estates was dated 14 August, that relating to divorce 20 September. An important step in the direction of the separation of church and state was also taken on 20 September, when the responsibility for maintaining the civil registers of births, deaths and marriages was transferred from clerical control to that of the municipalities. Entail (*substitution*) was forbidden by a decree of 25 August, finally confirmed by the Convention on 25 October.

[2] The deportation decree was of 26 August, the new civic oath was imposed by a law of 3 September.

Lückner's to Kellermann. The response to the traitorous surrender of the fortresses of Longwy on the 23rd and the imminence of the fall of Verdun at the end of the month, combined with the threat of fifth-column activity in the capital, was the September massacres in the Paris prisons.

In the elections to the National Convention the full effects of universal suffrage were distorted by illiteracy, fear and intimidation. In some departments three-quarters of those qualified to vote in the primary assemblies abstained, while many were debarred from the electoral assemblies by refusal to take the new civic oath to liberty and equality. In Paris all who had shown royalist or *Feuillant* sympathies were disenfranchised, all votes were cast in public and the electoral assembly was transferred to the Jacobin club. The result was that all twenty-four members of the Paris delegation were Jacobins, convinced republicans and supporters of the Commune—with Robespierre at the head of the poll and Marat as the last to be elected. Some of the Girondin leaders, such as Brissot, Petion and Condorcet, defeated in the capital, managed to find seats as representatives of the departments. Electors in the provinces were less subject to pressure from the radicals and were more inclined to vote for those who had risen to public prominence in the Constituent or Legislative Assemblies, irrespective of their affiliations. The Jacobins, however, were at a disadvantage because they were made the target of a smear campaign launched by Roland as Minister of the Interior. These factors and the indirect system of election made the social and professional composition of the Convention correspond closely to that of the Legislative Assembly and gave the Girondins a working preponderance in the new assembly.

The Convention held its first session on 20 September—the same day that Dumouriez and Kellermann stopped the Prussian invasion in its tracks at the battle of Valmy. At first the chances of political concord among the deputies appeared to be good. After Valmy the military dangers receded with the Prussian retreat, and the threat to the assembly's sovereign authority from the Paris Commune declined. The first act of the Convention—the abolition of the monarchy on 21 September—was virtually unanimous, and the proclamation of the republic inevitably followed. Early sources of possible dissension between the Jacobins and Girondins were accommodated, when it was agreed that persons and property should be guaranteed by the nation and that the republic should be 'one and indivisible'. The spectre of rural communism which had apparently been preached in the provinces by some of the commissioners of the Paris Commune and the bogey of 'federalism', which some Girondins, such as Buzot, were thought to favour, thus appeared to have been eliminated. The primary task of the Convention—the formulation of a new republican constitution—although formidable, seemed not to be insuperable.

Disunity, however, soon followed and the proceedings of the Convention were throughout bedevilled by the violent and irreconcilable conflicts between the Girondin deputies and the Jacobin members of the 'Mountain'. Although these groups or factions were in no sense disciplined political parties, what they were contending for was control of the Convention. The responsibility for the peculiar violence of these conflicts rests with the Girondins. It was they who plunged the assembly into bitter discord and rejected all efforts at reconciliation. Some of their differences with the Jacobins arose out of the perpetuation of the personal quarrels between Brissot and Robespierre carried over from the Legislative Assembly. Others developed out of Girondin recriminations over the 10th August and the September Massacres. The Jacobins were attacked as 'anarchists' and Marat, Danton and Robespierre were decried as 'Triumvirs' aiming at the establishment of a dictatorship. These accusations recoiled on those who made them, for they were condemned, not only by the more moderate elements in the assembly—the so-called 'phlegmatics', but also by the supporters of the Gironde in the provinces. Louvet's celebrated vendetta with Robespierre only served to emphasise the latter's ascendancy as leader of the 'Mountain'. Of greater substance was the division of opinion between the factions over the political importance of the capital—once more an issue raised by the supporters of Roland. The contention of Lasource that the capital should exercise no more influence than any other department reflected Girondin fears of the over-mighty preponderance of the Commune and of the unruly interventions of the Paris sections. The stubborn efforts made by Roland and Buzot to provide the Convention with a special guard drawn from the departments allowed their opponents to level against the Girondins the damaging, if baseless, charge of 'federalism'. Marxist historians, such as Soboul, however, have regarded these struggles as part of the class conflict.[1] Such an interpretation emphasises the undoubted connection between the Girondin group and the financiers, war-contractors and speculators of the time and the identification of the Jacobins with the interests and demands of the *sans-culottes*. Although any sharp distinction between the Girondins, as the defenders of the principle of *laissez-faire*, and the Montagnards, as reluctant protagonists of state intervention, would be exaggerated, the Girondins may, nevertheless, be rightly regarded as typical representatives of *la bourgeoisie possédante*.

The Jacobin counter-offensive to the Girondin campaign of personal abuse was the trial of Louis XVI. By this move the Jacobins sought, not only to strengthen the republican form of government, but also to embarrass and discredit their political opponents. Any attempt to delay the institution of legal proceedings against Louis could easily be misrepresented and it seemed probable that legal technicalities and the larger

[1] A. Soboul, *Précis d'histoire de la Révolution Française* (Paris, 1962), pp. 225–6.

issues of policy would divide and distract the Girondins. As soon, therefore, as the battle of Valmy robbed Louis of his potential value as a political hostage, the Jacobins did their best to expedite the trial. In the political contest which followed the Girondins were compelled to rely on temporising expedients, which revealed rather than concealed their hesitations, and on diversionary manœuvres, designed to confuse the main issues. All their efforts to stave off the trial were rendered futile by the discovery, on 20 November, of the iron chest in the Tuileries, with its damning disclosures of the king's dealings with the émigrés. Once Louis appeared before his judges—the members of the Convention—on 11 December, his conviction of the high political crimes of which he was accused was assured. His stubborn refusal to recognise the authority of the evidence against him created a bad impression. The chief plea of his leading defence counsel—de Sèze—that the king was inviolate under the terms of the constitution of 1791—proved a broken reed. Once it had become evident that the king could not escape a verdict of guilty the Girondins made two efforts to save his life. The first of these was the proposal, made on 27 December by Salle, that the sentence imposed by the assembly should not be carried out unless it was ratified by a popular referendum. This, however, called in question the sovereign authority of the Convention and naturally antagonised some sections of the assembly and it also had the effect of dividing the Girondins themselves—a striking example of their lack of discipline and cohesion as a political group. The final effort—after Louis had been found guilty and sentenced to death— was the proposal of a reprieve. This too failed and, on 21 January 1793, to the dismay of many of his subjects and the horror of countless sympathisers abroad, Louis XVI was executed. By their equivocal attitudes and votes in the final stages of the trial the Girondins had done much to dig their own political graves. Control over the uncommitted members of the Convention had already eluded them.

Between the fall of the monarchy and the final stages of the king's trial French foreign policy evolved rapidly under the pressure of events. From a cautious attitude of reserve in early August the Ministry of Foreign Affairs became in November a sounding board for revolutionary propaganda abroad and in December the Convention embarked on a course of aggressive territorial expansion. Successive challenges to the established order in Europe, the sanctity of international agreements and the economic and military security of the Netherlands led directly to the hostility of Great Britain and to the formation of the first European coalition against France.

So long as Danton exercised a preponderating influence in the provisional executive council, the foreign policy of the French government remained on the defensive. Once Danton had resigned his ministerial office at the end of September 1792, however, new factors conditioned the evolution of French foreign policy. These were, firstly the presence of Lebrun at the Ministry of Foreign Affairs, secondly a run of striking military successes for the French armies under their new leadership,[1] and thirdly the problem posed by the administration of foreign territories 'liberated' by French arms.

With the election of Lebrun as head of the Ministry of Foreign Affairs in August 1792 French foreign policy came under the control of a former revolutionary journalist who since the spring had been responsible, as an under-secretary, for the direction of France's relations with Britain, Holland and the Austrian Netherlands.[2] He had been given this appointment by Dumouriez because of his close association with the united group of democratic refugees from Liège and Belgium who were preparing, on French soil, for the establishment of an independent Belgian republic. Dumouriez's rapid advances in the Netherlands after Jemappes brought this objective within sight of achievement. At this point, however, the Belgian democrats were faced with the revival of the conservative Statist faction, whose leader, Van der Noot, had suggested the creation of a Belgian monarchy with a sovereign drawn from one of the princely houses of Orange, Brandenburg or Hanover. It was to offset this new danger that Lebrun induced the French executive council on 16 November 1792 to proclaim the freedom of the navigation of the river Scheldt. This new departure in French foreign policy was designed to wean the commercial interests in Antwerp from their leanings towards the monarchical cause in Belgium by assuring them of their future economic prosperity under French auspices and, more generally, to convince the Belgians that they need have no fears for their own independence as the result of French victories.[3] To proclaim the freedom of commerce on the Scheldt, however, which since the Treaty of Münster of 1648 had been closed to all nations except the Dutch, was not only to tamper unilaterally with one of the greatest international treaties, but also to infringe the rights and privileges of the United Provinces which both Great Britain and Prussia had guaranteed in 1788.[4] In order to win over the support of his own colleagues in the Executive Council Lebrun appealed, against international treaties, to the principles of natural law and it was on this basis that the executive act was vociferously approved by the Convention on 20 November.[5] On the 23rd French gunboats forced their way down the Scheldt estuary despite the protests of the Dutch States General, osten-

[1] The most spectacular success was Dumouriez's victory at Jemappes on 6 November, which enabled him to overrun the whole of Belgium in a few weeks.

[2] P. Muret, Le Département des Affaires Étrangères pendant la Révolution, 1787–1804 (Paris, 1877), pp. 161–4.

[3] P. Tassier, 'Aux Origines de la Première Coalition: Le Ministre Le Brun Tondu', Mélanges offerts à Louis Jacob. Revue du Nord, vol. XXXVI (1954), pp. 263–272.

[4] See above, ch. IX, p. 275.

[5] The contention was that international rivers, as the highways of commerce and civilisation, should by natural law be open to all nations.

sibly to reduce the fortress of Antwerp. The immediate threat to Holland and the ultimate naval threat to Britain could no longer be disregarded.

Meanwhile, on 19 November, in answer to various petitions from the Rhineland soliciting French protection, the Convention passed with acclamation a decree promising 'friendship and assistance' to all peoples wishing to recover their liberty. This decree seriously increased Pitt's anxieties as to the dangers to be anticipated from British radical societies and had an important immediate effect in causing the British government to repudiate negotiations which had been unofficially initiated at The Hague for a general pacification.[1] Pitt and the conservative 'Alarmists' regarded the opening of the Scheldt and the Edict of Fraternity as acts of deliberate provocation designed to drive Britain into war and, at the same time, to stimulate radical discontent inside the country. Precautionary measures to call out part of the militia and to increase Britain's state of naval preparedness were taken on 1 December and parliament was recalled on the 13th. Two days later, on 15 December, the Convention defined its policy in relation to territories conquered by French armies in a way that clearly indicated that it had virtually committed itself to the policy of annexation.[2] This decision was taken primarily for financial reasons—in order to stop the drain of French stocks of metallic currency to Belgium, where Dumouriez had been unable to meet his heavy military expenditure by means of local loans. On the initiative of Cambon, it was now declared that war expenditure incurred in the 'liberation' of subject people abroad would be defrayed by the introduction of French *assignats*, secured on the sequestrated property of clerical and noble estates. In conquered territories clerical tithes and feudal dues would be extinguished, political rights would be confined to the unprivileged classes, and provisional governments established under French control, exercised through special commissioners dispatched by the Executive Council. All previous French assurances to the Belgians that their independence would be respected had thus been jettisoned. These decisions would alienate not only Britain but the moderates, Catholics and counter-revolutionaries in Belgium. If the latter resisted, formal annexation would follow.[3] This was the policy of *guerre aux châteaux, paix aux chaumières*. The revolutionary

---

[1] In meetings with the French representative at The Hague, de Maulde, on 17 and 19 November the Grand Pensionary of the United Provinces, Van de Spiegel, discussed the possibility of a general pacification on the basis of a general recognition of the French republic and guarantees for the safety of the French royal family. These overtures were sponsored by Lord Auckland—British ambassador at The Hague—and had been approved by the British government. The maritime powers would have offered their mediation between France and Austria and Prussia (*H.M.C. Fourteenth Report. Appendix. Part V* (Dropmore Papers), pp. 334, 339 and 341).

[2] Savoy had actually been annexed on 27 November 1792.

[3] Annexation became the only possible policy for the French if counter-revolutions in the occupied territories were to be avoided (A. Soboul, *Précis d'histoire de la Révolution Française* (Paris, 1962), p. 236).

new order was now to be exported in the wake of conquering French armies and the costs of liberation were to be borne by the expropriation of the privileged.

As hostilities with Britain loomed nearer, however, Lebrun and the Girondins displayed signs of hesitation. Early in December the Executive Council suspended Dumouriez's plans for an attack on Holland. In his negotiations with the British government Lebrun made repeated efforts to allay its fears of the Edict of Fraternity by restrictive interpretation of its motivation.[1] Dumouriez was severely critical of the decree of 15 December and did his best to prevent its implementation in Belgium. By their attempts to adjourn the execution of the king the Girondin faction showed their apprehensions of a general war with the rest of Europe. Realising that a *guerre à outrance* would play into the hands of the *sans-culottes*, they increasingly expressed the same fears and anxieties as had formerly moved the *Feuillants*. When at the end of January 1793 Danton induced the Convention to pass the celebrated decree claiming for France her 'natural frontiers' on the Rhine, the Alps and the Pyrenees, his intention was not to extend but rather to set limits to revolutionary annexations.[2]

Unfortunately, from the middle of December 1792 French foreign policy slipped from the control of Lebrun and the Executive Council and was determined largely by the Convention. The question of the extension of hostilities with Europe, equally with the fate of Louis XVI, thus became a bone of contention between the political factions. The more complex the issues became, the more ambiguous and calculating was the attitude of both Girondins and Jacobins and the more divided the views expressed by both sides. Robespierre himself did not fully approve of the decree of 15 December promoted by the Jacobin Cambon, and he was critical of the policy of annexation. He did not, nevertheless, throw his weight against an extension of the conflict. Some of the Girondins, such as Kersaint, became the passionate advocates of a war with France's traditional enemy Britain, contending that both her colonial empire and her financial system could easily be laid in ruins. Brissot and other responsible leaders were afraid that if the Girondins committed themselves to last-minute negotiations with Pitt they would be accused by their opponents of treason and counter-revolution and would forfeit the support of the

---

[1] Lebrun contended that the decree only applied to states at war with France and that the assistance to be offered was not to discontented minorities, but to whole populations, who having freed themselves from foreign control, were threatened with subjugation.

[2] The doctrine of French 'natural frontiers', long thought by French historians such as Sorel to have had a long ancestry in French history, had only recently been invented. It was ventilated in the first instance not by the French, but by the Rhinelander J. G. Forster on 15 November 1792 in the effort to persuade the inhabitants of Mayence to favour their annexation by France (G. Zeller, 'La Monarchie d'Ancien Régime et les frontières naturelles', *Revue d'Histoire Moderne*, vol. VIII (1933), pp. 305–333; P. Sagnac, *Le Rhin Français pendant la Révolution et l'Empire* (Paris, 1917), p. 80; A. Soboul, *op. cit.* p. 236).

Plain in the assembly.[1] These were the reasons why Lebrun and the Executive Council were unable to meet the demands of the British government for the retraction of the offending decrees and adequate guarantees for the security of Holland. In this *impasse* war with Britain and Holland became unavoidable and the execution of the king merely had the effect of adding Spain to the list of France's enemies.[2] On 1 February 1793 the Convention declared war on Britain and the United Provinces and during March France found herself at war with most of Europe, with the exception of Russia and one or two Scandinavian powers.

[1] See D. Williams, 'The missions of David Williams and James Tilly Mathews to England 1793', *English Historical Review*, vol. LIII (1934), p. 659.

[2] J. Chaumié, *Les relations diplomatiques entre l'Espagne et la France de Varennes à la mort de Louis XVI* (1957), ch. xv.

APPENDIX: ESTIMATED GROWTH OF POPULATION IN EUROPE AND NORTH AMERICA IN THE EIGHTEENTH CENTURY[1]

(See footnote 1, page 25)

Mainland American Colonies	1,750/2,000	—	U.S.A. 4,000 (1790)
France	22,000 (1752–63)	24,000 (c. 1770)	26,900 (1801)
Russia[2]	19,000 (1762)	—	29,000 (1796)
Italy	15,484 (1750)	—	18,091 (1800)
Naples	3,953 (1765–6)	4,450 (1775–6)	4,964 (1801)
Papal States	2,189 (1769)	—	2,400 (1782)
Piedmont	1,795 (1750)	1,954 (1774)	—
Sicily	1,319 (1747)	—	1,660 (1798)
Lombardy	1,086 (1768)	—	1,154 (1799)
Tuscany	1,079 (c. 1750)	—	1,188 (c.1800)
Sardinia	360 (1751)	437 (1782)	461 (1821)
Venice	149 (1760)	141 (1776)	137 (1797)
Savoy	247 (1756)	—	422 (1801)
Spain[3]	9,308 (1768)	10,410 (1787)	10,541 (1797)
Austria	6,135 (1754)	7,937 (1784)	8,511 (1800)
Hungary (Inner)	1,718 (1720)	—	6,468 (1787)
England and Wales	6,140 (c. 1750)	7,531 (c. 1780)	9,156 (1801)
Ireland	3,191 (1754)	4,048 (1781)	4,753 (1791)
Scotland	1,266 (c. 1755)	—	1,678 (1801)
Poland	11,000/11,500 (1764)	—	—
Prussia[4]	3,617 (1763)	5,015 (1780)	5,844 (1793)
Certain Prussian Provinces	2,497 (1752)	3,487 (1778)	3,911 (1789)
Holland	—	—	2,078 (1795)
Belgium	—	2,273 (1784)	3,000 (1799–1800)
Brabant	445 (1755)	618 (1784)	—
Portugal	2,100 (1732)	—	2,900 (1800)
Sweden	1,781 (1750)	2,021 (1775)	2,347 (1800)

[1] Figures are given in thousands.
[2] The figure of 29 millions for 1796 does not include the population of the areas annexed to Russia under Catherine II.
[3] The Spanish census of 1797 was exceptionally deficient.
[4] The figure for Prussia includes the accessions of territory in 1772.

APPENDIX

Denmark	806 (1750)	843 (1775)	926 (1800)
Norway	591 (1750)	718 (1775)	883 (1800)
Finland	422 (1750)	610 (1775)	833 (1800)
Switzerland	1,200 (1700)	—	1,700 (1798)

SOURCES

Mainland American colonies: E. B. Greene and V. D. Harrington, *American population before the Federal Census of 1790* (N.Y. 1936), p. 6. U.S.A. (1790): *Federal Census*.

France from E. Levasseur, *La population Française*, I (Paris, 1889), pp. 213 and 216 ff., and E. Esmonin, 'L'abbé Expilly et ses travaux de statistique', *Revue d'histoire moderne*, IV (1957), p. 276.

Russia from P. I. Lyashenko, *History of the National Economy of Russia* (trans. New York, 1949), p. 273.

Italy as a whole from K. J. Belloch, *Bevölkerungsgeschichte Italiens*, III (Berlin, 1961), p. 354. Piedmont from Belloch, *op. cit.* III, p. 353. Naples from Belloch, *op. cit.* I (Berlin, 1937), p. 230; Sicily, Tuscany, and the Papal States from *ibid.* II (Berlin, 1939), pp. 152, 237 and 122. Lombardy from M. Romani, 'Il Movimento Demografica in Lombardia dal 1750 al 1850', *Economia e Storia*, IV (1955), p. 413. Sardinia from F. Corridore, *Storia documentata della popolazione di Sardegna, 1479–1901* (Turin, 1902), pp. 43, 47. Venice from D. Beltrami, *Storia della Popolazione di Venezia* (Padua, 1954), p. 59.

Savoy from R. Rousseau, *La population de la Savoie jusqu'en 1861* (Paris, 1960), pp. 220–1.

Spain from Domínguez Ortiz, *La sociedad española en il siglo XVIII* (Madrid, 1955), pp. 58–9.

Austria ('the lands and kingdoms represented in the Reichsrat') from *Annuaire international de statistique* (The Hague, 1916), p. 6, and A. Gürtler, *Die Volkzählungen Maria Theresias und Josef II, 1753–1790* (Innsbruck, 1909).

Hungary from G. Thirring, *Magyarország Népessége II Jósef Korában* (Budapest, 1938), p. 36; the population of Hungary as a whole, i.e. with inclusion of Transylvania, Croatia and the military frontier, was 9,516,000 in 1787 (*ibid.* p. 34). The estimate for the whole country in 1720 was 2,582,000 but S. Szabó (*Ungarisches Volk*, Budapest, 1944) considers that from 3 to 3½ millions would be nearer the mark.

England and Wales from J. Brownlee, 'The History of the Birth and Death Rates in England and Wales', *Public Health*, XXIX (1915–16), p. 228.

Ireland from K. H. Connell, *The Population of Ireland, 1750–1845* (Oxford, 1950), p. 25.

Scotland from J. G. Kyd, *Scottish Population Statistics*, Scottish Historical Society, third series, XLIV (1952), ix.

Poland from T. Korzon, *Wewnętrzne dzieje Polski za Stanisława Augusta, 1764–1794: badania historyczne ze stanowiska ekonomicznego i administracyjnego*, 2nd ed. (Cracow, 1897–8), I, p. 63.

Prussia (including the annexations of 1772) from O. Behre, 'Über den Anteil germanischer Völker an der Entwicklung der Statistik', *Allgemeines Statistiches Archiv*, vol. 17 (Tübingen, 1914), pp. 50–89.

Prussian Provinces from V. Inama-Sternegg and Häpke, 'Bevölkerungswesen' in *Handwörterbuch der Staatswissenschaft*, vol. II (4th ed. Jena, 1924), p. 672.

Holland (the Netherlands territory of 1931) from the commentary by J. C. Ramaer in *Geschiedkundige Atlas van Nederland, Het Koninkrijk der Nederlanden, 1815–1931* (The Hague, 1931), pp. 231–72.

Belgium from H. van Werveke, 'La Densité de la Population Belge au Cours des Âges', in *Studi in Onore di Armando Sapori* (Milan, 1957), p. 1428. Duchy of Brabant from A. Cosemans, *De Bevolking van Brabant in de XVIIde en XVIIIde Eeuw* (Brussels, 1939), p. 224.

Portugal from M. Reinhard, *Histoire de la Population Mondiale* (Paris, 1950), p. 149.

The Scandinavian countries from H. Gille, 'The Demographic History of the Northern European Countries in the Eighteenth Century', *Population Studies*, III (1949–50), p. 19.

Switzerland from W. Bickel, *Bevölkerungsgeschichte der Schweiz seit dem Ausgang des Mittelalters* (Zurich, 1947), pp. 49 ff.

INDEX

INDEX

Hungary (*cont.*)
labour services of peasants regulated by
Maria Theresa, 7, 281
awakening of Fourth Estate, 20
census (1784), 288
rebellion (1790), 423
Hutcheson, Francis, Scottish philosopher,
46
Hutton, James, Scottish geologist, 134

India, 548
loss of French colonial possessions in, 5
Anglo-French conflicts, 238
division of power between crown and
East India Company, 564
Mahratta War, 222, 548
Warren Hastings as Governor-General,
220, 221, 222, 225, 226, 545
Clive's 'dual' system, 219, 538
Lord Cornwallis as Governor-General,
225–8
struggle for power at Poona, 222–3;
Treaty of Salbai (1782), 222
the zamindars in Bengal, 220–1, 224–5,
227–8
trade, 231: with Britain, 34; East India
Company, 218–21, 538
North's Regulating Act, 220
Fox's East India Bill, 553–4
Pitt's India Act (1784), 555
see also India Act
India Act (1784), 555
terms, 14, 227
establishment of permanent Board of
Control, 223, 224
authority of Bengal government streng-
thened, 223
Industrial Revolution, 15–16, 563, 564
Ireland
concession of legislative independence to
Irish parliament, 14, 440, 551, 552
Dependency of Ireland Act (1719), 450
parliamentary reform, 564
Habeas Corpus Bill (1781), 551
conditions during War of American
Independence, 548, 550
Volunteer movement, 548–9
uprising (1798), 423
Declaratory Act modelled on that for
Ireland, 456
status of Irish parliament, 537
Irish immigration aggravates struggle for
employment in England, 564
trade, 555
proposed commercial treaty with Britain,
564
question of union, 564
population increases, 25, 26, 28, 32, 714
religion, 561

Italy
claims of Regalism fortified by spread of
'political' Jansenism, 19
problem of church and state, 389: the
Papacy not hostile to ideas of the Enlightenment, 389; factors hampering
economic advance, 389; changes made
by Pius VI, 389–90; quarrels between
church and state in Naples and Venice,
390; new climate of enlightened thought,
390; steps taken against Papal authority, 390; suppression of Jesuits in
Naples and Parma (1767), 391, 392, 393
Italian Jansenism, 392: too much claimed
for its influence, 392; inside church,
392; ebbing of its influence in Rome,
393; patrons of Jansenism, 393; synod
at Pistoia, 393, 394; diverse interests
of Jansenists, 394
comparison of states in Italy, 378–80
politics: legislative control in hands of a
few, 380; fragmented political system
in Italy, 380; unchanging political
structure, 381
economics: domination of 'economia
cittadina' of city states, 381; customs
barriers increased smuggling, 384 (reforms in customs system, 388, and of
corporations and guilds, 388, and of
legal institutions, 388); transition to
regional economy, 389
social structure, 384–5, 428
trade, 33: share of international trade,
381; industries, 381; grain trade, 383–
4; customs policies a brake on trade,
383
agriculture: products, 381–2; backwardness, 382; bad harvests, 382; poor
land, 382; methods, 383; fragmentation,
383; separate currencies, 383
education, 389
population increase, 25, 29, 381, 714
secret society 'the Philadelphians', 441
the Enlightenment: spread of new ideas,
385–6 (reforms, 388–9); cultural élite,
386; vigour of universities, 386; enlightened scholars, 386–7; impact of
enlightenment, 388 (strengthening of
central government, 388, centralisation
of judiciary, 388, fiscal reform, 388,
education, 389); pace of reform slows,
394–5
French Revolution, 395–6

James I & VI, king of Great Britain, 515
James II, king of Great Britain, 453
Jankovic, Serbian educationalist, 318
Jansenism, 19
influence in French *parlements*, 605

730

INDEX

Saint Germain, Claude Louis (*cont.*)
reforms, 567: espouses cause of lesser nobles, 207; attacks venality, 570–1; lays foundations of French revolutionary armies, 570; sets up recruiting depots, 571; improvements of recruitment, supply and manœuvre, 570; replaces lash by flat of sword, 212; establishment of cadet schools, 206; reforms halted, 214
Saint-Simon, Louis de Rouvroy, duc de, French socialist and writer, 623, 628
claims that *légistes* created and destroyed monarchy, 621
basic concept of predestined rise of middle classes, 626
St Vincent, John Jervis, First Earl, British admiral, 174
Salbai, Treaty of (1782), 222
Sandwich, John Montagu, Fourth Earl of, First Lord of the British admiralty, 181
reputation of corruption, 179, 491
admirals refuse to serve under him, 180
practical naval improvements, 180
Saratoga, Battle of (1777), 12, 210, 497, 503
Saxe, Maurice, comte de, Marshal of France, 194
Saxony, 33, 299
industry, 42, 44
Saxony, Prince Charles of, *see* Charles
Scandinavia
population rise, 25, 26, 28, 714–15
trade: increase in shipping, 38
Scheele, Carl Wilhelm (1742–86), German chemist
study of composition of air, 129
discovery of bleaching action of chlorine, 139
Schiller, Friedrich, German writer, 72, 73
Schubert, Franz, Austrian composer, 83, 95
resided and died in Vienna, 82
Science, 148
mathematics and mechanics, 115–16
astronomy, 116–18
improvements in scientific instruments, 118
physical sciences, 118–21: chemistry, 121–30; electricity, 130–1; meteorology, 131–2; geology, 132–4; cartography, 134–5, 141
societies and publications, 135–7
Sessé, Martin, Spanish botanist, 404
Seven Years War (1756–63), 4, 5, 6, 14, 36, 174, 183, 196, 204, 215, 241, 307, 321, 371, 521, 538
necessity for financial retrenchment and administrative reforms, 5
dictation of domestic policies by the war, 7, 279, 436

Sharp, Granville, English philanthropist, 249
Shelburne, William Petty, Second Earl of, later marquess of Lansdowne, English statesman, 2
view of royal proclamation on Canada of 1763, 522
signs separate peace with American colonists (1782), 268
Treaty of Versailles, 13, 505
hopes for American allegiance to common crown, 462
attempt to conclude commercial alliance with United States, 507, 564
Fox's attempt to keep him from office, 552
ministry, 553: compromise with East India Company, 542; disposal of numerous sinecures and useless offices, 559; dealings with Ireland, 564
fall from power, 506–7, 543
an impossible ally for Pitt, 555
Sieyès, Emmanuel Joseph, Abbé, French statesman, 692
pamphlet, *Qu'est-ce que le tiers état?*, 661
member of Committee of Thirty, 663
authority given to Legislative Assembly owes much to his influence, 681
and formulation of political pretensions of Constituent Assembly, 681
suspicious of direct democracy, 681
ideas for formation of new departments, 683
Silesia, Austrian, 8, 33, 299
industry, 42, 44
regulating decree (1771), 282
loss of, 279
Sindia, Mahadji, Maratha chieftain, 230
agrees to peace in Maratha Wars, 222
acts as guarantor for observance of Treaty of Salbai (1782), 222
treated as an independent prince by East India Company, 222
Cornwallis refuses him assistance, 228
death, 229
Smeathman, Henry, British naturalist, 249
Smith, Adam, Scottish economist
his theory of a natural order, 46
interest in agriculture, 47: programme of reform, 47–8; free trade, 48
contrast with the Physiocrats, 48
Spanish economic writers draw on his work, 49
less difference between Cameralists and Smith and Physiocrats than their language suggests, 52
sources of his ideas, 52
critical attitude to existing economic institutions, 52

743

DATE DUE